R. Gupta's®

National Testing Agency (NTA)

UGC-NET/JRF

Junior Research Fellowship & Assistant Professor Eligibility Exam

Library and Information Science

Previous Years' Papers

PAPER II

by

RPH Editorial Board

2027
EDITION

RAMESH PUBLISHING HOUSE, NEW DELHI

Published by

O.P. Gupta *for* Ramesh Publishing House

Admin. Office

12-H, New Daryaganj Road, Opp. Officers Mess,
New Delhi-110002 ✆ 23275224, 23245124

E-mail: info@rameshpublishinghouse.com
For Online Shopping: www.rameshpublishinghouse.com

Showroom

- Balaji Market, Nai Sarak, Delhi-110006 ✆ 23282525 📱 9354373464
- 4457, Nai Sarak, Delhi-110006

Book Code: R-2687

ISBN: 978-93-5477-655-7

Price: ₹ 680

Printed at: Deepak Offset, Delhi

CONTENTS

PREVIOUS PAPERS (SOLVED)

Previous Years' Paper

National Testing Agency (NTA)

UGC-NET Junior Research Fellowship & Assistant Professor Eligibility Exam

Library and Information Science, January-2026

(Exam held on 02-01-2026)

PAPER-II

1. Arrange the steps of the scientific research process in their most logical and systematic order:

A. Formulation of testable hypotheses based on research gaps

B. Conducting a comprehensive literature review to understand the background

C. Preparing and presenting the research report with findings and recommendations

D. Defining the research problem clearly and precisely

E. Collecting high-quality data according to the research design

Choose the *correct* answer from the options given below:

1. D, B, A, E, C 2. B, C, D, E, A
3. D, C, B, A, E 4. A, D, E, C, B

2. Given below are two statements: one is labelled as Assertion (A) and the other is labelled as Reason (R).

Assertion (A): Academic Social Networking (ASN) sites are promoting scholarly communication and it facilitates community to share, connect, and collaborate, both nationally and globally.

Reason (R): Unlike other social networking platforms, ASN sites are enhancing research funding opportunities for researchers.

In the light of the above statements, choose the ***most appropriate*** answer from the options given below:

1. Both (A) and (R) are true and (R) is the correct explanation of (A).
2. Both (A) and (R) are true, but (R) is not the correct explanation of A.
3. (A) is true, but (R) is false.
4. (A) is false, but (R) is true.

3. Match the Databases (List-I) with their Year of establishment (List-II).

List-I (*Items*)	List-II (*Year of Establishment*)
A. JSTOR (Launch)	I. 1950
B. JISC	II. 1955
C. ORBICOM	III. 1993
D. ERIC	IV. 1996

Choose the *correct* answer from the options given below:

1. A-I, B-II, C-III, D-IV
2. A-II, B-III, C-I, D-IV
3. A-II, B-IV, C-I, D-III
4. A-I, B-II, C-IV, D-III

4. Which of the following statements are true for Control Fields (00X) in MARC?

A. They are Fixed-Length Fields

B. They use Indicators to provide Field-Specific Meaning

C. They contain Coded Data Elements
D. They are always Repeatable
E. They do not contain Subfield Codes

Choose the ***correct*** answer from the options given below:

1. B, C, E only
2. A, D, E only
3. B, C, D only
4. A, C, E only

5. Which of the following statements correctly describe features of Geographical Indications (GIs)?

A. GIs are owned by individual inventor
B. GIs identify goods as originating from a specific territory
C. GIs protect technological innovation and invention
D. GIs are linked to qualities/characteristics due to geographical origin
E. GIs can be renewed indefinitely after registration

Choose the ***correct*** answer from the options given below:

1. A, C, D only
2. B, C, E only
3. B, D, E only
4. C, D, E only

6. The Quality Trilogy Process focussing on Planning, Control and Improvement was given by:

1. W. Edwards Deming
2. Philip Crosby
3. Joseph Juran
4. Kaoru Ishikawa

7. Who among the following blamed Web 2.0 for creating digital forest of mediocrity, embarrassing music and unreadable poems, essays and novels:

1. Andrew Keen
2. John Flintoff
3. Laura Turner
4. John Robb

8. What encoding schemes does Unicode use to represent characters?

A. UTF-8
B. UTF-16
C. UTF-32
D. UTF-64
E. UTF-128

Choose the ***correct*** answer from the options given below:

1. A, B only
2. A, B, C only
3. A, B, D, E only
4. B, C, D, E only

9. The PMB Integrated Library Management System (ILMS) was launched by:

1. Christopher Nolan
2. Richard S. Marcus
3. Francois Lemarchand
4. Robert L. Kusik

10. Which of the following is a disadvantage specific to Pre-Coordinate Systems compared to Post-Coordinate Systems?

1. High cognitive load on the user during retrieval
2. Limited flexibility in combining new concepts
3. Lack of need for controlled vocabulary
4. Unsuitability for printed indexes

11. In digital libraries, which strategy most effectively addresses the obsolescence risk during the storage phase of the information life cycle?

1. Implementing strict copyright checks before ingest
2. Using multiple redundant backup systems without format migration
3. Applying periodic format migration and emulation approaches
4. Restricting access to only the latest versions of digital content

12. As per the Indian Computer Emergency Response Team (CERT-In) guidelines on Information Security Practices for Government Entities, within how many hours must a cybersecurity incident be reported to CERT-In?

1. 12 hours
2. 6 hours
3. 24 hours
4. 48 hours

13. Which Section of the Information Technology Act deals with Identity Theft?

1. Section 66C
2. Section 66D
3. Section 67
4. Section 69

14. Which of the following best represents an ethical dilemma during the dissemination phase of the information life cycle?

1. Deciding which controlled vocabulary to use during indexing
2. Choosing long-term file formats for data curation
3. Deciding storage location based on cost constraints
4. Balancing Open Access with users, sensitive data

15. Arrange the following steps of Chain Indexing in their correct sequence:

A. Select links and isolates from the chain
B. Derive the chain of terms from the class number
C. Identify the class number of the document
D. Arrange the headings in alphabetical order for the index
E. Prepare subject heading entries (Main, Subordinate, Coordinate)

Choose the ***correct*** answer from the options given below:

1. D, A, E, C, B
2. C, A, B, D, E
3. C, B, A, E, D
4. B, C, A, D, E

16. ______ is recognized as the first person to introduce the idea of canonicalization.

1. Clifford Lynch
2. Kirchhoff
3. Trusted Digital Repositories (TDR)
4. Cornell University Library

17. Arrange the following ISBN elements in their correct sequence:

A. Registrant element
B. Prefix element
C. Check digit
D. Publication element
E. Registration group element

Choose the ***correct*** answer from the options given below:

1. B, E, D, A, C
2. B, A, E, D, C
3. E, B, A, D, C
4. B, E, A, D, C

18. The Multicultural Library Manifesto was primarily developed by ______.

1. ALA
2. SLA
3. IFLA
4. UNESCO

19. "Edanz" service is associated with which publisher?

1. Wiley
2. Elsevier
3. Springer
4. Sage

20. Given below are two statements: one is labelled as Assertion (A) and the other is labelled as Reason (R).

Assertion (A): RDF and RDFS are essential tools for building ontologies in the Semantic Web.

Reason (R): RDF provides a framework for describing resources, while RDFS extends RDF with vocabulary for defining classes and properties

In the light of the above statements, choose the ***most appropriate*** answer from the options given below

1. Both (A) and (R) are correct and (R) is the correct explanation of (A).
2. Both (A) and (R) are correct, but (R) is NOT the correct explanation of (A).
3. A is correct, but (R) is not correct.
4. A is not correct, but (R) is correct.

21. Match the OSI Layers List-I with Protocol/technology in List-II.

List-I (*OSI Layers*)	List-II (*Protocol/technology*)
A. Physical Layer	I. DNS (Domain Name System)
B. Network Layer	II. PPTP (Point-to-Point Tunnelling Protocol)
C. Session Layer	III. Fibre Optics
D. Application Layer	IV. ICMP (Internet Control Message Protocol)

Choose the ***correct*** answer from the options given below:

1. A-II, B-III, C-I, D-IV
2. A-III, B-IV, C-II, D-I
3. A-IV, B-II, C-III, D-I
4. A-IV, B-III, C-II, D-I

22. The ISO/IEC 27000 family of standards is primarily related to:

1. Information search and retrieval standard to uphold the quality of Content
2. Information security management
3. Environmental management
4. Green Library Building and Space Management

23. Arrange the following major committees/ commissions according to their chronological order of establishment:

A. Sankaran Committee on Health Science Libraries
B. UGC Library Committee (Ranganathan)
C. Advisory Committee for Libraries (Sinha Committee)
D. D.P. Chattopadhyaya Committee on NAPLIS
E. Bhore Committee on Medical Libraries

Choose the ***correct*** answer from the options given below:

1. C, B, E, D, A 2. D, A, C, E, B
3. E, C, B, A, D 4. C, A, B, E, D

24. Which of the following are considered "Soft" elements in the McKinsey 7S Model?

A. Shared Values B. Skills
C. System D. Staff
E. Strategy

Choose the ***correct*** answer from the options given below:

1. C, D, E only 2. A, D, E only
3. B, C, D only 4. A, B, D only

25. Which Part/Section of Colon Classification, 6th Revised Edition, is Enumerative:

1. Annexure
2. Rules
3. Schedules of Classification
4. Schedules of Classic and Sacred Books

26. To test Null Hypothesis, a researcher uses ______.

1. Regression Analysis
2. χ^2 (Chi Square)
3. ANOVA
4. Factorial Analysis

27. Match the terms in List-I with descriptions in List-II.

List-I (*Terms*)	List-II (*Descriptions*)
A. Intersubjectivity	I. This means occurring between or among two or more subjects or conscious minds
B. Insider/Outsider Perspective	II. The theory of how the inquiry should proceed
C. Participatory Action Research	III. Research that places a premium of the politics and power of knowledge production and uses
D. Methodology	IV. One way of thinking about the difference in the epistemologies of hermeneutics and naturalism

Choose the ***correct*** answer from the options given below:

1. A-II, B-III, C-I, D-IV
2. A-II, B-I, C-III, D-IV
3. A-I, B-IV, C-III, D-II
4. A-IV, B-II, C-I, D-III

28. Arrange the following character representation standards in chronological order:

A. Unicode B. ASCII
C. ISCII D. EBCDIC
E. Extended ASCII

Choose the ***correct*** answer from the options given below:

1. D, B, C, E, A 2. B, C, D, A, E
3. A, D, C, E, B 4. C, B, D, E, A

29. Which Section of the Information Technology Act provides conditional safe-harbour immunity to intermediaries?

1. Section 43A 2. Section 66
3. Section 79 4. Section 85

30. The three components of Victor Vroom's Expectancy Theory of Motivation are:

1. Expectancy, Instrumentality, Valence
2. Effort, Satisfaction, Motivation
3. Needs, Drives, Reinforcement
4. Equity, Instrumentality, Efficiency

31. Which of the following are features of the Qualitative Research paradigm?

A. The research is concerned with understanding the social phenomena from the participant's perspective
B. It seeks to establish relationships, among variables and explains the causes of changes in measured social facts
C. It is conducted in actual settings as the direct source of data and the researcher is the key instrument
D. It is concerned with the process rather than simply with outcomes or products
E. It attempts to establish universal context-free generalization

Choose the ***correct*** answer from the options given below:

1. C, D, E only 2. A, C, D only
3. A, B, C only 4. B, C, D only

32. Arrange the following steps of the software development lifecycle in logical sequence:

A. Testing and debugging
B. System Design
C. Requirements Analysis
D. Implementation Coding
E. Maintenance

Choose the ***correct*** answer from the options given below:

1. B, C, A, D, E 2. C, A, E, B, D
3. A, E, C, D, B 4. C, D, B, A, E

33. The acronym 'SLATES' used by Andrew McAfee to describe the features of Web 2.0 website is ______:

1. Seamless, List, Augment, Tag, Effort, Syndication
2. Simple, Linking, Arbitrary, Test, Extension, Syndication
3. Search, Link, Authoring, Tags, Extension, Signal
4. Sequence, Linking, Ability, Testable, Effortless, Signal

34. Arrange the following digital repositories in order of their establishment:

A. ScienceOpen
B. NDLTD (Networked Digital Library of Theses and Dissertations)
C. SSRN (Social Science Research Network)
D. HathiTrust Digital Library
E. DOAJ (Directory of Open Access Journals)

Choose the ***correct*** answer from the options given below:

1. B, A, E, C, D 2. C, B, E, D, A
3. C, E, B, A, D 4. E, C, D, A, B

35. Given below are two statements: one is labelled as Assertion (A) and the other is labelled as Reason (R).

Assertion (A): Taxonomies provide higher semantic precision than folksonomies.

Reason (R): They are developed through formal term governance and strict hierarchical relationships.

In the light of the above statements, choose the ***most appropriate*** answer from the options given below:

1. Both (A) and (R) are correct and (R) is the correct explanation of (A)
2. Both (A) and (R) are correct, but (R) is NOT the correct explanation of (A)
3. (A) is correct, but (R) is not correct
4. (A) is not correct, but (R) is correct

36. In the context of Change Management, Arrange the 5 Stages of Grief introduced by Dr. Elisabeth Kubler-Ross in 1969 in correct order:

A. Depression B. Denial
C. Acceptance D. Anger
E. Bargaining

Choose the *correct* answer from the options given below:

1. B, D, E, A, C 2. B, E, D, C, A
3. A, B, C, D, E 4. B, D, A, E, C

37. Poole's Index to Periodicals Literature was brought out by ______.

1. H.P. Luhn 2. F.W. Lancaster
3. Van Rijsbergen 4. William Frederick

38. Given below are two statements: one is labelled as Assertion (A) and the other is labelled as Reason (R).

Assertion (A): Data must be authentic before it can be of any value in historical research, yet proof of authenticity does not establish its value, it must also be accurate.

Reason (R): External criticism is, therefore, referred to as lower criticism of the data.

In the light of the above statements, choose the *most appropriate* answer from the options given below

1. Both (A) and (R) are correct and (R) is the correct explanation of (A).
2. Both (A) and (R) are correct, but (R) is NOT the correct explanation of (A).
3. (A) is correct, but (R) is not correct.
4. (A) is not correct, but (R) is correct.

39. Arrange the following Six Sigma stages in the correct sequence:

A. Control B. Measure
C. Define D. Improve
E. Analyse

Choose the *correct* answer from the options given below:

1. B, C, A, E, D 2. A, E, B, D, C
3. C, B, E, D, A 4. C, D, B, A, E

40. Match the Programming Languages List-I with their propounder in List-II.

List-I (*Programming Languages*)	**List-II (*Propounder*)**
A. Perl	I. Dennis Ritchie
B. C	II. Bjarne Stroustrup
C. Python	III. Larry Wall
D. C++	IV. Guido van Rossum

Choose the *correct* answer from the options given below:

1. A-II, B-III, C-I, D-IV
2. A-III, B-I, C-IV, D-II
3. A-IV, B-II, C-III, D-I
4. A-III, B-IV, C-II, D-I

41. Commercial Web Syndication can be categorized by:

A. Mirror of the whole scientific content
B. Business models
C. Types of content
D. Purpose of content
E. Methods for selecting distribution partners

Choose the *correct* answer from the options given below:

1. A, B, E only 2. B, C, E only
3. A, B, C only 4. A, C, D only

42. Given below are two statements: one is labelled as Assertion (A) and the other is labelled as Reason (R).

Assertion (A): Web 2.0, known as the "read-write" web, introduced interactive, collaborative platforms: its tools and techniques were selectively adopted by libraries, giving rise to the concept of Library 2.0.

Reason (R): Semantic Web is one of the important feature of Web 2.0.

In the light of the above statements, choose the *most appropriate* answer from the options given below:

1. Both (A) and (R) are correct and (R) is the correct explanation of (A).
2. Both (A) and (R) are correct, but (R) is NOT the correct explanation of (A).
3. (A) is correct, but (R) is not correct.
4. (A) is not correct, but (R) is correct.

43. Match the Major distributors of GNU/Linux Operating System List-I with their year of release in List-II.

List-I (*GNU-Linux based OS*)	List-II (*Year of release*)
A. Debian	I. 2000
B. SUSE Linux Enterprise Server	II. 1993
C. Ubuntu	III. 2003
D. Fedora	IV. 2004

Choose the ***correct*** answer from the options given below:

1. A-II, B-I, C-IV, D-III
2. A-III, B-I, C-IV, D-II
3. A-IV, B-III, C-II, D-I
4. A-III, B-IV, C-II, D-I

44. Match the terms in List-I with descriptions in List-II.

List-I (*Terms*)	List-II (*Descriptions*)
A. Experimental method	I. A detailed description of the way people believe and act in a particular society
B. Ex-post facto method	II. Studies designed to obtain information concerning the current status of phenomena.
C. Descriptive survey method	III. Studying the effect of manipulating independent variable on dependent variable under appropriate control imposed.
D. Ethnographic method	IV. Conducting a probe into casual factors on the basis of evidences manifested.

Choose the ***correct*** answer from the options given below:

1. A-II, B-I, C-III, D-IV
2. A-III, B-IV, C-I, D-II
3. A-IV, B-II, C-III, D-I
4. A-I, B-II, C-IV, D-III

45. Given below are two statements: one is labelled as Assertion (A) and the other is labelled as Reason (R).

Assertion (A): During the network communication, when an attacker is 'Eavesdropping', it is referred to as sniffing or snooping. This kind of eavesdropping is the biggest security problem that administrators face while managing the network.

Reason (R): 'Eavesdropping' can be avoided by using strong encryption services that are based on Cryptography.

In the light of the above statements, choose the ***most appropriate*** answer from the options given below:

1. Both (A) and (R) are correct and (R) is the correct explanation of (A).
2. Both (A) and (R) are correct, but (R) is NOT the correct explanation of (A).
3. (A) is correct, but (R) is not correct.
4. (A) is not correct, but (R) is correct.

46. How many Volumes did the 1st edition of the Imperial Gazetteer of India contain?

1. 5 volumes
2. 7 volumes
3. 9 volumes
4. 12 volumes

47. Who were the founders of Frontiers?

1. Lawrence Lessig and Kamila Lessig
2. Henry Markram and Kamila Markram
3. Kamila Shamsie and Vint Cerf
4. Tim Berners-Lee and Robert Cailliau

48. The acronym MUSTIE, used in academic libraries for weeding, stands for:

1. Misleading, Ugly, Superseded, Trivial, Irrelevant, Elsewhere
2. Musty, Useless, Smelly, Torn, Imperfect, Exhausted

3. Misleading, Useless, Suspended. Tedious, Intricate, Expanded
4. Misplaced, Unavailable, Short, Temporary, Incomplete, Expired

49. Select the correct combinations:

A. Central tendency - Mean
B. Regression curve - Hypothesis
C. Refinement of judgement — Delphi method
D. Absolute zero point - Likert Scale
E. Descriptive statistics - Median

Choose the *correct* answer from the options given below:

1. B, D only
2. D, E only
3. A, C only
4. A, B only

50. Match the ISDN Standards List-I with respective correct Interface in List-II.

List-I (*ISDN Standards*)	List-II (*Interfaces*)
A. Basic Rate Interface (BRI)	I. They are not part of ISDN interfaces
B. Primary Rate Interface (PRI)	II. An extension of ISDN offering Asynchronous Transfer Mode (ATM)
C. B-ISDN	III. A high-capacity ISDN interface providing 23B channels plus one 64 kbps D channel for a total of 1536 kbps
D. Symmetric DSL Interface (ADSL) and Ultra-Advanced Rate Interface (UARI)	IV. A standard ISDN interface providing two 64 kbps channels for voice and data transmission

Choose the *correct* answer from the options given below:

1. A-II, B-III, C-I, D-IV
2. A-III, B-I, C-IV, D-II
3. A-IV, B-II, C-III, D-I
4. A-IV, B-III, C-II, D-I

51. WAI-ARIA, the accessible web content to people with disabilities, is approved by ______.

1. World Health Organisation (WHO)
2. W3C
3. United Nations Convention on the Rights of People with Disabilities (CRPD)
4. Dept. of Empowerment of Persons with Disabilities, Govt. of India

52. The research approach of Max Weber, to understand how people create meanings in natural settings, is identified as:

1. Positive Paradigm
2. Critical Paradigm
3. Contextual Paradigm
4. Interpretative Paradigm

53. Match the Books in List-I with Authors in List-II.

List-I (*Books*)	List-II (*Authors*)
A. The Changing Academic Library	I. Jose-Marie Griffiths
B. Planning Public Library Building	II. John Budd
C. Introduction to Public Librarianship	III. Michael Dewe
D. Special Libraries	IV. Kathleen de la Pana McCook

Choose the *correct* answer from the options given below:

1. A-III, B-IV, C-I, D-II
2. A-IV, B-I, C-II, D-III
3. A-I, B-II, C-III, D-IV
4. A-II, B-III, C-IV, D-I

54. What is the primary objective of the Listing of Open Access Databases (LOADB)?

A. To create a single portal of web-enabled, linked databases
B. To curate a collection of subscription-based databases using A to Z list
C. To classify and categorize Open Access Databases

D. To provide access customised Institutional Repository Databases

E. To assess the use of Open Access Databases

Choose the *correct* answer from the options given below:

1. B, E only
2. A, D only
3. A, C only
4. B, D only

55. Match Discipline (List-I) with their contribution (List-II) to Information Science.

List-I (*Discipline*)	List-II (*Explanation*)
A. Cognitive Psychology	I. Information theory and transmission models
B. Communication Engineering	II. User-centred design and usability
C. Linguistics	III. Information-seeking behaviour models
D. Human-Computer Interaction	IV. Natural language processing and indexing

Choose the *correct* answer from the options given below:

1. A-I, B-III, C-II, D-IV
2. A-II, B-I, C-III, D-IV
3. A-III, B-I, C-IV, D-II
4. A-II, B-IV, C-I, D-III

56. Arrange the following stages of the reference interview in the correct sequence.

A. Discussing and Clarifying the Question

B. Establishing Rapport with the User

C. Developing Strategy for Successful Search

D. Finding the Information and Evaluating it

E. Follow up

Choose the *correct* answer from the options given below:

1. A, B, C, D, E
2. B, A, D, C, E
3. B, A, C, D, E
4. B, C, A, D, E

57. When implementing RFID in libraries, which frequency band is most commonly used:

1. 10.56 MHz and UHF at 780-960 MHz
2. 13.56 MHz and UHF at 860-960 MHz
3. 16.56 MHz and UHF at 680-760 MHz
4. 32.56 MHz and UHF at 960-1020 MHz

58. Fac-Back-OPAC was developed by:

1. Casey Durfee
2. Nagender Aneja
3. Paul Andrew Roth
4. Edwards Ross

59. Arrange the following open Access Initiatives/Policy Statements according to the year of their adoption/declaration at international level:

A. The Coalition of Open Access Policy Institutions

B. The Berlin Declaration on Open Access to Knowledge in the Sciences and Humanities

C. The Budapest Open Access Initiatives

D. Scholarly Publishing and Academic Resources Coalition

E. Scottish Open Education Declaration

Choose the *correct* answer from the following options:

1. A, D, C, E, B
2. D, C, B, A, E
3. C, A, D, E, B
4. C, D, E, B, A

60. 'The Charter Act' which is considered as an important landmark in the context of academic libraries was published in the year?

1. 1815
2. 1813
3. 1817
4. 1818

61. Given below are two statements: one is labelled as Assertion (A) and the other is labelled as Reason (R).

Assertion (A): POPSI depends on classification schedules to derive terms.

Reason (R): Because it follows the same chain-building process as Chain Indexing.

In the light of the above statements, choose the ***most appropriate*** answer from the options given below

1. Both (A) and (R) are correct and (R) is the correct explanation of (A)
2. Both (A) and (R) are correct, but (R) is NOT the correct explanation of (A)
3. (A) is correct, but (R) is not correct
4. (A) is not correct, but (R) is correct

62. Using an appropriate Parametric Test in a research project, the researcher finds evidence to reject the Null Hypothesis. In doing so, ______ is likely to happen.

1. Alpha error
2. Beta error
3. Sampling error
4. Non-responsive error

63. Normal Probability Curve should be ______.

1. Positively Skewed
2. Negatively Skewed
3. Leptokurtic Skewed
4. Nutrality Skewed

64. Which association is responsible for publishing the Library Bill of Rights?

1. IFLA
2. ASLIB
3. CILIP
4. ALA

65. Jean Piaget gave a theory of Cognitive Development of Humans on the basis of his ______.

1. Fundamental Research
2. Applied Research
3. Evaluation Research
4. Action Research

66. Match the List-I (Health Information Products Standards and Services) offered by the National Library of Medicine, USA with List-II (Description).

List-I (*Information Products*)	List-II (*Description*)
A. Unified Medical Language system (UMLS)	I. provides normalised names for clinical drugs
B. Value Set Authority Center (VSAC)	II. A set of files and software that brings together many health and biomedical standards
C. RxNorm	III. One of a suite of designated standards for the electronic exchange of clinical health information
D. SNOMED CT	IV. A repository and authoring tool for standard lists of codes and terms from biomedical vocabularies

Choose the ***correct*** answer from the options given below:

1. A-II, B-III, C-I, D-IV
2. A-IV, B-III, C-II, D-I
3. A-II, B-IV, C-I, D-III
4. A-III, B-IV, C-II, D-I

67. As per Colon Classification, which of the following Main Classes have only Levels and No Rounds:

1. B-Mathematics, P-Linguistics, Z-Law
2. C-Physics, J-Agriculture, X-Economics
3. z-Generalia, O-Literature, Z-Law
4. 2-Library Science, E-Engineering, I-Botany

68. Match the terms in List-I with descriptions in List-II.

List-I (*Terms*)	List-II (*Description*)
A. Interval/Ratio	I. Variables containing data that have only two categories
B. Ordinal	II. Variables whose categories cannot be rank Ordered
C. Nominal	III. Variables where the distances between the Categories are identical across the range
D. Dichotomous	IV. Variables whose categories can be rank Ordered, but the distances between the Categories are not equal across the range

Choose the ***correct*** answer from the options given below:

1. A-IV, B-II, C-I, D-III
2. A-I, B-III, C-II, D-IV
3. A-III, B-IV, C-II, D-I
4. A-IV, B-II, C-III, D-I

69. Match the Authors in List-I with the Concepts/Ideas associated in List-II.

List-I (*Authors*)	List-II (*Concepts/Ideas*)
A. George Marcus	I. Social organism
B. Clifford Greetz	II. Ethnography as writing or thick description
C. Bronislaw Malinowski	III. Classical ethnographic fieldwork associated with functionalism
D. Durkheim	IV. Multi-sited ethnography

Choose the ***correct*** answer from the options given below:

1. A-I, B-IV, C-II, D-III
2. A-IV, B-II, C-III, D-I
3. A-III, B-I, C-IV, D-II
4. A-II, B-III, C-I, D-IV

70. The United Nations Convention on the Rights of People with Disabilities (CRPD) came into force in ______.

1. May 2006
2. December 2007
3. May 2008
4. December 2008

71. Within the context of HTTP, which statement most accurately reflects the analytical distinction between cookies and cache?

1. Cookies primarily enhance network performance, whereas cache is responsible for enforcing authentication.
2. Cookies are designed to store client-specific information, whereas cache retains reusable server responses.
3. Both cookies and cache serve the primary function of ensuring data confidentiality during transmission.
4. Cache is exclusively generated by the user, whereas cookies are exclusively generated by the server

72. CeCILL Free Software License Agreement was initiated by:

A. CEA (Atomic Energy Commission)

B. CNRS (National Centre for Scientific Research)

C. NIACL (National Institute of Advanced Computing and Logic)

D. INRIA (National Institute for Research in Digital Science and Technology)

E. RID (Research Institute for Development)

Choose the ***correct*** answer from the options given below:

1. A, C, D only
2. A, B, D only
3. A, B, E only
4. A, B, C only

73. Given below are two statements: one is labelled as Assertion (A) and the other is labelled as Reason (R).

Assertion (A): A cross break is a numerical tabular presentation of data usually in frequency or percentage form in which variables are cross-partitioned to study relations between them.

Reason (R): The categories are set up according to the research hypothesis.

In the light of the above statements, choose the ***most appropriate*** answer from the options given below

1. Both (A) and (R) are correct and (R) is the correct explanation of (A).
2. Both (A) and (R) are correct, but (R) is NOT the correct explanation of (A).
3. (A) is correct, but (R) is not correct.
4. (A) is not correct, but (R) is correct.

74. Arrange these technologies by their reading range capability (shortest to longest):

A. Barcode B. QR Code
C. NFC D. RFID
E. Biometric scanner

Choose the ***correct*** answer from the options given below:

1. E, A, B, C, D 2. C, A, E, D, B
3. E, B, A, D, C 4. A, E, C, D, B

75. In which of the following methods of research, the independent variable has to be selected rather than manipulated?

1. Descriptive survey method
2. Ex post facto method
3. Experimental method
4. Exegetic method

76. The ISDN Basic Rate Interface (BRI) provides two 64 Kbps B channels and one 16 Kbps D channel. The B channels are used for:

1. Signaling and Control Information
2. Error Correction
3. Multiplexing
4. Voice and Data Traffic

77. AIFF (.aif. .aiff, .aifc) file format is mainly used for ______.

1. Text, Audio and Video compressed format
2. Audio and Video files
3. Compressed Video files
4. Audio files

78. Match the Digital Library Project List-I with their initiators in List-II.

List-I (*Digital Library Project*)	**List-II** (*Initiators*)
A. Citebase	I. DARPA and NSF
B. eScholarship Repository	II. National Center for Biotechnology Information
C. PubMed	III. California Digital Library
D. Networked Computer Science Technical Reference Library (NCSTRL)	IV. Southampton University

Choose the ***correct*** answer from the options given below:

1. A-II, B-III, C-I, D-IV
2. A-III, B-I, C-IV, D-II
3. A-IV, B-III, C-II, D-I
4. A-III, B-IV, C-II, D-I

79. e-Granthalaya 4.0 was developed using an ASP.NET 4.0 front-end with AJAX, JQUERY, and JSON and ______ at back-end.

1. MySQL 2. PostgreSQL
3. MS-SQL 4. SQLite

80. Arrange the steps in producing rotated entries in PRECIS correctly:

A. Generate secondary entries by rotating the lead term
B. Maintain original word order in all entries

C. Display entries in alphabetical order
D. Choose main entry based on role indicator
E. Link rotated entries back to the main entry

Choose the ***correct*** answer from the options given below:

1. B, A, C, E, D 2. C, D, A, B, E
3. D, E, B, A, C 4. D, B, A, E, C

81. Given below are two statements: one is labelled as Assertion (A) and the other is labelled as Reason (R).

Assertion (A): Performance measurement in libraries is limited to cost accounting and does not assess progress toward goals or user impact.

Reason (R): Evaluation in libraries judges the worth utility of services for target users and helps improve efficiency, quality, timeliness, and productivity relative to costs.

In the light of the above statements, choose the ***most appropriate*** answer from the options given below

1. Both (A) and (R) are correct and (R) is the correct explanation of (A).
2. Both (A) and (R) are correct, but (R) is NOT the correct explanation of (A).
3. (A) is correct, but (R) is not correct.
4. (A) is not correct, but (R) is correct.

82. DRIDE (Digital Repository of Information and Data for Evolution) advocates for community-adopted standards for metadata and persistent identifiers in concert with:

A. DataCite B. ORCID
C. ROR D. Arxiv
E. Funder Registry

Choose the ***correct*** answer from the options given below:

1. A, C, E only 2. B, C, D only
3. A, B, E only 4. B, D, E only

83. Arrange Ranganathan's five fundamental canons of classification in logical sequence of application:

A. Canon of Differentiation
B. Canon of Ascertainability
C. Canon of Consistency
D. Canon of Relevance
E. Canon of Permanence

Choose the ***correct*** answer from the options given below:

1. C, D, E, B, A 2. B, D, A, C, E
3. D, C, A, E, B 4. C, A, E, B, D

84. Which compression protocol is considered a lossless method for bitonal images?

1. LZW 2. GIF
3. TIFF-G4 4. JPEG

85. Which of the following is the time limit for providing information under RTI Act 2005. when it concerns the life or liberty of a person?

1. 24 hours 2. 48 hours
3. 15 days 4. 30 days

86. Match the Source List-I (Databases) with Publisher in List-II.

List-I (*Databases*)	List-II (*Publisher*)
A. The Serials Directory	I. EBSCO
B. Ebrary	II. Clarivate
C. ScienceDirect	III. Elsevier
D. Current Contents Connect	IV. ProQuest

Choose the ***correct*** answer from the options given below:

1. A-II, B-I, C-III, D-IV
2. A-III, B-IV, C-II, D-I
3. A-I, B-III, C-IV, D-II
4. A-I, B-IV, C-III, D-II

87. In a client-server digital library architecture, what is a key function of the server?

1. Controlling access to information, retrieving it, and sending it to the client.
2. Analyse and Display the information retrieved from the client
3. Requesting and receiving information from the client.
4. All data processing on the client's local machine

88. Arrange the following key Citation Indexes of Web of Science in their chronological order of introduction:

A. Science Citation Index (SCI)

B. Science Citation Index Expanded (SCIE)

C. Arts & Humanities Citation Index (AHCI)

D. Social Sciences Citation Index (SSCI)

E. Emerging Sources Citation Index (ESCI)

Choose the *correct* answer from the options given below:

1. A, C, B, E, D 2. B, E, D, A, C
3. D, C, B, A, E 4. A, D, C, B, E

89. Match the Semantic Web Technologies List-I with their respective purpose in List-II.

List-I (*Web Technologies*)	List-II (*Purpose*)
A. RDF	I. Ontology definition language
B. RDFS	II. Resource description framework
C. OWL	III. Query language for RDF
D. SPARQL	IV. Schema definition for RDF

Choose the *correct* answer from the options given below:

1. A-II, B-IV, C-I, D-III
2. A-I, B-II, C-IV, D-III
3. A-III, B-I, C-II, D-IV
4. A-IV, B-III, C-II, D-I

90. Given below are two statements: one is labelled as Assertion (A) and the other is labelled as Reason (R).

Assertion (A): RSS (Really Simple Syndication) uses XML files that automatically update information from websites.

Reason (R): An RSS feed reader fetches these XML files and converts them into an easy-to-read format, showing headlines, summaries, and update notices with links back to the original articles.

In the light of the above statements, choose the ***most appropriate*** answer from the options given below

1. Both (A) and (R) are correct and (R) is the correct explanation of (A).
2. Both (A) and (R) are correct, but (R) is NOT the correct explanation of (A).
3. (A) is correct, but (R) is not correct.
4. (A) is not correct, but (R) is correct.

Directions (Qs. No. 91 to 95): *Read the following passage and answer the question:*

Artificial Intelligence (AI) has reshaped information retrieval in libraries by enabling faster, more accurate, and context-aware access to resources. Traditional systems relied heavily on Boolean logic, keyword matching, and subject indexing, often demanding strong search skills. In contrast, AI-driven tools use Natural Language Processing (NLP), Machine Learning (ML), and semantic search to interpret user intent and retrieve results that match the user's context. For instance, instead of listing thousands of items for a term like "digital preservation," AI systems can identify whether the user needs theoretical insights, technological solutions, or case studies and prioritise accordingly. Chatbots and Virtual Reference Services (VRS) represent another major advancement. Earlier reference services were limited by staff availability and slower response times. AI-enabled chatbots now provide 24/7 scalable support, assisting users with catalogue navigation, database searching, and citation queries. Enhanced VRS also include voice-enabled interaction, multilingual help, and links to institutional repositories and e-learning platforms, expanding access for remote and diverse users. However, AI adoption introduces challenges. Ethical concerns include data privacy, dependence on automated systems, and algorithmic bias, which may unintentionally suppress unconventional research areas if tools are trained on mainstream datasets. Additionally, chatbots, despite their efficiency, cannot replicate human empathy, judgement, or critical thinking, making a hybrid approach that blends AI with human expertise the most sustainable model. For LIS professionals, integrating AI demands new competencies. Librarians must develop skills in digital ethics, algorithmic transparency, and data analytics while ensuring that AI tools are critically assessed. Their role increasingly includes evaluating AI systems to ensure they align with educational goals, rather than purely commercial interests. Balancing human expertise with AI capabilities remains central to ensuring equitable and meaningful access.

91. According to the passage, Chatbots cannot replicate which essential human quality?

1. Empathy and contextual judgement
2. Speed in answering questions
3. Skill in citation formatting
4. Ability to cross-search database

92. Which scenario illustrates a potential ethical risk of AI-driven retrieval in libraries?

1. Increase in subscription cost.
2. Algorithm bias suppressing unconventional research.
3. A user choosing between ILMS and Web Content.
4. Difficulty in cataloging AI tools.

93. According to the passage, what is the primary advantage of Chatbots in library services?

1. They provide empathetic human-like interaction.
2. Ability to create new digital resources.
3. They offer 24/7 support and scalable access.
4. Automatic correction of cataloging errors.

94. What key responsibility of librarians is emphasized in relation to AI tools?

1. Designing all AI Algorithms personally
2. Reducing collection to fit digital needs
3. Evaluating AI tools for educational alignment
4. Ensuring venders fellow commercial interests

95. What approach does the passage consider most sustainable for library services?

1. Full automation replacing staff
2. Outsourcing all technical operations
3. Maintaining only human reference desk
4. Blending AI tools with human expertise

Directions (Qs. No. 96 to 100): *Read the following passage and answer the question:*

In the 21st century, Information Literacy (IL) has expanded from basic library search skills to a broad framework essential for academic success, research integrity, and lifelong learning. UNESCO defines IL as the ability to recognise when information is needed and to locate, evaluate, and use information effectively. This foundational cycle remains relevant even as IL now incorporates media, digital, and data literacies, reflecting the interconnected nature of today's information environment. The Association of College and Research Libraries (ACRL) reshaped IL through its Framework for Information Literacy in Higher Education (2015). Moving beyond rigid "standards," it introduced six conceptual "frames," such as "Authority is Constructed and Contextual" and "Searching as Strategic Exploration". These frames encourage deeper critical engagement with information sources and help learners navigate challenges like misinformation, disinformation, and algorithmic bias. IL intersects closely with media literacy, which promotes the critical evaluation of messages across media platforms; digital literacy, which emphasises effective use of digital tools: and data literacy, which focuses on interpreting, analysing, and ethically using data. Together, these literacies enable learners to question credibility, context, and potential manipulation. Ethics remains central to IL. Issues such as plagiarism, improper attribution, and misuse of data highlight the need for students to understand citation practices and intellectual property rights. Librarians play a key instructional role, designing IL programs that balance technical skills with responsible scholarship. IL education increasingly interacts with AI. Tools like ChatGPT and AI-driven discovery systems support research but also raise concerns about accuracy and transparency. Librarians must therefore help students critically evaluate AI outputs, verify information, and distinguish between authoritative sources and machine-generated content, placing IL at the forefront of human-AI collaboration.

96. Why does the integration of AI tools like ChatGPT into IL education require a shift in librarians' roles?

1. Because librarians must teach students to critically assess AI outputs rather than accept them at face value.
2. Because AI tools fully replace traditional reference services.
3. Because AI tools guarantee accuracy and remove the need for source verification.
4. Because students can now rely exclusively on machine-generated summaries.

97. Why is UNESCO's definition of IL still relevant despite the rise of media and data literacies?

1. It prioritises cataloguing over critical thinking skills
2. It provides a universal cycle of recognizing, locating, evaluating, using information
3. It restricts IL to physical library contexts only
4. It discourages integration with other forms of literacy

98. According to the passage, how has the scope of Information Literacy evolved in the digital age?

1. It now integrates media, digital, and data literacies.
2. It remains limited to library catalogue search skills.
3. It only concerns citation management.
4. It is replaced entirely by AI literacy

99. What major shift did the ACRL Framework introduce?

1. Prescribed rule for using catalogue
2. A checklist for skill acquisition
3. More focus on hardware tools in libraries
4. Conceptual framework replacing rigid standards

100. Why is Data Literacy (DL) considered a crucial complement to Information Literacy (IL) today?

1. DL ensures exclusive use of quantitative data in decision-making
2. DL trains users to ethically interpret and analyse data for credibility and bias
3. DL eliminates the need for evaluating sources of information
4. DL focuses only on automating data collection processes

ANSWERS

1	2	3	4	5	6	7	8	9	10
1	2	*	4	3	3	2	2	3	2
11	**12**	**13**	**14**	**15**	**16**	**17**	**18**	**19**	**20**
3	2	1	4	3	1	4	3	4	1
21	**22**	**23**	**24**	**25**	**26**	**27**	**28**	**29**	**30**
2	2	3	4	4	2, 3	3	*	3	1
31	**32**	**33**	**34**	**35**	**36**	**37**	**38**	**39**	**40**
2	*	3	2	1	1	4	1	3	2
41	**42**	**43**	**44**	**45**	**46**	**47**	**48**	**49**	**50**
2	3	1	*	1	3	2	1	3	4

51	52	53	54	55	56	57	58	59	60
2	4	4	3	3	3	2	1	2	2
61	**62**	**63**	**64**	**65**	**66**	**67**	**68**	**69**	**70**
4	1	4	4	1	3	3	3	2	3
71	**72**	**73**	**74**	**75**	**76**	**77**	**78**	**79**	**80**
2	2	1	1	2	4	4	3	2	4
81	**82**	**83**	**84**	**85**	**86**	**87**	**88**	**89**	**90**
4	1	*	3	2	4	1	4	1	1
91	**92**	**93**	**94**	**95**	**96**	**97**	**98**	**99**	**100**
1	2	3	3	4	1	2	1	4	2

EXPLANATORY ANSWERS

1. • The scientific research process begins with defining the research problem clearly and precisely, because without a properly identified problem, the study lacks direction and purpose. A well-defined problem helps in setting the boundaries of the investigation and identifying what exactly needs to be studied.
   • After that, the researcher should conduct a comprehensive literature review. This step is necessary to understand earlier work, identify research gaps, avoid duplication, and build a theoretical base. Only after reviewing the available literature can the researcher know what remains unexplored.
   • The next logical step is formulation of testable hypotheses based on research gaps. Hypotheses are not framed in isolation; they arise from the research problem and the literature already studied. They give the research a predictive and testable direction.
   • Once hypotheses are ready, the researcher proceeds to collect high-quality data according to the research design. Data collection must come after conceptual preparation, because the method, tools, and variables depend on the problem and hypotheses already formulated.
   • Finally, the process ends with preparing and presenting the research report with findings and recommendations. This is the concluding stage where results are interpreted, organized, and communicated in a systematic academic form.

2. Assertion (A) is valid because Academic Social Networking (ASN) platforms such as ResearchGate, Academia.edu, and Mendeley are designed specifically for scholarly communication. They allow researchers to share publications, discuss research findings, build professional profiles, follow other scholars, and collaborate across institutions and countries. These functions significantly strengthen academic interaction and knowledge dissemination within the research community. The Reason (R) is also factually correct because ASN platforms can indirectly enhance opportunities related to research funding. By increasing the visibility of researchers, displaying citation metrics, showcasing publications, and enabling connections with collaborators or institutions, these platforms may help researchers become known to potential sponsors or collaborators. However, this aspect does not explain why ASN sites promote scholarly communication. The promotion of scholarly communication mainly arises from features such as publication sharing, networking tools, discussion threads, and collaborative interactions rather than funding opportunities. Therefore, while both statements are true individually, the Reason does not serve as the correct explanation of the Assertion.

3. • The given matching does not fit correctly because the actual establishment or launch years of these institutions/databases are not represented properly in the options. So none of the four options can be accepted as fully correct.

- JSTOR was launched in the mid-1990s, not in 1950 or 1955.

  JISC was established in 1993, so that part can match III, but the full option still fails because the other pairs do not align properly.
- ORBICOM is also a much later body and does not belong to 1950 in the proper historical sense given here.

  ERIC was established in the 1960s, not in 1993 or 1996. Therefore, the entire question contains mismatch in the year-pairing.
- Since the listed years do not correctly correspond to all the items in List-I, the most accurate response is NONE.

This is the safest and fully correct answer because no given option matches all pairs exactly.

4. In MARC, the 00X fields are control fields, and they have special structural features different from variable data fields. They are fixed-length fields, so statement A is correct. They are used for coded or control information rather than descriptive text, which makes statement C correct as well. These fields also do not contain subfield codes, so statement E is correct. Statement B is incorrect because control fields do not use indicators; indicators are used in variable fields. Statement D is also incorrect because control fields are not always repeatable. Therefore, the correct combination is A, C and E only, which is exactly given in option 4.

5. Geographical Indications are signs used on goods that identify them as originating from a specific geographical territory, so statement B is correct. They are also associated with qualities, reputation, or other characteristics that arise because of that geographical origin, so statement D is correct. Further, once registered, GIs can generally be renewed indefinitely for successive periods, which makes statement E correct. Statement A is incorrect because a GI is not owned by an individual inventor; it is linked to a community, association, or authorized producers of a region. Statement C is also incorrect because protection of technological innovation and invention belongs to patents, not GIs. Hence the correct set is B, D, E only.

6. The Quality Trilogy is a well-known concept in quality management proposed by Joseph Juran. It consists of three interconnected managerial processes: quality planning, quality control, and quality improvement. Quality planning involves identifying customers, determining their needs, and developing processes capable of meeting those needs. Quality control focuses on monitoring operations and ensuring that performance remains within acceptable standards through measurement and corrective action. Quality improvement aims at achieving breakthrough improvements by identifying root causes of problems and eliminating them permanently. Juran emphasized that managing quality requires a systematic managerial approach rather than only statistical techniques. His trilogy became a central framework in Total Quality Management and strongly influenced modern quality practices in manufacturing, services, and organizational management. Deming focused mainly on statistical process control and PDCA cycle, Crosby emphasized "zero defects," and Ishikawa contributed tools like cause-and-effect diagrams. Therefore the Quality Trilogy is specifically associated with Joseph Juran.

7. Andrew Keen, a British-American entrepreneur and author, strongly criticized the culture of Web 2.0 in his influential book The Cult of the Amateur (2007). He argued that Web 2.0 platforms encouraged user-generated content without adequate quality control, leading to what he described as a "digital forest of mediocrity." According to Keen, the internet allowed anyone to publish music, poems, essays, or opinions regardless of expertise, which in his view undermined professional journalism, literature, and cultural standards. His critique suggested that the democratization of publishing through blogs, social media, and collaborative platforms sometimes produced large amounts of low-quality or unverified information. While many scholars defend Web 2.0 for enabling participation and knowledge sharing, Keen's criticism became widely cited in discussions about digital culture, information quality, and the reliability of user-generated content online.

8. Unicode represents characters through several standardized encoding schemes designed to support global text processing.

- **UTF-8:** This is a variable-length encoding widely used on the internet. It uses one to four bytes per character and is backward compatible with ASCII, which makes it highly efficient for web technologies and modern operating systems.

- **UTF-16:** This encoding uses two or four bytes for characters and is commonly used in many programming environments such as Java and Windows systems. It efficiently represents characters in the Basic Multilingual Plane and supports extended characters using surrogate pairs.
- **UTF-32:** This encoding uses four bytes for every character, providing fixed-length representation and allowing direct indexing of characters, though it consumes more memory compared to UTF-8 and UTF-16.

Encodings like UTF-64 and UTF-128 are not defined or standardized by Unicode. Hence only UTF-8, UTF-16 and UTF-32 are valid Unicode encoding schemes.

9. The PMB Integrated Library Management System (ILMS) was developed and launched by Francois Lemarchand. It is a library automation system designed to support core library management operations such as cataloguing, circulation, acquisitions, and database management. Integrated Library Management Systems combine several library functions within a single computerized framework so that bibliographic records, user information, and transaction data can be managed efficiently. The PMB system gained recognition as an open-source library management solution and has been implemented in various libraries for managing digital catalogues and circulation services. Its development contributed to the broader movement toward automated and integrated library operations, which replaced earlier manual cataloguing and record-keeping systems.

10. In information retrieval systems, pre-coordinate indexing systems assign and arrange subject terms in a predetermined order at the time of indexing. This means the relationships among concepts are fixed when the index entry is created. Because the combinations are predetermined, users cannot easily combine new concepts or rearrange terms during retrieval. This lack of flexibility is the primary disadvantage of pre-coordinate systems compared to post-coordinate systems. In post-coordinate indexing, individual descriptors are assigned separately, and users combine them during the search process using logical operations such as AND, OR, and NOT. Pre-coordinate systems were historically suitable for printed indexes and catalogues, but their rigid structure limits dynamic searching capabilities in modern digital retrieval environments.

11. Digital information stored in libraries faces the risk of technological obsolescence because hardware, operating systems, and file formats continuously evolve. If digital files remain in outdated formats or rely on obsolete software, they may become unreadable even though the data itself still exists. The most effective preservation strategy during the storage phase is therefore periodic format migration and emulation. Format migration involves converting files from older formats into newer standardized formats so that they remain usable with current software. Emulation, on the other hand, recreates the original hardware or software environment so that old digital objects can still be accessed exactly as they were created. Together these methods ensure long-term accessibility of digital resources and are widely used in digital preservation frameworks such as the OAIS model. Other options such as copyright checks, simple backups without migration, or restricting access do not solve the fundamental problem of technological obsolescence.

12. According to the updated guidelines issued by the Indian Computer Emergency Response Team (CERT-In) in April 2022 regarding information security practices for government entities and organizations, cybersecurity incidents must be reported within six hours of noticing such incidents or being brought to notice about them. The directive was introduced to strengthen India's national cybersecurity response mechanism by ensuring rapid detection, reporting, and mitigation of cyber threats. Incidents that require reporting include unauthorized access to IT systems, data breaches, targeted scanning or probing of systems, attacks on servers or networks, ransomware incidents, identity theft, and other cyber intrusions. Quick reporting within this six-hour window allows CERT-In to analyze threats promptly, coordinate responses across affected organizations, and prevent wider systemic damage. The rule therefore forms a critical component of India's cybersecurity governance framework.

13. Identity theft is specifically addressed under Section 66C of the Information Technology Act, 2000 (as amended in 2008). This section deals with fraudulent or dishonest use of another person's electronic signature, password, or any other unique identification feature. If an individual uses someone else's digital identity or authentication credentials without authorization for unlawful purposes, it constitutes identity theft under this provision. The law prescribes punishment in the form of imprisonment that may extend to three years and also includes a monetary fine. This provision became particularly important with the growth of digital services, online transactions, and electronic authentication systems, where misuse of credentials such as passwords, digital signatures, or biometric identifiers can lead to serious financial and privacy violations.

14. During the dissemination phase of the information life cycle, information is shared with users through publications, repositories, databases, or other channels. An ethical dilemma often arises when institutions attempt to balance the principles of open access with the need to protect sensitive or confidential information. Open access promotes transparency, wider knowledge sharing, and equitable access to research outputs. However, some datasets may contain personal, confidential, or security-sensitive information that cannot ethically or legally be made fully public. Therefore, librarians and information professionals must carefully evaluate privacy concerns, data protection laws, intellectual property rights, and ethical responsibilities while deciding what information should be openly accessible and what should be restricted or anonymized. This tension between openness and protection of sensitive data represents a genuine ethical dilemma in information dissemination.

15. **C. Identify the class number of the document:** The first step in chain indexing is determining the correct classification number of the document using a classification scheme such as the Colon Classification. The class number represents the subject content of the document in a structured hierarchical form and becomes the starting point for deriving the subject chain.

B. Derive the chain of terms from the class number: After identifying the class number, the indexer traces the hierarchical chain embedded within that number. Each segment of the class number represents a broader-to-narrower conceptual relationship which forms the chain of subject terms.

A. Select links and isolates from the chain: From the derived chain, the indexer selects appropriate links (broader subject terms) and isolates (specific subject elements). These selected components represent the most meaningful subject access points for indexing.

E. Prepare subject heading entries (Main, Subordinate, Coordinate) Based on the selected links and isolates, different subject heading entries are prepared. These include the main heading, subordinate headings, and coordinate entries so that the document can be retrieved through multiple related subject approaches.

D. Arrange the headings in alphabetical order for the index: Finally, all the prepared subject entries are arranged alphabetically in the index. This step ensures systematic organization and enables users to locate the required subject entries quickly within the index structure.

16. Clifford Lynch is widely recognized for introducing and discussing the idea of canonicalization in the context of digital preservation and digital libraries. Canonicalization refers to transforming digital objects into a standardized or canonical form so that they can remain interpretable and usable even when technologies, file formats, or software environments become obsolete. Lynch argued that preserving the exact original digital environment is often impractical over long periods. Instead, repositories should maintain a normalized representation of the digital content that can be reliably migrated, re-rendered, or interpreted by future systems. This idea became influential in the development of long-term digital preservation strategies used in institutional repositories and digital archives. His work significantly shaped discussions on how digital repositories maintain authenticity, accessibility, and usability of digital objects across technological changes, which is why Clifford Lynch is credited with introducing the concept of canonicalization.

17. **B. Prefix element:** The ISBN system begins with a prefix element (currently 978 or 979), which identifies the number as part of the global ISBN system compatible with the EAN-13 barcode structure. This prefix ensures international standardization of book identification.

E. Registration group element: The second component identifies the country, geographical region, or language group participating in the ISBN system. For example, English-speaking countries share certain registration group numbers.

A. Registrant element: This element identifies the specific publisher or imprint responsible for the publication. Each publisher receives a unique registrant number allocated by the national ISBN agency.

D. Publication element: This element identifies a particular title or edition produced by the publisher. Each separate edition or format of a publication receives a different publication element.

C. Check digit: The final element is the check digit, which is mathematically calculated to validate the correctness of the entire ISBN number and detect transcription errors.

18. The Multicultural Library Manifesto was primarily developed by the International Federation of Library Associations and Institutions (IFLA). The manifesto emphasizes that libraries must serve culturally and linguistically diverse communities by providing equitable access to information regardless of cultural background, language, ethnicity, or nationality. It highlights the role of libraries in promoting intercultural dialogue, social inclusion, and equal participation in knowledge societies. The document encourages libraries to build collections representing different cultures, support multilingual services, and ensure that library staff possess cultural competencies necessary to serve diverse user groups. Although UNESCO endorsed and supported the dissemination of the manifesto, its primary development and advocacy were undertaken by IFLA within the global library community.

19. In the context of this objective question, Edanz is treated as associated with Sage. Multiple exam-oriented sources that address this exact question identify Sage as the expected answer. Edanz is an independent author-services company, but for this MCQ framing, the accepted association is with Sage Publications rather than Elsevier, Springer, or Wiley. Therefore, for this question, the answer should be marked as Option 4.

20. The Semantic Web relies on structured data representation so that machines can understand relationships between information resources. RDF (Resource Description Framework) provides the foundational model for describing resources using subject–predicate–object triples, allowing information to be expressed in a machine-readable graph structure. RDFS (RDF Schema) extends RDF by introducing vocabulary for defining classes, properties, hierarchies, and relationships among resources. Through constructs such as rdfs:Class, rdfs:subClassOf, and rdfs:domain and rdfs:range, RDFS enables the creation of structured knowledge models that resemble ontologies. Because RDF provides the basic descriptive framework and RDFS supplies the schema vocabulary needed to define conceptual relationships, together they serve as essential tools for constructing ontologies within the Semantic Web architecture. Therefore, the Reason correctly explains why RDF and RDFS are essential for ontology development.

21. **A. Physical Layer → III. Fibre Optics:**

The Physical layer of the OSI model deals with the transmission of raw bit streams over a physical medium. It defines hardware elements such as cables, connectors, transmission media, and signal modulation. Fibre optic technology is a physical transmission medium that carries data as light pulses through glass fibres. Hence it belongs to the Physical layer.

B. Network Layer → IV. ICMP (Internet Control Message Protocol)

The Network layer is responsible for logical addressing, routing, and packet forwarding between networks. ICMP operates at this layer and is used for error reporting, diagnostics, and network status messages (e.g., "Destination Unreachable" or "Time Exceeded"). Therefore ICMP corresponds to the Network layer.

C. Session Layer → II. PPTP (Point-to-Point Tunnelling Protocol)

The Session layer manages the establishment, maintenance, and termination of communication sessions between systems. PPTP establishes a secure communication tunnel and manages session-oriented communication between client and server, aligning it with the Session layer functionality.

D. Application Layer → I. DNS (Domain Name System)

The Application layer provides services directly to end-user applications such as email, file transfer, and domain name resolution. DNS translates domain names into IP addresses so that applications can locate network resources, making it an Application layer protocol.

22. The ISO/IEC 27000 family of standards is designed to provide a comprehensive framework for managing information security within organizations. These standards define requirements and best practices for establishing, implementing, maintaining, and continually improving an Information Security Management System (ISMS). The family includes standards such as ISO/IEC 27001, which specifies the formal requirements for an ISMS, and ISO/IEC 27002, which provides guidelines for information security controls. The purpose of these standards is to protect the confidentiality, integrity, and availability of information by addressing risks related to cyber threats, data breaches, unauthorized access, and system vulnerabilities. Organizations across sectors adopt ISO/IEC 27000 standards to strengthen data protection, manage security risks systematically, and ensure compliance with international information security practices.

23. E. Bhore Committee on Medical Libraries (1943): The Bhore Committee (Health Survey and Development Committee) was established in 1943 to evaluate health services in India. It emphasized the importance of medical libraries and information services for strengthening medical education and healthcare research.

C. Advisory Committee for Libraries (Sinha Committee) (1957): The Sinha Committee was formed to examine the development and coordination of library services in India and recommended measures for strengthening the national library system.

B. UGC Library Committee (Ranganathan) (1957): The University Grants Commission constituted a Library Committee under S.R. Ranganathan to study the condition of university libraries and recommend improvements in staffing, funding, and library services.

A. Sankaran Committee on Health Science Libraries (1965): This committee focused specifically on the development and improvement of health science libraries in India, including better coordination among medical library networks.

D. D.P. Chattopadhyaya Committee on NAPLIS (1986): The committee led by D.P. Chattopadhyaya examined the establishment of a National Policy on Library and Information System (NAPLIS) to strengthen the overall LIS infrastructure in India.

24. The McKinsey 7S Model identifies seven interdependent organizational elements required for effective organizational performance. These elements are divided into hard elements and soft elements. The soft elements are less tangible, culture-oriented, and difficult to define formally. They include Shared Values, Skills, Staff, and Style. Shared values represent the core beliefs and culture of the organization that guide behaviour and decision-making. Skills refer to the competencies and capabilities possessed by employees. Staff relates to the people within the organization and how they are developed and managed. On the other hand, System and Strategy are categorized as hard elements because they are more formal, structured, and easier to identify or modify. Therefore the soft elements among the given options are Shared Values, Skills, and Staff.

25. Colon Classification (6th Revised Edition) is fundamentally an analytico-synthetic (faceted) classification system where most subjects are constructed by synthesizing facets according to PMEST principles. However, within the structure of the scheme, the Schedules of Classic and Sacred Books with Special Names constitute an enumerative section. In this part, specific classic literary works, sacred texts, and well-known titles are assigned ready-made class numbers rather than requiring the classifier to build numbers through facet analysis. Because these works are frequently cited and historically significant, Ranganathan provided them in a pre-enumerated form to simplify classification and ensure uniformity in cataloguing across libraries. By contrast, the Schedules of Classification mainly provide the faceted framework for constructing class numbers, while Rules explain the procedures for synthesis and Annexures supply auxiliary tables. Therefore, the part of the Colon Classification (6th Revised Edition) that is considered enumerative is the Schedules of Classic and Sacred Books.

26. Both χ^2 (Chi Square) and ANOVA are used to test the Null Hypothesis: The null hypothesis (H_0) represents a statistical statement that there is no relationship, difference, or effect between variables in a population. Hypothesis testing in statistics uses different tests depending on the nature of the data and the research design. The Chi-Square (χ^2) test is a non-parametric statistical test mainly used for categorical data to determine whether there is a significant association between variables or whether observed frequencies differ from expected frequencies. It directly tests the null hypothesis that variables are independent or that observed frequencies do not significantly deviate from expected ones. ANOVA (Analysis of Variance) is a parametric statistical test used when comparing the means of three or more groups. It tests the null hypothesis that all group means are equal in the population. Both tests therefore begin with a null hypothesis and use statistical criteria to accept or reject it. Since the question asks generally which method is used to test the null hypothesis without specifying the type of variables, scale of measurement, or research design, both χ^2 and ANOVA correctly fit the requirement. Selecting only one would ignore another equally valid statistical method used for null hypothesis testing. Therefore the most accurate answer is NONE, because both options 2 and 3 are correct depending on the research situation.

27. **A. Intersubjectivity → I. This means occurring between or among two or more subjects or conscious minds**

Intersubjectivity refers to the shared understanding that emerges between individuals. It emphasizes how meanings and interpretations are formed through interaction among conscious subjects.

B. Insider/Outsider Perspective → IV. One way of thinking about the difference in the epistemologies of hermeneutics and naturalism

The insider–outsider perspective explains the difference between understanding a phenomenon from within a cultural or social group (insider) versus interpreting it from an external analytical viewpoint (outsider).

C. Participatory Action Research → III. Research that places a premium on the politics and power of knowledge production and uses

Participatory Action Research emphasizes collaboration between researchers and participants, focusing on empowerment, social change, and critical examination of knowledge production.

D. Methodology → II. The theory of how the inquiry should proceed

Methodology refers to the theoretical framework that explains how research should be conducted, guiding the choice of methods, techniques, and procedures.

28. The chronological sequence of the character representation standards does not perfectly match any of the given options due to ambiguity in the placement of Extended ASCII.

The correct historical development of these standards is generally understood as follows:

D. EBCDIC (1963): Extended Binary Coded Decimal Interchange Code was developed by IBM in 1963 for use in IBM mainframe computers. It was one of the earliest widely used character encoding schemes in commercial computing systems.

B. ASCII (1963–1967 standardization): The American Standard Code for Information Interchange (ASCII) was developed around 1963 and later standardized in 1967. It became the dominant 7-bit character encoding system used in computer systems and communication protocols.

C. ISCII (1988): The Indian Script Code for Information Interchange (ISCII) was introduced in 1988 to represent Indian language scripts in digital form.

E. **Extended ASCII (late 1980s):** Extended ASCII refers to several 8-bit extensions of ASCII, such as ISO-8859 variants and code pages. These appeared mainly in the 1980s, but they were not introduced as a single formally dated standard, which creates ambiguity in exact chronological placement relative to ISCII.

A. **Unicode (1991):** Unicode was introduced in 1991 to create a universal character encoding system capable of representing characters from virtually all writing systems of the world.

Because Extended ASCII does not have a single precise year of introduction and overlaps historically with other encoding developments, the exact chronological order among ISCII and Extended ASCII cannot be matched precisely with any option provided. None of the options correctly reflects the historically accepted sequence (EBCDIC → ASCII → ISCII/Extended ASCII → Unicode) without ambiguity. Therefore the most accurate answer is NONE.

29. Section 79 of the Information Technology Act, 2000 (as amended in 2008) provides conditional safe-harbour immunity to intermediaries. Intermediaries include internet service providers, web hosting services, search engines, online marketplaces, and social media platforms that transmit or host information on behalf of users. According to this provision, intermediaries are not held liable for third-party information hosted or transmitted through their platforms if they observe due diligence and comply with government guidelines. The immunity applies only when the intermediary does not initiate the transmission, select the receiver, or modify the content of the information. If an intermediary becomes aware of unlawful content and fails to remove it within the prescribed time, the protection may be withdrawn.

30. Victor Vroom's Expectancy Theory of Motivation explains how individuals decide to exert effort based on expectations about outcomes. The theory consists of three key components. Expectancy refers to the belief that increased effort will improve performance. Instrumentality refers to the belief that good performance will lead to desired rewards or outcomes. Valence represents the value or attractiveness that an individual places on the expected reward. According to Vroom, motivation occurs when individuals believe that their effort will result in performance, performance will lead to rewards, and those rewards are personally valuable. These three elements interact multiplicatively to determine the overall motivational force influencing behavior in organizations.

31. **A. The research is concerned with understanding the social phenomena from the participant's perspective**

Qualitative research focuses on understanding human experiences, meanings, and interpretations from the viewpoint of participants. Researchers attempt to explore how individuals perceive and interpret their social reality.

C. It is conducted in actual settings as the direct source of data and the researcher is the key instrument

Qualitative studies are typically carried out in natural or real-life settings such as communities, organizations, or institutions. The researcher personally collects and interprets data through observation, interviews, and interaction.

D. It is concerned with the process rather than simply with outcomes or products

Qualitative research emphasizes understanding the process, context, and dynamics behind social phenomena. Instead of only measuring outcomes, it studies how and why certain social patterns or behaviours occur.

32. The logical sequence of the Software Development Life Cycle (SDLC) steps does not match any of the given options.

The correct sequence of SDLC is:

C. **Requirements Analysis** – The process begins with gathering and analyzing user requirements to understand what the system should accomplish.

B. **System Design** – Based on requirements, the architecture and design of the system are prepared, including data structures, interfaces, and system components.

D. **Implementation Coding** – Developers translate the design into actual program code using programming languages.

A. Testing and Debugging – The developed system is tested to detect errors, verify functionality, and ensure that it meets specified requirements.

E. Maintenance – After deployment, the system undergoes maintenance to correct faults, improve performance, and adapt to changing requirements.

Thus the correct order should be C, B, D, A, E, which is not present in any of the provided options, therefore the correct answer is NONE.

33. The acronym SLATES, proposed by Andrew McAfee, describes the fundamental components of Enterprise 2.0 and Web 2.0 environments that enable collaborative knowledge sharing. Search allows users to easily locate information within digital systems. Link enables the creation of connections between resources and information objects. Authoring allows users to generate and publish content through blogs, wikis, and collaborative platforms. Tags help in organizing content through user-generated labels, enabling easier retrieval and categorization. Extension refers to systems recommending content automatically based on user behaviour and patterns. Signal involves technologies such as RSS feeds that notify users about updates or new content. Together, these six elements describe how Web 2.0 technologies facilitate collaborative knowledge creation and information discovery.

34. C. SSRN (Social Science Research Network) – 1994: SSRN was founded in 1994 as an online repository for preprints and working papers in social sciences, economics, law, and related disciplines.

B. NDLTD (Networked Digital Library of Theses and Dissertations) – 1996: NDLTD was initiated in 1996 to promote electronic theses and dissertations and improve access to graduate research worldwide.

E. DOAJ (Directory of Open Access Journals) – 2003: DOAJ was launched in 2003 to provide a comprehensive directory of high-quality peer-reviewed open access journals.

D. HathiTrust Digital Library – 2008: HathiTrust was established in 2008 as a large-scale collaborative digital repository created by major research libraries to preserve and provide access to digitized collections.

A. ScienceOpen – 2013: ScienceOpen was launched in 2013 as an open research platform integrating publishing, networking, and research discovery services.

35. Taxonomies are structured systems of classification in which terms are organized in hierarchical relationships such as broader term, narrower term, and related term. Because the vocabulary is controlled and relationships between terms are clearly defined, taxonomies provide higher semantic precision and consistency in information organization and retrieval. In contrast, folksonomies rely on user-generated tags that are created freely without formal control, which often leads to inconsistency, ambiguity, and lack of hierarchy. The Reason correctly explains why taxonomies provide higher semantic precision: they are developed through formal governance of terms and strict hierarchical relationships that ensure conceptual clarity and systematic organization of knowledge.

36. B. Denial – The first stage occurs when individuals initially refuse to accept or acknowledge the change. It acts as a psychological defense mechanism to buffer the immediate shock of a new reality.

D. Anger – When denial fades, frustration and resentment arise. Individuals may blame management, circumstances, or others responsible for the change.

E. Bargaining – At this stage individuals attempt to negotiate or seek compromises to reduce the perceived impact of the change. They may try to delay or modify the change.

A. Depression – As the reality of change becomes unavoidable, feelings of sadness, discouragement, and withdrawal may appear. Productivity and morale may decline.

C. Acceptance – In the final stage individuals come to terms with the change, adapt to the new situation, and begin to move forward productively.

37. Poole's Index to Periodical Literature was first compiled in 1848 by William Frederick Poole, an American librarian. It was the earliest comprehensive indexing tool designed to help readers locate articles in English-language periodicals. Before this index, accessing information from magazines and journals was extremely difficult because articles were not systematically indexed. Poole's work provided subject access to a wide range of periodical literature and became a pioneering development in bibliographic control and indexing. It greatly influenced later indexing and abstracting services used in libraries.

38. In historical research methodology, the evaluation of sources involves two important processes: external criticism and internal criticism. External criticism verifies the authenticity of a document by examining aspects such as authorship, date, handwriting, material, and origin. Because it focuses on establishing whether the source itself is genuine, it is also called lower criticism. However, even if a document is authentic, the information it contains may still be inaccurate, biased, or misleading. Therefore researchers must also apply internal criticism, which evaluates the accuracy and reliability of the content. The assertion correctly explains that authenticity alone does not establish value unless the information is accurate. The reason clarifies why authenticity is examined through external criticism, known as lower criticism. Thus the reason explains the assertion.

39. **C. Define** – The Six Sigma process begins by clearly defining the problem, project scope, objectives, and customer requirements.

B. Measure – Relevant data about the existing process is collected to determine current performance levels and establish baseline metrics.

E. Analyse – Data is analyzed to identify root causes of defects, inefficiencies, or variations in the process.

D. Improve – Solutions are developed and implemented to remove root causes and enhance process performance.

A. Control – Control mechanisms such as monitoring systems, standards, and documentation are established to sustain the improvements.

40. **A. Perl → III. Larry Wall** – Perl was created by Larry Wall in 1987 mainly for text processing, scripting, and system administration tasks.

B. C → I. Dennis Ritchie – The C programming language was developed by Dennis Ritchie at Bell Labs in the early 1970s and became one of the most influential programming languages.

C. Python → IV. Guido van Rossum – Python was developed by Guido van Rossum and first released in 1991, emphasizing readability and simplicity.

D. C++ → II. Bjarne Stroustrup – C++ was developed by Bjarne Stroustrup in 1985 as an extension of the C language incorporating object-oriented programming features.

41. **B. Business models** – Commercial web syndication is often categorized based on the business arrangements between content providers and distributors. These include subscription-based syndication, licensing models, revenue-sharing arrangements, and advertising-supported distribution models.

C. Types of content – Syndication can also be classified by the nature of the content being distributed, such as news feeds, blogs, multimedia, scholarly articles, or RSS feeds. Different content types require different syndication mechanisms and platforms.

E. Methods for selecting distribution partners – Another categorization relates to how distribution partners are chosen, such as open syndication networks, controlled partnerships, affiliate distribution channels, or platform-based content aggregation. These methods determine how and where the syndicated content reaches users.

42. The assertion correctly states that Web 2.0, often called the "read-write web," introduced interactive and collaborative platforms such as blogs, wikis, social networking sites, tagging systems, and user-generated content services. Libraries adopted many of these tools to enhance user participation, leading to the development of the concept known as Library 2.0, where users interact with library services through collaborative technologies. However, the reason is incorrect because the Semantic Web is associated with Web 3.0, not Web 2.0. The Semantic Web focuses on machine-understandable data, linked data, and ontologies that allow computers to interpret relationships between information resources. Therefore, the assertion is correct but the reason is incorrect.

43. A. Debian → II. 1993 – Debian was initiated in 1993 by Ian Murdock and became one of the earliest community-driven GNU/Linux distributions emphasizing free and open-source software principles.

B. SUSE Linux Enterprise Server → I. 2000 – SUSE introduced enterprise-level Linux server solutions around 2000, designed for stable and scalable business environments.

C. Ubuntu → IV. 2004 – Ubuntu was first released in 2004 by Canonical Ltd., aiming to provide a user-friendly Linux operating system for desktops and servers.

D. Fedora → III. 2003 – Fedora was launched in 2003 as a community-based Linux distribution sponsored by Red Hat, serving as an innovation platform for emerging Linux technologies.

44. The correct matching does not correspond to any of the given options.

A. Experimental method → III. Studying the effect of manipulating independent variable on dependent variable under appropriate control imposed.

The experimental method involves deliberate manipulation of an independent variable while controlling other variables to observe its effect on the dependent variable. It is used to establish cause–effect relationships.

B. Ex-post facto method → IV. Conducting a probe into causal factors on the basis of evidences manifested.

Ex-post facto research studies cause–effect relationships after events have already occurred. The researcher does not manipulate variables but analyzes existing evidence to identify possible causal factors.

C. Descriptive survey method → II. Studies designed to obtain information concerning the current status of phenomena.

The descriptive survey method collects data to describe present conditions, opinions, or characteristics of a population without manipulating variables.

D. Ethnographic method → I. A detailed description of the way people believe and act in a particular society.

Ethnographic research focuses on detailed observation and description of cultural patterns, beliefs, and behaviors of specific communities.

The correct mapping is therefore A-III, B-IV, C-II, D-I, which does not appear in any of the provided answer options. Hence the correct response is NONE.

45. Assertion (A) correctly states that during network communication an attacker may secretly intercept data packets travelling through the network. This interception is called eavesdropping, commonly known as sniffing or snooping, and it poses a significant security threat because sensitive information such as passwords, credentials, or confidential data can be captured.

Reason (R) is also correct because cryptographic encryption is the primary method used to protect data in transit. When strong encryption techniques are applied, intercepted packets become unreadable without the proper decryption keys.

The reason explains the assertion because it identifies the technical mechanism used to prevent or mitigate eavesdropping attacks. Encryption ensures confidentiality of transmitted data even if network traffic is intercepted.

46. The first edition of the Imperial Gazetteer of India was published in 1881 under the supervision of Sir William Wilson Hunter. This initial edition consisted of 9 volumes and was prepared as a comprehensive geographical and administrative reference describing British India. The work included detailed information about provinces, districts, towns, physical geography, population statistics, agriculture, trade, and historical background. It served as an important administrative and scholarly resource for understanding the political, economic, and social conditions of India during the colonial period. Later editions expanded significantly: the second edition (1885–1887) was enlarged to 14 volumes, and the well-known new edition (1908–1909) eventually grew to 26 volumes. Therefore, the first edition specifically contained nine volumes.

47. The academic publishing platform Frontiers was founded in 2007 by neuroscientist Henry Markram and Kamila Markram. Frontiers Media SA is known for its open-access scientific publishing model, which aims to make research freely available to the global community. The platform focuses on collaborative peer review and interdisciplinary research across fields such as neuroscience, medicine, engineering, and environmental sciences. Since its establishment, Frontiers has developed numerous open-access journals and has become one of the prominent publishers promoting open science and transparency in scholarly communication.

48. The acronym MUSTIE is widely used in academic libraries as a guideline for weeding or deselection of library materials. Each letter represents a criterion for removing items from the collection. M – Misleading refers to information that is inaccurate or outdated. U – Ugly refers to materials that are badly worn, damaged, or in poor physical condition. S – Superseded indicates that the content has been replaced by a newer or more authoritative edition. T – Trivial refers to works with little informational or literary value. I – Irrelevant indicates materials no longer related to the needs or objectives of the library's users. E – Elsewhere means the material is easily available in other accessible sources such as databases or nearby libraries. Using the MUSTIE criteria helps librarians maintain a relevant, accurate, and high-quality collection.

49. **A. Central tendency – Mean:** Measures of central tendency describe the central or typical value of a dataset. The mean is one of the most widely used measures of central tendency in statistics.

C. Refinement of judgement – Delphi method: The Delphi method is a structured forecasting and decision-making technique where expert opinions are gathered through multiple rounds of questionnaires. After each round, feedback is provided so that participants can refine their judgments.

50. **A. Basic Rate Interface (BRI) → IV**

BRI is the standard ISDN interface that provides two 64 kbps B channels for voice or data and one 16 kbps D channel for signaling, commonly summarized as 2B+D.

B. Primary Rate Interface (PRI) → III

PRI is a higher-capacity ISDN interface. In North America it typically provides 23 B channels plus one 64 kbps D channel, giving a total bandwidth of 1.544 Mbps (T1 line).

C. B-ISDN → II

Broadband ISDN (B-ISDN) is an advanced version of ISDN that supports Asynchronous Transfer Mode (ATM) technology to enable high-speed multimedia communication.

D. Symmetric DSL Interface (ADSL) and Ultra-Advanced Ra te Interface (UARI) → I

DSL technologies such as ADSL are not part of the ISDN interface standards, so they correspond to the description stating that they are not part of ISDN interfaces.

51. WAI-ARIA (Web Accessibility Initiative – Accessible Rich Internet Applications) is a technical specification developed and approved by the World Wide Web Consortium (W3C). It is part of the W3C Web Accessibility Initiative (WAI), which creates standards to make web content more accessible to people with disabilities. WAI-ARIA provides attributes that can be added to HTML elements so that assistive technologies such as screen readers can interpret dynamic web content, interactive widgets, and complex user interface components. By defining roles, states, and properties for web elements, WAI-ARIA improves accessibility for users with visual, auditory, cognitive, and motor impairments. Therefore the approval and standardization authority for WAI-ARIA is W3C.

52. Max Weber's research approach emphasized Verstehen, meaning interpretative understanding of human behaviour and social action. Weber believed that social sciences should focus on understanding how individuals create meaning within their social contexts rather than merely measuring observable facts. This perspective forms the basis of the interpretative paradigm, which studies social phenomena by examining human experiences, intentions, beliefs, and meanings in natural settings. The interpretative paradigm often uses qualitative methods such as interviews, observation, and ethnographic analysis to understand subjective interpretations of reality.

53. **A. The Changing Academic Library → II. John Budd:** John Budd wrote The Changing Academic Library, discussing

the transformation of academic libraries in response to technological and educational developments.

B. Planning Public Library Building → III. Michael Dewe: Michael Dewe authored Planning Public Library Buildings, which focuses on architectural planning, space design, and functional requirements for public libraries.

C. Introduction to Public Librarianship → IV. Kathleen de la Peña McCook: Kathleen de la Peña McCook wrote Introduction to Public Librarianship, a widely used text explaining the philosophy, services, and social role of public libraries.

D. Special Libraries → I. José-Marie Griffiths: José-Marie Griffiths contributed to literature related to special libraries and their management and services.

54. A. To create a single portal of web-enabled, linked databases: LOADB aims to provide a unified access point that links multiple open access databases so users can easily discover and navigate them.

C. To classify and categorize Open Access Databases: Another important objective is to organize open access databases into categories based on subject coverage and database type, making discovery and retrieval easier for researchers and librarians.

55. A. Cognitive Psychology → III. Information-seeking behaviour models

Cognitive psychology contributes theories explaining how users search for, interpret, and use information, forming the basis for information-seeking behaviour models.

B. Communication Engineering → I. Information theory and transmission models

Communication engineering contributes concepts such as signal transmission, noise, and Shannon's information theory, which are fundamental to information transfer systems.

C. Linguistics → IV. Natural language processing and indexing

Linguistics contributes to information science through language analysis, semantics, and computational processing of text, supporting indexing and natural language processing.

D. Human–Computer Interaction → II. User-centred design and usability

HCI contributes principles for designing interactive systems that are efficient, usable, and responsive to user needs in information retrieval and digital interfaces.

56. B. Establishing Rapport with the User – The reference interview begins with building a comfortable and cooperative relationship with the user so that the user feels confident in explaining the information need.

A. Discussing and Clarifying the Question – The librarian interacts with the user to clarify the exact nature, scope, and depth of the information required. This helps transform the user's initial query into a clearly defined information request.

C. Developing Strategy for Successful Search – After understanding the query, the librarian selects appropriate sources, tools, databases, or catalogues and plans a search strategy to locate the information efficiently.

D. Finding the Information and Evaluating it – The librarian retrieves relevant information resources and evaluates their reliability, relevance, and usefulness for the user's needs.

E. Follow up – Finally, the librarian confirms whether the information satisfies the user's need and offers further assistance if necessary. This stage ensures the effectiveness of the reference service.

57. Radio Frequency Identification (RFID) technology used in libraries generally operates within two frequency ranges. The High Frequency (HF) band at 13.56 MHz is the most widely adopted standard for library RFID systems because it supports short-range communication suitable for circulation, self-check systems, and security gates. In some advanced implementations, Ultra High Frequency (UHF) bands between 860–960 MHz are used to enable faster inventory control and longer read ranges. These frequency ranges are internationally standardized and widely implemented in modern RFID-based library management systems.

58. The Fac-Back-OPAC (Faceted Browsing OPAC) was developed by Casey Durfee. It is an interface designed to enhance the traditional Online Public

Access Catalogue (OPAC) by incorporating faceted browsing and navigation into library catalog searching. Faceted navigation allows users to refine search results using multiple attributes such as author, subject, format, publication date, language, and location. This approach improves information retrieval by enabling users to progressively narrow down large result sets through selectable facets. The system represents an important development in next-generation library catalog interfaces, aligning OPAC functionality with modern web search and e-commerce style filtering techniques to improve usability and discovery in library systems.

59. **D. Scholarly Publishing and Academic Resources Coalition (SPARC) – 1998:** SPARC was established in 1998 to promote open access and reform scholarly communication.

C. Budapest Open Access Initiative (BOAI) – 2002: The BOAI was one of the earliest global statements advocating free and unrestricted access to scholarly literature.

B. Berlin Declaration on Open Access to Knowledge in the Sciences and Humanities – 2003: This declaration expanded international commitment toward open access publishing and knowledge sharing.

A. The Coalition of Open Access Policy Institutions (COAPI) – 2011: COAPI was formed by universities adopting open access policies to collaborate on promoting institutional open access strategies.

E. Scottish Open Education Declaration – 2013: This declaration promoted open educational resources and open educational practices at the international level.

60. The Charter Act of 1813 is regarded as an important milestone in the development of education and academic libraries in India during the British colonial period. The Act renewed the charter of the East India Company but also introduced provisions related to education in India. It allocated one lakh rupees annually for the promotion of education and learning, encouraging the establishment of educational institutions and libraries. This financial provision laid an early foundation for institutional learning resources, which later contributed to the growth of academic libraries and educational infrastructure in India.

61. POPSI (Postulate-Based Permuted Subject Indexing), developed by G. Bhattacharyya, is an indexing system based on postulates and elementary categories rather than relying on classification schedules. It analyzes subjects using categories such as Discipline, Entity, Action, Property, and others derived from linguistic and conceptual analysis. Therefore, POPSI does not depend on classification schedules to derive terms, making the Assertion incorrect. However, POPSI does apply a chain-building approach similar to the conceptual linking used in Chain Indexing, where subject elements are arranged systematically to generate indexing strings. Hence the Reason is correct even though the Assertion is incorrect.

62. When a researcher rejects the Null Hypothesis (H_0) based on the results of a statistical test, there is a possibility that the null hypothesis is actually true but has been rejected due to sampling variation. This situation is called a Type I error or Alpha (α) error. It represents a false positive conclusion in hypothesis testing. Researchers control the probability of committing this error by setting a significance level (α) such as 0.05 or 0.01 before conducting the statistical test.

63. A Normal Probability Curve (NPC) is perfectly symmetrical. In such a distribution, the mean, median, and mode coincide at the center, and the distribution has zero skewness. Because there is no positive or negative skew, the distribution is considered neutral with respect to skewness. Among the given options, the term "neutrality skewed" represents this condition of zero skewness, which corresponds to the property of the normal distribution.

64. The Library Bill of Rights was adopted and published by the American Library Association (ALA) in 1939. It serves as a fundamental policy statement supporting intellectual freedom and opposing censorship in libraries. The document asserts that libraries should provide materials representing diverse viewpoints and should not exclude resources based on origin, background, or views of the authors.

65. Jean Piaget developed his theory of Cognitive Development through fundamental (basic) research. His studies focused on understanding the underlying processes through which children develop reasoning, perception, and intellectual abilities. Through systematic observation and experimentation, Piaget proposed stages such as sensorimotor, preoperational, concrete operational, and formal operational stages, contributing significantly to theoretical knowledge in psychology and education.

66. A. Unified Medical Language System (UMLS) → II. A set of files and software that brings together many health and biomedical standards

UMLS integrates numerous biomedical vocabularies and standards and provides tools to enable interoperability between different health information systems. It helps link different terminologies used in clinical and biomedical databases.

B. Value Set Authority Center (VSAC) → IV. A repository and authoring tool for standard lists of codes and terms from biomedical vocabularies

VSAC provides access to value sets used in clinical quality measures and electronic health records. It functions as a repository where standardized code sets from different vocabularies can be created and maintained.

C. RxNorm → I. Provides normalised names for clinical drugs

RxNorm offers standardized nomenclature for clinical drugs and links different drug vocabularies used in pharmacy management systems and electronic health records.

D. SNOMED CT → III. One of a suite of designated standards for the electronic exchange of clinical health information

SNOMED CT is a comprehensive clinical terminology used globally for recording patient data and enabling interoperability in electronic health information systems.

67.
- **z. Generalia** – In Colon Classification, the class Generalia mainly represents general works, encyclopaedias, and reference materials. Its structure is comparatively simple and does not involve the cyclic appearance of facets that would generate successive rounds. The arrangement proceeds through hierarchical levels rather than rounds.
- **O. Literature** – The facet formula of Literature is primarily Personality-based (for example language, form, author, work). These are represented as successive levels of the same category rather than repeated cycles of different categories. Because the Energy facet does not intervene, the mechanism that produces new rounds does not arise.
- **Z. Law** – The Law class is also largely dominated by Personality facets such as community, legal system, and subject of law. These facets occur as hierarchical levels within the same round, rather than initiating further rounds through Energy or Matter categories.

Therefore, these main classes are structured with levels only and without rounds in Colon Classification.

68. A. Interval/Ratio → III. Variables where the distances between the categories are identical across the range

Interval and ratio variables represent quantitative measurements where equal differences between values indicate equal intervals.

B. Ordinal → IV. Variables whose categories can be rank ordered, but the distances between the categories are not equal across the range

Ordinal variables indicate ranking or order but the intervals between ranks are not uniform.

C. Nominal → II. Variables whose categories cannot be rank ordered

Nominal variables represent categories without inherent ranking, such as gender, nationality, or types of institutions.

D. Dichotomous → I. Variables containing data that have only two categories

Dichotomous variables represent binary categories such as yes/no, true/false, or present/absent.

69. A. George Marcus → IV. Multi-sited ethnography

George Marcus introduced the concept of multi-sited ethnography, which studies cultural phenomena across multiple locations and contexts.

B. Clifford Geertz → II. Ethnography as writing or thick description

Clifford Geertz is known for the concept of "thick description", emphasizing deep interpretation of cultural practices and meanings.

C. Bronislaw Malinowski → III. Classical ethnographic fieldwork associated with functionalism

Malinowski pioneered intensive participant observation and fieldwork methods, linking them with functionalist anthropology.

D. Durkheim → I. Social organism

Émile Durkheim viewed society as a social organism where different institutions function together to maintain social order.

70. The United Nations Convention on the Rights of Persons with Disabilities (CRPD) was adopted by the United Nations General Assembly in December 2006 and came into force on 3 May 2008 after the required number of ratifications by member states. The convention aims to protect and promote the rights, dignity, and full participation of persons with disabilities in society. It establishes international standards to ensure equal opportunities, accessibility, non-discrimination, and inclusion in social, economic, and political life.

71. In HTTP architecture, cookies and cache serve fundamentally different purposes. Cookies are small pieces of data stored in the user's browser that contain client-specific information, such as session identifiers, login status, user preferences, and tracking information. They allow servers to recognize returning users and maintain session continuity across multiple requests. Cache, on the other hand, is used to store reusable server responses such as web pages, images, or scripts so that repeated requests can be served faster without contacting the server again. Caching improves network performance and reduces server load by reusing previously retrieved resources. Therefore, cookies manage client-related state information while cache improves efficiency by storing reusable responses.

72. A. CEA (Atomic Energy Commission) – The French Atomic Energy Commission contributed to the development of the CeCILL license to support open-source software within French research institutions.

B. CNRS (National Centre for Scientific Research) – CNRS participated in creating the CeCILL license to ensure compatibility with French law while promoting free software distribution.

D. INRIA (National Institute for Research in Digital Science and Technology) – INRIA played a major role in designing the CeCILL license, ensuring it aligned with open-source principles and the GNU GPL.

These three major French public research organizations jointly initiated the CeCILL Free Software License Agreement.

73. A cross break (cross-tabulation) is a statistical table used to analyze relationships between two or more variables. Data are arranged so that one variable is displayed across rows and another across columns, usually showing frequencies or percentages. This arrangement allows researchers to examine associations between variables and compare distributions across categories. The categories used in cross-break tables are typically structured according to the research hypothesis or analytical framework, which explains why specific variables and categories are selected for cross-partitioning. Hence the reason explains the assertion.

74. E. Biometric scanner – Biometric devices such as fingerprint or iris scanners generally require direct contact or extremely close proximity (0–2 cm) to capture biological patterns. Hence they represent the shortest effective reading range among the listed technologies.

A. Barcode – Barcode scanners operate using line-of-sight optical scanning and usually work within a short range of a few centimeters to roughly half a meter depending on the scanner type.

B. QR Code – QR codes can typically be read from slightly greater distances than linear barcodes because their two-dimensional matrix structure allows camera-based readers to capture information even when partially distorted or viewed from farther away.

C. NFC (Near Field Communication) – NFC technology works through very short-range radio communication, typically up to about 4–10 cm, designed intentionally for secure short-distance transactions such as contactless payments and access cards.

D. RFID – RFID has the largest reading range, which can vary from several centimeters in HF systems to several meters or even tens of meters in UHF or active RFID systems.

Therefore, arranged from shortest to longest reading range, the correct order is E, A, B, C, D.

75. In ex post facto research, the independent variable is not manipulated by the researcher but is instead selected after the event has occurred. The researcher studies the effects of existing conditions or past events to determine possible relationships between variables. Because the independent variable already exists and cannot be controlled experimentally, the researcher selects subjects based on their characteristics or past experiences and then analyzes the resulting differences. This distinguishes ex post facto research from experimental research, where the independent variable is deliberately manipulated.

76. In the ISDN Basic Rate Interface (BRI) configuration, the interface provides two 64 Kbps B (Bearer) channels and one 16 Kbps D (Delta) channel. The B channels are primarily used for carrying user information such as voice calls, data transmission, video communication, or other digital services. These channels operate independently and can support simultaneous communication sessions. The D channel, on the other hand, is mainly responsible for signaling and control information used to establish, manage, and terminate connections. Therefore, the B channels specifically handle voice and data traffic.

77. AIFF (Audio Interchange File Format) is a digital audio file format developed by Apple Inc. in 1988. The format uses file extensions such as .aif, .aiff, and .aifc and is designed primarily for storing high-quality uncompressed audio data. AIFF is widely used in professional audio editing, music production, and multimedia applications because it preserves sound quality without compression loss. Although the AIFC variant supports compression, the format is still mainly associated with audio files rather than video or multimedia formats.

78. **A. Citebase → IV. Southampton University**

Citebase was developed at the University of Southampton as a citation indexing service designed to analyze research impact using open-access repositories.

B. eScholarship Repository → III. California Digital Library

The eScholarship Repository was initiated by the California Digital Library (University of California system) to provide open access to scholarly publications produced by UC researchers.

C. PubMed → II. National Center for Biotechnology Information (NCBI)

PubMed is a widely used biomedical literature database maintained by the NCBI, part of the U.S. National Library of Medicine.

D. Networked Computer Science Technical Reference Library (NCSTRL) → I. DARPA and NSF

NCSTRL was an early digital library initiative funded by the Defense Advanced Research Projects Agency (DARPA) and the National Science Foundation (NSF) to provide distributed access to computer science technical reports.

79. e-Granthalaya 4.0, developed by the National Informatics Centre (NIC), Government of India, uses ASP.NET 4.0 as the front-end framework along with technologies such as AJAX, jQuery, and JSON for interactive web functionality. In this version, the back-end database was migrated to PostgreSQL, an open-source relational database management system. Earlier versions of e-Granthalaya (1.0–3.0) relied on Microsoft SQL Server, but version 4.0 shifted to PostgreSQL to support open-source architecture, improve scalability, and enable deployment on cloud environments such as the NIC National Cloud (Meghraj). This transition aligns the software with modern web-based and cloud-ready digital library management systems.

80. **D. Choose main entry based on role indicator:** In the PRECIS indexing system, the first step is selecting the main entry using role indicators, which identify the primary concept or subject within the statement.

B. Maintain original word order in all entries: PRECIS preserves the original syntactic order of words in the subject statement to maintain contextual meaning during indexing.

A. Generate secondary entries by rotating the lead term: Secondary access points are produced by rotating the lead term while maintaining the original word sequence to generate multiple subject access entries.

E. Link rotated entries back to the main entry: Each rotated entry is logically connected to the original entry so that users can trace the subject relationship and maintain conceptual consistency.

C. Display entries in alphabetical order: Finally, all generated entries are arranged alphabetically in the index to facilitate efficient retrieval by users.

81. Performance measurement in libraries is not limited only to cost accounting. Modern library performance measurement evaluates multiple aspects such as achievement of organizational goals, effectiveness of services, user satisfaction, and impact on users and communities. Tools such as performance indicators, benchmarking, service quality measures, and outcome assessment are commonly used. Therefore the Assertion is incorrect. The Reason is correct because evaluation in libraries examines the worth and utility of services for target users and aims to improve efficiency, quality, timeliness, and productivity relative to costs. Hence the correct option is that the assertion is false while the reason is true.

82. A. DataCite – Provides Digital Object Identifiers (DOIs) for research data, enabling persistent identification and citation of datasets.

C. ROR (Research Organization Registry) – Supplies persistent identifiers for research organizations, supporting interoperability in scholarly communication systems.

E. Funder Registry – Provides standardized identifiers for funding organizations, helping track funding information associated with research outputs.

DRIDE promotes community-adopted metadata standards and persistent identifiers aligned with these infrastructures.

83. The correct logical sequence of Ranganathan's five fundamental canons of classification is not represented exactly in the given options.

B. Canon of Ascertainability – The first requirement in classification is that the characteristic used for division must be clearly identifiable and objectively determinable. If the characteristic cannot be reliably ascertained, it cannot be used for classification.

D. Canon of Relevance – After selecting an ascertainable characteristic, it must also be relevant to the purpose of classification and the subject under consideration. Irrelevant characteristics should not be used for dividing classes.

A. Canon of Differentiation – The chosen characteristic must effectively divide the class into distinct and meaningful subclasses, ensuring that each subdivision represents a clear conceptual difference.

E. Canon of Permanence – The characteristic selected for division should be stable over time so that the classification system remains useful and does not require frequent changes.

C. Canon of Consistency – Finally, once a principle of division is adopted, it must be applied uniformly and consistently throughout the classification scheme.

Thus the correct logical order is B, D, A, E, C, which does not appear among the provided options. Therefore, the correct answer should be NONE.

84. TIFF Group 4 compression (TIFF-G4) is a lossless compression method specifically designed for bitonal (black-and-white) images, such as scanned documents and fax transmissions. It compresses data without losing image information, making it suitable for digital archiving and document imaging systems where exact reproduction of the original image is essential. Other formats like JPEG are lossy compression methods and therefore unsuitable for bitonal archival preservation.

85. Under the Right to Information (RTI) Act, 2005, when the requested information concerns the life or liberty of a person, the Public Information Officer must provide the information within 48 hours. This provision ensures urgent access to critical information in situations where delay could threaten an individual's safety or fundamental rights.

86. A. The Serials Directory → I. EBSCO – The Serials Directory is published by EBSCO Information Services and provides bibliographic information about serial publications worldwide, including journals, magazines, and newspapers.

B. Ebrary → IV. ProQuest – Ebrary is an e-book database originally developed by Ebrary Inc. and later acquired and managed by ProQuest, offering a large collection of academic e-books.

C. ScienceDirect → III. Elsevier – ScienceDirect is a major full-text scientific database operated by Elsevier, providing access to journals, books, and reference works across many disciplines.

D. Current Contents Connect → II. Clarivate – Current Contents Connect is a database produced by Clarivate Analytics (formerly part of Thomson Reuters), providing rapid access to tables of contents and bibliographic information from scholarly journals.

87. In a client–server digital library architecture, the server performs the central processing and management functions. It stores digital resources, manages databases, handles user authentication and authorization, retrieves requested information, and transmits the results back to the client. The client (user interface) sends requests and displays retrieved results, while the server manages the data and service logic. Therefore the server's key function is to control access to information, retrieve it, and deliver it to the client.

88. A. Science Citation Index (SCI) – 1964: Introduced by Eugene Garfield as the first citation index covering scientific literature.

D. Social Sciences Citation Index (SSCI) – 1973: Developed to cover citation data for journals in social science disciplines.

C. Arts & Humanities Citation Index (AHCI) – 1975: Added coverage for arts and humanities journals.

B. Science Citation Index Expanded (SCIE) – 1997 (online expansion): Expanded version of SCI available through Web of Science with broader journal coverage.

E. Emerging Sources Citation Index (ESCI) – 2015: Introduced to include emerging journals undergoing evaluation for inclusion in major citation indexes.

89. A. RDF → II. Resource Description Framework – RDF is the foundational framework used to represent information about resources on the Semantic Web using subject–predicate–object triples.

B. RDFS → IV. Schema definition for RDF – RDF Schema provides vocabulary and structure for defining classes, properties, and relationships within RDF data.

C. OWL → I. Ontology definition language – The Web Ontology Language allows the creation of complex ontologies describing relationships between concepts in the Semantic Web.

D. SPARQL → III. Query language for RDF – SPARQL is used to query and retrieve data stored in RDF format.

90. RSS (Really Simple Syndication) works by publishing XML-based feeds that automatically update whenever new content is posted on a website. These XML feeds contain structured information such as titles, summaries, publication dates, and links. An RSS feed reader or aggregator periodically retrieves these XML files and converts them into a readable interface for users. It displays headlines, summaries, and update notifications, allowing users to quickly access new content and follow links back to the original sources. Therefore both statements are correct and the reason explains how RSS feeds operate.

91. The passage clearly states that although AI chatbots and virtual reference services provide efficient and scalable support, they cannot replicate human empathy, judgement, or critical thinking. Human librarians can understand emotional cues, nuanced contexts, and complex research needs in ways that automated systems cannot. Therefore the essential human quality that chatbots cannot reproduce is empathy and contextual judgement.

92. The passage highlights ethical concerns associated with AI adoption in libraries, particularly algorithmic bias. If AI systems are trained mainly on mainstream datasets, they may unintentionally prioritise commonly cited or popular topics while overlooking unconventional or emerging research areas. This creates a risk that certain perspectives or innovative ideas may be suppressed in retrieval results.

93. One of the major advantages of AI-enabled chatbots mentioned in the passage is their ability to provide continuous support regardless of staff availability. Unlike traditional reference services that depend on working hours and staff presence, chatbots can assist users 24 hours a day and serve multiple users simultaneously. This scalability greatly improves access to library services for remote and diverse users.

94. The passage emphasizes that librarians must develop new competencies such as digital ethics, algorithmic transparency, and data analytics. A key responsibility highlighted is critically evaluating AI systems to ensure they support educational and research goals rather than merely serving commercial interests. Librarians act as mediators who assess whether AI tools align with institutional missions and user needs.

95. The passage concludes that the most sustainable model for library services is a hybrid approach combining AI capabilities with human expertise. While AI tools can enhance efficiency, speed, and accessibility, human librarians provide judgement, ethical oversight, and deeper intellectual guidance. Balancing these strengths ensures equitable, meaningful, and context-aware access to information resources.

96. The passage explains that AI tools such as ChatGPT and AI-driven discovery systems assist research but may raise concerns regarding accuracy, transparency, and reliability. Because AI-generated outputs can contain errors, bias, or incomplete interpretations, librarians must guide learners to critically evaluate AI-generated information, verify sources, and compare machine outputs with authoritative references. Therefore the role of librarians shifts from merely providing access to information toward teaching critical assessment and verification of AI outputs.

97. UNESCO's definition of Information Literacy remains relevant because it describes a fundamental cycle of information use. According to the passage, this cycle includes recognizing when information is needed, locating it, evaluating its credibility, and using it effectively. Even though modern IL now includes media, digital, and data literacies, these additional literacies still rely on the same core process. Thus the UNESCO definition continues to provide a universal conceptual foundation for information literacy.

98. The passage clearly states that Information Literacy in the digital age has expanded beyond traditional library search skills. It now includes media literacy (evaluating messages across media platforms), digital literacy (effective use of digital tools), and data literacy (interpreting and analysing data). These interconnected literacies help learners critically evaluate information in complex digital environments where misinformation and algorithmic bias are common.

99. The ACRL Framework for Information Literacy in Higher Education (2015) introduced a significant conceptual shift by replacing earlier rigid standards with six conceptual frames. These frames emphasize deeper understanding and critical thinking rather than a fixed checklist of skills. Concepts such as "Authority is Constructed and Contextual" and "Searching as Strategic Exploration" encourage learners to interpret information environments critically rather than simply applying procedural search techniques.

100. Data Literacy complements Information Literacy because modern information environments increasingly involve data-driven content and analysis. According to the passage, Data Literacy helps users interpret, analyse, and ethically use data, enabling them to identify potential bias, understand context, and judge credibility. This capability is essential when dealing with datasets, statistics, and algorithm-generated information in research and decision-making.

19. What is the principal purpose of ISO 25964-2?

1. To define MARC fields for multilingual thesauri.
2. To improve the internal structure of monolingual thesauri.
3. To support interoperability by mapping between heterogeneous vocabularies.
4. To translate thesauri into XML format for digital libraries.

20. Which of the following network architectures is associated with IBM?

1. TCP IP
2. Digital Network Architecture (DNA)
3. System Network Architecture (SNA)
4. Xerox Network Systems (XNS)

21. Which of the following is an example of a Platform as a Service (PaaS)?

1. Amazon Web Service (AWS)
2. Google App Engine
3. GoGrid
4. 3 Tera

22. Which visualization feature in Web of Science helps identify relationships between citing and cited articles?

1. Citation Network Graph
2. Citation Report
3. Research Impact Score
4. Journal Metrics Map

23. How many enhancements and bugfixes are in Koha 23.05.03?

1. 3 enhancements and 44 bugfixes
2. 3 enhancements and 41 bugfixes
3. 4 enhancements and 44 bugfixes
4. 4 enhancements and 43 bugfixes

24. For implementing Single Pair Ethernet (SPE) in modern digital libraries for IoT devices, which IEEE 802.3 project would most appropriately be referenced?

1. IEEE P802.3da
2. IEEE P802.3dk
3. IEEE P802.3dm
4. IEEE 802.2a

25. While using incoming server in SSL/TLS encryption, what is the part for setting up G-mail with MS outlook express?

1. 993 2. 635
3. 587 4. 349

26. In Goa Public Library Act, in the form of library cess, ₹ 0.50 is levied as surcharge on:

1. Per bulk liter of beer
2. Per proof liter of beer
3. Per bulk liter of India made foreign liquor
4. Per over proof liter of India made foreign liquor

27. How many core questions are provided in LibQUAL survey?

1. 18 2. 20
3. 22 4. 24

28. In the financial year 2023-24, under which Scheme Ministry of Finance, Government of India has allocated ₹ 5000 crore for development and strengthening of libraries at ward and village panchayat level?

1. National Mission on Library (NML)
2. Pradhan Mantri Adarsh Gram Yojana (PMAGY)
3. CAPEX
4. National Literacy Mission

29. Which is the fourth stage of Kuhlthau's model for information search process?

1. Exploration 2. Formulation
3. Collection 4. Closure

30. The project under which DSpace-CRIS was originally developed, was funded by:

1. University of Illinois-Urbana Champaign
2. Harvard University
3. Hong Kong University
4. Singapore University

31. What is the annual subscription amount of Journal of Indian Library Association (JILA) for its individual online subscription?

1. ₹ 1,000
2. ₹ 2,000
3. ₹ 2,500
4. ₹ 3,000

32. 'Technology Focus' is a periodic publication of:

1. BARC
2. ISRO
3. NIScPR
4. DRDO

33. In Chain Procedure the link which does not represent a subject with definite name is known as .... link.

1. Missing
2. Unsought
3. False
4. Sought

34. Under the UGC Plagiarism Regulations, what is the penalty for Level 2 plagiarism (40-60%)?

1. Rejection of the thesis or dissertation
2. Debarring the student from submitting a revised script for one year
3. Cancellation of the student's registration
4. No penalty

35. 'Entropy' is a measure of ....

1. Degree of relationship of Information
2. Quantity of relevant Information
3. Degree of relevance of Information
4. Degree of Uncertainty in Information

36. In modern library environments, CAS is increasingly integrated with:

1. Linked Open Data and RSS feeds
2. Z39.50 cataloguing systems
3. AACR2 descriptive cataloguing rules
4. MARC21 bibliographic format

37. As per the Annexure of Colon Classification, 6th Revised Edition, in the Main Class 'V' (History), an Isolate whose number ends with '19' is designated as a Host Class. In the Facet Formula of Host Class 'V:19', '[P], [P2]' represent:

1. [P] — Enumeration & (SD), [P2]- (GD)
2. [P]- (GD), [P2]- Enumeration & (SD)
3. [P] — (CD), [P2]- (GD)
4. [P] — (CD), [P2]- Enumeration & (GD)

38. As per the Annexure of Colon Classification, 6th Revised Edition, in which Main Classes the concept of Telescoped Facet was introduced?

1. J - Agriculture and KX-Animal Husbandry
2. D - Engineering and L - Medicine
3. T- Education and V - History
4. D- Engineering and S - Psychology

39. .... is an AI-powered app by Google that assists users with low or no vision by identifying food labels, images, text, and currency etc.

1. JAWS
2. Lookout
3. AVA
4. Voice Access

40. In the context of corporate libraries, what does the term 'Taxonomy' refer to?

1. The classification of employees based on their roles
2. A system for organizing and categorizing information and content
3. The financial structure of the organization
4. A method for calculating taxes

41. Arrange the steps of the 8 W's Literacy Model in correct order as given by Annettee Lamb:

A. Waving
B. Weaving
C. Watching
D. Webbing
E. Wiggling

Choose the **correct** answer from the options given below:

1. A, C, E, D, B
2. C, E, A, B, D
3. C, D, E, B, A
4. B, C, D, A, E

42. Arrange the following steps in application of POPSI in Logical Order:

A. Standardization
B. Formalisation

C. Preparation of EOC

D. Analysis

E. Modulation

Choose the **correct** answer from the options given below:

1. D, B, E, A, C
2. B, E, A, D, C
3. C, A, B, E, D
4. A, B, D, C, E

43. Arrange the following areas of access points in their proper sequence as given in ISBD:

A. Edition

B. Notes

C. Title

D. Publication

E. Material specific details

Choose the **correct** answer from the options given below:

1. B, D, A, C, E
2. D, A, B, E, C
3. A, C, E, B, D
4. C, A, E, D, B

44. Arrange the following open Access Initiatives/Policy Statements according to the year of their adoption/declaration at international level:

A. The Coalition of Open Access Policy Institutions

B. The Berlin Declaration on Open Access to Knowledge in the Sciences and Humanities

C. The Budapest Open Access Initiatives

D. Scholarly Publishing and Academic Resources Coalition

E. Scottish Open Education Declaration

Choose the **correct** answer from the options given below:

1. A, D, C, E, B
2. D, C, B, A, E
3. C, A, D, E, B
4. C, D, E, B, A

45. Arrange the following phases of disaster planning in appropriate sequence according to guidelines/principles of IFLA:

A. Preparedness

B. Recovery

C. Mitigation

D. Prevention

E. Response

Choose the **correct** answer from the options given below:

1. A, C, E, D, B
2. D, C, A, E, B
3. C, D, E, B, A
4. B, C, D, A, E

46. Arrange the following bibliographic utilities/ institutions according to their year of origin:

A. Resource Description and Access

B. Research Libraries Group

C. Ohio College Library Centre

D. Western Library Network

E. Library of Congress

Choose the **correct** answer from the options given below:

1. D, B, E, A, C
2. B, E, A, D, C
3. E, A, B, C, D
4. E, C, D, B, A

47. Arrange the Directors of National Library, Kolkata in ascending order of their posting:

A. Sudhendu Mandal

B. A.R. Bandyopadhyay

C. D.N. Banerjee

D. Harjit Singh

E. S.K. Chakravarti

Choose the **correct** answer from the options given below:

1. B, C, D, A, E
2. D, A, C, E, B
3. C, D, B, E, A
4. B, C, A, D, E

48. Arrange the following communication models in chronological order of their introduction:

A. Schramm's Interactive Model

B. Berlo's SMCR Model

C. Riley and Riley
D. Jakobsen's Model
E. Shannon and Weaver Model

Choose the **correct** answer from the options given below:

1. E, A, D, C, B
2. D, B, A, E, C
3. B, A, E, D, C
4. E, D, B, C, A

49. Arrange the following facets of Colon Classification as per the sequence in Facet Formula of any Main Class.

A. [P] B. Special
C. [2E] [3P] D. System
E. [E] [2P]

Choose the **correct** answer from the options given below:

1. E, B, D, A, C
2. C, D, B, E, A
3. D, B, A, E, C
4. D, E, A, C, B

50. Arrange the correct order in which the following commissions were set up:

A. K. Kasturirangan Committee
B. Yashpal Committee
C. Kothari Commission
D. Acharya Ramamurti Committee
E. Hari Gautam Committee

Choose the **correct** answer from the options given below:

1. D, C, A, B, E
2. C, B, E, A, D
3. D, A, C, E, B
4. C, D, B, E, A

51. Arrange the following Acts in chronological order:

A. Public Records Act
B. Antiquities and Art Treasures Act
C. Right to Information Act (RTI)
D. Indian Treasure Trove Act
E. Ancient Monuments and Archaeological Sites and Remains Act

Choose the **correct** answer from the options given below:

1. A, B, C, D, E
2. B, D, C, E, A
3. D, E, B, A, C
4. C, A, D, B, E

52. Sequence the actions for implementing a virtual reference service in a special library:

A. Train the staff
B. Launch service portal
C. Identify user needs
D. Monitor and improve service
E. Select virtual reference software

Choose the **correct** answer from the options given below:

1. C, E, A, B, D
2. A, C, E, B, D
3. A, C, B, E, D
4. D, A, C, E, B

53. Arrange the following occurrences in chronological ascending order (In year):

A. Dr. S.R. Ranganathan was appointed as National Research Professor of Library Science.
B. First time ILA became the member of IFLA.
C. ASLIB was acquired by MCB group, the holding company for emerald group publishing.
D. International institute of Documentation changed to International Federation of Documentation.
E. Online Europa Year Book started.

Choose the **correct** answer from the options given below:

1. C, D, B, A, E
2. D, B, A, E, C
3. A, D, B, E, C
4. B, D, A, E, C

54. Arrange the following in chronological order of occurrence year:

A. Introduction of Zero Base Budgeting system

B. MARC project completed
C. Publication of DDC 23rd edition
D. Typological study towards mode of formation of subjects
E. Starting of Browne charging system

Choose the **correct** answer from the options given below:

1. C, E, D, B, A
2. A, E, D, B, C
3. B, E, D, A, C
4. E, D, B, A, C

55. Arrange the following Protocols chronologically in order of their origin:

A. TCP/IP B. IPv6
C. HTTP D. FTP
E. HTTPS

Choose the **correct** answer from the options given below:

1. B, D, A, E, C
2. A, D, B, C, E
3. D, A, C, E, B
4. D, B, A, E, C

56. Which of the following are the component pillars of 'Knowledge Society' as reflected in UNESCO's Building Knowledge Societies:

A. Freedom of expression
B. Internet Governance
C. Quality Education for All
D. Respect for cultural and linguistic diversity
E. Information Society

Choose the **correct** answer from the options given below:

1. B, C and E only
2. A, B and D only
3. A, C and D only
4. B, D and E only

57. Which of the following are the necessary elements of an information society?

A. Confidentiality
B. Vulnerability
C. Integrity
D. Availability
E. Dishonesty

Choose the **correct** answer from the options given below:

1. B, C and D only
2. A, D and E only
3. B, C and E only
4. A, C and D only

58. Which of the following elements are mandatory in a MARC 21 bibliographic record?

A. Leader
B. Central Field (008)
C. ISBN (020)
D. Title Statement (245)
E. Publisher Statement (260/264)

Choose the **correct** answer from the options given below:

1. A and B only
2. A, B and D only
3. C and D only
4. A, B and E only

59. Controlled vocabularies fall broadly into following categories:

A. Subject Heading Lists
B. Thesauri
C. Folksonomies
D. Ontologies
E. Information Society

Choose the **correct** answer from the options given below:

1. A, C and D only
2. A, B and D only
3. B, D and E only
4. C, D and E only

60. Which of the following are review type services?

A. Current Awareness
B. Trend Reports
C. News Clippings
D. Geographical Sources
E. State of the Art Report

Choose the **correct** answer from the options given below:

1. C and D only 2. B and E only
3. B and D only 4. A and C only

61. Identify Indian patent databases from the list:

A. Patentscope B. inPASS
C. Patestate D. KIPO
E. The Lens

Choose the **correct** answer from the options given below:

1. A and B only 2. C and D only
3. D and E only 4. B and C only

62. Which of the following are functions of the National Knowledge Commission (NKC)?

A. Promote Open Access across the Nation
B. Promote a knowledge-driven society
C. Generate revenue through paid memberships
D. Advise the Government on matters related to higher education
E. Develop a nationwide digital library infrastructure

Choose the **correct** answer from the options given below:

1. B, C & E only
2. A, C & E only
3. B, C & D only
4. A, B & D only

63. The Global Open Access Portal (GOAP) is an initiative of:

A. UNESCO
B. IFLA-PAC
C. Indian Statistical Institute
D. Redalyc
E. WIPO

Choose the **correct** answer from the options given below:

1. A, B & D only
2. A, C & D only
3. B, D & E only
4. C, D & E only

64. In Colon Classification [P] (Personality) facet of the Main Class 'J – Agriculture' is made of the following components:

A. Part Array
B. Geographical Device
C. Genus/Species Number
D. Utility Array
E. Least Concrete

Choose the **correct** answer from the options given below:

1. D, A & C only
2. A, D & E only
3. B, A & C only
4. E, D & C only

65. Which of the following are Metadata harvesting tools?

A. OAI-PMH B. Apache Solr
C. Z39.50 D. SRU/SRW
E. OAI-ORE

Choose the **correct** answer from the options given below:

1. A, C & E only
2. B, C & D only
3. C & D only
4. A, D & E only

66. An academic librarian is tasked with implementing AI-driven services in a university library. Which of the following tools or technologies should they prioritize?

A. Machine Learning models for circulation forecasting
B. AI-enabled virtual reference assistants
C. Facial recognition for access cont. stacks
D. Auto-tagging of digital resources using NLP
E. Manual classification schemes like DDC

Choose the **correct** answer from the options given below:

1. A, B & D only
2. B, C & D only
3. C, D & E only
4. A, C & E only

67. Which of the following databases are commonly used in Health Science academic libraries?

A. PubMed
B. CINAHL
C. HeinOnline
D. ASME Journals
E. Scopus

Choose the **correct** answer from the options given below:

1. B, C & D only
2. A, C & D only
3. A, B & E only
4. A, D & E only

68. According to Edward Evans, which of the following are work analysis techniques?

A. PERT
B. GANTT Chart
C. Operation Research
D. Cost Effectiveness
E. Cost Benefit Analysis

Choose the **correct** answer from the options given below:

1. B and D are correct
2. B and C are correct
3. A and C are correct
4. A and E are correct

69. Which of the following are non-parametric tests?

A. Anova test
B. Spearman correlation coefficient
C. Z test
D. Chi-Square test
E. Kruskal-Wallis test

Choose the **correct** answer from the options given below:

1. A, B and C are correct
2. B, C and D are correct
3. A, C and E are correct
4. B, D and E are correct

70. Identify the principles for the implementation of the Canon of Helpful Sequence:

A. Principle of Spatial Contiguity
B. Principle of Increasing Literary Warrant
C. Principle of Modulation
D. Principle of Enumeration
E. Principle of Management

Choose the **correct** answer from the options given below:

1. B and D only
2. C and E only
3. A and D only
4. A and B only

71. Which of the following names are associated with post-coordinate indexing?

A. Mortimer Taube
B. Eugene Garfield
C. Calvin Mooers
D. W.E. Batten
E. Jorge E. Hirsch

Choose the **correct** answer from the options given below:

1. A, C and E only
2. B, C and D only
3. A, C and D only
4. B, D and E only

72. Identify the intellectual property related elements in Dublin Core Metadata.

A. Creator
B. Coverage
C. Publisher
D. Rights
E. Place

Choose the **correct** answer from the options given below:

1. A, C and D only
2. A, C and E only
3. B, C and D only
4. B, D and E only

73. Select the correct combinations:

A. William Martin — Information Society
B. Alvin Toffler — The Third Wave
C. S.C. Bradford — Classification
D. Karl Pearson — Webometrics
E. A.J. Walford — Guide to Reference Material

Choose the **correct** answer from the options given below:

1. A, B and E only
2. A, B and D only
3. C, D and E only
4. B, D and E only

74. Select the correct combinations:

A. Facts on File	News Digest
B. World of Learning	Directory
C. Concordance	Abstract
D. Willing' Press Guide	Periodical Directory
E. Books in Print	Index

Choose the **correct** answer from the options given below:

1. A, C and E only
2. A, B and D only
3. B, C and D only
4. B, D and E only

75. Select the correct combinations:

A. Wikipedia	Encyclopedia
B. Library Philosophy and Practice	e-journal
C. E-Granthalaya	e-book
D. E-PG Pathshala	Academic Source
E. SheRNI	Software

Choose the **correct** answer from the options given below:

1. A, B and D only
2. A, B and E only
3. B, C and D only
4. B, D and E only

76. Match ancient Library (List-I) with its country (List-II):

List-I (Ancient Library)	List-II (Country)
A. Bibliotheca Alexandria	I. Rome
B. Library of Ashurbanipal	II. Turkey
C. The Library of Pergamun	III. Iraq
D. Bibliotheca Ulpia	IV. Egypt

Choose the **correct** answer from the options given below:

1. A-IV, B-III, C-II, D-I
2. A-I, B-II, C-III, D-IV
3. A-II, B-IV, C-I, D-III
4. A-III, B-I, C-IV, D-II

77. Match the Library (List-I) with its University/ Institution of establishment (List-II):

List-I (Library)	List-II (University/ Institution)
A. Saraswati Bhawan Library	I. Tata Institute of Social Science
B. Sir Dorabji Tata Memorial Library	II. University of Hyderabad
C. Ratan Tata Library	III. Sampoornanand Sanskrit University
D. Indira Gandhi Memorial Library	IV. University of Delhi

Choose the **correct** answer from the options given below:

1. A-II, B-IV, C-III, D-I
2. A-III, B-I, C-IV, D-II
3. A-IV, B-II, C-I, D-III
4. A-II, B-III, C-I, D-IV

78. Match National Library of different countries (List-I) with its year of establishment (List-II):

List-I (National Library)	List-II (Year of Establishment)
A. Library of Congress	I. 1912
B. National Diet Library	II. 1948
C. National Library of Germany	III. 1800
D. National Library of Australia	IV. 1960

Choose the **correct** answer from the options given below:

1. A-II, B-I, C-IV, D-III
2. A-IV, B-III, C-II, D-I
3. A-III, B-II, C-I, D-IV
4. A-I, B-IV, C-III, D-II

79. Match the List-I with List-II in the context of Information Retrieval System:

List-I	List-II
A. Semantic Search Engine	I. Latent Semantic Indexing
B. Boolean Operators	II. Cognitive Model
C. Knowledge Retrieval Systems	III. Digital Logic
D. Algebraic IR Model	IV. Wolfram/Alpha

Choose the **correct** answer from the options given below:

1. A-I, B-III, C-II, D-IV
2. A-III. B-IV, C-II, D-I
3. A-IV, B-III, C-II, D-I
4. A-II, B-IV, C-III, D-I

80. Match the following e-governance initiatives (List-II) made in promotion, development and delivery of information services in different sectors (List-I):

List-I (Area)	List-II (Initiative)
A. Education	I. Compact
B. Transport	II. e-Choupal
C. Agriculture	III. Sarige
D. Taxation and Revenue	IV. Gyandoot

Choose the **correct** answer from the options given below:

1. A-IV, B-III, C-I, D-II
2. A-III, B-IV, C-I, D-II
3. A-I, B-II, C-III, D IV
4. A-IV, B-III, C-II, D-I

81. Match the MARC 21 elements (List-I) with corresponding tags (List-II):

List-I (Element)	List-II (Tag)
A. Personal Main Entry	I. 700
B. Personal subject Heading	II. 245
C. Personal Added Entry	III. 100
D. Bibliographic Title	IV. 600

Choose the **correct** answer from the options given below:

1. A-I, B-IV, C-II, D-III
2. A-II, B-I, C-III, D-IV
3. A-III, B-IV, C-I, D-II
4. A-IV, B-II, C-III, D-I

82. Match the Information Seeking Behaviour Model (List-I) with corresponding theories (List-II):

List-I (Model)	List-II (Theories)
A. Wilson Model of ISB	I. Tailored to Electronic Environment—the process consists of eight sub-processes
B. Derrin's Model of ISB	II. Association of feelings, thoughts and actions but not cognitive
C. Kuhlthous Model of ISB	III. Sense making approach-based on situation, gap and outcome-three key elements
D. Marchioninis Model of ISB	IV. Three fold view on information seeking context, system and information sources

Choose the **correct** answer from the options given below:

1. A-IV, B-III, C-II, D-I
2. A-III, B-II, C-I, D-IV
3. A-I, B-III, C-IV, D-II
4. A-II, B-IV, C-III, D-I

83. Match the Section of RTI Act (List-I) with its Provision in (List-II):

List-I (Section of Act)	List-II (Provision)
A. Section 4	I. Exemptions from Disclosure
B. Section 6	II. Penalties for non-compliance

C. Section 8	III. Procedure for requesting information
D. Section 10	IV. Obligation of public authorities

Choose the **correct** answer from the options given below:

1. A-IV, B-III, C-I, D-II
2. A-III, B-II, C-IV, D-I
3. A-I, B-III, C-II, D-IV
4. A-II, B-IV, C-I, D-III

84. Match the Knowledge Management Model (List-I) with its respective approach (List-II):

List-I (KM Model)	**List-II (Approach)**
A. Von Krogh and Roos	I. Sense-Making
B. WIIG	II. Synchronize
C. Nonaka and Takeuchi	III. Organizational Epistemology
D. Choo	IV. Socialization

Choose the **correct** answer from the options given below:

1. A-III, B-I, C-II, D-IV
2. A-IV, B-II, C-III, D-I
3. A-III, B-II, C-IV, D-I
4. A-I, B-III, C-II, D-IV

85. Match RSS feed components (List-I) with their respective functions (List-II):

List-I (RSS Component)	**List-II (Function)**
A. Channel	I. Multimedia file (audio/video) attachment
B. Item	II. Unique ID for each entry
C. Enclosure	III. Container of overall feed metadata
D. GUID	IV. Individual entry/article in a feed

Choose the **correct** answer from the options given below:

1. A-I, B-II, C-IV, D-III
2. A-III, B-I, C-II, D IV
3. A-III, B-IV, C-I, D-II
4. A-II, B-III, C-IV, D-I

86. Match the Canons of Classification (List-I) with the number of associated Canons (List-II):

List-I (Name of Canon)	**List-II (No. of Canons)**
A. Canons of Idea Plane	I. 4
B. Canons of Verbal Plane	II. 3
C. Canons of Notational Plane	III. 15
D. Canons of Book Classification	IV. 24

Choose the **correct** answer from the options given below:

1. A-II, B-III, C-I, D-IV
2. A-III, B-I, C-IV, D-II
3. A-IV, B-II, C-III, D-I
4. A-III, B-IV, C-II, D-I

87. Match the following technologies (List-I) with their propounder (List-II):

List-I (Technology)	**List-II (Propounder)**
A. Bar Code Technology	I. Ray Theories Ray Tag
B. RFID Technology	II. Sir William Herschel
C. Q.R. Code	III. Normen Joseph, Woodland and Bernard Silver
D. Biometric Technology	IV. Denson Wave

Choose the **correct** answer from the options given below:

1. A-II, B-IV, C-I, D-III
2. A-III, B-I, C-IV, D-II
3. A-IV, B-III, C-I, D-II
4. A-IV, B-I, C-II, D-III

88. Match Milestone in the history of Open Source Software (List-I) with the year (List-II):

List-I (OSS Milestone)	List-II (Year)
A. Richard Stallman formed GNU Project	I. 1998
B. Creation of Free Software Foundation	II. 1991
C. Development of Linux Kernel by Linus Torvalds	III. 1985
D. Open Source Initiatives formed by Eric Raymond	IV. 1983

Choose the **correct** answer from the options given below:

1. A-IV, B-III, C-II, D-I
2. A-I, B-IV, C-III, D-II
3. A-III, B-II, C-I, D-IV
4. A-IV, B-I, C-II, D-III

89. Match the MARC format data (List-I) with corresponding MARC TAG (List-II):

List-I (Format Data)	List-II (MARC Tag)
A. Physical Description Fixed Field	I. 887
B. Patent Control Information	II. 013
C. Creation/Reference Note	III. 007
D. Non-MARC Information Field	IV. 510

Choose the **correct** answer from the options given below:

1. A-III, B-I, C-II, D-IV
2. A-III, B-II, C-I, D-IV
3. A-III, B-II, C-IV, D-I
4. A-IV, B-II, C-III, D-I

90. Match the description of research (List-I) with its corresponding research methodology Term (List-II):

List-I (Description)	List-II (Research Term)
A. In-depth exploration of a specific case or phenomenon	I. Quantitative Research
B. Systematic investigation to establish relationships between variables	II. Survey Research
C. Gathering information from a population through questionnaires or interviews	III. Qualitative Research
D. Using numerical data and statistical analysis to draw conclusions	IV. Case Study

Choose the **correct** answer from the options given below:

1. A-III, B-I, C-II, D-IV
2. A-I, B-III, C-IV, D-II
3. A-II, B-IV, C-III, D-I
4. A-IV, B-II, C-I, D-III

Directions (Qs. No. 91-95): *Read the following passage and answer the question:*

The first significant date in the development of libraries for the public in India is 1808 when the Bombay Government initiated a proposal to register libraries which were to be given copies of books published from the "Funds for the Encouragement of Literature". By the middle of the 19th century, the three presidency towns of Bombay, Calcutta and Madras had their "public libraries", founded mostly with the active support and initiative of the Europeans in these towns. They were, of course, not public libraries in the full sense of the term. Founded in imitation of their western counterparts, the use of these libraries was confined to a thin upper layer of the society. Besides, they were subscription libraries and not free libraries, which alone can, nowadays, lay claim to the title of public libraries. The movement spread to the vast "hinterland" beyond the metropolises and grew particularly strong in the last two decades of the 19th century. By the end of the century, all the provincial capitals and even many of the district towns, at least in the three Presidencies, had their "public libraries". Even some of the Princely States, like Indore and Travancore-Cochin. had the distinction of having public libraries in their capitals. The shortcomings of the libraries in the three metropolises, mentioned above, clung more or less to the provincial, suburban and "mofussil" libraries as well. Due to apathy and the prevailing illiteracy in the country, the people were not prepared to take advantage of these institutions.

91. What primary characteristic differentiated early libraries in the presidency towns from modern public libraries?

1. They were funded by private donations.
2. They were subscription based rather than free.
3. They exclusively served Europeans.
4. They were exclusively located in the hinterland.

92. What factor significantly contributed to the spread of libraries in the last two decades of the 19th century?

1. Increased government funding for literature.
2. Expansion beyond metropolitan areas.
3. Decrease in illiteracy rates.
4. Direct imitation of western library models.

93. How did the early libraries in the presidency towns primarily serve the population according to the passage?

1. They were open to all socio-economic classes without charges.
2. They were accessible to a broad section of the society with subscription fee.
3. They primarily catered to a narrower upper layer of society.
4. They were managed by a local government and free of use.

94. According to the passage, what was a significant limitation faced by libraries in the provincial, suburban and 'mofussil' areas?

1. They lacked government support.
2. They were unable to attract European patrons.
3. They mirrored the shortcomings of metropolitan libraries.
4. They had an overabundance of library materials.

95. Which of the following statement is implied but not directly stated in the passage regarding public libraries in the 19th century?

1. They were initially designed to cater to all social classes equally.
2. The libraries in the Princely States were more advanced than those in metropolitan areas.
3. The early libraries often struggled due to the prevailing apathy and illiteracy among the populace.
4. Library usage increased significantly in the early years due to government intervention.

Directions (Qs. No. 96-100): *Read the following passage and answer the question:*

Integration of technology facilitates access to information and ideas by incorporating new digital technologies into the library environment. The public library today provides unprecedented community access to a wide variety of digital media, computer technology, and online services for reading, reference, research, entertainment, and communication.

Historically, the technological development of traditional print media to meet an ever increasing market demand correlated directly with the problem of growing library collections, and how best to house them. The evolution of reading materials from scroll to codex to book, papyrus to vellum to paper, and manuscript to print, gave rise to the parallel development of the library facility itself, from carrel to lectern to alcove to hall, and beyond. Quantitatively, increases in the capacity of libraries over time were dramatic, with volumes in large collections numbering in the hundreds in medieval times, the tens of thousands in the Renaissance era, and millions today. In the late twentieth century, the introduction of new digital media continued to expand this capacity, while offering the potential of reducing the physical size of collections and, subsequently, the library facility itself.

Today, the public library provides access to a combination of traditional print and new digital media, which are complementary of one another, rather than mutually exclusive. In addition to books, magazines, and newspapers, the library offers a wide selection of digital media available on disk or for downloading, including e-books, books on tape, CDs, and DVDs. For Internet access, personal computers are available to the public at dedicated stations, which are centrally located in open, common areas of the library. Wi-Fi services for laptop computers and other portable electronic devices provide additional remote access to the Internet in other non-dedicated areas of the library.

96. Which of the following best describes the correlation between the evolution of reading materials and library facilities?

1. The transition from scroll to codex led to the development of digital libraries.
2. The shift from papyrus to vellum to paper influenced the design of carrels, lecterns, alcoves and halls.
3. The advancement of manuscript to print media necessitated smaller library space.
4. The increase in library volumes from hundreds to millions directly led to digital media usages.

97. What inference can be made about the relationship between traditional print media and digital media in modern libraries?

1. Digital media has completely replaced traditional print media.
2. Traditional media and digital media are considered complementary resources.
3. Libraries have phased out traditional print media in favour of digital media.
4. Digital media has reduced the importance of traditional print collection.

98. Considering the historic context provided, why might libraries have developed from smaller to larger facilities over time?

1. The technological advancement in print media required more space for storage.
2. The introduction of digital media led to the need for larger physical spaces.
3. The increase in market demand for books decreased the need for larger facilities.
4. The physical space required for scroll was significantly more than for books.

99. Why might the combination of Wi-Fi services and dedicated computer stations be significant for modern library users?

1. It ensures that only patrons with portable devices can access the internet.
2. It allows users to access the internet from various locations within the library.
3. It restricts internet access to specific area, ensuring quitter study zone.
4. It replaces the need for any physical media collection within the library.

100. Based on passage, what might be a reason for the introduction of new digital media in libraries in the late twentieth century?

1. To reduce the financial costs associated with maintaining large physical collections.
2. To decrease the physical size of collections while expanding library capacity.
3. To replace all traditional print media with digital alternatives.
4. To limit public access to reading and research materials.

ANSWERS

1	**2**	**3**	**4**	**5**	**6**	**7**	**8**	**9**	**10**
2	4	4	2	1	3	4	2	2	3
11	**12**	**13**	**14**	**15**	**16**	**17**	**18**	**19**	**20**
2	1	2	2	2	4	3	4	3	3
21	**22**	**23**	**24**	**25**	**26**	**27**	**28**	**29**	**30**
1, 2	1	4	1	1	1	3	3	2	3
31	**32**	**33**	**34**	**35**	**36**	**37**	**38**	**39**	**40**
*	4	3	2	4	1	2	3	2	2
41	**42**	**43**	**44**	**45**	**46**	**47**	**48**	**49**	**50**
3	1	4	2	2	4	3	1	3	4
51	**52**	**53**	**54**	**55**	**56**	**57**	**58**	**59**	**60**
3	1	2	4	3	3	4	2	2	2
61	**62**	**63**	**64**	**65**	**66**	**67**	**68**	**69**	**70**
4	4	2	1	4	1	3	1	4	4
71	**72**	**73**	**74**	**75**	**76**	**77**	**78**	**79**	**80**
3	1	1	2	1	1	2	3	3	4
81	**82**	**83**	**84**	**85**	**86**	**87**	**88**	**89**	**90**
3	1	1	3	3	2	2	1	3	*
91	**92**	**93**	**94**	**95**	**96**	**97**	**98**	**99**	**100**
2	2	3	3	3	2	2	1	2	2

EXPLANATORY ANSWERS

1. Ranganathan's Second Law of Library Science—"Every reader his/her book"—focuses on identifying and fulfilling the information needs of each user. The phrase *"Know your community and its needs"* from the OCLC research report reinterprets this principle in a modern library context. It emphasizes that a librarian must study the community's demographic, educational, and cultural profile to select and organize materials that best serve its readers. Thus, the librarian's role extends beyond maintaining collections to actively connecting people with resources suited to their unique interests and requirements.

2. W.C. Berwick Sayers, a pioneer in library classification theory, developed the *Canons of Classification* that served as foundational principles for organizing knowledge systematically. These canons were later simplified into 29 principles, which outline clear logical and philosophical guidelines for classifying subjects. The 29 principles cover essential aspects such as consistency, exclusivity, relevance, coordination, subordination, and helpful sequence in classification design. This structured approach provided a scientific base for future classification systems like Ranganathan's *Colon Classification* and influenced modern bibliographic organization and subject cataloging techniques.

3. In information retrieval and document clustering, a normalized similarity measure is used to ensure that a document's similarity with itself always equals 1, representing perfect similarity. This normalization process adjusts raw similarity scores (which may vary due to document length or weighting factors) so that they fall within a uniform scale from 0 to 1. When normalization is applied, it eliminates the bias caused by differing document magnitudes, allowing consistent comparison across documents. Hence, in normalized similarity measures, the self-similarity of any document becomes exactly 1, making it mathematically and conceptually the most accurate representation of identity.

4. This type of online search allows the user to input any word, phrase, or sentence in natural language as a search query. The system scans every field of the document record—such as title, abstract, keywords, author, and even full text—without restriction to controlled vocabularies or subject headings. It provides flexibility and ease of access, as users can retrieve documents even without knowing the exact indexing terms used by the database. Free text searching underpins modern search engines and online databases, enabling broad retrieval through natural linguistic expression rather than strict classification codes.

5. The Cranfield Test, one of the earliest and most influential studies in information retrieval evaluation, was conducted under the supervision of Cyril W. Cleverdon at Cranfield College of Aeronautics in England. This experiment pioneered the empirical testing of retrieval systems using standardized document collections, fixed queries, and defined relevance judgments. It introduced the fundamental metrics of precision (accuracy of retrieved results) and recall (completeness of retrieval), which remain the cornerstone of performance evaluation in information retrieval research. The Cranfield approach later inspired large-scale experiments like TREC and CLEF.

6. In Ranganathan's classification theory, telescoping of arrays refers to the deliberate merging or compression of related subordinate categories into a single notation to save space and simplify schedules. This act technically violates the Canon of Hierarchy, which demands clear and explicit levels of classification, but Ranganathan allows this violation to honor the Law of Parsimony. The Law of Parsimony advocates for economy and simplicity in design, ensuring the classification system remains efficient, practical, and user-friendly by avoiding unnecessary repetition or expansion in notation.

7. This process involves surrogating, repackaging, and compacting the content of primary literature such as research papers, technical reports, and conference proceedings into concise, secondary information sources. Abstracting and indexing periodicals summarize the key ideas, concepts, and bibliographic details of original works, helping users locate relevant research efficiently. They act as secondary journals, bridging the gap between vast primary literature and the user's specific information needs. Examples include *Chemical Abstracts* and *Biological Abstracts,* which condense the original data for quick reference and retrieval.

8. *Poole's Index to Periodical Literature* was compiled and published by William Frederick Poole in 1848. It was the first major index to English-language periodicals, providing a systematic subject-based access to articles published in magazines and journals of the time. Poole's work laid the foundation for modern periodical indexing and bibliographic control, introducing the concept of cumulative indexing and subject arrangement, which significantly improved access to periodical content before the digital era.

9. When a user seeks nearly all relevant literature on a particular subject, the search strategy adopted is termed the exhaustive approach. This approach aims for maximum coverage and completeness of information, including both current and retrospective sources. It is typically employed in advanced research, systematic reviews, or thesis preparation where comprehensive background study is essential. Unlike the everyday or current approach, which focuses on recent materials, the exhaustive approach involves extensive database searches, bibliographies, reference tracking, and consultation of both print and electronic resources.

10. The International Federation of Library Associations and Institutions (IFLA) launched the "Sister Libraries" initiative for children's and young adult libraries. Its main objective is to build partnerships between libraries worldwide to promote cultural exchange, cooperative projects, and reading among young audiences. Through this network, libraries share experiences, conduct joint literacy events, and foster global understanding and collaboration among young readers across nations.

11. The phrase *"information tends to leak, and the more it leaks, the more we have"* perfectly illustrates the diffusive nature of information. This property refers to the spreading and dispersing tendency of information—once released, it travels, multiplies, and reaches more people without losing its value. Similar to how gases diffuse in all directions, information naturally expands in reach through communication channels, media, and networks. Hence, diffusion reflects the active process of dissemination and amplification of knowledge, not merely its potential for sharing.

12. In the AACR-II (R) (Anglo-American Cataloguing Rules, Second Edition, Revised), Part A deals with the description of materials, providing detailed instructions on the bibliographic elements required for cataloguing different types of resources. Within this part, Section 12 specifically addresses serial publications—those issued in successive parts bearing numeric or chronological designations (e.g., journals, annuals, periodicals). It outlines rules for recording title, numbering, publication details, and continuity to ensure consistent and precise cataloguing of serials across libraries.

13. In the Z39.50 information retrieval protocol, the BIB-1 Attribute Set plays the central role in enabling searching and retrieval of bibliographic records. It defines standardized attributes—such as use (field to search like author, title, subject), relation, structure, truncation, and completeness—allowing systems from different libraries and vendors to communicate and interpret queries uniformly. This standardization ensures interoperability across databases, making it possible for a user to search bibliographic data in one format and retrieve compatible results from another system seamlessly.

14. The Modern MARC initiative of the Library of Congress aims to evolve MARC rather than immediately replace it. Its primary goal is to align MARC with RDA (Resource Description and Access) principles and facilitate the transition toward linked data environments, such as BIBFRAME. This integration allows bibliographic data to become more web-compatible, structured, and machine-readable, ensuring that library metadata remains relevant in the semantic web era while supporting interoperability and data sharing.

15. When a local network operates on a non–TCP/IP protocol and needs to communicate with a TCP/IP-based network, a gateway functions as a protocol converter. Unlike a router or bridge, which forwards data within similar protocols, a gateway performs data translation, packet reformatting, and protocol conversion to ensure successful communication between dissimilar network architectures. Thus, it enables smooth interoperability between networks that otherwise could not exchange data directly due to differing communication standards.

16. The Developing Library Network (DELNET), headquartered in New Delhi, is one of India's largest resource-sharing library networks. It connects a vast number of academic, research, and public institutions across India and abroad to facilitate interlibrary loan, union catalogues, and access to shared databases. As of recent records, over 9,000 institutions—including universities, technical institutes, and research organizations—are members of DELNET. This extensive network significantly enhances cooperative access to information resources and supports the growth of a national and international knowledge-sharing ecosystem.

17. The KBART (Knowledge Bases and Related Tools) recommended practice, developed by NISO and UKSG, aims to improve the exchange of metadata related to electronic resources. It provides standardized formats and procedures for transferring holdings and entitlement data between publishers, aggregators, and library knowledge bases. The main purpose is to ensure that libraries maintain accurate and up-to-date access information in their link resolvers and discovery tools, thereby improving access management, title coverage accuracy, and user experience for e-resources.

18. The ALTO (Analyzed Layout and Text Object) XML schema, when used with METS (Metadata Encoding and Transmission Standard), serves to encode the physical layout and textual content of digitized documents. It captures information such as page structure, text blocks, lines, fonts, and spatial coordinates of text on scanned pages. This schema allows digital libraries to preserve both the visual and textual integrity of original materials, enabling accurate text retrieval, display, and reconstruction of documents like newspapers, manuscripts, and books in digital archives.

19. The ISO 25964-2 standard provides comprehensive guidance for achieving semantic interoperability among different thesauri and controlled vocabularies. Its principal purpose is to define models and methods for mapping equivalent, broader, narrower, or related concepts across heterogeneous vocabularies. This ensures smooth information exchange between databases, digital libraries, and knowledge management systems that use different subject terminologies, enabling unified search and retrieval across platforms and languages.

20. The System Network Architecture, developed by IBM, is a structured framework that defines the rules, protocols, and formats for data communication in IBM systems. Introduced in the 1970s, SNA established layered communication procedures similar to the later OSI model. It standardized how IBM mainframes and terminals interacted, ensuring reliability and compatibility across diverse network setups. SNA was a foundational architecture before the widespread adoption of TCP/IP and remains significant in the history of enterprise networking.

21. Both Amazon Web Services (AWS) and Google App Engine can be classified under the Platform as a Service (PaaS) model, although AWS also includes IaaS and SaaS components.

- **Google App Engine is a clear example of PaaS**—it offers developers a managed environment with built-in scalability, runtime environments, APIs, and deployment tools to create and host applications without managing servers.
- **Amazon Web Services (AWS)** provides several PaaS offerings within its ecosystem, such as AWS Elastic Beanstalk, AWS Lambda, and AWS Fargate, which deliver similar platform-level capabilities for developers.

Thus, both AWS and Google App Engine qualify as PaaS platforms, though AWS encompasses a broader range of cloud service models.

22. In the Web of Science database, the Citation Network Graph (also known as Citation Mapping) visually represents the relationships between citing and cited articles. It shows how one paper connects to earlier and later research, illustrating citation chains and academic influence. This helps researchers trace the intellectual lineage of ideas, identify clusters of related studies, and understand the evolution of a specific research topic across time.

23. The Koha 23.05.03 release, as per official Koha community documentation, includes 4 enhancements aimed at improving functionality and user experience, along with 43 bugfixes that address reported technical issues and performance inconsistencies. These updates enhance the system's stability, security, and efficiency, ensuring smoother operations in library management modules such as circulation, cataloguing, and OPAC services.

24. The IEEE P802.3da project under the IEEE 802.3 Ethernet Working Group is the most relevant for implementing Single Pair Ethernet (SPE) in modern digital libraries, particularly for IoT devices. It defines standards for 10 Mb/s Single Pair Multidrop Segments, enabling efficient, low-power, and space-saving data transmission over a single twisted pair. This makes it ideal for connecting sensors, access systems, and smart devices within library automation and intelligent infrastructure environments.

25. When configuring Gmail with MS Outlook Express using SSL/TLS encryption for the incoming mail server, the correct port number is 993. This port corresponds to IMAPS (Internet Message Access Protocol Secure), which allows the synchronization of emails across multiple devices while maintaining end-to-end encryption. If POP3 were used instead, the secure port would be 995. However, IMAP (port 993) is the preferred method since it keeps messages accessible on both the mail client and the Gmail server. Note that port 587 is reserved for the outgoing mail server (SMTP) under TLS.

26. Under Section 18 of the Goa Public Libraries Act, 1993, a library cess in the form of a surcharge on excise duty is levied at the rate of ₹ 0.50 per bulk liter of beer. This provision was designed to generate recurring revenue for the improvement and maintenance of the state's public library system. Although the cess amount has been revised in later amendments, the original levy structure clearly applied to beer measured in bulk liters, linking excise collections directly to library funding.

27. The LibQUAL+ survey, developed by the Association of Research Libraries (ARL), contains 22 core questions that evaluate the perceived quality of library services across three fundamental dimensions—Affect of Service, Information Control, and Library as Place. These standardized questions allow libraries to benchmark performance, identify service gaps, and measure user satisfaction. Beyond these 22 core items, the survey may include additional questions on general satisfaction, outcomes, and user comments to provide deeper insights into library performance.

28. In the Financial Year 2023–24, the Ministry of Finance, Government of India allocated ₹ 5000 crore for the development and strengthening of libraries at the ward and village panchayat level under the CAPEX (Capital Expenditure) initiative. This allocation formed Part-VII of the broader scheme titled "Special Assistance to States for Capital Investment 2023–24", through which ₹ 1.3 lakh crore was provided to states as a 50-year interest-free loan for capital infrastructure projects. The ₹ 5000 crore earmarked for libraries was specifically meant to enable states to create and upgrade physical and digital library infrastructure, thereby promoting knowledge access, digital literacy, and community education across rural India.

29. In Carol Kuhlthau's Information Search Process (ISP) model, the fourth stage is Formulation, which follows the Exploration stage. At this point, the user begins to clearly define and articulate the focus of their search. After an initial phase of uncertainty, users start identifying patterns and concepts, narrowing their topic to form a more structured understanding. This stage signifies the transition from confusion to clarity, as users refine search strategies and begin purposeful information gathering.

30. The DSpace-CRIS project was originally developed through funding from the Hong Kong University, aiming to enhance the DSpace digital repository by integrating Current Research Information System (CRIS) functionalities. This extension allows institutions to manage publications, research data, projects, and researcher profiles in one unified system. By combining DSpace's repository structure with CRIS capabilities, the system supports comprehensive research information management, visibility enhancement, and institutional performance tracking in academic environments.

31. The current individual online-only subscription for the *Journal of Indian Library Association (JILA)* is ₹ 1,500 per year, which does not match any of the listed options (₹ 1,000 / ₹ 2,000 / ₹ 2,500 / ₹ 3,000). Hence, none of the options is correct.

32. Technology Focus is a periodic magazine of the Defence Research & Development Organisation. It showcases indigenous R&D—systems, products, testbeds—and acts as DRDO's outreach vehicle to inform stakeholders and the public about technological milestones from its labs and clusters.

33. In Ranganathan's Chain Procedure, a false link is a link that does not denote a subject with a definite, nameable concept (e.g., connective/relational elements or artefacts produced by phase relations or notational devices). Because such links don't correspond to clear subject headings, they are excluded as entry points—unlike sought links (definite subjects that users would search under) and unsought links (valid subjects but not typically used as access points).

34. Under the UGC (Promotion of Academic Integrity and Prevention of Plagiarism in Higher Educational Institutions) Regulations, 2018, Level 2 plagiarism refers to similarity between 40% and 60% in the submitted academic work. The prescribed penalty for this level is cancellation of the submission and debarring the student from submitting a revised version for a period of one year. This rule applies to students, researchers, and scholars, ensuring academic honesty and discouraging unethical copying in research or theses.

35. In information theory, entropy is defined as a measure of the degree of uncertainty or randomness in information. Introduced by Claude E. Shannon, entropy quantifies how unpredictable or disordered a message or data source is. A higher entropy value indicates greater uncertainty, meaning more information is required to describe or predict the system. Conversely, low entropy reflects predictability and order. Hence, entropy is a mathematical representation of the amount of information contained within a communication system.

36. In modern digital library environments, Current Awareness Services (CAS) are being increasingly integrated with Linked Open Data (LOD) and RSS feeds to ensure real-time updates and automated information dissemination. LOD enhances interoperability by connecting bibliographic and research metadata across systems, while RSS feeds enable continuous updates on new publications, acquisitions, and research alerts.

This integration modernizes CAS by providing personalized, dynamic, and machine-readable updates to users through digital and web-based platforms.

37. In the Colon Classification (6th Revised Edition), for the Main Class 'V' (History), an isolate number ending in '19' designates a Host Class. Within its facet formula V:19, the symbols [P] and [P2] have defined roles:

- [P] represents the (GD) or *Geographical Division,* reflecting the spatial component of history.
- [P2] stands for *Enumeration and (SD)* or *Specific Division,* referring to the sequence or specialized detailing within that geography.

This arrangement allows historical subjects to be classified systematically by both geographic scope and detailed chronological or thematic subdivisions.

38. The Telescoped Facet concept was introduced as a new feature in the Annexure of the Colon Classification, 6th Revised Edition, specifically applied to the Main Classes T (Education) and V (History). A telescoped facet merges two or more facets that would normally appear separately into a compact form, thus simplifying complex notations without losing their meaning. This innovation improved classification efficiency and clarity, particularly in these disciplines where overlapping educational or historical facets frequently occur, enhancing both brevity and usability of notational expression.

39. Lookout is an AI-driven accessibility app developed by Google for individuals with low or no vision. It employs computer vision and artificial intelligence to identify and describe objects, text, food labels, currency, and scenes in real time using a device's camera. The app provides audio output to guide the user, offering independence in everyday activities such as reading documents, recognizing items, and navigating environments. It exemplifies Google's commitment to assistive technology for accessibility and inclusion.

40. In the context of corporate libraries, the term "Taxonomy" refers to a structured system for organizing and categorizing information, documents, and digital content. It provides a hierarchical framework of categories, subcategories, and relationships that help users easily locate and retrieve information. Corporate taxonomies are crucial for knowledge management, content tagging, and enterprise search, as they enable efficient organization of internal reports, policies, and data across business units. Unlike thesauri or ontologies, taxonomies primarily emphasize hierarchical classification for clarity and accessibility.

41. The 8W's Information Literacy Model proposed by Annette Lamb outlines a process-oriented approach to problem-solving and research. The correct sequence of the five key steps mentioned is:

C. **Watching:** Observing, identifying, and defining the problem or information need.

D. **Webbing:** Searching and exploring available resources and connections.

E. **Wiggling:** Evaluating, questioning, and filtering the gathered information critically.

B. **Weaving:** Synthesizing and organizing the information to form coherent understanding.

A. **Waving:** Presenting, sharing, and celebrating the newly created knowledge.

This sequence reflects a continuous cycle of inquiry, exploration, and communication in the learning process.

42. In the POPSI (Postulate-based Permuted Subject Indexing) system developed by Ganesh Bhattacharyya, the logical order of its application steps is as follows:

D. **Analysis:** Breaking down the subject to identify constituent concepts and their relationships.

B. **Formalisation:** Representing the analyzed concepts formally using postulates and logical expressions.

E. **Modulation:** Converting formalized expressions into a standard syntactic form suitable for indexing.

A. **Standardization:** Ensuring uniform terminology and structure across entries for consistency.

C. **Preparation of EOC (Entry of Combination):** Creating the final index entry (EOC) for retrieval.

This sequential process ensures logical precision, uniformity, and consistency in subject indexing.

43. The ISBD (International Standard Bibliographic Description) prescribes a structured sequence for bibliographic data presentation to ensure uniformity and global consistency. The correct order of the listed areas of description is:

C. Title and Statement of Responsibility Area

A. Edition Area

E. Material-Specific Details Area (applicable to specific materials like maps, serials, etc.)

D. Publication, Distribution, etc. Area

B. Notes Area

This order maintains logical flow from identifying the work to specifying its version, unique details, publication data, and additional descriptive notes.

44. The chronological order of major Open Access Initiatives and Policy Declarations at the international level is:

D. **Scholarly Publishing and Academic Resources Coalition (SPARC)** – established in 1998, promoting open access and reforming scholarly communication.

C. **Budapest Open Access Initiative (BOAI)** – adopted in 2002, formally defining and advocating for open access publishing.

B. **Berlin Declaration on Open Access to Knowledge in the Sciences and Humanities** – signed in 2003, expanding the BOAI principles.

A. **Coalition of Open Access Policy Institutions (COAPI)** – founded in 2011, supporting universities implementing OA policies.

E. **Scottish Open Education Declaration** – launched in 2013, emphasizing open education and learning resources.

This timeline reflects the evolution of the global open access movement from foundational advocacy to institutional and policy-level implementations.

45. According to IFLA's Guidelines for Disaster Risk Reduction and Management for Libraries, the proper sequence of disaster planning phases is:

D. **Prevention:** Identifying potential risks and taking steps to avert disasters before they occur.

C. **Mitigation:** Minimizing the impact of unavoidable hazards through protective measures.

A. **Preparedness:** Establishing response protocols, training, and resource planning to handle emergencies effectively.

E. **Response:** Implementing immediate action during or after a disaster to protect life, property, and resources.

B. **Recovery:** Restoring normal operations, salvaging materials, and learning from the event to improve future plans.

This systematic sequence ensures libraries can proactively safeguard collections and services against natural or man-made disasters.

46. The correct chronological sequence of origin for these major bibliographic utilities and standards is:

E. **Library of Congress (1800):** Established as the national library of the United States, it pioneered cataloguing and bibliographic standards used worldwide.

C. **Ohio College Library Center (1967):** Now known as OCLC, it began as a shared cataloguing network for Ohio colleges and grew into a global cooperative.

D. **Western Library Network (1974):** Formed to provide shared cataloguing and interlibrary cooperation among western U.S. libraries before merging into OCLC.

B. **Research Libraries Group (1974):** Founded by major research institutions to promote collaborative bibliographic control and resource sharing.

A. **Resource Description and Access (RDA) (2010):** Introduced as a new cataloguing code replacing AACR2, designed for the digital and linked data environment.

47. Based on the tenure periods of Directors of the National Library, Kolkata, the correct ascending order is:

C. **D.N. Banerjee (1992–1997):** Oversaw modernization efforts and bibliographic expansion projects.

D. **Harjit Singh (1998):** Served as interim director, contributing to organizational restructuring.

B. **A.R. Bandyopadhyay (1998–2000):** Initiated improvements in library services and staff training.

E. **S.K. Chakravarti (2001–2003):** Focused on digitization initiatives and reader service enhancement.

A. **Sudhendu Mandal (2004–2007):** Strengthened automation and technological integration, advancing library modernization.

This order accurately reflects the historical succession of directors according to their appointment years.

48. The correct chronological order of communication models is:

E. Shannon and Weaver Model (1949): The earliest linear model defining the basic process of sender, message, channel, and receiver.

A. Schramm's Interactive Model (1954): Introduced feedback and the idea of shared experience between sender and receiver.

D. Jakobson's Model (1960): Explained six functional aspects of communication, focusing on linguistic and contextual functions.

C. Riley and Riley Model (1961): Emphasized the influence of the social environment and feedback loops on communication.

B. Berlo's SMCR Model (1960): Expanded on Shannon-Weaver by adding detail to the sender, message, channel, and receiver components, focusing on human skills and attitudes.

Together, these models trace the evolution from simple linear transmission to interactive and socio-psychological perspectives in communication theory.

49. In Colon Classification (CC), the Facet Formula prescribes a specific and logical order for arranging facets within any main class. The correct sequence is:

D. System (Main Class Concept): The foundational idea or core system around which the subject is organized.

B. Special: Denotes specific or narrower aspects within the main system.

A. [P]: Refers to the Personality facet, representing the primary entity or focus of study.

E. [E][2P]: Denotes Energy and Property facets, indicating processes or characteristics associated with the subject.

C. [2E][3P]: Represents additional or compound energies and properties, elaborating further complexity.

This sequence ensures a hierarchical and logical build-up from the general system to more detailed and compound characteristics, maintaining Ranganathan's analytico-synthetic classification structure.

50. The correct chronological order in which these major education commissions/committees were constituted in India is:

C. Kothari Commission (1964–66): Led by D.S. Kothari, it provided a comprehensive framework for national education policy.

D. Acharya Ramamurti Committee (1990): Reviewed the implementation of the 1986 National Policy on Education and suggested decentralization reforms.

B. Yashpal Committee (2009): Recommended the creation of an overarching body for higher education and emphasized improving quality and autonomy.

E. Hari Gautam Committee (2014): Reviewed the functioning of the University Grants Commission (UGC) and suggested structural reforms.

A. K. Kasturirangan Committee (2017–2019): Drafted the National Education Policy 2020, promoting holistic and flexible learning frameworks.

This sequence traces the evolution of India's educational reform from the mid-20th century to the present policy era.

51. The chronological order of these important Acts related to information, archives, and cultural heritage in India is:

D. Indian Treasure Trove Act (1878): The earliest legislation dealing with the discovery and preservation of hidden or buried treasures of archaeological value.

E. Ancient Monuments and Archaeological Sites and Remains Act (1958): Enacted to protect and conserve ancient monuments and archaeological sites of national importance.

B. Antiquities and Art Treasures Act (1972): Introduced to regulate the export trade and prevent the smuggling of cultural property and artefacts.

A. Public Records Act (1993): Provides for the management, preservation, and access to public records by government offices and archives.

C. Right to Information Act (RTI) (2005): Empowers citizens to access information from public authorities to ensure transparency and accountability in governance.

This order represents the progression of India's legislative efforts from physical preservation of heritage to ensuring informational transparency.

52. The logical sequence for implementing a Virtual Reference Service (VRS) in a special library is as follows:

C. Identify user needs: The first step is to analyze the information requirements and digital behavior of target users to design a relevant VRS model.

E. **Select virtual reference software:** Based on identified needs, appropriate software (such as LibChat, Zoho Desk, or QuestionPoint) is selected for real-time and asynchronous support.

A. **Train the staff:** Librarians and information professionals must be trained in using the selected tools, communication protocols, and virtual reference ethics.

B. **Launch service portal:** The virtual reference platform is then officially launched and integrated into the library's website or digital services hub.

D. **Monitor and improve service:** Continuous assessment through feedback, analytics, and user satisfaction ensures sustained service quality and improvement.

This order ensures a structured implementation from planning to performance evaluation.

53. The chronological order of these events in library and information history is:

D. **International Institute of Documentation changed to International Federation of Documentation (FID) (1938):** Reflecting its expanded international role in documentation and information science.

B. **First time ILA became a member of IFLA (1953):** Marking India's active participation in international library cooperation.

A. **Dr. S.R. Ranganathan appointed as National Research Professor of Library Science (1962):** Recognizing his outstanding contributions to library and information science.

E. **Online Europa Year Book started (2000):** The digital edition of this international reference publication was launched for global access.

C. **ASLIB acquired by MCB Group, the holding company for Emerald Group Publishing (2005):** Reflecting a major transition in ownership of this UK-based professional library organization.

This sequence accurately reflects the historical progression of institutional and professional developments in the field.

54. The chronological order of the listed milestones is as follows:

E. **Starting of Browne Charging System (1895):** Introduced by Nina Browne, this was one of the earliest manual systems for recording book circulation in libraries.

D. **Typological Study Towards Mode of Formation of Subjects (1950):** Conducted by S.R. Ranganathan, this foundational study advanced subject analysis theory and led to the development of his facet theory.

B. **MARC Project completed (1968):** The Machine-Readable Cataloging (MARC) project was completed by the Library of Congress, revolutionizing bibliographic data automation.

A. **Introduction of Zero Base Budgeting system (1970):** Initiated in the U.S. by Peter Pyhrr and later adopted globally for rational financial planning.

C. **Publication of DDC 23rd Edition (2011):** Released by OCLC, this updated edition reflected the most recent classification developments.

This timeline traces the evolution from early manual library operations to theoretical, technological, and financial innovations in modern library management.

55. The correct chronological order of origin of these major Internet protocols is:

D. **FTP (File Transfer Protocol) (1971):** One of the earliest protocols, designed to transfer files between systems over a network.

A. **TCP/IP (Transmission Control Protocol/ Internet Protocol) (1974–1983):** Formed the foundation of the modern Internet, standardizing communication between different network systems.

C. **HTTP (Hypertext Transfer Protocol) (1989–1991):** Developed by Tim Berners-Lee for transferring hypertext documents, becoming the backbone of the World Wide Web.

E. **HTTPS (Hypertext Transfer Protocol Secure) (1994):** Introduced as a secure extension of HTTP, using SSL/TLS encryption to ensure data privacy and authenticity.

B. **IPv6 (Internet Protocol version 6) (1998):** Created to replace IPv4, providing a vastly larger address space and enhanced routing capabilities for the expanding Internet.

This order reflects the evolution of network communication from basic file exchange to the secure, scalable Internet framework used today.

56. According to UNESCO's "Building Knowledge Societies" (2005) framework, the three fundamental component pillars of a knowledge society are:

A. Freedom of expression: Ensures open access to information and ideas, a cornerstone of democratic knowledge exchange.

C. Quality Education for All: Promotes inclusive learning opportunities and skill development for active participation in the knowledge economy.

D. Respect for cultural and linguistic diversity: Encourages pluralism in knowledge creation and preservation of diverse cultural identities.

These pillars emphasize human rights, education, and cultural inclusion as the foundation for equitable and sustainable knowledge societies.

57. The necessary elements of an Information Society—which ensure secure, reliable, and accessible information systems—are:

A. Confidentiality: Protecting information from unauthorized access or disclosure.

C. Integrity: Ensuring data accuracy, completeness, and reliability throughout its lifecycle.

D. Availability: Guaranteeing that information and systems remain accessible to authorized users when needed.

Together, these three elements form the CIA triad, the cornerstone of information security and stability in an information-driven society.

58. A MARC 21 bibliographic record must include specific core elements essential for identification, structure, and retrieval of bibliographic information. These mandatory components are:

A. Leader: Always mandatory. The Leader (positions 00–23) defines the structure and processing characteristics of the record, including record length, status, and type of material.

B. Control Field (008): Mandatory. The Fixed-Length Data Elements field (008) provides coded data about the resource—such as language, date, format, and bibliographic level—used for machine processing and indexing.

D. Title Statement (245): Mandatory. The Title Statement uniquely identifies the resource by recording its title and usually the statement of responsibility. Without it, the record cannot properly describe or distinguish the item.

Fields like 020 (ISBN) and 260/264 (Publisher Statement) are conditionally required—they are included only when the information exists or is applicable to the type of material. Thus, the core mandatory elements in every complete MARC 21 bibliographic record are Leader, 008, and 245.

59. Controlled vocabularies are standardized systems used to ensure consistent description and retrieval of information. They fall broadly into three main categories:

A. Subject Heading Lists: Predefined lists of authorized subject terms (e.g., LCSH, Sears List).

B. Thesauri: Structured vocabularies showing hierarchical, associative, and equivalence relationships between terms (e.g., UNESCO Thesaurus).

D. Ontologies: Formal representations of knowledge domains defining entities and their relationships, used in semantic web and linked data systems.

Folksonomies (C) are user-generated tagging systems and not controlled, while Information Society (E) is unrelated to vocabulary control.

60. The review type services are designed to provide analytical and evaluative summaries of developments in a particular field. These include:

B. Trend Reports: Summarize emerging trends, progress, and direction of research or technology in a given area.

E. State of the Art Reports: Offer comprehensive, critical overviews of current knowledge and research developments on a specific topic.

By contrast, Current Awareness and News Clippings provide alerting or informational updates, and Geographical Sources refer to reference materials, not review services.

61. The Indian patent databases are:

B. inPASS (Indian Patent Advanced Search System): Managed by the Office of the Controller General of Patents, Designs & Trade Marks (CGPDTM) under the Government of India, inPASS provides access to Indian patent applications, granted patents, and their legal status information.

C. **Patestate:** An Indian patent analytics and search platform that compiles and provides access to domestic patent data for research, innovation, and policy tracking.

Other options are international databases: Patentscope (A) is from WIPO, KIPO (D) belongs to the Korean Intellectual Property Office, and The Lens (E) is a global open-access patent database.

62. The National Knowledge Commission (NKC), established in 2005 under the Government of India, was tasked with formulating policy recommendations to strengthen India's position as a knowledge-driven economy. Its key functions included:

A. **Promote Open Access across the Nation:** Encouraging open dissemination of research and public information.

B. **Promote a knowledge-driven society:** Advancing education, innovation, and technology to foster sustainable knowledge-based growth.

D. **Advise the Government on matters related to higher education:** Recommending reforms in university systems, curriculum standards, and academic excellence.

While NKC advocated for nationwide access to knowledge, developing the digital library infrastructure (E) was carried forward later through other dedicated projects like the National Digital Library of India (NDLI).

63. The Global Open Access Portal (GOAP) was launched as an initiative of UNESCO, designed to provide information on the global state of open access policies and practices. It was developed through collaboration with:

A. **UNESCO:** The primary implementing body overseeing the project's development and policy framework.

C. **Indian Statistical Institute:** Responsible for designing and developing the backend architecture of the new GOAP platform.

D. **Redalyc:** Along with AmeliCA, contributed to curating and designing the user interface and data presentation for the portal.

This partnership brought together expertise in open-access publishing, data analytics, and global coordination to strengthen knowledge accessibility worldwide.

64. In Colon Classification (CC), the [P] (Personality) facet of the Main Class 'J – Agriculture' is composed of three specific components:

D. **Utility Array:** Refers to the purpose or functional use of agricultural entities, such as crops grown for food, fibre, or medicinal value.

A. **Part Array:** Represents the specific physical part of a plant or agricultural product, such as root, leaf, flower, or seed.

C. **Genus/Species Number:** Denotes the biological classification or scientific identity of the plant or animal being studied in agriculture.

These elements together define the concrete and specific personality facet for agriculture, representing the essential object of study. The Geographical Device and Least Concrete are not structural components of the Personality facet in this class.

65. The principal metadata harvesting tools and protocols are:

A. **OAI-PMH (Open Archives Initiative – Protocol for Metadata Harvesting):** The most widely used protocol for harvesting metadata from multiple repositories for aggregation and indexing.

D. **SRU/SRW (Search/Retrieve via URL or Web Service):** Protocols for web-based metadata retrieval and exchange using standard queries.

E. **OAI-ORE (Open Archives Initiative – Object Reuse and Exchange):** A framework that extends OAI-PMH by enabling the exchange and reuse of compound digital objects and their metadata.

Apache Solr (B) is an indexing and search engine, not a harvester, while Z39.50 (C) is primarily a search and retrieval protocol rather than a metadata harvesting protocol.

66. For implementing AI-driven services in an academic library, the librarian should prioritize technologies that directly enhance information management, user interaction, and automation:

A. **Machine Learning models for circulation forecasting:** Predicts demand and optimizes resource allocation by analyzing borrowing trends.

B. **AI-enabled virtual reference assistants:** Chatbots or digital assistants powered by AI to provide real-time user support and answer queries efficiently.

D. Auto-tagging of digital resources using NLP (Natural Language Processing): Automates metadata generation, classification, and subject tagging for digital collections.

Facial recognition (C), while AI-based, raises ethical and privacy concerns in academic spaces, and manual classification schemes like DDC (E) are traditional, non-AI tools. Hence, A, B, and D best represent AI-driven innovations in libraries.

67. The most widely used databases in Health Science academic libraries include:

A. PubMed: A premier biomedical database managed by the U.S. National Library of Medicine, covering medical, life science, and clinical research literature.

B. CINAHL (Cumulative Index to Nursing and Allied Health Literature): Specializes in nursing, allied health, and healthcare management resources.

E. Scopus: A comprehensive multidisciplinary citation and abstract database that includes extensive coverage of health, medicine, and biomedical sciences.

In contrast, HeinOnline (C) focuses on law, and ASME Journals (D) are engineering-based, so they are not relevant to health science disciplines.

68. According to G. Edward Evans, the recognized work analysis techniques in library and information science are:

B. GANTT Chart: A project scheduling and monitoring tool that visually displays tasks against time, helping analyze workflow, task interdependencies, and progress in library operations.

D. Cost-effectiveness analysis: A decision-making tool used to evaluate the relative efficiency of different methods or projects by comparing their costs against measurable outcomes.

These techniques assist library managers in optimizing workflow efficiency and ensuring the most effective use of resources. Other methods such as PERT and Operations Research are broader management or analytical tools, not specifically categorized as work analysis techniques in Evans' context.

69. The non-parametric tests—used when data do not meet normal distribution assumptions—are:

B. Spearman Correlation Coefficient: Measures the rank-based relationship between two variables.

D. Chi-Square Test: Tests independence or goodness of fit between categorical data.

E. Kruskal-Wallis Test: A non-parametric alternative to one-way ANOVA, comparing medians across multiple independent groups.

Conversely, ANOVA (A) and Z Test (C) are parametric tests, requiring normally distributed interval or ratio data.

70. The Canon of Helpful Sequence, formulated by S.R. Ranganathan as a Canon for Array, ensures that the order of subjects or isolates in any classification scheme is logical and convenient for users. The two main principles guiding its implementation are:

A. Principle of Spatial Contiguity: This principle arranges entities according to their natural geographical proximity or physical relationship (e.g., arranging regions from west to east or north to south). It helps users locate related places or subjects in close sequence, reflecting natural adjacency.

B. Principle of Increasing Literary Warrant: This principle suggests organizing subjects in decreasing order of the amount of literature available on each topic. The subject with the most literature is placed first, making the scheme more practical for majority use and user demand.

These two principles ensure that the arrangement of classes or isolates in an array is both user-oriented and literature-based, aligning with Ranganathan's goal of maximizing retrieval efficiency and logical accessibility.

71. The key figures associated with post-coordinate indexing are:

A. Mortimer Taube: Introduced the Uniterm system, the earliest post-coordinate indexing method allowing subject terms to be combined at the retrieval stage.

C. Calvin Mooers: Developed the Zatocoding system, an early post-coordinate retrieval method using machine-readable codes and punched cards.

D. W.E. Batten: Contributed to refining post-coordinate systems and their practical applications in documentation services.

Eugene Garfield (B) is associated with citation indexing, and Jorge E. Hirsch (E) introduced the h-index—neither are linked to post-coordinate indexing.

72. In the Dublin Core Metadata Element Set (DCMES), the following elements address intellectual property and ownership aspects:

A. Creator: Identifies the person or organization primarily responsible for the creation of the content, establishing authorship and ownership.

C. Publisher: Indicates the entity responsible for publishing or distributing the resource, linking to ownership and copyright.

D. Rights: Specifies copyright, licensing terms, or access conditions related to the resource.

Elements like Coverage (B) and Place (E) describe spatial or temporal attributes rather than intellectual property, so the correct set is Creator, Publisher, and Rights.

73. The correct associations are:

A. William Martin → Information Society: William Martin authored *"The Information Society"*, exploring the social and economic transformation brought about by information and communication technologies.

B. Alvin Toffler → The Third Wave: Alvin Toffler's book *"The Third Wave"* describes the three waves of civilization—agricultural, industrial, and information-based—marking the rise of the information age.

E. A.J. Walford → Guide to Reference Material: A.J. Walford compiled and edited the multivolume *Guide to Reference Material,* a comprehensive bibliography of major reference sources.

S.C. Bradford is known for *Bradford's Law of Scattering,* not classification, and Karl Pearson is associated with statistics and correlation theory, not webometrics.

74. The correct matches are:

A. Facts on File → News Digest: A reference service that provides summaries and updates of current news and global events.

B. World of Learning → Directory: A directory listing universities, learned societies, and research institutions worldwide.

D. Willing's Press Guide → Periodical Directory: A comprehensive directory providing details about newspapers, magazines, and journals.

Concordance (C) lists word occurrences in texts (not abstracts), and Books in Print (E) is a bibliography, not an index, hence they are incorrect combinations.

75. The correct combinations are:

A. Wikipedia → Encyclopedia: A free, collaborative, web-based encyclopedia offering multilingual information on diverse topics.

B. Library Philosophy and Practice → e-journal: A peer-reviewed open-access e-journal publishing research in library and information science.

D. e-PG Pathshala → Academic Source: An academic initiative under the MHRD's National Mission on Education through ICT, offering high-quality postgraduate course materials online.

E-Granthalaya (C) is library management software, not an e-book, and SheRNI (E) (Scientific and Herbal Research Network of India) is a database, not software.

76. The correct historical matching of ancient libraries with their respective countries is:

A. Bibliotheca Alexandria → IV. Egypt: The most renowned library of the ancient world, located in Alexandria, Egypt, established during the reign of Ptolemy II around the 3rd century BCE.

B. Library of Ashurbanipal → III. Iraq: Situated in Nineveh (modern-day Iraq), this 7th-century BCE library was the royal collection of the Assyrian King Ashurbanipal, containing thousands of cuneiform tablets.

C. Library of Pergamum → II. Turkey: Located in Pergamum (modern Bergama, Turkey), it was a major center of Hellenistic learning, rivaling the Library of Alexandria.

D. Bibliotheca Ulpia → I. Rome: Established by Emperor Trajan in Rome, this library formed part of the Forum of Trajan and housed both Latin and Greek works.

77. The correct association between libraries and their institutions is:

A. Saraswati Bhawan → III. Sampoornanand Sanskrit University: Located in Varanasi, this library holds a vast collection of ancient Sanskrit manuscripts and rare works in Indian philosophy and linguistics.

B. Sir Dorabji Tata Memorial Library → I. Tata Institute of Social Sciences (TISS): This library, established in memory of Sir Dorabji Tata, supports research and academic programs in social sciences.

C. Ratan Tata Library → IV. University of Delhi: The main library for social sciences at the Delhi School of Economics, named after Ratan Tata.

D. Indira Gandhi Memorial Library → II. University of Hyderabad: The central library of the University of Hyderabad, providing modern facilities for research and higher studies.

78. The correct matching of national libraries with their year of establishment is:

A. Library of Congress → III. 1800: Founded in Washington, D.C., the Library of Congress is the national library of the United States and one of the largest libraries in the world.

B. National Diet Library → II. 1948: Established in Japan as the national parliamentary library to support legislative research and national documentation.

C. National Library of Germany → I. 1912: Formed as the *Deutsche Bücherei* in Leipzig, it became the unified national library for German publications.

D. National Library of Australia → IV. 1960: Established in Canberra, it serves as the repository for Australia's national documentary heritage.

79. The correct matching of information retrieval models and examples is:

A. Semantic Search Engine → IV. Wolfram/Alpha: A semantic search engine like Wolfram/Alpha interprets the meaning of queries and provides concept-based answers rather than keyword matches.

B. Boolean Operators → III. Digital Logic: Boolean logic forms the foundation of early information retrieval systems using AND, OR, and NOT operators to combine search terms logically.

C. Knowledge Retrieval Systems → II. Cognitive Model: Cognitive models simulate human thought processes to improve retrieval, interpreting user intent and domain knowledge.

D. Algebraic IR Model → I. Latent Semantic Indexing: This model applies algebraic and vector space techniques, such as matrix decomposition, to identify relationships between terms and documents for improved retrieval accuracy.

80. The correct association between areas and e-governance initiatives is:

A. Education → IV. Gyandoot: An e-governance initiative launched in Madhya Pradesh to provide rural education, information, and communication access through community-based information kiosks.

B. Transport → III. Sarige: A transport-related e-governance initiative in Karnataka, designed to manage and track public transport operations efficiently.

C. Agriculture → II. e-Choupal: An ITC initiative providing farmers with market information, weather forecasts, and agricultural best practices through rural digital kiosks.

D. Taxation and Revenue → I. Compact: A computerization project in the Indian Revenue Department aimed at streamlining accounting, taxation, and fund management in government offices.

81. The correct matching of MARC 21 bibliographic elements with their corresponding tags is:

A. Personal Main Entry → III. 100: Used for the primary author or creator of a work (main entry field).

B. Personal Subject Heading → IV. 600: Indicates a personal name used as a subject (e.g., for biographies or criticism).

C. Personal Added Entry → I. 700: Refers to additional authors or contributors other than the main entry.

D. Bibliographic Title → II. 245: Denotes the title statement of the resource, including subtitle and statement of responsibility.

This tagging structure ensures standardized bibliographic representation across library catalogues using MARC 21 format.

82. The correct matching of Information Seeking Behaviour (ISB) models with their corresponding theories is:

A. Wilson's Model of ISB → IV. Threefold view on information seeking – context, system, and information sources: Wilson's model (1981, revised 1996) conceptualizes information behaviour as influenced by multiple contexts (personal, social, environmental) and mediated by information systems and sources.

B. Dervin's Model of ISB → III. Sense-making approach – situation, gap, and outcome: Dervin (1983) proposed that individuals construct meaning through "sense-making," involving three elements—situation, gap, and outcome—to bridge their knowledge gaps.

C. Kuhlthau's Model of ISB → II. Association of feelings, thoughts, and actions but not cognitive: Kuhlthau's (1991) Information Search Process model emphasizes the affective, cognitive, and behavioral dimensions of information seeking, showing how emotions evolve through search stages.

D. Marchionini's Model of ISB → I. Tailored to electronic environment – process consists of eight subprocesses: Marchionini (1995) designed a model for online searching, consisting of eight dynamic subprocesses that reflect iterative human–computer interaction during digital information retrieval.

83. The Right to Information (RTI) Act, 2005 sections and their provisions correspond as follows:

A. Section 4 → IV. Obligation of public authorities: Mandates proactive disclosure of information by public authorities to promote transparency.

B. Section 6 → III. Procedure for requesting information: Specifies the process for citizens to request information from Public Information Officers (PIOs).

C. Section 8 → I. Exemptions from disclosure: Lists categories of information exempt from disclosure (e.g., national security, personal privacy, trade secrets).

D. Section 10 → II. Penalties for non-compliance: Provides for partial disclosure or severability of exempt information and also guides action in cases of refusal or delay, linked to penal sections (20) for non-compliance.

These sections collectively establish the framework for access, exemptions, and responsibilities under the RTI Act.

84. The correct association between Knowledge Management (KM) models and their approaches is:

A. Von Krogh and Roos → III. Organizational Epistemology: Their model focuses on the epistemological foundation of knowledge creation, emphasizing the role of organizations as knowledge-creating systems.

B. Wiig → II. Synchronize: Wiig's model stresses the systematic and synchronized management of knowledge to ensure that organizational knowledge is usable, complete, and aligned with objectives.

C. Nonaka and Takeuchi → IV. Socialization: Their SECI (Socialization, Externalization, Combination, Internalization) model describes how tacit and explicit knowledge interact dynamically within organizations; socialization is a core process of tacit knowledge sharing.

D. Choo → I. Sense-Making: Choo's model views organizations as "sense-making systems," where knowledge is used for decision-making, information seeking, and learning in dynamic environments.

85. The correct matching of RSS feed components with their functions is:

A. Channel → III. Container of overall feed metadata: The *channel* element contains general information about the RSS feed, such as title, link, description, and publication date—serving as the parent container for all items.

B. Item → IV. Individual entry/article in a feed: Each *item* represents a single post, news article, or update entry within the RSS feed.

C. Enclosure → I. Multimedia file (audio/video) attachment: The *enclosure* element is used to include external media files such as audio podcasts or video attachments.

D. GUID → II. Unique ID for each entry: The *GUID* (Globally Unique Identifier) provides a distinct identifier for every RSS item to differentiate updates and prevent duplication.

86. Dr. S.R. Ranganathan, in *Prolegomena to Library Classification* (3rd Edition, 1967), established a total of 43 Canons of Classification, distributed among the three planes of work (Idea, Verbal, and Notational) and an additional set for Book Classification. Their correct distribution and logic are as follows:

A. Canons of Idea Plane → III. 15: The Idea Plane represents the intellectual stage of classification—formulating concepts and defining their relationships. It includes 15 canons, divided into:

- 4 Canons for Characteristics
- 3 Canons for Succession of Characteristics
- 4 Canons for Array

- 2 Canons for Chain
- 2 Canons for Filiatory Sequence

These ensure logical structuring and interrelation among subjects.

B. Canons of Verbal Plane → I. 4: The Verbal Plane governs the linguistic representation of ideas—how classes and isolates are named. It has 4 canons:

- Canon of Context
- Canon of Enumeration
- Canon of Currency
- Canon of Reticence

These emphasize clarity, consistency, and relevance of terminology in classification.

C. Canons of Notational Plane → IV. 24: The Notational Plane focuses on constructing symbolic representations (notations) to express classified ideas. Ranganathan defined 24 canons, grouped under:

- Basic Canons (12)
- Canons for Mnemonics (5)
- Canons for Growing Universe (4)
- Canons for Book Classification (3)

These ensure that notation systems remain logical, expandable, and user-friendly.

D. Canons of Book Classification → II. 3: This set applies specifically to Book Numbers and Collection Numbers, dealing with how documents are organized physically. The 3 canons are:

- Canon of Book Number
- Canon of Collection Number
- Canon of Two-Fold Division (for separating Class Number and Book/Collection Number)

Hence, the total canonical framework of 43 canons integrates all planes and ensures both conceptual and physical organization in library classification systems.

87. The correct association of technologies with their propounders is:

A. Bar Code Technology → III. Norman Joseph Woodland and Bernard Silver: They invented the barcode in 1952, later commercialized by IBM for retail and inventory management.

B. RFID Technology → I. Ray Theories Ray Tag: RFID (Radio Frequency Identification) was developed through research on electromagnetic fields and tagging technology by Ray Tag and others, evolving in the mid-20th century.

C. QR Code → IV. Denso Wave: The QR (Quick Response) Code was invented in 1994 by Denso Wave, a subsidiary of Toyota, to track automotive components.

D. Biometric Technology → II. Sir William Herschel: He pioneered fingerprint identification in the 19th century, laying the foundation for modern biometric authentication systems.

88. The correct chronological mapping of milestones in Open Source Software (OSS) history is:

A. Richard Stallman formed GNU Project → IV. 1983: The GNU Project (GNU's Not Unix) was launched by Stallman to create a completely free operating system, marking the formal beginning of the free software movement.

B. Creation of Free Software Foundation → III. 1985: Founded by Stallman to support and promote free software development, licensing (GPL), and advocacy.

C. Development of Linux Kernel by Linus Torvalds → II. 1991: Linus Torvalds began developing the Linux kernel, which later became the foundation of many open-source operating systems.

D. Open Source Initiative formed by Eric Raymond → I. 1998: OSI was established to promote and protect open-source principles, introducing the term "open source" as distinct from "free software."

89. The correct correspondence between MARC format data and their MARC tags is:

A. Physical Description Fixed Field → III. 007: Field 007 contains coded data describing the physical characteristics of a resource, such as format, dimensions, and medium.

B. Patent Control Information → II. 013: Field 013 is used for patent document identification, including number and date details.

C. Creation/Reference Note → IV. 510: Field 510 cites references or bibliographic sources used in cataloging the record.

D. Non-MARC Information Field → I. 887: Field 887 stores metadata not conforming to MARC standards, often imported from external or legacy systems.

90. Correct mapping: A–IV, B–I, C–II, D–I.

- **A → IV (Case Study):** An in-depth exploration of a single case/phenomenon is, by definition, a case study.
- B → **I (Quantitative Research):** Establishing relationships between variables (e.g., correlation, regression, experiments) is a hallmark of quantitative designs.
- **C → II (Survey Research):** Collecting information from a population via questionnaires/structured interviews is survey research.
- **D → I (Quantitative Research):** Using numerical data and statistical analysis to draw conclusions is quantitative.

Because the correct mapping requires I twice (for B and D), none of the provided options matches this mapping; hence NONE.

91. The early libraries established in the presidency towns of Bombay, Calcutta, and Madras were modeled after European libraries but were not free. They required users to pay a subscription fee to access materials. Modern public libraries, however, are open and free to all, which marks the major distinction between them.

92. The passage clearly states that the library movement "spread to the vast hinterland beyond the metropolises" and became particularly strong in the last two decades of the 19th century. Thus, the major contributing factor was the expansion of libraries beyond the major presidency towns into provincial and district areas.

93. These early libraries were not open to all citizens. The passage mentions that the use of such libraries "was confined to a thin upper layer of society," meaning that only the educated elite had access, rather than the general public.

94. The provincial, suburban, and mofussil libraries suffered from the same problems as those in the presidency towns — limited accessibility and low public participation — due to general apathy and illiteracy in the population.

95. While not directly stated, the passage implies that despite the spread of libraries, people were not ready to use them because of "apathy and prevailing illiteracy." This indirect statement suggests that public libraries struggled for active engagement from the masses in the 19th century.

96. The passage highlights a direct historical parallel between the evolution of reading materials and the architectural development of libraries. As materials evolved—from scrolls to codices to books, and from papyrus to vellum to paper—the physical form and usability of these materials influenced how libraries were built. Hence, design features like carrels, lecterns, alcoves, and halls evolved to accommodate these changing reading formats and growing collections.

97. The passage explicitly states that print and digital media "are complementary of one another, rather than mutually exclusive." This means that libraries integrate both media types to serve varied needs—reading, research, and entertainment—without eliminating traditional resources.

98. Historically, as reading materials advanced from manuscripts to printed books, the quantity of volumes increased dramatically—from hundreds in medieval libraries to millions in modern times. This surge in the number of materials necessitated larger library facilities to house the growing collections.

99. The passage describes that libraries offer dedicated computer stations for Internet use in central areas and Wi-Fi for portable devices in non-dedicated spaces. This combination ensures that users can access the Internet conveniently from multiple locations—whether at fixed terminals or using their own devices.

100. The passage explains that the introduction of digital media in the late 20th century "continued to expand this capacity while offering the potential of reducing the physical size of collections." Thus, digital media allowed libraries to store and provide access to far more content without proportionately increasing their physical storage space.

Previous Years' Paper

National Testing Agency (NTA)

UGC-NET Junior Research Fellowship & Assistant Professor Eligibility Exam

Library and Information Science, January-2025

(Exam held on 16-01-2025)

PAPER-II

1. In Colour Classification (Ed. 6, Revised Ed.) 'y8' is used for:

A. Digest
B. Dictionary
C. Conference proceedings
D. Manual
E. Scope

Choose the ***most appropriate*** answer from the options given below:

1. A and C only 2. B and E only
3. E and A only 4. A and D only

2. What is the role of AI in Web 3.0?

1. AI is used only for improving user interfaces.
2. AI replaces the need for Blockchain in Web 3.0.
3. AI helps in understanding and processing unstructured data to deliver more personalized experiences.
4. AI is used only in search engine optimization.

3. SheRNI and Vidwan are the database services of ______.

1. DELNET 2. DESIDOC
3. INFLIBNET 4. NICNET

4. CERT-In (The Indian Computer Emergency Response Team) has been designated to perform the following functions:

A. Collection, analysis and dissemination of information on cyber incidents.
B. Forecast and alert of cyber security incidents.
C. Issue guidelines, activities, vulnerability notes and white papers relating to information security practices.
D. Emergence measures for handling national disaster management incidents.
E. Co-ordination of cyber incidents response activities.

Choose the ***most appropriate*** answer from the options given below:

1. A, C, D and E only
2. B, C, D and E only
3. A, B, C and E only
4. A, B, D and E only

5. Identify right statements about Folksonomies.

A. Folksonomy is a sub concept of social taxonomy.
B. Folksonomies are form of reader advisory service that is easy to use.
C. Folksonomy tagging and ranking have the same precision of professional cataloguing.
D. Folksonomies are being used with Social Media platforms of such as Flicker, Pinterest etc.

E. Folksonomies are a form of reader advisory service for classifier and classificationist both.

Choose the ***most appropriate*** answer from the options given below:

1. A, B and D only
2. B and D only
3. B, C and E only
4. A and E only

6. Arrange the following layers of semantic web from bottom to top:

A. Logic
B. Ontology
C. Proof
D. RDF
E. Trust

Choose the ***most appropriate*** answer from the options given below:

1. A, D, C, B, E
2. D, B, A, C, E
3. E, C, D, B, A
4. D, A, C, B, E

7. One criticism of h-index is that it can be biased in favour of:

1. Early career researcher
2. Researcher in fields with high citation rates
3. Researches with fewer publications
4. Researcher who publishes in low impact journals

8. Which of the following organizations is responsible for managing 'Open DOAR'?

1. The National Library of Medicine
2. University of Nottingham
3. The British Library
4. National Science Foundation

9. Abstract that provides important information about original, summerising the original, principal arguments and principal data, is known as:

1. Critical abstract
2. Indicative abstract
3. Informative abstract
4. Highlight abstract

10. Arrange the following in chronological order of their introduction:

A. Twitter
B. BlogSpot
C. ResearchGate
D. LinkedIn
E. Snapchat

Choose the ***most appropriate*** answer from the options given below:

1. B, D, A, C, E
2. D, B, C, E, A
3. B, A, D, E, C
4. E, B, C, D, A

11. What was the tenure of Dr. Ranganathan as ILA President?

1. 1937-1940
2. 1940-1942
3. 1944-1953
4. 1953-1955

12. One characteristic of information is, 'it is diffusive', it means:

1. It can be condensed and concentrated
2. It tends to leak
3. It is sharable
4. It is not reduced by use and share

13. Arrange the following steps in a logical sequence to be performed by acquisition module of any LMS.

A. Received documents
B. Duplicate checking
C. Preparing and mailing orders
D. Processing invoice and accessioning of documents
E. Verification and modification of actual bibliographic information

Choose the ***most appropriate*** answer from the options given below:

1. C, D, B, E, A
2. B, C, A, E, D
3. B, C, E, D, A
4. A, C, B, D, E

14. In which year DOI was launched?

1. 1996
2. 1998
3. 1999
4. 2003

15. Match the following theories of classification with their respective propounder.

List-I (Theory)	List-II (Propounder)
A. Descriptive Theory	I. J.D. Brown
B. One Place Theory	II. E.C. Richardson
C. Criteria of Classification	III. E.W. Hume
D. Literary Warrant	IV. Henry Bliss

Choose the ***correct*** answer from the options given below:

1. A-IV, B-I, C-II, D-III
2. A-II, B-III, C-IV, D-I
3. A-IV, B-III, C-II, D-I
4. A-III, B-IV, C-II, D-I

16. Arrange the following public library developments in India in chronological order.

A. Report submission of the National Policy on Library and Information System (NAPLIS)
B. Launch of the National Mission on Libraries (NML)
C. Enactment of the Public Libraries Act in Tamil Nadu
D. Establishment of the Raja Rammohan Roy Library Foundation (RRRLF)
E. Formation of the Delhi Public Library under UNESCO assistance.

Choose the ***most appropriate*** answer from the options given below:

1. C, E, A, B, D
2. D, A, C, B, E
3. C, E, D, A, B
4. D, C, A, B, E

17. Match the different types of storage technology with their unique characteristics.

List-I (Storage Technology)	List-II (Characteristics)
A. SSD	I. Uses magnetic platters
B. RAM	II. Non-volatile Flash memory
C. HDD	III. Volatile memory with quick access
D. ROM	IV. Permanent Firmware Storage

Choose the ***correct*** answer from the options given below:

1. A-II, B-III, C-I, D-IV
2. A-III, B-II, C-IV, D-I
3. A-I, B-III, C-II, D-IV
4. A-IV, B-I, C-III, D-II

18. In ISBD(M), bibliographical information is divided in _____ areas.

1. 5
2. 7
3. 8
4. 6

19. Which of the following are serious issues of Internet?

A. Obesity and depression
B. Age-inappropriate content
C. Social isolation
D. Abundant information resources
E. Global audience

Choose the ***most appropriate*** answer from the options given below:

1. A, C and E only
2. B, C and D only
3. C, D and E only
4. A, B and C only

20. Match the institutions with the name of the person on whom the central libraries of these institutions are named.

List-I (Institutions)	List-II (Names of Persons)
A. Indian Institute of Science, Bengaluru	I. Vikram Sarabhai
B. Indian Institute of Management, Ahmedabad	II. Sayaji Rao Gaikwad
C. Jawaharlal Nehru University, New Delhi	III. J.R.D. Tata
D. Banaras Hindu University, Varanasi	IV. Dr. B. R. Ambedkar

Choose the ***correct*** answer from the options given below:

1. A-IV, B-I, C-III, D-II
2. A-III, B-I, C-IV, D-II
3. A-III, B-IV, C-II, D-I
4. A-II, B-I, C-III, D-IV

21. What is the primary goal during the "preservation" phase of the information life cycle?

1. To ensure information is made accessible and used effectively.
2. To ensure that information is stored securely and backed up.
3. To archive and protect information for long term retention.
4. To delete outdated and unnecessary information.

22. Arrange the following according to their year of emergence.

A. ERNET
B. NKN
C. C-DOT
D. C-DAC
E. NMEICT

Choose the ***most appropriate*** answer from the options given below:

1. C, A, D, E, B
2. D, E, C, A, B
3. A, C, D, B, E
4. E, B, D, A, C

23. Which of the following platforms provide a mobile application for library patrons to track their book loans?

A. Tidal
B. Libby
C. Spotify
D. Overdrive
E. Borrow Box

Choose the ***most appropriate*** answer from the options given below:

1. A, C and E only
2. A, B and D only
3. B, D and E only
4. B, C and D only

24. Match the following institutions with their year of establishment.

List-I (Institutions)	List-II (Year of establishment)
A. IAEA	I. 1969
B. ICSSR	II. 1971
C. WIPO	III. 1957
D. UNISIST	IV. 1970

Choose the ***correct*** answer from the options given below:

1. A-IV, B-III, C-II, D-I
2. A-III, B-IV, C-II, D-I
3. A-III, B-I, C-IV, D-II
4. A-II, B-III, C-IV, D-I

25. Which is the correct sequence in the chronological order of their publication?

A. Jewett's Cataloguing Code
B. Cutter's Cataloguing Code
C. AACR
D. Classified Cataloguing Code
E. Anglo-American Joint Code

Choose the ***most appropriate*** answer from the options given below:

1. A, B, E, D, C
2. B, E, D, A, C
3. D, E, A, C, B
4. A, D, C, E, B

26. Arrange the following subjects according to the "Principle of increasing complexity" as per Colon Classification (Ed. 6th Rev. Ed.):

A. Biogeography
B. Anthropogeography
C. Political geography
D. Mathematical geography
E. Economic geography

Choose the ***most appropriate*** answer from the options given below:

1. A, C, D, B, E
2. B, C, E, A, D
3. D, A, B, C, E
4. A, B, C, D, E

27. What protocol is specifically designed for secure HTTP communication by adding SSL/TLS encryption?

1. FTP 2. SMTP
3. TCP/IP 4. SHTTP

28. Arrange the following acts according to their year of enactment:

A. The Information Technology Act
B. The Press and Registration of Books Act
C. The Right to Information Act (RTI)
D. Copyright Act
E. The Patent Act

Choose the ***most appropriate*** answer from the options given below:

1. B, C, D, E, A
2. D, B, A, C, E
3. E, D, B, A, C
4. B, D, E, A, C

29. Who authored the book "Towards Paperless Society"?

1. F.W. Lancaster 2. B.C. Vickery
3. C.W. Hanson 4. P.A. Atkinson

30. If an academic library reports a significant increase in the use of digital resources but a decline in the borrowing of print materials, what can be inferred?

A. The library users prefer digital formats for convenience.
B. The library's physical collection is outdated.
C. There is a lack of awareness about print resources among users.
D. The library has not focused on promoting its physical collection.
E. Digital resources are more accessible and easer to use compared to print materials.

Choose the ***most appropriate*** answer from the options given below:

1. A, B and D only
2. A, C and D only
3. A, C and E only
4. A, B and E only

31. Identify the correct option(s) among the following:

A. The "Deep Web" and the "Surface Web" are the same things.
B. Deep Web refers to web contents not indexed by search engines like Bing.
C. The Deep Web is legally used to protect personal information, whereas Surface Web is often used to engage in illegal activities.
D. Data in Deep Web is stored in a database which is not coded in HTML.
E. SSRN is an example of Deep Web contents.

Choose the ***most appropriate*** answer from the options given below:

1. A, C and D only
2. B, D and E only
3. B, C and D only
4. A, D and E only

32. Which of the following is an objective of the West Bengal Public Libraries Act, 1979?

1. To develop libraries as educational resources
2. To introduce library automation
3. To provide library services in rural areas
4. To establish a public library network

33. The structure of DOI (Digital Object Identifier) consists of ______.

1. A DOI consists only numeric code that uniquely identifies a document
2. A DOI consists alphanumeric code that uniquely identifies a document
3. A DOI is made up of a prefix and suffix. Prefix identifying the resistant and suffix is unique to the object
4. A DOI is a URL format and ends with a period

34. Information technology used with human intelligence simulation is used in the creation of:

1. Artificial Intelligence System
2. Machine Learning System
3. Learning Management System
4. Expert System

35. Arrange the following IPR related international treaties in the order of their adoption.

A. Berne Convention
B. TRIPS Agreement
C. Paris Convention
D. WIPO Copyright Treaty
E. Patent Cooperation Treaty

Choose the ***most appropriate*** answer from the options given below:

1. A, C, E, B, D
2. C, A, E, B, D
3. A, B, C, D, E
4. C, A, E, D, B

36. Match the following State Library Acts in order of their enactment.

List-I (States)	List-II (Year of enactment)
A. Mizoram	I. 2002
B. Odisha	II. 2009
C. Bihar	III. 1993
D. Arunachal Pradesh	IV. 2008

Choose the ***correct*** answer from the options given below:

1. A-III, B-I, C-IV, D-II
2. A-III, B-IV, C-II, D-I
3. A-I, B-II, C-IV, D-III
4. A-IV, B-III, C-II, D-I

37. Match the List-I with List-II.

List-I	List-II
A. IIT, Kanpur	I. MANTRA
B. C-DAC	II. SHIVA and SHAKTI
C. NCST, Mumbai	III. VYKARTA
D. CMU, USA & IISC, Bengaluru	IV. ANGLABHARTI

Choose the ***correct*** answer from the options given below:

1. A-III, B-I, C-II, D-IV
2. A-I, B-III, C-IV, D-II
3. A-IV, B-II, C-III, D-I
4. A-II, B-IV, C-I, D-III

38. How many entities does PREMIS data model has?

1. Two
2. Three
3. Four
4. Five

39. Match the following Standard Sub Divisions (Table-1) of DDC (19th edition) with their notation.

List-I (Standard Sub-division)	List-II (Notation)
A. Serials Publication	I. –07
B. Philosophy and Theory	II. –05
C. Collection	III. –01
D. Study and Teaching	IV. –08

Choose the ***correct*** answer from the options given below:

1. A-I, B-IV, C-II, D-III
2. A-II, B-III, C-IV, D-I
3. A-IV, B-III, C-I, D-II
4. A-I, B-II, C-III, D-IV

40. What is the correct difference between a web portal and a website?

1. A web portal allows users to personalize their experience while a website typically presents impersonalised information.
2. A portal does not provide access to external links, whereas website does.
3. A portal is designed only for e-commerce, whereas website is designed for information sharing.
4. A website requires a login to access content, while a web portal does not.

41. The development of ______ technologies in scholarly communication is transforming how research is shared and archived, particularly in terms of security and accessibility.

1. Artificial Intelligence
2. Blockchain
3. Internet of Things
4. Cloud computing

42. Match the Role Operators in PRECIS with the notations.

List-I (PRECIS Role Operators)	**List-II (Notations)**
A. Action	I. 0
B. Key System	II. 1
C. Location	III. 2
D. Performer	IV. 3

Choose the ***correct*** answer from the options given below:

1. A-IV, B-III, C-I, D-II
2. A-II, B-I, C-III, D-IV
3. A-III, B-II, C-I, D-IV
4. A-IV, B-I, C-II, D-III

43. Which type of plagiarism occurs when a person combines phrases or ideas from multiple sources into a single work without attribution?

1. Patch work plagiarism
2. Self-plagiarism
3. Verbatim plagiarism
4. Minimalistic plagiarism

44. Match the different network layers with their respective protocols/standards.

List-I (Network Layer)	**List-II (Protocols/ Standards)**
A. Application Layer	I. TCP, UDP protocols
B. Transport Layer	II. API, Sockets
C. Presentation Layer	III. FTP, HTTP
D. Session Layer	IV. Encryption, decryption

Choose the ***correct*** answer from the options given below:

1. A-II, B-III, C-I, D-IV
2. A-III, B-II, C-IV, D-I
3. A-III, B-I, C-IV, D-II
4. A-IV, B-I, C-III, D-II

45. Even being a member of "Advisory Committee for Libraries", who could not participate in committee work at all.

A. A.J. Mathai
B. T.D. Waknis
C. B.S. Kesavan
D. S.S. Saith
E. D.R. Kalia

Choose the ***most appropriate*** answer from the options given below:

1. A and E only
2. B and D only
3. C and E only
4. B and C only

46. Arrange the following metrics in chronological order of their year of inception:

A. SNIP
B. CiteScore
C. Eigenfactor
D. Crindes
E. Altmetric

Choose the *most appropriate* answer from the options given below:

1. C, A, E, B, D
2. D, B, C, A, E
3. B, E, D, C, A
4. E, A, C, D, B

47. Which of the following hold good with network cards?

A. This is the end port of any connection.
B. These cards are 4 bits, 12 bits and 20 bits.
C. A network card is called interface card.
D. It is a circuit board or chip which allows the computer to communicate to another computer network.
E. There are four types of modems.

Choose the *most appropriate* answer from the options given below:

1. C, D and E only
2. B, C and E only
3. A, B and D only
4. A, D and E only

48. Which of the following is an example of secondary source?

1. A court transcription
2. A biography of a famous scientist
3. A scientific experiment
4. A public speech by a political leader

49. Match the Digital Library Standards with their respective purpose.

List-I (Digital library standard)	List-II (Purpose)
A. Dublin Core	I. Digital Object Packaging
B. OAI-PMH	II. Persistent Identification
C. METS	III. Metadata Description
D. DOI	IV. Data Harvesting

Choose the *correct* answer from the options given below:

1. A-I, B-III, C-IV, D-II
2. A-II, B-IV, C-I, D-III
3. A-III, B-II, C-IV, D-I
4. A-III, B-IV, C-I, D-II

50. Match the canons with their respective purpose.

List-I (Canon)	List-II (Purpose)
A. Canon of Enumeration	I. Avoid unnecessary or excessive use of terminology
B. Canon of Currency	II. Notations should be simple and clear
C. Canon of Reticence	III. Terms based on latest developments
D. Cannon of Simplicity	IV. Terms should denote concepts in a structured manner

Choose the *correct* answer from the options given below:

1. A-II, B-III, C-I, D-IV
2. A-IV, B-III, C-II, D-I
3. A-III, B-IV, C-II, D-I
4. A-IV, B-III, C-I, D-II

51. Which of the following is another name for deliberate sampling?

1. Random sampling
2. Purpose sampling
3. Stratified sampling
4. Snowball sampling

52. Who is the winner of IFLA Green Library Award 2024?

1. Seoul Metropolitan Library, South Korea
2. West Vancouver Memorial Library, Canada
3. Missoula Public Library
4. Biblioteca EPM, Colombia

53. Who established the 'Mysore Oriental Library'?

1. King Chamarajendra Wodeyar
2. King Krishnaraja Wodeyar
3. King Narasraj Wodeyar
4. King Devraj Wodeyar

54. Which multiplexing technique divides the available bandwidth into fixed-size time slots?

1. Wave length Division Multiplexing (WDM)
2. Code Division Multiplexing (CDM)
3. Time Division Multiplexing (TDM)
4. Frequency Division Multiplexing (FDM)

55. What does the 'p'-value in hypothesis testing represents?

1. The likelihood that the null hypothesis is true
2. The probability of rejecting the null hypothesis, when it is true
3. The strength of the correlation between variables
4. The variance explained by the independent variable

56. Arrange the following Indexing Systems chronologically as per their inception.

A. PubMed B. Google Scholar
C. IEEXplore D. DOAJ
E. PsycInfo

Choose the ***most appropriate*** answer from the options given below:

1. E, A, C, D, B
2. A, E, B, D, C
3. C, E, D, A, B
4. B, C, A, D, E

57. Match the different profounders of digital archive platforms with the respective platforms created by them.

List-I (Propounders)	**List-II (Platform)**
A. Herbert Van de Sompel	I. ArXiv
B. Paul Ginsparg	II. Subversive Proposal
C. Michael S. Hart	III. Open Archive Initiative
D. Steven Harnad	IV. Project Guttenberg

Choose the ***correct*** answer from the options given below:

1. A-IV, B-II, C-III, D-I
2. A-III, B-I, C-II, D-IV
3. A-II, B-IV, C-III, D-I
4. A-III, B-I, C-IV, D-II

58. Which of the following statements are true about topologies in computer networks?

A. Star topology relies on a central hub for communication.
B. Mesh topology eliminates the need for a central node.
C. Bus topology is most fault tolerate topology.
D. Ring topology connects devices in a closed loop.
E. Tree topology is a hierarchical topology where multiple star networks are connected with central hub.

Choose the ***most appropriate*** answer from the options given below:

1. A, B, D and E only
2. A, C, D and E only
3. B, C, D and E only
4. A, B, C and D only

59. Which of the following are the necessary elements of an information society?

A. Confidentiality B. Vulnerability
C. Integrity D. Personality
E. Availability

Choose the ***most appropriate*** answer from the options given below:

1. A, C and E only
2. B, C and D only
3. C, D and E only
4. B, D and E only

60. Which organization is primarily responsible for promoting agricultural information systems globally?

1. World Bank
2. International Food Policy Research Institute
3. Food and Agricultural Organization
4. World Health Organization

61. Match the following databases with their metadata service provider.

List-I (Database)	List-II (Hosting Institutions/Body)
A. Aminer	I. Harvard University
B. Astrophysics Data System	II. DAI & University of Cologne
C. ATLA Religion Database	III. Tringhua University
D. Arachne	IV. EBSCO

Choose the ***correct*** answer from the options given below:

1. A-III, B-II, C-I, D-IV
2. A-IV, B-III, C-I, D-II
3. A-II, B-I, C-III, D-IV
4. A-III, B-I, C-IV, D-II

62. Which of the following accurately describe the process of digitisation in libraries?

A. It requires adherence to metadata standards for discoverability.
B. It involves converting analog materials to digital formats.
C. It ensures permanent access to all digital content without preservation efforts.
D. It involves selecting suitable hardware and software for the process.
E. It requires to get permission from National Digital Library of India (NDLI).

Choose the ***most appropriate*** answer from the options given below:

1. A, C, D and E only
2. B, C, D and E only
3. A, B, C and D only
4. A, B, D and E only

63. In Shannon and Weaver's model of communication, what is the primary function of the 'encoder'?

1. To interpret the message
2. To transmit the message
3. To convert the message into signals
4. To receive the message

64. A key challenge in scholarly communication today is the increasing concern about ______ in the academic publishing industry, particularly regarding access costs and "pay wall" model.

1. Open Access
2. Profitability
3. Ethics
4. Sustainability

65. According to IFLA, a green library takes into account.

A. Concern with Environment Management
B. Sustainable Economy
C. Social Sustainability
D. Cultural Sustainability
E. Sustainable Library Services

Choose the ***most appropriate*** answer from the options given below:

1. B, C, D and E only
2. A, B, C and E only
3. A, C, D and E only
4. A, B, C and D only

66. Arrange books published by Dr. S.R. Ranganathan in chronological order of their year of publication.

A. Elements of Library Classification
B. Prolegomena to Library Classification
C. Colon Classification
D. Library Manual
E. Classification and International Documentation

Choose the ***most appropriate*** answer from the options given below:

1. C, D, B, A, E
2. C, A, B, D, E
3. C, B, A, E, D
4. E, D, C, B, A

67. According to Colon Classification, which ACI is used to form class number for "Biography of Prime Minister"?

1. w
2. v
3. y7
4. y1

68. Which of the following retrieval metrics is a harmonic mean of recall and precision?

1. Cumulative gain
2. Discounted cumulative gain
3. Normalized discounted cumulative gain
4. F1 Score

69. Which of the following are true about document type definition (DTD)?

A. A DTD defines the structure and attributes of an XML document.

B. With DTD, independent group of people can agree on a standard for interchanging data.

C. If DTD is declared inside XML file, it must be wrapped inside the <!DTD> definition.

D. The Library of Congress has made available a DTD to convert MARC records to XML.

E. DTD is used to ensure the authenticity of data transmitted across the web.

Choose the ***most appropriate*** answer from the options given below:

1. A, B and D only
2. A, C and E only
3. B, D and E only
4. B, C and D only

70. Which of the following sources can be consulted to know the impact factor of journal publication?

A. EBSCO

B. Web of Science

C. Science Direct

D. SCOPUS

E. JSTORE

Choose the ***most appropriate*** answer from the options given below:

1. A, B and C only
2. B and E only
3. C and D only
4. B and D only

71. Which statement is not true about the difference between Mendeley and Zotero?

1. Mendeley has more extensive filtering options than Zotero
2. Mendeley offers broader accessibility options, Zotero is available as a website only
3. Mendeley provides more versatile support system including online chat, helping guides and a blog, Zotero mainly on its FAQ.
4. Mendeley's advantage over Zotero is direct reference formatting on the platform

72. Arrange the following databases according to their year of launch/inception in ascending order.

A. Hathi Trust
B. DOAJ
C. ScienceOpen
D. SSRN
E. NDLTD

Choose the ***most appropriate*** answer from the options given below:

1. A, C, B, E, D
2. D, E, B, A, C
3. A, B, C, D, E
4. B, E, A, C, D

73. In Universal Decimal Classification (UDC) connecting symbol square bracket [ ] is used for ______.

1. Language
2. Place
3. Form
4. Subgrouping

74. Kindly identify different awards given by CILIP.

A. Hugh Atkinson Memorial Award

B. Yoto Carnegie Award

C. Beta Phi Mu Award

D. Library Change Lives Award

E. Mentor of the year Award

Choose the *most appropriate* answer from the options given below:

1. A, B and C only
2. B, D and E only
3. C, D and E only
4. A, C and D only

75. The 'High Level Committee' of National Mission on Libraries was set up by Ministry of Culture wide notification no. 18-4/2009-Lib(Pt.) dated ______.

1. 2nd March 2012
2. 4th May 2012
3. 12th July 2012
4. 21st December 2012

76. Match the Principles of Facet Sequence with their description.

List-I (Principles)	List-II (Description)
A. Wall-Picture Principle	I. Suggests that a whole entity be treated a single unit
B. Whole-Organ Principle	II. Arranges facets based on their visual representation
C. Cow-Calf Principle	III. Specifies that one Facet should lead to a dependent Facet
D. Act and Action-Actor Tool Principle	IV. Defines the relationship between action and tool

Choose the *correct* answer from the options given below:

1. A-IV, B-III, C-II, D-I
2. A-II, B-IV, C-I, D-III
3. A-II, B-I, C-IV, D-III
4. A-III, B-IV, C-II, D-I

77. Which of the following are open access institutional repository?

A. Ashoka Trust for Research in Ecology and Environment.

B. JSTOR

C. CSIR-NIScPR online periodicals Directory

D. Krishikosh

E. Manupatra

Choose the *most appropriate* answer from the options given below:

1. A, B and D only
2. B, D and E only
3. A, C and D only
4. C, D and E only

78. Match the paradigms of programming languages with their respective feature.

List-I (Paradigm)	List-II (Feature)
A. Object-oriented	I. Based on mathematical functions
B. Functional	II. Sequential execution of instructions
C. Procedural	III. Encapsulation and inheritance
D. Declarative	IV. Describes what to do, not how to do it

Choose the *correct* answer from the options given below:

1. A-II, B-IV, C-I, D-III
2. A-IV, B-III, C-II, D-I
3. A-III, B-I, C-II, D-IV
4. A-I, B-II, C-III, D-IV

79. Presently International Federation of Library Associations and Institutions (IFLA) is having ongoing advisory committees as follows:

A. Committee on Standards

B. Committee on Public Libraries

C. Committee on Cultural Heritage

D. Committee on Copyright and other Legal Matters

E. Committee on Open Science and Scholarship

Choose the ***most appropriate*** answer from the options given below:

1. A, B, D and E only
2. B, C, D and E only
3. A, B, C and E only
4. A, C, D and E only

80. Identify the key attributes of ephemeral literature from the following.

A. Any transitory or printed matter
B. Not intended to be retained or preserved
C. Holding high archival value
D. Shorter lasting value
E. Materials with cultural importance

Choose the ***most appropriate*** answer from the options given below:

1. A, B and C only
2. B, D and E only
3. A, C and D only
4. A, B and D only

81. Which of the following are ISDN interface?

A. Asymmetric DSL Interface (ADSLI)
B. Basic Rate Interface (BRI)
C. Ultra-Advanced Rate Interface (UARI)
D. Primary Rate Interface (PRI)
E. Broadband-ISDN (B-ISDN) & ATM

Choose the ***most appropriate*** answer from the options given below:

1. A, B and C only
2. B, D and E only
3. B, C and D only
4. C, D and E only

82. Arrange the following library associations in chronological order of their establishment year.

A. Indian Library Association
B. Bengal Library Association
C. Punjab Library Association
D. Maharashtra Library Association
E. Madras Library Association

Choose the ***most appropriate*** answer from the options given below:

1. D, E, B, C, A
2. E, D, C, B, A
3. B, C, D, A, E
4. A, B, C, D, E

83. Which of the following is an example of utility software?

1. Microsoft PowerPoint
2. Disc Cleanup Tool
3. Adobe Illustrator
4. Skype

84. Which of the following models of scholarly publishing represents self-archiving?

1. Traditional model
2. Subversive model
3. Alternative model
4. Automated model

85. Which of the following is not true about OpenURL?

1. It enables user to retrieve the most appropriate copy of the web document
2. The Open URL system works in conjunction with CrossRef
3. SFX is an Open URL compliant link server
4. The OpenURL is a protocol for communication among multiple digital collections

86. Arrange the following stages of planning for retrospective conversion process.

A. Carefully draw documents procedures for efficient workflow.
B. Identify the necessary training for the staff.
C. Clearly identify the objectives.
D. Identify the equipments requirements.
E. Specify standards to be used.

Choose the ***most appropriate*** answer from the options given below:

1. A, B, C, D, E
2. B, D, C, E, A
3. A, E, B, D, C
4. C, A, E, D, B

87. How many indicator digits are used in CC-7?

1. 26 digits
2. 14 digits
3. 74 digits
4. 23 digits

88. The original issue of Oxford English Dictionary was issued under the title:

1. New English Dictionary on Historical Principles
2. International Dictionary of the English Language
3. Dictionary of English Language on Historical Principles
4. Comprehensive English Dictionary on Historical Principles

89. Browsewrap and Clickwrap are different methods used for:

1. Click and download the content
2. Browse and download the content under systematic download agreement
3. Just copy-paste the content with saving the document
4. It is license agreement between publisher and participating libraries

90. Which of the following is not true about Dianst as an architecture for digital library?

1. It is a protocol for service communication in digital library architecture.
2. It has structured document model.
3. It specifies operational characteristics of core digital service
4. It provides centralized architecture for digital library

Direction (Qs. No. 91 to 95): *Read the following passage and answer the questions.*

Artificial intelligence is the technology that drives robotics, driverless vehicles, drones, big data, and other technologies. AI is such an explosive revolution that companies are clamoring to spend billions of dollars of AI-related companies, because they know that AI is the future. It is in every facet of our lives from Siri and Cortana, to predicting diseases such a breast cancer and multiple sclerosis. It is being used to determine who is likely to commit a crime or default on a loan. It will continue to see expanded growth. It is used in every industry and its uses will continue to expand. There will be opportunities and challenges currently unheard of. Libraries will be more involved in AI through STEM (Science, technology, engineering, and maths) careers and collaborations with companies, university departments, workforce agencies, and others. As AI gains in popularity the general public will come to the library to obtain information on AI and what it means for their lives. They will also visit libraries to learn about retraining and other job-related opportunities.

91. Which of the following statement is not predicted in this paragraph?

1. Libraries will engage more with AI
2. Libraries will promote careers in science and technology
3. Libraries will work in partnership with many organisations
4. Libraries will become more popular places for general public

92. According to this paragraph, for which of the following purpose users will turn up in libraries?

1. To gather literature for research
2. To avail well maintained reading facilities
3. To upgrade their knowledge and skill
4. To connect other professionals in his domain

93. The opportunities of AI lies in almost all aspects of human lives. Which of the following is not true in this context?

1. Many areas of AI application are yet to explored
2. Research is in progress to find out further areas of AI application
3. The use of AI will further expand
4. Many opportunities of AI are not yet known

94. Libraries are going to be hub of information on AI and its applications. This is ______ in the paragraph.

1. stated
2. both stated and implied
3. stated, but not implied
4. neither stated, nor implied

95. Which of the following areas of AI application has not been depicted in this paragraph?

1. Business and finance
2. Health and medicine
3. Law and order
4. Education and research

Direction (Qs. No. 96 to 100): *Read the following passage and answer the questions.*

The library has become to emulate a space of distinction for what a city has to offer to its citizens in a democratic society, or as Manfrendini stated, public libraries epiotomize some of the few remaining genuine democratic spaces. Throughout history libraries have been affected by political shifts, changing power dynamics, growth and disintegration of empires, built up with gusto and enthusiasm, destroyed by wickedness and neglect. Libraries throughout history can be considered incredibly purposeful and anxiously useless, "channel order and chaos, house both print and digital, old and new, they can control and liberate the knowledge they contain". Libraries can be both an instrument to liberate to oppress and a tool for imperial conquest, assimilation and control. Libraries aim to encompass the whole memory of humankind make them vulnerable to complete erasure. Building where collections are housed can also be demolished, re-designed, or eliminated.

96. The paragraph projected libraries both as utilitarian and counter productive. Which of the following does not support the idea?

1. Order and chaos
2. Print and digital
3. Old and new
4. Generator and destroyer

97. Which of the following does not represent that libraries are instruments for oppression?

1. Colonialism
2. Integration
3. Domination
4. Homogenization

98. According to this passage, what is the reason for the extinction of libraries in the future?

1. Excessive use of technology
2. Excessive growth of collection
3. Inadequate manpower
4. Digitization of library materials

99. Which of the following is not a cause of disappearance of libraries?

1. Inactivity
2. Aggression
3. Imperialism
4. Competition

100. Which of the following is not a reason why Manfredini stated libraries as democratic spaces?

1. Freedom of choice
2. Equality in access
3. Pluralistic approach
4. Independence of power

ANSWERS

1. (4): In the Colour Classification (Ed. 6, Revised Ed.), specifically in the Bliss Bibliographic Classification system (BBC), the notation 'y8' is used to represent specific types of documents. According to the classification:

- A (Digest) and D (Manual) fall under the category represented by 'y8'.
- A Digest refers to a condensed collection or summary of information, while a Manual is a guidebook or handbook that provides instructions or guidelines.

- These are grouped under certain document-type classifications in BBC, and 'y8' corresponds to such practical and instructional materials.
- Other options like (B) Dictionary, (C) Conference proceedings, and (E) Scope are represented with different notations, not 'y8'.

2. (3):

- In Web 3.0, Artificial Intelligence (AI) plays a critical role in enhancing the functionality of the internet through semantic understanding, data integration, and intelligent automation.
- AI processes unstructured data (like text, video, audio, and social media content) to extract meaningful patterns.
- It helps deliver highly personalized and context-aware experiences by understanding user behaviour and preferences.
- AI technologies like Natural Language Processing (NLP), Machine Learning (ML), and Knowledge Graphs are heavily embedded in Web 3.0 to power applications like intelligent assistants, recommendation engines, and semantic search.

3. (3):

- SheRNI (Shared Resources National Information) and Vidwan are major scholarly information systems developed by the INFLIBNET Centre (Information and Library Network Centre), an autonomous Inter-University Centre of UGC (University Grants Commission) of India.
- Vidwan is a database of experts, researchers, and scientists in India, providing information about their academic and research profiles.
- SheRNI is a collaborative initiative aimed at creating a repository of e-resources including documents, data, and tools.
- These initiatives support academic networking and resource sharing among institutions.

4. (3): CERT-In (Indian Computer Emergency Response Team), under the Ministry of Electronics and Information Technology, performs the following functions:

A. Collection, analysis, and dissemination of information on cyber incidents to ensure preparedness.

B. Forecast and alert on potential or actual cyber threats or incidents.

C. Issue guidelines, vulnerability notes, and white papers to guide cybersecurity practices across various sectors.

E. Coordination of response activities to ensure collective and synchronized management of cyber incidents.

D. (Emergency measures for handling national disaster management incidents) falls under the mandate of NDMA (National Disaster Management Authority), not CERT-In.

Hence, option 3 is correct.

5. (2):

B. Folksonomies are a form of reader advisory service that is easy to use: True. Folksonomies allow users to add tags or keywords to online content, enabling easier navigation and retrieval based on popular, user-generated terms.

D. Folksonomies are being used with Social Media platforms such as Flickr, Pinterest, etc.: Correct. Platforms like Flickr and Pinterest extensively use tagging systems (folksonomies) for content classification.

Other statements are either inaccurate or misleading:

- A is incorrect because Folksonomy is not a sub-concept of social taxonomy; it's more of a bottom-up, user-generated classification system.
- C is incorrect since Folksonomy does not match the precision of professional cataloguing systems like Dewey Decimal Classification or Library of Congress Classification.
- E is incorrect as folksonomies are not intended as advisory services for classifiers or classificationists; they serve more as a user-centric tagging system.

6. (2): In the architecture of the Semantic Web, the layers are arranged in a stack from bottom to top, each building upon the previous one:

D. (RDF – Resource Description Framework): This is the foundation layer. It structures data in a machine-readable way using triples (subject-predicate-object).

B. (Ontology): On top of RDF, ontologies define the relationships between terms, enabling shared understanding and interoperability between data.

A. (Logic): This layer enables the reasoning over data and ontologies to infer new knowledge using rules.

C. (Proof): This layer is concerned with explaining and validating the reasoning carried out in the logic layer.

E. (Trust): At the top, this layer provides mechanisms to evaluate the reliability and trustworthiness of the data and its sources.

This layered model was proposed by Tim Berners-Lee, the inventor of the World Wide Web.

7. (2):

- The h-index is a metric that measures both the productivity and citation impact of a researcher's publications.
- One major criticism of the h-index is that it favours disciplines with naturally high citation frequencies, such as biomedical sciences or computer science.
- Fields like mathematics or philosophy tend to have lower citation rates, putting their researchers at a disadvantage even if their work is impactful.
- Thus, it introduces a bias not based on quality but on field-specific citation behaviours.

8. (2):

- OpenDOAR (Directory of Open Access Repositories) is a globally recognized service that provides a comprehensive list of academic open access repositories.
- It is maintained by the University of Nottingham, UK, particularly through its SHERPA services.
- OpenDOAR allows users to search and browse repositories, which improves access to freely available academic resources worldwide.
- It supports policy makers, repository administrators, and researchers with data on repository standards and openness.

9. (3):

- An Informative abstract provides a concise but complete summary of a research paper or article. It typically includes:
  - ❑ Purpose of the study
  - ❑ Principal arguments or hypotheses
  - ❑ Methodology used
  - ❑ Key results and conclusions
- It is self-sufficient — the reader can understand the key content of the paper without reading the full document.
- This contrasts with:
  - ❑ Indicative abstracts, which give only the scope or topic.
  - ❑ Critical abstracts, which also evaluate the document.
  - ❑ Highlight abstracts, which emphasize selected points rather than summarizing the entire work.

10. (1): Arranged in chronological order of their introduction:

B. (BlogSpot – 1999): Also known as Blogger, it was launched by Pyra Labs in 1999 and later acquired by Google.

D. (LinkedIn – 2003): A professional networking platform launched in 2003.

A. (Twitter – 2006): A microblogging platform created in March 2006.

C. (ResearchGate – 2008): A social networking site for researchers, launched in 2008.

E. (Snapchat – 2011): A multimedia messaging app first released in 2011.

This timeline reflects the evolution of social media and professional networking platforms, each catering to distinct user groups and purposes.

11. (3):

- Dr. S.R. Ranganathan, the father of Library Science in India, served as the President of the Indian Library Association (ILA) from 1944 to 1953.
- His tenure was marked by revolutionary contributions to library science in India, including the Five Laws of Library Science, Colon Classification, and development of library education.
- He played a pivotal role in shaping ILA's policies and framework during this crucial post-independence phase.

12. (2):

- When it is said that "Information is diffusive," it means that information spreads easily and tends to leak or move from one point to another, sometimes without control.

- Unlike physical goods, information cannot be confined easily; once released, it can flow to multiple users and platforms.
- This characteristic raises concerns in fields such as information security and confidentiality, especially in digital communication and data sharing.
- Hence, "diffusive" does not refer to mere shareability or non-reduction but emphasizes the natural tendency of information to disseminate.

13. (2): The logical sequence of steps in the Acquisition module of any Library Management System (LMS) is:

B. (Duplicate checking): Before placing any order, the system checks for duplicate items in the catalog to avoid redundant acquisitions.

C. (Preparing and mailing orders): After ensuring uniqueness, purchase orders are prepared and sent to vendors or suppliers.

A. (Received documents): Once the order is processed, the physical or digital items are received.

E. (Verification and modification of bibliographic information): After receipt, the documents are verified against order records, and metadata is updated if needed.

D. (Processing invoice and accessioning): Finally, invoices are processed, and documents are accessioned (entered into the collection officially).

This sequence ensures orderliness, financial control, and bibliographic accuracy.

14. (2):

- The Digital Object Identifier (DOI) system was officially launched in 1998 by the International DOI Foundation (IDF).
- DOI provides a permanent and unique digital identifier for objects such as research papers, datasets, and official publications.
- It is widely used in academic publishing and digital rights management, allowing for stable linking, citation tracking, and metadata integration.
- By 2024, over 260 million DOIs had been assigned, making it one of the most reliable tools in scholarly communication.

15. (1): Matching theories of classification with their respective propounders:

A. Descriptive Theory – IV. Henry Bliss:
Bliss emphasized the Descriptive Theory of classification, focusing on natural order and subject structure.

B. One Place Theory – I. J.D. Brown:
Proposed that a document should be classified at a single place, to simplify retrieval and avoid duplication.

C. Criteria of Classification – II. E.C. Richardson:
Discussed various criteria for classifying knowledge, such as by form, purpose, or discipline.

D. Literary Warrant – III. E.W. Hulme:
Introduced the principle of Literary Warrant, where the need for a subject in a classification system should be based on its existence in the literature.

This matching helps understand theoretical frameworks behind classification systems used in libraries and knowledge organization.

16. (3): The chronological development of public library systems in India is as follows:

C. (Enactment of the Public Libraries Act in Tamil Nadu – 1948): Tamil Nadu was the first Indian state to enact a Public Libraries Act, known as the Madras Public Libraries Act, 1948, laying the foundation for state-level public library legislation in India.

E. (Formation of the Delhi Public Library under UNESCO assistance – 1951): The Delhi Public Library was established as a pilot project by UNESCO in collaboration with the Government of India, meant to demonstrate the potential of public libraries in a democratic society.

D. (Establishment of the Raja Rammohan Roy Library Foundation – 1972): RRRLF was established by the Government of India as an autonomous organization to promote and support public libraries across the country.

A. (Report submission of the National Policy on Library and Information System – 1986): The NAPLIS report aimed to formulate a comprehensive national policy for library and information services to ensure uniformity and access nationwide.

B. (Launch of the National Mission on Libraries – 2014): The NML was initiated by the Ministry of Culture, focusing on modernizing libraries, networking, and digitization, particularly targeting public and school libraries.

17. (1): The correct matching of storage technologies with their unique characteristics is:

A. SSD – II. Non-volatile Flash memory: SSDs (Solid State Drives) use flash memory with no moving parts, offering faster access and reliability compared to HDDs.

B. RAM – III. Volatile memory with quick access: RAM (Random Access Memory) is volatile, meaning data is lost when power is off. It allows for very fast data access, crucial for active processes.

C. HDD – I. Uses magnetic platters: HDDs (Hard Disk Drives) function using spinning magnetic platters, making them slower but more cost-effective for bulk storage.

D. ROM – IV. Permanent Firmware Storage: ROM (Read-Only Memory) holds firmware and is non-volatile, used for storing programs that are not meant to be modified frequently, such as the BIOS.

18. (3): ISBD(M), which stands for International Standard Bibliographic Description for Monographic Publications, divides bibliographic information into eight standardized areas. These are:

1. Title and statement of responsibility area
2. Edition area
3. Material (or type of resource) specific details area
4. Publication, distribution, etc. area
5. Physical description area
6. Series area
7. Note area
8. Standard number and terms of availability area

This structure ensures uniformity and facilitates international exchange of bibliographic records.

19. (4): The serious issues of internet usage primarily include:

A. Obesity and depression: Prolonged screen time and reduced physical activity due to excessive internet usage are linked to obesity. Social comparison and cyberbullying can lead to depression, especially among teenagers.

B. Age-inappropriate content: The internet exposes users, particularly children, to violent, sexual, and misleading content, raising concerns about child safety online.

C. Social isolation: Excessive use of digital platforms can lead to reduced face-to-face interactions, fostering loneliness and reduced emotional bonding.

(D) and (E) (Abundant information resources and Global audience) are generally considered advantages, not issues.

20. (2): Matching central libraries with the names of eminent personalities they are named after:

A. Indian Institute of Science, Bengaluru – III. J.R.D. Tata: The J.R.D. Tata Memorial Library at IISc is named to honour the contributions of J.R.D. Tata to science and education in India.

B. Indian Institute of Management, Ahmedabad – I. Vikram Sarabhai: The Vikram Sarabhai Library at IIM Ahmedabad is named after the father of India's space program, recognizing his role in institutional development.

C. Jawaharlal Nehru University, New Delhi – IV. Dr. B.R. Ambedkar: The Dr. B.R. Ambedkar Central Library at JNU is a tribute to India's chief architect of the Constitution and a strong advocate of education.

D. Banaras Hindu University, Varanasi – II. Sayaji Rao Gaikwad: The Sayaji Rao Gaikwad Library at BHU honours the Maharaja of Baroda, who was a patron of education and libraries in pre-independence India.

21. (3):

- The primary goal of the "preservation" phase in the Information Life Cycle is to ensure that valuable information is archived and maintained in a stable and accessible form for long-term use.
- This involves:
  - ❑ Preventing data degradation or loss due to technological obsolescence, physical deterioration, or cyber threats.

- ❑ Implementing migration strategies to newer formats or storage media.
- ❑ Using climate-controlled environments, digital archiving tools, and redundancy backups.

- It is especially critical in archives, libraries, museums, and scientific institutions where preservation ensures intellectual and cultural continuity.

22. (1): The chronological emergence of the listed institutions and initiatives is:

C. (C-DOT – 1984): The Centre for Development of Telematics was established to develop indigenous telecom technologies for rural India.

A. (ERNET – 1986): The Education and Research Network was India's first internet service provider, primarily for educational and research purposes.

D. (C-DAC – 1988): The Centre for Development of Advanced Computing was created to develop India's first supercomputer – PARAM.

E. (NMEICT – 2009): The National Mission on Education through ICT focused on enhancing learning through ICT-based content and connectivity.

B. (NKN – 2010): The National Knowledge Network aimed at providing high-speed connectivity to educational and research institutions across India.

23. (3): The following platforms provide mobile applications for library patrons to track book loans, download eBooks/audiobooks, and manage digital borrowing:

B. (Libby): A user-friendly app by OverDrive for accessing eBooks and audiobooks from libraries.

D. (OverDrive): Provides access to a large catalog of digital media via public libraries.

E. (BorrowBox): An app for borrowing digital books and audiobooks, widely used by public libraries across multiple countries.

(A) Tidal and (C) Spotify are music streaming services, unrelated to library lending or book tracking.

24. (3): Matching institutions with their year of establishment:

A. IAEA – III. 1957: The International Atomic Energy Agency was founded in 1957 to promote peaceful use of nuclear energy.

B. ICSSR – I. 1969: The Indian Council of Social Science Research was established in 1969 to promote research in social sciences.

C. WIPO – IV. 1970: The World Intellectual Property Organization became a specialized UN agency in 1970 for protecting IP rights globally.

D. UNISIST – II. 1971: The UNISIST Programme was initiated in 1971 by UNESCO to develop a worldwide scientific and technical information system.

25. (1): Correct chronological order of cataloguing code publications:

A. Jewett's Cataloguing Code – 1850s: Charles C. Jewett's cataloguing rules were among the earliest standardized systems for libraries in the USA.

B. Cutter's Cataloguing Code – 1876: Charles A. Cutter introduced the Rules for a Dictionary Catalog, a more systematic and widely adopted approach.

E. Anglo-American Joint Code – 1908: A collaborative effort between British and American libraries, forming the basis of modern cataloguing practices.

D. Classified Cataloguing Code – 1934: Developed by S.R. Ranganathan, focusing on subject classification alongside bibliographic description.

C. AACR (Anglo-American Cataloguing Rules) – 1967: It further standardized cataloguing rules across English-speaking nations, updated later in AACR2 (1978).

26. (3): As per the Principle of Increasing Complexity in Colon Classification (6th Revised Edition), subjects are arranged from simple to complex. In the case of geography-related subjects:

D. Mathematical Geography: It is the simplest form, dealing with the measurement and mathematical principles of the Earth.

A. Biogeography: Adds biological complexity, studying the distribution of flora and fauna in relation to geography.

B. Anthropogeography: Introduces human elements, studying human interaction with the environment.

C. Political Geography: Adds institutional complexity, focusing on state boundaries, governance, and power dynamics.

E. Economic Geography: The most complex, as it integrates economic systems, trade, production, and socio-political elements across regions.

This progression reflects the Ranganathanian idea of building knowledge from basic to complex in a faceted classification system.

27. (4):

- SHTTP (Secure Hypertext Transfer Protocol) is specifically designed to provide secure transmission of individual messages over HTTP using SSL/TLS encryption.
- It ensures confidentiality, integrity, and authentication of web communications.
- It is different from HTTPS, which secures the entire HTTP session, while SHTTP can secure specific parts of the message.
- Other protocols listed:
  - ❑ FTP is for file transfers.
  - ❑ SMTP is used for email transmission.
  - ❑ TCP/IP is a suite of communication protocols but does not provide encryption on its own.

28. (4): Chronological order of enactment of the given Acts:

B. The Press and Registration of Books Act – 1867: The oldest press regulation law in India, governing the printing and publication of books and newspapers.

D. Copyright Act – 1957: Protects the rights of creators of literary, artistic, musical, and dramatic works.

E. The Patent Act – 1970: Provides a legal framework for granting exclusive rights to inventors for their inventions.

A. The Information Technology Act – 2000: Enacted to address issues related to cybercrime and electronic commerce.

C. The Right to Information (RTI) Act – 2005: Empowers Indian citizens to request information from public authorities, promoting transparency.

29. (1):

- F.W. Lancaster is the author of the book "Toward Paperless Society", published in 1978.
- The book was a visionary work that predicted the transformation of libraries and information systems from print-based to digital and electronic formats.
- Lancaster emphasized the increasing role of computers, databases, and networks in scholarly communication.
- This work remains significant in library and information science as it anticipated the future of digital information environments.

30. (3): If an academic library reports higher use of digital resources and reduced borrowing of print materials, the following inferences are valid:

A. The library users prefer digital formats for convenience: Users increasingly opt for anytime-anywhere access, making digital resources more attractive.

C. There is a lack of awareness about print resources among users: As users gravitate towards online databases and e-resources, they may overlook physical collections.

E. Digital resources are more accessible and easier to use compared to print materials: With advanced search ability, device compatibility, and remote access, digital formats are often more user-friendly.

(B) and (D) may be possible but are not necessarily direct inferences without further evidence (e.g., age or relevance of physical collection, promotion strategies).

31. (2):

B. Deep Web refers to web contents not indexed by search engines like Bing: Correct. The Deep Web includes content from databases, subscription services, and password-protected websites that are not indexed by standard search engines such as Google or Bing.

D. Data in Deep Web is stored in a database which is not coded in HTML: Correct. Much of the content in the Deep Web is stored dynamically in databases and not in static HTML pages, making it inaccessible to traditional crawlers.

E. SSRN is an example of Deep Web contents: Correct. The Social Science Research Network (SSRN) hosts academic papers and preprints that are not always fully indexed by search engines, and access often requires specific queries or institutional login.

(A) is incorrect: Deep Web and Surface Web are not the same; Surface Web is openly accessible and indexed, while Deep Web is not.

(C) is incorrect: The Deep Web includes legal and safe areas such as academic databases; it's the Dark Web that is often associated with illegal activity, not the Deep Web.

32. (4):

- The West Bengal Public Libraries Act, 1979 was enacted with the primary objective of establishing a statewide network of public libraries for systematic growth and coordinated management.
- It aimed to create a hierarchical structure of libraries including State Central Library, District Libraries, Sub-divisional Libraries, Town Libraries, and Rural Libraries.
- While automation and rural outreach are relevant today, the act's original intent was to ensure a well-organized network of library services throughout West Bengal.

33. (3):

- The Digital Object Identifier (DOI) is a permanent and unique alphanumeric string assigned to digital documents.
- Structure:
  - ❑ Prefix: Identifies the registrant or publisher (e.g., 10.1000)
  - ❑ Suffix: A unique code assigned to the individual item (e.g., abc123).
  - ❑ Example: 10.1016/j.inf.2020.101489
- It enables persistent linking and reliable citation of digital content across platforms, independent of URL changes.

34. (4):

- Expert Systems are computer programs that simulate human intelligence and decision-making by applying rules and reasoning from a specialized domain.
- They incorporate Information Technology and knowledge bases to solve complex problems typically requiring human expertise.
- Features:
  - ❑ Use of inference engines
  - ❑ Structured rule-based logic
  - ❑ Application in medical diagnosis, legal reasoning, engineering analysis, etc.
- While AI and Machine Learning are broader categories, Expert Systems are specific applications of AI where simulated intelligence mimics expert reasoning.

35. (2): Correct chronological order of international IPR-related treaties:

C. Paris Convention – 1883: One of the earliest international IP treaties, providing protection for industrial property including inventions and trademarks.

A. Berne Convention – 1886: Established to protect literary and artistic works across countries under copyright law.

E. Patent Cooperation Treaty (PCT) – 1970: Facilitates international patent filing with a single application across member states.

B. TRIPS Agreement – 1995: An agreement under the WTO that sets minimum standards for IP protection globally.

D. WIPO Copyright Treaty – 1996: Extends the Berne Convention, addressing digital copyright issues including online use and distribution.

This sequence shows the evolution of global intellectual property frameworks from foundational to modern digital concerns.

36. (1): Matching of State Library Acts with their year of enactment is:

A. Mizoram – III. 1993: The Mizoram Public Libraries Act was enacted in 1993, aiming to build a network of libraries in the state.

B. Odisha – I. 2002: The Odisha Public Library Act was passed in 2002 to provide a legal framework for library development in the state.

C. Bihar – IV. 2008: The Bihar Public Libraries Act came into force in 2008, reflecting the state's effort to strengthen library infrastructure.

D. Arunachal Pradesh – II. 2009: The Arunachal Pradesh Public Libraries Act was passed in 2009, one of the more recent among Indian states.

This order correctly reflects the chronological development of library legislation in these states.

37. (1): Matching of institutions and their notable language or technology projects:

A. IIT, Kanpur – III. VYKARTA: IIT Kanpur developed VYKARTA, a tool for Sanskrit computational analysis.

B. C-DAC – I. MANTRA: Centre for Development of Advanced Computing (C-DAC) developed MANTRA, a machine-aided translation system for Indian languages.

C. NCST, Mumbai – II. SHIVA and SHAKTI: National Centre for Software Technology worked on early Indian language text processing tools such as SHIVA and SHAKTI.

D. CMU, USA & IISc, Bengaluru – IV. ANGLABHARTI: ANGLABHARTI, a translation system for Indian languages, was developed through collaboration between Carnegie Mellon University (CMU) and IISc Bengaluru.

This mapping reflects significant contributions to Indian language processing technologies.

38. (4): The PREMIS (Preservation Metadata: Implementation Strategies) data model consists of five core entities, which are essential to digital preservation workflows:

1. Intellectual Entity – The abstract or conceptual object (e.g., a book).
2. Object – The actual digital file or bit stream.
3. Event – Actions taken with the digital object (e.g., migration, validation).
4. Agent – The person, organization, or software involved in the event.
5. Rights – The rights or permissions associated with the object.

These entities ensure that preservation metadata captures the full lifecycle and context of digital content.

39. (2): Correct matching of Standard Subdivisions from Table-1 of DDC (19th edition):

A. Serials Publication – II. –05: This notation is used for serial publications like journals or bulletins.

B. Philosophy and Theory – III. –01: This subdivision adds philosophical or theoretical context to any main class.

C. Collection – IV. –08: This is used when a work is a collection of various items or topics.

D. Study and Teaching – I. –07: This standard subdivision is used for educational or instructional material related to a subject.

These notations help in customizing classification numbers based on the content's specific focus.

40. (1):

- A web portal is an interactive platform that provides customized and user-specific content, often requiring authentication/login. It aggregates data from multiple sources and allows personalization, like dashboards, preferences, and restricted access.
- A website, in contrast, provides static or general information, mostly accessible to all users, without customization or login-based services.

Examples:

- ❑ Web portal: University intranet, banking portal.
- ❑ Website: Public news page, organization's homepage.

This distinction is fundamental in web architecture and user interface design.

41. (2):

- The development of Blockchain technologies is transforming scholarly communication by offering secure, immutable, and decentralized record-keeping mechanisms.
- In the context of research sharing and archiving, blockchain:
  - ❑ Ensures data integrity by creating tamper-proof records of research outputs.
  - ❑ Facilitates transparent peer review processes by recording timestamps and revisions.
  - ❑ Enhances accessibility and verification, making it easier to validate original contributions.
- Examples include platforms like ARTiFACTS and Springer Nature experiments with blockchain for tracking research provenance.

42. (3): Correct matching of PRECIS Role Operators with their respective notations:

A. Action – III. 2: Operator '2' is used in PRECIS (Preserved Context Indexing System) to denote the Action in the subject statement.

B. Key System – II. 1: Operator '1' is applied to highlight the primary system or concept discussed in the document.

C. Location – I. 0: Operator '0' identifies the geographical or spatial context (location) of the subject.

D. Performer – IV. 3: Operator '3' is used to denote the agent or person performing the action.

These role operators enable consistent indexing and retrieval of subjects by maintaining semantic relationships between concepts.

43. (1):

- Patchwork plagiarism occurs when a person copies phrases, ideas, or sections from multiple sources and stitches them together without proper citation.
- This type of plagiarism often involves:
  - ❑ Rewording some parts while keeping the core ideas identical.
  - ❑ Mixing content from various sources in a composite work that lacks originality.
- It is a serious academic offense as it deceptively presents borrowed material as original.
- Self-plagiarism, verbatim plagiarism, and minimalistic plagiarism differ in scope and nature of copying.

44. (3): Correct matching of Network Layers with their respective protocols/standards:

A. Application Layer – III. FTP, HTTP: This is the topmost layer of the OSI model and includes user-facing protocols like FTP (File Transfer Protocol) and HTTP (HyperText Transfer Protocol).

B. Transport Layer – I. TCP, UDP protocols: Responsible for end-to-end communication and reliability, using protocols like TCP (Transmission Control Protocol) and UDP (User Datagram Protocol).

C. Presentation Layer – IV. Encryption, decryption: This layer handles data translation, encryption, compression, ensuring data is readable across systems.

D. Session Layer – II. API, Sockets: Manages sessions and dialogues between systems, with tools like APIs and sockets facilitating this communication.

This structure follows the OSI model, ensuring standardized networking across platforms.

45. (1):

- Among the members of the Advisory Committee for Libraries, both A.J. Mathai and D.R. Kalia were officially included but could not actively participate in the committee's work.
- This may have been due to administrative constraints, other commitments, or health reasons.
- In contrast, members like T.D. Waknis, B.S. Kesavan, and S.S. Saith were known for their active involvement and contributions to the committee's recommendations on library policy.

The question emphasizes nominal membership vs. active contribution, a common scenario in government advisory bodies.

46. (1): Chronological order of inception for the listed research metrics:

C. Eigenfactor – 2007: Developed by researchers at the University of Washington, Eigenfactor measures journal influence based on citation networks, adjusting for citation quality and journal size.

A. SNIP (Source Normalized Impact per Paper) – 2010: Introduced by CWTS at Leiden University, SNIP normalizes citation impact by accounting for differences in citation behavior across disciplines.

E. Altmetric – 2011: Altmetric tracks the attention research outputs receive online, including mentions in social media, blogs, and news outlets—offering alternative impact measures.

B. CiteScore – 2016: Developed by Elsevier, CiteScore uses Scopus citation data to calculate the average number of citations per document.

D. Crindes – 2020s (Comparative Ranking Index of Dissertations): A relatively new metric designed for evaluating doctoral dissertations, developed for Indian academic environments.

This sequence accurately reflects when each metric was introduced to the scholarly ecosystem.

47. (1): Statements that are true for network cards (NICs):

C. A network card is called interface card: Correct. Network Interface Card (NIC) is the formal term, and it facilitates communication between a computer and a network.

D. It is a circuit board or chip which allows the computer to communicate to another computer network: Correct. It provides the hardware interface between the network and the system bus of the computer.

E. There are four types of modems: While this statement is technically not directly about NICs, it's factually correct. Common modem types include dial-up, DSL, cable, and fiber modems.

(A) is incorrect: The network card is not an end port; it acts as a connector but not necessarily the endpoint in networking terms.

(B) is incorrect: Network cards are typically measured by their data transfer rates (e.g., 100 Mbps, 1 Gbps), not in bits like 4, 12, or 20.

48. (2):

- A secondary source is one that interprets, analyzes, or summarizes primary sources.
- A biography is written by someone other than the subject and is based on primary documents, interviews, and historical records, making it a secondary source.
- Other options:
  - ❑ Court transcription – primary source
  - ❑ Scientific experiment – primary source
  - ❑ Public speech – primary source

49. (4): Correct matching of Digital Library Standards and their purposes:

A. Dublin Core – III. Metadata Description: Dublin Core is a set of 15 basic elements used for describing digital resources (title, creator, subject, etc.).

B. OAI-PMH – IV. Data Harvesting: The Open Archives Initiative Protocol for Metadata Harvesting is used for collecting metadata from digital repositories.

C. METS – I. Digital Object Packaging: The Metadata Encoding and Transmission Standard is used for organizing and packaging digital objects along with their metadata.

D. DOI – II. Persistent Identification: The Digital Object Identifier provides a permanent and unique identifier for digital documents, supporting citation and retrieval.

50. (4): Correct matching of Canons of Classification with their purposes:

A. Canon of Enumeration – IV. Terms should denote concepts in a structured manner: It ensures that terms are listed systematically, forming a structured subject arrangement.

B. Canon of Currency – III. Terms based on latest developments: It demands that classification schemes reflect current knowledge, updating terms as fields evolve.

C. Canon of Reticence – I. Avoid unnecessary or excessive use of terminology: This canon advises conciseness, discouraging overloading the schedule with too many terms.

D. Canon of Simplicity – II. Notations should be simple and clear: It ensures that notation systems are easy to understand and apply, avoiding complex or ambiguous symbols.

51. (2): Deliberate sampling, also known as purposive sampling, is a non-probability sampling technique where the researcher selects participants based on specific characteristics or qualities. This method is often used when a researcher wants to study a particular subset of a population that is especially knowledgeable about the subject of interest.

52. (3): The Missoula Public Library in the United States was awarded the IFLA Green Library Award 2024 in the Grand Scale Project category. The library was recognized for its innovative approach to sustainability, including housing third-party organizations focused on family development, STEM education, and media literacy. The building's design maximizes natural light and incorporates Indigenous art, reflecting a blend of modern innovation and ancient wisdom.

53. (1): The Mysore Oriental Library, now known as the Oriental Research Institute, was established in 1891 under the patronage of Maharaja Chamarajendra Wodeyar X. The institute was created to collect, preserve, and publish rare manuscripts in Sanskrit and Kannada, contributing significantly to the field of Indology.

54. (3): TDM is a multiplexing technique that divides the available bandwidth into fixed-size time slots, each allocated to a different signal or data stream. This method allows multiple signals to share the same transmission medium by transmitting them in rapid succession, one after the other, in their designated time slots.

55. (2): In hypothesis testing, the p-value represents the probability of obtaining test results at least as extreme as the observed results, assuming that the null hypothesis is true. A low p-value indicates that the observed data is unlikely under the null hypothesis, leading researchers to consider rejecting the null hypothesis. However, it's important to note that the p-value does not measure the probability that the null hypothesis is true or false.

56. (1): Chronological order of the indexing systems based on their year of inception:

E. PsycInfo – 1967: Developed by the American Psychological Association, PsycInfo is a comprehensive abstracting and indexing database for psychological literature.

A. PubMed – 1996: A free resource developed by the U.S. National Library of Medicine, PubMed provides access to MEDLINE and biomedical literature.

C. IEEE Xplore – 2000: Offers full-text access to journals, conference proceedings, and standards published by IEEE and IET.

D. DOAJ (Directory of Open Access Journals) – 2003: Aims to increase the visibility of peer-reviewed open access scholarly journals.

B. Google Scholar – 2004: A freely accessible search engine that indexes scholarly articles across disciplines, including theses, books, and abstracts.

This sequence reflects the evolution of digital scholarly indexing platforms from field-specific to multidisciplinary open access.

57. (4): Matching digital archive platform propounders with their creations:

A. Herbert Van de Sompel – III. Open Archive Initiative: He played a leading role in the creation of OAI-PMH, promoting interoperability among digital repositories.

B. Paul Ginsparg – I. ArXiv: Ginsparg created ArXiv.org in 1991 as an open-access archive for preprints in physics and other scientific fields.

C. Michael S. Hart – IV. Project Gutenberg: Hart is known for founding Project Gutenberg in 1971, the world's oldest digital library of free eBooks.

D. Steven Harnad – II. Subversive Proposal: In 1994, Harnad authored the Subversive Proposal, advocating for self-archiving of scholarly articles by researchers to ensure open access.

This matching highlights the pioneers of digital scholarship and their contributions to open knowledge systems.

58. (1): True statements about network topologies:

A. Star topology relies on a central hub for communication: Correct. All devices are connected to a central node; if the hub fails, communication breaks down.

B. Mesh topology eliminates the need for a central node: Correct. In a full mesh topology, every device connects directly to every other, ensuring redundancy and fault tolerance.

D. Ring topology connects devices in a closed loop: Correct. Each device has exactly two neighbours, forming a circle-like structure.

E. Tree topology is a hierarchical topology where multiple star networks are connected with central hub: Correct. It's a hybrid topology, combining features of star and bus topologies.

(C) is incorrect: Bus topology is not fault-tolerant—a failure in the main cable can shut down the entire network.

59. (1): Essential elements of an information society, especially in the context of information security (CIA triad):

A. Confidentiality: Ensures that information is accessible only to authorized users, protecting privacy and secrecy.

C. Integrity: Ensures the accuracy and trustworthiness of data, preventing unauthorized alterations.

E. Availability: Ensures that information and systems are accessible when needed by authorized users.

(B) Vulnerability and (D) Personality are not considered foundational pillars of information societies, particularly from a technical or cybersecurity standpoint.

60. (3):

- The Food and Agriculture Organization (FAO) of the United Nations is the primary international body responsible for promoting agricultural information systems globally.
- FAO works through initiatives like:
  - ❑ AGRIS (International System for Agricultural Science and Technology)
  - ❑ AIMS (Agricultural Information Management Standards)
- These platforms help improve access to agricultural knowledge, support rural development, and enhance food security by disseminating scientific and technical information.

61. (4): Correct matching of databases with their metadata service providers or hosting institutions:

A. Aminer – III. Tsinghua University: Aminer is a scholarly data platform for academic social networks and citation analysis, developed and maintained by Tsinghua University in China.

B. Astrophysics Data System – I. Harvard University: The SAO/NASA Astrophysics Data System (ADS) is hosted and managed by the Harvard-Smithsonian Center for Astrophysics.

C. ATLA Religion Database – IV. EBSCO: This theological and religious studies database is maintained by EBSCO Information Services in collaboration with ATLA (American Theological Library Association).

D. Arachne – II. DAI & University of Cologne: Arachne is an archaeological database and digital archive hosted by the German Archaeological Institute (DAI) and University of Cologne.

This alignment is based on verified institutional ownership and platform development history.

62. (3): Digitisation in libraries includes the following aspects:

A. It requires adherence to metadata standards for discoverability: Yes, using standards like Dublin Core, MODS, or METS ensures digital content is searchable and interoperable.

B. It involves converting analogy materials to digital formats: Correct. This includes scanning documents, photos, microfilms, etc., for digital preservation and access.

C. It ensures permanent access to all digital content without preservation efforts: Incorrect. While digitisation improves access, long-term access requires digital preservation practices such as format migration and regular backups.

D. It involves selecting suitable hardware and software for the process: Accurate. Scanners, OCR software, and digital asset management systems must be carefully selected for optimal output.

(E) is incorrect: Libraries do not need permission from NDLI to digitise their collections unless they are contributing to a specific NDLI partnership or initiative.

63. (3): In the Shannon and Weaver model of communication (1948):

- The encoder is the component responsible for converting the sender's message into signals, such as electrical pulses, sound waves, or binary code, depending on the medium.
- The encoder plays a critical role in bridging the gap between sender's intent and transmission system, allowing the message to travel through the channel to the receiver.

The model includes five components: Information Source → Encoder → Channel → Decoder → Receiver, and it also includes noise as a potential interference.

64. (4): A key concern in scholarly communication today is the sustainability of the academic publishing model:

- The dominance of subscription-based journals and high access costs creates barriers for researchers, especially in developing countries.

- The "paywall model" is being critically debated, as it limits access to publicly funded research.
- Although Open Access is a proposed solution, the article processing charges (APCs) in many OA journals still present a sustainability issue for authors.
- Thus, the challenge is to create a sustainable, equitable, and accessible system for scholarly knowledge dissemination.

65. (2): According to IFLA's concept of Green Libraries, the following are considered key components:

A. Concern with Environment Management: Green libraries implement eco-friendly infrastructure, waste reduction, and energy conservation practices.

B. Sustainable Economy: Green libraries support sustainable budgeting and procurement, minimizing wasteful spending.

C. Social Sustainability: Promotes community engagement, inclusion, and equity through library programs and design.

E. Sustainable Library Services: Libraries must design services that are environmentally conscious and future-ready, like digital lending, recycling policies, etc.

D. (Cultural Sustainability), while relevant in a broader context, is not explicitly stated in IFLA's green library sustainability framework as a primary pillar.

66. (3): Chronological order of books published by Dr. S.R. Ranganathan:

C. Colon Classification – 1933: This was Ranganathan's most pioneering work, introducing the facet-based system of classification.

B. Prolegomena to Library Classification – 1937: A theoretical exposition elaborating the philosophical foundations of classification.

A. Elements of Library Classification – 1945: This work focused on the structural elements and principles of classification schemes.

E. Classification and International Documentation – 1948: Discusses the role of classification in global documentation systems.

D. Library Manual – 1951: A practical guide for the management and functioning of libraries, aimed at practitioners.

This order reflects the progressive development of Ranganathan's classification theory and practical library science.

67. (3): According to Colon Classification (6th Revised Edition):

- The Auxiliary Class Indicator (ACI) y7 is used for biographical works.
- It specifically denotes the form of literature such as biography, autobiography, memoir, etc.
- Hence, for "Biography of Prime Minister," y7 is the correct ACI to represent the biographical nature of the subject.
- Other ACIs:
  - ❑ w – Year
  - ❑ v – Volume
  - ❑ y1 – Periodicals

68. (4):

- The F1 Score is the harmonic mean of precision and recall, commonly used in information retrieval and classification tasks.
- Formula:

$$\text{F1 Score} = \frac{2 \times \text{Precision} \times \text{Recall}}{\text{Precision} + \text{Recall}}$$

- It balances the trade-off between precision (exactness) and recall (completeness), particularly useful when there is class imbalance.

Other options:

- Cumulative Gain, DCG, and NDCG are related to ranking quality in information retrieval systems but are not harmonic means.

69. (1): Statements true about Document Type Definition (DTD):

A. A DTD defines the structure and attributes of an XML document: Correct. It specifies the legal building blocks of an XML document.

B. With DTD, independent group of people can agree on a standard for interchanging data: Correct. It enables data consistency across systems by defining a common structure.

D. The Library of Congress has made available a DTD to convert MARC records to XML: Correct. MARCXML is a schema provided by the Library of Congress for this purpose.

Incorrect statements:

C. The correct syntax is <!DOCTYPE>, not <!DTD>.

E. DTD ensures structure, not authenticity. Data authenticity is achieved through digital signatures or encryption, not DTD.

70. (4): To know the Impact Factor of a journal:

B. Web of Science: Impact Factor is published annually by Clarivate Analytics (previously under Thomson Reuters) in the Journal Citation Reports (JCR), which is part of Web of Science.

D. SCOPUS: Though it does not provide Impact Factor, it offers CiteScore, a comparable metric based on Scopus-indexed content. Many consider CiteScore alongside Impact Factor when evaluating journals.

Incorrect options:

(A) EBSCO, (C) ScienceDirect, and (E) JSTOR are content aggregators or databases, but they do not provide official Impact Factor data.

71. (4):

- This statement is not true. Both Mendeley and Zotero offer direct reference formatting features. Users can generate citations and bibliographies in multiple styles (APA, MLA, Chicago, etc.) directly through both platforms.
- Zotero has a plugin for word processors like Microsoft Word and LibreOffice, just like Mendeley, enabling real-time citation insertion and formatting.
- Thus, this particular point is not a valid differentiator between the two tools, making it the incorrect statement among the given options.

72. (2): Chronological order based on year of launch of the listed databases:

D. SSRN (Social Science Research Network) – 1994: One of the earliest platforms to distribute preprints in the social sciences.

E. NDLTD (Networked Digital Library of Theses and Dissertations) – 1996: A global initiative for electronic thesis and dissertation repositories.

B. DOAJ (Directory of Open Access Journals) – 2003: Aimed to index and promote peer-reviewed open access journals.

A. HathiTrust – 2008: A partnership of academic libraries for digitized book collections, especially those from Google Books and Internet Archive.

C. ScienceOpen – 2013: A research discovery and publishing platform promoting open access and post-publication peer review.

This sequence is correct from oldest to most recent in terms of database initiation.

73. (4):

- In Universal Decimal Classification (UDC), the square brackets [ ] are used to denote subgrouping or a composite subject relation.
- This helps create complex class numbers that represent relationships between different subjects without merging them into one facet.
- For example, [94(47+57)] would indicate historical study of combined regions (Russia + Central Asia).
- Other UDC symbols:
  - ❑ ( ) for place
  - ❑ = for language
  - ❑ " " for time or form

74. (2): Awards presented by CILIP (Chartered Institute of Library and Information Professionals) include:

B. Yoto Carnegie Award: Recognizes outstanding writing and illustration in children's books. It is organized by CILIP in partnership with Yoto.

D. Library Change Lives Award: Highlights the transformative impact of libraries on individual lives and communities.

E. Mentor of the Year Award: Part of CILIP's commitment to professional development, recognizing outstanding mentoring within the library profession.

Incorrect options:

A. Hugh Atkinson Memorial Award is presented by ALA (American Library Association).

C. Beta Phi Mu Award is also an ALA-administered award.

75. (2):

- The High-Level Committee of the National Mission on Libraries (NML) was constituted by the Ministry of Culture, Government of India, via Notification No. 18-4/2009-Lib(Pt.) dated 4th May 2012.
- This committee was entrusted with:
  - ❑ Formulating policy and operational plans for revamping public library services.
  - ❑ Suggesting models for library modernization, digitization, and improved infrastructure.
  - ❑ Ensuring alignment with Digital India and Knowledge Economy goals.

The notification marks a pivotal step in India's national-level library development planning.

76. (3): Matching Principles of Facet Sequence with their description:

A. Wall-Picture Principle – II. Arranges facets based on their visual representation: This principle draws an analogy from how pictures are arranged on a wall—typically from general to specific or background to foreground, guiding visual ordering of facets.

B. Whole-Organ Principle – I. Suggests that a whole entity be treated as a single unit: According to this principle, wholes are considered before parts in the sequence, i.e., organs before tissues.

C. Cow-Calf Principle – IV. Defines the relationship between action and tool: Though commonly interpreted as one concept leading to another, in this specific pairing, it aligns with dependent tools following the action.

D. Act and Action-Actor Tool Principle – III. Specifies that one facet should lead to a dependent facet: The actor/tool logically follows the action, hence is dependent on the main concept (act).

This principle sequence assists in building logical and semantically correct class numbers in Colon Classification.

77. (3): Correct list of open access institutional repositories:

A. Ashoka Trust for Research in Ecology and Environment (ATREE): Hosts an institutional repository providing open access to publications and data in ecological and environmental studies.

C. CSIR-NIScPR online periodicals directory: This repository from CSIR's National Institute of Science Communication and Policy Research offers open access to Indian scientific journals.

D. Krishikosh: A digital repository maintained by ICAR, provides open access to agricultural research outputs, theses, and publications.

Incorrect options:

B. JSTOR: Not an open access platform; subscription-based.

E. Manupatra: A paid legal research platform, not an institutional open access repository.

78. (3): Matching programming paradigms with their features:

A. Object-oriented – III. Encapsulation and inheritance: Core features of OOP include classes, objects, inheritance, and encapsulation, focusing on real-world modeling.

B. Functional – I. Based on mathematical functions: In functional programming, computation is treated as the evaluation of mathematical functions with no mutable state (e.g., Haskell, Lisp).

C. Procedural – II. Sequential execution of instructions: Follows a step-by-step procedure, breaking down a program into functions or routines (e.g., C, Pascal).

D. Declarative – IV. Describes what to do, not how to do it: Focuses on what the program should accomplish, leaving the how to the language processor (e.g., SQL, Prolog).

Each paradigm represents a distinct approach to software design and problem-solving.

79. (4): Currently active IFLA advisory committees include:

A. Committee on Standards: Focuses on the development and promotion of international standards in library and information services.

C. Committee on Cultural Heritage: Works to preserve documentary heritage, including archives, manuscripts, and library materials.

D. Committee on Copyright and other Legal Matters (CLM): Addresses legal and policy issues, especially intellectual property rights affecting libraries.

E. Committee on Open Science and Scholarship: Deals with issues relating to open access, research data management, and scholarly communications.

B. Committee on Public Libraries is not an advisory committee but falls under IFLA's professional units/sections, not the core advisory committee framework.

80. (4): Ephemeral literature is characterized by the following:

A. Any transitory or printed matter: These are usually temporary publications, like flyers, brochures, announcements, etc.

B. Not intended to be retained or preserved: Created for short-term utility, often discarded after use.

D. Shorter lasting value: Compared to books or periodicals, their value is often limited in duration and purpose.

Incorrect options:

C. Holding high archival value: Ephemeral materials are usually not preserved long-term unless they gain historical or research significance.

E. Materials with cultural importance: While some ephemeral items may acquire cultural value over time, this is not an inherent attribute of ephemeral literature.

81. (2): The Integrated Services Digital Network (ISDN) interfaces include:

B. Basic Rate Interface (BRI): Designed for home and small enterprise use, BRI offers two 64 Kbps bearer (B) channels and one 16 Kbps data (D) channel.

D. Primary Rate Interface (PRI): Used for larger organizations, PRI typically provides 23 B channels and 1 D channel in North America and 30 B + 1 D in Europe.

E. Broadband ISDN (B-ISDN) & ATM: B-ISDN was developed for high-speed data and multimedia transmission and supports Asynchronous Transfer Mode (ATM) technology.

Incorrect options:

A. ADSL Interface is related to DSL technology, not ISDN.

C. UARI is not a standard ISDN interface and appears to be fictitious or incorrectly stated.

82. (*)

83. (2):

- Utility software refers to system software designed to help analyze, configure, optimize, or maintain a computer.
- The Disc Cleanup Tool is a built-in Windows utility that helps free up disk space by removing temporary files, system cache, and unused programs.
- Other examples of utility software include antivirus programs, file compressors, and backup tools.

Incorrect options:

- Microsoft PowerPoint – Application software for presentations
- Adobe Illustrator – Graphic design software
- Skype – Communication software

84. (2):

- The Subversive Proposal (1994) by Stevan Harnad initiated the idea of self-archiving scholarly works by researchers.
- Under the subversive model, authors deposit preprints or postprints in institutional repositories or preprint servers like arXiv, SSRN, etc.
- It challenges the traditional paywall publishing model and promotes free access to scholarly content.

This model played a crucial role in the Open Access movement and inspired platforms like EPrints and DSpace.

85. (4):

- This statement is not true about OpenURL.
- OpenURL is not a communication protocol; rather, it is a standard format for transporting metadata about a resource from an information service to a link resolver.
- The main purpose is to enable users to locate the most appropriate version of a resource (e.g., full text, abstract, or library copy) via a context-sensitive linking system.

Correct statements:

- It enables retrieval of appropriate copy
- SFX is an OpenURL-compliant link resolver
- OpenURL works with CrossRef, helping resolve digital references to full texts.

86. (4): This is the correct sequence of planning stages for a retrospective conversion process (RECON):

C. Clearly identify the objectives: The first step is to define why the RECON project is being done, including scope, priorities, and desired outcomes.

A. Carefully draw documents procedures for efficient workflow: Once objectives are set, it's essential to define workflow procedures to ensure efficiency and consistency.

E. Specify standards to be used: Standards such as MARC 21, AACR2, RDA should be chosen to maintain bibliographic consistency and interoperability.

D. Identify the equipment requirements: After setting standards and procedures, identify the hardware and software tools needed for the project.

B. Identify the necessary training for the staff: Finally, ensure staff are trained in procedures, standards, and equipment to carry out the conversion effectively.

This systematic approach ensures a smooth and standardized RECON implementation.

87. (2):

- CC-7 (Colon Classification, 7th Edition) uses 14 indicator digits.
- These indicator digits are part of the class number construction process and are used for signifying facets, phases, isolates, and other details in the classification number.
- They help ensure precision and clarity in representing complex subjects and maintaining the faceted structure of the Colon Classification system.

88. (1):

- The Oxford English Dictionary (OED) was originally issued under the title "A New English Dictionary on Historical Principles".
- The first volume was published in 1884, and the full first edition was completed in 1928.
- It was revolutionary in its approach, presenting meanings and usage chronologically, based on historical principles, rather than alphabetically only.
- Later, the title evolved into the now-famous Oxford English Dictionary.

89. (4):

- Browsewrap and Clickwrap are two types of online license agreement mechanisms.
- Clickwrap agreements require users to actively click "I agree" to the terms before using a service.
- Browsewrap agreements imply consent through use of the website, even without explicitly clicking.
- These methods are used to establish legal agreements between publishers or content providers and users or libraries regarding access rights, use, and downloading of digital content.

90. (4):

- This statement is not true about DIENST (Distributed Interoperable ENgine for STandardized document delivery).
- DIENST is actually a distributed architecture, not a centralized one. It supports interoperability among digital libraries, allowing users to search across repositories using a unified interface.
- True features of DIENST:
  - ❑ Protocol for service communication
  - ❑ Structured document model
  - ❑ Defines core digital library services, such as search, retrieve, and submit.

Hence, the notion of it providing a centralized architecture is incorrect.

91. (4): This statement is not predicted in the passage.

- The passage mentions that the general public will come to the library to seek information on AI and to learn about retraining and job opportunities, but it does not explicitly or implicitly predict that libraries will become more popular as a result.
- The focus is on functions and services libraries may offer in the AI age, not on a rise in their popularity.

Correctly stated:

- Libraries will engage with AI (stated)
- Libraries will promote STEM careers (stated)
- Libraries will collaborate with external organizations (stated)

92. (3): According to the passage, users will turn to libraries:

- "to obtain information on AI and what it means for their lives", and
- "to learn about retraining and other job-related opportunities."

This indicates a clear focus on skill development and knowledge upgrading, particularly in the context of AI and emerging job markets.

The other options (literature, reading space, professional networking) are not mentioned or implied.

93. (2): This is not stated or implied in the paragraph.

- While the passage suggests that AI applications will continue to grow, and that many opportunities are currently unheard of, it does not mention any ongoing research being conducted to explore those areas.
- Statements 1, 3, and 4 are directly or indirectly supported:
    - "Many areas of AI application are yet to be explored" – Implied by "opportunities... currently unheard of"
    - "The use of AI will further expand" – Directly stated
    - "Many opportunities of AI are not yet known" – Also stated as "challenges currently unheard of"

94. (2): The paragraph both states and implies that libraries will become hubs of AI-related information and activity:

- Stated: "As AI gains in popularity the general public will come to the library to obtain information on AI..."
- Implied: By referencing collaboration with STEM fields, workforce agencies, and providing retraining resources, it's implied that libraries will serve as community centers of AI education and guidance.

Thus, the role of libraries in the context of AI is both explicitly mentioned and contextually suggested.

95. (4): Among the application areas of AI mentioned in the paragraph are:

- Health and medicine – "predicting diseases such as breast cancer and multiple sclerosis"
- Law and order – "determine who is likely to commit a crime"
- Business and finance – "default on a loan"

But education and research as direct application areas of AI are not discussed in the paragraph. Even though STEM education and training are mentioned in the context of library involvement, AI application in education and research itself is not depicted.

96. (4): This option does not directly appear in the passage, though the passage does talk about dualities like order/chaos, print/digital, and old/new.

- These dualities demonstrate how libraries are both purposeful and paradoxical, i.e., they balance utility and contradiction.
- However, the phrase "generator and destroyer" is not explicitly used or implied, hence it does not support the idea of libraries being both utilitarian and counterproductive as clearly as the others.

97. (4) This option does not clearly represent libraries as instruments for oppression in the way colonialism, integration, or domination do.

- The passage refers to libraries as tools of imperial conquest, assimilation, and control, which are forms of political or cultural oppression.
- While homogenization might occur as a by-product of such forces, it is not directly mentioned or emphasized in the passage as a method of oppression via libraries.
- Therefore, homogenization does not strongly support the idea of libraries being used for oppressive purposes in this context.

98. (2): This is the correct answer because it is the most accurately reflected cause of vulnerability as mentioned in the passage. The passage states: "Libraries aim to encompass the whole memory of humankind [which] makes them vulnerable to complete erasure."

- The phrase suggests that the ambition to collect everything—to house the entire memory of humankind—creates a risk of total loss, because the larger and more comprehensive a collection is, the more vulnerable it becomes to destruction, erasure, or collapse (especially in times of war, neglect, or disaster).

- This aligns conceptually with the idea of "excessive growth of collection", even though the exact phrase is not used.
- It is not digitization, technology, or inadequate manpower that is highlighted as a risk in this context.

Therefore, excessive growth of collection—in the sense of the ambitious scale of library collections—is indeed the correct reason inferred from the passage for why libraries may be vulnerable to extinction.

99. (1):

- The passage talks about libraries being destroyed by wickedness, neglect, or due to imperial motives (e.g., conquest, control).
- It also refers to demolition and elimination of library buildings.
- There is no mention of inactivity as a cause for the disappearance of libraries.
- Therefore, inactivity is not identified as a factor behind their decline or vanishing.

100. (3):

- Manfredini refers to libraries as "genuine democratic spaces" in the sense of:
  - ❑ Freedom of access
  - ❑ Equality of opportunity
  - ❑ Spaces open to all citizens
- However, the "pluralistic approach"—which typically refers to encouraging multiple ideologies, viewpoints, or cultural narratives—is not specifically stated or implied in the paragraph as a reason why libraries are considered democratic.
- Thus, this option does not directly align with the reasons cited for the democratic nature of libraries.

YOUR SPACE

YOUR SPACE

Previous Years' Paper

National Testing Agency (NTA)

UGC-NET Junior Research Fellowship & Assistant Professor Eligibility Exam

Library and Information Science, September-2024

(Exam held on 03-09-2024)

PAPER-II

1. Match the List-I with List-II.

List-I (Concept/Method)	**List-II (Explanation)**
(*a*) TQM Tools	I. Book repair and binding, Digitalization lab, Cafeteria
(*b*) Far end of the library	II. Direct-purchase of periodicals
(*c*) The Agency method	III. Newark charging system
(*d*) John Cotton Dane	IV. Pareto Analysis Charts

Choose the ***correct*** answer from the options given below:

	(*a*)	(*b*)	(*c*)	(*d*)
A.	II	III	IV	I
B.	I	IV	III	II
C.	IV	I	II	III
D.	II	I	III	IV

2. Arrange the following Web browsers based on their year of invention:

(*a*) Netscape Navigator
(*b*) Mozilla Firefox
(*c*) Mosaic
(*d*) Google Chrome

Choose the ***correct*** answer from the options given below:

A. (*c*), (*a*), (*b*), (*d*)
B. (*a*), (*b*), (*d*), (*c*)
C. (*b*), (*a*), (*c*), (*d*)
D. (*a*), (*b*), (*c*), (*d*)

3. Which of the following relations are found in subject headings?

(*a*) Subject relations
(*b*) Equivalence relations
(*c*) Hierarchical relations
(*d*) Phase relations
(*e*) Associative relations

Choose the ***correct*** answer from the options given below:

A. (*a*), (*b*), (*c*) only
B. (*c*), (*d*), (*e*) only
C. (*b*), (*c*), (*e*) only
D. (*b*), (*c*), (*d*) only

4. Arrange the following Year Books and Directories in ascending order from oldest to latest of their first publication.

(*a*) Europa World Yearbook
(*b*) Demographic Yearbook
(*c*) World of Learning
(*d*) Commonwealth Universities Yearbook

Choose the ***correct*** answer from the options given below:

A. (*a*), (*b*), (*c*), (*d*)
B. (*d*), (*c*), (*b*), (*a*)
C. (*b*), (*c*), (*a*), (*d*)
D. (*a*), (*d*), (*c*), (*b*)

5. Match the List-I with List-II.

List-I (Features of Information)	List-II (Information service)
(*a*) Inter disciplinary nature of information scatter	I. Indexing classification and storage systems, reference service
(*b*) Multiplicity of Languages	II. Information and data analysis and evaluation
(*c*) Wide variation in quality and reliability	III. Translation service
(*d*) Cumulation of information into vast quantities	IV. Indexing techniques to interlink subjects: Information analysis and enquiry service

Choose the ***correct*** answer from the options given below:

	(*a*)	(*b*)	(*c*)	(*d*)
A.	I	II	III	IV
B.	II	III	IV	I
C.	III	IV	I	II
D.	IV	III	II	I

6. What is the full form of RoMEO in Sherpa RoMEO?

A. Record of Master file for Open Archiving
B. Rights of Master MEtadata file for Open Archiving
C. Record MEtadata for Open Archiving
D. Rights MEtadata for Open Archiving

7. Probability distribution of all the possible means of random samples of a given sample size refers to:

A. Sampling distribution of mean
B. Distribution of sample
C. Distribution of population
D. Probability distribution of sample

8. Match the List-I with List-II

In respect of PRECIS, match the followin role operators with respective description

List-I (Role operators)	List-II (Description)
(*a*) *s*	I. Bound co-ordinate conce
(*b*) *t*	II. Two-way interaction
(*c*) *f*	III. Role definer
(*d*) *u*	IV. Author-attributed action

Choose the ***correct*** answer from the optio given below:

	(*a*)	(*b*)	(*c*)	(*d*)
A.	I	II	IV	III
B.	III	IV	I	II
C.	II	III	I	IV
D.	IV	I	III	II

9. Belkin is associated with:

A. Cataloguing B. Classification
C. Documentation D. Information theor

10. CERL stands for:

A. Consortium of European Researc Libraries
B. Community for European Researc Libraries
C. Consortium for East Asia Researc Libraries
D. Collection of European Researc Libraries

11. The word "Data" was originated fro ______ word.

A. Greek B. Latin
C. Spanish D. Persian

12. "Treatment for cancer in India" arrange th concepts of this title using facet sequenc formula of Dr. S.R Ranganathan:

(*a*) Treatment (*b*) Medicine
(*c*) India (*d*) Disease
(*e*) Cancer

Choose the ***correct*** answer from the options given below:

A. (*a*), (*b*), (*d*), (*e*), (*c*) only
B. (*d*), (*a*), (*e*), (*c*), (*b*) only
C. (*e*), (*c*), (*d*), (*b*), (*a*) only
D. (*b*), (*d*), (*e*), (*a*), (*c*) only

13. In which year, Delhi Public Library had introduced the mobile sendee for readers?

A. 1951 AD
B. 1953 AD
C. 1972 AD
D. 1996 AD

14. The SPSS has three views namely

(*a*) Help view
(*b*) Data view
(*c*) Output view
(*d*) Variable view
(*e*) Input view

Choose the ***correct*** answer from the options given below:

A. (*a*), (*d*) and (*e*) only
B. (*b*), (*b*) and (*e*) only
C. (*b*), (*c*) and (*d*) only
D. (*a*), (*b*) and (*c*) only

15. Which of the following are true for Resource Description Framework (RDF)?

(*a*) RDF is a standard model for data interchange on the web
(*b*) XML syntax is allowed for RDF data model
(*c*) RDF cannot merge data
(*d*) RDF allows structured data only
(*e*) RDF extends the linking structure of the web to use URI

Choose the ***correct*** answer from the options given below:

A. (*a*), (*b*) and (*c*) only
B. (*b*), (*c*) and (*d*) only
C. (*a*), (*c*) and (*d*) only
D. (*a*), (*b*) and (*e*) only

16. Tags in eXtensible Markup Language are case sensitive because:

A. these tags are fixed by the W3C
B. these tags are pre defined
C. these tags are standardized already
D. these tags are user defined

17. SHERNI of Information and Library Network is the expert profile network system that:

A. Connects the knowledge, skills and expertise of women across the field of Science, Humanities, Engineering only
B. Connects the knowledge, skills and expertise of women across the field of Library and Information Science only
C. Connects the knowledge, skills and expertise of women across the various field of studies only
D. Connects the knowledge, skills and expertise of women across the Social Science and Engineering only

18. Which of the following is an analytical information source?

A. Dictionary   B. Almanac
C. Directory   D. Monograph

19. Arrange the steps of PERT/CPM in chronological order.

(*a*) Determine the earliest and latest feasible event times
(*b*) Identify the precedence relationships among the activities
(*c*) Identify activities required by the project
(*d*) Determine the expected time requirement for each activity
(*e*) Develop a network diagram of activities and events or nodes showing precedence relationships

A. (*e*), (*b*), (*d*), (*a*), (*c*)
B. (*c*), (*b*), (*d*), (*e*), (*a*)
C. (*b*), (*c*), (*e*), (*d*), (*a*)
D. (*d*), (*a*), (*e*), (*b*), (*c*)

20. Which of the following are true in the context of Development Science Information System (DEVSIS)

(*a*) DEVSIS is related to the field of Science and Technology

(*b*) Devindex is the principal published product of the DEVSIS

(*c*) DEVSIS publishes periodic compendia under the title Devprofile

(*d*) INFOPLAN, a Latin American Planning Information Network has founded some regional DEVSIS centre.

(*e*) DEVSIS is a global decentralised mission-oriented information system.

Choose the ***correct*** answer from the options given below:

A. (*a*), (*b*), (*c*) and (*d*) only
B. (*b*), (*c*), (*d*) and (*e*) only
C. (*a*), (*c*), (*d*) and (*e*) only
D. (*a*), (*b*), (*d*) and (*e*) only

21. An estimate of loss of a few stacks of a library that is made on the basis of thorough checking is known as:

A. Stock taking by shelf register
B. Sample stock-verification
C. Stock taking by master record
D. Stock taking by Duplicate set of Book cards

22. Match the List-I with List-II.

List-I (Library Association)	List-II (Years of establishment)
(*a*) Gujarat Pustakalays Mandal	I. 1925
(*b*) Maharashtra Library Association	II. 1926
(*c*) Baroda State Library Association	III. 1921
(*d*) Bengal Library Association	IV. 1923

Choose the ***correct*** answer from the options given below:

	(*a*)	(*b*)	(*c*)	(*d*)
A.	I	II	IV	III
B.	IV	III	II	I
C.	III	I	IV	II
D.	III	IV	II	I

23. In early 1980s, the UCG established National Information Centres and Inter-University Centers to render reference and documentation services for promoting research in existing Institutes/Universities. Which of the following Universities had got inter-university centre?

A. Indian Institute of Science, Bangalore
B. Maharaja Sayajirao University, Baroda
C. SNDT Women's University, Bombay
D. Jawaharlal Nehru University, New Delhi

24. Which of the following is not a principle of library expenditure?

A. Principle of Economy
B. Principle of Maximum aggregate benefit
C. Principle of Advance Planning
D. Principle of Demand and Supply

25. Arrange the layers of Semantic Web Architecture in proper sequence from lower to higher

(*a*) RIF and SWRL
(*b*) UNICODE and URI
(*c*) OWL
(*d*) XML
(*e*) RDF

Choose the ***correct*** answer from the options given below:

A. (*c*), (*b*), (*a*), (*d*), (*e*)
B. (*a*), (*d*), (*b*), (*e*), (*c*)
C. (*b*), (*d*), (*e*), (*c*), (*a*)
D. (*d*), (*b*), (*a*), (*e*), (*c*)

26. Which of the following are metadata harvesting service providers:

(*a*) Udacity (http://www.udacity.com)

(*b*) Google scholar (http://scholar google. com)

(*c*) NCSTRL (http://www.ncstrl.org)
(*d*) NPTEL (http://www.nptl.iitm.ac.in)
(*e*) Search Digital Libraries (http://drtc.isibang.ac.in/sdc)

Choose the ***correct*** answer from the options given below:

A. (*a*), (*c*) and (*e*) only
B. (*a*), (*b*) and (*c*) only
C. (*b*), (*c*) and (*e*) only
D. (*b*), (*d*) and (*e*) only

27. Which of the following are true of Information:

(*a*) Information is a property of data
(*b*) Product of human brain
(*c*) Information may be abstract or concrete
(*d*) Information can not be creative
(*e*) Information is personal knowledge

Choose the ***correct*** answer from the options given below:

A. (*b*), (*c*) and (*d*) only
B. (*a*), (*b*) and (*c*) only
C. (*a*), (*c*) and (*d*) only
D. (*b*), (*c*) and (*e*) only

28. Who is the author of 'Basic Reference Sources'?

A. S.R. Ranganathan
B. Louis Shores
C. Dennis Grogan
D. Margaret Hutchins

29. 1 (one) nibble equals to how many bits?

A. 6 B. 4
C. 8 D. 2

30. Which of the following are true of Nalanda University.

(*a*) Nalanda University was established in 4th century B.C.
(*b*) Area of library was called Dharma Ganja
(*c*) Library was housed in three grand buildings
(*d*) The buildings were named as Ratna-Sagar, Ratna Pithika and Ratna Ranjaka
(*e*) Ratna Ranjaka was a nine storied building

Choose the ***correct*** answer from the options given below:

A. (*a*), (*c*) and (*d*) only
B. (*b*), (*c*) and (*d*) only
C. (*a*), (*b*) and (*e*) only
D. (*b*), (*c*) and (*e*) only

31. Which of the following is a neo conventional source of information?

A. Atlas B. Patent
C. Audio-visual D. Microform

32. Each surviving term of an Expressive Title is denoted by:

A. Supportive Term
B. Apparatus Term
C. Kernel Term
D. Fanciful Term

33. Match the List-I with List-II.

List-I (Departments of Industries)	**List-II (Purposes)**
(*a*) Small Industries Development Organisation (SIDO)	I. Receiving application for major assistance, examining technical feasibility and economic viability
(*b*) Small Industries Service Institute (SISI)	II. Coordinating overall policy, planning and rendering assistance and advisory services
(*c*) National Small Industries Corporation (NSIC)	III. Providing techno-economic services, management and technical training programs
(*d*) Small Entrepreneurs	IV. Infrastructure development and assistance in implementation of programs

Choose the ***correct*** answer from the options given below:

	(a)	(b)	(c)	(d)
A.	I	II	III	IV
B.	III	IV	I	II
C.	II	III	IV	I
D.	IV	I	II	III

34. Arrange the typical sections of a research paper in logical order:

(*a*) Brief summary
(*b*) Statistical analysis
(*c*) Areas for future research
(*d*) Research procedure
(*e*) Objective of the study

A. (*e*), (*b*), (*d*), (*a*), (*c*)
B. (*c*), (*a*), (*b*), (*e*), (*d*)
C. (*a*), (*e*), (*d*), (*b*), (*c*)
D. (*b*),. (*c*), (*a*), (*d*), (*e*)

35. The statistical test used to investigate the differences among the means of all the populations simultaneously is ______.

A. T-test
B. ANOVA
C. Correlation analysis
D. Chi-square test

36. The first ever library school in the world was started by:

A. Charles Ammi Cutter
B. A.D. Dickinson
C. Melvil Dewey
D. James Kaiser

37. Who was not a member of UCG panel on Library and Information Science for the Curriculum Development Committee 2001 headed by Prof. C.R. Karisiddappa:

A. Prof Harsha Parekh, SNDT Women's University
B. Prof T. Vishwanathan, INSDOC
C. Prof P.S.G Kumar, RTM Nagpur University
D. Prof M.K.R. Naidu, M.S. University

38. Arrange the sample size of population (N = 100) according to degree of accuracy with 0.05, 0.035, 0.025, 0.01 and 0.00 respectively.

(*a*) 80
(*b*) 94
(*c*) 89
(*d*) 100
(*e*) 99

Choose the ***correct*** answer from the options given below:

A. (*b*), (*d*), (*e*), (*a*), (*c*)
B. (*d*), (*b*), (*a*), (*c*), (*e*)
C. (*c*), (*a*), (*e*), (*b*), (*d*)
D. (*a*), (*c*), (*b*), (*e*), (*d*)

39. Match the List-I with List-II.

List-I (Languages)	List-II (Examples)
(*a*) Logic Programming Language	I. Prolog
(*b*) Front end programming Language	II. C#
(*c*) Back end programming Language	III. CSS
(*d*) Scripting Programming Language	IV. Bash

Choose the ***correct*** answer from the options given below:

	(a)	(b)	(c)	(d)
A.	I	IV	III	II
B.	I	III	II	IV
C.	II	IV	III	I
D.	III	I	II	IV

40. Which of the following are advantages of Mobile Library apps?

(*a*) Storage and display
(*b*) Quality assurance
(*c*) Allow users to set preferences
(*d*) Compatibility
(*e*) Load contents faster

Choose the ***correct*** answer from the options given below:

A. (*a*), (*b*), (*c*) only
B. (*b*), (*c*), (*d*) only
C. (*c*), (*d*), (*e*) only
D. (*a*), (*d*), (*e*) only

41. In what sequence one should consult the following information sources to understand about 'Referral Service' with its increasing extension and intention.

(*a*) Library Science with a Slant to Documentation
(*b*) Reference Service by S.R Ranganathan
(*c*) Harrod's Librarian's Glossary and Reference Book
(*d*) Encyclopedia of Library and Information Science

Choose the ***correct*** answer from the options given below:

A. (*a*), (*b*), (*c*), (*d*)
B. (*b*), (*c*), (*d*), (*a*)
C. (*c*), (*d*), (*b*), (*a*)
D. (*d*), (*a*), (*b*), (*c*)

42. Which of the technology drives are not part of SMAC system?

A. Social Media B. Mobile Computing
C. Data Analytics D. CMS

43. Who coined the term "Infoshere"?

A. Delphi B. Likert
C. Luciano Floridi D. Brophy

44. In ______ of job evaluation actual incident relevant to the work situation are taken into account and each employee is made to answer each incident to his supervisor.

A. Informal Plan Method
B. Self Rating Method
C. Mutual Rating Method
D. Critical Plan Method

45. Which of the following are true of Librarianship as a profession

(*a*) Needs a specialized knowledge
(*b*) Requires set of principles of professional ethics
(*c*) Information work is distinct from librarianship says Farradane
(*d*) Mainly an activity involving service against fee or fees
(*e*) The term information specialist does not include library professional

Choose the ***correct*** answer from the options given below:

A. (*a*), (*b*) and (*c*) only
B. (*b*), (*c*) and (*d*) only
C. (*c*), (*d*) and (*e*) only
D. (*b*), (*d*) and (*e*) only

46. Laney described the characteristics of ______ as data that cannot be processed by traditional data management tools.

A. Geospatial Data
B. Linked Data
C. Qualitative Data
D. Big Data

47. Which of the following data collection tools relates to the broader underlying emotions of a person's life experience?

A. focused interview
B. non-directive interview
C. clinical interview
D. telephonic interview

48. Sequence the following Act enacted by the Government of India logically from the date of their first enactment.

(*a*) The Geographical Indications of Goods (Registration and Protection) Act.
(*b*) The Patents Act
(*c*) The Designs Act
(*d*) The Trade and Merchandise Act

Choose the ***correct*** answer from the options given below:

A. (*a*), (*b*), (*c*), (*d*)
B. (*b*), (*c*), (*d*), (*a*)
C. (*d*), (*b*), (*a*), (*c*)
D. (*c*), (*d*), (*a*), (*b*)

49. Which of the following is not a digital library initiative:

A. Google Books Library Project
B. Digital Library Federation (DLF)
C. Web Library Project
D. Million Book Project

50. The first library act was enacted by:

A. Congress of the United States
B. British Parliament
C. Germany Parliament
D. Russian Governing Council

51. Webcasting is an example of ______.

A. Internet Technology
B. Web Technology
C. Push Technology
D. Communication Technology

52. The sources of information for the case study method includes:

(*a*) Confessions
(*b*) Observations
(*c*) Life histories
(*d*) Opinion polling
(*e*) Interview of individuals

Choose the ***correct*** answer from the options given below:

A. (*b*), (*c*), (*d*) and (*e*) only
B. (*a*), (*c*), (*d*) and (*e*) only
C. (*a*), (*b*), (*c*) and (*d*) only
D. (*a*), (*b*), (*c*) and (*e*) only

53. With specific reference to the establishment year, arrange the following consortium in ascending order.

(*a*) INDEST
(*b*) FORSA
(*c*) National Knowledge Research Consortium (NKRC)
(*d*) NGC-DAE Consortium

Choose the ***correct*** answer from the options given below:

A. (*a*), (*b*), (*c*), (*d*)
B. (*b*), (*c*), (*d*), (*a*)
C. (*b*), (*d*), (*a*), (*c*)
D. (*d*), (*b*), (*a*), (*c*)

54. Match the List-I with List-II.

List-I (E-Resource)	**List-II (Types)**
(*a*) Samarth	I. Subject gateway
(*b*) LIS-FORUM	II. Web portal
(*c*) Intute	III. Bulletin Board
(*d*) CBBS	IV. Discussion group

Choose the ***correct*** answer from the options given below:

	(*a*)	(*b*)	(*c*)	(*d*)
A.	II	IV	I	III
B.	III	I	II	IV
C.	II	IV	III	I
D.	IV	III	I	II

55. Which of the following are true of institutional source of information?

(*a*) No exclusive referral centre has been operating in India
(*b*) Clearing house cannot be considered as an institutional source of information
(*c*) A major part of information needed by social science researcher can be provided by institutional source
(*d*) A significant number of journals are published by learned societies
(*e*) Institutional sources may also be called as informal sources

Choose the ***most appropriate*** answer from the options given below:

A. (*a*), (*d*) and (*e*) only
B. (*b*), (*c*) and (*d*) only
C. (*c*), (*d*) and (*e*) only
D. (*a*), (*c*) and (*d*) only

56. MARC- 21 record communication format comprises of:

(*a*) Leader
(*b*) Directory
(*c*) Title
(*d*) Data Context
(*e*) Main Entry

Choose the ***correct*** answer from the options given below:

A. (*a*), (*b*) and (*c*) only
B. (*a*), (*b*) and (*d*) only
C. (*a*), (*c*) and (*d*) only
D. (*a*), (*b*) and (*e*) only

57. Which of the following are true of multimedia:

(*a*) There are six basic elements in multimedia
(*b*) A mobile user may use multimedia through SMS
(*c*) CAD/CAM can be used for designing engineering application
(*d*) Photoshops can be used for network development
(*e*) Common file types for audio include MP3, WAV and WMA

Choose the ***correct*** answer from the options given below:

A. (*a*), (*b*) and (*c*) only
B. (*c*), (*d*) and (*e*) only
C. (*b*), (*c*) and (*e*) only
D. (*a*), (*c*) and (*e*) only

58. Match the List-I with List-II.

List-I (Sources)	List-II (Editors)
(*a*) MC Graw Hill Dictionary of Scientific and Technical Terms, 1984	I. James Hastings
(*b*) ALA Glossary of Library and Information Science, 1983	II. David R Sills
(*c*) Encyclopedia of Religion and Ethics 1908-27	III. Cybil P Parker
(*d*) International Encyclopedia of Social Science, 1967	IV. Heartstill Young

Choose the ***correct*** answer from the options given below:

	(*a*)	(*b*)	(*c*)	(*d*)
A.	IV	III	II	I
B.	IV	I	III	II
C.	III	I	IV	II
D.	III	IV	I	II

59. Match the List-I with List-II.

List-I (Information Package Services)	List-II (Contents)
(*a*) Product Information Brochure	I. is a study of the salient features of products processes of competitors
(*b*) Comparative Product Profile	II. Provides the salient features of the products relevant to the industries
(*c*) Patent Information Services	III. Brings to the notice of the engineers the latest inventions of products formally
(*d*) Product Focus	IV. Provides exhaustive information on newly developed products of interest to the industry/organisation

Choose the ***correct*** answer from the options given below:

	(*a*)	(*b*)	(*c*)	(*d*)
A.	IV	I	III	II
B.	I	II	III	IV
C.	II	I	III	IV
D.	III	II	IV	I

60. Which of the following is not a limitation of chain indexing?

A. Chain indexing depends only on class number
B. Only last link is specific
C. False or Unsought link
D. It provides alternative approach to the classified file through reverse rendering

61. Match the List-I with List-II.

List-I (Modes of Formation of Subjects)	List-II (Description)
(*a*) Dissection	I. Construction by overlaying fact on facet
(*b*) Lamination	II. Connecting together two or more isolate ideas of same category
(*c*) Denudation	III. Cutting a universe of entities into parts of co-ordinate status
(*d*) Super imposition	IV. Progressive decrease of the extension and increase of the intension

Choose the ***correct*** answer from the options given below:

	(*a*)	(*b*)	(*c*)	(*d*)
A.	III	I	IV	II
B.	I	II	III	IV
C.	II	III	I	IV
D.	IV	I	III	II

62. Arrange the steps of performance appraisal in proper sequence.

(*a*) Performance improvement planning

(*b*) Compensation and rewarding good performance

(*c*) Performance feedback and evaluation

(*d*) Potential appraisal

(*e*) Performance reviewing or progress review

Choose the ***correct*** answer from the options given below:

A. (*a*), (*b*), (*d*), (*c*), (*e*)

B. (*e*), (*c*), (*b*), (*d*), (*a*)

C. (*d*), (*c*), (*a*), (*b*), (*e*)

D. (*b*), (*c*), (*a*), (*d*), (*e*)

63. A bidirectional wireless system that transmits data via LED or infrared light is:

A. Wi-Fi

B. Li-fi

C. Mobile communication

D. V-SAT

64. A cyclic recurrence of fundamental categories in the facet analysis of a subject is called:

A. Levels B. Rounds

C. Devices D. Isolates

65. Match the List-I with List-II

Match the following use and user studies with their investigations.

List-I	List-II
(*a*) Information metrics and user studies	I. Crawford
(*b*) Information Needs and uses	II. M.B. Line
(*c*) Organizational behaviour and information seeking	III. Carol Tenopir
(*d*) The information uses and needs of social scientists	IV. Auster Eithal

Choose the ***correct*** answer from the options given below:

	(*a*)	(*b*)	(*c*)	(*d*)
A.	II	I	IV	III
B.	III	IV	I	II
C.	I	II	III	IV
D.	III	I	IV	II

66. Who coined the term "Invisible college"?

A. B.C. Brooks B. Peter Drucker

C. J.H. Shera D. Diana Crane

67. Which of the following are true in connection with the Agricultural Network Information Centre (AgNIC):

(*a*) AgNIC was started in 1973

(*b*) National Agricultural Library of USA was involved as an alliance partner

(*c*) AgNIC has been renamed as AGRINDEX
(*d*) AgNIC has a web gateway providing immediate access to a cross-section of evaluated agriculture resources
(*e*) CB Pest database of occurrence and distribution of pesticides is available through AgNIC

Choose the ***correct*** answer from the options given below:

A. (*a*), (*b*) and (*d*) only
B. (*b*), (*c*) and (*d*) only
C. (*a*), (*b*) and (*c*) only
D. (*b*), (*d*) and (*e*) only

68. Match the List-I with List-II.

List-I (Citing indicators)	**List-II (Description)**
(*a*) Ibid.	I. Refers to the reference listed earlier by the same author
(*b*) Op.cit.	II. Refers to citation of sources with multiple authors
(*c*) Loc.cit.	III. Refers to the same author and serve in the immediately preceding reference
(*d*) et. al.	IV. Refers to foot note term-used to repeat the title and page number for a given work

Choose the ***correct*** answer from the options given below:

	(*a*)	(*b*)	(*c*)	(*d*)
A.	I	IV	III	II
B.	III	I	IV	II
C.	II	III	I	IV
D.	IV	II	III	I

69. Which of the following are types of MIS in an organisation?

(*a*) Executive support systems
(*b*) Management support systems
(*c*) Personnel support systems
(*d*) Software support systems
(*e*) Decision support systems

Choose the ***correct*** answer from the options given below:

A. (*a*), (*b*) and (*e*) only
B. (*a*), (*c*) and (*e*) only
C. (*b*), (*c*) and (*d*) only
D. (*c*), (*d*) and (*e*) only

70. Match the List-I with List-II.

List-I (Metrics)	**List-II (Term coined by)**
(*a*) Bibliometrics	I. Vassily and Mulchenko
(*b*) H-index	II. Almind and Ingwersen
(*c*) Webometrics	III. Pritchard
(*d*) Scientometrics	IV. J.E. Hirsh

Choose the ***correct*** answer from the options given below:

	(*a*)	(*b*)	(*c*)	(*d*)
A.	I	II	IV	III
B.	II	III	I	IV
C.	IV	I	III	II
D.	III	IV	II	I

71. Information communication process can be classified broadly into following four categories in terms of its level. Arrange them in decreasing level of involvement of number of people in the process.

(*a*) Interpersonal Communication
(*b*) Intra personal Communication
(*c*) Group Communication
(*d*) Mass Communication

Choose the ***correct*** answer from the options given below:

A. (*a*), (*b*), (*c*), (*d*)
B. (*b*), (*c*), (*a*), (*d*)
C. (*d*), (*c*), (*a*), (*b*)
D. (*b*), (*a*), (*c*), (*d*)

72. Which of the following is an implication of the first law of library science:

A. Compact shelving
B. Library extension service
C. Location of the library
D. Implementation of library act

73. A single schedule that lists all of the simple and compound subjects together with their readymade class number is called ______.

A. Faceted Classification
B. Analytico Synthetic Classification
C. Knowledge Classification
D. Enumerative Classification

74. Which of the following hold good with databases

(*a*) CAS Registry is a factual data base
(*b*) CAS react is a bibliographic data base
(*c*) PubMed is a full text data base
(*d*) ERIC is a numeric data base
(*e*) SCOPUS is a citation database

Choose the ***correct*** answer from the options given below:

A. (*b*), (*c*) and (*d*) only
B. (*a*), (*c*) and (*e*) only
C. (*c*), (*d*) and (*e*) only
D. (*a*), (*b*) and (*d*) only

75. The *data security measures include:*

(a) Book marking
(*b*) Antivirus protection
(*c*) Data encryption
(*d*) Firewall
(*e*) Data diddling

Choose the ***correct*** answer from the options given below:

A. (*b*), (*c*) and (*d*) only
B. (*a*), (*b*) and (*c*) only
C. (*a*), (*c*) and (*d*) only
D. (*c*), (*d*) and (*e*) only

76. The preliminary part of the research report may not include:

A. Table of Contents
B. List of tables
C. Preface
D. Importance of the problem under investigation

77. The term 'Reprography' was first introduced in ______.

A. India
B. Italy
C. Turkey
D. Germany

78. Which of the following are promotional methods of marketing?

(*a*) Mailshots
(*b*) Personal visits
(*c*) Newsletters
(*d*) Capacity Building
(*e*) Rehabilitation

Choose the ***correct*** answer from the options given below:

A. (*b*), (*c*) and (*d*) only
B. (*a*), (*b*) and (*c*) only
C. (*a*), (*b*) and (*d*) only
D. (*c*), (*d*) and (*e*) only

79. Which of the following is a computer program used to search website content and index, over the internet?

A. Search Engine
B. Web Browser
C. Web Crawler
D. Meta Search Engine

80. If all the non critical activities start as early as possible, the spare time is the ______.

A. Latest Finishing Time
B. Free Float
C. Total Float
D. Independent Float

81. Which of the following are related to INIS?

(*a*) Membership is open only to inter governmental organizations that deal with Nuclear research
(*b*) has its own International Nuclear Library Network

(*c*) INIS is multi-lingual in nature
(*d*) INIS was established in 1964
(*e*) NUCLEUS is IAEA's information resource portal

Choose the ***correct*** answer from the options given below:

A. (*a*), (*b*) and (*c*) only
B. (*b*), (*c*) and (*e*) only
C. (*c*), (*d*) and (*e*) only
D. (*a*), (*d*) and (*e*) only

82. Library pilgrimages are an example of:

A. Saraswati Pooja during Navaratri
B. Adult education program
C. Library cooperation
D. Library extension service

83. Match the List-I with List-II.

Match the following sections of RTI Act, 2015 with the description.

List-I (Section)	List-II (Description)
(*a*) 4	I. Third Party Inspection
(*b*) 11	II. Protection of action taken in good faith
(*c*) 15	III. Obligation of authority
(*d*) 21	IV. Constitution of State Information Commission

Choose the ***correct*** answer from the options given below:

	(*a*)	(*b*)	(*c*)	(*d*)
A.	I	II	III	IV
B.	II	III	IV	I
C.	III	I	IV	II
D.	IV	III	II	I

84. Which of the following is a Social Networking Service primarily used for non-social interpersonal communication?

A. Instagram
B. Reddit
C. Linkedin
D. Twitter/X

85. Arrange the steps used in POPSI in the logical sequence.

(*a*) Content Analysis
(*b*) Alphabetisation
(*c*) Modulation
(*d*) Preparation of entries
(*e*) Formalisation

Choose the ***correct*** answer from the options given below:

A. (*a*), (*e*), (*c*), (*d*), (*b*)
B. (*e*), (*a*), (*d*), (*c*), (*b*)
C. (*b*), (*a*), (*d*), (*c*), (*e*)
D. (*a*), (*b*), (*c*), (*d*), (*e*)

86. Which of the following are described as penalty for researchers in UGC (Promotion of Academic Integrity and Prevention of Plagiarism in Higher Educational Institutions) Regulations 2018.

(*a*) Researchers shall be asked to submit a revised script
(*b*) Researchers shall be asked to pay a penalty of Rs. 5000/-
(*c*) Researchers shall be debarred from submitting a revised script
(*d*) Researchers registration for the research degree shall be cancelled
(*e*) After there unsatisfactory plagiarism reports bailable arrest warrant will be issued.

Choose the ***correct*** answer from the options given below:

A. (*a*), (*b*) and (*c*) only
B. (*a*), (*c*) and (*e*) only
C. (*a*), (*c*) and (*d*) only
D. (*b*), (*c*) and (*e*) only

87. Arrange the following steps of information literacy scope and sequence model in the logical sequence of their operation.

(*a*) Find
(*b*) Assess
(*c*) Create
(*d*) Question
(*e*) Gather

Choose the ***correct*** answer from the options given below:

A. (*a*), (*b*), (*d*), (*c*), (*e*)
B. (*d*), (*a*), (*e*), (*c*), (*b*)
C. (*d*), (*e*), (*c*), (*a*), (*b*)
D. (*b*), (*a*), (*d*), (*c*), (*e*)

88. Match the List-I with List-II.

List-I (Technology)	List-II (Function)
(*a*) Barcode Technology	I. is implemented through a federation of registration agencies to uniquely identify an object.
(*b*) RFID	II. includes tolerance of mis-orientation and obscuration
(*c*) Flickering	III. is allowing users to read information on the screen but not capture it by screen dumping
(*d*) DOI	IV. is used for identification, location and tracking of items

Choose the ***correct*** answer from the options given below:

	(*a*)	(*b*)	(*c*)	(*d*)
A.	IV	II	III	I
B.	II	III	IV	I
C.	I	IV	III	II
D.	IV	II	I	III

89. The following have major initiatives in enhancing education and academic library system in India. Arrange them in reverse chronological order of their foundation

(*a*) All India Council for Technical Education (AICTE)

(*b*) National Council of Educational Research and Training (NCERT)

(*c*) National Institute of Educational Planning and Administration (NIEPA)

(*d*) State Council of Educational Research and Training (SCERT Delhi)

(*e*) University Grants Commission (UGC)

Choose the ***correct*** answer from the options given below:

A. (*a*), (*b*), (*c*), (*d*), (*e*)

B. (*d*), (*c*), (*b*), (*e*), (*a*)

C. (*a*), (*e*), (*b*), (*c*), (*d*)

D. (*d*), (*b*), (*a*), (*c*), (*e*)

90. 'Readers Digest' is an example for:

A. Scholarly journal

B. Trade journal

C. Popular/General interest periodical

D. Current source of information

Directions (Qs. No. 91 to 95): *Read the following passage and answer the following questions:*

Readability signifies easy comprehension of the text by a reader. There are three main aspects of readability: legibility of the text, easy flow of reading and easy comprehension. Thus, readability of a book is dependent on many factors, such as clarity of presentation in terms of language and illustration as also the ability of a reader in terms of his/her intellectual level, language proficiency and mental alertness. All authors may not have equal capability to produce 'readable' books. But they can certainly improve the readability of their books if they are able to know the readability level of the manuscripts that they have produced. For this, several experts have devised readability formulas to measure the readability of any text. Measurement of readability refers to the process of assessing the extent of ease in reading and understanding a written text.

Most readability formulas are based on one semantic factor, i.e., the difficulty of words and one syntactic factor, i.e., the difficulty of sentences. These formulas assume that longer sentences are harder sentences and longer words are harder words. Each readability formula measures text differently, but each formula typically assesses text only at the level of individual words and sentences, in a purely mechanical way. They measure certain attributes of words and sentences in isolation, ignoring other important attributes at the sentence level, including how writer has connected sentences into paragraphs. By applying scientific and mathematical principles, the readability principles aim to present an objective analysis about the readability of a particular text. Some of the commonly used readability formulas are: Dale-Chall readability formula (1948), PSK Readability Formula (1958), Gunning's FOG index (1964), FK Grade Level Formula (1975), and McAlpine EFLAW formula (2006). Word processor's tool analyzes the text supplied by a user and calculates the number of characters in the sentences, words and syllables and finds reading level and grade level of the text by applying any of the readability formulas used by it. Readability formulas have many advantages, but these are being often criticized as 'over-simplification and a critique of creative writing'. Indeed most great literary works may fail to pass the readability tests, though they are of very high quality. These formulas are more relevant for textbooks and subject books. While efforts should be made to have readability formulas which can give more accurate results, the authors should also be more alert to take prepublication readability tests of their creations so that we can have more readable books.

91. What indicator of difficulty is used as parameter in readability measurement formulas?

A. Difficulties in mechanical way of phonetics
B. Difficulties in text printing with clarity
C. Number of repeated editors of the written text
D. Length of word and sentences in the written text

92. What does the readability signify for a written text?

A. Readability of a written text signifies the style of printing
B. Readability signifies the ease in reading with which a reader can understand a written text
C. Readability signifies that ail authors have equal capabilities to write or produce readable books
D. Readability signifies transforming an illegible text to legible text

93. Which of the following is correct when readability formulas are arranged in reverse chronological order of their formation:

A. Dale-Chall Readability formula, PSK Readability Formula, FK Grade Level Formula, McAlpine EFLAW Formula.
B. McAlpine EFLAW Formula, PSK Readability Formula, FK Grade Level Formula, Dale-Chall Readability Formulas
C. McAlpine EFLAW Formula, FK Grade Level Formula, PSK Readability Formula, Dale-Chall Readability formula
D. McAlpine EFLAW Formula, Dale-Chall Readability formula, FK Grade Level Formula, PSK Readability Formula

94. Which of the following is not true in relation to the readability of written text?

A. Most literacy works of very high quality pass the readability test
B. One of the main aspects of readability is easy flow of reading
C. Readability formulas aim to present an analysis of a particular text scientifically
D. Readability formulas are relevant for textbooks

95. What are the factors to be considered for the future success of readability to produce more readable books?

A. Using mathematical calculations more and more mechanically towards bringing over-simplification in readability formulas
B. Making authors more alert to take pre-publication readability tests for their creations and improving accordingly
C. Publishing the criticism of the textbooks
D. Reading rapidly more and more books

Directions (Qs. No. 96 to 100): *Read the following passage and answer the following questions:*

Before the printing press, books were incredibly scare and precious. No technique of mass production being available, each book had be carefully copied by hand that took thousands of skilled man-hours in transcribing texts, handcrafting ornate covers, and illuminating colorful pages. Thus, in publicly accessible libraries, books were often shelved with chains for safeguarding the library's valuable collection from potential thieves while allowing the public to read simultaneously. The chains were fitted to the corner or cover of the books through ringlets, and were long enough to allow the books to be taken from their shelves and read. The books were typically shelved with their fore-edges facing the reader, rather than their spines. It was a wrong way of shelving as it made finding the right book more challenging. But it did allow the books to be lifted and opened without needing to be turned around. But with the introduction of the printing press, when duplicates became more readily available and significantly affordable, the practice of chaining books to shelve died out.

In England, the Francis Trigge Chained Library, established in Grantham in 1598, is claimed to be the first English public library in Wimborne Minister is the second largest chained library founded in 1686 with the donation from Rev. William Stone. Worldwide, only a few chained libraries have survived with their original furniture, chains and books. This includes the library built in the Church of Saint Walpurga in 1564, located in the small town of Zutphen in the Netherlands. The library is now the part of a museum that allows visitors to tour and view the library's original books, furniture and chains. Another chained library, the Biblioteca Malatestiana library in Cesena. Italy, founded in 1454 is significant for being first civil library in Europe open to the general public. In Ireland. Marsh's Library in Dublin, built in 1701, is a noninstitutional library, which is still housed in its original building. Interestingly, here it was not the books that were chained, but rather the readers were locked into cages to prevent rare volumes from 'wandering'. The oldest chain book written in the eighth century, found in the Mappa Mundiand Chained Library Museum located in Hereford, England, is the Hereford Gospels. However, the largest surviving example of a chained library is Hereford Cathedral Library in UK established in 1611 is now open to the public as a tourist attraction of museum with its chains and books intact.

96. Books, in a chained library, are shelved with chains because:

A. The owner of the library denied readers from reading books

B. The books are arranged with their spines facing the readers.

C. With the introduction of printing press, books cost were high due to beautifully printed or hate covers

D. Readers were allowed reading valuable collection safeguarding from potential thieves

97. Which of the following Chained Library is considered as the first English Public Library:

A. Mappa Mundiand Chained Library Museum, Hereford

B. Francis Trigge Chained Library, Grantham

C. Marsh's Library, Dublin

D. Hereford Cathedral Library, UK

98. Which one of the following is the oldest chained library in Europe?

A. Biblioteca Malatestiana, Cesena

B. Francis Trigge Chained Library, Grantham

C. Church Saint Zutphen Walpurga

D. Marsh's Library, Dublin

99. Which of the following library is the oldest chained book of the eighth century is available?

A. Mappa Mundiand Chained Library Museum, Hereford
B. Hereford Cathedral Library, UK
C. Church of Saint Walpurga Library, Zutphen
D. Francis Trigge Chained Library, Grantham

100. Which of the following is correct when chained libraries are arranged according to the reverse chronological order of their foundations:

A. Marsh's Library, Hereford Cathedral Library, Church of Saint Walpurga Library, Francis Trigge Chained Library, Biblioteca Malatestiana Chained Library.
B. Biblioteca Malatestiana Chained Library, Church of Saint Walpurga Library, Francis Trigge Chained Library, Hereford Cathedral Library, Marsh's Library.
C. Marsh's Library, Hereford Cathedral Library, Francis Trigge Chained Library, Church of Saint Walpurga Library, Biblioteca Malatestiana Chained Library
D. Biblioteca Malatestiana Chained Library, Church of Saint Walpurga Library, Hereford Cathedral Library, Francis Trigge Chained Library, Marsh's Library.

ANSWERS

1. **(C):** Total Quality Management (TQM) tools, such as Pareto Analysis Charts, are used to identify the most significant factors in a process, with the premise that 80% of problems are typically caused by 20% of the causes. This aligns with option IV for (*a*). The "Far end of the library" likely refers to physical or lesser-used areas and might include facilities like a book repair and binding site, digitalization lab, and cafeteria, fitting description I for (*b*). The "Agency method," aligns with description II, which involves direct-purchase activities such as the acquisition of periodicals, indicative of proactive library management. Finally, John Cotton Dana, noted for his contributions to library science and emphasizing public access and services, linked to Newark's charging system III, suggests a methodological approach, possibly in administrative or operational contexts in libraries.

2. **(A):** The correct chronological order of the invention of these web browsers starts with Mosaic, developed in 1993 as one of the first graphical web browsers which played a significant role in popularizing the World Wide Web. Netscape Navigator, which was derived from Mosaic and released in 1994, followed as a dominant browser before the rise of Internet Explorer. Mozilla Firefox, introduced in 2004, came from the Mozilla project, which was initiated by Netscape. Google Chrome, the youngest of the browsers, was launched in 2008 by Google and has since become the most widely used browser globally.

3. **(C):** Subject headings in library science employ various relational structures to organize and access information. Equivalence relations involve synonyms or near-synonyms to link terms that mean the same or nearly the same thing, enhancing the retrieval effectiveness. Hierarchical relations connect terms in a broader or narrower context, which helps in understanding the scope of a subject. Associative relations link subjects that are related conceptually but not hierarchically, aiding in exploring related subjects or interdisciplinary topics.

4. **(B):** The publication history of these reference works starts with the Commonwealth Universities Yearbook, first published in 1913. The World of Learning follows, with its first edition in 1947, providing a comprehensive guide to global educational institutions and scholarships. The Demographic Yearbook, initiated by the United Nations in 1948, annually provides statistical data on population changes. Finally, the Europa World Yearbook, beginning in 1959, offers detailed country profiles and international relations, making it the latest in this sequence.

5. **(D):** The interdisciplinary nature of information suggests its wide-reaching implications across various fields, necessitating indexing techniques that can interlink different subjects, fitting description (IV). The multiplicity of languages in global information necessitates translation services (III) to facilitate understanding and access. The varying quality and reliability of information require robust information and data analysis and evaluation methods (II) to maintain relevance and accuracy. Cumulation of vast quantities of information points towards comprehensive indexing, classification, and storage systems, along with reference and enquiry services, aligning with description (I).

6. **(D):** Sherpa RoMEO stands for Rights MEtadata for Open Archiving, which is a resource providing copyright and self-archiving information related to academic journal articles. It assists researchers in understanding what their rights are regarding the self-archiving of their works and how they can legally distribute and reuse these materials, particularly in relation to open access repositories.

7. **(A):** The sampling distribution of the mean is a probability distribution that quantifies the range and likelihood of various means from different samples of a given size drawn from the same population. This concept is crucial in inferential statistics as it underpins the central limit theorem, which states that the sampling distribution of the sample means approaches a normal distribution as the sample size increases, regardless of the population's shape.

8. **(B):** In the context of PRECIS (Preserved Context Index System), a system developed for subject indexing used in library and information science, each role operator has a specific function. 's' as a role definer (III) indicates the defining nature of the role in an index entry. 't' denoting author-attributed action (IV) points to the responsibility or authorship in the context of the content. 'f', representing a bound coordinate concept (I), implies a fixed relationship within the indexing system. 'u', indicating two-way interaction (II), suggests a reciprocal or interactive aspect within index entries.

9. **(D):** Nicholas Belkin is widely associated with documentation, specifically in the context of information retrieval and library science. His contributions primarily focus on the theoretical and practical aspects of documenting, organizing, and retrieving information. Belkin's work in developing user-centered approaches and his theories regarding the anomalous state of knowledge significantly advanced the field of documentation.

10. **(A):** CERL, or the Consortium of European Research Libraries, represents a collaboration among libraries and research institutions across Europe focused on the preservation and accessibility of European cultural heritage. This organization plays a critical

role in facilitating research through its extensive networks, sharing resources, and developing technologies pertinent to the archival materials held within member libraries.

11. **(B):** The word "Data" is derived from the Latin word "datum," which means "given" or "that which is given." This reflects its use in analysis and decision-making, where data represents facts or figures from which conclusions can be drawn or decisions made. The plural form of datum, "data" has been adopted in English and many other languages to represent information in numerical or categorical forms, essential for research, business, and governance. Understanding the etymology of "data" is crucial in grasifying its foundational role in the modern information-centric world, where it is synonymous with information that is systematically organized for analysis or used to reason and make decisions.

12. **(D):** Dr. S.R. Ranganathan's facet formula arranges concepts into a coherent order to facilitate information retrieval and organization in libraries. In the title "Treatment for cancer in India," the facet sequence would ideally place 'Medicine' as the discipline, followed by 'Disease' as the subject of interest within the field, and 'Cancer' as a specific form of the disease. 'Treatment' then specifies the aspect of cancer being addressed, and 'India' provides the geographical facet. This arrangement helps in categorizing the information logically, aiding librarians and researchers in navigating and retrieving relevant texts efficiently and accurately.

13. **(B):** Delhi Public Library introduced its mobile service for readers in 1953 AD. This innovative outreach was part of a broader initiative to extend library services beyond the physical confines of the institution, aiming to make books and reading materials more accessible to the general public, including those in remote areas. The mobile service effectively brought the library to people's doorsteps, promoting literacy and learning across various communities. The launch of this service marked a significant development in library services in India, demonstrating a commitment to education and accessibility, crucial for a nation with diverse and widespread populations.

14. **(C):** In SPSS (Statistical Package for the Social Sciences), a widely used software for statistical analysis, there are three primary views that facilitate data handling and analysis: Data view, Output view, and Variable view. The Data view allows users to enter and view data similarly to a spreadsheet, making it straightforward to input numerical and categorical data. The Output view displays results of analyses, including statistical tests, charts, and tables, providing a clear and organized presentation of outcomes. The Variable view is where the metadata about each variable is defined, such as variable type, label, and measurement level, which are critical for appropriate analysis setup and interpretation of data.

15. **(D):** The Resource Description Framework (RDF) is a framework designed for data interchange on the web, emphasizing flexibility and usability across different applications. It supports XML syntax, allowing for the integration with existing standards and facilitating the adoption of RDF in various environments. Additionally, RDF utilizes Uniform Resource Identifiers (URIs) to enable the linking of disparate data points across the web, thus extending the linking structure of the internet and

enhancing the capability of the web to function as a globally connected database. This makes RDF instrumental in semantic web initiatives, aiming to make web data machine-readable and interoperable.

16. (D): In XML (eXtensible Markup Language), tags are case sensitive, which means that tags such as <Item> and <item> are recognized as completely different elements. This case sensitivity arises because XML allows users to define their own tags according to their specific data structuring needs. The flexibility of tag definition in XML supports various types of data representation and ensures precise data handling and parsing in systems that use XML for data interchange, configuration, or storage. This characteristic underscores XML's utility in environments requiring customized data solutions, enhancing its applicability across different industries and use cases.

17. (C): SHERNI, as an expert profile network system, aims to connect the knowledge, skills, and expertise of women across a wide range of fields of study. This initiative is designed to promote collaboration and sharing of expertise among women professionals, thereby fostering an inclusive and supportive environment for professional growth and advancement. By linking women across diverse disciplines, SHERNI facilitates the exchange of ideas, mentoring opportunities, and the strengthening of professional networks, contributing to the empowerment of women in academia and industry.

18. (D): A monograph is an analytical information source that provides a detailed, comprehensive study of a specific subject or area of knowledge. Unlike dictionaries, almanacs, or directories, which offer brief entries, factual data, or listings, a monograph delves deeply into a topic, offering analysis, interpretation, and a synthesis of research. This makes it an invaluable resource for scholars and researchers seeking in-depth information and insights on particular subjects. Monographs are critical in academic settings where detailed examination and scholarly discussion are required.

19. (B): The correct sequence in PERT/CPM (Program Evaluation and Review Technique/Critical Path Method) starts with identifying the necessary activities for a project, establishing the order and dependencies among them. Then, estimating the time each activity will take is crucial for planning. Following this, a network diagram is developed to visually represent these activities and their precedence relationships. Finally, determining the earliest and latest times for each event helps in optimizing resources and timelines, ensuring project efficiency.

20. (B): The Development Science Information System (DEVSIS) was an initiative aimed at enhancing information sharing on science and technology with a focus on development, particularly in the Global South. Its principal outputs included Devindex, a comprehensive index of relevant literature, and Devprofile, which periodically compiled thematic analyses and reports. INFOPLAN's involvement in establishing regional DEVSIS centers highlights the collaborative nature of this network, which was designed to be decentralized and mission-oriented, addressing specific regional and developmental information needs through a globally coordinated effort.

21. (B): Sample stock-verification is an estimation technique used in libraries to assess the loss or misplacement of books without checking every single item. This method involves selecting a representative sample of the library's holdings and conducting a thorough check on these selected items. The results from this sample are then extrapolated to estimate the overall situation concerning missing or misplaced books. This approach is practical for larger libraries where checking every item would be too time-consuming and labor-intensive. It allows library management to understand the scope of the issue with reasonable accuracy and implement corrective measures efficiently.

22. (B): Correctly matching the library associations with their years of establishment, Gujarat Pustakalays Mandal was established in 1923, which aligns with IV. The Maharashtra Library Association was set up in 1921, corresponding with III. The Baroda State Library Association, established in 1926, matches with II. Finally, the Bengal Library Association, started in 1925, aligns with I. Understanding the sequence in which these library associations were formed highlights the progression of library science and advocacy across different regions in India, reflecting the varied focus and initiatives based on regional needs and historical contexts.

23. (D): In the early 1980s, the University Grants Commission (UGC) established National Information Centres and Inter-University Centers to enhance reference and documentation services, particularly to boost research capabilities in existing universities. Jawaharlal Nehru University (JNU) in New Delhi was among the universities that received an inter-university centre. This initiative was part of a broader effort to improve the research infrastructure and scholarly resources available to students and faculty members across India, fostering a stronger academic environment.

24. (D): The Principle of Demand and Supply is not typically considered a principle of library expenditure. Library budgets are generally guided by principles such as the Principle of Economy, which focuses on cost-effectiveness; the Principle of Maximum Aggregate Benefit, which aims to maximize the benefits derived from the available funds; and the Principle of Advance Planning, which involves forecasting future needs to ensure that the library can meet its users' demands. The Principle of Demand and Supply, more common in business and economics, does not align with the strategic financial management practices typically employed in library settings.

25. (C): The Semantic Web architecture is designed to allow data to be shared and reused across application, enterprise, and community boundaries. It is structured in layers, starting with UNICODE and URI at the base, which provide the foundational standards for encoding and identifying data. XML provides a flexible syntax for structured documents but does not provide semantics. RDF adds the semantic layer, allowing data to be linked and combined in various ways. OWL builds on RDF and provides a richer vocabulary for expressing meanings. RIF and SWRL are at the top, providing frameworks for rules that can be used with data defined in RDF and OWL.

26. (C): Metadata harvesting service providers are platforms or services that collect metadata from various sources to facilitate search and retrieval of digital content. Google Scholar, NCSTRL (Networked Computer Science Technical Reference Library), and Search Digital Libraries are examples of such service providers. They aggregate metadata from various repositories or publications, enhancing the discoverability of scholarly articles, technical reports, and other academic materials across different fields.

27. **(B):** Information is essentially derived from data, where it acts as a structured or meaningful output, hence it is a property of data. It is processed and conceptualized by the human brain, making it a cognitive product. Information can manifest in both abstract forms, such as ideas or theories, and concrete forms, like statistical data or factual content. These properties collectively underscore the multifaceted nature of information, serving various purposes and requiring different processing and presentation techniques depending on its intended use and audience.

28. **(B):** Louis Shores is recognized as the author of "Basic Reference Sources," a key work in the field of library and information science. This publication is essential in guiding librarians and information professionals in selecting and evaluating reference materials in various formats. Shores' contributions have been influential in the development of reference services, emphasizing the importance of a well-rounded and carefully curated collection of reference tools in libraries.

29. **(B):** In computing, a nibble is equal to 4 bits. This term is less commonly used than byte, which consists of 8 bits. The concept of a nibble is important in the context of digital computing and data storage, as it represents a unit that can encode a single digit in hexadecimal (base-16) notation—a compact format often used in programming and digital systems to simplify binary coding schemes.

30. **(D):** Nalanda University, one of the earliest universities in recorded history, housed its extensive library in three grand buildings known as Ratna-Sagar, Ratna Pithika, and Ratna Ranjaka. The area dedicated to the library was called Dharma Ganja, signifying its importance as a treasure house of knowledge in the Buddhist tradition. The library's architectural grandeur and the scope of its collections reflect the significance of knowledge and learning in ancient Indian culture, particularly in the Buddhist monastic educational system.

31. **(B):** A patent qualifies as a neo-conventional source of information, which typically refers to newer types of formal documentation that serve specific professional and technical needs. Patents contain detailed descriptions of new inventions and serve as a public disclosure of new technology, offering a wealth of information for research, development, and legal purposes. They are crucial for advancing technological innovation by providing exclusive rights to inventors for a period of time while simultaneously contributing to the public knowledge base.

32. **(C):** In the context of an expressive title, each surviving term that provides central meaning or core context is denoted as a "Kernel Term." These are the essential terms that capture the main subject matter or theme of the title. Kernel terms are pivotal in indexing and retrieval systems as they directly relate to the primary content and are used to enhance the precision in information retrieval, helping users find the most relevant documents based on the core themes or concepts.

33. **(C):** The alignment of departments of industries with their respective purposes is as follows: The Small Industries Development

Organisation (SIDO) coordinates overall policy, planning, and provides advisory services, which is a comprehensive role encompassing a range of support functions, aligning with (II). The Small Industries Service Institute (SISI) focuses on providing techno-economic services and management and technical training programs, which fits with (III). The National Small Industries Corporation (NSIC) is engaged in infrastructure development and assistance in the implementation of programs, fitting (IV). Small Entrepreneurs focus on the initial stages of a business, including receiving applications for major assistance and examining technical feasibility and economic viability, aligning with (I).

34. (C)

35. (B): ANOVA, or Analysis of Variance, is the statistical test designed to investigate differences among the means of all populations simultaneously. It is used when comparing three or more groups for statistical significance. ANOVA tests the null hypothesis that all groups are drawn from populations with the same mean, against the alternative hypothesis that at least one group is different. This method is crucial in various scientific studies where comparing multiple groups is necessary to understand broader patterns and influences.

36. (C): Melvil Dewey was instrumental in the founding of the first library school in the world, the School of Library Economy at Columbia College in 1887. This initiative marked a significant development in the field of library science, setting standards for the training of professional librarians and emphasizing the importance of organized and accessible library services. Dewey's contributions to library science are profound, including his development of the Dewey Decimal Classification system, which revolutionized library organization.

37. (C): Prof P.S.G Kumar from RTM Nagpur University was not a member of the UCG panel on Library and Information Science for the Curriculum Development Committee 2001 led by Prof. C.R. Karisiddappa. This panel included other prominent figures from the library and information science community tasked with revising and updating the curriculum to align with contemporary educational and professional demands. Prof Kumar's absence indicates the involvement of other experts who collectively contributed to refining the educational frameworks that prepare students for the evolving challenges in library and information sciences.

38. (D): Arranging the sample sizes according to degrees of accuracy involves aligning smaller sample sizes with less precise measurements and larger samples with more precise measurements. A sample size of 100 represents the most precise measurement (0.00 accuracy), while progressively smaller sizes correspond to less stringent accuracy requirements, such as 0.01 (99), 0.025 (94), 0.035 (89), and 0.05 (80).

39. (B): In programming languages, Prolog is a classic example of a logic programming language, known for its use in solving logical problems and in artificial intelligence. CSS, typically used in web development for styling, is best associated with front-end programming. C# is a versatile language used primarily for back-end programming, developing the logic and database interactions for software applications. Bash, often used for scripting, is notable for its use in writing short scripts for programming environments.

40. (C): Mobile library apps offer several significant advantages, including allowing users to set preferences for a personalized experience, compatibility with multiple device types and operating systems, and the ability to load contents faster, enhancing user engagement and accessibility. These features collectively improve the usability and functionality of library services, meeting the needs of modern library users who increasingly rely on digital platforms for information access and management.

41. (C): To understand the concept of 'Referral Service' effectively, starting with a broad and general resource like Harrod's Librarian's Glossary and Reference Book provides an initial foundational understanding of the term. Progressing to the Encyclopedia of Library and Information Science allows for a more detailed and comprehensive exploration of the topic. Following these, Reference Service by S.R. Ranganathan offers specific insights and practical applications within the field of librarianship. Lastly, Library Science with a Slant to Documentation can offer a specialized perspective, tying in documentation aspects to the referral services.

42. (D): SMAC is an acronym for Social, Mobile, Analytics, and Cloud. These are the four technologies that form a cohesive framework for modern business strategy. Social media facilitates interaction and communication, mobile computing enables on-the-go access to business resources, analytics provide insights from large data sets, and cloud technology offers scalable infrastructure. CMS, or Content Management System, while useful in digital strategies, does not fit into the SMAC model as it primarily deals with the creation and management of digital content rather than being a driving technology within the SMAC framework.

43. (C): Luciano Floridi, a philosopher and scholar of the philosophy of Information and Information Ethics, coined the term "Infosphere." This term represents an environment akin to a biosphere but composed of all informational processes, systems, and entities. The concept of the Infosphere extends to both analog and digital formats, encompassing any entity involved in the process of creating, managing, processing, and utilizing information. Floridi's work significantly contributes to our understanding of information ethics and the philosophical questions of digital existence and data handling in modern societies.

44. (D): In job evaluation, the Critical Plan Method involves the assessment of job performance through the use of critical incidents. This method requires employees to respond to specific, job-related incidents, presenting how they handled each situation to their supervisor. Each incident is analyzed to evaluate how effectively the employee performs crucial aspects of the job. This approach provides a practical and detailed analysis of performance, focusing on actual behaviors and outcomes rather than general competencies or abstract ratings.

45. (A): Librarianship as a profession requires specialized knowledge, particularly in the management, organization, and dissemination of information. It also adheres to a set of ethical principles that guide professional conduct and decision-making within the field. Jason Farradane made significant contributions to information science and was notable for distinguishing between general information work and the specific professional practices of librarianship, emphasizing the specialized nature of librarians' roles and the skills required to perform them effectively.

46. (D): Laney described the characteristics of Big Data as involving volumes of data that exceed the processing capability of traditional data management tools. Big Data is defined by three principal characteristics: volume (large amounts of data), velocity (speed of data flow), and variety (range of data types and sources). This complexity requires new technologies and approaches for effective management, analysis, and processing, making Big Data a distinct and challenging field within data science.

47. (C): The clinical interview is used extensively in psychological settings to delve deeply into an individual's emotions and experiences. It allows for a comprehensive and nuanced exploration of the psychological state of a person, facilitated by a trained professional who can interpret verbal and non-verbal cues. This method is particularly effective in identifying underlying emotional issues, mental health conditions, and the overall psychological well-being of individuals, making it an invaluable tool in clinical psychology and psychiatry. By enabling an in-depth understanding of a person's inner life, clinical interviews contribute significantly to effective diagnosis and treatment planning.

48. (C): The chronological order of these Acts starts with The Trade and Merchandise Act, which was among the earliest forms of intellectual property protection in India. The Patents Act followed, providing a structured framework for the protection of inventions. The Geographical Indications of Goods Act came later, aimed at safeguarding goods with specific geographical origin and qualities. Lastly, The Designs Act protects designs, ensuring creators can secure intellectual property rights for their unique designs.

49. (C): Among the listed options, the Web Library Project is not a recognized digital library initiative. Google Books Library Project, Digital Library Federation (DLF), and Million Book Project are well-known initiatives aimed at digitizing books and making them accessible online. They contribute significantly to the preservation and accessibility of literary and scholarly materials globally, enhancing the reach and utility of library resources.

50. (B): The first library act was enacted by the British Parliament. Known as the Public Libraries Act 1850, it allowed municipalities in England and Wales to establish public libraries. This legislation marked a significant step towards the development of free public libraries that were supported by public funding, reflecting a growing recognition of the importance of access to information and education for all members of society. This act set a precedent that many other countries followed, promoting the establishment of libraries as crucial public institutions.

51. (C): Webcasting is an example of push technology, where data is automatically delivered to the user without them requesting it specifically at that time. This contrasts with pull technology, where data transmission is initiated by the receiver. In webcasting, a live or pre-recorded video is broadcasted over the Internet to multiple users simultaneously, making it a practical application of push technology, as the content is streamed to users who have subscribed or chosen to view the broadcast.

52. (D): The case study method in research extensively relies on a variety of sources to gather comprehensive and in-depth information about a single case or a series of cases. This method typically includes sources such as confessions for personal insights, observations for objective data gathering, life histories to understand the broader personal and social context, and individual interviews that provide direct, detailed perspectives from the participants involved.

53. **(C):** When arranging the given consortiums by the year of establishment, FORSA comes first in 1984 as it is one of the earlier formed networks focusing on research and academic collaboration. UGC-DAE Consortium (1990) and INDEST (2003) follow respectively, each playing significant roles in facilitating academic and scientific research collaborations and resource sharing. The National Knowledge Research Consortium (NKRC) is the most recent established in 2009, further expanding the support for knowledge creation and dissemination among academic institutions.

54. **(A):** Matching the e-resources with their types, Samarth is identified as a Web portal designed to facilitate access to a variety of educational content and services online. LIS-FORUM is a discussion group where professionals within the library and information science community engage in discussions and information exchange. Intute, known as a subject gateway, provided a structured directory of web resources for education and research. CBBS represents a bulletin board system, an early form of online community and communication technology for posting news, messages, and discussions.

55. **(D):** Institutional sources of information, such as universities, research institutes, and learned societies, play a critical role in providing researchers, especially in the social sciences, with the necessary data and literature, including journal publications. In India, while there is no exclusive referral centre, many institutional sources effectively serve the purpose of central information resources, contributing significantly to academic and professional research.

56. **(B):** In the MARC-21 record format, the 'Leader' section at the beginning of the record provides essential control information that defines the parameters of the rest of the record. The 'Directory' follows, offering a map of the data fields present in the record, indicating their length and starting position. The 'Data Context', typically encapsulated in specific fields throughout the MARC record, includes additional contextual information that aids in the interpretation and processing of the bibliographic and cataloging data. This arrangement ensures that all necessary metadata is provided to facilitate accurate and efficient retrieval and management of library materials.

57. **(B):** CAD/CAM software is widely used in engineering to facilitate the design and manufacturing processes with high precision and efficiency, demonstrating its crucial role in multimedia applications in technical fields. Photoshop, although primarily a graphic design software, is mentioned here as a tool for network development, likely symbolizing its utility in creating graphical content for network design visualizations and presentations. Common audio file types such as MP3, WAV, and WMA are essential elements in multimedia for delivering audio content, highlighting multimedia's capability to handle various data formats efficiently, enhancing user experience across different platforms and applications.

58. **(D):** Matching the sources with their editors, the McGraw Hill Dictionary of Scientific and Technical Terms was edited by Sybil P. Parker. The ALA Glossary of Library and Information Science was managed by

Heartsill Young, a known figure in library science literature. James Hastings was responsible for the Encyclopedia of Religion and Ethics, an extensive reference work in its field. Lastly, the International Encyclopedia of the Social Sciences was edited by David L. Sills, marking significant contributions to the understanding of social sciences.

59. **(A):** In the context of information package services, Product Information Brochure provides exhaustive details about new products relevant to the industry or organization. Comparative Product Profile studies and outlines the salient features of competitors' products, aiding in strategic planning and marketing. Patent Information Services bring attention to the latest inventions, crucial for engineers and developers. Product Focus offers an analysis of product features, aiding industries in assessing market offerings.

60. **(D):** Chain indexing does not have a limitation of providing an alternative approach to the classified file through reverse rendering. In fact, this is one of its advantages, allowing users to approach indexing from multiple entry points within a classified arrangement, enhancing retrievability and user-friendliness. Chain indexing typically is limited by its dependency on class numbers, its specificity only at the last link of the indexing chain, and the potential for creating unsought or irrelevant links, which can complicate information retrieval.

61. **(A):** In the context of subject formation:

- Dissection (*a*) involves cutting a universe of entities into parts of coordinate status, accurately described as III.
- Lamination (*b*) overlays facts onto facets to build a composite view of a subject, fittingly described by I.
- Denudation (*c*) involves a progressive decrease in the extension and increase in the intension, perfectly matching description IV.
- Super imposition (*d*) connects together two or more isolated ideas of the same category, which is effectively summarized in II. These modes help in structuring and organizing subjects in a systematic and logical manner within knowledge management and library science.

62. **(B):** The sequence for performance appraisal processes begins with a performance reviewing or progress review (*e*), where initial assessments of an employee's work output and achievements are made. This is followed by performance feedback and evaluation (*c*), providing detailed insights into the employee's strengths and areas for improvement. Subsequently, compensation and rewarding good performance (*b*) serve as incentives for maintaining or improving performance levels. Potential appraisal (*d*) then assesses the employee's capabilities for future roles or promotions. Lastly, performance improvement planning (*a*) is conducted to outline specific steps for enhancing skills and competencies, ensuring ongoing development and alignment with organizational goals.

63. **(B):** Li-fi (Light Fidelity) is a bidirectional wireless communication technology that uses light waves instead of radio technology to transmit data. By utilizing LED or infrared light, Li-fi can achieve high-speed data transmission in a manner that remains confined to a controlled environment, providing security advantages over Wi-Fi. This technology is suitable for areas that are sensitive to electromagnetic interference, making it a promising solution for sectors like healthcare and aviation.

64. (B): In facet analysis, a cyclic recurrence of fundamental categories is termed as "Rounds." This term describes how fundamental concepts or categories in a structured subject classification system reappear through the analysis, allowing for a comprehensive and multi-dimensional exploration of subjects. This cyclical approach helps in identifying and organizing knowledge into a coherent structure that reflects the complexity and interrelatedness of different subject areas.

65. (D): Information metrics and user studies by Carol Tenopir (III) focus on quantitative assessments of how information is used, often involving statistical analyses of user engagement and behaviours. Information needs and uses by Crawford (I) explore the different ways information is sought and utilized across various contexts, providing insights into user preferences and requirements. Organizational behaviour and information seeking by Auster Eithal (IV) delve into how organizational structures influence information-seeking behaviours. Lastly, the information uses and needs of social scientists by M.B. Line (II) specifically examines how social scientists access and utilize information, highlighting the unique demands of this academic community.

66. (D): The term "Invisible College" was coined by Diana Crane. This concept refers to a network of researchers or academics who informally collaborate and communicate, often across different institutions and geographies. Invisible colleges facilitate the exchange of information and ideas, significantly influencing scientific and academic developments. They are termed "invisible" because these networks are not formalized and are often fluid and dynamic in nature.

67. (D): The Agricultural Network Information Centre (AgNIC) is a collaboration involving various institutions, including the National Agricultural Library of the USA, to provide a comprehensive online resource hub for agricultural information. This initiative includes access to evaluated resources and specialized databases like the CB Pest database, which provides data on the occurrence and distribution of pesticides, supporting the agriculture community by offering readily accessible, reliable information.

68. (B): In citing practices, "Ibid." (*a*) refers to the same source cited in the immediately preceding reference (III), typically used to streamline consecutive citations of the same work. "Op.cit." (*b*) indicates a reference listed earlier by the same author (I), used when the work has been cited previously but not immediately before the current citation. "Loc.cit." (*c*) repeats the title and page number for a work already cited (IV), used for direct repetition of a source. "et al." (*d*) is used when citing sources with multiple authors (II), indicating the inclusion of additional authors beyond the first named, streamlining the citation of works with numerous contributors.

69. (A): In the context of Management Information Systems (MIS) in organizations:

- Executive support systems (*a*) are designed to help senior executives make strategic decisions by providing relevant, concise, and up-to-date information.
- Management support systems (*b*) encompass a broader category that includes all systems that aid in management-level decision-making, planning, and control.
- Decision support systems (*e*) provide critical data analysis, projections, and

simulations to support complex decision-making processes, often incorporating statistical and analytical tools to assist managers in making informed choices.

70. (D): Correctly matching the metrics with the terms coined by:

- Bibliometrics (*a*), a term coined by Pritchard, refers to the quantitative analysis of written publications, such as books and articles.
- H-index (*b*), developed by J.E. Hirsh, measures both the productivity and citation impact of the publications of a scientist or scholar.
- Webometrics (*c*), introduced by Almind and Ingwersen, focuses on measuring aspects of the web that encompass not only citation analysis but also link analysis and web presence.
- Scientometrics (*d*), a term developed by Vassily and Mulchenko, is the study of measuring and analyzing scientific literature, focusing on the quantitative aspects of the production of research.

71. (C): When considering the level of involvement in terms of the number of people engaged in the communication process, mass communication involves the largest audience, as it is aimed at reaching a wide, general audience through mediums like television, radio, newspapers, and the internet. Group communication involves smaller, specific groups such as teams or committees. Interpersonal communication is more focused, involving interactions between two or more individuals, typically in a personal or professional setting. Intrapersonal communication involves a single individual, as it refers to internal thought processes and self-reflection.

72. (C): The first law of library science, "Books are for use," implies that libraries should be accessible and facilitate easy use of their resources. One direct implication of this law is the strategic location of the library. It should be situated where it is most accessible to its users, whether it's a public library positioned centrally for community access or an academic library located within the campus for student and faculty convenience. This positioning helps maximize usage and ensures that the library fulfills its purpose as a resource for information and learning.

73. (D): An enumerative classification system is one where subjects and their corresponding class numbers are listed directly in the schedules. This system is characterized by a pre-defined and comprehensive listing of subjects, where each subject is associated with a specific class number. This approach contrasts with faceted or analytico-synthetic classifications, which allow for the combination of facets to construct class numbers according to the characteristics of the material being classified. Enumerative classification provides a straightforward and user-friendly method, although it can lack the flexibility of other systems.

74. (B): Correct identifications in the context of database types include:

- CAS Registry, known for its comprehensive collection of chemical compounds, provides factual information about chemical substances including their properties and structures, classifying it as a factual database.
- PubMed offers access to a vast range of biomedical literature, much of it available in full-text format, making it a full-text database.
- SCOPUS is widely recognized as a citation database that indexes a wide

range of scientific articles and provides tools to track citations across a broad array of disciplines.

75. (A): Data security measures are essential to protect against unauthorized access and threats to information integrity. Antivirus protection software is crucial for defending against malware, viruses, and other malicious attacks. Data encryption enhances security by converting data into a secure format that is only accessible with a decryption key, ensuring data privacy and protection, particularly during transmission over networks. Firewalls serve as a barrier between secure internal networks and potentially insecure external networks, monitoring and controlling incoming and outgoing network traffic based on predetermined security rules.

76. (D): The preliminary part of a research report typically includes elements like the Table of Contents, List of Tables, and the Preface, which provide an organizational framework and introductory remarks. The Importance of the problem under investigation, while crucial to the body of the report where the research is outlined and discussed, is not typically part of the preliminary sections. These initial sections are meant to guide the reader through the document's structure and give acknowledgments or introductory thoughts, not to delve into the substantive content of the research.

77. (D): The term 'Reprography' was first introduced in Germany. It refers to the reproduction of graphics through mechanical or electrical means, including photocopying and microfilming. This technology became particularly important in the mid-20th century as a method for duplicating documents for industrial, educational, and administrative purposes. Germany's contributions to printing and photographic technologies played a significant role in the development and naming of reprographic processes.

78. (B): Mailshots, Personal visits and Newsletters are all promotional methods used in marketing to engage customers and increase visibility of products or services. Mailshots involve sending promotional material directly to potential customers via mail. Personal visits entail direct interaction with potential or existing customers, providing a personal touch that can enhance relationship building. Newsletters are regularly distributed publications that provide updates and information about a company's products or services, helping to keep the company top-of-mind among its customers. These methods are effective in promoting a business and maintaining ongoing customer engagement.

79. (C): A web crawler, also known as a spider or a robot, is a computer program that browses the World Wide Web in a methodical, automated manner. This tool is used by search engines to update their web content or indices of others' sites' web content. Web crawlers copy pages for processing by a search engine, which indexes the downloaded pages so users can search more efficiently. These tools are fundamental to the functioning of search engines, allowing them to provide up-to-date data in a rapidly changing internet environment.

80. (B): In project management, 'Free Float' refers to the amount of time that a task can be delayed without causing a delay to subsequent tasks or affecting the project's scheduled end date. This concept is important in scheduling where understanding the flexibility within project timelines can assist in resource allocation and risk management.

If all non-critical activities start as early as possible, the free float would represent the spare time available before these activities impact the overall timeline, thus providing a buffer that helps manage delays and coordinate activities without disrupting the project's overall timeline.

81. (B): The International Nuclear Information System (INIS) is a cooperative that hosts one of the world's largest collections of published information on the peaceful uses of nuclear science and technology. It is multi-lingual, reflecting the global participation and needs of its members. INIS does not restrict its membership only to intergovernmental organizations but is open to countries and international organizations interested in nuclear research. INIS hosts the International Nuclear Library Network, which enhances the sharing and dissemination of nuclear information globally. Additionally, NUCLEUS serves as the IAEA's central access point to its scientific, technical, and regulatory information resources, indicating the broader capacity of the agency to disseminate and manage nuclear knowledge effectively.

82. (D): Library pilgrimages are a form of library extension service where libraries organize visits to significant and historic libraries or related sites. This activity is part of broader efforts to engage the community, increase interest in library services, and promote the cultural and educational importance of libraries. Unlike traditional religious or educational activities, library pilgrimages specifically aim to connect library users and staff to their heritage and the broader library community, enriching their understanding of library science and history.

83. (C): Matching the sections of the RTI Act, 2015 with their correct descriptions:

- Section 4 mandates (III) the obligation of public authorities to maintain all their records duly cataloged and indexed to facilitate the right to information under the Act—ensuring transparency and accountability in the operation of the body.
- Section 11 deals with (I) the procedure involving third-party information, where a third party must be consulted before any information related to them is released under the RTI.
- Section 15 concerns (IV) the constitution of the State Information Commission, detailing the establishment and the function of these state-level bodies which are crucial in the implementation of the RTI Act.
- Section 21 provides (II) protection for actions taken in good faith under the Act, ensuring that officials who act according to the provisions of the RTI are not held liable for their actions in the execution of their duties.

84. (C): Linkedin is a social networking service that is primarily used for professional, non-social interpersonal communication. It serves as a platform for professional networking, including job postings, industry updates, and professional user profiles, facilitating career development and professional connectivity. Unlike other social media platforms that focus on personal expression or casual social interactions, LinkedIn emphasizes professional identity, engagements, and networks.

85. (A): In the Postulate Based Permuted Subject Indexing (POPSI) method, the sequence begins with content analysis (*a*), which involves examining the document to identify the subjects it covers. Formalisation (*e*) follows, where identified subjects are described using standard terms. Modulation (*c*) then involves adjusting these terms to fit the indexing system's structure. Preparation of entries (*d*) is next, where the formalized terms are organized into index entries. Finally, alphabetisation (*b*) is performed, arranging all entries in alphabetical order for ease of search and retrieval, completing the indexing process. This methodical approach ensures that information is systematically captured and organized, facilitating accurate and efficient information retrieval.

86. (C): (*a*) - Researchers shall be asked to submit a revised script, (*c*) - Researchers shall be debarred from submitting a revised script, (*d*) - Researchers registration for the research degree shall be cancelled: Under the UGC (Promotion of Academic Integrity and Prevention of Plagiarism in Higher Educational Institutions) Regulations 2018, penalties for plagiarism vary depending on the severity and extent of the misconduct. Common penalties include asking the researcher to submit a revised script if the plagiarism is at a lower level. For more severe cases, researchers may be debarred from submitting a revised script, and in the most serious cases, their registration for a research degree may be cancelled. These measures are intended to uphold academic integrity and deter academic dishonesty within higher education institutions.

87. (B): The logical sequence in the information literacy scope and sequence model starts with formulating a question or identifying a problem that needs resolution (Question). The next step involves finding potential sources of information (Find) and then gathering the necessary data from these sources (Gather). Once adequate information is gathered, it is used to create new knowledge or products (Create). Finally, the information or the created product is critically assessed (Assess) to ensure it meets the required standards and effectively addresses the initial question or problem.

88. (A): Matching the technologies with their functions:

- Barcode Technology (*a*) is used for identification, location, and tracking of items (IV). It encodes data visually and can be scanned electronically to retrieve information about the item it is attached to.
- RFID (*b*) includes tolerance of mis-orientation and obscuration (II), which allows for the tracking and identification of objects without the need for direct line-of-sight scanning.
- Flickering (*c*) is a technique used in digital rights management where information on a screen flickers at a rate that prevents it from being captured reliably by cameras or screen capture software, thus protecting the data from unauthorized copying (III).
- DOI (*d*) is implemented through a federation of registration agencies to uniquely identify objects (I) such as journal articles, data sets, and official documents, ensuring persistent identification and access.

89. (B): Following sequence lists the organizations in reverse chronological order based on their founding years. State Council of Education Research and Training (SCERT, Delhi) was established in 1988, followed by NIEPA in 1962 (originally established as the National Staff College for Educational Planners and Administrators), Nation Councilo of Education Research and Training (NCERT) in 1961, UGC in 1956, and AICTE in 1945. This arrangement highlights the evolution of educational and academic library system support organizations in India, showing the development of educational governance and policy over time.

90. (C): "Reader's Digest" is a popular general interest periodical that publishes a variety of content including human interest stories, humor, articles on health and personal finance, and condensed versions of books. It is designed for a broad audience rather than for a specialized or professional group. The magazine's format and content aim to entertain and inform a general readership, making it distinct from scholarly journals or trade journals, which target specific academic or industry audiences with more specialized content.

91. (D): Readability formulas commonly use the length of words and sentences as indicators of difficulty in written text. These formulas posit that longer words and sentences tend to make texts more complex and harder to understand. The semantic factor in these formulas considers the complexity of the vocabulary used, while the syntactic factor examines sentence structure. By measuring these aspects, the formulas attempt to quantify how easy or difficult a text is to read and comprehend, which helps in adjusting the text to suit the intended audience's reading level.

92. (B): Readability refers to how easily a piece of writing can be read and understood by a reader. It encompasses several aspects including the legibility of the text, the flow of reading, and the ease of comprehension. Factors influencing readability include the clarity of language and presentation, the intellectual level and language proficiency of the reader, and the structural aspects of the text itself such as vocabulary and sentence complexity. Enhancing readability is essential, especially in educational contexts, to ensure that information is accessible and comprehensible to all readers.

93. (C): Arranging the readability formulas in reverse chronological order of their introduction places the McAlpine EFLAW Formula first, introduced in 2006, followed by the FK Grade Level Formula from 1975, then the PSK Readability Formula from 1958, and finally the Dale-Chall Readability Formula from 1948. This sequence reflects the progression and development of readability assessment tools over time, each building on or diverging from earlier methodologies to better evaluate text complexity and readability.

94. (A): This statement is not true in relation to the readability of written text. Many literary works of high quality do not necessarily pass readability tests because these formulas typically measure text complexity based on word length and sentence structure rather than the depth of content or stylistic elements that often characterize great literature. Readability tests are more suited for assessing texts like textbooks and other educational materials where clarity and ease of understanding are prioritized over stylistic or thematic complexity.

95. (B): For the future success of readability to produce more readable books, it is crucial for authors to engage actively with readability assessments before publication. By utilizing readability tests, authors can gauge the accessibility of their work and make necessary adjustments to language, structure, and presentation to enhance understanding and engagement. This proactive approach helps in tailoring content to meet the needs and capabilities of the target audience, ensuring that the material is both accessible and effective in conveying the intended information or narrative.

96. (D): In the historical context of chained libraries, the chains were not meant to restrict access to the books but rather to prevent theft while allowing public access to these valuable resources. Books, being extremely rare and expensive before the widespread availability of the printing press, were significant investments for libraries. By chaining books to shelves or desks, libraries could safeguard their collections against potential theft while still permitting readers to access and read the books directly in the library. This system of chaining books highlights the balance between accessibility for education and protection of valuable assets.

97. (B): The Francis Trigge Chained Library in Grantham, established in 1598, is recognized as the first public library in England where books were made available to the public in a chained format. This library marked a significant development in public access to information, allowing broader segments of society to access educational materials, which had previously been confined mostly to private collections or institutions like universities. The establishment of this library represents a pivotal moment in the democratization of knowledge and the evolution of public libraries in England.

98. (A): The Biblioteca Malatestiana in Cesena, Italy, established in 1454, is significant for being the first public library in Europe and is known for its chained books. This library predates other notable chained libraries and stands out for its historical importance and its role in the development of public access to knowledge. Its foundation marks a crucial period in library history, where access to books began to extend beyond the elite and clergy to the general public, setting a precedent for the establishment of public libraries across Europe.

99. (A): The Mappa Mundiand Chained Library Museum in Hereford houses the Hereford Gospels, a notable manuscript from the eighth century. This ancient text, known for its historical and cultural significance, is preserved in one of the few remaining chained libraries. The preservation of such an old manuscript in its original chained setting provides invaluable insights into medieval bookmaking, religious art, and early literacy practices, making it a vital resource for historical and scholarly research.

100. (C): When arranging the chained libraries in reverse chronological order according to their foundation:

- Marsh's Library in Dublin, built in 1701, is the most recent among those listed.
- Hereford Cathedral Library in the UK was established in 1611.
- Francis Trigge Chained Library in Grantham started in 1598.
- The library at the Church of Saint Walpurga in Zutphen, Netherlands, was built in 1564.
- The Biblioteca Malatestiana in Cesena, Italy, founded in 1454, is the oldest. This order reflects the historical timeline of the establishment of chained libraries across Europe, showing the spread and evolution of this unique library format from Italy to other parts of Europe.

YOUR SPACE

YOUR SPACE

Previous Years' Paper

National Testing Agency (NTA)

UGC-NET Junior Research Fellowship & Assistant Professor Eligibility Exam

Library and Information Science, December-2023

(Exam held on 13-12-2023)

PAPER-II

1. National Mission on Libraries was set up by ________.

A. Ministry of Human Resource Development, GOI
B. Ministry of Culture, GOI
C. Ministry of IT, GOI
D. Ministry of Science and Technology, GOI

2. ________ is a routine knowledge about which the expert is conscious and often resides in short term memory.

A. Procedural knowledge
B. Declarative knowledge
C. Semantic knowledge
D. Episodic knowledge

3. IIPA stands for:

A. Indian Intellectual Property Administration
B. International Institute of Public Administration
C. International Intellectual Property Alliance
D. International Independent Property Administration

4. The origin of the discipline of Information Studies could be traced to the founding of ________.

A. UNESCO
B. International Institute of Bibliography
C. The British Library
D. American Library Association

5. 'Dr. S.R. Ranganathan : A Tribute' was published by:

A. Indian Library Association
B. The National Library, Kolkata
C. IASLIC
D. University of Madras

6. Who was not the founding member of ILA in 1933 ?

A. S. Bashiruddin
B. Wali Mohammad
C. T.C. Dutta
D. S.R. Ranganathan

7. Which of the following has implication on the first law of library science?

A. Location
B. Obligation of the state
C. Resource sharing
D. Method of circulation

8. The Report of the Advisory Committee for Libraries is also known as:

A. Parry Committee Report
B. Fyzee Report
C. Sinha Committee Report
D. Ekbote Committee Report

9. Best way to begin a search for information is:

A. Search Google
B. Define user's information needs
C. Search for sources
D. Some how start searching

10. Who called Tertiary sources as sources of information which are last to appear and mostly do not contain subject knowledge?

A. L. Shores B. W.A. Katz
C. C.W. Hanson D. Denis Grogan

11. Which of the following is not a non documentary source of information?

A. Database vendors
B. Extension workers
C. Product bulletins
D. Internet

12. Dr. S.R. Ranganathan was the president of ILA in the year:

A. 1950 B. 1960
C. 1945 D. 1940

13. The Chairman of the Advisory of Standard in IFLA is ______.

A. Deanna White B. Pat Riva
C. Victoria Owen D. Kalpana Dasgupta

14. The name of the Scheme of RRRLF designed to run in Public Private Partnership (PPP) mode is:

A. Development of Rural book deposit
B. Establishment of RRRLF children corner
C. Development of Library on wheel service
D. Creation of Divyangjan facilities for readers

15. RRRLF took initiation to develop District Youth Resource Centre (DYRC) in the year:

A. 2002-03 B. 2005-06
C. 2010-11 D. 2015-16

16. The Calcutta Public Library was opened to the public in 1936 in the residence of ______.

A. J.M. Stoqueler B. John Macfarlane
C. F.P. Strong D. J.A. Chapman

17. In which year, the Second edition of LC List of Subject Headings was published?

A. 1923 B. 1924
C. 1919 D. 1912

18. The form of revision adopted by DDC to resolve the conflict between change and stability is called:

A. Abridged Schedule
B. Phoenix Schedule
C. Augmented Schedule
D. Relative index

19. FRBR stands for:

A. Functional Requirements for Bibliography Records
B. Functional Requirements for Bibliographic Recordings
C. Functional Requirement for Bibliographic Records
D. Fundamental Requirements for Bibliographic Records

20. Identify the phase relation for the given title "Rural and the Urban folk culture".

A. Influence phase relation
B. Bias phase relation
C. Difference phase relation
D. General phase relation

21. Who among the following is not the main contributor to the Total Quality Management approach?

A. Philip B. Crosby
B. Mary Parker Follett
C. Joseph M. Juran
D. W. Edwards Deming

22. Which of the following is not the phase involved in development of a system in System Analysis?

A. System Implementation
B. System Design
C. System Analysis
D. System Monitoring

23. ________ is the process of devising the mechanism through which the efforts of the people are directed and coordinated towards goal achievement.

A. Staffing B. Leading
C. Controlling D. Organising

24. Which of the following is two-card system of charging and discharging?
A. Browne Issue System
B. Ledger System
C. Register System
D. Day book System

25. _________ uses unidirectional antennas that send signals in one direction.
A. Fiber optics B. Radio waves
C. Microwaves D. Infrared waves

26. _________ is a client server application that identifies each host on the internet with a unique user friendly name.
A. Telnet B. DNS
C. TCP D. IP

27. _________ translates a low level language program into Machine code.
A. Compiler B. Interpreters
C. Assembler D. Virus

28. Which of the following is not a part of a data packet?
A. Sender's IP address
B. Time and date of data packets
C. Identity number of the data packet
D. Header to identify the data packet

29. In India computers were used in Library work for the first time by _________.
A. Indian Statistical Institute, Calcutta
B. INSDOC, New Delhi
C. Indian Institute of Science, Bangalore
D. DRDO, New Delhi

30. The reading range of UHF tags is _________.
A. 0 cm to 10 cm
B. 1 feet to 1 Meter
C. 3-5 Meter
D. 7-10 Meter

31. _________ is an initiative to preserve the long tail of open access Journals.
A. JASPER B. CASPER
C. DIAPER D. MASPER

32. Econstar is a non-profit digital archiving service provided by:
A. Library of Congress
B. Australian National Library of Economics
C. German National Library of Economics
D. National Library of Economics, Netherland

33. Which of the following is also called "Cardinal Scale"?
A. Nominal Scale B. Ordinal Scale
C. Interval Scale D. Ratio Scale

34. _________ is mainly concerned with generalisations and with the formulation of a theory.
A. Quantitative Research
B. Fundamental Research
C. Applied Research
D. Qualitative Research

35. Which of the following is not a non probability sampling method?
A. Stratified Sampling
B. Convenience Sampling
C. Judgement Sampling
D. Quota Sampling

36. When the dependent variable is not free from the influence of extraneous variable(s), the relationship between the dependent and independent variables is said to be confounded by _________.
A. Extraneous variable
B. Discrete variable
C. Continuous variable
D. Non-continuous variable

37. Which of the following is not a function of AGRIS?
A. AGRIS is a co-operative system
B. Participating countries input the bibliographical references to literature
C. AGRIS processing Unit at Vienna processes the collected information
D. AGRIS follows decentralised processing of information for their purpose

38. Which of the following does take the pride of the becoming the first medical periodical in India not sponsored by any society or association?

A. Indian Journal of Medical Science
B. Indian Medical Record
C. Medical Record
D. The Indian Medical Gazette

39. Which of the following was not included in the Terms of Reference in the Project Agreement (between UNESCO and India) for the development of public library services in India in May 1951?

A. It shall provide public library services for the people of the city Delhi
B. The library shall keep itself abstained from carrying out the policy of UNESCO's public library Manifesto
C. It shall be in all countries where similar development of public libraries can be undertaken
D. It shall be a model for all public libraries developed in India

40. While Medical Library Association (MLA) has fostered excellence in the professional practice to enhance healthcare education and research, which of the following is not correct?

A. This association educates health information professional about how to handle health information
B. This association supports its professionals in promoting health information research
C. This association trains physicians
D. This association promotes access the worlds health science information

41. Which of the following are true of professional ethics in librarianship?

(*a*) ALA adopted a professional ethical code in 1938
(*b*) ILA has adopted a professional ethical code in 1957
(*c*) UK Professional ethical code was adopted in 1983
(*d*) AS1S - American Association for Information Science has published a draft ethical code in 1990

Choose the **correct** answer from the options given below:

A. (*a*), (*b*), (*c*) only
B. (*a*), (*b*), (*d*) only
C. (*a*), (*c*), (*d*) only
D. (*b*), (*c*), (*d*) only

42. Which of the following factors emphasize the need for public relations and publicity?

(*a*) Obligation of first law
(*b*) Obligation of second law
(*c*) Obligation of third law
(*d*) Obligation of fourth law

Choose the **correct** answer from the options given below:

A. (*a*), (*b*), (*c*) only
B. (*a*), (*c*), (*d*) only
C. (*a*), (*b*), (*d*) only
D. (*b*), (*c*), (*d*) only

43. Which of the following are true of categorization of users?

(*a*) Potential user is the one who needs information which cannot be provided by specific services
(*b*) Expected user is the one who is known to have intention of using certain information services
(*c*) Actual user is the one who has actually used an information service
(*d*) Beneficiary user is the one who derives measurable advantage from information services

Choose the **correct** answer from the options given below:

A. (*a*), (*b*), (*c*) only
B. (*b*), (*c*), (*d*) only
C. (*a*), (*c*), (*d*) only
D. (*a*), (*b*), (*d*) only

44. Which of the following holds good with geographical sources?
(*a*) Meriam Webster's Geographical dictionary was first published in 1949.
(*b*) Volume I of Gazetteer of India is titled as 'Country and People'.
(*c*) Rand McNally has published 'The New International Atlas'.
(*d*) Fodors Essential India is an atlas.

Choose the **correct** answer from the options given below:
A. (*a*), (*b*), (*c*) only
B. (*a*), (*c*), (*d*) only
C. (*b*), (*c*), (*d*) only
D. (*a*), (*b*), (*d*) only

45. Which of the following are true of Encyclopedia Americana?
(*a*) First edition was published in 1903-04.
(*b*) Edition published in 2005 contains 34 volumes.
(*c*) Contains short articles on specific subjects.
(*d*) Most of the articles are signed by contributors.

Choose the **correct** answer from the options given below:
A. (*a*), (*b*), (*c*) only
B. (*b*), (*c*), (*d*) only
C. (*a*), (*c*), (*d*) only
D. (*a*), (*b*), (*d*) only

46. Which of the following are the characteristics of primary sources?
(*a*) Represent a researcher's perspective
(*b*) Document events, people and viewpoint of particular time
(*c*) Widely scattered
(*d*) Reproduction of primary sources remain least important

Choose the **correct** answer from the options given below:
A. (*b*), (*c*), (*d*) only
B. (*a*), (*b*), (*c*) only
C. (*a*), (*c*), (*d*) only
D. (*a*), (*b*), (*d*) only

47. Direct methods for user education are:
(*a*) Orientation courses and lectures
(*b*) Conducting Library tours
(*c*) Reader-Librarian dialogue while rendering the reference service
(*d*) Audio-visual modules kept online
(*e*) Informal meetings at educational or cultural functions

Choose the **correct** answer from the options given below:
A. (*a*), (*b*), (*c*) and (*d*) only
B. (*a*), (*b*), (*c*) and (*e*) only
C. (*b*), (*c*), (*d*) and (*e*) only
D. (*a*), (*c*), (*d*) and (*e*) only

48. S.R. Ranganathan's Long Range Reference Service can be inferred through.
(*a*) Preparation
(*b*) Service
(*c*) Assimilation
(*d*) Automation
(*e*) Classification

Choose the **correct** answer from the options given below:
A. (*a*), (*b*) and (*c*) only
B. (*b*), (*c*) and (*d*) only
C. (*a*), (*d*) and (*e*) only
D. (*a*), (*b*) and (*e*) only

49. Objectives of resource sharing are:
(*a*) Reduction in all round cost
(*b*) Avoidance of duplication of resources, processing and maintenance costs
(*c*) Satisfying a large group of users irrespective of their academic streams
(*d*) Provision of greater access to information resources to a wide category of users
(*e*) Development of specialised areas of collection building

Choose the **correct** answer from the options given below:
A. (*a*), (*b*), (*c*), (*d*) only
B. (*b*), (*c*), (*d*) only
C. (*a*), (*b*), (*d*), (*e*) only
D. (*b*), (*c*), (*d*), (*e*) only

50. Which of the following systems are developed based on the basic principles of the post coordinate indexing system?

(*a*) Chain Indexing
(*b*) Peek-a-boo
(*c*) Edge-notched card
(*d*) Duel Directories

Choose the **correct** answer from the options given below:

A. (*a*), (*c*), (*d*) only
B. (*a*), (*b*), (*c*) only
C. (*b*), (*c*), (*d*) only
D. (*c*) and (*d*) only

51. The collation area of ISBD (M) includes:

(*a*) Pagination area
(*b*) Illustration statement
(*c*) Size
(*d*) Price

Choose the **correct** answer from the options given below:

A. (*a*), (*b*), (*d*) only
B. (*a*), (*b*), (*c*) only
C. (*b*), (*c*), (*d*) only
D. (*a*), (*c*), (*d*) only

52. The principles of proper abstracting include:

(*a*) Purpose (*b*) Scope
(*c*) Coverage (*d*) Conclusions

Choose the **correct** answer from the options given below:

A. (*a*), and (*d*) only
B. (*a*), (*b*), (*d*) only
C. (*b*), (*c*), (*d*) only
D. (*a*), (*b*), (*c*) only

53. Which of the following are advantages of stock taking?

(*a*) Helps librarian to replace the essential lost books
(*b*) Reveals the lost books
(*c*) Helps the library authorities to ascertain as to whether the library staff is dishonest, negligent and careless
(*d*) Cost of stock verification is not commensurate with the cost of books misplaced and is an added expenditure

Choose the **correct** answer from the options given below:

A. (*a*), (*c*), (*d*) only
B. (*a*), (*b*), (*c*) only
C. (*b*), (*c*), (*d*) only
D. (*a*), (*b*), (*d*) only

54. Job description implies the recording of the following data concerning each job analysed.

(*a*) Fixing the money value of job and comparing one job with another
(*b*) Principal duties to be performed and responsibilities involved are outlined
(*c*) Requisite materials, equipments, machinery and tools etc. are listed
(*d*) Conditions of work *i.e.* surroundings the time of work etc. are stated

Choose the **correct** answer from the options given below:

A. (*a*), (*b*), (*c*) only
B. (*b*), (*c*), (*d*) only
C. (*a*), (*c*), (*d*) only
D. (*a*), (*b*), (*d*) only

55. What are the requisite materials for Newark charging system for the book?

(*a*) Date slip (*b*) Date label
(*c*) Book pocket (*d*) Book card

Choose the **correct** answer from the options given below:

A. (*a*), (*c*), (*d*) only
B. (*a*), (*b*), (*c*) only
C. (*b*), (*c*), (*d*) only
D. (*a*), (*b*), (*d*) only

56. Every OS has ______ which permanently resides in the main memory of the computer to perform some of its basic functions.

(*a*) Interface (*b*) Kernel
(*c*) Nucleus (*d*) Compiler
(*e*) Shell

Choose the **correct** answer from the options given below:

A. (*a*) and (*b*) only
B. (*b*) and (*c*) only
C. (*c*) and (*d*) only
D. (*d*) and (*e*) only

57. When the sender and the receiver of an e-mail are on different systems, in order to send message over internet we need ________.

(*a*) Two UAs (*b*) Pair of MTAs
(*c*) MAA (*d*) NIME

Choose the **correct** answer from the options given below:

A. (*a*) and (*c*) only B. (*a*) and (*b*) only
C. (*b*) and (*d*) only D. (*c*) and (*d*) only

58. The AR App "Timescape : Kolkata" is developed by:

(*a*) University of Liverpool
(*b*) Jadavpur University
(*c*) British Library
(*d*) Calcutta University
(*e*) Mellon Foundation

Choose the **correct** answer from the options given below:

A. (*a*), (*b*), (*c*) only
B. (*b*), (*c*), (*d*) only
C. (*c*), (*d*), (*e*) only
D. (*b*), (*d*), (*e*) only

59. Which of the following are the types of content management system?

(*a*) Web content management system
(*b*) MIS
(*c*) Collaborative content management system
(*d*) Digital Research Repository system
(*e*) Unicode content management system

Choose the **correct** answer from the options given below:

A. (*a*), (*c*), (*e*) only
B. (*a*), (*b*), (*d*) only
C. (*a*), (*c*), (*d*) only
D. (*b*), (*c*), (*e*) only

60. National Digital Heritage Archive is a program that is a partnership between ________.

(*a*) National Library of New Zealand
(*b*) Library of Congress
(*c*) Ex Libris group
(*d*) Mellon Foundation
(*e*) Sun microsystems

Choose the **correct** answer from the options given below:

A. (*a*), (*b*), (*c*) only
B. (*b*), (*d*), (*e*) only
C. (*a*), (*c*), (*e*) only
D. (*c*), (*d*), (*e*) only

61. Which of the following are the challenges in adopting linked data in libraries?

(*a*) Terminology disparity that exists between the library and web based standards
(*b*) Complexity of linked data technologies such as RDF/XML
(*c*) Metadata openness and sharing
(*d*) Facet based navigation

Choose the **correct** answer from the options given below:

A. (*a*) and (*b*) only
B. (*b*) and (*c*) only
C. (*c*) and (*d*) only
D. (*a*) and (*c*) only

62. Which of the following are true about the "R" Software?

(*a*) R is an interpreted language
(*b*) Users can access through a command line interpreter
(*c*) R's capabilities are extended through user created package
(*d*) R is a commercial software

Choose the **correct** answer from the options given below:

A. (*b*), (*c*), (*d*) only
B. (*a*), (*c*), (*d*) only
C. (*a*), (*b*), (*d*) only
D. (*a*), (*b*), (*c*) only

63. A large number of manuscripts of different languages are found in Rampur Raza Library. Which are those languages?

(*a*) Arabic (*b*) Pali

(*c*) Bengali (*d*) Sanskrit

(*e*) Urdu

Choose the **correct** answer from the options given below:

A. (*a*), (*d*), (*e*) only

B. (*b*), (*c*), (*d*) only

C. (*c*), (*d*), (*e*) only

D. (*b*), (*d*), (*e*) only

64. Which of the following are true for Chicago Style manual of style?

(*a*) Chicago style manual was published first in the year 1896

(*b*) It is published by university of Chicago press

(*c*) It uses notes and bibliography style

(*d*) Title of the first edition was, "Manual of Style"

Choose the **correct** answer from the options given below:

A. (*a*), (*b*), (*c*) only

B. (*b*), (*c*), (*d*) only

C. (*a*), (*b*), (*d*) only

D. (*a*), (*c*), (*d*) only

65. Which of the following are true of telephonic interview?

(*a*) Most suitable for intensive surveys

(*b*) Faster than other methods of interview

(*c*) Replies can be recorded

(*d*) Questions have to be short and simple

Choose the **correct** answer from the options given below:

A. (*a*), (*b*), (*c*) only B. (*a*), (*c*), (*d*) only

C. (*a*), (*b*), (*d*) only D. (*b*). (*c*), (*d*) only

66. Match List-I with List-II.

List-I (Concept)	**List-II (Explanation)**
(*a*) Information society	I. Seeks to overcome the problem of digital divide
(*b*) Knowledge society	II. Investigates the properties and behaviour of information
(*c*) Information studies	III. Information is seen as a commodity
(*d*) Information science	IV. Emerged from cross fertilization of ideas

Choose the **correct** answer from the options given below:

	(*a*)	(*b*)	(*c*)	(*d*)
A.	I	II	III	IV
B.	II	III	IV	I
C.	III	I	IV	II
D.	IV	I	II	III

67. Match List-I with List-II.

List-I (Library Associations)	**List-II (Year of establishment)**
(*a*) Madras Library Association	I. 1928
(*b*) Andhra Desa Library Association	II. 1939
(*c*) Bengal Library Association	III. 1914
(*d*) Delhi Library Association	IV. 1925

Choose the **correct** answer from the options given below:

	(*a*)	(*b*)	(*c*)	(*d*)
A.	I	III	IV	II
B.	IV	III	I	II
C.	IV	II	I	III
D.	II	III	IV	I

68. Match List-I with List-II.

List-I (Purpose)	**List-II (Type of Portal)**
(*a*) Platform that focuses on the client through personalised access point	I. Information Portal
(*b*) For use within the company or organization	II. E-Commerce Portal

(*c*) Through which marketing can be promoted	III. Customer Portal
(*d*) Provides type of specialized information	IV. Corporate Portal

Choose the **correct** answer from the options given below:

	(*a*)	(*b*)	(*c*)	(*d*)
A.	I	II	III	IV
B.	I	IV	III	II
C.	III	II	IV	I
D.	III	IV	II	I

69. Match List-I with List-II.

List-I (Centres)	**List-II (Parent body)**
(*a*) NISCAIR	I. ICSSR
(*b*) DESIDOC	II. Ministry of Small Scale Industries
(*c*) NASSDOC	III. CSIR
(*d*) SENDOC	IV. DRDO

Choose the **correct** answer from the options given below:

	(*a*)	(*b*)	(*c*)	(*d*)
A.	I	II	III	IV
B.	II	III	IV	I
C.	III	IV	I	II
D.	IV	I	II	III

70. Match List-I with List-II.

List-I (Types of Abstracts)	**List-II (Explanation)**
(*a*) Descriptive abstract	I. Abstract of a paper which has not yet been written
(*b*) Listing abstract	II. General statement of the nature and scope of the document
(*c*) Slanted abstract	III. List the content of the document
(*d*) Pseudo abstract	IV. Oriented to serve a special group of users

Choose the **correct** answer from the options given below:

	(*a*)	(*b*)	(*c*)	(*d*)
A.	I	III	II	IV
B.	II	III	IV	I
C.	IV	III	II	I
D.	III	II	I	IV

71. Match List-I with List-II.

List-I (System)	**List-II (Usage)**
(*a*) PERT	I. used for the physical and logical descriptions of system
(*b*) DFD	II. generally two pairs of time/cost estimates a normal cost/time schedule and a crash cost/time schedule
(*c*) CPM	III. Event, Activity, Dummy activity, Merge event
(*d*) Libual	IV. based on users evaluation

Choose the **correct** answer from the options given below:

	(*a*)	(*b*)	(*c*)	(*d*)
A.	III	IV	I	II
B.	II	III	IV	I
C.	I	II	III	IV
D.	III	I	II	IV

72. Match List-I with List-II.

List-I (Types of firewall)	**List-II (User)**
(*a*) Packet filtering firewall	I. used in a situation in which the system administrators trust internal user
(*b*) Stateful packet inspection firewall	II. Applies a set of rules to each incoming and outgoing IP packet
(*c*) Application level Gateway	III. Also called application proxy tends to be more secure than packet filters

(*d*) Circuit level Gateway	IV. Tighten up the rules for TCP traffic by creating a directory of outbound TCP connections

Choose the **correct** answer from the options given below:

	(*a*)	(*b*)	(*c*)	(*d*)
A.	II	III	IV	I
B.	II	IV	III	I
C.	III	IV	I	II
D.	III	IV	II	I

73. Match List-I with List-II.

List-I (Content Management System)	List-II (Platform)
(*a*) TYPO3	I. Ruby
(*b*) Magnolia	II. PHP
(*c*) Umbraco	III. C#
(*d*) Radiant	IV. Java

Choose the **correct** answer from the options given below:

	(*a*)	(*b*)	(*c*)	(*d*)
A.	II	III	IV	I
B.	II	IV	III	I
C.	III	IV	I	II
D.	III	I	IV	II

74. Match List-I with List-II.

List-I (Metrix)	List-II (Characteristics)
(*a*) Cite Score	I. Weight value based on subject-field quality and reputation of Journal
(*b*) SJR	II. Calculates number of times article has been cited over 5 years
(*c*) Eigen factor	III. Provides insights into way people interact with individual pieces of research output
(*d*) Plum X metric	IV. Number of citations that a manuscript received over 3 years

Choose the **correct** answer from the options given below:

	(*a*)	(*b*)	(*c*)	(*d*)
A.	IV	I	III	II
B.	IV	I	II	III
C.	II	I	IV	III
D.	III	IV	II	I

75. Match List-I with List-II.

List-I (Centres/ programs)	List-II (Institute/campus where it was started initially)
(*a*) National Centre for Science Information	I. Gujarat University, Ahmedabad
(*b*) National Social Sciences Information Centre	II. SNDT Women's University, Bombay
(*c*) National Humanities Information Centre	III. MS University, Baroda
(*d*) Information and Library Network Centre	IV. Indian Institute of Science, Bangalore

Choose the **correct** answer from the options given below:

	(*a*)	(*b*)	(*c*)	(*d*)
A.	I	II	III	IV
B.	II	III	IV	I
C.	III	IV	I	II
D.	IV	III	II	I

76. Arrange the following concepts in the reverse order of their application:

(*a*) Wisdom (*b*) Data
(*c*) Information (*d*) Knowledge

Choose the **correct** answer from the options given below:

A. (*a*), (*d*), (*c*), (*b*) B. (*c*), (*b*), (*a*), (*d*)
C. (*a*), (*d*), (*b*), (*c*) D. (*a*), (*b*), (*c*), (*d*)

77. Arrange in sequence the steps of Browne Charging System.

(*a*) due date is stamped on the due date slip

(*b*) the call no. and borrower number are recorded in the daily circulation work

(*c*) Book card coupled with the readers pocket is filled in the charging tray behind the respective due date card by call number

(*d*) Counter assistant takes the book card out of the book pocket and slips it into the borrower's ticket

Choose the **correct** answer from the options given below:

A. (*b*), (*d*), (*a*), (*c*) B. (*d*), (*a*), (*c*), (*b*)
C. (*a*), (*b*), (*d*), (*c*) D. (*c*), (*a*), (*d*), (*b*)

78. Sequence the following in the order of their year of release:

(*a*) Intute (*b*) PLOS
(*c*) JISc (*d*) SciCentral

Choose the **correct** answer from the options given below:

A. (*c*), (*d*), (*b*), (*a*)
B. (*d*), (*c*), (*a*), (*b*)
C. (*c*), (*b*), (*a*), (*d*)
D. (*b*), (*c*), (*d*), (*a*)

79. Arrange the following functional phases of SDI service in a logical sequence.

(*a*) Modification
(*b*) Notification
(*c*) Selection
(*d*) Feedback

Choose the **correct** answer from the options given below:

A. (*c*), (*b*), (*d*), (*a*)
B. (*c*), (*d*), (*a*), (*b*)
C. (*b*), (*c*), (*d*), (*a*)
D. (*a*), (*b*), (*c*), (*d*)

80. Arrange the steps involved in POPSI to prepare the index entries in a logical sequence.

(*a*) Display of components
(*b*) Verbal representation
(*c*) Approach terms
(*d*) Alphabetical arrangement
(*e*) Cross reference

Choose the **correct** answer from the options given below:

A. (*b*), (*a*), (*c*), (*e*), (*d*)
B. (*a*), (*b*), (*d*), (*c*), (*e*)
C. (*c*), (*b*), (*a*), (*d*), (*e*)
D. (*e*), (*b*), (*d*), (*a*), (*c*)

81. Arrange in sequence the 5 stages of the Disaster Management cycle.

(*a*) Mitigation
(*b*) Recovery
(*c*) Response
(*d*) Preparedness
(*e*) Prevention

Choose the **correct** answer from the options given below:

A. (*d*), (*a*), (*c*), (*b*), (*e*)
B. (*a*), (*c*), (*b*), (*d*), (*e*)
C. (*b*), (*e*), (*a*), (*c*), (*d*)
D. (*e*), (*a*), (*d*), (*c*), (*b*)

82. Arrange the following Academic Social Networks according to their first release.

(*a*) Research Gate
(*b*) ORCiD
(*c*) Publon
(*d*) Zotero

Choose the **correct** answer from the options given below:

A. (*a*), (*b*), (*c*), (*d*)
B. (*b*), (*c*), (*d*), (*a*)
C. (*c*), (*d*), (*a*), (*b*)
D. (*d*), (*a*), (*b*), (*c*)

83. Arrange the steps of Data mining process in a proper logical sequence.

(*a*) Select suitable algorithm
(*b*) Prepare Data pattern
(*c*) Choose available analytical package
(*d*) Select of suitable databases from data warehouse

Choose the **correct** answer from the options given below:

A. (*b*), (*d*), (*a*), (*c*)
B. (*a*), (*b*), (*c*), (*d*)
C. (*a*), (*d*), (*c*), (*b*)
D. (*c*), (*a*), (*d*), (*b*)

84. Arrange the following steps in planning an Experimental Research in a logical order.

(*a*) Pilot study
(*b*) Conducting the experiment
(*c*) Research design
(*d*) Selecting the problem
(*e*) Selection of setting

Choose the **correct** answer from the options given below:

A. (*d*), (*e*), (*a*), (*b*), (*c*)
B. (*d*), (*e*), (*c*), (*a*), (*b*)
C. (*d*), (*e*), (*a*), (*c*), (*b*)
D. (*e*), (*d*), (*b*), (*a*), (*c*)

85. Arrange the following Commissions/ Committees that was setup for library development in a logical order.

(*a*) Mehrotra Committee
(*b*) Review Committee on Library Science
(*c*) Committee on National Network System for Universities/Libraries
(*d*) Education Committee

Choose the **correct** answer from the options given below:

A. (*a*), (*b*), (*c*), (*d*)
B. (*b*), (*d*), (*a*), (*c*)
C. (*c*), (*d*), (*a*), (*b*)
D. (*d*), (*a*), (*b*), (*c*)

86. Given below are two statements: one is labelled as Assertion (A) and the other is labelled as Reason (R).

Assertion (A): Archiving and preserving digital information resources are complex resource intensive process.

Reason (R): This applies to both *i.e.*, born digital and digitized information.

In the light of the above statements, choose the **most appropriate** answer from the options given below:

A. Both (A) and (R) are correct and (R) is the correct explanation of (A)
B. Both (A) and (R) are correct, but (R) is not the correct explanation of (A)
C. (A) is correct, but (R) is not correct
D. (A) is not correct, but (R) is correct

87. Given below are two statements:

Statement I: A website is a collection of webpages, images, videos and other digital assets and hosted on a particular domain.

Statement II: All publicly accessible websites collectively constitute the world wide web.

In the light of the above statements, choose the **most appropriate** answer from the options given below:

A. Both Statement I and Statement II are correct
B. Both Statement 1 and Statement II are incorrect
C. Statement I is correct, but Statement II is incorrect
D. Statement I is incorrect, but Statement II is correct

88. Given below are two statements: one is labelled as Assertion (A) and the other is labelled as Reason (R).

Assertion (A): Delegation of authority involves the establishment of authority relationship that provide both horizontal and vertical coordination between working units in an institution.

Reason (R): Mere delegation of authority does not absolve the delegation of responsibility for the consequences of such delegation. The risk involved in the decision should be the major criterion for delegation.

In the light of the above statements, choose the **most appropriate** answer from the options given below:

A. Both (A) and (R) are correct and (R) is the correct explanation of (A)
B. Both (A) and (R) are correct, but (R) is not the correct explanation of (A)
C. (A) is correct, but (R) is not correct
D. (A) is not correct, but (R) is correct

89. Given below are two statements:

Statement I: Electronic reference sources are most frequently updated than print sources.

Statement II: Use of electronic reference sources requires expensive infrastructure.

In the light of the above statements, choose the **most appropriate** answer from the options given below:

A. Both Statement I and Statement II are correct
B. Both Statement I and Statement II are incorrect
C. Statement I is correct, but Statement II is incorrect
D. Statement I is incorrect, but Statement II is correct

90. Given below are two statements:

Statement I: Modern library has to cater to the societal information needs.

Statement II: Library is a social institution.

In the light of the above statements, choose the most appropriate answer from the options given below:

A. Both Statement I and Statement II are correct
B. Both Statement I and Statement II are incorrect
C. Statement I is correct, but Statement II is incorrect
D. Statement I is incorrect, but Statement II is correct

Directions (Qs. No. 91-95): *Read the following passage and answer the following question:*

India has a long and venerable history in the field of higher education. In ancient times, the country was known to have been home to the oldest formal universities in world. These ancient universities were rich with library of contemporary reading materials like manuscripts. The nature of higher education in ancient India was considered as religious. The basic religions were Hinduism, Buddhism and Jainism. Religion based education in ancient India had a outstanding role in creating, transforming and transmitting knowledge to the people in society. The more striking of these ancient universities were Takshashila (Now in Pakistan), Nalanda (in the modern state of Bihar) and Ujjaini (in modern Madhya Pradesh). These were in the early times of Indian Civilization and attracted students from all parts of India, Central Asia, China and South East Asia. The Hindu Buddhist University of Takshashila, the oldest one, was probably established in 6th century BC. The role of Takshashila as a knowledge centre grew stronger day by day for nurturing students. Unfortunately, Takshashila University was destroyed by the White Huns (Ephthalites) around 460 AD. In 1193, Nalanda University and its library with 9 million manuscripts was sacked and burnt and totally destroyed by Bakhtiyar Khilji. This event not only ended the University, but was also followed by a rapid decline in the practice of Buddhism in India. In 1235, Sultan Iltutmish completely destroyed Ujjaini, a major knowledge centre for Mathematics, Literature, Philosophy and Astronomy. History of higher education in India and its library system had thus begun its journey quite with a bang, which had to face temporary hindrance in the forin of outside invasion. It is significant that at exactly the same time, half way across the world, Oxford University was being established. The libraries of Institutions of higher education are recognised as a most important agency of social change involved in the Human Resource Development of the Country. The socio-historical journey of higher education has been started with an ancient system of education in the Vedic period.

In pre British days Hindus and Muslims were educated through Patthsala and Madrassa respectively. The ideas and pedagogical methods of education during the colonial period from 1757 to 1947, were contested terrain. The commercial British East India Company ruled parts of India from 1764 to 1858. In 18th century a few company officials became Scholars of Sanskrit, Persian and Tamil and promoted 'Oriental' learning which was classical, devotic learning in indigenous Languages. However, they were outnumbered by Anglicists, those who denegrated 'Oriental' learning and advocated the introduction of institutions of western learning based upon the British curriculum with English as the medium of instruction. By the early 19th century, when English was made the official language of Government business, British policy promoted a cheap, trickle-down model for colonial education. When the British crown abolished company rule in 1858, Government universities existed at Bombay (Mumbai), Calcutta (Kolkata), and Madras (Chennai); about two thousand students studied at thirteen Government colleges in all of British India, and another 30,000 students were in Government Secondary Schools.

91. Which of the following was not practiced in religion-based education in Ancient Indian Universities?

A. Jainism B. Hinduism
C. Christianity D. Buddhism

92. The higher education and library system of Ancient India had venerable history that:

A. had faced a kind of impediment in the form of outside invasion
B. had witnessed attracting students restricted from Indian territory only
C. had promoted education with the financial support from ephthalities
D. had witnessed the non-religion based education for Indian students only

93. Which of the following is correct in respect of three universities and their libraries of Ancient India?

A. Sultan Iltutmish had demolished the Nalanda, Bakhtiyar Khilji had knocked down the Takshashila and White Huns destroyed the Ujjaini
B. Ujjaini was destroyed by Bakhtiyar Khilji, Nalanda was demolished by White Huns and Takshashila was ruined by Sultan Iltutmish
C. Sultan Iltutmish designed and created Ujjaini, White Huns developed Takshashila and Bakhtiyar khilji established Nalanda
D. Sultan Iltutmish had destroyed Ujjaini, White Huns had destroyed Takshashila and Bakhtiyar Khilji had destroyed totally Nalanda

94. Find the correct geographical location of the three universities of Ancient India?

A. Nalanda is in the modern state of Madhya Pradesh, Ujjaini is in modern Pakistan and Takshashila is in modern Bihar
B. Nalanda is in modern Rajasthan, Ujjaini is in modern Chhatisgarh and Takshashila is in Modern Bihar
C. Nalanda is in modern Bihar, Ujjaini is in modern Madhya Pradesh and Takshashila is in Pakistan
D. Nalanda is in modern Jharkhand, Ujjaini is in modern Uttarakhand and Takshashila is in modern Odisha

95. British policy promoted a cheap model for colonial education in India in nineteenth century.

A. by introducing an ancient system of Vedic education in the British Curriculum
B. by nurturing more the nature of the religion based higher education in ancient India.

C. by making English as the official language for government business in addition to making English as medium of instruction

D. by establishing Oxford university in UK

Directions (Qs. No. 96-100): *Read the following passage and answer the following question:*

Today Internet is possibly the most widely used information source in the world. With an aim to reach Internet to those who are still unreached, several tech farms have come forward with novel ideas. Google Sundar Pichai CEO started experimenting with project Loon, which plans to launch a series of balloons that can help people get connected by beaming Internet signals down to base stations in 2013. One year later, the north-eastern Brazil, it ran its first test, using Long-Term Evolution (LTE), also known as 4 G, to connect a school computer in a rural village to the Internet. And in March 2014, Facebook announced plans to make internet available to regions of the developing world by using drones and an array of low Earth orbiting satellites. Facebook founder and CEO Mark Zuckerberg also helped to create internet.org, a consortium of companies, working towards the same goal.

(The man who conceived the innovative idea of Outernet is Syed Karim, a library science drop-out and founder CEO of Outernet). Then came up Outernet Inc., a Chicago based datacast company, being incubated by a New York City- based non-profit organization, the Media Development Investment Fund, with a plan to launch hundreds of low-cost miniature satellites, known as *cubesats* (cube satellites), into orbit around the Earth to create the Outernet, a wireless connection to the web available for free to every person in the world. Each *cubesat* receives data from a network of ground stations around the world and transmits this information on a loop until new information is received. This means using the Outernet will be more like watching a programme broadcast on TV. Outernet users will build a priority list for the information they want and make suggestions for new contents. In addition to providing free access, the Outernet will also be universally available, allowing people to bypass censorship laws prevalent in many countries. The Outernet, as envisioned, would effectively be a one-way connection data would flow from feeders to the satellites which would broadcast to all below. As such, it would not provide e-mail or other chat facilities. But Internet-less users would be able to request for specific content by sending its operators an SMS text message or letter. Net-connected organizations can, however, pay a free to have their own materials added to broadcasts at specific times, providing a source of revenue.

96. Who among the following had conceived the innovative idea of outernet?

A. Mark Zuckerberg B. Syed Karim

C. Sundar Pichai D. Harlan Mandel

97. The outernet is envisioned to be effective for internet-less users.

A. by establishing a two way realtime connection effectively

B. by providing e-mail or other chat facilities as such

C. by sending an SMS text message or a letter to its operators to request for specific content

D. by establishing whatsapp connection

98. Which of the following is an initiative to provide internet facilities to the people who are unable to derive the benefit of it?

A. A plan of google to make internet available to regions of the developing world by using drones

B. A plan to connect a school computer in a rural village by Media Development Investment Fund

C. An initiative to launch computers more in numbers in different regions

D. An initiative of google that plans to launch a series of balloons to help people get connected by beaming internet signals down to base station

99. The plan of launching hundreds of low cost miniature satellites that would create outernet is to:

A. establish a wireless connection to the web available for free to every person in the world
B. use Long Term Evolution (LTE) to connect computers of rural village
C. find Google's digitisation to provide access to millions of books
D. scan millions of books and send them using e-mail facilities

100. Which of the following is true as far as functionalities of cubesats is concerned?

A. Outernet cubesat functions just opposite to watching a broadcast in television
B. Outernet users need not to build a priority list of their desired information
C. Data are received from a network of a ground station and transmitted on a loop until new information is received
D. Outernet will not be available universally by passing censorship laws prevalent in many countries.

ANSWERS

1. (B): The National Mission on Libraries, initiated by the Ministry of Culture, Government of India, is a comprehensive endeavour aimed at rejuvenating public libraries throughout the nation. Its multifaceted approach encompasses various key objectives, including the modernization and digitization of library resources to ensure accessibility in the digital age. This involves upgrading infrastructure, adopting state-of-the-art technologies, and implementing digitization initiatives to make literary and informational materials available online.

2. (B): Declarative knowledge refers to factual information that an individual consciously knows and can articulate, often residing in short-term memory. It encompasses factual knowledge about the world, including concepts, principles, facts, and rules. This type of knowledge can be easily verbalized and is typically stored and retrieved in a structured manner. Examples of declarative knowledge include historical events, scientific theories, mathematical formulas, and vocabulary definitions.

3. (C): IIPA most commonly refers to the International Intellectual Property Alliance, an influential coalition of trade associations representing the interests of American companies in copyright-protected industries, such as motion pictures, music, software, and pharmaceuticals. The IIPA lobbies governments around the world to enact and enforce strong intellectual property laws that protect the creative and innovative work of its members. The alliance argues that strong IP laws are essential to promote innovation and economic growth, as they provide creators and inventors with exclusive rights to their work, which incentivizes them to invest in research and development.

4. (B): The discipline of Information Studies can trace its roots back to the founding of the International Institute of Bibliography (IIB). Established in 1895 by Paul Otlet and Henri La Fontaine in Brussels, Belgium, the IIB aimed to create a comprehensive catalogue of all published works and facilitate access to information. Otlet, often regarded as a pioneer in information science, envisioned a global network of interconnected information repositories, which he called a "universal bibliography".

5. (B): "Dr. S.R. Ranganathan: A Tribute" was published by The National Library, Kolkata, to honour the legacy of Dr. S.R. Ranganathan, a pioneering figure in the field of library and information science.

Ranganathan, often referred to as the "Father of Library Science in India", made significant contributions to the development of library theory and practice worldwide. The tribute publication likely contains essays, articles, and reflections from scholars, professionals, and admirers of Ranganathan, highlighting his innovative ideas, theories, and methodologies that have shaped the field.

6. **(D):** S.R. Ranganathan was not a founding member of the Indian Library Association (ILA) in 1933. However, he became deeply involved in the association shortly after its formation and played a crucial role in shaping its direction and objectives. Ranganathan, often regarded as the "Father of Library Science in India", made significant contributions to the field of library and information science worldwide. He pioneered many innovative concepts and methodologies, including the Five Laws of Library Science, which have had a profound impact on library management and organization.

7. **(A):** The first law of library science, formulated by S.R. Ranganathan, states: "Books are for use". This principle emphasizes that libraries should make their resources readily available to users. In order to fulfill this core principle, libraries need to be situated in convenient locations that are accessible to their target communities. This means having a central location in a town or city, being close to public transportation hubs. By making it easy for users to get to the library, regardless of their physical location or limitations, the library is upholding the first law's commitment to user access.

8. **(C):** The Report of the Advisory Committee for Libraries is also known as the Sinha Committee Report, the Library Bill, or the Library Act. The committee was appointed in 1957 to study the status of public library development in India, and submitted its report in 1958. The committee's chairman, Dr. A.P. Sinha, was the Director of Public Instruction in Bihar at the time, which is why the committee is also known as the Sinha Committee.

9. **(B):** Before embarking on a search, it's crucial to understand exactly what information is required. This involves clarifying the specific topic or subject, identifying the scope of the search, determining the type of information needed (e.g., scholarly articles, books, statistics), and considering any relevant criteria or parameters. By defining the user's information needs upfront, one can tailor the search strategy more effectively, saving time and ensuring that the retrieved information is relevant and useful.

10. **(D):** Denis Grogan, a prominent figure in information science, is credited with coining the term "tertiary sources" to describe information sources that typically appear later in the research process and often lack in-depth subject knowledge. These sources, such as encyclopedias, dictionaries, and almanacs, primarily serve as starting points or gateways to finding primary and secondary sources. They offer concise summaries, overviews, or compilations of information, helping researchers get oriented to a topic, identify relevant keywords, and locate more authoritative resources.

11. **(C):** Product bulletins are a form of non-documentary source of information that typically provide details about specific products or services offered by companies or organizations. These bulletins often contain descriptions, specifications, features, pricing, and other relevant information about products or services. Unlike traditional documents such as books or articles, product bulletins are usually designed for promotional purposes or to inform potential customers about new offerings.

12. **(A, C):** Dr. S.R. Ranganathan was the president of the Indian Library Association (ILA) from 1944 to 1953. He was the first life member of the ILA. Ranganathan also founded the Mysore Library Association (now Karnataka State Library Association) and the Indian Association of Teachers of Library Science (IATLIS) (now, Indian Association of Teachers of Library and Information Science). During his tenure as ILA president, three journals merged to form ABGILA, first published in 1949 and continued until 1953.

13. **(C):** Victoria Owen is the Chairman of the Advisory of Standard in IFLA. The Advisory Committee on Standards (CoS) is responsible for improving the visibility, relevance, and uptake of IFLA Standards. The Chair of the CoS leads this work, and also coordinates the maintenance, storage, and access to standards. Her focus is on education that puts into practice the scholarship and principles of information policy, in particular copyright, access to knowledge, and the public interest.

14. **(C):** The "Development of Library on Wheel Service" is a scheme initiated by the Raja Rammohun Roy Library Foundation (RRRLF) to enhance library services through a Public-Private Partnership (PPP) mode. This innovative scheme aims to extend library services to underserved areas and marginalized communities by deploying mobile libraries equipped with books, reading materials, and other resources. These mobile libraries, often in the form of buses or vans, travel to various locations such as remote villages, urban slums, and areas lacking access to traditional library facilities.

15. **(B):** The Raja Rammohun Roy Library Foundation (RRRLF) initiated the development of District Youth Resource Centres (DYRC) in the year 2005-06. These centers were established with the objective of providing information and resources to empower and engage youth in various educational, recreational, and skill-building activities. DYRCs serve as hubs for young people to access a wide range of resources, including books, study materials, computers, internet facilities, and vocational training programs.

16. **(C):** The Calcutta Public Library was inaugurated to the public in 1836 at the residence of F.P. Strong. This marked a significant milestone in the history of library development in Calcutta (now Kolkata) and India as a whole. F.P. Strong, who was the then President of the Asiatic Society of Bengal, played a pivotal role in establishing the library, which aimed to provide access to books and knowledge to the general public. The library started with a modest collection of books and gradually expanded its holdings over the years.

17. **(C):** The second edition of the Library of Congress Subject Headings (LCSH) was published in 1919. The Library of Congress began creating subject headings for its own catalog in the late 19th century. The first edition, titled "Subject Headings Used in the Dictionary Catalogues of the Library of Congress", was printed in parts between 1909 and 1914. As the library's collection grew and subject terminology evolved, a need arose for a more comprehensive subject heading list. This resulted in the publication of the second edition in 1919.

18. **(B):** The form of revision adopted by the Dewey Decimal Classification (DDC) to address the tension between change and stability is known as the Phoenix Schedule. This approach involves the systematic review and updating of the classification system to accommodate new subjects, concepts, and developments while maintaining continuity with established principles and structures.

The term "Phoenix" symbolizes the cyclical nature of revision, wherein the classification system undergoes periodic renewal and rebirth to stay relevant and responsive to evolving knowledge domains and user needs.

19. **(C):** FRBR (Functional Requirements for Bibliographic Records) is a conceptual model developed by the International Federation of Library Associations and Institutions (IFLA) to describe the fundamental entities, attributes, and relationships involved in bibliographic data. It provides a framework for understanding the structure and organization of bibliographic records, aiming to improve consistency and interoperability among library catalogs and other information systems. FRBR defines four primary entities: Work, Expression, Manifestation, and Item, each representing distinct levels of intellectual or physical manifestation of a bibliographic resource.

20. **(D):** The phase relation for the title "Rural and the Urban folk culture" is general phase. General phase relations are vague and undefined, and include all other relations not included in any of the five other relations. In this context, the phase relation encompasses a comprehensive exploration of similarities, differences, interactions, and interdependencies between rural and urban folk cultures. It implies an investigation into how folk culture manifests, evolves, and adapts within distinct socio-cultural environments, encompassing aspects such as traditions, customs, beliefs, practices, arts, and expressions.

21. **(B):** Among the options provided, Mary Parker Follett is not typically considered a main contributor to the Total Quality Management (TQM) approach. While Follett was an influential management theorist known for her contributions to organizational theory and management philosophy, her work focused more on topics such as conflict resolution, power dynamics, and the integration of individuals within organizations. The main contributors to the TQM approach include Philip B. Crosby, Joseph M. Juran, and W. Edwards Deming, who are widely recognized for their theories and methodologies related to quality management and continuous improvement.

22. **(D):** Among the options provided, "System Monitoring" is not typically considered a phase involved in the development of a system in System Analysis. The phases involved in system development typically include System Analysis, System Design, and System Implementation, which encompass activities such as requirement gathering, designing the system architecture, and implementing the system respectively. System Monitoring, while important for the ongoing management and maintenance of the system, is not typically considered a distinct phase in the development process.

23. **(D):** Organizing is the process of structuring and arranging resources, including people, tasks, and activities, in a coordinated manner to achieve organizational goals effectively and efficiently. It involves determining the roles, responsibilities, and relationships among individuals and groups within the organization, as well as establishing communication channels and decision-making processes. Through organizing, managers create formal structures, such as departments, teams, and hierarchies, to clarify reporting relationships and ensure clarity in job assignments.

24. **(A):** Browne Issue System is a system, developed by Nina Browne in 1895, utilizes two cards to streamline the borrowing and returning process. One card is issued to the borrower, typically containing their identification information and borrowing privileges. The other card, known as a book card, is kept inside a pocket within the

book itself. This book card holds essential details about the specific item, such as title, author, and call number. When a borrower wishes to check out a book, the librarian retrieves both the borrower's card and the corresponding book card from the pocket.

25. **(C):** Microwaves utilize unidirectional antennas to send signals in one direction, making them particularly efficient for point-to-point communication over long distances. These waves have relatively short wavelengths, ranging from millimeters to meters, allowing for high-frequency transmission. Microwaves are commonly employed in various communication systems, including microwave communication links and satellite communication. In microwave communication links, directional antennas are used to transmit signals between two fixed points, such as communication towers or satellite ground stations, enabling high-speed data transfer over long distances with minimal signal loss.

26. **(B):** The Domain Name System (DNS) is a client-server application that translates domain names, which are user-friendly alphanumeric addresses, into corresponding IP addresses, which are numerical identifiers used by computers to communicate over the internet. DNS is a hierarchical and distributed naming system for computers, services, and other resources on the internet. It acts like a phonebook for the internet, translating human-readable domain names (like "google.com") into numerical IP addresses (like "142.250.184.196") that computers use to communicate. This translation allows users to access websites and online resources easily without needing to memorize complex IP addresses.

27. **(C):** An assembler is a software tool that translates a low-level assembly language program into machine code, which is the binary language understood by computer hardware. Assembly language is a human-readable mnemonic representation of machine code instructions, making it easier for programmers to write and understand code compared to directly working with binary instructions. The assembler processes the assembly language source code and generates the corresponding machine code, typically in the form of binary executable files or object files that can be further processed by a linker to create executable programs.

28. **(B):** Time and Date: While timestamps can be crucial for network troubleshooting or analysis, they are not typically embedded within individual data packets. Instead, timestamps are often associated with the overall data transfer process and recorded at specific points in the network (e.g., when a packet leaves a router or arrives at its destination). Therefore, sender's IP address, identity number (which could be a sequence number for tracking order within a larger data stream), and a header for identification are commonly found in data packets, while time and date are not essential components.

29. **(B):** The Indian National Scientific Documentation Centre (INSDOC) is considered a pioneer in library automation and is likely the first to use computers for library work in India. In 1964, INSDOC began using computers for information processing, including the IBM 1620 at IIT, Kanpur and Delhi University. In 1965, INSDOC computerized the author and subject indexes of "Indian Science Abstract". With the introduction of computers, INSDOC revolutionized library operations by automating various tasks such as cataloging, indexing, and document retrieval.

30. **(C):** The reading range of UHF tags is generally 3–5 meters. UHF (Ultra High Frequency) tags are a type of radio-frequency identification (RFID) tag that

use radio waves to wirelessly transmit data to readers or interrogators. UHF RFID technology is often used for tracking and identifying objects, assets, and individuals in various applications such as supply chain management, inventory tracking, access control, and logistics. The read range of RFID tags varies based on factors including: Type of tag, Type of reader, RFID frequency, and Interference in the surrounding environment or from other RFID tags and readers.

31. (A): JASPER (Journals Are Preserved for Ever), launched on World Preservation Day in 2020, is a collaborative effort between several key organizations in the scholarly communication landscape. Recognizing the importance of long-term archiving for open access journals, JASPER works to address the challenges faced by smaller publishers who may lack the resources or expertise to ensure the continued accessibility of their publications. Through partnerships with established digital preservation services like CLOCKSS and the Keepers Registry, JASPER provides a framework for open access journals to be deposited and maintained in secure, redundant archives.

32. (C): The German National Library of Economics, also known as the Leibniz Information Centre for Economics (ZBW), manages Econstar. This service is dedicated to the permanent preservation of literature in economics and related fields, ensuring continued access to valuable scholarly resources for researchers, students, and the general public. Econstar provides a platform for economists and researchers to deposit their work, making it accessible to a global audience and safeguarding it from potential loss or data corruption.

33. (C): An interval scale is also called a cardinal scale. An interval scale is a measurement scale that uses numerical labeling with the same difference between consecutive measurements. Interval scales have equal units of measurement, which allows researchers to interpret the order of scale scores and the distance between them. For example, temperature in Celsius or Fahrenheit is at an interval scale because zero is not the lowest possible temperature.

34. (B): Fundamental research, also known as basic or pure research, is primarily concerned with advancing knowledge and understanding in a particular field without specific practical applications in mind. It aims to explore fundamental principles, theories, and concepts to develop a deeper understanding of natural phenomena or social phenomena. Fundamental research often involves systematic investigation, experimentation, or analysis to generate new insights, theories, or hypotheses that contribute to the body of knowledge in a discipline.

35. (A): Stratified sampling is actually a probability sampling method, not a non-probability sampling method. It involves dividing the population into subgroups or strata based on certain characteristics, such as age, gender, or income level. Samples are then randomly selected from each stratum in proportion to their representation in the population, ensuring that each subgroup is adequately represented in the sample. This method allows for greater precision and control in estimating population parameters compared to simple random sampling.

36. (A): When the dependent variable (the variable being affected) is influenced by factors other than the independent variable (the variable being manipulated), the relationship between the two is said to be confounded by extraneous variables. They can influence the dependent variable independently of the independent variable, making it difficult to isolate the true effect of the independent variable on the dependent variable. As a result, the observed relationship between the independent and dependent variables may be misleading or even nonexistent.

37. (D): AGRIS is a centralized system for international cooperation in agricultural information. It functions as a global repository for bibliographic information on agricultural science and technology. Participating countries submit references to agricultural literature to a central database managed by the AGRIS Coordinating Centre, which is located at the Food and Agriculture Organization (FAO) headquarters in Rome, Italy. This centralized approach ensures consistency in data formatting and indexing, enabling users to search for information from a variety of sources using a single platform.

38. (A): The Indian Journal of Medical Sciences (IJMS) is the first medical periodical in India that is not sponsored by any society or association. It is an open-access, peer-reviewed journal that publishes high-quality articles in the fields of medicine and allied sciences, with an emphasis on scientific investigations. The IJMS is published quarterly and is intended to be suitable for primary care physicians and general practitioners. The journal served as a vital avenue for disseminating medical knowledge and advancements in various fields of medicine to practitioners, researchers, and students across India and beyond.

39. (B): The library shall keep itself abstained from carrying out the policy of UNESCO's public library Manifesto" was not included in the Terms of Reference in the Project Agreement between UNESCO and India for the development of public library services in India in May 1951. The Terms of Reference outlined specific objectives and guidelines for the development of public library services, emphasizing the provision of library services for the people, establishment as a model for public libraries in India, and expansion to other countries with similar development needs.

40. (C): The Medical Library Association (MLA) primarily focuses on supporting and developing the skills of health information professionals (HIPs), librarians, and information specialists who work in healthcare settings. These professionals play a vital role in ensuring the quality and accessibility of health information for patients, healthcare providers, researchers, and the public. The MLA provides a range of training programs, educational resources, and professional development opportunities to equip HIPs with the knowledge and expertise they need to effectively manage, organize, disseminate, and analyze health information.

41. (C):

(*a*) The American Library Association (ALA) adopted a professional code of ethics in 1938, known as the "Library Bill of Rights". This document outlines principles of intellectual freedom, equitable access to information, privacy rights, and ethical responsibilities of librarians.

(*c*) The United Kingdom established its professional ethical code for librarianship in 1983. This code, similar to those of ALA and ILA, outlines principles of professional conduct, intellectual freedom, confidentiality, and equitable access to information for librarians in the UK.

(*d*) The American Association for Information Science (ASIS) did publish a draft ethical code in 1990, and it was specifically focused on librarianship. ASIS is a professional organization primarily focused on information science, encompassing various disciplines and libraries.

42. (A):

(*a*) **Obligation of first law:** If we interpret the "First Law" as a general principle related to library services, it could indeed underscore the importance of making library resources accessible and known to the community through effective public relations and publicity efforts.

(*b*) **Obligation of second law:** It emphasizes the need for personalized services and resources tailored to individual library users. Public relations and publicity could contribute to understanding patrons' needs and interests better, aligning services and resources accordingly.

(*c*) **Obligation of third law:** Public relations and publicity efforts could aid in promoting specific collections, programs, or events that resonate with patrons' interests, ensuring that library resources effectively meet users' needs.

43. (B):

(*b*) **Expected User:** This refers to someone who shows an interest or intention to use a particular information service. This could involve browsing a library website, attending a workshop on information literacy, or expressing a need for information in a specific subject area.

(*c*) **Actual User:** This is someone who has demonstrably used an information service. This might involve borrowing books from a library, conducting a database search, or attending a library program.

(*d*) **Beneficiary User:** This describes someone who derives a measurable benefit from using an information service. This benefit could be increased knowledge, improved skills, problem-solving assistance, or enhanced decision-making based on the information obtained.

44. (A):

(*a*) **Merriam-Webster's Geographical Dictionary:** First published in 1949, Merriam-Webster's Geographical Dictionary is a well-regarded reference source for geographical information. It contains entries on a wide range of geographical features, including countries, cities, mountains, rivers, and lakes.

(*b*) **Gazetteer of India:** The Gazetteer of India, the first volume of which is titled "Country and People", is a comprehensive resource for information about India's geography, history, economics, politics, and culture.

(*c*) **Rand McNally's New International Atlas:** Rand McNally is a well-known company that has been publishing maps and atlases for over 150 years. Their New International Atlas is a comprehensive collection of maps of the world, including political maps, physical maps, and thematic maps.

45. (C):

(*a*) **First edition was published in 1903-04:** This statement aligns with historical records. The first edition of Encyclopedia Americana was published between 1903 and 1904.

(*c*) **Contains short articles on specific subjects:** Encyclopedia Americana is known for containing concise entries on a wide range of topics. These articles provide an overview of a subject and often serve as a springboard for further research.

(*d*) **Most of the articles are signed by contributors:** A hallmark of Encyclopedia Americana is that many of its articles are written and signed by recognized scholars and experts in their respective fields. This lends credibility and authority to the information presented.

46. (B):

(*a*) **Represent a researcher's perspective:** Primary sources are firsthand accounts or objects created at the time of the event or topic being studied. They represent the researcher's perspective but rather offer raw information.

(*b*) **Document events, people and viewpoint of particular time:** This is a key characteristic of primary sources. They provide firsthand accounts or evidence from the period under study, offering valuable insights into the perspectives and experiences of people during that time.

(*c*) **Widely scattered:** Primary sources can be scattered across various locations like libraries, archives, historical societies, museums, or even private collections. Finding these sources often requires extensive research and exploration.

47. (B):

(*a*) **Orientation courses and lectures:** These structured sessions provide an introduction to library layout, resources, services, and search strategies.

(*b*) **Conducting Library tours:** Guided tours allow users to explore the library physically, learn about different sections and collections, and gain insights into how to locate materials.

(*c*) **Reader-Librarian dialogue while rendering the reference service:** Interactive communication during reference interactions helps users clarify their information needs, identify relevant resources, and develop effective search strategies.

(*d*) **Informal meetings at educational or cultural functions:** These interactions promote library services and are specifically designed for library instruction.

48. (A):

(*a*) **Preparation:** Librarians or information professionals need to be well-prepared with a broad knowledge base and expertise in using various information resources to effectively conduct comprehensive searches for LRRS.

(*b*) **Service:** LRRS involves active engagement with the user to understand their information need and then delving into a wider range of resources to fulfill that need. This can involve using specialized databases, contacting subject experts, or consulting hard-to-find materials.

(*c*) **Assimilation:** Understanding the user's information need accurately is crucial for LRRS. The librarian needs to grasp the user's query, the context of their information seeking, and the specific type of information they require.

49. (C):

(*a*) **Reduction in all round cost:** Resource sharing allows libraries to avoid purchasing the same resources, reducing overall acquisition, processing, and maintenance costs.

(*b*) **Avoidance of duplication of resources, processing and maintenance costs:** This directly aligns with the objective of resource sharing. Libraries can leverage existing collections in other libraries instead of duplicating their own holdings.

(*d*) **Provision of greater access to information resources to a wide category of users:** Enhanced access to a broader collection of resources is a key benefit of resource sharing. It empowers users to find information beyond the limitations of a single library's collection.

(*e*) **Development of specialized areas of collection building:** Libraries can collaborate and specialize in collecting materials in specific subject areas.

This allows them to build stronger collections in their areas of expertise while relying on resource sharing to meet user needs outside those areas.

50. (C):

(*b*) **Peek-a-boo System:** This system uses cards with holes corresponding to indexing terms. Users can physically superimpose the cards to identify documents indexed with specific combinations of terms, reflecting the post-coordinate principle of combining terms during searching.

(*c*) **Edge-notched card:** Edge-notched card systems are developed based on the principles of post-coordinate indexing. Users can combine these cards to create complex queries, similar to the post-coordinate indexing approach.

(*d*) **Dual Directories:** Dual directories are also based on the principles of post-coordinate indexing. They consist of two separate directories—one for terms and one for document identifiers. Users can cross-reference these directories to locate documents containing specific terms.

51. (B):

(*a*) **Pagination:** The number of pages (or volumes) in a publication is a crucial element of the collation area. It provides users with information about the physical extent of the book.

(*b*) **Illustration Statement:** Information about illustrations, such as the number, type (e.g., plates, maps, figures), and presence or absence of colour printing, is valuable for users who may be looking for specific visual content within the publication.

(*c*) **Size:** The physical dimensions of the publication, typically expressed in height and width (e.g., centimeters), are another key element of the collation area.

52. (B):

(*a*) **Purpose:** Understanding the purpose of the abstract is crucial for proper abstracting. The abstract should succinctly convey the main objectives or goals of the original document.

(*b*) **Scope:** Proper abstracting involves defining the scope of the abstract, which includes determining the breadth and depth of the coverage. This ensures that the abstract accurately represents the content of the original document within specified boundaries.

(*d*) **Conclusions:** Including the main conclusions or findings of the original document in the abstract is important for summarizing its key insights. This helps readers quickly grasp the main outcomes or implications of the document.

53. (B):

(*a*) **Helps librarian to replace the essential lost books:** By identifying lost or missing books, librarians can take necessary steps to replace them, ensuring the completeness of the library's collection.

(*b*) **Reveals the lost books:** Stocktaking helps to identify any lost or missing books in the library's collection, allowing librarians to take appropriate action to recover or replace them.

(*c*) **Helps the library authorities to ascertain whether the library staff is dishonest, negligent, and careless:** It helps detect issues such as theft, negligence, or carelessness among library staff. Identifying such issues allows authorities to address them effectively.

54. (B):

(*b*) **Principal duties to be performed and responsibilities involved are outlined:** A core function of a job description is to clearly outline the main tasks, duties, and responsibilities associated with the position. This helps potential candidates understand the expectations of the role.

(*c*) **Requisite materials, equipments, machinery and tools etc. are listed:** Job descriptions may specify the tools, equipment, or software used in performing the job duties. This can help applicants assess if they have the necessary skills and experience to work with these tools.

(*d*) **Conditions of work i.e. surroundings the time of work etc. are stated:** The work environment, schedule, and any potential physical demands associated with the job are often included in a job description. This allows candidates to understand the work context and if the position aligns with their preferences.

55. (A):

(*a*) **Date slip:** A date slip is commonly used in library charging systems to indicate the due date for returning a book. It typically contains the borrower's name, the book's title, and the date it is due to be returned.

(*c*) **Book pocket:** A book pocket is a small envelope or pocket attached to the inside cover of a book. It is used to hold the borrower's library card or borrower's information, allowing for easy identification and tracking of the book's circulation history.

(*d*) **Book card:** A book card is a small card typically kept in the book pocket or affixed to the inside cover of a book. It contains information about the book, such as its title, author, call number, and circulation history.

56. (B):

(*b*) **Kernel:** The kernel is the core program of an operating system (OS). The kernel acts as an interface between the hardware and software components, managing resources like memory, processors, and devices.

(*c*) **Nucleus:** "Nucleus" is another term sometimes used to refer to the core resident part of an operating system. It essentially signifies the same functionality as the kernel.

57. (B):

(*a*) **Two UAs (User Agents):** User Agents are the software applications used by individuals to send, receive, compose, and manage email messages. When the sender and receiver are on different systems, each system would typically have its own User Agent.

(*b*) **Pair of MTAs (Mail Transfer Agents):** Mail Transfer Agents are responsible for routing and transferring email messages between mail servers. When the sender and receiver are on different systems, the message needs to pass through the respective Mail Transfer Agents of each system to be sent over the internet.

58. (A):

(*a*) **University of Liverpool:** This university provided expertise in digital humanities, augmented reality development, or historical research related to Kolkata.

(*b*) **Jadavpur University:** This university in Kolkata offered valuable insights into the city's history and cultural heritage, potentially contributing content or collaborating on the app's development.

(*c*) **British Library:** The British Library provided access to historical archives, photographs, or other resources related to Kolkata that were incorporated into the AR experience.

59. (C):

(*a*) **Web content management system (WCMS):** This is a widely used type of CMS designed to manage the creation, editing, and publishing of content on websites. It allows users with limited technical expertise to create and update web pages without needing to write code.

(*c*) **Collaborative content management system (CCMS):** This type of CMS focuses on facilitating collaboration among multiple users in creating and managing content. It allows for features like document version control, user permissions, and workflow management, making it suitable for teams working on shared projects.

(*d*) **Digital Research Repository system:** Digital research repositories share some functionality. They are systems used by universities, research institutions, or other organizations to store, manage, and disseminate digital research outputs like scholarly articles, data sets, or technical reports.

60. (C):

(*a*) **National Library of New Zealand:** The National Library serves as the custodian of New Zealand's documentary heritage and plays a central role in the NDHA program.

(*c*) **Ex Libris Group:** Ex Libris is a company that provides library management software and technology solutions. They likely partnered with the National Library to develop and implement the NDHA's technical infrastructure.

(*e*) **Sun Microsystems:** Sun Microsystems (now part of Oracle) was a computer hardware and software company. It's possible that Sun Microsystems provided hardware or software support for the NDHA in its early stages.

61. (A):

(*a*) **Terminology disparity that exists between that library and web-based standards:** Libraries often use specialized terminology and controlled vocabularies that may not align perfectly with web-based standards used in linked data.

(*b*) **Complexity of linked data technologies such as RDF/XML:** Linked data technologies, including RDF (Resource Description Framework) and XML (eXtensible Markup Language), can be complex and require specialized expertise for implementation and maintenance.

62. (D):

(*a*) **R is an interpreted language:** R code is interpreted line by line at runtime, unlike compiled languages that require pre-compilation of the entire program.

(*b*) **Users can access it through a command line interpreter:** The core functionality of R is accessed through a command-line interface.

(*c*) **R's capabilities are extended through user-created packages:** One of the strengths of R is the vast collection of user-contributed packages available on the Comprehensive R Archive Network (CRAN).

63. (A):

(*a*) **Arabic:** The library is known especially for its Arabic and Persian manuscripts. Arabic was a language of scholarship and administration during the Mughal era, and the Nawabs of Rampur who built the library were patrons of Islamic culture.

(*d*) **Sanskrit:** Sanskrit is a classical Indian language with a rich literary and philosophical tradition. The library holds manuscripts of Hindu religious texts or other works in Sanskrit.

(*e*) **Urdu:** Urdu is a Hindustani language that developed during the Mughal period. The Nawabs of Rampur used Urdu for courtly communication and documentation, and the library possess historical documents or literary works in this language.

64. (B):

(*b*) **It is published by the University of Chicago Press:** The University of

Chicago Press has been publishing the Chicago Manual of Style since its inception.

(*c*) **It uses notes and bibliography style:** The Chicago Manual of Style offers two main documentation styles: notes and bibliography (NB) and author-date. The NB style uses footnotes or endnotes to provide citations within the text, and a separate bibliography list for referencing all sources.

(*d*) **Title of the first edition was, "Manual of Style":** This is also correct. The first edition, published in 1906, was simply titled "A Manual of Style".

65. (D):

(*b*) **Faster than other methods of interview:** Telephonic interviews can be faster to conduct compared to in-person interviews, especially when scheduling interviews with geographically dispersed candidates.

(*c*) **Replies can be recorded:** With the interviewee's consent, telephonic interviews can be recorded. This allows the interviewer to focus on the conversation without taking detailed notes and can be helpful for later review.

(*d*) **Questions have to be short and simple:** Since telephonic interviews lack visual cues and rely solely on voice communication, questions tend to be more concise and direct compared to in-person interviews.

66. (C)	**67. (A)**	**68. (D)**
69. (C)	**70. (B)**	**71. (D)**
72. (B)	**73. (B)**	**74. (B)**
75. (D)		

76. (A):

(*a*) **Wisdom:** It involves applying knowledge and experience to make sound judgments and decisions. It goes beyond mere knowledge and understanding and requires a deeper level of reflection and insight.

(*d*) **Knowledge:** By analyzing and interpreting information, we gain knowledge and understanding of the subject matter. Knowledge answers the "how" and "why" questions.

(*c*) **Information:** Data is processed, organized, and contextualized to become information. Information answers basic questions like "who", "what", "where", and "when".

(*b*) **Data:** This is the raw, unprocessed information collected from various sources. It represents the foundation of the knowledge pyramid.

77. (D):

(*c*) When a book is borrowed, the book card is removed from the book and placed in the charging tray behind the appropriate due date card, typically sorted by call number (a classification system for library materials).

(*a*) The due date slip is part of the borrower's ticket or pocket. The librarian stamps the due date on this slip, indicating when the borrowed materials need to be returned.

(*d*) The librarian takes the book card from the charging tray and inserts it into a pocket or slot on the borrower's ticket. This keeps track of which books each borrower has checked out.

(*b*) The librarian might record the call number of the borrowed book and the borrower's identification number in a daily circulation log. This serves as a secondary record of borrowing activity.

78. (A):

(*c*) The Joint Information Systems Committee (JISC) was established on April 1, 1993. JISC is a membership community that supports higher education, research, and post-16 education.

(*d*) SciCentral was founded in 1997 and is headquartered in Morrisville, NC. The company is a private publisher that compiles research news from reputable sources.

(*b*) PLOS was founded in 2001 to accelerate progress in science and medicine by leading a transformation in research communication.

(*a*) Intute was formed in July 2006 after the merger of the eight semi-autonomous "hubs" that formed the Resource Discovery Network (RDN).

79. (A):

(*c*) **Selection:** The SDI system gathers information about the user's interests, preferred topics, keywords, or sources to create a user profile that guides the information selection process.

(*b*) **Feedback:** After the selection criteria are set up, the user might be presented with some initial information retrieved based on those criteria. They can then provide feedback on the relevance of this information.

(*d*) **Modification:** Based on the user's feedback and the system's performance in retrieving relevant information, adjustments might be made to the selection criteria. The goal is to optimize the system to deliver the most useful information to the user.

(*a*) **Notification:** Once the selection criteria are refined and the system is actively monitoring information sources, the user is notified when new content matching their interests is identified.

80. (A):

(*b*) **Verbal Representation:** The process starts with creating a clear and concise phrase (verbal representation) for each approach term. This phrase accurately captures the essence of the concept and helps users understand the content being indexed.

(*a*) **Display of Components:** Once the verbal representations are formulated, they are displayed alongside the corresponding approach terms. This is often done in a table format.

(*c*) **Approach Terms:** These are the key subject areas or concepts that the document deals with. Identifying these terms is crucial for creating meaningful index entries as they form the foundation for the entire indexing process.

(*e*) **Cross Reference:** After the initial index entries are established, cross-references are created. These are additional entries that point users to related terms or concepts within the index.

(*d*) **Alphabetical Arrangement:** Finally, all the index entries, including the main entries (approach terms + verbal representations) and cross-references, are arranged alphabetically based on the chosen heading term.

81. (D):

(*e*) **Prevention:** This is the ideal stage, which involves activities like building seawalls to prevent floods, enforcing earthquake-resistant building codes, or raising public awareness about fire safety.

(*a*) **Mitigation:** This involves strengthening infrastructure, creating evacuation plans, or stockpiling resources in preparation for potential emergencies.

(*d*) **Preparedness:** It involves training emergency personnel, conducting drills, and preparing emergency kits for individuals and communities.

(*c*) **Response:** This stage involves the immediate actions taken during and after a disaster which includes search and rescue operations, providing emergency shelter and food, and restoring essential services.

(*b*) **Recovery:** It involves reconstruction of damaged infrastructure, providing financial assistance to affected communities, and supporting social and economic recovery efforts.

82. (D):

(*d*) Zotero was first released in October 2006 as an add-on for the Firefox web browser, and then became a standalone application in 2011.

(*a*) Research Gate was launched on May 23, 2008. Research Gate is a social network and database for researchers from all fields of science.

(*b*) ORCID, or Open Researcher and Contributor ID, was incorporated as a nonprofit organization in Delaware, USA in August 2010.

(*c*) Publons was founded in 2012 by Andrew Preston and Daniel Johnston. Publons helps researchers gain credit for peer review and recognition for their contributions to scholarship throughout their career.

83. (A):

(*b*) **Prepare Data pattern:** In this step, the data is preprocessed, cleaned, and transformed to extract patterns or features relevant to the analysis.

(*d*) **Select of suitable databases from data warehouse:** After preparing the data, suitable databases from the data warehouse are selected to be used in the analysis.

(*a*) **Select suitable algorithm:** Once the data is ready and databases are selected, an appropriate data mining algorithm is chosen based on the objectives and characteristics of the dataset.

(*c*) **Choose available analytical package:** Finally, an available analytical package or software tool is chosen to apply the selected algorithm and perform the analysis.

84. (C):

(*d*) **Selecting the problem:** This is the initial step where the researcher identifies and selects the problem to be investigated through experimental research.

(*e*) **Selection of setting:** After identifying the problem, the researcher selects the appropriate setting or environment where the experiment will be conducted.

(*a*) **Pilot study:** Before conducting the main experiment, a pilot study is often conducted to test the feasibility and effectiveness of the research design and methodology.

(*c*) **Research design:** Once the pilot study is completed and any necessary adjustments are made, the researcher finalizes the research design, including the experimental variables, treatments, and procedures.

(*b*) **Conducting the experiment:** Finally, the main experiment is conducted according to the finalized research design, and data is collected for analysis.

85. (B):

(*b*) **Review Committee on Library Science (1961):** Chaired by Dr. S.R. Ranganathan, this committee recommended standards for teaching, examination, and research in library schools.

(*d*) **Education Commission (1964):** Also known as the Kothari Commission on Secondary Education, this commission was formed to evaluate India's educational system.

(*a*) **Mehrotra Committee (1983):** This committee recommended that 10% of a college's budget be allocated to library development.

(*c*) **Committee on National Network System for Universities/Libraries (1988):** This committee was formed in 1988.

86. (B): Both the assertion and reason are correct. The process of archiving and preserving digital information resources indeed involves complexity and resource-intensive efforts. Additionally, it applies to both born-digital content (created in digital format) and digitized information (converted from analog to digital format). However, the reason does not directly explain why archiving and preserving digital information resources are complex and resource-intensive.

87. (A): Statement I is accurate. A website is essentially a collection of webpages, which are digital documents created using a markup language like HTML. These webpages can contain text, images, videos, and other multimedia elements.

Statement II is also correct. The World Wide Web (WWW) refers to all of these publicly accessible websites that are interconnected by hyperlinks. Hyperlinks are essentially links embedded within webpages that, when clicked, take the user to another webpage, potentially on a completely different website.

88. (B): Assertion (A) is correct: When a task is delegated, it creates a connection between the delegator (who assigns the task) and the delegate (who receives the task). This fosters both horizontal coordination (between colleagues working on related tasks) and vertical coordination (between supervisor and subordinate).

Reason (R) is also correct: Delegation is about empowering others and improving efficiency. Someone shouldn't be afraid to delegate simply because there's a chance of a mistake. However, it's true that the delegator remains ultimately accountable for the task's outcome.

While both statements are true, the reason doesn't directly explain the assertion. Delegation creates coordination for various reasons, and risk assessment is just one aspect to consider when delegating effectively.

89. (A): Statement I is correct: Electronic reference sources are generally updated more frequently than print sources. This is because online resources can be easily modified and uploaded without the need for reprinting physical materials.

Statement II is also correct: While some electronic resources require subscriptions or access fees, the infrastructure needed to use them and it is necessarily expensive. Many libraries and institutions offer free access to online databases and resources.

90. (A): Statement I: Modern libraries go beyond just housing books. They offer a variety of resources, including electronic databases, internet access, multimedia resources, and programs and services that address the information needs of their communities. These needs can be educational, professional, recreational, or related to current events.

Statement II: Libraries are social institutions. They serve as public spaces where people can access information, gather for events, and connect with others. They play a vital role in fostering literacy, promoting lifelong learning, and providing a platform for social interaction and community engagement.

91. (C): The passage specifically mentions Hinduism, Buddhism, and Jainism as the prevalent religions in ancient India and the basis for religious education at that time. Christianity is not mentioned in the context of ancient Indian universities.

92. (A): The passage discusses how ancient Indian universities were destroyed by invaders, such as the White Huns and Bakhtiyar Khilji. This highlights how outside invasions posed a challenge to the flourishing educational system.

93. (D): Sultan Iltutmish had destroyed Ujjaini in 1235, bringing an end to a major center of knowledge for mathematics, literature, philosophy, and astronomy. The White Huns (Ephthalites) had destroyed Takshashila around 460 AD, disrupting the educational legacy of the Hindu Buddhist University, which was likely established in the 6th century BC. Finally, Bakhtiyar Khilji sacked and burned Nalanda University and its vast library of 9 million manuscripts in 1193.

94. (C): Nalanda was in Bihar, Ujjaini in Madhya Pradesh, and Takshashila in present-day Pakistan. These ancient centers of learning attracted scholars from across Asia and made significant contributions to various fields of study, including Buddhism, mathematics, literature, and astronomy.

95. (C): British policy in nineteenth-century colonial India promoted a cheap model for education by introducing English as the medium of instruction and making it the official language for government business. This facilitated the spread of Western education and ideas, which was a key aspect of British colonial control and influence.

96. (B): Syed Karim, as mentioned in the passage, is the individual who conceived the innovative idea of Outernet. He is described as a library science dropout and the founder CEO of Outernet Inc. The Outernet works by receiving data from a network of ground stations and transmitting it via satellites to users worldwide.

97. (C): The Outernet, as described in the passage, is envisioned to be effective for internet-less users by allowing them to request specific content by sending SMS text messages or letters to its operators. This means that users without internet access can still communicate their content preferences and needs to the Outernet operators, who will then prioritize and provide the requested information via the satellite broadcast system.

98. (D): The passage mentions Google's Project Loon, which involves launching a series of balloons into the stratosphere to provide internet access to remote and rural areas by beaming internet signals down to base stations. This initiative aims to reach people who are unable to access the internet by traditional means and to bridge the digital divide by providing internet facilities to underserved regions.

99. (A): The passage describes the plan to launch hundreds of low-cost miniature satellites, known as cubesats, to create the Outernet. The purpose of the Outernet is to establish a wireless connection to the web that is available for free to every person in the world. This initiative aims to provide universal access to information by broadcasting data from feeders to satellites, which then transmit it to users worldwide, bypassing censorship laws prevalent in many countries.

100. (C): According to the passage, cubesats receive data from a network of ground stations around the world and transmit this information on a loop until new information is received. This means that the data transmitted by cubesats is continuously circulated until updated or replaced with new information.

Previous Years' Paper

National Testing Agency (NTA)

UGC-NET Junior Research Fellowship & Assistant Professor Eligibility Exam

Library and Information Science, June-2023

(Exam held on 13-06-2023)

PAPER-II

1. The sector device is a device for:

A. Decreasing the capacity of an array with the aid of a digit

B. Increasing the capacity of a chain with the aid of an empty digit

C. Decreasing the capacity of a chain

D. Increasing the capacity of an array with the aid of an empty digit

2. The Law of Scattering was propounded by:

A. John J. Hubert

B. M.G. Kendall

C. Samuel Clement Bradford

D. G.K. Ziff

3. Match List-I with List-II.

List-I (Library Automation Software)	List-II (Unique Features)
(*a*) Maitreyee	(*i*) Based on INGRES
(*b*) Sanjay	(*ii*) Uses Postgre SQL
(*c*) libeys	(*iii*) Based on CDS/ISIS
(*d*) e-Granthalaya Version 40	(*iv*) Available-on different OSs

Choose the **correct** answer from the options given below:

	(*a*)	(*b*)	(*c*)	(*d*)
A.	(*ii*)	(*i*)	(*iv*)	(*iii*)
B.	(*ii*)	(*iii*)	(*iv*)	(*i*)
C.	(*i*)	(*iii*)	(*iv*)	(*ii*)
D.	(*iii*)	(*ii*)	(*iv*)	(*i*)

4. Which of the following elements are involved in Scientific Management?

(*a*) Force more on non-economic factors

(*b*) Science instead of rules of thumb

(*c*) Particular view of human behaviour

(*d*) Maximum output instead of restricted output

(*e*) The development of each person to his/her greatest efficiency

Choose the **correct** answer from the options given below:

A. (*a*), (*b*) and (*c*) only

B. (*b*), (*c*) and (*e*) only

C. (*c*), (*d*) and (*e*) only

D. (*b*), (*d*) and (*e*) only

5. Given below are two statements; one is labelled as Assertion (A) and other is labelled as Reason (R).

Assertion (A): AI technology usage in the library can allow library resources to be virtually reimagined.

Reason (R): Reimagination can't help the library to explore new ways to meet customer needs and support academic activities of anyone from anywhere.

In the light of the above statements. Choose the **correct** answer from the options given below:

A. Both (A) and (R) are true and (R) is the correct explanation of (A)
B. Both (A) and (R) are true, but (R) is not the correct explnation of (A)
C. (A) is true, but (R) is false
D. (A) is false, but (R) is true

6. Which of the following are subsystems of the library system, as identified by Hays and Becker?

(*a*) Acquisition Control
(*b*) Information Retrieval
(*c*) Serials Control
(*d*) Circulation Control

Choose the **correct** answer from the options given below:

A. (*a*), (*b*) and (*d*) only
B. (*a*), (*c*) and (*d*) only
C. (*b*), (*c*) and (*d*) only
D. (*a*), (*b*) and (*c*) only

7. DMCA stand for:

A. Digital Media Copyright Act
B. Digital Medium Copyright Act
C. Digital Millennium Copyright Act
D. Direct Millennium Copyright Act

8. Match List-I with List-II:

List-I (Description)	List-II (Year)
(*a*) Press & Registration of Book Act	(*i*) 1979
(*b*) Raja Ram Mohun Roy Library Foundation	(*ii*) 1919
(*c*) All India Public Library Association	(*iii*) 1972
(*d*) West Bengal Public Library Act	(*iv*) 1867

Choose the **correct** answer from the options given below:

	(*a*)	(*b*)	(*c*)	(*d*)
A.	(*iii*)	(*i*)	(*iv*)	(*ii*)
B.	(*iv*)	(*ii*)	(*iii*)	(*i*)
C.	(*iv*)	(*i*)	(*ii*)	(*iii*)
D.	(*iv*)	(*iii*)	(*ii*)	(*i*)

9. Arrange the five laws of library science as re-ordered by OCLC:

(*a*) Book are for use
(*b*) Every reader, his/her book
(*c*) Every book, its reader
(*d*) Save the time of the reader
(*e*) A library is a growing organism

Choose the **correct** answer from the options given below:

A. (*d*), (*b*), (*a*), (*c*), (*e*)
B. (*b*), (*c*), (*a*), (*e*), (*d*)
C. (*c*), (*b*), (*d*), (*a*), (*e*)
D. (*e*), (*d*), (*a*), (*b*), (*c*)

10. Who has said "Information is essentially found in answer to questions that begin with such words as who, what, where, when and how many?"

A. Gene Bellinger
B. T.S. Eliot
C. Ingetraut Dahlberg
D. Ackoff Russell

11. What is exact fieldname corresponding to the label 'LOC' in relation to LISA database?

A. Location
B. Library of Congress
C. Local Citation
D. Local Catalogue

12. Which of the following are true in the case of Patent Lens:

(*a*) It is open access
(*b*) It is a free full-text database
(*c*) It cover patents only published in India
(*d*) It covers patents and applications of WIPO, USPTO and EPO

Choose the **correct** answer from the options given below:

A. (*a*), (*c*) and (*d*) only
B. (*a*), (*b*) and (*d*) only
C. (*b*), (*c*) and (*d*) only
D. (*a*), (*b*) and (*c*) only

13. Which one of the following is a general assistive technology for users with all types of disability?

A. DAISY format readers
B. Reading software
C. Screen magnification software
D. Talking typing teachers-pro

14. Which of the following are true in relation of the Five Laws of Library Science?

(*a*) Ranganathan conceived the five laws in 1924
(*b*) First law was finalised only after the remaining four laws were framed
(*c*) Seconds law desires free book service for all
(*d*) Third law calls for closaed access

Choose the **correct** answer from the options given below:

A. (*a*), (*c*) and (*d*) only
B. (*a*), (*b*) and (*c*) only
C. (*a*), (*b*) and (*d*) only
D. (*b*), (*c*) and (*d*) only

15. Match List-I with List-II:

List-I (Layers of OSI Model)	List-II (Function)
(*a*) Physical layer	(*i*) Responsible for the delivery of a message from one process to another
(*b*) Transport layer	(*ii*) Responsible for dialog control and synchronization
(*c*) Session layer	(*iii*) Responsible for movement of individual bits from one node to next
(*d*) Application layer	(*iv*) Responsible for providing services to user

Choose the **correct** answer from the options given below:

	(*a*)	(*b*)	(*c*)	(*d*)
A.	(*ii*)	(*iii*)	(*i*)	(*iv*)
B.	(*iii*)	(*i*)	(*ii*)	(*iv*)
C.	(*iii*)	(*i*)	(*iv*)	(*ii*)
D.	(*ii*)	(*iii*)	(*iv*)	(*i*)

16. Sequence the following in the order of their inception:

(*a*) Internet-based communication
(*b*) Written communication
(*c*) Mass communication
(*d*) Telecommunication
(*e*) Oral communication

Choose the **correct** answer from the options given below:

A. (*a*), (*b*), (*d*), (*c*), (*e*)
B. (*a*), (*b*), (*c*), (*d*), (*e*)
C. (*e*), (*b*), (*c*), (*d*), (*a*)
D. (*b*), (*c*), (*d*), (*e*), (*a*)

17. Match List-I with List-II:

List-I (Subject)	List-II (Modes of Formation)
(*a*) Astrophysics	(*i*) Fission
(*b*) History and Economics	(*ii*) Agglomeration
(*c*) The influence of Physics on Biology	(*iii*) Fusion
(*d*) Metaphysics	(*iv*) Loose Assemblage

Choose the **correct** answer from the options given below:

	(*a*)	(*b*)	(*c*)	(*d*)
A.	(*ii*)	(*iv*)	(*iii*)	(*i*)
B.	(*i*)	(*iii*)	(*ii*)	(*iv*)
C.	(*iii*)	(*ii*)	(*iv*)	(*i*)
D.	(*iv*)	(*i*)	(*ii*)	(*iii*)

18. The term Knowledge-based Economy was coined by:

A. World Summit on Information Society
B. National Knowledge Commission
C. Organization for Economic Cooperation and Development
D. The World Network Society

19. Which of the following internet protocols are used to connect to Internet through telephone lines?

(*a*) SLIP (*b*) HTTP

(*c*) PPP (*d*) HTTPS
(*e*) SSL

Choose the **correct** answer from the options given below:

A. (*a*) and (*e*) only B. (*a*) and (*c*) only
C. (*b*) and (*d*) only D. (*c*) and (*e*) only

20. In case of Li-Fi which of the following are true:

(*a*) Distance of communication is greater then Wi-Fi
(*b*) The term Li-Fi was coined by Harold Haas
(*c*) Latest Verasion of Li-Fi was released by Hedy Lamarr
(*d*) Li-Fi cannot work in high data density environment

Choose the **correct** answer from the options given below:

A. (*a*) and (*b*) only
B. (*b*) and (*c*) only
C. (*c*) and (*d*) only
D. (*a*) and (*d*) only

21. The standards for Bibliographic Information Interchange and Communication are:

(*a*) ISO 2709 (*b*) ISO 2907
(*c*) Z39.50 (*d*) Z39.71
(*e*) Z39.70

Choose the **correct** answer from the options given below:

A. (*a*), (*b*) and (*e*) only
B. (*b*), (*c*) and (*e*) only
C. (*a*), (*c*) and (*d*) only
D. (*c*), (*d*) and (*e*) only

22. Which of the following functions of University Library are given by Wilson and Tauber?

(*a*) Conservation of Knowledge
(*b*) Teaching
(*c*) Leisure Study
(*d*) Publication
(*e*) Follow-up study

Choose the **correct** answer from the options given below:

A. (*a*), (*c*) and (*d*) only
B. (*a*), (*b*) and (*d*) only
C. (*b*), (*c*) and (*d*) only
D. (*c*), (*d*) and (*e*) only

23. Arrange the following Acts related to IPR in descending order of their year of enactment:

(*a*) The Patents Act
(*b*) The Biological Act
(*c*) The Copyright Act
(*d*) The Trademarks Act
(*e*) The Designs Act

Choose the **correct** answer from the options given below:

A. (*a*), (*b*), (*d*), (*c*), (*e*)
B. (*b*), (*e*), (*d*), (*a*), (*c*)
C. (*c*), (*a*), (*d*), (*b*), (*e*)
D. (*d*), (*e*), (*a*), (*b*), (*c*)

24. Which of the following are true for ACRL information Literacy Competency Standards?

(*a*) Applicable to higher education sector
(*b*) Rescinded in 2006
(*c*) Proposes five standards with 20 performance indicators
(*d*) The information literate student determines the nature and extent of information needs
(*e*) Bloom's Taxonomy of Educational objectives have been considered to map the outcomes

Choose the **correct** answer from the options given below:

A. (*a*), (*d*) and (*e*) only
B. (*b*), (*c*) and (*d*) only
C. (*c*), (*d*) and (*e*) only
D. (*a*), (*b*) and (*c*) only

25. Given below are two statements:

Statement I: Knowledge Management (KM) is a multidiciplinary approach to achieve organizational objectives by making best use of knowledge.

Statement II: KM focuses on improved performances competitive advantage, innovation and continuous improvement of the organisation through knowledge sharing.

In light of the above statements, choose the **most appropriate** answer from the options given below:

A. Both Statement I and Statement II are true.

B. Both Statement I and Statement II are false.

C. Statement I is true, but Statement II is false.

D. Statement I is false, but Statement II is true.

26. Which of the following are related to Semantic web Technology.

(*a*) RDF

(*b*) Ontologies

(*c*) URL

(*d*) Cloud seedling

(*e*) RFID

Choose the **correct** answer from the options given below:

A. (*a*), (*b*) and (*d*) only

B. (*b*), (*c*) and (*d*) only

C. (*a*), (*b*) and (*c*) only

D. (*c*), (*d*) and (*e*) only

27. Match List-I with List-II:

List-I (Knowledge)	List-II (Epistemological propositions)
(*a*) Empiricism	(*i*) Derived from culture hermeneutics
(*b*) Rationalism	(*ii*) Derived from consideration of goals and their consequences
(*c*) Historicism	(*iii*) Derived from observation, perception and experience
(*d*) Pragmatism	(*iv*) Derived from employing logic and reason over sensory experience

Choose the **correct** answer from the options given below:

	(*a*)	(*b*)	(*c*)	(*d*)
A.	(*ii*)	(*iii*)	(*i*)	(*iv*)
B.	(*iii*)	(*iv*)	(*i*)	(*ii*)
C.	(*iv*)	(*i*)	(*iii*)	(*ii*)
D.	(*i*)	(*iii*)	(*ii*)	(*iv*)

28. Which of the following web portals is not outcome of the recommendation of National Knowledge Commission:

A. ntm.org.in B. niscpr.res.in

C. nkn.gov.in D. nhp.gov.in

29. The survey of people to obtain insight to the relationship between variables and new ideas relating to the research problem is known as ______.

A. Population survey

B. Pilot survey

C. Experience survey

D. Census survey

30. Who among the following have distinguished "Primary document" as one of the type of documents?

(*a*) S.R. Ranganathan

(*b*) C.W. Hanson

(*c*) Denis Grogan

(*d*) F.W. Lancaster

(*e*) S.C. Bradford

Choose the **correct** answer from the options given below:

A. (*a*) and (*b*) only

B. (*b*) and (*c*) only

C. (*c*) and (*d*) only

D. (*d*) and (*e*) only

31. From the view point of the unit of measurement, categorical variables are further categorized into ______.

(*a*) Conceptual Variable

(*b*) Constant Variable

(*c*) Polytomous Variable

(*d*) Dichotomous Variable

Choose the **correct** answer from the options given below:

A. (*a*), (*b*) and (*d*) only
B. (*b*), (*c*) and (*d*) only
C. (*a*), (*c*) and (*d*) only
D. (*a*), (*b*) and (*c*) only

32. Who had used the term 'document bibliography' on a specialised subject to cover both bibliography and document list?

A. G. Bhattacharyya
B. S.R. Ranganathan
C. F.W. Lancaster
D. W.C.B. Sayers

33. Match List-I with List-II:

List-I (Methods)	List-II (Explanation/ Relation)
(*a*) Stock taking method	(*i*) Per capita method
(*b*) Budgeting	(*ii*) Shelf register or shelf list special columns
(*c*) Charging method	(*iii*) PPBS
(*d*) Method of assessment of financial needs	(*iv*) Browne system

Choose the **correct** answer from the options given below:

	(*a*)	(*b*)	(*c*)	(*d*)
A.	(*i*)	(*iv*)	(*ii*)	(*iii*)
B.	(*ii*)	(*iii*)	(*iv*)	(*i*)
C.	(*iii*)	(*iv*)	(*i*)	(*ii*)
D.	(*iv*)	(*i*)	(*ii*)	(*iii*)

34. Match List-I with List-II:

List-I (Concepts)	List-II (Description)
(*a*) Trends	(*i*) Diagrams, Pictures, Photographs, Cartoons, Slides, Films, Recording
(*b*) Current Awareness Services	(*ii*) Saving time of the researchers by crossing over the language barrier
(*c*) Translation Service	(*iii*) Providing the content page of the recent issues of periodicals
(*d*) Illustrations	(*iv*) Significant development of the past year for particular field

Choose the **correct** answer from the options given below:

	(*a*)	(*b*)	(*c*)	(*d*)
A.	(*i*)	(*ii*)	(*iii*)	(*iv*)
B.	(*ii*)	(*iii*)	(*iv*)	(*i*)
C.	(*iii*)	(*iv*)	(*i*)	(*ii*)
D.	(*iv*)	(*iii*)	(*ii*)	(*i*)

35. Given below are two statements:

Statement I: History of libraries must be studied in ralation to the educational, social, economic and political institutions of a society.

Statement II: The library kept itself abstained from developing on interlinked relationship with the society.

In the light of the above statements, choose the most appropriate answer from the options given below:

A. Both Statement I and Statement II are true.
B. Both Statement I and Statement II are false.
C. Statement I is true, but Statement II is false.
D. Statement I is false, but Statement II is true.

36. FaaS stands for ______.

A. Fix-as-a-Service
B. Fault repair-as-a-Service
C. Function-as-a-Service
D. FRBR-as-a-Service

37. The speed of DDS depends upon:

(*a*) Methods of receiving request for document
(*b*) Methods of processing the request by DDS provider

(*c*) Mode of delivery of documents
(*d*) Urgency for demanded document by the users

Choose the **correct** answer from the options given below:

A. (*a*), (*c*) and (*d*) only
B. (*a*), (*b*) and (*d*) only
C. (*a*), (*b*) and (*c*) only
D. (*b*), (*c*) and (*d*) only

38. In which of the following categories, the document entitled 'Prolegomena to Library Classification' written by S.R. Ranganathan belong to:

A. Reference book B. Journal article
C. Monograph D. Manual

39. Which of the following belong to the category of Assigned Indexing?

(*a*) KWOC (*b*) POPSI
(*c*) SCI (*d*) PRECIS
(*e*) Chain Inexing

Choose the **correct** answer from the options given below:

A. (*a*), (*b*) and (*c*) only
B. (*b*), (*c*) and (*d*) only
C. (*b*), (*d*) and (*e*) only
D. (*a*), (*d*) and (*e*) only

40. The term 'Webliography' was coined by:

A. Robert Collision B. James Frankel
C. Henry Connaway D. Tim Robert

41. Who has Conceptualised the term Change Management Iceberg?

A. Kurt Lewin
B. Prosci
C. Wilfried Kruger
D. Beckhard and Harris

42. A hypothesis should be:

(*a*) Capable of verification of facts
(*b*) Related to the existing body of knowledge
(*c*) Changed at any time
(*d*) Operationalisable

Choose the **correct** answer from the options given below:

A. (*a*), (*c*) and (*d*) only
B. (*a*), (*b*) and (*d*) only
C. (*b*), (*c*) and (*d*) only
D. (*a*), (*b*) and (*c*) only

43. Who has recognised three theories of reference services, namely minimal, middling and maximum?

A. Samuel Wilson B. Louis Shores
C. Denis Grogan D. Samuel Rothstein

44. Management By Objectives is based on the two main principals:

(*a*) Repetitive jobs
(*b*) Results orientation
(*c*) Particular view of human behaviour
(*d*) Jobs requiring frequent movement of people or equipment

Choose the **correct** answer from the options given below:

A. (*b*) and (*c*) only B. (*a*) and (*b*) only
C. (*a*) and (*d*) only D. (*b*) and (*d*) only

45. Arrange the following subject in an ascending order according to Colon Classification (7th edition):

(*a*) Mathematics (*b*) Physics
(*c*) Chemistry (*d*) Engineering

Choose the **correct** answer from the options given below:

A. (*c*), (*a*), (*d*), (*b*) B. (*a*), (*b*), (*d*), (*c*)
C. (*c*), (*b*), (*d*), (*a*) D. (*d*), (*c*), (*a*), (*b*)

46. Which of the following is not a designated National Library?

A. National Library of India
B. Library of Congress
C. British Library
D. Kungliga Biblioteket

47. The most frequently occuring observation in the data set is ______.

A. Median B. Mean
C. Mode D. Range

48. Which of the following are true of Maharaja Sayajirao Gaekwad III?

(*a*) He is regarded as Apostle of Indian Library Movement.

(*b*) He invited WA Borden for organizing the library system in his state.

(*c*) He is one of the founder members of the Indian Library Association.

(*d*) He was insiumental in opening the National Library of India.

(*e*) He played a vital role in providing matching grants to start village library.

Choose the **correct** answer from the options given below:

A. (*b*), (*c*) and (*d*) only
B. (*a*), (*b*) and (*c*) only
C. (*a*), (*b*) and (*e*) only
D. (*a*), (*b*) and (*d*) only

49. Arrange the following steps of Kuhlthau's (1991) Information Search Process model in reverse order of their stages of action.

(*a*) Collection
(*b*) Selection
(*c*) Formulation
(*d*) Exploration

Choose the **correct** answer from the options given below:

A. (*d*), (*a*), (*b*), (*c*) B. (*c*), (*d*), (*a*), (*b*)
C. (*b*), (*c*), (*d*), (*a*) D. (*a*), (*c*), (*d*), (*b*)

50. Organize the kinds of knowledge on the basis of their increasing complexity:

(*a*) Know-how (*b*) Know-why
(*c*) Know-what (*d*) Know-who

Choose the **correct** answer from the options given below:

A. (*a*), (*b*), (*c*), (*d*) B. (*c*), (*b*), (*a*), (*d*)
C. (*b*), (*d*), (*a*), (*c*) D. (*a*), (*c*), (*d*), (*b*)

51. Prenatal cataloguing is process in which:

A. the cataglogue cards are printed on the verso of the tile page.
B. the catalogue entires can be prepared when the book is published
C. the catalogue cards are printed before the book is published
D. the catalogue cards can be printed after the book is released

52. Which of the following are communication network?

(*a*) Public Data Network
(*b*) Integrated Services Digital Network
(*c*) Developing Library Network
(*d*) Public Telephone Network

Choose the **correct** answer from the options given below:

A. (*a*) and (*b*) only
B. (*c*) and (*d*) only
C. (*a*) and (*c*) only
D. (*b*) and (*d*) only

53. Which of the following is a group orientation programme?

A. Reading Circles
B. Display of new additions
C. Helping in location of documents
D. Publicity

54. Which of the following is a call number of the textbook "Cataloguing Manual AACR-II" by R.C. Sehgal?

A. 025.32 T
B. 0.25.32 SEH
C. 025.32 RLS
D. 0.25.32 SEH T

55. Match List-I with List-II:

List-I (Process)	List-II (Explanation)
(*a*) Mending	(*i*) Attaching of a new shelf back on a volume without binding
(*b*) Repairing	(*ii*) Strengthening of the structure of weekend volume
(*c*) Reinforcing	(*iii*) Major restoration not involving replacement
(*d*) Re-backing	(*iv*) Partial rehabilitation of worn volume

Choose the **correct** answer from the options given below:

	(a)	(b)	(c)	(d)
A.	(iv)	(iii)	(i)	(ii)
B.	(i)	(ii)	(iii)	(iv)
C.	(ii)	(iii)	(i)	(iv)
D.	(iii)	(iv)	(ii)	(i)

56. Which device was developed by A.G. Bell to demonstrate the use of electronic wireless communication through visible light media?

A. Photo diode B. Photo phone
C. Photo recorder D. Smart phone

57. The first President of the Indian Library Association was:

A. K.M. Asadullah
B. M.O. Thomas
C. Chaudhry Mohammad Walia
D. S.R. Ranganathan

58. Arrange the steps involved in hostorical research in the logical order:

(*a*) Identify the research topic
(*b*) Identify and locate primary/secondary sources
(*c*) Conduct a background literature review
(*d*) Evaluate the authenticity and accuracy of sources
(*e*) Analyse the data and develop narrative exposition of the finding

Choose the **correct** answer from the options given below:

A. (*a*), (*d*), (*c*). (*b*), (*a*)
B. (*d*), (*a*), (*b*), (*e*), (*c*)
C. (*a*), (*c*), (*b*), (*d*), (*e*)
D. (*b*), (*d*), (*c*), (*a*), (*e*)

59. Which of the following are true of Open DOAR?

(*a*) Open DOAR service was launched in 2005
(*b*) Use Plan X repository self assement tool
(*c*) Account Registration is not required
(*d*) Japan is the second largest participant country

Choose the **correct** answer from the options given below:

A. (*a*) and (*b*) only B. (*b*) and (*c*) only
C. (*c*) and (*d*) only D. (*a*) and (*d*) only

60. A document is to be called as Grey Literature when:

(*a*) The document is published with an ISBN.
(*b*) The document is not published commercially.
(*c*) The document is not ephemeral in nature.
(*d*) The document is protected by IPR.
(*e*) The document is not procured through normal book publication channels.

Choose the **correct** answer from the options given below:

A. (*a*), (*c*) and (*e*) only
B. (*b*), (*c*) and (*d*) only
C. (*c*), (*d*) and (*e*) only
D. (*b*), (*d*) and (*e*) only

61. Which type of Artificial Intelligence is treated as hypothetical Artificial Intelligence that surpasses human Intelligence and abilities?

A. Artificial Neo Intelligence
B. Artificial General Intelligence
C. Artificial Super Intelligence
D. Artificial Specific Intelligence

62. In which of method, jobs are evaluated by identifying specific compensable factors in job and assigning points to each factor according to its importance in fulfilling the objectives of the organisation?

A. Ranking System
B. Classification Method
C. Factor Comparison Method
D. Point System

63. Non-Sampling errors arise at state of:

A. Collection of data only
B. Writing research report
C. Distributing Questionnaire
D. Collection and preparation of data

64. Memory of the World Programme was estab-lished by ______.

A. IFLA B. SLA
C. UNESCO D. SCONUL

65. According to Botha, who is now using Facebook as an alternative to e-mail?

A. Generation X B. Generation Z
C. Generation Y D. Generation W

66. Which one of the following canons is not related to the verbal plane?

A. Canon of Context
B. Canon of Enumeration
C. Canon of Array
D. Canon of Currency

67. Which one of the following theories is based on the notion that individual attitude towards risk will vary?

A. Preference Theory
B. Scientific Management Theory
C. Herzberg Two-Factor Theory
D. Hierarchy of Needs Theory

68. Who among the following are the user community according to S.R. Ranganathan?

(*a*) Potential users
(*b*) Freshman
(*c*) Expected users
(*d*) Ordinary enquirer
(*e*) Specialist enquirer

Choose the **correct** answer from the options given below:

A. (*a*), (*b*), (*c*) only B. (*b*), (*c*), (*d*) only
C. (*c*), (*d*), (*e*) only D. (*b*), (*d*), (*e*) only

69. Which of the following is not documentation list?

A. Science Citation Index
B. Annual Review of Psychology
C. Fodor's Guide of India
D. Keesing's Record of World Events

70. MedIND is:

A. Bibliographic database of Bio-medical literature
B. Full-text peer reviewed Indian Bio-medical journal database
C. Open access archive of case study reports of patient
D. Union Catalog of Biomedical Serials in India

71. Given below are two statements:

Statement I: One of the impotant functions of R & D library is having a provision of reference service.

Statement II: the users have no time to use library as they are totally involved in research.

In light of the above statements, choose the **correct** answer from the options given below:

A. Both Statement I and Statement II are correct
B. Both Statement I and Statement II are incorect
C. Statement I is correct, but Statement II is incorrect
D. Statement I is incorrect, but Statement II is correct

72. KWIC index entries consists of ______.

(*a*) Key word (*b*) Context
(*c*) Contest (*d*) Concept
(*e*) Identification/location code

Choose the **correct** answer from the options given below:

A. (*a*), (*c*) and (*d*) only
B. (*a*), (*b*) and (*e*) only
C. (*b*), (*d*) and (*e*) only
D. (*c*), (*d*) and (*e*) only

73. Which was the following has created 'BibSonomy'?

A. MIT
B. Institute of Knowledge and Data Enginee-ring
C. Tata Consultancy Services
D. IBM

74. National Central Library Committee constituted in 1948 was headed by ______.

A. S. Radhakrishnan

B. S.R. Ranganathan

C. K.P. Sinha

D. M.D. Sen

75. Arrange the following programming in ascen-ding order according to their year of develop-ment.

(*a*) FORTRAN (*b*) Pascal

(*c*) BASIC (*d*) ALGOL

Choose the **correct** answer from the options given below:

A. (*d*), (*a*), (*c*), (*b*) B. (*c*), (*d*), (*a*), (*b*)

C. (*a*), (*d*), (*c*), (*b*) D. (*b*), (*c*), (*a*), (*d*)

76. Arrange the following Digital Assets Management Software ascending to the data of release of their first version

(*a*) Islandora (*b*) E Prints

(*c*) Fedora (*d*) DSpace

Choose the **correct** answer from the options given below:

A. (*b*), (*d*), (*a*), (*c*) B. (*b*), (*d*), (*c*), (*a*)

C. (*d*), (*b*), (*a*), (*c*) D. (*d*), (*c*), (*b*), (*a*)

77. Arrange the following different type of un-structured interviews based on the complexity of structure:

(*a*) Narrative (*b*) Focused Group

(*c*) Oral History (*d*) In-depth

Choose the **correct** answer from the options given below:

A. (*b*), (*a*), (*c*), (*d*)

B. (*a*), (*d*), (*b*), (*c*)

C. (*a*), (*b*), (*c*), (*d*)

D. (*c*), (*a*), (*b*), (*d*)

78. Dynamic Library Web OPAC enables users to:

(*a*) Renew book

(*b*) Access the content page of the materials

(*c*) Ask for copy of a document

(*d*) Return book

Choose the **correct** answer from the options given below:

A. (*a*), (*b*) and (*c*) only

B. (*a*), (*b*) and (*d*) only

C. (*a*), (*c*) and (*d*) only

D. (*b*), (*c*) and (*d*) only

79. Which of the following statement with reference to special libraries in India?

(*a*) There were no Scientific Libraries before World War II.

(*b*) Library of the Anthropological Survey of India, Calcutta, is rich in maps and reprints.

(*c*) The National Forest Library and Information Center is situated at Dehradun

(*d*) Indian Institute of Science Library is named after JRD Tata

(*e*) CSIR was formed after independence

Choose the **correct** answer from the options given below:

A. (*a*), (*b*) and (*c*) only

B. (*b*), (*c*) and (*d*) only

C. (*c*), (*d*) and (*e*) only

D. (*a*), (*c*) and (*e*) only

80. WIPO stand for:

A. Word Intellectuals Private Organisation

B. World Index Property Organ

C. World Intellectuals Property Organisation

D. World Internal Programme Organisation

81. Match List-I with List-II:

List-I (Information Sources)	List-II (Examples)
(*a*) Subject Periodical	(*i*) Keesing's Record of World Events
(*b*) Digesting Periodical	(*ii*) Knowledge Organisation
(*c*) Pamphlet Periodical	(*iii*) Library Literature
(*d*) Indexing Periodical	(*iv*) UNESCO's Alcohol & Substance Abuse: A Curse to Society

Choose the **correct** answer from the options given below:

	(a)	(b)	(c)	(d)
A.	(i)	(ii)	(iii)	(iv)
B.	(ii)	(i)	(iv)	(iii)
C.	(iii)	(i)	(iv)	(ii)
D.	(iv)	(iii)	(i)	(ii)

82. EBSDIC stands for:

A. Extended Binary Coded Decimal Inter-change Code

B. Extensible Binary Code and Decimal Inter-change Code

C. Extensible Binary Code Decimal Inter-change Code

D. Extension Binary Coded Decimal Inter-change Code

83. ______ are classified was white hat or black hat.

A. Attackers B. Hackers

C. Spammers D. Phishera

84. Given below are two statements: one is labelled as Assertion (A) and the other if labelled as Reason (R):

Assertion (A): A user is a systematic study of information requirements of users in order to facilitate meaningful exchange between information system and users which is now prefered over library survey.

Reason (R): Studies of information needs or information use behaviour focus upon a wider range of information sources and channels rather then simply litraries.

In light of the above statements, choose the **correct** answer from the options given below:

A. Both (A) and (R) are true and (R) is the correct explanation of (A)

B. Both (A) and (R) true, but (R) is NOT the correct explanation of (A)

C. (A) is true, but (R) is false

D. (A) is false, but (R) is true

85. Match List-I with List-II:

List-I (Types of Plagiarism)	List-II (Features)
(a) Clone	(i) Changing keywords but retaining the essential content of the source
(b) Find-Replace	(ii) Borrows generously from the writer's previous work without citation
(c) Remix	(iii) Submitting author's work word-for-word as one's own
(d) Recycle	(iv) Paraphrases from multiple sources

Choose the **correct** answer from the options given below:

	(a)	(b)	(c)	(d)
A.	(i)	(ii)	(iii)	(iv)
B.	(ii)	(iv)	(i)	(iii)
C.	(iii)	(i)	(iv)	(ii)
D.	(ii)	(iii)	(iv)	(i)

86. Which one of the following is a consortia in Agriculture Sciences?

A. FORSA B. CARLI

C. CeRA D. NISHTHA

87. The process of establishing the worth of a job in relation to other, jobs, in the organisation is known as:

A. Job enrichment

B. Job analysis

C. Job design

D. Job evaluation

88. Sinha Committee recommended the following Public Library System for India:

(a) National Library

(b) Parliament Library

(c) State Central Library

(d) Library of State Legislature

(e) District Cental Library

Choose the **correct** answer from the options given below:

A. (*b*), (*c*), (*d*) only
B. (*a*), (*c*), (*e*) only
C. (*c*), (*d*), (*e*) only
D. (*a*), (*b*), (*c*) only

89. ASTINFO stand for:

A. Association for Technical Information
B. Asian Scientific Technical Information Forum
C. African Social Traditional Information Forum
D. Regional Network for Exchange of Information and Experience in Science and Technology in Asia and Asia Pacific

90. START and STOP bits are sent _____ mode of transmission.

A. Asynchronous B. Synchronous
C. Lower overhead D. Higher throughput

Directions (Qs. No. 91 to 95): *Read the passage carefully and answer the questions that folow.*

In 1991, Le W Finks worte about the need for librarianship to develop a new code of ethics. In 1995, the ALA did just that. A perusal of the code leads to the conclusion that perhaps not all of his concerns were incorporated. Essential to Finks thesis is the belief that a code of ethics for librarians and information professionals must not be a hallow statement written to satisfy the public library boards. It must embody the principles and conviction that librarians have historically considered of value, and should "Focus on the way we do our work and whether or not we perform in a way that can honestly be called professional". Furthermore, as Johan Bekkar points out, since society judges a profession by its individual member, all members must follow a clearly defined set of ethical standards. In praticular ethical issues related to selection of materials and intellectual freedom should be carefully considered by librarians. Intellectual freedom hinges on the assumption that individuals choose the path their inquires take but this is often a false assumption. Professional codes require librarians to remain neutral and to provide the information a client request. Librarians should set aside their assumption and prejudices to make sure they won't destroy the fundamental principle that underlies librarianship; the social obligation to allow access to all perspectives.

91. Who should set aside their assumption and prejudices to make sure they won't destroy the fundamental principles?

A. Library and Information professionals
B. Society
C. ALA
D. User community

92. Which of the following is essential to 'Finks' thesis?

A. Code must be hollow statement
B. Code must be written to the public or library boards
C. Code must embody the principles and conviction considered as value
D. Librarians do not have professionalism

93. Who wrote about the needs for the code of ethics?

A. Lee W. Finks
B. American Library Association
C. Johan Bekker
D. Lee Kekker

94. In which year, did ALA develop the code of ethics?

A. 1991 B. 1995
C. 1994 D. 1999

95. Who pointed out that society judges a profession by its individual members?

A. Johan Bekker B. ALA
C. Lee W. Finks D. Johan Finks

Directions (Qs. No. 96 to 100): *Read the passage carefully and answer the following question.*

Reading is to the mind, what exercise is to the body, this line has been often used to describe the importance of reading. The joy of the reading cannot be expressed in the words. It's something which can be understood only through experience. A 2016 study revealed that people who read for atleast 30 minutes every days are likely to enjoy a longer life. Reading has many benefits, it teaches us new vocabulary, improves our focus and imagination, makes us smarter and most importantly, improve memory. Those who are habitual in reading feel comforted with books. It soothes and relieves tension and loneliness. People often get tired in their daily routine. Reading is something that can make forget other thinks that gives stress and gives one's mind complete relaxation, just like yoga. It exposes one to a world of imagination where nothing is impossible. In order to improve the reading habit amongst children particularly, motivation from parents and teachers is very necessary. Books are no doubt very faithful friends of a reader, they never betray, always accompany. We must never let it die out.

96. Reading is important to the:

A. Mind B. Exercise
C. Body D. Book

97. According to the 2016 study, who among the following are likely to enjoy a longer life?

A. Those who read hours together everyday
B. Those who read atleast thirty minutes a day
C. Those who read before they go to bed
D. Those who read early in the morning

98. Which of the following is compared with reading to proved complete relaxation?

A. Exercise B. Yoga
C. Friends D. Children

99. Which one of the following is a good friends of a reader?

A. People B. Children
C. Librarian D. Books

100. The joy of reading can be expressed through _______.

A. Exercise
B. Exhaling
C. Experience
D. Experiments

ANSWERS

1. (D): A sector device is a specialized tool designed to enhance the capacity of an array in computer programming by strategically inserting empty elements, often referred to as "sectors," within the existing array structure. Instead of traditional methods involving the creation of a new array and the copying of all elements, sector devices enable dynamic expansion without the need for such resource-intensive operations. This technology facilitates the efficient adaptation of arrays to changing storage requirements, optimizing memory usage by adding empty digits within the array, thus providing a flexible and memory-efficient solution for managing array capacities in various programming scenarios.

2. (C): The Law of Scattering, formulated by Samuel Clement Bradford, is a bibliometric principle that describes the distribution of scientific or bibliographic literature within a given field. Bradford observed that scholarly articles on a particular topic tend to cluster in a specific manner, forming a pattern of scattering. According to Bradford's Law, the literature on a subject can be divided into core journals, a first scattering zone, and a second scattering zone. The core journals contain a significant concentration of articles on the topic, while the first and second scattering zones represent diminishing concentrations of relevant literature.

3. (C)

4. (D): These elements collectively represent key principles of Scientific Management, as proposed by Frederick Taylor:

(*b*) **Science instead of rules of thumb:** This principle of Scientific Management emphasizes the use of scientific methods and analysis, replacing traditional rules of thumb or arbitrary decision-making with systematic observation and experimentation to determine the most efficient ways to perform tasks.

(*d*) **Maximum output instead of restricted output:** Scientific Management focuses on maximizing the productivity and output of workers. This involves identifying and implementing methods that lead to the highest level of efficiency and output in the given time.

(*e*) **The development of each person to his/her greatest efficiency:** This aspect involves recognizing the importance of training, development, and education for workers. Scientific Management advocates for enhancing individual skills and capabilities to achieve the highest level of efficiency and productivity in the workplace.

5. (C): Assertion (A): AI technology usage in the library can allow library resources to be virtually reimagined. - This statement suggests that the integration of AI technology can lead to a significant transformation in the way libraries operate. AI can introduce various advancements, such as virtual tours, personalized recommendations, and automated content creation, which collectively contribute to a virtual reimagining of library resources. This assertion is supported by the transformative capabilities that AI brings to information management and user interaction.

Reason (R): Reimagination can't help the library to explore new ways to meet customer needs and support academic activities of anyone from anywhere. - This reason posits that reimagination, particularly through AI, is not beneficial for libraries in meeting customer needs and supporting academic activities across diverse locations. However, this statement is contradicted by the reality that reimagination, especially with the aid of AI, is crucial for libraries to remain relevant and effective in a digital age. AI enables libraries to transcend physical limitations, offer personalized services, and create innovative programs that cater to a global audience.

6. (B): Identified subsystems of the library system as per Hays and Becker:

(*a*) **Acquisition Control:** This subsystem is concerned with the process of acquiring new materials for the library's collection. It involves activities such as selecting, ordering, receiving, and cataloging new books, journals, or other resources. Acquisition control ensures that the library continually updates and expands its collection to meet the needs of its users.

(*c*) **Serials Control:** The serials control subsystem focuses on the management of serial publications, which include periodicals, journals, magazines, and newspapers. This involves tasks like subscription management, tracking issues, handling renewals, and ensuring timely access to the latest editions. Effective serials control is crucial for providing users with up-to-date and relevant information.

(*d*) **Circulation Control:** Circulation control is a vital subsystem responsible for managing the borrowing and returning of library materials by patrons. It includes activities such as issuing library cards, tracking due dates, handling renewals, managing holds, and maintaining an accurate record of the circulation history. Circulation control ensures efficient access to library resources while maintaining proper inventory and security.

7. **(C):** The Digital Millennium Copyright Act (DMCA) is a U.S. copyright law enacted in 1998 to address the challenges posed by digital technologies to traditional copyright protection. The DMCA criminalizes the circumvention of technological measures employed to protect copyrighted materials, such as encryption and access controls. It also provides a safe harbor framework for online service providers, protecting them from liability for copyright infringement committed by their users if they adhere to certain prescribed conditions.

8. **(D)**

9. **(A): Reordering Ranganathan:** Shifting User Behaviors, Shifting Priorities is a book written by Lynn Silipigni Connaway and Ixchel Fanie and published by OCLC in 2014. In this book, they have changed the order of Ranganathan's Five Laws as follows:

   (*d*) Save the time of the reader

   (*b*) Every person his or her book

   (*a*) Books are for use

   (*c*) Every book, its reader

   (*e*) A library is a growing organism

10. **(D):** Russell L. Ackoff, a pioneering systems theorist, emphasized the idea that information is fundamentally obtained by addressing questions that start with interrogative words like who, what, where, when, and how many. This perspective underscores the role of questions in driving the search for knowledge and meaningful data. Ackoff's statement reflects the notion that information is not only a collection of facts but is, in fact, closely tied to the process of inquiry. By posing specific questions, individuals actively engage in seeking answers that contribute to the acquisition and understanding of information. Ackoff's insight highlights the dynamic and inquiry-driven nature of information retrieval and underscores the importance of asking the right questions to generate valuable and relevant information.

11. **(A):** In the LISA database, the 'LOC' field plays a crucial role in providing geographic context to the stored information. This field is dedicated to capturing details related to the location of publication for books, journals, or other materials, enabling users to discern the geographic origin of resources. Additionally, 'LOC' is used to specify the locations of conferences or events where presentations or papers were delivered, offering insight into the geographical scope of academic activities. Moreover, it serves to identify the geographic locations of organizations that produced reports or other documents, adding an extra layer of contextual information. By incorporating such geographic data, the 'LOC' field enhances the search capabilities of users, allowing them to refine queries based on location-specific criteria and fostering a better understanding of the global distribution and relevance of the available research and information in the LISA database.

12. **(B):**

   (*a*) **It is open access:** Patent Lens is an open-access platform, meaning that it provides unrestricted access to patent information for users without requiring a subscription or payment. This openness promotes transparency and allows a wide range of users, including researchers, inventors, and the general public, to access valuable patent-related data.

   (*b*) **It is a free full-text database:** Patent Lens not only provides access to patent metadata but also offers free access to the full text of patents. This includes detailed information within patent documents, allowing users to review and analyze the contents of patents without charge.

(*d*) **It covers patents and applications of WIPO, USPTO, and EPO:** Patent Lens indeed covers patents and applications from prominent patent offices, including the World Intellectual Property Organization (WIPO), the United States Patent and Trademark Office (USPTO), and the European Patent Office (EPO). This broad coverage ensures access to a diverse set of patent data.

13. (A): DAISY format readers are a general assistive technology for users with all types of disability. DAISY is a standard for accessible multimedia books. It's designed to be a complete audio substitute for print material and is specifically designed for use by people with "print disabilities", including blindness, impaired vision, and dyslexia. The primary goal of DAISY is to provide an alternative to traditional print material for people who face challenges in accessing standard printed text due to visual impairments, blindness, or conditions like dyslexia.

14. (B):

(*a*) **Ranganathan conceived the five laws in 1924:** This statement is accurate. S.R. Ranganathan, a renowned Indian librarian and library theorist, formulated the Five Laws of Library Science in 1924. These laws have since become foundational principles in library science, guiding librarians in the organization and management of library resources.

(*b*) **First law was finalized only after the remaining four laws were framed:** Ranganathan initially proposed the first four laws, and it was later that he formulated the fifth law. The First Law, "Books are for use," emphasizes the primary purpose of library resources, highlighting their role in serving the needs of library users. The subsequent laws further elaborate on principles related to readership, resource organization, and accessibility.

(*c*) **Second law desires free book service for all:** The Second Law, "Every reader his/her book," conveys the idea that libraries should strive to provide personalized access to library materials for every individual. It does not specifically mention "free" service but emphasizes inclusivity and accessibility.

The correct interpretation is that Ranganathan conceived the Five Laws of Library Science in 1924, the first law was finalized after the remaining four, the second law emphasizes access for all readers, and the third law promotes open access rather than closed access.

15. (B)

16. (C):

(*e*) **Oral communication:** This is the most ancient form of communication, dating back to prehistoric times when humans communicated through spoken language. It has been a fundamental and continuous aspect of human interaction.

(*b*) **Written communication:** The development of writing systems marked a significant advancement in communication, allowing information to be recorded, preserved, and transmitted across time and space Ancient civilizations like Sumer and Egypt contributed to the early forms of written communication.

(*c*) **Mass communication:** The inven-tion of the printing press in the 15th century by Johannes Gutenberg revolutionized communication. It enabled the mass production of written materials, making books, newspapers, and other printed items more accessible to a broader audience.

(*d*) **Telecommunication:** The 19th century saw the emergence of telecommunication technologies such as the telegraph and later the telephone. These innovations allowed near-instantaneous communication over long distances, greatly impacting global connectivity.

(*a*) **Internet-based communication:** The late 20th century witnessed the rise of the internet, a transformative force in communication. Internet-based communication encompasses email, online forums, social media, and various other platforms, enabling real-time global interaction and information sharing.

17. (C)

18. (C): The term "Knowledge-based Economy" was coined by the Organization for Economic Cooperation and Development (OECD). It refers to an economic system where the generation and exploitation of knowledge play a predominant part in the creation of wealth. In a knowledge-based economy, the focus shifts from traditional factors of production, such as natural resources or manual labour, to the production and use of knowledge, information, and innovation. This concept underscores the critical role of education, research, technology, and intellectual assets in driving economic growth and development. The OECD has played a significant role in shaping the discourse around knowledge-based economies, emphasizing the importance of policies that support innovation, education, and the effective utilization of information and communication technologies.

19. (B):

(*a*) **SLIP (Serial Line Internet Proto-col):** SLIP is an older communication protocol that was once used for establishing a connection to the internet over telephone lines. It operates at the data link layer of the OSI model and was designed for simplicity. However, due to its limitations and the advent of more advanced protocols like PPP, SLIP has become largely obsolete.

(*c*) **PPP (Point-to-Point Protocol):** PPP is a widely used and more advanced protocol for establishing a connection to the internet via various mediums, including tele-phone lines. It supports multiple network layer protocols, including IP (Internet Protocol), making it versatile for internet communication. PPP provides features such as error detection, encryption, and authentication, making it a more robust and secure choice compared to SLIP.

In the context of connecting to the internet through telephone lines, PPP is the more relevant and prevalent protocol. It ensures a reliable and secure link, allowing users to establish a connection and engage in internet activities. While SLIP was used in the past, PPP has largely replaced it due to its enhanced capabilities and compatibility with modern internet requirements.

20. (A):

(*a*) **Distance of communication is greater than Wi-Fi:** Li-Fi (Light Fidelity) is a wireless communication technology that utilizes visible light to transmit data. The range of Li-Fi is generally considered to be shorter compared to traditional Wi-Fi, which uses radio frequency signals. Visible light signals can be more easily obstructed by physical barriers, and they do not penetrate walls as effectively as radio signals. While Li-Fi has its advantages, such as higher data transfer rates, it may not be suitable for long-range communications or situations where line-of-sight is obstructed.

(*b*) **The term Li-Fi was coined by Harold Haas:** Professor Harald Haas is indeed credited with coining the term Li-Fi. He introduced the concept of Li-Fi in a TED Talk in 2011, where he demonstrated the transmission of data through flickering LED lights. Haas's research has been instrumental in developing and popularizing Li-Fi technology. The term "Li-Fi" is a play on words, combining "light" with "Wi-Fi" to describe a wireless communication system that uses visible light.

21. (C):

(*a*) **ISO 2709:** ISO 2709 is a standard for the format of bibliographic information interchange on magnetic tape. It specifies a structure for bibliographic records and data exchange between computer systems.

(*c*) **Z39.50:** This is another relevant standard, developed by the National Information Standards Organization (NISO) in the US. It defines data elements and tags for the interchange of bibliographic information in MARC (machine-readable cataloging) format.

(*d*) **Z39.71:** This standard also plays a role in bibliographic information interchange. It specifies a format for the identification and exchange of bibliographic data elements associated with electronic publica-tions.

22. (B): According to Wilson and Tauber, the university library plays crucial roles in conserving knowledge, supporting teaching activities, facilitating the publication of scholarly works, and contributing to the broader mission of the academic institution. The functions are closely aligned with the core mission of universities in education, research, and knowledge dissemination.

(*a*) **Conservation of Knowledge:** This function involves the preservation and conservation of knowledge resources, including books, journals, manuscripts, and other materials. The university library serves as a repository for a vast array of knowledge, ensuring that these resources are protected, maintained, and made available for current and future generations of scholars and students.

(*b*) **Teaching:** While the explicit mention of teaching as a function of the university library may not be as common in traditional library classifications, university libraries inherently support teaching activities. They provide essential resources for course materials, research support, and information literacy instruction. Librarians often collaborate with faculty to enhance students' research and information skills, contributing to the teaching mission of the university.

(*d*) **Publication:** The university library is involved in the dissemination of knowledge through various means, including publications. This can include managing institutional repositories, publishing research outputs, and supporting scholarly communication initiatives. Wilson and Tauber recognize the role of the library in the publication of academic and research materials.

23. (B):

(*b*) **The Biological Act (Biological Diversity Act):** Enacted in 2002, this Act aims to conserve biological diversity, ensure sustainable use of its components, and provide for fair and equitable sharing of benefits arising from the use of biological resources.

(*e*) **The Designs Act:** Enacted in 2000, this Act relates to the protection of industrial designs and provides for the registration and protection of designs in India. It governs the aesthetic aspects of products.

(*d*) **The Trademarks Act:** Enacted in 1999, this Act governs the regis-tration and protection of trademarks in India. It provides for the legal framework to protect distinctive marks associated with goods or services.

(*a*) **The Patents Act:** Enacted in 1970, the Patents Act is a key legislation governing patents in India. It outlines the criteria for patentability, the process of obtaining a patent, and the rights and obligations of patent holders.

(*c*) **The Copyright Act:** Enacted in 1957, the Copyright Act is a comprehensive legislation that provides for the protection of literary, artistic, and musical works. It grants exclusive rights to the creators of such works and regulates their use.

24. (A):

(*a*) **Applicable to higher education sector:** The ACRL (Association of College and Research Libraries) Information Literacy Competency Standards are indeed designed for the higher education sector. These standards provide a framework for assessing and developing information literacy skills among college and university students. Information literacy is crucial for students to navigate the complex information landscape, conduct effective research, and critically evaluate information sources.

(*d*) **The information literate student determines the nature and extent of information needs:** This statement reflects one of the key principles in the ACRL Information Literacy Competency Standards. It emphasizes that information literate students should be able to recognize when they need information, define the scope of their information needs, and formulate questions to guide the search process. This skill is foundational to effective information seeking and research.

(*e*) **Bloom's Taxonomy of Educational Objectives has been considered to map the outcomes:** Bloom's Taxonomy is a framework that classifies educational objectives into cognitive domains, ranging from lower-order thinking skills (e.g., remembering and understanding) to higher-order thinking skills (e.g., analyzing, evaluating, and creating). In the context of information literacy, the ACRL Information Literacy Competency Standards align with Bloom's Taxonomy by incorporating various cognitive levels in their standards and performance indicators. This alignment ensures that the outcomes cover a spectrum of cognitive skills, promoting a comprehensive approach to information literacy education.

25. (A): Statement I: "Knowledge Management (KM) is a multidisciplinary approach to achieve organizational objectives by making the best use of knowledge." This statement is generally true. Knowledge Management involves processes and strategies aimed at capturing, organizing, and leveraging an organization's collective knowledge to achieve its goals.

Statement II: "KM focuses on improved performances, competitive advantage, innovation, and continuous improvement of the organizations through knowledge sharing." This statement is also true. Knowledge Management aims to enhance organizational performance by fostering a culture of knowledge sharing, innovation, and continuous improvement. It is often linked to gaining a competitive advantage through effective use of knowledge resources.

Therefore, both statements align with the fundamental principles and goals of Knowledge Management.

26. (C):

(*a*) **RDF (Resource Description Framework):** RDF is a foundational technology in the Semantic Web. It provides a standardized framework for describing resources on the web in a way that can be understood by machines. RDF represents infor-mation in the form of subject-predicate-object triples, creating a graph-based structure that allows for the linking and connecting of data.

(*b*) **Ontologies:** Ontologies are formal representations of knowledge that define the relationships and properties of concepts within a particular domain. They provide a shared understanding and a common vocabulary for describing entities and their interrelations. Ontologies play a crucial role in the Semantic Web by enabling machines to understand and interpret the seman-tics of data.

(*c*) **URL (Uniform Resource Locator):** While URLs themselves are not a Semantic Web technology, they are an integral part of the web infrastructure and play a role in the Semantic Web context. URIs (Uniform Resource Identifiers), including URLs, are used to uniquely identify resources, including RDF resources. This identification is essential for creating links and connecting data on the Semantic Web.

27. (B)

28. (B): niscpr.res.in: This website belongs to the National Institute of Science Communication and Information Resources (NISCAIR), which falls under the Council of Scientific and Industrial Research (CSIR). While the NKC focused on education and knowledge creation, there could be overlaps or collaborations between its recommendations and existing CSIR initiatives like NISCAIR. Established in 2005, the NKC aimed to enhance India's access to knowledge and information through various initiatives. Specifically, the NKC advocated for the development of a web portal focused on scientific communication and information dissemination.

This recommendation led to the creation of the NISCAIR website in 2009 under the umbrella of the Council of Scientific and Industrial Research (CSIR). While other web portals might have benefited from the NKC's broader initiatives, NISCPR.res.in stands out as a tangible result of a specific recommendation, emphasizing the NKC's influence in fostering knowledge dissemination in the scientific domain.

29. (C): An experience survey involves gathering insights and knowledge from individuals with relevant experience to gain a better understanding of the relationship between variables and to generate new ideas related to a research problem. This survey method typically targets individuals who have direct experience or expertise in the subject matter under investigation. By leveraging the knowledge of these individuals, researchers aim to gather valuable qualitative information, perspectives, and insights that can contribute to refining research questions, formulating hypotheses, and guiding the overall research design. Experience surveys are particularly useful when exploring new or complex areas where the expertise of individuals can provide valuable qualitative data, helping researchers shape the direction and focus of their studies.

30. (B):

(*b*) **C.W. Hanson:** C.W. Hanson is recognized for his contributions to library and information science, particularly in the areas of infor-mation retrieval and understanding user needs. However, there is specific indication that he distinguished "primary documents" as a distinct category in the same way Denis Grogan did. Hanson's work often focused on the broader aspects of information retrieval systems and user-oriented approaches with a specific emphasis on categorizing documents into primary, secondary, or tertiary types.

(*c*) **Denis Grogan:** Denis Grogan is indeed associated with the concept of "primary documents." He emphasized the significance of original sources in research and distinguished them from secondary and tertiary sources. Grogan's contributions highlight the importance of recognizing primary documents as foundational and authentic sources of information, crucial for scholarly inquiry and understanding the context of historical events.

31. (B):

(*b*) **Constant Variable:** This term refers to a variable with a fixed value that doesn't vary across observations or units. It is often a numerical value that remains constant for all units in the dataset.

(*c*) **Polytomous Variable:** This term accurately describes a type of categorical variable with more than two distinct levels or categories. It is commonly used when a variable can take on three or more values, and each value represents a unique category.

(*d*) **Dichotomous Variables:** Dichotomous variables are a subset of categorical variables that specifically have exactly two possible categories or levels. The prefix "di-" means two, and these variables often represent binary outcomes.

32. (B): S.R. Ranganathan a renowned Indian librarian and philosopher, developed a comprehensive system for document classi-fication and organization. He advocated for "document bibliographies" as a specific type of bibliography focused on a particular subject or field. In his system, these bibliographies would go beyond just listing references and include detailed descriptions of the documents themselves, making them more informative and helpful for researchers. Beyond mere references, these specialized bibliographies focused on a particular subject area, immersing users in its resources with an added layer of detail. Unlike traditional bibliographies that simply list entries, document bibliographies delved into the documents themselves, offering summaries, descriptions, and critical insights.

This approach catered to researchers and scholars seeking a deeper understanding of their field's intellectual landscape. Instead of solely navigating a list of titles, they could explore summaries, identify relevant content within each document, and make informed choices about which resources to prioritize. Ranganathan positioned docu-ment bibliographies as valuable research companions, enriching the process of discovery and knowledge acquisition.

33. (B) **34. (D)**

35. (C): Statement I: This statement emphasizes the importance of studying the history of libraries in relation to various societal aspects such as education, social structures, economics, and politics. Understanding the historical context in which libraries evolved provides insights into their role and significance within a broader societal framework.

Statement II: Contrary to Statement I, Statement II suggests that the library kept itself abstained (isolated) from developing an interlinked relationship with society. This characterization is generally not accurate. Libraries, throughout history, have been integral parts of societies, evolving and adapting in response to societal changes. Libraries have actively engaged with educational, social, economic, and political institutions, contributing to and reflecting the dynamics of the societies they serve. Therefore, while Statement I aligns with the holistic perspective of studying library history, Statement II is not accurate in portraying libraries as detached from societal interlinkages.

36. (C): Function-as-a-Service (FaaS) is a cloud computing model that allows developers to deploy individual functions or pieces of code in the form of serverless functions. In FaaS, developers don't need to manage the underlying infrastructure or worry about server provisioning. Instead, they can focus solely on writing and deploying the specific functions they need, and the cloud provider automatically handles the execution and scaling of those functions based on demand. FaaS is particularly advantageous for its scalability, cost-effectiveness, and ease of use, making it a popular choice for building applications with event-driven architectures, microservices, and other scenarios where rapid and efficient execution of specific functions is crucial.

37. (C):

(*a*) **Methods of receiving request for a document:** While the method of receiving a request (email, web form, etc.) can influence user experience and potentially affect perceived speed, it doesn't directly impact the actual speed of DDS delivery.

(*b*) **Methods of processing the request by DDS provider:** This directly impacts the speed of document delivery. Internal processes like automated document retrieval, authorization checks, and notifica-tion systems can significantly affect how quickly a request is fulfilled.

(*c*) **Mode of delivery of documents:** Whether the document is delivered electronically (email, online plat-form) or physically (mail, courier) significantly influences delivery speed. Electronic delivery is typically much faster than physical delivery.

38. (C): The document "Prolegomena to Library Classification" by S.R. Ranganathan falls into the category of a monograph. A monograph is a scholarly work or book that focuses on a single subject, presenting a thorough and detailed examination of that topic.

In this case, Ranganathan's "Prolegomena" serves as a foundational work in the field of library science, specifically addressing the principles and theories related to library classification. As a monograph, it provides an extensive exploration of the subject matter, offering valuable insights, theories, and frameworks for understanding and implementing library classification systems. Monographs are distinguished by their in-depth treatment of a particular subject and are often considered authoritative works in their respective fields.

39. (C):

(*b*) **POPSI (Post-coordinate Indexing):** POPSI is a post-coordinate indexing system, where index terms are assigned to documents after the documents are created. In this approach, the indexer uses a thesaurus to select appropriate terms and combines them to represent the content of the document accurately. Post-coordinate indexing systems allow for flexibility and precision in representing complex subjects.

(*d*) **PRECIS (Preserved Context Index System):** PRECIS is an assigned indexing system designed to capture the essential concepts of a document while preserving the context in which they appear. Indexers identify significant concepts, assign appropriate terms, and maintain the hierarchical and relational structure of these concepts. PRECIS aims to provide a comprehensive and contextually rich representation of document content.

(*e*) **Chain Indexing:** Chain indexing is a technique where index terms are selected from the document's content, and these terms form a chain that represents the primary concepts in the document. Each term in the chain is linked to the next, creating a sequential structure. This method allows for the representation of the document's main ideas in a linked and easily navigable format.

40. (B): The term "webliography" is commonly used to describe online resources. Dr. James Frankel coined this term in 2000. A webliography is a list of websites or electronic works about a particular subject that have been used by a person writing an article. The term webliography is commonly used when discussing online resources. A webliography is a list of resources related to a specific topic that can be found on the World Wide Web. It is also known as a "Web bibliography". A webliography is similar to a bibliography, but it is limited to a collection of online resources rather than books and academic journals.

41. (C): The Change Management Iceberg, conceptualized by Wilfried Krüger, serves as a metaphorical representation of the dual dimensions involved in organizational change. Similar to an iceberg where only a fraction is visible above the waterline, the model illustrates that observable changes in structures and processes represent merely the tip of the iceberg. Beneath the surface lie the less apparent but crucial factors such as cultural dynamics, attitudes, and resistance to change. The model emphasizes the necessity of recognizing and addressing both the visible and hidden aspects to ensure successful organizational change. By acknowledging the complexity of the entire change landscape, organizations can navigate challenges more effectively and implement comprehensive strategies that encompass both the seen and unseen elements of the change process.

42. (B):

(*a*) **Capable of verification of facts:** This implies that a hypothesis should be formulated in a way that allows it to be tested and verified through empirical observation or experimentation. In scientific research, hypothesis are subjected to tests that can either support or refute them based on evidence and data.

(*b*) **Related to the existing body of knowledge:** A hypothesis should be rooted in the existing understanding of a subject. It builds upon the knowledge that already exists in a particular field and aims to contribute new insights or validate existing theories. This ensures that research is progressive and adds value to the scientific or academic community.

(*d*) **Operationalizable:** Operationalization involves defining how variables in a hypothesis will be measured or manipulated. A well-formulated hypothesis should be clear and specific enough that researchers can design experiments or collect data to test it. This clarity is essential for conducting meaningful research and drawing valid conclusions.

43. (D): Among those contributing to this discourse, Samuel Rothstein stands out for his seminal work in his 1955 book, "Guide to Reference Books." Here, he meticulously outlined three distinct theories of reference service, each offering a unique lens through which librarians interact with users and fulfill their information needs.

1. **Minimal Theory:** Focuses At the core of the minimal theory lies the notion of swift and efficient service. Librarians act as information way finders, guiding users to readily available resources and assisting them in locating basic factual information. The emphasis is on self-reliance, with users ultimately responsible for navigating the information landscape. This approach prioritizes speed and practicality, ensuring quick answers to straightforward queries.
2. **Middling Theory:** Moving beyond mere fact-finding, the middling theory champions a more collaborative relationship between librarian and user. Librarians actively engage with users, understanding their research goals and tailoring their assistance accordingly. They provide insightful recommendations, interpret complex information, and equip users with research skills for future independent exploration. This approach strikes a balance between efficiency and user empowerment, promoting deeper engagement with the information landscape.
3. **Maximum Theory:** Rothstein's maximal theory champions a transformative vision of reference service. Librarians transcend their role as information providers to become active partners in the user's learning journey. They engage in personalized research consultations, conduct in-depth literature searches, and offer tailored instruction and guidance. This approach fosters a dynamic and interactive learning environment, propelling users towards intellectual growth and lifelong learning habits.

44. (A): Two main principles of Management By Objectives (MBO):

(*b*) **Results orientation:** Management By Objectives places a strong emphasis on achieving specific and measurable results. This principle is aligned with the concept of setting SMART goals — goals that are Specific, Measurable, Achievable, Relevant, and Time-bound. In an MBO framework, individuals and teams collaborate to establish clear objectives that contribute to overall organizational goals. The focus is on outcomes rather than just following routine processes. By defining and pursuing measurable results, MBO aims to enhance organizational performance, productivity, and effectiveness.

(*c*) **Particular view of human behaviour:** This principle reflects the belief that individuals are more motivated and engaged when they actively participate in goal-setting processes. MBO recognizes that people thrive when they have a clear understanding of their roles and responsibilities and are involved in determining their own objectives. It encourages a sense of ownership and autonomy, assuming that employees are more likely to be motivated when they have a stake in the goals they are working towards. This aspect of MBO aligns with theories of motivation that highlight the importance of intrinsic motivation and self-determination in driving individual performance.

In essence, MBO combines a focus on concrete results with a human-centric approach that values employee involvement, motivation, and a sense of purpose in achieving organizational objectives.

45. (B): The Colon Classification, developed by S.R. Ranganathan, is a faceted classification system designed to organize and retrieve knowledge systematically. It uses facets to represent various aspects or characteristics of a subject. Each facet contributes to a composite class number that uniquely identifies a specific subject.

Mathematics (V1): This facet encompasses works related to pure mathematics, including mathematical theories and principles.

Physics (V2): This facet includes subjects related to the study of matter, energy, and the fundamental principles governing the physical world.

Engineering (V4): This facet is dedicated to works related to engineering disciplines, covering a wide range of applied sciences and practical applications.

Chemistry (V3): This facet includes subjects related to the study of matter, its composition, properties, and chemical reactions.

46. (B): The Library of Congress is not designated as a National Library. While the Library of Congress is a significant library in the United States and serves as the de facto national library for the U.S., it does not hold the formal title of the National Library. A designated National Library is typically a repository of a nation's intellectual and cultural heritage, serving as a central institution for collecting, preserving, and providing access to the nation's literature and knowledge. The National Library of India, located in Kolkata, plays a crucial role in preserving India's rich literary and cultural heritage. The British Library, based in London, is the national library of the United Kingdom and one of the world's largest libraries, housing a vast collection of books, manuscripts, and other materials. The Kungliga Biblioteket, or the Royal Library of Sweden, serves as the national library of Sweden, contributing to the preservation and dissemination of Swedish cultural and intellectual resources.

47. (C): The mode in a dataset is the value that appears most frequently. It is a measure of central tendency that provides insight into the most common observation or category. In a distribution, the mode identifies the peak or peaks, indicating where the data cluster the most. Unlike the mean (average) or median, the mode is not affected by extreme values or outliers, making it particularly useful for categorical data or distributions with multiple peaks. For example, in a dataset of test scores, the mode would be the score that occurs most frequently, giving a sense of the most prevalent performance level.

48. (C):

(*a*) **He is regarded as the Apostle of the Indian Library Movement:** Maharaja Sayajirao Gaekwad III, the ruler of the princely state of Baroda, is often referred to as the Apostle of the Indian Library Movement. During his reign (1875-1939), he played a pivotal role in promoting library development and education. His vision and efforts contributed significantly to the growth of libraries across the country.

(*b*) **He invited W.A. Borden for organizing the library system in his state:** Maharaja Sayajirao Gaekwad III recognized the importance of modernizing the library system in Baroda. To achieve this, he invited W. A. Borden, an American librarian, to organize and establish an efficient library system. Borden's expertise and collaboration with the Maharaja led to the improvement and expansion of libraries in the state.

(*e*) **He played a vital role in providing matching grants to start village libraries:** Maharaja Sayajirao Gaekwad III actively supported the establishment of libraries in villages. To encourage the growth of libraries at the grassroots level, he provided matching grants, creating an incentive for communities to initiate and maintain their own village libraries. This initiative contributed to increased literacy and knowledge dissemination in rural areas.

Maharaja Sayajirao Gaekwad III's contributions to the Indian Library Movement include being a visionary leader, inviting experts like W.A. Borden for library development, and promoting the creation of village libraries through financial support. His multifaceted efforts left a lasting impact on library infrastructure and education in India.

49. (D): Carol Kuhlthau's seminal ISP model outlines six stages of information seeking behaviour. When considering these stages in reverse order, a clear progression from information synthesis to initial task recognition emerges. Let's delve into this reversed sequence:

(*a*) **Collection:** This is the stage where the user actively gathers information pertinent to the focused perspective. At this point, uncertainty begins to subside as the individual's interest and involvement in the topic deepens. The act of collecting relevant information provides a sense of direction and purpose, contributing to a reduction in uncertainty.

(*c*) **Formulation:** In the formulation stage, the user has already established a focused perspective on the topic. This involves refining the research question and search terms. The uncertainty diminishes as confidence starts to increase. The user is transitioning from the initial exploration to a more targeted and informed approach to information seeking.

(*d*) **Exploration:** Exploration is the initial stage where users encounter inconsistent and sometimes incompatible information. During this stage, uncertainty, confusion, and doubt often increase. Users find themselves in the "dip" of confidence, navigating through the challenges of the early phases of the search process.

(*b*) **Selection:** This is the starting point where a general area, topic, or problem is identified. Initial uncertainty often gives way to a brief sense of optimism and a readiness to begin the search. Users are at the early stages of defining their information needs and shaping their search parameters.

50. (B):

(*c*) **Know-what:** This is the foundational level of knowledge, representing factual information about a subject. It involves knowing facts, data, or information without necessarily understanding the deeper context or implications.

(*b*) **Know-why:** Moving beyond factual knowledge, this level involves understanding the underlying principles or reasons behind the information. It requires a grasp of the cause-and-effect relationships and the logic behind certain phenomena.

(*a*) **Know-how:** This is practical knowledge that goes beyond under-standing to application. It involves the ability to use knowledge effectively in real-world situations, applying skills and know-what to solve problems or achieve specific goals.

(*d*) **Know-who:** This level of knowledge pertains to understanding the people or resources involved. It includes knowledge about experts, contacts, or sources that can provide additional information or support in a given context.

51. (C): Prenatal cataloguing involves the process of printing catalogue cards before a book is officially published. This proactive approach allows libraries to prepare catalog entries well in advance of a book's release. Typically, cataloguers work with publishers to gather relevant information about the book, such as author, title, subject headings, and other bibliographic details. With this information, catalogue cards are created and printed, enabling libraries to have a comprehensive record ready for the book's inclusion in their catalog immediately upon publication.

This method streamlines the cataloging workflow, facilitating quicker access to new materials for library patrons and ensuring a more efficient integration of the book into the library's collection.

52. (A):

(*a*) Public Data Network (PDN) is a broad term that encompasses various data transmission services provided to the public. PDNs facilitate communication and the exchange of information, including services like email, file transfer, and remote access. These networks are designed to handle different types of data applications and support connectivity for users to communicate and share information seamlessly.

(*b*) Integrated Services Digital Network (ISDN), on the other hand, is a telecommunications standard that provides a set of digital communi-cation services over traditional telephone copper wires. ISDN allows for the transmission of voice and data simultaneously, making it a versatile technology for integrated communications. It supports multiple channels, allowing users to use voice and data services concurrently on the same line.

53. (A): Reading circles can be considered a group orientation program when designed to facilitate the integration of individuals into a new environment or organization. In this context, reading circles involve a group of individuals coming together to read and discuss relevant materials, such as handbooks, policies, or introductory documents. This collaborative approach not only encourages a shared understanding of essential information but also promotes interaction and dialogue among participants. Reading circles can serve as an effective tool in the orientation process by fostering a sense of community, encouraging questions, and helping individuals absorb key information in a supportive group setting. This method allows newcomers to familiarize themselves with important materials and establish connections with their peers, contributing to a smoother integration into the organizational culture.

54. (D): The call number "025.32 SEH T" for the textbook "Cataloguing Manual AACR-II" by R.L. Sehgal is a library classification system that aids in the organization and retrieval of the book. The number 025.32 before the decimal point indicates the subject classification, possibly related to cataloging or information organization.

The letters "SEH" immediately after the decimal point represent the author's last name, identifying R.L. Sehgal as the author. The letter "T" at the end likely stands for the initial letter of the book's title, suggesting that the title begins with "T," possibly corresponding to "Cataloguing Manual AACR-II."

This unique call number serves as a specific address for the book within the library's collection, facilitating efficient location and retrieval by library users and staff.

55. (D)

56. (B): Alexander Graham Bell invented the Photo phone as a groundbreaking device to showcase the transmission of sound using light waves. Patented in 1880, the Photo phone utilized a technology where sound vibrations were converted into varying light patterns, which were then transmitted through a beam of sunlight. On the receiving end, a selenium photo detector (a primitive form of a photodiode) captured the variations in light intensity and converted them back into sound. This early experiment laid the foundation for the concept of wireless communication through visible light media, an idea that has evolved into modern optical communication technologies. The Photo phone marked an important step in the history of telecommunications, demonstrating the potential for transmitting audio signals without the need for physical wires.

57. (B): M.O. Thomas was the first president of the Indian Library Association (ILA). He was elected as the first President in 1933. He was a librarian at the University of Madras and contributed greatly to developing library services in India. Thomas played a significant role in the development of library services in India during his tenure as President. This likely involved advocating for policies, promoting professional development, and establishing standards for libraries. Thomas's leadership at the ILA during its formative years marks him as an important figure in the history of Indian libraries. The ILA was established on September 13, 1933 at the First All India Library Conference in Calcutta. The association offers a variety of services and programs to its members and others seeking technical support or advice.

58. (C):

(*a*) **Identify the research topic:** This is the starting point where you define the specific area or question you want to investigate in your historical research. It's crucial to have a clear and focused research topic to guide your efforts.

(*c*) **Conduct a background literature review:** Once you have your research topic, you need to review existing literature related to your subject. This involves exploring books, articles, and other scholarly works to understand the context of your research, identify key themes, and determine what is already known about the topic.

(*b*) **Identify and locate primary and secondary sources:** With a solid understanding of the existing literature, you can then identify and locate primary sources (such as original documents, letters, diaries) and secondary sources (interpretations and analyses by other scholars). This step is essential for gathering the raw material needed for your research.

(*d*) **Evaluate the authenticity and accuracy of sources:** Once you've gathered your sources, it's important to critically assess them. Consider the reliability, credibility, and context of each source. Evaluate whether the information provided is accurate and whether the source is trustworthy.

(*e*) **Analyze the data and develop a narrative exposition of the findings:** After ensuring the quality of your sources, you can move on to analyzing the data. This involves extracting meaningful patterns, themes, or insights from the collected information.

Once you've conducted your analysis, you can use it to construct a coherent narrative that presents your historical findings in a way that contributes to the understanding of the chosen topic.

These steps represent a systematic and logical progression in historical research, guiding researchers from the initial identification of a research topic to the development of a well-supported narrative based on critical analysis and evaluation of sources.

59. (D): Open DOAR service was launched in 2005. While OpenDOAR itself emerged in 2003, its complementary service, Open DOAR service, did begin operating in 2005. This automated notification system alerts repositories of updates and changes within the directory, making it a valuable tool for repository managers.

So, this statement is true. As of January 2024, Japan indeed holds the position of the second-largest participant country in OpenDOAR, boasting numerous academic and research repositories registered on the platform.

60. (D):

(*b*) **Not commercially published:** Unlike conventional books or journals, grey literature typically bypasses the established commercial publishing channels. This means it's not readily available through bookstores or subscription services. Instead, it might be found through institutional repositories, government websites, conference proceedings, or technical reports. This lack of commercial involvement often reflects the document's origin within non-profit organizations, research institutions, or government agencies, focusing on disseminating information within specific communities or fields rather than maximizing profit.

(*d*) **Protected by IPR (not always true):** While some grey literature might be protected by intellectual property rights like patents or copyrights, this isn't a defining characteristic. Many forms of grey literature, such as conference papers or technical reports, are freely accessible and shared without restriction. The focus lies on knowledge dissemination and collaboration within specific communities rather than exclusive ownership of the information.

(*e*) **Not procured through normal book publication channels:** As mentioned earlier, grey literature often utilizes non-traditional channels for distribution due to its bypassing of commercial publishing. This might involve online repositories, institutional websites, direct distribution by the producing organization, or presentations at conferences. This lack of reliance on established bookselling channels further underscores the document's origin outside the mainstream academic publishing circuit.

By combining these key features, it effectively captures the essence of grey literature. It's not about ephemerality, presence of ISBNs, or IPR protection, but rather about its origin, distribution channels, and primary purpose of knowledge dissemination within specific communities beyond the confines of traditional commercial publishing.

61. (C): Artificial Super Intelligence (ASI) refers to a theoretical level of artificial intelligence that surpasses human cognitive abilities across a broad range of tasks. It envisions a form of intelligence capable of outperforming the most brilliant human minds in virtually every intellectual and creative endeavor. Unlike Artificial General Intelligence (AGI), which aims to mimic human intelligence in all its facets, ASI goes beyond by potentially exhibiting intelligence and problem-solving capabilities far superior to those of any human being. The concept of ASI raises profound ethical and existential questions, as it suggests a level of intelligence that could fundamentally transform society, economies, and even the nature of human existence.

62. **(D):** The Point System is a job evaluation method where jobs are systematically assessed based on identified compensable factors, and points are assigned to each factor based on its significance in achieving organizational objectives. In this method, specific factors such as skill requirements, responsibility levels, and working conditions are determined, and a numerical value or point is allocated to each factor. The sum of these points reflects the overall value or worth of a particular job within the organization. The Point System provides a structured and quantitative approach to job evaluation, allowing organizations to establish a hierarchy of job values and facilitate decisions related to compensation, ensuring that remuneration aligns with the relative importance and complexity of different roles within the company.

63. **(D):** Non-sampling errors are inherent inaccuracies in research data that are not linked to the process of selecting a sample but can occur at any stage of the research process. These errors often arise during the collection and preparation of data, manifesting as measurement discrepancies, inaccuracies in recording information, or flaws in the research instruments. However, non-sampling errors are not confined to a specific phase; they can surface during questionnaire distribution, report writing, or any other research activity. Mitigating these errors requires vigilant quality control measures to ensure the accuracy and reliability of the collected data, underscoring the significance of thoroughness and precision throughout the entire research endeavor.

64. **(C):** The Memory of the World Programme was initiated by UNESCO (United Nations Educational, Scientific and Cultural Organization) in 1992 to safeguard and promote the world's documentary heritage. This program recognizes the importance of preserving and providing access to significant cultural documents, archives, and manuscripts. The primary goal is to raise awareness about the importance of documentary heritage and encourage the preservation of valuable materials that contribute to the collective memory of humanity. Through the Memory of the World Programme, UNESCO works to foster international cooperation in preserving and providing access to documentary heritage, ensuring that these cultural treasures are protected for future generations and remain accessible to the global community.

65. **(C):** According to Botha and others in 2011, Generation Y is using Facebook as an alternative to email. Generation Y includes people born between 1976 and 1999.

Botha, M. Farshid, and L. Pitt also say that Generation Y finds Facebook more convenient and time-saving. Email is a digital communication tool used to send messages, documents, and other information to specific recipients or groups. Facebook, in its early years, gained popularity among Millennials as a primary platform for connecting with friends, sharing updates, and communicating. While communication preferences can evolve, Millennials have played a significant role in shaping the digital landscape and influencing how people interact online.

66. **(C):** The Canon of Array is not directly related to the verbal plane but pertains

to the visual presentation or arrangement of elements. In the context of design and aesthetics, the Canon of Array involves organizing and structuring visual elements in a way that is aesthetically pleasing and effective. It is particularly relevant in fields like graphic design, where the placement, balance, and arrangement of images, text, and other visual components are crucial for conveying a message or creating a visually appealing composition. Unlike canons such as the Canon of Context, which involves understanding and interpreting the surrounding words or context of a passage, the Canon of Array focuses on the visual aspects and spatial relationships within a design or visual representation.

67. (A): Preference Theory is a concept rooted in economics and decision theory, asserting that individual attitudes towards risk differ, leading to varied preferences in decision-making. According to this theory, individuals exhibit different levels of risk aversion or risk-seeking behaviour based on their personal preferences, experiences, and psychological factors. In the realm of decision-making, people may make choices that reflect their tolerance for uncertainty or their willingness to take risks to achieve certain outcomes. This theory is particularly relevant in financial decision contexts where individuals weigh potential gains and losses, and it recognizes the subjective nature of risk perception, emphasizing that there is no one-size-fits-all approach to understanding how individuals respond to and navigate risk in their choices.

68. (D): According to S.R. Ranganathan's Five Laws of Library Science, the user community encompasses three distinct categories: Freshmen, Ordinary Enquirers, and Specialist Enquirers.

(*b*) Freshmen, representing new library users, require introductory sessions and comprehensive guidance to navigate the library's resources and services effectively. Ranganathan advocated for user-friendly interfaces, clear signage, and personalized assistance to foster a welcoming and supportive environment for first-time library patrons.

(*d*) Ordinary Enquirers, the most frequent users, seek general information or recreational reading materials. Ranganathan emphasized the importance of well-organized collections, intuitive search tools, and efficient circulation systems to facilitate their information retrieval needs and ensure a positive user experience.

(*e*) Specialist Enquirers, including researchers and academicians, demand in-depth and specialized information resources. Ranganathan envisioned libraries as repositories of comprehensive collections, encompassing rare documents and specialized databases, and advocated for the development of expert reference services to cater to their complex research objectives and support their intellectual pursuits.

By defining these user categories and recognizing their diverse needs, Ranganathan's classification system lays the foundation for a user-centric library environment. His principles continue to inform library practices worldwide, guiding librarians in their efforts to create accessible, efficient, and knowledge-rich spaces for all members of the user community.

69. (C): A documentation list typically comprises scholarly and reference materials that provide authoritative and comprehensive information. In the given options, "Fodor's Guide to India" stands out as it is not a documentation list but rather a travel guide. While the Science Citation Index, Annual Review of Psychology, and Keesing's

Record of World Events are examples of documentation lists commonly used in academic and research settings, Fodor's Guide to India serves a different purpose by offering travel-related information and recommendations for tourists exploring India.

Documentation lists are integral to academic research, aiding scholars and researchers in accessing credible sources for information and citation purposes.

70. (B): MedIND serves as a comprehensive resource in the field of biomedicine, offering a database of full-text articles from peer-reviewed Indian biomedical journals. Provided by the National Informatics Centre (NIC) in India, MedIND plays a crucial role in promoting access to scholarly research within the biomedical domain. Researchers, healthcare professionals, and individuals interested in biomedical literature can utilize MedIND to access and explore a diverse range of scientific articles published in Indian journals. The database contributes significantly to the dissemination of knowledge and facilitates the sharing of research findings within the Indian biomedical community, fostering advancements in healthcare and medical sciences.

71. (C): Statement I is correct because a key function of a Research and Development (R&D) library is to provide reference services. Reference services in a research library are essential for supporting the information needs of researchers and scholars. These services include helping users locate relevant literature, providing assistance in navigating databases, offering guidance on citation styles, and facilitating access to a wide range of resources that contribute to the research process.

On the other hand, Statement II is incorrect because it makes a sweeping assumption that users have no time to use the library as they are entirely involved in research. In reality, while researchers may be deeply engaged in their research activities, they often rely on library services to access crucial information, journals, databases, and other resources that contribute to the success of their research projects.

Many researchers actively utilize library resources to stay updated on the latest research trends, access relevant literature, and enhance the quality of their work.

72. (B): A KWIC (Key Word In Context) index is a type of index that presents key terms or keywords along with their contextual information, allowing users to quickly locate relevant information.

(*a*) **Key word:** The key word is the central term that the KWIC index entry is organized around. It represents the core concept or idea that the entry is intended to highlight. Users scanning the KWIC index look for these key words to quickly identify relevant topics or terms.

(*b*) **Context:** The context in a KWIC index entry provides additional words or phrases that surround the key word. This contextual information offers a brief snippet of the content in which the key term appears. It helps users understand how the term is used and provides a glimpse into the broader context of the information.

(*e*) **Identification/location code:** The identification or location code in a KWIC index entry serves as a reference to indicate where in the document or text the key term is located. It helps users pinpoint the specific location of the information, allowing for easy retrieval of the relevant content.

73. (B): BibSonomy was created by the Institute of Knowledge and Data Engineering at the University of Kassel in Germany. Launched in 2006, BibSonomy is a social bookmarking and publication-sharing system designed primarily for researchers. It enables users to collaboratively manage and share bookmarks, academic publications, and other scholarly resources. BibSonomy incorporates social tagging, making it a valuable tool for organizing and discovering content within academic communities. Researchers can collaboratively build and share bibliographies, explore resources relevant to their fields, and engage in knowledge exchange. The platform's focus on social collaboration distinguishes it as a resourceful tool in the academic and research community, fostering collective knowledge sharing and discovery.

74. (B): The National Central Library Committee established in 1948 was headed by the eminent librarian and information scientist, S.R. Ranganathan. Renowned as the "Father of Library Science in India," Ranganathan made significant contributions to the development of library systems and services in the country. As the head of the National Central Library Committee, he played a crucial role in shaping the vision and policies for the establishment of a central library in India. Ranganathan's influence extended beyond this committee, as he contributed to the formulation of key principles and standards in library science, leaving a lasting impact on the field of library and information science in India and globally.

75. (C):

(*a*) **FORTRAN (FORmula TRANslation, 1957):** Emerged as the first high level programming language, designed specifically for scientific and engineering calculations. Developed by IBM, it revolutionized numerical computation and remains influential in fields like physics, meteorology, and aerospace engineering. Its enduring popularity stems from its efficiency in handling complex mathematical equations and simulations.

(*d*) **ALGOL (ALGOrithmic Language, 1958):** Created as a language tailored for expressing algorithms clearly and concisely. Highly influential in language design, it introduced key concepts like block structure and recursion.

(*c*) **BASIC (Beginner's All-purpose Symbolic Instruction Code, 1964):** Developed at Dartmouth College to make programming accessible to students and non-experts. Designed for ease of learning and use, it became a popular choice for early personal computers.

(*b*) **Pascal (1970):** Named after mathematician Blaise Pascal, it was developed to promote structured programming principles and encourage clear, well-organized code. Widely used for teaching programming concepts due to its readability and emphasis on good coding practices. Influenced later languages like C++ and Java, which adopted its structured approach and focus on code maintainability.

76. (B):

(*b*) **E prints (2000):** Pioneer in the digital repository world, E prints pre-dates the formal DAMS acronym. Created by researchers at Cornell University, it focused on archiving scientific publications like preprints and conference papers, paving the way for open access to academic research.

(*d*) **Space (2002):** Developed by MIT Libraries and Hewlett-Packard, DSpace became a foundational open-source DAMS platform. Designed specifically for managing research output, it offered tools for archiving, indexing, and providing access to scholarly articles, datasets, and other research materials. Its open-source nature and flexibility led to widespread adoption by universities and research institutions worldwide.

(*c*) **Fedora (2003):** Initially developed by the Andrew W. Mellon Foundation, Fedora aimed to build a robust and modular infrastructure for managing digital objects of any kind. Its flexible architecture and emphasis on standards compliance made it popular for managing diverse collections in libraries, museums, and archives. It later evolved into Fedora Commons, a community-driven open-source platform.

(*a*) **Islandora (2004):** Born from the University of Florida, Islandora built upon the Drupal content management system to create a user-friendly DAMS platform. Focusing on customizable modules and community-driven development, it provided libraries and cultural institutions with tools for managing digital collections, showcasing them through engaging online exhibitions and promoting user interaction.

These four software programs represent pivotal moments in the evolution of DAMS solutions. They not only addressed the growing need for managing digital assets but also played a crucial role in advancing open access, fostering collaboration, and shaping the landscape of digital preservation for institutions across diverse sectors.

77. (D)

78. (A): Dynamic Library Web OPACs (Online Public Access Catalogs) have transformed library access, providing users with a convenient and flexible interface to navigate the library's resources. Beyond the traditional search and retrieval of bibliographic information, these modern systems offer a range of functionalities, empowering users to:

(*a*) **Renew Book:** This is a core feature of most OPACs. Whether through a dedicated "renew" button or automatic prompts, extending loan periods directly online saves users time and trips to the library. Some systems even offer bulk renewal options for multiple items, further enhancing convenience.

(*b*) **Access Content Page of Materials:** This option can have varied interpretations. While full-text access within the OPAC itself is less common, some systems offer "preview" functionalities for certain materials like journal articles or ebooks. These previews might provide snippets of text, tables of contents, or limited page views to give users a taste of the content before requesting the physical item or accessing it through dedicated digital platforms.

(*c*) **Ask for Copy of a Document:** This feature depends on the library's policies and technological infrastructure. Some OPACs might offer online request forms for document copies, allowing users to specify the desired material and preferred delivery method. However, libraries often handle copy requests through separate channels like email or in-person inquiries, particularly for complex requests or materials with copyright restrictions.

79. (B):

(*b*) **Library of the Anthropological Survey of India, Calcutta, is rich in maps and reprints:** This statement accurately captures the significance of this specialized library. Housing a treasure trove of maps and reprints related to anthropology, it serves as a vital resource for scholars and researchers in the field. The extensive collection provides valuable insights into cultural practices, geographic distributions, and historical dynamics, enriching research efforts and deepening our understanding of human societies.

(*c*) **The National Forest Library and Information Center is situated at Dehradun:** Established in 1906, the National Forest Library and Information Center in Dehradun stands as a leading repository of forestry knowledge in India. Its comprehensive collection of books, journals, maps, and other materials caters to the needs of students, researchers, and practitioners alike, guiding sustainable forest management practices and protecting India's rich biodiversity.

(*d*) **Indian Institute of Science Library is named after JRD Tata:** This statement, however, carries an error. While JRD Tata made invaluable contributions to the Indian Institute of Science, the library doesn't bear his name. Its official designation is simply the Indian Institute of Science Library. Recognizing the institute's dedication to scientific research and innovation, the library serves as a cornerstone of its knowledge infrastructure, supporting scholarly pursuits and nurturing future generations of scientists.

80. (C): WIPO, or the World Intellectual Property Organization, is a specialized agency of the United Nations established to promote and protect intellectual property (IP) rights globally. Founded in 1967, WIPO serves as a forum for international cooperation in the field of IP, bringing together member states and stakeholders to develop and harmonize policies, laws, and practices related to intellectual property. WIPO plays a crucial role in facilitating the protection of inventions, trademarks, copyright, and other forms of intellectual property on a global scale. The organization also provides services such as the registration of patents and trademarks, as well as dispute resolution mechanisms to address IP-related conflicts. WIPO's mission is to encourage innovation, creativity, and the fair use of intellectual property while balancing the interests of rights holders and the public.

81. (B)

82. (A): EBSDIC, or Extended Binary Coded Decimal Interchange Code, is a character encoding scheme that extends the earlier BCDIC (Binary Coded Decimal Interchange Code) and is commonly used in IBM mainframe computers. Introduced by IBM, EBCDIC represents characters using an 8-bit binary code, with each byte typically encoding one character. Unlike ASCII (American Standard Code for Information Interchange), which is widely used in personal computers, EBCDIC was primarily designed for mainframes. The "Extended" in EBCDIC signifies its expanded character set, accommodating a broader range of symbols, letters, and special characters. Despite its prevalence in legacy systems, EBCDIC is less common in modern computing environments, where ASCII and Unicode are more widely adopted.

83. (B): Hackers: All hackers possess technical skills related to computer systems and software. However, it's their intent and purpose that differentiates white hat and black hat hackers. While some use their skills for malicious purposes (black hat), others use them for good, such as identifying vulnerabilities to improve security (white hat).

84. (A)

85. (C)

86. (C): CeRA, or the Consortium for e-Resources in Agriculture, is a collaborative initiative in the field of Agriculture Sciences. It serves as a consortia platform aimed at providing electronic resources to the agricultural research and academic community. CeRA facilitates access to a wide range of digital resources, including research journals, databases, and other scholarly materials, enhancing the availability of agricultural information. This consortium brings together various institutions and organizations to pool resources, both financial and intellectual, to ensure comprehensive and efficient access to e-resources. By promoting collaboration and resource sharing, CeRA contributes to the advancement of research and knowledge dissemination in the field of agriculture.

87. (D): Job evaluation is the systematic process of determining the relative worth of different jobs within an organization. This process involves assessing and comparing the value of one job to another in terms of factors such as skills, responsibilities, effort, and working conditions. The primary goal of job evaluation is to establish a fair and consistent hierarchy of jobs based on their contribution to the organization. This process aids in developing a rational and equitable compensation structure, ensuring that employees are appropriately rewarded for their roles and responsibilities. Job evaluation is a key component of human resource management and is crucial for maintaining internal equity and transparency within an organization's job structure.

88. (B): The Sinha Committee proposed a comprehensive public library system for India, encompassing various levels and institutions. Considering the specific options presented:

(*a*) **National Library:** The establishment of a National Library was recommended to serve as a flagship institution at the national level. This library would house a comprehensive collection of books, documents, and resources, acting as a reservoir of knowledge and culture for the entire nation.

(*c*) **State Central Library:** The committee emphasized the need for State Central Libraries in each state. These libraries were envisioned as key institutions to promote literacy, education, and research at the state level. State Central Libraries play a pivotal role in coordinating library services and resources within their respective states.

(*e*) **District Central Library:** Recognizing the importance of local accessibility, the committee suggested the creation of District Central Libraries. These libraries were intended to cater to the informational and recreational needs of communities at the district level. District Central Libraries act as focal points for promoting reading habits and providing essential services to the local population.

89. (D): ASTINFO, or the Regional Network for the Exchange of Information and Experiences in Science and Technology in Asia and the Pacific, serves as a collaborative platform to facilitate the sharing of information and experiences in the realms of science and technology. This network, operating in the Asia and Pacific region, aims to foster cooperation and knowledge exchange among institutions and individuals involved in scientific and technological endeavors. By promoting the exchange of information and experiences, ASTINFO contributes to advancements in research, innovation, and technological development across the diverse countries and regions within Asia and the Pacific. The network plays a crucial role in building synergies, fostering partnerships, and enhancing the collective capacity for scientific and technological progress in the region.

90. (A): In asynchronous mode of transmission, START and STOP bits are employed to frame individual characters in a serial data stream. The asynchronous communication method allows data to be transmitted without the sender and receiver being synchronized in time. The START bit indicates the beginning of a character, alerting the receiver to prepare for incoming data. The actual data bits follow the START bit, and the STOP bit or bits mark the end of the character. The use of START and STOP bits aids in proper synchronization between the transmitting and receiving devices, enabling accurate interpretation of the data being transmitted. Asynchronous transmission is commonly used for its flexibility, as it does not require a constant clock signal, making it suitable for variable data rates and minimizing overhead compared to synchronous transmission.

91. (A): The passage emphasizes that librarians, specifically Library and Information professionals, should set aside their assumptions and prejudices to safeguard the fundamental principles of librarianship. The discussion revolves around the importance of a code of ethics for librarians and information professionals, highlighting that it should not be merely a superficial statement crafted to appease public library boards. Instead, the code should embody principles and convictions that librarians historically hold dear. The focus is on conducting professional work in a manner that aligns with these values. The passage also underscores the societal judgment of a profession based on the ethical standards followed by its individual members. In this context, ethical considerations related to material selection and intellectual freedom are particularly crucial, with the expectation that librarians remain neutral and provide information as requested, adhering to the social obligation of allowing access to diverse perspectives.

92. (C): Finks' thesis emphasizes that a code of ethics for librarians and information professionals should not be a superficial or hollow statement written merely to satisfy public library boards. Instead, the crucial aspect is that the code must embody the principles and convictions that librarians have historically regarded as valuable. Finks argues for a meaningful and substantive code that reflects the genuine values and beliefs of the profession. The emphasis is on the code being more than a token gesture and serving as a true reflection of the ethical foundations that librarians hold dear. This perspective underscores the need for a code of ethics that goes beyond appeasing external entities and truly guides the professional conduct of librarians based on their intrinsic values and principles.

93. (A): Lee W. Finks wrote about the necessity for the development of a new code of ethics for librarianship. In 1991, Finks expressed the need for this code to go beyond being a mere formality or a document written to please public library boards. According to his perspective, the code should embody the principles and convictions that librarians historically hold as valuable. Finks argued that the code of ethics should be a substantive reflection of the genuine values and beliefs within the profession, focusing on guiding the professional conduct of librarians based on these intrinsic principles. His stance underscores the importance of an authentic and meaningful code of ethics that truly represents the ethical foundations of librarianship.

94. (B): In 1995, the American Library Association (ALA) responded to the call for a new code of ethics by developing and implementing one. This initiative was a result of the recognition of the evolving landscape of librarianship and the need for a comprehensive and relevant ethical framework. The ALA's Code of Ethics serves as a guiding document for librarians and information professionals, outlining fundamental principles and values that should govern their professional conduct. The code emphasizes considerations related to intellectual freedom, material selection, and the overall social obligation to provide access to diverse perspectives. By establishing a clear and contemporary set of ethical standards, the ALA's Code of Ethics aims to ensure the integrity and professionalism of library services in a dynamic information environment.

95. (A): Johan Bekker emphasized the societal perception of a profession based on the actions and behaviour of its individual members. In the context of the passage, Bekker's point underscores the collective responsibility of professionals, suggesting that the ethical conduct of each member contributes to the overall reputation and judgment of the entire profession. His observation highlights the importance of maintaining a clearly defined set of ethical standards for all members to follow. This collective adherence to ethical principles ensures that the profession is viewed positively by society and reinforces the credibility and trustworthiness of the field as a whole. In particular, the passage emphasizes ethical considerations related to the selection of materials and intellectual freedom, suggesting that these aspects play a crucial role in shaping the public perception of the library and information profession.

96. (A): The passage emphasizes the profound importance of reading, comparing it to exercise for the body in its impact on the mind. The analogy suggests that just as exercise is crucial for physical well-being, reading is essential for mental health and development. The joy of reading, the passage contends, transcends verbal expression and can only be truly appreciated through personal experience. Reading is depicted as a source of comfort, capable of soothing and relieving tension and loneliness. The passage underscores the therapeutic nature of reading, likening it to a mental relaxation akin to yoga. Moreover, it emphasizes the crucial role of parental and teacher motivation in fostering a reading habit, particularly among children, and emphasizes the enduring companionship and loyalty offered by books.

97. (B): The passage cites a 2016 study revealing that individuals who engage in a daily reading habit of at least thirty minutes are likely to enjoy a longer life. This finding underscores the potential health benefits associated with regular reading. While the passage doesn't provide specific details about the study's methodology, the implication is that a moderate and consistent reading routine contributes positively to overall well-being. Reading is presented as a mindful activity that not only enriches the mind but also potentially contributes to longevity. The passage suggests that the act of reading, even for a relatively short duration each day, may have a positive impact on one's health and life expectancy, highlighting the multifaceted advantages of this intellectual pursuit.

98. (B): The passage draws a comparison between reading and yoga, asserting that reading, like yoga, offers complete relaxation to the mind. It highlights how engaging in the act of reading can serve as a mental reprieve from the stresses and challenges of daily life, similar to the calming effects of yoga on the body and mind. Both activities are depicted as sources of solace and relief, capable of soothing tension and loneliness. The analogy suggests that, just as yoga provides a holistic sense of relaxation for the body, reading offers a parallel sense of mental tranquility. By aligning reading with yoga in terms of its potential to bring about a state of complete relaxation, the passage underscores the therapeutic and rejuvenating aspects of the act of reading, positioning it as a valuable means to find solace and escape in the world of literature.

99. (D): The passage implies that a reader's good friend is none other than books. Books are depicted as faithful companions that never betray and always accompany the reader. This metaphorical representation underscores the unique and enduring relationship between individuals who enjoy reading and the written word. Books are seen as reliable sources of comfort, providing solace and relief from tension and loneliness. The passage suggests that the bond between a reader and books is unwavering and steadfast, emphasizing the trust and companionship found within the pages of literature. The portrayal of books as faithful friends reinforces the idea that reading is not just an intellectual pursuit but a deeply personal and enriching experience that brings a sense of loyalty and companionship to those who engage in it.

100. (C): The passage suggests that the joy of reading is an emotion that transcends verbal expression and can only be truly understood through personal experience. Unlike exercise, exhaling, or experiments, reading's profound impact on the mind is conveyed through the subjective and immersive experience it offers to individuals. The act of reading, delving into the worlds created by words on the pages, brings a unique and enriching joy that goes beyond mere words. This joy is deeply personal and varies from person to person, as it involves the intimate connection between the reader and the narrative. The passage encourages individuals to engage in the act of reading to fully comprehend and appreciate the delight it brings, highlighting the experiential nature of the joy derived from immersing oneself in the written word.

Previous Years' Paper (Solved)

National Testing Agency (NTA)

UGC-NET Junior Research Fellowship & Assistant Professor Eligibility Exam

LIBRARY & INFORMATION SCIENCE, March–2023

(Online exam held on 13-03-2023)

PAPER-II

Note: *This paper contains **hundred** (**100**) objective type questions of **two** (**2**) marks each. **All** questions are **compulsory**.*

1. _______ is a non-profit organization that enables the sharing and use of creativity and knowledge through free legal tools.

A. Creative Commons
B. Sherpa
C. Websites creation
D. Derivative Creation

2. Who said "Where is the information lost in data, knowledge lost in information and wisdom lost in knowledge"?

A. Richard Smiraglia
B. Ackoff Russel
C. Allan Frost
D. T.S. Eliot

3. _______ is the informal organizational communication network.

A. Invisible network
B. White Water Rapids
C. Calm Waters
D. Grapevine

4. On recommendations of National Knowledge Commission, which of the following is set up as the nodal agency for National Translation Mission?

A. English and Foreign Languages University, Hyderabad
B. Raja Rammohan Roy Library Foundation. Kolkata
C. Central Institute of Indian Languages, Mysuru
D. Raja Rammohan Roy National Agency for ISBN, New Delhi

5. During the Mughal period the Head Librarian was known as:

A. Darogha
B. Muhatin
C. Nizam
D. Kitabdar

6. First Public Library Act enacted in the pre-independent India.

A. Kolhapur Public Libraries Act (Karveer Vachan Mandir)
B. Madras Public Libraries Act
C. Baroda Public Libraries Act
D. Travancore Public Libraries Act

7. The first library committee for a university library in India was constituted at:

A. Madras University, Madras
B. Bombay University, Bombay
C. Banaras Hindu University, Varanasi
D. University of Calcutta, Calcutta

8. Who chaired the committee constituted to formulate NAPLIS in 1985?

A. P.B. Mangla
B. D.P. Chattopadhyaya
C. A. Neelameghan
D. A.C. Tikekar

9. The first commercial full-text legal information service is known as:
A. Manupatra
B. Manusmriti
C. Lexis Nexis
D. National Legal Service Authority

10. The abstracts in Indian Science Abstracts are arranged using:
A. Dewey Decimal Classification
B. Colon Classification
C. Library of Congress Classification
D. Universal Decimal Classification

11. In LISA database, what is the exact nomenclature used for the field representing the label 'NOFT'.
A. Nowhere
B. Anywhere
C. Anywhere except full text
D. Nowhere full text

12. The first abstracting periodical was published in the field of ________ .
A. Pharmaceutical Chemistry
B. Mathematical Sciences
C. Astrophysics and Atmospheric Services
D. Legal Sciences

13. Motion box is a ________ .
A. Knowledge sharing community
B. Video-sharing community
C. Audio-sharing community
D. Document sharing community

14. "Bibliophile" is a ________ .
A. Cataloguer
B. Classificationist
C. Information Specialist
D. Lover of books

15. GIS stands for:
A. Geological Informative Survey
B. Geographic Information System
C. Geographic Information Services
D. Geographic Information Software

16. Which of the following is not a form of index generally ?
A. Book index B. Periodical index
C. Newspaper index D. Music index

17. Which one of the following is not a vocabulary control ?
A. Classified Catalogue Code
B. Subject Headings
C. Classaurus
D. Thesaurus

18. Main entry in the catalogue contains:
A. Minimum Information about a documen
B. Nascent Information about a documen in brief
C. Maximum Information about a documen
D. Specific Information about a document

19. Which one of the following formats i followed in PRECIS to prepare inde entries?
A. Two-Line-Three-Part
B. One-Line-Two-Part
C. Two-Line-One-Part
D. Two-Line-Two-Part

20. Who developed the idea of Facet Analysis'
A. J.D. Brown B. Melvil Dewey
C. Henri la Fontaine D. S.R. Ranganatha

21. CPM was developed by ________ .
A. Koontz and Weihrich
B. United States Navy and Locknee Aircraft Corporation
C. DuPont Company
D. Dale D. McConkey

22. Which of the following is not a Huma Resource Planning technique?
A. Expert-Estimate Technique
B. Ranking Technique
C. Trend Projection Technique
D. Modelling Technique

23. Who among the following conducted a stud at Hawthorne, Illinois plant related to huma relations school?
A. Chester Barnard
B. Elton Mayo
C. Frederick Herzberg
D. Douglas McGregor

24. The collection development principle "Th best reading for the largest number at the lea cost" is given by:

A. McColvin B. Ranganathan
C. Melvil Dewey D. Drury

25. Who among the following introduced frequency modulation for mobile communication systems in 1935?
A. Edwin Armstrong B. Albert Einstein
C. Tim Burnerlee D. David Bohm

26. C is a ______ type of high level language.
A. Procedural Language
B. Non-procedural Language
C. Scientific Language
D. Business Language

27. Which type of Barcode printing is not long lasting?
A. Photo Composition Method
B. Laser Printing
C. Thermal Transfer Printing
D. Dot Matrix Printing

28. Which ot the "V" in big data is essential to have ways of detecting and correcting any false, incorrect or incomplete data?
A. Variety B. Velocity
C. Veracity D. Value

29. Which standard for data handling and interchange is used for structured documents?
A. PDF B. XML
C. JPEG D. GIF89A

30. Position detection pattern are arranged at ______ corners of QR code.
A. 1 B. 2
C. 3 D. 4

31. In SPSS, ______ is in the form of a spread sheet grid into which data can be entered.
A. Data Viewer B. Data Editor
C. Data dialog box D. Chart Editor

32. ________ provides a set of rules for assigning numerical values to answers obtained from respondents.
A. Questionnaire
B. Interview Schedule
C. Research Proposal
D. Code Book

33. Observing a group without interfering in its normal activities is referred as:
A. Observation under controlled conditions
B. Observation under unstructured conditions
C. Observation under natural conditions
D. Observation under structured conditions

34. Studies which are concerned with describing the characteristics of a particular individual or of a group is ________ .
A. Applied research
B. Descriptive research
C. Experimental research
D. Historical research

35. FORSA is a _______ .
A. Consortium
B. Open Educational Resources Portal
C. Automatic Abstracting Service
D. Federation of Library Associations

36. Open Educational Resources and course on Engineering and Technology are available at:
A. e-pg pathshala B. Diksha
C. NROER D. NPTEL

37. Secretariat libraries are part of _______ .
A. Chief Executive Officer's Personal Office
B. Government Secretariates
C. Corporate Offices
D. Public Libraries

38. Who defines hybrid library as "a cross breed which aims to meet the needs of new learning environment"?
A. Garrod and Oppenheim
B. Oppenheim and Smithson
C. Smithson and Garrod
D. Garrod, Oppenheim and Smithson

39. In Satellite Communication, multiple repeaters are known as ______
A. Detectors B. Modulators
C. Station D. Transponders

40. POST is performed by _________ .
A. Operating System B. Assembler
C. BIOS D. Linker

41. Basic requirements for copy rightability are:

(*a*) A work must be original

(*b*) A work must be reliable

(*c*) A work be fixed in a tangible form of expression

(*d*) A person must be a trustworthy

(*e*) A work must be a work of an authorship

Choose the correct answer from the options given below :

A. (*a*), (*b*) and (*c*) only

B. (*a*), (*c*) and (*d*) only

C. (*a*), (*c*) and (*e*) only

D. (*b*), (*c*) and (*d*) only

42. MOSCOW declaration refers to:

(*a*) Media and Information Literacy

(*b*) Information Consolidation

(*c*) Raising advocacy programmes

(*d*) International Conference held in 2012

(*e*) Organized by UNESCO

Choose the correct answer from the options given below:

A. (*a*), (*c*) and (*d*) only

B. (*b*), (*c*) and (*d*) only

C. (*b*), (*c*) and (*e*) only

D. (*a*), (*d*) and (*e*) only

43. Which of the following are true of CILIP?

(*a*) CILIP is the library and information association of Europe

(*b*) Membership is open to everyone working with information, knowledge, data or libraries

(*c*) The president is elected by members directly for two years

(*d*) CILIP was formed by the merger of Library Association and Institute of Information Scientists

(*e*) It has its headquarters at London

Choose the correct answer from the options given below:

A. (*a*), (*b*) and (*c*) only

B. (*b*), (*c*) and (*d*) only

C. (*b*), (*d*) and (*e*) only

D. (*c*), (*d*) and (*e*) only

44. Which of the following are identified categories of documents as suggested by S.R. Ranganathan?

(*a*) Primary document

(*b*) Neo Conventional document

(*c*) Meta document

(*d*) Non conventional document

(*e*) Secondary document

Choose the correct answer from the options given below:

A. (*a*), (*b*) and (*c*) only

B. (*b*), (*c*) and (*d*) only

C. (*c*), (*d*) and (*e*) only

D. (*d*), (*e*) and (*a*) only

45. Tools used for RSS Feeds include:

(*a*) Feedity **(*b*) Web RSS**

(*c*) Feed Fire **(*d*) Jot Spot**

(*e*) Edit me

Choose the correct answer from the options given below:

A. (*a*), (*b*) and (*c*) only

B. (*a*), (*c*) and (*d*) only

C. (*a*), (*d*) and (*e*) only

D. (*b*), (*c*) and (*d*) only

46. Which of the following can be treated as documentation list?

(*a*) Book review (*b*) News index

(*c*) Current contents (*d*) Treatise

(*e*) News digest

Choose the correct answer from the options given below:

A. (*a*), (*b*) and (*c*) only

B. (*d*), (*e*) and (*a*) only

C. (*b*), (*c*) and (*e*) only

D. (*b*), (*c*) and (*d*) only

47. Electronic Information Service is one that is:

(*a*) generated on the basis of digital information resource

(*b*) received by the user in digital format

(*c*) when downloaded printouts are delivered to the users by the library

(*d*) available in the 'form of access' through internet

Choose the most appropriate answer from the options given below:

A. (*a*), (*b*) and (*c*) only
B. (*b*), (*c*) and (*d*) only
C. (*a*), (*b*) and (*d*) only
D. (*c*), (*d*) and (*a*) only

48. Which of the following measures Lankes brought to assess the quality of digital reference services?

(*a*) Outcome measures
(*b*) Income measures
(*c*) Process measures
(*d*) Economic measures
(*e*) Electronic measures

Choose the correct answer from the options given below:

A. (*a*), (*b*) and (*c*) only
B. (*a*), (*c*) and (*d*) only
C. (*a*), (*c*) and (*e*) only
D. (*b*), (*c*) and (*d*) only

49. Biotechnology Information System covers:

(*a*) Genetic Engineering
(*b*) Electrical Engineering
(*c*) Chemical Engineering
(*d*) Immunology
(*e*) Neuro Informatics

Choose the correct answer from the options given below:

A. (*a*), (*b*) and (*c*) only
B. (*a*), (*c*) and (*d*) only
C. (*a*), (*d*) and (*b*) only
D. (*a*), (*d*) and (*e*) only

50. Sears list of Subject Headings include:

(*a*) Narrow Term
(*b*) Related term
(*c*) Broader Term
(*d*) Nearer Term
(*e*) Important Term

Choose the most appropriate answer from the options given below:

A. (*a*), (*d*) and (*e*) only
B. (*b*), (*d*) and (*e*) only
C. (*a*), (*b*) and (*c*) only
D. (*c*), (*d*) and (*e*) only

51. George Wilhelm Friedrich Hegol described the triadic scheme of knowledge classification into:

(*a*) Natural Science
(*b*) Logic Science
(*c*) Mental Science
(*d*) General Science
(*e*) Humanities

Choose the most appropriate answer from the options given below:

A. (*a*), (*b*) and (*d*) only
B. (*b*), (*c*) and (*e*) only
C. (*a*), (*b*) and (*c*) only
D. (*a*), (*b*) and (*e*) only

52. Which of the following are stages of Kurt Lewin's Change Management Model?

(*a*) Changing
(*b*) Unfreezing
(*c*) Preliminary Diagnosis
(*d*) Designing Autonomy

Choose the correct answer from the options given below:

A. (*a*) and (*b*) only B. (*b*) and (*c*) only
C. (*c*) and (*d*) only D. (*a*) and (*d*) only

53. Which of the following are basic components of any MBO system?

(*a*) Setting objectives
(*b*) Developing Action Plans
(*c*) Conducting periodic reviews
(*d*) Provision for jobs requiring trial operation

Choose the most appropriate answer from the options given below:

A. (*a*), (*b*) and (*d*) only
B. (*b*), (*c*) and (*d*) only
C. (*a*), (*b*) and (*c*) only
D. (*a*), (*c*) and (*d*) only

54. Which of the following are principles of Scientific Management?

(*a*) Job Analysis
(*b*) Unity of Command
(*c*) Division of Labour
(*d*) Stability of Tenure
(*e*) Maximum profits

Choose the most appropriate answer from the options given below:
A. (*a*), (*c*) and (*d*) only
B. (*b*), (*c*) and (*e*) only
C. (*a*), (*c*) and (*e*) only
D. (*b*), (*c*) and (*d*) only

55. Address space of the IP address is divided into following parts:
(*a*) Registry (*b*) Type prefix
(*c*) Identifier (*d*) Rest of Address
(*e*) Type identifier

Choose the correct answer from the options given below:
A. (*a*) and (*c*) only B. (*a*) and (*e*) only
C. (*b*) and (*d*) only D. (*c*) and (*d*) only

56. The presentation layer of OSI model has following functions:
(*a*) Reduces number of bits to be sent over the network
(*b*) Translates Data into standard format to be sent on the network
(*c*) Acts as a window for end users
(*d*) Inserts check points
(*e*) Prevents unauthorized users

Choose the correct answer from the options given below:
A. (*a*), (*b*) and (*c*) only
B. (*c*), (*d*) and (*e*) only
C. (*a*), (*b*) and (*e*) only
D. (*a*), (*b*) and (*d*) only

57. Digital signature can provide ______ for a message.
(*a*) Authentication
(*b*) Clarity
(*c*) Integrity
(*d*) Re-transmission
(*e*) Non-repudiation

Choose the most appropriate answer from the options given below:
A. (*a*), (*b*) and (*d*) only
B. (*b*), (*c*) and (*d*) only
C. (*c*), (*d*) and (*e*) only
D. (*a*), (*c*) and (*e*) only

58. Artificial Narrow Intelligence has the following features:
(*a*) Referred as weak AI
(*b*) Referred as strong AI
(*c*) Used in facial recognition
(*d*) Ability to solve any problem
(*e*) Used in cars

Choose the correct answer from the options given below:
A. (*a*), (*b*) and (*c*) only
B. (*b*), (*c*) and (*d*) only
C. (*b*), (*c*) and (*e*) only
D. (*a*), (*c*) and (*e*) only

59. DEITY has awarded the project entitled "Centre of Excellence for Digital Preservation" to which of the following agencies?
(*a*) C-DAC, Pune (*b*) C-DAC, Bengaluru
(*c*) C-DAC, Noida (*d*) C-DAC, Delhi
(*e*) IIT, Delhi

Choose the correct answer from the options given below:
A. (*a*) and (*b*) only B. (*a*) and (*c*) only
C. (*b*) and (*d*) only D. (*d*) and (*e*) only

60. DROMBORA was developed and released by:
(*a*) DCC
(*b*) DPE
(*c*) IIT, Bombay
(*d*) C-DAC, Bengaluru

Choose the correct answer from the options given below:
A. (*a*) and (*b*) only B. (*b*) and (*c*) only
C. (*c*) and (*d*) only D. (*a*) and (*d*) only

61. Webometric research includes longitudinal quantitative studies of:
(*a*) Web citation analysis
(*b*) Blog analysis
(*c*) Web pages
(*d*) Search engine designing

Choose the most appropriate answer from the options given below:
A. (*a*), (*b*) and (*d*) only
B. (*a*), (*c*) and (*d*) only

C. (*a*), (*b*) and (*c*) only
D. (*b*), (*c*) and (*d*) only

62. Impact Factor is used by _______ .
(*a*) Authors to select a right journal
(*b*) Libraries to make collection development decisions
(*c*) Academic institutions to access academic productivity
(*d*) Publishers to decide the journal price

Choose the most appropriate answer from the options given below:
A. (*b*), (*c*) and (*d*) only
B. (*a*), (*c*) and (*d*) only
C. (*a*), (*b*) and (*c*) only
D. (*a*), (*b*) and (*d*) only

63. The important measures of dispersion are:
(*a*) Mean
(*b*) Standard Deviation
(*c*) Mean Deviation
(*d*) Range

Choose the most appropriate answer from the options given below:
A. (*a*), (*b*) and (*c*) only
B. (*a*), (*c*) and (*d*) only
C. (*b*), (*c*) and (*d*) only
D. (*a*), (*b*) and (*d*) only

64. Which of the following are true of libraries of ancient India?
(*a*) Earliest written recorded materials found are the inscriptions on stone pillars of king Ashoka
(*b*) Nalanda library flourished till twelveth Century
(*c*) Ratna-Sagara is a seven-storied building
(*d*) Itsing visited Nalanda University
(*e*) Temple libraries existed before 10th Century A.D.

Choose the correct answer from the options given below:
A. (*b*), (*c*) and (*d*) only
B. (*a*), (*b*) and (*c*) only
C. (*a*), (*b*) and (*d*) only
D. (*c*), (*d*) and (*e*) only

65. Which of the following constitute Marketing Mix?
(*a*) Product
(*b*) Promotion
(*c*) Price
(*d*) Purchasing power
(*e*) Portability

Choose the correct answer from the options given below:
A. (*a*), (*b*) and (*d*) only
B. (*b*), (*c*) and (*e*) only
C. (*c*), (*d*) and (*e*) only
D. (*a*), (*b*) and (*c*) only

66. Match List-I with List-II.

List-I (Library Acts)	List-II (Features)
(*a*) Manipur Public Libraries Act	I. Bill drafted in 1959
(*b*) Kerala Public Libraries Act	II. No library cess
(*c*) Mizoram Public Libraries Act	III. Creation of state Library Service
(*d*) Karnataka Public Libraries Act	IV. Recognizes 4 categories of library

Choose the correct answer from the options given below:

	(*a*)	(*b*)	(*c*)	(*d*)
A.	I	II	III	IV
B.	III	I	IV	II
C.	II	I	IV	III
D.	IV	III	II	I

67. Match List-I with List-II.

List-I (Database/Sites)	List-II (Examples)
(*a*) Expert database	I. Scopus
(*b*) Online database	II. Twitter
(*c*) Numerical database	III. Census of India
(*d*) Social networking site	IV. Vidwan

Choose the correct answer from the options given below:

	(*a*)	(*b*)	(*c*)	(*d*)
A.	I	II	III	IV
B.	II	III	IV	I
C.	III	IV	I	II
D.	IV	I	III	II

68. Match List-I with List-II.

List-I (File/Format)	List-II (Standards for Data Handling)
(*a*) Page description	I. SGML
(*b*) Structured documents	II. RAM/RM
(*c*) Moving images	III. Post Script Level 2
(*d*) Audio format	IV. GIF89A

Choose the correct answer from the options given below:

	(*a*)	(*b*)	(*c*)	(*d*)
A.	I	III	IV	II
B.	I	III	II	IV
C.	II	III	I	IV
D.	III	I	IV	II

69. Match List-I with List-II.

List-I (Isolates/Facets)	List-II (Fundamental categories) CC 7th ed.
(*a*) Medicine	I. P
(*b*) Heart	II. E
(*c*) Morphology	III. BF
(*d*) Therapeutics	IV. MP

Choose the correct answer from the options given below:

	(*a*)	(*b*)	(*c*)	(*d*)
A.	II	III	I	IV
B.	III	I	IV	II
C.	I	II	III	IV
D.	IV	I	III	II

70. Match List-I with List-II.

List-I (Activities/Services)	List-II (Types of libraries)
(*a*) Story telling	I. Public libraries
(*b*) Community informations services	II. School libraries
(*c*) Theses collection	III. Industrial libraries
(*d*) R & D Activies	IV. University libraries

Choose the correct answer from the options given below:

	(*a*)	(*b*)	(*c*)	(*d*)
A.	I	II	III	IV
B.	IV	III	II	I
C.	II	I	IV	III
D.	III	IV	I	II

71. Match List-I with List-II.

List-I (Theory)	List-II (Propounders)
(*a*) Bureaucratic Organization	I. Henri Fayol
(*b*) Change Management Theory	II. Peter Drucker
(*c*) Administrative Management	III. Max Weber
(*d*) Management by Objectives	IV. Kurt Lewin

Choose the correct answer from the options given below:

	(*a*)	(*b*)	(*c*)	(*d*)
A.	IV	III	I	II
B.	I	IV	III	II
C.	II	III	IV	I
D.	III	IV	I	II

72. Match List-I with List-II.

List-I (Laws)	List-II (Explanation)
(*a*) Bradford's law	I. Author productivity
(*b*) Lotka's law	II. Sharing of one or more references by two documents
(*c*) Zip's law	III. Law of scattering
(*d*) Bibliographic coupling	IV. Usage of words by individuals

Choose the correct answer from the options given below:

	(*a*)	(*b*)	(*c*)	(*d*)
A.	I	II	IV	III
B.	II	I	III	IV
C.	III	I	IV	II
D.	IV	III	II	I

73. Match List-I with List-II.

List-I (Cryptography related terms)	List-II (Meaning)
(*a*) Plain text	I. Transforms the cipher text to plain text
(*b*) Cipher text	II. After the message is transformed
(*c*) Encryption	III. The original message before being transformed
(*d*) Decryption	IV. Transforms plain text to cipher text

Choose the correct answer from the options given below:

	(*a*)	(*b*)	(*c*)	(*d*)
A.	II	III	IV	I
B.	III	II	IV	I
C.	IV	III	II	I
D.	II	III	I	IV

74. Match List-I with List-II.

List-I (Questions pertaining to)	List-II (Attributes)
(*a*) Language	I. Leading personalities specialists, professionals, authors, less known persons
(*b*) Background	II. Location, description, distance, identification
(*c*) People	III. Definition, spelling pronounciation, abbreviations, synonyms, antonyms, signs, symbols
(*d*) Places	IV. General Information, self education, all about something about, something on

Choose the correct answer from the options given below:

	(*a*)	(*b*)	(*c*)	(*d*)
A.	I	II	III	IV
B.	III	IV	I	II
C.	II	III	IV	I
D.	IV	III	II	I

75. Match List-I with List-II.

List-I (Item)	List-II (Explanation)
(*a*) Budapest Treaty	I. Unified procedure for filing patent application in each of its member countries.
(*b*) Patent Cooperation Treaty	II. Common Classification for patents published, utility models and utility certificate
(*c*) International Patent Classification	III. Internationally agreed number for identification of data
(*d*) INID	IV. Applicants deposits the material in any one recognized institutions. It is not necessary to deposit again in other country

Choose the correct answer from the options given below:

	(*a*)	(*b*)	(*c*)	(*d*)
A.	III	II	I	IV
B.	II	I	III	IV
C.	IV	I	II	III
D.	I	III	II	IV

76. Arrange the following IPR Head Offices/Office of the Controller General alphabatically according to cities of their location.

(*a*) Rajiv Gandhi National Institute of Intellectual Property Right and Management

(*b*) Designs Office

(*c*) Trade Marks Registry

(*d*) Geographical Indications Registry

(*e*) Copyright Registry

Choose the correct answer from the options given below :

A. (*a*), (*b*), (*c*), (*d*), (*e*)

B. (*b*), (*c*), (*d*), (*e*), (*a*)

C. (*c*), (*d*), (*e*), (*a*), (*b*)

D. (*d*), (*e*), (*b*), (*c*), (*a*)

77. Sequence the following in the ascending order of their inception:

(*a*) ISBD (G)

(*b*) ISBD (M)

(*c*) IFLA Universal Availability of Publications

(*d*) IFLA Universal Bibliographic Control

(*e*) IFLA Program Development Group

Choose the correct answer from the options given below:

A. (*e*), (*d*), (*c*), (*b*), (*a*)

B. (*a*), (*b*), (*c*), (*d*), (*e*)

C. (*b*), (*c*), (*a*), (*e*), (*d*)

D. (*c*), (*a*), (*d*), (*b*), (*e*)

78. Arrange the following documents in reverse chronological order of their publication:

(*a*) Documentation and its Facets by S.R. Ranganathan

(*b*) Documentation by S.C. Bradford

(*c*) Traite de Documentation by Paul Otlet

(*d*) Documentation and Organization of Knowledge by J.H. Shera.

Choose the correct answer from the options given below:

A. (*b*), (*a*), (*d*), (*c*) B. (*a*), (*b*), (*c*), (*d*)

C. (*d*), (*a*), (*b*), (*c*) D. (*c*), (*b*), (*a*), (*d*)

79. Arrange the following based on their evolution:

(*a*) Consortia

(*b*) Library Cooperation

(*c*) Resource Sharing

(*d*) Networking

Choose the correct answer from the options given below:

A. (*a*), (*b*), (*c*), (*d*) B. (*b*), (*d*), (*a*), (*c*)

C. (*c*), (*d*), (*a*), (*b*) D. (*b*), (*c*), (*d*), (*a*)

80. Arrange the following classification schemes in an ascending order according to their year of development.

(*a*) Expensive Classification

(*b*) Library of Congress Classification

(*c*) Bibliographic Classification

(*d*) Subject Classification.

Choose the correct answer from the options given below:

A. (*a*), (*b*), (*c*), (*d*) B. (*d*), (*a*), (*b*), (*c*)

C. (*c*), (*a*), (*d*), (*c*) D. (*a*), (*b*), (*d*), (*c*)

81. Arrange the following search engines according to their year of launching in an ascending order.

(*a*) Yahoo (*b*) Google

(*c*) Bing (*d*) Hotbot

(*e*) Scirus

Choose the correct answer from the options given below:

A. (*e*), (*a*), (*d*), (*c*), (*b*)

B. (*a*), (*d*), (*b*), (*e*), (*c*)

C. (*e*), (*c*), (*a*), (*b*), (*d*)

D. (*a*), (*e*), (*d*), (*b*), (*c*)

82. Arrange the file formats based on the storage space required in ascending form.

(*a*) Text (*b*) Video

(*c*) Multimedia (*d*) Image

(*e*) Audio

Choose the correct answer from the options given below:

A. (*a*), (*e*), (*d*), (*b*), (*c*)

B. (*a*), (*d*), (*e*), (*c*), (*b*)

C. (*a*), (*e*), (*c*), (*b*), (*d*)

D. (*a*), (*d*), (*e*), (*b*), (*c*)

83. Arrange the following classes as per DDC scheme of classification.

(*a*) Ethics (*b*) Metaphysics

(*c*) Logic (*d*) Psychology

(*e*) Epistomology

Choose the correct answer from the options given below.

A. (*c*), (*a*), (*e*), (*d*), (*b*)

B. (*a*), (*c*), (*b*), (*d*), (*e*)

C. (*b*), (*e*), (*d*), (*c*), (*a*)

D. (*e*), (*d*), (*c*), (*b*), (*a*)

84. Organize the following in an ascending order from the date of their establishment

(*a*) Indian Institute of Science

(*b*) Allahabad University

(*c*) Connemara Public Library

(*d*) Bharat Heavy Electricals Ltd.
(*e*) The Roorkee College (New IIT, Roorkee)

Choose the correct answer from the options given below:

A. (*c*), (*a*), (*e*), (*d*), (*b*)
B. (*b*), (*c*), (*a*), (*e*), (*d*)
C. (*a*), (*c*), (*d*), (*b*), (*e*)
D. (*e*), (*b*), (*c*), (*a*), (*d*)

85. Arrange the basic steps of system analysis from the point of view of problem solving.

(*a*) Construction of models which formalize the alternatives
(*b*) Presentation of recommendations
(*c*) Determination of the cost/effectiveness of the alternatives
(*d*) Definition and formulation of the problem
(*e*) Development of alternative solutions

Choose the correct answer from the options given below:

A. (*a*), (*c*), (*b*), (*d*), (*e*)
B. (*d*), (*e*), (*a*), (*c*), (*b*)
C. (*e*), (*a*), (*b*), (*c*), (*d*)
D. (*c*), (*e*), (*b*), (*a*), (*d*)

86. Given below are two statements : One is labelled as Assertion (A) and the other is labelled as Reason (R).

Assertion (A): Conflict is a natural by-product of people's interactions in organizations and cannot be eliminated.

Reason (R): Conflict arises because organizational members have common goals.

In the light of the above statements, choose the most appropriate answer from the options given below.

A. Both (A) and (R) are correct and (R) is the correct explanation of (A)
B. Both (A) and (R) are correct, but (R) is not the correct explanation of (A)
C. (A) is correct, but (R) is not correct
D. (A) is not correct, but (R) is correct

87. Given below are two statements:

Statement I: Information seeking is purposive seeking of information as a consequence of a need to satisfy some goal of an individual.

Statement II: Information seeking pattern of an individual is a determinant of his/her information environment with which he/she is confronted.

In the light of the above statements, choose the correct answer from the options given below.

A. Both Statement I and Statement II are true
B. Both Statement I and Statement II are false
C. Statement I is true but Statement II is false
D. Statement I is false but Statement II is true

88. Given below are two statements:

Statement I: UDC is developed on the basis of first edition DDC.

Statement II: UDC has both enumerative and analytic-synthetic characters.

In the light of the above statements, choose the most appropriate answer from the options given below:

A. Both Statement I and Statement II are correct
B. Both Statement I and Statement II are incorrect
C. Statement I is correct but statement II is incorrect
D. Statement I is incorrect but Statement II is correct

89. Given below are two statements:

Statement I: Bacteria are programs that generally cause denial of service attack.

Statement II: Denial of service attack do not affect the existing files or programs.

In the light of the above statements, choose the most appropriate answer from the options given below:

A. Both Statement I and Statement II are correct
B. Both Statement I and Statement II are incorrect

C. Statement I is correct but statement II is incorrect
D. Statement I is incorrect but Statement II is correct

90. Given below are two statements: One is labelled as Assertion (A) and the other is labelled as Reason (R).

Assertion (A) : Libraries take part in consortia to get access to large number of electronic resources.

Reason (R) : College libraries invest huge amount of money for getting large number of e-collections.

In the light of the above statements, choose the most appropriate answer from the options given below.

A. Both (A) and (R) are correct and (R) is the correct explanation of (A)
B. Both (A) and (R) are correct, but (R) is not the correct explanation of (A)
C. (A) is correct, but (R) is not correct
D. (A) is not correct, but (R) is correct

Directions (Qs. No. 91-95): *Read The following passage and answer the questions.*

There are many reasons to tell stories to children. Pragmatically speaking, story telling is all about language. When children listen and focus on a story told to them, they are developing listening, comprehension and analytical skills. In terms of higher-level thinking, storytelling helps children recall details, summarize sequence and visualize and describe the settings and scenes. They can speculate on what will happen next and afterward, cite the clues that support their predictions. They can analyze the story structure, discuss plot elements and evaluate, debate and make their own judgements about why the characters behaved the way they did. They can compare and contrast other similar stories.

Finally, they can synthesize the experience in a creative way, perhaps acting out the story, writing an original tale using the same structure, or retelling the story from another character's point of view. All the strategies we use to analyze and evaluate other texts, both fiction and nonfiction, work just as well if not better, when a story is told.

Hearing stories also make a child want to read more of them. Storytelling helps turn kids into readers. But perhaps the best reason to tell stories is that it brings joy to the teller and listener alike.

91. Hearing stories make a child to _______.
A. Sleep peacefully
B. Stop thinking
C. Read more stories
D. Sit patiently

92. Best reason to tell stories is _______.
A. to keep children quiet
B. to impress children
C. to speculate future
D. to bring joy to the teller and listener

93. Storytelling is all about _______ .
A. Language
B. Story
C. Telling
D. Children

94. In terms of higher level thinking, the story-telling will help in _______.
A. developing listening skills
B. improving comprehension
C. developing analytical skills
D. Summarizing sequence

95. Storytelling helps kids to _______ .
A. help in predicting
B. help them in becoming story writers
C. turn them into readers
D. avoid classes

Directions (Qs. No. 96-100): *Read the following passage and answer the following questions:*

The existence of academic libraries during the medieval period of Indian history is not known, though the Muslim rulers did patronize libraries in their own places. A lone exception, however, was a library attached to a college at Bidar, having a collection of 3,000 books on different subjects. Aurangzeb got this library transferred to Delhi to merge it with his palace library. College libraries are the fore-runners of a modern university library.

Warren Hastings, Governor-General (1774-85), founded a Madrasa at Calcutta in 1781. Jonathan Duncan in 1792 stressed the need to collect books of the ancient valuable general learning and tradition. Lord Minto, Governor General (1807-13), in his minutes of the 6 March, 1811 wrote, Library be attached to each of the colleges under the charge of a learned native with a small establishment of servants for the care of manuscripts. Perhaps, this is the first statement on record concerning libraries in the academic set-up in India. Lord Auckland, Governor General of Indian (1836-40), further outlined the library policy in his minutes of the 24 November, 1839; make the greatest use of the college libraries which are now attached to many of our institutions. Library collections of the colleges thus started growing and by 1882 some of them crossed a thousand marks.

96. In which period of Indian history Muslim rulers patronized libraries?
A. Ancient Period
B. Medieval period
C. Post-industrial period
D. Pre-independence period

97. From which place to which place a college library did Aurangzeb shift?
A. Delhi to Bidar
B. Bidar to Calcutta
C. Bidar to Delhi
D. Calcutta to Delhi

98. Who founded Madrasa in 1781?
A. Aurangzeb
B. Jonathan Duncan
C. Lord Minto
D. Warren Hastings

99. Who of the following wrote a minute suggesting establishment of library in each college?
A. Warren Hastings B. Lord Auckland
C. Lord Minto D. Jonathan Duncan

100. Who outlined the library policy?
A. Lord Auckland B. Lord Minto
C. Jonathan Duncan D. Warren Hastings

ANSWERS

1. (A): Creative Commons is a global network that provides free, standardized legal tools to enable the sharing and use of creativity and knowledge within the boundaries of copyright law. It offers a range of licenses that allow creators to specify the permissions they grant to others regarding the use of their work. Creative Commons is a global network that provides free, standardized legal tools to enable the sharing and use of creativity and knowledge. The organization was founded in 2001 and is based in the United States.

2. (D): T.S. Eliot is credited with the quote "Where is the wisdom we have lost in knowledge? Where is the knowledge we have lost in information?" The wording you provided in the question slightly differs from the original quote, but it is likely a variation or adaptation of Eliot's words. T.S. Eliot was a renowned poet and playwright.

3. (D): The informal organizational communication network is commonly referred to as the "grapevine." The grapevine represents the informal channels through which information flows within an organization. It is characterized by unofficial,. unofficial and often unofficial communication that occurs through conversations, rumors, gossip and informal social interactions among employees. The grapevine can be a powerful and influential network for spreading information, both accurate and inaccurate, within an organization.

4. (C): Based on the recommendations of the National Knowledge Commission, the nodal agency for the National Translation Mission

Central Institute of Indian Languages, Mysuru. The National Translation Mission (NTM) was established to promote the translation of knowledge texts and other important literature from various languages in India. The Central Institute of Indian Languages (CIIL) was designated as the nodal agency to oversee and coordinate the activities of the NTM. CIIL, located in Mysuru, Karnataka, is an autonomous institution under the Ministry of Education, Government of India and is dedicated to the study and promotion of Indian languages.

5. (C): During the Mughal period, the Head Librarian was known as the "Nizam." So, the correct answer is option (C). The Nizam was in charge of the library and its administration, including the acquisition, cataloging and preservation of books and manuscripts in the Mughal Empire.

6. (A): The first Public Library Act enacted in pre-independent India was the Kolhapur Public Libraries Act, also known as the Karveer Vachan Mandir Act. So, the correct answer the Kolhapur Public Libraries Act. That was passed in 1904 in the princely state of Kolhapur, which is now part of Maharashtra. This act played a significant role in establishing a network of public libraries and promoting access to knowledge and education in the region.

7. (D): The first library committee for a university library in India was constituted at the University of Calcutta, Calcutta. The University of Calcutta, established in 1857, was one of the earliest universities in India and played a significant role in the development of higher education in the country. The formation of a library committee at the University of Calcutta reflects the importance placed on library services and the management of resources to support academic and research activities.

8. (B): The committee constituted to formulate the National Policy on Library and Information Systems (NAPLIS) in 1985 was chaired by : D.P. Chattopadhyaya. D.P. Chattopadhyaya, a renowned scholar and philosopher, chaired the committee responsible for formulating the national policy for libraries and information systems in India. The NAPLIS aimed to provide a comprehensive framework for the development, coordination and modernization of libraries and information systems in the country.

9. (C): The first commercial full-text legal information service is known as: Lexis Nexis. Lexis Nexis is a global provider of legal research and business information services. It offers a comprehensive collection of legal materials, including case laws, statutes, regulations, legal journals and more. Lexis Nexis has been widely used by legal professionals and researchers around the world for accessing and analyzing legal information.

10. (D): The abstracts in Indian Science Abstracts (ISA) are arranged using : Universal Decimal Classification (UDC). The Universal Decimal Classification is a widely used classification system that organizes knowledge into a systematic and hierarchical structure. ISA, as a bibliographic database for scientific literature, follows the UDC system for classifying and arranging abstracts based on subject content. The UDC system assigns a unique alphanumeric notation to each subject area, allowing for efficient organization and retrieval of information.

11. (C): In the LISA (Library and Information Science Abstracts) database, the exact nomenclature used for the field representing the label NOFT is: Anywhere except full text. The NOFT field in LISA denotes the availability of the full text of a particular document. When this label is assigned, it means that the document is indexed and accessible in the database, but the full text is not available within the database itself. The full text may be accessible through other means, such as another database, a separate subscription, or physical copies in libraries or repositories.

12. (A): The first abstracting periodical was published in the field of Pharmaceutical Chemistry. The first abstracting periodical specifically dedicated to the field of pharmaceutical chemistry was "Chemical Abstracts." It was first published in 1907 by the American Chemical Society and provided abstracts and indexing for research articles and literature in the field of chemistry, including pharmaceutical chemistry. Chemical Abstracts played a significant role in organizing and disseminating information in the field of pharmaceutical chemistry and set the foundation for abstracting and indexing services in various scientific disciplines.

13. (B): Motion box is a video-sharing community. Motion box is a platform where users can upload, share and view videos. It allows individuals and organizations to share their video content with others, similar to platforms like YouTube. Users can upload various types of videos, such as personal videos, educational content, tutorials and more. Motion box provides a platform for users to discover and engage with video content from different creators and communities.

14. (D): "Bibliophile" refers to a person who is an avid and passionate lover of books. A bibliophile is someone who collects, reads and cherishes books, often displaying a deep appreciation for the written word and the physical beauty of books themselves. Bibliophiles often seek out rare or unique editions, take joy in building personal libraries and derive immense pleasure from the act of reading and exploring different genres and subjects.

15. (B): GIS stands for: Geographic Information System. A Geographic Information System is a computer-based system used to capture, store, manipulate, analyze and present geospatial data. It combines hardware, software, data and methods to collect, manage and analyze geographic information. GIS allows users to visualize and understand patterns, relationships and trends in data related to geographic locations. It finds applications in various fields, including urban planning, environmental management, transportation, emergency response and natural resource management, among others.

16. (D): Music index is not generally considered a form of index. While book indexes, periodical indexes and newspaper indexes are common forms of indexes used to organize and provide access to information, a music index is not as prevalent. Music indexes, if they exist, are typically specialized tools used to catalog and access music compositions, recordings, or related materials. However, they are not as widespread or commonly encountered as book, periodical, or newspaper indexes.

17. (A): Classified Catalogue Code is not a vocabulary control technique. Vocabulary control refers to the methods and tools used to ensure consistent and standardized terminology in information organization and retrieval. The Classified Catalogue Code is a set of rules used for creating and organizing catalog entries in a library catalog. It primarily focuses on the organization and presentation of bibliographic information, rather than vocabulary control. While it does provide guidelines for subject cataloging, it is not specifically considered a vocabulary control technique.

18. (C): The main entry in the catalogue contains: Maximum Information about a document. The main entry provides the most comprehensive and detailed information about a document in the catalogue. It typically includes the author's name, title, edition, publication information and other relevant details that help identify and locate the document. The main entry serves as the primary access point for users searching for a particular document in the catalogue.

19. (A): The format followed in PRECIS to prepare index entries is: Two-Line-Three-Part. The PRECIS (Preserved Context Indexing System) is an indexing system developed by the British National Bibliography (BNB) to create concise and informative index entries for documents. In the Two-Line-Three-Part format, each index entry consists of two lines. The first line represents the lead or catchphrase, which is a brief summary of the content. The second line contains three parts: the qualifiers, the qualifiers' indicators and the main subject indicator. This format helps in providing a precise and structured representation of the document's content in the index entry.

20. (D): The idea of Facet Analysis was developed by: S.R. Ranganathan. S.R. Ranganathan, an Indian librarian and mathematician, made significant contributions to library science and information organization. He developed the concept of Facet Analysis as part of his work on classification systems. Facet Analysis involves breaking down a subject or topic into its component parts or facets and then systematically organizing and classifying the information based on these facets. Ranganathan's work on Facet Analysis and his development of the Colon Classification system had a profound influence on information organization and retrieval in libraries.

21. (C): The CPM (Critical Path Method) was developed by: DuPont Company. The Critical Path Method was initially developed by DuPont Company in the late 1950s as a project management technique to effectively schedule and control complex industrial construction projects. DuPont used the CPM to manage and optimize the shutdown and maintenance of chemical plants. The CPM methodology gained recognition and popularity beyond DuPont, becoming widely adopted in various industries for project planning and scheduling.

22. (B): The option that is not a Human Resource Planning technique is Ranking Technique. The ranking technique is not specifically considered a Human Resource Planning technique. It is a method used in decision-making processes to rank items or individuals based on certain criteria or attributes. In the context of Human Resource Planning, techniques such as the Expert-Estimate Technique, Trend Projection Technique and Modelling Technique are commonly used. These techniques involve analyzing data, trends and future projections to determine the human resource needs of an organization and develop appropriate strategies and plans.

23. (B): The study conducted at the Hawthorne Works in Illinois related to the human relations school was conducted by Elton Mayo. Elton Mayo, an Australian psychologist and organizational theorist, is known for his involvement in the Hawthorne studies. The Hawthorne studies were a series of experiments conducted between 1924 and 1932 at the Western Electric Hawthorne Works in Chicago. These studies examined the effects of various workplace conditions, including lighting and work hours, on worker productivity and morale. Elton Mayo's research and findings from the Hawthorne studies had a significant impact on the development of the human relations movement in management theory.

24. (C): The principle "The best reading for the largest number at the least cost" is given by Melvil Dewey. He was an American librarian and educator, is known for his significant contributions to library science, including the development of the Dewey Decimal Classification system. While Dewey is primarily associated with classification, he also emphasized the importance of providing access to the best and most widely useful reading materials for library users at an affordable cost. The principle reflects Dewey's belief in the democratic ideals of libraries and their role in promoting widespread access to knowledge and information.

25. (A): The person who introduced frequency modulation (FM) for mobile communication systems in 1935 is Edwin Armstrong. Edwin Armstrong, an American electrical engineer and inventor, is credited with the invention and development of FM technology. He patented his FM system in 1933 and demonstrated its effectiveness for mobile communication in 1935. FM became a breakthrough technology for broadcasting and communication due to its superior audio quality and resistance to noise and interference compared to other modulation techniques. Edwin Armstrong's contributions to FM technology revolutionized the field of telecommunications.

26. (A): Procedural Language: C is a widely used high-level programming language that falls under the category of procedural languages. Procedural languages are programming languages that follow a procedural or step-by-step approach to problem-solving. In C programs are structured as a sequence of procedures or functions that perform specific tasks. C provides features such as variables, control structures and functions, allowing programmers to write efficient and structured code. It is commonly used for system programming, embedded systems and developing applications.

27. (C): The type of Barcode printing that is not long-lasting is Thermal Transfer Printing. Thermal transfer printing involves the use of heat to transfer ink from a ribbon onto the label or barcode substrate. While thermal transfer printing is commonly used for barcode printing and offers high-quality prints, the durability of the printed barcode depends on the materials used. In some cases, thermal transfer prints may be prone to fading or degradation over time, particularly if the printed labels are exposed to harsh environmental conditions such as heat, light, or chemicals. Therefore, thermal transfer printed barcodes may not be as long-lasting as other printing methods like laser printing or photo composition method.

28. (C): The option that is essential to have ways of detecting and correcting any false, incorrect, or incomplete data in big data is Veracity. Veracity refers to the reliability and trustworthiness of the data. In the context of big data, the veracity aspect is crucial because data sources can be diverse and there is a risk of encountering inaccurate or incomplete information. It is essential to have methods and processes in place to assess the accuracy and quality of the data and to identify and correct any issues. Veracity ensures that the data used for analysis and decision-making is reliable and trustworthy, which is critical for extracting meaningful insights from big data.

29. (B): The standard for data handling and interchange used for structured documents is XML (eXtensible Markup Language). XML is a widely adopted standard for structuring and representing data in a format that is both human-readable and machine-readable. It allows for the organization and categorization of data elements using tags, making it suitable for structured documents. XML provides a flexible and extensible framework for describing and exchanging data across different systems and platforms. It is commonly used for document interchange, data integration and web services. PDF (Portable Document Format) is a file format primarily used for presenting and exchanging documents, but it is not specifically designed for structured data handling. JPEG and GIF89A are image file formats and are not primarily used for structured document handling or interchange.

30. (C): Position detection patterns are arranged at 3 corners of a QR code.

These position detection patterns consist of a square-shaped pattern of black and white modules that help the QR code reader identify and orient the code correctly. They are typically placed at the top left, top right and bottom left corners of the QR code. These patterns allow the QR code reader to determine the size, angle and position of the code, enabling accurate decoding of the information encoded within the QR code.

31. (A): In SPSS, the form of a spreadsheet grid into which data can be entered is called the Data Viewer.

The Data Viewer in SPSS is a separate window that displays the results of data analysis, including tables, charts and statistical outputs. It allows users to review and analyze the results of their statistical analyses.

32. (D): Code Book: A code book is a document that provides a set of rules or instructions for assigning numerical values to answers obtained from respondents in a research study. It serves as a reference guide for researchers, data analysts and coders involved in data coding and analysis.

The code book typically includes a list of questions or items from the questionnaire or interview schedule, along with the corresponding codes assigned to each possible response. The codes may be numerical or alphanumeric and are used to represent the different categories or levels of the variables being measured in the study.

The code book helps ensure consistency and standardization in data coding and analysis across different coders or researchers. It provides guidelines on how to interpret and code the responses accurately, facilitating data entry and subsequent statistical analysis. The code book is an important tool in quantitative research, particularly when dealing with large datasets and complex surveys.

33. (C): Observing a group without interfering in its normal activities is referred to as Observation under natural conditions.

In this type of observation, the researcher observes the group or individuals in their natural environment or real-life setting, without manipulating or controlling the conditions. The purpose is to understand and document the behaviors, interactions and dynamics of the group or individuals as they occur naturally, without any external interference or imposed structure.

Observation under natural conditions allows researchers to gather authentic and unbiased data, as it captures the group's or individuals' behavior in their everyday context. It is often used in qualitative research methodologies, such as ethnography, where the goal is to gain an in-depth understanding of social, cultural, or organizational phenomena.

34. (B): Descriptive research is a type of research that focuses on describing the characteristics, behaviors, attitudes and other relevant aspects of a particular individual or a group of individuals. It seeks to provide a comprehensive and accurate portrayal of the subject of study without attempting to manipulate or control variables.

Descriptive research is often used to gather information about a specific population, such as demographics, opinions, preferences, or behaviors. It involves collecting data through various methods, such as surveys, observations, interviews, or existing records and analyzing the data to summarize and describe the findings.

35. (A): FORSA refers to a consortium.

A consortium typically refers to an association or collaboration between multiple organizations or institutions that come together to achieve a common goal or objective. Consortia are often formed to leverage resources, share expertise and promote collaboration in specific areas such as education, research, or other fields.

36. (D): NPTEL (National Programme on Technology Enhanced Learning) is a popular platform in India that offers online courses and resources on Engineering and Technology. NPTEL provides video lectures, course materials, assignments and certification for learners interested in expanding their knowledge in these fields. It is a valuable resource for students, professionals and anyone interested in learning about engineering and technology-related topics.

37. (B): Secretariat libraries are part of Government Secretariates.

Secretariat libraries are libraries that are established within government secretariates or administrative offices. These libraries serve as information centers for government officials, employees and other stakeholders working in the secretariat or administrative departments. They provide access to relevant documents, reports, publications, legal materials and other resources needed for the functioning and decision-making processes of the government.

The main purpose of secretariat libraries is to support the information needs of the government officials and staff by providing them with access to accurate and timely information. They often have specialized collections that cater to the specific subject areas or functions of the government department or secretariat they serve. Secretariat libraries play a crucial role in facilitating research, policy-making and efficient governance within the government sector.

38. (B): Oppenheim and Smithson defined the concept of a hybrid library as "a cross breed which aims to meet the needs of the new learning environment." This definition highlights the evolving nature of libraries in response to the changing information landscape and the increasing integration of digital resources and technologies into traditional library services.

A hybrid library combines both physical and digital resources, services and technologies to provide users with a seamless and integrated learning and research environment. It incorporates traditional library collections, such as books, journals and other physical materials, along with digital resources, including electronic databases, e-books, e-journals and online learning platforms.

The concept of the hybrid library recognizes the importance of incorporating digital technologies and online resources into the library's infrastructure to enhance access, discovery and delivery of information. It reflects the need to adapt and transform libraries to meet the evolving needs of users in an increasingly digital and interconnected world.

39. (D): In Satellite Communication, multiple repeaters are known as Transponders.

A transponder in satellite communication refers to a device or unit that receives signals from an Earth station, amplifies them and retransmits them back to another location on Earth. Transponders are commonly used in satellite communication systems to facilitate the transmission of signals between the satellite and ground stations.

Multiple transponders are often used in satellites to handle and relay multiple communication channels simultaneously. Each transponder operates on a specific frequency or frequency band and is responsible for receiving, amplifying and retransmitting signals within its designated range.

Transponders play a vital role in satellite communication by enabling the relay of signals over long distances, facilitating communication between different geographic locations and providing essential connectivity for various applications such as television broadcasting, internet connectivity, telephony and data transmission.

40. (C): POST (Power-On Self Test) is performed by BIOS (Basic Input/Output System).

During the power-on sequence of a computer, the BIOS firmware takes control and performs the POST. The BIOS is responsible for initializing and configuring various hardware components in the computer system. As part of this initialization process, the BIOS conducts a series of self-tests to verify the functionality of key hardware components such as the CPU, memory, storage devices and peripheral devices.

The POST is executed by the BIOS to ensure that the hardware components are functioning properly before the operating system is loaded. If any errors or issues are detected during the POST, the BIOS may generate error codes or display error messages to indicate the problem.

Once the POST is completed without any critical errors, the BIOS hands over control to the bootloader, which then proceeds to load the operating system into memory and initiate the boot process.

41. (C): (*a*), (*c*) and (*e*) only.

The basic requirements for copyrightability are:

(*a*) **A work must be original:** Copyright protection applies to original works of authorship. This means that the work must be the result of the author's creativity and not a copied or derivative work.

(*c*) **A work must be fixed in a tangible form of expression:** Copyright protects works that are fixed in a tangible medium, such as a written document, a recorded audio or video file, or a digital file. It means that the work is captured or recorded in a way that it can be perceived, reproduced, or communicated.

(*e*) **A work must be a work of authorship:** Copyright protection applies to works that are the result of creative expression and authorship. This includes literary works, artistic works, musical works, dramatic works and other types of original creative expressions.

42. (A): (*a*), (*c*) and (*d*) only.

The MOSCOW Declaration refers to:

(*a*) **Media and Information Literacy:** The MOSCOW Declaration emphasizes the importance of media and information literacy (MIL) as a critical skill set in the digital age. MIL encompasses the ability to access, analyze, evaluate and create media and information in various forms.

(*c*) **Raising advocacy programs:** The MOSCOW Declaration also includes initiatives and efforts to raise advocacy for media and information literacy, promoting its importance and implementation in educational and societal contexts.

(*d*) **International Conference held in 2012:** The MOSCOW Declaration was adopted at the International Conference on Media and Information Literacy for Knowledge Societies held in Moscow in 2012. The conference brought together experts, policymakers and stakeholders to discuss MIL-related issues.

43. (C): (*b*), (*d*) and (*e*) only.

CILIP (Chartered Institute of Library and Information Professionals) is a professional association for librarians, information specialists and professionals working in the field of knowledge and information management. The following statements are true about CILIP:

(*b*) **Membership is open to everyone working with information, knowledge, data, or libraries:** CILIP membership is open to individuals working in various roles and sectors related to information and libraries, including librarians, information specialists, knowledge managers and data professionals.

(*d*) **CILIP was formed by the merger of Library Association and Institute of Information Scientists:** CILIP was created in 2002 through the merger of two prominent UK professional organizations, the Library Association and the Institute of Information Scientists.

(*e*) **It has its headquarters in London:** CILIP is headquartered in London, UK. The organization operates from its central office located in the city.

44. (B): (*b*), (*c*) and (*d*) only.

S.R. Ranganathan, an eminent librarian and information scientist, suggested different categories of documents based on their nature and characteristics. The following categories are associated with Ranganathan's classification:

(*b*) **Neo Conventional document:** This refers to documents that are newly created or emerging in response to changing technologies or formats.

(*c*) **Meta document:** This refers to documents that provide metadata or descriptive information about other documents, such as bibliographies, indexes and abstracts.

(*d*) **Non conventional document:** This refers to documents that do not fit into traditional formats or media, such as electronic documents, multimedia content and web resources.

45. (A): (*a*), (*b*) and (*c*) only.

RSS (Really Simple Syndication) feeds are used to subscribe to website content and receive updates in a standardized format. Various tools are available for managing and accessing RSS feeds. Among the options given:

(*a*) **Feedity:** Feedity is a tool that allows users to create RSS feeds for websites that do not have built-in feeds.

(*b*) **Web RSS:** Web RSS is a generic term referring to web-based RSS readers or aggregators that enable users to access and read RSS feeds directly from their web browsers.

(*c*) **Feed Fire:** Feed Fire is an RSS feed management service that provides tools for creating, publishing and managing RSS feeds.

46. (C): (*b*), (*c*) and (*e*) only.

A documentation list typically includes various types of documents that provide information and references. Among the options given:

(*b*) **News index:** A news index is a compilation or index of news articles, typically organized by subject or date.

(*c*) **Current contents:** Current contents refer to a list or compilation of recently published articles or research papers, often organized by topic or field.

(*e*) **News digest:** A news digest is a summary or compilation of news articles or stories, providing a condensed version of the original content.

47. (C): (*a*), (*b*) and (*d*) only.

An electronic information service is one that is:

(*a*) **Generated on the basis of digital information resource:** This means that the service is created using digital information sources, such as databases, websites, or digital content.

(*b*) **Received by the user in digital format:** The information is delivered to the user in a digital format, such as electronic documents, web pages, or multimedia files.

(*d*) **Available in the form of access through the internet:** The service is accessible to users through the internet, allowing them to connect and access the information remotely.

48. (B): (*a*), (*c*) and (*d*) only.

Lankes brought measures to assess the quality of digital reference services and they include:

(*a*) **Outcome measures:** These measures assess the outcomes or results of the digital reference service, such as user satisfaction, successful problem resolution, or the impact on user knowledge or behavior.

(*c*) **Process measures:** These measures evaluate the processes involved in delivering the digital reference service, including response time, accuracy of information provided, or the effectiveness of communication with users.

(*d*) **Economic measures:** These measures consider the economic aspects of the digital reference service, such as the cost-effectiveness, return on investment, or resource allocation.

49. (D): (*a*), (*d*) and (*e*) only.

The Biotechnology Information System covers:

(*a*) **Genetic Engineering:** It includes information related to the manipulation and modification of genes, DNA sequencing, gene expression and related techniques.

(*d*) **Immunology:** It encompasses the study of the immune system, including the response of the body to pathogens, immunotherapy, vaccines and other aspects related to immunological research.

(*d*) **Neuroinformatics:** It deals with the application of information and computational techniques to study the nervous system and brain-related processes, including neural networks, cognitive science, computational neuroscience and neuroimaging.

50. (C): (*a*), (*b*) and (*c*) only.

Sears List of Subject Headings includes:

(*a*) **Narrow Term:** It provides narrower or more specific terms or concepts related to the subject being described. For example, a narrow term for "Dogs" could be "Poodles" or "Terriers."

(*b*) **Related Term:** It includes terms that are closely related to the subject being described but may not be broader or narrower. These terms help in providing alternative or related entry points to the subject. For example, a related term for "Dogs" could be "Canines" or "Pets."

(*c*) **Broader Term:** It provides broader categories or concepts that encompass the subject being described. For example, a broader term for "Dogs" could be "Animals" or "Pets."

51. (C): (*a*), (*d*) and (*c*) only.

George Wilhelm Friedrich Hegel proposed a triadic scheme of knowledge classification, commonly known as the Hegelian system. According to Hegel, knowledge can be categorized into three main branches:

(*a*) **Natural Science:** This branch encompasses the study of the natural world, including physics, chemistry, biology, geology and other related disciplines.

(*b*) **Logic Science:** This branch deals with the study of reasoning, rationality and the principles of logical thinking. It includes formal logic, dialectics and philosophical reasoning.

(*c*) **Mental Science:** Also referred to as the Science of the Mind or Spirit, this branch focuses on the study of consciousness, self-awareness, subjective experience and human psychology.

52. **(A):** (*a*) and (*b*) only.

The correct stages of Kurt Lewin's Change Management Model are:

(*a*) **Changing:** This stage involves implementing the desired change by introducing new processes, structures, or behaviors. It includes planning, executing and monitoring the change.

(*b*) **Unfreezing:** This stage involves creating awareness and readiness for change by breaking down existing mindsets, beliefs and behaviors. It aims to create a sense of dissatisfaction with the current state.

53. **(C):** (*a*), (*b*) and (*c*) only.

The basic components of any Management by Objectives (MBO) system typically include:

(*a*) **Setting objectives:** This involves defining specific, measurable, achievable, relevant and time-bound (SMART) objectives for individuals or teams within an organization. These objectives serve as targets for performance and provide a clear direction for employees.

(*b*) **Developing action plans:** Once objectives are set, action plans are created to outline the specific steps and strategies required to achieve those objectives. Action plans define the tasks, responsibilities and timelines for implementation.

(*c*) **Conducting periodic reviews:** Regular and periodic reviews are essential in the MBO system. These reviews evaluate the progress towards achieving the objectives, identify any obstacles or challenges and make necessary adjustments to the action plans if needed.

54. **(C):** (*a*), (*c*) and (*e*) only

The principles of Scientific Management, developed by Frederick Winslow Taylor, include:

(*a*) **Job Analysis:** This principle involves analyzing and studying each job to determine the most efficient methods and techniques for performing it. It aims to identify the essential tasks, skills and requirements of a job and develop standardized procedures for optimal performance.

(*c*) **Division of Labor:** This principle suggests dividing work into specialized tasks and assigning them to individuals with the appropriate skills and abilities. By dividing work in this way, productivity and efficiency can be increased as each worker becomes highly proficient in their specific task.

(*e*) **Maximum Profits:** This principle emphasizes the goal of maximizing profits for the organization. Scientific Management aims to optimize productivity, reduce waste and improve efficiency, ultimately leading to higher profits.

55. **(C):** (*b*) and (*d*) only.

The address space of an IP address is divided into the following parts:

(*b*) **Type prefix:** This part of the IP address indicates the type or class of the IP address. It determines the range and format of the network and host portions of the address.

(*d*) **Rest of Address:** This part of the IP address represents the network and host portions, which uniquely identify the device within the network.

56. **(C):** (*a*), (*b*) and (*e*) only.

The presentation layer of the OSI model has the following functions:

(*a*) **Reduces the number of bits to be sent over the network:** The presentation layer can perform data compression techniques to reduce the size of the data to be transmitted, which helps in optimizing network bandwidth usage.

(*b*) **Translates data into a standard format to be sent on the network:** The presentation layer is responsible for transforming data from the application layer into a format that can be understood by the network. It handles tasks such as data encryption, decryption and data formatting.

(*e*) **Prevents unauthorized users:** The presentation layer can provide security mechanisms to ensure the confidentiality and integrity of the data being transmitted. It may include encryption and decryption of data to prevent unauthorized access.

57. (D): (*a*), (*c*) and (*e*) only.

Digital signatures can provide the following for a message:

(*a*) **Authentication:** A digital signature helps verify the identity of the sender and ensures that the message comes from the claimed source. It provides assurance that the message has not been tampered with during transmission.

(*c*) **Integrity:** A digital signature provides integrity by ensuring that the message has not been altered or modified in transit. If any changes are made to the message after it has been signed, the digital signature will be invalidated.

(*e*) **Non-repudiation:** A digital signature provides non-repudiation, which means that the sender cannot deny having sent the message. The digital signature serves as proof of the origin and authenticity of the message and the sender cannot later claim that they did not send it.

58. (D): (*a*), (*c*) and (*e*) only.

Artificial Narrow Intelligence (ANI), also known as weak AI, is characterized by the following features:

(*a*) **Referred as weak AI:** ANI is often referred to as weak AI because it is designed to perform specific tasks or solve specific problems within a limited domain. It lacks general intelligence or the ability to understand and learn any task.

(*c*) **Used in facial recognition:** ANI can be used in facial recognition systems to identify and authenticate individuals based on their facial features. It is one of the many applications of ANI in computer vision.

(*e*) **Used in cars:** ANI is utilized in various applications in the automotive industry, such as autonomous driving systems and driver assistance technologies. It allows cars to perceive their surroundings, make decisions and perform tasks without human intervention.

59. (B): (*a*) and (*c*) only.

The project entitled "Centre of Excellence for Digital Preservation" has been awarded to the following agencies:

(*a*) **C-DAC, Pune:** The Centre for Development of Advanced Computing (C-DAC) in Pune is one of the agencies awarded the project. C-DAC is a premier research and development organization under the Ministry of Electronics and Information Technology, Government of India.

(*c*) **C-DAC, Noida:** The Centre for Development of Advanced Computing (C-DAC) in Noida is another agency awarded the project.

60. (A): (*a*) and (*b*) only.

DROMBORA was developed and released by the following agencies:

(*a*) **DCC (Distributed Compiler Construction):** DROMBORA was developed by DCC, a research group working on distributed computing and communication.

(*b*) **DPE (Department of Public Enterprises):** DPE is associated with the development and release of DROMBORA.

61. (C): (*a*), (*b*) and (*c*) only.

Webometric research is a field of study that focuses on analyzing and measuring various aspects of the World Wide Web. It includes longitudinal quantitative studies of:

(*a*) **Web citation analysis:** This involves analyzing the links and citations between web pages to determine their impact and influence.

(*b*) **Blog analysis:** This involves studying blogs and their content to understand trends, opinions and discussions on specific topics.

(*c*) **Web pages:** This involves analyzing the content, structure and characteristics of web pages, including their design, usability and relevance.

62. (C): (*a*), (*b*) and (*c*) only.

The Impact Factor is a metric that measures the average number of citations received by articles published in a particular journal. It is primarily used by:

(*a*) **Authors to select a right journal:** Authors often consider the Impact Factor of a journal as an indicator of its reputation and influence within their field. They may choose to submit their research to journals with higher Impact Factors to increase the visibility and potential impact of their work.

(*b*) **Libraries to make collection development decisions:** Libraries may use the Impact Factor as one of the criteria for selecting journals to include in their collections. Journals with higher Impact Factors are often considered more valuable and relevant to the library's user community.

(*c*) **Academic institutions to assess academic productivity:** Academic institutions may use the Impact Factor as a measure of the research output and productivity of their faculty members. It can be used in tenure and promotion decisions, funding allocations and assessing the overall research performance of the institution.

63. (C): (*b*), (*c*) and (*d*) only.

The measures of dispersion are used to assess the variability or spread of data. The important measures of dispersion include:

(*b*) **Standard Deviation:** This measure quantifies the average amount of deviation or dispersion of individual data points from the mean. It provides a measure of how tightly or loosely the data points are clustered around the mean.

(*c*) **Mean Deviation:** This measure calculates the average absolute deviation of individual data points from the mean. It provides a measure of the average distance between each data point and the mean, regardless of the direction of deviation.

(*d*) **Range:** This measure represents the difference between the highest and lowest values in a dataset. It provides a simple measure of the spread of the data, but it does not consider the distribution of values within that range.

64. (C): (*a*), (*b*) and (*d*) only.

(*a*) **Earliest written recorded materials found are the inscriptions on stone pillars of king Ashoka:** This statement is true. The inscriptions on the stone pillars of King Ashoka provide some of the earliest written recorded materials in ancient India.

(*b*) **Nalanda library flourished till twelfth Century:** This statement is true. The library at Nalanda, one of the ancient universities in India, flourished until the twelfth century. It was renowned for its vast collection of Buddhist texts and manuscripts.

(*d*) **Itsing visited Nalanda University:** This statement is true. Itsing, a Chinese traveler and scholar, visited Nalanda University in the 7th century. He documented his observations and experiences in his travelogue.

65. **(D):** (*a*), (*b*) and (*c*) only.

The Marketing Mix, also known as the 4Ps of marketing, consists of four fundamental elements that are used to formulate a marketing strategy. These elements are:

(*a*) **Product:** This refers to the tangible or intangible goods or services that a company offers to meet the needs and wants of its target market.

(*b*) **Promotion:** This includes the activities and strategies used to communicate and promote the product to the target market. It involves advertising, sales promotions, public relations and other promotional tactics.

(*c*) **Price:** This refers to the amount of money that customers are willing to pay for the product. Pricing strategies are used to determine the optimal price point that balances profitability and customer value.

66. (C) **67. (D)** **68. (D)**

69. (B) **70. (C)** **71. (D)**

72. (C) **73. (B)** **74. (B)**

75. (C) **76. (D)** **77. (A)**

78. **(C):** (*d*), (*a*), (*b*), (*c*)

(*d*) **Documentation and Organization of Knowledge by J H Shera:** This document was published in 1973, making it the most recent publication among the given options.

(*a*) **Documentation and its Facets by S R Ranganathan:** This document was published in 1964, preceding Documentation and Organization of Knowledge.

(*b*) **Documentation by S C 'Bradford:** This document was published in 1948, prior to Documentation and its Facets.

(*c*) **Traite de Documentation by Paul Otlet:** This document was published first among the given options, in 1934, making it the earliest publication.

79. (D) **80. (D)**

81. **(B):** (*a*), (*d*), (*b*), (*e*), (*c*)

(*a*) **Yahoo:** Yahoo was launched in 1994 as a web directory and it later introduced its own search engine. It gained popularity as one of the early search engines.

(*d*) **Hotbot:** Hotbot was launched in 1996 and became known for its advanced search features and multimedia search capabilities.

(*b*) **Google:** Google was launched in 1998 and quickly became one of the most popular and widely used search engines worldwide. It revolutionized the search industry with its efficient search algorithms and emphasis on relevant search results.

(*e*) **Scirus:** Scirus, a specialized search engine for scientific information and research, was launched in 2001. It focused on indexing scholarly resources, including scientific websites, journals and conference papers.

(*c*) **Bing:** Bing, developed by Microsoft, was launched in 2009. It provides web search results along with additional features such as image and video search, news and integration with Microsoft services.

82. **(D):** (*a*), (*d*), (*e*), (*b*), (*c*)

(*a*) **Text:** Text files typically require the least amount of storage space compared to other file formats. They primarily consist of plain text characters and do not include embedded media or high-resolution graphics.

(*d*) **Image:** Image files can vary in size depending on factors such as resolution, color depth and compression. While some image formats may require less storage space, high-resolution images or images with complex graphics may require more storage space.

(*e*) **Audio:** Audio files, such as MP3 or WAV, generally require more storage space compared to text and image files. The size of an audio file depends on factors such as the audio quality, duration and the encoding format used.

(*b*) **Video:** Video files generally require the most storage space among the listed file formats. Videos can have high resolutions, frame rates and complex compression algorithms, resulting in larger file sizes. Formats like MP4 or MOV are commonly used for video files.

(*c*) **Multimedia:** Multimedia files, which can include a combination of text, images, audio and video, typically require more storage space than individual file formats. These files may be in formats such as MP4 or AVI and their size can vary depending on the content and quality of the media elements included.

83. (C)

84. (D): (*e*), (*b*), (*c*), (*a*), (*d*)

(*e*) **The Roorkee College (New IIT Roorkee):** It was established in 1847 as the Roorkee College of Civil Engineering. It later became the University of Roorkee and eventually the Indian Institute of Technology (IIT) Roorkee.

(*b*) **Allahabad University:** It was established in 1887 and is one of the oldest central universities in India.

(*c*) **Connemara Public Library:** It was established in 1896 and is one of the oldest libraries in India, located in Chennai (formerly known as Madras).

(*a*) **Indian Institute of Science:** It was established in 1909 in Bangalore (now Bengaluru) and is a premier institution for scientific research and higher education in India.

(*d*) **Bharat Heavy Electricals Ltd. (BHEL):** It was established in 1964 as a public sector undertaking (PSU) and is one of the largest engineering and manufacturing companies in India.

85. (B): (*d*), (*e*), (*a*), (*c*), (*b*)

(*d*) **Definition and formulation of the problem:** This step involves clearly understanding and articulating the problem that needs to be solved.

(*e*) **Development of alternative solutions:** In this step, different solutions or approaches to solving the problem are brainstormed and developed.

(*a*) **Construction of models which formalize the alternatives:** Models or representations of the alternative solutions are created to better understand and evaluate them.

(*c*) **Determination of the cost/effectiveness of the alternatives:** The costs and benefits of each alternative solution are assessed and evaluated to determine their feasibility and effectiveness.

(*b*) **Presentation of recommendations:** Based on the evaluation of the alternatives, recommendations are made on the best solution to implement.

86. (C): (A) is correct, but (R) is not correct.

Assertion (A) states that conflict is a natural by-product of people's interactions in organizations and cannot be eliminated. This is a widely accepted view in organizational theory. Conflict can arise due to various factors such as differences in goals, values, interests, or limited resources. It is considered a normal and inevitable part of organizational dynamics.

Reason (R) states that conflict arises because organizational members have common goals. However, this reason is not accurate as conflict can also arise when organizational members have divergent or conflicting goals.

Conflict can occur even when individuals or groups have different interpretations of goals or when there is a competition for limited resources.

87. **(A):** Both Statement I and Statement II are true.

Statement I is true because information seeking is indeed a purposeful activity where individuals actively seek information to fulfill their specific needs or goals.

Statement II is also true because an individual's information seeking pattern, which includes their preferences, behaviors and strategies for seeking information, influences the information environment they are exposed to. Different individuals may have different information environments based on their unique information seeking patterns.

88. **(D):** Statement I is incorrect and Statement II is correct.

UDC (Universal Decimal Classification) is not developed on the basis of the first edition of DDC (Dewey Decimal Classification). UDC has its own independent development and is not derived from DDC.

Statement II is correct because UDC does have both enumerative and analytic-synthetic characters. It combines the features of both approaches in its classification system, allowing for hierarchical enumeration of subjects as well as the ability to create new classes by combining different characteristics.

89. **(A):** Statement I and Statement II are correct.

Statement I states that bacteria are programs that generally cause denial of service attacks. This statement implies that bacteria refer to a type of malicious program that is often associated with carrying out denial of service attacks.

Statement II states that denial of service attacks do not affect the existing files or programs. This statement implies that during a denial of service attack, the focus is on disrupting the availability of a service or system rather than directly targeting and modifying existing files or programs.

90. **(C):** (A) is correct, but (R) is not correct.

Assertion (A) states that libraries take part in consortia to get access to a large number of electronic resources. This is a valid assertion as libraries often join consortia or cooperative agreements to pool their resources and provide access to a wider range of electronic resources and databases.

Reason (R) states that college libraries invest a huge amount of money to obtain a large number of e-collections. While it is true that libraries allocate budgets for acquiring electronic resources, the reason provided in Statement R does not directly explain Assertion A. The reason given in Statement R focuses on the investment of money, whereas Assertion A is about the participation of libraries in consortia for access to electronic resources.

91. (C)	**92. (D)**	**93. (A)**
94. (D)	**95. (C)**	**96. (B)**
97. (C)	**98. (D)**	**99. (C)**
100. (A)		

Previous Years' Paper (Solved)

National Testing Agency (NTA)

UGC-NET Junior Research Fellowship & Assistant Professor Eligibility Exam

LIBRARY & INFORMATION SCIENCE, July–2022

(Online exam held on 11-07-2022)

PAPER-II

Note: *This paper contains* ***hundred*** *(**100**) objective type questions of* ***two*** *(2) marks each.* ***All*** *questions are* ***compulsory****.*

1. The Marrakesh Treaty (2013) focusses on:
A. Providing access to published works by visually impaired persons
B. Providing access to published works for visually impaired persons
C. Providing access to unpublished works by visually impaired persons
D. Providing access to unpublished works for visually impaired persons

2. Which commission recommended the 'National Census of all Libraries'?
A. Radha Krishnan Commission
B. Kothari Commission
C. Chattopadhyaya Commission
D. National Knowledge Commission

3. The addition of Information as a sector in, "The Information Economy (1977)" was done by:
A. E. Machlup B. M.V. Porat
C. R.M. Hayes D. M.M. Parker

4. The study of signs and codes is called_______.
A. Semiotics B. Bionics
C. Cybernetics D. Altmetrics

5. In which year Berne convention was signed to forbid discrimination against foreign authors and also to establish uniform treatment for protection of copyrighted works?
A. 1952 B. 1852
C. 1963 D. 1863

6. The Big6 Model and approach was developed by _______.
A. S. Serap Kurbanoglu
B. W. Edwards Deming
C. D. Torrington and L. Hall
D. Mike Eisenberg and Bob Berkowitz

7. Who promulgated the Imperial Library Act, 1902?
A. Lord Curzon
B. Lord Mountbatten
C. Lord Canning
D. Lord Dalhousie

8. Who used the word Information Literacy in 1974?
A. James Herring
B. Zurkowski
C. John MacFarlane
D. Wilson

9. Fodor's essential India is:
A. Yearbook B. Travel Guide
C. Directory D. Handbook

10. JSTOR is:
A. General periodical database
B. Database of newspapers
C. Database of conference proceedings
D. Humanities and social sciences periodical database

* Exam of December 2021 & June 2022.

11. Who has classified the documentary sources of information into the following category "Conventional, Neo-conventional, Non-conventional and Meta documents"?

A. C.W. Hanson
B. Louis Shores
C. S.R. Ranganathan
D. Dennis Grogan

12. Propedia is part of:

A. Encyclopedia Americana
B. Encyclopedia Indica
C. Encyclopedia Britannica
D. McGraw Hill Encyclopedia of Science and Technology

13. Which kind of Library involves in Community Information Services?

A. Academic Library
B. Public Library
C. Government Library
D. Corporate Library

14. In which year, SMS was tested?

A. 1990 B. 1991
C. 1992 D. 1993

15. When was NICNET started functioning?

A. 1974 B. 1975
C. 1976 D. 1977

16. Who Publishes Medline?

A. NISCAIR B. AIIMS
C. ICMR D. NLM

17. The notations in colon classification (7th Edition) comprises ______ digits.

A. 71 B. 72
C. 73 D. 74

18. BIBFRAME stands for ______.

A. Bibliographical framework
B. Bibliograpic framework
C. Bibliography framework
D. Biography framework

19. According to the guidelines of ANSI/NISO Z39.14 the recommended length of abstract is of ______ words.

A. 150 B. 200
C. 250 D. 300

20. Which one of the following is not a information retrieval model based on the theories and fouls?

A. Linguistic model
B. Psychological model
C. Fuzzy logic model
D. Philosophical model

21. AgroVoc is a:

A. Controlled vocabulary
B. Classification Scheme
C. Catalog code
D. Full-text database

22. Raja Ram Mohan Roy Library Foundation comes under ______.

A. Ministry of Education, GOI
B. Ministry of Culture, GOI
C. Ministry of Culture, Govt. of West Bengal
D. Ministry of Education, Govt. of West Bengal

23. MIS is a mosaic of:

A. Management and Information System
B. Marketing and Information System
C. Materials and Information System
D. Machines and Information System

24. Health Management Information System Portal in India was launched in the year:

A. 2007 B. 2006
C. 2008 D. 2009

25. Which of them is the precedence diagrams used for disaster management programmes?

A. Control charts
B. Gantt charts
C. Digitally Accurate Response Tracking (DART)
D. Functional Task Analysis

26. In which of pricing strategy, the firm prices its product lower than others in the competition?

A. Skimming pricing strategy
B. Penetration pricing strategy
C. Geographic pricing strategy
D. Product line pricing strategy

27. Who has given Four-Framework model of leadership?

A. Robert Tannenbaum and Warren H. Schmidt
B. Bolman and Deal
C. W.J. Reddin
D. Robert R. Blake

28. Who propounded "Achievement motivation theory"?

A. Alderfer B. McClelland
C. Herzberg D. McGregor

29. Internet protocol version 6 supports _____ bit address.

A. 32 B. 64
C. 128 D. 256

30. ASCII uses ______ bits to code each character.

A. 7 B. 8
C. 9 D. 24

31. Which protocol is used by ping command?

A. TCP B. UDP
C. ARP D. ICMP

32. Which First version of e-Granthalaya was made available on cloud platform?

A. e-G 1.0 B. e-G 2.0
C. e-G 3.0 D. e-G 4.0

33. The characteristic, "volume" of Bigdata is related to ______.

A. size of data
B. type of data
C. speed of data processing
D. uncertainity of data

34. The language used by RDF is called:

A. RDF/XML B. HTML/RDF
C. RDF/HTML D. RDF/SGML

35. Which digitization program was initiated by National Library of India?

A. Down the memory lane
B. Dware Dware Gyan Sampada
C. Information for all
D. Aatma Nirbhar Bharat

36. In wireless communication, base station is connected to central Hub called

A. PSTN B. MSC
C. CO D. PBX

37. The scientific method of research is not based on:

A. Empirical evidence
B. Objective consideration
C. Probabilistic prediction
D. Subjectivity

38. Standard deviation is a/an ______.

A. Average amount of variation around the mode
B. Value that occurs most frequently in a distribution
C. Average amount of variation around the mean
D. Normal deviation around the mean

39. Deliberate sampling is also known as ______.

A. Random Sampling
B. Purposive Sampling
C. Systematic Sampling
D. Quota Sampling

40. A form of ethnography which applied to online or largely online communities is known as ______.

A. Network community
B. Meta ethnography
C. Netnography
D. Online assessment

41. The National Intellectual Property Rights Policy of India has been prepared by

(*a*) Ministry of Education
(*b*) Ministry of Commerce and Industry
(*c*) Ministry of Information and Broadcasting
(*d*) Department of Industrial Policy and Promotion

Choose the most appropriate answer from the options given below:

A. (*a*) and (*b*) only
B. (*b*) and (*c*) only
C. (*b*) and (*d*) only
D. (*a*) and (*d*) only

42. According to Goodman the information life cycle includes:
(*a*) Design and creation of records
(*b*) Restructuring of records
(*c*) Circulation, Access, Loan, Use
(*d*) Marketing

Choose the correct answer from the options given below:
A. (*a*) and (*b*) only B. (*a*) and (*c*) only
C. (*b*) and (*d*) only D. (*d*) and (*a*) only

43. Which of the following are kinds of extension service?
(*a*) Inter Library Loan
(*b*) Photocopy
(*c*) Reading circles
(*d*) Story hour for children
(*e*) Organising a book fair

Choose the most appropriate answer from the options given below:
A. (*c*), (*a*) and (*b*) only
B. (*b*), (*c*) and (*e*) only
C. (*c*), (*d*) and (*e*) only
D. (*a*), (*b*) and (*d*) only

44. Which of the following are the products/services of INFLIBNET?
(*a*) IndCat
(*b*) Shodh Shuddhi
(*c*) Vidyanidhi
(*d*) Vidyamitra

Choose the correct answer from the options given below:
A. (*a*), (*b*), (*d*) only B. (*a*), (*c*), (*d*) only
C. (*a*), (*b*), (*c*) only D. (*b*), (*c*), (*d*) only

45. The core collection of web of science includes
(*a*) Science Citation Index Expanded
(*b*) Social Sciences Citation Index
(*c*) Arts and Humanities Citation Index
(*d*) Agriculture, Biology and Environmental Science

Choose the correct answer from the options given below:
A. (*b*), (*c*), (*d*) only B. (*a*), (*b*), (*c*) only
C. (*a*), (*b*), (*d*) only D. (*a*), (*c*), (*d*) only

46. Identify the fact sources among the following:
(*a*) Whitaker's Almanac, London
(*b*) Statesman's Year Book, New York
(*c*) The Columbia Gazetteer of the World, New York
(*d*) Current Biography, New York

Choose the most appropriate answer from the options given below:
A. (*a*) and (*b*) only B. (*b*) and (*c*) only
C. (*c*) and (*d*) only D. (*d*) and (*a*) only

47. Web scale discovery services provide
(*a*) Content (*b*) Discovery
(*c*) Delivery (*d*) Blog contents

Choose the correct answer from the options given below:
A. (*a*), (*b*) and (*d*) only
B. (*b*), (*c*) and (*d*) only
C. (*c*), (*d*) and (*a*) only
D. (*a*), (*b*) and (*c*) only

48. Who were involved in coining the term, "RAID"?
(*a*) David Patterson
(*b*) William Katz
(*c*) Gorth A. Gibson
(*d*) Randy Katz
(*e*) John A. Gibson

Choose the correct answer from the options given below:
A. (*a*), (*b*) and (*c*) only
B. (*b*), (*c*) and (*d*) only
C. (*a*), (*c*) and (*d*) only
D. (*a*), (*b*) and (*d*) only

49. The object oriented programming is based on the following principles:
(*a*) Inheritance (*b*) Encapsulation
(*c*) Data Abstraction (*d*) Data filters

Choose the correct answer from the options given below:
A. (*a*), (*b*) and (*c*) only
B. (*b*), (*c*) and (*d*) only
C. (*a*), (*c*) and (*d*) only
D. (*a*), (*b*) and (*d*) only

50. The standards for bibliographic information interchange and communication are:

(*a*) ISO 2709 (*b*) Z 39.50

(*c*) Z 39.71 (*d*) CPM

(*e*) PEST

Choose the correct answer from the options given below:

A. (*a*), (*d*), (*e*) only B. (*b*), (*c*), (*d*) only

C. (*a*), (*b*), (*c*) only D. (*c*), (*d*), (*e*) only

51. Which of the following statistical packages are used for data analysis?

(*a*) MS-Excel

(*b*) SPSS

(*c*) MS-Access

(*d*) Mendeley

(*e*) R

Choose the correct answer from the options given below:

A. (*a*), (*c*), (*e*) only B. (*a*), (*b*), (*e*) only

C. (*c*), (*d*), (*e*) only D. (*b*), (*c*), (*e*) only

52. Which of the following are true of CILIP?

(*a*) Formerly known as ASLIB

(*b*) Formed in 2002

(*c*) Publishes LISA

(*d*) Headquarters at London

Choose the correct answer from the options given below:

A. (*b*), (*c*), (*d*) only B. (*a*), (*b*), (*d*) only

C. (*a*), (*c*), (*d*) only D. (*a*), (*b*), (*c*) only

53. Which of the following are elements of Job description?

(*a*) Job summary

(*b*) Job identification

(*c*) Job satisfaction

(*d*) Job activities and procedures

(*e*) Job motivation

Choose the most appropriate answer from the options given below:

A. (*b*), (*c*) and (*d*) only

B. (*a*), (*b*) and (*d*) only

C. (*a*), (*c*) and (*e*) only

D. (*b*), (*c*) and (*e*) only

54. Which of the following provides cloud based Koha to the libraries?

(*a*) Duraspace (*b*) Liblime

(*c*) Amazon (*d*) Informatics

Choose the correct answer from the options given below:

A. (*a*) and (*b*) only B. (*b*) and (*c*) only

C. (*b*) and (*d*) only D. (*a*) and (*c*) only

55. Expert system developed for rendering reference service are:

(*a*) POINTER (*b*) PLEXUS

(*c*) HAMLET (*d*) PANDORA

Choose the correct answer from the options given below:

A. (*a*) and (*b*) only B. (*b*) and (*c*) only

C. (*a*) and (*d*) only D. (*c*) and (*d*) only

56. Chemical Abstracts include

(*a*) Author Index (*b*) Keyword Index

(*c*) Patent Index (*d*) Region Index

(*e*) Publisher Index

Choose the correct answer from the options given below:

A. (*a*), (*c*) and (*d*) only

B. (*a*), (*b*) and (*d*) only

C. (*c*), (*d*) and (*e*) only

D. (*a*), (*b*) and (*c*) only

57. Primary role operators used in PRECIS are ______.

(*a*) Assembly

(*b*) Key System

(*c*) Action

(*d*) Performer of transitive action

(*e*) Part/Property

Choose the correct answer from the options given below:

A. (*a*), (*c*), (*e*) only B. (*c*), (*d*), (*e*) only

C. (*b*), (*c*), (*d*) only D. (*b*), (*d*), (*e*) only

58. Which of the following statements are correct in terms of PPBS?

(*a*) Combines programme budgeting and performance budgeting

(*b*) Scientific approach of budgeting

(*c*) Formula is used
(*d*) Incremental budget approach

Choose the most appropriate answer from the options given below:

A. (*a*) and (*d*) only B. (*b*) and (*d*) only
C. (*a*) and (*b*) only D. (*b*) and (*c*) only

59. Which of the following are associated with TQM?
(*a*) Prevention and Zero defects
(*b*) Directive
(*c*) Continuous improvement
(*d*) Based on slogans, exhortations and dependence on supervision
(*e*) Total participation

Choose the correct answer from the options given below:

A. (*a*), (*d*), (*e*) only B. (*d*), (*e*), (*c*) only
C. (*a*), (*c*), (*e*) only D. (*b*), (*c*), (*e*) only

60. BIOSIS provides information services to
(*a*) Social Science (*b*) Engineering
(*c*) Biology (*d*) Zoology
(*e*) Entomology

Choose the most appropriate answer from the options given below:

A. (*a*), (*b*) and (*c*) only
B. (*b*), (*c*) and (*d*) only
C. (*c*), (*d*) and (*e*) only
D. (*d*), (*e*) and (*a*) only

61. The qualities of a good notation are
(*a*) should convey order clearly
(*b*) should be numeric
(*c*) should be hospitable to new subjects
(*d*) should be alphabetic
(*e*) should be mnemonic

Choose the most appropriate answer from the options given below:

A. (*a*), (*b*), (*c*) only B. (*b*), (*c*), (*d*) only
C. (*c*), (*d*), (*e*) only D. (*a*), (*c*), (*e*) only

62. The main objective of the research is
(*a*) To gain familiarity with a phenomenon
(*b*) To test the hypothesis of a casual relationship between variables
(*c*) To get a research degree
(*d*) To get professional benefits
(*e*) To portrary accurately the characteristics of an individual/situation

Choose the correct answer from the options given below:

A. (*a*), (*b*), (*e*) only B. (*b*), (*c*), (*e*) only
C. (*c*), (*d*), (*e*) only D. (*a*), (*c*), (*d*) only

63. The characteristics of an hypothesis are :
(*a*) it should be clear and precise
(*b*) it should state the relationship between variables
(*c*) it should explain the earlier study results
(*d*) it should be consistance
(*e*) it must explain the facts that gave rise to the need for explanation

Choose the correct answer from the options given below:

A. (*a*), (*b*), (*c*) only B. (*b*), (*c*), (*d*) only
C. (*c*), (*d*), (*e*) only D. (*a*), (*b*), (*d*) only

64. Which of the following describes Special Library?
(*a*) Emphasis on handling of informational materials rather than educational materials
(*b*) Collection is delimited by subject area
(*c*) Service is provided to further the objectives of parent institution
(*d*) Any one can use the library

Choose the correct answer from the options given below:

A. (*a*), (*b*), (*c*) only B. (*b*), (*c*), (*d*) only
C. (*a*), (*c*), (*d*) only D. (*a*), (*b*), (*d*) only

65. Content Management System possess following characteristics
(*a*) It is a static system
(*b*) Provides an interface for content providers to add their content
(*c*) Knowledge of HTML is not mandatory
(*d*) It holds only unstructured data

Choose the correct answer from the options given below:

A. (*a*) and (*b*) only B. (*b*) and (*c*) only
C. (*c*) and (*d*) only D. (*a*) and (*d*) only

66. Arrange the following in ascending order according to their year of origin

(*a*) FRBR (*b*) CCF
(*c*) MARC21 (*d*) RDA

Choose the correct answer from the options given below:

A. (*b*), (*c*), (*a*), (*d*) B. (*d*), (*a*), (*b*), (*c*)
C. (*a*), (*b*), (*c*), (*d*) D. (*c*), (*a*), (*b*), (*d*)

67. Arrange the following in ascending order from the year of their inception

(*a*) AGRIS (*b*) Medline
(*c*) Ei-Compendex (*d*) BIOSIS

Choose the correct answer from the options given below:

A. (*d*), (*a*), (*b*), (*c*) B. (*a*), (*b*), (*c*), (*d*)
C. (*c*), (*d*), (*b*), (*a*) D. (*b*), (*d*), (*c*), (*a*)

68. Arrange the Public Libraries Act as per their year of Enactment in Ascending order

(*a*) Mizoram Public Libraries Act
(*b*) Goa Public Libraries Act
(*c*) Haryana Public Libraries Act
(*d*) Manipur Public Libraries Act

Choose the correct answer from the options given below:

A. (*a*), (*b*), (*d*), (*c*) B. (*c*), (*b*), (*a*), (*d*)
C. (*b*), (*c*), (*d*), (*a*) D. (*d*), (*c*), (*a*), (*b*)

69. Logical steps involved in providing SDI should be ______.

(*a*) Feedback (*b*) Notification
(*c*) User profiles (*d*) Database
(*e*) Matching

Choose the correct answer from the options given below:

A. (*a*), (*b*), (*c*), (*d*), (*e*)
B. (*b*), (*c*), (*d*), (*e*), (*a*)
C. (*c*), (*d*), (*e*), (*b*), (*a*)
D. (*d*), (*a*), (*b*), (*c*), (*e*)

70. Arrange in sequence the steps of automated acquisition

(*a*) Claims
(*b*) Cancellations
(*c*) Ordering
(*d*) Received item processing
(*e*) Received invoice processing

Choose the correct answer from the options given below:

A. (*e*), (*c*), (*b*), (*d*), (*a*)
B. (*b*), (*c*), (*d*), (*a*), (*e*)
C. (*c*), (*d*), (*e*), (*a*), (*b*)
D. (*d*), (*c*), (*a*), (*e*), (*b*)

71. Arrange the following in a logical order from beginning to end

(*a*) Selection of research problem
(*b*) Identification of research area
(*c*) Collection of data
(*d*) Research design
(*e*) Analysis of data

Choose the correct answer from the options given below:

A. (*a*), (*b*), (*d*), (*c*) and (*e*)
B. (*b*), (*d*), (*a*), (*e*) and (*c*)
C. (*b*), (*a*), (*d*), (*c*) and (*e*)
D. (*d*), (*b*), (*a*), (*c*) and (*e*)

72. Arrange the following content management software in an ascending form according to their first released version:

(*a*) Word press (*b*) Joomla
(*c*) Drupal (*d*) Magento

Choose the correct answer from the options given below:

A. (*c*), (*a*), (*d*), (*b*) B. (*a*), (*c*), (*b*), (*d*)
C. (*b*), (*a*), (*d*), (*c*) D. (*c*), (*a*), (*b*), (*d*)

73. Arrange the following in an ascending order from the dates of their first publication:

(*a*) Index Medicus
(*b*) Oxford English Dictionary
(*c*) Imperial Gazetteer of India
(*d*) Encyclopedia Americana

Choose the correct answer from the options given below:

A. (*b*), (*a*), (*c*), (*d*) B. (*a*), (*c*), (*d*), (*b*)
C. (*c*), (*d*), (*a*), (*b*) D. (*d*), (*b*), (*c*), (*a*)

74. Arrange the following programming languages in an ascending form according to their year of development:

(*a*) Cobol (*b*) C
(*c*) Java (*d*) FORTRAN

Choose the correct answer from the options given below:

A. (c), (d), (a), (b) B. (d), (a), (c), (b)
C. (c), (a), (d), (b) D. (a), (c), (d), (b)

75. Arrange the facets for the given title as per the facet formula of colon classification "Devaluation of Indian currency in 1970's":

(a) Devaluation
(b) India
(c) Paper Currency
(d) Money
(e) 1970's

Choose the correct answer from the options given below:

A. (a), (c), (b), (d), (e)
B. (b), (d), (e), (a), (c)
C. (d), (c), (a), (b), (e)
D. (d), (e), (b), (c), (a)

76. Match List-I with List-II:

List-I (Communication Model)	List-II (Year of origin)
(a) Charles E Osgood's Model	(i) 1956
(b) Harold D Lasswell's Model	(ii) 1954
(c) Shannon and Weaver's Model	(iii) 1948
(d) George Gerbner's Model	(iv) 1949

Choose the correct answer from the options given below:

	(a)	(b)	(c)	(d)
A.	(iv)	(iii)	(ii)	(i)
B.	(iii)	(ii)	(iv)	(i)
C.	(iii)	(iv)	(ii)	(i)
D.	(ii)	(iii)	(iv)	(i)

77. Match List-I with List-II:

List-I (Types of Library)	List-II (Characteristics)
(a) Special Library	(i) Duty of collecting the literary products of country
(b) Public Library	(ii) Serve to the need of personnel of parent body
(c) National Library	(iii) Aim is to help in research, teaching and extension
(d) Academic Library	(iv) Established under clear mandate of law

Choose the correct answer from the options given below:

	(a)	(b)	(c)	(d)
A.	(iii)	(ii)	(iv)	(i)
B.	(iv)	(iii)	(ii)	(i)
C.	(i)	(iv)	(iii)	(ii)
D.	(ii)	(iv)	(i)	(iii)

78. Match List-I with List-II:

List-I (Authors)	List-II (Books)
(a) Katz, A	(i) Science and technology : An introduction to literature
(b) Rowley JE	(ii) Reference service
(c) Dennis Grogan	(iii) Introduction to Reference work
(d) Ranganathan, SR	(iv) Abstracting and indexing

Choose the correct answer from the options given below:

	(a)	(b)	(c)	(d)
A.	(iii)	(iv)	(i)	(ii)
B.	(i)	(iii)	(iv)	(ii)
C.	(iii)	(i)	(ii)	(iv)
D.	(ii)	(iv)	(iii)	(i)

79. Match List-I with List-II:

List-I (File Extensions)	List-II (File Format)
(a) .wav	(i) structured
(b) .pdf	(ii) image
(c) .pcd	(iii) video
(d) .snd	(iv) audio

Choose the correct answer from the options given below:

	(a)	(b)	(c)	(d)
A.	(iv)	(i)	(ii)	(iii)
B.	(iii)	(ii)	(i)	(iv)
C.	(iii)	(i)	(ii)	(iv)
D.	(ii)	(i)	(iv)	(iii)

80. Match List-I with List-II:

List-I (Information centres)	List-II (Location)
(*a*) NICLAI	(*i*) Bangalore
(*b*) NICFOS	(*ii*) Lucknow
(*c*) NICMAP	(*iii*) Chennai
(*d*) Drugs and Pharmaceuticals	(*iv*) Mysore

Choose the correct answer from the options given below:

	(*a*)	(*b*)	(*c*)	(*d*)
A.	(*i*)	(*ii*)	(*iii*)	(*iv*)
B.	(*ii*)	(*iii*)	(*iv*)	(*i*)
C.	(*iii*)	(*iv*)	(*i*)	(*ii*)
D.	(*iv*)	(*iii*)	(*ii*)	(*i*)

81. Match List-I with List-II:

List-I (Propounders)	List-II (Theories)
(*a*) Herzberg	(*i*) Expectancy theory
(*b*) Vroom	(*ii*) Goal setting theory
(*c*) McClelland	(*iii*) Hygiene theory
(*d*) Edwin Locke	(*iv*) Achievement, Affiliation and Power need theory

Choose the correct answer from the options given below:

	(*a*)	(*b*)	(*c*)	(*d*)
A.	(*i*)	(*iv*)	(*iii*)	(*ii*)
B.	(*iv*)	(*i*)	(*ii*)	(*iii*)
C.	(*ii*)	(*iii*)	(*i*)	(*iv*)
D.	(*iii*)	(*i*)	(*iv*)	(*ii*)

82. Match List-I with List-II:

List-I (Classification Scheme)	List-II (Year)
(*a*) DDC	(*i*) 1904
(*b*) UDC	(*ii*) 1933
(*c*) CC	(*iii*) 1876
(*d*) LC	(*iv*) 1905

Choose the correct answer from the options given below:

	(*a*)	(*b*)	(*c*)	(*d*)
A.	(*iii*)	(*iv*)	(*ii*)	(*i*)
B.	(*i*)	(*iii*)	(*ii*)	(*iv*)
C.	(*ii*)	(*iv*)	(*iii*)	(*i*)
D.	(*iv*)	(*ii*)	(*i*)	(*iii*)

83. Match List-I with List-II:

List-I (OSI layer)	List-II (Functions of layer)
(*a*) Physical layer	(*i*) Concerned with orderly exchange of data between computers connected on LAN
(*b*) Network layer	(*ii*) Ensures data is received reliably by the receiver
(*c*) Transport layer	(*iii*) Supports mail transfer, file transfer, remote login etc.
(*d*) Application layer	(*iv*) Primarily concerned with data transmission speed

Choose the correct answer from the options given below:

	(*a*)	(*b*)	(*c*)	(*d*)
A.	(*iv*)	(*ii*)	(*i*)	(*iii*)
B.	(*iv*)	(*i*)	(*ii*)	(*iii*)
C.	(*ii*)	(*i*)	(*iii*)	(*iv*)
D.	(*iii*)	(*i*)	(*iv*)	(*ii*)

84. Match List-I with List-II:

List-I (Institute)	List-II (Type of Library)
(*a*) Tata Institute of Social Science Library	(*i*) Corporate Library
(*b*) Khudha Baksh Oriental Library	(*ii*) Academic Library
(*c*) BARC Library	(*iii*) Public Library
(*d*) TCS Library	(*iv*) R & D Library

Choose the correct answer from the options given below:

	(*a*)	(*b*)	(*c*)	(*d*)
A.	(*i*)	(*iii*)	(*ii*)	(*iv*)
B.	(*ii*)	(*iii*)	(*iv*)	(*i*)
C.	(*iii*)	(*i*)	(*iv*)	(*ii*)
D.	(*iv*)	(*ii*)	(*i*)	(*iii*)

85. Match List-I with List-II:

List-I (Methods)	List-II (Primary techniques)
(*a*) Analysis of historical records	(*i*) Observational behavioural scales, use of score cards
(*b*) Analysis of documents	(*ii*) Interactional recording possible use of A/V recorders
(*c*) Non participant direct observation	(*iii*) Statistical compilation, manipulation content analysis
(*d*) Participant observation	(*iv*) Recording of notes, content analysis

Choose the correct answer from the options given below:

	(*a*)	(*b*)	(*c*)	(*d*)
A.	(*i*)	(*iii*)	(*ii*)	(*iv*)
B.	(*iv*)	(*iii*)	(*i*)	(*ii*)
C.	(*ii*)	(*iv*)	(*iii*)	(*i*)
D.	(*iii*)	(*i*)	(*iv*)	(*ii*)

86. Given below are two statements:

Statement I: A natural language is developed for communication of ideas among human beings.

Statement II: An indexing language is a uncontrolled language.

In the light of the above statements, choose the **correct answer** from the options given below:

A. Both statement I and statement II are true
B. Both statement I and statement II are false
C. Statement I is true, but statement II is false
D. Statement I is false, but statement II is true

87. Given below are two statements : One is labelled as Assertion (A) and the other is labelled as Reason (R).

Assertion (A): Cloud computing is facilitating the libraries for pooling the resources.

Reason (R): Resource pooling has helped the libraries to share skilled manpower in cloud.

In the light of the above statements, choose the **correct answer** from the options given below.

A. Both (A) and (R) are true and (R) is the correct explanation of (A)
B. Both (A) and (R) are true, but (R) is NOT the correct explanation of (A)
C. (A) is true, but (R) is false
D. (A) is false, but (R) is true

88. Given below are two statements : One is labelled as Assertion (A) and the other is labelled as Reason (R).

Assertion (A): Public libraries in India emphasize on library cess.

Reason (R): The states not having Public Library Act do not have a provision of Library cess.

In the light of the above statements, choose the **correct answer** from the options given below:

A. Both (A) and (R) are true and (R) is the correct explanation of (A)
B. Both (A) and (R) are true, but (R) is NOT the correct explanation of (A)
C. (A) is true, but (R) is false
D. (A) is false, but (R) is true

89. Given below are two statements:

Statement I: Performance measurement is feedback mechanism to support decision making in libraries.

Statement II: Performance measurement is simply concerned with collecting data associated with pre-determined goals and quantitative in nature.

In the light of the above statements, choose the **most appropriate answer** from the options given below:

A. Both Statement I and Statement II are correct
B. Both Statement 1 and Statement II are incorrect
C. Statement I is correct, but Statement II is incorrect
D. Statement I is incorrect, but Statement II is correct

90. Given below are two statements : One is labelled as Assertion (A) and the other is labelled as Reason (R).

Assertion (A): A vibrant Intellectual property ecosystem is an asset for the intellectuals.

Reason (R): Intellectual property Rights protect the rights of the creators from misuse.

In the light of the above statements, choose the **most appropriate answer** from the options given below:

A. Both (A) and (R) are correct and (R) is the correct explanation of (A)

B. Both (A) and (R) are correct, but (R) is NOT the correct explanation of (A)

C. (A) is correct, but (R) is not correct

D. (A) is not correct, but (R) is correct

Directions (Qs. No. 91 to 95): *Read the given passage and answer the questions that follows:*

A century ago, library Services were focused on architecture, physical workflow design and urban planning. Planning the physical environment is still important, but more often than not, it serves as the backdrop for patrons operating in a world dominated by online information sources. The experience and preference of library users is being affected by other, non-library services such as Amazon, Google, Facebook, Twitter, and social question and answer sites, etc., Library catalogs have long been the point of discovery and delivery of content. People want to find information quickly and conveniently, and they expect the interface to be familiar to them. Unfortunately, libraries have not consistently employed their usage data to fully mobilize discovery services in the same way as Google. Providing seamless points of access to the content people discover through other online services could be a point of distinction for libraries. A study concluded that access— not discovery—is the major challenge for today's information seekers, who may be better served by online library catalogs that improve delivery and provide more links to more online content. It is true that services like Google help people discover content more quickly and conveniently, but their search results often leave them wanting more. When faced with sifting through a lot of content, people want search engines that return information relevant to their search queries in order to minimize their need to evaluate the content.

91. Major problem with tools like Google and Twitter is ______.

A. Relevancy of information

B. Query formulation

C. Dealing with huge content

D. Providing seemless points of access

92. Oldest discovery tool is ______.

A. Accession register B. Index

C. Catalogue D. Amazon

93. The discussion in the paragraph is centred around:

A. First Law of library science

B. Second Law of library science

C. Third Law of library science

D. Fourth Law of library science

94. A century ago library services were not focussed on:

A. On-line solutions

B. Planning

C. Physical work.flow

D. Architecture

95. Which of the following is a major challenge for today's information seekers:

A. Content delivery

B. Content access

C. Content discovery

D. Content availability

Directions (Qs. No. 96 to 100): *Read the given passage and answer the questions that follows:*

A reading culture is an environment where reading is championed, valued, respected, and encouraged. Reading lies at the heart of the curriculum, and it's of the upmost importance to a child's personal, social, and academic success, as well as their general wellbeing. Creating a reading culture should not be the responsibility of an individual. It takes dedication, perseverance, and effort. It's led by an enthusiastic and dedicated senior leadership team, and advocated by every pupil, parent, career, and staff member in the school community. If reading is to become a lifelong habit, then people must see themselves as participants in a community that views reading as a significant and enjoyable activity. Parents and the home environment are essential in fostering a love of reading. Where a reading culture exists, children read of their own free will, on a regular basis. Students select their own reading material, at a time and place of their choosing. They are willing and active participants, who anticipate the satisfaction they'll get from picking up a book.

To make sure children don't experience reading difficulty and demotivation, we should ensure students become fluent and engaged readers from an early age. Creating a reading culture where students are disaffected, hold negative attitudes, and whose reading ages are well below chronological, can be challenging, but not impossible. Building a strong reading culture puts reading at the forefront of school improvement. A creative and exciting reading culture not only breeds capable and committed readers, it boosts wellbeing, community connectedness, and student outcomes. Children will need high levels of literacy in so many aspects of their lives. Not only is reading required for success in future employment, an ability to read will help children in future relationships, when running a household, and when navigating all aspects of their personal lives. Only competent readers will be able to access the wonders of the curriculum, and thus improve their life chances.

96. Reading culture of children should be cultivated:
A. When they are interested to read
B. During their early age
C. When they become 12 years old
D. When they enter schools

97. What is the end result of reading culture?
A. Publication of more literature
B. Removal of demotivation
C. Improve life chances of individuals
D. One can select their own reading material

98. Which of the following is essential to build reading culture?
A. Good School
B. Automated Library
C. Strict teacher
D. Dedication, Perservarance

99. Creating reading culture breeds:
A. Rankholders
B. Appreciation from parents
C. Applause from publishers
D. Capable and committed readers

100. Where reading culture exists students ______ on their own.
A. Select reading materials
B. Prefer to go to school
C. Design curriculum
D. Play games

ANSWERS

1. (B): The Marrakesh Treaty to Facilitate Access to Published Works for Persons Who Are Blind, Visually Impaired or Otherwise Print Disabled, was adopted on June 27, 2013 by the member states of the World Intellectual Property Organization (WIPO). Prompting its adoption was the widespread recognition of the problem known as a "book famine," the situation where very few books are published in formats that are accessible to those who are blind and visually impaired. The goal of this treaty is increase access to printed materials for these persons around the world.

2. (D): The National Knowledge Commission 2007 has suggested the following for creating a knowledge society and to help libraries and librarians:

- **Set up a National commission on libraries:** To create an independent autonomous statutory body to address all the library related issues that require attention.

- **Prepare a National census of all libraries:** Collection of census data on libraries would provide baseline for planning. Survey of user needs and reading habits should be periodic at the national level as part of the National sample survey.
- **Revamp library and information science education, training and research facilities:** Establishing a well equipped institute for advance training and research in library and information science and services.
- **Re-assess staffing of libraries:** In the changed environment it is necessary to assess the manpower requirements for different types of libraries and department of library and information science, keeping in mind the job descriptions, qualifications, designations, pay scales, career advancement and service conditions.
- **Set up a central library fund:** A specified percentage of the central and state education budgets must be earmarked for libraries with initial funding of 1000 crores which may be matched by the private sector.
- **Modernize library management:** Libraries should be organized and the staff so trained that they become relevant to user communities in every aspect. Also to optimize resources efforts should be made to synergize the strengths of different types of libraries through innovative collaboration.
- **Encourage greater community participation in library management:** It is necessary to involve different stakeholders and user groups in the managerial decision-making process.

3. **(B):** The second intellectual strand focuses on the idea of an information sector, although not always with that name. One of the first economic studies in that area was Machlup's *The Production and Distribution of Knowledge in the United States* (1962). The famous book by the sociologist Daniel Bell, The Coming of Post-Industrial Society (1973), placed the idea of an information economy in the heads of a wide audience. The most comprehensive attempt to define precisely and to measure the information sector is the multivolume work by M. Porat, *The Information Economy: Definition and Measurement* (1977).

4. **(A):** Semiotics is the systematic study of sign processes (semiosis) and meaning making. Semiosis is any activity, conduct, or process that involves signs, where a sign is defined as anything that communicates something, usually called a meaning, to the sign's interpreter. The meaning car be intentional, such as a word uttered with a specific meaning; or unintentional, such as a symptom being a sign of a particular medical condition.

5. **(D):** The Berne Convention, adopted in 1886, deals with the protection of works and the rights of their authors. It provides creators such as authors, musicians, poets, painters etc. with the means to control how their works are used, by whom, and on what terms. It is based on three basic principles and contains a series of provisions determining the minimum protection to be granted, as well as special provisions available to developing countries that want to make use of them.

6. **(D):** The Big6 was developed by Mike Eisenberg and Bob Berkowitz to guide student through a process of conducting efficient and effective research. The Big6 is the most widely known and widely used approach to teaching information and technology skills in the world. Used in thousands of K-12 schools, higher education institutions, and corporate and adult training programs, the Big6 information problem-solving model is

applicable whenever people need and use information.

7. **(A):** The Calcutta Public Library was established in August, 1835. It was meant to serve the needs of "all ranks and classes without distinction". The Imperial Library was established in 1891. Lord Curzon, the Viceroy of India, promulgated the Imperial Library Act, 1902, amalgamating Calcutta Public Library with Imperial Library. Soon after independence, the Government of India renamed Imperial Library as the National Library. The National Library of Calcutta has not been able to provide national leadership in library matters.

8. **(B):** The term Information Literacy (IL) was first used by the president of US Information Literacy Associations - Prof. Paul G. Zurkowski in 1974. Information literacy is the ability to identify what information is needed, understand how the information is organized, identify the best sources of information for a given need, locate those sources, evaluate the sources critically and share that information. IL is the only way to enable people to make efficient, effective, creative, legal, ethical and strategic use of information for achieving their goals.

9. **(B): Fodor's:** Fodor's is a publisher of English-language travel and tourism information. It was founded in 1949 by Eugene Fodor who was a keen traveller.

   Travel Guide: A guidebook or travel guide is "a book of information about a place designed for the use of visitors or tourists". It contains information about sights, accommodations, restaurants, transportation, and activities. For example: Fodor's Essential India.

10. **(D):** JSTOR stands for journal storage. This is a wide-ranging database and archive of important scholarly journals spanning both multidisciplinary and discipline-specific collections. The Arts & Sciences Collections represent more than 600 journals in the arts, humanities, and social sciences. Because of JSTOR's archival mission, it is not a current issues database. JSTOR is a wide-ranging database containing back files from many scholarly journals.

11. **(C): S.R. Ranganathan Classification:** Based on the physical characteristics of documents S.R. Ranganathan classified documentary sources of information into four categories. These also reflect the chronological order of their development. They are:

    (*i*) **Conventional:** Books, periodicals, Map etc.;

    (*ii*) **Neo Conventional:** Standards, specification, patent etc.;

    (*iii*) **Non Conventional:** Audio visual, microcopy etc.;

    (*iv*) **Meta Document:** Direct records unmediated by human mind.

12. **(C):** Propedia is part of Encyclopedia Britannica. The first edition of Encyclopaedia Britannica was published in 1768-1771 in 3 volumes. The fourteenth edition published in 1929 was revised and reorganised till 1973. In 1974, the fifteenth edition was published as the "New Encyclopaedia Britannica" consisting of thirty volumes. It has three parts.

    I. Propaedia - 1 volume

    II. Micropaedia - 10 volumes

    III. Macropaedia - 19 volumes

13. **(B):** The public library is the dynamic and premiere community access point designed to proactively respond to a multitude of ever-changing information needs. These guidelines are framed to provide assistance to library and information professionals in most situations, to assist them in better developing effective services, relevant collections, and accessible formats within the context and requirements of the local community. In this exciting and complex information world it is important for library and information

professionals in search of knowledge, information and creative experience to succeed. We hope these guidelines will facilitate this search, ultimately enhancing the learning power and quality of life of people in the community the libraries serve.

14. (C): The first SMS message was sent on 3 December 1992, when Neil Papworth, a test engineer for Sema Group, sent "Merry Christmas" to the Orbitel 901 phone of colleague Richard Jarvis. SMS rolled out commercially on many cellular networks that decade and became hugely popular worldwide as a method of text communication. By the end of 2010, SMS was the most widely used data application, with an estimated 3.5 billion active users, or about 80% of all mobile phone subscribers.

15. (D): The National Informatics Centre (NIC) was established in 1976 by Narasimaiah Seshagiri under the Electronics Commission of India and later moved under the Planning Commission of India before coming under the Ministry of Electronics and Information Technology. NICNET started functioning in 1977.

NICNET stands for National Informatics Centre Network. National Informatics Centre (NIC) is an institution under the Government of India. It provides solutions in the area of e-governance particularly for the sectors that fall under Government of India. It supports NICNET.

16. (D): MEDLINE is the National Library of Medicine's (NLM) premier bibliographic database that contains references to journal articles in life sciences, with a concentration on biomedicine.

MEDLINE content is searchable via PubMed and constitutes the primary component of PubMed, a literature database developed and maintained by the NLM National Center for Biotechnology Information (NCBI).

17. (D): The notation in the CC-7 comprising of 74 digits (60 semantic and 14 indicator digits) has been divided into the following six species:

1. A/Z (Roman capitals) 26
2. Δ (Greek Delta) 01
3. 0/9 Indo-Arabic numerals 10
4. a/z Roman smalls (i, l, o excluded) 23
5. Indicator digits with anteriorising value 03
   * " ←
6. Ordinary indicator digits
   & ' . : ; , - = → + ( ) 11 = 74

18. (B): BIBFRAME (Bibliographic Framework) is a data model for bibliographic description. BIBFRAME was designed to replace the MARC standards, and to use linked data principles to make bibliographic data more useful both within and outside the library community.

19. (C): According to Guidelines for Abstracts, ANSI/NISO Z39, 14—1997, an abstract for a short communication should contain no more than 100 words, for an ordinary journal article no more than 250 words, and for a dissertation no more than 500 words.

20. (D): MODELS BASED ON THEORIES

Fuzzy Logic Model: An Information Retrieval System has software component that has the features and functions required to manipulate 'information' items versus a DBMS that is optimized to handle 'structured' data. Here information is regarded as fuzzy text. The term 'fuzzy' is used to imply the results from the minimal standards or controls on the creators of the text items. The author presents concepts, ideas and abstractions along with supporting facts. As such, there is minimal consistency in the vocabulary and styles of items.

Linguistic Model: In linguistic model for information retrieval, study the information retrieval from the point of view of the properties of language. Information retrieval is provided by features of natural language as well as artificial language the various ways of storage of information are essentially based on natural language.

Psychological Model: The psycholinguistic approaches to information retrieval led to the study of formation of concepts in human mind the way in which the human thinking process arranges the ideas, its presentation at the time of enquiry, and the type of retrieval cues it demands while searching has led to a cognitive research linked with computer communication processes.

21. **(A):** AGROVOC is a multilingual controlled vocabulary covering all areas of interest of the Food and Agriculture Organization of the United Nations (FAO), including food, nutrition, agriculture, fisheries, forestry and the environment. It is a collaborative effort, edited by a community of experts and coordinated by FAO. AGROVOC is made available by FAO as an RDF/SKOS-XL concept scheme and published as a linked data set aligned to 20 other vocabularies.

22. **(B):** RRRLF is a central autonomous organization established and fully financed by the Ministry of Culture, Government of India. RRRLF is registered under the West Bengal Societies Registration Act, 1961. It is the nodal agency of the Government of India to support public library services and systems and promote public library movement in the country commensurate with the objectives as embodied in its Memorandum of Association.

23. **(A):** Management Information Systems (MIS) is the study of people, technology, organizations, and the relationships among them. MIS professionals help firms realize maximum benefit from investment in personnel, equipment, and business processes. MIS is a people-oriented field with an emphasis on service through technology.

24. **(C):** Ministry of Health & Family Welfare, Government of India has put in place the Health Management Information System (HMIS) in 2008. Initially, HMIS started with uploading of district level consolidated figures in to the system. HMIS is a web-based Monitoring Information System of Ministry of Health & Family Welfare to monitor the National Health Mission and other National Health Programme and provide key inputs for policy formulation and appropriate programme interventions. HMIS is specially designed to assist health departments, at all levels, in managing and planning of health programmes.

25. **(C):** Precedence diagrams are designed to bridge the gap between manually operated planning systems like the Gantt chart and systems that are designed for computers, such as critical path method (CPM) and programme evaluation and review technique (PERT). However, these diagrams are rarely used as control tools in modern organizations. One of the most commonly used precedence diagrams is digitally accurate response tracking (DART), which is used in disaster management programmes.

26. **(B): Penetration pricing:** Penetration pricing is a pricing strategy where the price of a product is initially set low to rapidly reach a wide fraction of the market and initiate word of mouth. The strategy works on the expectation that customers will switch to the new brand because of the lower price.

27. **(B): Bolman and Deal's Four Frames Model**

Structural:

- This Frame focuses on the obvious 'how' of change.
- It's mainly a task-orientated Frame,
- It concentrates on strategy; setting measurable goals; clarifying tasks, responsibilities and reporting lines; agreeing on metrics and deadlines, and creating systems and procedures.

Human Resource:

- The FIR Frame places more emphasis on people's needs.
- It chiefly focuses on giving employees the power and opportunity to perform their jobs well, while at the same time, addressing their needs for human contact, personal growth, and job satisfaction.

Political

- The Political Frame addresses the problem of individuals and interest groups having sometimes conflicting (often hidden) agendas, especially at times when budgets are limited and the organisation has to make difficult choices.
- In this Frame, you will see coalition-building, conflict resolution work, and powerbase building to support the leader's initiatives.

Symbolic:

- The Symbolic Frame addresses people's needs for a sense of purpose and meaning in their work.
- It focuses on inspiring people by making the organisation's direction feel significant and distinctive.
- It includes creating a motivating vision and recognising superb performance through company celebrations.

28. (B): McClelland—Achievement Motivation Theory: It is also called the Three Needs Theory which motivate human behaviour. These three needs are: (*i*) Power (*ii*) Affiliation and (*iii*) Achievement. He was of the opinion that every employee requires the above needs but they differ in the degree of behaviour that motivates these needs.

(*i*) **Need for achievement (*n*-Ach):** a drive to excel, advance and grow;

(*ii*) **Need for power (*n*-Pow):** A drive to influencing others and situations;

(*iii*) **Need for affiliation (*n*-Aft):** A drive for friendly and close interpersonal relationships.

29. (C): Internet Protocol version 6 (IPv6) is the most recent version of the Internet Protocol (IP), the communications protocol that provides an identification and location system for computers on networks and routes traffic across the Internet. IPv6 was developed by the Internet Engineering Task Force (IETF) to deal with the long-anticipated problem of IPv4 address exhaustion, and is intended to replace IPv4. IPv6 uses 128-bit addresses, theoretically allowing 2128, or approximately 3.4×1038 total addresses.

30. (A): ASCII code: In order to easily exchange data between computers, coding of characters has been standardised. The most popular standard is known as ASCII (American Standard Code for Information Interchange). This code uses 7 bits to code each character. In addition to codes for characters, codes are defined in ASCII to convey information such as end of line, end of page, carriage return etc. to the computer. These codes are for non-printable control characters.

31. (D): Ping is a computer network administration software utility used to test the reachability of a host on an Internet Protocol (IP) network. It is available for virtually all operating systems that have networking capability, including most embedded network administration software. Ping operates by means of Internet Control Message Protocol (ICMP) packets. Pinging involves sending an ICMP echo request to the target host and waiting for an ICMP echo reply. The program reports errors, packet loss, and a statistical summary of the results, typically including the minimum, maximum, the mean round-trip times, and standard deviation of the mean.

32. (D): e-Granthalaya is a Digital Platform developed by National Informatics Centre, Ministry of Electronics and Information Technology, Government of India for Government Libraries for Automation of In-house activities as well as member services and Networking for resource sharing. e-Granthalaya 4.0 uses PostgreSQL-an Open Source DBMS as back-end database solution and is made available on NIC National Cloud (Meghraj) for Government Libraries on request basis with hosting of application and databases for online access.

33. (A): Characteristics of Big Data

- **Volume:** Size of data which is converting from terabytes to petabytes and so on.
- **Velocity:** Speed at which the data has arrived.
- **Variability:** Different speed of data from various sources.
- **Veracity:** Produces data of different pattern.

34. (A): RDF/XML is the standard XML syntax used to serialize the RDF data model. A collection of RDF statements can be represented in a variety of formats. However, XML is the preferable representation scheme because of software support. By using XML, RDF/XML satisfies requirements for character sets, tagging, XML namespaces, and URI technologies. RDF/XML supports the basic relational language layer.

35. (A): Down the Memory Lane: The National Library of India has initiated in late 1990s a digitization programme, known as 'Down the Memory Lane', to digitize rare books, manuscripts and other resources from its collection. The English books that were published prior to 1900 and Indian books published before 1920 were taken into consideration. Similarly, the Central Secretariat Library has initiated a programme to digitize government publications like, Gazette of India, Commission & Committee Reports, Annual Reports of the Ministries.

36. (B): The base stations, in turn, must be connected to a central hub called the Mobile Switching Center (MSC). The MSC provides connectivity between the Public Switched Telephone Network (PSTN) and the numerous base stations, and ultimately between all of the wireless subscribers in a system.

37. (D): The Scientific method is a process with the help of which scientists try to investigate, verify, or construct an accurate and reliable version of any natural phenomena. They are done by creating an objective framework for the purpose of scientific inquiry and analysing the results scientifically to come to a conclusion that either supports or contradicts the observation made at the beginning.

A method for being called a scientific method must have the following essential features:

- Objectivity
- Definiteness
- Verifiability
- Generality
- Predictability
- Modifiability and Dynamicity.

38. (C)

39. (B): Deliberate Sampling: This is also known as purposive, judgement sample. It involved the deliberate or convince selection of sample. It constitutes the representation of all universe, if data of petrol users is to be collected in relation to their reaction of quality of the petrol, than researcher may select few petrol pumps and conduct interview of the pet buyers. This is called convince sampling. In care of judgement sampling the judgement of the researcher is used for selecting sample.

40. (C): Netnography: A form of ethnography which is applied to online or largely online communities. It has mainly been used in relation to topics in the fields of marketing and retailing.

The term netnography is a portmanteau combining "Internet" or "network" with "ethnography". Netnography was originally developed in 1995 by marketing professor Robert Kozinets as a tool to analyze online fan discussions about the Star Trek franchise.

41. (C): Department of Industrial Policy & Promotion (DIPP), Ministry of Commerce, Government of India, has been appointed as the nodal department to coordinate, guide and oversee the implementation and future development of IPRs in India.

Objective of IPR Policy: There are seven major objectives:

- IPR, awareness, outreach, and promotion - awareness about the economic, social and cultural benefits of IPRs among the society.
- Create an atmosphere of inventibility and innovation - stimulate the generation of IPRs.
- Replace existing outdated laws - have strong and effective IPR laws, which balance the interests of rights owners with larger public interest.
- Human Capital Development for teaching, research and skill building in Intellectual Property Rights - strengthen and expand human resources, institutions and capacities.
- Administration and management of innovation - modernize and strengthen service-oriented IPR administration.
- Commercialization of IPRs - Get value for IPRs through commercialization.
- To combating IPR infringements by reinforcing the enforcement and adjudicatory mechanisms.

42. (B): The idea of an information life cycle is derived from records management, where the idea of document life cycle is central to the overall process. That cycle is set out by Goodman (1994).

The life cycle of records includes the following steps:

- design and creation of records;
- identification; authorization;
- verification, validation, auditing;
- circulation, access, loan, use;
- back-up procedures and disaster recovery plans;
- retention schedules and destruction.

43. (C): The Library extension services may be of internal or external type. The internal extension service includes orientation programmes and the external extension service includes the mobile library service, publicity programmes etc. Some of the main forms of extension services are as follows:

- Library Orientation/Library Tour
- Reading Circle, Study Circle
- Forming Friends of the Library Group
- Reading to Illiterates
- Meeting, Public Lectures and Talk.

44. (A): Information and Library Network (INFLIBNET) Centre, Gandhinagar is an Autonomous Inter-University Centre (IUC) of University Grants Commission, New Delhi (Ministry of Education, Govt. of India). It is a major National Programme initiated by the UGC in March 1991 as a project under the IUCAA, it became an independent Inter-University Centre in June 1996. INFLIBNET is involved in modernizing university libraries in India using the state-of-art technologies for the optimum utilisation of information. INFLIBNET is set out to be a major player in promoting scholarly communication among academicians and researchers in India.

Major service/products of INFLIBNET

- *E-Consortium:* e-ShodhSindhu; Shodh Shuddhi; N-LIST; Infistats; INFED.
- *Open Access Initiatives*-Shodhganga; Shodhgangotri; IR@INFLIBNET; INFO-PORT.
- *Projects & Services:* e-PG Pathshala; Vidwan Database; Vidya-Mitra; IRINS.
- *Library Automation:* IndCat:Union Catalogue; SOUL.

45. (B): The core collection of web of science includes:

- Science Citation Index Expanded.
- Social Sciences Citation Index.
- Arts & Humanities Citation Index.
- Conference Proceedings Citation Index-Science.
- Conference Proceedings Citation Index-Social Sciences & Humanities.
- Book Citation Index- Science.
- Book Citation Index- Social Sciences & Humanities.
- Emerging Science Citation Index.

46. (A)

47. (D): Web-scale discovery (WSD) systems bring the discovery layer technology developed to improve the search experience in next-gen OPACs and federated search systems together with a large, centralized index of content. This structure allows web-scale discovery to be more efficient and effective than federated search, and it provides a search experience capable of competing with Google and other commercial web search engines in terms of both scope and convenience.

The term *web scale* was used by Amazon and Google to describe the capacity and reach of their cloud computing and search platforms, as noted by Lorcam Dempsey (2007). In these contexts, it was meant to describe how these applications could adjust Web scale discovery services provide - Content; Discovery; Delivery

48. (C): The term "RAID" was invented by David Patterson, Garth A. Gibson, and Randy Katz at the University of California, Berkeley in 1987. In their June 1988 paper "A Case for Redundant Arrays of Inexpensive Disks (RAID)", presented at the SIGMOD Conference, they argued that the top-performing mainframe disk drives of the time could be beaten on performance by an array of the inexpensive drives that had been developed for the growing personal computer market. Although failures would rise in proportion to the number of drives, by configuring for redundancy, the reliability of an array could far exceed that of any large single drive.

49. (A): Object Oriented Programming is a language model that is organized around objects rather than actions and data rather than logic.

The four pillars of object-oriented programming are:

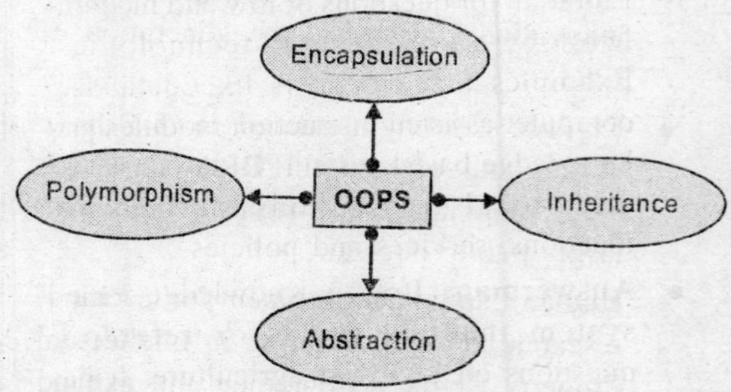

50. (C) **51. (B)** **52. (*)**

53. (B):

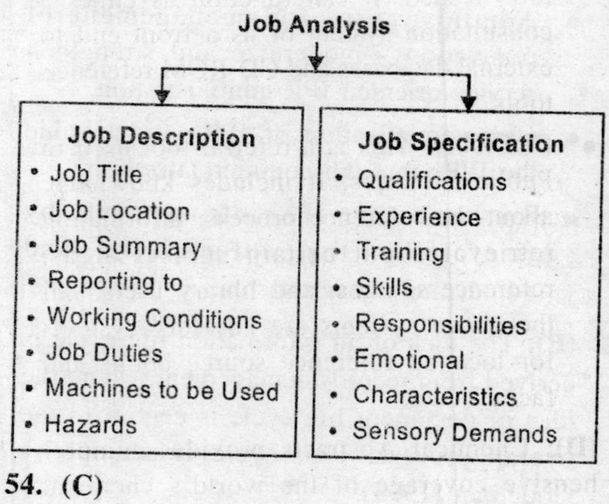

54. (C)

55. (A): Expert Systems in Reference Services: Reference service is one of vital services rendered in any library and the Expert System has to be used so as to substitute the reference librarian in the following ways:

- **Research:** It is a designed system that supplies clients with recommended sources to lookup for certain question. This is a system that teaches reference skills or computerized aid for practicing reference librarians and information specialists.
- **Pointer:** It is also known as knowledge based system but acting as computer assisted reference program. It directs patrons to reference sources.
- **Online Reference Assistance (ORA):** This system intended to stimulate the services of an academic reference Librarian for questions of low and medium level by using several technologies: Examples are videotext like database, computer assisted instruction modules and knowledge based system. ORA consist of directional transactions like library locations, services and policies.
- **Answerman:** It is a Knowledge based system that aid users for reference questions on topics of agriculture. It has series of menus that narrow down the subject of the questions and the type of tool needed. It can function as either a consultation system or as a front end to external databases and CD-ROM reference tools.
- **PLEXUS:** This is a referral tool used in Public Libraries. It includes knowledge about the reference process, information retrieval about certain subject areas, reference sources, and library users. All the above systems are advisory systems for locating reference source books and factual data.

56. **(D):** Chemical Abstracts provides comprehensive coverage of the world's chemical literature, and includes biochemistry, organic chemistry, macromolecular chemistry, applied chemistry and chemical engineering, physical, inorganic and analytical chemistry.

Chemical Abstracts Consists of Six Indexes:

- **General Subject Index:** This semiannual index covers subject concepts that do not refer to specific chemical substances in the corresponding Chemical Abstracts.
- **Author Index:** Authors, patentees, and patent assignees are listed in alphabetical order in this semiannual index with titles of their articles or patent specifications and abstract numbers.
- **Chemical Substance Index:** This semiannual index relates the Chemical Abstracts index names of chemical substances and their CAS Registry Numbers to Chemical Abstract abstract numbers for documents in which the substances are mentioned.

  Included with the Chemical Abstract name is a brief description of the document's context.
- **Formula Index:** This semiannual index relates the molecular formulas for chemical substances with the Chemical Abstracts chemical substance index names, CAS Registry Numbers, and corresponding abstract numbers.
- **Patent Index:** Entries are ordered alphabetically by a two-character code for the country of issue. Under each country the patent documents are listed in numerical order.
- **Index of Ring Systems:** Ring composition, ring size, and number of rings are listed providing a means for determining the systematic Chemical Abstract index names for specific ring systems as well as the non-systematic Chemical Abstract index names for cyclic natural products containing these ring systems.

57. **(C):** An important feature of the revised version of PRECIS is the provision of Codes for bringing expressiveness in the resulting index entries.

Three types of codes are there—Primary, Secondary, and Typographic codes.

Primary Operators	
Environment of core concepts	0 Location
Core concepts	1 Key System Thing when action not present. Thing towards which an action is directed, e.g., object of transitive action, performer of intransitive action 2 Action; Effect of action 3 Performer of transitive action (Agent, Instrument); Intake: Factor
Extra-core concepts	4 Viewpoint-as-form 5 Selected Instance: study region, study example, sample population 6 Form of document; Target user

58. (C): Planning Programming Budgeting System (PPBS): This method of budgeting was first proposed by USDOD (United States Department of Defence) (1961). Two key elements of PPBS are budgeting and systems analysis.

As an extension of programme budgeting, PPBS involves systems analysis, OR (Operation Research) and other cost-effectiveness processes to provide a more systematic and comprehensive comparison of costs and benefits of alterative approaches to a policy goal or programme objective. Planning, Programming and Budgeting System (PPBS) is a scientific approach. This establishes a rational basis to enable decision maker to choose between alternative programmes.

This method combines the functions of planning activities, programmes and services, translating them into tangible projects and finally presents the requirements in budgetary terms.

59. (C): "TQM is a management approach for an organization, centered on quality, based on the participation of all its members and aiming at long-term success through customer satisfaction, and benefits to all members of the organization and to society."

TQM requires six basic concepts:

- **A committed and involved management:** TQM is a continual long term activity that must be imbibed in the culture of the organization. Everything begins with the long-term-top-to-bottom-organization support. Management must participate in the quality program, establish a council to develop clear vision, set goals and direct the programs.
- **An unwavering focus on the customer:** Customers are the very purpose of any organization. Key to an effective TQM is orienting all activities towards the need of the customer, both internally and externally.
- **Effective involvement and achievement of the entire work force:** Implementing TQM is everyone's responsibility. Employees are the future of any organization. All personnel must be trained in TQM, its tools. They must be empowered to perform processes in an optimal manner.
- **Continuous improvement of the business and production processes:** All employees must continually strive to improve all business and production systems.
- **Treating Suppliers as Partners:** 40 to 60 % of the product cost is outsourced. So all supplier organizations have to be treated as extension of one's organisations.
- **Establish Performance measures:** Measure and prosper. Measures should be available to note downtimes, non-conformities and satisfaction of customers, absenteeism etc.

60. (C): BIOSIS is the major database in the biological sciences. Produced by Thomson

Reuters, it is available from multiple vendors. Includes conferences, patents, books, review articles, and more than 5,500 journals. Searchable via detailed BIOSIS indexing, MESH subject headings, and CAS Registry Numbers. Related products include *Biological Abstracts/RRM (Reports, Reviews, Meetings), BIOSIS Previews,* and *Zoological Record.* Back files available to 1926. This source is essential for all life sciences researchers. An essential tool for all users of the BIOSIS databases-Abstracts of Entomology; *Abstracts of Mycology; Zoological Record (ZR).*

61. (D): A notation is an ordered series of symbols representing terms. In a library classification scheme, the terms are ordered into classes and their sub-division. The symbols comprising a notation, therefore, stand in the place of classes and their sub-division to mechanise the process of sorting and replacement.

The qualities of a good notation are:

- should convey order clearly.
- should be hospitable to new subjects.
- should be alphabetic.

62. (A): The main aim of research is to find out the truth which is hidden and undiscovered. The purpose of research varies according to its subjects. Each research study has its own objectives. Though there are variety of objectives according to the varieties of subject. From a general point of view we can mention its objectives in the following way:

(*a*) To portray accurately the characteristics of a particular individual, situation or a group.

(*b*) To determine the frequency with which some things occur or with which it is associated with something else.

(*c*) To gain familiarity with a phenomenon or to achieve new insights into it.

(*d*) To test a hypothesis of a casual relationship between variables.

63. (D): Basic Characteristics of Hypothesis:

(*i*) Hypothesis should be clear and precise.

(*ii*) Hypothesis should be capable of being tested.

(*iii*) Hypothesis should state relationship between variables, if it happens to be a relational hypothesis.

(*iv*) Hypothesis should be limited in scope and must be specific.

(*v*) Hypothesis should be stated as far as possible in most simple terms so that the same is easily understandable by all concerned.

(*vi*) Hypothesis should be consistent with most known facts i.e., it must be consistent with a substantial body of established facts.

(*vii*) Hypothesis should be amenable to testing within a reasonable time.

(*viii*) Hypothesis must explain the facts that gave rise to the need for explanation.

64. (A): Special libraries often come to existence in order to meet an unsatisfied needs for information in an organization. They are responses to the information needs of geometrically expanding science and technology in the 20th century just as public and educational institutional libraries arose to serve the "universal education" concepts in that century. One of the earliest surveys of Special Libraries in the US (Schick and Howard, 1968) outlined the following criteria for identifying special libraries:

- The library must stress the handling of informational materials rather than recreational or educational materials;
- Generally, the library is part of a larger organization which has non-library objectives;
- The services of the library are limited to furthering the objectives of the sponsor and the collection of the library is delimited by the subject areas of particular interest of the sponsor.

- The librarian and his staff are the principal primary users of the library. It is their function to interpret the body of literature in the collection for the clientele.

65. (B)

66. (A): CCF is a structured format for creating bibliographical records and for exchanging records between groups of information agencies and libraries. An international symposium in Taormina, Sicily conducted by UNESCO was held in April 1978.

MARC is the acronym for Machine-Readable Cataloging. It defines a data format that emerged from a Library of Congress-led initiative that began nearly forty years ago. It provides the mechanism by which computers exchange, use, and interpret bibliographic information, and its data elements make up the foundation of most library catalogs used today. MARC became USMARC in the 1980s and MARC 21 in the late 1990s.

FRBR (Functional Requirements for Bibliographic Records) is a 1998 recommendation of the International Federation of Library Associations and Institutions (IFLA) to restructure catalog databases to reflect the conceptual structure of information resources.

Resource Description and Access (RDA) is a standard for descriptive cataloging initially released in June 2010, providing instructions and guidelines on formulating bibliographic data. Intended for use by libraries and other cultural organizations such as museums and archives, RDA is the successor to Anglo-American Cataloguing Rules, Second Edition (AACR2). In March 2012 the Library of Congress announced that it would fully implement RDA cataloging by the end of March 2013.

67. (C): Ei-Compendex is an engineering bibliographic database published by Elsevier. The name "Compendex" stands for COMPuterized ENgineering inDEX. It covers scientific literature pertaining to engineering materials. It started in 1884 under the name Engineering Index (Ei) and its first electronic bulletin was issued in 1967.

BIOSIS was founded in 1926 and aims to make life science information available to the scientific community through its bibliographic databases and related services.

MEDLARS (Medical Literature Analysis and Retrieval System) is a computerised biomedical bibliographic retrieval system. It was launched by the National Library of Medicine in 1964 and was the first large scale, computer based, retrospective search service available to the general public.

AGRIS, the International Information System for the Agricultural Sciences and Technology, was started in 1974 by the Food and Agriculture Organisation (FAO) of the United Nations. AGRIS became fully operational in 1975.

68. (D):

- Madras Public Libraries Act, 1948
- Andhra Pradesh Public Libraries Act, 1960
- Karnataka Public Libraries Act, 1965
- Megastar Public Libraries Act, 1967
- West Bengal Public Libraries Act, 1979
- Manipur Public Libraries Act, 1988
- Kerala Public Libraries Act, 1989
- Haryana Public Libraries Act, 1989
- Mizoram Public Libraries Act, 1993
- Goa Public Libraries Act; 1994.

69. (C): Hans Peter Luhn advanced the idea of selective dissemination of information (SDI) in 1958 which in due course formed the basis for planning a number of SDI systems by various bodies. The mechanised SDI system based on Luhn's design was first implemented in 1959 at the Advanced Systems Development Division of IBM Corporation at Yorktown Heights, New York. The success of the system emboldened others to follow suit and gradually the system spread all over the world.

Logical steps involved in providing SDI should be: User profiles; Database; Matching; Notification; Feedback.

70. (C) **71. (C)**

72. (D): A Web Content Management System (WCMS) is a software system that enables the users to create, manage and deploy content on web pages. The content includes text and embedded graphics, photos, audio and video. This application comprises of authoring tools, administration module and collaboration tools which enable the users to create and manage website content easily without any programming knowledge. There are simple readymade functions and modules which make it easier to manage and publish website content. A web content management system simplifies the process of publication of web-based content to a website. Most of the web content management systems are free and open source are characterised by ease of use and easy customisation as per needs. CMS in an ascending form according to their first released version:

- Drupal became an open source project in 2001.
- WordPress, content management system (CMS) developed in 2003.
- Joomla was the outcome of a fork of Mambo on 17 August 2005.
- Magento officially started development in early 2007.

73. (*) **74. (*)** **75. (C)**

76. (D):

- Harold D. Lasswell's Model (1948)
- Lasswell's Model (1948)
- Claude Shannon and Warren Weaver's Model (1949)
- Theodore M. Newcomb's Model (1953)
- Osgood's Model (1954)
- George Gerbner's Model (1956)
- Wilbur Schramm's Model (1971).

77. (D): A special library is a one, which is specializing in a particular subject or group of subjects or a particular form of documents. Some people even consider libraries serving the needs of special clientele (e.g. blinds, prisoners, patients, children, etc) as special libraries. A special library exists to serve its parent body. Therefore, aim of a special library is to further the interests of its parent body.

In this situation UNESCO manifesto states that "the public library should be established under clear mandate of law, so framed as to ensure nationwide provisions of public library service". So the public library should be wholly maintained from public funds, and no direct charge should be made to anyone for its service. To fulfil this objective there is no alternative to it.

A national library is that library which has the duty of collecting and preserving the literature of the nation within and outside the country. Thus, national libraries are those libraries whose community is the nation at large.

An academic library is a library that is attached to a higher education institution and serves two complementary purposes: to support the curriculum and the research of the university faculty and students. It is unknown how many academic libraries there are worldwide. An academic and research portal maintained by UNESCO links to 3,785 libraries.

78. (A) **79. (C)**

80. (C): Sectoral Information Centers

Acronym	Host Institution
NICLAI	Central Leather Research Institute, Madras
NICFOS	Central Food Technological Research Institute, Mysore
NICMAP	Central Manufacturing Technology Institute, Bangalore
NICDAP	Central Drug Research Institute, Lucknow
NICTAS	Ahmedabad Textile Industry's Research Association, Ahmedabad

Acronym	Host Institution
NICHEM	National Chemical Laboratory, Pune
NICAC	Central Glass and Ceramics Research Institute, Calcutta
NCB	Indian National Scientific Documentation Centre, New Delhi
NICRYS	University of Madras, Madras
NICDROM	National Aerospace Laboratory, Bangalore
NICMAN	Indian Institute of Management, Ahmedabad
NICMAS	National Institute of Oceanography

81. (D): Frederick Irving Herzberg was an American psychologist who became one of the most influential names in business management. He is most famous for introducing job enrichment and the Motivator-Hygiene theory.

Vroom's primary research was on the expectancy theory of motivation, which attempts to explain why individuals choose to follow certain courses of action and prefer certain goals or outcomes over others in organizations, particularly in decision-making and leadership.

McClelland's Human Motivation Theory states that every person has one of three main driving motivators: the needs for achievement, affiliation, or power. These motivators are not inherent; we develop them through our culture and life experiences. Achievers like to solve problems and achieve goals.

In 1960's, **Edwin Locke** put forward the Goal-setting theory of motivation. This theory states that goal setting is essentially linked to task performance.

82. (A): The Dewey Decimal Classification (DDC), colloquially known as the Dewey Decimal System, is a proprietary library classification system which allows new books to be added to a library in their appropriate location based on subject. It was first published in the United States by Melvil Dewey in 1876.

The Universal Decimal Classification (UDC) scheme of classification was developed in the year 1895 by the Belgium Barrister Paul Otlet and Nobel Prize winner Henri La Fountaine. The first edition appeared in French in 1905 as Manual du Repertoire Bibliographique Universel, which has 33,000 sub-divisions.

Colon Classification, system of library organization developed by the Indian librarian S.R. Ranganathan in 1933.

The first outline of the Library of Congress Classification was published in 1904 by Charles Martel and J.C.M. Hanson - the two fathers of Library of Congress Classification.

83. (B): Physical Layer: The lowest layer of the OSI reference model is the physical layer. It is responsible for the actual physical connection between the devices. The physical layer contains information in the form of bits. It is responsible for transmitting individual bits from one node to the next. When receiving data, this layer will get the signal received and convert it into 0s and 1s and send them to the Data Link layer, which will put the frame back together.

Network Layer: The network layer works for the transmission of data from one host to the other located in different networks. It also takes care of packet routing i.e. selection of the shortest path to transmit the packet, from the number of routes available. The sender & receiver's IP addresses are placed in the header by the network layer.

Transport Layer: The transport layer provides services to the application layer and takes services from the network layer. The data in the transport layer is referred to as Segments. It is responsible for the End to End Delivery of the complete message. The transport layer also provides the acknowledgement of the successful data transmission and re-transmits the data if an error is found.

Application Layer: At the very top of the OSI Reference Model stack of layers, we find the Application layer which is implemented by the network applications. These applications produce the data, which has to be transferred over the network. This layer also serves as a window for the application services to access the network and for displaying the received information to the user.

84. (B): Sir Dorabji Tata Memorial Library at TISS has been consistently making efforts to develop a strong collection of learning resources and to provide a human moderated access to knowledge. In its quest for excelence, library has achieved many milestones. Indian Library Association, New Delhi, conferred it with *"ILA - Dr. L. M. Padhya Best University Library Award"* for the year 2008, for the best practices being followed in the university library administration and for its excellent services. At individual levels also, library team members have been conferred with awards, fellowships, etc. Ever since the commencement of academic restructuring in 2004, library has enhanced its collection extensively. More than 25,000 new books have been added to the collection as library did an extensive collection development exercise considering the new programmes being introduced by the institute.

Khuda Bakhsh Oriental Library, in Patna, Bihar, is one of the national libraries of India. It was opened to the public on the 29th of October in 1891 by HMJ Sir Khan Bahadur Khuda Bakhsh. Its collection started with 4,000 of Bakhsh's own manuscripts, of which he inherited 1,400 from his father, Sir Mohammed Bakhsh, a lawyer from Patna. It is considered to have the best collection of Arabic, Persian, Urdu and Hindi Manuscripts and Literature. It is the 2nd Largest library in the world in term of Islamic literature collection. It is considered to be the most prominent Oriental Public library in the world.

BARC Library is a Research & Development Library. Because the Department of Atomic Energy (DAE) is one of the major scientific insitutions in India, the Bhabha Atomic Research Center (BARC; the principal R&D unit of the DAE) has a sophisticated Library and Information Services (L & IS) division. The heart of this division is the BARC library, which houses a large collection of nuclear literature, including 50,000 books, 1,600 periodical titles, and over 300,000 technical reports. It provides information services to the various nuclear establishments in India. There are excellent reprographic and printing facilities that are utilized to publish about 200 technical reports a year from the work being done at the center. The L&IS activity of BARC is the national link to INIS and it is thus able to access INIS's resources. The L&IS of BARC has been experimenting with computerization of many of its functions. An Automation for Storage and Retrieval of Information (AFSARI) system is being developed for SDI services, utilizing and H-400 computer programmed in COBOL.

TCS library is a corporate library. Services, Capgemini, Wipro, Tata Consultancy Services library, Mumbai, won the 2009 Special Library Association's Center of Excellence Award, the first time for an Asian library.

85. (B)

86. (C): Language is in part natural and in part conventional and between the two forms the difference is quantitative, not substantial. The more a language is natural, adapting itself greatly to sensitivity, the stronger it will be; more persistent in memory and more comprehensible, even though proportionally less definite. The natural language largely focuses on the stronger sentiments, which are those linked with the survival of the individual, and is particularly tied to fear. The conventional language is the one that the human beings build with their sentiments and has a "natural" origin: the human beings place linguistic ties between some things and ideas on which nature has placed none. The consequence is that the more pagan a mind is, using no part of its intellect, the more it would use the metaphorical property of language.

87. (C): Characteristics of Cloud Computing:

- **On-demand Self Service:** A consumer can request and receive access to a service offering, without an administrator or some sort of support staff having to fulfil the request manually.
- **Broad network Access:** The servers can be accessed from any location using any type of device - anywhere access and any-time.
- **Resource Pooling:** Resource can be storage, memory, network bandwidth, virtual machines, etc. which can be consumed by the cloud users. Resource Pooling means that multiple customers are serviced from the same physical resources.
- **Measured Services:** Pay according to the services you use.
- **Rapid Elasticity and Stability:** One of the great things about cloud computing is the ability to quickly provision resources in the cloud as organizations need them and then to remove them when they don't need them.
- **Easy maintenance:** Maintenance of the cloud is easier.
- **Security:** Copy of our data on various servers i.e., if 1 fails, data is safe on the other.

88. (A)

89. (C): Performance measurement systems can create an essential feedback and learning mechanism in support of key management decisions, especially when criteria measures institutionally focused performance. A successful system also functions as a communication and information system, particularly for senior staff and administration. Basically, performance assessment should allow; up-to-date job descriptions that will ensure staff members know what is expected of them; continuing communication between supervisors and staff; recognition of staff for doing well; and staff development processes (Lubans, 1999). Effective people management assists line managers in handling change management.

90. (A) **91. (A)** **92. (C)**

93. (D) **94. (A)** **95. (B)**

96. (B) **97. (C)** **98. (D)**

99. (D) **100. (A)**

Previous Years' Paper (Solved)

National Testing Agency (NTA)

UGC-NET Junior Research Fellowship & Assistant Professor Eligibility Exam

LIBRARY & INFORMATION SCIENCE, June–2021

(Online exam held on 24-11-2021)

PAPER-II

Note: *This paper contains **hundred (100)** objective type questions of **two (2)** marks each. **All** questions are **compulsory**.*

1. According to Copyright (Amendment) Act, 2012, in case of Photographs, the term of copyright is revised to:

A. 10 years B. 20 years
C. Omitted D. 60 years

2. According to the UGC (Promotion of Academic Integrity and Prevention of Plagiarism in Higher Educational Institutions) Regulation, 2018, if any person suspects plagiarism in any document, who should s/he report it to?

A. IAIP (Institutional Academic Integrity Panel)
B. DAIP (Departmental Academic Integrity Panel)
C. HHEI (Head of the Higher Education Institution)
D. UGC (University Grants Commission)

3. Under the RTI Act, 2005, which person cannot submit a complaint to the Central Information Commission or State Information Commission, as the case may be?

A. Who has been refused access to any information related under this act.
B. Who has been required to pay an amount of fee which s/he considers unreasonable.
C. Who approaches directly to CIS or SIC without approaching CPIO or SPIO as the case may be.
D. Who believes that s/he has been given incomplete, misleading or false information under this Act.

4. "Edanz", a journal suggester service is associated with which leading publisher?

A. Elsevier B. Sage
C. Springer D. Wiley

5. In UNESCO's conceptual model of Media Information Literacy (MIL), 2013, which one of the following circle represents:
"The information resources and the means by which information is communicated..."

A. Centre circle
B. The Second Circle from the Centre
C. The Third Circle from the Centre
D. The Final Circle

6. Which one of the following digital collections is not provided by the Library of Congress?

A. Chronicling America
B. Treasures in Full
C. Stereograph Cards
D. Civil War Glass Negatives and Related Prints

7. Which one of the following acts as a Nodal Agency for 'National Mission on Libraries' (NML) for administrative, logistics, planning and budgeting purposes?

A. National Library of India
B. Delhi Public Library
C. RRRLF
D. NISCAIR

8. According to UNESCO, what is the slogan for the World Book and Copyright Day 2020 observed globally?
A. Improve the Reading Habit
B. Books : A Window into the World during COVID-19
C. Books are for Use
D. Globalisation of Reading Material during COVID-19

9. Who devised the "Role Based Model of Digital Reference"?
A. R. D. Lankers
B. J. M. Wasik
C. M McClennen
D. G. G. Chowdhury and S. Chowdhury

10. Indian Standard 'IS 1553:1989' is related to:
A. Design of library furniture
B. Design of library building
C. Design of library van
D. Design of administrative buildings

11. Who was the Chief Editor of 'Webster's Third New International Dictionary of the English Language: Unabridged'?
A. M. R. Gould
B. Philip Babcock Gove
C. Edmund Herry
D. Michael Gorman

12. Who was the founder of Project Gutenberg?
A. Michael Hart B. M. Gutenberg
C. Joan M. Reitz D. Edmund Herry

13. Who among the following called "Reference Service" as a "personal intercourse between librarians and readers"?
A. S. R. Ranganathan
B. William A. Katz
C. Samuel Swett Green
D. Melvil Dewey

14. Who said, "a number of basic human needs can be identified from the social and psychological functions of the mass media"?
A. William Katz and Bill Katz
B. M. Sandelowski and H. Haas
C. E. Katz, M. Gurevitch and H. Haas
D. Sull H. Lee and Celia Hales Mabry

15. Mobile App, "BARD" is meant for people with:
A. Visual Impairment
B. Hearing Impairment
C. Speech and Language Disability
D. Mental Illness

16. "Reference and User Services Association" is a division of:
A. Association for Information Science and Technology
B. American Library Association
C. Medical Library Association
D. Society of American Archivists

17. According to S.R. Ranganathan, "Spot Subject" is a:
A. Subject formed by coupling two or more subjects
B. Subject of great extension and enormous intention
C. Subject of small extension and great intention
D. Subject of great extension and small intention

18. "The structure of a classification system on the basis of materials to be classified rather than on purely theoretical considerations" is known as:
A. Literature Search B. Taxonomy
C. Literal mnemonics D. Literary warrant

19. Which of the following is not a high-level class or entity in the BIBFRAME model?
A. BIBFRAME Work
B. BIBFRAME Instance
C. BIBFRAME Item
D. BIBFRAME Title

20. Who gave the concept of 'Mental Revolution'?
A. Henry Fayol B. Peter F. Drucker
C. F. W. Taylor D. Philip Crosby

21. Who authored the book *Practice of Management?*
A. Peter Drucker B. Henry Mintzberg
C. Henry Fayol D. Frederick Taylor

22. Which among the following is NOT a 'Process Theory' of motivation?
A. Expectancy theory B. Goal-setting theory
C. Content theory D. Equity theory

23. LibQUAL+ is a web-based survey offered by:
A. College and Research Libraries Association
B. Association of Research Libraries
C. Library Administration and Management Association
D. Special Libraries Association

24. A device that interconnects two or more networks and selectively interchanges packets of data between them is known as
A. Switch B. Gateway
C. Hub D. Router

25. .... is a suite of protocols that were developed by the Department of Defence to provide a highly reliable and fault-tolerant network infrastructure.
A. DHCP B. VPN
C. PPPoE D. TCP/IP

26. Lycos is a search engine which was originally started as a research project at:
A. Stanford University
B. Carnegie Mellon University
C. Harvard University
D. Virginia Tech

27. Theodor Holm Nelson founded Project Xanadu in the year
A. 1958 B. 1960
C. 1972 D. 1979

28. The first version of Unicode was
A. 8 bit encoding B. 16 bit encoding
C. 32 bit encoding D. 64 bit encoding

29. A type of attack in which a person or program disguises itself as another person or program to gain access to some resource is called
A. Masquerading B. Sniffing
C. Phishing D. Spooling

30. The first virus recorded, the *Creeper virus* was written by
A. Bob Thomas B. Whitman Diffie
C. Martin Hellman D. Fred Cohen

31. The first US patent for an active RFID tag with rewritable memory was awarded to:
A. Kevin Ashton B. Mario Cardullo
C. Sanjay Sharma D. David Brock

32. In the context of the spiral of Scientific Method, the verification phase is represented between which two cardinal point?
A. Nadir and Ascendent
B. Ascendent and Zenith
C. Descendent and Zenith
D. Descendent and Nadir

33. A researcher "X" published 5 manuscripts. Arranging the manuscripts in the descending order of their citations, the sequence of the citations appears as 21; 15; 13; 3; 2. What will be the h-Index of the researcher?
A. 13 B. 3
C. 21 D. 2

34. A publisher offers free access to articles for a week's or a month's time. Under which Open Access (OA) License will the accessibility option fall?
A. Green OA B. Bronze OA
C. Golden OA D. Platinum OA

35. 'Uptodate' (Kluwer) is:
A. A digital repository for health science researches in Europe
B. A directory of open access journals in health sciences
C. A resource for clinical decision support for health science professionals
D. An alert service from journals covered in a journal database

36. The International Council on Archives was founded in the year
A. 1943 B. 1948
C. 1952 D. 1956

37. The term 'Internet of Things' was first used by:
A. D. W. Lewis B. Bob Thomas
C. Kevin Ashton D. Jian Qin

38. National Centre for Children's Literature (NCCL) is related to
A. NCERT B. NBT
C. RRRLF D. CBSE

39. Which princely state passed Public Library Act prior to independence?
A. Rajputana B. Kolhapur
C. Kashmir D. Hyderabad

40. "The special library must, for instance, make much more use of what has come to be known as documentation than the general library" stated by whom:
A. Aksel G.S. Josephson

B. Paul Otlet
C. Richard H. Johnson
D. John Cotton Dana

41. Identify the recommendations made by National Knowledge Commission, 2005 to ensure sustained attention to the development of libraries.
(*a*) Implementation of Public Libraries Act in all states and UTs
(*b*) Reassess staffing of libraries
(*c*) Set up a central library fund
(*d*) Prepare a roadmap for holistic development of citizens

Choose the correct answer from the options given below:
A. (*b*) and (*c*) only B. (*a*) and (*d*) only
C. (*b*) and (*d*) only D. (*a*) and (*c*) only

42. As per UGC (Promotion of Academic Integrity and Prevention of Plagiarism in Higher Education Institutions) Regulations 2018, which penalties in case of plagiarism in academic and research publications shall be imposed?
(*a*) Similarity above 10% to 40%: Shall be asked to withdraw the manuscript
(*b*) Similarity above 30% to 40%: Shall be asked to withdraw the manuscript
(*c*) Similarity above 40% to 60%: Shall be denied a right to one annual increment
(*d*) Similarity above 40% to 60%: Shall be denied a right to two annual increments

Choose the correct answer from the options given below:
A. (*a*) and (*d*) only B. (*a*) and (*c*) only
C. (*b*) and (*c*) only D. (*c*) and (*d*) only

43. Which of the following Public Libraries Acts have the provision of library cess?
(*a*) Kerala (*b*) Manipur
(*c*) Haryana (*d*) Orissa

Choose the correct answer from the options given below:
A. (*a*) and (*c*) only B. (*b*) and (*c*) only
C. (*a*) and (*d*) only D. (*a*) and (*b*) only

44. Identify Mac Operating System of Apple:
(*a*) Sierra (*b*) Mojave
(*c*) Catalina (*d*) Debian
(*e*) Big Sur

Choose the correct answer from the options given below:
A. (*a*), (*b*), (*c*) and (*d*) only
B. (*a*), (*c*), (*d*) and (*e*) only
C. (*b*), (*c*), (*d*) and (*e*) only
D. (*a*), (*b*), (*c*) and (*e*) only

45. Which among the following are the examples of "Descriptive Metadata"?
(*a*) Finding aids
(*b*) Specialized Indexes
(*c*) Selection criteria for digitization
(*d*) Curatorial Information

Choose the correct answer from the options given below:
A. (*a*), (*b*) and (*c*) only
B. (*b*), (*c*) and (*d*) only
C. (*a*), (*c*) and (*d*) only
D. (*a*), (*b*) and (*d*) only

46. Semantic web is based on which of the following types of technologies?
(*a*) Resources Description Framework (RDF)
(*b*) Uniform Resource Identifier (URT)
(*c*) Ontologies
(*d*) Indentions

Choose the correct answer from the options given below:
A. (*a*), (*b*) and (*d*) only
B. (*a*), (*c*) and (*d*) only
C. (*a*), (*b*) and (*c*) only
D. (*b*), (*c*) and (*d*) only

47. Which of the following are the Product and Services of OCLC?
(*a*) E. Z. Proxy
(*b*) Librarians yellow pages
(*c*) Green Glass
(*d*) Cataloguing Distribution Service

Choose the correct answer from the options given below:
A. (*a*) and (*c*) only B. (*a*) and (*b*) only
C. (*b*) and (*c*) only D. (*c*) and (*d*) only

48. Which among the following options are true about the concept "Folksonomy"?
(*a*) It was coined by Thomas Vanderwal
(*b*) It was coined in 2009
(*c*) It was coined in 2004

(*d*) It was coined by Brian Acton
(*e*) It was coined by Jan Koum

Choose the correct answer from the options given below:

A. (*a*) and (*b*) only B. (*a*) and (*c*) only
C. (*b*) and (*d*) only D. (*d*) and (*e*) only

49. An important Academic Social Networking site, 'ResearchGate' was founded by

(*a*) Ijad Madisch (*b*) Soren Hofmayer
(*c*) Horst Fickenscher (*d*) Brian Acton
(*e*) Jan Koum

Choose the correct answer from the options given below:

A. (*a*), (*b*) and (*c*) only
B. (*a*), (*c*) and (*d*) only
C. (*b*), (*c*) and (*d*) only
D. (*c*), (*d*) and (*e*) only

50. In the context of dialogue between a user and computer through an interface, Tefko Saracevic's Stratified Model (1997) when viewed from the human side represents which strata:

(*a*) Content levels (*b*) Processing
(*c*) Cognitive (*d*) Affective
(*e*) Situational

Choose the correct answer from the options given below:

A. (*a*), (*b*) and (*c*) only
B. (*b*), (*c*) and (*d*) only
C. (*b*), (*d*) and (*e*) only
D. (*c*), (*d*) and (*e*) only

51. Which of the following are true about the Z39.50?

(*a*) It is an international (ISO 23950) standard
(*b*) The contextual Query Language is not based on Z39.50 semantics
(*c*) It was originally approved by the National Information Standards Organisation (NISO) in 1988
(*d*) It is maintained by IFLA

Choose the correct answer from the options given below:

A. (*a*) and (*b*) only B. (*a*) and (*c*) only
C. (*b*) and (*c*) only D. (*c*) and (*d*) only

52. Which of the following are not Posteriorising Common Isolates according to Colon Classification (sixth revised edition)?

(*a*) Institution (*b*) Learned Society
(*c*) Bibliography (*d*) Table

Choose the correct answer from the options given below:

A. (*a*) and (*b*) only B. (*a*) and (*c*) only
C. (*b*) and (*c*) only D. (*c*) and (*d*) only

53. Which of the following are the Data visualization software?

(*a*) Vosviewer (*b*) Zotero
(*c*) Minitab (*d*) NVivo

Choose the correct answer from the options given below:

A. (*b*), (*c*) and (*d*) only
B. (*a*), (*c*) and (*d*) only
C. (*a*), (*b*) and (*d*) only
D. (*a*), (*b*) and (*c*) only

54. Which of the following are 'TQM' tools?

(*a*) Histogram (*b*) Pie Chart
(*c*) Bar graph (*d*) Pareto Chart

Choose the correct answer from the options given below:

A. (*a*) and (*b*) only B. (*b*) and (*c*) only
C. (*a*) and (*d*) only D. (*c*) and (*d*) only

55. Identify web programming languages among the following

(*a*) Ruby (*b*) PL/1
(*c*) SQL (*d*) Python

Choose the correct answer from the options given below:

A. (*a*), (*b*) and (*c*) only
B. (*b*), (*c*) and (*d*) only
C. (*a*), (*c*) and (*d*) only
D. (*a*), (*b*) and (*d*) only

56. Which of these are based on Linux?

(*a*) Fedora (*b*) Solaris
(*c*) Ubuntu (*d*) Debian

Choose the correct answer from the options given below:

A. (*a*), (*b*) and (*c*) only
B. (*b*), (*c*) and (*d*) only
C. (*a*), (*c*) and (*d*) only
D. (*a*), (*b*) and (*d*) only

57. Identify open source library automation software:
(*a*) OPALS (*b*) LIBRARIAN
(*c*) KOHA (*d*) Evergreen ILS

Choose the correct answer from the options given below:
A. (*a*), (*b*) and (*c*) only
B. (*b*), (*c*) and (*d*) only
C. (*a*), (*c*) and (*d*) only
D. (*a*), (*b*) and (*d*) only

58. Select expert systems from among the following:
(*a*) DEEPIN (*b*) PROSPECTOR
(*c*) REACTOR (*d*) MYCIN

Choose the correct answer from the options given below:
A. (*a*), (*b*) and (*c*) only
B. (*b*), (*c*) and (*d*) only
C. (*a*), (*c*) and (*d*) only
D. (*a*), (*b*) and (*d*) only

59. An invitational metadata workshop organised at Dublin in 1995 and treated as the birthplace of contemporary metadata, was sponsored by
(*a*) National Centre for Super Computing Application (NCSA)
(*b*) Institute of Electrical and Electronics Engineering (IEEE)
(*c*) Online Computer Library Centre (OCLC)
(*d*) International Electrotechnical Commission (IEC)

Choose the correct answer from the options given below:
A. (*a*) and (*b*) only B. (*a*) and (*c*) only
C. (*b*) and (*c*) only D. (*b*) and (*d*) only

60. Which of the following are examples of Non-probability Sampling?
(*a*) Convenience Sampling
(*b*) Simple Random Sampling
(*c*) Quota Sampling
(*d*) Stratified Random Sampling

Choose the correct answer from the options given below:
A. (*a*) and (*b*) only B. (*a*) and (*c*) only
C. (*b*) and (*c*) only D. (*c*) and (*d*) only

61. Who among the following were members of the Advisory Committee for Libraries (1957)?
(*a*) B.S. Kesavan (*b*) S.R. Ranganathan
(*c*) P.N. Kaula (*d*) A.P. Srivastava
(*e*) D.R. Kalia

Choose the correct answer from the options given below:
A. (*a*) and (*b*) only B. (*a*) and (*c*) only
C. (*b*) and (*d*) only D. (*a*) and (*e*) only

62. Which among the following are examples of primary channels of communicating research?
(*a*) Journals (*b*) Encyclopedias
(*c*) Theses (*d*) Thesauri
(*e*) Biographies

Choose the correct answer from the options given below:
A. (*a*) and (*d*) only B. (*a*) and (*c*) only
C. (*b*) and (*d*) only D. (*c*) and (*e*) only

63. Which of the following are true about the Special Libraries Association (SLA)?
(*a*) SLA was formed in the year 1909
(*b*) John Cotton Dana was the founder President
(*c*) It has its headquarters in Chicago
(*d*) Publishes Science and Technology Libraries, a journal

Choose the correct answer from the options given below:
A. (*a*) and (*d*) only B. (*b*) and (*c*) only
C. (*a*) and (*b*) only D. (*c*) and (*d*) only

64. Which of the following are related to AGLINET?
(*a*) AGLINET is a voluntary network of agriculture libraries around the world
(*b*) AGLINET is consortia of agriculture university libraries of India
(*c*) AGLINET centres provide partner libraries with access to the literature originating in the country or the region
(*d*) AGLINET is a national network of agriculture libraries in India

Choose the correct answer from the options given below:
A. (*a*) and (*c*) only B. (*a*) and (*d*) only
C. (*b*) and (*d*) only D. (*c*) and (*d*) only

65. Which among the following represent, "Asynchronous" reference transactions?

(*a*) E-Mail
(*b*) Web Forms
(*c*) Video Conferencing
(*d*) Ask A Service
(*e*) Digital Reference Robots

Choose the correct answer from the options given below:

A. (*a*), (*b*) and (*d*) only
B. (*a*), (*b*) and (*c*) only
C. (*b*), (*c*) and (*d*) only
D. (*c*), (*d*) and (*e*) only

66. Match List I with List II

	List-I		***List-II***
(*a*)	Khuda Baksh Oriental Library	(*i*)	Tamil Nadu
(*b*)	Rampur Raza Library	(*ii*)	Bihar
(*c*)	Sarasvati Mahal Library	(*iii*)	Uttar Pradesh
(*d*)	Nehru Memorial Museum & Library	(*iv*)	Delhi

Choose the correct answer from the options given below:

	(*a*)	(*b*)	(*c*)	(*d*)
A.	(*iv*)	(*ii*)	(*iii*)	(*i*)
B.	(*ii*)	(*iii*)	(*i*)	(*iv*)
C.	(*i*)	(*ii*)	(*iii*)	(*iv*)
D.	(*iii*)	(*i*)	(*ii*)	(*iv*)

67. Match List I with List II

	List-I (Conference)		***List-II (Theme)***
(*a*)	69th IFLA General Conference and Council	(*i*)	Access Point Library, Media–information culture
(*b*)	73rd IFLA General Conference and Council	(*ii*)	Connections, Collaboration, Community
(*c*)	78th IFLA General Conference and Council	(*iii*)	Libraries now–Inspiring, Surprising, Empowering
(*d*)	82nd IFLA General Conference and Council	(*iv*)	Libraries for the future Progress Development and Partnership

Choose the correct answer from the options given below:

	(*a*)	(*b*)	(*c*)	(*d*)
A.	(*i*)	(*iii*)	(*iv*)	(*ii*)
B.	(*iv*)	(*ii*)	(*i*)	(*iii*)
C.	(*i*)	(*iv*)	(*iii*)	(*ii*)
D.	(*iv*)	(*i*)	(*iii*)	(*ii*)

68. Match List I with List II

	List-I (Author)		***List-II (Source)***
(*a*)	A.K. Das Gupta	(*i*)	*The Rise of Current Composite Bibliography*
(*b*)	AM Lewin Robinson	(*ii*)	*An Essay in Personal Bibliography*
(*c*)	T. Besterman	(*iii*)	*Systematic Bibliography*
(*d*)	Le Roy Harold Linder	(*iv*)	*The Beginnings of Systematic Bibliography*

Choose the correct answer from the options given below:

	(*a*)	(*b*)	(*c*)	(*d*)
A.	(*iii*)	(*iv*)	(*i*)	(*ii*)
B.	(*i*)	(*iii*)	(*iv*)	(*ii*)
C.	(*ii*)	(*i*)	(*iii*)	(*iv*)
D.	(*ii*)	(*iii*)	(*iv*)	(*i*)

69. Match List I with List II

	List-I		***List-II***
(*a*)	Strategic sharing	(*i*)	Maximising efficiency
(*b*)	Paradigmatic sharing	(*ii*)	Sharing between teachers and students
(*c*)	Directive sharing	(*iii*)	Establishing a novel distinguishable research approach
(*d*)	Social sharing	(*iv*)	Relationship and community-based activities

Choose the correct answer from the options given below:

	(*a*)	(*b*)	(*c*)	(*d*)
A.	(*ii*)	(*i*)	(*iii*)	(*iv*)
B.	(*i*)	(*iii*)	(*ii*)	(*iv*)
C.	(*iv*)	(*i*)	(*iii*)	(*ii*)
D.	(*iii*)	(*ii*)	(*iv*)	(*i*)

70. Match List I with List II:

List-I *(Metadata)*	*List-II* *(Examples)*
(*a*) Administrative Metadata	(*i*) Documentation of the physical condition of responses
(*b*) Preservation Metadata	(*ii*) Search Log
(*c*) Technical Metadata	(*iii*) Tracking of system response time
(*d*) Use Metadata	(*iv*) Selection criteria for digitization

Choose the correct answer from the options given below:

	(*a*)	(*b*)	(*c*)	(*d*)
A.	(*i*)	(*ii*)	(*iii*)	(*iv*)
B.	(*iv*)	(*i*)	(*iii*)	(*ii*)
C.	(*ii*)	(*iv*)	(*i*)	(*iii*)
D.	(*iii*)	(*iv*)	(*ii*)	(*i*)

71. Match List I with List II

List-I	*List-II*
(*a*) Member checking	(*i*) Attitude Ratings
(*b*) Likert scale	(*ii*) Virtual conversation
(*c*) Thurstone Equal Appearing Interval Scale	(*iii*) Bipolar scale
(*d*) Synchronous	(*iv*) Reverification of collected data and interpretations

Choose the correct answer from the options given below:

	(*a*)	(*b*)	(*c*)	(*d*)
A.	(*iv*)	(*iii*)	(*i*)	(*ii*)
B.	(*iii*)	(*iv*)	(*ii*)	(*i*)
C.	(*i*)	(*ii*)	(*iv*)	(*iii*)
D.	(*iii*)	(*ii*)	(*iv*)	(*i*)

72. Match List I with List II

List-I *(MARC Tag)*	*List-II* *(Field)*
(*a*) 020 tag	(*i*) Marks: a personal name main entry (author)
(*b*) 100 tag	(*ii*) Marks the physical description
(*c*) 300 tag	(*iii*) Marks a personal name added entry
(*d*) 700 tag	(*iv*) Marks the International Standard Book Number (ISBN)

Choose the correct answer from the options given below:

	(*a*)	(*b*)	(*c*)	(*d*)
A.	(*iv*)	(*i*)	(*ii*)	(*iii*)
B.	(*iv*)	(*ii*)	(*i*)	(*iii*)
C.	(*ii*)	(*iii*)	(*i*)	(*iv*)
D.	(*i*)	(*ii*)	(*iv*)	(*iii*)

73. Match List I with List II

List-I	*List-II*
(*a*) Quantitative Approach	(*i*) Gantt Chart
(*b*) Scientific Management	(*ii*) Bureaucratic Structure
(*c*) Behavioural Approach	(*iii*) PERT / CPM
(*d*) Organisational Approach	(*iv*) Theory X and Theory Y

Choose the correct answer from the options given below:

	(*a*)	(*b*)	(*c*)	(*d*)
A.	(*iii*)	(*ii*)	(*iv*)	(*i*)
B.	(*iii*)	(*iv*)	(*ii*)	(*i*)
C.	(*iv*)	(*ii*)	(*i*)	(*iii*)
D.	(*iii*)	(*i*)	(*iv*)	(*ii*)

74. Match List I with List II (Match the digital library initiative with the institution involved during their inception/creation):

List-I	*List-II*
(*a*) Alexandria Digital Library	(*i*) Cornell University
(*b*) arXiv	(*ii*) University of California
(*c*) Universal Digital Library	(*iii*) University of Illinois
(*d*) Project Gutenberg	(*iv*) Carnegie Mellon University

Choose the correct answer from the options given below:

	(*a*)	(*b*)	(*c*)	(*d*)
A.	(*i*)	(*ii*)	(*iii*)	(*iv*)
B.	(*iii*)	(*ii*)	(*i*)	(*iv*)
C.	(*ii*)	(*i*)	(*iv*)	(*iii*)
D.	(*iv*)	(*iii*)	(*i*)	(*ii*)

75. Match List I with List II

List-I	*List-II*
(*a*) Screen Magnification Software	(*i*) Microsoft Narrator
(*b*) Screen Reading Software	(*ii*) Vaachak

(*c*) Speech Synthesizer Software — (*iii*) Megadots

(*d*) Braille Translation Software — (*iv*) ChromeVis

Choose the correct answer from the options given below:

	(*a*)	(*b*)	(*c*)	(*d*)
A.	(*ii*)	(*iii*)	(*iv*)	(*i*)
B.	(*iii*)	(*iv*)	(*i*)	(*ii*)
C.	(*iv*)	(*i*)	(*ii*)	(*iii*)
D.	(*iv*)	(*ii*)	(*iii*)	(*i*)

76. Arrange the following software according to their year of origin in chronological order :

(*a*) DSpace (*b*) EPrints

(*c*) GSDL (*d*) Omeka

Choose the correct answer from the options given below:

A. (*c*), (*b*), (*a*), (*d*) B. (*d*), (*a*), (*b*), (*c*)

C. (*b*), (*c*), (*d*), (*a*) D. (*a*), (*b*), (*c*), (*d*)

77. As per APA Reference Style (6th ed.), for a journal article, which sequence of bibliographical elements is correct in the context of reference structure?

(*a*) Author of the article

(*b*) Title of the journal

(*c*) Title of the Article

(*d*) Year

(*e*) Pages

Choose the correct answer from the options given below:

A. (*a*), (*d*), (*c*), (*b*), (*e*)

B. (*a*), (*b*), (*c*), (*d*), (*e*)

C. (*a*), (*d*), (*b*), (*c*), (*e*)

D. (*a*), (*c*), (*b*), (*d*), (*e*)

78. Arrange the following e-learning initiatives related to higher education in India in chronological order:

(*a*) SWAYAM MOOCs

(*b*) eGyankosh

(*c*) ePG Pathshala

(*d*) NPTEL

Choose the correct answer from the options given below

A. (*a*), (*b*), (*c*), (*d*) B. (*b*), (*c*), (*d*), (*a*)

C. (*b*), (*d*), (*c*), (*a*) D. (*c*), (*d*), (*a*), (*b*)

79. Arrange the steps of the "Digital Reference Model" derived from Lankes (1998) and Virtual Reference Desk Project (1998) in the correct sequence:

(*a*) Triage

(*b*) Experts Answer Formulation

(*c*) Tracking

(*d*) Question Acquisition

(*e*) Resource creation

Choose the correct answer from the options given below:

A. (*a*), (*c*), (*b*), (*d*), (*e*)

B. (*c*), (*d*), (*b*), (*a*), (*e*)

C. (*e*), (*b*), (*c*), (*a*), (*d*)

D. (*d*), (*a*), (*b*), (*c*), (*e*)

80. Arrange the following Public Libraries Acts according to their year of enactment in ascending order:

(*a*) Gujarat (*b*) Chattisgarh

(*c*) Rajasthan (*d*) Goa

Choose the correct answer from the options given below

A. (*b*), (*a*), (*c*), (*d*) B. (*d*), (*a*), (*c*), (*b*)

C. (*d*), (*c*), (*a*), (*b*) D. (*a*), (*d*), (*c*), (*b*)

81. Arrange in sequence the following books authored by S. R. Ranganathan in order of their first publication.

(*a*) *Documentation Genesis and Development*

(*b*) *Library Manual*

(*c*) *Classified Catalogue Code*

(*d*) *Prolegomena to Library Classification*

Choose the correct answer from the options given below:

A. (*c*), (*d*), (*b*), (*a*) B. (*d*), (*c*), (*b*), (*a*)

C. (*d*), (*b*), (*c*), (*a*) D. (*c*), (*b*), (*d*), (*a*)

82. Arrange the following layers in their correct sequence in the OSI Model.

(*a*) Network Layer (*b*) Physical Layer

(*c*) Presentation Layer (*d*) Data Link Layer

(*e*) Application Layer

Choose the correct answer from the options given below:

A. (*d*), (*a*), (*c*), (*b*), (*e*)

B. (*a*), (*c*), (*e*), (*b*), (*d*)

C. (*b*), (*d*), (*a*), (*c*), (*e*)

D. (*c*), (*a*), (*b*), (*e*), (*d*)

83. Arrange the following reference and information sources according to their first year of publication:

(*a*) Europa Year - Book
(*b*) Whitaker's Almanac
(*c*) Guinness Book of World Records
(*d*) Statemen's Year - Book

Choose the correct answer from the options given below:

A. (*b*), (*d*), (*c*), (*a*) B. (*b*), (*a*), (*d*), (*c*)
C. (*d*), (*a*), (*b*), (*c*) D. (*d*), (*b*), (*a*), (*c*)

84. Arrange the following with their year of establishment in ascending order :

(*a*) American National Standards Institute
(*b*) International Telegraph Union
(*c*) Internet Engineering Task Force
(*d*) World Wide Web Consortium

Choose the correct answer from the options given below:

A. (*c*), (*d*), (*a*), (*b*) B. (*d*), (*a*), (*b*), (*c*)
C. (*a*), (*b*), (*c*), (*d*) D. (*b*), (*a*), (*c*), (*d*)

85. Arrange the following by their year of creation in ascending order :

(*a*) Moris Worm (*b*) Creeper Virus
(*c*) Storm Botnet (*d*) Animal (Trojan)

Choose the correct answer from the options given below:

A. (*a*), (*c*), (*d*), (*b*) B. (*c*), (*b*), (*a*), (*d*)
C. (*b*), (*d*), (*a*), (*c*) D. (*d*), (*a*), (*c*), (*b*)

86. Given below are two statements, one is labelled as Assertion (A) and the other is labelled as Reason R.

Assertion (A): e-Granthalaya can be customised by the library.

Reason (R): Libraries opting for e-Granthalaya have to pay NIC for hosting, maintenance etc.

In light of the above statements, choose the correct answer from the options given below:

A. Both (A) and (R) are true and (R) is the correct explanation of (A)
B. Both (A) and (R) are true, but (R) is not the correct explanation of A
C. (A) is true, but (R) is false
D. (A) is false, but (R) is true

87. Given below are two statements, one is labelled as Assertion (A) and the other is labelled as Reason (R).

Assertion (A): No need to have registration for the copyright works in India.

Reason (R): As per the Berne Convention, copyright protection is obtained automatically.

In light of the above statements, choose the correct answer from the options given below:

A. Both (A) and (R) are true and (R) is the correct explanation of (A)
B. Both (A) and R are true, but (R) is not the correct explanation of (A)
C. (A) is true, but (R) is false
D. (A) is false, but (R) is true

88. Given below are two statements:

Statement I: Yahoo can explore more count of web sites while searching a query than Metacrawler.

Statement II: Metacrawler is a Metasearch engine.

In light of the above statements, choose the most appropriate answer from the options given below

A. Both Statement I and Statement II are correct
B. Both Statement I and Statement II are incorrect
C. Statement I is correct, but Statement II is incorrect
D. Statement I is incorrect, but Statement II is correct

89. Given below are two statements, one is labelled as Assertion (A) and the other is labelled as Reason (R).

Assertion (A): Federated search was developed to provide simplified access to electronic content that libraries acquire.

Reason (R): INFEED supports access to e-resources in university libraries.

In light of the above statements, choose the most appropriate answer from the options given below:

A. Both (A) and (R) are correct and (R) is the correct explanation of (A)
B. Both (A) and (R) are correct but (R) is not the correct explanation of (A)

C. (A) is correct, but (R) is not correct
D. (A) is not correct, but (R) is correct

90. Given below are two statements, one is labelled as Assertion (A) and the other is labelled as Reason (R).

Assertion (A): A Web Portal is a specially designed website that brings information from diverse sources.

Reason (R): The majority of public libraries in India are using web portals.

In light of the above statements, choose the most appropriate answer from the options given below:

A. Both (A) and (R) are correct and (R) is the correct explanation of (A)
B. Both (A) and (R) are correct but (R) is not the correct explanation of (A)
C. (A) is correct, but (R) is not correct
D. (A) is not correct, but (R) is correct

Directions (Qs. No. 91-95): *Read the passage carefully and answer the questions that follows:*

Philosophy of science consists of epistemological problems as well as other kinds of philosophical problems related to science. Epistemology is an important philosophical subdiscipline concerned with the nature, sources and limits of knowledge. A crude classification of basic epistemologies is: Rationalism stresses the role of a priori theorising. Empiricism stresses observation. Historicism stresses the role of background knowledge. Pragmatism stresses the role of analysing values and goals.

Pragmatic view is probably the most relevant to information science. This sees living and acting in the world as constituting the a priori of human knowledge. Value-knowledge, factual knowledge and procedural knowledge are three types of knowledge. Having value-knowledge means knowing what fulfils the criteria of good values. Having factual knowledge means having true beliefs about the three worlds in which one is living. Having procedural knowledge means knowing how to carry out a specific act or act sequence. Knowledge can be unarticulated or articulated. Unarticulated knowledge is, for instance, tacit knowledge, familiarity, knowledge by acquaintance. The pragmatic view of knowledge is of special importance to Library and Information Science because it is connected to the societal role of LIS institutions, whether they are scientific or commercial; or public libraries serving democracy and enlightenment.

91. Which of the following branches of Philosophy studies the nature, origin, and limits of human knowledge?

A. Metaphysics B. Ethics
C. Epistemology D. Logic

92. Which one of the following methods states that knowledge comes primarily from the sensory experience?

A. Rationalism B. Historicism
C. Pragmatism D. Empiricism

93. Which of the following is not a reason for the pragmatic view of knowledge of special importance to library and information science?

A. Connected to the societal role of LIS institutions
B. Public libraries serving democracy and enlightenment
C. Living and acting in the world as constituting the 'a-priori' of human knowledge
D. Is a representation of reality or a 'Mirror of Nature'

94. 'Knowledge exercised in the performance of some task' is a

A. Procedural knowledge
B. Factual knowledge
C. Value knowledge
D. Social knowledge

95. Which one of the following knowledge types is difficult to transfer to another person?

A. Articulated knowledge
B. Social knowledge
C. Declarative knowledge
D. Tacit knowledge

Directions (Qs. No. 96-100): *Read the passage carefully and answer the questions that follows:*

In higher degree research, it is expected that no significant work is left in the Literature Review. Undergraduate research would be expected to discuss all of the most prominent research. A literature review is a critical discussion of all the significant available literature that contributes to the understanding of a subject. A literature review is a written document that presents a logically argued case. There are six steps in the literature review process: topic selection, literature search; developing an argument; literature survey; critique and write a review. The literature review process requires four separate skills such as the ability to search appropriate sources and scan the literature efficiently, to use manual and online methods, to identify and obtain a set of useful articles, chapters and books; the ability to judge a source based on a number of criteria, including the source itself, the author and the subject; the ability to examine and analyse the content of the literature systematically; and the ability to synthesize the various concepts and evidence a researcher has found into a structured piece of discursive prose that provides context and background on the research in the area.

96. At which stage the "review of literature" is usually a representative of the most "prominent research"?
A. Master's Level
B. PhD Level
C. Post Doc Level
D. Undergraduate Level

97. Which among the following is not a characteristic of "Review of Literature"?
A. Statistical Analysis
B. Understanding of the subject
C. In-depth knowledge
D. Arguments based on logic

98. The third step of the literature review process stresses on:
A. Logical arguments B. Writing
C. Topic selection D. Critique

99. Which among the following skills is required to synthesize concepts that can provide context and background of the research problem?
A. Ability to examine and analyse the context
B. Concept and evidence formulation
C. Potential to search appropriate sources
D. Judging a source

100. Evaluation of a source for the process of review does not depend on:
A. Source B. Author
C. Language D. Subject

ANSWERS

1	2	3	4	5	6	7	8	9	10
C	B	C	B	A	B	C	B	C	B
11	**12**	**13**	**14**	**15**	**16**	**17**	**18**	**19**	**20**
B	A	C	C	A	B	C	D	D	C
21	**22**	**23**	**24**	**25**	**26**	**27**	**28**	**29**	**30**
A	C	B	D	D	B	B	B	*	A
31	**32**	**33**	**34**	**35**	**36**	**37**	**38**	**39**	**40**
B	D	B	B	C	B	C	B	B	A
41	**42**	**43**	**44**	**45**	**46**	**47**	**48**	**49**	**50**
A	B	A	D	D	C	A	B	A	D
51	**52**	**53**	**54**	**55**	**56**	**57**	**58**	**59**	**60**
B	D	B	C	C	C	C	B	B	B
61	**62**	**63**	**64**	**65**	**66**	**67**	**68**	**69**	**70**
D	B	C	A	A	B	C	D	B	B
71	**72**	**73**	**74**	**75**	**76**	**77**	**78**	**79**	**80**
A	A	D	C	C	A	A	C	D	B
81	**82**	**83**	**84**	**85**	**86**	**87**	**88**	**89**	**90**
A	C	D	D	C	D	A	D	B	C
91	**92**	**93**	**94**	**95**	**96**	**97**	**98**	**99**	**100**
C	D	D	A	D	D	A	A	B	C

EXPLANATORY ANSWERS

1. Term of copyright in photographs—*Omitted by the Copyright (Amendment) Act, 2012 (27 of 2012), s. 13 (w.e.f. 21-6-2012).*

2. University Grants Commission (Promotion of Academic Integrity and Prevention of Plagiarism in Higher Educational Institutions) Regulation 2018— The Gazette notification states "Every Higher Educational institute (HEI) should establish mechanisms as to enhance awareness about responsible conduct of research and academic activities, to promote academic integrity and to prevent plagiarism". Some of the salient points are as follows:
   - Every student submitting a thesis shall submit an undertaking indicating that the document has been prepared by him/her, is original and free of any plagiarism.
   - The undertaking shall include the fact that specific sections (Abstract, Summary, Hypothesis, Observations, Results, Conclusions, and Recommendations) have been duly checked through an approved Plagiarism detection tool which will not have any similarities. It can exclude a common knowledge or coincidental terms (up to 14 consecutive words).
   - Each supervisor shall submit a certificate indicating that the work done by the researcher under him/her is plagiarism free.
   - If any faculty member suspects plagiarism, it should be reported to the Departmental Academic Integrity Panel (DAIP) which will investigate and submit recommendations to the Institutional Academic Integrity Panel (IAIP).
   - Students will be penalized according to quantity of plagiarism (Table).

Table: Levels of Plagiarism with corresponding penalty (UGC Guidelines)

Level	Extent of similarity	Penalty
0	≤ 10%	No Penalty
1	10-40%	Submission of revised script within 6 months
2	40-60%	Debarment from submitting revised script for 1 year
3	≥ 60%	Cancellation of student registration program

3. The Central Information Commission or State Information Commissions cannot receive applications for information directly from the citizens. Application for any information shall be filed before the Public Information Officer or the Assistant Public Information Officer. It is only when the citizen finds that there is any deficiency of service or refusal on the part of the latter to render the service that the applicant can file a complaint before the Information Commission. Petitions can be filed before the Information Commissions in two ways, one as a complaint and another by way of an appeal. Complaints are filed under section 18 and appeals under section 19(3) of the Act respectively.

6. In the early 1990s, the Library of Congress undertook a pilot program to digitize resources, establishing the National Digital Library Program. This encompassed 100 thematic collections at the Library of Congress and included partnerships with 23 external special collections. By 2000, more than 5 million items were online. This has grown

to more than 9 million items today. Many of the collections that were originally in American Memory have been migrated to self-standing sites, accessible through the Library of Congress.

Other significant collections and digital projects at the Library of Congress are Chronicling America, Performing Arts Encyclopedia, and the Prints and Photographs Online Catalog. Chronicling America makes available newspapers published between 1836 and 1922. More than 7 million pages are available, produced by the National Digital Newspaper Program. These represent 140,000 bibliographic titles and 900,000 separate library holdings records.

The Performing Arts Encyclopedia links users to sheet music, audio recordings, films, and photographs in various collections. These include access to imagery of creative writers' prose, poetry, correspondence, and iconography, and music associated with various events (the American Civil War, baseball). Also accessible are three-dimensional artifacts, such as musical instruments at the Library of Congress, and recordings of public domain music.

The Prints and Photographs Online Catalog highlights American history with its "Civil War Glass Negatives and Related Prints," including 7,000 different views and portraits made during the American Civil War (1861-1865) from original glass plate negatives by photographers Mathew B. Brady and Alexander Gardner, both influential in the dissemination of information about the war.

7. The National Knowledge Commission (NKC) in its Report to the Nation (2006-2009) made ten major recommendations on libraries. In pursuance of this, a High Level Committee to be called as National Mission on Libraries (NML) has been set up by the Government of India. Raja Rammohun Roy Library Foundation (RRRLF), an autonomous body under the Ministry of Culture will be the nodal agency for the National Mission on Libraries for administrative, logistics, planning and budgeting purposes.

9. McClennen's 'Roles in digital reference' defined a Role Based Model of Digital Reference. This model focuses on roles that are played by the participants based on the traditional process of librarian/patron interchange. The five roles are:

(*a*) *Patron:* person asking the question

(*b*) *Filterer:* this may be a person or an automatic process which filters the non-questions (for instance, repeat questions, inquiries about previous transactions, unclear, out-of-scope, or spam)

(*c*) *Answerer:* person who assists the patron with information needs

(*d*) *Administrator:* person who monitors workflow, clears the way for answerers and filterers to do their jobs, may assign questions and check answers for content

(*e*) *Coordinator:* person(s) responsible for defining and implementing policies and procedures that involve the operation on the service.

10. *Indian Library Standard:*

(1) Specifications for wooden shelving, cabinets (adjustable type)

IS: 4116 (reaffirmed-1998)

(2) Specifications for steel shelving cabinets

IS: 3312 (reaffirmed-1990)

(3) Design of library buildings-recommendations, relating to its primary elements

IS: 1553 (revised-1989)

(4) Specifications for library furniture and fittings

Part I Timber IS: 1829 (Part I)–1978 (reaffirmed-1991)

Part II Steel IS : 1829 (Part II)–1977 (affirmed-1998)

(5) Code of practice in library lighting

IS: 2672-1966 (reaffirmed-1990)

(6) Specification for mobile library van
IS: 2661-1975 (reaffirmed-1999)

(7) Guide for preparation of abstracts (1st rev.)
IS: 795-1976 (reaffirmed-1992)

(8) Guide for data elements and record format for computer based databases for bibliographic description of different kinds of documents
IS: 11370-1985 (reaffirmed-1998)

11. Webster's Third New International Dictionary of the English Language, Unabridged (commonly known as Webster's Third, or W3) was published in September 1961. It was edited by Philip Babcock Gove and a team of lexicographers.

12. Project Gutenberg (PG), founded by Michael Hart in 1971, is the oldest digitisation project. It is a volunteer effort to digitise, archive, and distribute cultural works. The project is named after Johannes Gutenberg, the 15th-century German printer who propelled the movable-type printing press revolution. The mission of the project is "to encourage the creation and distribution of e-Books". The project aims to make the items in its collection as free as possible, in long-lasting, open formats that can be used on almost any computer. The United States Declaration of Independence was the first Project Gutenberg e-text. The project started as an ambitious effort to develop a free public library of 10,000 public-domain e-books and now has more than 16,700 items in its collection, with new e-books posted most days. Earlier most text was entered manually but now image scanners and optical character recognition software is used. The status of the e-books is carefully verified according to U.S. copyright law. Material is added to the PG archive only after it has received a copyright clearance, and records of these clearances are saved for future reference.

The collection contains works of literature from the Western cultural tradition. In addition to literature like novels, poetry, short stories, and drama, the collection also includes cookbooks, reference works, issues of periodicals and a few non-text items such as audio files and music notation files. Most of the texts are in English, but there are also significant numbers in German, French, Italian, Spanish, Dutch. Finnish, Chinese, and many other languages. Project Gutenberg e-texts are made available in plain text, mainly using US-ASCII character encoding but frequently extended to ISO-8859-1. ASCII format was chosen to ensure easy access and readability. PG is made up entirely of volunteers who work on producing these ASCII texts. The Project Gutenberg Philosophy is to make information, books and other materials available to the general public in forms a vast majority of the computers, programs and people can easily read, use, quote, and search. The e-books can be freely downloaded and read, and redistributed for non-commercial use.

13. The first discussion of any type of direct service by librarians to help library users was in a paper presented by Samuel Swett Green at the first conference of the American Library Association in Philadelphia in 1876. His paper, "Personal Intercourse and Relations between Librarians and Readers in Popular Libraries," outlined the concept of the librarian interacting with and assisting the reader: he did not use the phrase "reference service" because that term had not yet been developed. His paper was published with a shorter title in the first volume of Library Journal and is universally recognized as the first professional discussion of what we now call reference service.

14. Katz, Gurevitch and Haas (1973) developed 35 needs taken from the social and psychological functions of the mass media and put them into five categories:

1. Cognitive needs, including acquiring information, knowledge and understanding.

2. Affective needs, including emotion, pleasure, feelings.
3. Personal integrative needs, including credibility, stability, status.
4. Social integrative needs, including interacting with family and friends; and
5. Tension release needs, including escape and diversion.

15. **BARD App:** Developer: Library of Congress, http://www.loc.gov/homepage/connect.html

The BARD Mobile App provides access to braille and talking books from the NLS (National Library Service for the Blind and Physically Handicapped), Library of Congress. BARD (Braille and Audio Reading Download) contains nearly 50,000 books, magazines, and music scores in audio and braille formats. The app allows blind and physically handicapped users to download these titles directly to their iPhone or iPad for convenient listening. If the device is connected to a Bluetooth Braille display, books can be read in braille.

16. The Reference and User Services Association (RUSA) is a division of the American Library Association. RUSA serves all types of libraries in reference, user services, adult readers advisory and collection development as well as resource sharing, genealogy and archives, business reference and reference technology.

RUSA has six specialty sections that are free to RUSA members: BRASS (Business Reference and Services Section), CODES (Collection Development and Evaluation Section) HS (History Section), ETS (Emerging Technologies Section), RSS (Reference Services Section) and STARS (Sharing and Transforming Access to Resources Section).

17. Ranganathan described subject as an organized set of ideas, whose extension and intension are likely to fall coherently within the field of interest and comfortably within the intellectual competence and the field of inevitable specialization of a normal person. The exposition of a subject may extend in print to several volumes at one extreme, or to only a single volume, or to an article in a periodical, or to a part, or a chapter, or a section of a book, or even to a single word at the other extreme. From the multi-volume document to single word, this is the range for suitable manifestation of a subject, i.e. a multi-volume document may belong to a single subject and a single word may also belong to a single subject. He categorized the subject in three main classes from the levels of exposition, i.e. macro-subject (great exteasion and small intension), micro-subject (small extension and great intension) and spot subject (very tiny extension and enormous intension). These categorization is however highly subjective and cannot segmentise well-defined groups or sets with sharp demarcation among them. As Ranganathan remarked, Macro subject, micro subject and spot subject are relative terms with their meaning loosely fixed by convention. The measures of their extension forms, so to speak, a continuous spectrum. The change-over from the range of macro subjects to that of micro subjects cannot be fixed to be at a sharp point in the spectrum. At the region of transition, it is difficult to distinguish between a macro subject and a micro subject.

18. Hulme theory of literary warrant immensely attracted the attention of later classificationists. E.A. Savage (1877-1966) revived the term. Hulme ragards books as "concrete aggregates of facts selected from the common stock of knowledge". What Hulme meant by concrete aggregates is that if there are books on the subject of electricity and magnetism there is literary warrant for providing a number for such a class named "electricity and magnetism". Literary warrant simply means that a subject cannot be listed in the scheme unless some literature has already appeared on it. Cr, the existing literature on a subject only justifies the inclusion of that subject in the scheme.

Hulme's principle of literary warrant greatly influenced the Library of Congress Classification (LC). Ranganathan also made use of this principle, but not exactly in the sense Hulme made, use of it. According to Ranganathan when the literature on a particular subject grows in size, there may arise a need for providing a separate class for it in the scheme. Ranganathan's principle of literary warrant states that "the subjects in an array of subjects or the isolates in an array of isolates may be arranged in the sequence of decreasing quantity of the documents published or anticipated to be published on them, except when any other overwhelming consideration rules it out." Hence, it requires that the various aspects of such a new subject should be so listed as to bring those aspects first on which more literature have appeared.

19. BIBFRAME: The BIBFRAME initiative is the future of bibliographic description in a networked and web-based world. The BIBFRAME initiative will:

- differentiate between conceptual content and the physical/digital manifestation(s);
- unambiguously identify information entities; and
- leverage and expose relationships among and between entities.

BIBFRAME model: A conceptual/practical model that has four high-level classes or entities:

- BIBFRAME work
- BIBFRAME instance
- BIBFRAME authority
- BIBFRAME annotation

20. The following principles are propounded by the Taylor:

- Scientific study and planning of the work
- Scientific selection, placement and training Standardisation—3rd point
- Division of responsibility between management and workers
- Functional foremanship
- Mental revolution
- Wage incentives

22. Content (or need) theories of motivation focus on factors internal to the individual that energise and direct behaviour. In general, such theories regard motivation as the product of internal drives that compel an individual to act or move toward the satisfaction of individual needs. Major content theories of motivation are Maslow's hierarchy of needs, Alderfer's ERG theory, Herzberg's motivator-hygiene theory, and McClelland's learned needs or three-needs theory.

Process (or cognitive) theories of motivation focus on conscious human decision processes as an explanation of motivation. The process theories are concerned with determining how individual behaviour is energised, directed, and maintained in the specifically willed and self-directed human cognitive processes. Process theories of motivation are based on early cognitive theories, which posit that behaviour is the result of conscious decision-making processes. The major process theories of motivation are expectancy theory, equity theory, goal-setting theory, and reinforcement theory.

23. LibQUAL+ is a web-based survey offered by the Association of Research Libraries that helps libraries assess and improve library services, change organizational culture, and market the library. The survey instrument measures library users' minimum, perceived, and desired levels of service quality across three dimensions: Affect of Service, Information Control, and Library as Place.

24. Routers: In an environment consisting of several network segments with different protocols and architecture, a bridge may not be adequate for ensuring fast communication among all of the segments. A complex network needs a device which not only knows the address of each segment, but also can determine the best path for sending data and filtering broadcast traffic to the local segment. Such a device is called a Router. Routers are both hardware and software devices. They can be cards that plug into a collapsed backbone, stand-alone devices or software that would run on a file server.

Purpose of Routers: The purpose of a router is to connect nodes across an Internetwork, regardless of the Physical Layer and Data Link Layer protocol that is used. Routers are hardware and topology-independent. Routers are not aware of the type of medium or frame that is being used (Ethernet, Token Ring, FDD1, etc.). Routers are aware of the Network Layer protocol that's used (e.g., Novell's IPX, Unix's IP, XNS, Apple's DDP, and so on)

25. TCP/IP stands for Transport Control Protocol/ Internet Protocol. It is a protocol suite used by most communications software, especially in the U.S. It came out of the work on ARPANet (predecessor to Internet). It is not so much of a model, but a base set of protocols. It comprises of four layers as shown in Fig.

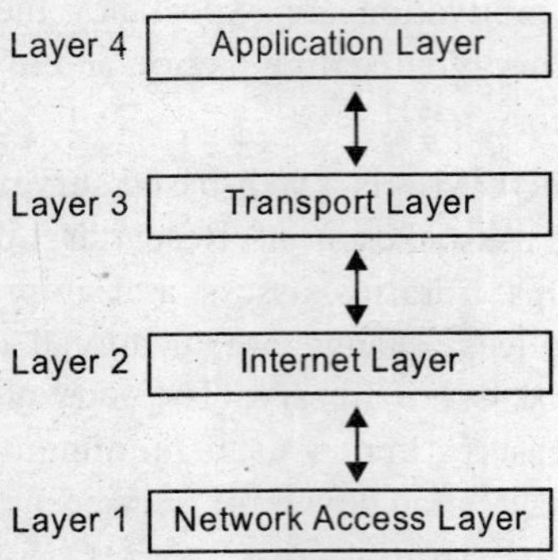

Fig. TCP/IP Layer

26. John Leavitt's LongLegs program provided the basis of Lycos. Michael Mauldin led a team from the Center for Machine Transition at Carnegie Mellon University that began development work on Lycos in May 1994. Lycos's name was based on the Latin term *Lycosidae lycosa*, the family name of a ground spider that hunts at night by chasing down prey rather than using a web. Similarly, Lycos's spider program gathered URLs at night. When it became available for public use on August 12, 1994, Lycos had a catalog of 54,000 documents. By January of 1995, the catalog expanded to 1.5 million documents. Lycos was licensed by Microsoft for its Microsoft Network in April 1995. The partnership was one of many by Carnegie Mellon that allowed use of Lycos but retained ownership of the search tool. In June 1995, however, CMG@Ventures purchased Lycos, forming a new company, Lycos, Inc. Mauldin received a minority take in the company that began providing advertising space to the emerging corporate market on the internet.

28. Unicode was primarily invented to overcome this problem. Unicode is a universal international standard character encoding that is capable of representing almost all characters in almost all human alphabets and writing systems around the world including English, Arabic, Chinese and more.

Unicode uses 16-bit (2 bytes) binary values for the representation of each character.

This allows for 65,536 different possible character combinations: enough to represent a wider range of character sets, characters for all languages.

Unicode can be implemented by different character encodings. The Unicode standard defines Unicode Transformation Formats (UTF): UTF-8, UTF-16, and UTF-32, and several other encodings. The most commonly used encodings are:

UTF-8, UTF-16, and UCS-2.

UTF-8: UTF-8 is the dominant encoding on the World Wide Web uses one byte for the first 128 code points, and up to 4 bytes for other characters. The first 128 Unicode code points represent the ASCII characters, which means that any ASCII text is also a UTF-8 text.

UCS-2: UCS-2 uses two bytes (16 bits) for each character but can only encode the first 65,536 code points.

UTF-32 (also referred to as UCS-4) uses four bytes to encode any given code point, Unicode defines different characters encodings, the most used ones being UTF-8, UTF-16 and UTF-32. UTF-8 is the most popular encoding in.

As Java was developed for multilingual languages it adopted the Unicode system.

30. The first recorded virus was in 1971 and it was called the Creeper Virus, which was written by Bob Thomas. What the Creeper virus did was it infected a remote computer by the ARPNET and copied itself displaying the message "I'M THE CREEPER: CATCH ME IF YOU CAN!". The first computer virus the Creeper infected and spread to PDP-10 mainframe, computers manufactured by Digital Equipment Corporation (DEC).

31. The earliest development of RFID technology dates back to World War II. Once radar was invented in 1935. German, Japanese, British, and American planes were detectable while they were still miles away. However, it was impossible to determine whether a plane was an enemy aircraft or friendly aircraft. The Germans discovered that if pilots rolled their planes on their approach to the airfield, it would change the radio signal reflected back, thus alerting the radar crew on the ground that they were German planes. This was the first passive RFID system. The British devised the first active RFID system by installing a transmitter on each plane. When the transmitter received signals from radio stations on the ground, friendly aircraft would broadcast a signal back identifying it as friendly aircraft. Uses of radio frequency communications continued to grow after World War II as a way to identify objects remotely. It developed as a technique to detect shoplifters in retail locations. The first patent for an active RFID tag with rewritable memory was awarded to Mario W. Cardullo on January 23, 1973. Charles Walton often referred to as the father of RFID technology, received U.S. Patent in August 1973 for a passive transponder or "key card" used to unlock a door without using a traditional key.

32. Scientific method involves various steps: Identify the problem, formulate the hypothesis, test the hypothesis, analysis the evidence, conclusion.

Dr. S.R. Ranganathan, Father of Library Science characterizes the development of any discipline by the Spiral. The Spiral given by Dr. S.R. Ranganthan is a way of describing the development and the phases through which a research enquire proceeds.

Infact, this is a system given by Ranganathan for describing the development of a new knowledge. He was very keen about how to conduct research for generating new knowledge or discipline. Ranganathan has characterised the working of Scientific method by a never ending spiral movement. He has added a chapter entitled Spiral of Scientific Method in second edition of his classic "Five Laws of Library Science (1957)". It is a visual representation of method of science; in which he explains, moves like a spiral where he means science is discovering new heights daily and discovering new knowledge. It is meant for continuous growth of knowledge which is open ended in nature.

To know each sequential step and their movement the spiral is divided into 4 cardinal points by 2 lines perpendicular to each other intersecting the centre. This also results in 4 points. The whole spiral moves in clockwise direction.

- The lowest point is known as Nadir
- The highest point is known as Zenith
- Last end of Horizontal line is known as Ascendency.

- Right end of horizontal line is known as Descendent
- **Nadir:** Accumulation of facts, obtained by observation, experimentation.
- **Ascendent:** Accumulation of inducted or empirical laws got out of the facts accumulated at the nadir.
- **Zenith:** The fundamental laws formulated with the aid of institution of some degree or other so as to comprehend all the inducted or empirical laws accumulated at ascendant.
- **Descendent:** The accumulation of the deducted laws got from the fundamental laws at Zenith

Spiral Works?

Four cardinal points give rise to 4 quadrants in Box I.

- Quadrant 1 corresponds to the stage in development of domain of the universe of knowledge, facts are found and recorded, primary senses are used.
- Quadrant 2 corresponds to the stage in which intellect is used, empirical laws are formulated.
- Quadrant 3 corresponds to the stage in which intuition is used, fundamental laws are seized and formulated.
- Quadrant 4 corresponds to the stage in which intellect is used, deduced laws are derived and recorded.

Table: Ranganathan's Spiral

Quadrant	Span/Situation	Phase of Research	Method/Tool
I	N-A South-West	Empirical	Experience and observation literature survey
II	A-Z North-West	Hypothesizing	Institution & Imagination
III	Z-D North-East	Deductive	Intellection/Logic/ Statistics
IV	D-N South-East	Verification	Applications/ Mathematics

33. The *h*-index was proposed by Jorge E. Hirsch, a physicist at the University of Carolina, San Diego, to measure concurrently the quality and quantity of scientific output of a scientist based on the highly cited papers of the author and the number of citations these papers have received from other articles. It was originally meant as a tool for determining theoretical physicists' relative quality (Hirsch 2005), which is sometimes also called the Hirsch index or Hirsch number. The *h* in *h*-index stands for Hirsch and 'highly cited'.

The *h*-index is computed based on the highly cited papers of the author and the number of citations these papers have received from other articles. The h-index gives a measure of the number of articles (*h*) of an author that have received at least (*h*) citations up to that lime. For instance, an *h*-index of 6 would mean that an author has 6 articles that have received at least 6 citations each.

34. Typically, an open access (OA) journal requires peer review and once a manuscript has been accepted, publications are immediately available electronically and are permanently free for anyone to access. Open Access publishing typically means the author pays an Article Processing Charge (APC) fee for this open access. These kinds of open access publications are labelled as gold open access journals. Often, institutions have agreements that reduce the fee amount for open access publishing. However, there are other categories associated with open access publishing. The term platinum or diamond open access publishing refers to open access journals that do not charge any APCs. Platinum open access journals are usually underwritten by a university or research entity. Green open access is a term that refers to when an author publishes an article in any category of journal and then self-archives a copy in a freely accessible institutional or online archive, often referred to as a repository which operates as a professional network. An example of such a repository is the archive Research Gate. Yet another open accessing term, bronze Open Access refers to articles that are free to read, but only on a publisher page. Bronze Open Access articles are not be available to scholars for later reuse or downloading. Finally, predatory open access journals are of questionable quality and merit. The Directory of Open Access Journal (DOAJ) is a database for open access publishing. According to this directory, the journals listed in DOAJ database have gone through a vetting process specific to the journals' peer review process and the specifications of the journals' editorial board.

36. The International Council of Archives (ICA) was founded in 1948 by the United Nations Educational Scientific and Cultural Organizations (UNESCO) to establish a worldwide organization for the archive profession. It was "created to improve worldwide standards of archival administration and practice and to advance archival theory." ICA has a global network of more than 1,400 institutional members in 190 countries, with current priorities being advocacy and promotion, automation and electronic records, disaster prevention and preservation, and education and training.

37. The actual term "Internet of Things" was first coined by Kevin Ashton in 1999 during his work at Procter & Gamble. Ashton worked on supply chain optimisation, and he wanted to attract senior management's attention to a new exciting technology called RFID. Partly because the Internet was the hottest new trend in 1999 and partly because it somehow made sense, he called his presentation "Internet of Things" or IoT.

38. The National Centre for Children's Literature (NCCL) was set up in 1993 as a coordinating agency to promote children's literature in all the languages of India. Set up by National Book Trust (NBT), India (an autonomous organisation of the Ministry of Human Resource Development, Govt. of India), this Centre helps in creation and translation of useful books for children. At the same time, it also works for monitoring, coordinating and aiding the publication of children's literature in the country.

The primary objective of this Centre is to collect and make available joyful Indian and foreign materials and expertise to publishers, authors, illustrators and others interested for rapid and balanced development of children's literature available to parents, teachers, ecucationists and planners. It involves public and private agencies for the purpose on regular basis. Major activities of the NCCL are as follows:

Training and Promotion

Research and Development

Information and Documentation

39. Kolhapur Princely State, in the Western India passed Public Libraries Act in 1945. Dr S.R. Ranganathan, father of Library Science, succeeded in the passage of this legislation and he was very keen about the development of effective public library system in India.

40. The SLA was founded in 1909 at an American Library Association (ALA) conference and the leading figure in its establishment was John Cotton Dana, noted public librarian and ALA leader. While Dana remained active and influential in SLA and the special libraries movement, they were only two of his many interests (Hanson, 1994). SLA was dominated by an activist group whose interests were only minimally concerned with traditional library materials and their service orientation to users was determinedly proactive. For the first 15 years of its existence, SLA members were constantly defining, justifying, and SLA members were constantly defining, justifying, and explaining themselves to ALA and the general library community. From the earliest uses of the term, only a few SLA leaders were satisfied with the term "special," but it stuck because no one could come up with a better one.

In one of the earliest discussions of the nature of special libraries, during the 1912 joint meeting with ALA at a session titled, "What Is a Special Library," several SLA members offered tentative definitions and examples. Aksel G.S. Josephson, of the Crerar Library in Chicago, noted: "The special library must, for instance, make much more use of what has come to be known as documentation than the general library." He added, later in his comments, "We might come to the point where special libraries will not even have whole books, but only such parts of many books as it needs, treating books as well as periodicals on the principle of documentation" (SLA Meeting Summary, 1912). Josephson was adopting the terminology developed by Paul Otlet, of the International Institute of Bibliography in Brussels, who had coined the term as early as 1903 to describe a new field of study.

41. Recommendations made by National Knowledge Commission, 2005 to ensure sustained attention to the development of libraries:

- Set up a National Commission on Libraries
- Prepare a National Census of all Libraries
- Revamp Library Information Science (LIS) Education, Training and Research facilities
- Re-assess staffing of libraries
- Set up a Central Library Fund
- Modernize library management, encourage greater community participation in library management
- Promote Information and Communication Technology (ICT) applications in all libraries
- Facilitate donation and maintenance of private collections
- Encourage Public Private Partnerships in LIS development

42. Penalties in case of plagiarism in research publications:

Level 0: Similarities up to 10% - Minor similarities, no penalty.

Level 1: Similarities above 10% to 40%: Shall be asked to withdraw manuscript.

Level 2: Similarities above 40% to 60%: Shall be asked to withdraw manuscript. Shall be denied a right to one annual increment. Shall not be allowed to be a supervisor to any new Master's. M.Phil. Student/scholar for a period of two years.

Level 3: Similarities above 60%: Shall be asked to withdraw manuscript. Shall be denied a right to two successive annual increments. Shall not be allowed to be a supervisor to any new Master's, M.Phil., Student/scholar for a period of three years.

Note 1: Penalty on repeated plagiarism : Shall be asked to withdraw manuscript and shall be punished for the plagiarism of one level higher than the lower level committed by him/her. In case where plagiarism of highest level is committed then the punishment for the same shall be operative.

In case level 3 offence is repeated then the disciplinary action including suspension/termination as per service rules shall be taken by the University.

Note 2: Penalty in case where the benefit or credit has already been obtained. If plagiarism is proved on a date later than the date of benefit or credit obtained as the case may be then his/her benefit or credit shall be put in abeyance for a period recommended and approved by the Committee constituted by the Vice-Chancellor.

45. Types of Metadata

Type	Definition	Examples
Administrative	Metadata used in managing and administering collections and information resources	• Acquisition information • Rights and reproduction tracking • Documentation of legal access requirements • Location information • Selection criteria for digitization
Descriptive	Metadata used to identify and describe collections and related information resources	• Cataloging records • Finding aids • Differentiations between versions • Specialized indexes • Curatorial information • Hyperlinked relationships between resources • Annotations by creators and users
Preservation	Metadata related to the preservation management of collections and information resources	• Documentation of physical condition of resources • Documentation of actions taken to preserve physical and digital versions of resources, e.g., data refreshing and migration • Documentation of any changes occurring during digitization or preservation
Technical	Metadata related to how a system functions or metadata behaves	• Hardware and software documentation • Technical digitization information, e.g., formats, compression ratios, scaling routines • Tracking of system response times • Authentication and security data, e.g., encryption keys, passwords
Use	Metadata related to the level and type of use of collections and information resources	• Circulation records • Physical and digital exhibition records • Use and user tracking • Content reuse and multiversioning information • Search logs • Rights metadata

Figure: Anne J. Gilliland, 'Different types of metadata and their functions'

46. Semantic Web: A collective term created by Tim Berners-Lee for technologies and concepts from the field of automatic processable metadata for resources connected through network structures. The vision of the semantic web is the augmentation of resources in the Web with unambiguous machine-readable descriptions about their content or functions. Existing web resources are extended without modifying their original function. Thus the boundary between human and automated understanding is abolished. Especially data collection from distributed sources is simplified and an automatic integration of data and application over the Web is possible. The structured, machine-readable metadata can be interpreted by means of inference rules. The most important semantic web technologies are the Resource Description Framework (RDF), the RDF Schema (RDFS) and the Web Ontology Language (OWL). All specifications are made by the World Wide Web Consortium (W3C).

RDF is a XML-based markup language for the description of resources in the Inter-, intra- and Extranet. RDF statements, called triples, describe a resource, which is identified by a URI (Uniform Resource Identifier), the characteristics of this resource, and the values of these characteristics.

48. Folksonomy is a term coined by Thomas Van der Waal in 2004 using a combination of two words, folks and taxonomy Folksonomy refers to a system of classification based on the practice of collaboratively creating and managing tags to annotate digital content. It has also been called collaborative tagging, social indexing, or social tagging.

49. ResearchGate, founded in 2008 by physicians Dr. Ijad Madisch (Boston) and Dr. Soren Hofmayer (Berlin), and computer scientist Horst Fickenscher (Berlin), is aimed at creating a working and discovering network among scientists, "Discover", "Communicate" and "Collaborate" are its main purposes.

50. Saracevic (1996) devised a model that also examined situational relevance, while examining the many types of relevance that are involved in search interaction. Stratified models help determine the range of abstraction levels that need to be considered when evaluating the effectiveness of a search system. Saracevic proposed a model of stratified interaction including hardware, software, searcher cognition, and situational levels, which suggests that the system and the searcher have equal influence on the outcome of the search. Any system involves hardware, processing, and data structures. For a given searcher, their interaction involves cognitive, affective, and situational levels, which represent their interpretation, motivation, and requirements, respectively. Figure presents a visualization of the stratified model. A core principle underlying the stratified model is that the search interaction is a dialog between the searcher and the search system at the surface level, with the expectation of merging and adaptation between the two agents over the course of the search process. The searcher (upper) side

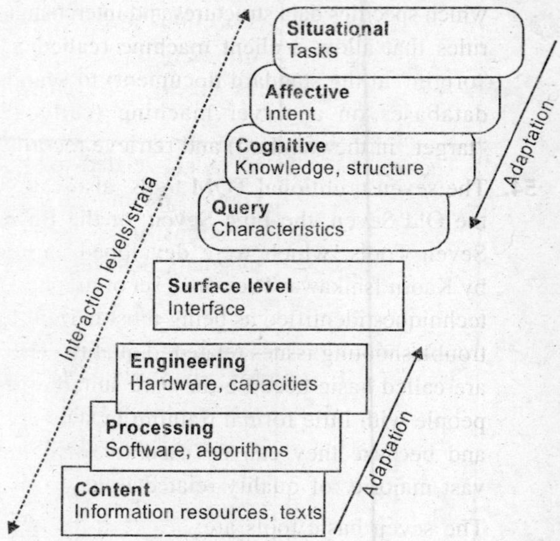

Fig. Stratified model of information retrieval interaction (adapted from Saracevic, 1996)

60. A non-probability sample is one in which a case in a sample is chosen in such a manner that it gives you information for the sample itself and makes it possible to generalize the findings for the population with certain degree of precision. Such a sample is also called a purposive sample. This kind of sampling is primarily used to collect information on market surveys to know the attitude, opinion, behaviour, reactions of individuals. There are many types of non-probability samples, including snowball sampling, Convenience, purposive/ judgment, Quota sampling, etc.

61. In 1957 the Government of India constituted an Advisory Committee for Libraries under the Chairmanship of Sri K.P. Sinha. The committee in its comprehensive report recommended for:

- Enactment of a Central Library Act by Government of India.
- Enactment of a State Library Act by each State.
- Authority for local bodies to levy a library cess as surcharge on property tax; and
- Provision for the Government of India grant equal to the library cess in a State.

63. **Special Libraries Association (SLA):** An organization with members worldwide whose members represent all kinds of libraries, including those from government, law, some academic divisional libraries, the business and financial world, nonprofit organizations, and others, "John Cotton Dana was the first president (1909-1911) and founder of Special Libraries Association (SLA)". "The Special Libraries Association (SLA) is a nonprofit global organization for innovative information professionals and their strategic partners. SLA serves more than 7,000 members in 75 countries in the information profession, including corporate, academic and government information specialists. SLA promotes and strengthens its members through learning, advocacy, and networking initiatives". "SLA is organized into 55 regional Chapters that elect officers, issue bulletins or meeting announcements, hold three to nine program meetings during a year, and initiate special projects".

64. The Agricultural Libraries Network (AGLINET) coordinated by the Food and Agriculture Organization of the United Nation (FAO), is a world-wide, voluntary network of international agricultural libraries with regional/country coverage and other comprehensive or specialized subject resource collections. All member libraries provide, upon request, access to the literature originating in the country or region or for a given specialization. AGLINET aims at combining resources for mutual and rational use through delivery of primary documents, by means of inter library loan provision of reproductions, bibliographic information; with appropriate regional and subject specialization. Member libraries include Agricultural libraries of national or regional importance with comprehensive collections and strong regional coverage; Libraries in special subject fields within the broad domain of agriculture with worldwide coverage.

AGLINET Network members include Libraries from Argentina, Australia, Belarus, Belgium, Benin, Botswana, Brazil, Bulgaria, Brazil, Canada, China Costa Rica, Czech republic, Denmark, Egypt, Estonia, Ethiopia, Finland, France, Germany, Hungary, India, Indonesia, Italy, Japan, Jordan, Kenya, Korea, Latvia, Lithuania, Malawi, Malaysia, Mexico, Netherlands, Nigeria, Norway, Philippines, Poland, Portugal, Russia, Slovenia, South Korea, Sprain, Sri Lanka, Sweden, Syria, Thailand, UK, Uruguay, USA, West Indies and Zambia (Satyanarayana *et al.* 2008).

65. Asynchronous digital reference is characterized by communication in one direction at a time, typically by e-mail or web forms. It involves the use of FAQs (frequently asked questions), e-resources, which are comprised of subject guides, lists, journals, and other content, and e-mail, which may be forms-based or address-based. According to Pomerantz *et al*. (2004), since the invention of the World Wide Web, there has been a great increase in the number of reference services utilizing asynchronous electronic communication media to conduct the reference transaction. The two broad categories of digital reference service models are as follows:

(*a*) Asynchronous transactions, which involves time delay between the question and answer.

(*i*) E-mail

(*ii*) Web forms

(*iii*) Ask-A services

(*b*) Synchronous transaction which takes place in 'real-time' with an immediate response to the query.

(*i*) Text-based chat

(*ii*) Chat reference using simple technologies

(*iii*) Chat reference using web contact centre software

(*iv*) Video-conferencing or web-cam services

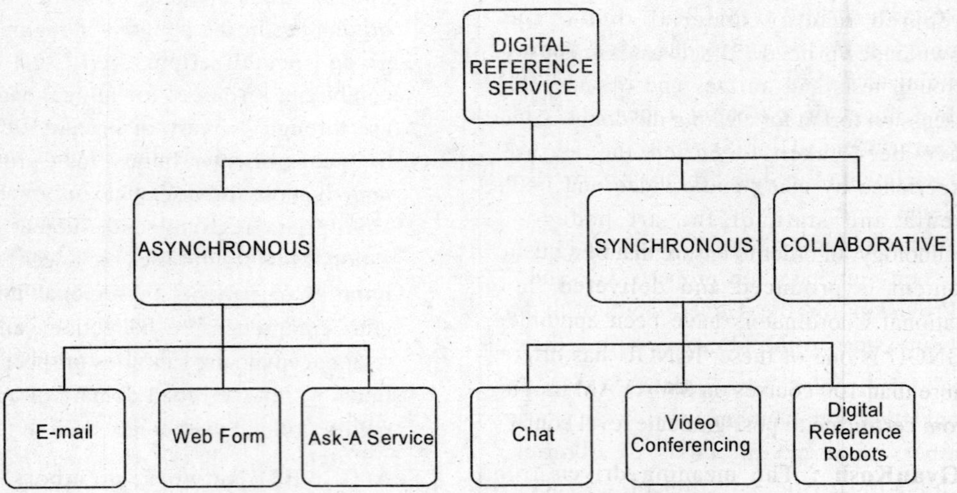

Fig. Topology of Digital Reference Service

78. MOOC is the new buzz word in educational scenario now. It stands for Massive Open Online Courses (MOOC). MOOC has not only bridged the gap between ODL and Conventional universities but also given an opportunity to learners beyond any geographical or administrative boundary to learn on will and choice. There are many popular MOOC platforms like Coursera , Edx, Futurelearn, etc. across the world and SWAYAM has emerged as Indian MOOC platform. Government of India has initiated SWAYAM in 2016 as a MOOC platform for Indian universities and institutions.

SWAYAM is designed to achieve the three cardinal principles of Education Policy viz., access, equity and quality. The objective of this effort is to take the best teaching learning resources to all, including the most disadvantaged. SWAYAM seeks to bridge the digital divide for students who have hitherto remained untouched by the digital revolution and have not been able to join the mainstream of the knowledge economy. This is done through a platform that facilitates hosting of all the courses, taught in classrooms from Class 9 till post-graduation to be accessed by anyone, anywhere at any time. All the courses are interactive, prepared by the best teachers in the country and are available, free of cost to any learner. More than 1,000 specially chosen faculty and teachers from across the country have participated in preparing these courses.

The courses hosted on SWAYAM are in 4 quadrants–(1) video lecture, (2) specially prepared reading material that can be downloaded/printed (3) self-assessment tests through tests and quizzes and (4) an online discussion forum for clearing the doubts. Steps have been taken to enrich the learning experience by using audio-video and multi-media and state of the art pedagogy/ technology. In order to ensure that best quality content is produced and delivered, nine National Coordinators have been appointed. IGNOU is one of these. IGNOU has offered more than 100 courses on SWAYAM ranging from certificate to post-graduate level courses.

eGyanKosh : The meaning driven from eGyanKosh is E = Electronic, Gyan = Knowledge and Kosh. eGyanKosh is a national digital repository. It is implemented and maintained by Indira Gandhi National Open University (IGNOU). Indira Gandhi National Open University (IGNOU) is a national open university that offers distance and open education in India and other countries. IGNOU has initiated the establishment of a National Digital Repository of learning resources eGyanKosh. IGNOU's learning resource repository, eGyanKosh, initiated in 2005 with the intention of digitizing self-instructional material, has emerged as one of the world's largest repositories, with more than 40,000 self-instructional text materials, and around 2,000 video lectures covering over 2,200 of the university's courses. The repository has become very popular in a short time and is being used the world over by student and teacher communities for its rich content. 'The site has already received over two million hits, with an average of 400 visits per day from all over the world. There are approximate 125,000 active registered users of the repository.

e-PG Pathshala: e-PG Pathshala is an initiative of the MHRD under its National Mission on Education through ICT (NME-ICT) being executed by the UGC. The content and its quality being the key component of education system, high quality, curriculum-based, interactive e-content in 77 subjects across all disciplines of social sciences, arts, fine arts and humanities, natural and mathematical sciences, linguistics and languages are being developed by the subject experts and other R&D institutes across the country. Every subject has a team of principal investigator, paper coordinators, content writers, content reviewers and multimedia team.

NPTEL: NPTEL (National Programme on Technology Enhanced Learning), started in 2003, is an initiative by seven Indian Institutes of Technology (IIT Bombay, Delhi, Guwahati, Kanpur, Kharagpur, Madras, and Roorkee) and Indian Institute of Science (IISc) for creating and providing course contents in engineering and science. This has been extended to also include social science subjects by bringing in many other institutions under this programme (NPTEL, n.d.).

79. 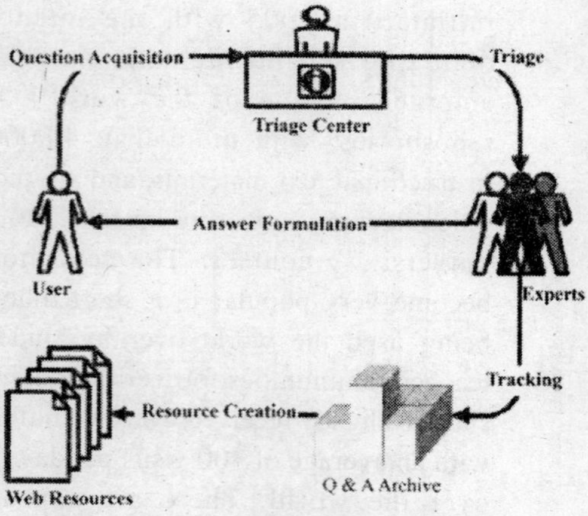

Fig. General Digital Reference Model

The above model is derived from Lankes (1998) and the Virtual Reference Desk (VRD)'s Project Ask-A software specifications document (Virtual Reference Desk Project 1998). This model consists of five steps:

(*a*) *Question acquisition* is a means of taking a patron's questions from e-mail, web forms, chat, or embedded applications.

(*b*) *Triage* is the assignment and routing of a question to a digital reference service, and to a reference or subject expert within a service. This step may be automated or conducted via human decision support. Triage also includes the filtering of repeated questions or out-of-scope questions.

(*c*) *Answer formulation* includes factors for creating good answers such as age and cultural appropriateness. Answers are also sent to the user at this point.

(*d*) *Tracking* is the quantitative and qualitative monitoring of repeat questions for trends. Tracking allows the identification of hot topics and may indicate where gaps exist in the collection.

Resource creation concerns the use of tracking data to build or expand collections and better meet users' information needs.

81. Arrange in sequence the following books authored by S.R. Ranganathan in order of their first publication.

(*a*) Documentation Genesis and Development, 1951

(*b*) Library Manual, 1951

(*c*) Classified Catalogue Code, 1934

(*d*) Prolegomena to Library Classification, 1937

82. The layers of the OSI Model are:

- Layer 1, physical layer, for transmission of bits on a link
- Layer 2, data-link layer (DLL), for transmission of frames on a link
- Layer 3, network layer, for transmission of packets across a subnet
- Layer 4, transport layer, for transmission of messages end to end between two hosts
- Layer 5, session layer, for set up and management of an end-to-end communication
- Layer 6, presentation layer, for formatting, encryption, and compression of data
- Layer 7, application layer, for network services (e-mail, file transfer, remote access, etc.)

83. Arrange the following reference and information sources according to their first year of publication:

(*a*) Europa Year - Book, 1926

(*b*) Whitaker's Almanac, 1868

(*c*) Guinness Book of World Records, 1955

(*d*) Statemen's Year - Book, 1864

84. Arrange the following with their year of establishment in ascending order :

(*a*) American National Standards Institute, 1918

(*b*) International Telegraph Union, 1965

(*c*) Internet Engineering Task Force, 1986

(*d*) World Wide Web Consortium, 1964

85. Arrange the following by their year of creation in ascending order :
(*a*) Moris Worm, 1988
(*b*) Creeper Virus, 1971
(*c*) Storm Botnet, 2007
(*d*) Animal (Trojan), 1975

87. The Copyright Act, 1957 protects original literary, dramatic, musical and artistic works and cinematograph films and sound recordings from unauthorized uses. Unlike the case with patents, copyright protects the expressions and not the ideas.

Acquisition of copyright is automatic and it does not require any formality. Copyright comes into existence as soon as a work is created and no formality is required to be completed for acquiring copyright. However, certificate of registration of copyright and the entries made therein serve as prima facie evidence in a court of law with reference to dispute relating to ownership of copyright.

Copyright under the Berne Convention must be automatic; it is prohibited to require formal registration. However, when the United States joined the Convention on 1 March, 1989, it continued to make statutory damages and attorney's fees only available for registered works.

88. Yahoo! was founded in 1994 and was started at Stanford University, USA by Jerry Wang and David Filo, who were Electrical Engineering graduate students when they created a website named 'Jerry and David's Guide to the World Wide Web'. The Guide was a directory of other websites, organized in a hierarchy, as opposed to a searchable index of pages. In this way it was not a search engine as such. In April 1994, Jerry and David's Guide to the World Wide Web was renamed "Yahoo!". The word "YAHOO" is an acronym for 'Yet Another Hierarchically Organized Oracle' or 'Yet Another Hierarchical Officious Oracle'. Oracle is the database management company of California USA. The yahoo.com domain was created on January 18, 1995.

MetaCrawler is a search engine. It is a registered trademark of InfoSpace and was created by Erik Selberg. It was originally a metasearch engine, as its name suggests. Throughout its lifetime it combined web search results from sources including Google, Yahoo!, Bing (formerly Live Search), Ask.com, About.com, MIVA, LookSmart and other search engine programs. MetaCrawler also provided users the option to search for images, video, news, business and personal telephone directories, and for a while even audio.

89. Federated search was developed to provide simplified and centralized access for all the new electronic content that libraries were acquiring. Access to this content was frequently "siloed" by a myriad of competing database products and online interfaces, resulting in user frustration and confusion with all the options on library webpages. Federated search, also known as metasearch or broadcast searching, utilizes communications standards (most frequently, Z39.50) to translate a single search query across multiple search platforms. Federated search products-including Metalib (Ex Libris), 360 Search (Serials Solutions), and Webfeat (Webfeat) came on the market in 2003 and 2004, allowing libraries to purchase a search tool that would allow searching of many databases simultaneously. Most OPAC products are Z39.50 compliant, making it possible for libraries to include the catalog data along with electronic database content.

Federated search was a leap forward, but it had its limitations. It was often slow to retrieve items across all the databases. Database subscriptions that had a low number of concurrent users allowed could frequently be tied up by federated searching if a library was not careful in its selection of resources to include. Vendors developed connectors to databases and electronic resources in high demand, but libraries with specialized collections often had to pay to have connectors built for their more unusual databases and electronic content sources. If a database changed its structure or interface, the related connector would break, and the database would no longer be available until the connector was updated. Of most concern was that federated search tools by their nature demanded a dumbing down of search queries to allow them to work across all the disparate search interfaces and database structures.

90. Web Portal (Web-Portal): Specially-designed Webpage of a Website that brings information together from diverse sources in a uniform way. Usually, each information source gets its dedicated area on the page for displaying information (a portlet); often, the user can configure which ones to display. Variants of portals include Mashups-Web application hybrids-and intranet "dashboards" for executives and managers.

Previous Years' Paper (Solved)

National Testing Agency (NTA)

UGC-NET Junior Research Fellowship & Assistant Professor Eligibility Exam

Library and Information Science, June-2020

(Online exam, held on 25/09/2020)

PAPER-II

Note: *This paper contains **hundred (100)** objective type questions of two (2) marks each. All questions are compulsory.*

1. Who developed the ABX model of communication?
A. Dean C. Barnlund
B. Westley & MacLean
C. Shannon & Weaver
D. Theodore M Newcomb

2. Who has developed the 'Geneva Declaration of Principles'?
A. WSIS B. UNESCO
C. IFLA D. WIPO

3. What is Marrakesh Treaty of WIPO?
A. Protection of Government Publications.
B. Protection of authors' rights in the digital environment.
C. Facilitates books for visually impaired.
D. Protection of Olympic symbol from commercial use.

4. When knowledge is derived by employing logic and reason over sensory experience, it is termed as:
A. Empiricism B. Rationalism
C. Historicism D. Pragmatism

5. Which Law of Library Science enunciated by S.R. Ranganathan has been reinterpreted by OCLC Research group as, "Develop the physical and technical infrastructure needed to deliver physical and digital material'?
A. 'Every reader his/her book'
B. 'Books are for use'
C. 'Save the time of the reader'
D. 'Every book its reader'

6. The theme of IFLAWLIC 2020, Dublin is:
A. 4th Industrial Revolution
B. World Wide Open Access
C. Library Services for Children
D. Joint Climate Change

7. The Calcutta Public Library was established largely at the initiative of
A. K.M. Asadullah B. Lord Curzon
C. F.P Strong D. J. H. Stocqueler

8. Who published 'DA2I 2019' series of reports?
A. ALA B. IFLA
C. UNESCO D. CILIP

9. Who is the publisher of The Statesman's Yearbook, 155th edition?
A. Palgrave Macmillan
B. Harper Collins
C. Simon & Schuster
D. Hachette Livre

10. What is ORCID?
A. Access to open access peer-reviewed journals.
B. Registry connecting research and researchers.
C. Commercial network for scientists and researchers.
D. Joint service of OAPEN and Open Edition.

11. What is Entrez?
A. Web portal for Engineering
B. Web portal for Health
C. Subject Gateway for Social Sciences
D. Subject Gateway for Humanities and Social Sciences

12. What is Library Thing?
A. Online Library of Education
B. Bibliography of Computer Science

C. Free books in humanities and Social Sciences
D. Online cataloguing service

13. In the FRSAD model, when 'themas' are semantically or conceptually connected and cooccurring but are not hierarchically related, the knowledge organization system may explicitly indicate and link them as:
A. Associative relationships
B. Instance relationships
C. Generic relationships
D. Perspective hierarchical relationships

14. Which of the following is a searching platform for academic and research publications?
A. Research Gate B. Google Scholar
C. Mendeley D. Academia

15. Which one of the following is NOT a bookmarking website?
A. Delicious.com B. Netvouz.com
C. Diigo.com D. Revish.com

16. 'Podcast' means
A. Blog post containing audio files
B. Blog post containing video files
C. Blog post containing audio and video files
D. Blog post containing image files.

17. Which one of the following is the special feature in the evaluation criteria of maps and atlases?
A. Synthetic search
B. Grid system
C. Citations
D. Credibility of the publisher

18. DESIDOC was formerly known as:
A. Bureau of Scientific Documentation.
B. Scientific information Bureau.
C. Scientific Information Center.
D. Defense Information Centre.

19. Some terms may be related to more than one broader term and more than one set of narrower terms.

Such relationship is called
A. Equivalence relationship
B. Instance relationship
C. Non-hierarchical relationship
D. Poly-hierarchical relationship

20. Which one of the following is NOT part of Administrative metadata?
A. Acquisition information
B. File characteristics
C. Relationship data
D. Use information

21. ISBD now contains how many areas of description?
A. Seven B. Eight
C. Nine D. Ten

22. A link in chain indexing system which does NOT represent a subject with a definite name, but represents a connecting symbol or a digit indicating any relation is known as
A. False link B. Missing Link
C. Sought Link D. Unsought Link

23. Which one of the following is the element of the marketing mix?
A. People B. Purchase
C. Power D. Product

24. Which one of the following is NOT an open-source discovery interface?
A. Blacklight
B. Vufind
C. extensible Catalog
D. Orchid

25. Who developed the 'Force Field Theory' of change?
A. Max Weber B. Frederick Herzberg
C. Kurt Lewin D. Elton Mayo

26. The practice of giving employees a high degree of control over their work is often considered as:
A. Job Engineering B. Job Enlargement
C. Job Enrichment D. Job Rotation

27. Who wrote the first hypertext solution "Memex"?
A. Vannevar Bush B. Judea Pearl
C. Tim Berners-Lee D. John McCarthy

28. Which one of the following is the IEEE standard for Wimax?

A. IEEE 802.3 B. IEEE 802.11
C. IEEE 802.15 D. IEEE 802.16

29. Telegraph Multiplexer was invented by:
A. S.F. B. Morse B. Emile Baudot
C. Grahm Bell D. Konrad Zuse

30. How many colour shades will be displayed in an 11-bite image?
A. 512 B. 256
C. 2048 D. 1024

31. OCLC released WorldCat on Blu-ray disc in which year?
A. 2008 B. 2009
C. 2010 D. 2011

32. The first public version of the content management system — 'Ghost' was released with which one of the following names?
A. Content Pro B. Typo3
C. Grav D. Kerouac

33. Which one of the following is the Linked Open Data project of Thomson Reuters?
A. UMBEL B. Open Calais
C. GRID D. Geo Names

34. Which one of these metadata sets is NOT predefined in GSDL?
A. Dublin Core B. PREMIS
C. RFC 1807 D. NZGLS

35. Which one of the following measures the impact of scholarship and research through online interaction?
A. Scientometrics B. Altmetrics
C. Bibliometrics D. Librametrics

36. Studies that are longitudinal and prospective in nature and collect information from the same respondents are known as:
A. Case Studies B. Cohort Studies
C. Panel Studies D. Trend Studies

37. Which one of the following is NOT a type of measurement scale?
A. Interval Scale B. Nominal Scale
C. Ordinal Scale D. Ratio Scale

38. In a sampling procedure, if you select every 10th name on a list or every 15th house on a street, it is known as:
A. Deliberate sampling
B. Simple random sampling
C. Systematic sampling
D. Stratified sampling

39. Who will be considered for the Access Point of the Main Entry for the following book according to AACR-11?
Title page: Buildings/by/Ralph E. Ellsworth
Shelving/by/Louis Kaplan
Strange warehouses/by/Je]rrold Orne
A. Buildings
B. Ellsworth, Ralph E.
C Kaplan, Louis
D. Orne, Jerrold

40. 'The Seven Faces of Information Literacy' was coined by:
A. Christini Susan Bruce
B. SCONUL
C. Steven Bob
D. Annette Lamb

41. Identify the intermediaries of an information industry among the following
(*a*) Invisible colleges
(*b*) Online Vendors
(*c*) Computer Programmers
(*d*) Students and Research Scholars

Choose the most appropriate answer from the options given below:
A. (*a*) and (*b*) only
B. (*b*) and (*c*) only
C. (*c*) and (*d*) only
D. (*a*) and (*d*) only

42. Which of the following are components of the Knowledge Pentagon as defined by the National Knowledge Commission (2006-2009)?
(*a*) Creation of Knowledge
(*b*) Knowledge Organization
(*c*) Knowledge Management
(*d*) Knowledge Application

Choose the correct answer from the options given below:
A. (*a*) and (*b*) only B. (*b*) and (*c*) only
C. (*a*) and (*d*) only D. (*b*) and (*d*) only

43. Which of the following are the component pillars of 'Knowledge Society' as reflected in UNESCO' s "Building Knowledge Societies'?
(*a*) Freedom of expression
(*b*) Internet Governance
(*c*) Quality Education for all
(*d*) Information Security

Choose the correct answer from the options given below:
A. (*a*) and (*b*) only B. (*b*) and (*c*) only
C. (*a*) and (*d*) only D. (*a*) and (*c*) only

44. Which of the following are e-PG Pathshala modules?
(*a*) e-Granth (*b*) e-Guru
(*c*) e-Pathya (*d*) e-Adhyayan

Choose the most appropriate answer from the options given below:
A. (*a*) and (*c*) only B. (*c*) and (*d*) only
C. (*b*) and (*d*) only D. (*a*) and (*d*) only

45. Identify the publications of National Library of India, Kolkata from the following:
(*a*) IndexTranslationum Indicarum
(*b*) Index Indiana
(*c*) Indian National Bibliography
(*d*) A Bibliography of Dictionaries and Encyclopedias in Indian Languages,1964

Choose the correct answer from the options given below:
A. (*a*) and (*b*) only B. (*b*) and (*d*) only
C. (*c*) and (*d*) only D. (*a*) and (*d*) only

46. Identify the components of the 'PLUS' model of Information Literacy from the following:
(*a*) People (*b*) Location
(*c*) Use (*d*) Search

Choose the correct answer from the options given below:
A. (*b*) and (*d*) only B. (*c*) and (*d*) only
C. (*b*) and (*c*) only D. (*a*) and (*c*) only

47. Which of the following are tertiary sources of Information?
(*a*) World List of Social Science Periodicals, UNESCO
(*b*) The Europa World of Learning
(*c*) Advances in Electrical & Computer Engineering
(*d*) Current Contents

Choose the correct answer from the options given below:
A. (*a*) and (*b*) only B. (*a*) and (*c*) only
C. (*b*) and (*d*) only D. (*c*) and (*d*) only

48. Which of the following are the Subject Gateways?
(*a*) BIOME
(*b*) Internet Public Library (iPL2)
(*c*) LIS Learning
(*d*) INFOPORT

Choose the correct answer from the options given below:
A. (*a*) and (*c*) only B. (*b*) and (*d*) only
C. (*a*) and (*b*) only D. (*a*) and (*d*) only

49. Which of the following are human sources of information?
(*a*) Patent attorneys
(*b*) Database Vendors
(*c*) Library Consultants
(*d*) Press and Media

Choose the most appropriate answer from the options given below:
A. (*a*) and (*b*) only B. (*b*) and (*c*) only
C. (*a*) and (*c*) only D. (*b*) and (*d*) only

50. Identify the online tools for cataloguing books:
(*a*) Library Thing (*b*) Good Reads
(*c*) Scoop (*d*) Reddit

Choose the correct answer from the options given below:
A. (*a*) and (*b*) only B. (*b*) and (*c*) only
C. (*c*) and (*d*) only D. (*b*) and (*d*) only

51. From the following, identify the mobile applications for image recognition developed by Google:
(*a*) Google Goggles (*b*) Google Specs
(*c*) Google Glass (*d*) Google Lens

Choose the correct answer from the options given below:
A. (*a*) and (*b*) only B. (*b*) and (*c*) only
C. (*c*) and (*d*) only D. (*a*) and (*d*) only

52. Which of the following are true about a folksonomy?

(*a*) It is a user-generated classification.

(*b*) It is an activity of collaborative categorization.

(*c*) It has precision in language and syndetic structure.

(*d*) It reflects general populace's language and needs.

Choose the correct answer from the options given below:

A. (*a*), (*b*) and (*d*) only

B. (*b*), (*c*) and (*d*) only

C. (*a*), (*b*) and (*c*) only

D. (*a*), (*c*) and (*d*) only

53. From the following, identify the core classes as given in the 'BIBFRAME model':

(*a*) Agents (*b*) Events

(*c*) Item (*d*) Subjects

Choose the correct answer from the options given below:

A. (*a*), (*b*) and (*c*) only

B. (*a*), (*b*) and (*d*) only

C. (*b*), (*c*) and (*d*) only

D. (*a*), (*c*) and (*d*) only

54. Which two of the following are benefits of the PEST analysis?

(*a*) Analysis of the larger quantity of data at ease is feasible.

(*b*) Heightened attention to Potential threats and dangers.

(*c*) Helps users to understand the relationship among activities.

(*d*) More effective long-term strategic planning.

Choose the correct answer from the options given below:

A. (*a*) and (*b*) only B. (*b*) and (*c*) only

C. (*c*) and (*d*) only D. (*b*) and (*d*) only

55. From the following, identify the Management Scientists who belong to the Classical Management Era:

(*a*) G.E. Mayo (*b*) F.W. Taylor

(*c*) Henri Fayol (*d*) D. McGregor

Choose the correct answer from the options given below:

A. (*a*) and (*b*) only B. (*b*) and (*c*) only

C. (*c*) and (*d*) only D. (*a*) and (*d*) only

56. Which of the following are principles of TQM?

(*a*) Stress on quantitative transactions only

(*b*) Non-adaptable to changes

(*c*) Customer focus

(*d*) Continuous Improvement

Choose the correct answer from the options given below:

A. (*a*) and (*b*) only B. (*b*) and (*c*) only

C. (*b*) and (*d*) only D. (*c*) and (*d*) only

57. Identify fifth-generation programming languages from the following

(*a*) Java (*b*) Mercury and OPS5

(*c*) PROLOG (*d*) SQL

Choose the correct answer from the options given below:

A. (*a*) and (*b*) only B. (*b*) and (*c*) only

C. (*c*) and (*d*) only D. (*a*) and (*d*) only

58. Name the scientists who developed the Google Search engine:

(*a*) Larry Page (*b*) David Filo

(*c*) Jerry Yang (*d*) Sergey Brin

Choose the correct answer from the options given below:

A. (*a*) and (*d*) only B. (*b*) and (*c*) only

C. (*a*) and (*c*) only D. (*b*) and (*d*) only

59. Identify unguided media of telecommunication from the following:

(*a*) Optical fibre cable

(*b*) Infrared

(*c*) Microwave

(*d*) Co-Axial cable

Choose the correct answer from the options given below:

A. (*a*) and (*c*) only B. (*b*) and (*c*) only

C. (*c*) and (*d*) only D. (*a*) and (*d*) only

60. Quality of a digital file is affected by:

(*a*) Dynamic range (*b*) Data architecture

(*c*) Resolution (*d*) Data integration

Choose the correct answer from the options given below:

A. (*a*) and (*c*) only B. (*b*) and (*d*) only

C. (*a*) and (*b*) only D. (*c*) and (*d*) only

61. Which of the following are proprietary file formats?

(*a*) MrSID (*b*) GIF
(*c*) RAR (*d*) TIFF

Choose the correct answer from the options given below:

A. (*a*) and (*b*) only B. (*b*) and (*d*) only
C. (*c*) and (*d*) only D. (*a*) and (*c*) only

62. Which of the following are suitable examples of IaaS?

(*a*) Eucalyptus (*b*) Open Nebula
(*c*) Fresh Books (*d*) Microsoft Azure

Choose the correct answer from the options given below:

A. A and B only B. B and C only
C. C and D only D. A and D only

63. From the following, identify the non-Parametric tests of hypotheses:

(*a*) Chi-square test (*b*) F-Test
(*c*) Signed Rank test (*d*) Rank Sum test

Choose the correct answer from the options given below:

A. (*a*) and (*b*) only B. (*b*) and (*c*) only
C. (*c*) and (*d*) only D. (*a*) and (*c*) only

64. Which of the following are formal experimental designs?

(*a*) Randomized block design
(*b*) Latin square design
(*c*) Before and after without control design
(*d*) Factorial design

Choose the correct answer from the options given below:

A. (*a*), (*c*) and (*d*) only
B. (*a*), (*b*) and (*d*) only
C. (*b*), (*c*) and (*d*) only
D. (*a*), (*b*) and (*c*) only

65. From the following, identify the System/Networks that came into existence in 1982:

(*a*) ERNET (*b*) FORSA
(*c*) ENVIS (*d*) CONCERT

Choose the correct answer from the options given below:

A. (*a*) and (*b*) only B. (*b*) and (*c*) only
C. (*c*) and (*d*) only D. (*a*) and (*d*) only

66. Match List I with List II

List-I **Library Consortia**	***List-II*** **Country/Place of origin**
(*a*) CURL	(*i*) South Africa
(*b*) EIFL	(*ii*) UK
(*c*) SANLIC	(*iii*) Europe
(*d*) CONCERT	(*iv*) Taiwan

Choose the correct answer from the options given below:

	(*a*)	(*b*)	(*c*)	(*d*)
A.	(*iii*)	(*ii*)	(*i*)	(*iv*)
B.	(*ii*)	(*iv*)	(*i*)	(*iii*)
C.	(*ii*)	(*i*)	(*iv*)	(*iii*)
D.	(*ii*)	(*iii*)	(*i*)	(*iv*)

67. Match List I with List II

List-I ***Books***	***List-II*** ***Authors***
(*a*) The Changing Academic Library	(*i*) Jose-Marie Griffiths
(*b*) Planning Public Library Buildings	(*ii*) John Budd
(*c*) Introduction to Public Librarianship	(*iii*) Michael Dewe
(*d*) Special Libraries	(*iv*) Kathleen de la Pena McCook

Choose the correct answer from the options given below:

	(*a*)	(*b*)	(*c*)	(*d*)
A.	(*ii*)	(*iii*)	(*iv*)	(*i*)
B.	(*ii*)	(*i*)	(*iii*)	(*iv*)
C.	(*iii*)	(*ii*)	(*i*)	(*iv*)
D.	(*i*)	(*iii*)	(*iv*)	(*ii*)

68. Match List I with List II

List-I ***Functional Explanation***	***List-II*** ***Type of bibliography***
(*a*) Study of the book as a physical entity	(*i*) Systematic bibliography
(*b*) Critical analysis of placing and timing of books	(*ii*) Descriptive bibliography
(*c*) Study of books as intellectual entities	(*iii*) Trade bibliography
(*d*) Book bibliographies	(*iv*) Historical bibliography

Choose the correct answer from the options given below:

	(a)	(b)	(c)	(d)
A.	(iii)	(ii)	(iv)	(i)
B.	(ii)	(iv)	(i)	(iii)
C.	(i)	(iii)	(ii)	(iv)
D.	(iv)	(i)	(iii)	(ii)

69. Match List I with List II

List-I *Reference Source*	*List-II* *Publisher*
(a) Statistical Yearbook of India	(i) INFA, New Delhi
(b) India, Who's Who	(ii) Ministry of Culture, Government of India
(c) India, A Reference Annual	(iii) Ministry of Statistics and Programme Implementation, Government of India
(d) Indian Literature Abroad	(iv) Publication Division, Ministry of Information and Broadcasting

Choose the correct answer from the options given below:

	(a)	(b)	(c)	(d)
A.	(iii)	(i)	(iv)	(ii)
B.	(ii)	(iii)	(i)	(iv)
C.	(i)	(iv)	(ii)	(iii)
D.	(iv)	(iii)	(i)	(ii)

70. Match List I with List II

List-I *IACR Products*	*List-II* *Types*
(a) Trend related publications	(i) Handbooks
(b) Condensing publications	(ii) Indexing periodicals
(c) Ready reference publications	(iii) State of the art report
(d) Trade and industry-related publications	(iv) Technical reports

Choose the correct answer from the options given below:

	(a)	(b)	(c)	(d)
A.	(i)	(ii)	(iii)	(iv)
B.	(ii)	(iii)	(iv)	(i)
C.	(iii)	(ii)	(i)	(iv)
D.	(iv)	(i)	(ii)	(iii)

71. Match List I with List II

List-I *Thinker*	*List-II* *Theory*
(a) Max Weber	(i) Human Relations
(b) Elton Mayo	(ii) Administrative Management
(c) F.W. Taylor	(iii) Theory of Bureaucracy
(d) Henri Fayol	(iv) Scientific Management

Choose the correct answer from the options given below:

	(a)	(b)	(c)	(d)
A.	(i)	(iii)	(ii)	(iv)
B.	(ii)	(i)	(iv)	(iii)
C.	(iii)	(i)	(iv)	(ii)
D.	(iv)	(i)	(ii)	(iii)

72. Match List I with List II

List-I *Programming Language*	*List-II* *Inventor*
(a) Java	(i) James A. Gosling
(b) C	(ii) Guido van Rossum
(c) Lisp	(iii) Dennis Ritchie
(d) Python	(iv) John McCarthy

Choose the correct answer from the options given below:

	(a)	(b)	(c)	(d)
A.	(ii)	(iii)	(iv)	(i)
B.	(iv)	(ii)	(iii)	(i)
C.	(iii)	(i)	(ii)	(iv)
D.	(i)	(iii)	(iv)	(ii)

73. Match List I with List II

List-I *Content Management Software*	*List-II* *Developers*
(a) Joomla	(i) Dries Buytaert
(b) Drupal	(ii) Hubert Burda Media
(c) Thunder	(iii) Open Source Matters
(d) Textpattern	(iv) Dean Allen

Choose the correct answer from the options given below:

	(a)	(b)	(c)	(d)
A.	(iii)	(iv)	(i)	(ii)
B.	(ii)	(iii)	(iv)	(i)
C.	(iii)	(i)	(ii)	(iv)
D.	(i)	(ii)	(iv)	(iii)

74. Match List I with List II

List-I *Law*	*List-II* *Explanation*
(a) Bradford's Law	(i) Number of journals/ journal citations
(b) Lotka's Law	(ii) Occurrence of words
(c) Zipf's Law	(iii) Author productivity
(d) Garfield's Law of Concentration	(iv) Law of scattering

Choose the correct answer from the options given below:

	(a)	(b)	(c)	(d)
A.	(iv)	(iii)	(ii)	(i)
B.	(iii)	(iv)	(i)	(ii)
C.	(ii)	(i)	(iii)	(iv)
D.	(i)	(ii)	(iv)	(iii)

75. Match List I with List II

List-I *Theories*	*List-II* *Theorist*
(a) MBO	(i) Kelley and Walker
(b) PEST	(ii) Peter Drucker
(c) CPM	(iii) Albert Humphrey
(d) SWOT	(iv) Francis Aguilar

Choose the correct answer from the options given below:

	(a)	(b)	(c)	(d)
A.	(iii)	(iv)	(i)	(ii)
B.	(ii)	(iv)	(i)	(iii)
C.	(i)	(ii)	(iv)	(iii)
D.	(iv)	(iii)	(ii)	(i)

76. Arrange in sequence, the following communication models in order of their emergence:

(a) The Dance Model of Harold Dwight Lasswell
(b) Circular Model of Lee Thayer
(c) SMCR Model of David Kenneth Berio
(d) Interactive Model of Wilbur Schramm

Choose the correct answer from the options given below

A. (a), (c), (b), (d) B. (c), (d), (a), (b)
C. (b), (d), (d), (c) D. (a), (a), (c), (b)

77. Arrange the following Public Libraries Acts according to their years of enactment in ascending order:

(a) Kerala (b) Andhra Pradesh
(c) Bihar (d) Mizoram

Choose the correct answer from the options given below:

A. (b), (a), (d), (c) B. (b), (d), (a), (c)
C. (a), (d), (b), (c) D. (a), (b), (d), (c)

78. Arrange in sequence the following geographical reference sources, in order of their first publication.

(a) The Statesman's Yearbook and World Gazetteer, Macmillan co.
(b) The Imperial Gazetteer of India
(c) Chamber's World Gazetteer
(d) Merriam-Webster's Geographical Dictionary

Choose the correct answer from the options given below:

A. (c), (d), (a), (b) B. (b), (d), (c), (a)
C. (d), (b), (a), (c) D. (a), (c), (b), (d)

79. Arrange the following Information Systems, according to their years of origin:

(a) INIS (b) AGRIS
(c) INSPEC (d) MEDLARS
(e) ENVIS

Choose the correct answer from the options given below

A. (c), (a), (b), (d), (e)
B. (d), (c), (a), (b), (e)
C. (b), (a), (c), (e), (d)
D. (a), (c), (e), (d), (b)

80. Arrange the steps that are required in a general framework for compiling any IACR product as stated by Prof. A. Chatterjee:

(a) Planning and preparation
(b) Determination of scope
(c) Initiation
(d) Processing and organization of information

Choose the correct answer from the options given below:

A. (*a*), (*b*), (*c*), (*d*) B. (*b*), (*c*), (*d*), (*a*)
C. (*a*), (*c*), (*b*), (*d*) D. (*c*), (*b*), (*a*), (*d*)

81. Arrange in sequence, the steps involved in the Newark Charging System:

(*a*) Book and Membership cards are handed over to borrower while the book card is kept in charging tray

(*b*) Putting date stamp on the borrower card after taking it out from the book

(*c*) Books are presented to counter assistant along with membership card

(*d*) Membership number of the borrower is put opposite to the due date

Choose the correct answer from the options given below:

A. (*d*), (*a*), (*b*), (*c*) B. (*b*), (*c*), (*a*), (*d*)
C. (*a*), (*d*), (*c*), (*b*) D. (*c*), (*b*), (*d*), (*a*)

82. Arrange in sequence, the following functional entities of the OASIS Reference Model that occur in the digital information life cycle:

(*a*) Administration
(*b*) Archival storage
(*c*) Access
(*d*) Digital management
(*e*) Ingest

Choose the correct answer from the options given below:

A. (*a*), (*b*), (*c*), (*d*), (*e*)
B. (*b*), (*c*), (*d*), (*e*), (*a*)
C. (*c*), (*a*), (*b*), (*e*), (*d*)
D. (*e*), (*b*), (*d*), (*c*), (*a*)

83. Arrange expert systems in their ascending order of development:

(*a*) Mycin
(*b*) ANSWER MAN
(*c*) DENDRAL
(*d*) Journal Expert Selector
(*e*) Prospector

Choose the correct answer from the options given below:

A. (*b*), (*d*), (*e*), (*a*), (*c*)
B. (*a*), (*c*), (*b*), (*e*), (*d*)
C. (*e*), (*b*), (*c*), (*d*), (*a*)
D. (*c*), (*a*), (*e*), (*b*), (*d*)

84. Arrange in sequence, the following major phases involved in a case study:

(*a*) Diagnosis and identification of causal factors as a basis for developmental treatment

(*b*) Recognition and determination of the status of the phenomenon

(*c*) Collection of data, the examination of the given phenomenon

(*d*) Application of remedial measures

Choose the correct answer from the options given below:

A. (*a*), (*b*), (*c*), (*d*) B. (*b*), (*c*), (*a*), (*d*)
C. (*a*), (*c*), (*d*), (*b*) D. (*c*), (*b*), (*a*), (*d*)

85. Arrange the following Public Library Acts according to their years of enactment in ascending order:

(*a*) Goa (*b*) Chhattisgarh
(*c*) Rajasthan (*d*) Odisha

Choose the correct answer from the options given below

A. (*a*), (*b*), (*d*), (*c*) B. (*a*), (*d*), (*c*), (*b*)
C. (*d*), (*c*), (*a*), (*b*) D. (*d*), (*b*), (*c*), (*a*)

86. Given below are two statements, one is labelled as Assertion A and other one labelled as Reason R.

Assertion (A) : The organizers of a public musical performance have to obtain permission from the composer for the sound recording used.

Reason (R) : It is necessary to obtain the licences from each and every right owner in the sound recording prior to such a performance in public.

In light of the above statements, choose the correct answer from the options given below:

A. Both A and R are true and R is the correct explanation of A
B. Both A and R are true, but R is NOT the correct explanation of A
C. A is true, but R is false
D. A is false, but R is true

87. Given below are two statements, one is labelled as Assertion A and other one labelled as Reason R.

Assertion (A) : Preparation of critical abstracts requires subject expertise and is a time-consuming job.

Reason (R) : In a critical abstract the abstractor includes his /her opinion and interpretations.

In light of the above statements, choose the most appropriate answer from the options given below:

A. Both A and R are correct and R is the correct explanation of A
B. Both A and R are correct, but R is NOT the correct explanation of A
C. A is correct, but R is not correct
D. A is not correct, but R is correct

88. Given below are two statements, one is labelled as Assertion A and other one labelled as Reason R.

Assertion (A) : Data normalization is intended to allow better matching.

Reason (R) : As users are always precise in the placement of such works as diacritics and commas.

In light of the above statements, choose the correct answer from the options given below:

A. Both A and R are true and R is the correct explanation of A
B. Both A and R are true, but R is NOT the correct explanation of A
C. A is true, but R is false
D. A is false, but R is true

89. Given below are two statements, one is labelled as Assertion A and other one labelled as Reason R.

Assertion (A) : In the present online environment, there is no need for librarians to evaluate reference sources on the web.

Reason (R) : There are publications which help the librarians to select and evaluate the reference collection for a particular library in print or online.

In light of the above statements, choose the most appropriate answer from the options given below:

A. Both A and R are correct and R is the correct explanation of A
B. Both A and R are correct, but R is NOT the correct explanation of A
C. A is correct, but R is not correct
D. A is not correct, but R is correct.

90. Given below are two statements, one is labelled as Assertion A and other one labelled as Reason R.

Assertion (A) : On decompression of a compressed zip file, the data loss is minimal.

Reason (R) : Zip data compression technique is based on lossy compression.

In light of the above statements, choose the correct answer from the options given below:

A. Both A and R are true and R is the correct explanation of A
B. Both A and R are true, but R is NOT the correct explanation of A
C. A is true, but R is false
D. A is false, but R is true

Directions (Q. No. 91-95): *Read the passage given below and answer the questions that follow.*

Communication on WhatsApp has been encrypted since 2016, which affords the app an aura of security and trust, and further distinguishes it from mainstream platforms that have been shown to compromise user privacy (Zanon, 2018). However, these claims must be measured against countering arguments. Research has argued that WhatsApp's end-to-end encryption is performative rather than being a core value of the company (Santos and Faure, 2018) - plus encryption does not necessarily mean that Facebook is not in a position to collect Whats App data (see Zanon, 2018). Yet other scholars identify encrypted chat apps as a 'safer' space for activists and ordinary citizens to share information and engage in civic and political networking and action, particularly in contexts where legacy media and other social media ave heavily censored and surveilled by the state [Khazraee and Losey, 2016; Dencik, et al, 2016 Hintz, et al, 2019) Despite the perception that end-to-end encryption means that surveillance is limited on WhatsApp, it also means that content circulates in a manner largely unregulated and unmoderated by the platform. This can be prob ematic, because as WhatsApp becomes an increasingly important channel for the dissemination of news (Newman, et al., 2018) and meme culture (Ballesteros Doncel, 2016; Ncube, 2016; Al Zidjaly, 2017), so does it play an important role in facilitating "information disorder" the spread of misinformation, disinformation, and malinformation in closed groups not subjected to any kind of platform moderation (Wardle and Derakshan, 2017).

91. Which one of the following is the primary reason for Whatsapp to get the trust of public?
A. User Privacy B. Free Service
C. Encryption D. Real-time sharing

92. Why WhatsApp encryption is performative as stated by Santos and Faure?
A. Facebook can collect WhatsApp data.
B. No end-to-end encryption.
C. Compromised user privacy.
D. No core value of the company.

93. Why is WhatsApp considered as a 'safer' space for citizens?
A. Heavily censored B. Encrypted chat app
C. State surveillance D. Easy sharing

94. Which one of the following is NOT perceived as end-to-end encryption?
A. Content is unregulated
B. Content is unmoderated
C. Unlimited Surveillance
D. Meme culture

95. According to Wardle and Derakshan, what is the reason for 'information disorder' of WhatApp?
A. Lack of platform moderation
B. Political networking
C. Increasingly a news channel
D. Encrypted conversations

Directions (Q. No. 96-100): *Read the following passage carefully and answer the questions that follow.*

More than two decades ago we entered a new world where a mouse no longer referred to Mickey; a floppy rarely described a hat and Apple and BlackBerry became proper nouns. We have now entered a universe where "twittering" is no longer the preserve of birds; communication in addition to food is "Delicious", and to have an avatar in a Second Life does not require the penance of an Asian mystic. We have, in short, entered the universe of Reference 2.0.

This universe has moved at such a fast clip that defining it and understanding its ramifications continue to skitter across many viewpoints. That goal of effective reference remains timeless, namely, the satisfaction of the user. However, the dramatic technology tools thrown up by Web 2.0 in which mass participation and web socialization have become both the norm and the expectation have added a new dimension to business as usual.

96. More than two decades ago, we entered a new world where:
A. A mouse referred to a longer Mickey
B. A floppy always described a rare hat
C. Apple became BlackBerry
D. Blackberry became a proper noun

97. We have now entered a universe where:
A. "Twittering" is not the preserve of birds
B. Communication is a delicious food
C. An avatar is not required in Second Life
D. Second Life is an Asian mystic

98. In this passage, what has moved at such a fast clip?
A. Universe of Knowledge
B. Universe of Reference 2.0
C. Universe of our world
D. Universe of second life

99. The goal of effective reference is to:
A. Remain timeless
B. Name the user
C. Satisfy the user
D. Skitter across many viewpoints

100. What has become both the norm and the expectation?
A. Dramatic technological tools
B. Web 2.0
C. Business
D. Mass participation

ANSWERS

1	2	3	4	5	6	7	8	9	10
D	A	C	B	B	*	D	B	A	B
11	**12**	**13**	**14**	**15**	**16**	**17**	**18**	**19**	**20**
B	D	A	B	D	A	B	B	D	C
21	**22**	**23**	**24**	**25**	**26**	**27**	**28**	**29**	**30**
C	A	D	D	C	C	A	D	B	C
31	**32**	**33**	**34**	**35**	**36**	**37**	**38**	**39**	**40**
A	D	B	B	B	C	*	C	B	A
41	**42**	**43**	**44**	**45**	**46**	**47**	**48**	**49**	**50**
A	C	D	B	D	C	A	D	C	A
51	**52**	**53**	**54**	**55**	**56**	**57**	**58**	**59**	**60**
D	A	B	D	B	D	B	A	B	A
61	**62**	**63**	**64**	**65**	**66**	**67**	**68**	**69**	**70**
D	A, D	C, D	B	B	D	A	B	A	C
71	**72**	**73**	**74**	**75**	**76**	**77**	**78**	**79**	**80**
C	D	C	A	B	D	A	B	B	D
81	**82**	**83**	**84**	**85**	**86**	**87**	**88**	**89**	**90**
D	*	D	B	B	A	A	C	D	C
91	**92**	**93**	**94**	**95**	**96**	**97**	**98**	**99**	**100**
C	A	B	C	A	D	A	B	C	D

EXPLANATORY ANSWERS

1. Newcomb's model of communication outlined some interesting facts with his ABX model, his model states that internal relations are interdependent. With A and B as the communicator and receiver and X being the social environment. Westley and Mac Lean's model is an extension of Theodore Newcomb's model. These models are specifically adopted for the mass media.

   Newcomb took a new approach to the communication process. The main purpose of this theory is to introduce the role of communication in a social relationship or society and to maintain social equilibrium within the social system. He published a new social approach in field of communication which is called –ABX system which was later known as Newcomb's model.

2. The World Summit on the Information Society (WSIS) is a unique two-phase United Nations (UN) summit that was initiated in order to create an evolving multi- stakeholder platform aimed at addressing the issues raised by information and communication technologies (ICTs) through a structured and inclusive approach at the national, regional and international levels. The goal of WSIS is to achieve a common vision, desire and commitment to build a people-centric, inclusive and development-oriented Information Society where everyone can create, access, utilize and share information. The UN General Assembly Resolution 56/183 (21 December 2001) endorsed the holding of the World Summit on the Information Society (WSIS) in two phases. The first phase took place in Geneva from 10 to 12 December 2003 and the second phase took place in Tunis, from 16 to 18 November 2005. In 2003, the number of participants was 11,000 representing 175 countries and

in 2005 the number of participants was more than 19,000 representing 174 countries.

3. The WIPO-administered Marrakesh Treaty makes the production and international transfer of specially-adapted books for people with blindness or visual impairments easier. It is establishing a set of limitations and exceptions to traditional copyright law.

   The Marrakesh Treaty was adopted on June 27, 2013, and entered into force on September 30, 2016.

4. Rationalism involves using logic and reasoning to acquire new knowledge. It has long been the rival of empiricism, the doctrine that all knowledge comes from, and must be tested by, sense experience. As against this doctrine, rationalism holds reason to be a faculty that can lay hold of truths beyond the reach of sense perception, both in certainty and generality. When knowledge is derived by employing logic and reason over sensory experience, it is termed as rationalism.

5. In 1931, Shiyali Ramamrita Ranganathan, a mathematician and librarian who is widely regarded as a founder of modern library science, proposed his Five Laws of Library Science. His five laws have provided powerful guidance for generations of librarians. As a framework for evaluating library programs, policies and strategies, there is probably not a single document as widely known, respected and referenced even today, more than 80 years after its publication.

   Ranganathan and his contemporaries, even in the 1930s, probably would have considered these changes to be part of his original doctrine. After all, there were magazines, newspapers, film and audio recordings in the 30s. Microfiche had come into commercial use the decade before, and in 1924 the Computing Tabulating-Recording Company changed its name to the International Business Machines Corporation-IBM-after having revolutionized the storage of data on punch cards. In short, there is no reason to suppose that Ranganathan didn't mean for books to be a stand-in for any and all media that a library might now, or ever, collect, catalog and circulate. The idea that we would one day encode information in digital format and share it using worldwide, interconnected computers probably would not have caused Ranganathan to change his language. "Books are for use" is simply too powerful a statement and too succinct to warrant much improvement.

7. J.H. Stocqueler proposed for the establishment of a public library and a resolution to this effect was passed which declared the existence of Calcutta Public Library in 1835. The Calcutta Public Library was subsequently merged with the Imperial Library and combining the collection of a number of secretariat libraries, the Imperial Library was opened to the public on January 1903. The National Library, Kolkata is the National Library of India and the National Repository. It is also a legal deposit library of India, where books published in the country are deposited under Delivery of Books Act, 1954.

8. Development and Access to Information (DA2I, 2019) is a series of reports, led by the International Federation of Library Associations and Institutions (IFLA) in partnership with the Technology and Social Change Group, University of Washington (TASCHA), that monitor the progress countries are making towards fulfilling their commitment to promote meaningful access to information (A2I) as part of the United Nations Sustainable Development Goals.

9. The Statesman's Year book 155th edition continues to be the reference work of choice for accurate and reliable information on every country in the world. Covering political, economic, social and cultural aspects, the Yearbook is also available online for subscribing institutions. Palgrave Macmillan is the publisher of The Statesman's Yearbook, 155th edition.

10. ORCID is a non-profit organization supported by a global community of member organizations, including research institutions, publishers, funders, professional associations, service providers, and other stakeholders in the research ecosystem. It is registry connecting research and researchers.

11. The Entrez Global Query Cross-Database Search System is a federated search engine, or web portal that allows users to search many discrete health sciences databases at the National Center for Biotechnology Information (NCBI) website. The NCBI is a part of the National Library of Medicine (NLM), which is itself a department of the National Institutes of Health (NIH), which in turn is a part of the United States Department of Health and Human Services. The name "Entrez" (a greeting meaning "Come in" in French) was chosen to reflect the spirit of welcoming the public to search the content available from the NLM.

12. Library Thing is an online service to help people catalog their books easily. You can access your catalog from anywhere-even on your mobile phone. Because everyone catalogs together, Library Thing also connects people with the same books, comes up with suggestions for what to read next, and so forth.

13. Functional Requirements for Subject Authority Data (FRSAD), previously known as Functional Requirements for Subject Authority Records (FRSAR), is a conceptual entity-relationship model developed by the International Federation of Library Associations and Institutions (IFLA) and published in 2010. It is a continuation of the work done on the FRBR model, detailing how "entities that serve as subjects of intellectual or artistic endeavor" can be related and controlled within the bibliographic universe. The model is intended to support global sharing and reuse of subject authority data.

14. Google Scholar is an academic search engine, and it is the clear number one when it comes to academic search engines. It's the power of Google searches applied to research papers and patents. It not only let's you find research papers for all academic disciplines for free, but also often provides links to full text PDF file. It is a searching platform for academic and research publications.

16. A podcast is an episodic series of spoken word digital audio files that a user can download to a personal device for easy listening. Streaming applications and podcasting services provide a convenient and integrated way to manage a personal consumption queue across many podcast sources and playback devices.

A podcast series usually features one or more recurring hosts engaged in a discussion about a particular topic or current event. Discussion and content within a podcast can range from carefully scripted to completely improvised. Podcasts combine elaborate and artistic sound production with thematic concerns ranging from scientific research to slice-of-life journalism. Many podcast series provide an associated website with links and show notes, guest biographies, transcripts, additional resources, commentary, and even a community forum dedicated to discussing the show's content.

17. **Grid System:** Latitude and longitude are essential to locate a particular place on the map. They are, represented by degrees, minutes and seconds. The advantage of this system helps in maintaining accuracy. Most maps are divided into grids or key reference squares. The grid system helps in the evaluation of maps. It is the special feature in the evaluation criteria of maps and atlases.

18. **Defence Scientific Information and Documentation Centre (DESIDOC):** DESIDOC started functioning in 1958 as Scientific Information Bureau (SIB). It was a division of the Defence Science Laboratory (DSL) which is presently called as Laser

Science & Technology Centre (LASTEC). The Defence Research and Development Organisation (DRDO) library which had its beginning in 1948 became a division of Scientific Information Bureau (SIB) in 1959. In 1967 SIB was reorganised with augmented activities and named Defence Scientific Information and Documentation Centre (DESIDOC). It still continued to function under the administrative control of Defence Science Laboratory (DSL). Defence Scientific Information and Documentation Centre (DESIDOC) became a self-accounting unit and one of the laboratories of DRDO on 29 July 1970. The Centre was functioning in the main building of Metcalfe House, a landmark in Delhi and a national monument. In August 1988 it moved to its newly built five-storied building in the same Metcalfe House complex. Since it became a self-accounting unit, DESIDOC has been functioning as a central information resource for DRDO. It provides science & technology information, based on its library and other information resources, to the DRDO headquarters, and its various laboratories at various places in India.

20. Administrative metadata comprises both technical and preservation metadata, and is generally used for internal management of digital resources. Administrative metadata may include information about rights and reproduction or other access requirements, selection criteria or archiving policy for digital content, audit trails or logs created by a digital asset management system, persistent identifiers, methodology or documentation of the imaging process, or information about the source materials being scanned. In general, administrative metadata is informed by the local needs of the project or institution and is defined by project-specific workflows. Administrative metadata may also encompass repository-like information, such as billing information or contractual agreements for deposit of digitized resources into a repository. Relationship data is not part of Administrative metadata.

21. The International Standard Bibliographic Description (ISBD) is a set of rules produced by the International Federation of Library Associations and Institutions (IFLA) to create a bibliographic description in a standard, human-readable form, especially for use in a bibliography or a library catalog. A preliminary consolidated edition of the ISBD was published in 2007 and the consolidated edition was published in 2011, superseding earlier separate ISBDs for monographs, older monographic publications, cartographic materials, serials and other continuing resources, electronic resources, non-book materials, and printed music.

The ISBD defines nine areas of description. Each area, except area 7, is composed of multiple elements with structured classifications. Elements and areas that do not apply to a particular resource are omitted from the description. Standardized punctuation (colons, semicolons, slashes, dashes, commas, and periods) is used to identify and separate the elements and areas. The order of elements and standardized punctuation make it easier to interpret bibliographic records when one does not understand the language of the description.

22. The concept of 'chain' is the foundation of chain indexing. A chain is deemed to be a structural manifestation of a subject. The term 'structure' in this context refers to the parts constituting a subject and their mutual interrelationship. It is a modulated sequence of sub-classes or isolates ideas. Since the chain expressed the modulated sequence of sub-classes more effectively in a notational scheme of classification of subjects, this method takes the class number of the document concerned as the base for deriving subject headings not only for specific subject entry but also for subject reference entries. The nature and structure of the classification scheme used to classify the subject of the document controls the structure of the subject headings drawn according to the chain procedure. The concept of 'chain' becomes operative only after the concept of a set 'links' about the structure of the subject is conceded. A chain should comprise a link of every order that lies between the first link and last link of the chain. The different types of links in chain indexing system are discussed below:

Sought Links (SL): Sought links denote the concepts (at any given stage of the λ chain) that the user is likely to use as access points.

Unsought Links (USL): Unsought links denote those concepts that are not likely to be used as access points by the user.

False Links (FL): False links are those that really do not represent any valid concept, mostly these are connecting symbols or indicator digits.

Missing Links (ML): Missing links represent those concepts that are not available in the preferred classification scheme, these are inserted by the indexer by means of verbal extension at the chain-with-gap corresponding to the missing isolate in the chain whenever there is such a need.

23. The marketing mix refers to the set of actions, or tactics, that a company uses to promote its brand or product in the market. The 4Ps make up a typical marketing mix - Price, Product, Promotion and Place. However, nowadays, the marketing mix increasingly includes several other Ps like Packaging, Positioning, People and even Politics as vital mix elements.

24. Open source discovery interface includes Blacklight, Vufind, Extensible catalog and Franklin which are not based on any index-based discovery services and are not capable of searching in open access and the community created central index is not incorporated in it unlike the commercial discovery system. Orchid is not an open-source discovery interface.

25. Force Field Analysis was created by Kurt Lewin in the 1940s. Lewin originally used it in his work as a social psychologist. Today, however, it is also used in business, for making and communicating go/no-go decisions.

The idea behind Force Field Analysis is that situations are maintained by an equilibrium between forces that drive change and others that resist change. For change to happen, the driving forces must be strengthened or the resisting forces weakened.

26. Job Enrichment is a job design technique that varies the concept of job enlargement. Job enrichment adds new sources of job satisfaction by increasing the level of responsibility of the employee in organization. While job enlargement is considered as horizontal restructuring method, job enrichment is considered as vertical restructuring method of moral excellence of giving the employee additional authority, autonomy, and control over the way the job is accomplished. Also called job enhancement or vertical job expansion.

27. Vannevar Bush was an American engineer, policymaker and science administrator, known primarily for his work on analog computing and his political role in the development of the atomic bomb.

In 1945, in the article **As We May Think** (the paper was originally written in 1939, but was originally published in the July 1945 issue of the magazine *The Atlantic Monthly*) Bush proposed a theoretical proto-hypertext system (an electromechanical device, called memex), which has influenced the development of subsequent hypertext and intellect augmenting computer systems.

28. WiMAX (a term originally devised as an abbreviation for Worldwide Interoperability for Microwave Access), is a revolutionary communications technology based on the IEEE 802.16 standard of the Institute of Electrical and Electronics Engineers (IEEE). This standard makes computer network applications mobile, at broadband speeds, with a new and growing family of internet-connected devices at speeds several times faster than current third-generation (3G) cellular speeds.

29. Jean-Maurice-Émile Baudot, French telegraph engineer and inventor of the first means of digital communication Baudot code, was one of the pioneers of telecommunications. He invented a multiplexed printing telegraph system that used his code and allowed multiple transmissions over a single line.The baud unit was named after him. The telegraph service trained him in the Morse telegraph and also sent him on a four-month course of instruction on the Hughes printing telegraph system, which was later to inspire his own system.

33. Calais is a service by Thomson Reuters that automatically extracts semantic information from web pages in a format that can be used on the semantic web. Calais was launched in January 2008, and is free to use. The technology is now available via the website of Refinitiv, a provider of financial market data and infrastructure founded in 2018 that is a subsidiary of London Stock Exchange Group.

The Calais Web service reads unstructured text and returns Resource Description Framework formatted results identifying entities, facts and events within the text. The service appears to be based on technology acquired when Reuters purchased ClearForest in 2007.

34. GSDL has four predefined metadata sets, such as Dublin core (DC), RFC 1807, New Zealand Government Locator Service (NZGLS), and Australian Government Locator Service (AGLS). New metadata sets can also be defined using Greenstone's Metadata Sets Editor (MSE).

The PREMIS maintenance activity is responsible for maintaining, supporting, and coordinating future revisions to the PREMIS data dictionary. The Preservation Metadata: Implementation Strategies Working Group, convened by OCLC and RLG, initially developed the PREMIS data dictionary as a specification with the goal of creating an implementable set of "core" preservation metadata elements, with broad applicability within the digital preservation community. Supporting XML schemas allow for implementation of the core metadata element set and are maintained in the Network Development and MARC Standards Office of the Library of Congress.

35. Altmetrics let us measure and monitor the reach and impact of scholarship and research through online interactions. Altmetrics stands for "alternative metrics." The "alternative" part references traditional measurements of academic success such as citation counts, journal prestige (impact factor), and author H-index. Altmetrics are meant to compliment, not totally replace, these traditional measures. Supporters of the altmetrics movement believe that doing so will give a more complete picture of how research and scholarship is used. However, there are limits to this approach and caution should be used to not rely on any one particular measure in evaluating the importance of scholarship.

36. Panel studies are similar to trend and cohort studies except that in addition to being longitudinal they are also prospective in nature and the information is always collected from the same respondents.

A panel survey involves a sample of people from a more significant population and is conducted at specified intervals for a more extended period.

One of the panel study's essential features is that researchers collect data from the same sample at different points in time. Most panel studies are designed for quantitative analysis, though they may also be used to collect qualitative data and analysis.

38. Systematic sampling is a type of probability sampling method in which sample members from a larger population are selected according to a random starting point but with a fixed, periodic interval. This interval, called the sampling interval, is calculated by dividing the population size by the desired sample size. Despite the sample population being selected in advance, systematic sampling is still thought of as being random if the periodic interval is determined beforehand and the starting point is random.. In a sampling procedure, if you select every' 10th name on a list or every 15th house on a street, it is known as systematic sampling.

40. Seven Faces of Information Literacy: The author (Christine Susan Bruce) has experienced different faces of information literacy at workplaces, these faces of information literacy have following characteristics:

- Varying emphases on technology;
- Emphasis on holding broad professional responsibilities, rather than specific skills;
- Social collaboration or interdependence between colleagues, rather than an emphasis on
- individual capability; Need for the partnership of information intermediaries;
- Emphasis on intellectual manipulation of information rather than technical skill with IT.

She further clarified that each face has three main components and these elements are essential and exists in each face. Two elements namely information technology and information use are present in all the faces and the third element is a unique element and which vary in each face depending on situation.

41. The information intermediaries may be of different types. Broadly, some of them are human experts or organisations, whereas some others are automated intelligent agents. The information intermediaries in various disciplines comprise information brokers, information consultants, online vendors, technological gatekeepers, invisible colleges, information filters, etc. In rural and semi-urban areas, extension workers, paramedical professionals, block development officers, social workers play a vital role as information intermediaries.

42. The National Knowledge Commission (NKC) is a high level advisory body to the Prime Minister of India with the objective of transforming India into a knowledge society. In its endeavour to transform the knowledge landscape of the country the NKC has submitted around 300 recommendation on 27 focus areas during its three and a half year term.

To meet 21st century challenges NKC was constituted in 13 June 2005 by the prime minister Dr. Manmohan Singh, under the chairmanship of Mr. Sam Pitroda (who led India's telecom revolution in the mid 1980s), to prepare a blueprint for reform of our knowledge related institutions & infrasturcture which would enable India to meet the challenges of the future.

Following components are:

Access to Knowledge: Access is one of the most fundamental issues in a knowledge society. Even if universities, research institutions and laboratories produce large amounts of knowledge, it will be of little use until the majority of the population actually possesses adequate means to acquire, absorb and communicate this knowledge.

Knowledge Concepts : Advances in knowledge and its applications are products of human endeavours; therefore it is of utmost importance that we nurture the skills and intellectual capacities of our largely youthful population in order to build a strong base of human capital that can transform India into a strong knowledge economy.

Knowledge Creation: Although India has the option of borrowing or buying new knowledge from abroad, it is important to create self-sufficiency by promoting indigenous research, especially in Science & Technology. S&T has the ability to accelerate the processes of other parallel knowledge objectives, leading to economic growth and security.

Knowledge Application : The creation of knowledge cannot be directionless. To derive maximum benefits from our intellectual assets, we must apply knowledge in fields like agriculture, industry, health, education etc. where productivity can be enhanced. Knowledge application is both a goal in itself and a facilitator of progress in these important sectors.

Knowledge Services: Investment in knowledge services will produce large-scale benefits for the common man. Technology has the potential to make government services and functioning more accountable, transparent and efficient. E-governance can change the way in which the citizens of India perceive and interact with the government.

43. UNESCO believes that the emergence of inclusive Knowledge Societies holds the key to sustainable human and economic development. By inclusive Knowledge Societies, UNESCO means societies in which people have the capabilities not just to acquire information but also to transform it into knowledge and understanding, which empowers them to enhance their livelihoods and contribute to the social and economic development of their communities. The concept of Knowledge Societies formed the centrepiece of UNESCO's contribution to WSIS, emphasising the importance of integrating technology and human development. The vision of Knowledge Societies articulated in this report was an important and original contribution to the discussions and outcomes of the WSIS. Since 2005, UNESCO has worked with governments and other stakeholders in its 193 Member-States and 11 Associate Members to build upon that vision, reaching beyond the recommendations set out in the WSIS documents, seeking lasting and sustainable progress towards social and economic development through inclusive Knowledge Societies. Four themes run through all of UNESCO's work to develop Knowledge Societies and implement the WSIS outcomes. These are:

1. Freedom of expression; 2. quality education for all 3. universal access to information and knowledge; and 4. cultural and linguistic diversity.

44. e-PG Pathshala is an initiative of the MHRD under its National Mission on Education through ICT (NME-ICT) being executed by the UGC.

e-Adhyayan: e-Adhyayan is a platform to provide 700+ e-Books for the Post-Graduate Courses. All the e-Books are derived from e-PG Pathshala courses. It also facilitates play-list of video content.

UGC MOOCs (Online Courses) : UGC-MOOCs is one of vertical to produce course on Post Graduate subjects in SWAYAM (Online Courses, An MHRD initiatives). UGC is one of the national coordinator of SWAYAM & INFLIBNET is technical partner for UGC-MOOCs.

e-Pathya (Offline Access): e-Pathya is one of the verticals of e-PG Pathshala which is software driven course / content package that facilitates students pursuing higher education (PG level) in distance learning as well as campus learning mode. It also facilitate offline access.

46. The PLUS model invented by James Herring, is an information literacy model which helps the school students to improve their learning by making them more information literate. It incorporates the elements of Purpose, Location, Use and Self-evaluation. The PLUS model is viewed as an iterative model and not a linear model as students may need to return to an earlier stage in the model during their information definition, search and use process.

48. Subject gateways are online sites that provide searchable and browsable catalogues of Internet based resources. Subject gateways satisfaction doesn't happen in a day—your business should continually find ways to improve processes and adapt your products and services as customer needs shift. As previously stated, the other Total Quality Management principles should help your business keep an eye toward continual improvement.

7. **Fact-based decision-making:** Analysis and data gathering lead to better decisions based on the available information. Making informed decisions leads to a better understanding of customers and your market.
8. **Communications:** Everybody in your organization needs to be aware of plans, strategies, and methods that will be used to achieve goals. There is a greater risk of failure if you don't have a good communication plan.

57. A fifth-generation programming language (5GL) is any programming language based on problem-solving using constraints given to the program, rather than using an algorithm written by a programmer. Most constraint-based and logic programming languages and some other declarative languages are fifth-generation languages.

While fourth-generation programming languages are designed to build specific programs, fifth-generation languages are designed to make the computer solve a given problem without the programmer. This way, the user only needs to worry about what problems need to be solved and what conditions need to be met, without worrying about how to implement a routine or algorithm to solve them. Fifth-generation languages are used mainly in artificial intelligence research.

Example : OPS5 and Mercury programming language.

58. Larry Page is an internet entrepreneur and computer scientist who teamed up with grad school buddy Sergey Brin to launch the search engine Google in 1998.

Larry Page's parents were both computer experts. Following in their footsteps, he studied computer engineering at Stanford University, where he met Sergey Brin. The duo developed a search engine that listed results according to the popularity of the pages and, with Page as CEO, Google became the world's most popular search engine after launching in 1998. Page and Brin later took charge of Google's new parent company, Alphabet, until stepping down from their everyday roles in late 2019. As a research project at Stanford University, Page and Brin created a search engine that listed results according to the popularity of the pages, after concluding that the most popular result would often be the most useful. They called the search engine "Google" after the mathematical term "googol," which refers to the No. 1 followed by 100 zeros, to reflect their mission to organize the immense amount of information available on the web.

59. Unguided Media of Transmission:

1. **Satellite Microwave Transmission:-** Transmitting data using electro radio waves through free space is called satellite communi-cation. In satellite communications there are many transponders (a device for receiving a radio signal and automatically transmitting a different signal) called frequency band. Satellites can be classified into two types: C-band: the frequency range of C-band satellite is from 3.7 to 4.2 GHz and from" 5.9 to 6.4 GHz. C-band are more reliable than Ku-band. Ku-band: the frequency range of Ku-band satellite is from 11 to 12 GHz.
2. **Radio wave transmission :** Its broadcast signals only in single direction which is in contrast with the microwave transmission that broadcast in both directions. One of the advantage of radio

wave transmissions is that it does not require any antennas. Radio waves are propagated using ground wave and sky wave. Radio waves performs modulation of electromagnetic waves using the frequency that is below the range of visible light.

3. **Terrestrial microwave transmission** : Microwave transmission make use of microwave link for transmitting information. Terrestrial microwave use large height antennas to cover long sight distances. It is more suitable for line-of-sight transmission link.

4. **Infrared wave transmission:** Infrared waves are electromagnetic waves that have the wavelength longer than visible light but shorter than radio wave. One of the advantage of infrared waves over other unguided media is that it cannot pass through walls due to which the security is more and the impairment such as interference is not present.

61. MrSID is a unique compression format for high-definition imagery and visual data, frequently used in geospatial industries. Although MrSID sounds like it may be a person, it's an acronym for Multi-Resolution Seamless Image Database.

The prototype for MrSID compression technology was developed at Los Alamos National Laboratory in 1992. LizardTech created a subsequent commercial version of the technology that was called the MrSID Generation 2 (MG2) format, which was released in 1998. LizardTech continued to develop and improve the compression technology to provide greater GIS functionality. The latest version of the MrSID file format, MrSID Generation 4 (MG4), was introduced in 2009.

RAR is a proprietary archive file format that supports data compression, error recovery and file spanning. It was developed in 1993 by Russian software engineer Eugene Roshal and the software is licensed by *win.rar GmbH.* The name *RAR* stands for *Roshal Archive.*

64. Formal Experimental Design

Completely randomized design: This design involves only two principles i.e., the principle of replication and the principle of randomization of experimental designs. Among all other designs this is the simpler and easier because its procedure and analysis are simple. The important characteristic of this design is that the subjects are randomly assigned to experimental treatments. For example, if the researcher has 20 subjects and if he wishes to test 10 under treatment A and 10 under treatment B, the randomization process gives every possible group of 10 subjects selected from a set of 20 an equal opportunity of being assigned to treatment A and treatment B. One way analysis of variance (one way ANOVA) is used to analyze such a design.

Randomized block design: In the R.B. Design, the principle of local control can be applied along with the other two principles of experimental designs. In the R.B. design, subjects are first divided into groups, known as blocks, such that within each group the subjects are relatively homogenous in respect to some selected variable. The number of subjects in a given block would be randomly assigned to each treatment. Blocks are the levels at which we hold the extraneous factor fixed, so that its contribution to the total variability of data can be measured. The main feature of the R.B. design is that, in this, each treatment appears the same number of times in each block. This design is analyzed by the two-way analysis of variance (two-way ANOVA) technique.

Latin squares design: The Latin squares design (L.S design) is an experimental design which is very frequently used in agricultural research. Since agriculture depends upon nature to a large extent, the condition of research and investigation in agriculture is

Historical bibliography is the Critical analysis of placing and timing of books.

71. At the end of the 19th century, it was German sociologist and author of The Protestant Ethic and the Spirit of Capitalism (1905), Max Weber who was the first to use and describe the term bureaucracy. This is also known as the bureaucratic theory of management, bureaucratic management theory or the Max Weber theory.

He believed bureaucracy was the most efficient way to set up an organisation, administration and organizations. Max Weber believed that Bureaucracy was a better than traditional structures. In a bureaucratic organisation, everyone is treated equal and the division of labour is clearly described for each employee.

According to Human Relations Approach, management is the Study of behaviour of people at work.This approach had its origin in a series of experiments conducted by Professor Elton Mayo and his associates at the Harvard School of Business at the Western Electric Company's Hawthorne Works, near Chicago.

F.W. Taylor or Fredrick Winslow Taylor is also known as the 'father of scientific management' proved with his practical theories that a scientific method can be implemented to management. Taylor gave much concentration on the supervisory level of management and performance of managers and workers at an operational level. Let's discuss in detail the five(5) principles of management by F.W Taylor.

Fayol called managerial skills "administrative functions." In his 1916 book, "Administration Industrielle et Générale," he shared his experiences of managing a workforce.

Fayol's book - and his 14 Principles of Management - helped to form what became known as Administrative Theory. It looks at the organization from the top down, and sets out steps for managers to get the best from employees and to run a business efficiently.

72. JAVA: James A Gosling, the father of Java, one of the world's most widely used programming languages, has talked with research scientist Lex Fridman about Java's origins and his motivations for creating a language that would be used on tens of billions of devices and become central to the development of Android at Google.

Gosling designed Java 25 years ago while at Sun Microsystems. In 2009, Java would be one of the key reasons Oracle acquired Sun. According to Oracle, today there are 51 billion active Java Virtual Machines (JVMs) deployed globally.

C PROGRAMMING: Dennis MacAlistair Ritchie was an American computer scientist. He created the C programming language and, with long-time colleague Ken Thompson, the Unix operating system and B programming language. He was the "R" in K&R C, and commonly known by his username dmr.

The history of LISP according to McCarthy's memory in 1978, presented at the ACM SIGPLAN History of Programming Languages Conference.

LISP history according to McCarthy's memory in 1978. This paper concentrates on the development of the basic ideas of LISP and distinguishes two periods - Summer 1956 through Summer 1958 when most of the key ideas were developed (some of which were implemented in the FORTRAN based FLPL), and Fall 1958 through 1962 when the programming language was implemented and applied to problems of artificial intelligence. After 1962, the development of LISP became multi-stranded, and different ideas were pursued in different places.

Python is an interpreted high-level general-purpose programming language. Python's design philosophy emphasizes code readability with its notable use of significant indentation. Its language constructs as well as its object-oriented approach aim to help programmers write clear, logical code for small and large-scale projects.

Python is dynamically-typed and garbage-collected. It supports multiple programming paradigms, including structured (particularly, procedural), object-oriented and functional programming. Python is often described as a "batteries included" language due to its comprehensive standard library.

Guido van Rossum began working on Python in the late 1980s, as a successor to the ABC programming language, and first released it in 1991 as Python 0.9.0. Python 2.0 was released in 2000 and introduced new features, such as list comprehensions and a garbage collection system using reference counting. Python 3.0 was released in 2008 and was a major revision of the language that is not completely backward-compatible and much Python 2 code does not run unmodified on Python 3. Python 2 was discontinued with version 2.7.18 in 2020.

73. Joomla: Open Source Matters, Inc. (OSM) is a not-for-profit formed under United States and New York state law that provides organizational, legal, and financial support for the Joomla! open-source project. OSM has been incorporated as a New York not-for-profit to ensure the Joomla project and future projects continue to exist beyond the participation of individual volunteers.

Drupal: Dries Buytaert is the original creator and project lead for the Drupal open source web publishing and collaboration platform. Buytaert serves as president of the Drupal Association, a non-profit organization formed to help Drupal flourish. He is also co-founder and chief technology officer of Acquia, a venture-backed software company that offers products and services for Drupal. Dries is also a co-founder of Mollom, a web service that helps you identify content quality and, more importantly, helps you stop website spam.

Thunder is a Drupal distribution for professional publishers. It consists of the current Drupal functionality, lots of handpicked publisher-centric modules with custom enhancements, and an environment which makes it easy to install, deploy and add new functionality.

In 2016, the German publisher Hubert Burda Media established the **Thunder** Coalition, which aims at joining forces amongst publishers by sharing code and innovation power.

As members of the Thunder Coalition, publishers, industry partners, and developers develop useful modules and extensions, use them for their own purposes and share them with the Coalition by publishing them under the GNU General Public License to further enhance Thunder.

Textpattern is a free and open-source content management system (CMS) based on PHP and MySQL, originally developed by Dean Allen and now developed by Team Textpattern. While it is often listed among weblogging tools, its aim is to be a general-purpose content management system suitable for deployment in many contexts.

74. Bradford's law begins with a regularity which is observed in the retrieval or use of published information. Broadly speaking, this regularity is characterized by both concentration and dispersion of specific items of information over different sources of information. Thus, for a search on some specific topic, a large number of the relevant articles will be concentrated in a small number of journal titles. The remaining articles will be dispersed over a large number of titles. Throughout the remaining discussion, journal articles will be used to represent the items retrieved and journals will be the sources. This is in keeping with most of the Bradford's law literature, although there is clear evidence that similar patterns occur for other kinds of items and sources.

Lotka's law is accepted as a benchmark for calculation of author's productivity in any field of knowledge. As per Lotka (1926), "in any field of knowledge, the number of authors making n contributions is about $1/n^2$ of those of the product concerned. This may be done on the basis of demands placed by them for some specific types of information.

- **Recognition/Assessment of user need:** The need for IACR work should be recognized/assessed before planning any IACR work through user study using some suitable method.
- **Identification of the subject area:** Basing on the needs of the target users, the subject area of the proposed IACR product is to be identified.
- **Identification of appropriate type of product:** The type of IACR product that will suit the needs of a particular user or user group has to be identified while making the user study.
- **Formation of working group:** Compilation of an IACR product can only be accomplished efficiently by the cooperation of several people with different specializations. A working group consisting of specialists in different fields should be formed, with a leader who will coordinate the work. The team leader will be adequately briefed, who can then initiate the work.

Determination of scope/product characteristics: At this stage, some essential characteristics of the product have to be determined as mentioned below:

- **Determination of subject scope:** Though the broad subject area has already been decided in the previous stage, it is necessary now to delineate the exact boundary of the subject concerned. "This involves the precise specification of a subject and would consist of recognizing each of the component ideas and the correct degree of interrelation among them, and expressing the totality of the subject coextensively and uniquely". This may also involve determination of depth of the component areas to be covered.
- **Demarcation of geographical area of coverage:** Where IACR product relates to any geographical area (e.g., area profile), the exact boundary of the geographical area to be covered has to be decided. In case of other IACR products too, it has to be decided as to the sources from and/or relating to which geographical area or areas are to be covered in the proposed product.
- **Fixing time limit/periodicity:** IACR products mostly cover current information. But on demand, retrospective information may also 222 Elements of Information Organization and Dissemination be covered. For products containing current information, it is necessary to decide the periodicity of the publication of the product. The decision regarding periodicity should be governed by the need of the users and the quantum of information available on the area of coverage.
- **Deciding packaging format and packaging medium:** The format and medium of packaging of the planned IACR product would vary from product to product. These should meet the requirements and comprehension level of the target users.

Planning and preparation: Planning and preparation work may include the following:

- **Deciding types of information sources to be consulted:** This involves decision regarding the types of information sources to be consulted for IACR work (e.g., journals, conference proceedings, etc. in case of an abstracting periodical) and also items, if any, in the selected sources that need to be excluded (e.g., book-reviews in newspapers while compiling a news digest).
- **Phasing/distribution of work:** This involves deciding about different phases in which the compilation work has to be

done and/or distribution of the tasks involved among the members of the working group.

- **Fixing time schedule for completion of compilation work:** A time schedule may be prepared and the members of the working group may be asked to adhere to the schedule so that the product can be brought out in time as delay may reduce its utility.

Processing and organization of information: The collected information should now be processed and organized to give a concrete shape to the product being compiled. This will involve analysis of the contents of selected sources or set of sources, identification and extraction of relevant information, compression or condensation of information, synthesis and restructuring of information, etc.

- **Arrangement of ideas/information:** At the time of synthesis and restructuring of information the question of arrangement or sequence will arise. It may be pointed out that one and the same set of ideas/ information can be arranged in several ways. The choice of the particular sequence should be based on its helpfulness to the users- intermediaries and/or end-users.

- **Integration of information:** After arrangement of the analyzed information/ ideas in a suitable sequence, these are to be integrated into an organized text. For this purpose, the target audience and their level, the intended use of the IACR product, the impact one desires of the product on the audience, and the peculiarities of the subject are some of the factors that need to be considered.

85. The following Public Library Acts according to their years of enactment in ascending order are:

- Goa Public Library Acts, 1993
- Odisha Public Library Acts, 2002
- Rajasthan Public Library Acts, 2006
- Chhattisgarh Public Library Acts, 2008

87. Preparation of critical abstracts requires subject expertise and is a time consuming job. A critical abstract is essentially a distillation of the most important components of a text. To succeed in this task, you must read the text carefully, take succinct but informed notes, think about your position/ beliefs in relation to the claims of the text, and then attempt to sift through all this information to create an effective presentation of the text and evaluation of its effectiveness to you, as a student of history.

88. Database normalization is the process of structuring a database, usually a relational database, in accordance with a series of so-called normal forms in order to reduce data redundancy and improve data integrity. It was first proposed by Edgar F. Codd as part of his relational model.

Normalization entails organizing the columns (attributes) and tables (relations) of a database to ensure that their dependencies are properly enforced by database integrity constraints. It is accomplished by applying some formal rules either by a process of synthesis (creating a new database design) or decomposition (improving an existing database design). The normalization of data is intended to allow better matching.

Identify and correct punctuation errors involving commas, apostrophes, colons and semicolons, parentheses and brackets, quotation marks, hyphens and dashes, question and exclamation marks, and periods.

89. With the advent of Internet, major libraries are now available online through internet and hence directly accessible from any part of the world. Librarians can have access to the catalogue of various libraries attached to the universities and colleges in the world and accordingly place a request for their users. The increase in the cost of documents for many disciplines in recent years has meant that the libraries have been able to provide less and less access to research literature through their in-house collection. Also with the financial constraints, the librarians and information professionals are seeking alternative means of providing access to journals. The problem of print journal and the concomitant development of computers and communication technologies have lead to the development of electronic alternatives to print journals, i.e., in various forms of electronic journals.

There are publications which help the librarians to select and evaluate the reference collection for a particular library in print or online. The libraries are service-oriented institutions. They exist to acquire, collect, organise and disseminate information, which is contained in different documents-print, audio, video and digital. The libraries acquire different documents, process them and make them available to the readers for use. They prepare and maintain tools like catalogue, shelf list, bibliographies to facilitate the use of books and other material by the readers. The libraries intend to convert potential visitors into the regular users. In order to achieve this, a human agency is needed to tell the users about the various resources and services offered by the libraries. The human agency or the staff of the library offers help to the readers in the form of reference service.

90. Lossless compression is a class of data compression algorithms that allows the original data to be perfectly reconstructed from the compressed data. By contrast, lossy compression permits reconstruction only of an approximation of the original data, though usually with greatly improved compression rates (and therefore reduced media sizes).

By operation of the pigeonhole principle, no lossless compression algorithm can efficiently compress all possible data. For this reason, many different algorithms exist that are designed either with a specific type of input data in mind or with specific assumptions about what kinds of redundancy the uncompressed data are likely to contain.

Lossless data compression is used in many applications. For example, it is used in the ZIP file format and in the GNU tool gzip. It is also often used as a component within lossy data compression technologies (e.g. lossless mid/side joint stereo preprocessing by MP3 encoders and other lossy audio encoders). Therefore, on decompression of a compressed zip file, the data loss is minimal.

Lossy compression is most commonly used to compress multimedia data (audio, video, and images), especially in applications such as streaming media and internet telephony. By contrast, lossless compression is typically required for text and data files, such as bank records and text articles. It can be advantageous to make a master lossless file which can then be used to produce additional copies from. This allows one to avoid basing new compressed copies off of a lossy source file, which would yield additional artifacts and further unnecessary information loss.

Previous Years' Paper (Solved)

National Testing Agency (NTA)

UGC-NET Junior Research Fellowship & Assistant Professor Eligibility Exam

Library and Information Science, December-2019*

PAPER-II

Note: *This paper contains* ***hundred*** *(**100**) objective type questions of* ***two*** *(**2**) marks each.* ***All*** *questions are* ***compulsory****.*

1. KB e-depot is maintained by:

A. National Library of India
B. National Library of Netherland
C. National Library of Germany
D. Library of Congress, USA

2. An attempt to make a computer resource unavailable to its intended user is called:

A. Denial of service attack
B. Virus attack
C. Worm attack
D. Bot-net attack

3. Which of the following is an example of 'Information Padding'?

A. Inclusion of a source in the bibliography which is relevent to your work and duly consulted
B. Inclusion of a source in the bibliography though not consulted, but required for further reading
C. Adding of necessary words or information to a speech or piece of work making the same more shorter
D. Adding of gratuitous and impertinent words or information to a work or piece of writing or speech extraneously making the same more longer

4. Which of the following information seeking behaviour model explains the activities viz initiation, selection, exploration, formulation, collection and presentation?

A. Kuhlthau's Model
B. Ellis' Model
C. Willson's Model
D. Krikelas Model

5. Which of the following is an example of 'microblogging'?

A. Word press B. Blogspot
C. Live journal D. Twitter

6. 'Research in Progress' database developed by INFLIBNET is known as:

A. Vidyanidhi B. Shodhganga
C. Shodhgangotri D. NDL

7. Identify the points related to Edward Deming's 14-points philosophy of TQM:

(*i*) Fair Wages
(*ii*) Division of Labour
(*iii*) Break Down Barriers
(*iv*) Eliminate Exhortation

Choose the correct answer from the following options:

A. (*iii*) and (*iv*) are correct
B. (*i*) and (*ii*) are correct
C. (*i*) and (*iii*) are correct
D. (*ii*) and (*iv*) are correct

8. Match the following:

	List-I		*List-II*
(*a*)	Barcode Technology	(*i*)	Ray Theories Ray tag
(*b*)	RFID Technology	(*ii*)	Sir William Herschel
(*c*)	QR code	(*iii*)	Norman Joseph Woodland and Bernard Silver
(*d*)	Biometric Technology	(*iv*)	Denson Wave

*Online exam held on 02-12-2019.

Choose the correct answer from the following options:

	(a)	(b)	(c)	(d)
A.	(ii)	(iv)	(i)	(iii)
B.	(iii)	(i)	(iv)	(ii)
C.	(iv)	(iii)	(i)	(ii)
D.	(iv)	(i)	(ii)	(iii)

9. Ex-Libris is an example of which type of cloud computing?
A. Software as a service
B. Infrastructure as a service
C. Platform as a service
D. Network as a service

10. Which of the following technologies use electronic waves at radio frequency for data transmission?
A. Li-fi B. Wi-fi
C. Optical cables D. Twisted pairs

11. **Assertion (A):** Glossary is an alphabetical list of technical terms on a particular subject.
Reason (R) : There is no difference between discipline-specific terms and general terms.

In the context of these two statements, which one of the following is true?
A. (A) is false, but (R) is true
B. (A) is true, but (R) is false
C. Both (A) and (R) are true
D. Both (A) and (R) are false

12. **Assertion (A):** Web search engines get their information by crawling from site to site.
Reason (R) : The "Spider" checks for the standard file name spider, Avi, addressed to it before sending certain information back to be indexed.

In the context of these two statements, which one of the following is true?
A. (A) is true, but (R) is false
B. (A) is false, but (R) is true
C. Both (A) and (R) are false
D. Both (A) and (R) are true

13. 'Altmetric' is not related to:
A. A record of bibliographic data on a subject
B. A record of attention
C. A measure of dissemination
D. An indicator of influence and impact

14. Match the following:

List-I	List-II
(a) Fundamentals of Reference Service	(i) A.J. Walford
(b) Introduction to Reference Works	(ii) S.R. Ranganathan
(c) Reference Service	(iii) F.N. Cheney and W.J. Williams
(d) Guide to Reference Books	(iv) William A. Katz

Choose the correct answer from the following options:

	(a)	(b)	(c)	(d)
A.	(ii)	(i)	(iv)	(iii)
B.	(iii)	(iv)	(i)	(ii)
C.	(iv)	(ii)	(iii)	(i)
D.	(iii)	(iv)	(ii)	(i)

15. Which Network protocol is involved in the execution of ping?
A. TCP B. ARP
C. ICMP D. BOOTP

16. INFOTERA is a global environmental information network of:
A. UNDP B. UNISIST
C. UNEP D. OECD

17. Conservative, moderate and liberal theories of reference service are propounded by:
A. S.R. Ranganathan B. James I. Wyer
C. W.A. Katz D. Krishan Kumar

18. Universal Bibliographic Control and International MARC (UBCIM) is a core activity of:
A. IFLA B. UNESCO
C. OCLC D. ALA

19. Which of the following publications are excluded from the scope of Indian National Bibliography?
(i) Maps

(*ii*) Guide to textbooks
(*iii*) First issue of a new periodical
(*iv*) Musical scores

Choose the correct answer from the following options:
A. (*i*), (*ii*) and (*iii*) are correct
B. (*i*), (*iii*) and (*iv*) are correct
C. (*ii*), (*iii*) and (*iv*) are correct
D. (*i*), (*ii*) and (*iv*) are correct

20. Dublin Core Metadata Element set version 1.1 consists of:
A. Fifteen elements
B. Eighteen elements
C. Twenty elements
D. Twenty two elements

21. Which of the budget methods emphasizes on identification of program objectives and the measurement of results?
A. ZBB B. Line budgeting
C. Item budgeting D. PPBS

22. Which of the following 'Change Management Model' has three stages namely, unfreezing, changing and refreezing?
A. Mary Parker Follett's Model
B. Kurt Lewin's Model
C. Henry Mintzberg's Model
D. Lillion Gilberth's Model

23. Bibframe 2.0 organises bibliographic information into three core levels of abstraction. Choose the correct answer from the options given below.
A. Work, Instance, Item
B. Work, Item, Agents
C. Work, Agents, Events
D. Events, Instance, Subjects

24. Arrange the following phases of Six Sigma in their correct sequence:
(*i*) Define (*ii*) Measure
(*iii*) Analyze (*iv*) Improve

Choose the correct answer from the following options:
A. (*i*), (*iii*), (*iv*) and (*ii*)
B. (*i*), (*ii*), (*iii*) and (*iv*)
C. (*iii*), (*i*), (*ii*) and (*iv*)
D. (*iii*), (*iv*), (*i*) and (*ii*)

25. "Haptics" is a form of non-verbal communication that uses":
A. Facial expression
B. Touch-to-communicate
C. Interpersonal space
D. Interpretation of symbols

26. The g-index was proposed by:
A. Jorge Hirsch B. Bill Smith
C. Leo Egghe D. Olle Persson

27. In universal decimal classification (Abridged English 3rd edition) symbol "......." indicates:
A. Relation sign
B. Common auxiliaries of place
C. Common auxiliaries of Race and Nationality
D. Common auxiliaries of Time

28. Match the following types of questions with corresponding explanations:

	List-I		*List-II*
(*a*)	Ranking item questions	(*i*)	When the language of questions is such that it may be interpreted in more than one way
(*b*)	Ambigous questions	(*ii*)	When answer to a question has been preconceived and classified into possible groups
(*c*)	Dichotomous questions	(*iii*)	Questions are given to record the preference of the respondent
(*d*)	Structural questions	(*iv*)	When reply to a question is given in form of one of the two alternatives

Choose the correct answer from the following options:

	(*a*)	(*b*)	(*c*)	(*d*)
A.	(*iii*)	(*i*)	(*iv*)	(*ii*)
B.	(*ii*)	(*iii*)	(*iv*)	(*i*)
C.	(*i*)	(*ii*)	(*iii*)	(*iv*)
D.	(*iv*)	(*ii*)	(*i*)	(*iii*)

29. Which of the following are Web-Zine?

(*i*) Email Magazine

(*ii*) E-conference

(*iii*) On-line Bulletin

(*iv*) Electronic News Letter

Choose the correct answer from the following options:

A. (*i*), (*iii*) and (*iv*) are correct

B. (*i*), (*ii*) and (*iii*) are correct

C. (*ii*), (*iii*) and (*iv*) are correct

D. (*i*), (*ii*) and (*iv*) are correct

30. Annual publication, listing a set of events forthcoming in the next year is known as:

A. Almanac B. Yearbook

C. Directory D. Handbook

31. What is the range for getting Gold level of certification under Leadership in Energy and Environmental Design (LEED)?

A. 40 - 49 B. 50 - 59

C. 60 - 79 D. 80 +

32. Arrange the following States in ascending order of the year of enactment of their respective public Library Acts:

(*i*) Kerala

(*ii*) Chhattisgarh

(*iii*) Goa

(*iv*) Uttarakhand/Uttaranchal

Choose the correct answer from the following options:

A. (*i*), (*iii*), (*iv*), (*ii*) B. (*ii*), (*iii*), (*i*), (*iv*)

C. (*iv*), (*i*), (*ii*), (*iii*) D. (*iii*), (*iv*), (*i*), (*ii*)

33. **Assertion (A)** : As the level of Recall decreases, the precision increases.

Reason (R) : Recall and Precision are not always inversely correlated.

In the context of these two statements, which one of the following is true?

A. (A) is false, but (R) is true

B. (A) is true, but (R) is false

C. Both (A) and (R) are true

D. Both (A) and (R) are false

34. Duraspace provides cloud-based services related to:

(*i*) D-space

(*ii*) NewGen Lib

(*iii*) E-Prints

(*iv*) Fedora Commons

Choose the correct answer from the following options:

A. (*i*) and (*ii*) are correct

B. (*ii*) and (*iii*) are correct

C. (*iii*) and (*iv*) are correct

D. (*i*) and (*iv*) are correct

35. Which of the following consortium supports e-resources exclusively for health sciences?

A. CeRA B. HELINET

C. FORSA D. NKRC

36. 'Index Indiana' is:

A. An index to Indian language periodical literature

B. An index to library science literature only

C. An index to English Language literature

D. An index to Reference material

37. The UK Committee on RDA (UKCOR) aims to:

(*i*) Represent the interests of LIS professional community of third world countries with regard to RDA.

(*ii*) Contribute to the RDA development program and to the maintenance and governance of RDA.

(*iii*) Ensure that representatives of the RDA European region are briefed on the position of the UK Community regarding all aspects of governance, development and maintenance of RDA.

(*iv*) Support implementation and development of RDA in UK.

Choose the correct answer from the following options:

A. (*i*), (*ii*) and (*iii*) are correct

B. (*ii*), (*iii*) and (*iv*) are correct

C. (*i*). (*iii*) and (*iv*) are correct

D. (*i*), (*ii*) and (*iv*) are correct

38. Arrange the following Library Associations according to ascending order of their year of establishment:

(*i*) IFLA (*ii*) SLA
(*iii*) CILIP (*iv*) ALA

Choose the correct answer from the following options:

A. (*iv*), (*ii*), (*i*), (*iii*) B. (*ii*), (*iv*), (*i*), (*iii*)
C. (*iv*), (*i*), (*ii*), (*iii*) D. (*iii*), (*ii*), (*iv*), (*i*)

39. CANMARC and US-MARC are merged together with:

A. CCF B. UNIMARC
C. UK-MARC D. MARC-21

40. According to S.R. Ranganathan "Wherever telescoping of array is done, the canon of Hierarchy is violated. This violation is deliberately done to satisfy:

A. Law of Parsimony
B. Law of Local Variation
C. Law of Symmetry
D. Law of Interpretation

41. Patent information system is located at:

A. Kanpur B. Lucknow
C. Nagpur D. Hyderabad

42. Which of the following steps are involved in the selection of documents for digitization?

(*i*) Checking for copyright
(*ii*) Checking the research significance of the document
(*iii*) Checking for price
(*iv*) Checking the condition of document

Choose the correct answer from the following options:

A. (*i*), (*ii*) and (*iii*) are correct
B. (*i*), (*iii*) and (*iv*) are correct
C. (*i*), (*ii*) and (*iv*) are correct
D. (*ii*), (*iii*) and (*iv*) are correct

43. Assertion (A) : Big Data is a product of data being generated constantly, automatically and rapidly.

Reason (R) : Due to the omnipresence of personal computing devices and smart phones, individuals generate massive amount of data through e-commerce, e-communication, social media, online searches and GPS Navigation.

In the context of these two statements, which one of the following is true?

A. (A) is true, but (R) is false
B. (A) is false, but (R) is true
C. Both (A) and (R) are true
D. Both (A) and (R) are false

44. ISBD was created and is maintained by:

A. OCLC
B. UNESCO
C. IFLA
D. Library of Congress

45. Which layer of the OSI Model is mostly concerned with the syntax of the data?

A. Session layer B. Presentation layer
C. Network layer D. Data link layer

46. Who proposed 'General System Theory of Communication'?

A. Robert T. Craig
B. W.R. Ashby
C. Shannon and Weaver
D. Ludwig Von Bertalanffy

47. Physical arrangement of computers in a Network is called:

A. Topology B. Routing
C. Bandwidth D. Switching

48. Which digital library software was developed at Cornell University?

A. FEDORA B. E-Prints
C. GSDL D. D-Space

49. Loss of signal power as light travel down the fibre is called:

A. Attenuation B. Propagation
C. Scattering D. Interpretation

50. Who was the first Librarian of National Library of India after independence?

A. K.M. Asadullah B. D.R. Kalia
C. B.S. Kesavan D. Kalpana Dasgupta

51. Identify the committee charged with the responsibility for Indian standards related to libraries.

A. Z-39 B. TC-46
C. BIS-LIB D. MSD-5

52. Match the following number of Table-1: Standard Subdivisions of Dewey Decimal Classification (19th Edition) with their correct terms:

List-I	*List-II*
(*a*) 0202	(*i*) Organizations and Management
(*b*) 0142	(*ii*) Synopses
(*c*) 06	(*iii*) Schools and Courses
(*d*) 071	(*iv*) Etymology

Choose the correct answer from the following options:

	(*a*)	(*b*)	(*c*)	(*d*)
A.	(*iv*)	(*iii*)	(*ii*)	(*i*)
B.	(*ii*)	(*i*)	(*iii*)	(*iv*)
C.	(*ii*)	(*iv*)	(*i*)	(*iii*)
D.	(*iii*)	(*ii*)	(*i*)	(*iv*)

53. Match the following:

List-I	*List-II*
(*a*) OCLC	(*i*) The Hague, Netherland
(*b*) INIS	(*ii*) Washington DC, USA
(*c*) IFLA	(*iii*) Viena, Austria
(*d*) MEDLARS	(*iv*) Dublin, Ohio

Choose the correct answer from the following options:

	(*a*)	(*b*)	(*c*)	(*d*)
A.	(*iv*)	(*iii*)	(*i*)	(*ii*)
B.	(*ii*)	(*i*)	(*iii*)	(*iv*)
C.	(*iii*)	(*ii*)	(*iv*)	(*i*)
D.	(*iii*)	(*i*)	(*ii*)	(*iv*)

54. Identify the electronic depository in which Librarians of the participating institutions have the right to put their words in managing the depository:

A. Portico B. LOCKSS
C. CLOCKSS D. PubMed

55. Which of the following is a technique of non-probability sampling?

A. Judgemental Sampling
B. Simple Random Sampling
C. Stratified Random Sampling
D. Cluster Sampling

56. Assertion (A) : INFLIBNET provides electronic document delivery service to all types of libraries in India.

Reason (R) : Due to inadequate ICT infrastructure, most of the libraries are not in a position to provide electronic document delivery service, to their clientele.

In the context of these two statements, which one of the following is true?

A. Both (A) and (R) are true
B. (A) is true, but (R) is false
C. Both (A) and (R) are false
D. (A) is false, but (R) is true

57. Which are the factors responsible for deterioration of Library Materials?

(*i*) Biological Factor
(*ii*) Electromagnetic Factor
(*iii*) Chemical Factor
(*iv*) Environmental Factor

Choose the correct answer from the options given below:

A. (*i*), (*ii*) and (*iv*) are correct
B. (*i*), (*iii*) and (*iv*) are correct
C. (*ii*), (*iii*) and (*iv*) are correct
D. (*i*), (*ii*) and (*iii*) are correct

58. 'Indian Library Review' is a blog of:

A. IASLIC
B. NISCAIR
C. INFLIBNET
D. National Library of India

59. Under RRRLF Financial Assistance Matching scheme, assistance is shared on matching basis between RRRLF and developed States as per the given ratio:

A. 70 : 30 B. 60 : 40
C. 90 : 10 D. 50 : 50

60. Which of the following routes is critical in CPM?

A. Shortest route
B. Longest route
C. Routes having simple activities
D. Routes having less important activity

61. Arrange the correct sequence of the following facets of Book Number according to Colon Classification (sixth reprint edition)

(*i*) Language Number
(*ii*) Volume Number
(*iii*) Copy Number
(*iv*) Form Number

Choose the correct answer from the following options:

A. (*i*), (*iv*), (*ii*) and (*iii*)
B. (*i*), (*ii*), (*iii*) and (*iv*)
C. (*iv*), (*i*), (*iii*) and (*ii*)
D. (*i*), (*iii*), (*ii*) and (*iv*)

62. Match the following:

List-I	***List-II***
(*a*) Judgemental Sampling	(*i*) Based on ability of the researcher to divide the sampling population into groups
(*b*) Snowball Sampling	(*ii*) Selecting a sample using networks
(*c*) Cluster Sampling	(*iii*) Each element in the population is given on equal and independent chance of selection
(*d*) Simple Random Sampling	(*iv*) Identification of person who can provide the best information

Choose the correct answer from the following options:

	(*a*)	(*b*)	(*c*)	(*d*)
A.	(*iv*)	(*ii*)	(*i*)	(*iii*)
B.	(*iii*)	(*iv*)	(*ii*)	(*i*)
C.	(*ii*)	(*i*)	(*iii*)	(*iv*)
D.	(*i*)	(*ii*)	(*iv*)	(*iii*)

63. Who among the following are the editors of ALA Glossary of Library and Information Science Fourth Edition?

(*i*) Michael Levine - Clark
(*ii*) Philip Babcock Gove
(*iii*) Toni M. Carter
(*iv*) L.M. Harrod

Choose the correct answer from the following options:

A. (*i*) and (*ii*) are correct
B. (*ii*) and (*iii*) are correct
C. (*i*) and (*iii*) are correct
D. (*i*) and (*iv*) are correct

64. Identify the publication years of different editions of AACR:

(*i*) 1967 (*ii*) 1970
(*iii*) 1978 (*iv*) 1988

Choose the correct answer from the following options:

A. (*i*), (*ii*) and (*iv*) are correct
B. (*i*), (*ii*) and (*iii*) are correct
C. (*ii*), (*iii*) and (*iv*) are correct
D. (*i*), (*iii*) and (*iv*) are correct

65. The concept of 'Information Encountering' (IE) was introduced in the domain information behaviour literature by Sanda Erdelez in 1997, where she proposed a conceptual framework for facilitating systematic study of IE. Identify the three key elements proposed by Erdelez in her study:

(*i*) Characteristics of the information user
(*ii*) Characteristics of information seeking habit
(*iii*) Characteristics of information environment
(*iv*) Characteristics of encountered information

Choose the correct answer from the following options:

A. (*i*), (*ii*) and (*iv*) are correct
B. (*ii*), (*iii*) and (*iv*) are correct
C. (*i*), (*ii*) and (*iii*) are correct
D. (*i*), (*iii*) and (*iv*) are correct

66. Which of the following are not the publications of Ministry of Information and Broadcasting, Government of India?

(*i*) Economic and Political Weekly

(*ii*) University News
(*iii*) Yojana
(*iv*) Vigyan Pragati

Choose the correct answer from the following options:
A. (*i*), (*ii*) and (*iii*) are correct
B. (*i*), (*iii*) and (*iv*) are correct
C. (*i*), (*ii*) and (*iv*) are correct
D. (*ii*), (*iii*) and (*iv*) are correct

67. "There is no significant difference in the proportion of male and female librarians in the study population", is an example of:
A. Hypothesis of point prevalence
B. Null-hypothesis
C. Hypothesis of association
D. Hypothesis of difference

68. Which of the following are the high-level classes or entities in the BIDFRAME model?
(*i*) Work (*ii*) Instance
(*iii*) Item (*iv*) Author

Choose the correct answer from the following options:
A. (*i*), (*ii*) and (*iii*) are correct
B. (*i*), (*ii*) and (*iv*) are correct
C. (*i*), (*iii*) and (*iv*) are correct
D. (*ii*), (*iii*) and (*iv*) are correct

69. What is 'Epilogue' in a thesis?
A. First Chapter B. Final Chapter
C. Title Page D. Appendix

70. Arrange the following information networks according to their year of launching.
(*i*) NICNET (*ii*) NKN
(*iii*) INFLIBNET (*iv*) ERNET

Choose the correct answer from the following options:
A. (*ii*), (*iii*), (*i*), (*iv*) B. (*i*), (*iv*), (*iii*), (*ii*)
C. (*iii*), (*iv*), (*ii*), (*i*) D. (*i*), (*iii*), (*ii*), (*iv*)

71. Identify the former Librarians of National Library of India from the names given below:
(*i*) D.N. Banerjee
(*ii*) Kalpana Dasgupta
(*iii*) R.K. Dasgupta
(*iv*) K.M. Asadullah

Choose the correct answer from the following options:
A. (*i*) and (*ii*) are correct
B. (*ii*) and (*iv*) are correct
C. (*i*) and (*iii*) are correct
D. (*iii*) and (*iv*) are correct

72. In data transfer process, which of the following is used for strengthening the signals:
A. Firewalls B. Hubs
C. Switching packets D. Repeater

73. Arrange the following according to their increasing storage capacity:
(*i*) Exabyte
(*ii*) Zettabyte
(*iii*) Petabyte
(*iv*) Yottabyte

Choose the correct answer from the following options:
A. (*iv*), (*ii*), (*i*), (*iii*) B. (*iii*), (*i*), (*ii*), (*iv*)
C. (*iii*), (*i*), (*iv*), (*ii*) D. (*iv*), (*iii*), (*i*), (*ii*)

74. Match the following notation of second summary of DDC (19th Edition) with their correct terms:

List-I	***List-II***
(*a*) 110	(*i*) Ethics (Moral Philosophy)
(*b*) 120	(*ii*) Epistemology Causation, Human kind
(*c*) 160	(*iii*) Meta Physics
(*d*) 170	(*iv*) Logic

Choose the correct answer from the following options:

	(*a*)	(*b*)	(*c*)	(*d*)
A.	(*iv*)	(*iii*)	(*ii*)	(*i*)
B.	(*iii*)	(*ii*)	(*i*)	(*iv*)
C.	(*ii*)	(*iii*)	(*iv*)	(*i*)
D.	(*iii*)	(*ii*)	(*iv*)	(*i*)

75. The method of communication in which transmission takes place in both the directions, but only in one direction at a time is called:
A. Simplex B. Full Duplex
C. Half Duplex D. Two-wire Circuits

76. Assertion (A) : The 'Schedule tool' of survey method helps the researcher to get information mostly from illiterates respondents.

Reason (R) : In the schedule method, the onus of filling up of the questionnaire usually lies with the respondents.

In the context of these two statements, which one of the following is true?

A. (A) is true, but (R) is false
B. Both (A) and (R) are true
C. (A) is false, but (R) is true
D. Both (A) and (R) are false

77. Identify the services of OCLC from the following:

(*i*) Infoport (*ii*) OJAS
(*iii*) First search (*iv*) Question point

Choose the correct answer from the following options:

A. (*i*) and (*ii*) are correct
B. (*ii*) and (*iv*) are correct
C. (*i*) and (*iii*) are correct
D. (*iii*) and (*iv*) are correct

78. Match the following authors with their corresponding books.

List-I	List-II
(*a*) A. Broadfield	(*i*) The foundations of Education for Librarianship
(*b*) J.H. Shera	(*ii*) A Philosophy of Librarianship
(*c*) Pierce Butler	(*iii*) Library Power : A New Philosophy of Librarian
(*d*) James Thomson	(*iv*) Introduction to Library Science

Choose the correct answer from the following options:

	(*a*)	(*b*)	(*c*)	(*d*)
A.	(*i*)	(*iii*)	(*iv*)	(*ii*)
B.	(*iv*)	(*i*)	(*iii*)	(*ii*)
C.	(*iii*)	(*i*)	(*iv*)	(*ii*)
D.	(*ii*)	(*i*)	(*iv*)	(*iii*)

79. Which of the following are network protocols?

(*i*) UDP (*ii*) SMTP
(*iii*) TCP (*iv*) Telnet

Choose the correct answer from the following options:

A. (*i*), (*ii*) and (*iv*) are correct
B. (*ii*),(*iii*) and (*iv*) are correct
C. (*i*), (*iii*) and (*iv*) are correct
D. (*i*), (*ii*) and (*iii*) are correct

80. Who is the creator of 'R' statistics?

A. Dale H. Bent and H.E. Garrett
B. Norman H. Nie and C. Had
C. Ross Inaka and Robert Gentleman
D. Harold Cramer and John C

81. Which of the following are Reference Style Management tools?

(*i*) Stata
(*ii*) Ref works
(*iii*) Mendeley
(*iv*) Zotero

Choose the correct answer from the following options:

A. (*i*), (*ii*) and (*iii*) are correct
B. (*ii*), (*iii*) and (*iv*) are correct
C. (*i*) and (*ii*) are correct
D. (*i*) and (*iv*) are correct

82. Who popularized the term 'Bibliomania'?

A. Ted Nelson
B. Thomas Frognall Dibdin
C. George Kingsley Zipf
D. Theodore Besterman

83. Who authored the book entitled 'Putting Knowledge to work'?

A. Pauline Atherton
B. Herman M. Weisman
C. S.C. Bradford
D. J.S. Brown

84. Identify the name of 'Editor-in-Chief' of Dewey Decimal Classification and Edition 23.

A. P. Green B. J. Martin
C. Joan S. Mitchell D. A. Kent

85. The UK Committee on RDA (UKCOR) is supported by:
(*i*) CILIP
(*ii*) The British Library
(*iii*) OCLC
(*iv*) UNESCO

Choose the correct answer from the following options:
A. (*i*) and (*iii*) are correct
B. (*ii*) and (*iv*) are correct
C. (*i*) and (*iv*) are correct
D. (*i*) and (*ii*) are correct

86. Arrange the following layers of Tiwana's KMS Architecture in order:
(*i*) Interface layer
(*ii*) Application layer
(*iii*) Access and Authentication layer
(*iv*) Collaborative, intelligence and Filtering

Choose the correct answer from the following options:
A. (*ii*), (*iii*), (*iv*), (*i*) B. (*iv*), (*ii*), (*iii*), (*i*)
C. (*i*), (*iii*), (*iv*), (*ii*) D. (*iii*), (*iv*), (*i*), (*ii*)

87. Assertion (A) : Consortia-based subscription of online resources now a days has become a practice in most of the University Libraries in India.

Reason (R) : Spiraling cost of publication, optimal utilization of resources at least efforts and cost coupled with growing expectations of users, have made such subscription redundant.

In the context of these two statements which one of the following is true?
A. (A) is false, but (R) is true
B. (A) is true, but (R) is false
C. Both (A) and (R) are true
D. Both (A) and (R) is false

88. Who introduced the term 'Literary Warrant'?
A. S.R. Ranganathan B. Wyndham Hulme
C. Melvil Dewey D. J.D. Brown

89. Match the following protocols with their creators:

List-I	*List-II*
(*a*) HTTP	(*i*) Eric Rescoria and Allan M. Schiffman
(*b*) SHTTP	(*ii*) Tim Berners–Lee
(*c*) FTP	(*iii*) Robert E. Kahn and Vintcerf
(*d*) SMTP	(*iv*) Abhay Bhusan

Choose the correct answer from the following options:

	(*a*)	(*b*)	(*c*)	(*d*)
A.	(*ii*)	(*iv*)	(*i*)	(*iii*)
B.	(*ii*)	(*iii*)	(*i*)	(*iv*)
C.	(*ii*)	(*i*)	(*iv*)	(*iii*)
D.	(*iv*)	(*i*)	(*ii*)	(*iii*)

90. Which of the following devices is used to connect different network segments and manage the traffic between them?
A. Switch B. Gateway
C. Bridge D. Repeater

Directions (Q. No. 91-95): *Read the passage given below and answer the questions which follow.*

Science provides the answer as to how to perform certain operations in order to secure given ends. But such knowledge is a two-edged sword. The same processes that led to the manufacture of aniline dyes set in motion physiological processes that ended in death for many of those who helped manufacture the dyes. The development of superior methods of keeping records basic to the growth of social science, may also be the means of strengthening the grip of a repressive political dictatorship. Today the use of radioactive-isotope therapy promises much for the reduction of disease, but these isotopes are products of the same scientific knowledge which produced the atomic bomb and which has made possible the even more destructive hydrogen bomb. Science as a mehod gives power, but this is a power which may be used for disapproved as well as approved ends.

Science, then can (1) offer a method of solving problems, *i.e.*, of achieving values; (2) offer *alternative* methods, so that relative costs can be calculated; (3) provide a means for predicting what the order consequences of a given course of action may be. If, for example, it is desired to clear a slum, it is good to be able not only to predict the financial and emotional costs of the specific program but also to know what other effects the slum clearance will have upon the community. This is a task to which only the scientific method may be successful applied.

Since science operates as a technique of problem solving, and since problems in this sense are formulated upon the basis of value judgements, then it is clear science and values are interrelated.

91. Which destructive product is made up by the use of radioactive-isotope?

A. Machine Gun B. Hydrogen Bomb
C. Robot D. Pistol

92. What is the benefit of 'Radioactive Isotope Therapy'?

A. Reduction of anxiety
B. Reduction of stress
C. Reduction of Disease
D. Reduction of psycho-fear

93. Which kind of process led to death for many who helped manufacture of the dyes?

A. Motion physiological process
B. Electromechanical process
C. Cognitive process
D. Psychological process

94. Which of the following strengthens the grip of a repressive political dictatorship?

A. Superior method of keeping records
B. Static in growth of social sciences
C. Inferior method of documentation
D. Fair political practice

95. Problems are formulated upon the basis of:

A. Market survey
B. Value Judgement
C. Review of literature
D. Pilot study

Directions (Q. No. 96-100): *Read the following passage carefully and answer the questions that follow.*

The term User Education is used interchangeably with 'library instruction', 'library orientation' and 'bibliographic instruction'. Neelameghan distinguishes user education, user orientation and user assistance. Roberts and Blandy prefer a broad term: library instruction. User education is a comprehensive service and a process of making the user self-reliant in locating, sorting and repacking information. This process may require two strategies: for general exposure, and for specific subject oriented—bibliographic instruction. The first visit to the library is mostly casual and in a sense this requires more frequent meetings with the user.

By the 1850s, US librarians instructed patrons on library use Samuel Greens attempt to initiate a reference desk in the public library in the 1870s. Luis Shore's library-college movement in the 1920s and Patricia Knapp's Montieth College programme in the 1960s are all significant. In 1949 the three-stage user education programme proposed by the UK library association's University and Research Section was a landmark. Ranganathan prescribed the role of an intermediary as a user-friendly reference librarian. Boon Fjallbrant and Stevenson Hopkins, Roberts and Blandy and others have made extensive historical assessments. Progress was slow, partly due to the problem of defining its place in the services; it was lost in the informational function or reference service. While lectures, tours and seminars are traditional methods, programmed learning, teaching machines, audiovisual tools and computer assisted learning (CAL) are the recent advances. User education is not merely a library tour or a brochure, it includes searching databases (local and global) and generally making the user less dependent on others.

A variety of media are used. One-to-one instruction is simple but expensive. Orientation by informal tour is traditional and effective, but it is time consuming and too general, and can cause boredom. Printed materials (leaflet, handout) describe services, tools and search strategies, but need frequent revision and may not be used. Displaying of posters, diagrams, etc can teaching skills, but requires a mediator. In workbooks, the audience is involved, which enables learning at the individual's pace and the educator can know the effect of learning.

96. What is Roberts and Blandy's most preferred term for 'User Education'?

A. Library orientation
B. Bibliographic instruction
C. Library instruction
D. User assistance

97. What are the traditional methods of imparting user education?

A. Lectures, tours and seminars
B. Teaching machines
C. Audio-visual tools
D. Programmed learning

98. Three stage of user education programme was proposed by:

A. S.R. Ranganathan
B. University and Research Section, UK Library Association
C. Samuel Green
D. Indian Library Association

99. User education as a service aims to:

A. Aid in understanding non-bibliographic instruction
B. Use appropriate referral source
C. Rely upon intermediary service
D. Make the user self-reliant in locating, sorting and repackaging information

100. Which of the following type of 'user-instruction' is relatively a costly proposition and less time consuming?

A. One to many instruction
B. Informal tour
C. One to one instruction
D. Classroom instruction

ANSWERS

1	**2**	**3**	**4**	**5**	**6**	**7**	**8**	**9**	**10**
B	A	D	A	D	C	A	B	A	B
11	**12**	**13**	**14**	**15**	**16**	**17**	**18**	**19**	**20**
B	A	A	D	C	C	B	A	D	A
21	**22**	**23**	**24**	**25**	**26**	**27**	**28**	**29**	**30**
D	B	A	B	B	C	D	A	A	A
31	**32**	**33**	**34**	**35**	**36**	**37**	**38**	**39**	**40**
C	A	B	D	B	A	B	A	D	A
41	**42**	**43**	**44**	**45**	**46**	**47**	**48**	**49**	**50**
C	C	C	C	B	D	A	A	A	C
51	**52**	**53**	**54**	**55**	**56**	**57**	**58**	**59**	**60**
D	C	A	C	A	D	B	D	D	B
61	**62**	**63**	**64**	**65**	**66**	**67**	**68**	**69**	**70**
A	A	C	D	*	C	B	A	B	B
71	**72**	**73**	**74**	**75**	**76**	**77**	**78**	**79**	**80**
B	D	B	D	C	A	D	D	D	C
81	**82**	**83**	**84**	**85**	**86**	**87**	**88**	**89**	**90**
B	B	A	C	D	C	B	B	C	C
91	**92**	**93**	**94**	**95**	**96**	**97**	**98**	**99**	**100**
B	C	A	A	B	C	A	B	D	C

EXPLANATORY ANSWERS

1. The Koninklijke Bibliotheek (National Library of the Netherlands) (KB) is the first national library in the world to start and own an operational system for the deposit and long-term preservation of digital publications. In 1994, the KB took the decision to include e-publications in its depository collection (e-Depot). Since then, research and development on long-term digitalization and archiving has been an important activity of KB. The e-Depot, an intrinsic part of Dutch National Library aims to ensure long-term preservation of digital objects. The KB has developed a specific workflow for archiving e-publications.

Elements of this workflow are: accept and preprocess; generate and resolve identifiers; search and retrieve publications and identify, authenticate and authorize users. The technical heart of the e-Depot system is IBM's DIAS (Digital Information and Archiving System). The KB ensures, libraries, publishers and end users that the information stored in the archive will outlast the transience or digital documents. In addition, the e-Depot offers publishers a durable check on archived formats as well as guidance on how to create the most durable electronic publications.

2. Denial-of-Service (DoS) Attack

A denial-of-service attack (DoS attack) or distributed denial of service attack (DDoS attack) is an attempt to make a computer resource unavailable to its intended users. Although the means to carry out, motives for, and targets of a DoS attack may vary, it generally consists of the concerted efforts to prevent an Internet site or service from functioning efficiently or at all, temporarily or indefinitely.

In computing, a *denial-of-service* (DoS) *attack* is an attempt to make a machine or network resource unavailable to its intended users, such as to temporarily or indefinitely interrupt or suspend services of a host connected to the Internet. A *distributed denial-of-service (DDoS)* attack is where the attack source is more than one, often thousands of, unique IP addresses. It is analogous to a group of people crowding the entry door or gate to a shop or business and not letting legitimate parties enter the shop or business, disrupting normal operations. Criminal perpetrators of DoS attacks often target sites or services hosted on high-profile Web servers such as banks and credit card payment gateways; but motives of revenge, blackmail, or activism can be behind other attacks.

3. Padding: Sometimes writers use a long and a large number of unnecessary words to impress their readers. Some writers have the habit of writing long sentences by inserting irrelevant words. When unnecessary words are added to make a speech or an article longer is called padding.

Example: If you are not sure how to spell 'recommendation' run a spell-check to verify it. In this sentence, the last part of the sentence is redundant and it is only padding the sentence. Trimming redundancies and word padding will make your writing emphatic and crisp.

Revised: If you are not sure how to spell **'recommendation'**, run a spell check.

4. Kuhlthau's Information Search Process: Kuhlthau's information search process (ISP) model in 1991 focuses on two aspects: affective and cognitive during the process of information searching. This ISP of Kuhlthau is a six-stage process of information seeking behaviour in library and information science. Kuhlthau identified the following stages in the information seeking process:

1. task initiation: uncertainty;
2. topic selection: confusion, sometimes anxiety;
3. prefocus exploration: confusion, frustration, sometimes threat and doubt;
4. focus formation: optimism, confidence of ability to complete task;
5. information collection: realization of extensive work to be done, direction, confidence;
6. presentation: relief, sometimes satisfaction and dissatisfaction.

Kuhlthau characterized the first stage, **initiation** as the stage when a person becomes aware that information will be needed to "complete an assignment". This stage of the information seeking process is filled with feelings of apprehension and uncertainty. In the next stage, **selection** where a person has chosen an idea, topic, or problem to proceed. At this point, the person is now less uncertain, and feels a sense of optimism and a readiness to start the information search process. The third stage, the **exploration process,** is when students or information seekers become confused when they encounter "inconsistent or incompatible" information. It is at this point that information seekers may become discouraged, express feelings of doubt and plan of abandoning their search process. Kuhlthau considers this stage as the most difficult stage. The fourth stage namely **focus formulation,** which is considered as the key point, states that a focused perspective is formed, and uncertainty gradually decreases, and clarity is achieved. The information seeker starts to evaluate the gathering information. At this point, a focused perspective begins to form and there is not as much confusion and uncertainty as in earlier stages formulation is considered to be the most important stage of the process. The information seeker will here formulate a personalized construction of the topic from the general information gathered in the exploration phase. The fifth stage, **collection** where information seeker gather the information which is relevant to the topic. At this point, the information seeker understands about the direction; he or she must have confidences. Consequently his/her uncertainty diminishes and becomes interested and deeply involved in the search process. At this point, confidence grows in the search process. The sixth stage, **presentation** is when the individual has completed the information search and information seekers prepare to present or use their findings that were found through the process. They experience relief and a sense of satisfaction if the search process is successful or disappointed if they feel that the search was a failure. Kuhlthau states that these stages of the ISP encompass three aspects—"the affective" *i.e.* feelings, the cognitive, thoughts, the physical actions.

Initiation	⇒	Uncertainty of getting information
Selection	⇒	Start the information search process
Exploration	⇒	Inconsistent information process
Focus	⇒	Uncertainty decreases formulation
Collection	⇒	Confidence grows and uncertainty Diminishes
Presentation	⇒	Completed the Search Process, *i.e.*, closure of searching

Fig. *Kuhlthau's six stages information Search Process*

5. **Microblogging** is a term in common use since 2006, when Twitter and Jaiku were launched. From an etymological perspective the word *'microblog'* (also, sometimes written with a hyphen: *micro-blog*) comes from the conjoining of the terms 'micro' and 'blog'. The first one is a common used prefix which

means 'small' whereas the second term represents a webpage with a continuous, regular and chronological series of information (text and/or multimedia content) about one or more subjects.

In other words, by microblog we understand a blog of small sizes, 'a severe space' with size constraints, as specifies Merriam Webster Dictionary, composed by posts of maximum of 140-200 characters, that may sometimes include links, images or video clips and are available to be read either by any internet or just by a group of people, named followers. The person who creates and maintains the entries is called 'microblogger', entries are called 'microposts' and the activity of writing is called 'microblogging'.

The 'lilliputian' character of the notes and the fact that they may be posted from wherever you are (online, by phone, ipads or tablets, sent as SMS, e-mail or instant messaging) has not only changed microblogging into a fast-food writing experience, circumventing the usual editorial rigor, but may be considered as a possible explanation for its popularity.

In a world of hundreds of microblogging platforms, the most popular applications include Twitter, Plurk, Edmodo, Tumblr, identi.ca, Yammer, Shoutem, Weibo in China or Cirip.eu as the most notable Romanian platform.

Summing up, we can state that microblogging is another form of social media, recognized as *Real-Time Web Publishing,* which has won an impressive audience acceptance and surprisingly changed online expression and interaction for millions of users.

6. **ShodhGangotri : Indian Research in Progress**

SbodhGangotri is an open access repository of Indian research in progress. Shodh is a Sanskrit word which means 'Research and Discovery' and Gangotri is one of the largest glaciers in the Himalayas and the source of origination of Ganga, the holiest and longest river in India. ShodhGangotri is an initiative by INFLIBNET in which research scholars/ supervisors are requested to deposit electronic version or their approved synopses or research proposal submitted by the research scholars to the Universities for registering themselves for PhD. Synopsis in Shodhgangotri later on mapped to full text theses in Shodhganga. When the full text thesis is submitted for a synopsis, a link will be provided from ShodhGangotri to Shodhganga.

ShodhGangotri reveals the trends and directions research in Indian Universities and helps in avoiding duplication of research. Users can search synopses in ShodhGangotri in terms of their Universities and Departments, issue date, name of researcher or supervisor, title and key words. Advanced search using Boolean logic is also possible.

7. TQM is an amalgam of the ideas evolving from Deming, Juran, Crosby, and others. TQM is the management philosophy that focuses on fulfilling customer expectations by providing quality services and product as a result of continuous improvement to the organizational processes.

W. Edwards Deming is the one person most identified with TQM. Deming, a statistician with experience teaching organizations in government and industry, developed a philosophy on how to use statistical process control to improve quality. The fourteen points of his management philosophy are anchored in statistical theory. A statistical study was used to provide a rational basis for TQM action using the scientific method and statistical theory.

W. Edwards Deming is known as the "guru of quality management." In postwar Japan, Deming taught Japanese industrialists statistical process control and quality concepts. His classic 1986 book describes how to do highquality, productive, and satisfying work. Deming's plan-do-check-act cycle of continuous improvement promoted the adoption of fourteen principles to make any organization efficient and capable of solving almost any problem.

Deming believed that removing fear from the workplace gives employees pride in their workmanship, which increases production. Deming also felt that when things go wrong, there is a 94 per cent chance that the system (elements under managerial control including machinery and rules) rather than the worker is the cause.

He believed that making changes in response to normal variations was unwise, and that a proper understanding of variation includes the mathematical certainty that variation will normally occur within a certain range. Deming's fourteen principles of transformation for improving the practice of management are:

1. Create constancy of purpose toward improvement of product and service.
2. Adopt a new philosophy for a new economic age.
3. Cease dependence on inspection to achieve quality.
4. Minimize total cost.
5. Improve constantly and forever.
6. Institute training on the job.
7. Institute leadership.
8. Drive out fear.
9. Break down barriers between departments.
10. Eliminate slogans.
11. Eliminate quotas.
12. Remove barriers to pride of workmanship.
13. Institute a vigorous program of education and self-improvement.
14. Involve everyone in the organization to work toward transformation.

9. Service Providers of Cloud Computing in Libraries

Ex Libris: Ex Libris is a well-known cloud service provider based in USA. They provide cloud solution in the field of libraries with all the software and hardware support needed to provide services to tbe users. Ex Libris is available for all type of libraries and also for consortia. Ex Libris is built on various standards and contains a number of features like compatibility with Unicode font, flexibility, migration of data, customization etc.

Polaris Library Systems: Polaris is one of the cloud based library automation system available in the market. The company also provides standard acquisition and processing system. Also, with a Polaris ILS Client License, the library can integrate various PC and print management systems at no extra cost. The systems uses a number of well known standards like MARC 21 for bibliographic data. XML, Z39.50 for information retrieval, Unicode etc.

Dura Cloud: Dura Cloud provides cloud solution for digital library services Dura Cloud is a sister concern of Duraspace that is a collaboration of the Dspace digital library software and Fedora Commons. Fedora Commons is a framework for digital repository.

It offers a complete solution for digital library with standard software and hardware solution. Dura Cloud also provides open source code and the code needs to be installed on your machine. Where in case if you use Dura Cloud storage and Software you have to subscribe Dura Cloud services with a nominal cost.

10. Li-Fi vs. Wi-Fi

- Both Wi-Fi and Li-Fi transmit data over the electromagnetic spectrum; Wi-Fi utilizes radio waves, whereas Li-Fi uses visible light.

- While there is a potential spectrum crisis as Wi-Fi is close to full capacity, Li-Fi has almost no limitations on capacity, because the visible light spectrum is 10,000 times larger than the entire radio-frequency spectrum.
- Li-Fi has the advantage of being useful in electromagnetic-sensitive areas, such as in aircraft cabins, hospitals and nuclear power plants without causing electromagnetic interference.
- Li-Fi is expected to be 10 times cheaper than Wi-Fi.

13. **Altmetrics** (or alternative metrics) provide article-level evidence of the societal impact of research, in terms of its mentions in social media (blogs, Facebook and Twitter), Wikipedia and other quasi-scholarly platforms, news sources and policy documents.

Altmetric, which examines each article's record of attention, measure of dissemination, and indicator of influence and impact.

Altmetrics can include:

- tweets, mentions, shares or links
- downloads, clicks or views
- saves, bookmarks, favourites, likes or upvotes
- mainstream media mentions
- reviews, comments, ratings, or recommendations
- adaptations or derivative works, and
- readers, subscribers, watchers, or followers.

Best uses: Altmetrics can help researchers understand how their outputs are being shared and discussed via social media and online, and may supplement the information gained from traditional indicators.

15. **The Internet Control Message Protocol (ICMP)**

The ICMP protocol is used to control messages. ICMP is an integral part of all IP prococol implementations. ICMP packets are used by user applications, such as ping, to diagnose network problems.

ICMP packets also may be generated by hosts to report network problems to other hosts on the network.

16. INFOTERRA is a component of EARTHWATCH, UNEP's programme for the critical assessment of the global environment. One of the first major activities of UNEP, initiated shortly after its establishment following the Stockholm Conference on the Human Environment (1972), INFOTERRA was set up to facilitate the exchange of environmental information within and between nations.

INFOTERRA is a decentralized international network incorporating diverse environmental information systems; its operation relies on a grid of government-designated national focal points.

INFOTERRA operations are based on the concept of referral. All INFOTERRA national focal points are equipped to refer an enquirer to the sources best able to provide the information sought. In other words, they act as switchboards to connect users with appropriate sources of environmental information.

Seventy developing countries constitute almost two-thirds of the total INFOTERRA partnership, providing between them nearly 25% of the total 7000 sources of environmental information registered in the INFOTERRA International Directory. Developing countries are valuable sources of information on such topics as renewable energy sources, biological control of certain diseases and other appropriate technological approaches, and their increased participation therefore makes a vast store of information and experience available. Since these same nations often lack well-established information channels, any tool for improving their ability to locate reliable sources and collect valid information can be of great value to them and promote the sharing of such information.

Moreover, through an international network like INFOTERRA, the developing world can profit from "no strings attached" information exchange with industrialized nations and hopefully avoid some of the technological errors of the more affluent societies. At the same time, INFOTERRA stimulates communication between countries at similar levels of development thus enabling developing countries to cooperate in solving common environmental problems and to avoid an unhealthy dependence on industrialized nations for their information needs.

17. Historically, reference services concept has become common among American librarians since 1876. Reference services theories appeared in 20th Century and there are three known types of reference services theories presented by James I. Wyer in 1930. These are Conservative Theory, Liberal Theory and Moderate Theory. Conservative theory persists on education and guidance instead of boundless help. This theory states that reference work is limited to use the ready reference sources to help the users. Liberal theory focuses on the maximum help and according to this theory, reference librarians must apply any approach to retrieve the information that users need. In fact reference librarians carry out the whole job and reference work takes a long time in many cases. The average of conservative theory and liberal theory is moderate theory which most of reference librarians prefer. In fact this theory results in high costs but the reference librarians can serve more readers.

18. The IFLA Universal Bibliographic Control and International MARC (UBCIM) Core Activity which was established thirty years ago came to an end in 2003. The objective of UBCIM was "to coordinate activities aimed at the development of systems and standards for bibliographic control at the national level and the international exchange of bibliographic data, including the support for professional activities of appropriate IFLA Sections and Divisions". UBCIM coordinated the development of the UNIMARC format and ensured publication of reports on projects related to international bibliographic and format standards and proceedings of relevant meetings and seminars.

The British Library hosted UBCIM from 1973 to 1989 and later Die Deutsche Bibliothek from 1990 to the beginning of 2003. The Biblioteca Nacional de Portugal took over the responsibility for both UNIMARC and *ICBC* (*International Cataloguing and Bibliographic Control,* a quarterly journal of IFLA, formerly of UBCIM).

19. Indian National Bibliography

It is India's most important bibliography. In this bibliography only current publications are included. The information included in bibliography is reliable and authentic. This bibliography covers current publications in 14 languages including English language. In it only those publications are included which are received by National Library, Kolkata under rhe Delivery of Books and Newspaper Act of 1954. (Act number 27 of 1954 as amended by Act number 99 of 1956).

Authority

(*a*) Its publication is done by Central Reference Library under Ministry of Research and Cultural Affairs at the National Library, Kolkata.

(*b*) Duration of Publication:

(*i*) The publication of first annual volumes was done in 1958.

(*ii*) It is published quarterly from 1958 to 1963.

(*iii*) From 1964 its publication was done monthly.

(*iv*) From 1967 to 1970 its publication was ceased.

(*v*) From 1971 to 1977 its publication was irregular.

(*vi*) From 1984 its publication is continuous and regular.

(*c*) Its general Editor was B.S. Kesavao.

(*d*) Indian National Bibliography is divided into two parts:

Part I - General Publication (with Index)
Part II - Government Publication (with Index).

Scope

(*a*) In Indian National Bibliography, current Indian publications covering 14 languages which are obtained under the Act of 1954, are given. The 14 languages are—Bengali, English, Hindi, Sanskrit, Urdu, Punjabi, Kannadda, Malayalam, Telugu, Tamil, Marathi, Gujarati, Assamese.

(*b*) The following types of publications have been excluded:

(*i*) Musical scores

(*ii*) Maps

(*iii*) Periodicals & newspapers (except the first issue of a new periodicals and the first issue of periodicals under new title).

(*iv*) Keys and Guides to textbooks

(*v*) Ephemeral material such as trade catalogue, telephone directory, reports and financial statements.

20. After MARC, Dublin Core is by far the most used descriptive metadata standard in the library domain. Dublin Core was first introduced in 1995 as an everyman metadata standard for the Web. It was hoped that many (if not most) Web page authors would adopt Dublin Core to describe the persistent Web-based information resources they created. Originally published as a draft for comment in 1995, Dublin Core initially consisted of only 13 properties (called *elements* or *fields* in Dublin Core documentation). These fields were designed to capture what the authors of the standard felt to be the essential descriptive attributes of Web-based information resources. The model embraced by the authors of Dublin Core was consciously bibliographic in scope and viewed Web-based information resources as being document-like (Lagoze 2001). Two more elements were added prior to the formal 1.0 release of Dublin Core in 1998.

21. Planning, Programming and Budgeting System (PPBS)

Planning, Programming and Budgeting System (PPBS) is used in governmental, non-profit or noncommercial organisations to enable them to make more informed decisions about resources allocation. These organisations' activities produce results that are often difficult to measure in monetary terms or that may take several years to be measured (although the related activities must continue to be funded annually). Thus, relating outputs to inputs is often extremely difficult.

PPBS differs from traditional non-profit and non-manufacturing budgets in the sense that the later are prepared as line item budgets whereas the former (PPBS) are prepared on the basis of programmes, *i.e.*, planned activities that have specified objectives. In PPBS, budgets for line/functional items for whole department are not presented. Instead, the expenses associated with specific programmes are detailed.

For instance, a railway authority may have the programme of total computerisation of its booking system, a municipal authority may have programmes of providing drinking water or providing health facilities in the city. Such programmes require greater coordination among several departments to make a specific programme successful.

PPBS is taken by extending the planning period beyond the one-year budget period. PPBS is the counterpart of the long-term planning process which is operated in profit oriented organisations. PPBS is based on a rational model of decision-making and involves the following stages:

1. Identify and define the objectives of programme.
2. Select performance or output measures to assess the effectiveness of the programme.
3. Identify and evaluate alternative methods of achieving the objectives laid down for each specific programme. For this, costs and benefits associated with each alternative course of action should be detailed.
4. Select the appropriate programmes on the basis of cost benefit analysis as done in (3).
5. Implement the selected alternative and monitor its performance to ensure that the objectives of the programmes are achieved given the resources allocated to those programmes.

22. Lewin's Three-Step Model

Kurt Lewin, the father of change processes, identified three phases in initiating and establishing any change—unfreezing, changing or moving, and refreezing. Kurt Lewin argued that successful change in organisations should follow these three steps: unfreezing the status quo, movement to a new state, and refreezing the new change to make it permanent. The status quo can be considered to be a state of equilibrium. To move from this equilibrium to overcome the pressures of both individual resistance and group conformity unfreezing is necessary.

Elements of Change and the Change Progress

By definition, change involves a sequence of organisational events or a psychological process that occurs over time. Kurt Lewin has suggested this sequence or process involves three basic stages—unfreezing, changing and refreezing.

1. Unfreezing occurs when recognition exists that some current state of affairs is inadequate. Crises and technological innovation are especially likely to stimulate unfreezing.
2. Change occurs when some program or plan is implemented to move the organisation and/or its members to a more adequate state or when new technology is introduced into the environment.
3. When refreezing occurs, the newly developed behaviours, attitudes or structures must be subjected to refreezing to become an enduring part of the organisational system.

23. Bibframe: Bibframe is developed by the Library of Congress, and it is considered the successor of MARC. BIBFRAME 2.0 organizes information into three core levels of abstraction.

Work—Work is considered the highest level of abstraction and reflects the essence of the item (author, language and subject content).

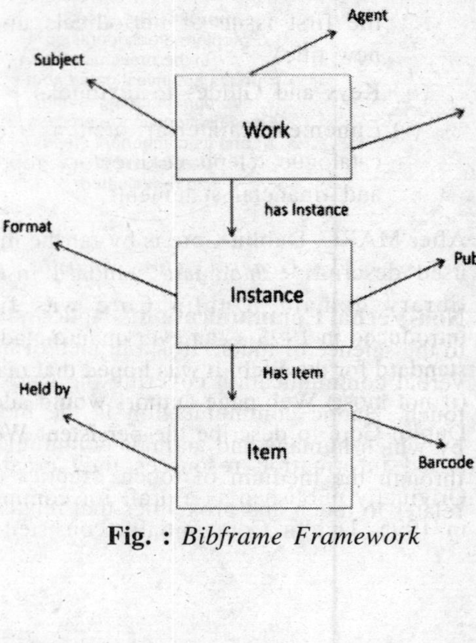

Fig. : *Bibframe Framework*

Instance: A work may one or more material formats and is reflected in an instance (publisher, place and format).

Item: Item is the actual physical or electronic copy of an instance (location, shelf mark, barcode, or radio-frequency identification (RFID) tag).

24. The DMAIC methodology is an important and central part of Six Sigma used to systematically improve process performance. It consists of five distinct phases that may overlap to some degree: define, measure, analyze, improve and control as shown in Figure.

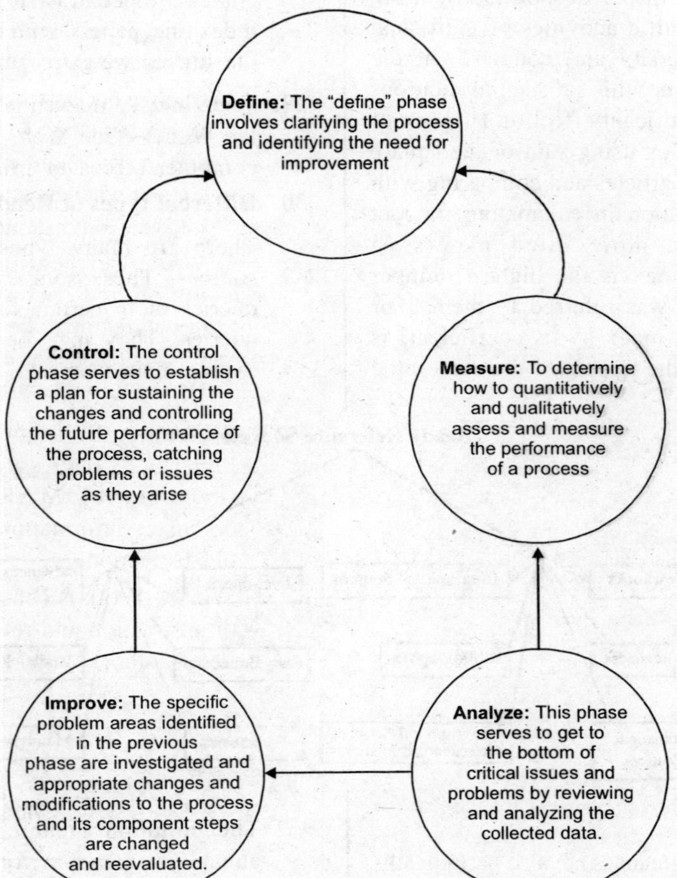

Fig. *General define, measure, analyze, improve, control (DMAIC) cycle.*

25. Non-Verbal Communication: Haptics relates to the science of touch. It is a branch of non-verbal communication covering the study of touch. Haptic communication is the means by which humans and animals communicate through the medium of touch. Haptics that relates to touch and proxemics that relates to space are closely related in business and personal communication, together they have much to convey. Touch can convey trust, encouragement, reassurance, dislike, etc. Any business communicator should, however, know the difference between a good touch and a bad touch, and avoid the wrong kind of touch.

26. G-Index: The G-Index was proposed by Leo Egghe for quantifying measurement of scientific output of physics science researchers and other researchers. His very aim was to improve and correct the limitations of H-index. One of the most important disadvantages of H-index is that the low count citations to paper do not contribute in ranking the scientific activities of individual or journal, university and country. On the other hand, papers with substantial citations also have no significant effect on H-index of researcher. G-Index using sum of the square of the number of articles and comparing with collection of citation in calculating, in fact highlighted the more cited papers of researchers. G-Index is the highest number of papers which was referred to them 2 or more times. This index by its coefficients is trying to reduce the impact of the most cited and low cited articles on conclusions and also remove one of the shortcomings of H-index.

To calculate the G-index, first of all, sort the papers in descending order based on the citation counts, then sum up the citations up to the point that the G paper would have G^2 citation. In contrast to the H-Index, in this index the papers with higher citations gain the higher weight.

29. Webzine: A magazine that is published on the World Wide Web. It can be read on the computer screen or printed out.

30. Different types of Ready Reference Sources

There are many types of ready reference sources. These sources satisfy fact-finding queries or in certain cases, material-finding queries. They may be grouped into six to twelve main classes:

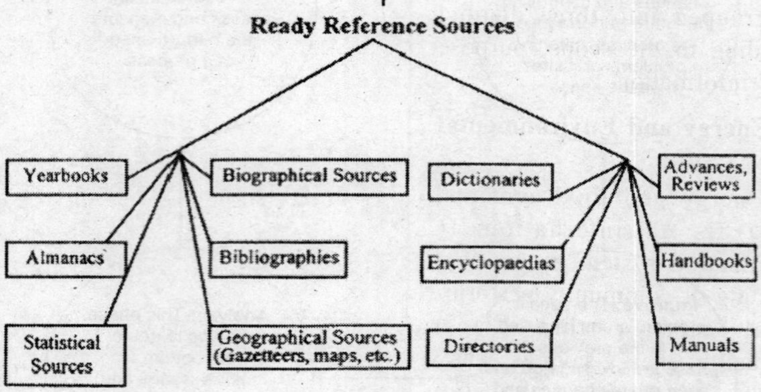

Almanacs

Like yearbooks, almanacs are also periodically published ready reference sources with similar objectives. Almanac literally means calendar of months and days containing astronomical and nautical information about the sun, moon, tides, anniversaries and so on. It is an annual calendar covering miscellaneous matters such as astronomical events, plenetary tables, astrological predictions and anecdotes. But the meaning of the word 'almanac' has undergone semantic change in recent days. The common meaning of almanac is an annual compendium of statistics and facts, both current and retrospective. It can broadly cover a particular region or subject or it can be limited to a particular nation, country or state. Thus, while the *Shorter Oxford English Dictionary* defines an almanac as "an annual table or book of tables, containing a calendar of months and days usually with astronomical data and information". Harrod's glossary calls it "a publication, usually annual, containing a variety of useful facts of a miscellaneous nature and statistical information." Librarians frequently use them as ready reference sources of statistics.

At this juncture, let us compare and contrast between the yearbooks and almanacs. Though they are two distinct types of reference books, still they are similar and closely related to each other in scope and use. They are always grouped together as ready reference sources. They have fixed periodicity and are published every year. The major distinction between the two is in coverage in the form of duration. A yearbook is an annual compendium of descriptive and statistical data of the past year whereas the almanac inevitably covers retrospective information too. Again a yearbook is published annually but almanacs vary in periodicity *e.g., Congressional Quarterly Almanac* or the *Almanac of American Politics* (biennial), *Almanac of Famous People* (irregular).

Almanacs are grouped into three distinct categories according to the scope, purpose and coverage of information.

31. Leadership in Energy and Environmental Design

Leadership in Energy and Environmental Design (LEED) is an internationally recognized certification system to measure how well a building or community performs across several metrics that affect environmental quality; energy savings; water efficiency; CO_2 emissions reduction; improved indoor environmental quality; stewardship of resources and sensitivity to their impacts; and innovation and design processes.

LEED was developed beginning in 1994 by a broad group of non-profit representatives, government agents, architects, engineers, developers, builders, product manufacturers and other industry leaders. A pilot certification program was released in 1998. Operated by the U.S. Green Building Council, LEED has become the defining certification system for ecologically sound building practices. Both new and retrofitted buildings can be LEED certified. LEED's primary goals are:

- Define 'green building' by establishing a common standard of measurement.
- Promote integrated, whole-building design practices.
- Recognize environmental leadership in the building industry.
- Stimulate green competition.
- Raise consumer awareness of green building benefits.
- Transform the building market.

The third version of the LEED certification (U.S. Green Building Council 2009) has 100 possible base points plus an additional 6 points for innovation and 4 points for undeserved regions. Scoring is subject to third-party verification. Once scored, buildings can qualify on four levels of LEED certification:

- Certified (40-49 points)
- Silver (50-59 points)
- Gold (60-79 points)
- Platinum (80 points or more)

LEED values thoughtful design of human habitats to promote more environmentally friendly habits.

33. The accuracy of any search query (or wordlist in a lexicon) is scored by the conflicting values of *recall* and *precision.* Recall refers to the per cent of relevant documents in the collection retrieved by the query, while precision refers to the per cent of retrieved documents that are actually relevant. A query which returns every document in the corpus will have a recall score of 100 per cent, but its precision score will be very low, while a query that is so narrow in scope that it returns only relevant documents must often trade recall, leaving out some peripherally relevant documents.

Recall and precision are important concepts when searching electronic archives, as search criteria must be restrictive enough so that most of the returned documents are relevant, while being broad enough to catch articles using slightly different terminology.

For example, searching for coverage of the Iraq War in a news archive using the keyword *Iraq* is likely to bring back nearly every document mentioning the war (high recall), but will also bring back many documents unrelated to the war (low precision). A search for *Iraq war civilian casualties* will most likely have fairly high precision, but would not return documents that used the phrase *women and children casualties* instead of the word *civilian*, or other wording to tally the dead, yielding poor recall. Recall and precision are therefore traditionally inversely related, with an increase in one invariably causing a decrease in the other.

34. **Dura Cloud:** Dura Cloud is a Cloud solution for digital library services. It is a managed service of Dura Space and is a not-for-profit organization providing services and technology for digitalization of content to be accessible for long term. Collaboration of the Dspace digital library software and Fedora Commons is known as Dura Space. D Space and Fedora Commons are two top open source solutions used by various libraries, research centers, and many other organizations involved in cultural heritage Fedora Commons offers solution for digital repository (Digital Library Solution) using standard software and hardware solution. Like other open source software's Dura Cloud also accommodate open source code and the code require to be installed on Computer System. Dura Cloud provides service for preservation of content simple and cost effective.

35. **Health Science Library and Information Network (HELINET)**

Health Science Library and Information Network (HELINET), an electronic resource sharing consortia concept adapted by Rajiv Gandhi Institute of Health Sciences, Karnataka (RGUHS) in 2001 to network all health scienct libraries in Karnataka. HELINET has grown to be the single largest library consortium in the country by membership.

36. **Index Indiana:** This was an ambitious project to trace the periodical literature appearing in the Indian Language periodicals. The first issue of the Index Indiana appeared as quarterly in 1977 and since 1981 it is being published as annual cumulated volumes. As a beginning 6 languages viz. Bengali, Hindi, Gujarati, Marathi, Tamil and Malayalam periodicals are covered. Indexing articles pertaining to Indian Literature, Social Science, Indian Systems of Medicine, Folk literature, Social Science, Philosophy etc. could be of great help to research scholars. For science and technology etc. such publications are already available. Due to lack of language competent professionals, certain languages goes unrepresented occasionally. Efforts are being to include all Indian languages.

This index is divided into three parts– classified part, subject index and author index. The entries are grouped in the classified part according to Dewey Decimal Classification system. The entries under the subject are further arranged by the author and wherever not available then by title. All the entries are serially numbered in the classified part. The name of the authors and titles are given in popular spelling in Roman but near to their transliterated forms without the use of any diacritical marks.

The subject and author indices are linked to these serial numbers.

37. The UK Committee on RDA (UKCoR) is the national committee in the UK responsible for contributing to the development and maintenance of the metadata standard Resource Description and Access (RDA).

The British Library and the Chartered Institute of Library and Information Professionals support the committee, and appoint representatives to the committee.

The committee:

- contributes to the RDA development programme, and to the maintenance and governance of RDA;
- represents the interests of the UK library and information professional community regarding all aspects of RDA;
- ensures that representatives of the RDA Europe Region are briefed on the position of the UK Community regarding all aspects of the governance, development and maintenance of RDA;
- supports implementation and development of RDA in the UK.

38. International Federation of Library Associations and Institutions (IFLA)

The International Federation of Library Associations and Institutions (IFLA) founded in 1927 with the aim of promoting international contacts among library associations and librarians, is a non-governmental professional organisation. In the first two decades, it had remained almost as a forum confirmed to leading librarians from Europe and America: In the post-war period; with a consultative status accorded by UNESCO, it began to develop, but slowly.

The International Conference on Cataloguing Principles held in Paris in 1961 gave some impetus to the growth of IFLA. After the Secretariat shifted to the Hague in 1971, IFLA (under the presidentship of Herman Liebaers) stepped up its activities and was able to enlist universal international membership.

At the present time, with some major projects and many smaller programmes, IFLA is quite active and is making worldwide impact towards promoting the cause of librarianship.

The broad objective of IFLA is to promote international understanding, cooperation; discussion, research and development in all fields of library activity including bibliography; information service and education of personnel and to provide a professional body through librarianship can be represented in matters of international interest.

Chartered Institute of Library and Information Professionals (CILIP)

CILIP (The Chartered Institute of Library and Information Professionals) is the leading professional body of library and information professionals in U.K. It came into existence in 2002 with the merger of the erstwhile Library Association (U.K.) and Institute of Information Science. CILIP provides practical support for members throughout their entire careers, helping them with their academic education, professional qualifications, job hunting and continuing professional development.

Objectives: The CILIP aims at: activism and enterprise to build its community, a strong voice to advance the profession and modern professionalism to develop the workforce. Its objectives are to:

- set, maintain, monitor and promote standards of excellence in the creation, management, exploitation and sharing of information and knowledge resources;
- support the principle of equality of access to information, ideas and works of the imagination which it affirms is fundamental to a thriving economy, democracy, culture and civilisation; and
- enable its members to achieve and maintain the highest professional standards in all aspects of delivering an information service, both for the professional and the public good.

American Library Association (ALA)

The American Library Association (ALA) has the uniqueness of being the oldest and largest library association in the world. It was founded in 1876 with its headquarters at Chicago.

A group of 103 library activists, at a meeting held in Philadelphia in the fall of 1876 to coincide with the nation's centennial celebrations, resolved on a motion moved by Melvile Dewey, the father of librarianship, to form the American Library Association. ALA, thus born, has been a success story by dedicated efforts of eminent librarians who steered the association in its formative periods, the ALA grew in strength steadily and became even in the early part of this century the national voice for library interests. Today, with a solid foundation, wide base expanding programmes and activities and social impact, ALA plays a dynamic role to foster American library interests with great success.

Objectives: ALA is an organisation of librarians and libraries having the following objectives:

- "Increase awareness and support for libraries by increasing their visibility in a positive context and by communicating why libraries are both unique and valuable;
- Update the image of libraries, librarians and all library staff for the 21st century, sustaining and strengthening their relevance;
- Bring renewed energy to the promotion of libraries and librarians; and
- Bring library messages to a more diverse audience.

SLA

The Special Libraries Association (SLA) was established in 1909 in New York at the initiative of some government departments, commercial organizations and research institutes. It is an international professional association for library and information professionals working in business, government, law, finance, non-profit and academic organizations and institutions. It is now an international organization with over 15,000 members in over 75 countries. SLA functions in a decentralized manner through 32 chapters and 16 divisions. The mission of SLA is "to advance the leadership role of SLA members in putting knowledge to work for the benefit of decision makers in corporations, government, the professions, and society as well as to shape the destiny of our information and knowledge based global society" and its motto is "Putting Knowledge to Work". SLA plays vital role in supporting professional knowledge workers in their work as they provide practical and utilitarian information, knowledge, and strategic learning to their identified knowledge customers and clients. The association has 58 regional chapters located throughout the world. SLA celebrated in centenary in 2009.

39. MARC: The MARC format was developed by the Library of Congress and released in 1968 as a standard structure for exchanging library cataloguing records. MARC is a specific implementation of ANSI/NISO Z39.2, the standard that specifies a record structure to accommodate bibliographic information. While MARC was developed for books, it can also be used for other print based formats such as serials and sheet music, as well as audiovisual and digital resources. It was widely adopted around the world, although national variants such as USMARC in the US, CAN/MARC in Canada, UKMARC in Britain and INDOMARC in Indonesia emerged whose paths diverged because of different national cataloguing practices and requirements. In order to facilitate international exchange of bibliographic data between national bibliographic agencies, and as a result of this proliferation of national formats, an international MARC format was developed which in principle would accept records in any MARC format and act as a common conversion format. This Universal MARC Format (UNIMARC) was established (in 1977) and maintained by the IFLA Permanent UNIMARC Committee (PUC); (more information on it can be found at http://www.ukoln.ac.uk/metadata/desire/overview/rev_17.htm).

US-MARC and the Canadian form of MARC (CAN/MARC) merged in 1997 to become MARC21, the current edition.

40. Basic Laws: Ranganathan formulated six basic laws. viz.,

1. Law of Interpretation
2. Law of Impartiality
3. Law of Symmetry
4. Law of Parsimony
5. Law of Local Variation
6. Law of Osmosis

1. Law of Symmetry: "The principle that of two entities in situations which admit of being regarded as symmetrical counterparts of each other, if one of the entities context, the other entry or situation should also be given a corresponding weight".

In case of a joint author's work, law of symmetry suggests that in the heading of the Main Entry, we are obliged to write the names of the two authors in the sequence in which they occur on the title pages. CCC prescribed the rules at the directive of law of symmetry in case of joint authors. No other code made such a provision.

2. Principle of Local Variation: This principle states that an international catalogue code should mark out the factors to be left in each national catalogue code. A national catalogue code should mark out the factors to be left to the care of each linguistic catalogue code in a multilingual country such as India. A national catalogue code or a linguistic catalogue code as the case may be should mark out the factors to be left to the care of the local catalogue codes in each individual library. The catalogue codes in each hierarchical line should be consistent with one another without any mutual contradiction; and each lower link in each hierarchical line should be a supplement to all the upper links taken together.

3. Principles of Osmosis: The principle state that when a change in the catalogue code or in the scheme of classification becomes necessary in difference to the canon of context on and after a chosen date, all the new accessions be catalogued and classified according to the new catalogue code and the new scheme of classification; just those of the old collection as are known to be in much use be recalculated and reclassified with an additional temporary staff, if necessary during the first few months; the new accessions and the recatalogued and reclassified books be kept in a new collection and similarly their catalogue cards too kept in a new collection; the rest of the old collection be kept as old collection and similarly their catalogue cards be kept as old collection; Reader's attention be invited by the Reference Librarian to the existence of the two collections; and if any book is taken out by a reader form the old collection, on its return by him, it be recatalogued and absorbed in the new collection and similarly with its catalogue cards.

4. Law of Parsimony: "Between two or more possible alternative rules bearing on a particular phenomenon, the one leading to overall economy of manpower, materials, money and time considered together with proper weightage is to be preferred."

This principle though brought in vogue by Ranganathan, it is in practice in many disciplines and suggested by various catalogue codes over a period of time. For examples the distinction made in RDC between 'full' and 'short' style in catalogue is a contribution of law of parsimony.

41. Office of the Patent Information System, Nagpur

Objectives: Government of India, Ministry of Commerce and Industry, Department of Industrial Policy and Promotion established Patent Information System (PIS), in the year 1980 with the following objectives.

- To obtain and maintain a comprehensive collection of patent specification and patent related literature on a worldwide basis to meet the needs for technological information, of various users in R&D establishments, Government Organizations, Industries, Business, Inventors and other users.
- To provide technological information contained in patents through, search services and patent copy supply service;

Functions: The PIS caters to user needs on the basis of patent documentation and computerized system for retrieval and dissemination of patent information.

44. The International Standard Bibliographic Descriptions (ISBD) date back to 1969, when the IFLA Committee on Cataloguing sponsored an International Meeting of Cataloguing Experts. This meeting produced a resolution that proposed the creation of standards to regularize the form and content of bibliographic descriptions. As a result, the Committee on Cataloguing put into motion work that ultimately would provide the means for a considerable increase in the sharing and exchange of bibilographic data. This work resulted in the concept of the International Standard Bibliographic.

The first of the ISBDs was the International Standard Bibliographic Description for Monographic Publications (ISBD(M)), which appeared in 1971.

45. Open Systems Interconnection Model

The open systems interconnection (OSI) model assumes seven layers of data communication functions over a telecommunication or a computer network. A layer in this model receives commands from and sends responses to the layer above it. This separation of the complicated process of communication simplifies the design and implementation of basic network functions. The layers in this model are as follows:

- *Physical Layer:* The main function of this layer is the transfer of data between the physical medium and the devices.
- *Data Link Layer:* This layer provides point-to-point data transfer between two connected devices. Doing so, it provides mechanisms for flow control and error detection and correction. It consists of two sub-layers: medium access control (MAC) and logical link control (LLC) layers. The MAC layer indulges in controlling network access and the LLC layer is responsible for error detection and flow control.
- *Network Layer:* The main task of this layer is to enable routing of data packets from a source node to a destination node.
- *Transport Layer:* This layer is responsible for correct end-to-end data transfer between two applications. The transmission control protocol (TCP) for connection-oriented and user datagram protocol (UDP) for connectionless communication are the two main protocols in this layer.
- *Session Layer:* Dialog management between two communicating entities is the main task performed in this layer.
- *Presentation Layer:* Syntax and context conversions between two communicating applications are handled in this layer.

47. Network Topology: Network Topology is the way computer systems or network equipment connected to each other.

Topologies may define both physical and logical aspect of the network. Both logical and physical topologies could be same or different in a same network. Topology can be referred as the physical arrangement of a computer system.

There are many types of Network Topologies: Bus Topology, Ring Topology, Star Topology, Mesh Topology, Tree Topology, Daisy Chain, Hybrid Topology; etc.

48. Fedora: The Fedora digital object repository management system is based on the Flexible Extensible Digital Object and Repository Architecture (Fedora). The system is designed to be a foundation upon which fullfeatured institutional repositories and other inter-operable web-based digital libraries can be built. Jointly developed by the University of Virginia and Cornell University, the system implements the Fedora architecture, adding utilities that facilitate repository management. The current version of the software provides a repository that can handle one million objects efficiently. Subsequent versions of the software will add functionality important for institutional repository implementations, such as policy enforcement, versioning of objects, and performance enhancement to support very large repositories.

49. Attenuation: Attenuation is the loss of optical power as light travels down a fiber. It is measured in decibels (dB/km). Over a set distance, a fiber with a lower attenuation will allow more power to reach its receiver than a fiber with higher attenuation.

While low-loss optical systems are always desirable, it is possible to lose a large portion of the initial signal power without significant problems. A loss of 50% of initial power is equal to a 3.0 dB loss. Any time fibers are joined together there will be some loss. Losses for fusion splicing and for mechanical splicing are typically 0.2 dB or less.

Attenuation can be caused by several factors, but is generally placed in one of two categories : intrinsic or extrinsic.

50. 1948 National Library Librarian: By an Act of Parliament the Government of India changed the name of the Imperial Library to National Library. B S Kesavan became the first Librarian of the National Library of Independent India.

51. Indian Standards Institution (ISI), now known as Bureau of Indian Standards (BIS) was established in the year 1947 primarily to improve quality of goods produced in the country. However, ISI/BIS has published a large number of standards, which relate to processes and procedures followed in the creation of knowledge artifacts (e.g. books, learned periodicals, technical manuals) or in exchange of information in a computer mediated environment. In addition, the importance of standard practices in library and documentation work was realised by the ISI, and it set up a technical committee known as EC 2: Documentation Committee, headed by an eminent person in the field Dr. S.R. Ranganathan.

This Committee is presently known as MSD 5: Documentation and Information Sectional Committee and is responsible for formulation of Indian standards on the following:

- Preparation of abstracts of periodical articles, reports, etc.
- Indexing work/preparation of subject indexes of books, etc.
- Bibliographic references.
- Cataloguing and classification terms.
- Automated information handling system.
- Transliteration.
- Book numbering (ISBN).
- Book production, illustration and printing processes.
- Style manual.

- Binding and any other aspects relevant to processing, handling and publication of documents.

The Committee works in close cooperation with other bodies responsible for formulating technical guidelines in related fields. They are:

ISO/TC 46 Information and documentation

ISO/TC 130 Graphic technology

ISO/TC 154 Processes, data elements and documents in commerce, industry and administration

ISO/TC 171 Document management applications.

53. Online Computer Library Center (OCLC)

Online Computer Library Center (OCLC), at www.oclc.org/home/, operates a computer network used by more than 2,400 libraries in the United States and Canada, of which more than 300 are U.S. federal libraries. Founded in 1967 as the Ohio College Library Center, it has grown rapidly into an international center for library automation.

To reflect its broadened geographic scope, the name was changed in 1977 to OCLC Inc., OCLC being the acronym by which it had already become known throughout the world. More than 3,800 remote computer terminals in the network are linked to OCLC's computer center in Dublin, Ohio. The OCLC is available only to institutions, through which individuals can use the resource.

Libraries use the OCLC system to catalog books, order custom-printed catalog cards, maintain location information on library materials, and arrange for interlibrary lending of materials.

The files contain more than 6 million records of books and other library materials such as U.S. government documents.

The researcher can use a terminal to check bibliographic information (e.g., author, title), find out whether his or her library owns the item, or locate items in other libraries. Most college and university libraries do not charge for these services.

International Atomic Energy Agency (IAEA)

The International Atomic Energy Agency (IAEA) is an international organization that seeks to promote the peaceful use of nuclear energy, and to inhibit its use for any military purpose, including nuclear weapons. The IAEA was established as an autonomous organisation on 29 July 1957. Though established independently of the United Nations through its own international treaty, the IAEA Statute, the IAEA reports to both the United Nations General Assembly and Security Council.

The IAEA has its headquarters in Vienna. The IAEA has two "Regional Safeguards Offices" which are located in Toronto, Canada, and in Tokyo, Japan.

The IAEA also has two liaison offices which are located in New York City, United States, and in Geneva, Switzerland.

In addition, the IAEA has three laboratories located in Vienna and Seibersdorf, Austria, and in Monaco.

The IAEA serves as an intergovernmental forum for scientific and technical cooperation in the peaceful use of nuclear technology and nuclear power worldwide.

The programs of the IAEA encourage the development of the peaceful applications of nuclear technology, provide international safeguards against misuse of nuclear technology and nuclear materials, and promote nuclear safety (including radiation protection) and nuclear security standards and their implementation.

MEDLARS (Medical Literature Analysis and Retrieval System): The Library's computer-based MEDLARS was established in January, 1964 to achieve rapid bibliographic access to NLM's vast store of biomedical information. The principal objective of MEDLARS is to provide references to the biomedical literature for researchers, clinicians, and other health professionals.

This is accomplished through:

1. preparation of citations for publication in *Index Medicus*, a comprehensive, subject-author index to articles from approximately 2,500 of the world's biomedical journals, and the *NLM Current Catalog,* a bibliographic listing of citations to publications cataloged by the Library;
2. compilation of other recurring bibliographies on specialized subjects of wide interest;
3. publication and distribution of selected searches (designated "Literature Searches") on a wide basis; and
4. provision of online search services through MEDLINE, TOXLINE, and other data bases.

Agreements with foreign institutions provide MEDLARS services to an international community of health scientists.

54. CLOCKSS (controlled LOCKSS) is, as its website says, "a not-for-profit joint venture between the world's leading academic publishers and research libraries whose mission is to build a sustainable, geographically distributed dark archive with which to ensure the long-term survival of Web-based scholarly publications for the benefit of the greater global research community."

A preservation service of Ithaka, Portico, like CLOCKSS, is a dark archive that aims to preserve published e-journals, e-books, and digital collections.

55. Sampling is the process of selecting a representative part of the population. Thus, a carefully carried out sampling process helps to draw a sample that represents the characteristics of the population from which the sample is drawn. There are several methods or techniques of sampling; however, basically sampling techniques are classified in two broad categories, *i.e.* probability and nonprobability sampling techniques.

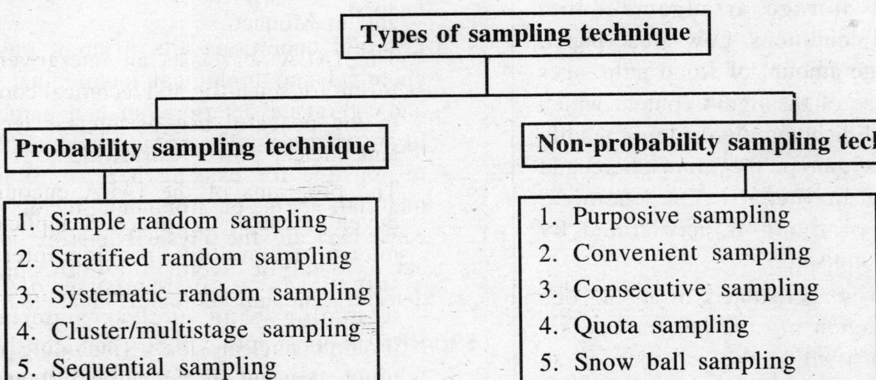

Figure: *Types of Sampling techinque*

57. The causes of deterioration of library materials may be grouped broadly under three categories:

1. Natural ageing
2. Intrinsic or inherent factors, and
3. External conditions.

Natural ageing indicates the gradual degradation or deterioration of the material. Obviously it affects the durability of the material. It is inevitable that each material is subject to natural decay. If the ingredients used in a particular material are of good quality, and the processes of manufacture are properly performed and no substance is used for any purpose which may cause deterioration in future under any condition, the material will be durable and long lasting and it will be capable for enduring any adverse condition.

In such a case natural ageing will take more time. If the basic ingredients are of poor quality, the substances used are such as may cause deterioration, and the manufacturing processes are not properly performed, the material will be less durable and natural decay or ageing will set in faster. Natural ageing does not refer to any external condition.

Paper is made of vegetable fibres and it is subject to the process of ageing; Paper as a product has mechanical resistance but it decreases with ageing and passage of time. The rate of ageing usually depends on the quality of raw materials from which the particular paper is made as well as on the condition of storage arrangement and environmental conditions. Low grade paper, containing large amount of wood pulp, ages quickly because of the lignin content which results in rapid disintegration. Lignin readily reacts with oxygen in the atmosphere and acids present in the air. The chemical degeneration of lignin is accelerated by humidity and moisture.

Cellulose pulp is also subject to ageing due to oxydising action of atmospheric oxygen, which is intensified in the presence of an alkali. Cellulose hydrolysis is caused by acid in atmosphere mixed with humidity. The acidity of paper has a considerable influence on the ageing of paper and thus on the durability of library materials. The ageing process in paper involves a degradation of cellulose fibres. When the long chain cellulose polymers are degenerated, and broken down to shorter chain molecules the mechanical strength of paper weakens. Both the physical and chemical factors and atmospheric conditions accelerate the process of ageing. All types of paper, irrespective of their ingredients, must deteriorate in course of time. Even the very good quality paper changes its condition with the passage of time, which makes it yellowish and causes subsequent embrittlement.

Intrinsic or inherent factors refer to the basic ingredients used in the manufacture of physical entity of library materials as well as the manufacturing processes. In case of paper these basic ingredients are low quality raw materials for paper pulp, chemicals used for processing of pulp, sizing and loading substances and processes involved in paper manufacture.

These things act as the root cause for physical and chemical effects for which durability of paper becomes affected even if without external cause or condition for deterioration. Since these causes are inherent to the material itself, these are intrinsic or inherent factors.

External conditions are different physical, chemical and biological factors that cause and aggravate deterioration and damage to library materials. The primary external factors responsible for causing hazards to library materials are the environmental factors which cause basically the physical deterioration and act as catalytic agents for both chemical deterioration and biological damage.

59. RRRLF boost public library services through funding assistant to the public libraries as per different scheme. There are two schemes of assistance:

1. Matching Scheme
2. Non Matching Scheme

Matching Scheme: Under this scheme help is provided from the sources shared on relevant grant basis with the states and/or

Union Territories Administration on the basis of developed state with the ratio of 50:50. underdeveloped and lagging states with the ratio of 60:40, and States of North-Eastern are have the ratio of 90:10. From 2005 it was implemented.

Scheme for Non Matching:

RRRLF gives full support under this scheme from its own sources to achieve following objectives.

Support for developing adequate collection of books and other materials through selection from the centre.

Support to voluntary institutions which provide public library and information services.

Support is given to libraries of children or children's department of general public library which also includes senior citizen section and women section.

Support is provided to public libraries for celebrating fifty years, hundred years, or one twenty five years of establishment.

Support for, gathering and agglomeration of library statistics through official or non official agencies.

Support to centrally Supported libraries.

Support for organizing seminars, conferences by national level library organizations.

60. A network is a graphical representation of a project, depleting the flow as well as the sequence of well-defined activities and events. A network path consists of a set of activities that connects the networking beginning event to the network terminal event. The longest path through the network is called the critical path and its length determines the minimum duration in which the said project can be completed.

63. Levine-Clark, Michael, and Toni M. Carter. ALA Glossary of Library and Information Science, 4th ed Chicago American Library Association, 2012. ISBN: 978-0-83891-111-2. This glossary includes specific words, jargon, and phases relevant to librarianship. The vocabulary covers materials, processes, and system definitions written by LIS experts. The fourth edition has been fully updated to include the latest technology and Internet terms related to LIS.

64. AACR has been revised periodically since its first publication in 1967. With the publication of the second edition of *AACR* (known as *AACR2*) in 1978, the body responsible for revisions was formally recognized as the *Joint Steering Committee* (JSC) for *Revision of AACR*. The constituent organizations represented on the JSC are the American Library Association, the Australian Committee on Cataloguing, the British Library, the Canadian Committee on Cataloguing, the Chartered Institute of Library and Information Professionals, and the Library of Congress. Many committees of professional library organizations meet to discuss concerns regarding *AACR* and provide suggestions to the JSC for consideration. Meetings at the ALA annual and midwinter conferences provide opportunities for non-committee members to hear about proposed changes and, on occasion, to comment on change proposals. In spite of the ability to comment and make suggestions, with each revision, catalogers complain about the repercussions of changes in the bibliographic record; however, each change has not been without merit. The incorporation of the "optional" rule in 1978 allowed catalogers the choice of following strict standards or adapting the standards to meet individual institutional needs. This was an important change in cataloging standards, as it allowed smaller libraries the freedom to catalog with less detail than was required of large research-oriented libraries.

The 1978 edition also included the much-needed updated rules for cataloging non-book materials. The 1988 revision was not considered a new edition *(AACR3),* because the basic premise and organization of the rules remains the same as the 1978 edition. That is, the basic code is the same but has merely been updated to reflect current theory and technology. The 1988 revision was the first to consider machine-readable cataloging developments that might affect the *AACR* rules, although examples were still given in the style of the manual catalog card. Two big changes in the 1988 revision were with respect to entries under pseudonyms and description of computer files. This was the edition of *AACR* that was responsible for the change of entering a work under "Seuss, Dr." instead of under "Geisel, Theodor:"

66. Yojana is a widely circulated theme based journal brought out by Publications Division, Ministry of Information & Broadcasting. Published in 13 languages, the journal has a combined circulation of about 2 lakhs and readership of over 8 lakhs. The journal provides a forum for discussion on subjects relating to planning and development and other socioeconomic issues of the country and also seeks to provide feedback to the policy makers. It is valued by scholars and students and analysts as well as common readers for in-depth analysis on various topics.

The journal during last one year has focused on contemporary issues like Demonetisation, GST, Social Security, Banking Reforms, Union Budget, India on the Move, MSMEs and Consumer Awareness. Eminent authors, with expertise in their respective fields, have been contributing to the journal. This includes Secretaries to the Government of India.

68. What is the BIBFRAME Model and BIBFRAME Vocabulary?

The BIBFRAME Model is a conceptual/ practical model that balances the needs of those recording detailed bibliographic description, the needs of those describing other cultural materials, and those who do not require such a detailed level of description.

There are three high-level classes, or entities, in the BIBFRAME Model:

- BIBFRAME Work
- BIBFRAME Instance
- BIBFRAME Item

BIBFRAME Work identifies the conceptual essence of something; a BIBFRAME Instance reflects the material embodiment of a Work. A BIBFRAME Item is an actual copy (physical or electronic) of an Instance.

The BIBFRAME Vocabulary is the key to the description of resources. Like the MARC format has a defined set of elements and attributes; the BIBFRAME Vocabulary has a defined set of classes and properties. A class identifies a type of BIBFRAME resource (much like a MARC field might bundle a single concept); properties serve as a means to further describe a BIBFRAME resource (much like MARC subfields more specifically identify aspects of the concept).

69. The 'epilogue' is very significant part of the thesis since it is the gist of the entire work. It is important because the evaluation of the thesis depends on it. It is the final impression the candidate can make upon the examiners and readers of the thesis. It is like playing the last ball that wins the match.

70. NICNET is a satellite based national informatics network established in 1987 at Seshagiri. Its aim has been to provide informatics services to State and Central Governments departments and its various organisations.

The National Knowledge Network in India (NKN) was conceived as a multi-gigabit pan-India network with the aim to provide a unified high speed network backbone, with an emphasis on scalability and a robust network architecture. The initial phase of

NKN was released to the users in April 2009 and to date it links 1357 institutes and leading national labs.

INFLIBNET: Information and Library Network (INFLIBNET) Centre is an autonomous Inter-University Centre (IUC) of the University Grants Commission (UGC) of India headquartered at Gujarat University Campus, Ahmedabad.

In April 1988, the University Grant Commission (UGC) constituted a committee under the chairmanship of Prof. Yash Pal, to work out the details of a university information library networking system. The report of this working group was published in December 1988 containing a project proposal for the establishment and development of an information and library network. Finally, in April 1991, INFLIBNET was initiated by the UGC.

Started as a project under the IUCAA, it became an independent Inter-University Centre in June 1996. INFLIBNET is a computer communication network of libraries and information centres of universities, institutions of national importance, Research and Development Institutions, bibliographical information centres, etc. It uses state-of-the-art technologies for optimising the capability in information handling and service and creating the infrastructure for the sharing of library and information resources and services among the academic and research institutions. INFLIBNET is set out to be a major player in promoting scholarly communication among academicians and researchers in India.

ERNET

ERNET (Education and Research Network) has made a significant contribution to the emergence of networking in the country. It practically brought the Internet to India and has built up national capabilities in the area of networking, especially in protocol software engineering. It has not only succeeded in building a large network that provides various facilities to the intellectual segment of Indian society, the research and education community, it has over the years become a trendsetter in the field of networking.

ERNET was initiated in 1986 by the Department of Electronics (DoE), with funding support from the Government of India and United Nations Development Program (UNDP), involving eight premier institutions as participating agencies–NCST (National Centre for Software Technology) Bombay, IISc (Indian Institute of Science) Bangalore, five IIT's (Indian Institutes of Technology) at Delhi, Bombay, Kanpur, Kharagpur and Madras, and the DoE, New Delhi. ERNET began as a multi protocol network with both the TCP/IP and the OSI-IP protocol stacks running over the leased-line portion of the backbone. Since 1995, however, almost all traffic is carried over TCP/IP.

74. The Dewey Decimal Classification (DDC) system is a general knowledge organization tool that is continuously revised to keep pace with knowledge. The system was conceived by Melvil Dewey in 1873 and first published in 1876. The DDC is published by OCLC Online Computer Library Center, Inc. OCLC owns all copyright rights in the Dewey Decimal Classification, and licenses the system for a variety of uses.

The DDC is the most widely used classification system in the world. Libraries in more than 135 countries use the DDC to organize and provide access to their collections, and DDC numbers are featured in the national bibliographies of more than 60 countries. Libraries of every type apply Dewey numbers on a daily basis and share these numbers through a variety of means (including WordCat, the OCLC Online Union Catalog). Dewey is also used for other purposes, *e.g.*, as a browsing mechanism for resources on the web.

The DDC has been translated into over thirty languages. Translations of the latest full and abridged editions of the DDC are completed, planned, or underway in Arabic, Chinese, French, German, Greek, Hebrew, Icelandic, Italian, Korean, Norwegian, Russian, Spanish, and Vietnamese.

Structure and Notation

The DDC is built on sound principles that make it ideal as a general knowledge organization tool: meaningful notation in universally recognized Arabic numerals, well-defined categories, well-developed hierarchies, and a rich network of relationships among topics. In the DDC, basic classes are organized by disciplines or fields of study. At the broadest level, the DDC is divided into ten *main classes,* which together cover the entire world of knowledge. Each main class is further divided into ten *divisions,* and each division into ten *sections* (not all the numbers for the divisions and sections have been used). The main structure of the DDC is presented in the DDC Summaries following this introduction. The headings associated with the numbers in the summaries have been edited for browsing purposes, and do not necessarily match the complete headings found in the schedules.

The *first summary* contains the ten main classes. The first digit in each three-digit number represents the main class. For example, 600 represents technology.

The *second summary* contains the hundred divisions. The second digit in each three-digit number indicates the division. For example, 600 is used for general works on technology, 610 for medicine and health, 620 for engineering, 630 for agriculture.

The *third summary* contains the thousand sections. The third digit in each three-digit number indicates the section. Thus, 610 is used for general works on medicine and health, 611 for human anatomy, 612 for human physiology, 613 for personal health and safety.

Arabic numerals are used to represent each class in the DDC. A decimal point follows the third digit in a class number, after which division by ten continues to the specific degree of classification needed.

Second Summary: The Hundred Divisions

000 Computer science, knowledge & systems

010 Bibliographies

020 Library & information sciences

030 Encyclopedias & books of facts

040 [Unassigned]

050 Magazines, journals & serials

060 Associations, organizations & museums

070 News media, journalism & publishing

080 Quotations

090 Manuscripts & rare books

100 Philosophy

110 Metaphysics

120 Epistemology

130 Parapsychology & occultism

140 Philosophical schools of thought

150 Psychology

160 Logic

170 Ethics

180 Ancient, medieval & eastern philosophy

190 Modern western philosophy

200 Religion

210 Philosophy & theory of religion

220 The Bible

230 Christianity & Christian theology

240 Christian practice & observance

250 Christian pastoral practice & religious orders

260 Christian organization, social work & worship

270 History of Christianity

280 Christian denominations
290 Other religions
300 Social sciences, sociology & anthropology
310 Statistics
320 Political science
330 Economics
340 Law
350 Public administration & military science
360 Social problems & social services
370 Education
380 Commerce, communications & transportation
390 Customs, etiquette & folklore
400 Language
410 Linguistics
420 English & Old English languages
430 German & related languages
440 French & related languages
450 Italian, Romanian & related languages
460 Spanish & Portuguese languages
470 Latin & Italic languages
480 Classical & modern Greek languages
490 Other languages
500 Science
510 Mathematics
520 Astronomy
530 Physics
540 Chemistry
550 Earth sciences & geology
560 Fossils & prehistoric life
570 Life sciences; biology
580 Plants (Botany)
590 Animals (Zoology)
600 Technology
610 Medicine & health
620 Engineering
630 Agriculture
640 Home & family management
650 Management & public relations
660 Chemical engineering
670 Manufacturing
680 Manufacture for specific uses
690 Building & construction
700 Arts
710 Landscaping & area planning
720 Architecture
730 Sculpture, ceramics & metalwork
740 Drawing & decorative arts
750 Painting
760 Graphic arts
770 Photography & computer art
780 Music
790 Sports, games & entertainment
800 Literature, rhetoric & criticism
810 American literature in English
820 English & Old English literatures
830 German & related literatures
840 French & related literatures
850 Italian, Romanian & related literatures
860 Spanish & Portuguese literatures
870 Latin & Italic literatures
880 Classical & modern Greek literatures
890 Other literatures
900 History
910 Geography & travel
920 Biography & genealogy
930 History of ancient world (to ca. 499)
940 History of Europe
950 History of Asia
960 History of Africa
970 History of North America
980 History of South America
990 History of other areas

75. Simplex, Half-Duplex, and Full-Duplex Data Transmission

The transmission of data between two devices can be characterized as simplex, half-duplex, and full-duplex. Simplex operation indicates that transmission can take place in only one direction from one device to the next. In this mode, one of the devices can transmit but cannot receive, or it receives but does not transmit.

Half-duplex operation indicates transmission in either direction, but it can take place in only one direction at a time. Full-duplex operation indicates transmission takes place in both directions simultaneously.

In networks where many devices are involved in communication, transmission uses multiple channels.

A channel is defined as a single path on a line through which signals flow. Lines are defined as the components and parts that extend between the terminals of the communicating devices.

79. Protocol: A set of rules used by computers network protocols in the operating system software or network applications to communicate with each other. Some of the commonly used protocols in the networking world are ATM, Ethernet, FTP, HTTP, IP, SMTP, TCP, TELNET, and UDP.

80. R is an open source programming language and software environment for statistical computing. The R language is widely used among statisticians and dataminers for developing statistical software and data analysis.

R is an implementation of the S programming language. The R language came to use quite a bit after S had been developed. One key limitation of the S language was that it was only available in a commercial package, S-PLUS. In 1991, R was created by Ross Ihaka and Robert Gentleman in the Department of Statistics at the University of Auckland. In 1993 the first announcement of R was made to the public.

A major advantage that R has over many other statistical packages and is that it's free in the sense of free software. R is both flexible and powerful. It has an amazing ecosystem for developers and it has wide range of packages for data access, data cleaning or munging, performing Analysis, creating Reports etc.

The primary R system is available from the Comprehensive R Archive Network, also known as CRAN. CRAN also hosts many add-on packages that can be used to extend the functionality of R. Over 6,789 packages are available on CRAN that have been developed by users and programmers around the world.

81. The various reference management software programs available these days differ in their emphasis on ease of use vs. functionality. As the functionality of a program increases, generally, the learning curve for the program becomes steeper.

Originally, reference managers helped researchers correctly format their citations. These tools have come a long way since then. However, with all the new options and features, deciding which citation tool works best requires background work and awareness. Among the various options available to the scientist, few common citation managers are RefWorks, Zotero, Mendeley, and EndNote.

EndNote: A tool for managing and publishing bibliographies, citations, and references.

Mendeley: A tool for reference management and for collaborating and sharing your work.

Zotero: A tool for managing and organize different resources and for sharing research.

RefWorks: A tool for managing and organizing bibliographies.

83. Pauline A. Atherton has critically examined the five laws of library science in her book entitled "Putting Knowledge to Work". According to her, the laws, "offer me (and my students) the guidance and the rationale we need when we critically review how we follow the cataloguing which prevail, how we evaluate the libraries we use, or work in, and how we work to improve the practice we follow and the library services we manage".

84.

Edition	Year	Editor
1	1876	Melvil Dewey
2	1885	Melvil Dewey
3	1888	Melvil Dewey
4	1891	May Seymour
5	1894	May Seymour
6	1899	May Seymour
7	1911	May Seymour
8	1913	May Seymour
9	1915	May Seymour
10	1919	May Seymour
11	1922	Jennie Dorkas Fellows
12	1927	Jennie Dorkas Fellows
13	1932	Jennie Dorkas Fellows
14	1942	Constantin Mazney
15	1951	Milton J. Ferguson
15 rev.	1952	Godfrey Dewey
16	1958	Benjamin A. Custer
17	1965	Benjamin A. Custer
18	1971	Benjamin A. Custer
19	1979	Benjamin A. Custer
20	1986	Dr J.P. Camaromi
21	1996	Miss J.S. Mitchell
22	2007	Miss J.S. Mitchell
23	2011	Miss J.S. Mitchell

86. Amrit Tiwana has given stress on communication, storage and retrieval technologies in KM. According to Tiwana while communications technology does provide for transfer and exchange of structured and formalized knowledge, it also provides and outlet for knowledge that cannot or has not yet been structured yet can be immediately applied. According to Tiwana there are seven layer in the system architecture of KM. Which are as follows:

INTERFACE LAYER Browser
ACCESS AND AUTHENTICATION LAYER Authentication, Recognition, Security, Firewalls, Tunneling
COLLABORATIVE INTELLIGENCE AND FILTERING Intelligent agent tools, Content personalization, Searching, Indexing and Meta tagging
APPLICATION LAYER Directories, Yellow pages, Collaborative work tools, Video-conference, DSS tools.
TRANSPORT LAYER Web, TCP/IP.deployment, Streaming audio, Document exchange, Video transport VPN, Electronic mail and POP/SMTP support.
MIDDLEWARE AND LEGACY INTEGRATION LAYER Wrapper tools such as TCL/TK or scripts to integrate legacy or Cross platform data.
REPOSITORIES Legacy date, Data Warehouse, Document bases, Discussion forums and others. Integration via the Web

88. Literary warrant analysis: The term "literary warrant" was first used in 1911 in an article by Wyndham Hulme. Hulme used the term specifically to refer to the fact that the vocabulary of the Library of Congress Classification was empirically based on the warrant supplied by the Library's collection rather than on the warrant supplied by other means such as classification theory and attempts to classify the whole body of knowledge, or by readers' requests. The literary warrant for professional practice, therefore, is made up of authoritative sources, which are recognised and valued by experts. Such authoritative sources may be found in the law, codes of ethics, standards, the professional and scholarly literature, oral and literary texts, and in domain experts. Analysis of the literary warrant for professional practice establishes the "mandates" for best practice, and identifies its conceptual and theoretical frames of reference.

Literary warrant simply means that a subject cannot be listed in the scheme unless some literature has already appeared on it. Hulme's principle of *literary warrant* greatly influenced the Library of Congress Classification (LC).

Ranganathan also made use of this principle, but not exactly in the sense Hulme made, use of it. According to Ranganathan, when the literature on a particular subject grows in size, there may arise a need for providing a separate class for, it in the scheme. Ranganathan's principle of literary warrant states that "the subjects in an array of subjects or the isolates in an array of isolates may be arranged in the sequence of decreasing quantity of the documents published or anticipated to be published on them, except when any other overwhelming consideration rules it out."

90. Bridges: A *bridge* is device that connects and controls the flow of traffic between two LANs, or two segments of the same LAN. The two LANs being connected can be alike or dissimilar. For example, a bridge can connect an Ethernet with a Token-Ring network. Bridges are protocol-independent. They simply forward packets without analyzing and re-routing messages.

Bridges operate at the Data Link layer of the OSI model and, like a repeater, attach two different network segments and pass data. The fundamental difference between a repeater and a bridge is that a repeater allows all data to pass through, whereas a bridge checks the data and determines whether they should be allowed to pass or not.

Previous Years' Paper (Solved)

National Testing Agency (NTA)

UGC-NET Junior Research Fellowship & Assistant Professor Eligibility Exam

Library and Information Science, June-2019*

PAPER-II

Note : *This paper contains* **hundred** *(***100***) objective type questions of* **two** *(2) marks each.* **All** *questions are* **compulsory**.

1. Match List-I with List-II:

List-I	List-II
(*a*) Cost effectiveness	(*i*) Cost of product service rendered by organisation
(*b*) Cost-benefit analysis	(*ii*) Determined by dividing the allotted cost of subsystem by its actual number of operations
(*c*) Cost analysis	(*iii*) Relationship between the benefits of product service and cost of providing it
(*d*) Unit cost	(*iv*) Relationship between level of performance and the cost involved in achieving the level

Choose the correct option from those given below:

	(*a*)	(*b*)	(*c*)	(*d*)
A.	(*iv*)	(*iii*)	(*i*)	(*ii*)
B.	(*i*)	(*ii*)	(*iv*)	(*iii*)
C.	(*ii*)	(*iii*)	(*iv*)	(*i*)
D.	(*iii*)	(*iv*)	(*ii*)	(*i*)

2. 'Law of Parsimony' belongs to the:

A. postulates

B. normative principles

C. rules

D. canons

3. The term 'Epigraph' means:

A. a motto or brief introduction prefixed to a book

B. spine of a book

C. essence of a subject

D. a pamphlet

4. Which of the following tools searches seamlessly across a wide range of local and remote content, provides relevance ranked results and has the ambitious goal of providing a single point entry into library's collections?

A. Web Scale Discovery Service

B. Web Reference Service

C. Union Catalogue

D. Web OPAC

5. Which of the following is a collaborative network of reference librarians?

A. Worldcat B. INFLIBNET

C. QuestionPoint D. Global Scholar

6. Under RRRLF (Financial) Assistance Matching Scheme, assistance will be shared on matching basis between RRRLF and North Eastern States at the ratio:

A. 80 : 20 B. 90 : 10

C. 50 : 50 D. 60 : 40

7. Arrange the following meta search engines in ascending order according to their year of launching.

(*a*) SeerX

(*b*) Skyscanner

(*c*) Kayak

(*d*) Metacrawler

*Online exam held on 20 June, 2019

Choose the correct answer from the options given below:

A. (*d*), (*b*), (*c*), (*a*)
B. (*d*), (*a*), (*b*), (*c*)
C. (*a*), (*b*), (*d*), (*c*)
D. (*a*), (*d*), (*c*), (*b*)

8. E-journal article can be identified with the help of:
A. Digital Open Identifier
B. Journal Source Identifier
C. Journal Article Identifier
D. Digital Object Identifier

9. Which of the following V's associated with Big Data is concerned with the integrity of data?
A. Volume B. Velocity
C. Variety D. Veracity

10. LOCKSS has been initiated by:
A. MIT Libraries
B. Stanford University
C. University of Waikato
D. Cambridge University

11. Who among the following coined the term Li-fi?
A. F.W. Lancaster B. Tim O'Relley
C. Harold Hass D. Mary Parker Follett

12. Assertion (A): E-Granthalaya is a freely available software.

Reason (R): E-Granthalaya can be customized depending on the requirement of libraries.

In the context of the above two statements, which one of the following is true?
A. (A) is true but (R) is false
B. (A) is false but (R) is true
C. Both (A) and (R) are false
D. Both (A) and (R) are true

13. Which of the following are the standards for encoding records?
(*a*) ONIX
(*b*) SGML
(*c*) W3C
(*d*) MARC 21

Choose the correct answer from the options given below:
A. (*a*), (*b*) and (*c*) B. (*a*), (*b*) and (*d*)
C. (*b*), (*c*) and (*d*) D. (*a*), (*c*) and (*d*)

14. Who has developed 'Bibexcel'?
A. Olle Persson B. Chris Argyris
C. Vroom D. Frederick Herzberg

15. Which Council has developed 'Leadership in Energy and Environmental Design (LEED)' rating system?
A. United States Green Building Council
B. United Kingdom Green Building Council
C. Canadian Green Building Council
D. Indian Green Building Council

16. Arrange the correct sequence of the sections of main entry in CCC (Ed. 5):
(*a*) Title section
(*b*) Leading section
(*c*) Note section
(*d*) Accession number

Choose the correct answer from the options given below:
A. (*b*), (*c*), (*d*), (*a*)
B. (*b*), (*a*), (*c*), (*d*)
C. (*a*), (*b*), (*c*), (*d*)
D. (*a*), (*c*), (*b*), (*d*)

17. In studying the relationship between smoking and cancer, if you assume that smoking is a cause of cancer and many factors affecting the relationship, such as number of cigarettes, the duration of smoking affect the extent of which smoking might cause cancer.

In the above example, the duration of smoking is which kind of variable?
A. Intervening variable
B. Extraneous variable
C. Independent variable
D. Dependent variable

18. Assertion (A): All academic libraries provide their services on mobile platform.

Reason (R): Academic community demands more library services through mobile app.

In the context of the above two statements, which one of the following is true?

A. Both (A) and (R) are true
B. Both (A) and (R) are false
C. (A) is false but (R) is true
D. (A) is true but (R) is false

19. The function carried out by firewall is to:

A. filter the IP packets
B. open parts to all IP
C. enable user privacy
D. enable anonymous surfing

20. 'Diffusion of innovation' theory is proposed by:

A. Judy Smith B. Eric Dezenhall
C. Peter Drucker D. Everett Rogers

21. Arrange the following information systems in ascending order according to their year of establishment:

(*a*) INIS
(*b*) AGRIS
(*c*) MEDLARS
(*d*) INSPEC

Choose the correct answer from the options given below:

A. (*b*), (*a*), (*c*), (*d*)
B. (*d*), (*c*), (*a*), (*b*)
C. (*a*), (*c*), (*d*), (*b*)
D. (*c*), (*d*), (*a*), (*b*)

22. Delphi method is related to:

A. conservation method
B. forecasting process based on panel of experts
C. planning of disaster management
D. method of recording bibliographic data

23. Identify the characteristics of 'fugitive material' from the following:

(*a*) Material printed in limited quantities
(*b*) Material having perpetual value
(*c*) Usually of immediate interest at the time of publication
(*d*) Materials not related to any programme or processed publications

Choose the correct answer from the options given below:

A. (*a*) and (*c*) B. (*a*) and (*b*)
C. (*b*) and (*c*) D. (*c*) and (*d*)

24. Assertion (A): Students are among the most prolific users of social network sites (SNS).

Reason (R): Social network sites always help in fulfilling their academic information needs.

In the context of the above two statements, which one of the following is true?

A. (A) is true but (R) is false
B. (A) is false but (R) is true
C. Both (A) and (R) are false
D. Both (A) and (R) are true

25. Who is the author of the book entitled, *The Third Wave?*

A. Daniel Bell B. Alvin Toffler
C. W.R. Ashby D. Robert T. Craig

26. Which ISBN element identifies the particular publisher or imprint?

A. Registrant element
B. Publication element
C. Registration group element
D. Check digit

27. Choose the key characteristics of 'Augmented Reality' (AR) system in library settings as identified by Sharon Maria S, Esposo-Betan and Jonathan F. Santos in their studies:

(*a*) Combines real and virtual
(*b*) Non-reciprocative and non-interactive application
(*c*) Registered 3D
(*d*) Interactive real time

Choose the correct answer from the options given below:

A. (*a*), (*b*) and (*c*) are correct
B. (*b*), (*c*) and (*d*) are correct
C. (*a*), (*c*) and (*d*) are correct
D. (*a*), (*b*) and (*d*) are correct

28. Identify the key salient features of 'Private Library' from the following:

(*a*) A library gives access to general public
(*b*) A library belonging to an individual

(*c*) A library not supported by taxation
(*d*) A library having statutory support

Choose the correct answer from the options given below:

A. (*b*) and (*d*) are correct
B. (*a*) and (*b*) are correct
C. (*b*) and (*c*) are correct
D. (*a*) and (*c*) are correct

29. Match List-I with List-II:

List-I (Class of IP)	***List-II (Supporting coverage)***
(*a*) Class A IP	(*i*) Supports small networks with fewer than 256 devices
(*b*) Class B IP	(*ii*) Reserved for multicast groups
(*c*) Class C IP	(*iii*) Supports large networks with many devices
(*d*) Class D IP	(*iv*) Supports medium-sized networks

Choose the correct option from those given below:

	(*a*)	(*b*)	(*c*)	(*d*)
A.	(*ii*)	(*i*)	(*iv*)	(*iii*)
B.	(*ii*)	(*i*)	(*iii*)	(*iv*)
C.	(*iii*)	(*iv*)	(*ii*)	(*i*)
D.	(*iii*)	(*iv*)	(*i*)	(*ii*)

30. In the formation of subjects, 'progressive decrease of extension and increase of intention of a basic subject' is known as:

A. lamination
B. denudation
C. dissection
D. loose assemblage

31. Any act by a conservator that involves a direct interaction between the conservator and the cultural material is called

A. archive conservation
B. instrumentive conservation
C. preventive conservation
D. interventive conservation

32. Which of the following information-seeking behaviour model explains the activities, viz., starting, chaining, browsing, monitoring, etc.?

A. Wilson's nested model
B. Ellis's model
C. Darvin's model
D. Kuhlthau's model

33. Arrange the following library softwares in ascending order according to their year of launching:

(*a*) Php-MyLibrary
(*b*) ABCD
(*c*) Koha
(*d*) NewGenLib

Choose the correct answer from the options given below:

A. (*c*), (*a*), (*b*), (*d*)
B. (*c*), (*b*), (*a*), (*d*)
C. (*c*), (*d*), (*a*), (*b*)
D. (*c*), (*a*), (*d*), (*b*)

34. Who among the following have developed the initial version of SPSS?

(*a*) Norman Nie
(*b*) C. Hadlai Hull
(*c*) Dale H. Bont
(*d*) John Chambers

Choose the correct answer from the options given below:

A. (*b*), (*c*) and (*d*)
B. (*a*), (*b*) and (*c*)
C. (*a*), (*b*) and (*d*)
D. (*a*), (*c*) and (*d*)

35. Which is NOT the part of Maslow's hierarchy of need?

A. Esteem need
B. Basic need
C. Security need
D. Psycho-physical need

36. Match List-I with List-II:

List-I (Authors)	***List-II (Works)***
(*a*) George Kingsley Zipf	(*i*) Documentation
(*b*) Samuel Clement Bradford	(*ii*) The Beginning of Systematic Bibliography

A. common auxiliaries of language
B. common auxiliaries of place
C. common auxiliaries of time
D. common auxiliaries of point of view

52. ZOTERO is a:
A. library management tool
B. statistical analysis tool
C. serials management tool
D. bibliographic reference management tool

53. Book Order Vigilance Pad (BOVP) was suggested by:
A. Paul Otlet B. Michael Gorman
C. Henry Fayol D. Melvil Dewey

54. The rejection of a null hypothesis, when it is true, is known as:
A. hypothesis of difference
B. hypothesis of association
C. type-I error
D. type-II error

55. Match List-I with List-II:

List-I	***List-II***
(*a*) FORSA	(*i*) Science and Technology
(*b*) NKRC	(*ii*) Medicinal Science
(*c*) HELNET	(*iii*) Agriculture
(*d*) CeRA	(*iv*) Astrophysics

Choose the correct option from those given below:

	(*a*)	(*b*)	(*c*)	(*d*)
A.	(*i*)	(*iii*)	(*iv*)	(*ii*)
B.	(*ii*)	(*i*)	(*iii*)	(*iv*)
C.	(*iv*)	(*i*)	(*ii*)	(*iii*)
D.	(*iii*)	(*ii*)	(*iv*)	(*i*)

56. NDL-India is developed and maintained by:
A. IIT, Gauhati B. IIT, Chennai
C. IIT, Roorkee D. IIT, Kharagpur

57. **Assertion (A):** 'Big deal' is a licensed package of journals that costs less to the subscriber.

Reason (R): The package usually includes some less relevant titles.

In the context of the above two statements, which one of the following is true?
A. (A) is true but (R) is false
B. (A) is false but (R) is true
C. Both (A) and (R) are true
D. Both (A) and (R) are false

58. The protocol used to provide security to e-mails is known as:
A. POP B. PGP
C. SNMP D. TCP

59. A customized website (often based on restrictions of domain articles) that immerses information from a wide array of sources in a consistent and unified manner is known as:
A. a collection of interlinked web pages
B. online portal
C. web portal
D. website

60. Which of the following components is NOT included in 'LAMP'?
A. Linux B. Apache
C. MySQL D. Pearl

61. HaaS is also known as:
A. SaaS B. IaaS
C. PaaS D. NaaS

62. A design that seeks to control conditions within which persons are observed and analyzed is known as:
A. experimental design
B. exploratory design
C. survey design
D. case study design

63. Identify the penalty in case of plagiarism at 'Level 2' in Academic and Research Publications as per UGC (Promotion of Academic Integrity and Prevention of Plagiarism in Higher Education Institutions) Regulation, 2018:
A. No penalty
B. Shall be denied a right to one annual increment
C. Shall be denied a right to two successive annual increments
D. Shall be denied a right to three successive annual increments

64. Which are the display elements of 'PRECIS'?
(*a*) Qualifier (*b*) Call Number
(*c*) Display (*d*) Lead

Choose the correct answer from the options given below:

A. (*a*), (*b*) and (*c*)
B. (*a*), (*b*) and (*d*)
C. (*a*), (*c*) and (*d*)
D. (*b*), (*c*) and (*d*)

65. Which of the following are non-probability sampling techniques?

(*a*) Purposive
(*b*) Convenience
(*c*) Snowball
(*d*) Simple random

Choose the correct answer from the options given below:

A. (*a*), (*b*) and (*d*)
B. (*b*), (*c*) and (*d*)
C. (*a*), (*c*) and (*d*)
D. (*a*), (*b*) and (*c*)

66. Identify the frequency of occurrence and the analysis of co-occurrence of descriptors assigned to journal articles:

A. Co-word analysis B. Word analysis
C. h-index D. g-index

67. The bit number as defined in IP Address in Internet Protocol Version 4 is:

A. 16 B. 128
C. 64 D. 32

68. Which software is used by INFLIBNET Access Management Federation (INFED) for authenticating authorized users to access the resources?

A. Koha B. Php-MyLibrary
C. Shibboleth D. NewGenLib

69. Match List-I with List-II:

List-I	*List-II*
(*a*) Repeaters	(*i*) Allows similar networks to communicate
(*b*) Gateways	(*ii*) Allows data to be transferred within the network
(*c*) Routers	(*iii*) Help in strengthening the signals
(*d*) Switches	(*iv*) Allows dissimilar networks to communicate

Choose the correct option from those given below:

	(*a*)	(*b*)	(*c*)	(*d*)
A.	(*ii*)	(*iii*)	(*iv*)	(*i*)
B.	(*iv*)	(*iii*)	(*ii*)	(*i*)
C.	(*iii*)	(*iv*)	(*i*)	(*ii*)
D.	(*iii*)	(*i*)	(*iv*)	(*ii*)

70. In which year 'Webster's Third New International Dictionary of the English Language' was published?

A. 1961 B. 1965
C. 1970 D. 1971

71. Assertion (A): Indian National Bibliography is not a comprehensive source of Indian publications.

Reason (R): National Library of India, Kolkata is entitled to receive one copy of each Indian publication under Delivery of Books Act.

In the context of the above two statements, which one of the following is true?

A. (A) is true but (R) is false
B. (A) is false but (R) is true
C. Both (A) and (R) are true
D. Both (A) and (R) are false

72. i10-index was created by:

A. Scimago Journal and Country Rank
B. Web of Science
C. Scopus
D. Google Scholar

73. Arrange the following libraries according to their year of foundation:

(*a*) Khuda Bakhsh Library, Patna
(*b*) Raja Library, Rampur
(*c*) Delhi Public Library, Delhi
(*d*) National Library of India, Kolkata

Choose the correct answer from the options given below:

A. (*b*), (*a*), (*d*), (*c*) B. (*a*), (*b*), (*c*), (*d*)
C. (*c*), (*a*), (*b*), (*d*) D. (*b*), (*c*), (*a*), (*d*)

74. The easiest way to bring Internet video to one's desktop or download is known as:

A. flogging B. podcasting
C. vodcasting D. blogging

75. Arrange the following States in ascending order of the year of enactment of their respective Public Library Acts:

(*a*) Arunachal Pradesh
(*b*) Uttar Pradesh
(*c*) Haryana
(*d*) Orissa

Choose the correct answer from the options given below:

A. (*d*), (*c*), (*b*), (*a*) B. (*c*), (*d*), (*b*), (*a*)
C. (*b*), (*d*), (*c*), (*a*) D. (*a*), (*c*), (*b*), (*d*)

76. Match List-I with List-II:

List-I	***List-II***
(*a*) Yearbooks	(*i*) Annual publication listing a set of events forthcoming in next year
(*b*) Directory	(*ii*) Information about events of previous year
(*c*) Almanac	(*iii*) Contains instructions or advice about a particular subject
(*d*) Handbook	(*iv*) A list of facts that contains an alphabetical index of names and addresses of persons or organizations

Choose the correct option from those given below:

	(*a*)	(*b*)	(*c*)	(*d*)
A.	(*iv*)	(*ii*)	(*iii*)	(*i*)
B.	(*ii*)	(*iv*)	(*iii*)	(*i*)
C.	(*i*)	(*iv*)	(*iii*)	(*ii*)
D.	(*ii*)	(*iv*)	(*i*)	(*iii*)

77. Which of the following are the parts of MARC record structure?

(*a*) Check digit
(*b*) Leader
(*c*) Directory
(*d*) Record terminator

Choose the correct answer from the options given below:

A. (*a*), (*c*) and (*d*) B. (*a*), (*b*) and (*d*)
C. (*a*), (*b*) and (*c*) D. (*b*), (*c*) and (*d*)

78. 'A number in DDC whithout meaning in itself, but used to introduce examples of the topic' is known as:

A. class number B. book number
C. hook number D. collection number

79. 'Internet Governance Guide for Libraries' is a publication of:

A. ALA B. IFLA
C. UNESCO D. OCLC

80. Match List-I with List-II:

List-I (e-depository)	***List-II (Year of establishment)***
(*a*) PMC	(*i*) 1999
(*b*) KB e-Depot	(*ii*) 2005
(*c*) Portico	(*iii*) 2000
(*d*) LOCKSS	(*iv*) 2003

Choose the correct option from those given below:

	(*a*)	(*b*)	(*c*)	(*d*)
A.	(*iii*)	(*iv*)	(*ii*)	(*i*)
B.	(*iv*)	(*ii*)	(*i*)	(*iii*)
C.	(*ii*)	(*iii*)	(*iv*)	(*i*)
D.	(*ii*)	(*iv*)	(*i*)	(*iii*)

81. World Intellectual Property Organisation (WIPO) is an agency of:

A. ALA B. IFLA
C. UNESCO D. United Nations

82. In data transfer process, which of the following has multiple bridges between different parts?

A. Firewalls B. Switching packets
C. Hubs D. Softwares

83. In binary number system, digit '22' is represented by:

A. 10111 B. 11000
C. 00111 D. 10110

84. Which of the search engines is merged with ScienceDirect?

A. CiteSeerX B. AltaVista
C. Dogpile D. Scirus

85. Which of the following are parts of 'SCONUL' Seven Pillars of Information Literacy Model?

(*a*) Gather (*b*) Scope
(*c*) Preserve (*d*) Present

Choose the correct answer from the options given below:

A. (*b*), (*c*) and (*d*) B. (*a*), (*c*) and (*d*)
C. (*a*), (*b*) and (*d*) D. (*a*), (*b*) and (*c*)

86. Arrange the following social networking tools according to their year of launching in ascending order:

(*a*) Twitter (*b*) Facebook
(*c*) LinkedIn (*d*) Pinterest

Choose the correct answer from the options given below:

A. (*b*), (*d*), (*a*), (*c*) B. (*d*), (*b*), (*a*), (*c*)
C. (*c*), (*b*), (*a*), (*d*) D. (*a*), (*c*), (*b*), (*d*)

87. Match List-I with List-II:

List-I	***List-II***
(*a*) Web portal	(*i*) Personal login and single access point
(*b*) Website	(*ii*) Enables users to see aggregated data from multiple applications
(*c*) Vertical Web portal	(*iii*) No login required
(*d*) Horizontal Web portal	(*iv*) Focus on a specific application or business function enabling users to see, edit and contribute

Choose the correct option from those given below:

	(*a*)	(*b*)	(*c*)	(*d*)
A.	(*i*)	(*iii*)	(*iv*)	(*ii*)
B.	(*iii*)	(*i*)	(*iv*)	(*ii*)
C.	(*iv*)	(*iii*)	(*i*)	(*ii*)
D.	(*ii*)	(*iii*)	(*i*)	(*iv*)

88. Multiplexing is used in:

A. packet switching B. circuit switching
C. data switching D. protocol switching

89. Arrange the following principles of management given by Henri Fayol in proper sequence:

(*a*) Division of work
(*b*) Unity of command
(*c*) Discipline
(*d*) Authority and responsibility

Choose the correct answer from the options given below:

A. (*a*), (*c*), (*d*), (*b*) B. (*a*), (*d*), (*c*), (*b*)
C. (*b*), (*c*), (*d*), (*a*) D. (*c*), (*d*), (*a*), (*b*)

90. Which of the following Public Library Acts does NOT have the provision of Library Cess?

(*a*) Kerala
(*b*) Karnataka
(*c*) West Bengal
(*d*) Maharashtra

Choose the correct answer from the options given below:

A. (*c*) and (*d*) B. (*b*) and (*d*)
C. (*a*) and (*b*) D. (*a*) and (*c*)

Directions (Qs. No. 91–95): *Read the passage given below and answer the question based on your understanding of the passage:*

When you travel around the world, you see tremendous variation in the standard of living. The average income in a rich country, such as the United States, Japan, or Germany, is more than ten times the average income in a poor country, such as India, Indonesia, or Nigeria. These large differences in income are reflected in large differences in the quality of life. People in richer countries have better nutrition, safer housing, better healthcare, and longer life expectancy as well as more automobiles, more telephones, and more televisions. Even within a country, these are large changes in the standard of living over time. In the United States over the past century, average income as measured by real GDP (gross domestic product) per person has grown by about 2 per cent per year. Although 2 per cent might seem small, this rate of growth implies that average income doubles every 35 years. Because of this growth, most Americans enjoy much greater economic prosperity than did their parents, grandparents, and great grandparents.

Growth rates very substantially from country to country. In recent history, some East Asian countries, such as Singapore, South Korea, and Taiwan, have experienced economic growth of about 7 per cent per year, at this rate, average income doubles every 10 years. Over the past two decades, China has enjoyed an even higher rate of growth—about 12 per cent per year, according to some estimates. A country experiencing such rapid growth can, in one generation, go from being among the poorest in the world to being among the richest. By contrast, some nations in sub-Saharan Africa, average income has been stagnant for many years. Zimbabwe has had one of the worst growth experiences: From 1991 to 2011, income per person fell by a total of 38 per cent.

What explains these diverse experiences? How can rich countries maintain their high standard of living? What policies should poor countries pursue to promote more rapid growth and join the developed world? These are among the most important questions in macroeconomics. As the Nobel-Prize-winning economist Robert Lucas put it. "The consequences for human welfare in questions like these are simply staggering: Once one starts to think about them, it is hard to think about anything else."

91. The subject domain in which Robert Lucas has acclaimed recognition is:
A. Chemistry B. Nuclear Physics
C. Economics D. Agriculture

92. In USA, average income of a person is measured by:
A. average GDP B. real GDP
C. GNP D. direct tax index

93. The country which enjoyed a higher rate of growth of 12% per year according to some estimates is:
A. USA B. Zimbabwe
C. Nigeria D. China

94. The reason as to why Americans enjoy much greater economic prosperity than did their parents is:
A. growth in average income
B. better nutrition and health care
C. growth in govt. jobs
D. growth in agriculture and its effective reform

95. The country which had experienced worst growth from 1991 to 2011 as income per person fell by a total of 38 per cent during the above period is:
A. Brazil B. Zimbabwe
C. China D. USA

Directions (Qs. No. 96–100): *Read the following passage carefully and answer the questions based on your understanding:*

Telecommunications (literally: communications at a distance) are always critical to human society. Even in ancient times, governments and military units relied heavily on telecommunications to gather information and to issue orders. The first type was with messengers on foot or on horseback; but the need to convey a short message over a large distance (such as one warning a city of approaching raiders) led to the use of fire and smoke signals. Using signal mirrors to reflect sunlight (heliography) was another effective way of telecommunication. Its first recorded use was in ancient Greece. Signal mirrors were also mentioned in Marco Polo's account of his trip to the Far East. These ancient visual communication technologies are, amazingly enough, digital. Fires and smoke in different configurations would form different codewords. On hills or mountains near Greek cities there were also special personnel for such communications, forming a chain of regenerative repeaters. In fact, fire and smoke signal platforms still dot the Great Wall of China. More interestingly, reflectors or lenses, equivalent to the amplifiers and antennas we use today, were used to directionally guide the light farther.

Naturally, these early visual communication systems were very tedious to set up and could transmit only several bits of information per hour. A much faster visual communication system was developed just over two centuries ago. In 1793 Claude Chappe of France invented and performed a series of experiments on the concept of 'semaphore telegraph'. His system was a series of signalling devices called semaphores, which were mounted on towers, typically spaced 10 km apart. (A semaphore looked like a large human figure with signal flags in both hands.) A receiving semaphore operator would transcribe visually, often with the aid of a telescope, and then relay the message from his tower to the next, and so on. This visual telegraph became the government telecommunication system in France and spread to other countries, including the United States. The semaphore telegraph was eventually eclipsed by electric telegraphy. Today, only a few remaining streets and landmarks with the name "Telegraph Hill" remind us of the place of this system in history. Still, visual communications (via Aldis lamps, ship flags, and heliographs) remained an important part of maritime communications well into the twentieth century.

96. Heliography was first used in:
A. Ancient Greece
B. China
C. France
D. United States of America

97. Who conducted a series of experiments on 'Semaphore Telegraph'?
A. Marco Polo B. Claude Shannon
C. Claude Chappe D. William Francis

98. What led the use of fire and smoke signals?
A. Large message over a short distance
B. An abridged message to war fighters
C. Short message over a large distance
D. Both short and large messages over a large distance

99. What is heliography?
A. Using signal mirror to reflect sunlight
B. Communication with a messenger on foot or on horseback
C. Semaphore telegraph
D. Maritime communication

100. What is replaced by amplifiers and antennas in the present scenario?
A. Regenerative repeaters
B. Telegraph
C. Smoke signal
D. Lenses

ANSWERS

1	2	3	4	5	6	7	8	9	10
A	B	A	A	C	B	A	D	D	B
11	**12**	**13**	**14**	**15**	**16**	**17**	**18**	**19**	**20**
C	A	B	A	A	B	B	C	A	D
21	**22**	**23**	**24**	**25**	**26**	**27**	**28**	**29**	**30**
D	B	A	A	B	A	C	C	D	B
31	**32**	**33**	**34**	**35**	**36**	**37**	**38**	**39**	**40**
D	B	D	B	D	B	C	A	A	A
41	**42**	**43**	**44**	**45**	**46**	**47**	**48**	**49**	**50**
A	C	B	C	A	B	C	A	C	C
51	**52**	**53**	**54**	**55**	**56**	**57**	**58**	**59**	**60**
A	D	B	C	C	D	C	*	C	D
61	**62**	**63**	**64**	**65**	**66**	**67**	**68**	**69**	**70**
B	A	B	C	D	A	D	C	C	A
71	**72**	**73**	**74**	**75**	**76**	**77**	**78**	**79**	**80**
B	D	A	C	B	D	D	C	B	A
81	**82**	**83**	**84**	**85**	**86**	**87**	**88**	**89**	**90**
D	C	D	D	C	C	A	B	B	A
91	**92**	**93**	**94**	**95**	**96**	**97**	**98**	**99**	**100**
C	B	D	A	B	A	C	C	A	D

EXPLANATORY ANSWERS

2. Normative principles which are widely applicable to cataloging are (1) Law of interpretation (2) Law of impartiality (3) Law of symmetry (4) Law of parsimony and (5) Law of local variation.

Law of Impartiality: The principle that between two or more claimants—say, for use as heading—the preference of any one should be made only on sufficient grounds, and not arbitrarily.

***Law of Symmetry*:** The principle that, of two entities or situations which admit to being regarded as symmetrical counterparts of each other, if one of the entities or the situations is given weight in any particular context, the other entity or situation should also be given a corresponding weight.

Law of Parsimony: The principle that between two or more possible alternative rules bearing on a particular phenomenon, the one leading to overall economy of man-power, material, money, and time considered together with proper weightage is to be preferred.

Law of Local Variation: The principle that the international catalogue code should mark out the factors to be left to the care of each national catalogue code; a national catalogue code should mark out the factors to be left to the care of each linguistic catalogue code in a multi-lingual country such as India; a national catalogue code or a linguistic catalogue code, as the case may be, should mark out the factors to be left to the care of the local catalogue code of each individual library; the catalogue codes in each hierarchical line should be consistent with one another without any mutual contradiction; and each lower link in each hierarchical line should be a supplement to all the upper links taken together.

3. Epigraph: The inscription on a temple, or the motto prefixed to a book. *Epigraphy,* is the study or knowledge of inscriptions, a science auxiliary to history. The epigraphic side of a coin is that on which the image and the inscription are impressed; *monepigraphic* is the name given to it if it has only an inscription; *anepigraphic* if it has only an image.

4. Web-scale discovery tools, or services, allow a user to "search seamlessly across a wide range of local and remote content and provide relevance-ranked results" and additionally to have "the ambitious goal of providing a single point of entry into a library's collections". Perhaps more succinctly, Jason Vaughn suggests web-scale discovery "can be considered as deep discovery within a vast ocean of content". The structure of a web-scale discovery tool employs a central index (or, variously, base index or unified index) of content that has been preharvested, from which a user can search across localized collections, open access resources, and subscription-based resources, all using a feature-rich discovery) layer. Currently, the four major vendors of web-scale discovery tools that offer both a central index and a discovery layer are EBSCO (EBSCO Discovery Service), ProQuest (Serials Solutions' Summon), OCLC (World-Cat Local), and Ex Libris (Primo Central Index). The central index, as is in the case of the major vendors mentioned previously, is a collection of citations and full text from publishers, subscription databases, and opensource collections, as well as MARC records from library catalogues. Metadata from local collections that have been digitized, in addition to content from institutional repositories, may further enhance the central index. The discovery layer, or the user interface, allows for interactive search and display of content within a library system, such as a web-scale discovery index. Of course, discovery layers are not entirely a new concept within libraries—many discovery layer interfaces are currently deployed as end user search interfaces for online public access catalogues. Web-scale discovery services have unique and distinct qualities that make them desirable to libraries: they allow for simple, single searching across the central index; they are responsive and quick; they typically offer a variety of methods for refining search results, such as facets and sorting capabilities; they provide relevance ranked search results; and they allow the user to connect directly with full text whenever appropriate.

In addition to their robust search capabilities that empower the concept of discovery for the end user, web-scale discovery services exhibit an extremely powerful system for indexing an amazing array of content, regardless of where the service is hosted. In addition to integrated library system records, a web-scale discovery service can index a library's digital collections, content from institutional repositories, in addition to other locally created and hosted digital content. Increasingly, this allows libraries the opportunity to uncover for users "hidden" or deep content that may otherwise go undiscovered in general searching. Further, preindexed and remotely hosted content, including e-books, full-text journals, article abstracts, and open access content, the sum of which can seem astronomical to many libraries, can vastly improve resource discovery by the end user in groundbreaking ways. In short, web-scale discovery services provide a unique, seamless, and rapid method for discovery and delivery of relevance ranked content from a vast and rich index.

5. Collaborative reference services combine digital library services among a group of libraries to combine expertise and availability. This helps libraries provide services at every hour of the day without the added pressure on human and technical resources. Examples of vendor-based consortium products are QuestionPoint, LSSI and Docutek. Vendors of these and similar services typically offer the same thing; quality reference assistance at any hour online with the benefit of some type of management software for administrators to organize the virtual data for assessment and other purposes. These virtual collaborations help intercept reference questions at any time by multiple librarians.

In the early 2000s, online services such as Ask Jeeves (now known as simply Ask.com because most people missed the P.G. Wodehouse reference to Jeeves the butler), were claiming millions of answered questions daily, free of charge. While there is a plethora of databases available for a reference librarian to use, the licenses usually stipulate that they only be used by current faculty, students, and staff of that institution. This can prove to be frustrating if you offer your virtual reference service to the community at large—sending full-text items from these licensed, subscription-based services is not allowed.

Libraries, feeling compelled to compete with Internet services such as Ask.com, wanted users to remember that their library also had answers for free. In addition, they wanted reference services that accommodated users as much as the commercial sites did. Thus, the marker for collaborative chat began. Interactive virtual reference services, where a librarian and patron interact in real time, actually migrated into the library field in 1999 to 2000 through the use of commercial business customer service software called eGain that the consortium 24/7 (now part of OCLC) and LSSI (now tutor.com) modified for library purposes. The QuestionPoint virtual reference system is a collaborative reference service formed by the Library of Congress (LOC) and OCLC (Online Computer Library Center). According to the LOC's Global Reference Network website, QuestionPoint "provides libraries with access to a growing collaborative network of reference librarians in the United States and around the world" (www.loc.gov/rr/digiref). This service is purchased by libraries and added to their websites so that patrons can interact with a qualified library staff member at any hour—regardless of whether the staff member is from the patron's library or not. The service was created to "enable reference librarians to share their resources and expertise with each other and with their patrons free of charge in unprecedented ways" (www.loc.gov/rr/digiref). OCLC also developed QuestionPoint Enhanced, a higher-end product with voice and video, but as seen with similar products providing VoIP software, unreliability and instability create disadvantages for users and librarians alike.

In short, The QuestionPoint service, available at www.QuestionPoint.org, provides libraries with access to a growing collaborative network of reference librarians in the United States and around the world. Library patrons can submit questions at any time of the day or night through their library's Website. The questions will be answered online by qualified library staff from the patron's own library or may be forwarded to a participating library around the world. The service, which is available to libraries by subscription, will enable reference librarians to share their resources and expertise with each other and with their patrons free of charge in unprecedented ways.

6. RRRLF has adopted certain schemes of Matching and Non-matching assistance.

State/U.T. has to participate in the Matching programmes of the RRRLF by contributing matching share on a pre-determined basis.

50:50, for the states having developed library system.

60:40 (40% is the state share and 60% is the central share) for the states having moderately developed Library System.

90:10 for north eastern states (90% is the central share and 10% is the state share).

Financial Assistance under Matching schemes are provided out of the total fund created with the State Contribution and the corresponding Central Share. In case of Non-Matching schemes assistances are provided from the Central Government Plan fund only.

Sharing of Assistance Central : State

50:50	60:40	90:10
Andhra Pradesh	Himachal Pradesh	Assam
Gujarat	Odisha	Manipur
Karnataka	Rajasthan	Meghalaya
Kerala	Andaman & Nicobar	Nagaland
Maharashtra	Chandigarh	Sikkim
Tamil Nadu	Dadra & Nagar Haveli	Tripura
West Bengal	Goa	Arunachal Pradesh
Puducherry	Uttarakhand	Mizoram
	Bihar	
	Haryana	
	Jammu & Kashmir	
	Madhya Pradesh	
	Punjab	
	Uttar Pradesh	
	Delhi	
	Lakshadweep	
	Jharkhand	
	Chattishgarh	

8. Digital libraries facilitate easy referencing and citations and ensure the preservation of access to the intellectual content of electronic information resources through the use of a unique identifier known as Digital Object Identifier (DOI). Digital Object Identifier is an open standard for creating an alphanumeric name that identifies digital content of mostly scholarly publications contents such as electronic book or journal article. The DOI is an essential feature of electronic information resources which serves as an identifier and a control mechanism for digital objects as it does not change, even if its location changes. With the aid of the Digital Object Identifier (DOI), the intellectual property of information resources domiciled in digital libraries' collection are properly managed. The main impetus of the Digital Object Identifier (DOI) system is to provide publishers with a method by which the intellectual property right issues associated with their materials can be managed.

9. Big Data describes innovative techniques and technologies to capture, store, distribute, manage and analyze datasets that traditional data management methods are unable to handle. The concept of "Big Data" was first defined by Laney in his research note. Laney described the characteristics of big data as which cannot be processed by traditional data management tools. Three Vs were first used to characterize the Big Data. With further study on big data, the "Three V's" have been expanded to "Five V's": volume, velocity, variety, veracity (integrity of data), value (usefulness of data) and complexity (degree of interconnection among data structures).

Gordon-Murname specifically addresses the rise in big data and in her article "Big Data: A Big Opportunity for Librarians." Gordon-Murname points out four key areas: (1) organization, (2) search and access of internal datasets, (3) awareness of external data sources, and (4) to serve as authorities on copyright and intellectual property issues for the management of research data.

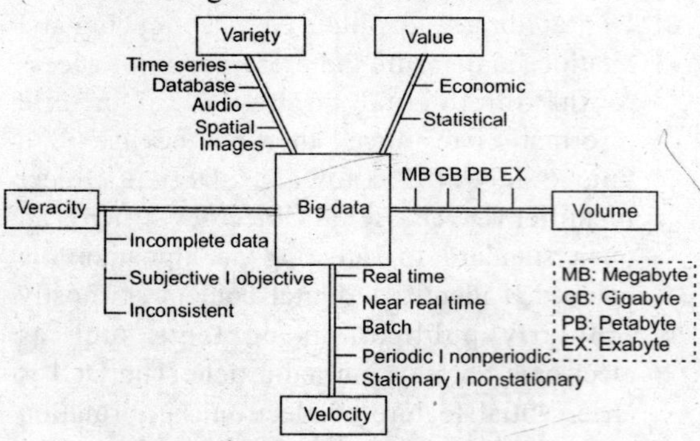

Fig.: *Five Vs of big data*

Big data consists of multidimensional, multimodal data sets and can be characterized by five Vs. Figure shows the five Vs.

- **Volume:** This refers to the huge amount of data that needs to be processed, stored, and analyzed. This requires developing algorithms that are scalable.
- **Velocity:** This is the indication of how quickly data is to be analyzed. Some challenges include processing the data in near real time or virtually real time.
- **Variety:** This is related to the different types of structured or unstructured data. The integration of different types of data is paramount.
- **Veracity:** This is the indication of the integrity of the data. Therefore, a robust and predictive algorithm capable of handling noise and incomplete data and information is needed for decision-making.
- **Value:** This is an important feature in big data. It mainly refers to the worth of the information being managed. Value also includes the discovery of knowledge and high return of investment.

10. Presently, two major long-term preservation programmes are available to academic libraries, researcher institutions and scholarly publishers, namely LOCKSS and CLOCKSS. The LOCKSS Programme, initiated in 1999 at the Stanford University Libraries is an open-source, library-led digital preservation system built on the principle of "Lots of Copies Keep Stuff Safe". LOCKSS follows a few unique principles that are vital to successful long-term preservation. Those principles are:

- Decentralized and distributed preservation (Lots of Copies Keep Stuff Safe).
- Give libraries local custody and control of their assets.
- Preserve the publisher's original authoritative version.
- Perpetual access—guaranteed and seamless.
- Affordable and Sustainable.

In LOCKSS Program, libraries are building and preserving collections of OA titles and subscribed e-journals and e-books, using the LOCKSS software. The collaborative collections become part of the Global LOCKSS Network. Libraries can also participate in Private LOCKSS Networks to preserve manuscripts and image collections, data sets, and government document collections.

The CLOCKSS (Controlled LOCKSS) initiative, launched in 2005 as a nonprofit venture, is a partnership of libraries and publishers committed to ensuring long-term access to scholarly work in digital format. It maintains the CLOCKSS Archive for long-term preservation of scholarly contents archived by its members. CLOCKSS has provision of permanent preservation of abandoned and orphaned contents with a Creative Commons license to ensure these contents remain available forever. CLOCKSS runs on LOCKSS technology. While LOCKSS is an open network, CLOCKSS is a closed system. These two systems are also experimenting with open file formats, which are device independent or software independent for future retrieval of archived contents.

11. Li-Fi, or light fidelity, is a new way to establish wireless communication links using the LED lighting networks. It is a bidirectional, high-speed and fully networked wireless communications similar to Wi-Fi. It uses visible light communication or infra-red and near ultra-violet (instead of radio frequency waves) spectrum. Light-emitting diodes (LEDs) are used as a medium to deliver networked, mobile, high-speeu communication in a similar manner to Wi-Fi.

The term Li-Fi was coined by Harald Hass from the University of Edinburgh in the United Kingdom.

Li-Fi vs. Wi-Fi

- Both Wi-Fi and Li-Fi transmit data over the electromagnetic spectrum: Wi-Fi utilizes radio waves, whereas Li-Fi uses visible light.
- While there is a potential spectrum crisis as Wi-Fi is close to full capacity, Li-Fi has almost no limitations on capacity, because the visible light spectrum is 10,000 times larger than the entire radio-frequency spectrum.
- Li-Fi has the advantage of being useful in electromagnetic-sensitive areas, such as in aircraft cabins, hospitals and nuclear power plants without causing electromagnetic interference.
- Li-Fi is expected to be 10 times cheaper than Wi-Fi.

13. Metadata must be encoded in order to allow for data transmission. Each piece of metadata—whether it is a single discrete statement or part of a larger metadata record-should be encoded separately so that it may be identified, parsed and accessed as needed, and so that it may be displayed in a meaningful way. Encoding also allows for integration of many languages and scripts within our data. We accomplish encoding by assigning tags, numbers, letters or words (*i.e.,* codes) to discrete pieces of metadata. In actual work situations, the encoding is often set up as a template or workform into which the pieces of information are inserted. Standard codes are used so that records will be interchangeable. Many of today's encoding schemes are derivatives of (1) the MARC format, (2) the Standard Generalized Markup Language (SGML), or (3) the extensible Markup Language (XML). These include the following:

MARC-based standards:

- MARC 21—the version of the Machine-Readable Cataloging formats now used by most English-speaking countries for their library bibliographic records;
- Universal MARC (UNIMARC)—designed for international interchange among several different countries' versions of MARC, but also adopted by some countries as their official MARC version:
- Various international versions of the MARC formats, such as IBERMARC (used in Spain and Portugal) and RusMARC (used in Russia).

SGML/XML document type definitions (DTDs) and schemas:

- Text Encoding Initiative (TEI)—for encoding literary texts;
- Hypertext Markup Language (HTML/XHTML)—for encoding Web pages;
- Encoded Archival Description (EAD)—for encoding archival finding aids; and
- Online Information exchange (ONIX)—for encoding publishers' records.

MARC and XML-based standards:

- MARCXML scheme–for encoding MARC 21 records using XML–based encoding; and
- Metadata Object Description Schema (MODS)–an XML encoding standard, based on the MARC 21 bibliographic format, that uses language-based rather than numeric codes.

These encoding standards are used as a container for resource descriptions ranging from a single metadata statement to an entire metadata record, some of which (*e.g.*, an archival finding aid) can be quite lengthy. The next level of container holds more than one record and can provide a means for linking together metadata for different kinds of resources (*e.g.*, metadata for resources that are linked with metadata for persons and organizations responsible for them and, perhaps, linked with metadata for other information resources). One such framework is the Metadata Encoding and Transmission Standard (METS) developed to hold metadata aimed at managing, preserving, displaying and exchanging digital objects.

14. Olle Persson was a professor in Library and Information Science at Umea University (Sweden) where he also obtained his Ph.D. in sociology in 1980. He was among the first in Europe to develop bibliometrics for indicators of scientific and technological activity, impact and collaboration as well as cognitive mapping of research fields. His work has been documented in a large number of journal articles. Among other things he has developed a software (Bibexcel) for bibliometric analysis.

15. The U.S. Green Building Council (USGBC) developed the Leadership in Energy and Environment Design (LEED) rating system to help in improving the quality of buildings and to minimize the impact of these buildings on the environment. The rating system is intended to blend the structure with the environment, reduce operating costs, and aid in marketing the structure for resale. LEED certification for green buildings requires that the project meet the fundamentals of green construction established by the USGBC, and score a minimum number of points in a LEED rating system. LEED acknowledges four levels of certification, including Certified, Siiver, Gold, and Platinum.

Key areas of the construction process covered by the LEED rating system include: integrative process, location and transportation, sustainable sites, water efficiency, energy and atmosphere, material and resources, indoor environmental quality, performance, innovation, and regional priority.

16. CCC recognizes the following kinds of entries in a classified catalogue:

Main entry

Book index entry

Class index entry

Cross reference entry

Cross reference index entry

The main entry and cross reference entry are number entries. Therefore, these form part of the classified part.

Book index entry, class index entry and cross reference index entry are word entries.

Therefore, these are included in the alphabetical part.

A main entry in CCC consists of the following sections:

- Leading section
- Heading section
- Title section
- Note section; if any
- Accession number
- Tracing section.

The Leading section consists of call number of the document and is always written in pencil.

The Heading section consists of authorship.

The Title section consists of title, edition and collaborators.

Other information is provided in the note section, if required.

The tracing section is given on the book of the main entry. It indicates which entries is addition to the main entry have been prepared for the given book. The purpose is to enable the removal of catalogue cards related to a main entry at the time of the weeding of a book from a library.

17. Extraneous variables are inconsistent or improper variables or factors in research environment which may affect the dependent variable(s) but are uncontrolled or not manipulated by us. Extraneous variables could damage the validity of our study making it impossible to know whether the effects were caused by independent and moderator variables or some extraneous factor. Since they cannot be controlled, we consider them while interpreting results. The murmur of students, parents education, socio-economic status, family history, interest in topic, time, preference for teaching style, personality, working capacity of teachers, etc. are extraneous variable. Intervening variables are abstract processes not directly observable but linked with independent and dependent variables whereas extraneous variables are factors in research environment which may affect dependent variable and are uncontrolled.

19. **Packet-filtering firewall:** A technique used to control network access by monitoring outgoing and incoming packets and allowing them to pass or halt based on the source and destination Internet Protocol (IP) addresses, protocols, and ports.

20. The diffusion of innovation theory was developed by E.M. Rogers to explain how a new idea or product gains acceptance and diffuses (or spreads) through a specific population or subset of an organization. A key point of this theory is that adoption of any innovation does not happen all at once for all members of the targeted population; rather, it is a drawn out process with some people quicker to adopt the innovation than others.

22. Delphi assessment is a group process involving a panel of 'experts' who attempt to forecast future outcomes in situations where there is no direct knowledge, or at least a great deal of uncertainty. It is an intuitive procedure which relies on the subjective probabilities that participants attach to the likelihood of future events; it is also iterative in nature, so that individual opinion can be modified by the influence of other group members. The Delphi method attempts to generate collective expert opinion by making two substitutions: expert judgement for direct knowledge, and group for individual. Linstone and Turoff note a significant convergence of responses for almost all forecast statements within three rounds of the process, and considerable stability of opinion thereafter.

23. **Fugitive material:** Publications such as pamphlets, posters, performance and exhibit programs, and duplicated material produced in small quantities, that are of immediate, local, or transitory interest and therefore difficult for libraries to collect and catalogue.

26. ISBNs were ten digits long until 2007, when a new global standard, using 13 digits, was introduced. Under the system which started on 1 January 2007, the 13 digits are always divided into five parts, separated by spaces or hyphens. The four parts following the prefix element can be of varying length and are as shown below.

- **Prefix element:** For the foreseeable future this will be 978 or 979.
- **Registration group element:** Identifies a national, geographic, or national grouping. It shows where the publisher is based.
- **Registrant element:** Identifies a specific publisher or imprint.
- **Publication element:** Identifies a specific edition of a specific title in a specific format.

- **Check digit:** The final digit which mathematically validates the rest of the number.

Following the change on 1 January 2007 existing ten-digit numbers must be converted by prefixing them with '978' and the check digit must be recalculated using a Modulus 10 system with alternate weights of 1 and 3.

27. Augmented reality (AR) and mixed reality (MR) are two approaches for advanced human-computer interaction (HCI) that emerged in the last fifteen years. Azuma defines augmented reality (AR) as a variation of Virtual Reality (VR). While VR technologies present to the user a completely synthetic environment without a relation to the real world (the users perceives only the virtual world), in an AR world the user can see the real world with its artifacts together with virtual objects superimposed upon or composited with the real world.

Obviously, AR supplements and enhances reality, rather than completely replacing it. Azuma defines three characteristics of AR systems:

(*i*) they combine real and virtual,

(*ii*) they are interactive in real time, and

(*iii*) they are registered in 3-D.

30. Ranganathan's Modes of Formation of Knowledge

Dissection "is cutting a universe of entities into parts of coordinate status, even as we cut a slice of bread into strips." When the parts are ranked, they form an array. Each part is termed as a "Lamina".

Example: Botany, Agriculture, Zoology constitute the dissected members of the universe of Basic Subjects.

Lamination "is a construction by overlaying facet on facet, even as we make a sandwich by laying a vegetable layer over a layer of bread When the basic layer is a Basic Subject and the other layers are isolates, a compound subject is formed."

Example: In the subject "Agriculture of Corns", the two layers, Agriculture and Corn lie on both the ends of the Basic Subject Agriculture and isolate idea Corns. There can be more layers of this type.

Denudation "is the progressive decrease of the extension and increase of the intension (or the depth) of a Basic Subject or an isolate idea, even as we scoop the flesh of a soft fruit from deeper and deeper layers or as we excavate a well". In the words of Shera denudation is "the exposure of a new area of knowledge by erosion or divestment through research or enquiry."

Example: Philosophy, Logic, and Symbolic logic.

Loose Assemblage "is the assembling together of two or more subjects."

Example: General relation between Political Science and Economics.

Superimposition "is connecting together two or more isolate ideas belonging to the same universe of isolate ideas. The need for this usually arises when an entity is eligible to as isolate idea on the basis of two or more quasi isolate ideas."

Example: Sociology of Rural Poor.

31. Preservation and Conservation of library Materials: The library houses the document by considering the long-term preservation of the items while still allowing the end user to access the material easily. But all library collections experience damage from use and decay from aging. So, there is a need of preservation and conservation of library materials.

Books and other materials suffer damage or deterioration because of several groups of factors, some inherent in the materials and others beyond the control of the library. Library holdings may begin to deteriorate because of the organic materials from which they are made. Each type of material - paper, glue, plastic, etc. that goes into the

on their perceptions of IE experiences: *super-encounterers, encounterers, occasional encounterers,* and *nonencounterers.*

In her follow-up work, Erdelez (2000) addressed the characteristics of the Internet and the Web as IE environments. The information richness of the Web and the ease of manipulation of electronic information might seem to be advantageous for IE. Erdelez, however, reported that this may be true only for users at the middle and lower end of the IE spectrum. The super-encounterers in her study reported a high level of apprehension about the Web as an IE environment. A related study by Erdelez & Rioux (2000) explored the use of the Web for encountering information useful to other people.

Through the above empirical research, Erdelez confirmed that IE is an integral element of users' overall information behaviour and a very rich topic for study. After additional conceptual refining, Erdelez recently identified IE as a specific type of OAI and defined it as *an instance of accidental discovery of information during an active search for some other information.* This view of IE, while narrower than the one presented in her initial study, allows for the presence of other types of OAI that yet need to be identified and defined.

42. The types of reference services are mainly grouped in two heads viz. ready reference service and Long range reference service. But different scholars identified different types based on the queries solved or information provided.

James I Wyer (1931) identified and proposed three theories of reference service *i.e.* conservative, moderate and liberal. Where as Samuel Rothstein called them minimum, middling, and maximum.

(*i*) **Conservative:** It includes giving occasional personal assistance to the inexperienced and bewildered reader. It limits the help to pointing the way only and so it is traditional in nature.

(*ii*) **Moderate:** The moderate reference service goes beyond providing mere instruction to actually helping the reader in using the book or finding the document and facts, etc.

(*iii*) **Liberal:** It includes the provision of the full and direct supply of reliable information to the readers.

44. WAMP is an open source software used to run dynamic Web sites on the Windows environment. The WAMP package principal components are: Apache Web server, MySQL, database management system, PHP (or Perl/Python) scripting languages and PhpMyAdmin.

46. A histogram consists of a series of rectangles drawn next to each other without any space between them, each representing the frequency of a category or subcategory. Their height is in proportion to the frequency they represent. The height of the rectangles may represent the absolute or proportional frequency or the percentage of the total. A histogram can be drawn for both categorical and continuous variables.

Figures 1 and 2 shows a two-dimensional and three-dimensional histograms respectively.

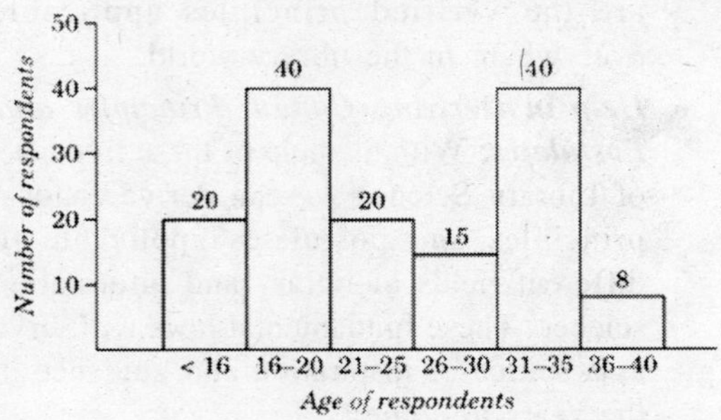

Fig. 1. *Two-dimensional histogram*

Age of respondent	*Number of respondents*
< 16	20
16-20	40
21-25	20
26-30	15
31-35	40
36-40	8

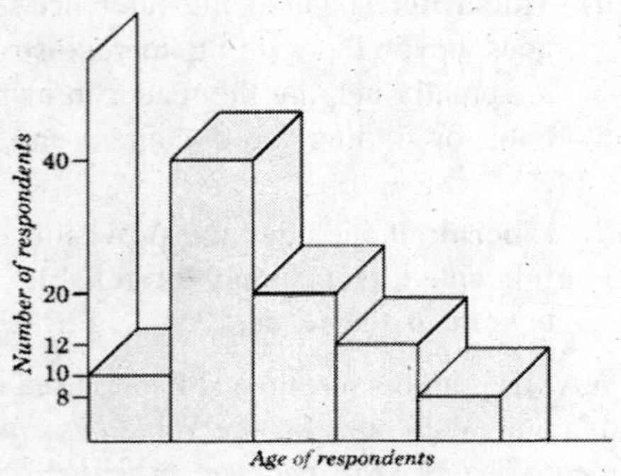

Fig. 2. *Three-dimensional histogram*

Age of respondent	*Number of respondents*
10-15	10
16-20	40
21-25	20
26-30	12
31-35	8

47. Usefulness of the five laws is as follows:

- ***Act as Fundamental Laws:*** The five laws of library science are fundamental laws of library and information science and are applicable to any problem in the areas of library science, library service and library practice. Five laws are guiding norms; these are the verified principles applicable everywhere in the library world.
- ***Help in Deriving Canon, Principles and Postulates:*** With the help of these five laws of Library Science we can derive canons, principles and postulates applicable in different fields of library and information science. These fundamental laws will serve as a source of inspiration and guidance in the years to come.
- ***Resolve Conflict Between Cannons:*** The laws of library science help in solving any conflict that may arise during the functioning of libraries. The five laws serve as a higher court.
- ***Caution:*** So in case of conflict between canons of cataloguing, classification etc., an appeal is made to the five laws of library science to resolve the conflict.
- ***Guiding Rules:*** The laws of library science guide the staff in decision making about what is right and what is wrong in a given situation. As such Ranganathan's five laws of library science have found universal acceptance as Pentagon of Library Philosophy.

48. Paul Otlet, a Belgian bibliographer, peace activist and information science pioneer, with colleague Henri La Fontaine, in 1904 created the Universal Decimal Classification (UDC) system based on the American Dewey Decimal cataloging system. Otlet actively promoted the adoption of the UDC in Europe by cataloging more than bibliographic information about books and articles; he sought to expand the UDC system to include other media such as photographs, drawings, and films. It was fundamentally a paper-based system of index cards that contained information on the 14 million multimedia items classified and accessed using the UDC. This system was unique in that its cross-index was an analog precursor of the hypertext links found in websites today.

49. The Special Libraries Association is a not-for-profit corporation founded in 1909 as a response to a growing number of special libraries. It is an international association of librarians who work in special libraries serving such areas as business, industry, research, government, universities, and cultural institutions. They are focused on the strategic use of information. There are more than 9,000 members. SLA has fifty-six regional chapters and twenty-six divisions representing various subject fields and interests, including biomedical and life sciences, business and finance, competitive intelligence, engineering, government information, legal, petroleum and energy resources, pharmaceuticals, social science, and transportation. There are also numerous caucuses, which are information groups that foster discussion and interaction among members with common interests.

Caucus areas include archives and preservation, information futurists, natural history, and user experience. SLA is sustained by five core values: leadership, service, innovation and continuous learning, results and accountability, and collaboration and partnering.

SLA is engaged in a variety of activities to support special libraries, including providing continuing education programs and advocacy for special librarians within special libraries. The Association is also engaged in political advocacy externally regarding national and international information policies. The monthly magazine of SLA is *Information Outlook*, which serves as a major professional continuing education tool for special librarians (sla.org).

50. The famous 'big6' information problem-solving model raised by Eisenberg and Berkowitz (1990) pointed out the essential information skills, that is task definition, information seeking strategies, location and access, use of information, synthesis and evaluation. The 'Big6' model is widely adopted in information literacy studies and considered as essential skills for information professio-nals.

51. **Common auxiliary signs**

+ (plus) for co-ordination, addition

/ (stroke) for consecutive extension

: (Colon) for relation

[ ] (Square brackets) for sub-grouping.

: : (Double colon) for order fixing.

Independentauxiliary tables

= For language

(01/09) form (data form, handbook, pamphlets, theses, articles, dictionaries etc.)

(1/9) Place, country.

(= ..) race

"..." time.

52. Zotero is open source reference management software that allows users to manage bibliographic data and related search materials. Features include web browser integration, online syncing, generation of in-text citations, and footnotes and bibliographies. It is also integrated with word processors Microsoft Word. LibreOffice, OpenOffice.org Writer and NeoOffice. Zotero offers ways to connect and collaborate with other researchers as well, through Zotero Groups and Zotero People. Zotero is primarily a Mozilla Firefox browser plugin, but Zotero Standalone and Zotero Connectors allow users to use the software with Mac OSX, PCs and Linux and Google Chrome and Apple Safari, respectively.

54. There are two types of error associated with hypothesis testing that the marketing researcher needs to be aware of when forming conclusions based on the data analysis. The first type of error is termed Type I. Type I error is associated with rejecting the null hypothesis and accepting the alternative hypothesis in error. This type of error, frequently called alpha (α), occurs when the sample data lead to rejection of a null hypothesis that is in fact true. The probability of such an error is termed the level of significance. The level of significance is equivalent to the amount of risk regarding the accuracy of the test that the researcher is willing to accept. In other words, the level of significance is the probability that the rejection of the null hypothesis is in error.

56. The Union Human Resource Development Minister, Prakash Javadekar launched the new digital initiative of HRD Ministry 'National Digital Library of India (NDLI)' on the occasion of National Reading Day (NRD) in New Delhi on June 19, 2018. The library has been developed by IIT Kharagpur. It is a single window platform that collects and collates metadata from premier learning institutions in India and abroad, as well as other relevant sources.

57. **Big deal:** A *publisher's licensed* package of journals that costs less to the subscriber/ *licensee* than would the sum of the *titles* (3)

purchased individually. The packages usually include some less relevant titles (3) along with the most desired *titles* (3). A big deal may be leveraged when negotiated for a consortium or group of *libraries* (3) to include a larger number of *titles* (3) than the group could afford if subscribing individually.

59. A web portal is a customized website that immerses information from a wide array of sources in a consistent and uniformed manner.

For example, web portals are served in the form of dashboards for company executives and managers. How the content on a portal should be organized and presented depends largely on the requirements of the end users?

A web portal may be customized based on the restrictions of domain searches. An enterprise portal usually has a consistent design and has the capability to interact with applications and databases.

There are various types of web portals depending on the usage and content restrictions. Some of them are:

- Government and federal portals
- Corporate and enterprise portals
- Cultural and trade portals
- Stock and financial portals
- Search portals
- Tender and bidding portals
- Domain specific portals.

61. Cloud computing offers computing infrastructure, platform and application delivered 'as-a-service'. Those services are considered as primary *cloud computing services* and are referred to as:

- Infrastructure-as-a-Service (IaaS)
- Platform-as-a-Service (PaaS)
- Software-as-a-Service (SaaS)

These services are generally pronounced as 'i-a-a-s', 'pass' and 'saas' respectively. They are the driving forces behind the growth of cloud computing. Clubbed together these three service models are commonly referred as SPI (Service-Platform-Infrastructure) model. Cloud service providers arrange these services for the cloud consumers.

Infrastructure-as-a-Service: Cloud computing allows access to computing resources in a virtualized environment popularly referred as 'the Cloud'. *Infrastructure-as-a-Service* delivers virtualized-hardware (not physical, but simulated software) resources to consumers known as virtual resources or virtual components. It provides the facility of remotely using virtual processor, memory, storage and network resources to the consumers. These virtual resources can be used just like physical (hardware) resources to build any computing setup (like virtual machine or virtual network). For this reason, IaaS is also referred as *Hardware-as-a-Service* (HaaS).

64. PRECIS (PREserved Context Index System) is a system of subject indexing which provides a full subject statement at each significant point of entry into the index. The context of the terms is always preserved and each index entry is coextensive with the subject indexed. All entries except one have a two-line structure reflecting the following pattern:

LEAD QUALIFIER
DISPLAY

66. Co-Word Analysis: This is a technique of analyzing a set of documents to evaluate their strength of linkage by measuring the extent to which they share important key words or terms. The co-word analysis examines co-occurrences of key words and terms extracted from publication titles or their full text. The co-occurrences of key words measure the degree of cognitive linkage among a set of documents. The co-word frequency array (matrix) can be further analyzed via cluster analysis, multi-dimensional scaling, and network analysis to construct a co-word map.

67. IPv4 ADDRESSES:

- An IPv4 address is a 32-bit address that uniquely and universally defines the connection of a device (for example, a computer or a router) to the Internet.

- IPv4 addresses are unique. They are unique in the sense that each address defines one, and only one, connection to the Internet. Two devices on the Internet can never have the same address at the same time.

68. INFLIBNET Access Management Federation (INFED), the first Federation in India, has adopted Shibboleth, a standard-based open source software, for authenticating authorized users from colleges and universities and provide them seamless access to e-resources from anywhere, anytime.

The INFLIBNET Centre, as one of its core mandates, provides access to scholarly e-resource to universities and colleges in India under the e-ShodhSindhu. The INFED is being set-up as a centralized agency to coordinate with member institutions in the process of implementation of user authentication and access control mechanism distributed across participating institutions using standardized rules and metadata for exchange of attributes.

70. Webster's Third New International Dictionary of the English Language, published by the Merriam-Webster Company in 1961 (NID3), is the only other relatively complete unabridged English dictionary of recent times. It differs from the Oxford English Dictionary in that it does contain very large numbers of technical words, going far beyond just those that have moved out into common parlance. It has some 450,000 entries. It replaced Webster's New International Dictionary of 1934 (NID2), which remains the largest of all English dictionaries, having over 600,000 entries. NID3 was shortened (at the same time that over 100,000 new entries were included, which means that 250,000 entries were dropped from NID2) mainly to make it possible to bind it by machine.

72. i10-index is the number of publications with at least 10 citations. In July 2011, Google Scholar started a tool, which allows scholars to keep track of their own citations and also produces an h-index and an i10-index.

74. A video podcast (shortened to 'vodcast') includes video clips, web television series. A wide and vast amount of matter can be created with connection to the internet. This communication through the online service takes it to a new level. Video has become extremely popular online and are short clips of video. Video podcasts are also being used for web television. commonly known as web TV, which is growing as a digital entertainment game. The web TV vodcasts typically are short ranging from 2 to 9 minutes per episode. They are used for advertising, video blogs, amateur filming, journalism and convergence with traditional media.

77. A MARC record consists of three main sections: the leader, the directory and the variable fields.

The Leader: It consists of data elements containing coded information and it is identified by relative character position. The leader is fixed in length in a string of 24 characters, 00 to 23. It occurs in the beginning of each MARC record.

The Directory: It contains the tag, starting location, and length of each field within the record. It serves as road map of the data contents area. Directory information is dynamically gathered and stored in a place between the Leader and the Data contents sections. The Directory is generated programmatically by computer for locating data fields with the help of their address, which is a string of 12 numeric characters. The size of directory area varies depending on the number of times the address repeats in the directory. The directory ends with a field terminator character.

Variable fields/Data Content: The data content of a record is divided into variable fields. MARC 21 format describe two types of variable fields, viz. variable control fields and variable data fields. Control and data fields are distinguished only by structure. The data fields are separated by the field terminator which is a pre-determined special character such #,@, etc. The data content resides in the final section of a Record, and ends with the Record Terminator.

78. **Hook number:** A number in the DDC without meaning in itselt: but used to introduce examples of the topic. Hook numbers have headings that begin with "Miscellaneous," "Specific," or "Other"; and do not contain add notes, including notes, or class-here notes. Standard subdivisions are always bracketed under hook numbers.

81. Under the umbrella of the United Nations (U.N.), the World Intellectual Property Organization (WIPO) was created in 1967 to promote the protection of intellectual property throughout the world.

82. A nub is the most basic of the hardware devices that interconnect multiple nodes. Hubs have multiple ports to which nodes connect. When a packer arrives at one port, it is sent to all the ports of the hub except for the port of entry. The bandwidth available for usage by all devices connected to a hub is equal to its total port speed. Bandwidth describes the amount of data that can travel from one network point to another within a specified time. For example, a five-port 10/100-megabit-per-second (Mbps) hub has five network ports that can transmit data at 10 Mbps or 100 Mbps, depending on the client NIC configuration. If five nodes are connected to this hub at 10 Mbps, those five nodes must share the 10 Mbps of bandwidth. If one node is sending large amounts of data, it decreases the available bandwidth for the other four nodes.

83. The binary system uses two digits (0 and 1) to represent numbers. This is similar to how data is stored inside the computer memory. Similar to the decimal system, the value of the number represented by this system is equal to the sum of the product of each digit multiplied by rwo raised to the power of the location of that digit. For example, the binary number 10110 is equivalent to the decimal number 22. This can be seen by writing $10110 \Rightarrow 1 \times 2^4 + 0 \times 2^3 + 1 \times 2^2 + 1 \times 2^1 + 0 \times 2^0 \Rightarrow 22$

To convert from decimal to binary representation, we start by dividing the decimal number by the largest power of 2 that it can be divided by. We then take the remainder and divide by the next-highest power of 2 possible. We repeat this process until the remainder is zero. For example, consider converting the decimal number 59 into binary representation.

Example: Represent the decimal number 59 in binary form

Solution: We start by dividing 59 by 32, which is the largest power of 2 that we can divide 59 into. We take the remainder, which is 27, and then divide by the next-largest power of 2, which in this case is 16. The remainder after the second division operation is 11. This process is continued until we get a remainder of 0 when we divide 1 by 1. The details are shown here, where *r* is the remainder after each division.

$$59/32 = 1\ r\ 27$$
$$27/16 = 1\ r\ 11$$
$$11/8 = 1\ r\ 3$$
$$3/4 = 0\ r\ 3$$
$$3/2 = 1\ r\ 1$$
$$1/1 = 1\ r\ 0$$

The binary equivalent is then formed by arranging the quotients to form the binary number, So $59 \Rightarrow 111011$.

84. Scirus is the most comprehensive science-specific search engine on the Internet. Driven by the latest search engine technology, Scirus searches over 370 million science-specific Web pages, enabling you to quickly:

- Pinpoint scientific, scholarly, technical and medical data on the Web.
- Find the latest reports, peer-reviewed articles, patents, pre-prints and journals that other search engines miss.

- Offer unique functionalities designed for scientists and researchers.

Searches more than 370 million science-related pages, Scirus helps you quickly locate scientific information on the Web:

- Filters out non-scientific sites. For example, if you search on REM, Google finds the rock group—Scirus finds information on sleep, among other things.
- Finds peer-reviewed articles such as PDF and PostScript files, which are often invisible to other search engines.

85. The Society of College, National and University Libraries (SCONUL) developed a model to describe information literacy competencies in 1999. SCONUL identified seven main "pillars" of skills and competencies. The first pillar was the ability to recognize a need for information; the second pillar was the ability to distinguish ways in which the information need could be filled; the third pillar was the ability to construct search strategies to locate information; the fourth pillar was the ability to locate and access information; the fifth pillar was the ability to compare and evaluate information acquired from different sources; the sixth pillar was the ability to organize and communicate the information to others; and the seventh and final pillar was the ability to synthesize from existing information and build on it, thus contributing to the creation of new knowledge (SCONUL, 1999).

Given the changing information landscape, SCONUL revised its model in 2011 and provided a new model, also with seven pillars, as a generic core model of information literacy for higher education. This model is now known as the *SCONUL Seven Pillars of Information Literacy: Core Model for Higher Education.* The new seven pillars are:

- Manage
- Present
- Identify
- Scope.
- Evaluate
- Gather
- Plan

88. In general, a medium can carry only one signal at any moment in time. For multiple signals to share one medium, the medium must somehow be divided, giving each signal a portion of the total bandwidth. Multiplexing (also known as MUXing) is a method by which multiple analog message signals or digital data streams are combined into one signal over a shared medium. The basic aim of the Multiplexing is to share an expensive resource by putting-up multiple signals on the same channel. For example, in telecommunications, several telephone calls may be carried using one wire. Multiplexing originated in telegraphy in the 1870s, and is now widely applied in different streams of communications. When several communication channels are needed between the same two points, significant economics may be realized by sending all the messages on one transmission facility—called multiplexing.

Thus, Multiplexing refers to the ability to transmit data coming from several pairs of equipment (transmitters and receivers) called *low-speed channels* on a single physical medium (called the *high-speed channel*). Whereas, a *multiplexer* is the multiplexing device that combines the signals from the different transmitters and sends them over the *high-speed channel.* A *demultiplexer* is the device which separates signal received from a *high-speed channel* into different signal and sends them to receivers.

There are four basic multiplexing techniques:

- Frequency Division multiplexing (FDM)
- Time Division Multiplexing (TDM)
- Code Division Multiplexing (COM)
- Space-Division Multiplexing (SDM)
- Frequency Division Multiplexing: Band-width is divided into different smaller frequency bands (range).
- Time Division Multiplexing (TDM) (Time slots are allocated to message signals in an non overlapping manner in the time domain so that individual messages can be recovered from time synchronized switches)

- **Quadrature Carrier/amplitude Multiplexing (QAM):** Two message signals are transmitted in the same frequency band. The recovery is possible due to the carrier signals being orthogonal.
- Code Division Multiplexing (CDM) users occupy the same frequency band but modulate their messages with different codes TDMA FDMA CDMA when used for multiple access TDMA, FDMA, e.g., GSM, FM, AM, Wireless networks.

Circuit switching is defined as a mechanism applied in telecommunications (mainly in PSTN) whereby the user is allocated the full use of the communication channel for the duration of the call. That is if two parties wish to communicate, the calling party has to first dial the numbers of the called party. Once those numbers are dialed, the originating exchange will find a path to the terminating exchange, which will in turn find the called party. After the circuit or channel has been set up, then communication will take place, then once they are through the channel will be cleared. This mechanism is referred to as being connection-oriented.

Voice being a very vital medium of human communication, telephone was invented. It permitted long distance voice communication. The need of a user to talk to a desired person out of many persons on a real time basis leads to the concept of establishing a direct path between the caller and the called users. Circuit switching was conceived to be an appropriate technique for the purpose. Telephone systems use circuit switching largely to date because it serves the purpose very well. However, a major drawback of circuit switching is the requirement of a dedicated path between the calling and the called parties. This means reserving resources like the chain of switches and transmission media over the entire path.

89. Principles of Management: Henri Fayol suggested the fourteen principles of management which are given below:

(*i*) **Division of work:** Division of work means division of the total task into compact jobs and allocating these compact jobs to different persons so that an employee can concentrate on only one type of work. It helps to improve efficiency by avoiding wastage of time and effort caused by change from one type of work to another. When an individual does the same job repeatedly he acquires speed and accuracy in performance. In the words of Henri Fayol, "The worker always on the same post, the manager always concerned with the same matters, acquire an ability, sureness and accuracy which increases their output". Division of work is applicable to all kinds of work, technical as well as managerial.

(*ii*) **Authority and responsibility:** Authority is the right to get work done from others and responsibility is the obligation to perform the assigned task. Anyone who exercises authority must accept responsibility for his work. Similarly, one who is held responsible should be given the necessary authority. Authority and responsibility are co-existent and they must go hand in hand. Authority without responsibility leads to irresponsible behaviour while responsibility without authority will make a person ineffective. Therefore, there should be parity between authority and responsibility.

(*iii*) **Discipline:** Discipline implies obedience, respect of authority and observance of the established rules and regulations. Discipline is essential for the smooth running of every organisation. According to Fayol, good supervision at all levels, clear and fair rules and built-in system of penalties will help to maintain discipline.

(*iv*) **Unity of command:** According to this principle an employee should receive orders from one superior only and be accountable to him. No person can serve several masters at the same time. If a subordinate has more than one boss, dual command will undermine authority, weaken discipline, divide loyalty and create confusion, delays, etc. Principle of unity of command is very relevant in large and modern organisations as it helps in smooth working of people.

Violating of the principle of unity of command leads to the following adverse effects.

(*a*) Overlapping of orders and instructions.

(*b*) Confusion and indiscipline.

(*c*) Duplication of work.

(*d*) Divided loyalty and disobedience.

(*e*) Lack of responsibility.

(*f*) Disrespect for superiors.

(*v*) Unity of direction: There should be one head and one plan for a group of activities having the same objective. In other words, each group of activities with the same objective must have one plan of action and must be under the control of one superior. Without unity of direction unity of action and co-ordination of efforts are not possible.

Unity of direction should be differentiated from unity of command. Unity of command relates to the functioning of people whereas unity of direction is concerned with the activities. Unity of direction does not automatically lead to unity of command though there cannot be unity of command without unity of direction. Unity of direction relates to the functioning of the whole organisation.

(*vi*) Subordination of individual interest to general interest: An organisation is bigger than an individual. Therefore, the interests or goals of the organisation must prevail upon the personal interests of individuals. In order to achieve supremacy of group or common interests, managers must set a good example and they must be firm but reasonable in dealing with subordinates. Constant supervision is necessary to prevent promotion of personal interests at the cost of the organisation.

In order to achieve subordination of individual interest to common interest, is necessary that employees are honest sincere and loyal. Mutual difference and clash of interests can be reconcile through mutual agreement.

(*vii*) Remuneration: The remuneration payable to workers must be fair, reasonable and satisfactory both to the employees and the employer. It must reward effort so as to motivate higher productivity. The amount of remuneration and the method of wage payment should both be fair and rewarding.

(*viii*) Centralisation: According to Fayol, everything that increases the importance of subordinates' role is decentralisation and everything that reduces it is centralisation. Centralisation and decentralisation is a matter of proportion and the right proportion between them should be decided keeping in view the circumstances of the particular case. There should be a proper balance between centralisation and decentralisation.

(*ix*) Scalar chain: It refers to the chain of superiors ranging from the ultimate authority (top) to the lowest rank (bottom). Normally, the prescribed chain of command should be followed and communications should flow through the established chain of command. However, to facilitate quick communication between two links in the chain, a gang plank (direct contact) may be created.

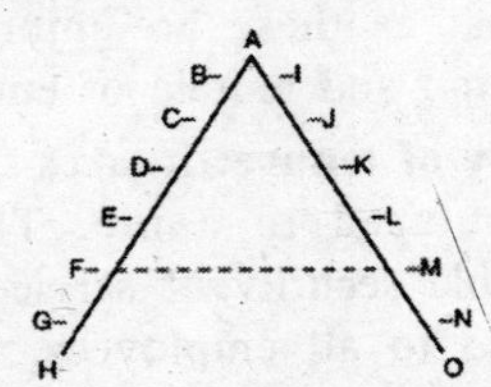

In this figure, the scalar chain is represented by the double ladder HAQ. Any communication from F to M will flow upwards A through E, D, C and B and then downwards through I, J, K and L. A gang plank represented by the dotted line between F and M may be created to avoid delays and difficulties in communication.

Gang plank should not, however, be a normal practice because it undermines the established lines of authority. Moreover, F and M should inform their respective superiors about the direct communication among them.

The idea of gang plank indicates that principles of management are general and flexible guidelines rather than hard and fast laws.

(x) Order: There must be material and social order in an enterprise. Material order implies "a proper place for everything and everything in its right place. Similarly, social order means "a place for everyone and everyone in his appointed place". The right man in the right job is very important for the successful functioning of an organisation.

Violation of the principle of order causes the following adverse effects.

(*a*) Confusion and chaos in the organisation.

(*b*) Wastage of resources.

(*c*) Increase in cost of operations.

(xi) Equity: Management should treat the employees with justice and kindness. There should be equity of treatment in dealing with subordinates and no discrimination should be made between them. Nepotism and favouritism should not exist as these are injurious to the motivation and morale of employees.

(xii) Stability of tenure: It takes time to learn and get used to a job. Therefore, a reasonable security of service should be provided to all employees. Stability of tenure helps to develop loyalty and attachment on the part of employees. Unnecessary labour turnover or change of personnel increases cost of selection and training and spoils the image of the firm.

Violation of this principle causes the following adverse effects:

(*a*) A feeling of insecurity among employees.

(*b*) Reduction in the efficiency of employees.

(*c*) Disturbance in work routine.

(xiii) Initiative: Employees at all levels should be encouraged to think out and execute the assigned tasks in a better way. Initiative is a source of strength for an organisation. Therefore, subordinates should be inspired to suggest improvements in the formulation and implementation of plans.

(xiv) Esprit de corps: There must be team spirit and co-operation among the members of an organisation. 'Unity of strength' and the strength of an enterprise lies in the co-operation and harmony in individual efforts. Group efforts are more than the aggregate of individual contributions on account of esprit de corps.

Strong motivation, recognition of contributions made by employees, mutual cooperation, constructive approach by managers and effective coordination help to achieve espirit de corps in an organisation.

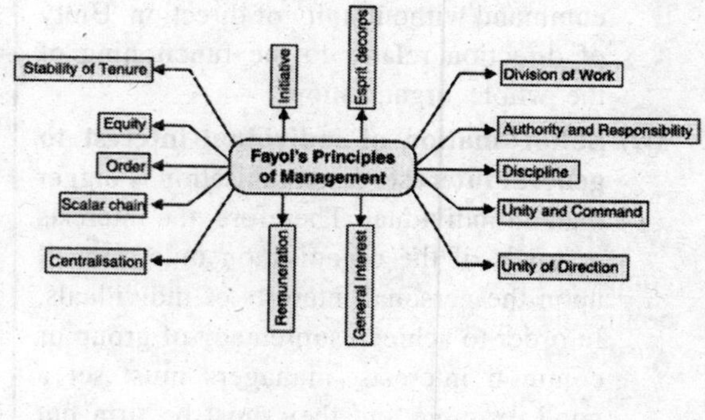

National Testing Agency (NTA)

UGC-NET Junior Research Fellowship & Assistant Professor Eligibility Exam

Library and Information Science, December-2018*

PAPER-II

Note : *This paper contains* ***hundred (100)*** *objective type questions of* ***two*** *(2) marks each.* ***All*** *questions are* ***compulsory***.

1. According to S.R. Ranganathan, reference service provided using a chain of books, periodicals and other materials is called as:
A. Long Range Reference Service
B. Reach-me-down Service
C. Short Range Reference Service
D. Information and Referral Service

2. Who said "Management is the art of getting things done through people"?
A. Mary Parker Follett
B. F.W. Taylor
C. Lillian Gilbreth
D. Henry Mintzberg

3. Which of the following canon implies, according to Dr. S.R. Ranganathan, that each class number should represent one and only one subject or isolate idea?
A. Canon of Hierarchy
B. Canon of Mnemonics
C. Canon of Homonym
D. Canon of Relativity

4. Decimal number '100' is represented in binary as:
A. 01010011 B. 00100111
C. 11101100 D. 01100100

5. Which of the following models of communication is also called ABX model of communication?
A. Westley and MacLean's model of communication
B. Theodore M. Newcomb's model of communication
C. George Gerbner's model of communication
D. Wilbur Schramm and Osgood model of communication

6. = 00 in UDC denotes:
A. Translated documents
B. Untranslated documents
C. Multilingual documents
D. Artificial languages

7. In the context of user studies, a Librarian's study on "How well the human-computer-networks interaction works"? can be categorized as:
A. Philosophical-analytic approach
B. Cognitive approach
C. User-centered approach
D. Physical approach

8. Who was the first Librarian of the Imperial Library, India?
A. John Macfarlane
B. Khan Bahadur M.A. Asadulla
C. J.A. Chapman
D. Harinath De

9. 'UNIMARC' is a contribution of:
A. IFLA B. LC
C. UNESCO D. OCLC

10. Identify from the following which publication is ***not*** excluded from Indian National Bibliography.
A. Ephemerals
B. Musical scores
C. Maps
D. First issue of a new periodical

*Held on 18 December, 2018

11. In PRECIS 'f' and 'g' in secondary operators represent:
A. Coordinate concepts
B. Extra core concepts
C. Special classes of action
D. Core concepts

12. Copyright Office, Govt. of India functions under the Ministry of:
A. Law and Justice
B. Information and Broadcasting
C. Commerce and Industry
D. Culture

13. On which of the following themes does 'The Europa World of Learning 2017' contain introductory essays?
A. Accreditation
B. The role of higher education in national development
C. Academic freedom
D. The role of gender in access to and participation in higher education

14. In spiral of scientific method, the 'Hooke's Law' is an example of:
A. Verification phase
B. Empirical phase
C. Deductive phase
D. Hypothesizing phase

15. Creative Common offers CC0 (CC-Zero) for:
A. Users B. Vendors
C. Copyright holders D. Publishers

16. Who developed information literacy logo?
A. IFLA/UNESCO B. ALA/ACRL
C. IFLA/ALA D. LC/OCLC

17. In which year did IFLA launch 'International Advocacy Programme' (IAP)?
A. 1996 B. 2016
C. 2010 D. 2012

18. A set of best practices for publishing and interlinking structured data on the web is known as:
A. Unmarked data B. Distributed data
C. Linked data D. Web data

19. 'Touchpoint' end-user discovery service is provided by:
A. SLA B. OCLC
C. LC D. ALA

20. Vidya Mitra, integrated e-content portal of INFLIBNET is a web-based portal consisting of all e-content developed under:
A. NME–ICT
B. Swayam–Prabha
C. ICSSR Data Service
D. Unnat Bharat Abhiyan

21. Which among the following are the characteristics of 'informative abstracts'?
(*i*) Orientation to serve specific group.
(*ii*) Detailed information about content of the original.
(*iii*) May not need to consult the original.
(*iv*) Reviews the document.
Choose the correct answer from the code given below:
Code:
A. (*iii*) and (*iv*) are correct
B. (*ii*) and (*iii*) are correct
C. (*ii*) and (*iv*) are correct
D. (*i*) and (*iii*) are correct

22. Which of the following are Object-based-logical data models?
(*i*) Hierarchical model.
(*ii*) Network model.
(*iii*) Entity relationship model.
(*iv*) Functional model.
Choose the correct answer from the code given below:
Code:
A. (*i*) and (*iii*) are correct
B. (*ii*) and (*iii*) are correct
C. (*i*) and (*iv*) are correct
D. (*iii*) and (*iv*) are correct

23. Which of the following are the different types of longitudinal study?
(*i*) Cohort Study
(*ii*) Correlational Study
(*iii*) Panel Study
(*iv*) Trend Study

Choose the correct answer from the code given below:

Code:

A. (*i*), (*iii*) and (*iv*) are correct
B. (*i*), (*ii*) and (*iii*) are correct
C. (*ii*), (*iii*) and (*iv*) are correct
D. (*i*), (*ii*) and (*iv*) are correct

24. Which of the following can be categorized as administrative roles of an LIS professional?

(*i*) Knowledge organizer
(*ii*) Resource allocator
(*iii*) Disseminator of information
(*iv*) Subscription negotiator

Choose the correct answer from the code given below:

Code:

A. (*ii*) and (*iii*) are correct
B. (*i*) and (*iv*) are correct
C. (*ii*) and (*iv*) are correct
D. (*i*) and (*iii*) are correct

25. Which of the following statements are true to define cost-benefit analysis?

(*i*) Evaluation of alternatives in relation to their costs.
(*ii*) Maintaining the present performance level while reducing the costs of operating the system.
(*iii*) Holding operating costs constant while raising the average performance level.
(*iv*) Rank variant alternatives appropriate to a given set of objectives.

Choose the correct answer from the code given below:

Code:

A. (*iii*) and (*iv*) are correct
B. (*i*) and (*iii*) are correct
C. (*ii*) and (*iii*) are correct
D. (*i*) and (*iv*) are correct

26. Which of the following are free and open source Content Management Systems?

(*i*) Text pattern (*ii*) Concrete 5
(*iii*) Content verse (*iv*) Kentico

Choose the correct answer from the code given below:

Code:

A. (*ii*) and (*iv*) are correct
B. (*ii*) and (*iii*) are correct
C. (*i*) and (*iii*) are correct
D. (*i*) and (*ii*) are correct

27. Which of the following are the characteristics of Google's 'featured snippets' in search?

(*i*) Full text answer to a query
(*ii*) Quick direct answer to a query
(*iii*) Extracted from a web page
(*iv*) Displayed at the bottom of a search

Choose the correct answer from the code given below:

Code:

A. (*ii*) and (*iii*) are correct
B. (*i*) and (*ii*) are correct
C. (*i*) and (*iv*) are correct
D. (*ii*) and (*iv*) are correct

28. Empty Digit means a digit

(*i*) with ordinal value
(*ii*) without semantic value
(*iii*) without ordinal value
(*iv*) with semantic value

Choose the correct answer from the code given below:

Code:

A. (*ii*) and (*iii*) are correct
B. (*i*) and (*ii*) are correct
C. (*i*) and (*iii*) are correct
D. (*iii*) and (*iv*) are correct

29. Which of the following are open access LIS journals from India?

(*i*) SRELS Journal of Information Management
(*ii*) Annals of Library and Information Studies, NISCAIR
(*iii*) Journal of Library and Information Science, DLIS, Delhi University
(*iv*) DESIDOC Journal of Library and Information Technology

Choose the correct answer from the code given below:

Code:

A. (*ii*) and (*iv*) are correct
B. (*ii*) and (*iii*) are correct
C. (*i*) and (*iv*) are correct
D. (*i*) and (*ii*) are correct

30. Identify the independent variables in the statement "Will students who are taught by a team of three teachers learn more science than students taught by one individual teacher."

(*i*) One teacher (*ii*) Learn more science
(*iii*) Taught (*iv*) Three teachers

Choose the correct answer from the code given below:

Code:

A. (*ii*) and (*iii*) are correct
B. (*i*) and (*iii*) are correct
C. (*i*) and (*iv*) are correct
D. (*i*) and (*ii*) are correct

31. Identify the correct objectives of an Enterprise Information System (EIS) from the following.

(*i*) To increase employee productivity
(*ii*) To advance the cost of IT and optimize the manual input of data
(*iii*) To maximize duplication of company data and demote the work quality
(*iv*) To ensure greater employee collaboration and efficiency

Choose the correct answer from the code given below:

Code:

A. (*i*) and (*iv*) are correct
B. (*ii*) and (*iv*) are correct
C. (*i*) and (*ii*) are correct
D. (*ii*) and (*iii*) are correct

32. Which of the following are considered as standard channels of scholarly communication?

(*i*) Handbooks (*ii*) Wikis
(*iii*) Working Papers (*iv*) Research Report

Choose the correct answer from the code given below:

Code:

A. (*i*) and (*iv*) are correct
B. (*i*) and (*iii*) are correct
C. (*ii*) and (*iv*) are correct
D. (*iii*) and (*iv*) are correct

33. Which of the following documents on information literacy are developed by IFLA?

(*i*) Guidelines for Information literacy assessment
(*ii*) Information literacy guidelines and competencies for Under Graduates
(*iii*) Guidelines for Information literacy for lifelong learning
(*iv*) Framework for Information literacy for Higher Education

Choose the correct answer from the code given below:

Code:

A. (*i*) and (*ii*) are correct
B. (*iii*) and (*iv*) are correct
C. (*i*) and (*iii*) are correct
D. (*ii*) and (*iii*) are correct

34. Identify the correct Sound File Formats.

(*i*) .MOV (*ii*) .WAV
(*iii*) .MID (*iv*) .MPG

Choose the correct answer from the code given below:

Code:

A. (*i*) and (*ii*) are correct
B. (*i*), (*ii*) and (*iii*) are correct
C. (*iii*) and (*iv*) are correct
D. (*ii*) and (*iii*) are correct

35. Identify the features of 'HTML'.

(*i*) Ease of creating new references
(*ii*) Users' interactivity
(*iii*) Ease of tracing references
(*iv*) Ease of customising documents

Choose the correct answer from the code given below:

Code:

A. (*i*), (*ii*) and (*iii*) are correct
B. (*i*), (*ii*) and (*iv*) are correct
C. (*ii*), (*iii*) and (*iv*) are correct
D. (*i*), (*iii*) and (*iv*) are correct

36. Which of the following are sampling errors?

(*i*) Framing errors (*ii*) Process errors
(*iii*) Response errors (*iv*) Tabulation errors

Choose the correct answer from the code given below:

Code:

A. (*i*) and (*ii*) are correct
B. (*iii*) and (*iv*) are correct
C. (*i*) and (*iii*) are correct
D. (*ii*) and (*iv*) are correct

37. Chi-square test is used by researchers to test which of the following?

(*i*) Judging the significance of several measures

(*ii*) Test the significance of population variation

(*iii*) Test the significance of the difference amongst more than two sample means at the same time

(*iv*) Test the significance of association between two attributes

Choose the correct answer from the code given below:

Code:

A. (*ii*) and (*iii*) are correct

B. (*ii*) and (*iv*) are correct

C. (*i*) and (*ii*) are correct

D. (*iii*) and (*iv*) are correct

38. Identify the correct features of the Classification Research Group, London (CRG) from the following:

(*i*) CRG was one of the most significant contributors to sociological research and theory.

(*ii*) The theoretical work of the group involved in the study of facet analysis, relational operators and theory of integrative levels.

(*iii*) It is the basis of the dynamic theory of Ranganathan.

(*iv*) CRG was interested in first piecing together individual elements and then determining the areas of knowledge they form.

Choose the correct answer from the code given below:

Code:

A. (*ii*) and (*iv*) are correct

B. (*i*) and (*ii*) are correct

C. (*i*) and (*iii*) are correct

D. (*iii*) and (*iv*) are correct

39. Which of the following entities have been introduced by Functional Requirements for Subject Authority Records (FRASAR) working group?

(*i*) Strings (*ii*) Nomen

(*iii*) Thema (*iv*) Integers

Choose the correct answer from the code given below:

Code:

A. (*iii*) and (*iv*) are correct

B. (*i*) and (*ii*) are correct

C. (*i*) and (*iii*) are correct

D. (*ii*) and (*iii*) are correct

40. Identify from the following the correct salient traits of "Invisible College":

(*i*) It is based on Francis Bacon's principle that "Knowledge is power".

(*ii*) It aims to acquire knowledge through experimental investigation.

(*iii*) It is not to be seen as a precursor to the Royal Society, UK.

(*iv*) It is a club of intellectuals with less than 14 core members.

Choose the correct answer from the code given below:

Code:

A. (*ii*) and (*iv*) are correct

B. (*ii*) and (*iii*) are correct

C. (*i*) and (*ii*) are correct

D. (*iii*) and (*iv*) are correct

41. Match the following colour codes by JISC funded RoMEO project with their respective standardised approach to different rights.

List-I	***List-II***
(*a*) Blue	(*i*) Archiving of pre and post print
(*b*) Gold	(*ii*) Can archive post-print
(*c*) Green	(*iii*) Can archive pre-print
(*d*) Yellow	(*iv*) Open access publishing

Code:

	(*a*)	(*b*)	(*c*)	(*d*)
A.	(*iv*)	(*iii*)	(*ii*)	(*i*)
B.	(*ii*)	(*iv*)	(*i*)	(*iii*)
C.	(*ii*)	(*i*)	(*iv*)	(*iii*)
D.	(*i*)	(*ii*)	(*iii*)	(*iv*)

42. Match the following ISO standards with their respective fields.

List-I	***List-II***
(*a*) ISO 2146 : 2010	(*i*) Computer applications in terminology–terminological mark up framework

(*b*) ISO/TR 11219 : 2012	(*ii*) Library performance indicators
(*c*) ISO 11620 : 2014	(*iii*) Registry services for libraries and related organisations
(*d*) ISO 16642 : 2017	(*iv*) Qualitative conditions and basic statistics for library buildings

Code:

	(*a*)	(*b*)	(*c*)	(*d*)
A.	(*iv*)	(*ii*)	(*iii*)	(*i*)
B.	(*iii*)	(*i*)	(*iv*)	(*ii*)
C.	(*i*)	(*ii*)	(*iii*)	(*iv*)
D.	(*iii*)	(*iv*)	(*ii*)	(*i*)

43. Match the following types of management with coresponding library operational activity.

List-I	***List-II***
(*a*) Total Quality Management	(*i*) Taking measures for occupational health of library staff
(*b*) Change Management	(*ii*) Teamwork on digital library project
(*c*) Risk Management	(*iii*) Analysis of user feedback
(*d*) Participative Management	(*iv*) Introducing RFID for library circulation operations

Code:

	(*a*)	(*b*)	(*c*)	(*d*)
A.	(*ii*)	(*iii*)	(*i*)	(*iv*)
B.	(*i*)	(*iii*)	(*iv*)	(*ii*)
C.	(*iv*)	(*ii*)	(*iii*)	(*i*)
D.	(*iii*)	(*iv*)	(*i*)	(*ii*)

44. Match the following character positions with their respective descriptions as given in MARC:

List-I	***List-II***
(*a*) 00–04	(*i*) Record length
(*b*) 06	(*ii*) Type of Record
(*c*) 07	(*iii*) Kind of data
(*d*) 08	(*iv*) Type of control

Code:

	(*a*)	(*b*)	(*c*)	(*d*)
A.	(*i*)	(*ii*)	(*iii*)	(*iv*)
B.	(*ii*)	(*i*)	(*iii*)	(*iv*)
C.	(*iii*)	(*ii*)	(*iv*)	(*i*)
D.	(*iv*)	(*ii*)	(*i*)	(*iii*)

45. Match the following numerical values, used as collection indicators, with their respective depth levels as defined in the IFLA Guidelines on Acquisition and Collection Development.

List-I	***List-II***
(*a*) 0	(*i*) Comprehensive level
(*b*) 1	(*ii*) Study or Instructional Support Level
(*c*) 3	(*iii*) Minimal Information Level
(*d*) 5	(*iv*) Out of Scope

Code:

	(*a*)	(*b*)	(*c*)	(*d*)
A.	(*iv*)	(*iii*)	(*ii*)	(*i*)
B.	(*i*)	(*ii*)	(*iii*)	(*iv*)
C.	(*ii*)	(*iv*)	(*iii*)	(*i*)
D.	(*iii*)	(*ii*)	(*i*)	(*iv*)

46. Match the following 'information phrases' with their appropriate descriptions.

List-I	***List-II***
(*a*) Information hunger	(*i*) Motivation or addiction to learning new information
(*b*) Information appetite	(*ii*) Excessive word count and details that make it harder for people to extract useful information
(*c*) Information pollution	(*iii*) Less access to information and vulnerable to all kinds of pressures
(*d*) Information poor	(*iv*) Eager to discuss and learn information in a group

Code:

	(*a*)	(*b*)	(*c*)	(*d*)
A.	(*i*)	(*iv*)	(*ii*)	(*iii*)
B.	(*i*)	(*iii*)	(*ii*)	(*iv*)
C.	(*ii*)	(*i*)	(*iv*)	(*iii*)
D.	(*iv*)	(*ii*)	(*i*)	(*iii*)

47. Match the following memory measurement units with their corresponding equivalence:

List-I	***List-II***
(*a*) 1024 EB	(*i*) 1 BB
(*b*) 1024 ZB	(*ii*) 1 ZB
(*c*) 1024 YB	(*iii*) 1 GpB
(*d*) 1024 BB	(*iv*) 1 YB

Code:

	(a)	(b)	(c)	(d)
A.	(iii)	(iv)	(i)	(ii)
B.	(ii)	(i)	(iii)	(iv)
C.	(ii)	(iv)	(i)	(iii)
D.	(i)	(iii)	(ii)	(iv)

48. Match the following quality assessment measures with corresponding explanation.

List-I	List-II
(a) Effectiveness	(i) Deriving best practices
(b) Efficiency	(ii) Value provided
(c) Benchmark	(iii) Desired result provided
(d) Impact	(iv) Cost effectiveness

Code:

	(a)	(b)	(c)	(d)
A.	(iii)	(iv)	(i)	(ii)
B.	(ii)	(i)	(iii)	(iv)
C.	(iii)	(i)	(iv)	(ii)
D.	(iv)	(iii)	(ii)	(i)

49. Match the following motivation theories of management with their corresponding propounders.

List-I	List-II
(a) Hierarchy of Needs theory	(i) Victor Vroom
(b) Motivation-Hygiene theory	(ii) David McClelland
(c) Learned Need Theory	(iii) Abraham Maslow
(d) Expectancy Theory	(iv) Frederic Herzberg

Code:

	(a)	(b)	(c)	(d)
A.	(iii)	(iv)	(ii)	(i)
B.	(iii)	(i)	(iv)	(ii)
C.	(iii)	(ii)	(iv)	(i)
D.	(iv)	(ii)	(iii)	(i)

50. Match the following in the context of a digital library.

List-I	List-II
(a) Migration	(i) Replicating the functionality of an obsolete system
(b) Refreshing	(ii) Transfer of data between two types of same storage system
(c) Emulation	(iii) Concerned with longevity of digital information
(d) Digital Sustainability	(iv) Transferring data to newer system

Code:

	(a)	(b)	(c)	(d)
A.	(iii)	(iv)	(ii)	(i)
B.	(ii)	(iii)	(iv)	(i)
C.	(iv)	(ii)	(i)	(iii)
D.	(i)	(iii)	(ii)	(iv)

51. Match the following management approaches with the person associated with it.

List-I	List-II
(a) Administrative	(i) Hugo Münsterberg
(b) Behavioural	(ii) Henry Fayol
(c) Quantitative	(iii) Peter Drucker
(d) Composite	(iv) Herbert A. Simon

Code:

	(a)	(b)	(c)	(d)
A.	(iv)	(iii)	(i)	(ii)
B.	(i)	(iii)	(ii)	(iv)
C.	(iii)	(ii)	(iv)	(i)
D.	(ii)	(i)	(iv)	(iii)

52. Match the following terms with their corresponding explanations.

List-I	List-II
(a) Compound Subject	(i) Subject of small extension and great intension
(b) Complex Subject	(ii) A subject with a basic subject and one or more isolate ideas as component subjects
(c) Micro Subject	(iii) Subject of very tiny extension and enormous intension
(d) Spot Subject	(iv) Subject formed by coupling two or more subjects

Code:

	(a)	(b)	(c)	(d)
A.	(iv)	(i)	(ii)	(iii)
B.	(i)	(iii)	(ii)	(iv)
C.	(iii)	(i)	(iv)	(ii)
D.	(ii)	(iv)	(i)	(ii)

53. Match the following books with their authors.

List-I	*List-II*
(*a*) Classification, Theoretical and Practical	(*i*) E.W. Hulme
(*b*) A Manual of Classification	(*ii*) J. Mills
(*c*) A Modern Outline of Library Classification	(*iii*) E.C. Richardson
(*d*) Principles of Book Classification	(*iv*) W.C.B. Sayers

Code:

	(*a*)	(*b*)	(*c*)	(*d*)
A.	(*ii*)	(*i*)	(*iv*)	(*iii*)
B.	(*iii*)	(*iv*)	(*ii*)	(*i*)
C.	(*i*)	(*ii*)	(*iii*)	(*iv*)
D.	(*iv*)	(*iii*)	(*ii*)	(*i*)

54. Match the following information literacy models with their developers.

List-I	*List-II*
(*a*) Big 6 Model	(*i*) Trevor Bond
(*b*) Eight WS Model	(*ii*) Mike Eisenberg and Bob Berkowitz
(*c*) PLUS Model	(*iii*) James Herring
(*d*) SAUCE Model	(*iv*) Annette Lamb

Code:

	(*a*)	(*b*)	(*c*)	(*d*)
A.	(*i*)	(*ii*)	(*iii*)	(*iv*)
B.	(*ii*)	(*iv*)	(*iii*)	(*i*)
C.	(*iii*)	(*ii*)	(*iv*)	(*i*)
D.	(*ii*)	(*iii*)	(*iv*)	(*i*)

55. Match the following awards with the Association that instituted them.

List-I	*List-II*
(*a*) Prof. Kaula Best Librarian Award	(*i*) IATLIS
(*b*) Prof. Joginder Singh Ramdev Lifetime Achievement Award	(*ii*) IASLIC
(*c*) Librarian of the Year Award	(*iii*) SIS
(*d*) A.S. Raizada Memorial Young Information Scientist Award	(*iv*) ILA

Code:

	(*a*)	(*b*)	(*c*)	(*d*)
A.	(*iv*)	(*i*)	(*ii*)	(*iii*)
B.	(*iii*)	(*ii*)	(*i*)	(*iv*)
C.	(*ii*)	(*iii*)	(*iv*)	(*i*)
D.	(*i*)	(*iv*)	(*iii*)	(*ii*)

56. Match the following types of abstracts with their respective function.

List-I	*List-II*
(*a*) Critical abstract	(*i*) Oriented to serve a specific group
(*b*) Indicative abstract	(*ii*) Comprehensive description of the document
(*c*) Informative abstract	(*iii*) Alerts the user with content of the document
(*d*) Slanted abstract	(*iv*) Evaluates the document

Code:

	(*a*)	(*b*)	(*c*)	(*d*)
A.	(*i*)	(*iv*)	(*iii*)	(*ii*)
B.	(*iii*)	(*ii*)	(*iv*)	(*i*)
C.	(*iv*)	(*iii*)	(*ii*)	(*i*)
D.	(*ii*)	(*iii*)	(*i*)	(*iv*)

57. Match the following modes of formation of subjects with their corresponding subject.

List-I (*Mode of formation*)	*List-II* (*Subject*)
(*a*) Lamination	(*i*) Management Science
(*b*) Loose Assemblage	(*ii*) Astrophysics
(*c*) Distillation	(*iii*) Arteries of arms
(*d*) Fusion	(*iv*) Statistical Analysis for Railway Manager

Code:

	(*a*)	(*b*)	(*c*)	(*d*)
A.	(*i*)	(*iii*)	(*iv*)	(*ii*)
B.	(*iii*)	(*iv*)	(*i*)	(*ii*)
C.	(*iii*)	(*ii*)	(*iv*)	(*i*)
D.	(*ii*)	(*iv*)	(*i*)	(*iii*)

58. Match the following characteristics with their notation as they appear in Table 1 K (Common auxiliaries of general characteristics) in UDC, standard edition.

List-I	*List-II*
(*a*) 02	(*i*) Common auxiliaries of Materials
(*b*) 03	(*ii*) Common auxiliaries of Persons and Personal Characteristics

(*c*) 04 (*iii*) Common auxiliaries of Properties

(*d*) 05 (*iv*) Common auxiliaries of Relations, Processes and Operations

Code:

	(*a*)	(*b*)	(*c*)	(*d*)
A.	(*iii*)	(*i*)	(*iv*)	(*ii*)
B.	(*ii*)	(*iii*)	(*i*)	(*iv*)
C.	(*i*)	(*ii*)	(*iii*)	(*iv*)
D.	(*iv*)	(*iii*)	(*i*)	(*ii*)

59. Match the following reference questions with corresponding service.

List-I	***List-II***
(*a*) In which country was acupuncture originated?	(*i*) Current awareness service
(*b*) What measures are taken by the Government of India for control of Malaria in the last decade?	(*ii*) Long range reference service
(*c*) How will you find out 'Ignited Minds' by A.P.J. Abdul Kalam in the library?	(*iii*) Ready reference service
(*d*) Asking for a list of newly added books to the library	(*iv*) User orientation

Code:

	(*a*)	(*b*)	(*c*)	(*d*)
A.	(*iii*)	(*ii*)	(*iv*)	(*i*)
B.	(*iii*)	(*i*)	(*ii*)	(*iv*)
C.	(*iv*)	(*iii*)	(*ii*)	(*i*)
D.	(*ii*)	(*iii*)	(*i*)	(*iv*)

60. Match the following types of Knowledge Discovery in Databases (KDD) with their respective activity.

List-I	***List-II***
(*a*) Text mining	(*i*) Aggregates related items
(*b*) Web usage mining	(*ii*) Structuring the input, deriving patterns
(*c*) Web content mining	(*iii*) Discovering hyper-links for ranking
(*d*) Web structure mining	(*iv*) Discover patterns of visited pages

Code:

	(*a*)	(*b*)	(*c*)	(*d*)
A.	(*i*)	(*iii*)	(*ii*)	(*iv*)
B.	(*iii*)	(*ii*)	(*iv*)	(*i*)
C.	(*iv*)	(*i*)	(*iii*)	(*ii*)
D.	(*ii*)	(*iv*)	(*i*)	(*iii*)

61. Arrange the following Associations according to ascending order of their year of establishment.

(*i*) ILA (*ii*) ALA

(*iii*) CILIP (*iv*) IFLA

Choose the correct answer from the code given below:

Code:

A. (*ii*), (*iv*), (*i*), (*iii*) B. (*iv*), (*i*), (*ii*), (*iii*)

C. (*i*), (*iii*), (*iv*), (*ii*) D. (*ii*), (*iii*), (*i*), (*iv*)

62. Arrange the following libraries according to their year of establishment.

(*i*) Bibliotheque Publique (Pondicherry) (Now Romain Rolland Library)

(*ii*) Connemara Public Library, Madras

(*iii*) Asafia Public Library, Hyderabad (Now State Central Library, Hyderabad)

(*iv*) Publica Livraria, Panaji (Goa) (Now Krishnadas Shama Central Library)

Choose the correct answer from the code given below:

Code:

A. (*iii*), (*ii*), (*iv*), (*i*) B. (*i*), (*iv*), (*iii*), (*ii*)

C. (*i*), (*ii*), (*iii*), (*iv*) D. (*iv*), (*iii*), (*i*), (*ii*)

63. Arrange the following metadata standards in order of their year of development.

(*i*) Resource Description and Access

(*ii*) Resource Description Framework

(*iii*) Metadata Object Description Scheme

(*iv*) Text Encoding Initiative

Choose the correct answer from the code given below:

Code:

A. (*iii*), (*i*), (*iv*), (*ii*) B. (*ii*), (*iii*), (*i*), (*iv*)

C. (*iv*), (*ii*), (*iii*), (*i*) D. (*ii*), (*iv*), (*i*), (*iii*)

64. Arrange the following States in ascending order of the year of enactment of their respective Public Library Acts.

(*i*) Manipur
(*ii*) Lakshadweep
(*iii*) Karnataka
(*iv*) Arunachal Pradesh

Choose the correct answer from the code given below:

Code:

A. (*ii*), (*iv*), (*iii*), (*i*) B. (*i*), (*ii*), (*iii*), (*iv*)
C. (*iv*), (*i*), (*ii*), (*iii*) D. (*iii*), (*i*), (*ii*), (*iv*)

65. Arrange the following steps of procedure for classifying a simple book as mentioned in CC 7th edition.

(*i*) Title in Kernel terms
(*ii*) Expressive title
(*iii*) Title in Facet Numbers
(*iv*) Title in Standard terms

Choose the correct answer from the code given below:

Code:

A. (*i*), (*ii*), (*iii*), (*iv*) B. (*ii*), (*iv*), (*i*), (*iii*)
C. (*i*), (*ii*), (*iv*), (*iii*) D. (*ii*), (*i*), (*iv*), (*iii*)

66. Arrange the following terms 'letter-by-letter'.

(*i*) Lead compounds (*ii*) Leadership
(*iii*) Leading edges (*iv*) Lead oxide

Choose the correct answer from the code given below:

Code:

A. (*i*), (*iv*), (*iii*), (*ii*) B. (*i*), (*ii*), (*iii*), (*iv*)
C. (*i*), (*iii*), (*iv*), (*ii*) D. (*ii*), (*i*), (*iv*), (*iii*)

67. Arrange the following important international events according to the date and month of their observations/celebration every year by UNESCO.

(*i*) World Teachers Day
(*ii*) International Day for the Universal Access to Information
(*iii*) International Literacy Day
(*iv*) World Book and Copyright Day

Choose the correct answer from the code given below:

Code:

A. (*ii*), (*i*), (*iii*), (*iv*) B. (*ii*), (*iii*), (*i*), (*iv*)
C. (*iv*), (*i*), (*ii*), (*iii*) D. (*iv*), (*iii*), (*ii*), (*i*)

68. Arrange the following webmails according to the first year of launching.

(*i*) Yahoo mail (*ii*) Hush mail
(*iii*) G mail (*iv*) Proton mail

Choose the correct answer from the code given below:

Code:

A. (*ii*), (*iii*), (*i*), (*iv*) B. (*iv*), (*iii*), (*ii*), (*i*)
C. (*iii*), (*i*), (*iv*), (*ii*) D. (*i*), (*ii*), (*iii*), (*iv*)

69. Arrange the following components in the order of their significance as stated by E.J. Coates.

(*i*) Material (*ii*) Part
(*iii*) Action (*iv*) Thing

Choose the correct answer from the code given below:

Code:

A. (*iii*), (*ii*), (*iv*), (*i*) B. (*iv*), (*ii*), (*i*), (*iii*)
C. (*ii*), (*i*), (*iii*), (*iv*) D. (*i*), (*iii*), (*iv*), (*ii*)

70. Arrange in order the following pillars of SCONUL Seven Pillars of 'Information Literacy Model'.

(*i*) Plan (*ii*) Manage
(*iii*) Gather (*iv*) Scope

Choose the correct answer from the code given below:

Code:

A. (*iv*), (*iii*), (*i*), (*ii*) B. (*iv*), (*i*), (*iii*), (*ii*)
C. (*iii*), (*iv*), (*i*), (*ii*) D. (*i*), (*iv*), (*ii*), (*iii*)

71. Arrange the following four stages of Carol Kuhlthau's (1991) six stage model of Information Search Process.

(*i*) Formulation (*ii*) Selection
(*iii*) Collection (*iv*) Exploration

Choose the correct answer from the code given below:

Code:

A. (*iv*), (*iii*), (*ii*), (*i*) B. (*iii*), (*ii*), (*i*), (*iv*)
C. (*ii*), (*iv*), (*i*), (*iii*) D. (*i*), (*ii*), (*iii*), (*iv*)

72. Arrange the following books authored by S.R. Ranganathan in order of the year of their first publication.

(*i*) Headings and Canons
(*ii*) Elements of Library Classification
(*iii*) Prolegomena to Library Classification
(*iv*) Philosophy of Library Classification

Choose the correct answer from the code given below:

Code:

A. *(iv)*, *(iii)*, *(i)*, *(ii)* B. *(iii)*, *(ii)*, *(iv)*, *(i)*
C. *(ii)*, *(iii)*, *(i)*, *(iv)* D. *(iii)*, *(i)*, *(ii)*, *(iv)*

73. Arrange the following library automation softwares according to the year of their first release.

(i) e-Granthalaya *(ii)* NewGenLib
(iii) Soul *(iv)* Koha

Choose the correct answer from the code given below:

Code:

A. *(ii)*, *(i)*, *(iv)*, *(iii)* B. *(i)*, *(ii)*, *(iii)*, *(iv)*
C. *(ii)*, *(iii)*, *(i)*, *(iv)* D. *(iii)*, *(i)*, *(ii)*, *(iv)*

74. Arrange the following steps of "Change process" as mentioned by John Kotter.

(i) Creating a vision for change
(ii) Creating urgency
(iii) Removing obstacles
(iv) Forming a powerful coalition

Choose the correct answer from the code given below:

Code:

A. *(ii)*, *(iii)*, *(iv)*, *(i)* B. *(i)*, *(ii)*, *(iii)*, *(iv)*
C. *(ii)*, *(iv)*, *(i)*, *(iii)* D. *(i)*, *(iii)*, *(ii)*, *(iv)*

75. Arrange the following indexing techniques according to their year of origin.

(i) COMPASS *(ii)* SLIC
(iii) KWIC *(iv)* Systematic Indexing

Choose the correct answer from the code given below:

Code:

A. *(i)*, *(iii)*, *(iv)*, *(ii)* B. *(iv)*, *(iii)*, *(ii)*, *(i)*
C. *(iv)*, *(ii)*, *(i)*, *(iii)* D. *(ii)*, *(i)*, *(iii)*, *(iv)*

76. Assertion (A) : Consider for example that 'A' writes down '7' on a paper with small font size and uses FAX machine to transfer the page to 'B'. 'B' sees a distorted '7' and decodes as '9'.

Reason (R) : Disruptive functioning of FAX machine.

In the context of these two statements, which one of the following is correct?

Code:

A. (A) is false, but (R) is true.
B. (A) is true, but (R) is false.
C. Both (A) and (R) are true.
D. Both (A) and (R) are false.

77. Assertion (A) : The entry element in Leading Section has the potency to decide the position of an entry among the various entries in a catalogue.

Reason (R) : The potency of entries, sorted letter by letter or digit by digit goes on increasing rightwards and upwards.

In the context of these two statements, which one of the following is correct?

Code:

A. Both (A) and (R) are true.
B. Both (A) and (R) are false.
C. (A) is true, but (R) is false.
D. (A) is false, but (R) is true.

78. Assertion (A) : Employers of library and information personnel remain responsible for providing staff development programmes and support for continuing education.

Reason (R) : Professional and continuing education of the librarian is indispensable to ensure adequate services.

In the context of these two statements, which one of the following is correct?

Code:

A. (A) is false, but (R) is true.
B. Both (A) and (R) are true.
C. (A) is true, but (R) is false.
D. Both (A) and (R) are false.

79. Assertion (A) : The emergence of the information economy, in an interdependent world, played an insignificant role in the development of transborder dataflow.

Reason (R) : Most of the data transmitted in transborder dataflow belongs to business and finance using both publicly and privately available channels.

In the context of these two statements, which one of the following is correct?

Code:

A. Both (A) and (R) are false.

B. Both (A) and (R) are true.
C. (A) is false, but (R) is true.
D. (A) is true, but (R) is false.

80. Assertion (A) : All the main classes enumerated in Colon Classification, Ed. 6 are coordinate.
Reason (R) : C.C. has secured the mutual exclusiveness of the classes by avoiding the overlapping of subdivisions.

In the context of these two statements, which one of the following is correct?
Code:
A. Both (A) and (R) are false.
B. (A) is true, but (R) is false.
C. (A) is false, but (R) is true.
D. Both (A) and (R) are true.

81. Assertion (A) : In Colon Classification Ed. 6, Posteriorising Common Isolate 'Profession (b)' is an Energy Common Isolate.
Reason (R) : It is a manifestation of action.
In the context of these two statements, which one of the following is correct?
Code:
A. Both (A) and (R) are false.
B. Both (A) and (R) are true.
C. (A) is false, but (R) is true.
D. (A) is true, but (R) is false.

82. Assertion (A) : Resource Description and Access (RDA) lacks potential to revolutionize library cataloguing in spite of its expansive element sets and vocabularies.
Reason (R) : RDA is primarily designed as a content standard.

In the context of these two statements, which one of the following is correct?
Code:
A. (A) is false, but (R) is true.
B. (A) is true, but (R) is false.
C. Both (A) and (R) are false.
D. Both (A) and (R) are true.

83. Assertion (A) : IFLA advocates for copyright reform at WIPO.
Reason (R) : Outdated copyright laws prevent libraries from performing their basic functions.

In the context of these two statements, which one of the following is correct?
Code:
A. (A) is false, but (R) is true.
B. Both (A) and (R) are false.
C. Both (A) and (R) are true.
D. (A) is true, but (R) is false.

84. Assertion (A) : In Unicode, the character encoding reflects the way the coded character set is mapped to bytes for manipulation in a computer.
Reason (R) : Unicode is a standard that defines all the characters needed for writing the majority of living languages in use on computer.
In the context of these two statements, which one of the following is correct?
Code:
A. Both (A) and (R) are false.
B. Both (A) and (R) are true.
C. (A) is true, but (R) is false.
D. (A) is false, but (R) is true.

85. Assertion (A) : Patents provide incentives to individuals by recognizing their creativity.
Reason (R) : Patent provides patent owners with lifetime protection for their inventions.
In the context of these two statements, which one of the following is correct?
Code:
A. (A) is true, but (R) is false.
B. Both (A) and (R) are false.
C. Both (A) and (R) are true.
D. (A) is false, but (R) is true.

86. Assertion (A) : All LIS journals published in India are rigorously peer reviewed.
Reason (R) : Peer reviewing is seen as a key quality control mechanism for a reputed journal to keep it amongst the best in its subject field.

In the context of these two statements, which one of the following is correct?
Code:
A. (A) is true, but (R) is false.
B. (A) is false, but (R) is true.
C. Both (A) and (R) are true.
D. Both (A) and (R) are false.

87. Assertion (A) : PRECIS was originally developed by the British National Bibliography, replacing the chain indexing, to provide subject index for UK/MARC records.

Reason (R) : Chain index was not successful for production of subject index by computer.

In the context of these two statements, which one of the following is correct?

Code:

A. (A) is false, but (R) is true.
B. Both (A) and (R) are true.
C. (A) is true, but (R) is false.
D. Both (A) and (R) are false.

88. Assertion (A) : Researchers in the behavioural sciences can describe variables in ratio scale form.

Reason (R) : Ratio scales have an absolute or true zero measurement.

In the context of these two statements, which one of the following is correct?

Code:

A. (A) is true, but (R) is false.
B. Both (A) and (R) are true.
C. (A) is false, but (R) is true.
D. Both (A) and (R) are false.

89. Assertion (A) : 'Social tagging' technique used in some libraries allows students to tag books and other information resources with their own search terms.

Reason (R) : Introducing social tagging methods to the traditional library settings usually helps to improve 'patron use' of library and acquire knowledge.

In the context of these two statements, which one of the following is correct?

Code:

A. (A) is true, but (R) is false.
B. Both (A) and (R) are false.
C. (A) is false, but (R) is true.
D. Both (A) and (R) are true.

90. Assertion (A) : Infringement of copyright of digital materials is not a concern for rights owners.

Reason (R) : The cost of copying electronic resources are trivial and the copies can be easily disseminated.

In the context of these two statements, which one of the following is correct?

Code:

A. Both (A) and (R) are false.
B. Both (A) and (R) are true.
C. (A) is false, but (R) is true.
D. (A) is true, but (R) is false.

91. Assertion (A) : Users, more or less, have same access points and can broaden up or narrow down their search, both in OPAC and Card Catalogue.

Reason (R) : In OPAC, almost every single part of the bibliographic record is accessible through keyword searching which its traditional counterpart cannot.

In the context of these two statements, which one of the following is correct?

Code:

A. Both (A) and (R) are true.
B. Both (A) and (R) are false.
C. (A) is true, but (R) is false.
D. (A) is false, but (R) is true.

92. Assertion (A) : e-Shodhsindhu develops a formidable collection of e-journals, e-journal archives and e-books on perpetual access basis.

Reason (R) : Perpetual access facilitates the participating university libraries to access all journals right from their first issue.

In the context of these two statements, which one of the following is correct?

Code:

A. Both (A) and (R) are false.
B. (A) is true, but (R) is false.
C. (A) is false, but (R) is true.
D. Both (A) and (R) are true.

93. Assertion (A) : The newly emerging libraries are being designed to become active agents of learning.

Reason (R) : Participative new media tools and learning commons are transforming the library's physical and virtual spaces into collaborative work areas.

In the context of these two statements, which one of the following is correct?

Code:

A. Both (A) and (R) are false.
B. (A) is true, but (R) is false.
C. Both (A) and (R) are true.
D. (A) is false, but (R) is true.

94. Assertion (A) : In an information economic society, much of the returns to information are distributive.

Reason (R) : Private returns to information can often exceed social returns.

In the context of these two statements, which one of the following is correct?

Code:

A. (A) is false, but (R) is true.
B. Both (A) and (R) are false.
C. Both (A) and (R) are true.
D. (A) is true, but (R) is false.

95. Assertion (A) : Compound terms in a thesaurus are more exact and specific than single terms used in combination to represent the same concept.

Reason (R) : Compound terms are able to prevent false drops and to ensure good precision.

In the context of these two statements, which one of the following is correct?

Code:

A. (A) is true, but (R) is false.
B. Both (A) and (R) are true.
C. Both (A) and (R) are false.
D. (A) is false, but (R) is true.

Directions (Qs. No. 96-100): *Read the passage given below and answer the questions based on your understanding of the passage.*

School lunches are a common topic when Japanese reminiscence about their school life. There is even a small museum in the Ministry of Education, Culture, Sports, Science and Technology in Japan (MEXT) where the typical school lunches of each generation are replicated. This exhibition receives favourable reviews from visitors, who make comments like, "It was great for conversation with my child", and, "It brought back memories of those days". In Japan "eating from the same pot" signifies fellowship and bonds, and this phrase can be applied all around the country in the case of school lunches. This article looks into the School Lunch Service, which the Japanese hold so close to their hearts.

Modern school lunch services are widely defined as any sustenance given to children under school administration, but in Japan, it originated from local civilian efforts to provide lunch for poor children at the end of the 19th century. Later on, before and during world wars, school lunches were recommended by the Ministry of Education (MOE) as a way of improving the physical health of school children. Starting from the more accessible major cities, school lunches were provided with the goal of reaching out to as many children as possible, but it was only after the establishment of the School Lunch Law, proclaimed and enacted in 1954 under reconstruction following World War II, that the Japanese school lunch program gained lawful authority and was provided nationwide.

The beginning of charity school lunch services in Japan can be traced to 1889, where lunches were provided by a Buddhist confederation for poverty-stricken children in an elementary school in Tsuruoka City, Yamagata Prefecture. The majority of school lunches in the *Meiji* (1868–1912) and *Taisho* (1912–1926) periods were limited to impoverished children and had the effect of encouraging them to attend school. Several examples were also seen in Akita, Shizuoka, Iwate and other prefectures, which were funded by school or district budgets as well as private donations. The meals usually consisted of a white-rice ball and *miso* (soy bean paste), with occasional pickled vegetables, or hot soups. In a documentary photo, recipient children can be seen eating in the corner of the school kitchen, while better-off classmates ate their packed home-made lunches in the classrooms.

96. From where was the concept of 'modern school lunch' originated in Japan?

A. Human Rights Organizations
B. MOE, Japan

C. Private School Management
D. The efforts of the local civilians

97. What does the phrase, "eating from the same pot" signify in Japan?
A. Fellowship and bonds
B. Famishment
C. Stretch to each other's heart
D. Fellowship and unfetter

98. What does the meal in school lunch usually contain?
A. A ball of Ramen noodles served in a soy sauce or miso soup
B. White-rice ball and miso with occasional picked vegetables, or hot soups
C. A ball of sushi and sashimi with vinegar mix (made with sugar and salt)
D. Tempura, a Japanese fried snack

99. What was the key goal of introducing school lunches by the MOE in Japan?
A. To worsen the physical health of school children
B. To control starvation
C. To improve the quality of primary education
D. To reach out to as many children as possible

100. Who was the first beneficiary to avail the charity school lunch service provided by Buddhist confederation for poverty-stricken children in Japan in 1889?
A. Higher Secondary Schools in Meiji and Taisho
B. Upper Primary School in Akita, Shizuoka, Iwate
C. Higher Secondary students in Tsuruoka City, Yamagata Prefecture
D. Elementary School in Tsuruoka City, Yamagata Prefecture

ANSWERS

1	2	3	4	5	6	7	8	9	10
A	A	C	D	B	C	C	A	A	D
11	**12**	**13**	**14**	**15**	**16**	**17**	**18**	**19**	**20**
A	C	D	B	C	A	B	C	B	A
21	**22**	**23**	**24**	**25**	**26**	**27**	**28**	**29**	**30**
B	D	A	C	D	D	A	B	A	C
31	**32**	**33**	**34**	**35**	**36**	**37**	**38**	**39**	**40**
A	D	C	D	D	C	B	A	D	C
41	**42**	**43**	**44**	**45**	**46**	**47**	**48**	**49**	**50**
B	D	D	A	A	A	C	A	A	C
51	**52**	**53**	**54**	**55**	**56**	**57**	**58**	**59**	**60**
D	D	B	B	A	C	B	A	A	D
61	**62**	**63**	**64**	**65**	**66**	**67**	**68**	**69**	**70**
A	B	C	D	D	B	D	D	B	B
71	**72**	**73**	**74**	**75**	**76**	**77**	**78**	**79**	**80**
C	B	D	C	B	C	C	B	C	C
81	**82**	**83**	**84**	**85**	**86**	**87**	**88**	**89**	**90**
A	A	C	B	A	B	B	C	D	C
91	**92**	**93**	**94**	**95**	**96**	**97**	**98**	**99**	**100**
D	B	C	C	B	D	A	B	D	D

EXPLANATORY ANSWERS

1. **Dr. S.R. Ranganathan's Classification:** Dr. S.R. Ranganathan identified two aspects of reference work—Ready reference service and Long range reference service.

   1. **Ready Reference Service:** Most of the ready reference services are of the nature of fact finding types that can be finished in a very short time—in a moment if possible. The librarian generally uses reference book for providing such kind of services. The need of ready reference services arises from the fact of the complex nature of a reference book, its artificiality, and arrangement of information.

   2. **Long Range Reference Service:** The long range Reference Service is based on consulting every possible source of information to arrive at the required information; as such, it is not possible to render this type of service immediately. The time needed may range from half an hour to weeks. The search in the long range reference service starts at the reference books and then goes to the ordinary books, pamphlets, reports, articles in periodicals, etc. If the information is not available in the library, then the search can even go to other local libraries and occasionally to the other libraries in the country. According to S.R. Ranganathan, reference service provided using a chain of books, periodicals and other materials is called as Long Range Reference Service.

3. The dynamic theory of library classification, developed by Ranganathan between 1948 and 1955, was presented for the first time in the second edition of has Prolegomena to Library Classification, published in 1957. A more advanced version of this theory appeared in 1967 in the shape of the third edition of the Prolegomena. This dynamic theory has provided a sound and stable methodology for designing a scheme of library classification. This has also helped the classificationists to keep pace with the developments in the universe of knowledge to design more stable schemes of classification. The formulation of a dynamic theory of library classification was marked by the recognition and separation of three planes of work: the Idea Phine, the Verbal Plane and the Notational Plane. Before this was done, lack of capacity in the Notational Plane inhibited free work in the Idea Plane. Nor was the Notational Plane cultivated. On the other hand, there was reluctance to cultivate it. There was even opposition to attention being paid to it. The use of popular terms with all their homonyms and synonyms in the Verbal Plane caused confusion in the Idea Plane. Thus, the separation of work in the three planes laid bare the paramountancy of the work in the Idea Plane and the need to allow it to develop unhindered on its own right.

5. The New Comb's model of communication was introduced by Theodore M Newcomb of the University of Michigan in 1953. He gives different approach to the communication process. The main purpose of this theory is to introduce the role of communication in a social relationship (society) and to maintain social equilibrium within the social system. He does not include the message as a separate entity in his diagram, implying it only by use of directional arrows. He concentrates on the social purpose of communication, showing all communication as a means of sustaining relationships between people. Sometimes it's called as an "ABX" model of communication.

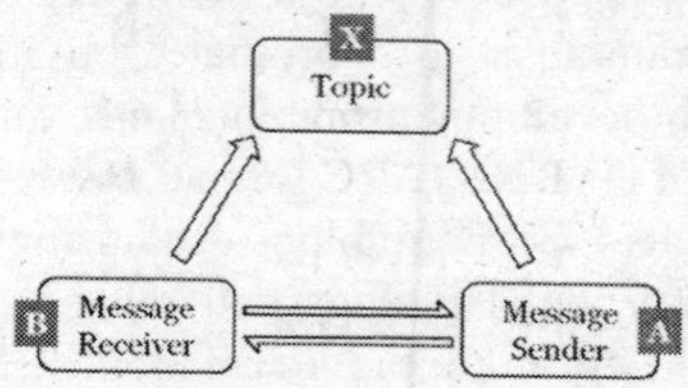

The Newcomb's Model

The Newcomb's model works in a triangular format or A-B-X system

A–Sender; B–Receiver; X–Matter of Concern

The relationship between A and B is like student and teacher, government and public or newspaper and readers. Sender and Receiver may work in a same flow but the same time some factor like "X" may affect their flow of relationship. "X" it may be third persons, issue, topic or policy.

6. **MULTILINGUAL DOCUMENTS:** Denote multilingual documents either by = 00 or by the auxiliaries of the individual languages in ascending numeric order, *e.g.*

53 (035) = 00

Multilingual handbook of physics

53 (035) = 111 = 112.2 = 133.1 Handbook of physics in English, French and German.

8. John Macfarlane, Assistant Librarian of the British Museum, London, was appointed the first Librarian of the Imperial Library. After his death, the polyglot scholar Harinath De took over the charge of the library. J.A. Chapman succeeded him in 1911. During Chapman's term, the library experienced remarkable growth and improvement. After his retirement, Khan Bahadur M.A. Asadulla was appointed librarian and he continued in office till July, 1947.

9. Succeeding to the IFLA UBCIM Strategic Programme, the IFLA UNIMARC Strategic Programme was established in 2003 with the responsibility for the maintenance and development of the Universal MARC format (UNIMARC), originally created by IFLA to facilitate the international exchange of bibliographic data.

The purpose of the UNIMARC Strategic Programme is to coordinate activities aimed at the development, maintenance and promotion of the UNIMARC format, now a set of four formats—Bibliographic, Authorities, Classification and Holdings and related documentation, through the Permanent UNIMARC Committee (PUC). For a brief overview of the history, aims and general structure of UNIMARC see UNIMARC: an introduction. Understanding the UNIMARC format.

11. PRECIS is a system of subject indexing in which the initial string of terms organised according to the scheme of role operators, is computer manipulated in such a way that each sought term in the string functions as the approach term while preserving the full context of the document. Entries are restructured at every step in such a way that the user can determine from the format of the entry which terms set the approach term into its context and which terms are context dependent on the approach term.

Schema of Role Operators

Primary Operators		
Environment of core concepts	0	Location
Core concepts	1	Key System *Thing when action not present. Thing towards which an action is directed, e.g., object of transitive action, performer of intransitive action.*
	2	Action; Effect of action
	3	Performer of transitive action (Agent, Instrument); Intake; Factor
Extra-core concepts	4	Viewpoint-as-form
	5	Selected Instance: study region, study example, sample population
	6	Form of document; Target user
Secondary Operations		
Co-ordinate concepts	f	'Bound' co-ordinate concept
	g	Standard co-ordinate concept
Dependent elements	p	Part; Property
	q	Member of quasi-generic group
	r	Assembly
Special classes of action	s	Roll definer; Directional property
	t	Author-attributed action
	u	Two-way interaction

12. The Registrar of Copyrights is the head of the Copyright Office under the Department of Industrial Policy and Promotion of the Ministry of Commerce and Industry and in-charge of implementation of Copyright Act. The appointment of the Registrar is done by the central government. The registrar of copyrights is also the secretary of the copyright board.

14. At the nadir is the problem to be solved. In this first quadrant (called empirical phase) data is collected empirically and the problem may be refined further. Data may be collected by any means described in section 3.2 of the unit on descriptive research. In experimental method the data is collected by means of many meters, scopes and other instruments. Data may be qualitative or quantitative. In the second quadrant (called hypothesis phase) the data is collected, tabulated, classified and analysed. It is known as data processing. From the analysed data cause-effect inferences are drawn or state of-the-art *i.e.,* ground situation is assessed. Here hypothesis is drawn by using inductive logic and intuition. In the third quadrant (called deductive phase) laws are deduced with the help of deductive logic. The fourth quadrant is also known as the verification phase. Here the laws formulated in the third quadrant are tested and verified; and further some higher generalisation may be drawn. Statistical techniques may be used for verification and to support or disprove the hypothesis.

15. CC0 enables scientists, educators, artists and other creators and owners of copyright or database-protected content to waive those interests in their works and thereby place them as completely as possible in the public domain, so that others may freely build upon, enhance and reuse the works for any purposes without restriction under copyright or database law.

In contrast to CC's licenses that allow copyright holders to choose from a range of permissions while retaining their copyright, CC0 empowers yet another choice altogether—the choice to opt out of copyright and database protection, and the exclusive rights automatically granted to creators—the "no rights reserved" alternative to our licenses.

16. The aim of writing this marketing manual is to promote the use of the Information Literacy IFLA—UNESCO logo. The logo was selected from an international competition with the objective of creating an image that would strengthen communication between participants in Information Literacy (IL) programs: those who fund them, the institutions and organizations; those who facilitate the programs, the trainers; and those who benefit from developing information competencies, the learners. The adoption and use of the logo by information literacy pro-fessionals will make it an easily recognizable symbol for IL across countries, and will therefore, make IL communication easier.

17. The IFLA International Advocacy Programme (IAP) is a capacity-building programme launched in 2016, designed to promote and support the role libraries can play in the planning and implementation of the UN 2030 Agenda and the SDGs.

Objectives:

- Raise the level of awareness on the SDGs of library workers at community, national and regional levels, and to promote the important role libraries can play in development by contributing to the UN 2030 Agenda and the SDGs;
- Increase the participation of library associations and public library representatives in advocacy work at national and regional levels to secure sustainable public access to information through library services and programmes.

In the context of the IAP, 'advocacy' involves *"the actions individuals or organizations undertake to influence decision-making at the local, regional, state, national, and international levels that help create a desired policy or funding change in support of public libraries".*

18. Linked Data is about using the Web to connect related data that wasn't previously linked, or using the Web to lower the barriers to linking data currently linked using other methods. More specifically, Wikipedia defines Linked Data as "a term used to describe a recommended best practice for exposing, sharing, and connecting pieces of data, information, and on the Semantic Web using URIs and RDF."

19. TouchPoint is a patron interface developed by SISIS Informationssysteme, acquired by OCLC in 2005. OCLC does not continue to perform ongoing development of this product, though it does remain in use, often as a front-end interface for CBS union catalogs.

20. Vidya-mitra is an online learning portal for all the e-content projects developed under the NME-ICT (National Mission on Education through Information and Communication Technology), MHRD. The portal facilitates searching and browsing of all content hosted on a platform wherein a learner can easily access the desired material including audio/ video learning material, textual material, multimedia-enriched materials, etc. through a single interface. Moreover, features of faceted search, My-Space and usage statistics, project-wise access are also incorporated in this portal.

Objectives:

- Develop an Open Education Repository (OER) consisting of formidable collection of e-content from across all Govt (MHRD) sponsored e-content projects;
- Enriched metadata for all e-content projects;
- Provide access to all e-content through a single platform that facilitates search and browse through a user friendly interface;
- Platform and browser independent access with seamless streaming; and
- Promote usage of e-content amongst students and peers.

21. One common type of abstract is an informative abstract. If you are writing an abstract for a strictly-structured document like an experiment, investigation, or survey, you will write an informative abstract. An informative abstract is made up of four parts:

- Purpose
- Methodology
- Results
- Conclusions

The purpose section of an informative abstract should state either the reason for or the primary objectives of the experiment or investigation. The purpose section of an informative abstract might also contain the hypothesis of the experiment.

The methodology section of an informative abstract should describe the techniques used in conducting the experiment. This section should give only as much detail as is necessary to understand the experiment; the abstract should not focus entirely on research methods unless that is the primary focus of the original document.

The results section of an informative abstract should relate the observations and/or data collected during the experiment. This section should be concise and informative, and only the most important results need be included.

The conclusion section of an informative abstract should state the evaluation or analysis of the experiment results. It should also briefly state the implications of these results. This conclusion section might also state whether the driving hypothesis of the experiment was correct.

22. Object-based logical models are used in describing data at logical level and view level. Logical level and view level are used to retrieve the data. Logical level describes what data are stored in the database and what relationships exist among those data. Logical level is used by DBA, who must decide what information is to be kept in the database. View level describes only part of the entire database to be viewed by the user of the database hiding the details of the information stored.

Object-Based Logical Models are Described in the Different Following Models:

- The Entity-Relationship Model
- The Object-Based Logical Model
- The Semantic Data Model
- The Functional Data Model.

23. Longitudinal research is a type of correlational research that involves looking at variables over an extended period of time. This type of study can take place over a period of weeks, months, or even years. In some cases, longitudinal studies can last several decades.

There are three major types of longitudinal studies:

- **Panel Study:** Involves sampling a cross-section of individuals.
- **Cohort Study:** Involves selecting a group based on a specific event such as birth, geographic location or historical experience.
- **Retrospective Study:** Involves looking to the past by looking at historical information such as medical records.

24. Experienced librarians may take administrative positions such as library or information center director. Similar to the management of any other organization, they are concerned with the long-term planning of the library, and its relationship with its parent organization (the city or county for a public library, the college/university for an academic library, or the organization served by a special library). In smaller or specialized libraries, librarians typically perform a wide range of the different duties. Sometimes depending upon the nature of work they had to perform, they may be named as Cataloguing Librarian; Metadata Librarian; Application Specialist; Collections Librarian; Electronic Resources Librarian; Research Instruction Librarian; Reference Librarian; Legal research Law Librarian; Prospect researcher; Information broker; Records manager; Archivist; Indexer; Information architect; Curator; Teacher-librarian; etc.

26. Concrete5 is an open-source content management system (CMS) for publishing content on the World Wide Web and intranets. Concrete5 is designed for ease of use, for users with a minimum of technical skills. It enables users to edit site content directly from the page. It provides version management for every page, similar to wiki software, another type of web site development software. Concrete5 allows users to edit images through an embedded editor on the page.

Text-pattern CMS is an elegant content management system that is free, open source software. Web designers, developers, publishers and bloggers love its flexibility and extensibility. It has a powerful, sophisticated engine that can be infinitely tuned to suit whatever type of website you can imagine.

28. Digit: A single character in a notation (whether semantic or indicator) say 9, A, or + : , etc.

Empty Digit: A digit having only ordinal value and without any semantic value. In the CC 0, 9, z and Z are empty digits in lower order arrays.

Empty-Emptying Digit: A digit which is both empty and emptying U, W and Y are Empty-Emptying digits in the CC. These are used for interpolation in an array.

Empty Digit: A digit which takes away the semantic power of the preceding digit but allows it to retain its ordinal value. T, V and X are Emptying Digits. For example K in KX has nothing to do with Zoology, but KX will file between K and L. In fact KX becomes a fused pair treated de jure as a single digit.

29. List of open access Library and Information Science (LIS) Journals in India.

- Annals of Library and Information Studies (ALIS) formerly known as Annals of Library Science in 1954, Annals of Library Science and Documentation in 1964 and Annals of Library and Information Studies in 2001. ISSN 0972-5423 (Print) ISSN 0975-2404 (Online).

- DESIDOC Journal of Library and Information Technology (DJLIT) formerly known as DESIDOC Bulletin of Information Technology (DBIT) ISSN 0974-0643 (Print) ISSN 0976-4658 (Online).
- Informatics Studies (IS) An International Scholarly Journal (Select issues and papers available for Open Access) ISSN 2320-530X.
- The International Journal of Library and Information Studies (IJLIS) ISSN 2231-4911 (Online).

30. Independent and dependent variables:

- Independent variable is presumed to affect is called the dependent variable.
- The nature of dependent variable "depends on" what the independent variable does to it, how it affects it.

Examples:

- A researcher studying the relationship between childhood success in mathematics and adult career choice is likely to refer to the former as the independent variable and subsequent career choice as the dependent variable, even though success is not manipulated.
- "Will students who are taught by a team of three teachers learn more science than students taught by one individual teacher?"
- Independent variable is the number of teachers.
- Amount of science learning is dependent.

32. Scholarly communication is the process by which academics, scholars, and researchers share and publish their research findings so that they are available to the wider academic community and beyond.

Common methods of scholarly communication include writings in a scholarly journals, books, E-only journals, reviews, preprints and working papers, encyclopedias, dictionaries, and annotated content, data, blogs, discussion forums, professional and scholarly hubs and conference papers. Other forms, particularly in the arts and humanities include multimedia formats such as sound and video recordings. At the outset, the goal of most e-journal editors was the education of those who subscribed to their publication. Through this medium, users had an incentive to access the Internet and to become familiar with navigating the Web. The editors' goals were similar to those of the library. Both wanted to provide access to journals, in order to help readers and patrons gain the knowledge to conduct further online research independently. Over time the role of the e-journal has transformed from an innovative education tool, to the primary means for delivery of scholarly content.

34. The Audio Files category includes compressed and uncompressed audio formats, which contain waveform data that can be played with audio playback software. This category also includes MIDI files, musical scores, and audio project files, which typically do not contain audio data. Common audio file extensions include .WAV, .AIF, .MP3, and .MID.

Waveform Audio (.wav): Waveform Audio (.wav) is a common file format. Created by Microsoft and IBM, WAV was one of the first audio file types developed for the PC. WAV files are defined as lossless, meaning that files are large and complete; nothing has been lost. Professionally recorded CDs aré also a lossless audio source.

Audio Interchange File (.aif, .aifc or .aiff.): Audio Interchange File (.aif, .aifc or .aiff.) was developed for the Macintosh computer to store audio files.

MPEG-1 Audio Layer 3 (.mp3): MPEG-1 Audio Layer 3 (.mp3) is a common, compressed WAV file. MPEG-1 files are about one-twelfth the size of WAV files. This is why MP3 players can accommodate hundreds of songs on a tiny chunk of storage space.

Musical Instrument Digital Interface (.midi): Musical Instrument Digital Interface (.midi) is commonly used for computer keyboards and other computer-based musical tools. MIDI files contain musical notes, rhythm notation and other information often needed by a composer.

37. The Chi Square statistic is commonly used for testing relationships between categorical variables. The null hypothesis of the Chi-Square test is that no relationship exists on the categorical variables in the population; they are independent.

The Chi-Square statistic is most commonly used to evaluate Tests of Independence when using a crosstabulation. Crosstabulation presents the distributions of two categorical variables simultaneously, with the intersections of the categories of the variables appearing in the cells of the table. The Test of Independence assesses whether an association exists between the two variables by comparing the observed pattern of responses in the cells to the pattern that would be expected if the variables were truly independent of each other. Calculating the Chi-Square statistic and comparing it against a critical value from the Chi-Square distribution allows the researcher to assess whether the observed cell counts are significantly different from the expected cell counts.

38. The Classification Research Group (CRG), formed in the UK in 1952, has been one of the most significant contributors to classification research and theory in the latter half of the 20th century. The theoretical work of the Group has involved the study of facet analysis, relational operators, and the theory of integrative levels. The CRG opposed the traditional top-down approach to classification, whereby areas of knowledge are predetermined and then broken down into their constituent elements. The CRG was interested in first piecing together individual elements and then determining the areas of knowledge they form. The CRG looked towards the theory of integrative levels to provide them with the basis for this bottom-up approach to classification. This paper explores and evaluates the CRG's efforts to apply the theory of integrative levels to the construction of bibliographic classification systems.

39. The FRSAR Working Group proposes a generalisation of FRBR, as seen in Figure 1. This diagram is based on the original FRBR Figure 2 that depicts the "subject" relationships between works and entities in Group 1, Group 2, and Group 3. A new entity, family, added by FRAD in Group 2, is also reflected in this general framework. The entities in the third group represent an additional set of entities that serve as the subjects of works. The group includes, according to the FRBR model, concept (an abstract notion or idea), object (a material thing), event (an action or occurrence), and place (a location).

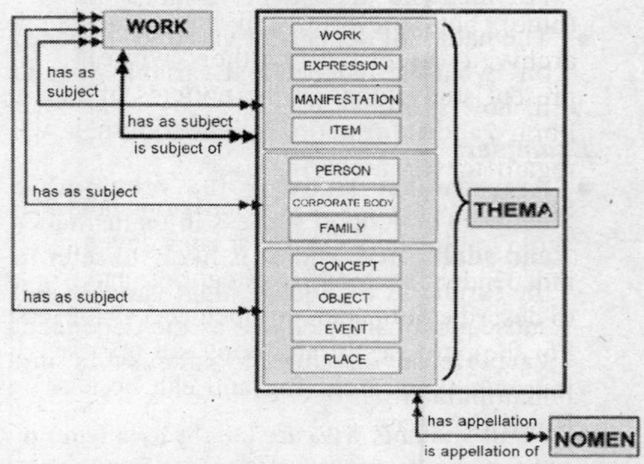

Fig.1: *FRSAD's relation to FRBR (With the addition of FRAD entity family)*

The FRSAR Working Group introduced the following two entities:

Thema: Any entity used as a subject of a work.

Nomen: Any sign or sequence of signs (alphanumeric characters, symbols, sound, etc.) that a thema is known by, referred to, or addressed as.

The Functional Requirements for Subject Authority Data (FRSAD) model is presented as:

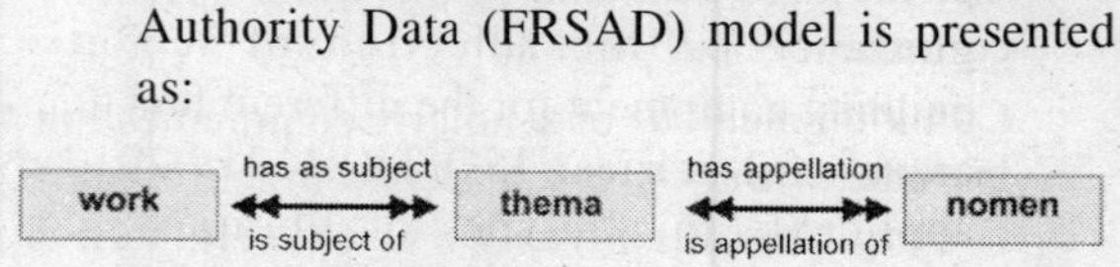

Fig.2: *FRSAD conceptual model*

41. The RoMEO project aimed to develop simple rights metadata by which academics could protect their research papers in an open-access environment and also to develop a means by which OAI data and service providers could protect their open access metadata. RoMEO proposed to show how such rights solutions might be disclosed and harvested under OAI-PMH. The RoMEO project was divided into two phases: a data-gathering phase and a development phase. The project team produced a series of six studies based on their work3. The SHERPA/RoMEO database is being redeveloped and renamed the Copyright Knowledge Bank. However, it will still assign a colour to individual publishers indicating whether pre-prints can be self-archived (yellow), post-prints can be self-archived (blue), both pre-print and post-print can be archived (green) or neither (white)4. The present study looks at the policies of various library and information science journals with regard to self archiving.

Sometimes open access discussions talk about "gold" publishers. This is a later development independent of RoMEO categories, and is used to describe publishers of open access journals. For the purposes of archiving, all open access journals allow archiving and can be taken as RoMEO "green".

42. ISO 2146:2010 establishes the rules for registries operating in a network environment to provide the information about collections, parties, activities and services needed by libraries and related organizations to manage their collections and deliver information and documentation services across a range of applications and domains.

ISO/TR 11219:2012 specifies data for the planning of library buildings. It also provides guidance on the selection of technical building equipment for the different functional areas of libraries. ISO/TR 11219:2012 is applicable to all types of libraries in all countries, but especially to academic and public libraries.

ISO 11620:2014 is applicable to all types of libraries in all countries. However, not all performance indicators apply to all libraries. Limitations on the applicability of individual performance indicators are listed in the scope clause of the description of each indicator. Performance indicators can be used for comparison over time within the same library. Comparisons between libraries can also be made, but only with caution. Comparisons between libraries will need to take into account any differences in the constituencies of the libraries and library attributes, with a good understanding of the indicators used, limitations to comparisons, and careful interpretation of the data.

ISO 16642:2017 specifies a framework for representing data recorded in terminological data collections (TDCs). This framework includes a metamodel and methods for describing specific terminological markup languages (TMLs) expressed in XML. The mechanisms for implementing constraints in a TML are defined, but not the specific constraints for individual TMLs.

44. Important Bibliographic Elements in the Marc 21 Record Leader:

The Leader (24 characters in length)

- 400-04 - Length of record
- 405 - Record status
- 406 - Type of record
- 407 - Bibliographic level
- 408 - Type of control
- 409 - Character encoding
- 417 - Encoding level
- 418 - Description conventions

Numbers and Codes (OXX):

- 001 Control Number
- 003 System Identification
- 005 Date and Time of Latest Transaction
- 007 Physical Description Fixed Field
- 008 Fixed-Length Data Elements
    - ❑ 00-05 Date record entered on file
    - ❑ 06 Type of publication date
    - ❑ 07-14 1st and 2nd dates
    - ❑ 15-17 Place of publication code
    - ❑ 35-37 Language code
    - ❑ 38 Modification code

45. This booklet is a brief guide on how to write a collection development policy, making use of the Conspectus methodology. It is the result of the recognition by the IFLA Acquisition and Collection Development Section that its worldwide members lacked a handy introduction to this important subject. The guide is intended to be of particular value to staff new to collection development and in areas where there is little written tradition of collection development.

Collection depth indicators: The collection depth indicators, or levels, are numerical values used to describe a library's collecting activity and goals. Three aspects of collection management are considered: current collection level, acquisition commitment, and collection goal.

Collection depth indicator definitions:

0 = out of scope

1 = minimal information level

2 = basic information level

3 = study or instructional support level

4 = research level

5 = comprehensive level

47. Memory Measurement Units

1 Bit = Binary Digit

8 Bits = 1 Byte

1024 Bytes = 1 KB (Kilo Byte)

1024 KB = 1 MB (Mega Byte)

1024 MB = 1 GB (Giga Byte)

1024 GB = 1 TB (Terra Byte)

1024 TB = 1 PB (Peta Byte)

1024 PB = 1 EB (Exa Byte)

1024 EB = 1 ZB (Zetta Byte)

1024 ZB = 1 YB (Yotta Byte)

1024 YB = 1 (Bronto Byte)

1024 Brontobyte = 1 (Geop Byte)

Note: Geop Byte is The Highest Memory Measurement Unit.

49. Maslow's hierarchy of needs is a theory in psychology proposed by Abraham Maslow in his 1943 paper "A Theory of Human Motivation" in Psychological Review. Maslow's hierarchy of needs is used to study how humans intrinsically partake in behavioural motivation. Maslow used the terms "physiological", "safety", "belonging and love", "social needs" or "esteem", and "self-actualization" to describe the pattern through which human motivations generally move. This means that in order for motivation to occur at the next level, each level must be satisfied within the individual themselves. Furthermore, this theory is a key foundation in understanding how drive and motivation are correlated when discussing human behaviour. Each of these individual levels contains a certain amount of internal sensation that must be met in order for an individual to complete their hierarchy. The goal in Maslow's theory is to attain the fifth level or stage: self-actualization.

The **two-factor theory** states that there are certain factors in the workplace that cause job satisfaction while a separate set of factors cause dissatisfaction, all of which act independently of each other. It was developed by psychologist Frederick Herzberg.

McClelland's Needs Theory was proposed by a psychologist David McClelland, who believed that the specific needs of the individual are acquired over a period of time and gets molded with one's experience of the life. McClelland's Needs Theory is sometimes referred to as Three Need theory or Learned Needs Theory.

Vroom's Expectancy Theory was proposed by Victor. H. Vroom, who believed that people are motivated to perform activities to achieve some goal to the extent they expect that certain actions on their part would help them to achieve the goal.

50. Refreshing: Refreshing is the transfer of data between two types of the same storage medium so that there are no changes or alteration of data, e.g. Transferring data from an old backup DVD to a new one.

Replication: Creating duplicate copies of data on one or more systems is called replication.

Data that exists as a single copy in only one location is highly vulnerable to software or hardware failure, intentional or accidental alteration, and environmental disasters like fire, flooding, etc. Digital data is more likely to survive if it is replicated in several locations.

Migration: Migration is the transferring of data to newer system environments. This may include conversion of resources from one file format to another (*e.g.*, conversion of PDF to EPUB), from one operating system to another (*e.g.*, Windows to Linux), from one programming language to another (*e.g.*, C to C++) or from one medium to another (*e.g.*, data backup on disk) so the resource remains fully accessible and functional.

Emulation: Emulation is the replicating of functionality of an obsolete system. Emulating softwares, *i.e.*, emulators program the newer system in such a way that even older, obsolete platform and operating systems can be accessible on the same new system. Emulators may be built for applications, operating systems, or hardware platforms, *e.g.*, Simics, CPU Sim and GXemul are some of the full-system emulaters.

Digital Sustainability: In encompasses building an infrastructure and approach that emphasizes on continued maintenance and development to facilitate access and availability in the future.

51. Administrative Approach: Two of the proponents of this approach are Henri Fayol (1841-1925) and Max Weber (1864-1920). Other notable figures are Lyndall Urwick (1891-1983) and Chester Barnard (1886-1961).

Henri Fayol was both a practitioner/manager and a thinker about management. He believed his success was due to skills he developed over the years as well as his ideas about what it takes to be an effective manager. He published his "principles" in 1916 in *Administration Industrielle et Generale* (Fayol, 1962).

Behavioural Approach: There is a connection between the scientific management and behavioural approaches. As we noted earlier, Lillian Gilbreth's book addressed industrial psychology, not scientific management and its importance to effective management. Hugo Munsterberg (1863-1916) is probably the best candidate for being the founder of the behavioural approach to management. His book *Psychology and Industrial Efficiency* makes the case for applying psychology to the workplace (Munsterberg, 1913). He proposed three major foci: identifying the person with the proper characteristics to perform the job (skills, attitudes, physical abilities), developing methods to identify the ideal psychological condition for engaging in a task, and creating optimal motivational influences on the worker. He drew on scientific methods, specifically conducting experiments to accomplish the field's goals. His work led to the development of pre-employment skills testing.

Composite Approaches: We end this brief review of management approaches with a discussion of Peter Drucker (1909–2005) and Henry Mintzberg (1939–). Each has had a long and distinguished career as a scholar and a teacher of management. They are not associated with any particular management approach, but rather they draw from the vast array of options available to contemporary managers. If anything, they are closest to the contingency approach.

Management Science/Quantitative Approach: There are a variety of subfields within management science or the quantitative approach. Operations research, decision analysis, simulation, forecasting, game theory, mathematical modelling, management information systems, project management, and data mining are but a few of the variations.

A major figure in management in general and in management science in particular was Herbert A. Simon (1916–2001). He was an early leader in the fields of quantitative modelling of human behaviour, artificial intelligence, and problem-solving strategies (simulation). His book *Administrative*

Behavior (Simon, 1947) focused on the behavioural and cognitive processes involved when people engage in rational decision making.

53. E.C. Richardson (1860-1939): American librarian and bibliographer. Author of *Classification, theoretical and practical* (1st ed. in 1901; further eds. In 1912 & 1930), the first major book on classification theory in (Anglo-American) L(I)S. Richardson's theory provides a historically influential early attempt at synthesizing ontology and epistemology in a single classification scheme.

William Charles Berwick Sayers, an English librarian and teacher of S.R. Ranganathan made a remarkable contribution to the development of the theory of classification. He is referred to as the first grammarian of library classification. He is responsible for interpreting and systematising the ideas of other theoreticians. He never designed any classification scheme, though, through his theory he has shown the way for others in the designing of classification schemes. His theory of book classification first appeared in 1915 under the title "Canons of Classification". He expanded the outline of the theory contained in this book in three other books, viz., Grammar of Classification, Introduction to Library Classification, and Manual of Library Classification.

E.W. Hulme was the librarian of the Patent Office Library, London. In 1911-1912, he published his book Principles of Book Classification in the library Association Record. His principles influenced the later theories of book-classification.

Jack Mills (1918 - 9 July 2010) was a British librarian and classification researcher, who worked for more than sixty years in the study, teaching, development and promotion of library classification and information retrieval, principally as a major figure in the British school of facet analysis which builds on the traditions of Henry E. Bliss and S.R. Ranganathan.

Bibliography of Jack Mills' works

A modern outline of library classification;

The new Bliss Classification; "Catalogue and Index;

A new edition of Bliss Catalogue and index; Number building and filing order in BC." Bliss classification bulletin;

54. The Big 6 Model is a process model for information problem-solving. It integrates information search and use skills along with technology tools in a systematic process to find, use, apply, and evaluate information for specific needs and tasks. The Big 6 was developed by Mike Eisenberg and Bob Berkowitz and is the popular approach to teaching information and technology skills for schools and HEIs in the world.

Eight WS Information literacy model was developed by Annette Lamb in the early 1990s. It is an eight-phase model for project and community based learning on the web/ internet. A project and community based learning environment involves wondering about a topic, wiggling through information, and weaving elements together. This model was used to stimulate student interest and focus on the student's perspective in information inquiry on the web. This model states and describes eight phases of information inquiry skills which are needed to be developed among students in the digital environment to complete a project.

PLUS information skills process model is developed by James E. Herring in 1991 at Scotland. It is an information literacy model which encourages pupils to identify purpose, to locate relevant sources, to use the ideas and information found effectively and to reflect on their own information skills through self evaluation.

SAUCE Model:

- Trevor Bond's model is known as the SAUCE model.
- Trevor Bond provides ongoing support with planning and training as part of ICT PD.

- Many schools in our area are working with the SAUCE model.

Elements of Model:

- S–Setting the scene...It provides a context for the learning, and involves initial interaction with the task and identification of prior knowledge.
- A–Acquire...Acquiring the knowledge (and validating it).
- U–Use...Application of the knowledge in the context of the task.
- C–Communicate...Presentation.
- E–Evaluate...Evaluation of process.

55. The Indian Association of Teachers of Library and Information Science **(IATLIS),** a national professional organization to further the cause of library education in India was founded on 19th Dec. 1969. Two new awards, namely IATLIS-Prof. S.P. Narang Research Promotion Award, and IATLIS-Prof. Jogindar Singh Ramdev Lifetime Achievement Award have been instituted in addition to already existing two awards.

The Indian Association of Special Libraries and Information Centres **(IASLIC)** is a non-profit organisation based in India that supports development in the entire field of special librarianship in India. The IASLIC undertakes supports, coordinate research and studies, conducts short term training courses; organises general/special meetings, and hold seminars and conferences in alternate years on current problems of Libraries and Information services and other allied areas are selected as themes for discussions on thesis occasions. IASLIC has instituted a national level S.M. Ganguly-IASLIC Award for the Librarian of the Year since 1993, sponsored by Late S.M. Ganguly.

Young Information Scientist Award: The Society instituted The Young Information Scientist Award in 1989 in the memory of Late Shri A.S. Raizada, Founder Secretary of SIS, to Young Information Scientists for their outstanding contribution in their profession. So far many Young Information Scientists have been awarded Raizada Memorial Award.

ILA-Kaula Best Librarian Award 2018: The Award, instituted by Prof. P.N. Kaula Endowment for Library and Information Science, Guntur (AP), is for the professionals in the field of LIS in India. The Award carries a shawl, citation and memento.

61. **The American Library Association (ALA)** is the oldest and largest library association in the world. Founded on October 6, 1876 during the Centennial Exposition in Philadelphia, the mission of ALA is "to provide leadership for the development, promotion and improvement of library and information services and the profession of librarianship in order to enhance learning and ensure access to information for all."

The **International Federation of Library Associations and Institutions (IFLA)** is the leading international body representing the interests of people who rely on libraries and information professionals. An independent, non-governmental, not-for-profit organization, IFLA was founded in Scotland in 1927 and maintains headquarters at the National Library of the Netherlands in The Hague.

Indian Library Association (ILA) was established on September 12, 1933 registered under the societies Registration Act (XXI of 1860), on the occasion of the First All India Library Conference held at Calcutta (now Kolkata). The ILA is the largest and renowned professional body in the field of Library and Information Science in India with a membership of more than 7000. The headquarter of ILA situated in Delhi, India.

The **Chartered Institute of Library and Information Professionals (CILIP)** is a professional body for librarians, information specialists and knowledge managers in the United Kingdom. Since 2017, it has been branded CILIP: The library and information association. CILIP in Scotland is an independent organisation which operates in Scotland on behalf of CILIP.

62. The **Romain Rolland Library,** founded in 1827 as the Bibliotheque Publique, is one of the oldest Libraries of India located in the union territory of Puducherry. In the year 1966 when the birth centenary of the Great French Scholar, Romain Rolland who was also a contemporary and a close friend of Mahatma Gandhi was celebrated, the Library was renamed after him and ever since it is known as 'Romain Rolland Library'.

Krishnadas Shama Goa State Central Library a State-of-art edifice situated near Panjim bus stand at Patto. The Library is named after Krishnadas Shama founder of Konkani Prose and known as Father of Konkani literature, to recognize his contribution in the field of literature in 16th century. The State Central Library was established in the year 1832 and was shifted to the new building in the year 2012.

The **State Central Library Hyderabad,** known as the State Central Library (SCL) earlier known as Asafia Library, is a public library in Hyderabad, Telangana. The building was constructed in 1891 with the help of chief engineer of Nizam - Nawab Khan Bahadur Mirza Akbar Baig. It is one of the most imposing structures in the city and was granted heritage status in 1998 by INTACH, Hyderabad.

Connemara Public Library at Egmore in Chennai, Tamil Nadu, India, is one of the four National Depository Libraries which receive a copy of all books, newspapers and periodicals published in India. Established in 1890, the library is a repository of centuries-old publications, wherein lie some of the most respected works and collections in the country. It also serves as a depository library for the UN.

63. The **Text Encoding Initiative (TEI)** is a consortium which collectively develops and maintains a standard for the representation of texts in digital form. Its chief deliverable is a set of Guidelines which specify encoding methods for machine-readable texts, chiefly in the humanities, social sciences and linguistics. Since 1994, the TEI Guidelines have been widely used by libraries, museums, publishers, and individual scholars to present texts for online research, teaching, and preservation.

The **Resource Description Framework (RDF)** is a family of World Wide Web Consortium (W3C) specifications originally designed as a metadata data model. It has come to be used as a general method for conceptual description or modelling of information that is implemented in web resources, using a variety of syntax notations and data serialization formats. It is also used in knowledge management applications. RDF was adopted as a W3C recommendation in 1999.

The Library of Congress' Network Development and MARC Standards Office, with interested experts, developed the **Metadata Object Description Schema (MODS)** in 2002 for a bibliographic element set that may be used for a variety of purposes, and particularly for library applications.

Resource Description and Access (RDA), is the new catalouging standard that will replace AACR2. RDA offers libraries the potential to change significantly how bibliographic data is created and used. Published in July 2010, RDA is now available, and certain libraries have started using it for their current catalouging workflow. The Library of Congress has announced full implementation of RDA for 31 March 2013.

64. The public library legislation made its impact on the development of public libraries in India. The library movement helped to set up a number of private libraries in urban and rural areas initially, the public library legislation provided the public library services on a sound financial foundation with governmental support and library cess. The Kolhapur Public Libraries Act (1945) was the first library act in India and it was followed by Madras state (presently Tamil Nadu) in 1948, Andhra Pradesh (1960), Karnataka (1965), Maharashtra (1967), West Bengal (1979), Manipur (1988), Kerala (1989), Haryana (1989), Mizoram

(1993), Goa (1994), Gujarat (2002), Odisha (2002), Uttaranchal (2006) and Rajasthan (2006).

67. **World Book and Copyright Day** is a celebration to promote the enjoyment of books and reading. Each year, on 23 April, celebrations take place all over the world to recognize the scope of books—a link between the past and the future, a bridge between generations and across cultures. On this occasion, UNESCO and the international organizations representing the three major sectors of the book industry—publishers, booksellers and libraries, select the World Book Capital for a year to maintain, through its own initiatives, the impetus of the Day's celebrations.

International Literacy Day, celebrated annually on 8 September, is an opportunity for Governments, civil society and stakeholders to highlight improvements in world literacy rates, and reflect on the world's remaining literacy challenges. The issue of literacy is a key component of the UN's Sustainable Development Goals and the UN's 2030 Agenda for Sustainable Development.

The **International Day for the Universal Access to Information** (commonly called the Access to Information Day) is an international day of recognition designated by the UNESCO General Conference to be held on 28 September.

World Teachers' Day, also known as International Teachers Day, is held annually on October 5. World Teachers' Day aims to focus on "appreciating, assessing and improving the educators of the world" and to provide an opportunity to consider issues related to teachers and teaching.

68. **Yahoo! Mail** is an email service launched in 1997 through the American parent company Yahoo!. Yahoo Mail provides four different email plans: three for personal use (Basic, Plus, and Ad Free) and another for businesses. Hush Communications was founded in 1998, and in May 1999 we launched **Hush mail,** the world's premier end-to-end encrypted free email service. We believe communication should be kept private, and we offer a way for individuals and businesses to do this easily and affordably.

Gmail is a free email service developed by Google. Users can access Gmail on the web and using third-party programs that synchronize email content through POP or IMAP protocols. Gmail started as a limited beta release on April 1, 2004 and ended its testing phase on July 7, 2009.

ProtonMail is an end-to-end encrypted email service founded in 2014 at the CERN research facility by Andy Yen, Jason Stockman, and Wei Sun. ProtonMail uses client-side encryption to protect email contents and user data before they are sent to ProtonMail servers, unlike other common email providers such as Gmail and Outlook.com.

69. The most significant term in a compound subject heading is the one that is most readily available to the memory of the enquirer. From this, Coates has developed the idea of Thing and Action like Kaiser's Concrete and Process.

A 'Thing' is whatever one can think, that is to say whatever can be thought as a static image. It is the image that comes straight into our mind, *i.e.* which we can visualize first. It includes not only the names of physical objects but systems and organisations of a mental kind, *e.g.* Democracy. An Action refers to anything in action or process denotes by term/word.

Among 'Thing' and 'Action', thing is more significant than Action. So the subject heading would be: Thing/Action. Coates also added the idea of Material. A Material is a state images produced by names of Things and names of Material. A Thing is made up of certain Material and the Material follows the Thing. A Thing has a boundary (*i.e.* shape) but the Material has none and for this reason the name of the Material is of low significance than the name of a Thing. On the other hand, the image of a Material is made of some static seeming properties—such as, colour, hardness, smoothness, etc. (*i.e.* the image of a material is produced due to its colour, hardness, smoothness, etc.) and is rated higher in the significance than the name of an action. Therefore, the significant order is Thing—Material—Action like Personality—Matter—Energy of Ranganathan. Part is a component of a thing. Hence, it depends on the thing to which they belong and, thus, giving us the order of significance: Thing—Part—Material—Action.

70. SCONUL was founded in 1950 as the Standing Conference of National and University Libraries. In 1994 when British polytechnics became universities it merged with COPOL, the Council of Polytechnic Librarians, and in 2001 it extended its membership to libraries of Colleges of Higher Education and changed to its current name.

These seven model are:

Sl. No.	***Pillars***	***An Information Literate Person***
1.	Identify	• *Able to identify a personal need of information.*
2.	Scope	• *Able to understand and assess current knowledge and identify gaps.*
3.	Plan	• *Able to construct strategies for locating information and data.*
4.	Gather	• *Able to locate and access the information and data they need.*
5.	Evaluate	• *Able to review the research process and compare and evaluate the information and data.*
6.	Manage	• *Able to organize information Professionally and ethically*
7.	Present	• *Able to apply the know-ledge gained: presenting the results of their research, synthesizing new and old information and data to create new know-ledge and disseminating it in a variety of ways.*

71. The **information Search Process (ISP)** is a six-stage process of information seeking behaviour in library and information science. The ISP was first suggested by Carol Kuhlthau in 1991. It describes the thoughts, feelings and actions of the searcher, and is often used to describe students. The model of the ISP is articulated in a holistic view of information seeking from the user's perspective in six stages:

- **Initiation,** when a person first becomes aware of a lack of knowledge or understanding and feelings of uncertainty and apprehension are common.
- **Selection,** when a general area, topic, or problem is identified and initial uncertainty often gives way to a brief sense of optimism and a readiness to begin the search.
- **Exploration,** when inconsistent, incompatible information is encountered and uncertainty, confusion, and doubt frequently increase and people find themselves "in the dip" of confidence.
- **Formulation,** when a focused perspective is formed and uncertainty diminishes as confidence begins to increase.
- **Collection,** when information pertinent to the focused perspective is gathered and uncertainty subsides as interest and involvement deepens.
- **Presentation,** when the search is completed with a new understanding enabling the person to explain his or her learning to others or in someway put the learning to use.

74. John Kotter, leadership and change management professor at Harvard Business School, introduced his ground-breaking 8-Step Change Model in his 1995 book, "Leading Change". Built on the work of Kurt Lewin, the model sets out the 8 key steps of the changes process, arguing that neglecting any of the steps can be enough for the whole initiative to fail.

Step One: Create Urgency

Step Two: Form a Powerful Coalition

Step Three: Create a Vision for Change

Step Four: Communicate the Vision

Step Five: Remove Obstacles

Step Six: Create Short-Term Wins

Step Seven: Build on the Change

Step Eight: Anchor the Changes in Corporate Culture

80. Colon classification is a general classification scheme, designed by Dr. S.R. Ranganathan. He applied this scheme during 1932. Ist edition was found 1933. It is up to VIIth edition. Ist edition in 1933, IInd edition in 1939, IIIrd edition in 1950, IVth edition in 1952, Vth edition in 1957, VIth edition in 1960, reprinted in 1963, 1964, 1967, 1976 and 1989 VIIth edition in 1987.

The VIIth edition is an in-completed one. So we are following the VIth edition by only for the practical applicable.

C.C. has secured the mutual exclusiveness of the classes by avoiding the overlapping of subdivisions.

82. The Resource Description and Access (RDA) standard, due to be released this coming summer, has included since May, 2007 a parallel effort to build Semantic Web enabled vocabularies. This article describes that effort and the decisions made to express the vocabularies for use within the library community and in addition as a bridge to the future of library data outside the current MARC-based systems. The authors also touch on the registration activities that have made the vocabularies usable independently of the RDA textual guidance. Designed for both human and machine users, the registered vocabularies describe the relationships between FRBR, the RDA classes and properties and the extensive value vocabularies developed for use within RDA.

RDA is being developed as a new standard for resource description and access designed for the digital world. Built on foundations established by the **Anglo-American Cataloguing Rules** (AACR), RDA will provide a comprehensive set of guidelines and instructions on resource description and access covering all types of content and media. The new standard is being developed for use primarily in libraries, but consultations are being undertaken with other communities (archives, museums, publishers, semantic web, etc.) in an effort to attain an effective level of alignment between RDA and the metadata standards used in those communities.

83. Copyright and intellectual property issues and laws have long been recognized important to the library profession. A volunteer-driven committee, the CLM was created to advise and represent the IFLA on matters of international copyright law.

- The CLM produces legal briefs and is the representative for the IFLA at meetings of the World Intellectual Property Organization (WIPO). The CLM's activities for the WIPO involve:
- Copyright limitations and exceptions for libraries and archives.
- Copyright limitations and exceptions for visually impaired persons.
- Relations with WIPO Secretariat.
- Opposition to the Broadcast Treaty at WIPO.
- Development Agenda at WIPO.
- Preservation of Traditional Knowledge at WIPO.

Copyright laws are meant to balance the public interest in accessing information with the rights of authors, artists, and publishers. In some countries, copyright laws include provisions so libraries and archives can provide public access to the world's knowledge—but in many countries, these exceptions apply only to resources that exist in traditional formats. Outdated copyright laws increasingly prevent libraries and archives from performing their most basic functions, simply because resources are now digital.

84. **Unicode** is a universal character set, *i.e.* a standard that defines, in one place, all the characters needed for writing the majority of living languages in use on computers. It aims to be, and to a large extent already is, a superset of all other character sets that have been encoded.

Text in a computer or on the Web is composed of characters. Characters represent letters of the alphabet, punctuation, or other symbols.

The character encoding reflects the way the coded character set is mapped to bytes for manipulation in a computer. The picture below shows how characters and code points in the Tifinagh (Berber) script are mapped to sequences of bytes in memory using the UTF-8 encoding.

The code point values for each character are listed immediately below the glyph (*i.e.*, the visual representation) for that character at the top of the diagram. The arrows show how those are mapped to sequences of bytes, where each byte is represented by a two-digit hexadecimal number.

85. A patent is the granting of a property right by a sovereign authority to an inventor. This grant provides the inventor exclusive rights to the patented process, design, or invention for a designated period in exchange for a comprehensive disclosure of the invention. Government agencies typically handle and approve applications for patents. In the United States, the U.S. Patent and Trademark Office handles applications and approvals.

In the United States, most patents are valid for 20 years from the date the application was filed with the U.S. Patent and Trademark Office. U.S. patents are only valid in the United States. Patents provide an incentive for companies or individuals to continue developing innovative products or services without the fear of infringement. For example, large pharmaceutical companies can spend millions of dollars on research and development. Without patents, their medicines can be easily duplicated and sold by companies that issue no outlays for R&D.

87. PRECIS is generally considered as one of the most ambitious late twentieth century attempts to create an indexing system from scratch. A major break-through in the field of subject indexing was achieved by Classification Research Group (CRG), London and Derek Austin came out with a new method of subject indexing called PRE served Context Index System (PRECIS) in the early 1970s for the British National Bibliography (BNB). When the BNB began in 1950, it used chain indexing system for about 20 years. However it was not, for various reasons, ideal for a computerised system, and in 1971, when BNB had developed the MARC system in the United Kingdom and was also engaged in using computers for the production of BNB itself, chain indexing was replaced by PRECIS.

PRECIS is a system of subject indexing in which the initial string of terms organised according to the scheme of role operators, is computer manipulated in such a way that each sought term in the string functions as the approach term while preserving the full context of the document. Entries are restructured at every step in such a way that the user can determine from the format of the entry which terms set the approach term into its context and which terms are context dependent on the approach term.

92. e-ShodhSindhu was formed with merger of three consortia, namely UGC-INFONET Digital Library Consortium, NLIST and INDEST-AICTE Consortium in December 2015. e-ShodhSindhu continues to provide current as well as archival access to more than 10,000+ core and peer-reviewed journals (including journals available through NLIST) and a number of bibliographic, citation and factual databases in different disciplines from a large number of publishers and aggregators to its member institutions including centrally-funded technical institutions, universities and colleges that are covered under 12(B) and 2(f) Sections of the UGC Act.

Previous Years' Paper (Solved)

UGC-NET Junior Research Fellowship & Assistant Professor Eligibility Exam

Library and Information Science, July-2018*

PAPER-II

Note : *This paper contains* ***hundred (100)*** *objective type questions of* ***two (2)*** *marks each.* ***All*** *questions are* ***compulsory****.*

1. What is the meaning of the term "Information Iceberg"?
A. 1/3 Non-visible and 2/3 Visible
B. 1/3 Visible and 2/3 Non-visible
C. 1/4 Non-visible and 3/4 Visible
D. 1/4 Visible and 3/4 Non-visible

2. What is the name of the committee responsible for Indian standards related to libraries?
A. TC 46 B. MSD 5
C. BIS - LIB D. Z 39

3. 'World Book and Copyright Day' is celebrated on:
A. 22nd August B. 23rd April
C. 23rd March D. 20th March

4. "To make at least one in every household e-literate" is thrust area of policy (# 7) included in:
A. National Knowledge Commission, 2005
B. National Policy on Information Technology, 2012
C. National Education Policy, 1992
D. National Policy on Library and Information Systems, 1986

5. Identify which one of the Five Laws of Library Science that Ranganathan remarked as 'trivial truism' in his writing "Library Science and Scientific Method".
A. First Law B. Second Law
C. Third Law D. Fifth Law

6. 'Wikipedia' owned by the non-profit "Wikipedia Foundation" was launched on January 15, 2001 by:
A. Jimmy Wells and Larry Sanger
B. Jimmy Wells and Vincent J. Aceto
C. Larry Sanger and W. Kathy
D. William A. Ford and W. Kathy

7. 'Anukriti' is a:
A. Bibliographic India Website
B. Indexing India Website
C. Translating India Website
D. Abstracting India Website

8. Ezproxy is a product of:
A. UTLAS
B. OCLC
C. RLIN
D. Library of Congress

9. Which of the following is **not** a classical model of information retrieval?
A. Boolean B. Cluster
C. Probabilistic D. Vector-space

10. Who criticized the concept of main entry as 'a relic of outdated technology'?
A. Michael Gorman
B. Robert L. Maxwell
C. Pat Oddy
D. Tom Delsey

11. Identify the odd one out:
A. Reference entry
B. Centred entry
C. Analytical entry
D. Added entry

*Held on 8 July, 2018

12. 'Path-Goal Theory of Leader Effectiveness' is developed by:
A. Douglas McGregor
B. William Ouchi
C. Robert House
D. Abraham Maslow

13. 'Ambra' an innovative open source platform (for publishing open access resource articles) is developed by:
A. OCLC B. DOAJ
C. PLOS D. WDL

14. The term 'Weblog' was coined by:
A. E. Williams B. Jack Dorsey
C. Jorn Barger D. Peter Merholz

15. Which of the following is not file hosting service?
A. One Drive B. Google Drive
C. Live Drive D. Xbox Live

16. VuFind is the tool used for:
A. Library Automation
B. Digital Library System
C. Library Resource Discovery System
D. Institutional Repository

17. Which one is the correct 'Binary number' for Decimal '115'?
A. 1100011 B. 1010111
C. 1111111 D. 1110011

18. Research method based on the consensus opinions of panel of experts and judgements is known as:
A. Historical method
B. Case study method
C. Delphi method
D. Interview method

19. A probability which is **not** associated with the occurrence of an event is expressed as a number between:
A. +1 and –1 B. 1 and < 1
C. –1 and 0 D. 0 and 1

20. What is the name of the initiative taken by the UGC to provide a 24×7 online store house of all academic awards issued by different academic institutions all over the country?
A. National Mission on Education Through Information and Communication Technology (NMEICT)
B. National Academic Depository (NAD)
C. HEI Online Registration Portal
D. Swayam Prabha

21. Wersig and Neveling gave which of the following approaches for defining information?
(*a*) The Action Approach
(*b*) The Message Approach
(*c*) The Process Approach
(*d*) The Structural Approach
Code:
A. (*a*), (*b*), (*c*) are correct.
B. (*b*), (*c*), (*d*) are correct.
C. (*a*), (*c*), (*d*) are correct.
D. (*a*), (*b*), (*d*) are correct.

22. Why a Library Association should have a code of "professional conduct"?
(*a*) Prescribes standards of behaviour expected for the member
(*b*) Sets out standards and duties which a professional is expected to observe
(*c*) Standards can be used as a point of reference while dealing with disciplined procedures against members
(*d*) Standards help to demean the image of the Association and de-ameliorate funding and ensure better functioning of libraries.
Code:
A. (*a*), (*b*) and (*d*) are correct.
B. (*b*), (*c*) and (*d*) are correct.
C. (*a*), (*b*) and (*c*) are correct.
D. (*a*), (*c*) and (*d*) are correct.

23. Which of the following states do **not** have provision of library cess in their respective Public Library Acts?
(*a*) West Bengal (*b*) Tamil Nadu
(*c*) Kerala (*d*) Manipur
Code:
A. (*a*) and (*d*) are correct.
B. (*a*), (*b*) and (*c*) are correct.
C. (*b*) and (*c*) are correct.
D. (*b*) and (*d*) are correct.

24. National Knowledge Commission (2005) had the following members from the library and Information profession:

(*a*) P.B. Mangla
(*b*) C.R. Karisiddappa
(*c*) Kalpana Das Gupta
(*d*) A.R.D. Prasad

Code:

A. (*a*), (*b*), (*c*) are correct.
B. (*a*), (*b*), (*d*) are correct.
C. (*a*), (*c*), (*d*) are correct.
D. (*b*), (*c*), (*d*) are correct.

25. Which of the following are the features of Classic IR Model?

(*a*) documents are represented by index terms
(*b*) all terms are equally useful
(*c*) index term cannot be weighted
(*d*) there is an assumption that terms are mutually independent

Code:

A. (*a*) and (*b*) are correct.
B. (*c*) and (*d*) are correct.
C. (*a*) and (*c*) are correct.
D. (*a*) and (*d*) are correct.

26. Vocabulary in a data base is controlled by:

(*a*) Thesaurus Files
(*b*) Import Files
(*c*) Standard Files
(*d*) Authority Files

Code:

A. (*a*) and (*b*) are correct.
B. (*c*) and (*d*) are correct.
C. (*a*) and (*d*) are correct.
D. (*b*) and (*c*) are correct.

27. Pre-coordinate indexing systems comprise:

(*a*) NEPHIS
(*b*) SLIC
(*c*) Peek-a-boo
(*d*) Edge - Notched card

Code:

A. (*a*) and (*b*) are correct.
B. (*a*) and (*d*) are correct.
C. (*b*) and (*c*) are correct.
D. (*c*) and (*d*) are correct.

28. Identify the correct statement from the following:

(*a*) In uniterm indexing system, terms are recorded in numerical file according to the system known as terminal digit posting.
(*b*) Main activities of TREC are divided into Routing and Tracks
(*c*) Recall and precision tend to vary in searching
(*d*) False drops in post coordinate indexing system cannot be eliminated

Code:

A. (*a*) and (*b*) are correct.
B. (*c*) and (*d*) are correct.
C. (*a*) and (*c*) are correct.
D. (*b*) and (*d*) are correct.

29. What will be the correct filing order of the following documents classified according to Colon classification, (6th reprint edition)?

(*a*) 23.44 Academic library system in India
(*b*) 23; 43 : 51.44 Classification of books in academic libraries in India
(*c*) 23 : 62 Lending services in academic libraries
(*d*) 23n4451, N82 Journal of Academic Libraries (published from New Delhi since 1982)

Code:

A. (*b*), (*c*), (*a*), (*d*)
B. (*d*), (*b*), (*c*), (*a*)
C. (*b*), (*c*), (*d*), (*a*)
D. (*d*), (*a*), (*c*), (*b*)

30. According to Ranganathan's classified catalogue code (5th edition), in which among the following cases the initial article is to be omitted?

(*a*) In rendering the name of a conference
(*b*) In rendering the name of a government
(*c*) In rendering the name of a series
(*d*) In rendering the name of an institution

Code:

A. (*a*) and (*b*) are correct.
B. (*b*) and (*d*) are correct.
C. (*a*), (*c*) and (*d*) are correct.
D. (*b*), (*c*) and (*d*) are correct.

31. Which of the following theories are related to motivation of employees:

(*a*) Theory 'Z' of the Japanese style of Management propounded by William Ouchi

(*b*) Theory 'X' and Theory 'Y' of Douglas McGregar

(*c*) Max Weber's Theory of Bureaucratic Management

(*d*) Maslow's Hierarchy of Needs Theory

Code:

A. (*a*), (*b*) and (*d*) are correct.
B. (*b*), (*c*), (*d*) are correct.
C. (*a*), (*b*), (*c*) are correct.
D. (*a*), (*c*), (*d*) are correct.

32. Identify the ways in which the library can benefit from the TQM as stated by Jurow and Barnard:

(*a*) Breaking down interdepartmental barriers.

(*b*) Redefining the beneficiaries of library services as internal customers (staff) and external customers (patrons).

(*c*) More inclined to short-term goals and defiant to changes to suit users needs.

(*d*) Reaching a state of continuous improvement.

Code:

A. (*a*), (*b*) and (*c*) are correct.
B. (*b*), (*c*) and (*d*) are correct.
C. (*a*), (*c*) and (*d*) are correct.
D. (*a*), (*b*) and (*d*) are correct.

33. Identify the cases that require an application for a new ISSN number:

(*a*) Change in the publication's medium

(*b*) Change in publisher

(*c*) Change in the frequency of publication

(*d*) Change in publication title

Code:

A. (*a*) and (*b*) are correct.
B. (*c*) and (*d*) are correct.
C. (*a*) and (*d*) are correct.
D. (*b*) and (*c*) are correct.

34. Identify the key salient traits of Soft data:

(*a*) human intelligence

(*b*) certain and definite

(*c*) opinions and contradictions

(*d*) no scope for constructive criticisms

Code:

A. (*a*) and (*b*) are correct.
B. (*c*) and (*d*) are correct.
C. (*a*) and (*c*) are correct.
D. (*b*) and (*d*) are correct.

35. Identify the components of 'LAMP' given below:

(*a*) Linux (*b*) Acrobat

(*c*) MYSQL (*d*) Pearl

Code:

A. (*b*) and (*c*) are correct.
B. (*a*) and (*c*) are correct.
C. (*a*) and (*d*) are correct.
D. (*b*) and (*d*) are correct.

36. Identify the features of proprietary software:

(*a*) Continuity and Development

(*b*) Ease of use

(*c*) Transparency

(*d*) Documentation and Support

Code:

A. (*a*), (*b*) and (*d*) are correct.
B. (*b*), (*c*) and (*d*) are correct.
C. (*a*), (*b*) and (*c*) are correct.
D. (*a*), (*c*) and (*d*) are correct.

37. Which of the following research methods are used in a study of scattering of periodicals?

(*a*) Biobibliometric study

(*b*) Bibliometric study

(*c*) Citation analysis study

(*d*) Altmetric study

Code:

A. (*a*) and (*d*) are correct.
B. (*b*) and (*c*) are correct.
C. (*a*) and (*c*) are correct.
D. (*a*), (*b*) and (*c*) are correct.

38. Information seeking behaviour (ISB) essentially refers to and concerned with:

(*a*) De-recognition of some needs perceived by the user.

(*b*) The strategies and actions undertaken to locate discrete knowledge elements.

(*c*) The experiment conducted on usefulness of library collection with reference to a non-purposive and conscious need of a particular piece of information.
(*d*) Interactive utilization of three basic resources such as people, information and system.

Code:

A. (*a*) and (*b*) are correct.
B. (*c*) and (*d*) are correct.
C. (*a*) and (*c*) are correct.
D. (*b*) and (*d*) are correct.

39. A virtual library:
(*a*) Presupposes a physical existence.
(*b*) Collection of resources available on one or more computer systems with a single interface or entry point to the collection.
(*c*) Does not provide access to entire content of a (digital) library via internet.
(*d*) Provides user assistance services such as reference, inter library loan, etc.

Code:

A. (*a*) and (*b*) are correct.
B. (*b*) and (*c*) are correct.
C. (*b*) and (*d*) are correct.
D. (*a*) and (*c*) are correct.

40. Which of the following are review type services?
(*a*) Current Awareness List
(*b*) Trend Reports
(*c*) News clippings
(*d*) State of the Art Report

Code:

A. (*a*) and (*b*) are correct.
B. (*a*) and (*d*) are correct.
C. (*b*) and (*d*) are correct.
D. (*b*) and (*c*) are correct.

41. Match the following Sections of Copyright Act 1957 (India) with their correct explanation:

List-I	List-II
(*a*) Section 55	(*i*) Offence of infringement of copyright
(*b*) Section 63	(*ii*) Enhanced penalty on second and subsequent convictions
(*c*) Section 63 A	(*iii*) Civil remedies for infringement of copyright
(*d*) Section 64	(*iv*) Power of police to seize infringing copies

Code:

	(*a*)	(*b*)	(*c*)	(*d*)
A.	(*iii*)	(*ii*)	(*i*)	(*iv*)
B.	(*iii*)	(*i*)	(*ii*)	(*iv*)
C.	(*ii*)	(*iii*)	(*i*)	(*iv*)
D.	(*ii*)	(*iv*)	(*iii*)	(*i*)

42. Match the following intellectual property rights concepts with their relevant features:

List-I	List-II
(*a*) Copyright	(*i*) Commercial source indicators and distinctive signs
(*b*) Patents	(*ii*) A treaty between Government and inventor
(*c*) Trade Secrets	(*iii*) Economic rights
(*d*) Trademarks	(*iv*) Information used in operation of a business invaluable to afford the potential economic utility

Code:

	(*a*)	(*b*)	(*c*)	(*d*)
A.	(*i*)	(*ii*)	(*iii*)	(*iv*)
B.	(*iii*)	(*ii*)	(*iv*)	(*i*)
C.	(*iv*)	(*iii*)	(*ii*)	(*i*)
D.	(*ii*)	(*iv*)	(*i*)	(*iii*)

43. Match the President of IFLA with his/her tenure:

List-I	List-II
(*a*) Sinikka Sipila	(*i*) 2015 - 2017
(*b*) Ellen Tise	(*ii*) 2017 - 2019
(*c*) Donna Scheeder	(*iii*) 2011 - 2013
(*d*) Gloria Perez Salmeron	(*iv*) 2013 - 2015

Code:

	(*a*)	(*b*)	(*c*)	(*d*)
A.	(*i*)	(*ii*)	(*iii*)	(*iv*)
B.	(*ii*)	(*i*)	(*iv*)	(*iii*)
C.	(*iii*)	(*iv*)	(*i*)	(*ii*)
D.	(*iv*)	(*ii*)	(*iii*)	(*i*)

44. Match the following:

List-I	List-II
(*a*) Library Journal	(*i*) Reed Business Information
(*b*) Library Quarterly	(*ii*) Emerald Group Publishing Ltd
(*c*) Library Review	(*iii*) John Hopkins University Press
(*d*) Library Trends	(*iv*) University of Chicago Press

Code:

	(*a*)	(*b*)	(*c*)	(*d*)
A.	(*i*)	(*ii*)	(*iii*)	(*iv*)
B.	(*iv*)	(*i*)	(*iii*)	(*ii*)
C.	(*i*)	(*iv*)	(*ii*)	(*iii*)
D.	(*iv*)	(*iii*)	(*ii*)	(*i*)

45. Match the following queries with their appropriate category of reference sources:

List-I	List-II
(*a*) Enrolment of students in a university	(*i*) Year Book
(*b*) Weather of Denmark	(*ii*) Statistical sources
(*c*) Number of foreigners visited World Book Fair in 2016	(*iii*) Directory
(*d*) Number of Hospitals in Singapore	(*iv*) Geographical sources

Code:

	(*a*)	(*b*)	(*c*)	(*d*)
A.	(*iv*)	(*iii*)	(*i*)	(*ii*)
B.	(*i*)	(*iii*)	(*ii*)	(*iv*)
C.	(*ii*)	(*iv*)	(*i*)	(*iii*)
D.	(*iii*)	(*iv*)	(*i*)	(*ii*)

46. Match the following titles with their class numbers according to CC 6th edition:

List-I	List-II
(*a*) Small pox	(*i*) L293 : 46
(*b*) Fever	(*ii*) L : 414
(*c*) Diabetics	(*iii*) L35 : 4261
(*d*) Malaria	(*iv*) L : 4231

Code:

	(*a*)	(*b*)	(*c*)	(*d*)
A.	(*i*)	(*iv*)	(*ii*)	(*iii*)
B.	(*iv*)	(*ii*)	(*i*)	(*iii*)
C.	(*ii*)	(*iii*)	(*i*)	(*iv*)
D.	(*iii*)	(*iv*)	(*i*)	(*ii*)

47. Match the following Search Engines with their corresponding subjects/or scientific research discovery information they offer:

List-I	List-II
(*a*) Vadlo	(*i*) Web resources including Twitter and Job Posting
(*b*) Mamma	(*ii*) Life Science Literature
(*c*) Athenus	(*iii*) World's Known Living Languages
(*d*) Ethnologue	(*iv*) Science and Engineering

Code:

	(*a*)	(*b*)	(*c*)	(*d*)
A.	(*i*)	(*iii*)	(*iv*)	(*ii*)
B.	(*iii*)	(*iv*)	(*ii*)	(*i*)
C.	(*ii*)	(*iv*)	(*iii*)	(*i*)
D.	(*ii*)	(*i*)	(*iv*)	(*iii*)

48. Match the following number of Anteriorising common isolates (Applicable before space facet) of colon classification (6th reprint edition) with their correct terms:

List-I (Number)	List-II (Term)
(*a*) Y^1	(*i*) Synopsis
(*b*) Y^3	(*ii*) Case study
(*c*) Y^7	(*iii*) Digest
(*d*) Y^8	(*iv*) Program of instruction

Code:

	(*a*)	(*b*)	(*c*)	(*d*)
A.	(*iv*)	(*i*)	(*ii*)	(*iii*)
B.	(*iv*)	(*ii*)	(*iii*)	(*i*)
C.	(*i*)	(*ii*)	(*iv*)	(*iii*)
D.	(*i*)	(*ii*)	(*iii*)	(*iv*)

49. Match the following MARC fields with their corresponding descriptions:

List-I	List-II
(*a*) 020	(*i*) Electronic Location and Access
(*b*) 250	(*ii*) Edition Statement
(*c*) 440	(*iii*) Series
(*d*) 856	(*iv*) ISBN

Code:

	(*a*)	(*b*)	(*c*)	(*d*)
A.	(*i*)	(*ii*)	(*iii*)	(*iv*)
B.	(*iv*)	(*ii*)	(*iii*)	(*i*)
C.	(*iv*)	(*iii*)	(*ii*)	(*i*)
D.	(*ii*)	(*i*)	(*iv*)	(*iii*)

50. Match the following popular social networking sites with their corresponding founders:

List-I	List-II
(*a*) Blog	(*i*) Tim Vanderhook and Justin Timberlake
(*b*) Wikis	(*ii*) Google
(*c*) Linkedin	(*iii*) Word Cunningham
(*d*) Myspace	(*iv*) Reid Hoffman and his friends

Code:

	(*a*)	(*b*)	(*c*)	(*d*)
A.	(*ii*)	(*iii*)	(*iv*)	(*i*)
B.	(*i*)	(*ii*)	(*iii*)	(*iv*)
C.	(*iv*)	(*iii*)	(*ii*)	(*i*)
D.	(*iii*)	(*i*)	(*iv*)	(*ii*)

51. Match the following:

List-I	List-II
(*a*) Chester Carlton	(*i*) e - Book
(*b*) Brewstu Kable	(*ii*) Xerox Copier
(*c*) Michael S. Hart	(*iii*) NDLTD
(*d*) Edward Fox	(*iv*) Internet Archive

Code:

	(*a*)	(*b*)	(*c*)	(*d*)
A.	(*ii*)	(*iv*)	(*i*)	(*iii*)
B.	(*iv*)	(*iii*)	(*ii*)	(*i*)
C.	(*iv*)	(*i*)	(*iii*)	(*ii*)
D.	(*i*)	(*ii*)	(*iii*)	(*iv*)

52. Match the following domains of application with their corresponding metadata schemes:

List-I	List-II
(*a*) ETD domain	(*i*) METS
(*b*) Image domain	(*ii*) CCO
(*c*) Cultural objects	(*iii*) ConCore
(*d*) Learning objects	(*iv*) VRA-Core

Code:

	(*a*)	(*b*)	(*c*)	(*d*)
A.	(*i*)	(*ii*)	(*iii*)	(*iv*)
B.	(*i*)	(*ii*)	(*iv*)	(*iii*)
C.	(*iii*)	(*ii*)	(*i*)	(*iv*)
D.	(*i*)	(*iv*)	(*ii*)	(*iii*)

53. Match the following:

List-I	List-II
(*a*) Infomix	(*i*) Image software
(*b*) Omni page	(*ii*) Remote login software
(*c*) Tiff viewer	(*iii*) DBMS software
(*d*) Team viewer	(*iv*) OCR software

Code:

	(*a*)	(*b*)	(*c*)	(*d*)
A.	(*ii*)	(*i*)	(*iii*)	(*iv*)
B.	(*iii*)	(*iv*)	(*i*)	(*ii*)
C.	(*i*)	(*ii*)	(*iii*)	(*iv*)
D.	(*iv*)	(*iii*)	(*ii*)	(*i*)

54. Match the following:

List-I (Term)	List-II (Explanation)
(*a*) Data mart	(*i*) Specific analytic technique that examining large pre-existing databases in order to generate new information.
(*b*) Data silo	(*ii*) Systems that integrate data from databases across an entire enterprise, used to guide decisions.
(*c*) Data warehouse	(*iii*) Is a lower-cost, scaled-down version of a data warehouse that can be implemented in a much shorter time.
(*d*) Data mining	(*iv*) Stand alone data stores available for a specific function.

Code:

	(*a*)	(*b*)	(*c*)	(*d*)
A.	(*ii*)	(*iv*)	(*i*)	(*iii*)
B.	(*i*)	(*iii*)	(*iv*)	(*ii*)
C.	(*iv*)	(*iii*)	(*i*)	(*ii*)
D.	(*iii*)	(*iv*)	(*ii*)	(*i*)

55. Match the following terms with their corresponding descriptors:

List-I	List-II
(*a*) Term List	(*i*) Ontologies
(*b*) Categories	(*ii*) System software
(*c*) Relationship List	(*iii*) Taxonomy
(*d*) Emulators	(*iv*) Glossaries

Code:

	(*a*)	(*b*)	(*c*)	(*d*)
A.	(*ii*)	(*iii*)	(*iv*)	(*i*)
B.	(*iii*)	(*ii*)	(*i*)	(*iv*)
C.	(*iv*)	(*i*)	(*ii*)	(*iii*)
D.	(*iv*)	(*iii*)	(*i*)	(*ii*)

56. Match the following:

List-I	List-II
(*a*) Muktabodha	(*i*) Research Gate
(*b*) Net First	(*ii*) Online citation and reference management tool
(*c*) Zotero	(*iii*) Abstracting and indexing database of OCLC
(*d*) R.G. Score	(*iv*) Digital Library of Indology

Code:

	(*a*)	(*b*)	(*c*)	(*d*)
A.	(*iv*)	(*iii*)	(*ii*)	(*i*)
B.	(*iv*)	(*ii*)	(*iii*)	(*i*)
C.	(*ii*)	(*i*)	(*iv*)	(*iii*)
D.	(*iii*)	(*ii*)	(*i*)	(*iv*)

57. Match the following communication concepts with corresponding explanations:

List-I	List-II
(*a*) Kinesics communication	(*i*) Use of touch to communication
(*b*) Haptics communication	(*ii*) Use of Interpersonal space
(*c*) Proxemics communication	(*iii*) Facial Expression, gestures, eye movement
(*d*) Iconics communication	(*iv*) Interpretation of symbolism

Code:

	(*a*)	(*b*)	(*c*)	(*d*)
A.	(*i*)	(*iii*)	(*ii*)	(*iv*)
B.	(*iii*)	(*iv*)	(*ii*)	(*i*)
C.	(*ii*)	(*iii*)	(*i*)	(*iv*)
D.	(*iii*)	(*i*)	(*ii*)	(*iv*)

58. Match the following:

List-I Types of Research	List-II Focus
(*a*) Ethnographic	(*i*) Present events
(*b*) Evaluative	(*ii*) Social behaviour
(*c*) Descriptive	(*iii*) Causation
(*d*) Experimental	(*iv*) Judgement about quality

Code:

	(*a*)	(*b*)	(*c*)	(*d*)
A.	(*ii*)	(*iv*)	(*i*)	(*iii*)
B.	(*iv*)	(*iii*)	(*ii*)	(*i*)
C.	(*ii*)	(*iii*)	(*iv*)	(*i*)
D.	(*iv*)	(*ii*)	(*i*)	(*iii*)

59. Match the following:

List-I Countries	List-II Name of the Library
(*a*) Egypt	(*i*) Library of Ashurbanipal
(*b*) Turkey	(*ii*) Villa of Papyri
(*c*) Italy	(*iii*) Library of Pergamum
(*d*) Iraq	(*iv*) Royal Library of Alexandria

Code:

	(*a*)	(*b*)	(*c*)	(*d*)
A.	(*iv*)	(*ii*)	(*iii*)	(*i*)
B.	(*iv*)	(*iii*)	(*ii*)	(*i*)
C.	(*i*)	(*iii*)	(*iv*)	(*ii*)
D.	(*iii*)	(*ii*)	(*i*)	(*iv*)

60. Match the following:

List-I	List-II
(*a*) Dr. Zakir Husain Library	(*i*) Indian Institute of Science, Bangalore
(*b*) J.R.D. Tata Library	(*ii*) Jamia Millia Islamia, Delhi
(*c*) Sayaji Rao Gaekwad Library	(*iii*) IIM, Ahmedabad
(*d*) Vikram Sarabhai Library	(*iv*) B.H.U. Varanasi

Code:

	(*a*)	(*b*)	(*c*)	(*d*)
A.	(*iv*)	(*iii*)	(*i*)	(*ii*)
B.	(*ii*)	(*i*)	(*iv*)	(*iii*)
C.	(*i*)	(*ii*)	(*iii*)	(*iv*)
D.	(*ii*)	(*iii*)	(*i*)	(*iv*)

61. Arrange the following IPR related Acts in India according to their year of enactment:

(*a*) The Copy Right Act
(*b*) The Design Act
(*c*) Information Technology Act
(*d*) Trade and Merchandise Marks Act

Code:

A. (*a*), (*b*), (*d*), (*c*) B. (*b*), (*a*), (*d*), (*c*)
C. (*c*), (*b*), (*d*), (*a*) D. (*d*), (*a*), (*b*), (*c*)

62. Arrange the following Padma Shri award recipients in chronological of their year of the award:
(*a*) Bellari Shamanna Kesavan
(*b*) Shiyali Ramamrita Ranganathan
(*c*) Prithvi Nath Kaula
(*d*) Iyyanki Venkata Ramanayya
Code:
A. (*a*), (*b*), (*c*) and (*d*)
B. (*a*), (*d*), (*b*) and (*c*)
C. (*b*), (*a*), (*d*) and (*c*)
D. (*b*), (*d*), (*a*) and (*c*)

63. Arrange the following Public Libraries Acts according to their year of enactment:
(*a*) Bihar Public Libraries Act
(*b*) Uttaranchal Public Libraries Act
(*c*) Haryana Public Libraries Act
(*d*) Orissa Public Libraries Act
Code:
A. (*b*), (*d*), (*a*), (*c*)
B. (*a*), (*b*), (*c*), (*d*)
C. (*d*), (*c*), (*b*), (*a*)
D. (*c*), (*d*), (*b*), (*a*)

64. Arrange the following laws of Library Science enunciated by S.R. Ranganathan in a sequence as recorded by L.S. Connaway and I.M. Faniel for OCLC Project.
(*a*) Library is a growing organism
(*b*) Save the time of the readers
(*c*) Books are for use
(*d*) Every book its reader
Code:
A. (*b*), (*c*), (*d*), (*a*)
B. (*c*), (*d*), (*a*), (*b*)
C. (*a*), (*b*), (*c*), (*d*)
D. (*d*), (*a*), (*b*), (*c*)

65. Arrange the following Information Sources according to their first year of Publication:
(*a*) Ulrich's International Periodical Directory
(*b*) Guide to Indian Periodical Literature
(*c*) Library Literature
(*d*) Indian Science Abstracts
Code:
A. (*a*), (*c*), (*b*), (*d*) B. (*b*), (*c*), (*d*), (*a*)
C. (*c*), (*a*), (*b*), (*d*) D. (*d*), (*a*), (*b*), (*c*)

66. Arrange the following according to the year of their first publication:
(*a*) Bibliotheca Universalis by Konard Gesner
(*b*) Catalogue of Books in the 15th century by the British Museum
(*c*) The Bibliographic Instructive Rare Books by G.E. Bura
(*d*) Union catalogue of learned periodical Publications in South Asia by S.R. Ranganathan
Code:
A. (*a*), (*b*), (*d*), (*c*)
B. (*b*), (*a*), (*d*), (*c*)
C. (*a*), (*c*), (*b*), (*d*)
D. (*d*), (*a*), (*c*), (*b*)

67. Arrange the following e-book sites according to the chronological order of their origin:
(*a*) Project Gutenberg
(*b*) Open Library
(*c*) Google Books
(*d*) DOAB
Code:
A. (*a*), (*c*), (*b*), (*d*)
B. (*b*), (*a*), (*c*), (*d*)
C. (*c*), (*b*), (*d*), (*a*)
D. (*d*), (*c*), (*a*), (*b*)

68. Arrange the following entities according to FRBR Model:
(*a*) Item
(*b*) Expression
(*c*) Work
(*d*) Manifestation
Code:
A. (*c*), (*b*), (*d*), (*a*)
B. (*d*), (*a*), (*b*), (*c*)
C. (*c*), (*d*), (*a*), (*b*)
D. (*c*), (*a*), (*b*), (*d*)

69. Find out the correct sequence of the following forms of Main Class Literature according to Colon Classification (sixth reprint edition):
A. Poetry, Fiction, Campu, Oration
B. Poetry, Fiction, Oration, Campu
C. Poetry, Oration, Fiction, Campu
D. Fiction, Poetry, Campu, Oration

70. Which of the following Sections Constitute the parts of main entry according to CCC (Ed.5)?
(*a*) Leading Section
(*b*) Title Section
(*c*) Format Section
(*d*) Note Section
Code:
A. (*a*), (*b*) and (*c*) are correct.
B. (*a*), (*b*) and (*d*) are correct.
C. (*b*), (*c*) and (*d*) are correct.
D. (*a*), (*c*) and (*d*) are correct.

71. Which of the following are the features of Vector Space Model IR ?
(*a*) Complex model based on non-linear algebra
(*b*) Term weights are not binary
(*c*) Allows computing a continuous degree of similarity between queries and documents
(*d*) Do not allow ranking documents according to their possible relevance
Code:
A. (*a*) and (*b*) are correct.
B. (*b*) and (*c*) are correct.
C. (*c*) and (*d*) are correct.
D. (*a*) and (*d*) are correct.

72. Arrange the following work components of WINISIS according to the order of sequence of approach:
(*a*) FST (*b*) FDT
(*c*) Print Format (*d*) Worksheet
Code:
A. (*b*), (*d*), (*c*), (*a*)
B. (*b*), (*c*), (*d*), (*a*)
C. (*a*), (*b*), (*c*), (*d*)
D. (*d*), (*c*), (*b*), (*a*)

73. Arrange the following according to their year of origin:
(*a*) Myspace (*b*) MOSAIC
(*c*) Friendster (*d*) Blogger
Code:
A. (*b*), (*c*), (*a*), (*d*)
B. (*a*), (*d*), (*c*), (*b*)
C. (*b*), (*d*), (*c*), (*a*)
D. (*d*), (*b*), (*c*), (*a*)

74. Arrange the filters as proposed by Robert S. Tylor that may be employed by Librarians to approximate the higher information needs of individuals.
(*a*) Personal characteristics of the inquirer
(*b*) Relationship of inquiry description to file organisation
(*c*) Objective and motivation
(*d*) Determination of the subject
Code:
A. (*c*), (*a*), (*b*), (*d*) B. (*d*), (*c*), (*a*), (*b*)
C. (*a*), (*c*), (*b*), (*d*) D. (*d*), (*b*), (*a*), (*c*)

75. Arrange the names of the following librarians of Library of Congress in the chronological order of their period of service in LC:
(*a*) Carla Hayden
(*b*) John James Beckley
(*c*) James H. Billington
(*d*) George Waterston
Code:
A. (*b*), (*d*), (*c*), (*a*) B. (*a*), (*b*), (*c*), (*d*)
C. (*a*), (*b*), (*d*), (*c*) D. (*b*), (*a*), (*d*), (*c*)

76. Assertion (A) : Information, not data, is the fundamental fuel of the current Big Data Phenomenon.
Reason (R) : The reason behind the quick expansion of Big Data is the extensive degree to which data are created, shared and utilised in recent times.
Code:
A. (A) is false, but (R) is true.
B. (R) is false, but (A) is true.
C. Both (A) and (R) are false.
D. Both (A) and (R) are true.

77. Assertion (A) : Preprint archives, such as arxiv and SSRN rapidly achieved prominence in the field of scholarly communication.
Reason (R) : These archives contain Preprint along with DOI.
Code:
A. Both (A) and (R) are true.
B. Both (A) and (R) are false.
C. (A) is false, but (R) is true.
D. (A) is true, but (R) is false.

78. Assertion (A) : There has been a demand for data exchange between library catalogues and databases with records of documentary information.

Reason (R) : Interoperatability leads to information reuse as a requisite to access data, and takes into account quality, contents, knowledge, products and services.

Code:

A. Both (A) and (R) are true.
B. Both (A) and (R) are false.
C. (A) is true, but (R) is false.
D. (A) is false, but (R) is true.

79. Assertion (A) : Inclusion of DOAJ implies the quality of an open access journals.

Reason (R) : DOAJ is an online directory that indexes and provides access to open access and peer viewed journals. Besides DOAJ has tightened the listing criteria.

Code:

A. Both (A) and (R) are true.
B. Both (A) and (R) are false.
C. (A) is false, but (R) is true.
D. (A) is true, but (R) is false.

80. Assertion (A) : In the Information Retrieval domain, Probabilistic Model is becoming unpopular.

Reason (R) : Probabilistic Model fails to provide accurate estimate for the first run probabilities since index terms are not weighted and terms are assumed mutually independent.

Code:

A. (A) is true, but (R) is false.
B. Both (A) and (R) are true.
C. (A) is false, but (R) is true.
D. Both (A) and (R) are false.

81. Assertion (A) : System effectiveness may be evident while evaluating an IR system but cost effectiveness may not be satisfactory.

Reason (R) : A cost effectiveness study of an IR system is the evaluation in terms of how to satisfy the users' information requirements in the most efficient and economical way.

Code:

A. (A) is false, but (R) is true.
B. (A) is true, but (R) is false.
C. Both (A) and (R) are true.
D. Both (A) and (R) are false.

82. Assertion (A) : Principle of canonical sequence is mainly followed to arrange the array of subjects in a classification scheme.

Reason (R) : This principle sets the proviso that when subjects in an array of subjects are traditionally referred to in a specific sequence, it will be convenient to conform to this traditional sequence.

Code:

A. Both (A) and (R) are true.
B. (A) is false, but (R) is true.
C. Both (A) and (R) are false.
D. (A) is true, but (R) is false.

83. Assertion (A) : TREC is credited for bringing the concept of the evaluation of IR system.

Reason (R) : TREC series of IR experiment has drawn attention of the LIS professionals all over the world for providing an open testing event and standard evaluation scenario.

Code:

A. Both (A) and (R) are false.
B. Both (A) and (R) are true.
C. (A) is false, but (R) is true.
D. (A) is true, but (R) is false.

84. Assertion (A) : As is true for an organisation, effective leadership is crucial for success, as poor managerial leadership may mar the organisational goals.

Reason (R) : Patterns of poor managerial leadership create low morale, poor organisational climate, distrust towards supervisors among subordinates, lack of team work and consensus building and shared goals, etc. which are the clear indicators of a wrong person attained a managerial leadership position.

Code:

A. (A) is true, but (R) is false.
B. (A) is false, but (R) is true.
C. Both (A) and (R) are true.
D. Both (A) and (R) are false.

85. Assertion (A) : Netiquette mandates that you do your best to act within the laws of cyberspace and society.

Reason (R) : Failing to respect others privacy and impolite way of communication in considered breach of Netiquette.

Code:

A. Both (A) and (R) are false.
B. Both (A) and (R) are true.
C. (A) is true, but (R) is false.
D. (A) is false, but (R) is true.

86. Assertion (A) : Serial crisis led to the formation of library consortia around the world.

Reason (R) : Serial crisis arises due to the situation in which budget of the library for subscription of Journals remains static in spite of rising subscription cost of Journals which in turn affect the collection development policy of the libraries.

Code:

A. Both (A) and (R) are true.
B. Both (A) and (R) are false.
C. (A) is true, but (R) is false.
D. (A) is false, but (R) is true.

87. Assertion (A) : Plagarism is the wrongful appreciation and stealing and publication of another author's language, thought, ideas or expressions.

Reason (R) : Plagarism is in itself a crime, and thus constitute copyright infringement.

Code:

A. (A) is true, but (R) is false
B. (A) is false, but (R) is true.
C. Both (A) and (R) are false.
D. Both (A) and (R) are true.

88. Assertion (A) : The Mendeley is one of the most preferred online reference managers which can store bibliographic records as well as full text documents and help in creating bibliographical references in any popular citation style like APA, MLA, or Chicago style.

Reason (R) : Web-based solutions related to online reference management have become freely available to the global researchers engaged in collaborative research project.

Code:

A. Both (A) and (R) are false.
B. Both (A) and (R) are true.
C. (A) is false, but (R) is true.
D. (A) is true, but (R) is false.

89. Assertion (A) : Dr. Eugene Garfields original invention still continues to serve as a reliable and efficient guide to the sprawling world of research.

Reason (R) : Garfield was not only honoured for his work in developing the field of Citation Analysis, but also his subsequent contribution in founding ISI (1960) that developed and launched SCI (1964) consequently led to the development of numerous citation databases of first order including 'Web of Science', all of which brought him an idiomatic identity in the research world till the date.

Code:

A. (A) is true, but (R) is false.
B. (A) is false, but (R) is true.
C. Both (A) and (R) are true.
D. Both (A) and (R) are false.

90. Assertion (A) : In technical writing, style manuals and citation standards are essential in structuring and maintaining uniformity of research report.

Reason (R) : The Quality of research can be achieved only by standardising the structure of research report, but not by the content.

Code:

A. Both (A) and (R) are true.
B. Both (A) and (R) are false.
C. (A) is true, but (R) is false.
D. (R) is true, but (A) is false.

91. Assertion (A) : Delphi Techniques in Social Science Research do not give weightage to consensus.

Reason (R) : Consensus opinions expressed by the panel of experts is valuable in drawing inferences.

Code:

A. (A) is true, but (R) is false.
B. (A) is false, but (R) is true.
C. Both (A) and (R) are true.
D. Both (R) and (A) are false.

92. Assertion (A) : In social research, a high proportion of refusals to answer a research always occurs solely due to inadequate interview instructions or poor interview training.

Reason (R) : Within the questionnaire or interview, even a substantive number of questions often remain unanswered making difficult for the researcher to state an exact figure and forcing him to restudy the questions carefully as fault might lie upon a poor transition.

Code:

A. (A) is true, but (R) is false.
B. (A) is false, but (R) is true.
C. Both (A) and (R) are true.
D. Both (A) and (R) are false.

93. Assertion (A) : In recent times, it is easier to copy, and paste the contents from a digital documents for which people knowingly avoid to credit the sources. Increased access to digital documents has provided a means for increase of plagiarism.

Reason (R) : Software assisted detection tools like ithenticate, turnitin etc. now allow vast collection of online documents to be compared to each other making successful detection of plagiarism.

Code:

A. Both (A) and (R) are false.
B. (A) is true, but (R) is false.
C. (R) is true, but (A) is false.
D. Both (A) and (R) are true.

94. Assertion (A) : F.W. Lancaster's cocksure prediction of a paperless society by the end of 20th century holds no good.

Reason (R) : Transition from print dominance to paperless ascendancy, change from scroll to codex and introduction of movable type were not only the few historical shifts, but were also hugely significant innovations. Inspite of rapid technological changes, the future libraries will still accommodate a very large print collection. However, the propelling vision of an information driven paperless society, though seems inevitable to avoid space, staff, and cost crunch, may buy more time to become a reality.

Code:

A. (A) is true, but (R) is false.
B. (A) is false, but (R) is true.
C. Both (A) and (R) are true.
D. Both (A) and (R) are false.

95. Assertion (A) : The curriculum of LIS education in India is mostly unsteady as local LIS requirements vary.

Reason (R) : Adoption of UGC model syllabus is not mandatory for the LIS schools in India.

Code:

A. (A) is true, but (R) is false.
B. (A) is false, but (R) is true.
C. Both (A) and (R) are true.
D. Both (A) and (R) are false.

Direction (Qs. 96-100): *Read the following passage carefully and answer the questions based on your understanding:*

In the agentic sociocognitive view, people are self-organizing, proactive, self-reflecting, and self-regulating, not just reactive organisms shaped and shepherded by external events. People have the power to influence their own actions to produce certain results. The capacity to exercise control over one's thought processes, motivation, affect, and action operates through mechanisms of personal agency. Human agency has been conceptualized in at least three different ways – as either autonomous agency, mechanically reactive agency or emergent interactive agency. The notion that humans operate as entirely independent agents has few serious advocates, although it is sometimes invoked in caricatures of cognitive theories of human behaviour.

The tools for the exercise of agency are derived, in large part, from experiences but what is created by their generative use is not reducible to those experiences. Human action, being socially situated, is the product of a dynamic interplay of personal and situational influences.

A second approach to the self system is to construe it as mechanically reactive agency. It is an internal system through which external influences operate mechanistically on action, but individuals exert no motivative, self-reflective, self-reactive, creative or directive influence on the process. The self system is merely a repository for implanted structures and a conduit for external influences. The more dynamic models operating holistically include multilevel neural networks. However, a diverse mix of parallel distributed neural activity cannot remain fragmented. It requires an integrative system. Given the proactive nature of human functioning, such a system must have agentic capabilities as well as integrative reactive ones. Agentic functions get lodged in a hidden network operating without any consciousness. Consciousness is the very substance of phenomenal and functional mental life. It provides the information base for thinking about events, planning, constructing courses of action and reflecting on the adequacy of one's thinking and actions. There is an important difference between being conscious of the experiences one is undergoing, and consciously producing given experiences. For example, consciousness of one's heart rate and consciously and intentionally doing things known to elevate one's heart rate illustrate the difference between passive undergoing and agentic doing. The purposive accessing and deliberative processing of information to fashion efficacious courses of action represent the functional consciousness. Consciousness cannot be reduced to an epiphenomenon of the output of a mental process realized mechanically at nonconscious lower levels. In the connectionist line of theorizing, sensory organs deliver up information through their diverse pathways to the hidden network acting as the cognitive agent that does the construing, planning, motivating and regulating. However, stripped of consciousness and agentic capability of decision and action, people are mere automatons undergoing actions devoid of any subjectivity, conscious regulation, phenomenological life, or personal identity.

96. In the agentic socio-cognitive view, "human action" is the product of :

A. A dynamic interplay of personal and situational influences
B. Personal determinants and mechanisms of human functioning
C. Social bespoke and practices
D. Schematic processing of experiences and memory representation

97. Why the second approach to the 'self system' is construed by the author as "mechanically reactive agency"?

A. An external system through which internal influences operate mechanically.
B. An internal system through which external influences operate mechanically on action having no directive influence exerted by the individuals on process.
C. An external system through which external influences operate mechanically on action.
D. An external system through which external influences operate in which individuals exert direct influence on the process.

98. According to the agentic view of "Personality", what does the 'self system' meant to the author?

A. A Repository for implanted structures and a conduit for internal influences.
B. A Repository for implanted structures and a conduit for external influences.
C. An archive for preserving unusual human instincts.
D. A Pen-stock to restrict the flow of unusual and instant human behaviour.

99. What does 'consciousness' conceptually meant to the author?

A. A demonstration of physical condition based on situation
B. The very substance of phenomenal and functional mental life
C. The rigid state of mental condition.
D. A Spiritual state of mind

100. How does the author differentiate between "passive undergoing" and "agentic doing" ?

A. Conscious of the experiences one is undergoing and consciously producing given experiences.
B. Conscious of the experiences one is undergoing, but fail to use the given experiences.
C. Conscious of the past experience and their wrongful use irrelevant to need.
D. Unconscious of the experience and their non-intentional use.

ANSWERS

1	2	3	4	5	6	7	8	9	10
*	B	B	B	A	A	C	B	B	A
11	12	13	14	15	16	17	18	19	20
B	C	C	C	D	C	D	C	D	B
21	22	23	24	25	26	27	28	29	30
B	C	A	C	D	C	A	C	D	C

31	32	33	34	35	36	37	38	39	40
A	D	C	C	B	A	B	D	C	C
41	**42**	**43**	**44**	**45**	**46**	**47**	**48**	**49**	**50**
B	B	*	C	D	B	D	A	B	A
51	**52**	**53**	**54**	**55**	**56**	**57**	**58**	**59**	**60**
A	D	B	D	D	A	D	A	B	B
61	**62**	**63**	**64**	**65**	**66**	**67**	**68**	**69**	**70**
*	C	D	A	A	C	A	A	B	B
71	**72**	**73**	**74**	**75**	**76**	**77**	**78**	**79**	**80**
B	A	C	B	A	D	D	A	A	B
81	**82**	**83**	**84**	**85**	**86**	**87**	**88**	**89**	**90**
C	A	C	C	B	A	D	B	C	C
91	**92**	**93**	**94**	**95**	**96**	**97**	**98**	**99**	**100**
B	B	D	B	C	A	B	B	B	A

* Error in Question/Option

EXPLANATORY ANSWERS

2. Committee number "MSD 5" having the name "Documentation and Information" is responsible for Indian standards related to libraries.

Bureau of Indian Standards is the National Standards Body of India, engaged in Standardization activity in various fields through its fourteen Division Councils, which includes Management and Systems Division Council (MSDC). Under this Division, Documentation and Information Sectional Committee, MSD 5 is engaged in standardization activity in the field of practices relating to libraries, documentation and information centers. Various areas of standardization cover, indexing and abstracting services, bibliographic formats, conservation and preservation of print and non-print medium, archives, information science, document imaging applications, data processing etc. Other areas relate to processing and handling of documents, besides coordination with related international committees for standardization *i.e.* ISO, with a view to disseminate its knowledge and promote its application. Standards play an active role in effective and efficient management of various practices, processes and systems. It is a tool for effective management of documentation and information systems.

3. World Book and Copyright Day is a celebration to promote the enjoyment of books and reading. Each year, on 23rd April, celebrations take place all over the world to recognize the scope of books—a link between the past and the future, a bridge between generations and across cultures. On this occasion, UNESCO and the international organizations representing the three major sectors of the book industry—publishers, booksellers and libraries, select the World Book Capital for a year to maintain, through its own initiatives, the impetus of the Day's celebrations.

23rd April is a symbolic date in world literature. It is the date on which several prominent authors, William Shakespeare, Miguel Cervantes and Inca Garcilaso de la Vega all died. This date was a natural choice for UNESCO's General Conference, held in

Paris in 1995, to pay a world-wide tribute to books and authors on this date, encouraging everyone to access books.

4. The National Policy on Information Technology 2012 aims to leverage Information & Communication Technology (ICT) to address the country's economic and developmental challenges. The policy is rooted in the conviction that ICT has the power to transform the lives of people.

The thrust areas of the policy include:

1. To increase revenues of IT and ITES (Information Technology Enabled Services) Industry from 100 Billion USD currently to 300 Billion USD by 2020 and expand exports from 69 Billion USD currently to 200 Billion USD by 2020.
2. To gain significant global market-share in emerging technologies and Services.
3. To promote innovation and R&D in cutting edge technologies and development of applications and solutions in areas like localization, location based services, mobile value added services, Cloud Computing, Social Media and Utility models.
4. To encourage adoption of ICTs in key economic and strategic sectors to improve their competitiveness and productivity.
5. To provide fiscal benefits to SMEs and Startups for adoption of IT in value creation.
6. To create a pool of 10 million additional skilled manpower in ICT.
7. To make at least one individual in every household e-literate.
8. To provide for mandatory delivery of and affordable access to all public services in electronic mode.
9. To enhance transparency, accountability, efficiency, reliability and decentralization in Government and in particular, in delivery of public services.
10. To leverage ICT for key Social Sector initiatives like Education, Health, Rural Development and Financial Services to promote equity and quality.
11. To make India the global hub for development of language technologies, to encourage and facilitate development of content accessible in all Indian languages and thereby help bridge the digital divide.
12. To enable access of content and ICT applications by differently-abled people to foster inclusive development.
13. To leverage ICT for expanding the work-force and enabling life-long learning.
14. To strengthen the Regulatory and Security Framework for ensuring a Secure and legally compliant Cyberspace ecosystem.
15. To adopt Open standards and promote open source and open technologies.

6. Wikipedia is a free-access, free-content Internet encyclopedia, supported and hosted by the non-profit Wikimedia Foundation. Those who can access the site can edit most of its articles. Wikipedia is ranked among the ten most popular websites and constitutes the Internet's largest and most popular general reference work. Jimmy Wales and Larry Sanger launched Wikipedia on January 15, 2001. Sanger coined its name, a portmanteau of wiki and encyclopedia. Initially only in English, Wikipedia quickly became multilingual as it developed similar versions in other languages, which differ in content and in editing practices.

7. The Planning Commission had already granted a major project in the area of translation to the Central Institute of Indian Languages (CIIL), Mysore under the title 'Anukriti'. The translation website titled Anukriti: Translating India was designed to function as a translation service and information site in all the Indian languages. The idea of creating such a website was conceived by three institutions devoted to the development of Indian languages—

Central Institute of Indian Languages (MHRD), Mysore, Sahitya Akademi and National Book Trust, New Delhi.

8. Ezproxy is a web proxy server used by libraries to give access from outside the library's computer network to restricted-access websites that authenticate users by IP address. This allows library patrons at home or elsewhere to log in through their library's Ezproxy server and gain access to resources to which their library subscribes, such as bibliographic databases.

The software was originally written by Chris Zagar in 1999 who founded Useful Utilities LLC to support it. OCLC announced in January, 2008 that it had acquired the product and was hiring Zagar as a full-time consultant for a year. Zagar is a librarian who serves as a systems librarian at the Estrella Mountain Community College, a part of the Maricopa Community Colleges in Arizona. He won the 2006 LITA/Brett Butler Entrepreneurship Award for his work with Ezproxy.

10. Some catalouging experts, among them Michael Gorman, criticized AACR1 for its emphasis on the concept of main entry, which Gorman called "a relic of outdated technology" made obsolete by computer-based catalougs with multiple access points for all works contained in the database. Part II of AACR2, rules for access points and headings, addresses itself to these problems, and in some instances makes substantive and worthwhile contributions toward solving them.

Rules for form of personal names in AACR2 are fundamentally the same as in AACR1, which followed the guidelines of the Paris Principles in most cases. However, AACR1 rules for both form and choice of entry for corporate bodies were not considered satisfactory. AACR2 rules for entry under corporate body show the influence of Eva Verona's definitive study of corporate bodies, in limiting main entry under corporate heading to works of an administrative nature dealing with the corporate body, its staff, its resources, or official statements recording the collective thought or activity of the body. Entry under government heading is limited to administrative regulations, decrees, laws, court rules, legislative hearings, treaties, charters and constitutions.

12. The path-goal theory, also known as the path-goal theory of leader effectiveness or the path-goal model, is a leadership theory developed by Robert House, an Ohio State University graduate, in 1971 and revised in 1996. The theory states that a leader's behaviour is contingent to the satisfaction, motivation and performance of his or her subordinates. The revised version also argues that the leader engages in behaviours that complement subordinate's abilities and compensate for deficiencies. According to Robert House and John Antonakis, the task-oriented elements of the path-goal model can be classified as a form of instrumental leadership.

13. Ambra is an innovative Open Source platform for publishing Open Access research articles. It provides features for post-publication discussion and versioned articles that allows for a "living" document around which further scientific discoveries can be made. The platform is in active development by PLOS (Public Library of Science) and is licensed under the MIT License.

Ambra is currently used for by the following journals and publishing platforms:

- *PLOS ONE*
- *PLOS Medicine*
- *PLOS Biology*
- *PLOS Computational Biology*
- *PLOS Pathogens*
- *PLOS Genetics*
- *PLOS Neglected Tropical Diseases*
- *PLOS Collections*

14. Jorn Barger is an American blogger, best known as editor of *Robot Wisdom,* an influential early weblog. Barger coined the term *weblog* to describe the process of "logging the web" as he surfed. He has also written extensively on James Joyce and artificial intelligence, among other subjects; his writing is almost entirely self-published.

15. Xbox Live is not file hosting service. Xbox Live is an online multiplayer gaming and digital media delivery service created and operated by Microsoft. It was first made available to the Xbox system in November, 2002. An updated version of the service became available for the Xbox 360 console at the system's launch in November 2005, and a further enhanced version was released in 2013 with the Xbox One. The service was extended in 2007 on the Windows platform, named Games for Windows—Live, which makes most aspects of the system available on Windows computers.

16. VuFind is a library resource portal designed and developed for libraries by libraries. The goal of VuFind is to enable your users to search and browse through all of your library's resources by replacing the traditional OPAC to include:

- Catalogue Records
- Locally Cached Journals
- Digital Library Items
- Institutional Repository
- Institutional Bibliography
- Other Library Collections and Resources

VuFind is completely modular so you can implement just the basic system, or all of the components. And since it's open source, you can modify the modules to best fit your need or you can add new modules to extend your resource offerings.

17. **Binary Number System:** Information within the computer is normally represented in binary form, because it is convenient to use circuits which have two clearly defined states. Thus a transistor can be fully conducting or non-conducting and magnetic material can be saturated, in one direction or the other to represent the two binary states 0 or 1. In the binary system the successive digit positions represent the powers of 2 in increasing significance. Thus, the decimal number 115 is represented in binary form as:

$1110011 = 1(2^6) + 1(2^5) + 1(2^4) + 0(2^3) + 0(2^2) + 1(2^1) + 1(2^0)$

The conversion is performed by successive subtraction of the highest power of 2 less than the decimal number. The conversion of decimal 115 to binary proceeds as follows:

$$115 - 2^6 = 115 - 64 = 51$$

$$51 - 2^5 = 51 - 32 = 19$$

$$19 - 2^4 = 19 - 16 = 3$$

3 is less than 2^3
and less than 2^2

$$3 - 1^1 = 3 - 2 = 1$$

$$1 - 2^0 = 1 - 1 = 0$$

Hence, number contains

$1(2^6)$	1000000
$1(2^5)$	100000
$1(2^4)$	10000
$0(2^3)$	0000
$0(2^2)$	000
$1(2^1)$	10
$1(2^0)$	1
Sum	1110011

18. The name "Delphi" derives from the Oracle of Delphi, although the authors of the method were unhappy with the oracular connotation of the name, "smacking a little of the occult". The Delphi method is based on the assumption that group judgements are more valid than individual judgements.

Delphi is based on the principle that forecasts (or decisions) from a structured group of individuals are more accurate than those from unstructured groups. The experts answer questionnaires in two or more rounds. After each round, a facilitator or change agent provides an anonymised summary of the experts' forecasts from the previous round as well as the reasons they provided for their judgements.

20. The vision of National Academic Depository (NAD) is born out of an initiative to provide an online store house of all academic awards. National Academic Depository (NAD) is a 24 × 7 online store house of all academic awards viz. certificates, diplomas, degrees, marksheets etc. duly digitised and lodged by academic institutions/boards/eligibility assessment bodies. NAD not only ensures easy access to and retrieval of an academic award but also validates and guarantees its authenticity and safe storage.

National Academic Depository comprises of two interoperable digital depositories viz. CDSL Ventures Limited (CVL) and NSDL Database Management Limited (NDML). These digital depositories have ensured hardware, network facilities and software of prescribed quality for smooth and secured operationalisation of NAD.

The Union Cabinet has approved establishing a digital depository of academic awards to be known as National Academic Depository (NAD) on the pattern of securities depository in its meeting held on 27th October, 2016.

21. Wersig and Neveling consider information much more comprehensively, adopting six different approaches:

1. **The Structural Approach** (matter oriented) in which information is seen as structures of the world or static relations between physical objects which may be perceived or not;
2. **The Knowledge Approach,** which records knowledge that is built up on the basis of perception of the structure of the world. This approach is not recommended because knowledge and information are used as synonyms;
3. **The Message Approach** in which information is recorded as symbols oriented in a physical career. This approach is used only by those concerned with the mathematical theory of communication;
4. **The Meaning Approach** where the semantic content of a message is accepted as information;
5. **The Effect Approach** or the **Recipient-Oriented Approach,** which states that information occurs only as a specific effect of a process;
6. **The Process Approach** where information is seen as a process, which, for example, occurs in the human mind when a problem and useful data are brought together.

The substance of these approaches is that information is a social process, and can be understood if it is in relation to needs either as reduction of uncertainty caused by a communication of data or as data used for reducing uncertainty.

23. West Bengal Public Libraries Act, 1979: The important features of this Act are given below:

1. Constitution of a State Library Council with the Minister in Charge of Library Service; as its Chairman, for advising the Government on the matters of public library system.
2. Representative from the employees of the libraries as a member in the State Library Council.
3. Constitution of a Department of Libraries to supervise and direct the matters of Public.
4. Constitution of Local Library Authority for each district, The District Magistrate of the District shall be the Ex-officio Chairman of the Local Library Authority.
5. Provision for Constitution of Executive Committee for Local Library. Authority (LLA).
6. The Government is empowered/to appoint District Library Officers and District Librarians in districts: The Government, after consultation with the Authority, may place the District-Libraries in charge of District Librarian. He shall manage library affairs subject to the control of the Authority.

7. No provision for Library Cess. The financial management for local libraries by the Local Library Authority.

Manipur Public Libraries Act, 1988: The Salient features of the Manipur Public Libraries Act are given hereunder:

1. Constitution of a State Library Committee, to advise the State Government on all matters arising under this Act and to exercise and perform such other powers and duties as maybe prescribed.
2. Constitution of a Department of Public Libraries.
3. Provision for Constitution of Executive Committee for District Library Authority.
4. Constitution of District Library Authority in each District, as a corporate body, for the purpose of organising and administering public library service in the district.
5. Constitution of 'Library Fund' formed mainly with the contribution of the State Government.
6. No Library cess.

24. National Knowledge Commission (2005) had the following members from the Library and Information profession:

- Smt. Kalpana Dasgupta (Chairperson)
- Dr. S. Arunachalam
- Mr. K.K. Banerjee
- Mr. K. Jayakumar
- Dr. H.K. Kaul
- Mr. K.K. Kochukoshy
- Mr. Manoj Kumar K.
- Prof. S. Mandal
- Prof. P.B. Mangla
- Dr. T.A.V. Murthy
- Dr. Harsha Parekh
- Dr. A.R.D. Prasad

26. Vocabulary in a data base is controlled by:

- **AUTHORITY FILE:** Most libraries maintain a subject authority file consisting of subject authority records in order to ensure uniformity and consistency in subject heading terminology and cross-references. The process of creating subject authority records and maintaining subject authority file is called subject authority control. A subject authority record is made when subject headings are established and used for the first time. ALA Glossary has defined the subject authority file as: "A set of records indicating the authorized forms of terms used as subject headings in a particular set of bibliographic records; the references made to and from the authorized forms; and the information used, and its sources, in the establishment of the headings and the determination of the references to be made".
- **THESAURUS:** The word 'thesaurus' comes from Greek term 'thesauros' meaning a storehouse or treasury of words. The Oxford English Dictionary defines 'thesaurus' as a archaeological term "a treasury of temple, etc." and quotes its use in 1736 as a treasury or store house of knowledge. Dictionary defines it as "a book of words or of information about a particular field or a set of concepts, specially a dictionary of synonyms". A dictionary lists words along with their meanings; synonyms, etc. in alphabetical order, but a thesaurus assembles all words related to an idea at one place. Modern usage may be said to date from 1852 when Peter Mark Roget thought of his thesaurus as a classification of ideas. Roget's Thesaurus had nothing to do with information retrieval. But his novel idea was later profitably employed in the compilation of thesaurus for information retrieval.

28. Uniterm Indexing System

- Developed by Mortimer Taube in 1953.
- It is a simple post-coordinate indexing system.
- It creates index entries for each unit term identified by the indexer.

- In fact, a card is prepared for each term that is considered to be an appropriate index term for a given document.
- The term is posted on top of the card.
- The card is divided into ten columns, 0 to 9.
- The document number (*i.e.,* the accession number or number of the given document being indexed) is written on the card by a technique known as 'terminal digit posting'.
- The number is written in a column based on the right-most digit in the document number.

Recall & Precision: The most important parameters used for evaluating on indexing system are: Recall and Precision. The term recall refers to a measure of whether or not a particular item is retrieved or the extent to which the retrieval of wanted item occur. Lancaster therefore states that recall and precision tend to vary inversely in searching. By this we mean that when we broaden a search to achieve better recall, precision tends to go down.

31. Theory Z of Ouchi is Dr. William Ouchi's so-called "Japanese Management" style popularized during the Asian economic boom of the 1980s.

For Ouchi, 'Theory Z' focused on increasing employee loyalty to the company by providing a job for life with a strong focus on the well-being of the employee, both on and off the job. According to Ouchi, Theory Z management tends to promote stable employment, high productivity, and high employee morale and satisfaction.

Theory X and Theory Y are theories of human work motivation and management. They were created by Douglas McGregor while he was working at the MIT Sloan School of Management in the 1950s, and developed further in the 1960s. McGregor's work was rooted in motivation theory alongside the works of Abraham Maslow, who created the hierarchy of needs. The two theories proposed by McGregor describe contrasting models of workforce motivation applied by managers in human resource management, organizational behaviour, organizational communication and organizational development.

Theory X explains the importance of heightened supervision, external rewards, and penalties, while Theory Y highlights the motivating role of job satisfaction and encourages workers to approach tasks without direct supervision. Management use of Theory X and Theory Y can affect employee motivation and productivity in different ways, and managers may choose to implement strategies from both theories into their practices.

Maslow's Hierarchy of Needs Theory: Abraham Maslow is well renowned for proposing the Hierarchy of Needs Theory in 1943. This theory is a classical depiction of human motivation. This theory is based on the assumption that there is a hierarchy of five needs within each individual. The urgency of these needs varies. These five needs are as follows:

1. Physiological needs
2. Safety needs
3. Social needs
4. Esteem needs
5. Self-actualization need

32. Total Quality Management: BSI/ISO Standards define total quality management as "a management philosophy enabling all activities through which the needs of the customer and the community and the objectives of the organization are satisfied in the most efficient and cost effective way by maximising the potential of all employees in a continuing drive for improvement."

"Total Quality Management is a way of managing to improve the effectiveness, efficiency, flexibility and competitiveness of a business as a whole. It involves whole companies getting organised and committed to quality in each department, each activity and each person, at each level."

"TQM" is "a system of continuous and centered on the needs of customers". Key components of total quality management are employee involvement and training, problem solving teams, statistical methods, long term goals and thinking and recognition that the system, not people, produces inefficiencies. Libraries can benefit from Total Quality Management in three ways:

(*i*) breaking down interdepartmental barriers;
(*ii*) redefining the beneficiaries of library services as internal customers (staff) and external customers (patrons); and
(*iii*) reaching a state of continuous improvement.

33. An International Standard Serial Number (ISSN) is an eight-digit serial number used to uniquely identify a serial publication, such as a magazine. The ISSN is especially helpful in distinguishing between serials with the same title. ISSN are used in ordering, catalouging, interlibrary loans, and other practices in connection with serial literature. The ISSN system was first drafted as an International Organization for Standardization (ISO) international standard in 1971 and published as ISO 3297 in 1975. ISO subcommittee TC 46/SC 9 is responsible for maintaining the standard.

When a serial with the same content is published in more than one media type, a different ISSN is assigned to each media type. For example, many serials are published both in print and electronic media. The ISSN system refers to these types as print ISSN (p-ISSN) and electronic ISSN (e-ISSN), respectively. Conversely, as defined in ISO 3297:2007, every serial in the ISSN system is also assigned a linking ISSN (ISSN-L), typically the same as the ISSN assigned to the serial in its first published medium, which links together all ISSNs assigned to the serial in every medium.

35. LAMP is an archetypal model of web service stacks, named as an acronym of the names of its original four open-source components: the Linux operating system, the Apache HTTP Server, the MySQL relational database management system (RDBMS), and the PHP programming language. The LAMP components are largely interchangeable and not limited to the original selection. As a solution stack, LAMP is suitable for building dynamic web sites and web applications.

Since its creation, the LAMP model has been adapted to other componentry, though typically consisting of free and open-source software. For example, an equivalent installation on the Microsoft Windows family of operating systems is known as WAMP and an equivalent installation on macOS is known as MAMP.

39. Virtual Library is another kind of Digital Library which provides portal to information that is available electronically elsewhere. This is referred so to emphasize that the Library does not itself hold content. Librarians have used this term for a decade or more to denote a Library that provides access to distributed information in electronic format through pointers provided locally.

A Virtual Library has been defined by Gapen (1993) as, "the concept of remote access to the contents and services of libraries and other information resources, combining an on-site collection of current and heavily used materials in both print and electronic form, with an electronic network which provides access to, and delivery from, external worldwide library and commerical information and knowledge sources".

The speedy and wide access to current information contents makes virtual libraries a global symbol of the information access paradigm.

The Virtual Library has changed the traditional focus of librarians on the selection, cataloguing and management of information resources such as books and periodicals. The virtual library is putting emphasis on access without the need to allow for the time required by these technical processes.

Virtual Libraries have induced libraries, scholars, publishers and document delivery vendors to develop new partnerships that are working for the good of scholarly communication in both developed and developing countries.

Features of a Virtual Library

1. It provides speedy and wide access to updated information in a global manner.
2. It has changed the traditional library system of cataloguing only book materials.
3. Cataloguing of NBM (Non Book Materials) includes not only databases but also websites.
4. Greater emphasis is on access and not on collection.
5. Time saving.
6. It results in a creation of digital divide because only developed countries with strong funds for automation and fulfilling infrastructural requirements for Virtual Library can afford to support Virtual Library services.

41. The Copyright Act 1957 (as amended by the Copyright Amendment Act 2012) governs the subject of copyright law in India. The Act is applicable from 21 January 1958. Important section of the Copyright Act 1957.

Section 1.	Short title, extent and commencement.
Section 2.	Interpretation.
Section 3.	Meaning of publication.
Section 5.	When work deemed to be first published in India.
Section 17.	First owner of copyright.
Section 18.	Assignment of copyright.
Section 19.	Mode of assignment.
Section 27.	Term of copyright in sound recording.
Section 35.	Control over the copyright society by the author and other owners of rights.
Section 41.	Provisions as to works of certain international organisations.
Section 55.	Civil remedies for infringement of copyright.
Section 56.	Protection of separate rights.
Section 57.	Author's special rights.
Section 63.	Offences of infringement of copyright or other rights conferred by this Act.
Section 63A.	Enhanced penalty on second and subsequent convictions.
Section 63B.	Knowing use of infringing copy of computer programme to be an offence.
Section 64.	Power of police to seize infringing copies.
Section 65.	Possession of plates for purpose of making infringing copies.
Section 65A.	Protection of technological measures.
Section 78.	Power to make rules.
Section 79.	Repeals, savings and transitional provisions.

42. Copyright is a legal right, existing in many countries, that grants the creator of an original work exclusive rights to determine whether, and under what conditions, this original work may be used by others. This is usually only for a limited time. Copyright is one of two types of intellectual property rights, the other is industrial property rights. The exclusive rights are not absolute but limited by limitations and exceptions to copyright law, including fair use. A major limitation on copyright on ideas is that copyright protects only the original expression of ideas, and not the underlying ideas themselves.

Most jurisdictions recognize copyright limitations, allowing "fair" exceptions to the creator's exclusivity of copyright and giving users certain rights. The development of digital media and computer network technologies have prompted reinterpretation of these exceptions, introduced new difficulties in enforcing copyright, and inspired additional challenges to the philosophical basis of copyright law. Simultaneously, businesses with great economic dependence upon copyright, such as those in the music business, have advocated the extension and expansion of copyright and sought additional legal and technological enforcement.

A patent is a government-granted monopoly on an invention to an inventor or their assignee for a limited period of time in exchange for a public disclosure of an invention. The term "limited period of time" mean the maximum period during which patent can be maintained into force.

Patents are exclusively national affairs, so patent that was issued in one country cannot provide protection of the invention in the any other countries in the world. However some countries have concluded treaties under which patents can be granted, and these patents automatically become valid in all treaty members.

Trade Secrets: The precise language by which a trade secret is defined varies by jurisdiction, as do the particular types of information that are subject to trade secret protection. Three factors are common to all such definitions:

A trade secret is information that

- is not generally known to the public;
- confers economic benefit on its holder because the information is not publicly known; and
- where the holder makes efforts to maintain its secrecy.

In international law, these three factors define a trade secret under article 39 of the Agreement on Trade-Related Aspects of Intellectual Property Rights, commonly referred to as the TRIPS Agreement.

Similarly, in the United States Economic Espionage Act of 1996, "A trade secret has three parts: (1) information; (2) reasonable measures taken to protect the information; and (3) which derives independent economic value from not being publicly known."

A **trademark, trade mark,** or **trade-mark** is a recognizable sign, design, or expression which identifies products or services of a particular source from those of others, although trademarks used to identify services are usually called service marks. The trademark owner can be an individual, business organization, or any legal entity. A trademark may be located on a package, a label, a voucher, or on the product itself. For the sake of corporate identity, trademarks are often displayed on company buildings. It is legally recognized as a type of intellectual property.

43.

IFLA Presidents	**Tenure**
Gloria Perez-Salmeron	2017-2019
Donna Scheeder	2015-2017
Sinikka Sipilä	2013-2015
Ingrid Parent	2011-2013
Ellen Tise	2009-2011
Claudia Lux	2007-2009
Alex Byrne	2005-2007
Kay Raseroka	2003-2005
Christine Deschamps	1997-2003
Robert Wedgeworth	1991-1997
Hans-Peter Geh	1985-1991
Else Granheim	1979-1985
Preben Kirkegaard	1974-1979
Herman Liebaers	1969-1974
Sir Frank Francis	1963-1969
Gustav Hofmann	1958-1963
Pierre Bourgeois	1951-1958
Wilhelm Munthe	1947-1951
Marcel Godet	1936-1947
William Warner Bishop	1931-1936
Isak G.A. Collijn	1927-1931

44. Library Journal is an American trade publication for librarians. It was founded in 1876 by Melvil Dewey. It reports news about the library world, emphasizing public libraries, and offers feature articles about aspects of professional practice. It also reviews library-related materials and equipment.

Its "Library Journal Book Review" does pre-publication reviews of several hundred popular and academic books each month. *Library Journal's* original publisher was Frederick Leypoldt, whose company became R.R. Bowker. Reed International (later merged into Reed Elsevier) purchased Bowker in 1985; they published *Library Journal* until 2010, when it was sold to Media Source Inc., owner of the Junior Library Guild and *The Horn Book Magazine.*

The Library Quarterly was established in January 1931, the year that Lee Pierce Butler joined the University of Chicago Graduate Library School, which was where library science as the academic study of the relationship between books and users was originally conceived. Thus, its publication history parallels the existence of library science as a field of academic research. The emergence of a journal devoted expressly to research in library science was met with conflict in the discipline according to the journal's first editor, William M. Randall. The controversy revolved around whether research and scientific method was needed in the field.

Library Review is an academic journal which was established in 1927. This journal focuses on social sciences, specific to library and information sciences. The journal is published nine times a year by Emerald Group Publishing. The editor-in-chief is Judith Broady-Preston (Aberystwyth University). In January 2018, 'Library Review' was renamed 'Global Knowledge, Memory and Communication' using the acronym 'GKMC'.

Library Trends is a quarterly peer-reviewed academic journal founded in 1952 and published quarterly by the Johns Hopkins University Press. It covers international developments and future directions in the fields of library and information science. It includes analysis of research and writing, critical opinion, and reviews. Each issue is devoted to a single topic of interest. *Library Trends* is available electronically via EBSCO, Academic OneFile (Gale), WilsonWeb (Wilson Library Literature & Information Science Full Text), IDEALS, and Project MUSE.

46.

L:414	Fever
L:423	Pox
L:4231	Small pox
L:4232	Chicken pox
L:4233	Measles
L:4631	Scurvy
L:4632	Beriberi
L14:485	Ascites
L2161:423	Mumps
L24:451	Anorexia
L25:4241	Typhoid
L25:4242	Bacillary dysentery
L25:4251	Cholera
L25:4371	Tapeworm
L35:4113	Pernicious
L35:4114	Splenic
L35:4115	Leucernia
L35:4231	Typhus
L35:4261	Malaria
L35:4262	Sleeping sickness
L37:411	Arteriosclerosis
L25:452	Diarrhoea
L25:474	Dysentery (general)
L291:453	Jaundice
L292:481	Gallstone
L2927:481	Biliary colic
L293:46	Diabetes

47. VADLO is brought to you by Life in Research, LLC., a company founded by two biology scientists who wish to make it easier to locate biology research related information on the web.

The *FASTEST* growing search engine in Biology, VADLO caters to all branches of life sciences.

Protocols category lets you search for methods, techniques, assays, procedures, reagent recipes, plasmid maps, etc. Products category allows searching for commercially available life sciences research reagents. Powerpoints category finds powerpoint files for presentations, seminars, lectures and talks. Bioinformatics category caters calculators, servers, prediction tools, sequence alignment and manipulation tools, primer design etc.

VADLO is a large fig tree characterized by aerial roots that eventually become accessory trunks. This allows it to grow horizontally to amazing proportions. Aerial roots provide for convenient swings to the kids, who, along with eager birds, also enjoy the ripe red figs on VADLO, called Teta.

Mamma.com is a global Meta search engine. It provides extensive web search and fetches results from top search engines. If you need information on latest news and updates, images, videos and twitter then this is the best place to surf online.

Athenus.com is the search engine of choice for scientists and engineers seeking resources in science and engineering on the web.

The Athenus search engine indexes hundreds of thousands of subject-specific web sites, publications, news and other resources, providing users with the most current, most focused collection of topic-specific material on the Internet.

Athenus.com has its origins in 'Engwho: The Engineering Search Engine', launched in 1999 as a public service to the engineering and science community. Despite being run on a shoestring budget by a tiny team, Engwho quickly flourished and developed a loyal following in both industry and academia.

In 2004, Engwho changed hands and was acquired by think new. The new ownership committed to provide the financial, technological and human resources required to adequately meet the growing requirements of the engineering and science search community. In April 2004, the Engwho site was officially relaunched as Athenus.com.

It is the mission of Athenus.com to continue to provide the best search tools available for the engineering and science community. In addition, we shall undertake to provide cutting edge services, advocacy and information relevant to our community in the most responsible of manners.

Ethnologue: *Languages of the World* is an annual reference publication in print and online that provides statistics and other information on the living languages of the world. It was first issued in 1951, and is now published annually by SIL International, a U.S.-based, worldwide, Christian non-profit organization. SIL's main purpose is to study, develop and document languages to promote literacy and for religious purposes.

As of 2019, *Ethnologue* contains web-based information on 7,111 languages in its 22nd edition, including the number of speakers, locations, dialects, linguistic affiliations, autonyms, availability of the Bible in each language and dialect described, a cursory description of revitalization efforts where reported, and an estimate of language viability using the Expanded Graded Intergenerational Disruption Scale *(EGIDS)*.

48. Anteriorising Common Isolate

Number	*Term*
a	Bibliography
b	Concordance
d	Table
e	Formula
f	Atlas
k	Cyclopaedia
m	Periodical
n	Serial
p	Conference proceedings

v	History
w	Biography
	General
	Individual
	Autobiography
	Ana
	Letters
x	Works (Collection or Selection)
	General
	Individual
*y*1	Programme of instruction
*y*2	Syllabus
*y*3	Synopsis
*y*4	Scope
*y*7	Case Study
*y*8	Digest

49. MARC Fields

001 Control number
003 Control number identifier
005 Date and time of latest transaction
006 Fixed-length data elements—additional material characteristics
007 Physical description fixed field
008 Fixed length data elements
020 ISBN
022 International Standard Serial Number (ISSN)
037 Source of acquisition
041 Language code
043 Geographic area code
050 Library of Congress call number
110 Main entry—Corporate name (less frequent under AACR2 rules)
250 Edition Statement
256 Computer file characteristics
263 Projected publication date (indicates a CIP—Cataloguing in Publication—record)
306 Playing time
440 Series
508 Creation/production credits note
510 Citation/references note (review sources)
511 Participant or performer note
586 Awards note
656 Index term—Occupation
730 Added entry—Uniform title
852 Location
856 Electronic location and access

50. Reid Garrett Hoffman CBE is an American internet entrepreneur, venture capitalist and author. Hoffman was the co-founder and executive chairman of LinkedIn, a business-oriented social network used primarily for professional networking.

Howard G. "Ward" Cunningham is an American computer programmer who developed the first wiki. A pioneer in both design patterns and extreme programming, he started programming the software WikiWikiWeb in 1994 and installed it on the website of the software consultancy he started with his wife Karen, Cunningham & Cunningham (commonly known by its domain name, c2.com), on March 25, 1995, as an add-on to the Portland Pattern Repository.

Blogger is a blog-publishing service that allows multi-user blogs with time-stamped entries. It was developed by Pyra Labs, which was bought by Google in 2003. The blogs are hosted by Google and generally accessed from a subdomain of blogspot.com. Blogs can also be served from a custom domain owned by the user (like www.********.com) by using DNS facilities to direct a domain to Google's servers.

Tim Vanderhook serves as the Chief Executive Officer and Chief Executive Officer of Specific Media at Myspace. LLC. Mr. Vanderhook is the co-founder Specific media, Inc., an affiliate of Myspace LLC in July 1999 and serves as its Chief Executive officer and President. Mr. Vanderhook also co-founded specific media UK Ltd. and serves as its Chief Executive officer.

51. The xerographic process, which was invented by **Chester Carlson** in 1938 and developed and commercialized by the Xerox Corporation, is widely used to produce high-quality text and graphic images on paper.

Carlson originally called the process electro photography. It's based on two natural phenomena: that materials of opposite electrical charges attract and that some materials become better conductors of electricity when exposed to light. Carlson invented a six-step process to transfer an image from one surface to another using these phenomena.

Brewster Kahle is an American computer engineer, Internet entrepreneur, internet activist, advocate of universal access to all knowledge, and digital librarian. Kahle founded the Internet Archive and Alexa. In 2012 he was inducted into the Internet Hall of Fame.

Michael Stern Hart (March 8, 1947 - September 6, 2011) was an American author best known as the founder of Project Gutenberg, a project to make electronic books (e-Book) freely available via the Internet.

Edward Fox serves as Executive Director and Chairman of the Board for NDLTD. He began work on ETDs in 1987 when some involved in SGML (a precursor to HTML and XML) were considering its application to dissertations. He received a B.S. from MIT in 1972 and then completed his M.S. and Ph.D. (1983) at Cornell University, working with Gerard Salton ("the father of information retrieval"). At Virginia Tech since Aug. 1983, he is a Professor of Computer Science and is Director of the Digital Library Research Laboratory. He served as a Board member of the Computer Research Association (CRA).

53. Stands for **"Database Management System."** In short, a DBMS is a database program. Technically speaking, it is a software system that uses a standard method of catalouging, retrieving, and running queries on data. The DBMS manages incoming data, organizes it, and provides ways for the data to be modified or extracted by users or other programs. Some DBMS examples include MySQL, PostgreSQL, Microsoft Access, SQL Server, FileMaker, Oracle, RDBMS, dBASE, Clipper, and FoxPro.

OmniPage was one of the first OCR programs to run on personal computers. It was developed in the late 1980s and sold by Caere Corporation, a company headed by Robert Noyce. The original developers were Philip Bernzott, John Dilworth, David George, Bryan Higgins, and Jeremy Knight. Caere was acquired by ScanSoft in 2000. ScanSoft acquired Nuance Communications in 2005, and took over its name.

Tagged Image File Format, abbreviated TIFF or TIF, is a computer file format for storing raster graphics images, popular among graphic artists, the publishing industry, and photographers. TIFF is widely supported by scanning, faxing, word processing, optical character recognition, image manipulation, desktop publishing, and page-layout applications. The format was created by Aldus Corporation for use in desktop publishing.

TeamViewer is a popular piece of software used for Internet-based remote access and support. TeamViewer software can connect to any PC or server, so you can remote control your partner's PC as if you were sitting right in front of it. For the remote session to work the partner has to start a small application, which does not require installation or administrative rights.

TeamViewer 6 is the latest version of the software and works with Windows, Mac, Linux operating systems and Mobile (Android, Apple iPad, Apple iPhone) devices.

56. Over the last two decades, the Muktabodha Indological Research Institute (MIRI) has created a vast online digital library, including many searchable e-texts, which is respected and utilized by scholars around the world. Over 2,600 manuscripts have been digitally preserved and made freely available to Indologists, scholars of religion, and practitioners worldwide through the MIRI online Digital Library. In this way, MIRI provides the global community with an invaluable resource for research and study.

NetFirst Database - OCLC Contains bibliographic citations—complete with summary descriptions and subject headings--describing Internet accessible resources, including World Wide Web pages, interest groups, library catalougs, FTP sites, Internet services, Gopher servers, electronic journals, and newsletters. Records contain location information that can be used to connect users to resources of interest.

Zotero is a free and open-source reference management software to manage bibliographic data and related research materials (such as PDF files). Notable features include web browser integration, online syncing, generation of in-text citations, footnotes and bibliographies, as well as integration with the word processors Microsoft Word, LibreOffice Writer and Google Docs. It is produced by the Center for History and New Media at George Mason University.

ResearchGate is a social networking site for scientists and researchers to share papers, ask and answer questions, and find collaborators. ResearchGate publishes a citation impact measurement in the form of an "RG Score". RG score is not a citation impact measure. RG Scores have been reported to be correlated with existing citation impact measures, but have also been criticized as having questionable reliability and an unknown calculation methodology.

57. Kinesics or kinesic communication is all about communication through body movements, such as gestures and facial expressions. It is all about non-verbal behaviour using any part of the body. It also includes communicating using the body as a whole.

In popular culture, we call this 'body language'. In fact, the founder of kinesics, American anthropologist Ray Birdwhistell (1918–1994), never used the term 'body language'. He did not like the term, insisting that our bodies do not convey what linguists define as 'language.'

Haptic communication is a form of non-verbal communication and the way by which people and animals communicate via touching. Touch is the most effective means to communicate feelings and emotions.

The withholding of touch may communicate a variety of negative feelings.

Proxemics Distances: We all have varying definitions of what our "personal space" is, and these definitions are contextual and depend on the situation and the relationship. Scholars have identified four zones for US Americans, which are public, social, personal, and intimate distance. Even within a particular zone, interactions may differ depending on whether someone is in the outer or inner part of the zone.

Iconic systems are systems of communication in which icons or symbols are used to represent words or linguistic concepts. Iconic systems are a type of augmentative communication. Iconic systems can be part of a picture exchange system (*e.g.,* PECS) or used in augmentative communication devices. Iconic systems are hypothesized to facilitate communication by a recognition process (*e.g.,* the user recognizes the icon as a picture of the object).

58. Descriptive research describes a social situation, social events, social systems, social structures, etc. Its main purpose is to describe the state of affairs as it exists. For instance, a study of drug abuse would cover questions like the extent of drug abuse among college students, the nature of drugs taken, the causes of taking drugs, the sources of drugs, the effects of taking drugs, etc.

Experiments are, theoretically, the purest way of dealing with the problem of cause and effect. Therefore, the experiment is the most sophisticated way of getting at the problems of 13 explanation. Ideally, in this type of research the researcher would like to show that X causes Y. In order to show that X causes Y the researcher will have to demonstrate that X was both a necessary and a sufficient cause of Y. *i.e.,* the researcher will have to show that X must occur in order for Y to follow, and that Y is the result of X, or nothing else.

Ethnography is a qualitative method for collecting data often used in the social and behavioural sciences. Data are collected through observations and interviews, which are then used to draw conclusions about how societies and individuals function.

Evaluation is a set of research methods and associated methodologies with a distinctive purpose. They provide a means to judge actions and activities in terms of values, criteria and standards. At the same time evaluation is also a practice that seeks to enhance effectiveness in the public sphere and policy making. In order to improve as well as judge, there is a need to explain what happens and would have to be done differently for different outcomes to be achieved.

59. The **Villa of the Papyri** is named after its unique library of *papyri* (or scrolls), discovered in 1750, but is also one of the most luxurious houses in all of Herculaneum and in the Roman world. Its luxury is shown by its exquisite architecture and by the very large number of outstanding works of art discovered, including frescoes, bronzes and marble sculpture which constitute the largest collection of Greek and Roman sculptures ever discovered in a single context.

The **Library of Pergamum** in Pergamum, Turkey, was one of the most important libraries in the ancient world. Founded sometime prior to the Hellenistic Age, Pergamum or Pergamon was an important ancient Greek city, located in Anatolia. It is now the site of the modern Turkish town, Bergama. Ruled by the Attalid dynasty, the city rose to prominence as an administrative center under King Eumenes II of Pergamum, who formed an alliance with the Roman Republic, severing ties with the Macedonians.

The Royal Library of Ashurbanipal has sometimes been described as the 'first library' in the world, or the 'oldest surviving royal library in the world'. The library was discovered by archaeologists who were excavating at the site of Nineveh, today known as Kuyunjik. As this was the imperial capital of the Neo-Assyrian Empire during the reign of Ashurbanipal, the library has been attributed to this ruler.

The Great Library of Alexandria in Alexandria, Egypt, was one of the largest and most significant libraries of the ancient world. The Library was part of a larger research institution called the Mouseion, which was dedicated to the Muses, the nine goddesses of the arts.

60. Dr Zakir Husain Library is the university's central library. Established in 1920, it was named after Dr. Zakir Husain, former President of India and Jamia's former Vice-Chancellor in 1973.

The J.R.D. Tata Memorial Library (JRDTML) completed its centenary year of establishment in 2011. Started in 1911, the library was one of the earliest central facilities to have been started by the Institute for teaching and research. Initially, the library was housed in the majestic main building. The library moved into the present premises in January 1965, built out of grants provided by University Grants Commission (UGC) in commemoration of the golden jubilee celebrations of the Indian Institute of Science, Bangalore in 1959. In 1995, the library was renamed as "J.R.D. Tata Memorial Library".

The Sayaji Rao Gaekwad Library, also known as the Central Library, is the main library of Banaras Hindu University (BHU) in Varanasi, Uttar Pradesh in India. Established in 1917, it is listed in the Survey of Manuscripts in India. The present building of the library was built in 1941 on pattern of British Museum, at the suggestion of Pandit Madan Mohan Malaviya, the founder of university, after his return from the Round Table Conference, London in 1931, with a donation from the Sayajirao Gaekwad III, Maharaja of Baroda State from 1875 to 1939, known for establishing libraries throughout his state.

The Vikram Sarabhai Library (VSL) is named after Dr. Vikram Sarabhai, world renowned physicist and founding Director of IIMA. It was set up in 1962 and is one of the best management libraries in Asia. The library is open 24 × 7. Our mission is to facilitate convenient and user friendly access to current, global and relevant information by identifying, acquiring, organizing and retrieving information in various formats (print & non print) to serve the information needs of the academic fraternity of IIMA to meet their teaching, research, consulting, training and learning requirements.

62. Dr. S.R. Ranganathan a tribute on the Librarian's Day Shiyali Ramamrita Ranganathan, Father of Library and Information Science movement in India, was born on 12 August, 1892 to Ramamrita at Shiyali in The Tanjur district of Madras State, in the state of Tamil Nadu. The Government of India awarded Padmashri to Dr. S.R. Ranganathan in 1957 for valuable contributions to Library Science.

Bellary Shamanna Kesavan was the first National Librarian of independent India (1947-1962). He is also known as *Father of Indian National Bibliography* as it was first brought out in his leadership on 15 August 1958. Later, he became the first Director of the Indian National Scientific Documentation Centre (INSDOC) at New Delhi (1963-1969). In recognition of his great service to the nation, the Government of India honoured him with Padma Shri.

Iyyanki Venkata Ramanayya has been called the "Architect of Public Library Movement in India". He is the first Indian to be awarded the Kaula Gold Medal. His efforts regarding development of public library system in India is worth appreciating and that is the reason he is recognized as the "Architect of Public Library Movement in India" and was awarded by Indian Govt. with Padmashri in 1972.

Prithvi Nath Kaula was a librarian, Library and Information Sciences specialist and author who worked with the Banaras Hindu University in Varanasi, India. Kaula was also the recipient of the Padma Shri award in the year 2004.

63. Sixteen states of India have put into state book their Public Libraries Act. The chronological sequence is as follows:

1. Tamil Nadu (Then called Madras Public Libraries Act, 1948).
2. Andhra Pradesh (The Hyderabad Public Libraries Act, 1955, as a result of reorganisation of the states merged in Andhra Pradesh Public Libraries Act, 1960).
3. Karnataka (The Karnataka Public Libraries Act, 1965).
4. Maharashtra (The Kolhapur Public Libraries Act was passed in 1945. After states reorganisation, state of Kolhapur was merged with Maharashtra State. The Maharashtra Public Libraries Act, 1967 came into being in 1967).
5. West Bengal (West Bengal Public Libraries Act, 1979).
6. Manipur (Manipur Public Libraries Act, 1988).
7. Kerala (Kerala Public Libraries Act, 1989).
8. Haryana (Haryana Public Libraries Act, 1989).
9. Mizoram (Mizoram Public Libraries Act, 1993).
10. Goa (Goa Public Libraries Act, 1994).
11. Gujarat (Gujarat Public Libraries Act, 2001).

12. Orissa (Orissa Public Libraries Act, 2001).
13. Uttaranchal (Uttaranchal Public Libraries Act, 2005).
14. Rajasthan (Rajasthan Public Libraries Act, 2006).
15. Uttar Pradesh (Uttar Pradesh Public Libraries Act, 2006).
16. Bihar (Bihar State Public Libraries and Information Centres Act, 2008).

67. Project Gutenberg (PG) is a volunteer effort to digitize and archive cultural works, to "encourage the creation and distribution of eBooks". It was founded in 1971 by American writer Michael S. Hart and is the oldest digital library. Most of the items in its collection are the full texts of public domain books.

Google Books: The Publisher Program was first known as Google Print when it was introduced at the Frankfurt Book Fair in October, 2004. The Google Books Library Project, which scans works in the collections of library partners and adds them to the digital inventory, was announced in December, 2004.

Open Library is an online project intended to create "one web page for every book ever published". Created by Aaron Swartz, Brewster Kahle, Alexis Rossi, Anand Chitipothu, and Rebecca Malamud, Open Library is a project of the Internet Archive, a non profit organization. Open Library lunched in 2006. It has been funded in part by grants from the California State Library and the Kahle/Austin Foundation. Open Library provides online access to many public domain and out-of-print books.

The Directory of Open Access Books (DOAB) will officially launch at the Open Access Monographs in the Humanities and Social Sciences Conference in the British Library on 1 July, 2013. DOAB will be launched by Bas Savenije, Chairman of the Board of the OAPEN Foundation and Director General of the Dutch National Library.

68. Group 1 entities are the foundation of the FRBR model:

- ***Work*** is a "distinct intellectual or artistic creation." For example, Beethoven's Ninth Symphony apart from all ways of expressing it is a work. When we say, "Beethoven's Ninth is magnificent!" we generally are referring to the work.
- ***Expression*** is "the specific intellectual or artistic form that a work takes each time it is 'realized.'" An expression of Beethoven's Ninth might be each draft of the musical score he writes down (not the paper itself, but the music thereby expressed).
- ***Manifestation*** is "the physical embodiment of an expression of a work. As an entity, manifestation represents all the physical objects that bear the same characteristics, in respect to both intellectual content and physical form." The performance the London Philharmonic made of the Ninth in 1996 is a manifestation. It was a physical embodiment even if not recorded, though of course manifestations are most frequently of interest when they are expressed in a persistent form such as a recording or printing. When we say, "The recording of the London Philharmonic's 1996 performance captured the essence of the Ninth," we are generally referring to a manifestation.
- ***Item*** is "a single exemplar of a manifestation. The entity defined as item is a concrete entity." Each copy of the 1996 pressings of that 1996 recording is an item. When we say, "Both copies of the London Philharmonic's 1996 performance of the Ninth are checked out of my local library," we are generally referring to items.

70. Parts of main entry according to CCC (Ed. 5): The Main entry in the classified catalogue has different sections. They are:

(*i*) **Leading Section:** This is made up of the call number of the document you are cataloguing. It is entered on the first horizontal line starting from the first indention. The class number and the book number are separated by two spaces. The call number is to be written with pencil. For the simple reason that it is liable to change.

(*ii*) **Heading Section:** The name of the author is entered in this section. When we say the name of the author, it can be single personal author, joint personal authors, corporate author(s), pseudonym(s), collaborator(s) and in few cases can also be the title of the document.

(*iii*) **Title Section:** Title is to be written from the next horizontal line after the heading and it starts from the second indention and continuation from the first indention. Edition statement, collaborators if any, will be part of the title statement. This section can be divided into three parts—title, edition and collaborators. The title is written in running hand.

(*iv*) **Accession Number Section:** In the Main Entry accession number is given on the bottom most line starting from the first indention. Full stop is not used where, call or class number forms a section, after directing section and after the accession number section.

(*v*) **Tracing Section:** The purpose of tracing is to show what additional entries for a given document have been prepared. This information is given on the back of the Main Entry Card, Tracing consists of Cross Reference Entry, Class Index Entry, Book Index Entry and Cross Reference Index Entry.

71. Vector Space Model: Often weighted systems are discussed as vectorised information systems. This association comes from the SMART system at Cornell University, created by Dr. Gerald Salton [1979]. The system emphasises weights as a foundation for information detection and stores these weights in a vector form. In systems, based upon a vector model, the semantics of every item are represented as a vector. A vector is a one-dimensional set of values, where the order/position of each value in the set is fixed and represents a particular domain. Each vector represents a document and each position in a vector represents a different unique word (processing token) in the database. There are two approaches to the domain of values in the vector—binary and weighted. The value assigned to each position is the weight of that term in the document. A value of zero indicates that the word is not in the document. Queries can be translated into the vector form. Search is accomplished by calculating the distance between the query vector and the document vector. The use of weights also provides a basis for determining the rank of an item.

72. Components of Winisis database: Winisis database comprises of a set of records and each record contains a set of fields such as author, title etc. A field in a record is a container of data elements. Winisis database has a master file containing all the records of the database. An inverted file functions as an index to the master file for faster access to any record.

In order to create a Winisis database with any chosen fields, you need to define the following components.

- **Field Definition Table (FDT):** The FDT defines the fields such as Author, Title, Publisher etc. of the records in the database and their characteristics. FDT determines the nature of data entry worksheet.
- **Data Entry Worksheet(s):** The worksheet is the screen layout used to create and/or update the records of the database. Winisis provides a specially designed editor to create the worksheet.
- **Print Format (PFT):** The PFT is the format for display or printing of records.
- **Field Selection Table(s) (FST):** FST defines fields that can be searched in the database. Search is made possible by creating an inverted file of terms indexed from the fields chosen for search.

73. **MOSAIC—***Multi-lingual Orientation Service Association for Immigrant Communities—* became a non-profit society in 1976, and was formally registered as a charity in 1978. MOSAIC was founded from the union of two grass-roots agencies which had sprung up in response to unaddressed community needs in 1972. Both *Multilingual Social Service,* and *Language Aid for Ethnic Groups,* began as "Local Initiative Projects", and developed in response to the ongoing challenges faced by Vancouver's many non-English-speaking immigrants.

Blogger is a blog-publishing service that allows multi-user blogs with time-stamped entries. It was developed by Pyra Labs, which was bought by Google in 2003. The blogs are hosted by Google and generally accessed from a subdomain of blogspot.com.

Friendster was a social gaming site based in Kuala Lumpur, Malaysia. It was originally a social networking service website. After the relaunch of Friendster as a social gaming platform in June 2011, the number of registered users reached over 115 million.

Myspace is a social networking website offering an interactive, user-submitted network of friends, personal profiles, blogs, groups, photos, music, and videos. Myspace founded in 1 August, 2003.

74. Robert Saxton Tylor (1918-2009) was an influential library scholar and information scientist who served as Dean of the Syracuse University School of Information Studies from 1972 to 1981. His research and publications focused attention on users of information systems and services.

They may be briefly stated as follows:

1. determination of subject;
2. objective and motivation;
3. personal characteristics of inquirer;
4. relationship of inquiry description to file organization;
5. anticipated or acceptable answers.

75. **John James Beckley (1757-1807):** 1st Librarian of Congress 1802-1807 John Beckley was the first Librarian of Congress, albeit a part-time one. When the position of Librarian was established on January 26, 1802, President Thomas Jefferson asked his friend and political ally John Beckley—who also was serving as the Clerk of the House of Representatives-to fill the post.

George Waterston (1783-1854): 3rd Librarian of Congress 1815-1829 George Waterston served as Librarian of Congress from March 21, 1815 until May 28, 1829. Appointed by President James Madison, he was the first Librarian who did not also serve simultaneously as Clerk of the House of Representatives; thus, even though he followed John Beckley and Patrick Magruder in the position, he is sometimes called the first Librarian of Congress.

James H. Billington (1929-2018): 13th Librarian of Congress 1987-2015 James Hadley Billington was sworn in as the Librarian of Congress on September 14, 1987. He is the 13th person to hold the position since the Library was established in 1800. Billington was nominated by President Ronald Reagan, and his appointment was unanimously approved by the U.S. Senate.

Carla Diane Hayden (born August 10, 1952) was sworn in as the 14th Librarian of Congress on September 14, 2016. Hayden, the first woman and the first African American to lead the national library, was nominated to the position by President Barack Obama on February 24, 2016, and her nomination was confirmed by the U.S. Senate on July 13.

77. According to Wikipedia, the preprint is a "version of a scholarly or scientific paper that precedes publication in a peer-reviewed scholarly or scientific journal". Preprint archives, such as arXiv and SSRN, rapidly achieved prominence in both the hard and social sciences as rapid access to new work became a priority. It's wonderful to have those platforms, but what are best practices for libraries and other content providers in working with them? Should preprints be assigned DOIs? What relationship should exist between pre-prints and discovery services? What is the interoperability with link resolvers like? What are the implications for citation practices?

When a article is published, the author may wish to indicate this in the abstract listing for the article. For this reason, the journal reference and DOI (Digital Object Identifier) fields are provided for articles. Additionally, a report number field is provided for institutional report numbers.

You can add journal-ref, DOI and report number information to your articles via the journal reference facility on your user page. Note that no new article version will be generated when journal reference, DOI or report number information is added.

79. The DOAJ (Directory of Open Access Journals) was launched in 2003 at Lund University, Sweden, with 300 open access journals. Today, the independent database contains ca. 12000 open access journals covering all areas of science, technology, medicine, social science and humanities.

DOAJ is a membership organisation and membership is available in 3 main categories: Publisher, Ordinary Member and Sponsor. A DOAJ Membership is a clear statement of intent and proves a commitment to quality, peer-reviewed open access. DOAJ is co-author to the Principles of Transparency and Best Practice in Scholarly Publishing (Principles) and DOAJ members are expected to follow these principles as a condition of membership. DOAJ reserves the right to reject applications for membership, or revoke membership if a member or sponsor is found to contravene the Principles.

DOAJ is a community-curated list of open access journals and aims to be the starting point for all information searches for quality, peer reviewed open access material. To assist libraries and indexers keep their lists up-to-date, we make public a list of journals that have been accepted into or removed from DOAJ but we will not discuss specific details of an application with anyone apart from the applicant. Neither will we discuss individual publishers or applications with members of the public unless we believe that, by doing so, we will be making a positive contribution to the open access community.

89. **Eugene Eli Garfield** (September 16, 1925 - February 26, 2017) was an American linguist and businessman, one of the founders of bibliometrics and scientometrics. He helped to create *Current Contents, Science Citation Index* (SCI), *Journal Citation Reports,* and *Index Chemicus,* among others, and founded the magazine *The Scientist.*

Garfield founded the Institute for Scientific Information (ISI), which was located in Philadelphia, Pennsylvania. ISI formed a major part of the science division of Thomson Reuters. In October 2016, Thomson Reuters completed the sale of its intellectual property and science division; it is now known as Clarivate Analytics.

Garfield is responsible for many innovative bibliographic products, including *Current Contents*, the *Science Citation Index* (SCI), and other citation databases, the *Journal Citation Reports,* and *Index Chemicus.* He is the founding editor and publisher of *The Scientist,* a news magazine for life scientists. In 2003, the University of South Florida School of Information was honoured to have him as lecturer for the Alice G. Smith Lecture. In 2007, he launched HistCite, a bibliometric analysis and visualization software package.

Previous Paper (Solved)

UGC-NET-Junior Research Fellowship & Assistant Professor Exam

Library and Information Science, November-2017*

PAPER-II

Note: *This paper contains **fifty** (**50**) objective type questions of **two** (**2**) marks each. **All** questions are **compulsory**.*

1. DELNET was initially supported by:
A. RRRLF B. NISSAT
C. NIC D. INSDOC

2. Who wrote the Foreword to the first edition of 'The Five Laws of Library Science'?
A. B.I. Palmer
B. Henry E. Bliss
C. P.S. Sivaswamy Aiyer
D. W.C. Berwick Sayers

3. 'Keesing's Record of World Events' is published from:
A. London B. France
C. Germany D. Japan

4. The 'Letter by Letter' Method of alphabetization in Dictionary catalogue is known as:
A. Nothing before something
B. Something before nothing
C. All through
D. Something after more

5. International Standard Name Identifier (ISNI) consists of:
A. 10 digits B. 12 digits
C. 13 digits D. 16 digits

6. Identify the symbol of 'Spiritual Experience and Mysticism' as given by CC:
A. Δ B. Σ
C. 4 D. MZA

7. Which of the following is indicated in the third digit of DDC Third Summary?
A. Schedule B. Class
C. Section D. Division

8. 'Cannon of Reticence' is a canon for:
A. Idea Plane
B. Verbal Plane
C. Notational Plane
D. Both Idea and Notational Planes

9. Positive Correlation occurs when:
A. Two variables move in opposite direction
B. Both variables move in a zigzag way
C. Two variables move in the same direction
D. Both variables are constant

10. Ex-post facto study is a type of:
A. Diagnostic design
B. Quasi-experimental design
C. Descriptive design
D. Historical design

11. Who proposed Big Six Information Literacy Skills?
A. C.D. Ferguson
B. G. Dunsire
C. E.A. Fox
D. M.B. Eisenberg and R.E. Berkowitz

12. Which of the following statements are **wrong** with reference to INB?
(*a*) Excludes musical scores
(*b*) First appeared in 1951
(*c*) Classified part follows CC, but DDC numbers assigned at the bottom
(*d*) The main entries are in Roman Script
Code:
A. (*a*) and (*b*) are correct
B. (*b*) and (*c*) are correct
C. (*c*) and (*d*) are correct
D. (*a*) and (*d*) are correct

*Held on 5 November, 2017

13. The protection of non-personal data in Transborder Data Flow uses which of the following legal instruments?
(*a*) Copyright
(*b*) Patent
(*c*) Bandwidth
(*d*) Trademark
Code:
A. (*a*), (*b*) and (*c*) are correct
B. (*b*), (*c*) and (*d*) are correct
C. (*a*), (*c*) and (*d*) are correct
D. (*a*), (*b*) and (*d*) are correct

14. From which universities S.R. Ranganathan was awarded D. Litt (Honoris Causa)?
(*a*) University of Delhi
(*b*) University of Madras
(*c*) University of London
(*d*) University of Pittsburgh
Code:
A. (*a*) and (*b*) are correct
B. (*a*) and (*c*) are correct
C. (*b*) and (*c*) are correct
D. (*a*) and (*d*) are correct

15. Information about recent floods in Bihar can be found in:
(*a*) Asian Recorder
(*b*) Data India
(*c*) India; a reference annual
(*d*) Statistical Abstract, India
Code:
A. (*a*) and (*b*) are correct
B. (*a*) and (*c*) are correct
C. (*a*), (*b*) and (*c*) are correct
D. (*b*), (*c*) and (*d*) are correct

16. Which of the following questions fall under the category of ready reference service?
(*a*) Population of Varanasi
(*b*) Height of Qutub Minar
(*c*) Concept of Symbiosis
(*d*) Collection development in university libraries
Code:
A. (*a*), (*b*) and (*d*) are correct
B. (*a*), (*b*) and (*c*) are correct
C. (*b*), (*c*) and (*d*) are correct
D. (*a*), (*c*) and (*d*) are correct

17. Identify the basic parts of Colon Classification:
(*a*) Rules
(*b*) Schedule of classification
(*c*) Schedule of classics and sacred books
(*d*) Geographical schedule
Code:
A. (*a*), (*b*) and (*d*) are correct
B. (*a*), (*b*) and (*c*) are correct
C. (*b*), (*c*) and (*d*) are correct
D. (*a*), (*c*) and (*d*) are correct

18. Identify the budget heads of non-recurring budget:
(*a*) Periodical subscription
(*b*) Maintenance of equipment
(*c*) Building extension
(*d*) Infrastructure development
Code:
A. (*a*) and (*b*) are correct
B. (*b*) and (*c*) are correct
C. (*c*) and (*d*) are correct
D. (*a*), (*c*) and (*d*) are correct

19. Which of the following are non-parametric tests?
(*a*) Anova test
(*b*) Spearman correlation coefficient
(*c*) Z-test
(*d*) Chi-Square test
Code:
A. (*b*) and (*d*) are correct
B. (*b*) and (*c*) are correct
C. (*a*), (*b*) and (*d*) are correct
D. (*a*), (*b*) and (*c*) are correct

20. Which of the following are work analysis techniques according to Edward Evans?
(*a*) PERT - CPM
(*b*) GANTT - Charts
(*c*) Operation research
(*d*) Cost-effectiveness
Code:
A. (*d*) and (*b*) are correct
B. (*b*) and (*c*) are correct
C. (*a*) and (*c*) are correct
D. (*c*) and (*d*) are correct

21. Transborder Data Flow includes (in the definition given by United Nations) movements across national boundaries:
(*a*) Machine-readable data for processing, storage or retrieval
(*b*) Media products (mass diffusion)
(*c*) Machine-readable data or magnetic tapes
(*d*) Machine-readable data on discs
Code:
A. (*a*), (*b*) and (*c*) are correct
B. (*b*), (*c*) and (*d*) are correct
C. (*a*), (*c*) and (*d*) are correct
D. (*a*), (*b*) and (*d*) are correct

22. Which of the following are the Canons for characteristics as enunciated by S.R. Ranganathan?
(*a*) Canon of Relevance
(*b*) Canon of Permanance
(*c*) Canon of Differentiation
(*d*) Canon of Interpetation in Chain
Code:
A. (*b*), (*c*), (*d*) are correct
B. (*a*), (*b*), (*c*) are correct
C. (*a*), (*c*), (*d*) are correct
D. (*a*), (*b*), (*d*) are correct

23. Arrange the following libraries in the chronological sequence of their emergence:
(*a*) Rampur Raza Library, UP
(*b*) Asiatic Society Library, Bombay
(*c*) Connemara Public Library, Chennai
(*d*) Sarasvati Mahal Library, Tanjore
Code:
A. (*a*), (*b*), (*c*), (*d*) B. (*b*), (*c*), (*d*), (*a*)
C. (*c*), (*d*), (*a*), (*b*) D. (*d*), (*c*), (*b*), (*a*)

24. Arrange the following printing technologies according to their emergence:
(*a*) Movable type
(*b*) Dot-Matrix printer
(*c*) Woodblock printing
(*d*) Screen printing
Code:
A. (*d*), (*c*), (*b*) and (*a*)
B. (*c*), (*a*), (*d*) and (*b*)
C. (*c*), (*d*), (*b*) and (*a*)
D. (*d*), (*a*), (*b*) and (*c*)

25. Arrange the following steps of digital preservation in their sequential order:
(*a*) Refreshing
(*b*) Encapsulation
(*c*) Emulation
(*d*) Data archiving
Code:
A. (*c*), (*b*), (*d*), (*a*) B. (*d*), (*b*), (*a*), (*c*)
C. (*a*), (*d*), (*b*), (*c*) D. (*a*), (*c*), (*b*), (*d*)

26. Arrange in sequence the following steps followed in Programming:
(*a*) Programme Code
(*b*) Programme Documentation
(*c*) Program Test
(*d*) Programme Design
Code:
A. (*a*), (*b*), (*c*), (*d*) B. (*d*), (*a*), (*c*), (*b*)
C. (*b*), (*c*), (*d*), (*a*) D. (*d*), (*c*), (*b*), (*a*)

27. Arrange the following Open Access Initiatives/ Policy Statements according to the year of their adoption/declaration at international level.
(*a*) The Coalition of Open Access Policy Institutions (COAPI)
(*b*) The Berlin Declaration on Open Access to Knowledge in the Sciences and Humanities (BDOAKS and H)
(*c*) The Budapest Open Access Initiatives (BOAI)
(*d*) Scholarly Publishing and Academic Resources Coalition (SPARC)
Code:
A. (*a*), (*b*), (*c*), (*d*) B. (*d*), (*c*), (*b*), (*a*)
C. (*b*), (*a*), (*d*), (*c*) D. (*c*), (*d*), (*b*), (*a*)

28. Match the following indexing/abstracting publications with the corresponding institution:

List-I	***List-II***
(*a*) Indian Citation Index	(*i*) ICMR
(*b*) INSPEL (Retrospective, 1970)	(*ii*) ICAR
(*c*) Med Ind	(*iii*) Diva Enterprises, Delhi
(*d*) Indian Animal Science Abstracts	(*iv*) NASSDOC

Code:

	(a)	(b)	(c)	(d)
A.	(ii)	(iii)	(iv)	(i)
B.	(iii)	(iv)	(i)	(ii)
C.	(i)	(ii)	(iii)	(iv)
D.	(iv)	(i)	(ii)	(iii)

29. Match the following terms with the corresponding authors who coined them:

List-I	List-II
(a) Knowledge Economy	(i) Mikhailov, Chernyi and Gilyarevskii
(b) Documentation	(ii) Calvin Mooers
(c) Informatics	(iii) Paul Otlet
(d) Information Retrieval	(iv) Peter Drucker

Code:

	(a)	(b)	(c)	(d)
A.	(ii)	(iii)	(iv)	(i)
B.	(i)	(iv)	(ii)	(iii)
C.	(iv)	(iii)	(i)	(ii)
D.	(iii)	(i)	(ii)	(iv)

30. Match the following:

List-I	List-II
(a) Bibliography	(i) Number of people recently died of dengue in Delhi
(b) Biography	(ii) Number of volumes of a book
(c) Statistical Source	(iii) Number of siblings of Mahatma Gandhi
(d) Newspaper Digest	(iv) Number of primary schools in Mumbai

Code:

	(a)	(b)	(c)	(d)
A.	(iv)	(ii)	(i)	(iii)
B.	(ii)	(i)	(iii)	(iv)
C.	(ii)	(iii)	(iv)	(i)
D.	(iii)	(iv)	(ii)	(i)

31. Match the fundamental categories with corresponding examples:

List-I	List-II
(a) Asia	(i) Matter
(b) Book Selection	(ii) Personality
(c) Microfilms	(iii) Energy
(d) University Libraries	(iv) Space

Code:

	(a)	(b)	(c)	(d)
A.	(iv)	(iii)	(i)	(ii)
B.	(iii)	(ii)	(iv)	(i)
C.	(ii)	(iii)	(i)	(iv)
D.	(i)	(iv)	(ii)	(iii)

32. Match the following ACI symbols (CC 6th edition) with their corresponding Isolates:

List-I	List-II
(a) p	(i) Conference
(b) k	(ii) Encyclopedia
(c) w	(iii) Biography
(d) n	(iv) Serials

Code:

	(a)	(b)	(c)	(d)
A.	(ii)	(iv)	(iii)	(i)
B.	(i)	(ii)	(iii)	(iv)
C.	(ii)	(i)	(iii)	(iv)
D.	(iv)	(iii)	(ii)	(i)

33. Match the following NISO (National Information Standard Organisation) standards with their corresponding descriptions applicable to Libraries:

List-I	List-II
(a) Z39.2	(i) Guidelines for Abstracts
(b) Z39.4	(ii) ISSN
(c) Z39.9	(iii) Guidelines for Indexes and Related Information Retrieval devices
(d) Z39.14	(iv) Information for interchange format

Code:

	(a)	(b)	(c)	(d)
A.	(iv)	(iii)	(ii)	(i)
B.	(i)	(ii)	(iii)	(iv)
C.	(ii)	(iv)	(iii)	(i)
D.	(iii)	(i)	(ii)	(iv)

34. Match the following devices with their mediums/system:

List-I	List-II
(a) Pen drive	(i) Web server device
(b) I-pad	(ii) Communication device

(*c*) Wi-Fi modem	(*iii*) Tablet run on iOS mobile operating system
(*d*) Cloud computing	(*iv*) Storage device

Code:

	(*a*)	(*b*)	(*c*)	(*d*)
A.	(*ii*)	(*iv*)	(*i*)	(*iii*)
B.	(*iv*)	(*iii*)	(*ii*)	(*i*)
C.	(*i*)	(*iv*)	(*ii*)	(*iii*)
D.	(*iii*)	(*ii*)	(*i*)	(*iv*)

35. Match the following Web tools with their corresponding features:

List-I	***List-II***
(*a*) Web 1.0	(*i*) People Centric and participative/bi-directional
(*b*) Web 2.0	(*ii*) Linking and Integrating Global files
(*c*) Web 3.0	(*iii*) Man-Machine Interaction with critical mass of participation and use of Al
(*d*) Web 4.0	(*iv*) Static and mono-directional

Code:

	(*a*)	(*b*)	(*c*)	(*d*)
A.	(*iv*)	(*i*)	(*ii*)	(*iii*)
B.	(*i*)	(*ii*)	(*iii*)	(*iv*)
C.	(*iv*)	(*iii*)	(*ii*)	(*i*)
D.	(*iii*)	(*i*)	(*iv*)	(*ii*)

36. Match the following research methods with their corresponding explanation:

List-I	***List-II***
(*a*) Formalized research	(*i*) Interpretation of abstract ideas
(*b*) Conceptual research	(*ii*) Survey and fact finding enquiries
(*c*) Descriptive research	(*iii*) Formulation of theory
(*d*) Fundamental research	(*iv*) Substantial structure and hypothesis to be tested

Code:

	(*a*)	(*b*)	(*c*)	(*d*)
A.	(*i*)	(*ii*)	(*iii*)	(*iv*)
B.	(*ii*)	(*iii*)	(*iv*)	(*i*)
C.	(*iii*)	(*iv*)	(*i*)	(*ii*)
D.	(*iv*)	(*i*)	(*ii*)	(*iii*)

37. Assertion (A): Extending the library's reach through strategic partnership, collaborative relationship is an important goal for any academic library.

Reason (R) : Partnerships do not allow participating organisations to yield efficiency.

Code:

A. (A) is true but (R) is false.
B. (A) is false, but (R) is true.
C. Both (A) and (R) are true.
D. Both (A) and (R) are false.

38. Assertion (A): Science rests itself upon a series of postulates or assumptions which are themselves fundamentally unproved and unprovable.

Reason (R) : One can only assert that these postulates are true, can believe them, but cannot prove them as they deal with the validity of human knowledge.

Code:

A. (A) is true, but (R) is false.
B. (A) is false, but (R) is true.
C. Both (A) and (R) are true.
D. Both (A) and (R) are false.

39. Assertion (A): Implementation of TQM in Libraries is quite challenging.

Reason (R) : Some of the key essentials, like open and cooperative culture and employees responsiveness for customer's satisfaction, required for successful implementation of TQM, are very much noticed in a library.

Code:

A. (A) is true, but (R) is false.
B. (A) is false, but (R) is true.
C. Both (A) and (R) are true.
D. Both (A) and (R) are false.

40. Assertion (A): Web 2.0 has wholly wiped out the digital divide, particularly with regard to individual ability, access to and engagement with technology.

Reason (R) : Use of Web 2.0 in learning and teaching is still in an embryonic state.

Code:

A. (A) is true, but (R) is false.
B. (A) is false, but (R) is true.
C. Both (A) and (R) are true.
D. Both (A) and (R) are false.

41. Assertion (A): It is not economical to store and read video data from secondary storage devices.

Reason (R) : Video data require enormous disk storage as image compression ratio is high.

Code:

A. (A) is true, but (R) is false
B. (A) is false, but (R) is true
C. Both (A) and (R) are true
D. Both (A) and (R) are false

42. Assertion (A): Participatory action research follows the conventional model of pure research in which members of the communities under study are treated as passive subjects.

Reason (R) : In participatory action research no member of the communities under study participate throughout the research process.

Code:

A. (A) is true, but (R) is false.
B. (A) is false, but (R) is true.
C. Both (A) and (R) are true.
D. Both (A) and (R) are false.

43. Assertion (A): The mean is a measure of dispersion.

Reason (R) : The mean is based on every obervation and is representative of the whole population.

Code:

A. (A) is true, but (R) is false.
B. Both (A) and (R) are true.
C. (A) is false, but (R) is true.
D. Both (A) and (R) are false.

44. Assertion (A): Access to e-collection of a library via Login and password recognition is mostly used than access via IP-address.

Reason (R) : Access via IP-address presents a challenge in controlling the distribution of password to non-affiliates.

Code:

A. (A) is true, and (R) is false
B. Both (A) and (R) are true
C. (A) is false and (R) is true
D. Both (A) and (R) are false

45. Assertion (A): Interlibrary loan departments in libraries will be affected in positive ways by the development of Massive Digital Libraries.

Reason (R) : Because the increased availability of online resources will considerably reduce the need for sending books through traditional mail resulting in the decrease of the workloads of the inter-library loan departments.

Code:

A. (A) is true, but (R) is false.
B. Both (A) and (R) are true.
C. (A) is false, but (R) is true.
D. Both (A) and (R) are false.

Directions (Qs. No. 46-50): *Read the passage given below and answer the questions based on your understanding of the passage.*

The medical community is not homogeneous. We have a wide range of kinds of work and, hence, we have a wide range of kinds of needs for information. Therefore, solutions for better access by investigators to information that they need might not help practicing physicians at all.

Science in medicine and the practice of medicine differ greatly. How they differ was described succinctly by Peter Mere Latham well over a century ago : "Medicine is a strange mixture of speculation and action. We have to cultivate a science and to exercise an art. The calls of science are upon our leisure and our choice; the calls of practice are of daily emergence and necessity". Latham's point is well made, but it is not quite detailed enough for our considerations here. Let me sketch out how the information needs of investigators and physicians differ.

1. An investigator usually poses one question (or faces one problem) at a time and works on it for a long period. A physician constantly faces a quick succession of problems that call for rapid solutions.
2. The investigator's problem is usually narrow and readily defined. The problems dealt with by the physician tend to be highly various and fogged by many uncertainties.
3. An investigator's earnings are not tightly coupled to how he spends time from minute to minute and hour to hour. A physician's earnings are tightly coupled to every day's working hours and how they are spent.

These differences lead to differences in kinds of information needs and searches.

1. The investigator tends to need an exhaustive search of information sources ("the literature") but at infrequent intervals. The time available for the search is relatively large and can be carried out at relatively low cost in "purchase" and in "time-cost".
2. The physician needs quick access to valid information of immediate and high utility. The time available for a search is small. The "time-cost" for a search is high. The physician has to work mainly with thoroughly digested concepts and with most of the needed data carried in his head; the brain has a very rapid access time. Additional facts needed for clinical decisions must be accessed very rapidly. Both investigator and physician occasionally have needs like those of the other. The investigator may need quick access to a small and specific piece of technical information; the physician may be willing occasionally to embark on a broad search to deal with a rare problem. Further, both have ongoing needs for general awareness of new developments that may come eventually to have high utility.

These differences seem to me to determine how investigators and physicians use or do not use various kinds of information materials and sources.

Investigators tend to use reports of specific and individual research efforts-journal articles. They tend to carry out searches themselves or to assign them to close professional associates. They have time to assess and to digest individual papers. Synoptic information, such as that in review articles, is used mainly for orientation to a new problem.

46. How do Peter Mere Latham differentiate calls of 'Science' (in Medicine) from that of the 'practice' (of medicine)?

A. The calls of science are upon one's leisure and choice, where as the calls of practice are of daily emergence.

B. 'Medicine' is a non exotic mixture of certainty, while practice of medicine is an infrequent phenomenon.

C. Science is not a study of the natural world, where as practice is based on facts learned through a formal study.

D. Science is not a method of reconciling practical ends with scientific laws, where as 'practice' do not allow repeated exercise to make one proficient.

47. How Lathams differentiates the information needs of Investigators from that of Physicians.

A. An Investigator unconventionally faces with multiple problems at a single point of time and works on it for a long period, while a physician constantly faces slow-witted succession of problems that hardly warrant rapid solution.

B. An investigator ordinarily faces one

question/problem at a time which is usually narrow and rapidly defined, while a physician constantly faces a quick succession of varied problems fogged by many uncertainties.

C. Earnings of an Investigator are strictly coupled to how he spends time from minute to minute, whereas a Physician's earnings are not tightly coupled to every day working hours.

D. Information needs of Investigators are solely academic, where as the needs of Physicians are both academic and utilitarian.

48. Who tends to need quick access to valid Information of immediate and high quality?

A. An Investigator B. A Screwball

C. A Physician D. A Teacher

49. Why 'time cost' for a search made by a Physician is higher?

A. Slow access to invalid information.

B. Access to information that are distant in need and of less utility.

C. Exhaustive search of information sources.

D. Rapid access to high quality information needed for clinical decision.

50. Why the Investigators tend to carryout searches themselves?

A. They have time to assess and digest individual papers.

B. They are unaware of appropriate information sources.

C. They have no access to information/ literature they need.

D. They cannot afford time to search, identify, and digest the articles of high quality.

ANSWERS

1	**2**	**3**	**4**	**5**	**6**	**7**	**8**	**9**	**10**
B	C	A	C	D	A	C	B	C	B
11	**12**	**13**	**14**	**15**	**16**	**17**	**18**	**19**	**20**
D	B	D	D	A	B	B	C	A	A
21	**22**	**23**	**24**	**25**	**26**	**27**	**28**	**29**	**30**
C	B	A	B	D	B	B	B	C	C
31	**32**	**33**	**34**	**35**	**36**	**37**	**38**	**39**	**40**
A	B	A	B	A	D	A	C	A	B
41	**42**	**43**	**44**	**45**	**46**	**47**	**48**	**49**	**50**
B	D	C	D	B	A	B	C	D	A

EXPLANATORY ANSWERS

1. DELNET or **Developing Library Network** was started at the India International Centre Library in January 1988 and was registered as a society in 1992. It was initially supported by the National Information System for Science and Technology (NISSAT), Department of Scientific and Industrial Reseach, Government of India. It was subsequently supported by the National Informatics Centre, Department of Information Technology, Ministry of Communications and Information Technology, Government of India and the Ministry of Culture, Government of India.

3. Keesing's was founded in 1931 with the intention of creating a lasting archive of original, accurate, and objective articles on the world's political, social, and economic events. The team of writers and editors based in Cambridge, UK creates concise, clear articles published every month that provide readers with a digestible, detailed summary of global news. Keesing's Record of World Events, available from Keesing's World News Archive, is a news digest, compiling the world's most significant political, social and economic events by the end of the month following that in which they occurred. Events covered include elections and changes of government; wars, treaties, appointments, and diplomacy; terrorism and issues of internal security; legislation, budgets, economic developments and international agreements; actions by the UN and other international organisations; natural disasters, environmental issues, and scientific discoveries.

4. **Letter by Letter method of alphabetization** is a method in which a reference work's entries are arranged in the sequence of the letters and not words and where multi-word entries are treated as single words. For example, 'linear function' is followed by 'linearity' and not 'linear market'. Letter-by-letter alphabetization is commonly used by scholarly publishers and is the familiar arrangement found in dictionaries and encyclopedias.

5. The **International Standard Name Identifier (ISNI)** is an identifier for uniquely identifying the public identities of contributors to media content such as books, television programmes, and newspaper articles. Such an identifier consists of 16 digits. It can optionally be displayed as divided into four blocks. It was developed under the auspices of the International Organization for Standardization (ISO) as Draft International Standard 27729; the valid standard was published on 15 March 2012. The ISO technical committee 46, subcommittee 9 (TC 46/SC 9) is responsible for the development of the standard.

6. **Colon classification (CC)** is a system of library classification developed by S. R. Ranganathan. It was the first ever faceted (or analytico-synthetic) classification. The first edition was published in 1933. Since then six more editions have been published. It is especially used in libraries in India. Its name "colon classification" comes from the use of colons to separate facets in class numbers. However, many other classification schemes, some of which are completely unrelated, also use colons and other punctuations in various functions.

7. **DDC Third Summary:** The Dewey Decimal Classification (DDC) system is a general knowledge organization tool that is continuously revised to keep pace with knowledge. The system was conceived by Melvil Dewey in 1873 and first published in 1876. The main structure of the DDC is presented in the DDC Summaries. The third summary contains the thousand sections. The third digit in each three-digit number indicates the section. Thus, 610 is used for general works on medicine and health, 611 for human anatomy, 612 for human physiology, 613 for personal health and safety.

8. S.R. Ranganathan provided a completly new direction to the concept of classification originally formulated by Sayers. Ranganathan formulated 43 canons and grouped them into three planes of work. (*i*) Canons for Idea Plane (15). (*ii*) Canons for Verbal Plane (4). (*iii*) Canons for Notational Plane (24).

   The four canons for Verbal Plane deal with the language and terminology aspects in a scheme of classification. The terminology used in the scheme should clearly indicate the context in which a particular term has been used and what aspects it comprehends. The terms used to denote concepts should be current and noncritical. The four canons are:

   (*i*) Canon of Context
   (*ii*) Canon of Enumeration
   (*iii*) Canon of Currency
   (*iv*) Canon of Reticence

9. **Positive correlation:** It is a relationship between two variables in which both variables move in tandem. A positive correlation exists when one variable decreases as the other

variable decreases, or one variable increases while the other increases. In statistics, a perfect positive correlation is represented by 1, while 0 indicates no correlation and negative 1 indicates a perfect negative correlation.

10. A quasi-experimental design is one that looks a bit like an experimental design but lacks the key ingredient — random assignment. Ex-post-facto study or after-the-fact research is a category of research design in which the investigation starts after the fact has occurred without interference from the researcher. The majority of social research, in contexts in which it is not possible or acceptable to manipulate the characteristics of human participants, is based on ex-post-facto research designs.

11. **The Big 6:** The Big 6 is a process model of how people of all ages solve an information problem. The process is a systematic approach to information problem-solving that relies upon critical thinking skills. Mike Eisenberg (Dean Emeritus and Professor - University of Washington Information School) and Bob Berkowitz (School Library Media Specialist with the Wayne Central School District, Ontario Center, NY) developed this process which guides students through information problem-solving as well as provides a basic framework for teaching and promoting information literacy. The Big 6 process encourages teaching partnerships of library media specialists and classroom teachers. The big six information library skills proposed by M. B. Eisenberg and R. E. Berkowitz are *Task Definition*, *Information Seeking Strategies*, *Location and Access*, *Use of Information*, *Synthesis* and *Evaluation*.

12. **Indian National Bibliography (INB):** It has been conceived as an authoritative bibliographical record of current Indian publications in Assamese, Bengali, English, Gujarati, Hindi, Kannada, Malayalam, Marathi, Odiya, Punjabi, Sanskrit, Tamil, Telugu and Urdu languages, received in the National Library, Kolkata under the Delivery of Books and Newspapers, (Public Libraries) Act, 1954. The following types of publications are excluded:

(*a*) Maps
(*b*) Musical scores
(*c*) Periodicals and Newspapers (except the first issue of a new periodical and the first issue of a periodical under a new title)
(*d*) Keys and Guides to Textbooks
(*e*) Ephemeral and other such materials.

13. **Transborder data flow:** It is the transmission over computer-communicational systems of automated data to be processed and stored in foreign data processing systems. A number of issues, including privacy protection and data security, arise in various transborder data flow (TDF) situations and are discussed in this paper, especially the potential effects on TDF of national privacy protection laws and pending international agreements. Sets of associated technical requirements are examined.

14. **S.R. Ranganathan** (12 August 1892 – 27 September 1972) was a mathematician and librarian from India. His most notable contributions to the field were his five laws of library science and the development of the first major faceted classification system, the colon classification. He is considered to be the father of library science, documentation, and information science in India and is widely known throughout the rest of the world for his fundamental thinking in the field. His birthday is observed every year as the National Librarian's Day in India. Dr. Ranganathan recevied D. Litt Degree from the Delhi and Pittsburgh universities, in recognition of unique service to library science and was also the recipient of Rao Sahib and Padmashri awards from the Government of India.

15. **Asian Recorder** is an information digest. It contains the information about what is happening in Asia and other events related to Asian countries that are going on outside Asia and also news related with sports inside Asia. **Data Portal of India** is a platform for single-point access to datasets and apps published by Ministries/Departments/Organisations of the Government of India. It combines and expands the best features of India's and the U.S. government's data.gov project.

17. Colon classification (CC) is a system of library classification developed by S. R. Ranganathan. It was the first ever faceted (or analytico-synthetic) classification. The first edition was published in 1933. Since then six more editions have been published. It is especially used in libraries in India. Its name "colon classification" comes from the use of colons to separate facets in class numbers. However, many other classification schemes, some of which are completely unrelated, also use colons and other punctuations in various functions.

19. Non-parametric inferential statistical methods are mathematical procedures for statistical hypothesis testing which, unlike parametric statistics, make no assumptions about the probability distributions of the variables being assessed. The most frequently used tests include:

Anderson–Darling Test: tests whether a sample is drawn from a given distribution.

Statistical bootstrap methods: Estimates the accuracy/sampling distribution of a statistic

Cochran's Q: Tests whether *k* treatments in randomized block designs with 0/1 outcomes have identical effects.

Cohen's kappa: Measures inter-rater agreement for categorical items.

Spearman's rank correlation coefficient: Measures statistical dependence between two variables using a monotonic function.

Squared ranks test: Tests equality of variances in two or more samples.

Kuiper's test: Tests whether a sample is drawn from a given distribution, sensitive to cyclic variations such as day of the week.

Logrank test: Compares survival distributions of two right-skewed, censored samples.

20. Cost-effectiveness: Relationship between monetary inputs and the desired outcome, such as between the expenditure on an advertising campaign and increase in sales revenue.

GANTT Charts: A **Gantt chart** is a type of bar chart that illustrates a project schedule. Gantt charts illustrate the start and finish dates of the terminal elements and summary elements of a project. Terminal elements and summary elements comprise the work breakdown structure of the project. Modern Gantt charts also show the dependency (*i.e.*, precedence network) relationships between activities.

21. The views expressed here do not necessarily reflect those of the organization with which the author is currently affiliated. For a broader discussion of transborder data flows see the UN document "Transnational Corporations and Transborder Data Flows: An Overview" on which this article is based.

Broadly defined, transborder data flows are movements across national boundaries of machine-readable data for processing, storage, or retrieval. Such movements can be effected by nonelectronic means such as magnetic tapes, discs, punched cards, or other media. Increasingly, however, electronic means are used. In these cases, transnational computer-communication systems are established: that is, arrangements whereby one or several sophisticated computers in one or several countries are linked to affiliated computers in other countries and through them, or directly, to remote terminals.

22. S.R. Ranganathan was instrumental in revolutionising the Theory of Classification. He propounded certain fundamental ideas and concepts, which are the basis for the development of the Theory of Classification. 141- consistently advocated that library classification should conform to the Laws of Library Science. He worked vigorously towards the most helpful and filiatory sequence of classes in a scheme of classification based on the concept of Facet Analysis and Fundamental Categories. He totally rejected the earlier schemes, based purely on enumeration. His laws, canons and principles of library classification have been presented in his Prolegomena to Library Classification. Basic Laws: Ranganathan formulated six basic laws, viz.,

(*a*) Law of Interpretation
(*b*) Law of Impartiality
(*c*) Law of Symmetry
(*d*) Law of Parsimony
(*e*) Law of Local Variation
(*f*) Law of Osmosis

These basic laws govern the thinking process in general. These may be invoked when two or more Laws of Library Science or Canons for Classification lead to conflicting or equally valid different decisions.

23. Rampur Raza Library: The **Rampur Raza Library** located in Rampur, Uttar Pradesh, India is a repository of Indo-Islamic cultural heritage and a treasure-house of knowledge established in the last decades of 18th century, and built up by successive Nawabs of Rampur and now managed by Government of India.

Asiatic Society Library, **Bombay:** Asiatic Society of Bombay Library started in 1804 by Sir James Mackintosh along with the start up of Literary Society of Bombay in those days. The library of the Society has over a hundred thousand books out of which 15,000 are classified as rare and valuable. It also has priceless artifacts and over 3,000 ancient manuscripts in Persian, Sanskrit and Prakrit, mostly on paper but some on palm leaf. The numismatic collection of 11,829 coins includes a gold coin of Kumaragupta I, a rare gold mohur of Akbar and coins issued by Shivaji. Its map collection comprises 1300 maps.

Connemara Public Library, Chennai: Connemara Public Library at Egmore in Chennai, Tamil Nadu, India, is one of the four National Depository Libraries which receive a copy of all books, newspapers and periodicals published in India. Established in 1890, the library is a repository of centuries-old publications, wherein lie some of the most respected works and collections in the country. It also serves as a depository library for the UN.

24. Woodblock printing: Woodblock printing is a technique for printing text, images or patterns used widely throughout East Asia and originating in China in antiquity as a method of printing on textiles and later paper. Most European uses of the technique for printing images on paper are covered by the art term woodcut, except for the block-books produced mainly in the 15th century in India.

Movable type: Movable type is a weblog publishing system developed by the company Six Apart. It was publicly announced on September 3, 2001; version 1.0 was publicly released on October 8, 2001. The current version is 6.3.2.

Screen printing: Screen printing is a printing technique whereby a mesh is used to transfer ink onto a substrate, except in areas made impermeable to the ink by a blocking stencil. Screen printing first appeared in a recognizable from in China during the Song Dynasty (960-1279 AD). It was then adapted by other Asian countries like Japan, and was furthered by creating newer methods.

Dot-Matrix printer: A dot matrix printer is an impact printer that prints using a fixed number of pins or wires. A variation on the Dot-matrix printer was the cross hammer dot printer, patented by Seikosha in 1982.

25. Refreshing: *Refreshing* is the transfer of data between two types of the same storage medium so there are no bitrot changes or alteration of data. For example, transferring census data from an old preservation CD to a new one.

Emulation: *Emulation* is the replicating of functionality of an obsolete system. According to van der Hoeven, "Emulation does not focus on the digital object, but on the hard- and software environment in which the object is rendered. It aims at (re)creating the environment in which the digital object was originally created."

Examples are having the ability to replicate or imitate another operating system.

Encapsulation: This method maintains that preserved objects should be self-describing, virtually "linking content with all of the information required for it to be deciphered and understood". The files associated with the digital object would have details of how to interpret that object using "logical structures called "containers" or "wrappers" to provide a relationship between all information components that could be used in future development of emulators, viewers or converters through machine readable specifications. The method of encapsulation is usually applied to collections that will go unused for long periods of time.

Data archiving: Data archiving is the process of moving data that is no longer actively used to a separate storage device for long-term retention. Archive data consists of older data that is still important to the organization and may be needed for future reference, as well as data that must be retained for regulatory compliance. Data archives are indexed and have search capabilities so files and parts of files can be easily located and retrieved.

26. A program is a list of instructions that contains data for a computer to follow. Different programs are written with different languages. An editing program is made with a different programming "language" than one that uses graphics. Programming is complicated process, below is general overview of this 5 step procedure.

Clarify/Define the Problem: Knowing the objective is the first consideration. Is it a payroll or editing program? Knowing who the end user will be also important. Determining the inputs and outputs is next. How will the program operate and what data is needed to make it happen. After this has been decided feasibility is the next consideration.

Program design: The activity of progressing from a specification of some required program to a description of the program itself. Most phase models of the software life cycle recognize program design as one of the phases.

Program code: In programming, code (noun) is a term used for both the statements written in a particular programming language - the source code, and a term for the source code after it has been processed by a compiler and made ready to run in the computer - the object code.

Program test: A system of checking before running any problem in which a sample problem of the same type with a known answer runs.

Program documentation: Program documentation is a kind of documentation that gives a comprehensive procedural description of a program. It shows as to how software is written. Program documentation describes what exactly a program does by mentioning about the requirements of the input data and the effect of performing a programming task.

27. Scholarly Publishing and Academic Resources Coalition (SPARC): The SPARC is an international alliance of academic and research libraries developed by the Association of Research Libraries in 1998 which promotes open access to scholarship. SPARC Europe was established with LIBER in 2001.

The Budapest Open Access Initiatives (BOAI): The BOAI is a public statement of principles relating to open access to the research literature, which was released to the public on February 14, 2002. It arose from a conference convened in Budapest by the Open

Society Institute on December 1–2, 2001 to promote open access – at the time also known as *Free Online Scholarship*.

The Berlin Declaration on Open Access to Knowledge in the Sciences and Humanities (BDOAKS and H). The BDOAKS and H is a major international statement on open access and access to knowledge. It emerged from a conference on open access hosted in the Harnack House in Berlin by the Max Planck Society in 2003.

The Coalition of Open Access Policy Institutions (COAPI): The COAPI is a membership organization that has been working since 2011 to advance the promotion, passage, and implementation of Open Access policies at institutions of higher education.

28. Indian Citation Index (ICI) is a comprehensive multidisciplinary citation index for the research journals published from India. Indian Citation Index is developed by The Knowledge Foundation (a registered society) with the support of M/s Diva Enterprises Pvt. Ltd. India provides a significant contribution to the global knowledge but is not covered and evaluated enough in the present international tools.

The National Social Science Documentation Centre (NASSDOC), a constituent unit of the Indian Council of Social Science Research (ICSSR), was established in 1969. The objective of the NASSDOC is to provide library and information support services to social science researchers.

From 1986 to 31st March 2009, **National Informatics Centre (NIC)** and **Indian Council of Medical Research (ICMR)** had collaborated to setup ICMR-NIC Centre for Biomedical Information. The Centre, known as Indian Medlars Centre, provided information support services to medical research community. It also produced two important resources:

- A bibliographic database - IndMED - by indexing about 100 Indian medical journals.
- A portal - medIND - providing free full text access to 62 Indian medical journals.

For continuing the maintaining, updating and improvising these two important national resources, ICMR funded a new project (National Databases of Indian Medical Journals) in 2010.

Indian Animal Science Abstract: It is a journal published by Directorate of Information and Publications of Agriculture, Indian Council of Agricultural Research (ICAR), New Delhi.

29. Knowledge Economy: The knowledge economy is the use of knowledge to generate tangible and intangible values. Technology and, in particular, knowledge technology help to incorporate part of human knowledge into machines. This knowledge can be used by decision support systems in various fields to generate economic value. Knowledge economy is also possible without technology.

The term was popularized by Peter Drucker as the title of Chapter 12 in his book *The Age of Discontinuity* (1969), that Drucker attributed to economist Fritz Machlup, originating in the idea of "scientific management" developed by Frederick Winslow Taylor.

Documentation: Paul Otlet was a Belgian author, entrepreneur, visionary, lawyer and peace activist; he is one of several people who have been considered the father of information science, a field he called "documentation". Otlet created the Universal Decimal Classification, one of the most prominent examples of faceted classification.

Informatics: The term 'informatics' was first advanced formally by the Director of VINITI, A. I. Mikhailov, and his colleagues A. I. Chernyi and R. S. Gilyarevskii, in their paper

Informatics—new name for the theory of Scientific Information published at the end of 1966.

Information Retrieval: Calvin Northrup Mooers (1919 – December 1, 1994), was an American computer scientist known for his work in information retrieval and for the programming language TRAC.

30. Bibliography: Bibliography as a discipline, is traditionally the academic study of books as physical, cultural objects; in this sense, it is also known as bibliology. A volume is a physical book in codex format. It may be printed or manuscript. The term may be used to identify a single book that is part of a larger collection. The term is also used as an identifier for a sequence of periodicals, generally based on a single calendar year.

Biography: A biography, or simply bio, is a detailed description of a person's life. It involves more than just the basic facts like education, work, relationships, and death; it portrays a person's experience of these life events.

Siblings of Mahatma Gandhi had two older brothers, Laxmidas and Karsandas, and an older sister, Raliatbehn. Statistical source: Statistical sources are works that often present data in charts, graphs, tables, etc.

Primary school: A primary school (or elementary school in American English) is a school in which children receive primary or elementary education from the age of about five to twelve, coming after preschool and before secondary school. (In some countries there is an intermediate stage of middle school between primary and secondary education).

31. Postulates: We have now a set of postulates to guide the design of classification. The attributes "True" and "False" do not apply to postulates. The only attributes applicable to them are "Helpfulness" and "Unhelpfulness". The following set of postulates have proved helpful. There are five and only Five Fundamental Categories—viz., Time, Space, Energy, Matter, and Personality.

Time: Perhaps the fundamental category "Time" gives the least difficulty in its identification. It is in accordance with what we commonly understand by that term. The usual Time Isolate Ideas—such as millennium, century, decade, year, and so on—are its manifestations. Time Isolate Ideas of another kind—such as day and night, seasons such as summer and winter, time with meteorological quality such as, wet, dry, and stormy—are also taken as manifestations of the fundamental category "Time".

Space: The fundamental category "Space" comes next to "Time" in difficulty in its identification. It is in accordance with what we commonly understand by that term. The surface of the earth, the space inside it, and the space outside it, are manifestations of the fundamental category "Space". The usual Geographical Isolate Ideas—such as continents, countries, and counties—and water formations—such as oceans and seas—are taken to be its manifestations.

Energy: Even otherwise, the identification of the fundamental category "Energy" is a little more difficult than that of "Space" or "Time". Generally speaking, its manifestation is an action of one kind or another. The action may be among and by all kinds of entities—inanimate, animate, conceptual, intellectual, and intuitive. Till now, we have been taking Morphology, Physiology, Disease, Ecology, Hygiene, and some other isolate ideas also as manifestations of the fundamental category "Energy". It was difficult to see only "Action" in them.

Matter: The identification of the fundamental category "Matter" is more difficult than even of "Energy". Its manifestations are taken to be of two kinds—Material and Property. It may look strange that property should be taken alongwith material. But let us take a table as an example. The table is made of the material, timber or steel, as the case may be. The material is intrinsic to the table, but is not the table itself. Moreover, the same material can figure also in several other entities. So also, the table has the property of being two and a half ft. high and the property of having a soft top or a hard top. The property is intrinsic to the table, but not the table itself. Moreover, the same property can figure also in several other entities. Each of the isolate ideas Morphology, Physiology, Disease, etc., mentioned in the preceding section and now being excluded from the manifestations of the fundamental category "Energy", admit of being looked upon as Property. As such, they are now regarded as manifestations of the fundamental category "Matter".

Personality: The fundamental category "Personality" presents the greates difficulty in its identification. It is too elusive. It is ineffable.

32. **ACI Symbols (CC 6th Edition):** Colon classification (CC) is a system of library classification developed by S. R. Ranganathan. It was the first ever faceted (or analytico-synthetic) classification. The first edition was published in 1933. Since then six more editions have been published. It is especially used in libraries in India.

    Its name "colon classification" comes from the use of colons to separate facets in class numbers. However, many other classification schemes, some of which are completely unrelated, also use colons and other punctuation in various functions. In CC, facets describe "personality" (the most specific subject), matter, energy, space, and time (PMEST). These facets are generally associated with every item in a library, and so form a reasonably universal sorting system.

33. **National Information Standard Organization (NISO):** The National Information Standard Organization (NISO) is a United States non-profit standards organization that develops, maintains and publishes technical standards related to publishing, bibliographic and library applications. It was founded in 1939. Examples of NISO standards include:

    - Z39.2: Bibliographic records Information Interchange Format (IIF) encoding mostly used with MARC standards
    - Z39.29: Bibliographic References; last version is Z39.29-2005 (R2010)
    - Z39.5: Journal title abbreviations, resulting in the 1969 publication of the American National Standard for the Abbreviation of Titles of Periodicals
    - Z39.50: A protocol for accessing bibliographic databases
    - Z39.83: NISO Circulation Interchange Protocol (NCIP) for library catalogue data exchange
    - Z39.84: Digital Object Identifier (DOI)
    - Z39.85: Dublin Core
    - Z39.86: Specifications for the Digital Talking Book: DAISY Digital Accessible Information System
    - Z39.87: Technical Metadata for Digital Still Images - MIX
    - Z39.88: OpenURL

34. **Pen Drive:** Pen Drive is a "USB Flash Drive". Pen Drive is also a "Removable Storage Device" with an integrated Universal Serial Bus (USB) interface. In the past time, people use the "Floppy Disk" to transfer any document from one computer to another computer.

    iPad: iPad is a line of tablet computers designed, developed and marketed by Apple Inc., which runs the iOS mobile operating system. The first iPad was released on April 3, 2010. The user interface is built around the device's multi-touch screen, including a virtual keyboard. All iPads can connect via

Wi-Fi; some models also have cellular connectivity.

Wi-Fi modem: Wi-Fi is a wireless networking technology that allows computers and other devices to communicate over a wireless signal. It describes network components that are based on one of the 802.11 standards developed by the 1EEE and adopted by the Wi-Fi Alliance.

Cloud computing: Cloud computing is an information technology (IT) paradigm that enables ubiquitous access to shared pools of configurable system resources and higher-level services that can be rapidly provisioned with minimal management effort, often over the Internet. Cloud computing relies on sharing of resources to achieve coherence and economy of scale, similar to a public utility.

In the PaaS models, cloud providers deliver a computing platform, typically including operating system, programming language execution environment, database, and web server.

35. Web 1.0: Web 1.0 is the first generation of the web. Web 1.0 was mainly a read-only web. Web 1.0 was static and somewhat mono-directional. Businesses could provide catalogs or brochures to present their productions using the web and people could read them and contacted with the businesses. Web 1.0 is simply an information portal where users passively receive information without being given the opportunity to post reviews, comments, and feedback.

Web 2.0: It is 2nd generation of the www that focused on the ability for people to collaborate and share information online. Web 2.0 is the name used to describe the second generation of the World Wide Web, where it moved static HTML pages to a more interactive and dynamic Web experience. Web 2.0 encourages participation, collaboration, and information sharing. Examples of Web 2.0 applications are Youtube, Wiki, Flickr, Facebook, and so on.

Web 3.0: In Web 3.0, computers can interpret information like humans and intelligently generate and distribute useful content tailored to the needs of users. One example of Web 3.0 is Tivo, a digital video recorder. Its recording program can search the web and read what it finds to you based on your preferences.

Web 4.0: The Web is evolving far beyond Web 2.0 to Web 4.0. Web 4.0 is described as the symbiotic web in which the human mind and machines can interact symbiotically, including Medicine 4.0 and its links to human city interaction.

36. Formalized research: To formalize means to give formal standing or endorsement to; make official or legitimate by the observance of proper procedure. Therefore, a research which has been given formal standing or endorsement or which has been made official or legitimate by the observance of proper procedure is known as formalized research.

Conceptual research: Conceptual research is that related to some abstract idea(s) or theory. It is generally used by philosophers and thinkers to develop new concepts or to reinterpret existing ones.

Descriptive research: Descriptive research is used to describe characteristics of a population or phenomenon being studied. It does not answer questions about how/when/why the characteristics occurred. Rather it addresses the "what" question. The characteristics used to describe the situation or population are usually some kind of categorical scheme also known as descriptive categories. For example, the periodic table categorizes the elements.

Fundamental research: Fundamental research, also called Basic research, or Pure research, is a scientific research aimed to improve scientific theories for improved understanding or prediction of natural or other phenomena. Applied research, in turn, uses scientific theories to develop technology or techniques to intervene and *alter* natural or other phenomena. Though often driven by curiosity, fundamental research fuels applied science's innovations. The two aims are often coordinated in research and development.

38. **Postulates:** A postulate (also sometimes called an axiom) is a statement that is agreed by everyone to be correct. This is useful for creating proofs in mathematics and science, and postulates are often the basic truth of a much larger theory or law.

    Assumptions: The act of assuming, or taking to or upon oneself; the act of taking up or adopting.

39. **TQM application:** Theories form the backdrop for TQM. Actual difficulties are faced when it is implemented in libraries/information centers. The theories are basically intended for business organizations. Implementing the strategies for TQM in libraries and information centers is quite challenging. A different model needs to be developed for the service sector like libraries/information centers. This section discusses the basic elements of TQM for libraries and information centers and steps to be followed for their implementation.

40. **Web 2.0:** Web 2.0 refers to World Wide Web websites that emphasize user-generated content, usability (ease of use, even by non-experts), and interoperability (this means that a website can work well with other products, systems, and devices) for end users. The term was popularized by Tim O'Reilly and Dale Dougherty at the O'Reilly Media Web 2.0 Conference in late 2004, though it was coined by Darcy DiNucci in 1999. Web 2.0 does not refer to an update to any technical specification, but to changes in the way Web pages are designed and used.

    Web 2.0 is the term given to describe a second generation of the World Wide Web that is focused on the ability for people to collaborate and share information online. Web 2.0 basically refers to the transition from static HTML Web pages to a more dynamic Web that is more organized and is based on serving Web applications to users.

41. **Secondary storage device:** Alternatively referred to as **external memory**, **secondary memory**, and **auxiliary storage**, a **secondary storage device** is a non-volatile device that holds data until it is deleted or overwritten. Secondary storage is about two orders of magnitude cheaper than primary storage. Consequently, hard drives (a prime example of secondary storage) are the go-to solution for nearly all data kept on today's computers.

42. **Participatory action research:** Participatory action research (PAR) is an approach to research in communities that emphasizes participation and action. It seeks to understand the world by trying to change it, collaboratively and following reflection. PAR emphasizes collective inquiry and experimentation grounded in experience and social history.

    Pure research: Pure research is a scientific research aimed to improve scientific theories for improved understanding or prediction of natural or other phenomena. Applied research, in turn, uses scientific theories to develop technology or techniques to intervene and *alter* natural or other phenomena. Though often driven by curiosity, fundamental research fuels applied science's innovations. The two aims are often coordinated in research and development.

43. As such, measures of central tendency are sometimes called measures of central location. They are also classed as summary statistics. The mean (often called the average) is most likely the measure of central tendency that you are most familiar with, but there are others, such as the median and the mode.

    The mean can be defined in terms of exact mathematical operations and we have no scope to use our judgement in its computation or evaluation. The mean is based on every observation and hence is representative of the whole population or sample. The mean is not very much affected by the sampling fluctuations. The mean lends itself to algebraic treatment. For example, if we are given *m* means of *m* different samples of a population, we can compute the mean of *m* means using an algebraic formula. The mean is very easy to compute.

45. Interlibrary loan: Interlibrary loan (abbreviated **ILL**, and sometimes called interloan, interlending, document delivery, or document supply) is a service whereby a patron of one library can borrow books, DVDs, music, etc. and/or receive photocopies of documents that are owned by another library. The user makes a request with their home library; which, acting as an intermediary, identifies libraries with the desired item, places the request, receives the item, makes it available to the user, as well as arranges for its return. The lending library usually sets a due date and overdue fees of the material borrowed. Although books and journal articles are the most frequently requested items, some libraries will lend audio recordings, video recordings, maps, sheet music, and microforms of all kinds. In some cases, nominal fees accompany the interlibrary loan services.

PAPER-III

Note: *This paper contains* ***Seventy five (75)*** *objective type questions of* ***two (2)*** *marks each.* ***All*** *questions are* ***compulsory.***

1. Identify the author of 'Essays of an Information Scientist' from among the following:
   A. F.W. Lancaster
   B. Derek J. de Solla Price
   C. Eugene Garfield
   D. B.C. Vickery

2. Who has coined the term 'Information Society' from the following?
   A. B.C. Brookes B. Fritz Machlup
   C. B.C. Vickery D. N.J. Belkin

3. Dance's Helical Spiral communication model is a:
   A. Classical B. Linear
   C. Non-Linear D. Multi-dimentional

4. What was the theme of IFLA World Library and Information Congress 2017?
   A. Connections. Collaboration. Community
   B. Dynamic Libraries : Access, Development and Transformation
   C. Libraries, Citizens, Societies : Confluence for knowledge
   D. Libraries. Solidarity. Society

5. Which of the following is a collaborative network of Reference Librarians?
   A. World Cat B. eSS
   C. Question Point D. Global Scholar

6. Resource Description and Access (RDA) is divided into how many sections?
   A. 9 B. 10
   C. 11 D. 12

7. p, q, r in the schema of operators in PRECIS belong to:
   A. Core elements
   B. Extra-core concepts
   C. Dependent elements
   D. Special classes of action

8. According to APA Style Manual, a section at the end of a paper that includes information that is too detailed for the text of the paper itself and would "burden the reader" or be "distracting" or "in appropriate" is called:
   A. Appendix B. Bibliography
   C. References D. Tables

9. Who coined the word "Management theory jungle"?
   A. Henry Fayol B. F.W. Taylor
   C. Heinz Weihrich D. Harold Koontz

10. Which of the following cases require the application of a new ISSN?
A. Change in publisher
B. Change in publication medium and title
C. Change in location of publication
D. Change in editorial policy

11. Which of the following organisations have introduced "Dig by"- a new mobile application available as a part of 'Worldshare Management Service'?
A. Library of Congress
B. NISCAIR
C. OCLC
D. UTLAS

12. Percentage (%) sign is used in an URL to represent:
A. Space B. Date
C. Time D. Person

13. FRBRoo version 2 is based on:
A. FRBR model alone
B. FRAD model alone
C. FRBR and FRAD models only
D. FRBR, FRAD and FRSAD models

14. Which one of the following is **not** Image format?
A. TIFF B. MPEG
C. JPEG D. GIF

15. Which of the following does not come under the domain of Descriptive bibliometrics (Descriptive Studies)?
A. Geographical Distribution of Documents
B. Nature of Information Conveyed
C. Subject Distribution
D. Medium of Communication

16. 'Half-life' in the context of literary growth is used to indicate:
A. Rate of obsolescence
B. Rate of growth
C. Degree of scatter
D. Information explosion

17. Which sampling method is not suitable, if unit members are homogeneous?
A. Simple random B. Cluster
C. Stratified D. Systematic

18. Hermeneutics, principle is primarily related with:
A. Interpretation of texts
B. Interrelation between data and knowledge
C. Human experience
D. Human behaviour

19. How many Working Groups are constituted under National Mission on Libraries, India?
A. Two B. Three
C. Four D. Five

20. Who is responsible for development and maintenance of UGC official website?
A. MHRD B. Do E
C. NIC D. INFLIBNET

21. Which of the following are the necessary elements of an information society?
(*a*) Confidentiality
(*b*) Vulnerability
(*c*) Integrity
(*d*) Availability
Code:
A. (*b*), (*c*) and (*d*) are correct
B. (*a*), (*b*) and (*c*) are correct
C. (*a*), (*c*) and (*d*) are correct
D. (*a*), (*b*) and (*d*) are correct

22. Which of the following components are essential for National Information Policy?
(*a*) Legislation framework
(*b*) E-Journal consortium
(*c*) Digital repositories
(*d*) National bibliography
Code:
A. (*a*) and (*b*) are correct
B. (*a*) and (*d*) are correct
C. (*b*) and (*c*) are correct
D. (*b*) and (*d*) are correct

23. SWAYAM, the free online education was developed by:
(*a*) IIT, Madras
(*b*) AICTE
(*c*) IIM, Ahmedabad
(*d*) MHRD, Govt. of India
Code:
A. (*b*) and (*d*) are correct
B. (*c*) and (*d*) are correct
C. (*a*) and (*b*) are correct
D. (*a*) and (*d*) are correct

24. Which of the following are the activities of National Mission on Libraries?

(*a*) CIP Project
(*b*) Capacity Building
(*c*) Library Assistance Programme
(*d*) Setting up of Model Libraries

Code:

A. (*a*) and (*d*) are correct
B. (*b*) and (*d*) are correct
C. (*b*) and (*c*) are correct
D. (*c*) and (*d*) are correct

25. Which of the following indicate the purpose of reference list in a thesis/dissertation?

(*a*) Allows author to credit the work of others that directly influenced the present work.
(*b*) Gives interested readers the information necessary to identify and retrieve the sources.
(*c*) An expansive list that covers works that are consulted.
(*d*) Recommends to the interested readers the works that are not cited in the text.

Code:

A. (*a*) and (*b*) are correct
B. (*b*) and (*c*) are correct
C. (*c*) and (*d*) are correct
D. (*b*) and (*d*) are correct

26. Which of the following are the products of Chemical Abstract services?

(*a*) Sci Finder
(*b*) Sci Val
(*c*) Methods Now
(*d*) Analytical Services

Code:

A. (*a*) and (*c*) are correct
B. (*b*) and (*d*) are correct
C. (*a*), (*b*) and (*c*) are correct
D. (*b*), (*c*) and (*d*) are correct

27. Which of the following roles does a library have in the information transfer cycle?

(*a*) Information organization and control
(*b*) Primary distribution
(*c*) Secondary publication
(*d*) Secondary distribution

Code:

A. (*b*) and (*d*) are correct
B. (*b*) and (*c*) are correct
C. (*a*) and (*d*) are correct
D. (*a*) and (*b*) are correct

28. Who among the following are associated with established theories of reference service?

(*a*) C.M. Winchell
(*b*) James I Wyer
(*c*) Daniel Brophy
(*d*) Samuel Rothstein

Code:

A. (*a*) and (*b*) are correct
B. (*b*) and (*d*) are correct
C. (*c*) and (*d*) are correct
D. (*a*) and (*c*) are correct

29. Which of the following are related to 'Sugamya Pustakalaya'?

(*a*) An online platform that makes accessible the content available to 'print disabled people'.
(*b*) Created by Department of Empowerment of persons with disabilities (Divyangjan) Ministry of Social Justice and Empowerment, GOI.
(*c*) Powered by TCS Access.
(*d*) Maintained by National Association for the Blind (India).

Code:

A. (*a*), (*b*) and (*d*) are correct
B. (*a*), (*b*) and (*c*) are correct
C. (*b*), (*c*) and (*d*) are correct
D. (*a*), (*c*) and (*d*) are correct

30. 'Entropy' in the context of 'Information Science' is:

(*a*) Measure which cannot be normalised by dividing it by information length.
(*b*) Measure of unpredictability of the state or equivalently, of its average information content.
(*c*) Average amount of information produced by a probabilistics stochastic source of data.
(*d*) Way to measure diversity.

Code:

A. (*a*), (*b*) and (*d*) are correct
B. (*a*), (*b*) and (*c*) are correct
C. (*a*), (*c*) and (*d*) are correct
D. (*b*), (*c*) and (*d*) are correct

31. Controlled vocabularies fall broadly into following categories:

(*a*) Subject Heading Lists
(*b*) Thesauri
(*c*) Folksonomies
(*d*) Ontologies

Code:

A. (*a*) and (*c*) are correct
B. (*b*), (*c*) and (*d*) are correct
C. (*a*), (*b*) and (*d*) are correct
D. (*c*) and (*d*) are correct

32. Which of the following are the components of a barcode symbol?

(*a*) Antenna (*b*) Quiet zone
(*c*) Transponder (*d*) Start character

Code:

A. (*a*) and (*c*) are correct
B. (*b*) and (*c*) are correct
C. (*b*) and (*d*) are correct
D. (*a*) and (*d*) are correct

33. 'Embargo' in the context of 'Book Trade' is:

(*a*) a limitation on access, to older resources by the publishers.
(*b*) perpetual ban on the access of the given resources of a publisher.
(*c*) a limitation on access to resources placed by publishers.
(*d*) a limitation on access to the resources usually to prevent the cancellation of individual subscription.

Code:

A. (*c*) and (*d*) are correct
B. (*a*) and (*b*) are correct
C. (*a*) and (*c*) are correct
D. (*a*), (*c*) and (*d*) are correct

34. Which of the following are Research Information Management System?

(*a*) Pure (*b*) Quetext
(*c*) Converis (*d*) VIVO

Code:

A. (*a*), (*b*) and (*d*) are correct
B. (*a*), (*b*) and (*c*) are correct
C. (*a*), (*c*) and (*d*) are correct
D. (*b*), (*c*) and (*d*) are correct

35. Which of the following are the open access initiatives of INFLIBNET?

(*a*) Shodhganga
(*b*) e-Shodh Sindhu
(*c*) Infoport
(*d*) IndCat

Code:

A. (*a*) and (*b*) are correct
B. (*b*) and (*c*) are correct
C. (*c*) and (*d*) are correct
D. (*a*) and (*c*) are correct

36. Which of the following are embedded processors?

(*a*) Micro Controller
(*b*) Digital Signal Processor
(*c*) Cor 2 extreme
(*d*) Intel Xeon

Code:

A. (*a*), (*b*) and (*d*) are correct
B. (*b*), (*c*) and (*d*) are correct
C. (*a*), (*b*) and (*c*) are correct
D. (*a*), (*c*) and (*d*) are correct

37. Jubilee (JISC User Behaviour in Information Seeking : Longitudinal Evaluation of Electronic Information Services) seeks to:

(*a*) Predict, monitor and characterise ISB in relation to EIS (Electronic Information Services).
(*b*) Provide illuminative and contextual pictures built up overtime to users and non-users.
(*c*) Evaluate materials of rarity in nature.
(*d*) Adjudge the quality of hard copies of e-reference tools served to readers in a given library over a period of time.

Code:

A. (*c*) and (*d*) are correct
B. (*a*) and (*b*) are correct
C. (*b*) and (*c*) are correct
D. (*a*) and (*d*) are correct

38. Arrange the following state Public Library Acts according to their year of enactment:
(*a*) Chhattisgarh Public Libraries Act
(*b*) Haryana Public Libraries Act
(*c*) Odisha Public Libraries Act
(*d*) Lakshadweep Public Libraries Act
Code:
A. (*b*), (*c*), (*d*), (*a*) B. (*d*), (*b*), (*c*), (*a*)
C. (*c*), (*b*), (*d*), (*a*) D. (*a*), (*b*), (*c*), (*d*)

39. Arrange in sequence the following public libraries according to their year of origin.
(*a*) Connemara Public Library
(*b*) Delhi Public Library
(*c*) Calcutta Public Library
(*d*) Baroda Central Library
Code:
A. (*c*), (*a*), (*d*), (*b*) B. (*c*), (*d*), (*b*), (*a*)
C. (*a*), (*b*), (*d*), (*c*) D. (*a*), (*d*), (*b*), (*c*)

40. Arrange the following laws/principles from lower to higher level as propounded by S.R. Ranganathan.
(*a*) Fundamental Laws
(*b*) Canons
(*c*) Principles
(*d*) Basic Laws
Code:
A. (*c*), (*b*), (*a*), (*d*) B. (*a*), (*b*), (*c*), (*d*)
C. (*b*), (*d*), (*a*), (*c*) D. (*d*), (*c*), (*b*), (*a*)

41. Arrange year-wise development of the following indexing systems:
(*a*) Relational Indexing by J.E.L. Farradane
(*b*) Chain Indexing by S.R. Ranganathan
(*c*) Subject Indexing by J.E. Coates
(*d*) PRECIS by Derek Austin
Code:
A. (*b*), (*a*), (*c*), (*d*) B. (*a*), (*b*), (*c*), (*d*)
C. (*c*), (*d*), (*b*), (*a*) D. (*d*), (*c*), (*a*), (*b*)

42. Arrange, from among the following, the areas of access-points in their proper sequence as given in ISBD.
(*a*) Notes
(*b*) Series
(*c*) Edition
(*d*) Material Specific details
Code:
A. (*a*), (*b*), (*c*), (*d*) B. (*c*), (*d*), (*b*), (*a*)
C. (*b*), (*c*), (*d*), (*a*) D. (*d*), (*c*), (*b*), (*a*)

43. Arrange the following connecting symbols of CC-6th ed. according to their increasing ordinal value:
(*a*)) (arrester)
(*b*) ← (backward arrow)
(*c*) → (forward arrow)
(*d*) 0 (zero)
Code:
A. (*b*), (*c*), (*d*), (*a*) B. (*a*), (*b*), (*c*), (*d*)
C. (*c*), (*d*), (*b*), (*a*) D. (*d*), (*a*), (*c*), (*b*)

44. Identify the correct sequence of indicator digits of Intra Facet Phase Relation as used in CC (6th edition).
A. j k m n r B. j k m r o
C. i j k m n D. j k m n q

45. Arrange in sequence the following subject classes according to their occurance in the schedules of DDC, 21st Ed.
(*a*) Food Technology
(*b*) Public Finance
(*c*) General Encyclopaedias
(*d*) Bibliographies
Code:
A. (*d*), (*b*), (*c*), (*a*) B. (*d*), (*c*), (*b*), (*a*)
C. (*c*), (*b*), (*a*), (*d*) D. (*c*), (*a*), (*b*), (*d*)

46. Arrange in sequence the Maslow's hierarchy of needs:
(*a*) Social
(*b*) Esteem
(*c*) Physiological
(*d*) Safety
Code:
A. (*c*), (*d*), (*a*), (*b*) B. (*d*), (*b*), (*a*), (*c*)
C. (*d*), (*a*), (*c*), (*b*) D. (*c*), (*a*), (*b*), (*d*)

47. Arrange in sequence the following document titles alphabetically word by word:
(*a*) Bookfinder
(*b*) Bookkeeping made simple
(*c*) Bookbytes
(*d*) Books that changed the world

Code:

A. (*a*), (*b*), (*c*), (*d*) B. (*b*), (*c*), (*d*), (*a*)
C. (*c*), (*a*), (*b*), (*d*) D. (*c*), (*d*), (*a*), (*b*)

48. Arrange the steps of the 8W'S Literacy Model in correct order as given by Annette Lamb:
(*a*) Webbing
(*b*) Wishing
(*c*) Wondering
(*d*) Weaving

Code:

A. (*c*), (*a*), (*b*) and (*d*)
B. (*b*), (*a*), (*c*) and (*d*)
C. (*c*), (*a*), (*d*) and (*b*)
D. (*c*), (*b*), (*a*) and (*d*)

49. Match the following sources with their corresponding functions:

List-I	***List-II***
(*a*) Counter	(*i*) Tracking e-resources usage statistics
(*b*) Affinity string	(*ii*) Impact factor
(*c*) Link resolver	(*iii*) Tracking online usage by user categories
(*d*) Journal of citation report	(*iv*) Number of times users' connectivity to a resource

Code:

	(*a*)	(*b*)	(*c*)	(*d*)
A.	(*iii*)	(*iv*)	(*i*)	(*ii*)
B.	(*ii*)	(*iv*)	(*iii*)	(*i*)
C.	(*i*)	(*iii*)	(*iv*)	(*ii*)
D.	(*iv*)	(*ii*)	(*i*)	(*iii*)

50. Match the following consortiums with their corresponding locations:

List-I	***List-II***
(*a*) UGC-DAE Consortium	(*i*) Manesar (Gurgaon)
(*b*) ERMED-India Consortium	(*ii*) Gandhinagar, (Ahmedabad)
(*c*) DeLCON-DBT's E-Library Consortium	(*iii*) Indore
(*d*) e-Shodh Sindhu	(*iv*) New Delhi

Code:

	(*a*)	(*b*)	(*c*)	(*d*)
A.	(*iii*)	(*iv*)	(*i*)	(*ii*)
B.	(*iv*)	(*iii*)	(*ii*)	(*i*)
C.	(*i*)	(*ii*)	(*iii*)	(*iv*)
D.	(*ii*)	(*i*)	(*iv*)	(*iii*)

51. Match the following leading Abstracting and Indexing tools/Databases with their corresponding Publishers/Content Providers:

List-I	***List-II***
(*a*) LISA	(*i*) NISCAIR
(*b*) ILSA	(*ii*) EBSCO
(*c*) LISTA	(*iii*) IASLIC
(*d*) Indian Science Abstracts	(*iv*) ProQuest

Code:

	(*a*)	(*b*)	(*c*)	(*d*)
A.	(*iv*)	(*iii*)	(*ii*)	(*i*)
B.	(*i*)	(*ii*)	(*iii*)	(*iv*)
C.	(*ii*)	(*iv*)	(*i*)	(*iii*)
D.	(*iii*)	(*i*)	(*iv*)	(*ii*)

52. Match the following threats to 'information society' with the corresponding concept:

List-I	***List-II***
(*a*) Compromises intellectual property	(*i*) Confiscation of equipment or information
(*b*) Deliberate acts of theft	(*ii*) Unauthorized access to data
(*c*) Deliberate acts of information extortion	(*iii*) Piracy
(*d*) Deliberate acts of espionage or trespass	(*iv*) Blackmail of information disclosure.

Code:

	(*a*)	(*b*)	(*c*)	(*d*)
A.	(*iii*)	(*iv*)	(*i*)	(*ii*)
B.	(*iv*)	(*ii*)	(*iii*)	(*i*)
C.	(*i*)	(*ii*)	(*iii*)	(*iv*)
D.	(*iii*)	(*i*)	(*iv*)	(*ii*)

53. Match the following:

List-I	***List-II***
(*a*) Political Map	(*i*) Features of land
(*b*) Route Map	(*ii*) Roads and bridges, etc.

(*c*) Physical Map	(*iii*)	Limiting territorial boundaries
(*d*) Thematic Map	(*iv*)	Mining, agriculture, etc.

Code:

	(*a*)	(*b*)	(*c*)	(*d*)
A.	(*iv*)	(*i*)	(*ii*)	(*iii*)
B.	(*i*)	(*ii*)	(*iii*)	(*iv*)
C.	(*iii*)	(*ii*)	(*i*)	(*iv*)
D.	(*ii*)	(*iii*)	(*i*)	(*iv*)

54. The MARC Field 264 has different second indicator values to indicate separate data elements in RDA. Match these second indicator values with the respective data elements:

List-I	***List-II***
(*a*) –0	(*i*) Distribution statement
(*b*) –1	(*ii*) Publication statement
(*c*) –2	(*iii*) Manufacture statement
(*d*) –3	(*iv*) Production statement

Code:

	(*a*)	(*b*)	(*c*)	(*d*)
A.	(*iv*)	(*ii*)	(*i*)	(*iii*)
B.	(*iii*)	(*ii*)	(*iv*)	(*i*)
C.	(*ii*)	(*iv*)	(*iii*)	(*i*)
D.	(*i*)	(*ii*)	(*iii*)	(*iv*)

55. Match the following mechanisms of information processing with corresponding service as given by S. Seetharama:

List-I	***List-II***
(*a*) Announcement	(*i*) Translation Service
(*b*) Evaluation	(*ii*) Current Awareness Service
(*c*) Document access	(*iii*) Indexing Service
(*d*) Accretion	(*iv*) State-of-the-art report

Code:

	(*a*)	(*b*)	(*c*)	(*d*)
A.	(*iii*)	(*ii*)	(*iv*)	(*i*)
B.	(*ii*)	(*iv*)	(*i*)	(*iii*)
C.	(*i*)	(*iii*)	(*ii*)	(*iv*)
D.	(*iv*)	(*i*)	(*iii*)	(*ii*)

56. Match the following queries with corresponding type of reference service:

List-I	***List-II***
(*a*) Communication with Library Staff through VoIP	(*i*) Asynchronous reference service
(*b*) Reference query through e-mail	(*ii*) Online reference service
(*c*) Use of e-resources seeking answers	(*iii*) Virtual Reference Desk
(*d*) Webforms	(*iv*) Reference interview

Code:

	(*a*)	(*b*)	(*c*)	(*d*)
A.	(*iv*)	(*iii*)	(*i*)	(*ii*)
B.	(*i*)	(*ii*)	(*iv*)	(*iii*)
C.	(*iii*)	(*i*)	(*ii*)	(*iv*)
D.	(*ii*)	(*iv*)	(*iii*)	(*i*)

57. Match the following with corresponding explanation:

List-I	***List-II***
(*a*) Embargo	(*i*) Publisher's list of new titles
(*b*) Big Deal	(*ii*) Authorization for regular shipment of new editions of specific products
(*c*) Front List	(*iii*) Publisher's restriction one-resource access
(*d*) Standing order	(*iv*) Large bundled e-journal package of single publisher on discounted price

Code:

	(*a*)	(*b*)	(*c*)	(*d*)
A.	(*iii*)	(*iv*)	(*i*)	(*ii*)
B.	(*i*)	(*iv*)	(*iii*)	(*ii*)
C.	(*iv*)	(*ii*)	(*i*)	(*iii*)
D.	(*ii*)	(*iii*)	(*i*)	(*iv*)

58. Match the following NISO (National Information Standard Organisation) standards with their corresponding descriptions applicable to Libraries:

List-I	***List-II***
(*a*) Z 39.41	(*i*) Dublin core Metadata Element set

(*b*) Z 39.63 (*ii*) Syntax for Digital Object Identifier (DOI)

(*c*) Z 39.84 (*iii*) Inter library loan data elements

(*d*) Z 39.85 (*iv*) Printed information on spines

Code:

	(*a*)	(*b*)	(*c*)	(*d*)
A.	(*i*)	(*ii*)	(*iii*)	(*iv*)
B.	(*iii*)	(*ii*)	(*iv*)	(*i*)
C.	(*iv*)	(*iii*)	(*ii*)	(*i*)
D.	(*ii*)	(*i*)	(*iii*)	(*iv*)

59. Match the following:

List-I	***List-II***
(*a*) Counter	(*i*) Article metric
(*b*) PLoS ALMs	(*ii*) Author metric
(*c*) ORC ID	(*iii*) All metric
(*d*) Social Media citations	(*iv*) Journal metric

Code:

	(*a*)	(*b*)	(*c*)	(*d*)
A.	(*iii*)	(*iv*)	(*i*)	(*ii*)
B.	(*iv*)	(*i*)	(*ii*)	(*iii*)
C.	(*ii*)	(*iv*)	(*iii*)	(*i*)
D.	(*i*)	(*iv*)	(*ii*)	(*iii*)

60. Match the following Office Products with their corresponding Producers/Organisations:

List-I	***List-II***
(*a*) Open Office	(*i*) IBM
(*b*) MS-Office	(*ii*) Apache Foundation
(*c*) Lotus Note	(*iii*) Apple
(*d*) iWork	(*iv*) Microsoft Corporation

Code:

	(*a*)	(*b*)	(*c*)	(*d*)
A.	(*i*)	(*ii*)	(*iii*)	(*iv*)
B.	(*ii*)	(*iv*)	(*i*)	(*iii*)
C.	(*i*)	(*iv*)	(*iii*)	(*ii*)
D.	(*iv*)	(*ii*)	(*i*)	(*iii*)

61. Match the following statements with corresponding research process:

List-I	***List-II***
(*a*) What is the role of MOOCs in imparting LIS education?	(*i*) Hypothesis
(*b*) EDUCAUSE (2013) "Selective institutions can be democratized via MOOCs".	(*ii*) Analytical statement
(*c*) MOOCs programmes will replace distance Learning in LIS	(*iii*) Formulation of the problem
(*d*) Though MOOCs is advantageous, majority respondents preferred distance learning	(*iv*) Literature study

Code:

	(*a*)	(*b*)	(*c*)	(*d*)
A.	(*iii*)	(*iv*)	(*i*)	(*ii*)
B.	(*ii*)	(*iii*)	(*iv*)	(*i*)
C.	(*iv*)	(*ii*)	(*iii*)	(*i*)
D.	(*i*)	(*ii*)	(*iv*)	(*iii*)

62. Match the following Online Survey Development Cloud based Software Applications/tools with their corresponding founders:

List-I	***List-II***
(*a*) Survey Monkey	(*i*) Christian Vanek and Scott Mc Daniel-(Colorado, USA)
(*b*) Type Form	(*ii*) Gordon Tan-Brisbane (Austria)
(*c*) Client Heartbeat	(*iii*) Robert Munoz and David Okuniev-Barcelona (Spain)
(*d*) Survey Gizmo	(*iv*) Ryan Finley-Sanmateo, California (USA)

Code:

	(*a*)	(*b*)	(*c*)	(*d*)
A.	(*i*)	(*ii*)	(*iii*)	(*iv*)
B.	(*iv*)	(*iii*)	(*ii*)	(*i*)
C.	(*ii*)	(*iv*)	(*i*)	(*iii*)
D.	(*iii*)	(*i*)	(*iv*)	(*ii*)

63. Match the following with their corresponding year of launching:

List-I	***List-II***
(*a*) National Mission on Manuscripts	(*i*) 2003
(*b*) National Mission on Libraries	(*ii*) 2007
(*c*) National Mission on Monuments and Antiquities	(*iii*) 2012
(*d*) National Knowledge Network	(*iv*) 2010

Code:

	(a)	(b)	(c)	(d)
A.	(i)	(iii)	(ii)	(iv)
B.	(iv)	(iii)	(ii)	(i)
C.	(iii)	(ii)	(i)	(iv)
D.	(ii)	(iv)	(iii)	(i)

64. Assertion (A): The copyright system, born and bred for print technology, faces a technological revolution in its environment.

Reason (R) : The old print technology's broadcast model of one to many communication is replaced with many to many global connectivity.

Code:

A. (A) is true, but (R) is false.
B. (A) is false, but (R) is true.
C. Both (A) and (R) are true.
D. Both (A) and (R) are false.

65. Assertion (A): Avoidance of difficult reference questions are usually an outcome of momentary panic in the face of a seemingly impenetrable question.

Reason (R) : Reference never adhere to few helpful tips such as developing handy-referral systems, both with in and outside the reference area, and fail to establish a context for the questions to counter such panic attack.

Code:

A. (A) is true, but (R) is false.
B. (A) is false, but (R) is true.
C. Both (A) and (R) are false.
D. Both (A) and (R) are true.

66. Assertion (A): In collection development, pamphlets do not require frequent review like books and journals.

Reason (R) : Pamphlet's information value is likely to be short lived, their physical format is usually flimsy and subject to rapid deterioration.

Code:

A. (A) is true, but (R) is false.
B. (A) is false, but (R) is true.
C. Both (A) and (R) are true.
D. Both (A) and (R) are false.

67. Assertion (A): The content-based indexing techniques enable identification of wanted persons in photographs of crowds.

Reason (R) : The content-based indexing system uses all sorts of characteristics of the image to guess what it is about.

Code:

A. (A) is true, but (R) is false.
B. (A) is false, but (R) is true.
C. Both (A) and (R) are false.
D. Both (A) and (R) are true.

68. Assertion (A): In Gold Open Access, costs are not transferred to authors.

Reason (R) : Gold Open Access journals publish peer-reviewed articles without paid subscription barriers for their readers.

Code:

A. (A) is true, but (R) is false.
B. (A) is false, but (R) is true.
C. Both (A) and (R) are true.
D. Both (A) and (R) are false.

69. Assertion (A) : In recent years, QR codes have become ubiquitous and may replace the use of bar codes.

Reason (R) : QR is a two - dimensional code with large capacity for storage. These codes hold information both horizontally and vertically and can be scanned by users with their smart phones at ease.

Code:
A. (A) is true, but (R) is false.
B. (A) is false, but (R) is true.
C. Both (A) and (R) are true.
D. Both (A) and (R) are false.

70. Assertion (A): Librarians usually prefer to provide access to e-content for the users via a proxy server, allowing authorized library users to access content from outside the physical confines of a library.

Reason (R) : Proxy-server access is possible without IP-address recognition.

Code:
A. Both (A) and (R) are true.
B. Both (A) and (R) are false.
C. (A) is true, but (R) is false.
D. (A) is false, but (R) is true.

71. Assertion (A): 'Web Assembly', a standard that enables applications to run securely in browsers (without the use of Plug-ins) is a people-friendly application in using Web.

Reason (R) : A web language transforms the way people use their devices and the web making applications are more accessible to people at ease all over the globe.

Code:
A. (A) is true, but (R) is false.
B. Both (A) and (R) are true.
C. (A) is false, but (R) is true.
D. Both (A) and (R) are false.

72. Assertion (A): Grounded Theory methods in Qualitative research start from same set of assumptions as traditional Quantitative research design.

Reason (R) : The inductive nature of these Grounded Theory methods allows the key issues emerge rather than force them into pre conceived categories.

Code:
A. (A) is true, but (R) is false.
B. Both (A) and (R) are true.
C. Both (A) and (R) are false.
D. (A) is false, but (R) is true.

73. Assertion (A): The fundamental need of a hypothesis is to guide sound research.

Reason (R) : Without hypothesis, research is focused and do not become a random empirical wandering.

Code:
A. (A) is true, but (R) is false.
B. (A) is false, but (R) is true.
C. Both (A) and (R) are true.
D. Both (A) and (R) are false.

74. Assertion (A): Traditional Knowledge Resource Classification (TKRC) is an innovative structured classification system useful for the systematic arrangement, dissemination and retrieval of all subjects.

Reason (R) : It is structured, based on International Patent Classification.

Code:
A. (A) is true, but (R) is false.
B. Both (A) and (R) are true.
C. (A) is false, but (R) is true.
D. Both (A) and (R) are false.

75. Identify the resource sharing and document delivery principles as given by IFLA.

(*a*) Each country should accept responsibility for providing access to its own publications to any other country.
(*b*) Supplying libraries should accept requests submitted in hardcopy only.
(*c*) From the moment a library dispatches an item to a requesting library until it returns the supplying library is responsible for any loss or damage incurred.
(*d*) Each country should aim to develop an efficient national resource sharing system.

Code:
A. (*a*) and (*b*) are correct.
B. (*b*) and (*c*) are correct.
C. (*a*) and (*d*) are correct.
D. (*b*) and (*d*) are correct.

ANSWERS

1	2	3	4	5	6	7	8	9	10
C	B	C	D	C	B	C	A	D	B
11	**12**	**13**	**14**	**15**	**16**	**17**	**18**	**19**	**20**
C	A	D	B	B	A	B	A	C	D
21	**22**	**23**	**24**	**25**	**26**	**27**	**28**	**29**	**30**
C	B	A	B	A	A	C	B	B	D
31	**32**	**33**	**34**	**35**	**36**	**37**	**38**	**39**	**40**
C	C	A	C	D	A	B	A	A	A
41	**42**	**43**	**44**	**45**	**46**	**47**	**48**	**49**	**50**
A	B	B	A	B	A	C	C	C	A
51	**52**	**53**	**54**	**55**	**56**	**57**	**58**	**59**	**60**
A	D	C	A	B	C	A	C	B	B
61	**62**	**63**	**64**	**65**	**66**	**67**	**68**	**69**	**70**
A	B	A	C	A	B	D	B	B	C
71	**72**	**73**	**74**	**75**					
B	D	A	C	C					

EXPLANATORY ANSWERS

1. Eugene Garfield: Eugene Garfield (1925–2017) was an American scientist and publisher. In 1960, Garfield set up the Institute for Scientific Information which produced, among many other things, the Science Citation Index and fulfilled his dream of a multidisciplinary citation index. The impact of this is incalculable. Without Garfield's pioneering work, the field of scientometrics would have had a very different landscape, and the study of scholarly communication would have been considerably poorer. Transcript of an Interview of Garfield conducted by Henry Small in September, 2007 is published here for the first time. It begins with a discussion of his childhood and education. He recollects memories of his career from jobs at Welch Medical Library, Smith, Kline & French, teaching at University of Pennsylvania, and starting of Eugene Garfield Associates and Institute of Scientific Information. His research, and development of products that revolutionized knowledge management scenario are described. His views on Informatics, NGOs, economic aspects of Open Access, quality of resrach, impact factors, and Big science are discussed. The interview reveals the life a person born to poor uneducated parents; facing the challenges of academic and business world becoming one of the greatest masters of the universe of knowledge developing magical products that can ensure quality of scientific and scholarly research.

2. Fritz Machlup, professor of economics at Princeton University and a president of the American Association of University Professors, had already secured his reputation in mainstream economics when, in 1962, he published what is regarded as the first major *apologia* for the information society. *The Production and Distribution of Knowledge in the United States* is believed to contain the original proof of the startling proposition that an advanced industrial society, namely the USA, was on the way to developing a new type of economy, the 'information economy'. This proposition involved two interrelated empirical claims: first, that a significant and inexorably growing section of the gross national product of the USA can be attributed to information activities; and second, that the numerically dominant sector of the US workforce is now engaged in information-centred occupations. In the hands of Machlup's followers, these claims about an information *sector* or *economy* evolved into the information *society* thesis, as a result of the economistic assuption, implicit in the well-established terms 'agrarian society' and 'industrial society', that the nature of a society is a function of itş economic setup. Whether or not the pioneer himself actually espoused that broader agenda is one of the questions this chapter will have to consider.

3. **Helical Spiral Communication Model:** In 1967, Frank Dance proposed the communication model called Dance's Helix Model for a better communication process. The name helical comes from "Helix" which means *an object having a three-dimensional shape like that of a wire wound uniformly around a cylinder or cone.* He shows communication as a dynamic and non-linear process. Dance's model emphasized the difficulties of communication. Frank Dance uses the form of a Helix to describe communication process. He developed this theory based on a simple helix which gets bigger and bigger as it moves or grows. The main characteristic of helical model of communication is that it is evolutionary.

4. The **IFLA World Library and Information Congress (WLIC):** The IFLA World Library and Information Congress (WLIC) is an international event for the library and information services sector. It brings together over 3,500 participants from more than 120 countries. It sets the international agenda for the library profession and offers opportunities for networking and professional development. The 83rd World Library and Information Congress will take place in Wroclaw, Poland, from 19-25 August 2017. "Libraries, Solidarity, Society." A straight forward yet powerful message that resonates with a singular truth in a country where the most powerful union movement of the past century was born and went on to change the face of history.

5. **Reference Librarian:** A librarian employed in a reference department who is responsible for providing helpful information in response to questions posed by users of the library. Reference service may be delivered in person or by phone or e-mail or virtual reference (chat).

6. The RDA cataloging guidelines divide into two basic parts: attributes (Sections 1-4) and relationships (Sections 5-10). Supplementary materials at the end consist of appendixes, a glossary, and an index (RDA 0.5). As of this writing, most chapters in RDA Sections 4, 7, and 10—those chapters covering Group 3 entities (COEvPl)—remain undeveloped and are not yet included in the RDA standard.

7. **Schema of Role Operators.** Derek William Austin, PRECIS: a manual of concept analysis and subject indexing British Library, Bibliographic Services Division, 1984.

Primary Operators		
Environment of core concepts	0	Location
Core concepts	1	Key system
		Things when action not present.
		Things towards which an action is directed, e.g. object of transitive action, performer of intransitive action
	2	Action; Effect of action
	3	Performer of transitive action (agent, instrument); Intake; Factor
Extra-core concepts	4	Viewpoint-as-form
	5	Selected instance; study region, study example, sample population
	6	Form of document; Target user
Secondary Operators		
Co-ordinate concepts	f	"Bound" co-ordinate concept
	g	Standard co-ordinate concept
Dependent elements	p	Part; Property
	q	Member of quasi-generic group
	r	Assembly
Special classes of action	s	Role definer: Directional property
	t	Author attributed action
	u	Two-way interaction

9. **Management Theory Jungle:** It was Harold Koontz who introduced the concept of Management Theory Jungle. 'Management Theory Jungle' was made in an environment where the development of management theory had escalated over a period of two decades. This has resulted to confusion and conflict which many theories have entangled in it. As such, it is seen as a jungle.

   Koontz defined the management theory jungle by identifying and classifying major management theory. Six schools of thoughts were identified. They included the management process, empirical, human behaviour, social system, decision theory and the mathematical school. He said that each school had something to offer to management theory but suggested one should not confuse content with tools. For example, the field of human behaviour should not be judged the equivalent of the field of management, nor should a focus on decision making or mathematics be considered as encompassing the entire area of analysis. Therefore, each of these schools would provide insight and methods to aid manager in performing task, hence were tools not school.

10. **ISSN:** The **ISSN** or International Standard Serial Number identifies a serial publication, such as a newspaper, magazine, or academic journal, or blog; it is the periodical counterpart of the ISBN for a book. It does not identify a particular issue or a particular article in an issue.

    It is an eight-digit serial number used to uniquely identify a serial publication. The ISSN is especially helpful in distinguishing between serials with the same title. ISSN is used in ordering, cataloging, interlibrary loans, and other practices in connection with serial literature.

    The ISSN system was first drafted as an International Organization for Standardization (ISO) international standard in 1971 and published as ISO 3297 in 1975.

11. **OCLC** is introducing Dig by, a new mobile app that will soon be available as part of World Share Management Services, the cloud-based library services platform. Dig by is specifically designed to increase the efficiency, accuracy and independence of student library workers. The intuitive design of the Dig by app provides student workers with clear instructions for handling pull-list and reshelving tasks. Dig by lets student workers scan library materials right in the stacks—saving them time and reducing their reliance on paper slips.

12. URL Encoding: One potential problem with the query string is using characters that aren't allowed in a URL. The list of characters that are allowed in a URL is much shorter than the list of allowed characters in an HTML document. All characters must be alphanumeric or one of a small set of special characters. Some browsers tolerate certain additional special characters (Internet Explorer is notoriously lax), but many do not.

Furthermore, some characters have special meaning. For example, the ampersand (&) is used to separate multiple query string parameters, the plus sign (+) is an alternate way to represent a space, and the number sign (#) is used to point to a specific bookmark in a web page. If you try to send query string values that include any of these characters, you'll lose some of your data.

If you're concerned that the data you want to store in the query string may not consist of URL-legal characters, you should use URL encoding. With URL encoding, special characters are replaced by escaped character sequences starting with the percent sign (%), followed by a two-digit hexadecimal representation. The only exception is the space character, which can be represented as the character sequence %20 or the + sign.

You can use the methods of the HttpServerUtility class to encode your data automatically. For example, the following shows how you would encode a string of arbitrary data for use in the query string. This replaces all the nonlegal characters with escaped character sequences.

13. FRBRoo is an interpretation of the FR family of models using object-oriented methodology. It is not the same as the three existing entity-relationship models, FRBR, FRAD and FRSAD, nor is it the same as the consolidated entity-relationship model currently under development. But the ontology described in FRBRoo is based on the three entity-relationship models, FRBR, FRAD and FRSAD. The original FRBRoo version 1 was published in 2009 and was based on FRBR alone. Version 2 of FRBRoo is based on all three FR models. FRBRoo version 2.2 underwent a world-wide review in 2015.

14. MPEG is the abbreviated form of Moving Picture Expert Group, which works on the standards for compression of digital movies. MPEG was first proposed in 1991. It is actually a family of standards for compressed digital movies, and is still evolving. One may think of a digital movie as a sequence of still images displayed one after another at video rate. However, this approach does not take into consideration the extensive redundancy from frame to frame. MPEG takes advantage of that redundancy to achieve even better compression. The MPEG standards actually consist of three main parts: video, audio and systems. The MPEG systems part coordinates between the video and audio parts, as well as coordinating external synchronization for playing.

15. In the *sample reference*, **Nicholas and Ritchie (1978) distinguish** between descriptive bibliometrics and behavioral bibliometrics (bibliometrics, behavioral). The latter often involves the study of citations. On the other hand, descriptive bibliometrics collects information such as:

1. Bodies responsible for the production and transmission of the information.
2. Form of transmission (e.g., journal, monograph).
3. Medium of communication (e.g., article, letter).
4. Nature of information conveyed-subject and language characteristics.
5. Timing and frequency with which information is conveyed.
6. Amount of information conveyed.
7. Geographical origin.

16. In 1960 Robert E. Burton and R.W. Kebler wrote "The 'Half-Life' of some Scientific and Technical Literatures," in which they compared the rate of obsolescence of scientific literature with that of radioactive substances. The authors noted upon their research "A short half-life, which is equivalent to rapid obsolescence, is the result of rapidly changing techniques or interest within a subject field."

Half-life as explained by Maurice B. Line was "half the active life," and this was usually interpreted "as meaning the time during which one-half of the currently active literature was published."

The results of many of the half-life studies varied so greatly that they did not project a possible general application. There also were discrepancies as to meanings. This was Maurice Line's explanation of the process. If the average number of articles in each journal remained constant, and the number of journals doubled, "the probability of citation is twice as great." "The so-called 'half-life' of a literature is (therefore) compounded of its obsolescence rate and its growth rate." Line then proceeded to develop mathematical expressions for determining a half-life corrected because of the two rates.

17. **Cluster Sampling:** This type of method is very useful in lowering the field cost as this method is a very practical and easily opera table method. Here the population is divided into a number of groups and these groups are referred to as the clusters and further these clusters are referred to as the primary sampling units. This method involves first of all the identification of the cluster, according to which clusters may be units like districts, talukas, city blocks, schools etc. Clusters should be homogeneous in the internal characteristics. Then further in this method, determination of the number of the stages is to be done.

18. Hermeneutics as the methodology of interpretation is concerned with problems that arise when dealing with meaningful human actions and the products of such actions, most importantly texts. As a methodological discipline, it offers a toolbox for efficiently treating problems of the interpretation of human actions, texts and other meaningful material. Hermeneutics looks back at a long tradition as the set of problems it addresses have been prevalent in human life, and have repeatedly and consistently called for consideration: interpretation is a ubiquitous activity, unfolding whenever humans aspire to grasp whatever *interpretanda* they deem significant. Due to its long history, it is only natural that both its problems, and the tools designed to help solve them, have shifted considerably over time, along with the discipline of hermeneutics itself. The article focuses on the main problem areas and presents some proposals that have been put forward for tackling them effectively.

19. The **National Mission on Libraries India,** an initiative of the Ministry of Culture under the Government of India, works to modernise and digitally link nearly 9,000 libraries across India to provide readers access to books and information. The scheme was approved on 28 November, 2013 and the President of India, Pranab Mukherjee launched the National Mission on Libraries on 3 February, 2014 at Rashtrapati Bhavan.

Mission has four working groups for its main advisory function. These are:

- Upgrade of existing public libraries, college libraries, school libraries, and shifting the use of school libraries as community libraries chaired by Shri B S Baswan.
- Library and Information Science education, training and research facilities chaired by Professor ARD Prasad.
- Setting up the National Virtual Library, networking and ICT application in libraries, chaired by Dr. H K Kaul.
- National Census of Libraries, Content Creation and Community Information Centers, chaired by Dr. Subbiah Arunachalam.

20. **INFLIBNET:** An Inter-University Centre of UGC the INFLIBNET serves towards modernization of Libraries, serves as Information Centre for transfer and access of information, supporting scholarships and learning and academic pursuits through a

National Network of Libraries in around 264 Universities, Colleges and R&D Institutions across the country.

21. **Confidentiality, integrity and availability,** also known as the **CIA triad**, is a model designed to guide policies for information security within an organization. The model is also sometimes referred to as the AIC triad (availability, integrity and confidentiality) to avoid confusion with the Central Intelligence Agency. The elements of the triad are considered the three most crucial components of security. In this context, confidentiality is a set of rules that limits access to information, integrity is the assurance that the information is trustworthy and accurate, and availability is a guarantee of reliable access to the information by authorized people.

22. **National Information Policy:** A National Information Policy is a set of decisions taken by a government, through appropriate laws and regulations, to orient the harmonious development of information transfer activities in order to satisfy the information needs of the company. A National Information Policy needs provision of necessary means or instruments such as financial, personnel, institutional for concrete implementation.

    Legislation Framework: A set of ideas, rules, or beliefs from which involve or relate to the process of making and passing laws.

    National Bibliography: National bibliographies are non-commercial publications that attempt to list everything produced in a country "under the auspices of a national library or other governmental agency" . The items usually come to the agency through a national copyright law that demands legal deposit. National bibliographies are primarily used "to identify and verify, to locate, and to select". As Gorman and Howe point out in *Collection Development for Libraries*, national bibliographies are found in most countries that have an organized publishing trade. For instance, the National Library of Canada has compiled *Canadiana*, the national bibliography of Canada, since 1950.

23. **SWAYAM:** SWAYAM or Study Webs of Active-Learning for Young Aspiring Minds is a programme initiated by Government of India and designed to achieve the three cardinal principles of Education Policy, *viz.,* access, equity and quality. The objective of this effort is to take the best teaching learning resources to all, including the most disadvantaged. SWAYAM seeks to bridge the digital divide for students who have hitherto remained untouched by the digital revolution and have not been able to join the mainstream of the knowledge economy.

    The courses hosted on SWAYAM will be in 4 quadrants – (1) video lecture, (2) specially prepared reading material that can be downloaded/printed, (3) self-assessment tests through tests and quizzes and (4) an online discussion forum for clearing the doubts. Steps have been taken to enrich the learning experience by using audio-video and multi-media and state of the art pedagogy/ technology. In order to ensure best quality content are produced and delivered, seven National Coordinators have been appointed: They are NPTEL for engineering, UGC for post-graduation education, CEC for undergraduate education, NCERT & NIOS for school education, IGNOU for out of the school students and, for management studies.

    SWAYAM platform is indigenously developed by Ministry of Human Resource Development (MHRD) and All India Council for Technical Education (AICTE) with the help of Microsoft and would be ultimately capable of hosting 2000 courses and 80000 hours of learning: covering school, under-graduate, post-graduate, engineering, law and other professional courses.

24. **National Mission on Libraries:** National Knowledge Commission has recommended setting up of a National Mission on Libraries

to ensure sustained attention to development of libraries. Accordingly, Ministry of Culture set up a High Level Committee *i.e.*, National Mission on Libraries, vide notification no. 18-4/2009-Lib (Pt.) dated 4th May, 2012. In order to achieve the objectives, High Level Committee held a number of meetings and formulated the scheme called "National Mission on Libraries: Upgradation of Libraries providing Service to the Public" which includes the following four components:

(*i*) Creation of National Virtual Library of India;
(*ii*) Setting up of NML Model Libraries;
(*iii*) Quantitative & Qualitative Survey; and
(*iv*) Capacity Building.

28. In some instances—as a consequence of the utilization of subject specialist staff, the development of improved tools and techniques for bibliographic control and enhanced access to recorded information, and the growing informational needs of technical and research clienteles—reference service has developed in scope far beyond the minimal level of "assistance to readers." As noted in the opening paragraph of this article, however, the extent and character of available reference service varies markedly at present both among individual libraries and among different types and sizes of libraries.

Writing in 1930, James Ingersoll Wyer, seeking to elucidate a "theory of reference work," reported the existence of "three distinct conceptions of it." Thirty years later, in what has become a classic paper, Samuel Rothstein suggested that reference service as practiced in contemporary libraries continued to reflect Wyer's three distinct conceptions, which the earlier author had characterized as "conservative," "moderate," and "liberal," and which Rothstein termed "minimum," "middling," and "maximum". In 1977, this taxonomy remains apt in describing reference and information services as they exist across the range of libraries in the United States.

29. Union Government on 24 August, 2016 launched Accessible E-Library 'Sugamya Pustakalaya' for Divyang under Prime Minister's Accessible India Campaign (Sugamya Bharat Abhiyan). The e-library was jointly launched by Union Ministers Ravi Shankar Prasad, Prakash Javadekar and Thawar Chand Gehlot. Sugamya Pustakalaya is an online platform that makes accessible content available to print disabled people. It houses more than 2 lakh books in diverse subjects and languages and multiple accessible formats. The e-library was created by Department of Empowerment of Persons with Disabilities (Divyangjan), Ministry of Social Justice and Empowerment in collaboration with member organizations of Daisy Forum of India and powered by TCS Access.

30. **Information entropy** is defined as the average amount of information produced by a stochastic source of data. The measure of information entropy associated with each possible data value is the negative logarithm of the probability mass function for the value. Thus, when the data source has a lower-probability value (*i.e.*, when a low-probability event occurs), the event carries more "information" ("surprisal") than when the source data has a higher-probability value. The amount of information conveyed by each event defined in this way becomes a random variable whose expected value is the information entropy. Generally, *entropy* refers to disorder or uncertainty, and the definition of entropy used in information theory is directly analogous to the definition used in statistical thermodynamics. The concept of information entropy was introduced by Claude Shannon in his 1948 paper "A Mathematical Theory of Communication".

Entropy is a measure of *unpredictability* of the state, or equivalently, of its *average information content*. To get an intuitive understanding of these terms, consider the example of a political poll. Usually, such polls happen because the outcome of the poll is not already known. In other words, the outcome of the poll is relatively *unpredictable*, and actually performing the poll and learning the results gives some new *information*; these are just different ways of saying that the a *priori* entropy of the poll results is large. Now, consider the case that the same poll is performed a second time shortly after the first poll. Since the result of the first poll is already known, the outcome of the second poll can be predicted well and the results should not contain much new information; in this case the a *priori* entropy of the second poll result is small relative to that of the first.

31. **Controlled vocabularies** provide a way to organize knowledge for subsequent retrieval. They are used in subject indexing schemes, subject headings, thesauri, taxonomies and other forms of knowledge organization systems. Controlled vocabulary schemes mandate the use of predefined, authorised terms that have been preselected by the designers of the schemes, in contrast to natural language vocabularies, which have no such restriction.

    In computer science and information science, an **ontology** is a formal naming and definition of the types, properties, and interrelationships of the entities that really exist in a particular domain of discourse.

    An ontology (in information science) compartmentalizes the variables needed for some set of computations and establishes the relationships between them.

32. **Barcode symbol**: Barcode symbols are dark bars or stripes (some narrow some wide) printed side-by-side on merchandise and other items. Each bar represents a number, and together they represent a code that can be read by machines called bar code readers or scanners (such as those used at supermarket checkout counters). The data read by the reader is passed on to a computer which matches the code with the stored information such as the item's name, price, size, quantity in stock.

    Quiet zone: A Quiet zone is an area of the library used for quiet study. It is located on the first floor of the library. In the Quiet zone, mobile phones should be switched off or to silent; students should use headphones to listen or watch media, and use a quiet speaking voice for any conversation.

    Start character: The start and stop characters of a barcode symbology are used to identify the beginning and end points of the symbol. The start and stop characters are not transmitted with the barcode and are not included in any check digit calculations.

33. **Embargo:** An "embargo" originally meant a governmental ban on the movements of other nations' ships in and out of its ports, or a prohibition on trade with a foreign nation. In book publishing, an embargo means that the publishing company won't release advance copies of the book to the media—and that if members of the media get a copy of the book before its publication date, they're not allowed to review it before that date.

34. Pure and Converis are parts of broader sets of research management and analytics services from, respectively, Elsevier (Elsevier research intelligence) and Thomson Reuters (Research management and evaluation). Each is a recent acquisition, providing an institutional approach alongside the aggregate, network level approach of each company's broader research analytics and management services.

    Symplectic is a member of the very interesting Digital Science portfolio. Digital Science is a company set up by Macmillan Publishers to incubate start-ups focused on scientific workflow and research productivity. These include, for example, Figshare and Altmetric.

    Other products are also relevant here. As RIM is an emerging area, it is natural to expect some overlap with other functions. For example, there is definitely overlap with backoffice research administration systems—Ideate from Consilience or solutions from infoEd Global, for example. And also with more publicly oriented profiling and expertise systems on the front office side.

With respect to the latter, Pure and Symplectic both note that they can interface to VIVO. Furthermore, Symplectic can provide "VIVO services that cover installation, support, hosting and integration for institutions looking to join the VIVO network". It also provides implementation support for the Profiles Research Networking Software.

As I discuss further below, one interesting question for libraries is the relationship between the RIMs or CRIS and the institutional repository. Extensions have been written for both Dspace and Eprints to provide some RIMs-like support. For example, Dspace-Cris extends the Dspace model to cater for the Cerif entities. This is based on work done for the Scholar's Hub at Hong Kong University.

35. **INFLIBNET:** The Information and Library Network (INFLIBNET) Centre was established as a project of IUCAA in 1991 and was recognized and as an independent, autonomous Inter-University Centre (IUC) of the University Grants Commission (UGC) in May 1996. Major activities and services of the Centre include automation of academic libraries and information centres, creation of union databases of resources (IndCat) available in academic libraries, promote resource sharing among academic libraries, promote information access and transfer, support scholarship, learning and academic pursuits. The Centre acts as a nodal agency for networking of libraries and information centres in universities, institutions of higher learning and R&D institutions in India with an aim to promote scholarly communication. Open access initiatives taken-up by the Centre includes OJAS, a platform offered to faculty and researchers in universities to host their open-access journals, and three institutional repositories, namely ShodhGanga, ShodhGangotri and IR@INFLIBNET. InfoPortal: A Subject Gateway to Indian Electronic Resources is designed and developed by the INFLIBNET Centre to serve as a comprehensive gateway to all Indian scholarly content. The gateway open-up the Indian scholarly content scattered over the Internet through an integrated interface that support search, browse and multiple listing of more than 1,700 e-resources. The InfoPortal uses "Subject Gateway Management System (SGMS)" as hosting platform. The SGMS, designed and developed at the INFLIBNET Centre, facilitates entry of Internet resources and extending its access to users. SGMS supports browsing of Internet resources by Dewey Decimal Classification (DDC) Scheme.

37. **Jubilee Project by JISC:** JUBILEE (JISC User Behaviour in Information seeking: Longitudinal Evaluation of Electronic Information Services) is one of two large-scale projects funded by the UK Joint Information Systems Committee (JISC) under the JISC's MEUB Framework. It began in August 1999, and has since been extended to also include the further education sector, and is about to expand again to include Adult and Community Learning. JUBILEE is undertaking a holistic, longitudinal monitoring and evaluation, which seeks to predict, monitor and characterise information-seeking behaviour in relation to EIS, and is providing illuminative and contextualised pictures built up over time, of users and non-users in different disciplines.

38. **Haryana Public Libraries Act:** Haryana Public Library Act, 1989 was passed by the Haryana Vidhan Sabha on Monday September 11, 1989 by them education minister Smt. Sushma Swaraj.

Odisha Public Libraries Act: The following Act of the Odisha Legislative Assembly having been assented to by the Governor on the 28th

February 2002: An act to provide for the establishment of a network of public libraries in the state of Odisha and to maintain, regulate, guide, control, supervise, integrate and consolidate the libraries in the state as also to provide for a comprehensive rural and urban library service in the state and for matters connected therewith or incidental thereto. This Act may be called in Odisha Public Libraries Act, 2001.

Lakshadweep Public Libraries Act: This Act came into being in 2007. Lakshadweep became a Union Territory in 1956. Even though the Central Library of Lakshadweep was located in the Secretariat, its sprouts were extended in almost all islands as reading rooms-cum-libraries.

Chhattisgarh Public Libraries Act: Chattisgarh means 36 forts. There was a demand for a separate State from 1964 which was finally fulfilled in 2000. There are District libraries set up in all the districts by the former Madhya Pradesh State Government. The Public Libraries Act of this State was already passed in 2008 but it is not yet implemented.

39. **Calcutta Public Library:** Calcutta Public Library was established in 1836. It was run in Metcalf Hall. It was not a Government institution.

Connemara Public Library: Connemara Public Library at Egmore in Chennai, Tamil Nadu, India, is one of the four National Depository Libraries which receive a copy of all books, newspapers and periodicals published in India. Established in 1890, the library is a repository of centuries-old publications, wherein lie some of the most respected works and collections in the country.

Baroda Central Library: The Cental Library was actually born in Laxmi Vilas Palace of Maharaja Sayajirao Gaekwad, who was the pioneer of public library movement in India that began in 1906.

Delhi Public Library: Delhi Public Library is a national depository library in the Indian state of Delhi. The library has 35 branches across the state. The Library was established on 27 October 1951 as a pilot project sponsored by UNESCO and the Government of India.

In February 1950, the Indian government and UNESCO agreed to initiate the project, and the library was officially opened on 27 October 1951, by then Prime Minister Jawaharlal Nehru.

40. In discussing Ranganathan's approach to the design, development and use of information systems and services, it is useful to bear in mind his holistic approach. With a view to securing consistency and integrity in designing and developing information systems, he proposed a range of normative principles (51, 64), a typology as well as a hierarchy among them, and formulated guildelines for their application. The typology of Ranganathan's normative principles may be summarized as follows:

Level 1: Basic Laws (Law of Symmetry, Law of Impartiality, Law of Context/Local Variation, Laws of Interpretation and Law of Parsimony), applicable to intellectual work in all areas of the universe of knowledge;

Level 2: Fundamental Laws, (e.g., Laws of Physics, Laws of Biology, and the Five Laws of Library Science postulated by Ranganathan) applicable to a discipline as a whole;

Level 3: Canons, (e.g., Canons of Classification in Library Science) applicable to a branch of a discipline; and

Level 4: Principles (e.g., Principles of Facet Sequence in Classification), applicable to a subdivision of a branch of a discipline.

Additionally, Ranganathan provided several postulates for use at one or more of the above levels.

The principal functions of the normative principles is to guide research and development from the micro to the macro level, to serve as criteria for assessing the helpfulness of findings or innovations in library and information systems and services. Any problem or conflict that may arise, for example when more than one principle appears applicable at one level (e.g., the Canons of Classification), it may be resolved by applying the principles of higher levels.

41. Chain Indexing: Chain Indexing or Chain Procedure is a mechanical method to derive subject index entries or subject headings from the class number of the document. It was developed by Dr. S.R. Ranganathan. He first mentioned this in his book "Theory of Library Catalogue" in 1938.

Relational Indexing by J.E.L. Farradane: It is an indexing system developed by J.E.L. Farradane, which involves the identification of the relationship between each pair of terms of a given subject statement and representation of those relations by ***relational*** operators. In this indexing system, two or more isolates are linked by relational operators.

Subject Indexing by J.E. Coates: Subject indexing is the act of describing or classifying a document by index terms or other symbols in order to indicate what the document is about to summarize its content or to increase its findability. In other words, it is about identifying and describing the subject of documents. Indexes are constructed, separately, on three distinct levels: terms in a document such as a book; objects in a collection such as a library; and documents (such as books and articles) within a field of knowledge. It was developed by J.E. Coates.

PRECIS came into existence in 1968. It has been developed by Derek Austin. It was the result of long research which was undertaken by the Classification Research Group (CRG, London). After testing it thoroughly, it was introduced in BNB in 1971. The BNB since its inception in 1950 has been using Ranganathan's Chain Procedure for preparing its alphabetical index. It is supposed to be free from all the limitations which chain procedure was suffering from. It may not be the best indexing system but it is believed to be better one.

42. ISBD: The International Standard Bibliographic Description (ISBD) is a set of rules produced by the International Federation of Library Associations and Institutions (IFLA) to create a bibliographic description in a standard, human-readable form, especially for use in a bibliography or a library catalog. A preliminary consolidated edition of the ISBD was published in 2007 and the consolidated edition was published in 2011, superseding earlier separate ISBDs for monographs, older monographic publications, cartographic materials, serials and other continuing resources, electronic resources, non-book materials, and printed music. IFLA's ISBD Review Group is responsible for maintaining the ISBD.

One of the original purposes of the ISBD was to provide a standard form of bibliographic description that could be used to exchange records internationally. This would support IFLA's Universal Bibliographic Control program.

46. Maslow's hierarchy of needs: Maslow's hierarchy of needs is a theory in psychology proposed by Abraham Maslow in his 1943 paper "A Theory of Human Motivation" in *Psychological Review*. Maslow subsequently extended the idea to include his observations of humans' innate curiosity. His theories parallel many other theories of human developmental psychology, some of which focus on describing the stages of growth in humans. Maslow used the terms "physiological", "safety", "belonging and love", "esteem", "self-actualization", and "self-transcendence" to describe the pattern that human motivations generally move through. The goal of Maslow's Theory is to attain the sixth level or stage: self transcendent needs.

Maslow studied what he called exemplary people such as Albert Einstein, Jane Addams, Eleanor Roosevelt, and Frederick Douglass rather than mentally ill or neurotic people, writing that "the study of crippled, stunted, immature, and unhealthy specimens can yield only a cripple psychology and a cripple philosophy." Maslow studied the healthiest 1% of the college student population.

Maslow's theory was fully expressed in his 1954 book *Motivation and Personality*. The hierarchy remains a very popular framework in sociology research, management training and secondary and higher psychology instruction.

48. The 8 W's Literacy Model was developed by Annette Lamb in the early 1990s.

Steps in model with a description of each step: Here are the 8 steps with detail about each in terms of specific use in information gathering and information sharing:

- ***Watching*** (Exploring) asks students to explore and become observers of their environment. It asks students to become more in tune to the world around them from family needs to global concerns.
- ***Wondering*** (Questioning) focuses on brainstorming options, discussing ideas, identifying problems, and developing questions.
- ***Webbing*** (Searching) directs students to locate, search for, and connect ideas and information. One piece of information may lead to new questions and areas of interest. Students select those resources that are relevant and organize them into meaningful clusters.
- ***Wiggling*** (Evaluating) is often the toughest phase for students. They're often uncertain about what they've found and where they're going with a project. Wiggling involves evaluating content, along with twisting and turning information looking for clues, ideas, and perspectives.
- ***Weaving*** (Synthesizing) consists of organizing ideas, creating models, and formulating plans. It focuses on the application, analysis, and synthesis of information.
- ***Wrapping*** (Creating) involves creating and packaging ideas and solutions. Why is this important? Who needs to know about this? How can I effectively convey my ideas to others? Many packages get wrapped and rewrapped before they're given away.
- ***Waving*** (Communicating) is communicating ideas to others through presenting, publishing, and sharing. Students share their ideas, try out new approaches, and ask for feedback.
- ***Wishing*** (Assessing) is assessing, evaluating, and reflecting on the process and product. Students begin thinking about how the project went and consider possibilities for the future.

50. The UGC-DAE Consortium for Scientific Research (UGC-DAE CSR) is an autonomous institution established by the UGC, New Delhi with headquarters at Indore and Centers at Indore, Mumbai and Kolkata. This Consortium also has a Node near IGCAR at Kalpakkam. The UGC-DAE CSR coordinates research from scientists/teachers from all Indian Universities on major facilities like Dhruva reactor, Variable Energy Cyclotron, INDUS-I etc. established by the Department of Atomic Energy. In addition, the Centers are also having many advanced research facilities including in the areas of condensed matter physics etc.

Electronic Resources in Medicine **(ERMED-India)** Consortium, Managed by National

Medical Library, New Delhi, India. National Medical Library's Electronic Resources in Medicine Consortium is an initiative taken by DGHS & MOHFW to develop nation wide electronic information resources in the field of medicine for delivering effective health care. 39 centrally funded Government Institutions including 10 DGHS libraries + 28 ICMR Libraries and AIIMS library are selected at the initial stage as its core members. The MOHFW aims to provide fund required for the purchase of electronic journals under the NML-ERMED consortium project.

The DBT's Electronic Library Consortium **(DeLCON)**, & National Brain Research Centre in Manesar. The 'DBT's Electronic Library Consortium (DeLCON)' is major project of the 'Department of Biotechnology (DBT)' to bring qualitative change in their research Institutions. It was launched in January, 2009 with the 10 DBT member Institutions with a large number of high impact online journals. It is a national initiative for providing access to scholarly electronic resources including full-text and bibliographic databases in all the life science subject disciplines to DBT Institutional community.

The e-Shodh Sindhu: The INDEST-AICTE Consortium was set up by MHRD on the recommendation of an Expert group constitued by the Ministry. IIT Delhi was designated as Consortium Headquarter to coordinate activities. AICTE has been releasing grant to IIT Delhi in the name of the consortium being the subscription for providing e-journal package to AICTE supported technical institutes since 2009-10. As per the directive of MHRD released during the end of 2015, it was decided that the subscription of e-resources shall be looked after by e-Shodh Sindhu. INFLIBNET Centre, Gandhinagar, Gujarat from 2016 onwards. The e-Shodh Sindhu, INFLIBNET Centre, Gandhinagar, Gujarat is accordingly providing e-resources to the existing 94 beneficiaries of AICTE supported technical institutes since 2016 and the subscription are being paid by AICTE annually. A list of 94 AICTE supported Govt./ Govt. Aided institutes under e-Shodh Sindhu, INFLIBNET Centre, Gandhinagar, Gujarat is attached.

51. Library and Information Science Abstracts (LISA): LISA is an international abstracting and indexing service designed for library professionals and other information specialists. "LISA provides bibliographic information about past and present developments in librarianship, information science, online retrieval, publishing and information technology. LISA currently abstracts over 440 periodicals from more than 45 countries and in more than 20 different languages."

The Indian Association of Special Libraries and Information Centres (IASLIC): IASLIC is a non-profit organisation based in India that supports development in the entire field of special librarianship in India. The IASLIC undertakes supports, coordinate research and studies, conducts short term training courses; organises general/special meetings, and hold seminars and conferences in alternate years on current problems of Libraries and Information services and other allied areas are selected as themes for discussions on these occasions. IASLIC Publication is IASLIC Bulletin, IASLIC NewsLetter and ILSA.

Library, Information Science & Technology Abstracts™ (LISTA): LISTA is available FREE to any library-compliments of EBSCO Publishing. LISTA indexes more than 560 core journals, nearly 50 priority journals, and nearly 125 selective journals; plus books, research reports and proceedings. Subject coverage includes librarianship, classification, cataloging, bibliometrics, online information retrieval, information management and more. Coverage in the database extends back as far as the mid-1960s.

Indian Science Abstracts (ISA): ISA is a bibliographical database published by NISCAIR, CSIR. This database provides abstracts of research articles, short communications, review articles, and informative articles published in current Scientific and technical periodicals, as well as Indian standards and thesis. It is a leading bibliographical database in India covering entire spectrum of Science and Technology including Intellectual Property Rights, Management and Library & Information Science published in India and covers the information since 2009.

52. Piracy: In the context of intellectual property, piracy refers to the unauthorized use of protected material, especially material protected by copyright.

Blackmail: Blackmail is an act, often criminal, involving unjustified threats to make a gain—most commonly money or property—or cause loss to another unless a demand is met. It is coercion involving threats to reveal substantially true or false information about a person to the public, a family member, or associates, or threats of physical harm or criminal prosecution.

Blackmail of information disclosure. It means unjustified threat to disclose information on anything, *e.g.*, property, official data, etc.

Unauthorized access of data piracy: It is an act of illegally gaining access into any computer, network, etc, or promoting such activity, and the illegal copying, distribution, or use of data. It is such a profitable "business" that it has caught the attention of organized crime groups in a number of countries.

53. Political Map: A map that represents the political subdivisions of the world, of continents, or of major geographic regions. Political maps are divided into general, or survey, maps and specialized maps. General political maps show the political divisions of the area being mapped, that is, the location of countries and the area they occupy. They also show major political centers, strategic points, and lines of communication of international and national significance. Specialized political maps treat specific political problems and political events. General political maps are most common.

A road map or **route map** is a map that primarily displays roads and transport links rather than natural geographical information. It is a type of navigational map that commonly includes political boundaries and labels, making it also a type of political map. In addition to roads and boundaries, road maps often include points of interest, such as prominent business or buildings, tourism sites, parks and recreational facilities, hotels and restaurants, as well as airports and train stations. A road map may also document non-automotive transit routes, although often these are found only on transit maps.

A **physical map** focuses on the geography of the area and will often have shaded relief to show the mountains and valleys. Typical colours are blues, greens and browns. Many rivers, mountains and lake features are usually labelled. Cities, towns, countries and other political features are often labelled as well its just not the focus of the map or the first thing you notice.

Thematic maps: A map that displays the spatial distribution of an attribute that relates to a single topic, theme, or subject of discourse. Usually, a thematic map displays a single attribute (a "univariate map") such as soil type, vegetation, geology, land use, or land ownership. For attributes such as soil type or land use ("nominal" variables), shaded maps that highlight regions ("polygons") by employing different colours or patterns is generally wanted. For other attributes (like population density—a "metric" variable), a shaded map in which each shade corresponds to a range of population densities is generally wanted.

54. The MARC field 264: MARC field 264 (formerly known as the publication, distribution, field in AACR2) is the home for many different RDA elements. MARC field 264 will replace field 260 so that each of the different types can be coded explicitly. Use the 264 field for RDA cataloging. Converting 260 fields in AACR2 records to 264 is not required, but for any new AACR2 cataloging use the 264 field.

264 Indicator 2

0 – Production
1 – Publication
2 – Distribution
3 – Manufacture
4 – Copyright notice date

55. However remarkable changes are evident in special libraries that centered on current literature in specific subject areas. They have adopted different mechanisms to offer services to target groups after assessing their information requirements. S. Seetharama has listed some of the basic mechanisms and the corresponding services provided by an information centre of a research/scientific/ industrial organizations as follows:

Mechanism Service	Service
1. Reference/Referral	Reference Service
2. Announcement	Current Awareness Services
3. Accretion	Indexing and abstracting services
4. Evaluation	State-of-the-art report,/Trend Report, Critical Compilation and Reviews etc
5. Document access	Reprographic and translation services.
6. Promotion/Liaison	Liaison services; Technical equiry service

56. Voice-over IP: Voice-over IP (VoIP) allows users to talk to each other over the Internet, instead of telephone lines, and is accessible from many parts of the world. Some VoIP services include video conferencing as well. Many VoIP services, such as Skype, are available at low or no cost, require minimal equipment, and can be used from mobile devices. During an exploration of new services to offer, librarians at the University of North Carolina at Chapel Hill asked scientists to suggest potential new service areas. One surprising but easy-to-implement suggestion was consultations with librarians via Skype.

E-mail: In addition to sending and receiving messages, a few things can be done to enhance e-mail functionality. Setting up mailing lists for groups of staff members and groups of patrons offers a quick way to share information with groups of individuals. Prewritten messages that answer frequently asked questions can be saved and reused as needed, making it easy to answer frequently asked questions. E-mailing news and updates on topics such as health policy to hospital administrators on a regular basis is one way hospital librarians use e-mail to increase the library's visibility and highlight services and resources.

Web forms: Most reference librarians know how hard it can sometimes be to discover just what the user at the desk really wants. The literature about the reference interaction is full of examples of miscommunication and misunderstandings (on the part of both librarian and user). In an online reference setting, the librarian can structure the user's request for help somewhat by having the user fill out a form asking the kind of clarifying questions use during reference interviews. With a click of a button the user can send the form to the library.

Use of e-resources seeking answers – Online reference service: An electronic resource is defined as a resource which requires computer access or any electronic product that delivers a collection of data, be it text referring to full text bases, electronic journals, image collections, other multimedia products and numerical, graphical or time based, as a commercially available title that has been published with an aim to being marketed. These may be delivered on CD ROM, on tape, via internet and so on.

59. **COUNTER:** This COUNTER Code of Practice provides a framework for the recording and exchange of online usage statistics for the major categories of e-resources (journals, databases, books, reference works, and multimedia databases) at an international level. In doing so, it covers the following areas: data elements to be measured; definitions of these data elements; content and format of usage reports; requirements for data processing; requirements for auditing; guidelines to avoid duplicate counting when intermediary gateways and aggregators are used.

PLOS ALMs: Article-Level Metrics (ALMs) help guide understanding of the influence and impact of work before the accrual of academic citations. All PLOS journal articles display PLOS ALMs—quantifiable measures that incorporate both academic and social metrics to document the many ways in which both scientists and the general public engage with published research. PLOS ALMs are presented on the metrics tab on every published article. In addition, a signpost in the upper right provides summary metrics of citations, views, shares and bookmarks.

ORCID: An ORCID (Open Researcher and Contributor iD) is a unique, persistent identifier for researchers that helps distinguish your research activities and outputs from those of other researchers with similar names to ensure you get credit for your work. It aims to connect researchers with all their research outputs, including publications, grants and datasets. ORCID is a non-profit organisation supported by a global community of organisations including universities, publishers, funders, professional associations, and other stakeholders in the research ecosystem. Together, this global community has turned ORCID into a tool that links the many available author ID numbers under a single identifier and allows researcher data to be shared between systems.

Social media citations – All metric: Social media citations: Social media: It is a media for social interaction, using highly accessible and scalable communication techniques. It is the use of web-based and mobile technologies to turn communication into interactive dialogue.

60. **Apache OpenOffice (AOO)** is an open-source office productivity software suite. It is one of the successor projects of OpenOffice.org and the designated successor of IBM Lotus Symphony. Apache OpenOffice is a close cousin of LibreOffice and NeoOffice. It contains a word processor (Writer), a spreadsheet (Calc), a presentation application (Impress), a drawing application (Draw), a formula editor (Math), and a database management application (Base).

Microsoft Office is an office suite of applications, servers, and services developed by Microsoft. It was first announced by Bill Gates on 1 August 1988, at COMDEX in Las Vegas. Initially a marketing term for a bundled set of applications, the first version of Office contained Microsoft Word, Microsoft Excel, and Microsoft PowerPoint. Over the years, Office applications have grown substantially closer with shared features such as a common spell checker, OLE data integration and Visual Basic for Applications scripting language. Microsoft also positions Office as a development platform for line-of-business software under the Office Business Applications brand. On 10 July 2012, Softpedia reported that Office is used by over a billion people worldwide.

IBM Notes (formerly Lotus Notes) and IBM Domino (formerly Lotus Domino) are the client and server, respectively, of a collaborative client-server software platform sold by IBM. IBM Notes provides business collaboration functions, such as email, calendars, to-do lists, contacts management, teamrooms, discussion forums, file sharing, microblogging, instant messaging, blogs, and user directories. Lotus Development Corporation originally developed "Lotus Notes" in 1989. IBM bought the Lotus Corporation in 1995 and it became known as the Lotus Development division of IBM. As of 2015 it forms part of the IBM Software and Systems Group under the name "IBM Collaboration Solutions".

iWork is an office suite of applications created by Apple Inc. for its macOS and iOS operating systems, and also available cross-platform through the iCloud website.

It includes Keynote, a presentation program; the word processing and desktop publishing application Pages; and the spreadsheet application Numbers.

61. **MOOCs-LIS Education – Formulation of the problem:** MOOCs-LIS Education: Massive Open Online Courses (MOOCs) are revolutionizing the field of higher education by giving a new learning opportunity for aspiring students, faculty and universities in many subject areas including Library and Information Science (LIS). The MOOCs like in other areas have made a beginning in Library and Information Science [LIS]. The objectives of the LIS courses are to provide a balanced training, integrating theory with practical exercises, and to cover all aspects of professional work with equal emphasis embracing new frontiers of librarianship.

EDUCAUSE 2013 – Literature study: EDUCAUSE 2013: The EDUCAUSE Annual Conference is the premier gathering for higher education IT professionals. It provides content and exploration of today's toughest technology issues facing campuses around the world, and convenes some of the brightest minds in the community. EDUCAUSE Center for Analysis and Research (ECAR) at EDUCAUSE 2013 recommended to educate the students about MOOCs; most students are unaware of them. Institutions have a fleeting opportunity to contextualize MOOCs for students in a way that will mesh with the institution's own MOOC strategy.

MOOCs programmes – Hypothesis: There is every possibility that MOOCs programmes will replace distance learning in LIS because of various reasons, viz., discussion forums, cohorting, interactive, student engagement and persistence, personalization, data analytics and learning dashboards, the user experience, a sustainable business model, etc.

Distance learning – Analytical statement: Distance education or distance learning is the education of students who may not always be physically present at a school. Traditionally, this usually involved correspondence courses wherein the student corresponded with the school via post. Today it involves online education.

62. **Survey Monkey** is an online survey development cloud-based software as a service company, founded in 1999 by Ryan Finley. Survey Monkey provides free, customizable surveys, as well as a suite of paid back-end programs that include data analysis, sample selection, bias elimination, and data representation tools. In addition to providing free and paid plans for individual users, SurveyMonkey offers more large-scale enterprise options for companies interested in data analysis, brand management, and consumer-focused marketing. Since releasing its enterprise in 2013, business-focused services, SurveyMonkey has grown dramatically, opening a new headquarters in San Mateo.

Typeform: Typeform is a Barcelona-based online software as a service (SaaS) company that specializes in online form building. Its main software creates dynamic forms based on user needs. Typeform's software has been used by Apple Inc., Airbnb, Uber and Nike, Inc. Typeform produces millions of forms every month. Typeform was founded in 2012 by Robert Muñoz and David Okuniev. Typeform's software was released in Alpha phase by invitation only.

Client Heartbeat is a web-based tool for helping IT Managed Service Providers (MSP's) track their client's levels of satisfaction. It allows you to regularly survey your customers, but what makes it unique is it allows you to benchmark your performance against others in your industry and region. It was founded by Gordon Tan.

Survey Gizmo is a software company based in Boulder, Colorado in the United States, founded in 2006. The company provides Software as a service online survey software. The company was founded by partners Christian Vanak and Scott McDaniel in 2006.

63. National Mission on Manuscripts – 2003: The National Mission for Manuscripts was established in February 2003, by the Ministry of Tourism and Culture, Government of India. A unique project in its programme and mandate, the Mission seeks to unearth and preserve the vast manuscript wealth of India. India possesses an estimate of ten million manuscripts, probably the largest collection in the world.

National Mission on Libraries – 2012: National Mission on Libraries, *i.e.,* High Level Committee, has been set up by Ministry of Culture, Government of India in 2012 in pursuance of National Knowledge Commission recommendations for sustained attention for development of Libraries and Information Science Sector.

National Mission on Monuments and Antiquities – 2007: On 15th August, 2003, then Prime Minister of India made an announcement for setting up of a National Mission on India's Tangible Heritage. Accordingly, the National Mission on Monuments and Antiquities was launched on 19th March 2007.

The objective for undertaking the National Mission on Monuments & Sites and Antiquities is to develop a national database with a view to enhance access to the students, scholars, researchers and to the general public and preserve it for the posterity. The main emphasis should be to improve awareness about cultural inheritance and encourage their use for educational and research purposes for lifelong learning.

National Knowledge Network – 2010: National Knowledge Network (NKN) is a multi-gigabit National Research and Education Network (NREN), whose purpose is to provide a unified high speed network backbone for educational institutions in India. The NKN is a hierarchical network divided into three basic layers – ultra-high speed CORE, Distribution and Edge. The NKN backbone will be created by multiple bandwidth providers and the edges can be provided by any service provider.

In March 2010, the Cabinet Committee on Infrastructure (CCI) approved the establishment of the National Knowledge Network (NKN).

64. The Copyright System: Copyright is a legal right created by the law of a country that grants the creator of an original work exclusive rights for its use and distribution. This is usually only for a limited time. The exclusive rights are not absolute but limited by limitations and exceptions to copyright law, including fair use. A major limitation on copyright is that copyright protects only the original expression of ideas, and not the underlying ideas themselves. Copyright is a form of intellectual property, applicable to certain forms of creative work.

The copyright system, born and bred for print technology, for a technological revolution in its environment. Digitization and global networks have heightend the interdependence of copyright production systems, markets, and the laws the govern them. The old broadcast model of one-to-many communication is replaced with many-to-many global connectivity.

67. **Content-based indexing technique:** Content-based retrieval of multimedia database calls for content-based indexing techniques. Different from conventional databases, where data items are represented by a set of attributes of elementary data types, multimedia objects in multimedia databases are represented by a collection of features; similarity of object contents depends on context and frame of reference; and features of objects are characterized by multimodal feature measures. These lead to great challenges for content-based indexing.

    On the other hand, there are special requirements on content-based indexing: To support visual browsing, similarity retrieval, and fuzzy retrieval, nodes of the index should represent certain meaningful categories. That is to say that certain semantics must be added while performing indexing.

69. QR codes are the most popular from of 2D barcodes around and have become extremely popular in the marketing world. Users scan the barcode using an application on their phone which utilises the phone's camera.

    The barcodes are mainly being used for easily communicating web links to people so they can quickly get access to a long web-link without having to type it in. They can also be used to dial numbers and send messages.

    QR codes have only become really popular in 2011 because of the rise in the number of smartphone users and the increasing popularity and usability of the mobile web. A variety of applications are available to read QR codes and in some handsets this functionality is pre-installed. From a security perspective, QR codes represent a risk. The user often has no view at all of what the QR code links through to, which could easily be something malicious. A lot of companies have rushed into implementing this functionality for making things more convenient for people without thinking about security properly.

    One example of a poor and insecure implementation of QR codes was the Verrus paybyphone parking service which encouraged people to scan a QR code to pay for their parking quickly over the web. The QR code took users straight to a mobile site which asks users to enter their credit card details. The site is so astonishingly easy to spoof that it is scary, partly because screen space is so confined that the user can't see the whole of the URL (which might actually lead to a malicious site instead of the real Verrus one). An attacker could easily stick a replacement QR code over the top of the original code on the parking sign, taking the user to their malicious payment site instead. There was no description whatsoever near the sign's QR code about what it was supposed to do. There were a whole host of other attacks that could potentially take place too.

70. A proxy server is a service that libraries use to authenticate their users to provide access to many online databases and publisher websites. Using a proxy service allows library resource vendors to authenticate users from a single point-of-access regardless of where they are located, on-campus or from their home computer.

    To avoid having to provide users with an individual or institutional login and password, most database and publisher websites authenticate users by IP address. Sometimes vendors will limit access to a range of IP addresses—on a single campus, for example. But for users outside of the physical campus, you must provide a known IP address (or set of IP addresses). This is accomplished by routing users through a proxy server so that the access requests come from its IP address(es) which are recognized by the vendor. The content is then returned to the proxy server and routed back to the original user.

Because libraries can't let everyone access their resources via EZproxy, they must authenticate their users before access. EZproxy allows user login itself, but EZproxy also provides a method of authentication using your institution's single sign-on (SSO) server. Today, most proxies are web proxies, facilitating access to content on the World Wide Web, providing anonymity and may be used to bypass IP address blocking.

75. IFLA's International Resource Sharing and Document Delivery: Principles and Guidelines for Procedure, first agreed to by IFLA in 1954, was revised in February, 2009. It contains eight principles and guidelines; copyright is number six. It advises: "Due regard must be given to the copyright laws of the supplying country. While material requested on international ILL may often fall within 'fair use' or 'fair dealing' provisions, responsibility rests with the supplying library to inform the requesting library of any copyright restrictions which might apply." It continues in sections:

- Each supplying library should be aware of, and work within, the copyright laws of its own country. In addition, the supplying library should ensure that any relevant copyright information is made available and communicated to requesting libraries.
- Lending, and limited copying for purposes such as education, research or private study, are usually exceptions within national copyright legislation. The supplying library should inform the requesting library of these exceptions.
- The requesting library should pay due regard to the copyright laws of the supplying library's country.

Previous Paper (Solved)

UGC-NET-Junior Research Fellowship & Assistant Professor Exam

Library and Information Science, January-2017*

PAPER-II

Note: *This paper contains* ***fifty*** *(**50**) objective type questions of* ***two*** *(**2**) marks each.* ***All*** *questions are compulsory.*

1. Number of working days of National Library of India in a year
A. 350 days B. 360 days
C. 362 days D. 365 days

2. Lotka's law deals with
A. Frequency of occurrence of words in a text.
B. Productivity of authors in terms of scientific papers.
C. Scattering of articles over different journals.
D. Growth of articles in journals.

3. The large volumes of high velocity, complex and variable data are termed as
A. Big data
B. Linked data
C. Semantic data
D. Ontology-based data

4. Sony unveiled the first Blu-ray Disc (BD) prototypes in
A. September 1982 B. August 1985
C. October 2000 D. November 2005

5. ISO 26324 : 2012 is a standard for
A. RFID in Libraries
B. DOI
C. Dublin Core
D. Inter Library Transaction

6. ISO 2108 standard is related to :
A. International Standard Serial Number
B. International Standard Book Number
C. International Technical Report Number
D. International Standard for Patents Number

7. The Browne charging system does not include
A. Reader's ticket B. Book card
C. Date slip D. Transaction slip

8. In CC '1' is used for Unity, God, World, First in evolution, etc., as a
A. Seminal mnemonic
B. Schedule mnemonic
C. Alphabetical mnemonic
D. Syntactical mnemonic

9. Identify the mode of formation of the subject 'Agriculture of Corn':
A. Agglomeration B. Denudation
C. Fusion D. Lamination

10. The number of successive characteristics forming the basis of its derivation from the Universe of Knowledge is known as:
A. Order of an array
B. Order of a class
C. Open array
D. Collateral array

11. What is the third part of colon classification?
A. Schedules
B. Rules
C. Classic and sacred books
D. Index

12. Subject entry which refers from the name of a class to its class number is known as:
A. Class Index Entry
B. Consolidated Entry
C. Cross Reference Entry
D. Subject Analytical Entry

*Held on 22/01/2017

13. The license for accessing the'Europa World of Learning Online' is available through

A. Routledge – (Taylor and Francis)
B. SpringerOpen
C. Sage Publications
D. Elsevier

14. What is the periodicity of 'Annals of Library and Information Studies' published by NISCAIR, India?

A. Monthly B. Bi-monthly
C. Quarterly D. Bi-annual

15. 'Facet publishing' is a division of

A. American Library Association
B. Canadian Library Association
C. Chartered Institute of Library and Information Professionals
D. International Federation of Library Associations

16. Who differentiated information and knowledge in the following way?

"Information is piecemeal, fragmented, particular; whereas knowledge is structural, coherent and universal"

A. B.C. Brooks and N.J. Belkin
B. S.G. Faibisoff and D.P. Ely
C. F. Machlup and U. Mansfield
D. J.H. Shera

17. Which of the following key terms of references assigned to National Knowledge Commission (NKC) constituted in June 2005 under the Chairmanship of Sam Pitroda for preparing a blue print to reform knowledge-related institutions and their infrastructure?

(*a*) Build Excellence in Education System and increase India's competitive advantage in the field of knowledge.
(*b*) Establishment of one "Knowledge Pool" (KP) in each state capital and to check the drop-out rate of school going children in acquiring knowledge.
(*c*) Promote creation of knowledge in S & T Labs and improve management of institutions engaged in IPR activities.
(*d*) Promote knowledge applications in Agriculture and Industry and use of knowledge capabilities in making Government effective, transparent, and accountable.

Codes:

A. (*b*), (*c*) and (*d*) are correct
B. (*a*), (*b*) and (*d*) are correct
C. (*a*), (*c*) and (*d*) are correct
D. (*a*), (*b*) and (*c*) are correct

18. In which of the following places the zonal offices of RRRLF are located?

(*a*) Delhi (*b*) Trivandrum
(*c*) Mumbai (*d*) Hyderabad

Codes:

A. (*a*) and (*d*) are correct
B. (*a*) and (*c*) are correct
C. (*b*) and (*d*) are correct
D. (*b*) and (*c*) are correct

19. Which of the following can be used to measure the research output of an individual?

(*a*) h-index (*b*) Benchmark
(*c*) g-index (*d*) Bookmarks

Codes:

A. (*a*) and (*b*) are correct
B. (*b*) and (*c*) are correct
C. (*a*) and (*c*) are correct
D. (*c*) and (*d*) are correct

20. Identify from the following the Silver Halide process used in reprography:

(*a*) Exposure (*b*) Miniature
(*c*) Developing (*d*) Rinsing

Codes :

A. (*a*), (*b*) and (*d*) are correct
B. (*b*), (*c*) and (*d*) are correct
C. (*a*), (*c*) and (*d*) are correct
D. (*d*), (*b*) and (*c*) are correct

21. Identify the type of 'metadata' held by D space for archiving contents:

(*a*) Descriptive
(*b*) Configured
(*c*) Structural
(*d*) Administrative

Codes:

A. (*a*), (*b*), (*c*) are correct
B. (*b*), (*c*), (*d*) are correct
C. (*a*), (*b*), (*d*) are correct
D. (*a*), (*c*), (*d*) are correct

22. Which of the following are 'Special Auxiliary Subdivisions' of UDC ?

(*a*) Apostrophe (*b*) Sub-grouping
(*c*) Colon (*d*) Point-naught

Codes:

A. (*a*) and (*d*) are correct
B. (*a*) and (*b*) are correct
C. (*b*) and (*c*) are correct
D. (*c*) and (*d*) are correct

23. What are the constituent elements of Simon's Flow Chart that are the components of management system?

(*a*) Planning (*b*) Staffing
(*c*) Motivating (*d*) Innovating

Codes:

A. (*a*), (*b*) and (*d*) are correct
B. (*a*), (*c*) and (*d*) are correct
C. (*d*), (*b*) and (*c*) are correct
D. (*a*), (*b*) and (*c*) are correct

24. Which of the following are the characteristics of not-for-profit organizations according to Edward G. Evans?

(*a*) Financial sources derived from outside funding sources rather than from sales of service.
(*b*) Have clear indicator of effect, i.e., profit or loss.
(*c*) Organizations are public rather than private.
(*d*) Funding preferences for collaborative projects.

Codes:

A. (*a*), (*b*) and (*d*) are correct
B. (*a*), (*c*) and (*d*) are correct
C. (*b*), (*c*) and (*d*) are correct
D. (*a*), (*b*) and (*c*) are correct

25. Which of the following are the criteria for defined open standard in W3C (2006)?

(*a*) Transparency and Impartiality
(*b*) Maintenance and Relevance
(*c*) Availability and Openness
(*d*) Security and Preservation

Codes:

A. (*a*), (*b*), (*d*) are correct
B. (*b*), (*c*), (*d*) are correct
C. (*a*), (*c*), (*d*) are correct
D. (*a*), (*b*), (*c*) are correct

26. A Blog usually provides

(*a*) a commentary on a particular subject.
(*b*) a personal online diary.
(*c*) an online brand advertising of a particular individual or company.
(*d*) an exclusive pre-paid publishing tool and non-instructional and non-illustrative resource for the scribes.

Codes:

A. (*a*), (*c*) and (*d*) are correct
B. (*b*), (*c*) and (*d*) are correct
C. (*a*), (*b*) and (*c*) are correct
D. (*a*), (*b*) and (*d*) are correct

27. Which of the following are pillars of information literacy according to SCONUL seven pillars of information literacy?

(*a*) Find (*b*) Gather
(*c*) Identify (*d*) Manage

Codes:

A. (*a*), (*b*) and (*c*) are correct
B. (*b*), (*c*) and (*d*) are correct
C. (*a*), (*c*) and (*d*) are correct
D. (*a*), (*b*) and (*d*) are correct

28. Identify from the following, the digital library projects were implemented by C-DAC (Agency) Noida:

(*a*) Creation of Vidwan database
(*b*) Print your own book – Mobile Digital Library
(*c*) Creation of Shodhsindhu
(*d*) Creation of Digital Library of Books in President House

Codes:

A. (*a*) and (*b*) are correct
B. (*b*) and (*c*) are correct
C. (*c*) and (*d*) are correct
D. (*b*) and (*d*) are correct

29. Which of the following are the objectives of RRRLF?

(*a*) To act as referral centre
(*b*) To act as clearing house
(*c*) To promote reading habit
(*d*) To promote library movement

Codes:

A. (*a*), (*b*) are correct
B. (*b*), (*c*) are correct
C. (*a*), (*d*) are correct
D. (*c*), (*d*) are correct

30. Identify the sequence of the 'title' and 'statement of responsibility' area from the following:

(*a*) Title proper
(*b*) Parallel title
(*c*) General Material Designation (GMD)
(*d*) Statement of responsibility

Codes:

A. (*a*), (*c*), (*b*) and (*d*)
B. (*c*), (*b*), (*a*) and (*d*)
C. (*d*), (*c*), (*b*) and (*a*)
D. (*b*), (*a*), (*c*) and (*d*)

31. Arrange the following according to their year of origin/publication:

(*a*) Cause and effect diagram
(*b*) MBO
(*c*) Pareto Principle
(*d*) POSDCORB

Codes:

A. (*a*), (*b*), (*c*), (*d*)
B. (*b*), (*c*), (*d*), (*a*)
C. (*c*), (*d*), (*a*), (*b*)
D. (*d*), (*a*), (*b*), (*c*)

32. Arrange the following Public Libraries Acts' according to their year of enactment:

(*a*) Gujarat Public Libraries Act
(*b*) Chhattisgarh Public Libraries Act
(*c*) Goa Public Libraries Act
(*d*) Rajasthan Public Libraries Act

Codes:

A. (*a*), (*c*), (*b*), (*d*) B. (*d*), (*b*), (*a*), (*c*)
C. (*c*), (*a*), (*d*), (*b*) D. (*d*), (*b*), (*c*), (*a*)

33. Match the following:

List–I	List–II
(*a*) Sample	(*i*) Height, weight
(*b*) Variable	(*ii*) Cluster
(*c*) Range	(*iii*) Square root of variance
(*d*) Standard deviation	(*iv*) Difference in score distribution

Codes:

	(*a*)	(*b*)	(*c*)	(*d*)
A.	(*iii*)	(*ii*)	(*i*)	(*iv*)
B.	(*ii*)	(*i*)	(*iv*)	(*iii*)
C.	(*i*)	(*iii*)	(*ii*)	(*iv*)
D.	(*iv*)	(*ii*)	(*i*)	(*iii*)

34. Match the following:

List–I	List–II
(*a*) Basic Research	(*i*) Problem of gaps in periodical collection in J.N.U. Library
(*b*) Applied Research	(*ii*) Use of measurement technique in Library Science
(*c*) Action Research	(*iii*) Use of Library in public schools in Delhi
(*d*) Survey Research	(*iv*) Five laws of Library

Codes:

	(*a*)	(*b*)	(*c*)	(*d*)
A.	(*iv*)	(*ii*)	(*i*)	(*iii*)
B.	(*ii*)	(*iv*)	(*i*)	(*iii*)
C.	(*iii*)	(*ii*)	(*iv*)	(*i*)
D.	(*i*)	(*ii*)	(*iii*)	(*iv*)

35. Match the following States with their corresponding E-Government initiatives:

List–I	List–II
(*a*) Kerala	(*i*) Akshaya
(*b*) M.P. (Dhar)	(*ii*) Banglar Mukh
(*c*) Maharashtra	(*iii*) Gyandoot
(*d*) West Bengal	(*iv*) Information Junction

Codes:

	(*a*)	(*b*)	(*c*)	(*d*)
A.	(*i*)	(*iii*)	(*iv*)	(*ii*)
B.	(*ii*)	(*i*)	(*iii*)	(*iv*)
C.	(*iv*)	(*iii*)	(*ii*)	(*i*)
D.	(*iii*)	(*ii*)	(*iv*)	(*i*)

36. Match the following:

List–I	List–II
(*a*) Web of Science	(*i*) Chemical Abstract Service (CAS)
(*b*) Web Junction	(*ii*) Elsevier
(*c*) Scopus	(*iii*) OCLC
(*d*) SciFinder	(*iv*) Thomas Reuters

Codes:

	(*a*)	(*b*)	(*c*)	(*d*)
A.	(*ii*)	(*iii*)	(*iv*)	(*i*)
B.	(*iv*)	(*i*)	(*iii*)	(*ii*)
C.	(*iii*)	(*iv*)	(*ii*)	(*i*)
D.	(*iv*)	(*iii*)	(*ii*)	(*i*)

37. Match the following:

List–I	List–II
(*a*) ABCD	(*i*) Georgia (USA)
(*b*) KOHA	(*ii*) New Zealand
(*c*) Weblis	(*iii*) Brazil
(*d*) Evergreen	(*iv*) Poland

Codes:

	(*a*)	(*b*)	(*c*)	(*d*)
A.	(*iii*)	(*ii*)	(*i*)	(*iv*)
B.	(*iv*)	(*ii*)	(*i*)	(*iii*)
C.	(*iii*)	(*iv*)	(*i*)	(*ii*)
D.	(*i*)	(*ii*)	(*iv*)	(*iii*)

38. Match the following:

List–I	List–II
(*a*) Library Finance	(*i*) Regular Grant
(*b*) Non-plan Grant	(*ii*) Funds given for building, Infrastructure & Machinery
(*c*) Non-Recurring Grant	(*iii*) Sources of Income and Expenditure
(*d*) Plan Grant	(*iv*) Funds given for project under annual/ 5 year plan

Codes:

	(*a*)	(*b*)	(*c*)	(*d*)
A.	(*ii*)	(*iii*)	(*i*)	(*iv*)
B.	(*i*)	(*iv*)	(*iii*)	(*ii*)
C.	(*iii*)	(*i*)	(*ii*)	(*iv*)
D.	(*ii*)	(*i*)	(*iv*)	(*iii*)

39. Match the following Main Entry fields with their corresponding tag as are given numbers in MARC 21:

List–I	List–II
(*a*) 100	(*i*) Main Entry–Uniform Title
(*b*) 110	(*ii*) Main Entry–Meeting Name
(*c*) 111	(*iii*) Main Entry–Personal Name
(*d*) 130	(*iv*) Main Entry–Corporate Name

Codes:

	(*a*)	(*b*)	(*c*)	(*d*)
A.	(*iii*)	(*iv*)	(*ii*)	(*i*)
B.	(*iv*)	(*iii*)	(*ii*)	(*i*)
C.	(*i*)	(*iii*)	(*iv*)	(*ii*)
D.	(*ii*)	(*iv*)	(*i*)	(*iii*)

40. **Assertion (A):** There is a connection between the concept of uncertainty and relevance in IR.

Reason (R): In IR both uncertainty and relevance are totally ruled out as part of query document matching.

Codes:

A. (A) is true, but (R) is false
B. (A) is false, but (R) is true
C. Both (A) and (R) are true
D. Both (A) and (R) are false

41. **Assertion (A):** Electronic indexing and abstracting services are not advantageous over print.

Reason (R): Electronic indexes work on much the same principles as print.

Codes:

A. (A) is true, but (R) is false
B. (A) is false, but (R) is true
C. Both (A) and (R) are false
D. Both (A) and (R) are true

42. **Assertion (A):** The efforts of contemporary libraries in using static A-Z lists (as a part of their ERM system) to facilitate access for users who wanted to limit their searches to e-content has failed to yield results.

Reason (R): Such lists maintained locally are, by necessity, more detailed and elaborate, as increase of titles made the maintenance of such lists more labour intensive and complicated.

Codes:

A. (A) is true, but (R) is false
B. (A) is false, but (R) is true
C. Both (A) and (R) are true
D. Both (A) and (R) are false

43. **Assertion (A):** Libraries contribute to capacity building, which is essential to community development.

Reason (R): Library programmes and services can influence a person's desire for life-long learning, which is an important component of capacity building.

Codes:

A. (A) is true, but (R) is false
B. (A) is false, but (R) is true
C. Both (A) and (R) are true
D. Both (A) and (R) are false

44. **Assertion (A):** A collaborative culture is an important condition for knowledge transfer between individuals.

Reason (R): Knowledge transfer does not require individuals to come together to interact, exchange, and share ideas and knowledge with one another.

Codes:

A. (A) is true, but (R) is false
B. (A) is false, but (R) is true
C. Both (A) and (R) are true
D. Both (A) and (R) are false

45. **Assertion (A):** Right to Information Act in India mandates timely response to citizen requests for information sought.

Reason (R): The basic object of the Right to Information Act is to empower the citizens, promote transparency and accountability.

Codes:

A. (A) is true, but (R) is false
B. (A) is false, but (R) is true
C. Both (A) and (R) are true
D. Both (A) and (R) are false

Directions (Qs. No. 46-50) : *Read the passage given below and answer the questions based on your understanding of the passage.*

The idea and phrase "serious leisure' comes from Stebbins' interviewees, who used the word "serious" to underline the extent of their passion for a favourite leisure activity. In this case, the term embodies positive qualities such as importance and sincerity, rather than negative traits such as gravity or anxiety. Whereas casual leisure supplies pleasure, and project-base leisure delivers a temporary reward, serious leisure generates deep and enduring sensations of fulfilment.

There are six defining characteristics to all serious leisure. First, there is the occasional need to persevere, as when mountain climbers push through exhaustion to reach a peak. Second, is that of finding a leisure career in the activity, with turning points and a sense of advancement. Third, serious leisure takes significant personal effort based on specially acquired knowledge, training, experience, or skill. In this quality, serious leisure is the opposite of its casual counterpart, which requires no expertise. Fourth, there are eight durable benefits or outcomes to serious leisure: self-actualization, self-enrichment, self-expression, regeneration or renewal of self, feelings of accomplishment, enhancement of self-image, social interaction and belongingness, and lasting physical products of the activity. Fifth, serious leisure participants tend to identify strongly with their chosen pursuits, and may be quick to assert their affiliation. Sixth, a unique ethos, or spirit of the community, exists around each serious leisure activity.

There are three main types of serious leisure : amateurism, volunteering, and hobbies. Amateurs operate in the fields of art, science, sport, and entertainment.

46. One of the six defining characteristics of serious leisure is

A. amateurism
B. requires no expertise
C. pleasure
D. spirit of the community

47. One of the three main types of serious leisure is

A. hobbies B. sport
C. entertainment D. art

48. Which is not one of the eight durable benefits of serious leisure?

A. Self-expression B. Renewal of self
C. Social interaction D. Unique ethos

49. The word 'serious' in the phrase 'serious leisure' expresses the idea of

A. gravity B. anxiety
C. sincerity D. pleasure sensations

50. A temporary reward comes from

A. casual leisure
B. project-based leisure
C. serious leisure
D. enduring sensations of fulfilment

ANSWERS

1	2	3	4	5	6	7	8	9	10
C	B	A	C	B	B	D	A	D	B
11	**12**	**13**	**14**	**15**	**16**	**17**	**18**	**19**	**20**
C	A	A	C	C	C	C	B	C	C
21	**22**	**23**	**24**	**25**	**26**	**27**	**28**	**29**	**30**
D	A	A	B	D	C	B	D	*	A
31	**32**	**33**	**34**	**35**	**36**	**37**	**38**	**39**	**40**
C	C	B	A	A	D	A	C	A	A
41	**42**	**43**	**44**	**45**	**46**	**47**	**48**	**49**	**50**
B	A	C	A	C	D	A	D	C	B

* Error in Question

EXPLANATORY ANSWERS

1. The National Library is the largest library in India, situated at Kolkata. It serves as a prominent repository of all reading and information materials produced in India as well as abroad concerning India.

Lord Curzon established the Imperial library at Kolkata by merging Calcutta public Library and the Imperial Library in 30th January,1903. After Independence, the Government of India changed the name of the Imperial Library to the National Library, with the enactment of the Imperial Library (Change of Name) Act, 1948.

Designated as an institution of national importance under the Ministry of Culture, the National Library is designated to collect, disseminate and preserve the printed material produced in the country. It is the recipient library under the Delivery of Books and Newspapers (Public Libraries) Act, 1954 and the repository library in South Asia. National Library of India works 362 days in a year.

2. Alfred J. Lotka was an American scientist who published in 1926 an article 'The frequency distribution of scientific productivity'. He has been quoted since 1949 for his so-called 'law of scientific productivity', which is an inverse power function describing the rate of productivity in terms of published scientific articles over time. 'Lotka's law' is a misconceived term and could be better coined 'Lotka's formula', but for reasons of its general use, the term 'law' is maintained hereafter.

3. Big Data, a term that describes large volumes of high velocity, complex and variable data that require advanced technologies to capture, store, distribute and analyze information, is at a tipping point, with billions being spent to turn mountains of information into valuable insights for businesses. But there is more to Big Data than numbers and insights.

4. In the middle of 1990s, commercial HDTV sets finally started to appear in a larger market. However, there was no good, cheap way to record or play back HD content. There was no cheap storage medium that could store that amount of data, except JVC's Digital VHS and Sony's HDCAM. Nevertheless, it was well known that using lasers with shorter wavelengths would yield optical storage with higher density. When Shuji Nakamura invented practical blue laser diodes, it was a sensation, although a lengthy patent lawsuit delayed commercial introduction.

Sony started two projects applying the new diodes: UDO (Ultra Density Optical) and DVR Blue (together with Pioneer), a format of rewritable discs which would eventually become Blu-ray (more specifically, BD-RE). The core technologies of the formats are essentially similar.

The first DVR Blue prototypes were unveiled at the CEATEC exhibition in October 2000. Because the Blu-ray Disc standard places the data recording layer close to the surface of the disc, early discs were susceptible to contamination and scratches and had to be enclosed in plastic cartridges for protection. In February 2002, the project was officially announced as Blu-ray, and the Blu-ray Disc Association was founded by the nine initial members.

5. ISO 26324:2012 specifies the syntax, description and resolution functional components of the digital object identifier system, and the general principles for the creation, registration and administration of digital object identifier (DOI) names.

ISO 26324:2012 defines the syntax for a DOI name, which is used for the identification of an object of any material form (digital or physical) or an abstraction (such as a textual work) where there is a functional need to distinguish it from other objects.

6. The purpose of ISO 2108:2005 is to establish the specifications for the International Standard Book Number (ISBN) as a unique international identification system for each product form or edition of a monographic publication published or produced by a specific publisher. It specifies the construction of an ISBN, the rules for its assignment and use, the metadata to be associated with the ISBN allocation, and the administration of the ISBN system. ISO 2108:2005 is applicable to monographic publications and certain types of related products that are available to the public. Examples of applicable and non-applicable products are provided.

8. Seminal mnemonics means specified digit should be seminally equivalent to entire schedule, that means, the same concept is represented by the same term and also same number in entire schedule. If any conflict occurs, then we simply say that particular classification schedule ignore this concept. In colon classification of entire schedule is divided into seminal mnemonics such as:

Number Meaning

1. Fundamentals, preliminary, persons
2. Structure, parts, forms, constitute
3. Function, syntax, method analysis
4. Fault, disease, pathology
5. Liquid, blood, environment
6. Money, finance, evolution, movement
7. Personality, composition, growth, produce
8. Management, organization

9. This paper describes research related to manufacturing of composite parts and resin infusion preforms with new materials based on a fungal mycelium-based binder developed and patented by Ecovative Design, LLC (Green Island, NY). Mycelium, the vegetative part of a fungus, acts like a natural, self-assembling glue that digests and binds securely to natural reinforcement materials and agricultural byproducts with essentially no added energy. Laminate structures can consist of natural reinforcement layers (*e.g.*, jute textile, kenaf mat) bound by mycelium, while sandwich structures have laminate skins and core made of agricultural byproducts all bound with together with mycelium. These structures can be used as is or as preforms for infusion with natural resin (*e.g.*, epoxidized linseed oil) to significantly increase strength and stiffness.

11. The sixth edition was published in the year 1960 and was reprinted in the year 1963. The noticeable change was the removal of Greek letters and replacement of the concept of Empty, Emptying and emptying digits. The indicator digit for time was replaced by 'single inverted comma. Levels in the Time and Space facets were introduced. In this edition, CC was divided into three parts:

Part 1 dealt with Rules. Each main class of the scheme had an individual chapter devoted to it. These chapters tell you how the class number is constructed and how it is to be used. There is an index to this part of the scheme.

Part 2 constitutes the main body of the scheme and is the part with which you will be more concerned. It contains the schedules of classification.

Part 3 is the schedules of Classics and Sacred books with special names. Here Indian Classics and sacred books are dealt.

12. Class Index Entries (CIE) are to serve as alphabetical index to the Class Numbers representing the 'works'. A CIE has to consist of three sections, viz., Leading Section, Second Section and Index Number. Alphabetical subject headings derived from the Class Number, applying Chain Procedure have to occupy the Leading Section. A directing statement "For documents in this Class and its Subdivisions see the Classified Part of the catalogue under the Class Number" has to be the content of Second Section. The Class Number denoting the heading written in the Leading Section shall be the Index Number.

14. Annals of Library and Information Studies is a leading quarterly journal in Library and Information Studies publishing original papers, survey reports, reviews, short communications, and letters pertaining to library science, information science and computer applications in these fields. It is an open access academic journal, published since 1954 by the CSIR-National Institute of Science Communication and Information Resources (CSIR-NISCAIR) formerly Indian National Scientific Documentation Centre.

15. Facet Publishing, the commercial publishing and bookselling arm of CILIP: the Chartered Institute of Library and Information Professionals, is the leading publisher of books for library and information professionals worldwide. Our business has a long-standing global profile. We sell books all over the world and the Facet brand is recognised as the home of quality content for the information professions. Our list contains several award-winning titles and our books regularly receive positive reviews in the top LIS journals.

16. The term "knowledge" is broadly used and seldom defined. It has become a buzzword associated with artificial intelligence and expert systems. A better understanding of the term may be gained by comparing knowledge and information. Machlup and Mansfield provide three distinctions between the two concepts.

(1) Information is piecemeal, fragmented, particular, whereas knowledge is structured, coherent, and often universal. (2) Information is timely, transitory, perhaps even ephemeral, whereas knowledge is of enduring significance. (3) Information is a flow of messages, whereas knowledge is a stock, largely resulting from the flow, in the sense that the "input" of information may affect the stock of knowledge by adding to it, restructuring it, or changing it in any way (though, conceivably, information may leave knowledge unchanged). These distinctions are mutually compatible, though they often relate to different aspects of the cognitive processes or states involved.

17. National Knowledge Commission, was an Indian think-tank charged with considering possible policies that might sharpen India's comparative advantage in the knowledge-intensive service sectors. As per Government Notification of 13th June 2005, the following are the Terms of Reference of the National Knowledge Commission (NKC).

- Build excellence in the educational system to meet the knowledge challenges of the 21st century and increase India's competitive advantage in fields of knowledge.
- Promote creation of knowledge in S&T laboratories.
- Improve the management of institutions engaged in intellectual property rights.
- Promote knowledge applications in agriculture and industry.
- Promote the use of knowledge capabilities in making government an effective, transparent and accountable service provider to the citizens and promote widespread sharing of knowledge to maximize public benefit.

18. Raja Rammohun Roy Library Foundation (RRRLF), Kolkata was established by the government to promote and support public library movements in the country by providing adequate library services through assistance and by developing reading habits all over the country. It was established in 1972, the bicentenary year of the birth of Raja Rammohun Roy. Raja Rammohun Roy Library Foundation (RRRLF) is an autonomous organisation under the Ministry of Culture. It is the nodal agency of the Government of India to support public library services and systems and promote public library movement in the country. It has headquarters at Kolkata and four zonal offices: Mumbai, Chennai, New Delhi and Kolkata.

21. Metadata has been a buzzword in the digital library community for several years. As systems and schemas are being developed, several categories of metadata have been defined and named. Although the concepts behind the different categories of metadata are fairly consistent, there is some variance in how different groups (and individuals) categorize types of metadata, and there is often an overlap between the different categories. For the purposes of D Space I have chosen to define the following categories of metadata:

Descriptive Metadata provides identification and a description of an object. It is used primarily for search and retrieval purposes, providing information about the contents of an object. It provides fields for table-driven searching, as well as a description of the intellectual contents and a physical description of the object.

Structural Metadata provides information about the relationships between different parts of an object. It binds together components of complex information objects.

Administrative Metadata provides information used in managing and administering information resources within a system or a federation of systems. Typical examples of administrative metadata are information about rights and reproduction, legal requirements, version control, access restrictions, and statistical and audit trails.

Preservation Metadata provides information about the physical specification of an object's creation, its format and condition, hardware and software requirements to render it, its transformation into other formats (change history or "provenance") and its authenticity (fixity). The purpose of preservation metadata is to help future generations interpret and recreate the information objects.

22. Each main UDC class may also contain tables called special auxiliaries which express aspects that are recurrent, but in a limited subject range. These are usually facets of concepts related to operations, techniques, processes, materials, agents, etc. They are listed only in particular sections of the main tables. Special auxiliary numbers can be recognized as they all begin with one of these three specific symbols/indicators: .0 (point nought), - (hyphen) or ' (apostrophe). Any UDC number beginning with any of these symbols can be combined with any other UDC number in its designated area of application.

25. Using the W3C (2006) process as a model, we define the following set of requirements that a provider of technical specification must follow to qualify for the adjective Open Standard.

- Transparency (due process is public, and all technical discussions, meeting minutes, are archived and referencable in decision making)
- Relevance (new standardization is started upon due analysis of the market needs, including requirements phase, *e.g.*, accessibility, multi-linguism, etc.)
- Openness (anybody can participate, and everybody does: industry, individual, public, government bodies, academia, on a worldwide scale)
- Impartiality and consensus (guaranteed fairness by the process and the neutral hosting of the W3C organization, with equal weight for each participant)
- Availability (free access to the standard text, both during development and at final stage, translations, and clear IPR rules for implementation, allowing open source development in the case of Internet/Web technologies)
- Maintenance (ongoing process for testing, errata, revision and permanent access).

26. Many blogs provide commentary on a particular subject or topic, ranging from politics to sports. Others function as more personal online diaries, and others function more as online brand advertising of a particular individual or company. A typical blog combines text, digital images, and links to other blogs, web pages, and other media related to its topic. The ability of readers to leave publicly viewable comments, and interact with other commenters, is an important contribution to the popularity of many blogs. However, blog owners or authors often moderate and filter online comments to remove hate speech or other offensive content. These blogs are referred to as edublogs. Microblogging is another type of blogging, featuring very short posts.

27. In 1999, The SCONUL Working Group on Information Literacy published "Information skills in higher education: a SCONUL position paper" (SCONUL, 1999), introducing the Seven Pillars of Information Skills model. Since then, the model has been adopted by librarians and teachers around the world as a means of helping them to deliver information skills to their learners. The model was revised in 2011, and then reviewed in 2015. Seven Pillars of Information Literacy core is:

- Identify
- Scope
- Plan
- Gather
- Evaluate
- Manage
- Present.

28. Digital Library is a mission to create a portal for the Digital Library of India which will foster creativity and free access to all human knowledge. As a first step in realizing this mission, it is proposed to create the Digital Library with a free-to-read, searchable collection of one million books, predominantly in Indian languages, available to everyone over the Internet.

Digital Library Projects

- Mega Centre for Digital Library
- Mobile Digital Library : Dware Dware Gyan Sampada
- Digital Library at President's House
- Digital Library at Nagari Pracharini Sabha Varanasi
- Digital Library at Uttaranchal
- GyanNidhi : Multilingual Parallel Corpus in Indian Languages
- Digital Library at Gujarat Vidyapeeth, Ahmedabad
- Digitization of Libraries.

31. The Pareto principle states that, for many events, roughly 80% of the effects come from 20% of the causes. Management consultant Joseph M. Juran suggested the principle and named it after Italian economist Vilfredo Pareto, who noted the 80/20 connection while at the University of Lausanne in 1896, as published in his first paper, "Cours d'économie politique".

POSDCORB An acronym representing the functional responsibilities of a chief executive officer, as formulated by Luther Gulick and Lyndall Urwick in their 1937 paper on administrative management theory. The acronym stands for Planning, Organizing, Staffing, Directing, Coordinating, Reporting, and Budgeting.

Ishikawa diagrams (also called fishbone diagrams, herringbone diagrams, cause-and-effect diagrams, or Fishikawa) are causal diagrams created by Kaoru Ishikawa (1968) that show the causes of a specific event. Common uses of the Ishikawa diagram are product design and quality defect prevention to identify potential factors causing an overall effect.

Management by objectives (MBO) is a management model that aims to improve performance of an organization by clearly defining objectives that are agreed to by both management and employees. According to the theory, having a say in goal setting and action plans should ensure better participation and commitment among employees, as well as alignment of objectives across the organization. The term was first outlined by management guru Peter Drucker in 1954 in his book "The Practice of Management".

32. Library Legislation: Public Libraries Acts in India

- The Tamil Nadu Public Libraries Act, 1948
- Andhra Pradesh Public Libraries Act, 1960
- Karnataka Public Libraries Act, 1965
- The Maharashtra Public Libraries Act, 1967
- The West Bengal Public Libraries Act, 1979
- Manipur Public Libraries Act, 1988
- Kerala Public Libraries Act, 1989
- Haryana Public Libraries Act, 1989
- Mizoram Public Libraries Act, 1993
- Goa Public Libraries Act, 1993
- Orissa Public Libraries Act, 2002
- Gujarat Public Libraries Act, 2001
- Uttaranchal Public Libraries Act, 2005
- Rajasthan Public Libraries Act, 2006
- Chattisgarh Public Libraries Act, 2008

33. Sample: In statistics and quantitative research methodology, a data sample is a set of data collected and/or selected from a statistical population by a defined procedure. The elements of a sample are known as sample points, sampling units or observations. Several types of random samples are simple random samples, systematic samples, stratified random samples, and cluster random samples.

A **variable** is any characteristic, number, or quantity that can be measured or counted. A variable may also be called a data item. Age, sex, height, weight and business income and expenses, country of birth, capital expenditure, class grades, eye colour and vehicle type are examples of variables. It is called a variable because the value may vary between data units in a population, and may change in value over time.

In statistics, the **range** of a set of data is the difference between the largest and the smallest values. However, in descriptive statistics, this concept of range has a more complex meaning. The range is the size of the smallest interval which contains all the data and provides an indication of statistical dispersion. It is measured in the same units as the data. Since it only depends on two of the observations, it is most useful in representing the dispersion of small data sets.

The **standard deviation** of a random variable, statistical population, data set, or probability distribution is the square root of its variance. It is algebraically simpler, though in practice less robust, than the average absolute deviation. A useful property of the standard deviation is that, unlike the variance, it is expressed in the same units as the data.

36. Web of Science is an online subscription-based scientific citation indexing service originally produced by the Institute for Scientific Information (ISI), now maintained by Clarivate Analytics (previously the Intellectual Property and Science business of Thomson Reuters), that provides a comprehensive citation search.

Web Junction is a division of OCLC funded by a grant from the Bill and Melinda Gates Foundation, which provides training services to librarians.

Scopus is a bibliographic database containing abstracts and citations for academic journal articles. It covers nearly 22,000 titles from over 5,000 publishers, of which 20,000 are peer-reviewed journals in the scientific, technical, medical, and social sciences. It is owned by Elsevier and is available online by subscription.

Chemical Abstracts Service (CAS) is a division of the American Chemical Society. It is a source of chemical information. CAS is located in Columbus, Ohio, United States. CAS databases are available via two principal database systems, STN, and SciFinder. SciFinder is a database of chemical and bibliographic information. Originally, a client application, a web version was released in 2008.

37. ABCD is a non-profit entity founded in 1999 in Brazil with the purpose of offering easy access to information required by IBD patients and promoting experience exchange between patients and professionals involved.

KOHA is a New Zealand Maori custom which can be translated as gift, present, offering, donation or contribution.

Weblis A Web-based integrated library system developed by the Institute for Computer and Information Engineering of Poland with support from UNESCO.

Project **Evergreen** completed its first 2015 "Healthy Turf Healthy Kids" project, renovating the entranceway to Wallace Park in Mableton, Georgia.

39. MARC 21 was designed to redefine the original MARC record format for the 21st century and to make it more accessible to the international community. MARC 21 has formats for the following five types of data: Bibliographic Format, Authority Format, Holdings Format, Community Format, and Classification Data Format.

MARC 21 Code List for Field Identification

- 100 - Personal names
- 110 - Corporate names
- 111 - Meeting names
- 130 - Uniform titles
- 140 - Bibliographic titles
- 150 - Topical terms
- 151 - Geographic names
- 155 - Genre/form terms.

44. Collaboration is an indispensable component in a culture that is friendly to Knowledge Management. This component implies that people are willing to cooperate with each other, which is a basis for the successful share of knowledge. Goh, for example, remarks that a collaborative culture is an important condition for knowledge transfer between individuals and groups. In this research, collaboration readiness represents the first of the three variables that measure the success of the impact of Micro-Bargaining strategies on Knowledge Management.

The recognition of willingness to cooperate as a key factor for the success of organisations is not new. Already in 1937, Chester Barnard stressed in his book "The Functions of the Executive" that every system is constituted by three universal elements: (1) willingness to cooperate, (2) common purpose and (3) communication. More recently, Frank and Fahrbach have underlined the importance of collaboration between people as a "critical aspect of systems in general and organizations in particular". Collaboration may produce collective or public goods, which are available for all the members of the community. From a constructivist perspective, interactions with other are internalised and transformed, creating new understanding. Through collaboration, individuals create new knowledge and acquire skills that they have not had before. Therefore, many authors suggest collaboration as the unique way to succeed in the knowledge economy.

45. Right to Information Act 2005 mandates timely response to citizen requests for government information. Right to Information empowers every citizen to seek any information from the Government, inspect any Government documents and seek certified photocopies thereof. Right to Information also empowers citizens to officially inspect any Government work or to take sample of material used in any work.

The basic object of the Right to Information Act is to empower the citizens, promote transparency and accountability in the working of the Government, contain corruption, and make our democracy work for the people in real sense. An informed citizenry will be better equipped to keep necessary vigil on the instruments of government and make the government more accountable to the governed.

PAPER-III

Note: *This paper contains* ***Seventy five (75)*** *objective type questions of* ***two (2)*** *marks each.* ***All*** *questions are compulsory.*

1. Index Indiana, an index to Indian Periodical Literature is being compiled by
A. Central Reference Library, Kolkata
B. National Library of India
C. NISCAIR
D. IASLIC

2. According to OCLC research report 'Know your community and its needs' is the rephrasing of which law of Ranganathan?
A. First Law   B. Second Law
C. Third Law   D. Fourth Law

3. Identify the document which is published by H.W. Wilson.
A. Europa World Yearbook 55th ed. 2014
B. The International Who's Who 78th ed. 2014
C. Sears list of subject Headings 20th ed. 2010
D. Ulrich's Periodicals Directory 53rd ed. 2015

4. 'Open Journal System' is an example of which of the following open access models?
A. Green   B. Red
C. Gold   D. Platinum

5. When was the final 'ISBD Consolidation Edition' published by IFLA?
A. 2008   B. 2009
C. 2010   D. 2011

6. According to S.R. Ranganathan the canons for chain are:
A. Canon of Ascertainability
B. Canon of Recall Value
C. Canon of array and filitary sequence
D. Canon of decreasing extension and modulation

7. In Colon Classification (6th edition) 'LB' denotes
A. Special   B. System
C. Canonical Class   D. Rounds

8. According to AACR 2R who will be considered for the access point of the Main Entry for the document entitled 'Adventures of Tom Sawyer by Mark Twain; rewritten for young readers by Felix Sutton.
A. Sawyer, Tom   B. Twain, Mark
C. Mark Twain   D. Sutton, Felix

9. 'Time and Motion' study was enunciated by ________
A. Edward Evans
B. Frank and Lillian Gilbreth
C. Harrington Emerson
D. G. McGregor

10. Which RFID component is attached to the Book/item for identification?
A. Barcode   B. Antenna
C. Reader   D. Tag

11. What is RJ45?
A. A network cable connector
B. A node
C. An electronic coupler
D. A video display unit

12. SIP, the communication protocol for signalling and controlling multimedia communication stands for
A. Signalling Information Protocol
B. Internet Session Protocol
C. Sound Initiation Protocol
D. Session Initiation Protocol

13. The Fifth Anniversary of the general release of OCLC World Share Management Service– the first-ever cloud-based Cooperative Library Management System (that selected 500 libraries spanning six continents) was celebrated on:
A. July 01, 2015   B. July 03, 2015
C. May 01, 2016   D. August 12, 2016

14. Which of the following is a measure of dispersion?
A. Geometric mean
B. Median

C. Mode

D. Root Mean Square Deviation

15. If 'r' is a rank of a word and 'f' is its frequency, then $rf = c$, where 'c' is a constant. Which law is this?

A. Bradford's law B. Lotka's law

C. Narain's law D. Zipf's law

16. VIDWAN (INFLIBNET) is

A. an open source software

B. an Association of Intellectuals

C. a Programming Language

D. a Database of Experts and a network of Researchers and Scientists at national level

17. Which of the following rights are granted for 'Literary works' according to Copyright Law of India?

(*a*) To make translation

(*b*) To use in reporting current events

(*c*) To make any adaptation

(*d*) To use for the purpose of research

Codes:

A. (*a*) and (*c*) are correct

B. (*a*) and (*b*) are correct

C. (*b*) and (*c*) are correct

D. (*b*) and (*d*) are correct

18. Identify from the following the features of tacit knowledge:

(*a*) Resides in human mind

(*b*) Cannot be articulated

(*c*) Tangible

(*d*) Easily accessible

Codes:

A. (*a*) and (*c*) are correct

B. (*b*) and (*c*) are correct

C. (*a*) and (*b*) are correct

D. (*c*) and (*d*) are correct

19. Which of the following are the examples of Web-based learning and education?

(*a*) Answer Tips

(*b*) Moodle

(*c*) Revish

(*d*) Campus bug

Codes:

A. (*a*), (*b*) and (*d*) are correct

B. (*a*), (*b*) and (*c*) are correct

C. (*b*), (*c*) and (*d*) are correct

D. (*a*), (*c*) and (*d*) are correct

20. Which of the following are the two sections stated in 'IFLA Digital Reference Guidelines'?

(*a*) Collaborative Virtual Reference

(*b*) The Administration of Digital Reference Service

(*c*) The Practice of Digital Reference

(*d*) Online Tools for Libraries

Codes:

A. (*a*) and (*c*) are correct

B. (*b*) and (*c*) are correct

C. (*b*) and (*d*) are correct

D. (*a*) and (*d*) are correct

21. Which of the following sites are offered by Britannica Library, a product of Encyclopaedia Britannica?

(*a*) Children

(*b*) Young Adult

(*c*) Patron

(*d*) Reference Centre

Codes:

A. (*a*), (*b*) and (*c*) are correct

B. (*a*), (*b*) and (*d*) are correct

C. (*b*), (*c*) and (*d*) are correct

D. (*d*), (*c*) and (*a*) are correct

22. Identify the key attributes of 'Digest' from the following:

(*a*) Significant ideas on one document area arranged separately in an unhelpful sequence.

(*b*) A Methodically arranged compendium or summary of literary, historical, legal, scientific or other written matters.

(*c*) Informative in nature and contains brief description of more than one document.

(*d*) Often prepared by a non-subject specialist without understanding and assimilating the contents of documents.

Codes:

A. (*a*) and (*b*) are correct
B. (*a*) and (*c*) are correct
C. (*a*) and (*d*) are correct
D. (*b*) and (*c*) are correct

23. Which of the following communication channels are used frequently in Virtual Reference Service?

(*a*) Bulletin Board
(*b*) Instant Messaging
(*c*) R.S.S.
(*d*) Voice-Over-I.P.

Codes:

A. (*a*) and (*b*) are correct
B. (*b*) and (*c*) are correct
C. (*b*) and (*d*) are correct
D. (*a*), (*b*) and (*d*) are correct

24. Identify the affinitive/associative relationship of the following:

(*a*) Genus-Species
(*b*) Translations
(*c*) Genetic
(*d*) Concurrent

Codes:

A. (*a*) and (*b*) are correct
B. (*b*) and (*c*) are correct
C. (*c*) and (*d*) are correct
D. (*a*) and (*d*) are correct

25. Which of the following are the components of a master database in acquisition system/ module?

(*a*) Membership Master
(*b*) Vendor Master
(*c*) Currency Master
(*d*) Transaction Master

Codes:

A. (*a*) and (*b*) are correct
B. (*a*), (*b*) and (*d*) are correct
C. (*b*), (*c*) and (*d*) are correct
D. (*b*) and (*c*) are correct

26. Which of the following are types of random samples?

(*a*) Cluster sampling
(*b*) Purposive sampling
(*c*) Stratified sampling
(*d*) Systematic sampling

Codes:

A. (*a*), (*c*) and (*d*) are correct
B. (*b*), (*c*) and (*d*) are correct
C. (*a*), (*b*) and (*c*) are correct
D. (*a*), (*b*) and (*d*) are correct

27. Who among the following devised the 'Critical Path Method'?

(*a*) Morgan R. Walker
(*b*) Clank Sedore
(*c*) Blake William
(*d*) James E. Kelley

Codes:

A. (*a*) and (*b*) are correct
B. (*a*) and (*d*) are correct
C. (*b*) and (*c*) are correct
D. (*c*) and (*d*) are correct

28. Which of the following databases is available for scientific community free of cost?

(*a*) Inspec
(*b*) ERIC
(*c*) IEEE Xplore
(*d*) PubMed

Codes:

A. (*a*) and (*b*) are correct
B. (*a*) and (*c*) are correct
C. (*b*) and (*d*) are correct
D. (*c*) and (*d*) are correct

29. Which of the following are protocol standards?

(*a*) z39.50
(*b*) z39.71
(*c*) z39.05
(*d*) z39.81

Codes:

A. (*a*), (*b*), (*c*) are correct
B. (*b*), (*c*) and (*d*) are correct
C. (*a*), (*c*) and (*d*) are correct
D. (*a*), (*b*) and (*d*) are correct

30. Which of the following are the Semantic Web technologies?

(*a*) SKOS (*b*) AJAX
(*c*) SPARQL (*d*) UTF

Codes:

A. (*a*) and (*b*) are correct
B. (*a*) and (*c*) are correct
C. (*a*), (*b*) and (*c*) are correct
D. (*b*), (*c*) and (*d*) are correct

31. Which of the following are the features of Operations Research?

(*a*) Aid in decision making
(*b*) Handles decision tables
(*c*) Optimization of Performance
(*d*) Used as motivational technique

Codes:

A. (*a*), (*b*) are correct
B. (*a*), (*c*) are correct
C. (*b*), (*d*) are correct
D. (*c*), (*d*) are correct

32. Which of the following are discrete distributions?

(*a*) Beta
(*b*) Exponential
(*c*) Geometric
(*d*) Poisson

Codes:

A. (*a*) and (*b*) are correct
B. (*b*) and (*c*) are correct
C. (*a*) and (*c*) are correct
D. (*c*) and (*d*) are correct

33. Identify the criteria for evaluation of qualitative research:

(*a*) Objectivity
(*b*) Reliability
(*c*) Divisibility
(*d*) Validity

Codes :

A. (*a*), (*b*) and (*d*) are correct
B. (*b*), (*c*) and (*d*) are correct
C. (*a*), (*c*) and (*d*) are correct
D. (*a*), (*b*) and (*c*) are correct

34. TRAILS-9 is

(*a*) A process or an assessment tool for real time assessment of Information Literacy Skill of the student-learners.
(*b*) A tool or process used by the School Librarians to produce evidence of Library's impact on student achievements to share with stake-holders.
(*c*) A tool to adjudge the quality of library services offered, but not to demonstrate the value of the Library's contribution.
(*d*) A tool funded by ILILE (Institute for Library & Information Literacy Education) based on Ohio-K12 Library Academic Content Standards.

Codes:

A. (*b*), (*c*) and (*d*) are correct
B. (*a*), (*b*) and (*d*) are correct
C. (*a*), (*c*) and (*d*) are correct
D. (*a*), (*b*) and (*c*) are correct

35. Which of the following are the sources to lookup for DOI?

(*a*) Central Search List
(*b*) DOI Handbook
(*c*) Registration Agencies
(*d*) Search results using a search engine

Codes:

A. (*a*) and (*b*) are correct
B. (*c*) and (*d*) are correct
C. (*a*) and (*c*) are correct
D. (*a*) and (*d*) are correct

36. Arrange in sequence the following types of activity according to Ellis's model of information-seeking behaviour :

(*a*) Browsing
(*b*) Chaining
(*c*) Differentiating
(*d*) Extracting

Codes:

A. (*a*), (*b*), (*c*), (*d*)
B. (*b*), (*a*), (*c*), (*d*)
C. (*c*), (*d*), (*b*), (*a*)
D. (*d*), (*a*), (*b*), (*c*)

37. Arrange in sequence the evolution of reference service:

(*a*) Reference work with subject specialization.

(*b*) Aid Reader/Assistance to Reader
(*c*) Long Range Reference Service.
(*d*) 'Personal relation between librarians and readers'

Codes:
A. (*b*), (*c*), (*d*), (*a*)
B. (*a*), (*c*), (*b*), (*d*)
C. (*d*), (*b*), (*a*), (*c*)
D. (*c*), (*d*), (*b*), (*a*)

38. Arrange the following class numbers according to Colon Classification, 6th edition.
(*a*) 2 (*b*) 2 Ob T
(*c*) 2 'N (*d*) 2k

Codes:
A. (*d*), (*a*), (*b*) and (*c*)
B. (*a*), (*b*), (*d*) and (*c*)
C. (*b*), (*a*), (*c*) and (*d*)
D. (*c*), (*b*), (*a*) and (*d*)

39. Arrange in sequence the following phases of disaster planning according to guidelines/ principles of IFLA:
(*a*) Preparedness
(*b*) Prevention
(*c*) Recovery
(*d*) Response

Codes:
A. (*a*), (*b*), (*c*), (*d*)
B. (*b*), (*a*), (*d*), (*c*)
C. (*c*), (*a*), (*b*), (*d*)
D. (*d*), (*c*), (*b*), (*a*)

40. Arrange the following bibliographic utilities according to their year of origin :
(*a*) Ohio College Library Center
(*b*) Washington Library Network
(*c*) UTLAS
(*d*) RLIN

Codes:
A. (*a*), (*b*), (*c*), (*d*)
B. (*a*), (*c*), (*d*), (*b*)
C. (*a*), (*b*), (*d*), (*c*)
D. (*a*), (*d*), (*c*), (*b*)

41. Arrange the steps of Big 6 skill information literacy model in correct order as given by M. Eisenberg and B. Berkowitz.
(*a*) Evaluation
(*b*) Location and Access
(*c*) Information seeking strategies
(*d*) Synthesis

Codes:
A. (*a*), (*b*), (*d*) and (*c*)
B. (*b*), (*a*), (*c*) and (*d*)
C. (*c*), (*b*), (*d*) and (*a*)
D. (*b*), (*a*), (*d*) and (*c*)

42. Arrange the following committees according to their year of Constitution?
(*a*) Committee on National Network System for University Libraries.
(*b*) K.P. Sinha Committee
(*c*) Review Committee on Library and Information Science
(*d*) D.P. Chattopadhyaya Committee on National Policy of Library and Information Services.

Codes:
A. (*b*), (*c*), (*d*), (*a*)
B. (*c*), (*d*), (*a*), (*b*)
C. (*d*), (*a*), (*b*), (*c*)
D. (*a*), (*b*), (*c*), (*d*)

43. Arrange in sequence the following components of Tom Wilson's Expanded Model in sequential order of their occurrence:
(*a*) Information seeking behaviour
(*b*) Context of information need
(*c*) Passive attention and search
(*d*) Intervening variables

Codes:
A. (*b*), (*d*), (*a*), (*c*)
B. (*a*), (*b*), (*d*), (*c*)
C. (*c*), (*b*), (*d*), (*a*)
D. (*a*), (*c*), (*b*), (*d*)

44. Match the following:

List–I	List–II
(*a*) David Ellis	(*i*) Process
(*b*) James Krikelas	(*ii*) Complex
(*c*) Tom Wilson	(*iii*) Descriptive
(*d*) Alan Foster	(*iv*) Cognitive

Codes:

	(a)	(b)	(c)	(d)
A.	(ii)	(iii)	(iv)	(i)
B.	(iv)	(ii)	(i)	(iii)
C.	(iii)	(i)	(iv)	(ii)
D.	(i)	(iv)	(iii)	(ii)

45. Match the following management concepts with their corresponding propounders :

List–I	List–II
(a) Quality Trilogy Process	(i) Philip B. Crosby
(b) Quality Management Maturity Grid	(ii) W. Edwards Deming
(c) 14 points for management	(iii) J.M. Juran
(d) Fishbone diagram	(iv) Kaoru Ishikawa

Codes :

	(a)	(b)	(c)	(d)
A.	(iii)	(i)	(ii)	(iv)
B.	(i)	(ii)	(iii)	(iv)
C.	(iv)	(iii)	(ii)	(i)
D.	(iii)	(ii)	(iv)	(i)

46. Match the following:

List–I	List–II
(a) Maslow, A	(i) Two factor theory
(b) Alderfer, C.P.	(ii) Acquired-needs theory
(c) Frederick Herzberg	(iii) ERG Theory
(d) David McClelland	(iv) Hierarchy of needs

Codes:

	(a)	(b)	(c)	(d)
A.	(i)	(iii)	(iv)	(ii)
B.	(ii)	(iv)	(i)	(iii)
C.	(iv)	(iii)	(i)	(ii)
D.	(iii)	(ii)	(iv)	(i)

47. Match the following:

List–I	List–II
(a) Instagram	(i) Facebook
(b) Face Time	(ii) Apple
(c) Tumbir	(iii) Google
(d) Picasa	(iv) Yahoo

Codes:

	(a)	(b)	(c)	(d)
A.	(iv)	(i)	(iii)	(ii)
B.	(i)	(ii)	(iv)	(iii)
C.	(ii)	(iv)	(iii)	(i)
D.	(iv)	(ii)	(i)	(iii)

48. Match the following:

List–I	List–II
(a) Crowd Funding	(i) Public assistance through donations
(b) Crowd sourcing	(ii) Collaborative milieu of knowledge dissemination
(c) Hathi Trust	(iii) Re-setting priorities due to financial constraints
(d) Social and Cultural hubs	(iv) Collaborative huge collection of digital resources

Codes:

	(a)	(b)	(c)	(d)
A.	(ii)	(iv)	(i)	(iii)
B.	(i)	(iii)	(iv)	(ii)
C.	(ii)	(iii)	(iv)	(i)
D.	(i)	(iv)	(ii)	(iii)

49. Match the following:

List–I	List–II
(a) Portico	(i) Preserves scholarly publications in dark archives to be accessed under emergent situation
(b) Lockss	(ii) Non-profit service that allows libraries to collect e-contents for digital preservation
(c) Clockss	(iii) Non-profit digital preservation service for participating libraries
(d) Chorus	(iv) Clearinghouse for the open resources of the U.S.

Codes:

	(a)	(b)	(c)	(d)
A.	(i)	(ii)	(iii)	(iv)
B.	(iv)	(iii)	(ii)	(i)
C.	(ii)	(iv)	(i)	(iii)
D.	(iii)	(ii)	(i)	(iv)

50. Match the following Library Automation Software Products with their corresponding developers:

List–I	List–II
(a) Genesis G4	(i) Innovative Interfaces
(b) VERSO	(ii) ExLibris
(c) Aleph	(iii) Auto Graphics
(d) Millennium	(iv) Library Resource Management System

Codes:

	(a)	(b)	(c)	(d)
A.	(iv)	(iii)	(ii)	(i)
B.	(i)	(ii)	(iii)	(iv)
C.	(iii)	(iv)	(ii)	(i)
D.	(ii)	(i)	(iv)	(iii)

51. Match the following Gateways with their corresponding subjects:

List–I	List–II
(a) AHDS	(i) Urban Design
(b) ALTIS	(ii) Forestry Food, Veterinary & Agricultural Sciences
(c) NOVAGate	(iii) Hospitality, Leisure, Sports & Tourism
(d) RUDI	(iv) Arts and Humanities

Codes:

	(a)	(b)	(c)	(d)
A.	(iii)	(i)	(iv)	(ii)
B.	(ii)	(iii)	(iv)	(i)
C.	(iv)	(iii)	(ii)	(i)
D.	(i)	(ii)	(iii)	(iv)

52. Match the following:

List–I	List–II
(a) Meta-analysis	(i) The most theoretical form of desk research, clarify terms, concepts
(b) Conceptual analysis	(ii) To assess the extent to which concepts and issues are mentioned or not
(c) Content analysis	(iii) Quantitative methods for describing and analysis patterns of recorded communication
(d) Bibliometric analysis	(iv) Quantitative data by statistical analysis

Codes:

	(a)	(b)	(c)	(d)
A.	(ii)	(i)	(iv)	(iii)
B.	(iii)	(ii)	(i)	(iv)
C.	(i)	(iv)	(iii)	(ii)
D.	(iv)	(i)	(ii)	(iii)

53. Match the following:

List–I	List–II
(a) Nominal Scale	(i) Places events in order and exhibits their relation
(b) Ordinal Scale	(ii) Classifies Objects/ Observations
(c) Ratio Scale	(iii) Involves Judges to rank items into categories
(d) Differential Scale	(iv) Represents the actual amount of variable – theoretically unobtainable

Codes:

	(a)	(b)	(c)	(d)
A.	(ii)	(i)	(iv)	(iii)
B.	(i)	(ii)	(iii)	(iv)
C.	(iii)	(i)	(iv)	(ii)
D.	(iv)	(iii)	(ii)	(i)

54. Match the following:

List–I	List–II
(a) Impact Factor	(i) Cited during the current year
(b) SNIP	(ii) Duration of citations to article in a journal
(c) Immediacy Factor	(iii) Cited during the recent two years
(d) Cited Half Life	(iv) Citation based on the number of citations in a field

Codes:

	(a)	(b)	(c)	(d)
A.	(iii)	(iv)	(i)	(ii)
B.	(i)	(iii)	(ii)	(iv)
C.	(ii)	(i)	(iv)	(iii)
D.	(iv)	(i)	(ii)	(iii)

55. Match the following:

List–I	List–II
(a) Systematic Sample	(i) Population specified by traits, discretionary and inexpensive
(b) Stratified Sample	(ii) Scattered population
(c) Cluster Sample	(iii) Heterogeneous Population
(d) Quota Sample	(iv) Too large population

Codes:

	(a)	(b)	(c)	(d)
A.	(iv)	(iii)	(ii)	(i)
B.	(i)	(ii)	(iii)	(iv)
C.	(iii)	(i)	(iv)	(ii)
D.	(ii)	(iv)	(i)	(iii)

56. Match the following:

List–I	List–II
(a) Ibid	(i) See
(b) Loc.Cit.	(ii) Previously used reference
(c) Op.Cit.	(iii) Same reference cited immediately above
(d) Vide	(iv) Same page cited (in the place cited)

Codes:

	(a)	(b)	(c)	(d)
A.	(iii)	(iv)	(ii)	(i)
B.	(iv)	(ii)	(i)	(iii)
C.	(ii)	(i)	(iii)	(iv)
D.	(i)	(iii)	(iv)	(ii)

57. Match the type of services suitable for the queries given below:

List–I	List–II
(a) Alert service	(i) Can I have details of Lok Sabha elections 2009?
(b) Documentation service	(ii) Who won Wimbledon Singles in 2015?
(c) Retrospective Search Service	(iii) Let me Know the forthcoming conferences on Green Libraries?
(d) Reference service	(iv) Let me have a comprehensive list of articles published on genome in 2016.

Codes:

	(a)	(b)	(c)	(d)
A.	(ii)	(iii)	(i)	(iv)
B.	(iv)	(ii)	(i)	(iii)
C.	(i)	(iv)	(ii)	(iii)
D.	(iii)	(iv)	(i)	(ii)

58. Match the following:

List–I	List–II
(a) W.A. Katz	(i) Documentation and Information
(b) B. Guha	(ii) Introduction to reference work 2 V.
(c) S. Seetharama	(iii) Documentation and its facets
(d) S.R.Ranganathan	(iv) Information Consolidation and repackaging : Framework, Methodology, Planning

Codes:

	(a)	(b)	(c)	(d)
A.	(iii)	(ii)	(iv)	(i)
B.	(i)	(iii)	(ii)	(iv)
C.	(ii)	(i)	(iv)	(iii)
D.	(iv)	(ii)	(i)	(iii)

59. Match the following:

List–I	List–II
(a) Literary Warrant	(i) Melvil Dewey
(b) Alternative Location	(ii) H.E. Bliss
(c) Decimal Fraction Notation	(iii) S.R. Ranganathan
(d) Seminal Mnemonics	(iv) E.W. Hulme

Codes:

	(a)	(b)	(c)	(d)
A.	(iv)	(ii)	(i)	(iii)
B.	(ii)	(i)	(iii)	(iv)
C.	(i)	(iii)	(ii)	(iv)
D.	(iii)	(ii)	(iv)	(i)

60. Match the following symbols/signs used in UDC standard edition:

Signs/Symbols	Meaning
(a) $\rightrightarrows$ Double arrow	(i) Examples of combination
(b) ◇ Diamond	(ii) Including
(c) □ Square	(iii) See also
(d) ≅ Approximately equal to	(iv) subdivide as

Codes:

	(a)	(b)	(c)	(d)
A.	(iii)	(i)	(ii)	(iv)
B.	(i)	(ii)	(iii)	(iv)
C.	(ii)	(i)	(iv)	(iii)
D.	(iv)	(iii)	(ii)	(i)

61. Match the following:

List–I	List–II
(a) The Crisis in Cataloguing	(i) Michael Gorman
(b) Headings and Canons: Comparative Study of Five Catalogue Codes	(ii) Raymond Knox Olding
(c) Our Enduring Values: Librarianship in the 21st century	(iii) Andrew D. Osborn
(d) Readings in library Cataloguing	(iv) S.R. Ranganathan

Codes:

	(a)	(b)	(c)	(d)
A.	(iii)	(iv)	(i)	(ii)
B.	(i)	(iv)	(ii)	(iii)
C.	(ii)	(i)	(iii)	(iv)
D.	(iii)	(iv)	(ii)	(i)

62. Assertion (A): 'Information Economy' which is based on the premise that, information has economic value and as such requires an 'Information Market Place' in which such value can be exchanged, holds no good in the contemporary information age.

Reason (R): Information as a valuable resource occupies a slum dwelling in the town of economics, as this economic reality runs counter to the popular and historic notion that, "information is free".

Codes:

A. (A) is true, but (R) is false
B. (A) is false, but (R) is true
C. Both (A) and (R) are true
D. Both (A) and (R) are false

63. Assertion (A): Libraries should serve as a local centre of information and knowledge and be a local gateway to national and global knowledge.

Reason (R): Libraries must modernize their collection, services and collaborate with other institutions to develop a community-based information system.

Codes:

A. (A) is true, but (R) is false
B. (A) is false, but (R) is true
C. Both (A) and (R) are true
D. Both (A) and (R) are false

64. Assertion (A): Some modern users are quite apprehensive about virtual reference service chat.

Reason (R): They fear negative judgements from librarians and advisors arising from the content of the chat transcript.

Codes:

A. (A) is true, but (R) is false
B. (A) is false, but (R) is true
C. Both (A) and (R) are true
D. Both (A) and (R) are false

65. Assertion (A): In recent years, the explosion of information in electronic format has placed a significant burden on the small public libraries.

Reason (R): E-resources are expensive, both in licensing cost and in the technology needed to support them to which small public libraries can hardly afford.

Codes:

A. (A) is true, but (R) is false
B. (A) is false, but (R) is true
C. Both (A) and (R) are true
D. Both (A) and (R) are false

66. Assertion (A): In the digital environment, the University libraries in India need not build their reference collection.

Reason (R): 'Question Point' of OCLC provides a complete virtual reference management system for subscription.

Codes:

A. (A) is true, but (R) is false
B. (A) is false, but (R) is true
C. Both (A) and (R) are false
D. Both (A) and (R) are true

67. Assertion (A): Libraries market their products and services to overcome the problems of under-utilization of their information resources and services.

Reason (R): Libraries are under-utilized because they do not provide access to electronic resources.

Codes:

A. (A) is true, but (R) is false
B. (A) is false, but (R) is true
C. Both (A) and (R) are true
D. Both (A) and (R) are false

68. Assertion (A): In RDA the 'rule of 3", to provide upto three authors, is now the main instruction.

Reason (R): RDA does not encourage access to the names of persons and corporate bodies important to the users.

Codes:

A. (A) is true, but (R) is false
B. (A) is false, but (R) is true
C. Both (A) and (R) are true
D. Both (A) and (R) are false

69. Assertion (A): Application of six sigma in library management is a quality programme that improves customers' experience and lowers costs.

Reason (R): Six phases of sigma are necessary in all library operations.

Codes:

A. (A) is true, but (R) is false
B. (A) is false, but (R) is true
C. Both (A) and (R) are true
D. Both (A) and (R) are false

70. Assertion (A): A library needs to generate a satisfied customer base which is supportive of library programmes.

Reason (R): If a library's resources and services are measured upto customer's expectations, then repeat use cannot be ensured.

Codes:

A. (A) is true, but (R) is false
B. (A) is false, but (R) is true
C. Both (A) and (R) are true
D. Both (A) and (R) are false

71. Assertion (A): Podcasting, once an obscure method of spreading information, has become a recognised medium for distributing audio contents – be it corporate or for personal use.

Reason (R): Podcasts, though similar to radio programs, are primarily audio files which the listeners can play at their convenience, using devices that have become more common than portable broadcast receivers.

Codes:

A. (A) is true, but (R) is false
B. (A) is false, but (R) is true
C. Both (A) and (R) are true
D. Both (A) and (R) are false

72. Assertion (A): Open-ended questions are suitable to glean more and candid information from the respondents seeking on a specific aspect.

Reason (R): Open-ended questions provide an opportunity to go beyond the closed option of 'Yes' or 'No' as it enables to express one's own ideas more candidly.

Codes:

A. Both (A) and (R) are false
B. Both (A) and (R) are true
C. (A) is false, but (R) is true
D. (A) is true, but (R) is false

73. Assertion (A): An information literate generally has the potential to determine the nature and extent of the information needed.

Reason (R): An information literate can define and articulate the need better than an information illiterate.

Codes:

A. (A) is true, but (R) is false
B. (A) is false, but (R) is true
C. Both (A) and (R) are true
D. Both (A) and (R) are false

74. Assertion (A): Majority of State Public Library Acts enacted from 1990s have provision for Library fund with contributions from State and Central Governments.

Reason (R): Library Cess is inadequate to manage public libraries.

Codes:

A. (A) is true, but (R) is false
B. (A) is false, but (R) is true
C. Both (A) and (R) are false
D. Both (A) and (R) are true

75. Assertion (A): Most of the LIS professionals in India are yet to recognise fully the significance of Web-based OPAC services.

Reason (R): Although some libraries in India have started to develop their own websites and portals with enhanced features of Web-based OPACs, but none of these libraries are yet to have their library page and lack federated search facilities.

Codes:

A. (A) is true, but (R) is false
B. (A) is false, but (R) is true
C. Both (A) and (R) are true
D. Both (A) and (R) are false

ANSWERS

1	2	3	4	5	6	7	8	9	10
A	B	C	D	D	D	B	D	B	D
11	**12**	**13**	**14**	**15**	**16**	**17**	**18**	**19**	**20**
A	D	*	D	D	D	A	C	A	B
21	**22**	**23**	**24**	**25**	**26**	**27**	**28**	**29**	**30**
B	D	C	C	D	A	B	C	D	B
31	**32**	**33**	**34**	**35**	**36**	**37**	**38**	**39**	**40**
B	D	A	B	B	B	C	A	B	C
41	**42**	**43**	**44**	**45**	**46**	**47**	**48**	**49**	**50**
C	A	A	C	A	C	B	B	D	A
51	**52**	**53**	**54**	**55**	**56**	**57**	**58**	**59**	**60**
C	D	A	A	A	A	D	C	A	A
61	**62**	**63**	**64**	**65**	**66**	**67**	**68**	**69**	**70**
A	C	C	C	C	B	A	D	A	A
71	**72**	**73**	**74**	**75**					
C	B	C	D	A					

* Error in Question

EXPLANATORY ANSWERS

1. Index Indiana, an Index Periodical Literature is being compiled by Central Reference Library, Kolkata. This was an ambitious project to trace the periodical literature appearing in the Indian Language periodicals. The first issue of the Index Indiana appeared as quarterly in 1977 and since 1981 it is being published as annual cumulated volumes. As a beginning 6 languages *viz.*, Bengali, Hindi, Gujarati, Marathi, Tamil and Malayalam periodicals are covered.

2. Ranganathan's Second Law is clearly applicable today and carries with it on expanded charge in the new digital environment in which libraries are operating. "Every person his or her book" is now *know your community and its needs*, with the reinterpretation calling for new services from libraries and new skills from librarians along with continuing the key practices of today. Knowing your community and its needs is a key step in developing these new programs and moving in new directions will help libraries remain transformational places, as central to our shared future as they have been to our shared past.

4. Open access (OA) journals are scholarly journals that are available online to the reader "without financial, legal, or technical barriers other than those inseparable from gaining access to the internet itself." They remove price barriers and most permission barriers. While open access journals are freely available to the reader, there are still costs associated with the publication and production of such journals. Some are subsidised, and some require payment on behalf of the author.

Some open access journals are subsidised and are financed by an academic institution, learned society or a government information centre. Others are financed by payment of article processing charges by submitting authors, money typically made available to researchers by their institution or funding agency. Sometimes, these are two referred to respectively as "gold" and "platinum" models to emphasize their distinction, although other times "gold" OA is used to refer to both paid and unpaid OA.

5. The International Standard Bibliographic Description (ISBD) is a set of rules produced by the International Federation of Library Associations and Institutions (IFLA) to create a bibliographic description in a standard, human-readable form, especially for use in a bibliography or a library catalogue. A preliminary consolidated edition of the ISBD was published in 2007 and the consolidated edition was published in 2011, superseding earlier separate ISBDs for monographs, older monographic publications, cartographic materials, serials and other continuing resources, electronic resources, non-book materials, and printed music. IFLA's ISBD Review Group is responsible for maintaining the ISBD.

6. According to S.R. Ranganathan, the canons for chain are:

Canon of Decreasing Extension: While moving down a chain from its first link to its last link, the intension of the classes should increase, and the extension of the classes should decrease.

Canon of Modulation: A chain of classes should comprise one class of each and every order that lies between the orders of the first link and the last link of the chain.

7. Colon classification (CC) is a system of library classification developed by S. R. Ranganathan. It was the first ever faceted (or analytico-synthetic) classification. The first edition was published in 1933. Since then six more editions have been published. It is especially used inlibraries in India. Up to the sixth edition of

CC, systems and specials were enumerated along with the concerned main classes. However, they have been separately defined.

Systems: The term system basic subjects denote a division of a main class expounded after a school of thought.

B6-M8 Hyperbolic geometry, where B6 is geometry and M8 means the 1880s. The number stands for a system of geometry expounded in the 1880s.

L-B Ayarveda. B is 999 to 1000 BC - a system of medicine that came into being prior to 1000, BC.

9. A time and motion study is a business efficiency technique combining the Time Study work of Frederick Winslow Taylor with the Motion Study work of Frank and Lillian Gilbreth. It is a major part of scientific management (Taylorism).

10. Radio-frequency identification (RFID) uses electromagnetic fields to automatically identify and track tags attached to objects. The tags contain electronically stored information. Passive tags collect energy from a nearby RFID reader's interrogating radio waves. Active tags have a local power source such as a battery and may operate at hundreds of meters from the RFID reader. Unlike abarcode, the tag need not be within the line of sight of the reader, so it may be embedded in the tracked object. RFID is one method for Automatic Identification and Data Capture (AIDC).

11. RJ45 is a type of connector commonly used for Ethernet networking. It looks similar to a telephone jack, but is slightly wider. Since Ethernet cables have an RJ45 connector on each end, Ethernet cables are sometimes also called RJ45 cables. The "RJ" in RJ45 stands for "registered jack," since it is a standardized networking interface. The "45" simply refers to the number of the interface standard.

12. The Session Initiation Protocol (SIP) is a communications protocol for signalling and controlling multimedia communication sessions. The most common applications of SIP are in Internet telephony for voice and video calls, private IP telephone systems, as well as instant messaging over Internet Protocol (IP) networks.

15. Next, we need to discuss a phenomenon commonly known as Zipf's Law, named after the Harvard linguistic professor George Kingsley Zipf. This models the occurrence of distinct objects or events in particular sorts of collections and is most famous for describing a number of patterns in the distributions of linguistic units, such as words and phonemes in texts. So, suppose we consider a natural language corpus, such as a book or collection of magazines written in English. Suppose also that we decide to go about counting of the frequency of the words in the book or magazines and list them. That is to say we count the number of occurrences of words like 'the', 'and', 'of' and so on. Finally, consider that we arrange the words we find in decreasing order of the frequency of their occurrence, so that the most frequent work has rank 1, the next most frequent rank 2, and so on. Zipf's Law now tells us the approximate constraining relationship between the frequency of a word in a corpus and its rank in our list. Accordingly, this relationship can be written down as:

$$rf = c.$$

Where r is the rank of a word-type, f is the frequency of occurrence of the word-type and c is some constant dependant on the corpus.

16. VIDWAN is the premier database of profiles of scientists/researchers and other faculty members working at leading R & D Organisation and other Academic Institutions involved in teaching and research in India. It provides important information about expert's background, contact address, skills and accomplishments.

The database is being developed by INFLIBNET Centre, Infocity, Gandhinagar. The database offers expertise of various subject from Nation's leading institutions. Attempt has been made to provide access to relevant and accurate information collected from various sources. Web enabled interface has been incorporated to facilitate the search and update names listed in the database. On Expert Database, you are not limited to publishing a static Profile(s). Our members can take advantage of many "value - added" offerings such as having Books and Articles published on the personal website and linked to their Profile(s).

17. Copyright is a right given by the law to creators of literary, dramatic, musical and artistic works and producers of cinematograph films and sound recordings. In fact, it is a bundle of rights including, *inter alia*, rights of reproduction, communication to the public, adaptation and translation of the work. There could be slight variations in the composition of the rights depending on the work.

18. Unwritten, unspoken, and hidden vast storehouse of knowledge held by practically every normal human being, based on his or her emotions, experiences, insights, intuition, observations and internalized information. Tacit knowledge is integral to the entirety of a person's consciousness, is acquired largely through association with other people, and requires joint or shared activities to be imparted from on to another. Like the submerged part of an iceberg it constitutes the bulk of what one knows, and forms the underlying framework that makes explicit knowledge possible. Concept of tacit knowledge was introduced by the Hungarian philosopher-chemist Michael Polanyi (1891-1976) in his 1966 book 'The Tacit Dimension.' Also called informal knowledge.

20. The purpose of these guidelines is to promote digital reference best practices on an international basis. The online environment is uniquely suited to consortial models of work and to the development of shared resources. Libraries in different countries may have different traditions of public service, which both affect their current reference practices and their patrons' expectations. But it is also important to recognize that new technologies will enable librarians to redefine the scope of their public services. These guidelines attempt to create some common standards from diverse traditions in the hope that this will allow the worldwide community of librarians to freely explore the possibilities.

Some issues raised in these guidelines may ultimately warrant additional consideration and expansion-issues such as the management of change: how does the administrator of a digital reference project mitigate the impact of new models of work on an institution's staff, schedule, and clients? Additional work might also be done to determine the exact funding requirements for these efforts in a variety of different communities, with respect to staffing, resource acquisition, and equipment.

21. Britannica Library gives your library three sites in one: Children, Young Adults, and the Reference Center for older students and adults. Patrons can choose the age-appropriate level that works best for them and will find it easy to conduct research, complete homework assignments, and work on special projects. They can even store their research in their own personal my Britannica account. Remote access is included, and Britannica Library works splendidly on any device—PC, laptop, tablet, or smart phone.

23. **Virtual Reference:** Reference service which is initiated electronically, often in real time; patrons employ computers or other Internet technology to communicate with reference staff, without being physically present. Communication channels used frequently in virtual reference include chat, video-conferencing, voice over internet protocol (VoIP), co-browsing, e-mail and instant messaging.

26. Sampling Methods can be classified into one of two categories : Probability Sampling and Non-probability Sampling.

Probability Sampling

In probability sampling, it is possible to both determine which sampling units belong to which sample and the probability that each sample will be selected. The following sampling methods are examples of probability sampling:

1. Simple Random Sampling (SRS)/ purposive sampling
2. Stratified Sampling
3. Cluster Sampling
4. Systematic Sampling
5. Multistage Sampling

Non-probability Sampling

The following sampling methods that are listed in your text are types of non-probability sampling that should be avoided:

1. volunteer samples
2. haphazard (convenience) samples.

27. The critical path method (CPM) is a project modelling technique developed in the late 1950s by Morgan R. Walker of DuPont and James E. Kelley Jr. of Remington Rand. Kelley and Walker related their memories of the development of CPM in 1989. Kelley attributed the term "critical path" to the developers of the Program Evaluation and Review Technique which was developed at about the same time by Booz Allen Hamilton and the U.S. Navy. The precursors of what came to be known as Critical Path were developed and put into practice by DuPont between 1940 and 1943 and contributed to the success of the Manhattan Project.

28. **ERIC** (Educational Resources Information Center) is the world's most widely used index to educational-related literature. Established in 1966, ERIC is supported by the US Department of Education's Office of Educational Research and Improvement and is administered by the U.S. National Library of Education (NLE).

ERIC is the largest education database in the world-containing over 1.5 million records of journal articles, research reports, curriculum and teaching guides, conference papers, dissertations and theses, and books.

PubMed: The premier biomedical database. PubMed provides international coverage of English- and foreign-language journals in the areas of medicine, nursing, allied health, and the basic life sciences.

29. **Z39.50** is an international standard client-server, application layer communications protocol for searching and retrieving information from a database over a TCP/IP computer network. It is covered by ANSI/NISO standard Z39.50, and ISO standard 23950. The standard's maintenance agency is the Library of Congress.

Z39.71 An associated standard is Z39.71, governing holdings statements for bibliographic items, which is of special interest because it governs the syntax of serials holdings information in MARC records.

30. The Semantic Web is a Web of Data—of dates and titles and part numbers and chemical properties and any other data one might conceive of. The collection of Semantic Web technologies (RDF, OWL, SKOS, SPARQL, etc.) provides an environment where application can query that data, draw inferences using vocabularies, etc.

32. Statistical inference requires assumptions about the probability distribution (*i.e.*, random mechanism, sampling model) that generated the data. For example for a t-test, we assume that a random variable follows a normal distribution. For discrete data key distributions are: Bernoulli, Binomial, Poisson and Multinomial. A more or less thorough treatment is given here. The mathematics is for those who are interested. But the results and their applications are important.

Recall, a *random variable* is the outcome of an experiment (*i.e.*, a random process) expressed as a number. We use capital letters near the end of the alphabet (X, Y, Z, etc.) to denote random variables. Random variables are of two types: discrete and continuous. Here, we are interested in distributions of discrete random variables.

33. The methods used by quantitative and qualitative researchers to establish trustworthiness differ in many ways. For qualitative researchers, the methods used to establish trustworthiness include credibility, transferability, dependability, and confirmability. For quantitative researchers, the methods used to establish trustworthiness include internal validity, external validity, reliability, and objectivity.

34. TRAILS is a knowledge assessment with multiple-choice questions targeting a variety of information literacy skills based on 3rd, 6th, 9th, and 12th grade standards. The assessment items are based on the American Association of School Librarians' Standards for the 21st-Century Learner and those from the Common Core State Standards Initiative that have been adopted by most states.

Initial support for TRAILS was provided through the University Libraries' grant partnership with the Institute for Library and Information Literacy Education (ILILE), which was a Federally funded initiative of the Institute of Museum and Library Services (IMLS) and the US Department of Education. ILILE was established to provide local, regional, and national leadership in fostering successful collaboration among K-12 teachers and school librarians who are concerned with advancing library and information literacy in the K-12 school curriculum. Grant partners at Kent State University include the College and Graduate School of Education, Health, and Human Services; the School of Library and Information Science; and University Libraries.

35. This is the web site of the International DOI Foundation (IDF), a not-for-profit membership organization that is the governance and management body for the federation of Registration Agencies providing Digital Object Identifier (DOI) services and registration, and is the registration authority for the ISO standard (ISO 26324) for the DOI system. The DOI system provides a technical and social infrastructure for the registration and use of persistent interoperable identifiers, called DOIs, for use on digital networks. Crossref offers a DOI search for journal articles, books, and chapters. Simply cut and paste the reference list into their search box. The form will take any reference style, although it works most reliably with standard styles.

36. David Ellis-Investigated the behaviour of researchers in the physical and social sciences and engineers and research scientists through semi-structured interviews using a grounded theory approach, with a focus on describing the activities rather than a process.

These initial investigations produced six key activities within the information seeking process:

- Starting (activities that form the information search)
- Chaining (backwards or forwards—following references in initial information sources)
- Browsing (semi-directed search)
- Differentiating (filtering and selecting sources based on judgement of quality and relevance)
- Monitoring (keeping track of developments in an area)
- Extracting (systematic extraction of material of interest from sources).

40. OCLC began in 1967, as the Ohio College Library Center, through a collaboration of Ohio University presidents, vice-presidents, and library directors who wanted to create a cooperative, computerized network for Ohio Libraries.

Originally known as the **Washington Library Network,** WLN was formed in the early 1970s to support resource-sharing activities by libraries in the state of Washington. Its first project was a batch-processed union catalogue produced in 1972.

Although its impact in the United State has been limited, the University of Toronto Library Automated System (UTLAS) was a fourth major online bibliographic networking system to have emerged on the North American continent during the 1970s.

41. Developed by Mike Eisenberg and Bob Berkowitz, the Big 6 is the most widely known and widely used approach to teaching information and technology skills in the world. Used in thousands of K-12 schools, higher education institutions, and corporate and adult training programs, the Big 6 information problem-solving model is applicable whenever people need and use information. The Big 6 integrates information search and use skills along with technology tools in a systematic process to find, use, apply, and evaluate information for specific needs and tasks.

The Big 6 is a process model of how people of all ages solve an information problem. From practice and study, we found that successful information problem-solving encompasses six stages:

1. Task Definition
2. Information Seeking Strategies
3. Location and Access
4. Use of Information
5. Synthesis
6. Evaluation.

42. The central government appointed in 1957 an Advisory Committee for Libraries under the chairmanship of **K.P. Sinha**. The Sinha Committee submitted its report in 1958.

Review Committee on Library Science (1961) : Chairman **Dr. S.R. Ranganathan**. Regarding standard for teaching, Curriculum, Qualification of the student for each course, Guidelines for conducting examination and lay down minimum standard for passing.

In October 1985, the government of India constituted a committee under the chairmanship of Professor **D.P. Chattopadhyaya** to formulate the National Policy on Library and Information System (NAPLIS). The final report of the Committee was submitted to the Minister of Human Resource Development, Government of India, vide letter of May 30, 1986, for its final approval. NAPLIS (1986) has recommended a policy on public library system, including these extracts:

Committee on National Network set up for Universities/Libraries (1988) : Chairman **Prof. Yash Pal**. The Chairman of committee suggested measure for networking of libraries and information centre in Universities, Information Centre, Colleges.

44. Descriptive Models: The first class of models we may call *descriptive*. These simply list the factors and activities involved in the aspects of information behaviour being considered; they may be presented graphically or just as a list. The model, developed in two stages (Ellis, 1989; Ellis, Cox and Hall, 1993), identified eight features of behaviour within information seeking.

James Krikelas (1983) was the first to develop an information seeking model derived from published Library and Information Science (LIS) literature about information needs and uncertainty. The Krikelas model can be reassessed considering the advances taking place in today's online environment. The internal and external source preferences which are important part of the model have taken new form. The advanced online tools and techniques can help the researcher in capturing information, organizing and eventually collaborating with others to fulfill the information giving and gathering process.

Tom Wilson later built upon his original model in order to understand the personal circumstance, social role, and environmental context in which an information need is created. This new model, altered in 1994 incorporated Ellis' stages of information-seeking: starting, browsing, differentiating, monitoring, extracting, verifying and ending. It also displayed the physiological, affective, and cognitive needs that give rise to information seeking behavior.

Complex Models: The models considered so far all tend to explain information behaviour as a linear, ordered set of stages, and to focus on specifically information-related action and cognition. In the fourth and last category are a group of more elaborate models, which we might call *complex*. These introduce a greater degree of context and an increased number of perspectives, and are typically non-linear or multi-directional, rather than having a single sequence of steps.

The non-linear nature of information seeking in the real world has been most clearly captured in the model devised by Alan Foster, another British academic originally from the Sheffield school and now at Aberystwyth.

45. The Quality Trilogy explained by Juran is: Any organization taking up a journey in Quality Management will have to have three Processes in place, which are: (*i*) Quality Planning (*ii*) Quality Control and (*iii*) Quality Improvement.

The Quality Management Maturity Grid (QMMG) is an organizational maturity matrix conceived by Philip B. Crosby first published in his book Quality is Free in 1979. The QMMG is used by a business or organization as a benchmark of how mature their processes are, and how well they are embedded in their culture, with respect to service or product quality management.

W. Edwards Deming's 14 Points on Quality Management, a core concept on implementing total quality management, is a set of management practices to help companies increase their quality and productivity.

Ishikawa diagrams (also called fishbone diagrams, herringbone diagrams, cause-and-effect diagrams, or Fishikawa) are causal diagrams created by Kaoru Ishikawa (1968) that show the causes of a specific event.

46. Maslow's **hierarchy of needs** is a theory in psychology proposed by Abraham Maslow in his 1943 paper "A Theory of Human Motivation" in Psychological Review. Maslow subsequently extended the idea to include his observations of humans' innate curiosity.

ERG theory is a theory in psychology proposed by Clayton Alderfer. Alderfer further developed Maslow's hierarchy of needs by categorising the hierarchy into his ERG theory (Existence, Relatedness and Growth). The existence group is concerned with providing the basic material existence requirements of humans.

The two-factor theory (also known as Herzberg's motivation-hygiene theory and dual-factor theory) states that there are certain factors in the workplace that cause job satisfaction, while a separate set of factors cause dissatisfaction.

David McClelland achievement and acquired needs theory. He proposed that an individual's specific needs are acquired over time and are shaped by one's life experiences.

47. **Instagram** was acquired by Facebook in April 2012. The popularity of Instagram has sparked an engaging community, including dedicated "trends", in which users post specific types of photos on specific days of the week with a hashtag representing a common theme.

Face Time is a proprietary video-telephony product developed by Apple Inc. FaceTime Audio is an audio-only version.

Tumblr is a micro-blogging and social networking website founded by David Karp in 2007, and owned by Oath Inc. On May 20, 2013, it was announced that Yahoo and Tumblr had reached an agreement for Yahoo.

Picasa is a discontinued image organiser and image viewer for organising and editing digital photos, plus an integrated photo-sharing website, originally created by a company named Lifescape in 2002. In July 2004, Google acquired Picasa from Lifescape and began offering it as freeware.

49. **Portico**, a not-for-profit digital preservation service, is among the largest community-supported digital archives in the world. Working with libraries and publishers, Portico preserves e-journals, e-books, and other electronic scholarly content to ensure researchers and students will have access to it in the future.

The **LOCKSS** system is the first and only mechanism to apply the traditional purchase-and-own library model to electronic materials. The LOCKSS system allows librarians at each institution to take custody of and preserve access to the e-content to which they subscribe, restoring the print purchase model with which librarians are familiar.

CLOCKSS is a not-for-profit joint venture between the world's leading academic publishers and research libraries whose mission is to build a sustainable, geographically distributed dark archive with which to ensure the long-term survival of Web-based scholarly publications for the benefit of the greater global research community.

Called Chorus: the Clearing house for the Open Research of the United States—the partnership would use publishers' existing infrastructure to identify and provide free access to peer-reviewed articles based on publicly supported research. The proposal comes as an August deadline looms for federal agencies to comply with the new policy.

50. **Genesis G4** by Library Resource Management Systems. Windows SQL library software that includes circulation, cataloguing, online catalogue (WebOPAC2), Reporting, etc. Having two great library software systems, G4 network suite or Hosted Internet Services both are Dynamic, highly versatile, easy-to-use by all types of libraries. Driven by Librarians who have told us what they need and wish for in a program; we include features as "Free" Point and Click MARC record retrieval, record enrichment, multi-collection capabilities even Textbook control, remote Web-based product support sessions.

Auto-Graphics Releases New Version of VERSO® ILS Software at ALA Midwinter 2012. System Enhancements Provide Additional Functionality to Meet the Needs of Large Complex Library Systems and Consortia.

Ex Libris Group is an Israeli software company that develops integrated library systems and other library software. The company is headquartered in Jerusalem, and has ten other offices around the world. The company claims to serve the 20 top universities worldwide as rated by Times Higher Education.

Millennium Software Productions is India's leading developer and provider of advanced solutions through innovative web-based products to the global market. We are a true blue technology company and not a mere back office support or service provider.

51. **The Arts and Humanities Data Service (AHDS)** was a United Kingdom national service aiding the discovery, creation and preservation of digital resources in and for research, teaching and learning in the arts and humanities. It was established in 1996 and ceased operation in 2008.

ALTIS aims to provide a trusted source of selected, high quality internet information for students, lecturers, researchers and practitioners in the areas of hospitality, leisure, sport and tourism. ALTIS is created by a core team of information specialists and subject experts based at the University of Birmingham, in partnership with key organisations throughout the UK.

The Nordic Forestry, Veterinary and Agricultural University Network **(NOVA)**, is a university cooperation aimed at supporting the understanding of major global challenges in a Nordic context.

RUDI (Resource for Urban Design Information) began in January 1996 and is run jointly by the Engineering Research and Development Centre at the University of Hertfordshire, and the Library of Oxford Brookes University. RUDI is concerned with all aspects of urban design, but in particular physical design, within the Western cultural context.

52. **Meta-analysis** deals with quantitative data by statistical analysis. It is difficult to perform this kind of analysis on the literature of the information sciences, because of the lack of comparable numeric data sets. Some library and information papers are unhelpfully termed as meta-analyses, when they are in fact 'only' qualitative, or semi-quantitative, literature reviews.

Conceptual or Philosophical analysis, perhaps the most theoretical form of desk research, sets out to analyse and clarify terms, concepts and issues within the information sciences.

Historical analysis analyses the historical development of issues within the library and information disciplines and professions. The most common form of this has been the description of the development of libraries and information institutions. These have been joined by analyses of the development of systems, services, processes, and concepts, and by studies of information phenomena in society.

Content analysis is a diverse form of analysis, always involving some kind of quantitative assessment of the content of a set of documents, to assess the extent to which concepts and issues are mentioned, or not (White and Marsh, 2006). It may include a qualitative dimension, to record *how* concepts and issues are described.

Bibliometrics and **webliometrics** are quantitative methods for describing and analysing patterns of recorded communication. They are used to carry out research into such topics as: size and growth of information within disciplines; significant sources, authors, institutions and countries; linkages and influence between information producers; and changes in communication patterns.

54. **Impact Factor:** The Journal Impact Factor is published each year by Thomson Reuters. It is a measure of the number of times an average paper in a particular journal is cited during the preceding two years.

SNIP: Source-Normalised Impact per Paper (SNIP) measures contextual citation impact by weighting citations based on the total number of citations in a subject field. This unique perspective enables direct comparison of sources in different subject fields. The impact of a single citation is given higher value in subject areas where citations are less likely, and vice versa.

Immediacy Factor: The Immediacy Factor is the average number of times an article is cited in the year it is published. The journal Immediacy Factor indicates how quickly articles in a journal are cited.

Cited Half-life: Median age of the articles that were cited in the JCR year. Half of a journal's cited articles were published more recently than the cited half-life. The cited Half-life measures all of the cites earned by a publication (across all cited years) during the JCR year (*i.e.*, citing year = JCR year).

55. **Systematic sampling** is a type of probability sampling method in which sample members from a larger population are selected according to a random starting point and a fixed periodic interval. This interval, called the sampling interval, is calculated by dividing the population size by the desired sample size. Despite the sample population being selected in advance, systematic sampling is still thought of as being random if the periodic interval is determined beforehand and the starting point is random.

Stratified sampling works best when a heterogeneous population is split into fairly homogeneous groups. Under these conditions, stratification generally produces more precise estimates of the population percents than estimates that would be found from a simple random sample.

Cluster sampling studies a cluster of the relevant population. It is a design in which the unit of sampling consists of multiple cases *e.g.*, a family, a class room, a school or even a city or a school system. Cluster sampling is also known as area sampling. Some authors consider it synonymous with multistage sampling.

Quota sampling method is a non-probability sampling and it can be defined as "a sampling method of gathering representative data from a group". Application of quota sampling ensures that sample group represents certain characteristics of the population chosen by the researcher. Quota sampling can be divided into two groups: controlled and uncontrolled. Controlled sampling involves introduction of certain restrictions in order to limit researcher's choice of samples. Uncontrolled sampling, on the other hand, resembles convenience sampling method in a way that researcher is free to choose sample group members according to his/her will.

56. **Ibid-**(Latin, short for ibidem, meaning "in the same place") is the term used to provide an endnote or footnote citation or reference for a source that was cited in the preceding endnote or footnote. The previous reference should be immediately visible, *e.g.*, within the same paragraph or page.

Loc.Cit -(Latin, short for loco citato, meaning "in the place cited") is a footnote or endnote term used to repeat the title and page number for a given work (and author). Loc. Cit. is used in place of Ibid. When the reference is not only to the work immediately preceding, but also refers to the same page. Therefore, loc.

Op. cit. is an abbreviation of the Latin phrase opere citato, meaning "in the work cited." It is used in an endnote or footnote to refer the reader to a previously cited work, standing in for repetition of the full title of the work.

Vide-see; consult (used as an instruction in a text to refer the reader to a specified passage, book, author, etc., for further information).

59. **E. Wyndham Hulme** proposed the concept of literary warrant as the basis of book classification and the definition of subject classes, wherein classes and names of classes would be derived from existing literature rather than a pre-conceived philosophical order of sciences, the predominant and favoured type of classification system in Hulme's day. The methods of establishing classes by literary warrant are described and its relationship to what Hulme called "statistical bibliography" is explored.

Henry Evelyn Bliss was the author of a classification system he called Bibliographic Classification which is often abbreviated to BC and is sometimes called Bliss Classification. Another of the important features of Bliss's work is his ideas on "Alternative Location." This simply means that Bliss provided provisions in his system for the possible different shelf locations of certain materials.

Melvil Dewey: The Dewey Decimal Classification (DDC), or Dewey Decimal System, is a proprietary library classification system first published in the United States by Melvil Dewey in 1876. It has been revised and expanded through 23 major editions, the latest issued in 2011, and has grown from a four-page pamphlet in 1876.

S.R. Ranganathan proposed four kinds of mnemonic devices for use in constructing isolate numbers and whole class numbers. They are: Seminal mnemonics, systematic mnemonics, scheduled mnemonics, and verbal mnemonics 1521. These concepts can be usefully applied in database design, especially integrated databases and vocabulary control tools.

60. NOTATION AND LAYOUT: The UDC notation is a mix of decimal numbers, punctuation signs, and symbols with permissible use of alphabets, or other non-UDC symbols. The use of decimal notation has made it a truly international classification with many technical advantages. It is hierarchical, expressive, hospitable, mnemonic, faceted and synthetic. Layout of the abridged edition (2003) explained here is that of the pocket edition (1999). In this edition instead of verbal signs, following symbols independent of language have been used to give notes and instructions under an entry in the schedules.

Symbol	Name	Meaning
	Double Arrow	See Also
◇	Diamond	Examples numbers combinations
□	Square	Inclusion note (it reads including)
|	Sideline	Special auxiliaries
#	Hash	Non-UDC extensions
≅	Approximately equal to	Subdivide as
A/Z	Alphabets	Alphabetical divisions

61. Dr. Andrew Osborn: This paper identifies the text of Dr. Andrew Osborn's 1941 "The Crisis in Cataloging" as a place where a shift in the shared set of assumptions governing cataloguing rules and practices occurs. Cataloging from 1930-1942 was in a state of change and confusion. Dr. Osborn functioned as a "gatekeeper" who understood and integrated the available intellectual discourse on American Pragmatism and introduces it to Librarianship.

S.R. Ranganathan: Dynamic theory of cataloguing. With the aid of this theory. Ranganathan made, in the *Headings and Canons*, a comprehensive study (in 1955) of five catalogue codes: the Anglo-American code, the classified catalogue code, Cutter's rules, Prussian instructions, and the Vatican code.

Michael Gorman: Our Enduring Values: Librarianship in the 21st century (2000) ALA in this work, Gorman attempts to define the role of both library and librarians, discussing the core values of the profession. Gorman proposes eight values of librarianship which he believes are the principles which underpin the profession and, in turn, underpin democracy. The books consider the role of the library today, librarianship in the 21st century, what patrons and communities want from their libraries, the effects of new and changing technology on libraries, and ways to maintain the core values of librarianship into the future.

Raymond Knox Olding received his education at the University of Adelaide. He entered librarianship in 1946 and was elected a professional member of the Library Association of Australia in 1956. In 1956 F W Cheshire published *Reading in Library Cataloguing*, edited and introduced by R.K. Olding. This book has since gone into several overseas editions and has attracted very favourable comment both in Australia and abroad.

68. RDA relies on cataloguer's judgement to make some decisions about how much description or access is warranted. For example, the "rule of 3" to only provide up to three authors, composers, etc. is now an option, not the main instruction, so RDA encourages access to the names of persons and corporate bodies and families important to the users. RDA ties every descriptive and access element to the relevant FRBR user tasks: find, identify, select, and obtain in order to develop cataloguer's judgement to know not only *what* identifying characteristic to provide, but *why* they are providing it—to meet a user need.

Previous Paper (Solved)

UGC-NET-Junior Research Fellowship & Assistant Professor Exam

Library and Information Science, July-2016*

PAPER-II

Note: *This paper contains* ***fifty (50)*** *objective type questions of* ***two (2)*** *marks each.* ***All*** *questions are compulsory.*

1. Who identified the eight central values of librarianship?
A. Margaret Mann B. Michael Gorman
C. David Hume D. S.R. Ranganathan

2. Which of the following organizations declared 17th May as "World Information Society Day"?
A. IFLA
B. World Summit on the Information Society (WSIS)
C. World Health Organization (WHO)
D. UNESCO

3. 'Bibliographic Coupling' was first advocated by
A. B.K. Sen B. S.R. Ranganathan
C. M.M. Kessler D. S.C. Bradford

4. By which mode 'Management Science' and 'Research Methodology' are formed?
A. Agglomeration B. Fusion
C. Cluster D. Distillation

5. 'Prefix' element of ISBN consists of _____ number of digits.
A. 3 B. 5
C. 4 D. 2

6. Who defined notation as shorthand sign?
A. S.R. Ranganathan
B. Benjamin A. Custer
C. Immanuel Kant
D. E.C. Richardson

7. Which of the search strategy is useful to increase recall output?
A. Proximity operators
B. Boolean operators 'NOT'
C. Truncation
D. Boolean operators 'AND'

8. The 'Right to Information Bill' was enacted by the Parliament of India on
A. 5th May 2005
B. 15th June 2005
C. 12th October 2005
D. 22nd June 2005

9. Who was the first Director of Raja Ram Mohan Roy Library Foundation?
A. B.S. Kesvan B. D.R. Kalia
C. B.P. Barua D. S. Bashruddin

10. In Ranganathan's terminology 'Latent Facet' is a
A. Facet added at the end
B. Hidden Facet
C. Important Facet
D. Current of all Facets

11. 'Transactional Model of Communication' was suggested by
A. Peter Drucker B. George Zipf
C. Dean Barnlund D. A.C. Kessler

12. Research Methodology involving the construction of theory through analysis of data is known as
A. Sampling Theory
B. Grounded Theory
C. Ideal Theory
D. Basic Theory

* *Held on 10 July, 2016.*

13. Chapter 12 of AACR-2 has changed its name in AACR-2R, 2002. Identify the changed name.

A. Integrated Resources
B. Continuing Resources
C. Periodical Resources
D. Online Resources

14. Identify the persons who contributed to the development of TQM.

(*a*) Philip B. Crosby (*b*) Kaoru Ishikawa
(*c*) Joseph Juran (*d*) Michael Gorman

Codes:

A. (*a*), (*b*), (*c*) are correct
B. (*b*), (*c*), (*d*) are correct
C. (*a*), (*c*), (*d*) are correct
D. (*a*), (*b*), (*d*) are correct

15. Identify the correct statements associated with Universal Decimal Classification Scheme (UDC).

(*a*) It is a faceted classification scheme.
(*b*) Paul Otlet and Henry La Fontaine are associated with it.
(*c*) It has relative index.
(*d*) It uses pure notation.

Codes:

A. (*a*), (*b*) are correct B. (*b*), (*c*) are correct
C. (*c*), (*d*) are correct D. (*a*), (*d*) are correct

16. In which of the following studies, a researcher is required to examine some specific sub-population, as they change time?

A. Trend Study
B. Cohort Study
C. Cross Sectional Study
D. Panel Studies

17. Which of the following are associated with UNESCO Programme?

(*a*) General Information Programme (PGI)
(*b*) World Scientific Information System (UNISIST)
(*c*) Universal Availability of Publications (UAP)
(*d*) International Standard Bibliographic Description (ISBD)

Codes:

A. (*a*), (*b*) are correct B. (*a*), (*c*) are correct
C. (*a*), (*d*) are correct D. (*b*), (*c*) are correct

18. Collection development principles are given by:

(*a*) C.A. Cutter (*b*) Melvil Dewey
(*c*) S.R. Ranganathan (*d*) B.S. Kesvan

Codes:

A. (*a*), (*b*) are correct B. (*b*), (*c*) are correct
C. (*c*), (*d*) are correct D. (*b*), (*d*) are correct

19. 'Product lifecycle' is helpful in

(*a*) deciding marketing strategies best fitted to particular stages in the development of service activities.
(*b*) maintaining that all products or services follow distinctive pattern overtime.
(*c*) dealing with the historical aspect of the product.
(*d*) dealing with the stages of product life-cycle.

Codes:

A. (*a*), (*b*), (*d*) are correct
B. (*a*), (*b*), (*c*) are correct
C. (*b*), (*c*), (*d*) are correct
D. (*a*), (*c*), (*d*) are correct

20. PMEST in colon classification of S.R. Ranganathan is

(*a*) decreasing order of concreteness.
(*b*) decreasing order of association.
(*c*) decreasing order of classification.
(*d*) decreasing order of fundamental categories.

A. (*a*), (*b*) are correct B. (*a*), (*d*) are correct
C. (*a*), (*c*) are correct D. (*b*), (*d*) are correct

21. Information under section 2(f) of the 'Right to Information Act, 2005' means any material in any form, thus includes

(*a*) Records, Documents, Memos, E-mails, Papers.
(*b*) Opinions, Advices, Press Releases, Circulars, Samples.
(*c*) Orders, Log books, Contracts, Reports.
(*d*) Book Chapters, Journal Articles, Sale Deeds, Reprints, Snapshots of Consort.

Codes:

A. (*a*), (*c*) and (*d*) are correct
B. (*b*), (*c*) and (*d*) are correct
C. (*a*), (*b*) and (*d*) are correct
D. (*a*), (*b*) and (*c*) are correct

22. The objectives of Metadata are:
(*a*) Unique identification
(*b*) Authentification of records
(*c*) To eliminate the duplicate record
(*d*) To arrange the collection.
Codes:
A. (*a*) and (*d*) are correct
B. (*a*) and (*b*) are correct
C. (*b*) and (*d*) are correct
D. (*a*) and (*c*) are correct

23. Identify the following Institutional Archives/ Repositories available free:
(*a*) Project MUSE
(*b*) Web of Science
(*c*) e-prints
(*d*) Open DOAR
Codes:
A. (*a*) and (*b*) are correct
B. (*b*) and (*d*) are correct
C. (*c*) and (*d*) are correct
D. (*a*) and (*c*) are correct

24. Identify the following basic steps as advocated by William Edwards for implementing TQM:
(*a*) Assessment of organisation's culture and training process for the top management.
(*b*) Formation of Quality Council.
(*c*) Dissemination of information through established communication system and integration of TQM tools, techniques and training.
(*d*) Filtering and censoring Information.
Codes:
A. (*b*), (*c*) and (*d*) are correct.
B. (*a*), (*b*) and (*c*) are correct.
C. (*a*), (*c*) and (*d*) are correct.
D. (*a*), (*b*) and (*d*) are correct.

25. Identify the Audio File Format for Digital libraries:
(*a*) .tif (*b*) .jfif
(*c*) .aif (*d*) .ra
Codes:
A. (*c*) and (*d*) are correct.
B. (*b*) and (*d*) are correct.
C. (*a*) and (*b*) are correct.
D. (*b*) and (*c*) are correct.

26. The available options for extending Wiki vary depending on the software that runs the site. Identify the correct options available to users using "Media Wiki".
(*a*) GISWiki kWBreadCrumbs
(*b*) Bibwiki
(*c*) YouTube Tag and FireStats
(*d*) pbwikiGS
Codes:
A. (*a*), (*b*) and (*c*) are correct.
B. (*b*), (*c*) and (*d*) are correct.
C. (*a*), (*c*) and (*d*) are correct.
D. (*a*), (*b*) and (*d*) are correct.

27. Deliberate Sampling is known as
(*a*) Purposive Sampling
(*b*) Sequential Sampling
(*c*) Probability Sampling
(*d*) Non-probability Sampling
Codes:
A. (*a*) and (*d*) are correct
B. (*a*) and (*c*) are correct
C. (*a*), (*b*) and (*d*) are correct
D. (*b*), (*c*) and (*d*) are correct

28. Arrange the following indexing journals according to the year of their first publication:
(*a*) Engineering Index, New York
(*b*) Humanities Index, New York
(*c*) Index Medicus, Bethesda
(*d*) Agrindex, Rome
Codes:
A. (*d*), (*c*), (*a*) and (*b*) B. (*c*), (*b*), (*d*) and (*a*)
C. (*a*), (*c*), (*b*) and (*d*) D. (*c*), (*a*), (*b*) and (*d*)

29. Arrange the following Dublin core elements in descending order:
(*a*) Contributor (*b*) Identifier
(*c*) Relation (*d*) Right
Codes:
A. (*d*), (*c*), (*b*), (*a*) B. (*a*), (*d*), (*b*), (*c*)
C. (*a*), (*b*), (*d*), (*c*) D. (*a*), (*b*), (*c*), (*d*)

30. Identify the correct elements of 'AIDA' model in Marketing Communication.
A. Attraction, Investigation, Direction, Action
B. Attention, Intuition, Desire, Acquisition
C. Attention, Interest, Desire, Action
D. Abstract, Institution, Diversity, Action

31. Arrange the following museums according to the year of their establishment:

(*a*) Nehru Memorial Museum and Library, Delhi

(*b*) National Museum, Delhi

(*c*) Indian Museum, Calcutta

(*d*) National Gandhi Museum, Delhi

Codes:

A. (*d*), (*a*), (*c*), (*b*) B. (*c*), (*b*), (*d*), (*a*)

C. (*b*), (*c*), (*d*), (*a*) D. (*a*), (*d*), (*c*), (*b*)

32. Arrange the following international standards developed in the broader context of 'Information Organisation' in their respective year of development:

(*a*) ISO-999 (*b*) ISO-214

(*c*) ISO-2788 (*d*) ISO-5963

Codes:

A. (*c*), (*b*), (*d*), (*a*) B. (*a*), (*b*), (*c*), (*d*)

C. (*b*), (*c*), (*d*), (*a*) D. (*d*), (*c*), (*b*), (*a*)

33. Match the following:

List-I	***List-II***
(*a*) Pareto Chart	(*i*) Pictorian representation of stages in a process
(*b*) Fish Bone Diagram	(*ii*) Tool of recording variables
(*c*) Flow chart	(*iii*) Identifies the intensity of each problem in the production line
(*d*) Check-sheet	(*iv*) Identifies the relationship between the defects or problems and their root causes

Codes:

	(*a*)	(*b*)	(*c*)	(*d*)
A.	(*i*)	(*iii*)	(*iv*)	(*ii*)
B.	(*iv*)	(*i*)	(*ii*)	(*iii*)
C.	(*iii*)	(*iv*)	(*ii*)	(*i*)
D.	(*iii*)	(*iv*)	(*i*)	(*ii*)

34. Match the following:

List-I	***List-II***
(*a*) New Gen Lib	(*i*) 1984
(*b*) LIBSYS	(*ii*) 2000
(*c*) Koha	(*iii*) 2005
(*d*) Open Biblio	(*iv*) 2002

Codes:

	(*a*)	(*b*)	(*c*)	(*d*)
A.	(*ii*)	(*i*)	(*iii*)	(*iv*)
B.	(*ii*)	(*i*)	(*iv*)	(*iii*)
C.	(*iii*)	(*i*)	(*ii*)	(*iv*)
D.	(*iv*)	(*iii*)	(*ii*)	(*i*)

35. Match the following:

List-I	***List-II***
(*a*) Gujarat Public Libraries Act	(*i*) 1965
(*b*) Chhattisgarh Public Libraries Act	(*ii*) 1993
(*c*) Karnataka Public Libraries Act	(*iii*) 2009
(*d*) Goa Public Libraries Act	(*iv*) 2001

Codes:

	(*a*)	(*b*)	(*c*)	(*d*)
A.	(*i*)	(*iv*)	(*iii*)	(*ii*)
B.	(*ii*)	(*i*)	(*iv*)	(*iii*)
C.	(*iv*)	(*ii*)	(*iii*)	(*i*)
D.	(*iv*)	(*iii*)	(*i*)	(*ii*)

36. Match the following:

List-I	***List-II***
(*a*) Key to a given collection	(*i*) Abstract
(*b*) Key to literary sources on a subject	(*ii*) Index
(*c*) Representation of subject concept	(*iii*) Catalogue
(*d*) Condensation of a document	(*iv*) Bibliography

Codes:

	(*a*)	(*b*)	(*c*)	(*d*)
A.	(*iv*)	(*ii*)	(*iii*)	(*i*)
B.	(*iii*)	(*ii*)	(*i*)	(*iv*)
C.	(*iii*)	(*iv*)	(*ii*)	(*i*)
D.	(*i*)	(*iii*)	(*ii*)	(*iv*)

37. Match the following:

List-I (AACR-II)	***List-II (Connecting Symbols)***
(*a*) The size of the document	(*i*) Colon
(*b*) Statement of Responsibility	(*ii*) Plus
(*c*) Between place and the name of the publishers	(*iii*) Semicolon
(*d*) Accompanying material	(*iv*) Diagonal slash

Codes:

	(a)	(b)	(c)	(d)
A.	(i)	(iii)	(iv)	(ii)
B.	(ii)	(iv)	(iii)	(i)
C.	(iv)	(iii)	(i)	(ii)
D.	(iii)	(iv)	(i)	(ii)

38. Match the following:

List-I	*List-II*
(a) Subject Classification	(i) J. Atchinson
(b) Thesaurofacet	(ii) S.R. Ranganathan
(c) Classaurus	(iii) J.D. Brown
(d) APUPA	(iv) G. Bhattacharya

Codes:

	(a)	(b)	(c)	(d)
A.	(iv)	(iii)	(ii)	(i)
B.	(i)	(ii)	(iii)	(iv)
C.	(iii)	(i)	(iv)	(ii)
D.	(ii)	(iv)	(i)	(iii)

39. Match the following:

List-I	*List-II*
(a) Classical School	(i) John Cotton Dana
(b) X and Y Theory	(ii) Henry Fayol
(c) Newark Charging System	(iii) Peter Drucker
(d) MBO	(iv) Douglas McGregor

Codes:

	(a)	(b)	(c)	(d)
A.	(i)	(iii)	(iv)	(ii)
B.	(iii)	(iv)	(i)	(ii)
C.	(ii)	(iv)	(i)	(iii)
D.	(iii)	(ii)	(iv)	(i)

40. Assertion (A) : Selection of e-resources requires utmost care and caution in order to make the same user-centric.

Reason (R) : Availability of seamless online products in the market coupled with abundant internet resources at no cost made the e-resources redundant.

Codes:

A. (A) is false, but (R) is true.
B. Both (A) and (R) are false.
C. (A) is true, but (R) is false.
D. Both (A) and (R) are true.

41. Assertion (A) : Results from popular web search engines are usually having high recall, but an indexing database can provide high precision.

Reason (R) : Indexing databases use controlled vocabulary which is a carefully selected list of words and phrases which are used to tag units of information (document or work) so that they may be more easily retrieved.

Codes:

A. Both (A) and (R) are true.
B. (A) is true, but (R) is false.
C. Both (A) and (R) are false.
D. (R) is true, but (A) is false.

42. Assertion (A) : Management is the efficiency in climbing the ladder of success.

Reason (R) : Leadership determines whether the ladder is leaning towards right wall.

Codes:

A. (A) is true, but (R) is false.
B. (A) is false, but (R) is true.
C. Both (A) and (R) are true.
D. Both (A) and (R) are false.

43. Assertion (A) : Web 2.0 is a good set of economic, social and technological trend that collectively form the basis of the next generation of the Internet.

Reason (R) : More than just the latest technology buzzword, Web 2.0 is a transformative force that is propelling libraries towards a new way to offer services.

Codes:

A. (A) is true, but (R) is false.
B. (A) is false, but (R) is true.
C. Both (A) and (R) are true.
D. Both (A) and (R) are false.

44. Assertion (A) : Consortia subscriptions are not always beneficial to libraries as publishers bundle irrelevant titles to inflate the number of titles for better price during negotiations.

Reason (R) : In bundled titles, libraries have not to pay for the titles which are not core to them.

Codes:

A. (A) is true, but (R) is false.
B. (R) is true, but (A) is false.
C. Both (A) and (R) are true.
D. Both (A) and (R) are false.

45. Assertion (A) : Chain procedure is a systematic and almost mechanical method of deriving subject headings.

Reason (R) : It does not always operate well only with a faceted scheme of classification.

Codes:

A. (A) is true, but (R) is false.
B. (A) is false, but (R) is true.
C. Both (A) and (R) are false.
D. Both (A) and (R) are true.

Directions (Qs. No. 46-50) : *Read the passage given below and answer the questions based on your understanding of the passage.*

One of the major features of the World Wide Web is the capability to create links between pages. These links are often viewed as analogues of citations in scientific publications (*e.g.*, ROUSSEAU, 1997; BJORNEBORN & INGWERSEN, 2001; CRONIN, 2001). Links can lead to a different site or may lead to a page in the same site. Links for which the source and the target of the page are within the same site or domain are called self-links. Instead of counting self-links, we count self-sitations - the number of pages on the site having a link or links pointing to the same site. The difference between self-links and self-sitations is that for self-sitations a page with several self-links is counted with multiplicity one. The reason for counting self-sitations instead of self-links is technical: commercial search engines report the number of pages with self-links and not the number of self-links. The term-sitation has been coined by ROUSSEAU (1997). In this paper we develop the measures self-linking and self-linked, which correspond to the classical measures for journals: self-citing and self-cited. We calculate these rates for a number of academic institutions on the Web. Self-links seem to be more problematic than self-citations (of authors in scientific publications), because self-links are often inserted for navigational purposes.

46. Self-links denote:
A. Links between two websites.
B. Links between two authors.
C. Links between source and the target of the page within the same site or domain.
D. Links between two articles written by two different authors.

47. Commercial search engines report
A. the number of pages with self-links.
B. the number of self-links.
C. the number of sites.
D. the total number of total citations.

48. Self-linking and self-linked measures calculate their rates for
A. number of academic institutions on the web.
B. number of websites on the web.
C. number of databases available on a given site.
D. number of subject gateways on the web.

49. Links in domain can lead to
(*a*) different sites on www.
(*b*) page in the same site.
(*c*) page in the different sites.
(*d*) all available e-documents.

Codes:

A. (*a*) and (*c*) are correct
B. (*a*) and (*b*) are correct
C. (*b*) and (*d*) are correct
D. (*c*) and (*d*) are correct

50. Reason for counting self-sitations is:
A. Academic B. Classificatory
C. Technical D. Non-technical

ANSWERS

1	2	3	4	5	6	7	8	9	10
B	B	C	D	A	D	C	B	C	B
11	**12**	**13**	**14**	**15**	**16**	**17**	**18**	**19**	**20**
C	B	B	A	A	B	A	B	A	B
21	**22**	**23**	**24**	**25**	**26**	**27**	**28**	**29**	**30**
D	B	C	B	A	A	A	D	A	C
31	**32**	**33**	**34**	**35**	**36**	**37**	**38**	**39**	**40**
B	A	D	C	D	C	D	C	C	C
41	**42**	**43**	**44**	**45**	**46**	**47**	**48**	**49**	**50**
A	C	C	A	A	C	A	A	B	C

EXPLANATORY ANSWERS

1. Michael Gorman (Born 6 March 1941, Witney, Oxfordshire) is a British-born librarian, library scholar and editor/writer on library issues noted for his traditional views. During his tenure as president of the American Library Association (ALA), he was vocal in his opinions on a range of subjects, notably technology and education. He currently lives in the Chicago area with his wife, Anne Reuland, a librarian at Loyola University.

Gorman's principles of librarianship derive from core liberal, democratic and humanist values. A key influence is S.R. Ranganathan, whom he regarded as "the greatest figure of librarianship in the 20th century." He maintains that it is through focusing on core professional values that librarians will facilitate personal growth and enhance the success of their institutions.

2. World Information Society Day was proclaimed to be on 17 May by a United Nations General Assembly resolution, following the 2005 World Summit on the Information Society in Tunis.

3. The concept of *bibliographic coupling* was introduced by M. M. Kessler of MIT in a paper published in 1963, and has been embraced in the work of the information scientist Eugene Garfield. It is one of the earliest citation analysis methods for document similarity computation and some have questioned its usefulness, pointing out that two works may reference completely unrelated subject matter in the third. Furthermore, bibliographic coupling is a retrospective similarity measure, meaning the information used to establish the similarity relationship between documents lies in the past and is static, *i.e.,* bibliographic coupling strength cannot change over time, since outgoing citation counts are fixed.

8. Right to Information (RTI) is an Act of the Parliament of India to provide for setting out the practical regime of right to information for citizens and replaces the erstwhile Freedom of Information Act, 2002. Under the provisions of the Act, any citizen of India may request information from a "public authority" (a body of Government or "instrumentality of State") which is required to reply expeditiously or within thirty days. The Act also requires every public authority to computerise their records for wide dissemination and to proactively certain categories of information so that the citizens need minimum recourse to request for information formally. This law was passed by Parliament on 15 June 2005 and came fully into force on 12 October 2005.

9. Raja Ram Mohan Roy Library Foundation (RRRLF), Kolkata was established by the government to promote and support public library movements in the country by providing adequate library services through assistance and by developing reading habits all over the country. It was established in 1972, the bicentenary year of the birth of Raja Ram Mohan Roy.

Raja Ram Mohan Roy Library Foundation (RRRLF) is an autonomous organization under the Ministry of Culture. It is the nodal agency of the Government of India to support public library services and systems and promote public library movement in the country. It has headquarters at Kolkata and four zonal offices: Mumbai, Chennai, New Delhi and Kolkata. B.P. Barua was first director of Raja Ram Mohan Roy Library Foundation.

11. Dean Barnlund proposed a transactional model of communication in 1970 for basic interpersonal communication which articulates that sending and receiving of messages happens simultaneously between people which is popularly known as Barnlund's Transactional Model of Communication. The model has been further adapted and reformed by other theorists as General Transactional Model. The model shifted from the trend of linear model to dynamic and two way communication model. Barnlund's Transactional Model is a multi-layered feedback system. This is a continuous process where the sender and the receiver interchange their places and both are equally important. The message passing takes place with a constant feedback being provided from both parties. A feedback for one is the message for the other.

12. Grounded theory (GT) is a systematic methodology in the social sciences involving the construction of theory through the analysis of data.Grounded theory is a research methodology which operates almost in a reverse fashion from social science research in the positivist tradition. Unlike positivist research, a study using grounded theory is likely to begin with a question, or even just with the collection of qualitative data. As researchers review the data collected, repeated ideas, concepts or elements become apparent, and are tagged with *codes,* which have been extracted from the data. As more data are collected, and as data are re-reviewed, codes can be grouped into concepts, and then into categories. These categories may become the basis for new theory. Thus, grounded theory is quite different from the traditional model of research, where the researcher chooses an existing theoretical framework, and only then collects data to show how the theory does or does not apply to the phenomenon under study.

14. Total Quality Management (TQM) in the Department of Defense is a strategy for continuously improving performance at every level, and in all areas of responsibility. It combines fundamental management techniques, existing improvement efforts, and specialized technical tools under a disciplined structure focused on continuously improving all processes. Improved performance is directed at satisfying such broad goals as cost, quality, schedule, and mission need and suitability. Increasing user satisfaction is the overriding objective. The TQM effort builds on the pioneering work of Dr. W.E. Deming, Dr. J.M. Juran, Philip B. Crosby and Kaoru Ishikawa, and benefits from both private and public sector experience with continuous process improvement.

18. Library collection development is the process of meeting the information needs of the people (a service population) in a timely and economical manner using information resources locally held, as well as from other organizations. According to The International

Federation of Library Association and Institutions (IFLA), acquisition and collection development focuses on methodological and topical themes pertaining to acquisition of print and other analogue library materials (by purchase, exchange, gift, legal deposit) and the licensing and purchase of electronic information resources. Collection development principles are given by Melvil Dewey and S.R. Ranganathan.

20. The PMEST-System leads back to the so-called "Colon Classification" developed by the Indian librarian S.R. Ranganathan (1872-1972). He originated a system of five fundamental categories (Personality, Matter, Energy, Space, Time) in order of decreasing concreteness to focus on subjects, topics and objects. He developed this faceted classification system in respect to put books in order, I abuse it just a little to put my presentation in order : Many people think, the essence of cognition is classification and the classification system, which is used, does influence the complying view on things. And so I do. That's why I do...it that way.

21. Section 2(f) in the Right To Information Act, 2005 : (f) 'information' means any material in any form, including records, documents, memos, e-mails, opinions, advices, press releases, circulars, orders, logbooks, contracts, reports, papers, samples, models, data material held in any electronic form and information relating to any private body which can be accessed by a public authority under any other law for the time being in force.

22. Metadata is "data (information) that provides information about other data." Three distinct types of metadata exist: descriptive metadata, structural metadata, and administrative metadata.

- Descriptive metadata describes a resource for purposes such as discovery and identification. It can include elements such as title, abstract, author, and keywords.
- Structural metadata is a metadata about containers of metadata and indicates how compound objects are put together, *e.g.,* how pages are ordered to form chapters.
- Administrative metadata provides information to help manage a resource, such as when and how it was created, file type and other technical information, and who can access it.

23. In a survey for Open DOAR in early 2006, Peter Millington discovered that about two thirds of Open Access repositories did not have publicly stated policies for the permitted re-use of deposited items or for such things as submission of items, long term preservation etc. This complicates matters for organisations wishing to provide search services, which in turn reduces the visibility and impact of these repositories.

This output option generates the source code for an e-prints static HTML page for your site's policies. This will be displayed using your normal e-prints template layout. For a real life example, please see the Nottingham e-prints Policies web page.

25. Simplified Guidelines/File Format recommendations:

- **Audio:** Highly recommended: AIFF (.aif, .aiff) or WAV (.wav). Moderately recommended: MP3 (.mp3), AAC (.mp4, .mp4a, .aac), FLAC (.flac) or ALAC (.m4a).
- **Video:** Highly recommended: Uncompressed Quicktime Movie (.mov); uncompressed AVI (.avi). Moderately recommended: MPEG-1, MPEG-2 or MPEG-4 encoded video (.avi, .mpg, .mpeg, .mov, .mkv, .mp4).
- **Virtual Reality/3D:** Highly recommended; X3D (*.x3d). Please talk with a Northwestern Digital Librarian to determine best output settings and format.

- **Image:** Highly recommended: Full colour images @ 600 dpi or higher saved as JPEG2000 Lossless (.jp2) or TIFF 24-bit, uncompressed (.tif, .tiff). Moderately recommended; lossy compressed formats limited to JPEG (.jpg, .jpeg), JPEG2000 (.jp2), TIFF (.tif, .tiff), or PNG (.png) at highest quality possible.
- **Test:** Highly recommended: Open Document Text (.odt), UTF-8 Unicode text (.txt), or PDF/A (.pdf). Moderately recommended: Rich Text Format (.rtf).

27. Deliberate Sampling is known as Purposive Sampling and Non-probility Sampling. A purposive sample is where a researcher selects a sample based on their knowledge about the study and population. The participants are selected based on the purpose of the sample, hence the name.

Non-probability sampling is a sampling technique where the odds of any member being selected for a sample cannot be calculated. It's the opposite of probability sampling, where you can calculate the odds. In addition, probability sampling involves random selection, while non-probability sampling does not–it relies on the subjective judgement of the researcher.

29. The Dublin Core Metadata Element Set is a vocabulary of fifteen properties for use in resource description. The name 'Dublin' is due to its origin at a 1995 invitational workshop in Dublin, Ohio; 'core' because its elements are broad and generic, usable for describing a wide range of resources. The fifteen element 'Dublin Core' described in this standard is a part of a larger set of metadata vocabularies and technical specifications maintained by the Dublin Core Metadata Initiative (DCMI).

The Dublin Core Metadata Element Set in the descending order : 1. Rights, 2. Coverage, 3. Relation, 4. Language, 5. Source, 6. Identifier, 7. Format, 8. Type, 9. Date, 10. Contributor, 11. Publisher, 12. Description, 13. Subject, 14. Creator, 15. Title.

30. The acronym AIDA stands for Attention, Interest, Desire and Action. These are the four stages that a consumer goes through while watching or viewing an advertisement. According to Lewis, first and foremost, the role of an advertisement is to attract the customers. Once an ad grabs attention, it has to invoke interest towards the product in the minds of the consumers. After creating an interest, the ad has to bring desire in consumers' mind to use the product and finally the consumer has to take a favourable action towards the product by ultimately purchasing the product.

The Process of AIDA:

- **Attention:** Attention is usually grabbed by the use of image, colour, layout, typography, size, celebrity, model, etc.
- **Interest:** Once attention is grabbed, it's necessary to create interest in the viewers' mind so that they will read more about the brand being advertised. By the use of an attractive sub head, interest can be invoked.
- **Desire:** The element of desire is usually created by the use of body copy where you write in detail about the necessity of buying the brand, thereby explaining the features of the brand, facts and figures.
- **Action:** Towards the end, the contact information of the brand will be given where they expects the viewers to take action immediately. It can be in the form of shop address, toll free numbers or website address.

31. The Indian Museum is the largest and oldest museum in India and has rare collections of antiques, armous and ornaments, fossils, skeletons, mummies, and Mughal paintings. It was founded by the Asiatic Society of Bengal in Kolkata (Calcutta), India, in 1814.

The founder curator was Nathaniel Wallich, a Danish botanist.

The National Museum in New Delhi, also known as the National Museum of India, is one of the largest museums in India. Established in 1949, it holds variety of articles ranging from pre-historic era to modern works of art. If functions under the Ministry of Culture, Government of India.

The National Gandhi Museum or Gandhi Memorial Museum is a museum located in New Delhi, India showcasing the life and principles of Mahatma Gandhi. The museum first opened in Mumbai, shortly after Gandhi was assassinated in 1948. The museum relocated several times before moving to Rajghat, New Delhi in 1961.

The Nehru Memorial Museum & Library (NMML) established in the memory of Jawaharlal Nehru (1889-1964) is an autonomous institution under the Ministry of Culture, Government of India.

32. **ISO 2788** was the ISO international standard for monolingual thesauri for information retrieval, first published in 1974 and revised in 1986. The official title of the standard was *"Guidelines for the establishment and development of monolingual thesauri"*.

ISO 214 Commitment to abstracting standards has a very significant role in information retrieval. The present research aimed to evaluate the rate of Commitment to ISO 214 Standard among the Persian abstracts of approved research projects at School of Health Management and Medical Informatics, Isfahan University of Medical Sciences, Isfahan, Iran.

The ISO 5963 standard Methods for examining documents, determining their subjects and selecting indexing terms, for example, defines "subject" as follows: "Any concept or combination of concepts representing a theme in a document". (This definition and standard is also clearly document-oriented.)

ISO 999 (Information and Documentation–Guidelines for the content, organization and presentation of indexes) is an ISO standard which provides the information industry with guidelines for the content, organisation and presentation of indexes to a wide range of documents including books, Periodicals, electronic documents, films, images, maps, and three-dimensional objects.

34. NewGenLib is an integrated library management system developed by Verus Solutions Pvt. Ltd. Domain expertise is provided by Kesavan Institute of Information and Knowledge Management in Hyderabad, India. NewGenLib version 1.0 was released in March 2005.

LIBSYS Ltd., a New Delhi based software company, is engaged in providing software solution since 1984. Continuous growth for over 2 decades, has made LIBSYS the most trusted brand for libraries in India. Its wide acceptance in market strengthens its popularity as the most field proven library system with unmatched depth in functionality and features. We take pride in being the pioneer and market leader for library automations in India.

Koha was created in 1999 by Katipo Communications for the Horowhenua Library Trust in New Zealand, and the first installation went live in January 2000.

Open Biblio was created in 2002 by Dave Stevens, who was interested in creating an easy-to-use, well-documented, easy-to-install library system. The current maintainer is Hans van der Weij.

36. An abstract is a brief summary of a research article, thesis, review, conference proceeding or any in-depth analysis of a particular subject and is often used to help the reader quickly ascertain the paper's purpose. When used, an abstract always appears at the beginning of a manuscript or typescript, acting as the point-of-entry for any given academic paper or patent application. Abstracting and indexing services for various academic disciplines are aimed at compiling a body of literature for that particular subject.

Index: An index is an indicator or measure of something, and in finance, it typically refers to a statistical measure of change in a securities market. In the case of financial markets, stock and bond market indices consist of an imaginary portfolio of securities representing a particular market or a portion of it. In reference to mortgages, it refers to a benchmark interest rate created by a third party.

Catalogue: A library catalog or library catalogue is a register of all bibliographic items found in a library or group of libraries, such as a network of libraries at several locations. A bibliographic item can be any information entity (*e.g.,* books, computer files, graphics, realia, cartographic materials, etc.) that is considered library material (*e.g.,* a single novel in an anthology), or a group of library materials (*e.g.,* a trilogy), or linked from the catalog (*e.g.,* a webpage) as far as it is relevant to the catalog and to the users (patrons) of the library.

Bibliography, as a discipline, is traditionally the academic study of books as physical, cultural objects; in this sense, it is also known as bibliology. Carter and Barker (2010) describe bibliography as a twofold scholarly discipline the organized listing of books (enumerative bibliography) and the systematic description of books as physical objects (descriptive bibliography).

38. **James Duff Brown** (1862-1914) was a British librarian, information theorist, music biographer and educationalist. Most of his life was spent in London.

Publications

- 1886: Biographical Dictionary of Musicians
- 1898: Manual of Library Classification and Shelf Arrangement
- 1906: Subject Classification (1st ed. 1906; 2nd ed. 1914 ; 3rd ed. (rev. by J. D. Stewar) 1939)
- 1912: Library Classification and Cataloguing

G. Bhattacharya : The classaurus developed by G. Bhattacharya of Documentation Research and Training Centre, Bangalore has only one section consisting of separate schedules for different facets, but the schedules incorporate within themselves the feature of both classification scheme and a thesaurus. The Index of the classaurus is a usual alphabetical index.

Thesaurofacet (Aitchison *et al.* 1969, Aitchison 1970) is commonly taken to be the first faceted thesaurus. It divided information fairly equally between the classified display and the alphabetical listing. Another style follows the BSI ROOT Thesaurus in providing all information in the classified display (Aitchison *et al.* 2000). Other prominent faceted thesauri include the Alcohol and other Drug Thesaurus (AOD), while the (US) National Library of Medicine controlled vocabulary thesaurus (MeSH) contains various faceted elements.

Dr S.R. Ranganathan who is our father of Library and Information Science in India has enunciated a fundamental principle, known as APUPA pattern. APUPA pattern is one of the methods of arrangement of books in Classification. As per this method documents are classified into three type, viz, Umbral, Penumbral and Alien. Umbral document implies the totally relevant document which is the main interest of the reader. Penumbral document satisfies the marginal interest of the reader. This type is partially relevant and someway related to Umbral document. Alien document is totally non-relevant and thus is not required by the reader. So, we can recognize the pattern of every helpful sequence of the books as Alien- Penumbral-Umbral-Penumbral- Alien - *i.e.,* APUPA arrangement.

39. Henery Fayol (1841-1925) is generally hailed as the founder of the classical management school not because he was the first to investigate managerial behaviour, but because he was the first to systematize it. Fayol believed that sound management falls in to certain patterns that can be identified and analyzed. From this basic insight, he drew up a blueprint for a cohesive doctrine of management, one that retains much of its force to this day.

Theory X and Theory Y are theories of human motivation and management. They were created and developed by Douglas McGregor at the MIT Sloan School of Management in the 1960s. These theories describe two contrasting models of workforce motivation applied by managers in human resource management, organizational behaviour, organizational communication and organizational development. According to the models, the two opposing sets of general assumptions of how workers are motivated form the basis for two different managerial styles. Theory X stresses the importance of strict supervision, external rewards, and penalties: in contrast, Theory Y highlights the motivating role of job satisfaction and encourages workers to approach tasks without direct supervision.

MBO stands for Management by Objectives, a phrase coined by Peter Drucker in his book "The Practice of Management," published in 1954. MBO measures the performance of employees as compared to typical standards for the job. The belief is that, if employees help determine those standards, they will be more likely to fulfill them.

John Cotton Dana (1856-1929) librarian, author; born in Woodstock, Vt. He graduated from Dartmouth College and held a series of positions before becoming head of the Denver (Colo.) Public Library (1889)where he established the nation's first children's reading room. While working in the Newark, N.J., library system(1902-29) he established the "Newark charging system," a simplified lending process, and cofounded the business library. He also helped found the Newark Museum Association and the Port of New York Authority. He wrote over 500 books and articles on librarianship and museum operations.

PAPER-III

Note: *This paper contains* ***Seventy five (75)*** *objective type questions of* ***two (2)*** *marks each.* ***All*** *questions are compulsory.*

1. Which law of the Library Science, as enunciated by Dr. Ranganathan, covered the words children, blind and the crippled, artisans, neo-literates, farmers, factory workers, and many more under the ambience of Public Library Service?
A. First Law B. Second Law
C. Fourth Law D. Fifth Law

2. Chapter – 9 of AACR-2 has changed its name in AACR 2R 2002. Identify the changed name.
A. Computer Files
B. Electronic Resources
C. Machine Readable Data Files
D. Computer Resources

3. Which of the following Associations had suggested that, for every 3000 persons there should be one public library and India with 1.2 billion population requires 3,30,000 libraries?
A. IASLIC B. IFLA
C. ALA D. ASLIB

4. Who, among the following, had visualized the establishment of Village Knowledge Centres (VKCs) in 2.3 lakh Panchayats to empower the villagers with knowledge?
A. Jawaharlal Nehru
B. Dr. S.R. Ranganathan
C. Dr. Abdul Kalam
D. C.V. Raman

5. In1930, who theorized that reference work may be conservative, moderate and liberal?
A. James I. Wyer B. William A. Katz
C. S.R. Ranganathan D. S. Rothestein

6. The term 'Exponential Growth' refers to
A. Linear Growth
B. Normal mode of distribution
C. Geometric Progression
D. Arithmetic Progression

7. Which of the following sections of the 'Right to Information Act', 2005 (India) grants exemption from disclosure of information?
A. Section – 5(2) B. Section – 6
C. Section – 8 D. Section – 11

8. The World Digital Library (WDL) is an international collaboration led by
A. IFLA, with support of Library of Congress
B. CILIP, with support of UNESCO
C. CILIP, with support of IFLA
D. Library of Congress, with support of UNESCO

9. Which of the following is the first book authored by S.R. Ranganathan?
A. Library Manual
B. Five laws of Library Science
C. Prolegomena to Library Classification
D. Colon Classification

10. Journalseek is an
A. Online database covering academic journals articles.
B. Online database covering abstracts.
C. Online database of freely available journal information.
D. Subscription agent for freely available journals.

11. Which of the following types of publication is/are included in the INB?
A. Guides to Textbooks
B. Maps
C. The first issue of a periodical
D. Back volumes of periodicals

12. Who has been referred to as 'First Grammarian of library classification'?
A. S.R. Ranganathan B. E.W. Hulme
C. Melvil Dewey D. W.C.B. Sayers

13. 760 tag in MARC format marks
A. The Edition
B. The Publication Information
C. Main Series Entry
D. A Topical Subject Heading

14. The '12 Rules for Relational Database' were given by

A. Edgar F. Codd B. Larvy Page
C. J. Bill Gates D. Linus Tolward

15. Which among the following is free Audio Book Site?

A. Ebrary B. Virtua
C. Google Books D. Librivox

16. Bench marking, SWOT analysis and Environmental Scanning activities should occur continually and consistently in Library's strategic planning process to ensure that

A. the organisation is competitive and enabled to meet future needs as they occur.
B. not to modify or update mission statements of the organisation periodically.
C. to keep the library stakeholders under cloud about the forward movement of the organisation.
D. to derecognise the faster movement of technology.

17. The term 'Gang Plank' is associated with _____ administrative principle.

A. Remuneration B. Stability of Tenure
C. Scalar Chain D. Division of Labour

18. 'Instagram' is acquired by _____.

A. Whatsapp B. Yahoo
C. Facebook D. Google

19. An e-resource consortium 'CeRA' is working in the field of

A. Agriculture B. Astronomy
C. Astrophysics D. Anthropology

20. LOCKOSS (software), an international community initiative by

A. MIT Library
B. Stanford University
C. University of Waikato
D. University of Southampton

21. Identify the principal findings of Vilfredo Pareto study on application of 'Pareto Chart' in social research.

(*a*) Small percentage of population accounted for a large proportion of wealth.
(*b*) 80% of results are due to 20% causes and 80% of the profit of an organisation came from 20% of its products.
(*c*) Large percentage of population accounted for a small proportion of wealth.
(*d*) 20% of causes are responsible for 80% of quality problems.

Codes:

A. (*a*), (*b*) and (*d*) are correct.
B. (*a*), (*b*) and (*c*) are correct.
C. (*b*), (*c*) and (*d*) are correct.
D. (*a*), (*c*) and (*d*) are correct.

22. Which of the following important objectives included in 29 objectives laid down by RRRLF for its operation?

(*a*) To promote library movement in the country.
(*b*) To enunciate a national library policy and to work towards its adoption by the central and state governments.
(*c*) To propagate the adoption of library legislation in the country.
(*d*) To maintain a database of qualified librarians.

Codes:

A. (*a*), (*b*) and (*c*) are correct.
B. (*b*), (*c*) and (*d*) are correct.
C. (*a*), (*c*) and (*d*) are correct.
D. (*a*), (*b*) and (*d*) are correct.

23. Identify the key features of Emptying Digit from the following:

(*a*) Helps in intrapolation between two consecutive ordinal numbers.
(*b*) Deprives the preceding digit of its semantic value in a digit group.
(*c*) Deprives the preceding digit of its semantic value in a digit group but does not retain the ordinal value allotted to it.
(*d*) When it occurs as an initial digit, it deems semantically poor digit.

Codes:

A. (*a*) and (*c*) are correct.
B. (*a*) and (*b*) are correct.
C. (*a*) and (*d*) are correct.
D. (*b*) and (*d*) are correct.

24. Which of the following are not published by US National Library of Medicine?
(*a*) eMedicine (*b*) Pubmeth
(*c*) PubMed (*d*) Medline Plus
Codes:
A. (*a*) and (*b*) are correct.
B. (*a*) and (*d*) are correct.
C. (*c*) and (*d*) are correct.
D. (*b*) and (*d*) are correct.

25. 'E-Shodh Sindhu' emerged by the merger of
(*a*) INDEST (*b*) INFONET
(*c*) NICNET (*d*) N-LIST
Codes:
A. (*a*), (*c*), (*d*) are correct.
B. (*a*), (*b*), (*c*) are correct.
C. (*b*), (*c*), (*d*) are correct.
D. (*a*), (*b*), (*d*) are correct.

26. Identify the websites for best practices: as viewed by June L. Power:
(*a*) Library Success
(*b*) Second Life Library 2.0
(*c*) LISNews.org
(*d*) Bloomington Delivery Service
Codes:
A. (*a*), (*c*), (*d*) are correct.
B. (*a*), (*b*), (*c*) are correct.
C. (*b*), (*c*), (*d*) are correct.
D. (*a*), (*b*), (*d*) are correct.

27. Identify the principles for the implementation of the canon of helpful sequence:
(*a*) Principle of spatial contiguity
(*b*) Principle of increasing literary warrant
(*c*) Principle of modulation
(*d*) Principle of enumeration
Codes:
A. (*a*) and (*b*) are correct.
B. (*a*) and (*c*) are correct.
C. (*b*) and (*d*) are correct.
D. (*a*) and (*d*) are correct.

28. Identify the popular modes of staff development practised in libraries:
(*a*) Planned rotation
(*b*) Deputing staff to conferences and seminars
(*c*) Sponsoring for refresher courses
(*d*) Making them members of other libraries
Codes:
A. (*a*), (*b*), (*c*) are correct.
B. (*b*), (*c*), (*d*) are correct.
C. (*a*), (*b*), (*d*) are correct.
D. (*a*), (*c*), (*d*) are correct.

29. In thesaurus SN (Scope Note) provides
(*a*) related terms
(*b*) restriction in usage of description
(*c*) brief descriptions of sense or framework in which the terms should be used
(*d*) clarification of ambiguity
Codes:
A. (*a*), (*b*) and (*c*) are correct.
B. (*a*), (*b*) and (*d*) are correct.
C. (*b*), (*c*) and (*d*) are correct.
D. (*a*), (*c*) and (*d*) are correct.

30. A sound marketing plan contains
(*a*) an analysis of macro-environment
(*b*) a SWOT analysis
(*c*) a brief statement of mission
(*d*) an analysis of advertising
Codes:
A. (*a*), (*b*) and (*c*) are correct.
B. (*a*), (*c*) and (*d*) are correct.
C. (*b*), (*c*) and (*d*) are correct.
D. (*a*), (*b*) and (*d*) are correct.

31. LANs are distinguished from other types of Networks by the following characteristics:
(*a*) Full time connectivity to local service.
(*b*) Unlimited geographic operation.
(*c*) Data transfer rate.
(*d*) Low cost and cabling transmission media.
Codes:
A. (*b*), (*c*), (*d*) are correct.
B. (*a*), (*b*), (*c*) are correct.
C. (*a*), (*c*), (*d*) are correct.
D. (*a*), (*b*), (*d*) are correct.

32. Which of the following are the different layers of UNIX operating system?
(*a*) Kernel (*b*) Shell
(*c*) Format (*d*) Application
Codes:
A. (*a*), (*b*) and (*d*) are correct.
B. (*b*), (*c*) and (*d*) are correct.
C. (*a*), (*c*) and (*d*) are correct.
D. (*a*), (*b*) and (*c*) are correct.

49. Match the following authors with the subjects they are associated with:

List-I	*List-II*
(*a*) Peter Suber	(*i*) Management
(*b*) H.E. Bliss	(*ii*) Information Technology
(*c*) Henry Fayol	(*iii*) Classification
(*d*) Tim Berners Lee	(*iv*) Open Access Movement

Codes:

	(*a*)	(*b*)	(*c*)	(*d*)
A.	(*iv*)	(*iii*)	(*i*)	(*ii*)
B.	(*iii*)	(*ii*)	(*i*)	(*iv*)
C.	(*i*)	(*iii*)	(*iv*)	(*ii*)
D.	(*ii*)	(*iv*)	(*iii*)	(*i*)

50. Match the following:

List-I	*List-II*
(*a*) Invenio	(*i*) Course Management System
(*b*) Moodle	(*ii*) Content Management System
(*c*) Share Point	(*iii*) Digital Library System
(*d*) PhpMyAdmn	(*iv*) Web Database Management

Codes:

	(*a*)	(*b*)	(*c*)	(*d*)
A.	(*iii*)	(*i*)	(*ii*)	(*iv*)
B.	(*iv*)	(*i*)	(*ii*)	(*iii*)
C.	(*ii*)	(*i*)	(*iii*)	(*iv*)
D.	(*iv*)	(*iii*)	(*ii*)	(*i*)

51. Match the following:

List-I	*List-II*
(*a*) Histogram	(*i*) Signs and symbols
(*b*) Bar Charts	(*ii*) Data in Circle
(*c*) Pie Chart	(*iii*) Length of the bar
(*d*) Pictogram	(*iv*) Frequency distribution

Codes:

	(*a*)	(*b*)	(*c*)	(*d*)
A.	(*iv*)	(*iii*)	(*ii*)	(*i*)
B.	(*iii*)	(*iv*)	(*ii*)	(*i*)
C.	(*i*)	(*iii*)	(*ii*)	(*iv*)
D.	(*ii*)	(*i*)	(*iii*)	(*iv*)

52. Match the following:

List-I	*List-II*
(*a*) Facebook	(*i*) Video Networking site
(*b*) Research Gate	(*ii*) Social Networking site
(*c*) Oovoo	(*iii*) Academic Networking site
(*d*) Flickr	(*iv*) Photo Networking site

Codes:

	(*a*)	(*b*)	(*c*)	(*d*)
A.	(*i*)	(*iii*)	(*ii*)	(*iv*)
B.	(*iv*)	(*i*)	(*ii*)	(*iii*)
C.	(*ii*)	(*iii*)	(*i*)	(*iv*)
D.	(*iii*)	(*iv*)	(*i*)	(*ii*)

53. Match the following:

List-I	*List-II*
(*a*) Qualitative research	(*i*) Studies different units or culture or social groups
(*b*) Quantitative research	(*ii*) Describes reality as experienced by groups, communities, individuals, etc.
(*c*) Longitudinal research	(*iii*) Employs measurement and statistical analysis
(*d*) Comparative research	(*iv*) Study of the problem or phenomenon over a period of time

Codes:

	(*a*)	(*b*)	(*c*)	(*d*)
A.	(*i*)	(*iv*)	(*iii*)	(*ii*)
B.	(*ii*)	(*iii*)	(*iv*)	(*i*)
C.	(*iii*)	(*ii*)	(*i*)	(*iv*)
D.	(*iv*)	(*i*)	(*ii*)	(*iii*)

54. Match the following:

List-I	*List-II*
(*a*) Ezproxy	(*i*) A community awareness programme
(*b*) Geek the Library	(*ii*) Access and authentification software
(*c*) Outside the box	(*iii*) Online learning place for libraries
(*d*) Web junction	(*iv*) Library focussed community entertainment initiative

Codes:

	(*a*)	(*b*)	(*c*)	(*d*)
A.	(*ii*)	(*i*)	(*iv*)	(*iii*)
B.	(*ii*)	(*i*)	(*iii*)	(*iv*)
C.	(*iv*)	(*iii*)	(*ii*)	(*i*)
D.	(*iii*)	(*i*)	(*iv*)	(*ii*)

55. Match the following:

List-I	List-II
(a) Bhuvan 3D	(i) Operating System
(b) Ubuntu	(ii) ERMS
(c) Urkund	(iii) Geoportal
(d) CORAL	(iv) Anti-plagiarism software

Codes:

	(a)	(b)	(c)	(d)
A.	(i)	(iv)	(iii)	(ii)
B.	(iv)	(ii)	(i)	(iii)
C.	(iii)	(i)	(iv)	(ii)
D.	(iii)	(iv)	(ii)	(i)

56. Match the following:

List-I (Examples)	List-II (Type of Relation)
(a) Relation between political science and history	(i) Influencing
(b) Geopolitics	(ii) Intra-array general relation
(c) Medical Jurisprudence	(iii) Bias
(d) Chemical relation between silver and gold	(iv) General

Codes:

	(a)	(b)	(c)	(d)
A.	(ii)	(iii)	(iv)	(i)
B.	(i)	(iv)	(ii)	(iii)
C.	(iv)	(i)	(iii)	(ii)
D.	(iv)	(i)	(ii)	(iii)

57. Match the following:

List-I	List-II
(a) Super-imposition Device	(i) Treatment of eye disease in children
(b) Subject Device	(ii) Use of '1' for Unity, God, World
(c) Systems & Specials	(iii) Agricultural countries
(d) Mnemonic Device	(iv) British-India

Codes:

	(a)	(b)	(c)	(d)
A.	(iv)	(iii)	(i)	(ii)
B.	(iv)	(iii)	(ii)	(i)
C.	(ii)	(iii)	(i)	(iv)
D.	(i)	(iv)	(ii)	(iii)

58. Match the following:

List-I	List-II
(a) Abstractor	(i) Credible Authors and Publishers
(b) Classifier	(ii) Strong subject base and command over language
(c) Reference Librarian	(iii) Thought contents of documents
(d) Collection Development Manager	(iv) Inquisitive and good psychologists

Codes:

	(a)	(b)	(c)	(d)
A.	(ii)	(iv)	(i)	(iii)
B.	(ii)	(iii)	(iv)	(i)
C.	(iii)	(ii)	(iv)	(i)
D.	(iv)	(ii)	(iii)	(i)

59. Match the following:

List-I	List-II
(a) Greenpilot	(i) Library of Congress
(b) Kalasampada	(ii) Indira Gandhi National Centre for Arts
(c) Gallica	(iii) German National Library of Medicine
(d) SACO	(iv) Bibliotheque Nationale de France

Codes:

	(a)	(b)	(c)	(d)
A.	(i)	(ii)	(iii)	(iv)
B.	(ii)	(iv)	(i)	(iii)
C.	(iii)	(ii)	(i)	(iv)
D.	(iii)	(ii)	(iv)	(i)

60. Assertion (A) : In recent time, it is easier to copy and paste the contents from a digital document for which people knowingly avoid to credit the source. Hence, increased access to digital documents has provided a means for increase of plagiarism.

Reason (R) : Software-assisted detection tools like iThenticate, Turnitin, etc., now allow vast collections of online documents to be compared to each other making successful detection of plagiarism.

Codes:

A. Both (A) and (R) are false.
B. (A) is true, but (R) is false.
C. (R) is true, but (A) is false.
D. Both (A) and (R) are true.

61. Assertion (A) : Maximum use of library resources is the motto of the library.

Reason (R) : It satisfies the fifth law of library science.

Codes:

A. Both (A) and (R) are true.
B. Both (A) and (R) are false.
C. (A) is true, but (R) is false.
D. (A) is false, but (R) is true.

62. Assertion (A) : Not all bibliographic records require a uniform title.

Reason (R) : Most published works are published only once and are never republished and translated.

Codes:

A. Both (A) and (R) are true.
B. Both (A) and (R) are false.
C. (A) is true, but (R) is false.
D. (A) is false, but (R) is true.

63. Assertion (A) : A controlled vocabulary may take some form of classification scheme.

Reason (R) : In a controlled vocabulary semantically related terms are not linked.

Codes:

A. Both (A) and (R) are true.
B. Both (A) and (R) are false.
C. (A) is true, but (R) is false.
D. (A) is false, but (R) is true.

64. Assertion (A) : RDA replaces the General Material Designations (GMD).

Reason (R) : The problem with the GMDs was inconsistent categorization.

Codes:

A. Both (A) and (R) are true.
B. (A) is true, but (R) is false.
C. (A) is false, but (R) is true.
D. Both (A) and (R) are false.

65. Assertion (A) : Precision is the fraction of the documents retrieved that are relevant to the user's information need.

Reason (R) : In practical situations, recall and precision are always inversely related.

Codes:

A. (A) is false, but (R) is true.
B. (A) is true, but (R) is false.
C. Both (A) and (R) are true.
D. Both (A) and (R) are false.

66. Assertion (A) : Dictionary catalogue is very easy to consult.

Reason (R) : Dictionary catalogue consists of author and title entries only.

Codes:

A. (A) is false, but (R) is true.
B. (A) is true, but (R) is false.
C. Both (A) and (R) are true.
D. Both (A) and (R) are false.

67. Assertion (A) : Authority work deals with formulation and recording of authorised access points.

Reason (R) : Without authority control, the burden is placed on user.

Codes:

A. Both (A) and (R) are true.
B. Both (A) and (R) are false.
C. (A) is true, but (R) is false.
D. (A) is false, but (R) is true.

68. Assertion (A) : Google search is considered as the biggest threat to contemporary libraries.

Reason (R) : Now-a-days, users taking help from Reference Librarian for factual queries have considerably decreased.

Codes:

A. Both (A) and (R) are true.
B. Both (A) and (R) are false.
C. (A) is true, but (R) is false.
D. (A) is false, but (R) is true.

69. Assertion (A) : Commercial Library Management Softwares need to be discouraged in libraries to make the contemporary librarians free from the dictate of commercial vendors.

Reason (R) : Open source softwares (OSS) are more flexible and are free from much recurring expenditure and wider user base of OSS helps in problem solving better.

Codes:

A. Both (A) and (R) are true.
B. Both (A) and (R) are false.
C. (A) is true, but (R) is false.
D. (A) is false, but (R) is true.

70. Assertion (A) : Online survey tools such as Survey Monkey and Question Pro have made data collection, analysis and result extraction much easier and simpler.

Reason (R) : Though these tools are being used widely without any doubt in recent time, but social research cannot rely always on the results from an online survey because of their inherent limitations.

Codes:

A. Both (A) and (R) are true.
B. Both (A) and (R) are false.
C. (A) is true, but (R) is false.
D. (R) is true, but (A) is false.

71. Assertion (A) : Technical writing, style manuals and citation standards are essential in structuring the research report.

Reason (R) : The quality of research can be achieved only by standardizing the structure of a research report.

Codes:

A. (A) is true and (R) is false.
B. (A) is false and (R) is true.
C. Both (A) and (R) are true.
D. Both (A) and (R) are false.

72. Assertion (A) : Total quality in organization usually depends upon the skill and competency of library staff.

Reason (R) : Quality management is an information-based management system where professional education alone helps the employee to take decisions judiciously.

Codes:

A. (A) is false, but (R) is true.
B. Both (A) and (R) are true.
C. (A) is true, but (R) is false.
D. Both (A) and (R) are false.

73. Assertion (A) : Libraries must have a well defined collection development policy to make their collection balanced, rational and user-friendly.

Reason (R) : Exponential growth of e-resources, their spiralling cost and decreasing budget of libraries have made consortium based system imminent.

Codes:

A. Both (A) and (R) are true.
B. Both (A) and (R) are false.
C. (A) is true, but (R) is false.
D. (A) is false, but (R) is true.

74. Assertion (A) : There are no problems in a retrieval system in which indexers use natural language terms to describe subject matter.

Reason (R) : The complete text of a document may be stored in a machine readable form.

Codes:

A. Both (A) and (R) are true.
B. Both (A) and (R) are false.
C. (A) is true, but (R) is false.
D. (A) is false, but (R) is true.

75. Assertion (A) : There is no distinction between needs and demands for information services.

Reason (R) : In many situations, the non-active users of a given information service may greatly outnumber the active users.

Codes:

A. Both (A) and (R) are true.
B. Both (A) and (R) are false.
C. (A) is true, but (R) is false.
D. (A) is false, but (R) is true.

ANSWERS

1	2	3	4	5	6	7	8	9	10
B	B	B	C	A	C	C	D	B	C
11	**12**	**13**	**14**	**15**	**16**	**17**	**18**	**19**	**20**
C	D	C	A	D	A	C	C	A	B
21	**22**	**23**	**24**	**25**	**26**	**27**	**28**	**29**	**30**
A	A	B	A	D	B	A	A	C	A
31	**32**	**33**	**34**	**35**	**36**	**37**	**38**	**39**	**40**
C	A	B	C	A	*	B	C	B	C
41	**42**	**43**	**44**	**45**	**46**	**47**	**48**	**49**	**50**
C	B	C	B	A	D	A	A	A	A
51	**52**	**53**	**54**	**55**	**56**	**57**	**58**	**59**	**60**
A	C	B	A	C	C	A	B	D	D
61	**62**	**63**	**64**	**65**	**66**	**67**	**68**	**69**	**70**
C	A	C	A	C	B	A	D	A	A
71	**72**	**73**	**74**	**75**					
A	C	A	D	D					

EXPLANATORY ANSWERS

2. AACR-2R Chapter 9 has been reissued, although "a number of the rules within the chapter do not contain any changes." LC began to apply these revised rules to items cataloged after Nov. 30, 2001. The greatest temptation regarding some of the changes to Chapter 9 is to apply these changes to material in other formats. Do not do this. The changes listed in this section apply only to materials cataloged under Chapter 9. The biggest change is that the entire "Computer files" chapter has been renamed "Electronic resources" and that this terminology change has been made throughout AACR-2R.

4. Dr. A P J Abdul Kalam said the concept of creating village knowledge centre (VKC) was essential for the rural transformation and to become a developed nation by 2020.

"VKC is one of the essential components for realising our goal of graduating into a knowledge society and lead to the transformation of the nation into a developed country before 2020," Kalam said while inaugurating the convocation of National virtual academy for rural transformation.

5. Reference services concept has become common among American librarians since 1876. Reference services theories appeared in 20th century. There are three types of Reference services theories presented by James Wyer In 1930. There were conservative theory, liberal theory and moderate theory. Conservative theory persists on education and guidance instead of boundless help. This theory states that reference work is limited to use the ready reference sources to help the users. Liberal theory focuses on the maximum help. According to this theory reference librarians must apply any approaches to retrieve the information that users need. In fact reference librarians carry out the whole job and reference work takes a long time in many cases. The average of conservative theory and liberal theory is moderate theory which most of reference librarians prefer. In fact this theory results in high costs but the reference librarians can serve more readers (Moradi, 1373). Besides Wyer, other librarianship scientists presented reference services theories. All of them tried to identify the reference services in libraries.

6. Exponential growth occurs when the growth rate of the value of a mathematical function is proportional to the function's current value, resulting in its growth with time being an exponential function. Exponential decay occurs in the same way when the growth rate is negative. In the case of a discrete domain of definition with equal intervals, it is also called geometric growth or geometric decay, the function values forming a geometric progression. In either exponential growth or exponential decay, the ratio of the rate of change of the quantity to its current size remains constant over time.

7. Section 8 in The Right To Information Act, 2005

Section-8. Exemption from disclosure of information.-

1. Notwithstanding anything contained in this Act, there shall be no obligation to give any citizen,-

(*a*) information, disclosure of which would prejudicially affect the sovereignty and integrity of India, the security, strategic, scientific or economic interests of the State, relation with foreign State or lead to incitement of an offence;

(*b*) information which has been expressly forbidden to be published by any court of law or tribunal or the disclosure of which may constitute contempt of court;

(*c*) information, the disclosure of which would cause a breach of privilege of Parliament or the State Legislature;

(*d*) information including commercial confidence, trade secrets or intellectual property, the disclosure of which would harm the competitive position of a third party, unless the competent authority is satisfied that larger public interest warrants the disclosure of such information;

(*e*) information available to a person in his fiduciary relationship, unless the competent authority is satisfied that the larger public interest warrants the disclosure of such information;

(*f*) information received in confidence from foreign government;

(*g*) information, the disclosure of which would endanger the life or physical safety of any person or identify the source of information or assistance given in confidence for law enforcement or security purposes;

(*h*) information which would impede the process of investigation or apprehension or prosecution of offenders;

(*i*) cabinet papers including records of deliberations of the Council of Ministers, Secretaries and other officers: Provided that the decisions of Council of Ministers, the reasons thereof, and the material on the basis of which the decisions were taken shall be made public after the decision has been taken, and the matter is complete, or over: Provided further that those matters which come under the exemptions specified in this section shall not be disclosed;

(*j*) information which relates to personal information the disclosure of which has not relationship to any public activity or interest, or which would cause unwarranted invasion of the privacy of the individual unless the Central Public Information Officer or the State Public Information Officer or the appellate authority, as the case may be, is satisfied that the larger public interest justifies the disclosure of such information: Provided that the information, which cannot be denied to the Parliament or a State Legislature shall not be denied to any person.

2. Notwithstanding anything in the Official Secrets Act, 1923 (19 of 1923) nor any of the exemptions permissible in accordance with sub-section (1), a public authority may allow access to information, if public interest in disclosure outweighs the harm to the protected interests.

3. Subject to the provisions of clauses (a), (c) and (i) of sub-section (1), any information relating to any occurrence, event or matter which has taken place, occurred or happened twenty years before the date on which any request is made under section 6 shall be provided to any person making a request under that section: Provided that where any question arises as to the date from which the said period of twenty years has to be computed, the decision of the Central Government shall be final, subject to the usual appeals provided for in this Act.

8. The World Digital Library (WDL) is a project of the U.S. Library of Congress, carried out with the support of the United Nations Educational, Cultural and Scientific Organization (UNESCO), and in cooperation with libraries, archives, museums, educational institutions, and international organizations from around the world.

The WDL makes available on the Internet, free of charge and in multilingual format, significant primary materials from all countries and cultures.

The principal objectives of the WDL are to:

- Promote international and intercultural understanding;
- Expand the volume and variety of cultural content on the Internet;
- Provide resources for educators, scholars, and general audiences;
- Build capacity in partner institutions to narrow the digital divide within and between countries.

9. Siyali Ramamrita Ranganathan (S.R.R.) 12 August 1892 - 27 September 1972) was a mathematician and librarian from India. His most notable contributions to the field were his five laws of library science and the development of the first major faceted classification system, the colon classification. He is considered to be the father of library science, documentation, and information science in India and is widely known throughout the rest of the world for his fundamental thinking in the field. His birthday is observed every year as the National Library Day in India.

10. JournalSeek is an online database covering academic journals. It includes journals published by over 5400 publishers. The database includes journal descriptions and links to the journals' homepages.

11. The Indian National Bibliography has been conceived as an authoritative bibliographical record of current Indian publications in Assamese, Bengali, English, Gujarati, Hindi, Kannada, Malayalam, Marathi, Oriya, Punjabi, Sanskrit, Tamil, Telugu and Urdu languages, received in the National Library, Kolkata under the Delivery of Books and Newspapers, (Public Libraries) Act, 1954 (Act No. 27 of 1954 as amended by Act No. 9 of 1956).

The following types of publications are excluded:

(*i*) Maps

(*ii*) Musical scores

(*iii*) Periodicals and Newspapers (except the first issue of a new periodical and the first issue of a periodical under a new title)

(*iv*) Keys and Guides to Textbooks

(*v*) Ephemeral and other such materials.

12. William Charles Berwick Sayers, an English librarian and teacher of S.R. Ranganathan made a remarkable contribution to the development of the theory of classification. He is referred to as the first grammarian of library classification. He is responsible for interpreting and systematising the ideas of other theoreticians. He never designed any classification scheme, though, through his theory he has shown the way for others in the designing of classification schemes. His theory of book classification first appeared in 1915 under the title "Canons of Classification". He expanded the outline of the theory contained in this book in three other books, viz., *Grammar of Classification* (Ed.2, 1915; Ed.4, 1935), *Introduction to Library Classification* (Ed.1,1918; Ed.9,1958) and *Manual of Library Classification* (ed.l, 1926; Ed.3, 1955; Ed.4, 1967 and Ed.5, 1975, revised by Arthur Maltby). It has now been revised by Rita Marcella and Robert Newton in 1994.

13. MARC-Information concerning the related main series when the target item is a subseries (vertical relationship). When a note is generated from this field, the introductory phrase *Main series:* or *Subseries of:* may be generated based on the field tag for display.

14. Dr E.F. Codd, also known to the world as the 'Father of Database Management Systems' had propounded 12 rules which are in-fact 13 in number. The rules are numbered from zero to twelve. According to him, a DBMS is fully relational if it abides by all his twelve rules. Till now, only few databases abide by all the eleven rules. His twelve rules are fondly called 'E.F. Codd's Twelve Commandments'. His brilliant and seminal research paper 'A Relational Model of Data for Large Shared Data Banks' in its entirety is a visual treat to eyes.

15. LibriVox is a group of worldwide volunteers who read and record public domain texts creating free public domain audiobooks for download from their website and other digital library hosting sites on the internet. It was founded in 2005 by Hugh McGuire to provide "Acoustical liberation of books in the public domain" and the LibriVox objective is "To make all books in the public domain available, for free, in audio format on the internet".

On 6 August 2016, the project completed project number 10,000. Most releases are in the English language, but many non-English works are also available. There are multiple affiliated projects that are providing additional content. LibriVox is closely affiliated with Project Gutenberg from where the project gets some of its texts, and the Internet Archive that hosts their offerings.

17. Gang plank: For overcoming this limitation of scalar chain, Henery Fayol introduced the concept of 'Gang Plank'. According to this concept, two executives of the organization of different department at the same level can communicate directly in case of emergency, so that speedy decisions and actions could be taken. In case of the above example, if employee 'C' has to contact employee 'G', he can easily and directly communicate the information to 'G' using this Gang plank ('C' → 'G'). This reduces a lot of time and helps in effective performance.

18. Facebook is a social networking company that has acquired more than 50 companies, including WhatsApp. The WhatsApp acquisition closed at a steep $19 billion; more than $40 per user of the platform. Facebook also purchased the defunct company ConnectU in a court settlement and acquired intellectual property formerly held by rival Friendster. The majority of the companies acquired by Facebook are based in the United States, and in turn, a large percentage of these companies are based in or around the San Francisco Bay Area. Facebook has also made investments in LuckyCal and Wildfire Interactive.

Most of Facebook's acquisitions have been 'talent acquisitions' and acquired products are often shut-down. Facebook CEO Mark Zuckerberg has stated that "We have not once bought a company for the company. We buy companies to get excellent people... In order to have a really entrepreneurial culture one of the key things is to make sure we're recruiting the best people. One of the ways to do this is to focus on acquiring great companies with great founders.". The Instagram acquisition, announced on 9 April, 2012, appears to be the first exception to this pattern.

19. Consortium for e-Resources in Agriculture (CeRA) is an e-Consortium of Agricultural Libraries under the Indian Council of Agricultural Research for National Agricultural Research System (NARS) libraries. This article describes the background, main features, advantages and use of e-journals (subscribed by CeRA) by the users of NARS institutes/ universities. Besides covering the use of e-journals, the article also examines the utilization and satisfaction levels of users accessing e-journals. Lastly, some cost avoidance analysis and research productivity analysis are also highlighted.

20. LOCKSS (Lots of Copies Keep Stuff Safe), established in 1998 under the auspices of Stanford University, develops and supports open-source software for digital preservation based on a distributed network of preservation appliances running a sophisticated voting protocol. Originally designed to preserve scholarly journals, the LOCKSS technology is now being used to preserve electronic theses and dissertations, government documents, books, blogs, websites, image collections, etc. The LOCKSS Program also runs its own preservation network.

Prior to implementing a LOCKSS system, some questions need to be considered carefully in order to make sure the content is verified, evaluated, and auditable by users. The user must ask questions such as, "What are your procedures?", "What are your methods?", "How is this system evaluated?", and "What is your disaster preparedness program?". These questions will enable the user to evaluate the system, create a successful maintenance plan for their materials, and enable the system to be reinforced by a carefully evaluated support structure.

The source code for the entire LOCKSS system carries BSD-style open-source licenses and is available from SourceForge. LOCKSS is a trademark of Stanford University.

22. **Raja Ram Mohan Roy Library Foundation (RRRLF):** The year 1972 was the year of celebration of the bicentenary of Raja Ram Mohan Roy, a great social reformer. The government of India decided that a library foundation would be the best tribute to the memory of Raja Ram Mohan Roy, who spent his life in fighting against forces that shackle and retard the progress of a society. Thus,

Raja Ram Mohan Roy Library Foundation was set up by the government of India in 1972 as an autonomous body under the then Department of Culture, Ministry of Education and Social welfare with its headquarters in Calcutta.

RRRLF functions as a promotional agency, an advisory and consultancy organization, a funding body for public library development in India. Some important objectives are:

- To promote library movement in the country.
- To enunciate a national library policy and to help build up a national library system.
- To provide financial and technical assistance to libraries.
- To provide financial assistance to organisations, regional or national engaged in the promotion of library development.
- To publish appropriate literature and to act as a clearing house of ideas and information on library development in India and abroad.
- To promote research in problems of library development.
- To advise the government on all matters pertaining to the library development in the country.

24. The National Library Medicine (NLM) in Bethesda, Maryland, is a part of the National Institutes Health, U.S. Department of Health and Human Services (HHS). Since its founding in 1836 as the library of the U.S. Army Surgeon General, NLM has played a pivotal role in translating biomedical research in to practice. It is the world's largest biomedical library and the developer of electronic information service that deliver trillion of bytes of data to million of users every day. Scientists health professionals, and the public in the United States and around the globe search the Library's online information resources more than 1 billion times each year.

The Library is open to all and has many services and resources - for scientists, health professionals, historians, and the general public. NLM has nearly 22 million books, journals, manuscripts, audio-visuals, and other forms of medical information on its shelves, making it the largest health–science library in the world.

Important Events in NLM History–

- 1836 : Library of the office of the Surgeon General of the Army (the present National Library of Medicine) established.
- 1879 : First volume of Index Medicus Published.
- 1952 : Army Medical Library renamed Armed Forces Medical Library.
- 1967 : Toxicology Information Program established at NLM in response to recommendations of the President's Science Advisory Committee.
- 1972 : Toxline, an online bibliographic service covering pharmacology and toxicology, become operational.
- 1986 : Grateful Med-PC-based, user-friendly software for accessing MEDLARS–was introduced to the health community.
- 1993 : NLM's Internet World Wide Website (www.nlm. nih. gov) appeared.
- 1997 : Web based access to NLM's MEDLINE became available free of charge.
- 1998 : Medline Plus created to provide access to consumer health information.
- 2000 : PubMed Central, a free archive of biomedical and life sciences journal literature, launched. In keeping with NLM's legislative mandate to collect and preserve the biomedical literature, PMC serves as a digital counterpart to NLM's extensive print journal collection.
- 2006 : NIH Medline plus magazine launched to provide Americans with reliable, up-to-date health information in a consumer-friendly format.
- 2010 : Mobile Medlineplus released and Emergency Access Initiative (EAI) launched. Vocabulary standards supported

or developed by NLM (LOINC, RxNorm, SNOMED CT) include in rule specifying certification criteria for electronic health record systems that Medicare and Medicaid providers must use to be eligible for "meaningful use" incentives included in the American Recovery and Revitalization Act of 2009.

25. **e-ShodhSindhu** : Based on the recommendation of an Expert Committee, the MHRD has formed e-ShodhSindhu merging three consortia initiatives, *viz.,* UGC-INFONET Digital Library Consortium, NLIST and INDEST-AICTE Consortium.The e-ShodhSindhu will continue to provide current as well as archival access to more than 15,000 core and peer-reviewed journals and a number of bibliographic, citation and factual databases in different disciplines from a large number of publishers and aggregators to its member institutions including centrally-funded technical institutions, universities and colleges that are covered under 12(B) and 2(f) Sections of the UGC Act.

31. LAN (Local Area Network) refers to a particular region interconnected by multiple computers into computer groups. "A region" refers to the same office, the same building, the same company and in the same schools, generally within a radius of several kilometres. You can provide different services like document management, application software sharing, printer sharing, scanner sharing, workgroup scheduling, e-mail and fax communications services and other VOIP and unified communication.

LAN has the following characteristics:

- Coverage area is generally a few kilometres.
- Using different dedicated transmission medium you can achieve the transmission rate of 1 Mb/s to 100 Mbit / sec or higher, with the further development of LAN technology is currently being developed towards higher speed (*e.g.,* 155 Mbps, 655 Mbps and 1000 Mbps, etc.).
- In LAN you can run the multiple devices to share a transmission medium.
- You can use the different topology mainly bus and ring in LAN.
- The communication quality is better in LAN, the transmission error rate is low as compared to WAN.
- LAN supports a variety of communications transmission medium such as Ethernet cable (thin cable, thick cable, and twisted pair), fiber and wireless transmission.
- A LAN usually has low cost, installation, expansion and maintenance and LAN installation is relatively simple, good scalability.

32. In general, the UNIX operating system is made up of three parts; the kernel, the shell, and the programs.

The kernel : If we think of the UNIX operating system in terms of layers, the kernel is the lowest layer. It interfaces directly with the computer hardware and is responsible for allocating and managing the resouces available to programs. It allocates processor time and memory to each program and determines when each program will run. The kernel also provides an interface to programs whereby they may access files, the network, and devices.

The shell : The shell acts as an interface between the user and the kernel. When a user logs in, the login program checks the username and password, and then starts another program called the shell. The shell is a command line interpreter (CLI). It interprets the commands the user types in and executes them. The commands are themselves programs. Once programs terminate, control is returned to the shell and the user receives another prompt ($ on our systems), indicating that another command may be entered.

The programs : One of the main features of UNIX is that it includes a variety of small programs to meet various needs. Typically, each of these programs does one thing and does it well. This modular design allows the functionality of small programs to be mixed and matched. As you become more familiar with UNIX, you will find that this design provides you great flexibility and power to accomplish almost any task. Typically these programs operate on top of the shell, but they may also interface directly with the kernel.

33. Web 3.0 Technologies in today's Internet dominated world, every business organization has recognized the need for having an effective Web 3.0 site. In the present always-on world, a company's website plays a very critical role in competing with others and in attaining success. The following are some of the technologies employed in Web 3.0: Artificial Intelligence. • Automated reasoning. • Cognitive architecture. • Composite applications. • Distributed computing. • Knowledge representation. • Ontology (computer service). • Recombinant text. • Scalable vector graphics. • Semantic Web. • Semantic wiki, and • Software agent. • Some of the examples of Web 3.0 sites are iGoogle, Net Vibes, Dig, Flicker, Delicious.

37. Radhakrishnan education commission (1948-49): University education commission 1948-49 also know as Radhakrishnan commission which was the first education commission set up in independent india.

Ranganathan Committee : This is a detailed study of the college library situation in India. It points out that in India the importance of library in higher education was emphasized by many educationists, experts and committees from 1950 and of them Ranganathan Committee (1958) of UGC.

K.P.Sinha Committee : As per the Recommendation at a Seminar on 'Role of Libraries in Social Education' organized by India Adult Education Association at Delhi in the year 1955, the Ministry of Education, the Government of India appointed Library Advisory Committee in 1957 to report on the status of public library development in the country. The Library Advisory Committee or Sinha Committee, after its chair, the late Dr. K.P. Sinha, who was at that time Director of Public Instruction in Bihar. This committee recommended the need for library legislation for each state. It is the first report of the Post Independent India which deals extensively with the issues related to the development of public libraries in India.

Indian Education Commission (1964-1966), popularly known as Kothari Commission, was an ad hoc commission set up by the Government of India to examine all aspects of the educational sector in India, to evolve a general pattern of education and to advise guidelines and policies for the development of education in India. It was formed on 14 July 1964 under the chairmanship of Daulat Singh Kothari, then chairman of the University Grants Commission. The terms of reference of the commission was to formulate the general principles and guidelines for the development of education from primary level to the highest and advise the government on a standardized national pattern of education in India.

44.
- The .dbf file extension represents the dBASE database file. The file type was introduced in 1983 with the introduction of dBASE II. The file structure has evolved over the years to include many more features and capabilities and has introduced various other files to help support data storage and manipulation. The current .dbf file level is called Level 7. The .dbf format is supported by a number of database products.
- DB is a database file format for Windows. DB files store data information, usually stored in a series of tables, table fields, and field data values. The information is then stored and organized according to

the data model, the most common model structure being the relational model. DB files can be created using database software like Microsoft Access and Filemaker Pro. DB files can be exported in .CSV format using these programs.

- The dbk file extension is associated with dBase database management system from dataBased Intelligence developed for various platforms and operating systems.

  A dbk file contains database backup created in the program.

46. ANDHRA PRADESH : The state Andhra was formed on 1st October, 1953, comprising Telugu speaking areas of the erstwhile Madras Presidency. Later Andhra and Telangana areas merged as Andhra Pradesh State from 1st November 1956 under the States Reorganization Act of 1956. Its capital is Hyderabad. When Andhra Pradesh was formed, the Madras Public Libraries Act of 1948 was in force in Andhra area and Hyderabad Public Libraries Act 1955 was in force in Telangana area. So, both the Acts were amalgamated, modified, brought up to date, and passed as an integrated act, *i.e.,* Andhra Pradesh Public Libraries Act, 1960, which came into force from 1st April 1960, for entire Andhra Pradesh. A separate and independent directorate has been established in the year 1961. It is under the Administrative control of Hon'ble Minister of School Education of Primary Education. This act was later amended in 1964, 1969, 1987 and in 1989. Andhra Pradesh has a good Public Library system with State Central Library, Regional Libraries, District Central Libraries and branches and a full time Director to control the system.

ARUNACHAL PRADESH : Part of the original North-East Frontier Agency (NEFA) was reconstituted to form the Arunachal Pradesh State on 20th February 1987. After the formation of the State, in 1978 the Secretariat Library was converted into the State Central Library. Presently there are one State Central Library, its two branches, 16 District Libraries, 3 Divisional Libraries, 13 Sub-divisional Libraries, 26 Block Libraries and 30 Circle Libraries. Mobile library service was introduced in the capital city through automobile van. There are District Libraries in all district headquarters. However, there is no initiative for the Public Library Act so far.

ODISHA : Odisha has a significant historical background harping back to the reign of the Kalinga Dynasty. It was made a province during British rule in 1936. With Independence, the Princely states in and around Odisha were merged into the State. Having a rich cultural tradition, Odisha had libraries from an early period. During the Fifth Five-year Plan, the Government of Odisha (then) started district libraries in all district headquarters. A new building was constructed for the State Central Library, named after Hare Krishna Mehatab, at Bhubaneswar. During the seventh Plan period, a proposal has been made to set up sub-divisional libraries and local libraries. The Utkal Library Association, formed in 1944, played a great role in sprouting the seed of library legislation in Odisha. This association has submitted a draft of the Library Act on the floor of the Odisha Legislative Assembly as a private Bill, which was introduced in the House on 25th March 1988.

WEST BENGAL : After many changes, the State of West Bengal in its present form came into existence from 1956. Its capital is Kolkata and it has 18 districts with an area of 88,752 sq. km. Kumar Munindra Deb Roy Mahasay of Bansberia Raj, a pioneer of the Indian Library movement, was a lover of books and libraries. He made modifications to the Model Act drafted by Dr S R Ranganathan to suit Bengal and tried to introduce it in the Assembly. The Bengal Library Association gave a draft of the Bill to the new Government. Shri Partha De, who later became the First Minister for Library Services of the State, personally took a lot of trouble in enacting the law. The Bengal Public Libraries Act was passed in the Assembly on 12th September 1979.

47. IFLA - The International Federation of Library Associations and Institutions (IFLA) is the leading international body representing the interests of library and information services and their users. It is the global voice of the library and information profession.

Founded in Edinburgh, Scotland, in 1927 at an international conference, we celebrated our 75th birthday at our conference in Glasgow, Scotland in 2002. We now have over 1300 Members in approximately 140 countries around the world. IFLA was registered in the Netherlands in 1971. The Royal Library, the national library of the Netherlands, in The Hague, generously provides the facilities for our headquarters.

OCLC : The Online Computer Library Center (OCLC) is a nonprofit cooperative organization "dedicated to the public purposes of furthering, access to the world's information and reducing information costs". It was founded in 1967 as the Ohio College Library Center. OCLC and its member libraries cooperatively produce and maintain WorldCat, the largest online public access catalog (OPAC) in the world. OCLC has completed a year-long renovation to its headquarters in Dublin, Ohio, a project to not only repair the 35-year-old structure but also to purposefully update the environment to support a vibrant, innovative space for staff and member libraries.

RLIN : The Research Libraries Group (RLG) was a U.S.-based library consortium. They developed the Eureka interlibrary search engine, the Red Light Green database of bibliographic descriptions, and ArchiveGrid, a database containing descriptions of archival collections. RLG was founded by a group of major research libraries in 1974, two years after OCLC, another library consortium, was founded. A major reason for RLG's establishment was dissatisfaction among research institutions with OCLC's record keeping.

The Research Libraries Group's conspectus is still posted at the Library of Congress. This is a helpful scale for judging an academic collection's depth.

The founding libraries were New York Public Library and the university libraries of Columbia, Harvard and Yale. RLG moved its offices to Stanford University in 1978 and adopted Stanford Library's BALLOTS computerized processing system. This system evolved into the online database, RLIN. RLIN was generally only for use by library specialists. In 1993 RLG developed Eureka as a user-friendly interface for use by non-librarians. RLG expanded its membership to other research libraries throughout the U.S. and in 1992 the British Library became the first non-North American member.

In June 2006, RLG merged with OCLC. Its catalog became a part of OCLC's WorldCat. Its current programs joined with OCLC Research to become OCLC Programs and Research . Eureka databases were migrated to OCLC's FirstSearch service. The office was relocated from Mountain View, California to San Mateo, California.

UTLAS Inc., had its beginnings in the mid-1960s at the university of Toranto, where it started as one of Canada's most ambitions library data processing efforts. The university spum off UTLAS as a separate nonprofit corporation in 1971.

49. Peter Suber, widely considered to be the de facto leader of the worldwide open-access movement, is Director of the Harvard Office for Scholarly Communication, Director of the Harvard Open Access Project, Faculty Fellow at the Berkman Center, Senior Researcher at SPARC, and Research Professor of Philosophy at Earlham College. He is the author of *Open Access* (MIT Press), named by *Choice* as an Outstanding Academic Title for 2013.

Henry Evelyn Bliss was the author of a classification system he called *Bibliographic Classification* which is often abbreviated to BC and is sometimes called Bliss Classification. He was named one of the 100 most important leaders in the field of Library and Information Science in the 20th century by American Libraries in December 1999, which praised his "subject approach to information" as "one of the most flexible ever conceived." Despite these praises, Bliss was "met with apathy and even derision in his efforts" during his lifetime.

Henri Fayol was a French mining engineer, mining executive, author and director of mines who developed a general theory of business administration that is often called Fayolism. He and his colleagues developed this theory independently of scientific management but roughly contemporaneously. Like his contemporary, Frederick Winslow Taylor, he is widely acknowledged as a founder of modern management methods.

Tim Berners Lee, also known as TimBL, is an English computer scientist, best known as the inventor of the World Wide Web. He made a proposal for an information management system in March 1989, and he implemented the first successful communication between a Hypertext Transfer Protocol (HTTP) client and server via the Internet sometime around mid-November of that same year.

50. Invenio is an open source software library management package that provides the tools for management of digital assets in an institutional repository. The software is typically used for open access repositories for scholarly and/or published digital content and as a digital library.

Invenio is developed by the CERN Document Server Software Consortium and is freely available for download.

Moodle is a free and open-source software learning management system written in PHP and distributed under the GNU General Public License. Developed on pedagogical principles, Moodle is used for blended learning, distance education, flipped classroom and other e-learning projects in schools, universities, workplaces and other sectors.

With customizable management features, it is used to create private websites with online courses for educators and trainers to achieve learning goals. Moodle (acronym for modular object-oriented dynamic learning environment) allows for extending and tailoring learning environments using community sourced plugins.

SharePoint is a web-based application that integrates with Microsoft Office. Launched in 2001, SharePoint is primarily sold as a document management and storage system, but the product is highly configurable and usage varies substantially between organizations.

PhpMyAdmin is one of the most popular applications for MySQL databases management. It is a free tool written in PHP. Through this software you can create, alter, drop, delete, import and export MySQL database tables. You can run MySQL queries, optimize, repair and check tables, change collation and execute other database management commands.

All the SiteGround clients can manage their MySQL databases through the preinstalled PhpMyAdmin software which is integrated in cPanel. Check our PhpMyAdmin hosting for more details.

In this tutorial we will show how to use PhpMyAdmin and manage your MySQL databases through it.

51. • A histogram is a graphical representation of the distribution of numerical data. It is an estimate of the probability distribution of a continuous variable (quantitative variable) and was first introduced by Karl Pearson. To construct a histogram, the first step is to "bin" the range of values—that is, divide the entire range of values into a series of intervals—and then count how many values fall into each interval. The bins are usually specified as consecutive, non-overlapping intervals of a variable. The bins (intervals) must be adjacent, and are often (but are not required to be) of equal size.

- A bar chart or bar graph is a chart or graph that presents grouped data with rectangular bars with lengths proportional to the values that they represent. The bars can be plotted vertically or horizontally. A vertical bar chart is sometimes called a Line graph.

  A bar graph is a chart that uses either horizontal or vertical bars to show comparisons among categories. One axis of the chart shows the specific categories being compared, and the other axis represents a discrete value. Some bar graphs present bars clustered in groups of more than one.

- A pie chart (or a circle chart) is a circular statistical graphic which is divided into slices to illustrate numerical proportion. In a pie chart, the arc length of each slice (and consequently its central angle and area), is proportional to the quantity it represents. While it is named for its resemblance to a pie which has been sliced, there are variations on the way it can be presented. The earliest known pie chart is generally credited to William Playfair's Statistical Breviary of 1801.

  Pie charts are very widely used in the business world and the mass media. However, they have been criticized, and many experts recommend avoiding them, pointing out that research has shown it is difficult to compare different sections of a given pie chart, or to compare data across different pie charts. Pie charts can be replaced in most cases by other plots such as bar chart, box plot or dot plots.

- A pictogram, also called a pictogramme pictograph, or simply picto, and in computer usage an icon, is an ideogram that conveys its meaning through its pictorial resemblance to a physical object Pictographs are often used in writing and graphic systems in which the characters are to a considerable extent pictorial in appearance. A pictogram may also be used in subjects such as leisure, tourism and geography.

  Pictography is a form of writing which uses representational, pictorial drawings, simila to cuneiform and, to some extent hieroglyphic writing, which also uses drawings as phonetic letters o determinative rhymes. Some pictograms such as Hazards pictograms, are element of formal languages.

52.

- Facebook is an American for-profi corporation and online social media and social networking service based in Menlo Park, California. The Facebook website wa launched on February 4, 2004, by Mark Zuckerberg, along with fellow Harvard College students and roommates, Eduardo Saverin, Andrew McCollum, Dustin Moskovitz, and Chris Hughes.

- ResearchGate is a social networking site for scientists and researchers to share papers ask and answer questions, and find collaborators. According to a study b Nature and an article in Times Highe Education, it is the largest academic socia network in terms of active users, althoug other services have more registered user and more recent data suggests that almos as many academics have Google Schola profiles.

- ooVoo is a video chat and an instan messaging client developed by ooVoo LLC for Microsoft Windows, Windows Phone Mac OS X, Android, iOS and Facebook. I was released in 2007, and is similar in som ways to Microsoft's Skype.

- Flickr (pronounced "flicker") is an image hosting and video hosting website and web services suite that was created by Ludicorp in 2004 and acquired by Yahoo on March 20, 2005. In addition to being a popular website for users to share and embed personal photographs, and effectively an online community, the service is widely used by photo researchers and by bloggers to host images that they embed in blogs and social media.

54. • EZproxy is a web proxy server used by libraries to give access from outside the library's computer network to restricted-access websites that authenticate users by IP address. This allows library patrons at home or elsewhere to log in through their library's EZproxy server and gain access to bibliographic databases and the like to which their library subscribes.

- The software was originally written by Chris Zagar in 1999 who founded Useful Utilities LLC to support it. The software is sometimes confused with generic proxy server software designed to control web access. It is sometimes referred to as a "proxy referral" server to distinguish it.

- Geek the Library was a campaign designed to highlight the vital role of public libraries and raise awareness about the critical funding issues many libraries face. This campaign was developed based on the research findings included in From Awareness to Funding: A study of library support in America. This study, published by OCLC in 2008, found that increasing funding support for public libraries requires changing community perceptions.

- Welcome to the learning management site for WebJunction's continuing education opportunities. Access to Web Junction's library-specific courses and webinar archives is available for free to all library workers and volunteers. Through the generous support of OCLC, the Gates Foundation, and many state library agencies across the U.S., WebJunction provides timely and relevant learning content for you to access anytime, from anywhere.

- All new learners will need to create an account. Begin by selecting "Log in" at the top right of this page, and then "Create new account." Once you've created your new account, explore the catalog of library-focused self-paced courses and webinars. Certificates of completion will be available to you after you have completed any course or webinar that you enroll in from the catalog.

55. • Bhuvan, is a software application which allows users to explore a 2D/3D representation of the surface of the Earth. The browser is specifically tailored to view India, offering the highest resolution in this region and providing content in four local languages. A beta version was launched on 12 August 2009.

Apart from visualization Bhuvan provides timely disaster support services (domestic and international), free satellite data and a products download facility, and rich thematic datasets. Bhuvan is using a crowdsourcing approach to enrich its maps and collect point of interest data. It also acts as a platform for hosting government data (example - Karnataka Forest Department datasets).

- Plagiarism detection is the process of locating instances of plagiarism within a work or document. The widespread use of computers and the advent of the Internet has made it easier to plagiarize the work of others. Most cases of plagiarism are found in academia, where documents are typically essays or reports. However, plagiarism can be found in virtually any field, including novels, scientific papers, art designs, and source code. Detection of plagiarism can be either manual or software-assisted. Manual detection requires substantial effort and excellent memory, and is impractical in cases where too many documents must be compared, or original documents are not available for comparison. Software-assisted detection allows vast collections of documents to be compared to each other, making successful detection much more likely. The practice of plagiarizing by use of sufficient word substitutions to elude detection software is known as rogeting.

- Ubuntu is a community driven question and answer website for the Ubuntu operating system. It is part of the Stack Exchange Network, running the same software as Stack Overflow. Members gain reputation based on the community's response (through voting) to their questions and answers. Reputation signifies trust for users in the answers they give. Privileges are given based on reputation levels, with users with the highest reputation having similar privileges to moderators. The site came out of public beta on 10 October 2010, launching alongside Ubuntu 10.10.

- CORAL is an electronic resource management system built by the University of Notre Dame's Hesburgh Libraries. The first module, Licensing, was released as open source software in the summer of 2010 and we have continued releasing new modules since then. It is designed to be both simple and highly customizable—each module can be installed independently or used together depending on your library's needs. If you do decide to install the entire suite, easy access to linked records helps make sense of the electronic resource through the entire life cycle.

59. • The online portal Greenpilot is a service provided by the German National Library of Medicine, ZB MED.

The project is funded by the German Research Foundation and gets its technical support from Averbis Ltd. The portal first went online May 29, 2009 and currently runs in the updated beta version. In the context of the 'Germany - Land of Ideas' (Deutschland - Land der Ideen) initiative under the patronage of the President of Germany Horst Köhler the ZB MED was awarded the distinction 'Selected Landmark 2009' (Ausgewählter Ort 2009).

- KALASAMPADA-Recognizing the need to encompass and preserve the distributed fragments of Indian art and culture, and to serve as a major resource centre for the arts, the Indira Gandhi National Centre for the Arts (IGNCA) in collaboration with Ministry of Communication and Information Technology, initiated a project, KALASAMPDA (Digital Library: Resources of Indian Cultural Heritage), for the development of databank of cultural heritage. Kalasampada facilitating the scholars (users) to access and view the materials including over couple of lakhs of manuscripts, over a lakhs of slides, thousands of rare books, rare photographs, audio and video along with highly researched publications of the IGNCA, from a single window.

- Gallica est la bibliothèque numérique de la Bibliothèque nationale de France. En libre accès, elle regroupe des livres numérisés, des cartulaires, des revues, des photos et une collection d'enluminures.

- SACO : The Subject Authority Cooperative Program (SACO) enables member institutions to submit subject heading proposals for inclusion in Library of Congress Subject Headings (LCSH), and classification number proposals for inclusion in Library of Congress Classification (LCC) schedules.

Previous Papers (Solved)

UGC-NET/JRF & Assistant Professor Exam
LIBRARY AND INFORMATION SCIENCE, December-2015

PAPER-II

Note : *This paper contains **fifty (50)** objective type questions of **two (2)** marks each. All questions are **compulsory.***

1. The Class Index entries which are derived from the class number of a document in classified catalogue are based upon:
A. Unsought Links B. Missing Links
C. False Links D. Sought Links

2. Mode of formation of subject 'Oceanography' is:
A. Distilization B. Cluster
C. Agglomeration D. Loose Assemblage

3. 'Half-life' in Information Science relates to:
A. Rate of obsolescence
B. Rate of growth
C. Degree of scatter
D. Information explosion

4. As per Indian Copyright Law, Copyright is granted for (Literary Work):
A. Fifty years after the book is published
B. Fifty years after the death of the author
C. Sixty years after the book is published
D. Sixty years after the death of the author

5. Who chaired the Committee set up in October 1984 to formulate the 'National Policy for Library and Information System' constituted by the Dept. of Culture, Govt. of India?
A. Dr. S.R. Ranganathan
B. Dr. C.D. Deshmukh
C. B.S. Kesavan
D. Prof. D.P. Chattopadhya

6. Ratnasagar, Ratnaranjaka and Ratnodadhi Library buildings were the part of:
A. Vikramashila Learning Centre
B. Takshashila Learning Centre
C. Nalanda Learning Centre
D. Vallabhi Learning Centre

7. What type of information sources are Almanacs?
A. Ready Reference B. Dictionary
C. Directory D. Bibliographics

8. Which of the following is not an essential feature of an e-book?
A. Mostly cost effective
B. Scope for online purchase
C. Search information at ease
D. Access at slow pace

9. A database contains 100 records on a particular topic. A search was conducted and 80 records were retrieved. Of the 80 records retrieved, 60 were relevant. What is the recall?
A. 60 B. 75
C. 45 D. 80

10. Who was the teacher of S.R. Ranganathan at London?
A. J.D. Brown
B. A. Panizzi
C. W.C. Berwick Sayers
D. Melvil Dewey

11. The seven basic statistical tools for quality control was advocated by:
A. Joseph Jurnan B. Phillip Kotler
C. Kaoru Ishikawa D. C.A. Cutter

12. Which layer of 'OSI' Model occurs between 'Network' and 'Physical'?
A. Data Link B. Transport
C. Session D. Presentation

13. 'Number Twenty (20)' is represented in binary digit as:
A. 00111100 B. 00001010
C. 0001110 D. 00010100

14. Action research is:
A. An applied research
B. A Longitudinal research
C. A research carried out to solve immediate problems
D. Simulative research

15. Lotka's Law relates to:
A. Scattering of Periodicals
B. Obsolescence of Literature
C. Seepage of Information
D. Scientific Productivity

16. According to Dr. S.R. Ranganathan 'Library Civics and Hygiene' means:
(*a*) Library behaviour (*b*) Library Layout
(*c*) Physique of Book (*d*) Care of Book
Codes:
A. (*a*), (*b*) and (*d*) are correct
B. (*d*), (*b*) and (*c*) are correct
C. (*a*), (*c*) and (*d*) are correct
D. (*a*), (*b*) and (*c*) are correct

17. Which of the following are not the Working Groups under National Mission on Libraries?
(*a*) National Census of Libraries, Content Creation and Community Information Centres.
(*b*) Setting up of National Virtual Library, Networking and ICT Applications in Libraries.
(*c*) Library and Information Science Research, Development and Accreditation.
(*d*) Upgradation of the Existing Academic Libraries, University and Research Libraries.
Codes:
A. (*a*), (*b*) are correct B. (*b*), (*c*) are correct
C. (*c*), (*d*) are correct D. (*a*), (*d*) are correct

18. Which among the following are true about publication element of ISBN?
(*a*) Variable Length (*b*) Upto 5 digits
(*c*) Fixed Length (*d*) Upto 6 digits
Codes:
A. (*a*), (*d*) are correct
B. (*a*), (*b*), (*d*) are correct
C. (*b*), (*c*), (*d*) are correct
D. (*a*), (*c*) are correct

19. Which of the following are uses of work analysis?
(*a*) Simplifying the procedures
(*b*) Line of authority
(*c*) Improvement in various processes
(*d*) Unity of Command
Codes:
A. (*b*), (*d*) are correct
B. (*a*), (*b*), (*c*) are correct
C. (*a*), (*d*) are correct
D. (*a*), (*c*) are correct

20. Which of the following are Impact Printers?
(*a*) Inkjet (*b*) Line
(*c*) Dot Matrix (*d*) Laser
Codes:
A. (*b*), (*c*) are correct
B. (*a*), (*b*), (*c*) are correct
C. (*a*), (*d*) are correct
D. (*c*), (*d*) are correct

21. Following are some of the problems with "Difficult Materials" usually faced by the users as advocated by Dr. S.R. Ranganathan:
(*a*) Books with different numbers.
(*b*) Books with different styles and standards.
(*c*) Books in various forms of exposition.
(*d*) Books with different sizes and colours.
Codes:
A. (*a*) and (*c*) are correct
B. (*b*) and (*d*) are correct
C. (*c*) and (*d*) are correct
D. (*b*) and (*c*) are correct

22. According to Dr. S.R. Ranganathan, which of the following items are not considered as fugitive materials?
(*a*) Newspaper-clippings
(*b*) Books
(*c*) Pamphlets
(*d*) Reports
Codes:
A. (*a*) and (*c*) are correct
B. (*b*) and (*d*) are correct
C. (*a*) and (*b*) are correct
D. (*b*) and (*c*) are correct

23. Which of the following are the demerits of MBO System?
(*a*) Superior-subordinate relationships
(*b*) Over simplification
(*c*) More coordination
(*d*) All variables are not taken into account
Codes:
A. (*a*) and (*b*) are correct
B. (*a*) and (*d*) are correct
C. (*b*) and (*c*) are correct
D. (*b*) and (*d*) are correct

24. In Classified Catalogue Code of Ranganathan the conflict of authorship includes:
(*a*) Person versus Person
(*b*) Person versus Corporate body
(*c*) Government versus Institution
(*d*) Person versus Publisher
Codes:
A. (*a*), (*b*) and (*c*) are correct
B. (*a*), (*b*) and (*d*) are correct
C. (*b*), (*c*) and (*d*) are correct
D. (*d*), (*c*) and (*a*) are correct

25. Which of the services are being offered by National Library, Kolkata?
(*a*) Lending
(*b*) Bibliographic
(*c*) NL connect
(*d*) Online reference services
Codes:
A. (*a*), (*b*) are correct
B. (*a*), (*d*) are correct
C. (*b*), (*d*) are correct
D. (*c*), (*d*) are correct

26. Which of the following are the level of problems in communication process identified by Warren Weaver?
(*a*) Technical (*b*) Semantic
(*c*) Effective (*d*) Interpreter
Codes:
A. (*a*), (*c*), (*d*) are correct
B. (*a*), (*b*), (*c*) are correct
C. (*b*), (*c*), (*d*) are correct
D. (*a*), (*b*), (*d*) are correct

27. Which of the following are special features of geographical sources?
(*a*) scale (*b*) revision
(*c*) rpm (*d*) projections
Codes:
A. (*a*) and (*d*) are correct
B. (*a*) and (*b*) are correct
C. (*c*) and (*d*) are correct
D. (*a*) and (*c*) are correct

28. Arrange in sequence the evolution of Intel Processors:
(*a*) Pentium (*b*) 8008
(*c*) 486 TM CPU (*d*) 80286
Codes:
A. (*d*), (*b*), (*c*), (*a*) B. (*b*), (*d*), (*c*), (*a*)
C. (*c*), (*b*), (*a*), (*d*) D. (*a*), (*d*), (*b*), (*c*)

29. Arrange in sequence the basic components of MBO system:
(*a*) Conducting reviews
(*b*) Setting objectives
(*c*) Appraising performance
(*d*) Developing action plans
Codes :
A. (*b*), (*a*), (*c*) and (*d*)
B. (*b*), (*d*), (*a*) and (*c*)
C. (*a*), (*b*), (*d*) and (*c*)
D. (*c*), (*a*), (*d*) and (*b*)

30. Arrange the following in chronological order:
(*a*) ISBD (*b*) MARC
(*c*) CCF (*d*) RDA
Codes:
A. (*a*), (*c*), (*d*), (*b*) B. (*b*), (*a*), (*c*), (*d*)
C. (*c*), (*b*), (*a*), (*d*) D. (*d*), (*a*), (*b*), (*c*)

31. Arrange the following Public Libraries Acts according to their year of enactment:
(*a*) Maharashtra Public Libraries Act
(*b*) Karnataka Public Libraries Act
(*c*) Odisha Public Libraries Act
(*d*) Mizoram Public Libraries Act
Codes:
A. (*c*), (*a*), (*b*), (*d*) B. (*b*), (*a*), (*c*), (*d*)
C. (*a*), (*b*), (*d*), (*c*) D. (*b*), (*a*), (*d*), (*c*)

32. Identify the **correct** sequence according to the year of first publication:
A. Library and Information Science Abstract, Biological Abstract, Chemical Abstract

B. Chemical Abstract, Biological Abstract, Library and Information Science Abstract

C. Biological Abstract, Chemical Abstract, Library and Information Science Abstract

D. Chemical Abstract, Library and Information Science Abstract, Biological Abstract

33. Arrange the following publications of S.R. Ranganathan in their year of first publication:

(*a*) Reference Service

(*b*) Colon Classification

(*b*) Five Laws of Library Science

(*d*) Prolegomena to Library Classification

Codes:

A. (*c*), (*a*), (*b*), (*d*) B. (*a*), (*b*), (*d*), (*c*)

C. (*c*), (*b*), (*d*), (*a*) D. (*b*), (*c*), (*a*), (*d*)

34. Match the following:

List-I	**List-II**
(*a*) IndCat	(*i*) Access for e-resources
(*b*) Shodhganga	(*ii*) Digital Library Consortium
(*c*) N-list	(*iii*) Indian ETD repository
(*d*) UGC Infonet	(*iv*) Online Union Catalogue of Indian Universities

Codes:

	(*a*)	(*b*)	(*c*)	(*d*)
A.	(*iii*)	(*ii*)	(*iv*)	(*i*)
B.	(*ii*)	(*i*)	(*iii*)	(*iv*)
C.	(*i*)	(*iv*)	(*ii*)	(*iii*)
D.	(*iv*)	(*iii*)	(*i*)	(*ii*)

35. Match the following:

List-I	**List-II**
(*a*) Rules for Dictionary Catalogue	(*i*) S.R. Ranganathan
(*b*) PMEST	(*ii*) Kaiser
(*c*) Systematic Indexing	(*iii*) Cutter
(*d*) Nested Phrase Indexing System	(*iv*) T.C. Carven

Codes:

	(*a*)	(*b*)	(*c*)	(*d*)
A.	(*iii*)	(*i*)	(*ii*)	(*iv*)
B.	(*iii*)	(*i*)	(*iv*)	(*ii*)
C.	(*ii*)	(*i*)	(*iii*)	(*iv*)
D.	(*i*)	(*iii*)	(*ii*)	(*iv*)

36. Match the following:

List-I	**List-II**
(*a*) Likert type	(*i*) Test of significance of the difference between variables
(*b*) Chi-square	(*ii*) Test of Measurement
(*c*) ANOVA	(*iii*) Summation Scale
(*d*) Test of Validity	(*iv*) Test of significance

Codes:

	(*a*)	(*b*)	(*c*)	(*d*)
A.	(*ii*)	(*iv*)	(*i*)	(*iii*)
B.	(*iii*)	(*iv*)	(*i*)	(*ii*)
C.	(*iii*)	(*ii*)	(*iv*)	(*i*)
D.	(*iii*)	(*i*)	(*ii*)	(*iv*)

37. Match the following:

List-I	**List-II**
(*a*) Turnitin	(*i*) Electronic Resource Management Software
(*b*) Drupal	(*ii*) Usage Statistics Software
(*c*) CORAL	(*iii*) Antiplagiarism Software
(*d*) SUSHI	(*iv*) Content Management Software

Codes:

	(*a*)	(*b*)	(*c*)	(*d*)
A.	(*iii*)	(*iv*)	(*ii*)	(*i*)
B.	(*ii*)	(*iv*)	(*i*)	(*iii*)
C.	(*iv*)	(*iii*)	(*ii*)	(*i*)
D.	(*iii*)	(*iv*)	(*i*)	(*ii*)

38. Match the following:

List-I	**List-II**
(*a*) Nadir to Ascendant	(*i*) Verification phase
(*b*) Ascendant to Zenith	(*ii*) Deductive phase
(*c*) Zenith to Descendant	(*iii*) Hypothesing phase
(*d*) Descendant to Nadir	(*iv*) Empirical phase

Codes:

	(*a*)	(*b*)	(*c*)	(*d*)
A.	(*iii*)	(*ii*)	(*i*)	(*iv*)
B.	(*iv*)	(*iii*)	(*ii*)	(*i*)
C.	(*ii*)	(*i*)	(*iv*)	(*iii*)
D.	(*i*)	(*iv*)	(*iii*)	(*ii*)

39. Match the following Intellectual Property Rights Acts of India with the year of their enactment:

List-I	List-II
(*a*) The Design Act	(*i*) 1970
(*b*) The Copyright Act	(*ii*) 1958
(*c*) The Trade and Merchandise Mark Act	(*iii*) 1911
(*d*) The Patents Act	(*iv*) 1957

Codes:

	(*a*)	(*b*)	(*c*)	(*d*)
A.	(*iii*)	(*ii*)	(*iv*)	(*i*)
B.	(*i*)	(*iv*)	(*ii*)	(*iii*)
C.	(*ii*)	(*iii*)	(*i*)	(*iv*)
D.	(*iii*)	(*iv*)	(*ii*)	(*i*)

40. Assertion (A): Inter-library loan services are still a necessity in the information explosion regime.

Reason (R): None of the libraries are self sufficient with respect to their holding.

Codes:

A. Both (A) and (R) are true
B. (A) is true, but (R) is false
C. Both (A) and (R) are false
D. (A) is false, but (R) is true

41. Assertion (A): Open Access Publication Model involves zero cost.

Reason (R): Open Access increases the visibility of the publication, as they are available to the users for free.

Codes:

A. Both (A) and (R) are true
B. (A) is true, but (R) is false
C. (A) is false, but (R) is true
D. Both (A) and (R) are false

42. Assertion (A): Controlled Vocabulary based on Indexing requires intellectual ability to assign keywords to the thought contents of the documents in such a way that these selected terms could effectively represent the contents.

Reason (R): Retrieval Systems based on Natural Language-based Indexing such as Google gives maximum precision.

Codes:

A. Both (A) and (R) are true
B. (A) is true, but (R) is false
C. (A) is false, but (R) is true
D. Both (A) and (R) are false

43. Assertion (A): Buying e-Journals is advantageous to a Library as Librarians do not have to follow up the missing issues.

Reason (R): Perpetual access takes care of missing issues.

Codes:

A. Both (A) and (R) are true
B. (A) is true, but (R) is false
C. (A) is false, but (R) is true
D. Both (A) and (R) are false

44. Assertion (A): The Product of the relative frequency of occurrence of a word and its rank is equal to a constant.

Reason (R): The above statement is known as Bradford's Law of scattering.

Codes:

A. (A) is false, but (R) is true
B. (A) is true, but (R) is false
C. Both (A) and (R) are true
D. Both (A) and (R) are false

45. Assertion (A): Most of the institutions around the world use 'impact factors' for measuring institutional productivity.

Reason (R): All the articles published in an 'Impact factor' Journals will be of equal quality.

Codes:

A. Both (A) and (R) are true
B. (A) is true, but (R) is false
C. (A) is false, but (R) is true
D. Both (A) and (R) are false

Direction (Qs. No. 46-50): *Read the passage given below and answer the questions based on your understanding of the passage.*

The vital role played by information and communication technologies in the development of digital environment revolutionized the way libraries handle information for centuries. The ICTs offer increased efficiency in terms of time, human resources and cost; improved quality of information, greater flexibility and responsiveness, increased access and sharing, enhanced degree of user interaction to specific information, review and modify the needs as per the situation. More specifically the Internet takes firm roots in information storage, processing and dissemination and provides global access. The users prefer the ease of use, portability, affordability and access to a wide range of subjects on the net over the rule bound library environment. However, on the other hand, electronic environment is not rosy, as it appears to be. The major issue is content organization. The information is poorly structured on the web while libraries have successful methods for information processing and retrieval. The content mapping, semantic web and ontology are under experimental stages for the purpose of effective organization and retrieval of web resources. Hence, users are apparently in need of librarians to assist them to access pertinent and precise information. Therefore it is high time for library professionals to remodel themselves and act as aggregators, and knowledge managers through web based services tailor-made to the user information requirements. In this context, Six Sigma applications have an immense value.

Service is the ability of an organisation to constantly and consistently exceed the customer's expectations. Improving customer service in libraries involves making a commitment to assess users' needs and developing action plans that implement user friendly processes. LICs are implementing the same through user studies or surveys to ascertain the level of user satisfaction, seek their opinions and suggestions and improve their service base based on the findings. However, they are not documenting the policies, processes, procedures and important tools of these programmes. Further, they don't have a mechanism to identify the latent and dormant users and their needs. This shows that there is a necessity to apply proved management techniques like Six Sigma to analyse the current service programmes and to suggest for their improvement. It is a fact that there is vast difference between the desired and perceived information needs of library users. The traditional metrics have limitations and hence adoption of Six Sigma is useful as it measures quality capability.

46. What is the impact of ICTs on Library and Information Centres?

A. All libraries are digitized

B. Increased manpower

C. Improved Finances

D. Enhanced information access and sharing

47. What is the user's preference in networked environment?

A. Exhaustive information

B. Access to diversified information at ease

C. Cost effective information

D. Both A and C

48. Why do the user needs assistance from librarian to access information on the Web?

A. Semantically connected

B. Ontologically structured

C. Poorly structured

D. Inaccurate information

49. What is to be done to improve customer service in Library and Information Centres?

A. Assess user needs

B. User friendly processes

C. Strategic policies

D. Both A and B

50. How Six Sigma does lead to quality service in libraries?

A. Assess the quality of service

B. Perceives user needs

C. Suggests tools and techniques to organize data

D. Provides tailor-made services

ANSWERS

1	2	3	4	5	6	7	8	9	10
D	B	A	D	D	C	A	D	A	C
11	**12**	**13**	**14**	**15**	**16**	**17**	**18**	**19**	**20**
C	A	D	C	D	C	C	A	D	A

21	22	23	24	25	26	27	28	29	30
D	B	D	A	A	B	A	B	B	B
31	**32**	**33**	**34**	**35**	**36**	**37**	**38**	**39**	**40**
D	B	C	D	A	B	D	B	D	A
41	**42**	**43**	**44**	**45**	**46**	**47**	**48**	**49**	**50**
C	B	B	B	B	D	B	C	D	A

EXPLANATORY ANSWERS

2. Cluster is a mode of formation of subject 'Oceanography'. Cluster analysis is a useful data mining method to obtain detailed information on the physical state of the ocean. The primary objective of this study is to develop a new spatio-temporal density-based algorithm for clustering physical oceanographic data. This study extends the regular spatial cluster analysis to deal with spatial data at different epochs. It also presents the sensitivity of the new algorithm to different parameter settings.

3. The term and notion of the "half-life" index number of literature obsolescence, as well as their borrowing from nuclear physics and adaptation into the literature of literature obsolescence, has up to now been attributed to the librarian Burton and the physicist Kebler and to their famous 1960 journal article. A consideration is given to the analogy between the half-life of radioactive substances and the rate of obsolescence of scientific literature. The validity of this analogy suggests the possibility of more accurate prognostications concerning the period of time, during which scientific literature may be used and hence might help to guide the planning of library collections and technical information services.

4. The Copyright Act, 1957 (as amended by the Copyright Amendment Act 2012) governs the subject of copyright law in India. The Indian copyright law protects literary works, dramatic works, musical works, artistic works, cinematograph films and sound recordings. In literature, if the author dies sixty years after the publication of his book and someone wants the copyright of that book to publish it in any form, then the copyright may be granted to the person seeking it.

5. Chaired by K.P. Sinha, The Sinha Committee in 1957 appointed National Policy on Libraries and Information System or NAPLIS under the Chairmanship of Prof. D.P. Chattopadhyay who was appointed by the Ministry of HRD, Government of India, the Empowered Committee (1988) to consider the recommendations of NAPLIS, Advisory Committee for Libraries (1959), Planning Commission Working Group on Libraries and Informatics (1885-90), National Commission on Libraries and Information Service etc.

6. For over 800 years Nalanda University or Nalanda Learning Centre was one of the best learning centres in the world. Students from across the globe came here to study in one of the greatest libraries in the world. The library was spread over three buildings, namely Ratnasagara, Ratnadadhi and Ratnaranjaka, each having nine storeys high and had a huge collection of books that covered various subjects ranging from religion, literature, astrology, astronomy, medicine and much more.

7. Almanacs are annual publications that include such information as weather forecasts, farmers' planting dates, timetables, and tabular information often arranged according to the calendar. Astronomical data and various statistics are found in almanacs, such as the times of the rising and setting of the sun and moon, eclipses, hours of full tide, church festivals, and so on. Thus, Almanacs are the information source of ready reference, which can be obtained within a moment just by flipping through the pages.

8. An eBook or digital book is an *electronic* version of a traditional print book that can be read by using a personal computer or by using an eBook reader. Access at slow pace is not an essential feature of an e-book; rather it has such beneficial features as it is mostly cost-effective, information can be searched and obtained with ease and there is scope for online purchase besides other advantages that can be gained from it.

9. The method of PRECISION & RECALL is applied here. Precision and recall are the basic measures used in evaluating search strategies. As shown in the first two figures given below, these measures assume: There is a set of records in the database which is relevant to the search topic Records are assumed to be either relevant or irrelevant (these measures do not allow for degrees of relevancy). The actual retrieval set may not perfectly match the set of relevant records.

RECALL is the ratio of the number of relevant records retrieved to the total number of relevant records in the database. It is usually expressed as a percentage.

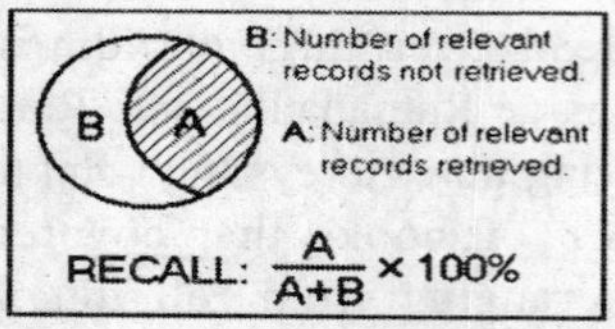

$$\text{Recall} = \frac{60}{60+40} \times 100 = 60$$

Here, A = 60

B = 100 − 60 = 40.

10. S.R. Ranganathan (12 August 1892 – 27 September 1972) was a mathematician and librarian from India. His most notable contributions to the field were his five laws of library science and the development of the first major analytico-synthetic classification system, the colon classification. He is considered to be the father of library science, documentation, and information science in India and is globally known for his fundamental thinking in the field.

In London, Ranganathan studied at the School of Librarianship, University College, London, under W.C. Berwick Sayers (1881-1960), the chief librarian of the Croydon Public Library. Sayers' stint as a perfect librarian was eclipsed by his landmark success as a writer and teacher of librarianship, particularly in the field of library classification.

11. **Kaoru Ishikawa** (July 13, 1915 - April 16, 1989) was a Japanese organisational theorist, Professor at the Faculty of Engineering at The University of Tokyo, noted for his quality management innovations.

Ishikawa's **Seven Basic Tools of Quality** is a designation given to a fixed set of graphical techniques identified as being most helpful in troubleshooting issues related to quality. They are called *basic* because they are suitable for people with little formal training in statistics and because they can be used to solve the vast majority of quality-related issues.

The seven tools are:

- Cause-and-effect diagram (also known as the "fishbone" or Ishikawa diagram)
- Check sheet
- Control chart
- Histogram
- Pareto chart
- Scatter diagram
- Stratification (alternately, flow chart or run chart)

12. The Open Systems Interconnection Model (OSI Model) is a conceptual model that characterises and standardises the communication functions of a telecommunication or computing system without regard to their underlying internal structure and technology.

Its goal is the interoperability of diverse communication systems with standard protocols. The model partitions a communication system into abstraction layers. The original version of the model defined seven layers.

Among the seven layers, the data link layer provides node-to-node data transfer—a link between two directly connected nodes. It detects and possibly corrects errors that may occur in the physical layer. It, among other things, defines the protocol to establish and terminate a connection between two physically connected devices. It also defines the protocol for flow control between them.

13. Decimal Binary Conversion:—

2	20	0
2	10	0
2	5	1
2	2	0
	1	

$\therefore (20)_{10} = (10100)_2$

In 16 bit format

$(20)_{10} = (00010100)_2$.

14. Action research is either research initiated to solve an immediate problem or a reflective process of progressive problem solving led by individuals working with others in teams or as part of a "community of practice" to improve the way they address issues and solve problems. There are two types of action research:

(*i*) Participatory action research

(*ii*) Practical action research.

Denscombe (2010, p. 6) writes that an action research strategy's purpose is to solve a particular (immediate) problem and to produce guidelines for best practice.

15. Alfred J. Lotka published in 1926 an investigation of the statistical distribution of the productivity of authors based on Chemical Abstracts. He found an approximate mathematical formula according to which most authors (60%) only contribute one document while a very small number of authors contribute a large amount of the total production of documents. The approximation is: The number of authors each contributing n articles is proportional to $1/n^2$. If 100 authors each produce 1 article in a given period, 25 authors produces each 2 articles, 11 produces each 3 etc. In other words:

The number of authors making n contributions is about $1/n^a$ of those making one contribution, where a is often nearly 2.

This law is often termed "the inverse square law of scientific productivity" and is (with Bradford's law of scattering and Zip's law) regarded one of the three classical bibliometric laws. The Lotka's law is one of the varieties of special applications of Zipf's law that describes the frequency of publication by authors in any given field.

Munch-Petersen (1981) is a Danish investigation of Lotka's law concerning the distribution of authors of fiction prose translated into Danish in the period 1800-1899.

16. According to Dr. S.R. Ranganathan, 'Library Civics and Hygiene' means Library behaviour, Physique of Book and Care of Book.

Library Behaviour: Library behaviour is premised upon certain decorum and discipline that must be followed while in library. Queue system, walking quietly, maintaining silence, adhering to the policy of live and let live besides fulfilling other civic responsibilities reflect the requisite library behaviour in the library.

Physique of Book: Physique of a book includes demonstration with a partially bound book, turning pages carefully by upper right-hand corner, using bookmarks, taking books from the shelves without injuring backs, putting them back the right way up, back outward, putting books in a safe place at home or library.

Care of Book: Care of a book comprises a few aspects that a visitor or a reader in a library must be aware of and must follow some DOs & DO NOTs. Books are a fragile object. So they must be handled carefully lest their pages are torn or separated from the bindings by rough handling. If the shelves are opened with more power and abruptness than required, their handles may come out. Therefore, in each and every act care must be taken to add further life to the books and library items.

17. The National Mission on Libraries India, an initiative of the Ministry of Culture under the Government of India, works to modernise and digitally link nearly 9,000 libraries across India to provide readers access to books and information.

The Mission has the following four working groups for its main advisory function:

(*i*) Upgrade of existing public libraries, college libraries, school libraries, and shifting the use of school libraries as community libraries chaired by Shri B.S. Baswan.

(*ii*) Library and Information Science education, training and research facilities chaired by Professor A.R.D. Prasad.

(*iii*) Setting up the National Virtual Library, networking and ICT applications in libraries, chaired by Dr. H.K. Kaul.

(*iv*) National Census of Libraries, Content Creation and Community Information Centres, chaired by Dr. Subbiah Arunachalam.

However, with a noticeable difference, the following do not come in the Working Groups under National Mission on Libraries:

(*i*) Library and Information Science Research, Development and Accreditation.

(*ii*) Upgradation of the Existing Academic Libraries, University and Research Libraries.

18. An ISBN is an International Standard Book Number. Each ISBN consists of 5 elements with each section being separated by spaces or hyphens. Three of the five elements may be of varying length:

(*i*) **Prefix element:** Currently this can only be either 978 or 979. It is always 3 digits in length.

(*ii*) **Registration group element:** This identifies the particular country, geographical region, or language area participating in the ISBN system. This element may be between 1 and 5 digits in length.

(*iii*) **Registrant element:** This identifies the particular publisher or imprint. This may be up to 7 digits in length.

(*iv*) **Publication element:** This identifies the particular edition and format of a specific title. This may be up to 6 digits in length

(*v*) **Check digit**: This is always the final single digit that mathematically validates the rest of the number. It is calculated using a Modulus 10 system with alternate weights of 1 and 3.

20. Impact printer refers to a class of printers that work by banging a head or needle against an ink ribbon to make a mark on the paper. This includes dot-matrix printers, daisy-wheel printers, and line printers. In contrast, laser and ink-jet printers are *non-impact printers.* The distinction is important because impact printers tend to be considerably noisier than non-impact printers, but are useful for multi-part forms such as invoices.

22. Fugitive material or Grey Literature is produced on all levels of government, academics, business and industry in print and electronic formats, but it is not controlled by commercial publishers. Thus, the books and reports published by commercial publishers are not considered as fugitive materials.

23. Management by Objectives (MBO) is a personnel management technique where managers and employees work together to set, record and monitor goals for a specific period of time. Organisational goals and planning flow top-down through the organisation and are translated into personal goals for organisational members. The technique was first championed by management expert Peter Drucker and became commonly used in the 1960s.

Besides merits, there are some demerits of MBO as well. Over simplification is one of the demerits of MBO. Some tasks are so simple that setting goals makes little sense and becomes more of silly, annual ritual. Another demerit can be exemplified as all variables are not taken into account. The organisation often fails to take into account environmental factors that hinder goal achievement, such as lack of resources or management support.

25. Among the seven services offered by National Library, Kolkata, the two are elucidated below:

LENDING SERVICES

Local Membership: A limited number of books are lent out to readers under certain terms and conditions. To make use of this facility one has to become the member of the Lending division, applying on a prescribed lending form. Two books can be borrowed at a time for a period of 14 days, which can be extended for another 14 days either by phone, or by post or by personal visit. Membership of the Lending division is free, but the borrower has to deposit the amount equal to one and half time of the price of the book. A fine of Re. 1 is charged per book per day for late return. When the borrower wishes to cancel the membership, he/she gets back the money, through a cheque, without any deduction.

Bibliographic Services: Research scholars, Government agencies, universities and national level institutions may make use of this facility. Selected lists of reading materials or bibliographies are prepared by the library on request. Special bibliographies are prepared to augment the exhibitions, which the National Library holds. Compilation of exhaustive bibliographies on special topics are under way. The library provides bibliographies and/or bibliographic statistics to national and international organisations. The library provides support to the Central Reference Library, Kolkata, in compiling the Indian National Bibliography.

26. Following are the levels of problems in communication process as identified by Warren Weaver:

The ***technical problems*** are concerned with the accuracy of transference from sender to receiver of sets of symbols (written speech), or of a continuously varying signal (telephonic or radio transmission of voice or music), or of a continuously varying two-dimensional pattern (television), etc.

The ***semantic problems*** are concerned with the identity, or satisfactorily close approximation, in the interpretation of meaning by the receiver, as compared with the intended meaning of the sender. This is a very deep and involved situation, even when one deals only with the relatively simpler problems of communicating through speech.

The ***effectiveness problems*** are concerned with the success with which the meaning conveyed to the receiver leads to the desired conduct on his part. It may seem at first glance undesirably narrow to imply that the purpose of all communication is to influence the conduct of the receiver. But with any reasonably broad definition of conduct, it is clear that communication either affects conduct or is without any discernible and probable effect at all.

27. Scale: The relationship between distance on a map and actual distance on the earth. Scale may be represented by words (e.g., "one inch equals one mile"), a ratio or fraction (e.g., 1:63,360), or a divided bar. Bar scale is best to use when enlarging or reducing the size of a map, since the scale size will change with the map size. A map showing a small area in detail (such as a street map of a neighbourhood) is a "large scale" map, while a map showing a large area without much detail (such as the world or a continent) is a "small scale" map (think about fractions here!). Types of Scale Verbal words one inch equals one mile Number ratio or fraction 1:63,360 Graphic divided bar or line (like a ruler), usually showing miles or kilometres.

Type of Scale

Verbal	words	one inch equals one mile
Number	ratio or fraction	1:63,360
Graphic	divided bar or line (like a ruler), usually showing miles or kilometers	0 500 miles 0 500 kilometers

Projections: Projections are among the special features of geographical sources. It is impossible to accurately depict the spherical Earth on a flat surface without distorting shape, area, distance, or direction (try peeling an orange and flattening it out!), so cartographers use different projections to preserve selected properties (shape, size, distance, direction), while others get distorted.

28. Following are the Intel Processors in evolutionary sequence with brief explanation:

Introduced in 1972, the **Intel 8008** ("*eight-thousand-eight*" or "*eighty-oh-eight*") is an early byte-oriented microprocessor designed and manufactured by Intel. It was an 8-bit CPU with an external 14-bit address bus that could address 16KB of memory. Originally known as the **1201**, the chip was commissioned by Computer Terminal Corporation (CTC) to implement an instruction set of their design for their Datapoint 2200 programmable terminal.

Introduced on 1 February 1982, the **Intel 80286** (also marketed as the **iAPX 286** and often called **Intel 286**) is a 16-bit microprocessor. It was the first 8086-based CPU with separate, non-multiplexed, address and data buses and also the first with memory management and wide protection abilities. The 80286 used approximately 134,000 transistors in its original nMOS (HMOS) incarnation and, just like the contemporary 80186, it could correctly execute most software written for the earlier Intel 8086 and 8088 processors.

Intel's venerable **486 CPU** is now 15-year-old. Intel began working on the 486 in the early 1980s, and introduced the chip in April of 1989. The 486 was essentially an improved, modified version of the 386. The 32-bit 486 was initially manufactured on a one-micron process, and was introduced at speeds of 25 and 33MHz. All 486 chips except for the "sx" versions came with a built-in floating-point unit and contained 8 KB of cache memory.

Pentium is a brand used for a series of x86-compatible microprocessors produced by Intel since 1993. In its current form, Pentium processors are considered entry-level products that Intel rates as "two stars", meaning that they are above the low-end Atom and Celeron series but below the faster Core i3, i5 and i7 lines as well as the high-end Xeon processors.

29. The basic components of MBO system are explained below in arranged sequence:

Setting objectives: Setting objectives is a joint undertaking that should be mutually agreed upon by the responsible individual and his superior.

Developing action plans: The development of action plans is often deleted by management. A manager has the responsibility for identifying the steps involved in planning. The necessary tools and activities must be outlined and specific responsibilities assigned. Available resources are made known, and an estimated time for completion of the task is proposed.

Conducting reviews: Conducting reviews is an annual review for which the performance review meeting is a process where manager and employee work together to assess the degree to which the employee has attained agree-upon goals, and work together to overcome any difficulties encountered. Also called performance appraisal meeting, or performance evaluation meeting, it usually refers to an annual meeting.

Appraising performance: It is also an annual appraisal report. The annual performance appraisal differs from a periodical review in that it is a holistic approach to the individual's performance. The first task is to review the mutually agreed upon objectives that the individual is responsible for. The actual results are determined and a measure of results against predetermined performance standards is observed.

30. MARC (Machine Readable Cataloguing): MARC standards are a set of digital formats for the description of items catalogued by libraries, such as books. Working with the Library of Congress, American computer scientist Henriette Avram developed MARC in the 1960s to create records that could be read by computers and shared among libraries. By 1971, MARC formats had become the national standard for dissemination of bibliographic data in the United States, and the international standard by 1973.

ISBD (International Standard Bibliographic Description): The ISBD is useful and applicable for descriptions of bibliographic resources in any type of catalogue. In this edition, the stipulations for cataloguing the various resources have been made more consistent with each other and brought up to date.

CCF (Common Communication Format): CCF is a structure format for creating bibliographical records and for exchanging records between groups of information agency and libraries. An international symposium in Taormina, Sicily conducted by UNESCO was held in April 1978. On the recommendations of the symposium, UNESCO / PGI formed the adhoc group on the establishment of a Common Communication Format (CCF).

RDA Implementation: As of April 1, 2013, the U.S. Library of Congress and the British Library are using RDA as their official descriptive cataloguing standard. The announcements in this regard have already been made from the Library of Congress and the British Library.

31. During the last six decades, 14 (fourteen) Public Library Bills were enacted in different states of India, four of which are given below in chronological order of the year of their enactment:

- Karnataka Public Libraries Act, 1965
- Maharashtra Public Libraries Act, 1967
- Mizoram Public Libraries Act, 1993
- Odisha Public Libraries Act, 2001.

32. ***Chemical Abstracts***, which started its publication from 2007, is a periodical index that provides summaries and indexes of disclosures in recently published scientific documents. Approximately 8,000 journals, technical reports, dissertations, conference proceedings, and new books, in any of 50 languages, are monitored yearly, as are patent specifications from 27 countries and two international organisations. *Chemical Abstracts* ceased print publication on January 1, 2010.

Biological Abstracts is a database produced by Thomson Reuters through its subsidiary BIOSIS. It includes abstracts from peer-reviewed academic journal articles in the faculties of biology, biochemistry, biotechnology, botany, pre-clinical and experimental medicine, pharmacology, zoology, agriculture, and veterinary medicine published since 1926.

Library and Information Science Abstracts (LISA) is an international abstracting and indexing tool designed for library professionals and other information specialists. LISA covers the literature in Library and information science (LIS) since 1969 and currently abstracts 440+ periodicals from 68+ countries and in 20+ languages.

33. Published in 1931, ***The Five laws of library science*** is a theory proposed by S.R.

Ranganathan that provides the details about the principles of operating a library system.

First edition published in 1933, ***Colon classification (CC)*** is a system of library classification developed by S. R. Ranganathan. It was the first ever faceted (or analytico-synthetic) classification.

Published in 1967, ***Prolegomena to Library Classification*** has the discussion by the author about how classification schemes like the Dewey and Library of Congress systems work. They organise knowledge (in books and other things) by deciding what the book is about and then giving it a call number and putting it in order with other books.

Published in 2006, ***Reference Service*** is undertaken by using a historical methodology. It was evident from the literature review that Ranganathan had established that reference service was the most important work and served as the hub of all library practices.

34. **(*a*)** **IndCat: Online Union Catalogue of Indian Universities** is unified Online Library Catalogues of books, theses and journals available in major university libraries in India. The union database contains bibliographic description, location and holdings information for books, journals and theses in all subject areas available in more than 174 university libraries across the country. The IndCat is a major source of bibliographic information that can be used for inter-library loan, collections development as well as for copy cataloguing and retro-conversion of bibliographic records.

(*b*) The **Shodhganga@INFLIBNET** Centre provides a platform for research students to deposit their Ph.D. theses and make it available to the entire scholarly community in open access. The repository has the ability to capture, index, store, disseminate and preserve ETDs submitted by the researchers.

(*c*) **N-LIST** (National Library and Information Services Infrastructure for Scholarly content), being jointly executed by the UGC-INFONET Digital Library Consortium, INFLIBNET Centre and the INDEST-AICTE Consortium, IIT Delhi provides for (i) cross-subscription to e-resources subscribed by the two Consortia, i.e. subscription to INDEST-AICTE resources for universities and UGCINFONET resources for technical institutions; and (ii) access to selected e-resources to colleges. The N-LIST project provides access to e-resources to students, researchers and faculty from colleges and other beneficiary institutions through server(s) installed at the INFLIBNET Centre.

(*d*) Launched in December 2003, the UGC-Infonet Digital Library Consortium is proved to be a recipe to university libraries which have been discontinuing subscription of scholarly journals because of "Serials Crisis". The Consortium provides current as well as archival access to more than 7500+ core and peer-reviewed journals and 11 bibliographic databases from 26 publishers and aggregators in different disciplines.

35. (*a*) Born in Boston, Charles Ammi Cutter (1837–1903) was an American librarian. The format of the catalogue we have today was largely set forth in Charles A. Cutter's *Rules for a Dictionary Catalogue*, originally published in 1875. In that work, Cutter suggested that the catalogue should "enable a person to find a book of which either the author, the title, or the subject is known." These suggestions mirror the typical indices found in the majority of catalogues today.

(*b*) The Colon Classification (CC) of S.R. Ranganathan uses 42 main classes that are combined with other letters, numbers and marks in a manner resembling the Library of Congress Classification to sort a publication. CC uses five primary categories or facets, to further specify the sorting of a publication, which collectively are called PMEST. The acronym is explained below:

Personality, the most specific or focal subject.

Matter or property, the substance, properties or materials of the subject.

Energy, including the processes, operations and activities.

Space, which relates to the geographic location of the subject.

Time, which refers to the dates or seasons of the subject.

(*c*) Julius Otto Kaiser (1968–1927) was a special librarian and indexer who developed, in last years of the 19th, and the first years of the 20th centuries, an innovative method of subject indexing known as systematic indexing (SI). SI is based on "concretes" and "processes" to govern the form of subject headings and subdivisions.

(*d*) Nested Phrase Indexing System (NEPHIS) by Timothy C. Craven is a system of computer aided permuted subject indexing designed to be as easy as possible for the indexer, for the programmer, and for the user of the index. The indexer needs to learn only four commands in order to be able to construct any input string. However, the permutations produced are browsable, while providing a complete description of even quite complicated subjects. The program is cheap to run, requiring only an input file and an output file and 1k of core.

36. (*a*) A **Likert type scale** is a psychometric scale commonly involved in research employing questionnaires. It is the sum of responses on several Likert items. Since many Likert scales pair each constituent Likert item with its own instance of a visual analogue scale, an individual item is itself sometimes erroneously referred to as a scale, with this error creating pervasive confusion in the literature and parlance of the field.

(*b*) A **chi-squared test**, also referred to as χ^2 **test** (or **chi-square test**), is any statistical hypothesis test in which the sampling distribution of the test statistic is a chi-square distribution when the null hypothesis is true. Chi-squared tests are often constructed from a sum of squared errors, or through the sample variance. Test statistics that follow a chi-squared distribution arise from an assumption of independent normally distributed data, which is valid in many cases due to the central limit theorem. A chi-squared test can then be used to reject the null hypothesis that the data are independent.

(*c*) The **one-way analysis of variance (ANOVA)** is used to determine whether the mean of a dependent variable is the same in two or more unrelated, independent groups. However, it is typically only used when you have three or more independent, unrelated groups, since independent-samples t-test is more commonly used when you have just two groups. If you have two independent variables, you can use at two-way ANOVA.

(*d*) **Test of Validity** is an indicator of how much meaning can be placed upon a set of test results. In psychological and educational testing, where the importance and accuracy of tests merit vital importance, test validity is crucial. Test validity incorporates a number of different validity types, including criterion validity, content validity and construct validity. If a research project scores highly in these areas, then the overall test validity will be high.

37. (*a*) **Turnitin**, which was first launched in 1997, is an Internet-based Anti-plagiarism Software created by iParadigms, LLC. Typically, universities and high schools buy licenses to submit essays to the Turnitin website, which checks the documents for unoriginal content. The results can be used to identify similarities to existing sources or can be used in formative assessment to help students learn how to avoid plagiarism and improve their writing. Students may be required by schools to submit essays to Turnitin, as a deterrent to plagiarism.

(*b*) **Drupal** is a free and open-source content-management framework written in PHP and distributed under the GNU General Public License. It is used as a back-end framework for at least 2.1% of all Web sites worldwide ranging from personal blogs to corporate, political, and government sites. It is also used for knowledge management and business collaboration.

(*c*) **CORAL** is an electronic resource management system built by the University of Notre Dame's Hesburgh Libraries. The first module, Licensing, was released as open source software in the summer of 2010 and they have continued releasing new modules since then. It is designed to be both simple and highly customisable – each module can be installed independently or used together depending on one's library's needs.

(*d*) **SUSHI** is Usage Statistics Software. Its primary benefit is that it automates a tedious and repetitive process. Current practice for statistics retrieval calls for library staff to go to each individual publisher's website and manually retrieve statistical data.

39. (*a*) **The Patents and Designs Act, 1911** is an Act of the Bangladesh National Assembly. This Act extends to the whole of Bangladesh and came into force from 1 January 1912. It primarily provides some definitions pertaining to this Act, *i.e.* definitions of 'Attorney General', 'Copyright', 'Design', 'Patent', 'Manufacture' and so on.

(*b*) **The Copyright Act, 1957** was the first post-independence copyright legislation in India, which has been amended six times since 1957. Copyright is a bundle of rights given by the law to the creators of literary, dramatic, musical and artistic works and the producers of cinematograph films and sound recordings. The rights provided under this law include the rights of reproduction of the work, communication of the work to the public, adaptation of the work and translation of the work.

(*c*) **The Trade and Merchandise Marks Act, 1958** is an Act to provide for the registration and better protection of trademarks and for the prevention of the use of fraudulent marks on merchandise.

(*d*) **The Patent Act, 1970** is a country's legislation that controls the use of patents. The government started encouraging the growth of drug manufacturing by Indian companies in the early 1960s, and with the Patents Act in 1970. This patent act removed composition patents from foods and drugs, and though it kept process patents, these were lessened to a period of five to seven years.

40. Inter-library loan (ILL and sometimes called inter-loan, inter-lending, document delivery, or document supply) is a service whereby a user of one library can borrow books or receive photocopies of documents that are owned by another library. The statement in **Assertion (A)** is true, as ILL services are still a necessity in the information explosion regime. The statement in **Reason (R)** is also true, as the libraries due to not being self-sufficient, have no option but to depend upon others in respect of their holding.

41. Open Access Publishing means providing content free online to readers while supporting operations by financial models that permit this free electronic distribution. However, it does not mean that no cost involves to start or run such publishing business. Thus, the statement given in **Assertion (A)** is false. However, the statement in **Reason (R)** is true because open access encourages more readers' visibility of the publication, as they are available free of cost.

42. Controlled vocabularies provide a way to organise knowledge for subsequent retrieval. They are used in subject indexing schemes, subject headings, thesauri, taxonomies and other forms of knowledge organisation systems. Controlled vocabulary schemes mandate the use of predefined, authorised terms that have been pre-selected by the designers of the schemes, in contrast to natural language vocabularies, which have no such restriction. The statement given in **Assertion (A)** is true. The statement in **Reason (R)** is false, because Retrieval Systems based on Natural Language-based Indexing has no business with Google.

43. The statement given in **Assertion** (A) is true, because buying e-journals is advantageous to a Library as Librarians do not need to follow up the missing issues. Whichever issue the Librarian wants to view, can be accessed in a click of the mouse. The statement, "Perpetual access takes care of missing issues" in **Reason (R)** is false, as it has no relevance to the care of missing issues.

44. In studying human behaviour as a natural phenomenon, Zipf devoted a great amount of effort to analysing language statistically. The motivation behind this study was, of course, Zipf's strong desire to establish laws, which could successfully describe complex areas of human behaviour, of which language is the most important. The statistical analysis performed on a large amount of data collected by Zipf resulted in at least one significant contribution: the establishment of a general law, which could describe many aspects of human behaviour. Zipf's basic premise is that there are certain underlying principles controlling such sociological factors as the use of words, and that these principles are similar over a wide variety of social phenomena. Thus, with respect to language the law reads, 'The product of the relative frequency of occurrence of a word and its rank is equal to a constant (F X R = C).' Hence, the statement in **Assertion** (A) is true.

The statement in **Reason (R)** is false, because it's Zipf's law which is elucidated in **(A)**; not Bradford's Law of scattering as mentioned in **(R)**.

45. The **impact factor (IF)** of an academic journal is a measure reflecting the average number of citations to recent articles published in that journal. In any given year, the impact factor of a journal is the average number of citations received per paper published in that journal during the two preceding years. For example, if a journal has an impact factor of 3 in 2008, then its papers published in 2006 and 2007 received 3 citations each on average in 2008. Thus, the statement in **Assertion (A)** is true. However, the statement in **Reason (R)** is false, as it has no relevance to the statement in **(A)**, nor is the statement **(R)** true from any point of view.

46. With the advancement in distributed computing and collaborative software technologies, information sharing and privacy related issues are gaining interest of researchers related to digital information creation, management, and distribution. So the impact of Information & Communication technologies in the development of digital environment has been such as Collaborative information sharing environment requires enhanced information sharing among users while privacy laws demand for the protection of user's information from unauthorised access and usage. Keeping this trade-off in view, there is a need for a flexible and enhanced information-sharing model that preserves the privacy of user's information.

47. Today, what matters the most in information-search is having easy access to the diversified information, especially the information one needs to access without any hassle to meet the pertinent requirements. It is possible if more specifically the Internet takes firm roots in information storage, processing and dissemination and provides global access. Thus, the users prefer the ease of use, portability, affordability and access to a wide range of subjects on the net over the rule-bound library environment.

48. The adoption of information & communication technologies (ICTs) by librarians have enabled the users to find the desired information by easy access which is poorly structured on the web; whereas libraries have successful methods for information processing and retrieval. The content mapping, semantic web and ontology are under experimental stages for the purpose of effective organisation and retrieval of web resources.

49. For smooth functioning of users' devices and resultantly easy access to the information they need and access depend upon customer service as well. Service is the ability of an organisation to constantly and consistently exceed the customer's expectations. Improving customer service in libraries involves making a commitment to assess users' needs and developing action plans that implement user-friendly processes. LICs are implementing the same through user studies or surveys to ascertain the level of user satisfaction, seek their opinions and suggestions and improve their service base based on the findings.

50. Six Sigma is a set of techniques and tools for process improvement that helps analyse the current service programs and suggest for improvement. It is true that there is a huge difference between the desired and perceived information needs of library users. The traditional metrics have limitations and hence adoption of Six Sigma is useful as it measures quality capability. Today, Six Sigma is used in many industrial sectors.

PAPER-III

Note: *This paper contains* ***seventy five (75)*** *objective type questions of* ***two (2)*** *marks each.* ***All*** *questions are* ***compulsory****.*

1. Digital collection developed for capturing the intellectual output of a single or multi institution is called as:

A. Digital Library B. Digital archive
C. Digital repository D. Digital publishing

2. INFLIBNET initiative for 'Integrated e-content ports : Gateway to All Learners' is named as:

A. e-PG Pathshala B. IR@INFLIBNET
C. INFOPORT D. e-Acharya

3. International Literacy Day is celebrated on:

A. 8th July B. 9th August
C. 8th September D. 18th September

4. SCONUL stands for:

A. The Council of National and University Libraries
B. Scientific National University Libraries
C. The Scientific Conference on National and University Libraries
D. The Standing Conference on National and University Libraries

5. The key factor that enforces uniformity throughout retrieval system is:

A. Controlled vocabulary
B. Search strategy
C. User profile
D. Database

6. Which of the following is **not** an example of non-random sampling?

A. Snowball Sampling
B. Convenience Sampling

C. Quota and Purposive Sampling
D. Census

7. According to S.R. Ranganathan, the reference service aimed at freshman is called:
A. General Help to General Reader
B. Short Range Reference Service
C. Long Range Reference Service
D. Initiation

8. Which one of the following is the implementing agency for 'capacity building' activity of National Mission on Libraries?
A. Delhi Public Library
B. Raja Ram Mohun Roy Library Foundation
C. National Library of India
D. Documentation, Research and Training Centre

9. When an author has not registered his/her work under copyright but legally proceeded over dispute of ownership. What is the validity of ownership?
A. No ownership without Registration
B. It may not be legally tenable
C. Ownership is automatic
D. Both A and B are correct

10. "Guide for the Preparation and Publication of Abstracts" was published by:
A. IFLA B. FID
C. OCLC D. UNESCO

11. What type of directory is the "Times of India Directory and Yearbook including Who's Who"?
A. General B. Special
C. Professional D. Trade

12. Folksonomy is a:
A. System in which users apply public tag to microdocuments only
B. System in which users apply public tag to online items
C. System in which users do not apply public tag to online items
D. System in which users apply public tag to only print items

13. What is intercalation in UDC?
A. Prefix of auxiliary B. Suffix of auxiliary
C. Infix of auxiliary D. Super-impose

14. The first order of division of classes in DDC is based on:
A. Jewett's system of classification
B. System of Paris Book Sellers
C. The Fixed Location System
D. Francis Bacon's three fountains of learning

15. Identify the service that is made available through Web 3.0 Technologies:
A. Message Board B. FOAF
C. Flikr D. Mashup

16. Who propounded the 'theory of human relation'?
A. Renis Likert B. Elton Mayo
C. Barnard D. None of the above

17. What is Dynamic HTML?
A. Asynchronous Web Development Technique
B. Collection of technologies to create interactive, animated website
C. Dynamic Web Page
D. Digital Signal Processor

18. Which one is **not** used as transmission media for voice/data communication?
A. Copper wire B. Co-axial cables
C. Plastic wire D. Optic wire

19. Ministry of Education, Government of Delhi will be rendered according to Classified Catalogue Code (CCC) as:
A. Ministry of Education (Delhi)
B. Delhi, (Education (Ministry of -)
C. Delhi, Ministry of Education
D. DELHI, EDUCATION (Ministry of -)

20. Which of the following memories has the shortest access time?
A. Optical Memory
B. Magnetic Core Memory
C. RAM
D. Cache Memory

21. Page Maker is an example of:
A. Operating System
B. Electronic Spread Sheet
C. Geometrical Software
D. Publishing Software

22. Which of the following are the Special Auxiliaries of Universal Decimal Classification (Medium Edition 1993)?
(*a*) Point of view .00
(*b*) Materials –03
(*c*) Point-not series .0/.9
(*d*) Hyphen series –1/–9
Codes:
A. (*a*) and (*d*) are correct
B. (*a*) and (*c*) are correct
C. (*c*) and (*d*) are correct
D. (*b*) and (*d*) are correct

23. Which of the following are linear models of communication?
(*a*) Dance's Helical model
(*b*) Lasswell model
(*c*) W. Schramm's Interactive model
(*d*) Becker's Mosaic model
Codes:
A. (*a*) and (*c*) are correct
B. (*c*) and (*d*) are correct
C. (*b*) and (*c*) are correct
D. (*a*) and (*d*) are correct

24. A copyright law usually aims at the following features:
(*a*) Stimulate creative authorship
(*b*) Public availability of intellectual works
(*c*) Freedom of access to information
(*d*) Profit making by publishers
Codes:
A. (*a*) and (*b*) are correct
B. (*a*) and (*c*) are correct
C. (*b*) and (*d*) are correct
D. (*a*), (*b*) and (*c*) are correct

25. By 2002, which of the following states have enacted their respective Public Library Acts?
(*a*) Haryana
(*b*) Uttar Pradesh
(*c*) Mizoram
(*d*) Rajasthan
Codes:
A. (*a*) and (*c*) are correct
B. (*a*), (*b*) and (*c*) are correct
C. (*b*) and (*d*) are correct
D. (*c*) and (*d*) are correct

26. Which of the following types of publications are excluded in INB?
(*a*) Maps
(*b*) First issue of periodical
(*c*) Newspapers
(*d*) Books in regional languages
Codes:
A. (*b*) and (*c*) are correct
B. (*c*) and (*d*) are correct
C. (*a*) and (*c*) are correct
D. (*d*) and (*a*) are correct

27. Which of the following are the elements of marketing mix?
(*a*) Selling
(*b*) Place
(*c*) Purchasing
(*d*) Product
Codes:
A. (*a*) and (*b*) are correct
B. (*b*) and (*c*) are correct
C. (*c*) and (*d*) are correct
D. (*b*) and (*d*) are correct

28. ALA's newly labelled Public Awareness Campaign "Libraries Transform" launched by ALA President Sari Feldman aims to focus on:
(*a*) the critical role the Public Libraries play in digital age;
(*b*) the change of perception that libraries are just quiet places to do research, find book and read;
(*c*) transforming the lives of all through education and life-long learning;
(*d*) to undermine the role of school, academic and special libraries;
Codes:
A. (*a*), (*b*) and (*c*) are correct
B. (*a*), (*b*) and (*d*) are correct
C. (*b*), (*c*) and (*d*) are correct
D. (*a*), (*c*) and (*d*) are correct

29. Which of the following are the synthetic features of 'Dewey Decimal classification'?
(*a*) Relative Index
(*b*) Enumeration of Schedules
(*c*) Tables
(*d*) Add to Instruction

Codes:
A. (*a*) and (*b*) are correct
B. (*b*) and (*c*) are correct
C. (*c*) and (*d*) are correct
D. (*a*), (*c*) and (*d*) are correct

30. Which of the following are the management theories related to motivation?
(*a*) Maslow Theory of Needs
(*b*) Drucker Theory
(*c*) McGreger Theory of X and Y
(*d*) Fayol Theory
Codes:
A. (*a*), (*b*) and (*c*) are correct
B. (*b*), (*c*) and (*d*) are correct
C. (*a*), (*b*) and (*d*) are correct
D. (*a*), (*c*) and (*d*) are correct

31. Which of the following are the techniques of Total Quality Management (TQM)?
(*a*) Quality circles
(*b*) Empowerment
(*c*) Bureaucratic set up
(*d*) Participative management
Codes:
A. (*a*), (*c*) and (*d*) are correct
B. (*a*), (*b*) and (*d*) are correct
C. (*b*), (*c*) and (*d*) are correct
D. (*a*), (*c*) and (*b*) are correct

32. Which of the following are the parts of a URL (Uniform Resource Locator)?
(*a*) Protocol
(*b*) Media Access Control
(*c*) Domain name
(*d*) Path
Codes:
A. (*a*), (*b*) and (*c*) are correct
B. (*b*), (*c*) and (*d*) are correct
C. (*a*), (*c*) and (*d*) are correct
D. (*b*) and (*c*) are correct

33. Which of the following tools index cited references?
(*a*) D - Space
(*b*) SCOPUS
(*c*) JCCC
(*d*) Google Scholar
Codes:
A. (*a*) and (*c*) are correct
B. (*b*) and (*c*) are correct
C. (*a*) and (*d*) are correct
D. (*b*) and (*d*) are correct

34. Null hypothesis is based on which of the following assumptions?
(*a*) No relationship between the two variables in the total population
(*b*) Relationship between the two variables in the total population
(*c*) Variables are related after having statistically rejected
(*d*) Variables are related before statistical analysis
Codes:
A. (*a*) and (*d*) are correct
B. (*a*) and (*c*) are correct
C. (*a*) and (*b*) are correct
D. (*b*) and (*d*) are correct

35. The ancient Nalanda learning center had which of the following buildings for libraries?
(*a*) Ratnasagara
(*b*) Ratnaranjaka
(*c*) Ratangarbha
(*d*) Ratnamanjari
Codes:
A. (*a*) and (*b*) are correct
B. (*b*) and (*c*) are correct
C. (*c*) and (*d*) are correct
D. (*d*) and (*a*) are correct

36. Identify the **correct** sequence of the Abraham Maslow's hierarchy of needs:
(*a*) Esteem
(*b*) Belonging
(*c*) Safety
(*d*) Physiological
Codes:
A. (*b*), (*c*), (*d*) and (*a*)
B. (*c*), (*b*), (*d*) and (*a*)
C. (*d*), (*b*), (*c*) and (*a*)
D. (*d*), (*c*), (*b*) and (*a*)

37. According to S.R. Ranganathan the steps in classifying documents include the following analysis of the title. Arrange the steps in the sequential order:
(*a*) Expressive title
(*b*) Kernel title
(*c*) Analysed title
(*d*) Transformed title

Codes:
A. (*a*), (*b*), (*c*) and (*d*)
B. (*b*), (*c*), (*d*) and (*a*)
C. (*c*), (*d*), (*a*) and (*b*)
D. (*d*), (*a*), (*b*) and (*c*)

38. Arrange the following units of computer memory in an ascending order:
(*a*) Zettabyte (*b*) Exabyte
(*c*) Yottabyte (*d*) Petabyte
Codes:
A. (*a*), (*b*), (*d*) and (*c*)
B. (*b*), (*c*), (*a*) and (*d*)
C. (*d*), (*b*), (*a*) and (*c*)
D. (*c*), (*a*), (*b*) and (*d*)

39. Arrange in sequence the following steps involved in testing a hypothesis according to C.R. Kothari.
(*a*) Selecting random sample and computing appropriate value
(*b*) Calculating and comparing the probability
(*c*) Selecting significant level
(*d*) Making formal statement
Codes:
A. (*b*), (*c*), (*d*) and (*a*)
B. (*a*), (*b*), (*c*) and (*d*)
C. (*c*), (*a*), (*b*) and (*d*)
D. (*d*), (*c*), (*a*) and (*b*)

40. Arrange the following Acts according to the year of their respective enactments:
(*a*) Digital Millennium Copyright Act
(*b*) Right to Information Act (India)
(*c*) Information Technology Act (India)
(*d*) Indian Copyright Act
Codes:
A. (*d*), (*a*), (*c*) and (*b*)
B. (*d*), (*b*), (*c*) and (*a*)
C. (*a*), (*d*), (*b*) and (*c*)
D. (*b*), (*c*), (*a*) and (*d*)

41. Arrange in sequence the following repository libraries according to their year of establishment:
(*a*) Connemera Public Library, Chennai
(*b*) Delhi Public Library, Delhi
(*c*) Asiatic Society Library, Mumbai
(*d*) Central Reference Library, Kolkata

Codes:
A. (*d*), (*a*), (*c*) and (*b*)
B. (*a*), (*b*), (*c*) and (*d*)
C. (*b*), (*d*), (*a*) and (*c*)
D. (*c*), (*a*), (*b*) and (*d*)

42. Arrange the following Catalogue Codes according to their first publication year :
A. CCC, AA code, ALA code, AACR-I
B. ALA code, CCC, AA code, AACR-I
C. AA code, ALA code, CCC, AACR-I
D. AACR-I, CCC, AA code, ALA code

43. Arrange in sequence the steps involved in Browne Charging Procedure:
(*a*) Stamping the date slip
(*b*) Identification of borrower
(*c*) Slipping the book card in reader's ticket
(*d*) Arrange cards in juxta position
Codes:
A. (*a*), (*d*), (*b*) and (*c*)
B. (*b*), (*c*), (*a*) and (*d*)
C. (*c*), (*b*), (*d*) and (*a*)
D. (*d*), (*a*), (*c*) and (*b*)

44. Arrange in sequence the following E-Journal Consortia in India according to their year of establishment:
(*a*) National Knowledge Resource Consortium
(*b*) IIM Library Consortium
(*c*) Consortium for e-Resources in Agriculture
(*d*) INDEST-AICTE Consortium
Codes:
A. (*c*), (*a*), (*d*) and (*b*)
B. (*a*), (*d*), (*b*) and (*c*)
C. (*b*), (*d*), (*c*) and (*a*)
D. (*d*), (*b*), (*a*) and (*c*)

45. Match the following:

List-I	List-II
(*a*) Protocols	(*i*) Work Station
(*b*) Device Drivers	(*ii*) Electronic/Radio Signals
(*c*) Node	(*iii*) Manages Network Services
(*d*) Transmission Media	(*iv*) Languages that allow computers to communicate

Codes:

	(a)	(b)	(c)	(d)
A.	(iv)	(iii)	(i)	(ii)
B.	(iii)	(iv)	(ii)	(i)
C.	(i)	(ii)	(iv)	(iii)
D.	(ii)	(i)	(iii)	(iv)

46. Match the following:

List-I	List-II
(a) Bus	(i) Nodes connected to hub
(b) Star	(ii) Each node connects to every other
(c) Ring	(iii) Nodes connected to backbone
(d) Mesh	(iv) Each node connected to the next

Codes:

	(a)	(b)	(c)	(d)
A.	(iv)	(ii)	(iii)	(i)
B.	(iii)	(i)	(ii)	(iv)
C.	(iii)	(i)	(iv)	(ii)
D.	(i)	(iv)	(ii)	(iii)

47. Match the following:

List-I	List-II
(a) Readers Advisory Service	(i) Market Survey Report
(b) Referral Service	(ii) Preparation of Trend Report
(c) Review Service	(iii) Helping reader in selection of right book
(d) Digest Service	(iv) Directing the user to the source of information

Codes:

	(a)	(b)	(c)	(d)
A.	(i)	(iii)	(iv)	(ii)
B.	(ii)	(iv)	(i)	(iii)
C.	(iv)	(iii)	(ii)	(i)
D.	(iii)	(iv)	(ii)	(i)

48. Match the following organizations with their contribution to information literacy:

List-I	List-II
(a) CILIP	(i) Information Literacy Model of Eight Competencies
(b) SCONUL	(ii) Guidelines for Information Literacy for Life Long Learning
(c) ACRL	(iii) Information Literacy Competency Standards for Higher Education
(d) IFLA	(iv) Seven Pillars of Information Literacy

Codes:

	(a)	(b)	(c)	(d)
A.	(iii)	(iv)	(i)	(ii)
B.	(i)	(iv)	(iii)	(ii)
C.	(ii)	(iv)	(i)	(iii)
D.	(ii)	(iv)	(iii)	(i)

49. Match the following Information Seeking Behaviour models with corresponding theories:

List-I	List-II
(a) Wilson Model of ISB	(i) Tailored to Electronic Environment–the process consists of eight sub-processes.
(b) Dervin's Model of ISB	(ii) Association of feelings, thoughts and actions but not cognitive.
(c) Kuhlthaus Model of ISB	(iii) Sense making approach–based on situation, gap and outcome–three key elements.
(d) Marchioninis ISB Model	(iv) Three fold view on information seeking context, system and information sources.

Codes:

	(a)	(b)	(c)	(d)
A.	(iv)	(iii)	(ii)	(i)
B.	(iii)	(ii)	(i)	(iv)
C.	(i)	(iii)	(iv)	(ii)
D.	(ii)	(iv)	(iii)	(i)

50. Match the following:

List-I	List-II
(a) Descriptive research	(i) Critical evaluation of available facts or information
(b) Applied research	(ii) Surveys and fact finding enquiries

(*c*) Empirical research — (*iii*) Relies on experience or observation alone

(*d*) Analytical research — (*iv*) Finding a solution to an immediate social problem

Codes:

	(*a*)	(*b*)	(*c*)	(*d*)
A.	(*ii*)	(*iii*)	(*iv*)	(*i*)
B.	(*ii*)	(*iv*)	(*iii*)	(*i*)
C.	(*i*)	(*ii*)	(*iv*)	(*iii*)
D.	(*i*)	(*iv*)	(*iii*)	(*ii*)

51. Match the following:

List-I	List-II
(*a*) Day book system	(*i*) Each per book
(*b*) Ledger system	(*ii*) Browne system
(*c*) One card	(*iii*) Note down transactions
(*d*) Two card system	(*iv*) One page per borrower

Codes:

	(*a*)	(*b*)	(*c*)	(*d*)
A.	(*ii*)	(*iii*)	(*iv*)	(*i*)
B.	(*iii*)	(*iv*)	(*i*)	(*ii*)
C.	(*iv*)	(*i*)	(*ii*)	(*iii*)
D.	(*i*)	(*ii*)	(*iii*)	(*iv*)

52. Match the following:

List-I	List-II
(*a*) Nominal Data	(*i*) Level of satisfaction regarding library facilities
(*b*) Ordinal Data	(*ii*) Frequency of use of internet by different user groups
(*c*) Interval Data	(*iii*) Ranking of library services by users
(*d*) Ratio	(*iv*) Gender details of library users

Codes:

	(*a*)	(*b*)	(*c*)	(*d*)
A.	(*i*)	(*iii*)	(*ii*)	(*iv*)
B.	(*iv*)	(*ii*)	(*i*)	(*iii*)
C.	(*iii*)	(*ii*)	(*iv*)	(*i*)
D.	(*iv*)	(*iii*)	(*i*)	(*ii*)

53. Match the following:

List-I (Commissions)	List-II (Opinions)
(*a*) D.S. Kothari Commission	(*i*) It is right and proper that university should provide great libraries.
(*b*) Radhakrishnan Commission	(*ii*) The library is second to instructional staff.
(*c*) Calcutta Commission	(*iii*) Nothing could be more damaging to a department than neglecting its library.
(*d*) Truman's Commission	(*iv*) The library is the heart of university work.

Codes:

	(*a*)	(*b*)	(*c*)	(*d*)
A.	(*i*)	(*iii*)	(*ii*)	(*iv*)
B.	(*iii*)	(*iv*)	(*i*)	(*ii*)
C.	(*ii*)	(*i*)	(*iv*)	(*iii*)
D.	(*iv*)	(*ii*)	(*iii*)	(*i*)

54. Match the following:

List-I	List-II
(*a*) Books in print	(*i*) ProQuest
(*b*) The statesman's year book	(*ii*) Microsoft
(*c*) Ulrich's International Periodical Directory	(*iii*) Palgrave MacMillan
(*d*) Encarta Encyclopedia	(*iv*) R.R. Bowker

Codes:

	(*a*)	(*b*)	(*c*)	(*d*)
A.	(*ii*)	(*iv*)	(*i*)	(*iii*)
B.	(*iii*)	(*iv*)	(*i*)	(*ii*)
C.	(*i*)	(*iv*)	(*ii*)	(*iii*)
D.	(*iv*)	(*iii*)	(*i*)	(*ii*)

55. Match the following:

List-I	List-II
(*a*) Statistical Analysis	(*i*) Pritchard
(*b*) Statistical Bibliography	(*ii*) S.R. Ranganathan
(*c*) Librametry	(*iii*) E.W. Hulme
(*d*) Bibliometrics	(*iv*) Francis Cole

Codes:

	(a)	(b)	(c)	(d)
A.	(iv)	(iii)	(ii)	(i)
B.	(iii)	(iv)	(i)	(ii)
C.	(i)	(ii)	(iii)	(iv)
D.	(ii)	(iii)	(i)	(iv)

56. Match the following:

List-I	List-II
(a) F. Rider	(i) FRBR
(b) E.J. Coates	(ii) Citation Indexing
(c) IFLA	(iii) International classification
(d) Eugene Garfield	(iv) BTI Indexing

Codes:

	(a)	(b)	(c)	(d)
A.	(iii)	(iv)	(i)	(ii)
B.	(iv)	(i)	(ii)	(iii)
C.	(i)	(ii)	(iii)	(iv)
D.	(ii)	(iii)	(iv)	(i)

57. Match the following:

List-I	List-II
(a) Browne	(i) OCLC
(b) SWOT analysis	(ii) Digital Library Software
(c) Worldcat	(iii) Charging System
(d) Greenstone	(iv) Management Practice

Codes:

	(a)	(b)	(c)	(d)
A.	(iv)	(i)	(iii)	(ii)
B.	(i)	(ii)	(iv)	(iii)
C.	(iii)	(iv)	(i)	(ii)
D.	(ii)	(i)	(iii)	(iv)

58. Match the following:

List-I	List-II
(a) Cumulative Books in Print	(i) Bibliography of Periodicals
(b) Ulrich International Periodical Directory	(ii) Trade bibliography
(c) World of Learning	(iii) Biographical source
(d) Who's Who in India	(iv) Directory

Codes:

	(a)	(b)	(c)	(d)
A.	(ii)	(i)	(iv)	(iii)
B.	(i)	(ii)	(iii)	(iv)
C.	(iii)	(i)	(iv)	(ii)
D.	(i)	(iii)	(iv)	(ii)

59. Match the following:

List-I	List-II
(a) Bibliographic service	(i) E-mail to user with links to latest e-journals
(b) Alert service	(ii) Translated copy of a document
(c) Condensation service	(iii) Compilation of audio records by a singer
(d) Support service	(iv) Abstracting selected and analysed information

Codes:

	(a)	(b)	(c)	(d)
A.	(iv)	(i)	(iii)	(ii)
B.	(i)	(iv)	(ii)	(iii)
C.	(iii)	(ii)	(i)	(iv)
D.	(iii)	(i)	(iv)	(ii)

60. Assertion (A): LIS professionals are ultimately bestowed with the responsibility of building the image of the profession.

Reason (R): The measure of the image is the service they render and not their financial gains.

Codes:

A. Both (A) and (R) are true
B. (A) is true, but (R) is false
C. Both (A) and (R) are false
D. (A) is false, but (R) is true

61. Assertion (A): Five Laws of Library Science are the normative principles that are capable of countering any problem faced by the Librarians.

Reason (R): Normative principles are not only considered to be the correct way of doing something, but also determines norms or standards in day-today library practice.

Codes:

A. Both (A) and (R) are false
B. (A) is true, but (R) is false
C. (A) is false, but (R) is true
D. Both (A) and (R) are true

62. Assertion (A): A recent feature that have been incorporated to Integrated Library Management Software is self-checking or self-issue of books option in the circulation module using RFID technology.

Reason (R): Application of RFID technology is economically viable and suitable to all types of libraries.

Codes:

A. Both (A) and (R) are true
B. (A) is false, but (R) is true
C. (A) is true, and (R) is false
D. Both (A) and (R) are false

63. Assertion (A): POP is the main internet standard for electronic mail transmission.

Reason (R): The Post Office Protocol (POP) is a protocol used by local e-mail clients to retrieve e-mail from a remote server over TCP/ IP connection.

Codes:

A. Both (A) and (R) are true
B. Both (A) and (R) are false
C. (A) is true, but (R) is false
D. (A) is false, but (R) is true

64. Assertion (A): Institutional Repositories (IRs) no more remain an inaccessible resource for the contemporary researchers as they not only open up their scholarly output to the entire world, but also maximized their visibility and impact of these outputs.

Reason (R): Repositories adhere to an internationally agreed set of technical standards by which they pose the metadata of each item and their contents on the Web and as such are interoperable.

Codes:

A. Both (A) and (R) are true
B. Both (A) and (R) are false
C. (A) is true, but (R) is false
D. (A) is false, but (R) is true

65. Assertion (A): An example for an array of geographical divisions can be Asia, India, Bihar, Patna.

Reason (R): An Array is a series of coordinate sub-divisions which are obtained by dividing a class or division according to a single characteristics.

Codes:

A. Both (A) and (R) are true
B. Both (A) and (R) are false
C. (A) is true, but (R) is false
D. (A) is false, but (R) is true

66. Assertion (A): Increased access to digital documents led to substantial increase in Plagiarism.

Reason (R): Most of the people are ignorant of the procedures in citing the digital documents.

Codes:

A. Both (A) and (R) are true
B. Both (A) and (R) are false
C. (A) is true, but (R) is false
D. (A) is false, but (R) is true

67. Assertion (A): Information reflects the synergic combination of medium and message.

Reason (R): There is no difference between conduit and content.

Codes:

A. Both (A) and (R) are true
B. Both (A) and (R) are false
C. (A) is true, but (R) is false
D. (A) is false, but (R) is true

68. Assertion (A): The Library users have easy and more access to information in networked environment than in print environment.

Reason (R): There is no distortion from barriers to communication process in networked environment.

Codes:

A. Both (A) and (R) are true

B. (A) is true, but (R) is false

C. Both (A) and (R) are false

D. (A) is false, but (R) is true

69. Assertion (A): UDC is more suitable for special libraries compared to DDC scheme of classification.

Reason (R): UDC can better accommodate new complex subjects compared to DDC.

Codes:

A. Both (A) and (R) are true

B. Both (A) and (R) are false

C. (A) is true but, (R) is false

D. (A) is false but, (R) is true

70. Assertion (A): In DDC only 'Add to' device provides an opportunity to expand a given number.

Reason (R): DDC is a purely enumerative scheme of classification without synthetic features.

Codes:

A. (A) is false, but (R) is true

B. (A) is true, but (R) is false

C. Both (A) and (R) are true

D. Both (A) and (R) are false

71. Assertion (A): Impact factor is the only method for evaluating the performance of an individual researcher.

Reason (R): Impact factor helps Libraries in their Journal subscription.

Codes:

A. (A) is true, but (R) is false

B. (A) is false, but (R) is true

C. Both (A) and (R) are false

D. Both (A) and (R) are true

72. Assertion (A): All public libraries in India are maintained from cess.

Reason (R): UNESCO Manifesto recommended that public libraries should be "maintained wholly from public funds".

Codes:

A. Both (A) and (R) are true

B. Both (A) and (R) are false

C. (A) is true, but (R) is false

D. (A) is false, but (R) is true

73. Assertion (A): FRBR is very important development towards global sharing of information.

Reason (R): FRBR outlines the relationship between many different interpretations or expressions.

Codes:

A. Both (A) and (R) are false

B. Both (A) and (R) are true

C. (A) is true, but (R) is false

D. (A) is false, but (R) is true

74. Assertion (A): Most Information Retrieval (IR) systems that used qualitative research techniques explored information seeking and retrieval behaviour of users.

Reason (R): The qualitative research methods help to explore human behaviour.

Codes:

A. Both (A) and (R) are false

B. (A) is false, but (R) is true

C. Both (A) and (R) are true

D. (A) is true, but (R) is false

75. Assertion (A): AACR-2 instructs that no information should be added to catalogue from other than the title page.

Reason (R): The main source of cataloguing information is the "Title Page" and the "Verso of the title page".

Codes:

A. Both (A) and (R) are true

B. (A) is true, but (R) is false

C. (A) is false, but (R) is true

D. Both (A) and (R) are false

ANSWERS

1	2	3	4	5	6	7	8	9	10
C	D	C	D	A	D	D	B	C	D
11	**12**	**13**	**14**	**15**	**16**	**17**	**18**	**19**	**20**
A	B	C	D	B	B	B	C	D	D
21	**22**	**23**	**24**	**25**	**26**	**27**	**28**	**29**	**30**
D	C	C	A	A	C	D	A	C	A
31	**32**	**33**	**34**	**35**	**36**	**37**	**38**	**39**	**40**
B	C	D	B	A	D	A	C	D	A
41	**42**	**43**	**44**	**45**	**46**	**47**	**48**	**49**	**50**
D	C	B	C	A	C	D	B	A	B
51	**52**	**53**	**54**	**55**	**56**	**57**	**58**	**59**	**60**
B	D	B	D	A	A	C	A	D	A
61	**62**	**63**	**64**	**65**	**66**	**67**	**68**	**69**	**70**
D	C	D	A	D	A	C	B	A	B
71	**72**	**73**	**74**	**75**					
B	D	B	C	C					

EXPLANATORY ANSWERS

1. A **digital repository** is a mechanism for managing and storing digital content. Repositories can be subject or institutional in their focus. Putting content into an institutional repository enables staff and institutions to manage and preserve it, and therefore derive maximum value from it. A repository can support research, learning, and administrative processes. Repositories use open standards to ensure that the content they contain is accessible in that it can be searched and retrieved for later use. The use of these agreed international standards allows mechanisms to be set up which import, export, identify, store and retrieve the digital content within the repository.

2. The INFLIBNET Centre has developed a web-based interface called "**e-Acharya**: Integrated e-Content Portal" for all e-content projects, developed / funded under the National Mission of Education through ICT. There are more than 50 projects on e-content under NME-ICT, which are developed / being developed in various subject disciplines (science, arts, engineering, social science, etc) through various Indian institutes / universities / colleges.

3. **September 8**, which is celebrated across the world as International Literacy Day, was proclaimed by UNESCO on November 17, 1965. Its aim is to shed light on the importance of literacy to individuals, communities and societies. On International Literacy Day each year, UNESCO reminds the international community of the status of literacy and adult learning globally.

4. The Standing Conference on National and University Libraries (SCONUL) was founded in 1950 for the benefit of their libraries and their users with the aims to promote the sharing and development of good practice; to influence policy makers and encourage debate and to raise the profile of higher education and national libraries. In 1994, when British

In 1994, Adobe Systems acquired Aldus and PageMaker. And then, its newer versions continued to be in market.

23. Lasswell model of communication (also known as Lasswell's communication model) is a **linear model** that describes an act of communication by defining who said it, what was said, in what channel it was said, to whom it was said, and with what effect it was said. It is regarded by many communication and public relations scholars as "one of the earliest and most influential communication models." The model was developed by American political scientist and communication theorist Harold Lasswell in 1948 while he was a professor at Yale Law School.

W. Schramm's Interactive model is a linear model of communication that views communication as a process taking place between a sender (transmitter) and a receiver: there will be also a message, and a medium through which the message can be transmitted (Schramm, 1948). The receiver may have a method of sending feedback on the message, to confirm that the message has been correctly received and understood.

24. The main aim of copyright law is not so much to protect the interests of the authors/creators, but rather to promote the progress of science and the useful arts—that is—knowledge. To accomplish this purpose, copyright ownership **stimulates** authors/creators in their efforts for creativity by granting them a temporary monopoly, or ownership of exclusive rights for a specified length of time.

One of the features of the aim of Copyright Act is such as it generally gives the owner of copyright the exclusive right to do and to authorise others to have access to authors'/creators' intellectual works made **available in the public**.

25. After being carved of the State of Punjab on 1st November 1966, **Haryana** state of India started the State Central Library in 1967 and district libraries in all the districts and municipal libraries in municipal towns. All these libraries are managed under the administrative control of Director of Higher Education. The public Library Act was passed in the state in 1989.

In 1987, **Mizoram** became a full-fledged state of India and the Government of Assam started a sub-divisional library at Aizawl in 1964. The State library was established at Aizawl after the formation of Mizoram and two district libraries at Lunglei and Siha. The Young Mizo Association (YMA) and other voluntary organisations started the village libraries with government's assistance. The YMA provides staff, buildings, equipment to these village libraries. In 1980, the State Library prepared the draft of Mizoram Public Library Bill and submitted it to the Government for necessary action. The Government eventually passed Mizoram Public Library Act in 1993, which was implemented until 2002.

26. Indian National Bibliography (INB) reflects the nation's cultural heritage and preserves it for the future generation. It also plays a major tool for national bibliographic control. Government of India entrusted Central Reference Library (CRL), Kolkata, Govt. of India, Ministry of Culture, to publish the INB, an authoritative bibliographical record of current Indian publications. INB is unique when compared with other National bibliographies since 14 languages come under one umbrella. It publishes first issue of periodical, books in regional languages and so on as said above, but it does not publish such things as maps and newspapers etc.

27. The term "marketing-mix", which was first coined by Neil Borden, the president of the American Marketing Association in 1953, is a business tool used in marketing and by marketers. It is often crucial when determining a product or brand's offer, and is often associated with the **four Ps**: *price*, *product*, *promotion*, and *place*.

Place is an element of marketing mix that refers to providing the product at a place which is convenient for consumers to access. A **product**, which is also an element of marketing mix, is seen as an item that satisfies what a consumer demands. A product may consist of a tangible good or an intangible service.

28. Founded in 1876, the American Library Association (ALA) is a non-profit organisation based in the United States that promotes libraries and library education internationally. With more than 62,000 members, ALA is the oldest and largest library association in the world.

On October 29, 2015, the American Library Association (ALA) President Sari Feldman officially launched Libraries Transform, a national public awareness campaign in Chicago that is highlighting the transformative nature of USA's national libraries, and thus, an effort is being made to elevate the critical role libraries play in the digital age.

30. Maslow Theory of Needs was developed by Abraham Maslow in 1940-50s USA, and this Hierarchy of Needs theory is still valid for understanding human motivation, management training, and personal development. Indeed, Maslow's ideas surrounding the Hierarchy of Needs, concerning the responsibility of employers to provide a workplace environment that encourages and enables employees to fulfil their own unique potential (self-actualisation), are today more relevant than ever.

Drucker Theory developed by Peter Drucker is Management by Objectives (MBO), which he expounded in his 1954 book *The Practice of Management*. MBO deals with a certain type of interaction, specific to a manager and his/her employee. MBO is based on the thinking that various hierarchies within companies need to be integrated. There was a need for commitment, responsibility, maturity and also for a common challenge. Here MBO becomes a process by which the objectives of an organisation are agreed to and decided between the management and the employees, this way the employees understand what is expected of them and help set their own individual goals.

McGreger Theory of X and Y theories of human motivation and management were created and developed by Douglas McGregor at the MIT Sloan School of Management in the 1960s. These theories describe two contrasting models of workforce motivation applied by managers in human resource management, organisational behaviour, organisational communication and organisational development. McGregor's 'Theory X' stresses the importance of strict supervision and external rewards and penalties; and 'Theory Y' highlights the motivating role of job satisfaction and allows scope for workers to approach tasks creatively.

31. Total Quality Management (TQM) comprises organisation-wide efforts to install and make permanent a climate in which an organisation continuously improves its ability to deliver high-quality products and services to customers.

A **Quality Circle** is a group of workers who do the same or similar work, who meet regularly to identify, analyse and solve work-related problems. Normally small in size, the group is usually led by a supervisor or manager and presents its solutions to management; where possible, workers implement the solutions themselves in order to improve the performance of the organisation and motivate employees.

Empowerment in context of TQM refers to empowering the employees to take up the task with responsibility and accomplish it successfully to the best satisfaction of the management. Thus, employee empowerment requires that the individual is held responsible for accomplishing the whole task, thereby becoming a process owner; he is not only responsible but also accountable.

Participatory Management is the practice of empowering members of a group, such as employees of a company or citizens of a community, to participate in organisational decision-making. It is used as an alternative to traditional vertical management structures, which has shown to be less effective as participants are growing less interested in their leader's expectations due to a lack of recognition of the participant's effort or opinion.

32. **Protocol** is a part of Uniform Resource Locator (URL). The first part of the URL is called a *protocol identifier* and it indicates what protocol to use. The second part is called a *resource name*, which specifies the IP address or the domain name where the resource is located. The protocol identifier and the resource name are separated by a colon and two forward slashes.

Domain name locates an organisation or other entity on the Internet. For example, the domain name www.totalbaseball.com locates an Internet address for "totalbaseball.com" at Internet point 199.0.0.2 and a particular host server named "www." The "com" part of the domain name reflects the purpose of the organisation or entity (in this example, "commercial") and is called the top-level domain name.

Path is a part of URL points to a file system location by following the directory tree hierarchy expressed in a string of characters in which path components, separated by a delimiting character, represent each directory. The delimiting character is most commonly the slash ("/"), the backslash character ("\"), or colon (":"), though some operating systems may use a different delimiter. Paths are essential in the construction of URLs.

33. Owned by Elsevier, **Scopus** is a bibliographic database containing abstracts and citations for academic journal articles. It covers nearly 22,000 titles from over 5,000 publishers, of which 20,000 are peer-reviewed journals in the scientific, technical, medical, and social sciences (including arts and humanities). It is available online by subscription. Searches in Scopus also incorporate searches of patent databases.

Google Scholar is a freely accessible web search engine that indexes the full text or metadata of scholarly literature across an array of publishing formats and disciplines. Released in beta in November 2004, the Google Scholar index includes most peer-reviewed online journals of Europe and America's largest scholarly publishers, plus scholarly books and other non-peer reviewed journals.

34. In inferential statistics, the term "**null hypothesis**" usually refers to a general statement or default position that there is no relationship between two measured phenomena, or no difference among groups. Rejecting or disproving the null hypothesis—and thus concluding that there are grounds for believing that there is a relationship between two phenomena (*e.g.* that a potential treatment has a measurable effect)—is a central task in the modern practice of science, and gives a precise criterion for rejecting a hypothesis. Thus, null hypothesis is based on two assumptions, that there is no relationship between the two variables in the total population; and variables are related after having statistically rejected.

35. The ancient Nalanda learning centre or Nalanda University, in Magadha region of present Bihar state, was a major centre of learning facilitated with hostels, libraries and other amenities a learning centre ought to have. **Ratnasagara**, **Ratnaranjaka** and **Ratnadadhi** were three huge multi-storeyed library buildings. Though the exact number of volumes available in the Nalanda library is not known, it is estimated to have been in the hundreds of thousands.

36. Maslow posited a **hierarchy of human needs** based on two groupings: deficiency needs and growth needs. Within the deficiency needs, each lower need must be met before moving to the next higher level. Once each of these needs has been satisfied, if at some future time a deficiency is detected, the individual will act to remove the deficiency. The first four levels are:

1. **Physiological:** hunger, thirst, bodily comforts, etc.
2. **Safety/security:** out of danger
3. **Belongingness and Love:** affiliate with others, be accepted
4. **Esteem:** to achieve, be competent, gain approval and recognition.

38. The following units of computer memory are arranged below in ascending order with their explanation:

The **petabyte** is a multiple of the unit byte for digital information. The prefix *peta* indicates the fifth power of 1000 and means 10^{15} in the International System of Units (SI), and therefore 1 petabyte is one quadrillion (short scale) bytes, or 1 billiard (long scale) bytes. The unit symbol for the petabyte is PB.

The **exabyte** is a multiple of the unit byte for digital information. The prefix *exa* indicates multiplication by the sixth power of 1000 (10^{18}) in the International System of Units (SI). Therefore, one exabyte is one quintillion bytes (short scale). The symbol for the exabyte is EB.

The **zettabyte** is a multiple of the unit byte for digital information. The prefix *zetta* indicates multiplication by the seventh power of 1000 or 10^{21} in the International System of Units (SI). A zettabyte is one sextillion (one long scale trilliard) bytes. The unit symbol is ZB.

The **yottabyte** is a multiple of the unit byte for digital information. The prefix *yotta* indicates multiplication by the eighth power of 1000 or 10^{24} in the (SI), and therefore one yottabyte is one septillion (one long scale quadrillion) bytes. The unit symbol for the yottabyte is YB.

40. The Indian **Copyright Act, 1957** (as amended by the Copyright Amendment Act 2012) governs the subject of copyright law in India. The history of copyright law in India can be traced back to its colonial era under the British Empire. The Copyright Act, 1957 was the first post-independence copyright legislation in India and the law has been amended six times since 1957.

The **Digital Millennium Copyright Act (DMCA)** is a United States copyright law that implements two 1996 treaties of the World Intellectual Property Organisation (WIPO). It criminalises production and dissemination of technology, devices, or services intended to circumvent measures (commonly known as digital rights management or DRM) that control access to copyrighted works.

The **Information Technology Act, 2000** (also known as **ITA-2000**, or the **IT Act**) is an Act of the Indian Parliament (No 21 of 2000) notified on 17 October 2000. It is the primary law in India dealing with cybercrime and electronic commerce. It is based on the *United Nations Model Law on Electronic Commerce 1996* (UNCITRAL Model) recommended by the General Assembly of United Nations by a resolution dated 30 January 1997.

The **Right to Information Act** (**RTI**) is an Act of the Parliament of India *"to provide for setting out the practical regime of right to information for citizens"* and replaces the erstwhile Freedom of information Act, 2002. Under the provisions of the Act, any citizen may request information from a "public authority" (a body of Government or "instrumentality of State") which is required to reply expeditiously or within thirty days.

41. Established in **1804** by Sir James Mackintosh, the **Asiatic Society of Mumbai** (formerly *Asiatic Society of Bombay*) is a learned society in the field of Asian studies based in Mumbai. It can trace its origin to the Literary Society of Bombay, which first met in Bombay on November 26, 1804.

Established in **1890, Connemara Public Library, Chennai** (formerly *Madras*), is one of the four National Depository Libraries which receive a copy of all books, newspapers and periodicals published in India.

Established in October 1951 as a pilot project sponsored by UNESCO and Govt. of India, **Delhi Public Library** is a national depository library in the Indian state of Delhi. The library has 35 branches across the state.

In the early years of its formation the **Central Reference Library, Kolkata** (formerly *Calcutta*) CRL functioned under the Administrative charge of the Librarian, National Library. This arrangement went on until August 1970 when a new Librarian for CRL was appointed with independent charge. The CRL functions today as a separate subordinate office of the Ministry of Culture, Govt. of India.

42. First published in **1908, Anglo-American Code (AA code)** had though appeared in the same year of 1908 as the first successful product of British and American co-operation, it owes its origin to various 19th century codes.

Published in **1939** by the **American Library Association (ALA),** the Library Code of Ethics is a guideline for librarians and other library associates on how to uphold the values that libraries symbolise. Since its creation, it has been updated three times.

Published in **1964,** Dr. Ranganathan's **Classified Catalogue Code (CCC)** is primarily a subject catalogue arranged on the basis of notation (Margret Man). A common reader approaches the catalogue by author or title. Keeping this fact in view, he defined classified catalogue as a catalogue in which some entries are number entries and some are word entries.

The most influential code is the **Anglo-American Catalogue Rules I (AACR-I); Author and Title Entries,** first published in **1908** and revised in **1967**. A further revision was published in 1978 as ***Anglo-American Cataloguing Rules,*** second edition; it is commonly referred to as *AACR2*.

43. The **Browne Issue System** is an old library system for loaning books. When a book is lent to a member of a library, the librarian takes the identification of the borrower by taking the borrower's card (cards are tickets organised in trays) and removes the book's own card.

The two cards are filed together this date is stamped in the book. These cards/tickets have date of issue, and within date by the key on the card.

When the book is returned, the user's card is removed from the file of the day indicated by the stamp and given back, and the book card is replaced in the book.

Whilst the filed cards reveals as to which user has a particular book, or which books a particular reader has borrowed; this is only true whilst the loan continues. Afterwards no record of the transaction remains there.

44. Formed in **2000,** the **IIM Consortium** had its first meeting in Calicut. The objective was to ensure among the IIMs, optimum utilisation and enhancement of the resources, and to minimise the expenditure by consortia based subscriptions to the commonly subscribed databases and journals.

The **"Indian National Digital Library in Engineering Sciences and Technology (INDEST)** Consortium" was set up in **2003** and the IIT Delhi has been designated as the Consortium Headquarters to coordinate its activities. The Consortium was renamed as INDEST-AICTE Consortium in December 2005 with the AICTE playing a pivotal role in enrolling its approved engineering colleges and institutions as members of the Consortium for selected e-resources at much lower rates of subscription.

Consortium for e-Resources in Agricultural Libraries was launched successfully on **30 April 2008** at its headquarters at IARI. Consortium for e-Resources in Agriculture (CeRA) provides access to about 2,900 scholarly journals including almost 300 journals in veterinary science and related fields such as dairy science and technology, biotechnology, and fisheries.

The National Knowledge Resource Consortium (NKRC), established in year **2009,** is a network of libraries and information centres of 40 CSIR and 26 DST laboratories. The NKRC is the national platform to allocate core S&T online resources (7000+ online journals and 18 major global databases like Web of Science, SciFinder, Science Direct) to all 23 DST and 40 CSIR laboratories in a substantive cost effective manner.

45. (*a*) In telecommunications, a communications **protocol** is a system of rules that allow two or more entities of a communications system to transmit information via any kind of variation of a physical quantity. These are the rules or standard that defines the syntax, semantics and synchronisation of communication and possible error recovery methods. Protocols may be implemented by hardware, software or a combination of both.

(*b*) A **device driver** that manages network services is a program to control a particular type of device that is attached to computer. There are device drivers for printers, displays, CD-ROM readers, diskette drives, and so on. A device driver essentially converts the more general input/output instructions of the operating system to messages that the device type can understand.

(*c*) Workstation **nodes** and unmanaged server nodes can be brought online to run job and be taken offline manually or automatically with the specification of a weekly availability policy in the node template. They can automatically become available to run cluster jobs according to a weekly availability policy that one configures (for example, every night on weekdays and all day on weekends).

(*d*) A **transmission** medium is a material substance that can propagate energy waves. Cable radio (also called "cable FM", from 1928) and cable television (from 1932): both via coaxial cable, originally serving principally as transmission media for programming produced at either radio or television stations, but later expanding into a broad universe of cable-originated channels.

46. (***a***) **Bus:** Bus topology uses one main cable to which all nodes are directly connected. The main cable acts as a backbone for the network. One of the computers in the network typically acts as the computer server.

(***b***) **Star:** In star topology, each computer is connected to a central hub using a point-to-point connection. The central hub can be a computer server that manages the network, or it can be a much simpler device that only makes the connections between computers over the network possible.

(*c*) **Ring:** In ring topology, the computers in the network are connected in a circular fashion, and the data travels in one direction. Each computer is directly connected to the next computer, forming a single pathway for signals through the network.

(*d*) **Mesh:** In mesh topology, every node has a direct point-to-point connection to every other node. Since all connections are direct, the network can handle very high-volume traffic. It is also robust because if one connection fails, the others remain intact. Security is also high since data travels along a dedicated connection.

48. (*a*) **Chartered Institute of Library and Information Professionals (CILIP):** Formed in 2002, CILIP is the leading professional body for librarians, information specialists and knowledge managers in the United Kingdom. Its vision is a fair and economically prosperous society underpinned by literacy, access to information and the transfer of knowledge. CILIP has developed an information literacy model that contains the following eight competencies/understandings that an individual needs to be information literate:

- *A need for information*
- *The resources available*
- *How to find information*
- *Need to evaluate results*
- *How to work with or exploit results*
- *Ethics and responsibility of use*
- *How to communicate or share your finding*
- *How to manage your findings.*

(*b*) **Society of College, National and University Libraries (SCONUL):** SCONUL aims to promote excellence in library services in higher education and national libraries across the UK and Ireland. It developed the Seven Pillars of Information Literacy model in 1999, and the most recent version was published in 2011. The latest version recognises that becoming information literate "is not a linear process"; rather, individuals can take different paths to become information literate and may learn different skills at different points.

The following 'lenses' have been created, which take the seven pillars and observe them through the eyes of individuals engaged in the following types of activities:

- *Research lens*
- *Digital Literacy lens*
- *Open Educational Resources lens*
- *Evidence-based practice healthcare lens*

(*c*) **Association of College & Research Libraries (ACRL):** Founded in 1940, ACRL is the higher education association for librarians. Representing over 11,000 academic and research librarians and interested individuals, ACRL develops programs, products and services to help academic and research librarians learn, innovate and lead within the academic community. It updates the information literacy competency standards for higher education so that they reflect the current thinking on such things as the creation and dissemination of knowledge, the changing global higher education and learning environment, the shift from information literacy to information fluency, and the expanding definition of information literacy to include multiple literacy, e.g., transliteracy, media literacy, digital literacy, etc.

(*d*) **International Federation of Library Associations and Institutions (IFLA):** IFLA is the leading international body representing the interests of library and information services and their users. It is the global voice of the library and information profession. Guidelines on Information Literacy for Lifelong Learning of IFLA have been compiled by the Information Literacy Section (InfoLit) of IFLA with the aim of providing a pragmatic framework for those professionals who need or are interested in starting an information literacy program.

49. (*a*) **Wilson's** various models of information behaviour (Wilson 1981, 1999, Wilson & Walsh 1996) were developed over time. Wilson presented a series of interrelated models in his 1981 paper, which has become one of the most cited publications in the field reproduced in figures. One of them suggests a three-fold view of information seeking: the context of the seeker, the 'system' employed (which might be manual or machine and navigated either personally or by an intermediary), and the information resources that might be drawn upon.

(*b*) **Dervin's** Model of ISB has the concept of sense-making approach on situation, gap and outcome-three key elements. Sense-making considers how we (attempt to) make sense of uncertain situations. Her description of sense-making consisted of the definition of how we interpret information to use for own information relation decisions. She described sense-making as a method through which people make sense of their worlds in their own language.

(*c*) **Kuhlthau's** work complements that of Ellis by attaching to stages of the 'information search process' the associated feelings, thoughts and actions, and the appropriate information tasks. This association of feelings, thoughts and actions clearly identify Kuhlthau's perspective as phenomenological, rather than cognitive.

(*d*) **Marchionini's** ISB Model, a more integrated model, is all about better to capture the processes users apply in an electronic search. This model was designed as a generic construct to describe the information seeking processes from any electronic information source. It focuses specifically on the information search processes of electronic system users, and their actual information seeking activities. This model has been widely cited in studies on search behaviour and search queries.

50. (*a*) **Descriptive Research** refers to the type of research question, design, and data analysis that will be applied to a given topic. Descriptive studies are aimed at finding out "what is," so observational and survey methods are frequently used to collect descriptive data (Borg & Gall, 1989). Studies of this type might describe the current state of multimedia usage in schools or patterns of activity resulting from group work at the computer.

(*b*) **Applied Research** aims at finding a solution for an immediate problem faced by a society, or an industrial/business organisation. The problems to be solved may consist of different types – it may be social, medical, environmental, technical and other various types of problems, which can be remedied immediately by dint of Applied research. Psychologists working in human factors or industrial/organisational fields often do this type of research.

(*c*) **Empirical Research** can be defined as "research based on experimentation or observation (evidence)". Such research is conducted to test a hypothesis. The word empirical means information gained by experience, observation, or experiment. The central theme in scientific method is that all evidence must be empirical which means it is based on evidence. In scientific method, the word "empirical" refers to the use of working hypothesis that can be tested using observation and experiment.

(*d*) **Analytical Research** is a specific type of research that involves critical thinking skills and the evaluation of facts and information relative to the research being conducted. A variety of people including students, doctors and psychologists use analytical research during studies to find the most relevant information. From analytical research, a person finds out critical details to add new ideas to the material being produced.

51. (*a*) **Day book system or Book-keeping** is the recording of financial transactions, and is part of the process of accounting in business. Transactions include purchases, sales, receipts, and payments by an individual person or an organisation/ corporation.

(*b*) In **Ledger system**, the statement of financial position and the statement of income and comprehensive income are both derived from the general ledger. Generally, each account in the general ledger consists of one page for one borrower. The general ledger is where posting to the accounts occurs. Posting is the process of recording amounts as credits (right side), and amounts as debits (left side), in the pages of the general ledger.

(*c*) In **One card system**, only one card is issued per person for each book, regardless of residency status. Library cards are for the sole use of the individual to whom the card has been issued and are not to be loaned to others.

(*d*) **Two Card system** or **Browne Issue System** is an old library system for lending books. When a book is lent to a member of a library, the librarian takes the identification of the borrower by taking the borrower's card (cards are tickets organised in trays) and removes the book's own card. The two cards are filed together this date is stamped in the book. These cards/tickets have date of issue, and within date by the key on the card. When the book is returned, the user's card is removed from the file of the day indicated by the stamp and given back, and the book card is replaced in the book.

53. (*a*) **Indian Education Commission (1964-1966)**, popularly known as **Kothari Commission**, was an ad hoc commission set up by the Government of India to examine all aspects of the educational sector in India, to evolve a general pattern of education and to advise guidelines and policies for the development of education in India. The Kothari Commission on Education mentioned, "No university, college, or department, should be set up without taking into accounts its library needs in terms of staff, books, journals, space, etc. Nothing could be more damaging to a growing department than to neglect its library or to give it a low priority..."

(*b*) After Independence, the most significant action of the Government of India in the field of education was the appointment of the **University Education Commission (UEC)** also known as **Radhakrishnan Commission** under the chairmanship of Dr. S. Radhakrishnan in 1948. The Commission was appointed, to report on Indian University Education and suggest improvements and extensions that may be desirable to suit the country's present and future requirement. The UEC has submitted its report in 1949. Library was also considered playing a major role in educational uplift. In this respect, the Radhakrishnan Commission observed that the library is the heart of all the university's work.

(*c*) The **Calcutta University Commission** was appointed in 1917-1919, result of which unravelled the fact that the system of university education in Bengal was wholly inadequate to meet the modern needs of the Presidency. It lacked the adequate libraries for students. In order to achieve the aims of the university, library was kept in one of the dire requirements. So it was recommended it is right and proper that the universities should provide great libraries and great laboratories of research with great scholars to direct them.

(*d*) The US President **Truman** appointed a Presidential Commission on Higher Education in the summer of 1946, urging, "We should now re-examine our system of higher education in terms of its objectives, methods, and facilities; and in the light of the social role it has to play." The Commission laid huge emphasis on improving the standard of education. President Truman's Commission on Higher Education said, "The Library is second only to the instructional staff in its importance for high quality instruction and research."

54. (*a*) **Books in Print** is the leading bibliographic database for publishers, retailers and libraries around the world, which helps people search the marketplace, find the right title, and explore all known format options. Its publishers, R.R. Bowker LLC ("**Bowker**") is an American limited liability company based in New Providence, New Jersey, and incorporated in Delaware.

(*b*) **The Statesman's Yearbook** is a one-volume reference book providing information on the countries of the world. It is published by **Palgrave Macmillan**.

(*c*) **Ulrich's Periodicals Directory** (ISSN 0000-0175, and ISSN 0000-2100), which is produced by **ProQuest**, is the standard library directory and database providing information about popular and academic magazines, scientific journals, newspapers and other serial publications.

(*d*) **Encarta Encyclopedia** was a digital multimedia encyclopedia published by **Microsoft Corporation** from 1993 to 2009. Originally available for sale on multiple CDs or a DVD, it was later also available on the World Wide Web via an annual subscription – although later many articles could also be viewed free online with advertisements.

55. (*a*) **A Statistical Analysis of the Literature** by the British zoologist, **Prof. Francis Joseph Cole** focuses on the idea of using the number of published scientific research products to measure activity in this area. The publication is primarily concerned with patent issues – to grant, on what basis is awarded for how long, and among other territorial inclusion of the works themselves. This work has become a key area for bibliometrics.

(*b*) **Statistical Bibliography** in relation to the growth of modern civilisation consists of two lectures delivered in the University of Cambridge in May, 1922, by **E.W. Hulme**, B.A., Sandars Reader in Biblography, sometime Librarian of the Patent Office. His first two lectures dealt with the thesis of human mind in its practical application to library work and the compilation of subject bibliographies. Here, statistical bibliography is considered in relation to the growth of modern civilisation.

(*c*) **From Librametry to informetrics: An Overview and Ranganathan's Contributions** mentions selected informetrics techniques with examples from library and information field. Discusses briefly the contributions of **Dr. S.R. Ranganathan** to quantification in library work and service; some of the applications appear to be intuitive with a view to improving information services to users, making the services more user-friendly and enhancing efficiency of library and information management. Ranganathan suggested the term Librametry in 1948.

(*d*) The term, ***bibliometrics*** was coined by Alan Pritchard in a paper published in 1969, titled ***Statistical Bibliography*** or ***Bibliometrics***. He defined the term as "the application of mathematics and statistical methods to books and other media of communication". Bibliometrics is the statistical analysis of bibliographic data, commonly focusing on citation analysis of research outputs and publications, i.e. how many times research outputs and publications are being cited. Bibliometric analysis is becoming an increasingly important way to measure and assess research impact of individuals, groups of individuals or institutions.

56. (*a*) **Arthur Fremont Rider** (May 25, 1885 – October 26, 1962) was an American writer, poet, editor, inventor, genealogist, and librarian. Rider's ***International Classification*** and early editions of the DDC are broad classifications. Rider's *International Classification* is an example of an enumerative classification organisation. Enumerative classifications are contemptuously called since spot and park organisations. An Approximately Enumerative scheme for classification consists of a big schedule enumerating mainly of the subjects of the past, the present, and the anticipatable future, and in addition some schedules of general isolates.

(*b*) The ***British Technology Index*** is a publication of the Library Association. First published in 1962 under the editorship of **E. J. Coates**, it is a monthly subject indexing, with annual cumulations, and it aims to provide access to technical papers in over three hundred British journals. Since January 1972 an author index has been included.

(*c*) The ***Functional Requirements for Bibliographic Records*** **(FRBR)** Review Group reports to the **IFLA** Cataloguing Section. All reports are posted on the **IFLA** website. Members of the FRBR Review Group are elected by members of the Cataloguing Section Standing Committee. There can be neither less than 8, nor more than 10 members. The chair is appointed for a two-year term from among the members by the chair of the Cataloguing Section. A regular term of service lasts 4 years, with one renewal allowed, and can be restricted to 2 years or extended beyond 8 years under certain circumstances.

(*d*) **Eugene Garfield** (born September 16, 1925) is an American linguist and businessman, one of the founders of bibliometrics and scientometrics. He is responsible for many innovative bibliographic products, and the ***Science Citation Index*** **(SCI)**, is one of them. The creation of the *Science Citation Index* made it possible to calculate impact factor, which supposedly measures the importance of scientific journals. It led to the unexpected discovery that a few journals like *Nature* and *Science* were core for all of hard science. The same pattern does not happen with the humanities or the social sciences

58. (*a*) The main purpose of ***Trade bibliographies*** is to list titles that are currently available from a whole series of publishers, within a geographic area. For example, Whitaker's *Books in Print* concentrates on materials published in Great Britain, while Canadian *Books in Print* contains everything that is currently available from Canadian publishing houses. If a desired book is out of print, a librarian may decide to replace it with an alternative title, or place it on a desiderata or wish list.

(*b*) ***Ulrich's Periodicals Directory*** (ISSN 0000-0175, and ISSN 0000-2100) is the standard library directory and database providing information about popular and academic magazines, scientific journals, newspapers and other serial publications.

(*c*) Now in its 65th edition, ***The Europa World of Learning*** is one of the world's leading reference works in the form of **Directory**. Updated to the highest editorial standards, entries are sourced directly from the organisations to ensure accurate and reliable information. The accreditation status of every university and college is verified before its entry is approved. Every type of academic institution is covered therein.

(*d*) Published in Delhi, ***Who's Who in India*** is a **biographical source** that that gives information about the persons holding the highest offices as well as respectable positions at the Executive, Judiciary, and Legislature levels in the country. Sometimes, proprietors and CEOs of big and widely known companies are also included in India's Who's is Who. Users can get the detailed profiles of the President, Vice President, Prime Minister, Chief Ministers, Members of Parliament, Governors and Chief Justice of India etc.

59. (*a*) In most countries, and also notably in UNESCO, there has developed in recent years, a growing awareness of the importance of ***bibliographical services***, not as ends in themselves but as a means of contributing to the efficiency and economy of studies and activity in all fields of education, science, culture and entertainment. Compilation of audio records by a **singer** also comes under bibliographic service.

(*b*) An email **alert service** is an option by which an email is sent according to an alert request specified by the Internet user. An email alert may concern any required information, including the latest e-journals, which can be accessed through their respective **links**. Email alerts are, for instance, frequently used on real estate websites or job boards and on ecommerce sites for product availability etc.

(*c*) **Condensation service** is abstracting selected and analysed information. Through the process of **abstraction**, a programmer hides all but the relevant data about an object in order to reduce complexity and increase efficiency, and that is done through condensation service.

(*d*) **Support service** in translation work is the service that helps in **translating** the copy of a document.

60. The statement in **Assertion (A)** is true, as LIS professionals' true professionalism premises on doing justice to their responsibility and skills, with which they provide their service. Thus, they can build the image of the profession by discharging their duties with full responsibility while utilising the skills they have.

The statement in **Reason (R)** is also true, as the professionals' image can be gauged by the quality of service they render, not by their financial gains.

61. The **Five laws of library science** is a theory proposed by S.R. Ranganathan in 1931, detailing the principles of operating a library system. The statement in **Assertion (A)** is true, as these laws are the normative principles that are proved capable of countering any problem faced by the librarians. Many librarians worldwide accept them as the foundations of their philosophy. Thus, the statement in **Reason (R)** is also true because normative principles not only help the librarians do their assigned tasks impeccably, but also help them determine norms or standards in day-to-day library practice.

62. **RFID** (Radio Frequency IDentification) is the latest technology to be used in library theft detection systems. RFID-based systems move beyond security to become tracking systems that combine security with more efficient tracking of materials throughout the library, including easier and faster charge and discharge, inventorying, and materials handling. So it is truly said in **Assertion (A)** that the use of RFID technology has helped a lot in self-checking or self-issue of books option in the circulation module. However, as mentioned in **Reason (R)** that application of RFID technology is economically viable and suitable to all types of libraries, is false.

63. In computing, the **Post Office Protocol (POP)** is an application-layer Internet standard protocol used by local e-mail clients to retrieve e-mail from a remote server over a TCP/IP connection. POP has been developed through several versions, with version 3 (**POP3**) being the last standard in common use before largely being made obsolete by the more advanced IMAP. It's true definition of POP as given in **Reason (R)**. However, the statement about POP in **Assertion (A)** is false; it does not have relevance with the use or importance of POP.

64. Institutional Repositories (IRs) are online archive of an institution's scholarly papers, deposited by their authors. Institutional Repositories may include a variety of research output of an organisation such as datasets, administrative documents, course notes, learning objects, or conference proceedings. IRs provide scholars with a common platform so that everyone in the institution can contribute scholarly material to promote cross-campus interdisciplinary research. In the light of above definition of IR and as defined both in **Assertion (A)** and **Reason (R)** are true.

66. The statement in **Assertion (A)** is true, as nowadays many people, who are claiming to be author, have resorted to plagiarism. The reason behind the substantial increase in plagiarism is easy and increased access to digital documents, through which they extract the desired information (by copying them) and simply paste them instead of using their own diction and writing. The statement in **Reason (R)** is true as well, because a majority of the people do not know how to cite the digital documents.

67. The statement in **Assertion (A)** is true because the information, which we obtain from different sources, are made available by synergic combination of medium and message.

A **conduit** is a pipe, duct or a channel through which anything is conveyed. In other words, it can also be regarded as a means of communication, while **content** means the substance or significance of a written work, especially as contrasted with its form. Besides, content also have some other meanings. Thus, it will be wrong to say that there is no difference between conduit and content. So the statement in **Reason (R)** is false.

68. The digital information environment has dramatically changed the way that faculty and students access information offered by academic libraries. Libraries around the world are playing a major role for themselves in this "digital revolution" by negotiating for and providing networked electronic services that publishers and vendors formerly sell as print materials. These include electronic indexes and abstracts, reference materials, electronic journals, and electronic books, just to name a few. Thus, the statement in **Assertion (A)** is true. But it will be wrong to say that there is no distortion from barriers to communication process in networked environment. So the statement in **Reason (R)** is false.

72. In India, all the public libraries are maintained by voluntary organisations for a fairly long time, Some are maintained by Regional and District Libraries and assists the libraries at the Gram Panchayat level. The Education Department of the Puducherry Government is now maintaining 64 Branch Libraries in rural areas. Therefore, the statement given in **Assertion (A)** is false.

However, the statement in **Reason (R)** is true, as UNESCO manifesto recommended that public libraries should be maintained wholly from public funds.

73. Functional Requirements of Bibliographic Records (FRBR) is a broadly defined approach to cataloguing which takes into account the inter-relationships among different entities. To pursue global sharing of information resources RDA is being developed in line with a set of objectives and principles which are based on the IME ICC (IFLA Meeting of Experts on an International Cataloguing Code) draft Statement of International cataloguing principles. Thus, the statement in **Assertion (A)** is true. FRBR outlines the relationship among many different interpretations or expressions as stated in **Reason (R)**, is also true.

75. As per **AACR – 2**, the chief source of information is the title page. If there is no title page, the part of the item supplying the most complete information is to be used, whether this is the cover (excluding a book jacket), half title page, caption, colophon, running title or other part. If information traditionally given on the title page is given on facing pages without repetition or with only partial repetition, it is to be considered that these pages are kept together as the chief source. Separate title pages are not to be combined nor are the title pages to be added. When no statement of responsibility is given on the chief source, but information appears prominently on the title page verso, pages preceding the title page, or cover, the information is transcribed as remainder of title and enclosed in square brackets. So in the light of the above information, the statement given in **Assertion (A)** is false while the statement in **Reason (R)** is true.

Previous Paper (Solved)

UGC–NET Library and Information Science, June–2015

PAPER-II

Note : *This paper contains* ***fifty*** *(**50**) objective type questions, each question carries* ***two*** *(**2**) marks. All questions are compulsory.*

1. S.M.C.R Communication model was developed by:
A. David K Berlo B. Harold Lasswell
C. W. Schramm D. Charles Osgood

2. Who suggested the 'Seven Lamps of Conduct' as must for library professional?
A. Joint Council of Library Association in India (JOCLAI)
B. Indian Library Association
C. S.R. Ranganathan
D. R.L. Mettal

3. DARE, which is a UNESCO database, provides information for:
A. Social Sciences B. Applied Sciences
C. Law D. Pure Sciences

4. Which type of information need can be satisfied with Review and State-of-the-Art Reports?
A. Everyday B. Exhaustive
C. Current D. Catching up

5. The Principle which states that if the facet B in a subject will not be operative without the concept behind A is conceded then B should follow A is known as:
A. Principle of later in time
B. Principle of gradual evolution
C. Principle of bottom upwards
D. Wall-picture principle

6. The principle which states 'that between two or more possible alternatives bearing on a particular phenomenon the one leading to overall economy is to be preferred' is known as:
A. Law of symmetry
B. Law of Parsimony
C. Law of Osmosis
D. Law of Impartiality

7. The records associated with genealogy file might reasonably be arranged in a:
A. Clustered files
B. Tree-structured files
C. Hashed files
D. Indexed files

8. What is the purpose of cookies?
A. Identify Users on the server
B. Act as buffer store
C. Connects database
D. Develops dynamic webpages

9. "Rank × frequency = constant" formula describes the essence of:
A. Impact factor B. Zipf's Law
C. Fuzzy query D. Lotka Law

10. Name the Indian Librarian who was honoured with the title of 'Khan Bahadur' in 1935 by the British Government?
A. S.R. Ranganathan B. B.S. Kesavan
C. K. M. Asadullah D. K. Issac

11. NALANDA, the digital library is an initiation of:
A. DRTC
B. IISC Bangalore
C. National Institute of Technology, Calicut
D. NISCAIR

12. Six Sigma in quality management was developed by:

A. Motorola B. IBM

C. Honey well D. GENPACT

13. In Binary Number System digit '11' is represented by:

A. 1010 B. 00001011

C. 110011 D. 00010110

14. Arrange the following elements of ISBN in proper order:

(*a*) Check Digit

(*b*) Registration Group Element

(*c*) Publication Element

(*d*) Registrant Element

Codes:

A. (*a*), (*c*), (*b*), (*d*) B. (*c*), (*a*), (*d*), (*b*)

C. (*d*), (*b*), (*a*), (*c*) D. (*b*), (*d*), (*c*), (*a*)

15. Identify the correct sequence of user tasks that are supported by the structure of FRBR, RDA, 0.2 version:

A. Identify, Select, Obtain, Find

B. Find, Identify, Select, Obtain

C. Select, Identify, Find, Obtain

D. Find, Select, Identify, Obtain

16. Which of the following are formal means of communication?

(*a*) Adhoc talks (*b*) Reports

(*c*) Blogs (*d*) Meetings

Codes:

A. (*a*), (*b*) and (*c*) are correct

B. (*b*) and (*c*) are correct

C. (*b*) and (*d*) are correct

D. (*a*), (*b*) and (*d*) are correct

17. Identify parts of social science citation Index.

(*a*) Corporate Index

(*b*) Permuterm Subject Index

(*c*) Source Index

(*d*) Title Index

Codes:

A. (*a*), (*b*) and (*c*) are correct

B. (*b*), (*c*) and (*d*) are correct

C. (*c*), (*d*) and (*a*) are correct

D. (*d*), (*a*) and (*b*) are correct

18. Which of the following display racks are used to display print periodical publications?

(*a*) Kardex

(*b*) Step-type

(*c*) Pigeon-hole type

(*d*) Inclined type

Codes:

A. (*a*), (*b*) and (*c*) are correct

B. (*b*), (*c*) and (*d*) are correct

C. (*a*), (*c*) and (*d*) are correct

D. (*a*), (*b*) and (*d*) are correct

19. Which of the following elements are associated with Dervin's Model of Information Seeking Behaviour?

(*a*) Situation

(*b*) Extracting

(*c*) Gap

(*d*) Browsing

Codes:

A. (*a*) and (*b*) are correct

B. (*b*) and (*c*) are correct

C. (*a*) and (*c*) are correct

D. (*b*) and (*d*) are correct

20. Which of the following are the salient features of UDC - IME?

(*a*) Minimum three digits in a class number

(*b*) Main class 4 is vacant

(*c*) Notation is independent of any language or scripts

(*d*) More suitable to micro documents

Codes:

A. (*a*), (*b*) and (*c*) are correct

B. (*a*), (*b*) and (*d*) are correct

C. (*b*), (*c*) and (*d*) are correct

D. (*a*), (*c*) and (*d*) are correct

21. Which of the following are advantageous features of Portable Document Format (PDF)?

(*a*) More compatibility

(*b*) Easy Editing

(*c*) Supports image format

(*d*) Good compression ratio

Codes:

A. (*a*) and (*b*) are correct

B. (*b*) and (*c*) are correct

C. (*c*) and (*d*) are correct

D. (*d*) and (*a*) are correct

22. Which of the following sampling techniques offer an 'equal probability selection method'?
(*a*) Simple random sampling
(*b*) Quota sampling
(*c*) Purposive sampling
(*d*) Proportional stratified sampling
Codes:
A. (*a*) and (*b*) are correct
B. (*b*) and (*c*) are correct
C. (*a*) and (*c*) are correct
D. (*a*) and (*d*) are correct

23. Identify the three information activities presented by James Krikelas (1983) as the foundation of his ISB model:
(*a*) Information gathering
(*b*) Information seeking
(*c*) Information computing
(*d*) Information giving
Codes:
A. (*a*), (*b*) and (*d*) are correct
B. (*b*), (*d*) and (*a*) are correct
C. (*b*), (*c*) and (*d*) are correct
D. (*a*), (*c*) and (*d*) are correct

24. Arrange in sequence the following state Public Library Acts according to the year of their enactment.
(*a*) West Bengal
(*b*) Orissa
(*c*) Arunachal Pradesh
(*d*) Karnataka
Codes:
A. (*d*), (*a*), (*b*), (*c*) B. (*b*), (*a*), (*d*), (*c*)
C. (*c*), (*b*), (*d*), (*a*) D. (*d*), (*b*), (*c*), (*a*)

25. Arrange the following books by S.R. Ranganathan according to their publication year.
(*a*) Colon classification
(*b*) Elements of library classification
(*c*) Philosophy of library classification
(*d*) Prolegomena to library classification
Codes:
A. (*a*), (*d*), (*b*), (*c*) B. (*c*), (*d*), (*b*), (*a*)
C. (*b*), (*c*), (*d*), (*a*) D. (*d*), (*c*), (*b*), (*a*)

26. Arrange the following in the order of their development:
(*a*) DOS
(*b*) MACOS
(*c*) LINUX
(*d*) UBUNTO
Codes:
A. (*a*), (*b*), (*c*), (*d*) B. (*b*), (*c*), (*d*), (*a*)
C. (*a*), (*c*), (*b*), (*d*) D. (*b*), (*d*), (*a*), (*c*)

27. Identify the correct chronological order in which the following were established:
A. National Library of India (Kolkata), Delhi Public Library, Documentation Research and Training Centre, Raja Ram Mohan Roy Library Foundation
B. Delhi Public Library, Documentation Research and Training Centre, Raja Ram Mohan Roy Library Foundation, National Library of India (Kolkata)
C. Documentation Research and Training Centre, Raja Rammohan Roy Library Foundation, Delhi Public Library, National Library of India (Kolkata)
D. Raja Ram Mohan Roy Library Foundation, National Library of India (Kolkata), Delhi Public Library, Documentation Research and Training Centre

28. Match the following:

List-I	List-II
(*a*) W. Edward Deming	(*i*) Quality Control Circles
(*b*) Elton Mayo and others	(*ii*) Statistical Process Control
(*c*) Kaoru Ishikawa	(*iii*) Hawthorne Studies
(*d*) Shigeo Shingo	(*iv*) Zero defect

Codes:

	(*a*)	(*b*)	(*c*)	(*d*)
A.	(*ii*)	(*iii*)	(*i*)	(*iv*)
B.	(*iii*)	(*i*)	(*iv*)	(*ii*)
C.	(*iv*)	(*ii*)	(*iii*)	(*i*)
D.	(*i*)	(*iv*)	(*iii*)	(*ii*)

29. Match the following:

List-I	List-II
(*a*) A pictograph that stands for an individual word	(*i*) Petroglyphs
(*b*) A pictograph that stands for an individual idea	(*ii*) Petrograms
(*c*) Pictographs drawn or painted on rocks	(*iii*) Ideogram
(*d*) Pictographs incised or carved on rocks	(*iv*) Logogram

Codes:

	(*a*)	(*b*)	(*c*)	(*d*)
A.	(*iii*)	(*ii*)	(*i*)	(*iv*)
B.	(*ii*)	(*iii*)	(*iv*)	(*i*)
C.	(*iv*)	(*iii*)	(*ii*)	(*i*)
D.	(*i*)	(*iv*)	(*iii*)	(*ii*)

30. Match the following:

List-I	List-II
(*a*) Ecological Theory of Human Information Behaviour	(*i*) Sanda Erdelez
(*b*) Everyday Life Information Seeking	(*ii*) Williamson
(*c*) Information Encountering	(*iii*) Nicholas J. Belkin
(*d*) Anamalous State of Knowledge (ASK)	(*iv*) Reijo Sarolainen

Codes:

	(*a*)	(*b*)	(*c*)	(*d*)
A.	(*ii*)	(*iv*)	(*i*)	(*iii*)
B.	(*ii*)	(*i*)	(*iii*)	(*iv*)
C.	(*i*)	(*iv*)	(*ii*)	(*iii*)
D.	(*iv*)	(*i*)	(*iii*)	(*ii*)

31. Match the following:

List-I	List-II
(*a*) Annals of Library and Information Studies	(*i*) S.R.E.L.S., Bangalore
(*b*) Journal of Information Management	(*ii*) Delhi Library Association
(*c*) Herald of Library Science	(*iii*) NISCAIR, Delhi
(*d*) Library Herald	(*iv*) P.N. Kaula Endowment, Lucknow

Codes:

	(*a*)	(*b*)	(*c*)	(*d*)
A.	(*ii*)	(*iii*)	(*iv*)	(*i*)
B.	(*iii*)	(*i*)	(*iv*)	(*ii*)
C.	(*iii*)	(*ii*)	(*i*)	(*iv*)
D.	(*i*)	(*iii*)	(*iv*)	(*ii*)

32. Match the following:

List-I	List-II
(*a*) Barack Hussein Obama-II	(*i*) Gazetteer
(*b*) GDP Growth in last year	(*ii*) Who is who
(*c*) Universities in U.K.	(*iii*) Year Book
(*d*) Area of Ganjam District	(*iv*) World of Learning

Codes:

	(*a*)	(*b*)	(*c*)	(*d*)
A.	(*i*)	(*ii*)	(*iii*)	(*iv*)
B.	(*ii*)	(*iii*)	(*iv*)	(*i*)
C.	(*iv*)	(*ii*)	(*i*)	(*iii*)
D.	(*iii*)	(*iv*)	(*ii*)	(*i*)

33. Match the following:

List-I	List-II
(*a*) Illiad	(*i*) "Collective collection" of world libraries
(*b*) QuestionPoint	(*ii*) Cost effective training and staff development programme
(*c*) WebJunction	(*iii*) High quality reference service
(*d*) WorldCat	(*iv*) Interlibrary loan operation

Codes:

	(*a*)	(*b*)	(*c*)	(*d*)
A.	(*iv*)	(*iii*)	(*ii*)	(*i*)
B.	(*iii*)	(*ii*)	(*i*)	(*iv*)
C.	(*ii*)	(*i*)	(*iv*)	(*iii*)
D.	(*i*)	(*iv*)	(*iii*)	(*ii*)

34. Match the following:

List-I	List-II
(*a*) Nominal scale	(*i*) Temperature measurement

(*b*) Ordinal scale	(*ii*) Gender as variable		
(*c*) Interval scale	(*iii*) Ranking of library services		
(*d*) Ratio scale	(*iv*) Mass of a body		

Codes:

	(*a*)	(*b*)	(*c*)	(*d*)
A.	(*iii*)	(*iv*)	(*ii*)	(*i*)
B.	(*ii*)	(*iii*)	(*iv*)	(*i*)
C.	(*ii*)	(*iii*)	(*i*)	(*iv*)
D.	(*i*)	(*iv*)	(*iii*)	(*ii*)

35. Match the following:

List-I	**List-II**
(*a*) My SQL	(*i*) Language
(*b*) Apache	(*ii*) Server
(*c*) Perl	(*iii*) User Interface
(*d*) API	(*iv*) RDBMS

Codes:

	(*a*)	(*b*)	(*c*)	(*d*)
A.	(*ii*)	(*iv*)	(*iii*)	(*i*)
B.	(*iv*)	(*ii*)	(*i*)	(*iii*)
C.	(*i*)	(*ii*)	(*iii*)	(*iv*)
D.	(*iii*)	(*i*)	(*ii*)	(*iv*)

36. Match the following:

List-I	**List-II**
(*a*) Real time communication	(*i*) Bulletin Boards
(*b*) Telnet	(*ii*) Subscribed Membership
(*c*) USENET	(*iii*) Video conferencing
(*d*) Listserv	(*iv*) Remote Login

Codes:

	(*a*)	(*b*)	(*c*)	(*d*)
A.	(*ii*)	(*iii*)	(*iv*)	(*i*)
B.	(*iii*)	(*iv*)	(*i*)	(*ii*)
C.	(*iv*)	(*ii*)	(*i*)	(*iii*)
D.	(*iii*)	(*i*)	(*ii*)	(*iv*)

37. Assertion (A): Computers are tools that can help to create more Knowledge.

Reason (R): Knowledge is mechanical hence developed in computers.

Codes:

A. Both (A) and (R) are true
B. (A) is true, but (R) is false
C. Both (A) and (R) are false
D. (A) is false, but (R) is true

38. Assertion (A): Users need to have training in accessing to a large number of E-journals through consortia.

Reason (R): Most of the users are not aware of using Web-resources.

Codes:

A. (A) is true, but (R) is false
B. (A) is false, but (R) is true
C. Both (A) and (R) are false
D. Both (A) and (R) are true

39. Assertion (A): There is no need for distinct geographical sources like Gazetteers, maps, atlas, etc.

Reason (R): Some of the general reference sources like encyclopaedias, yearbooks, almanacs also include geographical information.

Codes:

A. Both (A) and (R) are true
B. Both (A) and (R) are false
C. (A) is true, but (R) is false
D. (A) is false, but (R) is true

40. Assertion (A): Boolean Logic allows a user to logically relate multiple concepts together to define what information is needed.

Reason (R): If the operators (AND, OR, NOT) are interpreted in their normal interpretation, they act too restrictive or too general.

Codes:

A. Both (A) and (R) are true
B. Both (A) and (R) are false
C. (A) is true and (R) is false
D. (A) is false and (R) is true

41. Assertion (A): While using OPAC user need to have some understanding of inverted files and search strategies.

Reason (R): Online catalogues place the responsibility for a search strategy on the user.

Codes:

A. (A) is true but (R) is false
B. Both (A) and (R) are true
C. Both (A) and (R) are false
D. (A) is false, but (R) is true

42. Assertion (A): Median is simply the middle value when the data have been arranged in an ascending or descending order.

Reason (R): Median refers to the middle value in a distribution.

Codes:

A. (A) is true, but (R) is false
B. (A) is false, but (R) is true
C. Both (A) and (R) are false
D. Both (A) and (R) are true

43. Assertion (A): Open access publication model involves zero cost.

Reason (R): Open access increases the visibility of the publication, as they are available to the users for free access.

Codes:

A. Both (A) and (R) are true
B. (A) is true but (R) is false
C. (A) is false but (R) is true
D. Both (A) and (R) are false

44. Assertion (A): Questionnaire is often used in surveys as the primary data collection tool.

Reason (R): Questionnaires prevent personal contact with respondents.

Codes:

A. Both (A) and (R) are true
B. Both (A) and (R) are false
C. (A) is true but (R) is false
D. (A) is false but (R) is true

45. Assertion (A): When the data is skewed, the arithmetic mean calculated is misleading.

Reason (R): Even when the data is skewed, the arithmetic mean gives some valuable information but needs to be interpreted in right manner.

Codes:

A. (A) is true, but (R) is false
B. Both (A) and (R) are true
C. Both (A) and (R) are false
D. (A) is false, but (R) is true

Directions (Qs. 46-50): *Read the passage given below and answer the questions based on your understanding of the passage.*

In British Columbia (B.C.) there are no public libraries on reserve, and the libraries that do exist on reserve are generally small, underfunded band council collections, and band school libraries. In Ontario, the provincial government contributes to the development of public libraries in First Nations Communities. However in 2001-2002, only 52 of 141 First Nation libraries in Ontario received operating grants, and because the operating grants are based on population size many small communities are underfunded. Among First Nations Communities, libraries are not always a priority when there are pressing needs in the areas of rights and title claims, infrastructure, education, and health. A First Nations library worker explains: "We need all our money to fund our land claims. If we don't have land, we don't have community. If we don't have community, we don't need a library."

The Library Services for Saskatchewan's Aboriginal Peoples Committee is composed of Aboriginal and public sector representatives who meet six times a year to advise on the implementation of the recommendations.

Public libraries in urban centers tend not to differentiate between Aboriginal people and the general population. As a consequence urban Aboriginal peoples are often not well served. There are exceptions, such as the Albert Library branch of the Regina Public Library and the Spadina branch of the Toronto Public that work.

46. Which of the following reflects the position of libraries In British Columbia?

A. There are no libraries on reserve
B. Public libraries on reserve are under funded
C. Band school libraries exist on reserve
D. There are 141 First Nations libraries

47. In Ontario in 2001-2002:

A. Only 52 first Nations libraries existed
B. Only 141 first nations libraries received operating grants
C. Many small communities are underfunded
D. Majority of First Nations libraries received operating grants

48. Among First Nations Communities
A. libraries are always priority
B. sometimes rights and title claims are pressing needs
C. there are no pressing needs for education and health
D. they need a library even when they do not have land

49. Which of the following is true about public libraries in urban centres?
A. Public libraries in urban centres tend to differentiate between aboriginal people and the general population
B. Urban aboriginal people are often well served by public library
C. The Albert library branch of the Rijina public library does not work closely with local urban aboriginal communities.
D. Spadina Branch of the Toronto Public library works closely with local aboriginal communities.

50. Which of the following is not true about the library services for Saskatchewan's Aboriginal Peoples Committee?
A. It has aboriginal representatives
B. It has public sector representatives
C. They meet once a year
D. They advise on the implementation of the recommendation

ANSWERS

1	2	3	4	5	6	7	8	9	10
A	D	A	D	D	B	B	A	B	C
11	**12**	**13**	**14**	**15**	**16**	**17**	**18**	**19**	**20**
C	A	B	D	B	C	A	B	C	C
21	**22**	**23**	**24**	**25**	**26**	**27**	**28**	**29**	**30**
C	D	A,B	A	A	A	A	A	C	A
31	**32**	**33**	**34**	**35**	**36**	**37**	**38**	**39**	**40**
B	B	A	C	B	B	B	D	D	A
41	**42**	**43**	**44**	**45**	**46**	**47**	**48**	**49**	**50**
B	D	C	C	B	C	C	B	D	C

SOME SELECTED EXPLANATORY ANSWERS

1. The S.M.C.R Model, developed by David K. Berlo and used in training programs of the National Project in Agricultural Communications, emphasizes the psychological nature of communication as it affects both the source and the receiver in any communication situation. Although other models have also emphasized the psychological nature of communication, the S-M-C-R Model has the special characteristics of providing an analysis of messages and of sensory channels in communication.

2. R.L. Mettal has suggested the 'Seven Lamps of Conduct' as must for library professional. They are
1. Impersonal Book Selection
2. Service Before Self
3. Split-mind
4. Sympathetic Behaviour
5. Tact
6. Industry
7. Scholarship

3. The DARE Database offers over 11,000 worldwide references to
- social science research and training institutes

- social sciences specialists
- social science documentation and information services
- social science periodicals

The database also contains special references to peace, human rights and international law research institutes.

5. **Wall-picture Principle:** Introduced by Ranganathan, this principle figuratively expresses a dependency. It states that "if two facets A and B of a subject are such that the concept behind B will not be operative unless the concept behind A is conceded, even as a mural picture is not possible unless the wall exists to draw on, then the facet A should precede the facet B".

6. **Law of parsimony** says that between two or more possible alternative bearing on a particular phenomenon, the one leading to overall economy of man-power, material, money and time considered together with proper weight age—is to be preferred.

   The law says that the possible those alternatives may be preferred which may be more helpful to users together overall economy in library classification.

8. A cookie is a piece of information in the form of a very small text file that is placed on an internet user's hard drive. It is generated by a web page server, which is basically the computer that operates a web site. The information the cookie contains is set by the server and it can be used by that server whenever the user visits the site. A cookie can be thought of as an internet user's identification card, which tell a web site when the user has returned.

9. Zipf's law state that "The frequency of a word is inversely proportional to its statistical rank." i.e. "Rank × Frequency = Constant".

10. **Khalifa Mohammad Asadullah** (1890 - 1949) was a pioneer of the library movement in the Indian subcontinent before 1947. He was also the first prominent librarian to opt for Pakistan at the time of independence in 1947. He was honoured with the title of Khan Bahadur in 1935.

11. NALANDA Digital Library initiated in 1999 at National Institute of Technology, Calicut, is one of the largest digital libraries in the country. NALANDA helps members of the NIT in meeting their academic and research needs by providing timely and up-to-date information with value added services in all the areas of science, engineering, and technology.

12. Six Sigma is a business management strategy originally developed by Motorola in 1986. Six Sigma seeks to improve the quality of process outputs by identifying and removing the causes of defects (errors) and minimising variability in manufacturing and business processes.

13.

2	11	1
2	5	1
2	2	0
	1	

$\therefore (11)_{10} = (1011)_2$.

14. An International Standard Book Number consists of 4 parts (if it is a 10 digit ISBN) or 5 parts (for a 13 digit ISBN):

    The parts of a 10-digit ISBN and the corresponding EAN 13 and barcode. Note the different check digits in each. The part of the EAN 13 labeled "EAN" is the Bookland country code.

    for a 13-digit ISBN, a prefix element - a GS1prefix: so far 978 or 979 have been made available by the registration group element, (language-sharing country group, individual country or territory) the registrant element, the publication element, and a checksum character or check digit.

    The 13 digit ISBN separates its parts (prefix element, registration group, registrant, publication and check digit) with either a hyphen or a space. Other than the prefix and the check digit, no part of the ISBN has a fixed number of digits.

The 10 digit ISBN also separated its parts (registration group, registrant, publication and check digit) with either a hyphen or a space.

15. RDA's principles are based on FRBR and the *Functional Requirements for Authority Data* (FRAD) both of which influenced the revision of the Paris Principles into the Statement of International Cataloguing Principles. The principles of RDA are to find, identify, select, obtain, and understand and moreover to provide relationships between multiple entities from other resources, authors, and publishers to works, editions, and corporate bodies.

16. In an organization, there are basically two ways of Communication namely:

- Formal and
- Informal communication
- Communication takes place through the formal channels of the organization structure along the lines of authority established by the management. Such communications are generally in writing and may take any of the forms; policy; manuals: procedures and rule books; memoranda; official meetings; reports, etc.

17. The *Science Citation Index* (SCI) provides access to current and retrospective bibliographic information; author abstracts, and cited references found in leading scholarly science and technical journals covering more than 100 disciplines.

It consists of following components: (*i*) Source Index, (*ii*) Permuterm Subject Index and (*iii*) Citation Index.

In Source Index: The *Source Index* provides full bibliographical record for the documents indexed in SCI - the other parts or indexes of SCI refer back to *Source Index* for complete record identification or information.

Permuterm Subject Index: It is called a natural language index because it uses current language (terminology) in the form of words from the title of articles listed in the *Source Index*, as subject headings.

Citation Index: The Citation Index, lists by first author, year of publication, and journal title and location (volume and pagination) every published and unpublished work cited in the references of articles published by the SCI's source journals during the year.

18. For displaying periodicals, usually periodical display racks are used. These display racks are of three kinds:

(*a*) **Step type:** Step type periodicals are displayed stepwise in this kind of rack.

(*b*) **Pigeon-hole type:** This is the most popular type of display rack in libraries especially in the libraries subscribing to a large number of periodicals. This type of rack has two parts, one being a cupboard in the bottom and other pigeon-holes at the top.

(*c*) **Inclined type:** This type of display rack is considered to be the best type and is an improvement over the earlier pigeon-hole type of rack. This is a box type of rack with horizontal shelves, each covered with wooden planks with an inclination to the shelf plank.

19. Dervin's sense-making framework comprises four basic elements: a *situation* in time and space defining the context in which information problems arise; a *cognitive gap* which identifies the difference between the contextual situation and the desired situation; an *outcome;* and a *cognitive bridge* involving some closing of the gap between the situation and outcome. In this model, the user is portrayed as moving through a situation in which he or she may experience a moment of discontinuity or gap.

20. The Universal Decimal Classification (UDC) is a bibliographic and library classification developed by the Belgian bibliographers Paul Otlet and Henri La Fontaine at the end of the

19th century. UDC provides a systematic arrangement of all branches of human knowledge organized as a coherent system in which knowledge fields are related and inter-linked.

Salient features of UDC-IME:

(*i*) Main Class 4 is vacant

(*ii*) Notation is independent of any language or scripts

(*iii*) More suitable to micro documents

21. Portable Document Format (PDF) is a file format used to present documents in a manner independent of application software, hardware, and operating systems.

Advantages of PDF: Quickly and Easily Created, Securable, Compact and Able to Compress Large Files, Supports Image Format, Self-contained.

22. Proportional stratified sampling is one of the most commonly applied forms of stratified sampling. If you choose to select your sample using stratified random sampling you can be confident that your sample will also be representative of the population on *all other variables* that are not used as stratification variables because you are still using simple random sampling within each population stratum. It is important to note that *proportional stratified sampling is an equal probability of selection method* (EPSM), which means that every individual in the population has an equal chance of being included in the sample. As a result, proportional stratified sampling produces samples that are representative of the population from which they are drawn.

24. Dr S.R. Ranganathan, father of Library Science, succeeded in the passage of this legislation and he was very keen about the development of effective public library system in India. The first Public Library Act was passed in India in 1948.

- Karnataka Public Libraries Act — 1965.
- Pachim Banga Public Libraries Act (Previously known as West Bengal Public Libraries Act) — 1979.
- Orissa Public Libraries Act — 2002.
- Arunachal Public Libraries Act — 2009.

25. Dr S.R. Ranganathan, father of the Indian library movement, was the most prolific writer and librarian of his time. His exemplary dedication and uncanny insights won him the acclaims of his peers the world over.

His major books on classification are:

- *Colon Classification:* Madras Library Association, Madras, 1933. The last edition done by Ranganathan was the 6th (1959), again issued with amendments in 1963, and published by Asia Publishing House, Bombay.
- *Prolegomena to Library Classification:* Madras Library Association, Madras, 1937. (Now in its 3rd Ed.) (1967) published by Asia Publishing House, Bombay. Its 2nd Ed. (1957) was brought out by the Library Association, London.
- *Elements of Library Classification:* NK Publishing House, Pune, 1945. (Now in its 3rd Ed., 1967), published by Asia Publishing House, Bombay.
- *Philosophy of Library Classification:* Ejnar Munksgaard, Copenhagen, 1951.

26. (*i*) MS-DOS was wide spread in 1982 when 50 companies licensed MS-DOS. Software and hardware manufacturers build on this binary standard at this time.

(*ii*) On January 24, 1984, Apple Computer Inc. introduced the Macintosh personal computer, later retroactively renamed to the Macintosh 128K model. The operating system of early Macintosh is named "System Software" or "System", and its ensuing series was later renamed to Mac OS after 7.5.

(*iii*) Linux is a Unix-like and mostly POSIX-compliant computer operating system (OS) assembled under the model of free and open-source software development and distribution. The defining component of Linux is the Linux kernel, an operating system kernel first released on 5 October 1991 by Linus Torvalds.

(*iv*) Ubuntu is a Debian-based Linux operating system and distribution, with Unity as its default desktop environment for personal computers including smartphones in later versions. Ubuntu also runs network servers. Ubuntu was released on 20 October 2004.

27. The Calcutta Public Library began its journey on 21st March 1836. The Library was established for reference and lending, open to all, irrespective of class, colour & nationalities, on the self-financing principle.

The Calcutta Public Library was subsequently merged with the Imperial Library and combining the collection of a number of secretariat libraries, the Imperial Library was opened to the public in January in 1903.

After Independence of India, the National Library came into being in place of Imperial Library by the "Imperial Library (Change of Name) Act" in 1948. It was accorded a special status of an institution of national importance in the Article 62 in the 7th Schedule of the Union list of the Constitution of India and Maulana Abul Kalam Azad, the then Union Minister of Education opened the Library to Public on 1st February 1953.

Delhi Public Library is a national depository library in the Indian state of Delhi. The library has 35 branches across the state. The Library was established on 27 October 1951 as a pilot project sponsored by UNESCO and the Government of India.

Documentation Research and Training Centre (DRTC) was established in January 1962 as a division of the Indian Statistical Institute.

Raja Rammohan Roy Library Foundation (RRRLF) was established in May, 1972 by the Department of Culture, Govt. of India to spread library services all over the country in cooperation with State Governments, Union Territory Administrations and Organisations working in the field.

28. (*i*) Quality circles originated in Japan in 1962; Kaoru Ishikawa has been credited with their creation.

(*ii*) William Edward Deming has helped to develop the sampling techniques still used by the U.S. Deming championed the work of Walter Shewhart, including Statistical Process Control, Operational Definitions, and what Deming called The Shewhart Cycle which had evolved into PDSA.

(*iii*) Elton Mayo's team conducted a number of experiments involving six female workers. These experiments are often referred to as the Hawthorne experiments or Hawthorne studies as they took place at The Hawthorne Works of the Western Electric Company in Chicago.

(*iv*) Shigeo Shingo was primarily an engineer. He developed Zero Quality Control (ZQC), an innovative approach in the era of quality control and other tools used by the Poka Yoke, a system of inspection the source.

29. (*i*) Petroglyphs are images created by removing part of a rock surface by incising, picking, carving, or abrading. Outside North America, scholars often use terms such as "carving", "engraving", or other descriptions of the technique to refer to such images.

(*ii*) Petrogram : a drawing or painting on rock, especially one made by a member of a prehistoric people.

(*iii*) Ideogram or ideograph is a graphic symbol that represents an idea or concept, independent of any particular language, and specific words or phrases.

(*iv*) Logographic systems, or logographies, are writing systems in which each symbol represents a concept rather than a sound, as in syllabaric or phonographic systems.

33. (*i*) WorldCat represents a "collective collection" of the world's libraries, built through the contributions of librarians, expanded and enhanced through individual, regional and national programs.

(*ii*) WebJunction works with a number of supporting organizations to provide cost-effective training and staff development programs that are convenient to access and easy to manage.

(*iii*) OCLC operates QuestionPoint, a service which lets students and others doing research directly query library professionals. It deliver high quality reference services.

(*iv*) Illiad is an interlibrary loan borrowing system designed and implemented in the University Libraries at Virginia Tech.

34. (*a*) Variables at a nominal scale of measurement are, typically, those such as gender, political affiliation, colour, etc. The values of these variables are qualitative, simple "labels", with no real quantitative difference between them.

(*b*) An ordinal datum helps us to distinguish relationships in terms of rank-order. Feelings or opinions are frequently measured in terms of ordinal data. For instance, a user may be asked to rank the importance of different library services. Thus, the ordinal scale of measurement yields information about the ordering of categories, but does not indicate the magnitude of differences between observations.

(*c*) On an interval scale, measurements are not only classified and ordered therefore having the properties of the two previous scales, but the distances between each interval on the scale are equal right along the scale from the low end to the high end.

(*d*) "A ratio scale is an interval scale in which distances are stated with respect to a rational zero rather than with respect to, for example, the mass of the body".

35. (*a*) MS SQL Server is a Relational Database Management System (RDBMS) developed by Microsoft Inc. Its primary query languages are:

- T-SQL.
- ANSI SQL.

(*b*) The Apache HTTP Server, colloquially called Apache is the world's most used web server software. Originally based on the NCSA HTTPd server, development of Apache began in early 1995 after work on the NCSA code stalled.

(*c*) Perl is a programming language developed by Larry Wall, especially designed for text processing. It stands for Practical Extraction and Report Language. It runs on a variety of platforms, such as Windows, Mac OS, and the various versions of UNIX.

(*d*) In computer programming, an application programming interface (API) is a set of routines, protocols, and tools for building software applications. An API expresses a software component in terms of its operations, inputs, outputs, and underlying types.

40. Boolean logic allows a user to logically relate multiple concepts together to define what information is needed. Typically the Boolean functions apply to processing tokens identified anywhere within an item. The typical Boolean operators are **AND, OR,** and **NOT**. These operations are implemented using set intersection, set union and set difference procedures. Issues arise when Boolean queries are associated with weighted index system. Some of the issues are associated with how the logic (AND, OR, NOT) operators function with weighted values and how weights are associated with the query terms. If the operators are interpreted in their normal interpretation, they act too restrictive or too general (i.e., AND and OR operators respectively).

42. The median is simply the middle value in a set of results that have been arranged in ascending or descending order. The mean is calculated from adding up all the values and dividing by the number of values to give the 'average' value.

The mode is useful if the data contains very similar numbers, such as shoe size. The median is used where the data is discrete and is often used in conjunction with the range.

45. When the arithmetic mean is used to calculate it can be misleading because the salaries can be widely spread. Thus it may happen that 10% of the class have gotten excellent job offers while half the class is without jobs. Even in such a scenario, the mean salary can be a good number, but it hides facts behind it. The median becomes a much better measure of the salaries of the students in this case.

However, in some cases, even when the data is skewed, the arithmetic mean gives some valuable information about the data but it needs to be interpreted in the right manner.

PAPER-III

Note: *This paper contains* ***seventy five (75)*** *objective type questions of* ***two (2)*** *marks each.* ***All*** *questions are compulsory.*

1. The protection of copyright in the care of films, photographs, anonymous, pseudonymous publications and works of governments, the 60 years period is counted from:

A. the date of birth of creator
B. year following the death of creator
C. the date of publication
D. as per statement of author

2. International Standard Music Number (ISMN) for print music is promoted, coordinated and supervised by:

A. International Agency for ISMN, London
B. International Standards Agency for Music, Sydney
C. Standards Agency for Music International, Paris
D. The International ISMN Agency, Berlin

3. In which year the WIPO Copyright Treaty was adopted?

A. 1995 B. 1996
C. 1997 D. 1998

4. Which one of the following data bases has not originated from USA?

A. BIOSIS
B. MEDLARS
C. Chemical Abstracts
D. INSPEC

5. The knowledge to which we have valid, conscious, introspective access under all circumstances is called:

A. Explicit knowledge
B. Semi tacit knowledge
C. Tacit knowledge
D. Predictive knowledge

6. 'Working Papers' fall under the category of:

A. Books B. Monographs
C. News papers D. Grey Literature

7. Who developed the theory of Information Supply and Indexing based on five axioms (doctorines) such as - definability; order; sufficient degree of order; predictability; and Fidelity?

A. Robert Fugmann B. William Cooper
C. E. Garfield D. Calvin Moores

8. Which of the viceroys was associated with the imperial library Act?

A. Lord Curzon B. Lord Minto
C. Lord Willington D. Lord Vipin

9. Identify the full form of the acronym FAIFE (IFLA)

A. Full-text Access to Information for Free Expression
B. Full-text Access to Internet for Free E-resources
C. Free Archives on Internet for Free Expression
D. Freedom of Access to Information and Freedom of Expression

10. Boolean Logic was propounded by:

A. P.K. Boole B. G.R. Boole
C. K.S. Boole D. George Boole

11. The 'Other Title Information' in statement of Responsibility Area in AACR II is preceded by a:

A. Semicolon B. Hyphen
C. Dash D. Colon

12. The term 'Partial Comprehension' in the Theory of Classification is known as:
A. Denudation
B. Fission
C. Lamination
D. Agglomeration kind-I

13. According to AACR-2 the source from which the title proper is taken is known as:
A. Chief Source of Information
B. Preferred Source of Information
C. Prescribed Source of Information
D. Referred Source of Information

14. SYNTOL stands for:
A. Syntactic Term On Line
B. Syntagmatic Term On Line
C. Syntagmatic Organisation Language
D. Syntactic Organising Language

15. Herzberg's 'two factor theory' deals with:
A. Staff recruitment B. Leadership
C. Decision making D. Motivation

16. In 'Open System Interconnect (OSI) Model' the layer between 'Network' and 'Physical' is:
A. Data link B. Transport
C. Application D. Presentation

17. The term indicating a distinct intellectual or artistic creation is:
A. Item B. Title
C. Expression D. Work

18. In a questionnaire, an item that directs participants to different follow-up questions depending on their response is called:
A. Contingency question
B. Response set
C. Secondary question
D. Filter question

19. Lok Sabha Secretariate Library Service is called as:
A. Lok Sabha Library
B. Legislators Library Services
C. LARRDIS
D. M.P. Library Services

20. The term literary warrant was introduced by:
A. W.B. Sayers B. S.R. Ranganathan
C. Melvil Dewey D. E.W. Hulmes

21. Sarda Ranganathan chair in Library science was announced in 1957 at the centenary celebration of:
A. University of Delhi
B. University of Madras
C. University of Bombay
D. Banaras Hindu University

22. Identify the statements which are true about e-books in an online environment:
(*a*) e-books are dependent on equipment to be used
(*b*) e-books offer seamless access
(*c*) all publishers produce the e-books equivalent of their print books
(*d*) e-books allows highlighting of contents.
Codes:
A. (*a*), (*b*), (*c*) are correct
B. (*b*), (*c*), (*d*) are correct
C. (*a*), (*c*), (*d*) are correct
D. (*a*), (*b*), (*d*) are correct

23. Which of the following are examples of collaborate virtual reference service?
(*a*) Ask A Librarian
(*b*) Wikis
(*c*) Folksonomies
(*d*) Question Point : 24/7 Reference
Codes:
A. (*b*) and (*c*) are correct
B. (*a*) and (*b*) are correct
C. (*a*) and (*d*) are correct
D. (*a*) and (*c*) are correct

24. Which of the following institutions are established by Dr. S.R. Ranganathan?
(*a*) INSDOC, Delhi
(*b*) DRTC, Bangalore
(*c*) Sarada Ranganathan Endowment, Bangalore
(*d*) National Library, Kolkata

Codes:

A. (*a*) and (*b*) are correct
B. (*b*) and (*d*) are correct
C. (*a*) and (*c*) are correct
D. (*b*) and (*c*) are correct

25. Descriptive technologies required to add meaning to the content of web documents include:

(*a*) Resource Description Framework (RDF)
(*b*) RFID
(*c*) Extensible Markup Language (XML)
(*d*) Barcode Technology

Codes:

A. (*b*) and (*c*) are correct
B. (*a*) and (*c*) are correct
C. (*c*) and (*d*) are correct
D. (*a*) and (*b*) are correct

26. Which of the following devices may be used for securing extrapolation in chain?

(*a*) Decimal fraction device
(*b*) Gap device
(*c*) Inversion device
(*d*) Isolate indicator device

Codes:

A. (*a*) and (*b*) are correct
B. (*b*) and (*c*) are correct
C. (*c*) and (*d*) are correct
D. (*a*) and (*c*) are correct

27. Which of the following are social book marking services?

(*a*) Facebook (*b*) Dropbox
(*c*) Favorites (*d*) Delicious

Codes:

A. (*a*) and (*b*) are correct
B. (*b*) and (*c*) are correct
C. (*a*) and (*c*) are correct
D. (*b*) and (*d*) are correct

28. Web-Junction is:

(*a*) a place where Public Library Staff gather to build knowledge, skills and support that they need to power relevant vibrant Libraries;
(*b*) on Online Learning Community launched by OLLC in 2003 for Library staff;
(*c*) providing free training resources on Library Management technology and services;
(*d*) an Offline platform that provides hands-on training in web-based applications to LIS students only of USA.

Codes:

A. (*a*), (*b*) and (*c*) are correct
B. (*b*), (*c*) and (*d*) are correct
C. (*a*), (*c*) and (*d*) are correct
D. (*a*), (*b*) and (*d*) are correct

29. The search in a Boolean query may be expanded by the following methods:

(*a*) Using thesaurus or list of related terms
(*b*) Stemming or reduction of a word to its root form
(*c*) Using literals
(*d*) Specifying number of terms

Codes :

A. (*a*) and (*d*) are correct
B. (*b*) and (*c*) are correct
C. (*c*) and (*d*) are correct
D. (*a*) and (*b*) are correct

30. RDA replaces the General Material Designations and the class of materials are to represented by:

(*a*) Content type (*b*) Carrier type
(*c*) Media type (*d*) Context type

Codes:

A. (*a*), (*b*) and (*c*) are correct
B. (*b*), (*c*) and (*d*) are correct
C. (*a*), (*b*) and (*d*) are correct
D. (*a*), (*c*) and (*d*) are correct

31. Which of the following are features of Micro subjects?

(*a*) A basic subject with isolate ideas
(*b*) Subject of great extension and small intension
(*c*) Subject of small extension and greater intension
(*d*) Subject usually embodied in the form of an article in a periodical, or a part or chapter or section of a book

Codes:

A. (*a*) and (*b*) are correct

B. (*c*) and (*a*) are correct
C. (*c*) and (*d*) are correct
D. (*b*) and (*d*) are correct

32. Which of the following are the features of "Folksonomy"?
(*a*) Keyword indexing
(*b*) Collaborative tagging
(*c*) Posts in chronological order
(*d*) Audio files
Codes:
A. (*a*) and (*b*) are correct
B. (*a*) and (*c*) are correct
C. (*b*) and (*d*) are correct
D. (*c*) and (*d*) are correct

33. Which of the following concepts are related to each other?
(*a*) Unity of command
(*b*) Factor of planning
(*c*) Espirit de crops
(*d*) Management by objectives
Codes:
A. (*c*) and (*d*) are correct
B. (*a*) and (*c*) are correct
C. (*b*) and (*d*) are correct
D. (*a*) and (*b*) are correct

34. Which of the following are synchronous communication tools?
(*a*) Instant Messaging
(*b*) Blog
(*c*) Video conferencing
(*d*) Bulletin Board
Codes:
A. (*a*) and (*b*) are correct
B. (*a*) and (*c*) are correct
C. (*b*) and (*c*) are correct
D. (*b*) and (*d*) are correct

35. Net-Neutrality in India:
(*a*) is the outcome of the absence of any law governing net-neutrality in India;
(*b*) requires that all internet users be treated differently and unfairly by user, content, site platform, application, type of attached equipment or mode of communication;
(*c*) is emerged due to reported violation of the net-neutrally principles by the Indian ISPs;
(*d*) came to public debate after a mobile Telephony Service Provider in India announced to levy additional charges for making voice calls (VoIP) from its network using apps like, 'WhatsApp', Skype, etc.
Codes:
A. (*a*), (*c*) and (*d*) are correct
B. (*b*), (*c*) and (*d*) are correct
C. (*a*), (*b*) and (*d*) are correct
D. (*a*), (*b*) and (*c*) are correct

36. 'Information Filtering System' is primarily designed for:
(*a*) unstructured or semi-structured data;
(*b*) delivery of information to people who need it;
(*c*) removal and selection of data or an object from an incoming stream for a given profile;
(*d*) location and inclusion of data or object in the stream.
Codes:
A. (*a*), (*b*) and (*c*) are correct
B. (*b*), (*c*) and (*d*) are correct
C. (*a*), (*c*) and (*d*) are correct
D. (*a*), (*b*) and (*d*) are correct

37. The arithmetic mean is the most commonly used statistical mean to measure:
(*a*) Average
(*b*) Central tendency of data
(*c*) Sum of data points
(*d*) Nature of distribution of data
Codes :
A. (*a*) and (*c*) are correct
B. (*a*) and (*b*) are correct
C. (*c*) and (*d*) are correct
D. (*b*) and (*d*) are correct

38. Which of the following organizations are associated with the development of public libraries?
(*a*) UNESCO (*b*) RRRLF
(*c*) INFLIB NET (*d*) DRTC

Codes:

A. (*a*) and (*b*) are correct
B. (*a*) and (*d*) are correct
C. (*c*) and (*d*) are correct
D. (*b*) and (*d*) are correct

39. Which of the following are access authentication methods for digital collection?

(*a*) Shibboleth (*b*) Open ID
(*c*) Open URL (*d*) Counter

Codes:

A. (*a*) and (*b*) are correct
B. (*a*) and (*c*) are correct
C. (*b*) and (*c*) are correct
D. (*b*) and (*d*) are correct

40. Identify the principles of PRECIS:

(*a*) Context dependency
(*b*) Formalisation
(*c*) Modulation
(*d*) One-to-one relationship

Codes:

A. (*a*) and (*b*) are correct
B. (*a*) and (*c*) are correct
C. (*a*) and (*d*) are correct
D. (*b*) and (*d*) are correct

41. Arrange the following according to the year of first publication:

(*a*) Medical Subject Headings
(*b*) Sears List of Subject Headings
(*c*) Library of Congress Subject Headings
(*d*) AGROVOC

Codes:

A. (*b*), (*a*), (*d*), (*c*) B. (*c*), (*b*), (*a*), (*d*)
C. (*b*), (*a*), (*c*), (*d*) D. (*a*), (*c*), (*d*), (*b*)

42. Arrange the following codes of ethics in the order of their development:

(*a*) Librarian's Canons of Ethics, First code of ethics for Librarianship in USA.
(*b*) Code of Ethics - ALA.
(*c*) Code of Professional Conduct - LA, UK
(*d*) Code of Ethics for Librarians and Information workers - IFLA

Codes:

A. (*a*), (*b*), (*c*), (*d*) B. (*b*), (*a*), (*c*), (*d*)
C. (*d*), (*b*), (*a*), (*c*) D. (*c*), (*a*), (*b*), (*d*)

43. Identify the correct sequence of entities in Group 1 of Functional Requirements of Bibliographic Records (FRBR), RDA 0.2 version:

A. Expression, Works, Items, Manifestation
B. Works, Items, Expression, Manifestation
C. Works, Expression, Manifestation, Item
D. Works, Expression, Item, Manifestation

44. Arrange the following landmarks in the Library Movement of India in proper sequence:

(*a*) First All India Library Conference (Calcutta)
(*b*) First All India Public Library Conference (Madras)
(*c*) First Public Library Act Enacted in Madras
(*d*) First Library Association in India (Andhra Desa Library Association)

Codes:

A. (*d*), (*b*), (*a*), (*c*) are correct
B. (*b*), (*d*), (*c*), (*a*) are correct
C. (*c*), (*b*) (*d*), (*a*) are correct
D. (*a*), (*c*), (*b*), (*d*) are correct

45. Arrange the following steps given in sample Design in proper sequence:

(*a*) Source List
(*b*) Size of the Sample
(*c*) Sampling Unit
(*d*) Parameters of Interest

Codes:

A. (*c*), (*a*), (*b*), (*d*) B. (*d*), (*b*), (*c*), (*a*)
C. (*b*), (*d*), (*a*), (*c*) D. (*a*), (*c*), (*d*), (*b*)

46. Arrange the following libraries according to their year of foundation:

(*a*) Bibliothèque nationale de France
(*b*) British Library
(*c*) Imperial Library
(*d*) Library of Congress

Codes :

A. (*a*), (*b*), (*c*), (*d*) B. (*a*), (*c*), (*d*), (*b*)
C. (*a*), (*c*), (*b*), (*d*) D. (*a*), (*d*), (*c*), (*b*)

47. Arrange in chronological order the following initiatives of the UGC for the Development of academic Libraries in India:

(*a*) Sponsor of National Information Centres
(*b*) Matching Gants for College Libraries
(*c*) Appointment of Library Committee on 'University and College Libraries' (Chairman : S.R. Ranganathan)
(*d*) Establishment of Information and Library Network (INFLIBNET)

Codes:

A. (*c*), (*b*), (*a*), (*d*) B. (*b*), (*a*), (*c*), (*d*)
C. (*c*), (*a*), (*b*), (*d*) D. (*d*), (*b*), (*a*), (*c*)

48. Match the following:

List-I	List-II
(*a*) Update (A magazine)	(*i*) Association of College and Research Libraries
(*b*) Information Outlook (an online digital magazine)	(*ii*) American Library Association
(*c*) Reference and User Service Quarterly (RUSQ)	(*iii*) Special Library Association (USA)
(*d*) Choice (A monthly journal)	(*iv*) Chartered Institute of Library and Information Professionals (CILIP)

Codes:

	(*a*)	(*b*)	(*c*)	(*d*)
A.	(*ii*)	(*iv*)	(*i*)	(*iii*)
B.	(*iii*)	(*ii*)	(*iv*)	(*i*)
C.	(*iv*)	(*iii*)	(*ii*)	(*i*)
D.	(*iii*)	(*ii*)	(*i*)	(*iv*)

49. Match the following:

List-I	List-II
(*a*) Loose Assemblage	(*i*) Organometallic Chemistry
(*b*) Agglomeration	(*ii*) Physics for Engineers
(*c*) Fusion	(*iii*) Indology
(*d*) Clustering	(*iv*) Natural Sciences

Codes:

	(*a*)	(*b*)	(*c*)	(*d*)
A.	(*ii*)	(*iv*)	(*i*)	(*iii*)
B.	(*iii*)	(*ii*)	(*i*)	(*iv*)
C.	(*i*)	(*iii*)	(*ii*)	(*iv*)
D.	(*iv*)	(*i*)	(*iii*)	(*ii*)

50. Match the following:

List-I	List-II
(*a*) Indian Electronic Thesis and Dissertation Database	(*i*) Ekaswa
(*b*) Database of Indian Experts	(*ii*) TKDL
(*c*) Indian Patent database	(*iii*) Shodhganga
(*d*) Database of Indian Ancient Knowledge	(*iv*) Vidwan

Codes:

	(*a*)	(*b*)	(*c*)	(*d*)
A.	(*iii*)	(*ii*)	(*iv*)	(*i*)
B.	(*ii*)	(*iv*)	(*i*)	(*iii*)
C.	(*iii*)	(*iv*)	(*i*)	(*ii*)
D.	(*iv*)	(*ii*)	(*iii*)	(*i*)

51. Match the following MARC 21 elements with corresponding tags:

List-I	List-II
(*a*) Personal Main Entry	(*i*) 700
(*b*) Personal Subject Heading	(*ii*) 245
(*c*) Personal Added Entry	(*iii*) 100
(*d*) Bibliographic Title	(*iv*) 600

Codes:

	(*a*)	(*b*)	(*c*)	(*d*)
A.	(*i*)	(*iv*)	(*ii*)	(*iii*)
B.	(*ii*)	(*i*)	(*iii*)	(*iv*)
C.	(*iii*)	(*iv*)	(*i*)	(*ii*)
D.	(*iv*)	(*ii*)	(*iii*)	(*i*)

52. Match the following:

List-I	List-II
(*a*) Physical Description	(*i*) 3 XX
(*b*) Main Entry Level	(*ii*) 1 XX
(*c*) Control Fields	(*iii*) 70 X to 75 X
(*d*) Added Entry	(*iv*) 00 X

Codes:

	(*a*)	(*b*)	(*c*)	(*d*)
A.	(*i*)	(*ii*)	(*iv*)	(*iii*)
B.	(*ii*)	(*iii*)	(*i*)	(*iv*)
C.	(*iii*)	(*iv*)	(*ii*)	(*i*)
D.	(*iv*)	(*iii*)	(*i*)	(*ii*)

53. Match the following:

List-I	List-II
(*a*) Folksonomy	(*i*) Tim Wu
(*b*) Web log	(*ii*) Thomas Vander Waal
(*c*) Net Neutrality	(*iii*) Tim Berners Lee
(*d*) Semantic Web	(*iv*) John Barger

Codes:

	(a)	(b)	(c)	(d)
A.	(i)	(iii)	(iv)	(ii)
B.	(iii)	(ii)	(iv)	(i)
C.	(ii)	(iv)	(i)	(iii)
D.	(iv)	(i)	(iii)	(ii)

54. Match the following:

List-I	List-II
(a) NATIS	(i) IFLA
(b) NIP/NITS	(ii) Dept. of Culture, Govt. of India
(c) CONPOLIS, 1985	(iii) UNESCO
(d) National Policy on Library and Information System (India) 1986	(iv) Raja Ram Mohan Roy Library Foundation

Codes:

	(a)	(b)	(c)	(d)
A.	(i)	(ii)	(iii)	(iv)
B.	(ii)	(iii)	(iv)	(i)
C.	(iii)	(i)	(ii)	(iv)
D.	(iv)	(iii)	(ii)	(i)

55. Match the following:

List-I	List-II
(a) Elton Mayo	(i) Scientific School
(b) Henry Fayol	(ii) Behavioural School
(c) Abraham Maslow	(iii) Classical Style of Management
(d) F.W. Taylor	(iv) Human Relations School

Codes:

	(a)	(b)	(c)	(d)
A.	(iv)	(iii)	(ii)	(i)
B.	(iii)	(iv)	(i)	(ii)
C.	(ii)	(iii)	(iv)	(i)
D.	(i)	(iv)	(ii)	(iii)

56. Match the following:

List-I	List-II
(a) Web page	(i) Navigation
(b) Web server	(ii) Internet storage
(c) Web site	(iii) HTML Doc.
(d) Web browser	(iv) Collection of pages

Codes:

	(a)	(b)	(c)	(d)
A.	(iii)	(ii)	(iv)	(i)
B.	(iii)	(iv)	(ii)	(i)
C.	(i)	(iii)	(iv)	(ii)
D.	(i)	(iv)	(ii)	(iii)

57. Match the following:

List-I	List-II
(a) Central Tendency	(i) Ratio Scale
(b) Regression Curve	(ii) Delphi Method
(c) Refinement of Judgement	(iii) Mean
(d) Absolute zero point	(iv) Relationship between two variables

Codes:

	(a)	(b)	(c)	(d)
A.	(ii)	(iii)	(iv)	(i)
B.	(i)	(iv)	(iii)	(ii)
C.	(iv)	(ii)	(i)	(iii)
D.	(iii)	(iv)	(ii)	(i)

58. **Assertion (A):** There is no difference between Knowledge Management and Information Management.

Reason (R): Knowledge and Information are sometimes used synonymously and inter changeably.

Codes:

A. (A) is true, but (R) is false
B. Both (A) and (R) are true
C. (A) is false but (R) is true
D. Both (A) and (R) are false

59. **Assertion (A):** Keeping one's skills and knowledge current is the ethical obligation of a reference librarian.

Reason (R): It is the responsibility of the reference librarian to satisfy the current information needs of users.

Codes:

A. Both (A) and (R) are true
B. (A) is true but (R) is false
C. (A) is false but (R) is true
D. Both (A) and (R) are false

60. **Assertion (A):** The controlled vocabulary system is more difficult to search than the natural language system.

Reason (R): A natural language system has the major advantage that it is completely specific.

Codes:

A. Both (A) and (R) are true
B. Both (A) and (R) are false
C. (A) is true but (R) is false
D. (A) is false but (R) is true

61. Assertion (A): The Anomalous State of Knowledge (ASK) model is based on the understanding that, given such an anomaly the user is probably unable to state precisely what is needed to resolve the lack of information.

Reason (R): The ASK can be used to formulate an appropriate search strategy.

Codes:

A. Both (A) and (R) are true
B. Both (A) and (R) are false
C. (A) is true but (R) is false
D. (A) is false but (R) is true

62. Assertion (A): FRAD defines its users some what more narrowly than FRBR.

Reason (R): Functional Requirement for Authority Data (FRAD) takes the same entitles found in FRBR and extends them to the authority context.

Codes:

A. Both (A) and (R) are true
B. Both (A) and (R) are false
C. (A) is true but (R) is false
D. (A) is false but (R) is true

63. Assertion (A): The implication of the Recall Precision curve is that if we try to improve Recall, we can only do so at the expense of precision.

Reason (R): Recall precision curve represents the average performance of any given system.

Codes :

A. Both (A) and (R) are true
B. Both (A) and (R) are false
C. (A) is true but (R) is false
D. (A) is false but (R) is true

64. Assertion (A): Pre-coordinate systems are basically one-place systems.

Reason (R): Pre-coordinate systems avoid the need for the citation or significance order.

Codes :

A. Both (A) and (R) are true
B. Both (A) and (R) are false
C. (A) is true but (R) is false
D. (A) is false but (R) is true

65. Assertion (A): If the library is to be automated, system analysis is not needed.

Reason (R): System analysis identifies the flow of work.

Codes:

A. Both (A) and (R) are true
B. (A) is false but (R) is true
C. Both (A) and (R) are false
D. (A) is true but (R) is false

66. Assertion (A): Web-OPAC is a computerized library catalogue available to the readers on-line.

Reason (R): It can be searched by the users within the four walls of the library only.

Codes:

A. (A) is true but (R) is false
B. (A) is false but (R) is true
C. Both (A) and (R) are true
D. Both (A) and (R) are false

67. Assertion (A): Structured Query Language (SQL) is a query language used for accessing and modifying information in a database.

Reason (R): SQL allows precise specification of the value for attributes of terms to be retrieved.

Codes :

A. (A) is false and (R) is true
B. (A) is true and (R) is false
C. Both (A) and (R) are true
D. Both (A) and (R) are false

68. Assertion (A): LOCKSS is a peer to peer preservation system based on the existence of multiple low cost persistent caches of e-Journals, contents hosted at, different institutions licensed to "own" such content.

Reason (R): Participating institutions cooperate through Membership in the LOCKSS Alliance, which is a collaborative network based on the Commercial software model.

Codes:

A. (A) is true, but (R) is false
B. (A) is false but (R) is true
C. Both (A) and (R) are true
D. Both (A) and (R) are false

69. Assertion (A): The Central ideas guiding Qualitative Research are same as those in Quantitative Research.

Reason (R): An essential feature of Qualitative Research is the recognition and analysis of different perspectives.

Codes:

A. Both (A) and (R) are true
B. Both (A) and (R) are false
C. (A) is true but (R) is false
D. (A) is false but (R) is true

70. Assertion (A): The h-index of a scientist is 10, if 10 of his/her papers have at least 10 citations each.

Reason (R): h-index is the only measure to assess a researcher's output.

Codes :

A. (A) is true, but (R) is false
B. (A) is false but (R) is true
C. Both (A) and (R) are true
D. Both (A) and (R) are false

71. Assertion (A): One-way ANOVA is a technique used to compare means of three or more samples.

Reason (R): The two group case can be covered by a t-test.

Codes:

A. Both (A) and (R) are true
B. (A) is true but (R) is false
C. (A) is false but (R) is true
D. Both (A) and (R) are false

72. Assertion (A): While taking 'dumb' page image and producing 'smart' e-text that is added to collection of a digital library, Optical Character Recognition (OCR) does not need any manual intervention.

Reason (R): Optical Character Recognition (OCR) process is entirely automatic.

Codes :

A. (A) is true but (R) is false
B. (A) is false but (R) is true
C. Both (A) and (R) is true
D. Both (A) and (R) are false

73. Assertion (A): RSS feeds automatically allow to view breaking news content from any number of web sites in single interface.

Reason (R): RSS feeds are not helpful to offer user alert services.

Codes :

A. Both (A) and (R) are false
B. Both (A) and (R) are true
C. (A) is false but (R) is true
D. (A) is true but (R) is false

74. Assertion (A): Word of mouth is one of the promotion techniques which does not require any money to be spent if used for the promotion if LIS products and services.

Reason (R): Word of mouth technique is hardly used in libraries.

Codes :

A. Both (A) and (R) are true
B. Both (A) and (R) are false
C. (A) is true but (R) is false
D. (A) is false but (R) is true

75. Assertion (A): Marketing segmentation helps libraries in achieving their goals and objectives as it is easy to decide which type of library service is needed by which type of user.

Reason (R): Libraries do not do segmentation of their users to apply marketing strategy in promoting LIS products and services.

Codes:

A. Both (A) and (R) is true
B. Both (A) and (R) is false
C. (A) is true but (R) is false
D. (R) is true but (A) is false

ANSWERS

1	2	3	4	5	6	7	8	9	10
C	D	B	D	A	D	A	A	D	D
11	**12**	**13**	**14**	**15**	**16**	**17**	**18**	**19**	**20**
D	D	A	C	D	A	D	A	C	D
21	**22**	**23**	**24**	**25**	**26**	**27**	**28**	**29**	**30**
B	D	C	D	B	A	D	A	D	A
31	**32**	**33**	**34**	**35**	**36**	**37**	**38**	**39**	**40**
C	A	B	B	A	A	B	A	A	C
41	**42**	**43**	**44**	**45**	**46**	**47**	**48**	**49**	**50**
B	A	C	A	A	D	A	C	A	C
51	**52**	**53**	**54**	**55**	**56**	**57**	**58**	**59**	**60**
C	A	C	C	A	A	D	C	A	D
61	**62**	**63**	**64**	**65**	**66**	**67**	**68**	**69**	**70**
C	A	A	C	B	A	C	A	D	A
71	**72**	**73**	**74**	**75**					
A	B	D	A	C					

SOME SELECTED EXPLANATORY ANSWERS

1. **Duration of Copyright:** The Copyright prescribes the protection for limited period of time. The Copyright protection lasts for 60 years normally and this period is counted from the year following the death of the author in the case of original literary, dramatic, musical and artistic works. In cases of work of cinematograph films, sound recordings, photographs, posthumous publications, anonymous and pseudonymous publications, works of government etc., the periods of 60 year period is counted from the date of publication of the same.

2. The International ISMN Agency is located in Berlin, Germany. The International ISMN Agency promotes, coordinates and supervises the world-wide use of the ISMN system. It acts as the Registration Authority for this ISO Standard (ISO 10957).

   The Agency approves the definition and structure of the national agencies and allocates ranges of publisher IDs to them.

3. The World Intellectual Property Organization Copyright Treaty (WIPO) is an international treaty on copyright law adopted by the member states of the World Intellectual Property Organization (WIPO) in 1996.

5. Explicit knowledge is knowledge that can be readily articulated, codified, accessed and verbalized. It can be easily transmitted to others. Most forms of explicit knowledge can be stored in certain media.

6. Grey literature is a type of information or research output produced by organisations, outside of commercial or academic publishing and distribution channels. Common grey literature publication types include reports, wørking papers, government documents, and evaluations.

7. Robert Fugmann has developed a theory of information supply and indexing ased on five axioms: Definability, Order, Sufficient Degree of Order, Predictability, and Fidelity. Although part of a theory of indexing, three of these axioms relate directly to searching. The

Axiom of Definability states: "The compilation of information relevant to a topic can be delegated only to the extent to which an inquirer can define the topic in terms of concepts and concept relatios." The last two axioms address factors affecting performance, that is, precision and recall ratios. The Axiom of Predictability states that performance depends on the degree to which the query formulation predicts the modes in which concepts and their relations are expressed in the database, and the Axiom of Fidelity states that performance depends on the fidelity with which concepts and their relations are expressed in the database.

8. The Imperial Library was established in 1891. Lord Curzon, the Viceroy of India, promulgated the Imperial Library Act, 1902, amalgamating Calcutta Public Library with Imperial Library. Soon after independence, the Government of India renamed Imperial Library as the National Library.

9. FAIFE is an initiative within IFLA to defend and promote the basic human rights defined in Article 19 of the United Nations Universal Declaration of Human Rights. The FAIFE Committee furthers freedom of access to information and freedom of expression in all aspects, directly or indirectly, related to libraries and librarianship.

10. In mathematics and mathematical logic, Boolean algebra is the branch of algebra in which the values of the variables are the truth values *true* and *false*, usually denoted 1 and 0 respectively. Boolean algebra was introduced by George Boole in his first book *The Mathematical Analysis of Logic* (1847), and set forth more fully in his *An Investigation of the Laws of Thought* (1854).

11. **Colon:** Use judgment to determine whether the colon is part of that title proper or whether it separates the title proper from the other title information.

13. "Titles always have been a problem with audiovisual material. There may be several forms of a title on an item, or even completely different titles on the same item. By first specifying a chief source of information for each type of material, the designers of AACR2 helped ensure the uniformity of bibliographic records. When we catalog a sound disc, for example, we are told the chief source of information is the disc label(s). We take the title proper from it."

14. SYNTOL stands for "Syntagmatic Organization of Language".

15. Frederick Herzberg, a behavioural scientist proposed a two-factor theory or the motivator-hygiene theory. According to Herzberg, there are some job factors that result in satisfaction while there are other job factors that prevent dissatisfaction. Herzberg's 'two factor theory' deals with motivation.

16.

Description of OSI layers

OSI Model				
	Layer	**Data unit**	**Function**	**Examples**
Host layers	7. Application	Data	High-level APIs, including resource sharing, remote file access, directory services and virtual terminals	HTTP, FTP, SMTP, SSH, TELNET
	6. Presentation		Translation of data between a networking service and an application, including character encoding, data compression and encryption/decryption	HTML, CSS, GIF
	5. Session		Managing communication sessions, i.e. continuous exchange of information in the form of multiple back-and-forth transmissions between two nodes	RPC, PAP, SSL, SQL
	4. Transport	Segments/ Datagram	Reliable transmission of data segments between points on a network, including segmentation, acknowledgement and multiplexing	TCP, UDP, NETBEUI

	Layer	Data unit	Function	Examples
Media layers	3. Network	Packet	Structuring and managing a multi-node network, including addressing, routing and traffic control	IPv4, IPv6, IPsec, AppleTalk, ICMP
	2. Data link	Frame	Reliable transmission of data frames between two nodes connected by a physical layer	PPP, IEEE 802.2, L2TP, MAC, LLDP
	1. Physical	Bit	Transmission and reception of raw bit streams over a physical medium	Ethernet physical layer, DSL, USB, ISDN, DOCSIS

17. The terms *work, expression, manifestation,* and *item* are used as follows:

The term *work* refers to a distinct intellectual or artistic creation i.e., the intellectual or artistic content.

The term *expression* refers to the intellectual or artistic realization of a work in the form of alpha-numeric, musical or choreographic notation, sound, image, object, movement, etc., or any combination of such forms.

The term *manifestation* refers to the physical embodiment of an expression of a work.

The term *item* refers to a single exemplar or instance of a manifestation.

18. A contingency question also called a filter question is an item that directs participants to different follow-up questions depending on their response. It allows the researcher to "filter out" participants from questions that these participants cannot or should not attempt to answer. It also is a good idea to limit the number of contingency questions in a questionnaire because participants might become confused or agitated.

19. A library for the exclusive use of members of the Central Legislative Assembly was set up in 1921. It continued to be a small library, meeting the limited requirements of members in those days. After India achieved Independence in 1947, the expansion of the library was considered in order to meet the growing requirements of the Central Legislature in the new set up. The year 1950 saw the setting up of a Research and Reference Branch in the then Parliament Secretariat. Over the years, the organisation grew into what is today known as Parliament Library and Reference, Research, Documentation and Information Service (LARRDIS).

20. E. Wyndham Hulme proposed the concept of literary warrant as the basis of book classification and the definition of subject classes, wherein classes and names of classes would be derived from existing literature rather than a preconceived philosophical order of sciences, the predominant and favoured type of classification system in Hulme's day.

21. In 1957, during the centenary celebrations of the Madras University, S.R.R. donated his life's savings of ₹ 100,000 with which an endowment chair known as Sarada Ranganathan Professionship in Library Science was created. The students of this stream have taken leading part at all levels of activity - local, national and international.

22. Hawkins states that "an e-book is the contents of a book made available in an electronic form." An e-book is an "integration of the classical print structure with an electronic environment giving additional value added features that paper cannot provide". Some of the advantages are timely and cost efficient distribution; the ability to search and interact with the text easily; and widespread accessibility through the Internet. E-books are dependent on equipment to be used and it offer seamless access. It also allow highlight of contents.

The main disadvantages for downloadable e-books to standard hardware and those remaining on the provider's web site include reading from PC screens; unattractive formats;

and download times dependent on the speed of data lines.

24. With the view to ensuring the continuance of research and high level of teaching in Library and Information Science, Dr. S.R. Ranganathan formed Library Research Groups/Circles, initiated and nurtured the Documentation Research and Training Centre (DRTC), Bangalore, as a division of the Indian Statistical Institute, Kolkata, and he established the Sarada Ranganathan Endowment for Library Science, with a small contribution from his former students, augmented by the royalty from the sale of his books. The Endowment is registered as a charitable trust with the Treasurer of Charitable Endowments Government of India.

25. The semantic Web applies a set of technologies that include a *Resource Description Framework* (RDF), a *Web Ontology Language* (OWL), and the *Extensible Markup Language* (XML). Wikipedia describes the interaction of these technologies in the following manner:

These technologies are combined in order to provide descriptions that supplement or replace the content of Web documents. Thus, content may manifest as descriptive data stored in Web-accessible databases, or as markup within documents (particularly, in Extensible HTML (XHTML) interspersed with XML, or, more often, purely in XML, with layout/rendering cues stored separately). The machine-readable descriptions enable content managers to add meaning to the content, thereby facilitating automated information gathering and research by computers.

26. Hospitality in Chain can be secured by two devices mainly by — Gap device and decimal fraction device.

27. Dropbox and Delicious are widely used social bookmarking services that allow all users to freely tag and save sites that they choose in order to share them with others at a future date. Unlike the old system of having to save such sites on individual computers as "Favorites," this service manages saved webpages from a centralized source that can be accessed from anywhere.

28. Web-Junction is the place where public library staff gather to build the knowledge, skills and support we need to power relevant, vibrant libraries.

Web-Junction values community, collaboration, and support for lifelong learning. These values ensure that all libraries—regardless of size, type, or geographic location—can effectively use and share resources towards common goals.

Since its launch in 2003, Web-Junction has helped more than 80,000 library staff build the job skills they need to meet the challenges of today's libraries. Membership is free, all are welcome, and it's always on.

30. RDA introduces a new approach to the categorization of technical and content aspects of a resource. RDA replaces the general material designations (GMDs) and the class of materials concept with a grid or framework that consists of three elements: content type, media type and carrier type. The information that the GMDs communicated was useful information. The problem with the GMDs and with the class of materials concept was inconsistent categorization. The categories, used as terms in the GMDs and as class of material chapters, represented attributes at the level of work, expression, and manifestation. The GMD also intruded into the middle of the title statement, thus making it difficult to move beyond a single term.

31. Micro subject embodied in the form of an article in a periodical, or a part or chapter or section of a book. It is a classification scheme at depth level or a micro subject. It treats and lists the subjects of smaller extension and of greater intension.

32. Folksonomy, also known as collaborative tagging, social classification, social indexing and social tagging, is formed by all the web users in a way of contributing tags. And it may be one of the right ways in which the bottleneck of the content-based recommendation mentioned abov can be handled.

33. The phrase espirit de corps means the spirit of loyalty and devotion which unites the members of the group. It also means unity of command or regard for the honer of the group to which one belongs. Harmoy among the personnel is a source of strength, unity among the personnel can be accomplished through proper communication and coordination.

34. As opposed to asynchronous communication tools, synchronous communication tools, such as instant messaging, VOIP, and video conferencing, require the users to be connected at the same time. Interacting via these tools is similar to participating in a telephone conversation, in that all parties interact in real time.

35. As of August 2015, there were no laws governing net neutrality in India, which would require that all Internet users be treated equally, without discriminating or charging differentially by user, content, site, platform, application, type of attached equipment, or mode of communication. There have already been a few violations of net neutrality principles by some Indian service providers. The government has once again called in for comments and suggestions regarding net neutrality as of 14 August, and has given the people one day to post their views on the mygov forum. After this, the final decision regarding the debate will be made.

The debate on network neutrality in India gathered public attention after Airtel, a mobile telephony service provider in India, announced in December 2014 additional charges for making voice calls (VoIP) from its network using apps like WhatsApp, Skype, etc.

36. An information filtering system is an information system designed for unstructured or semistructured data. This contrasts with a typical database application that involves very structured data, such as employee records.

Information filtering is a name used to describe a variety of processes involving the delivery of information to people who need it.

'Information Filtering System' is primarily designed for removal and selection of data or an object from an incoming stream for a given profile.

37. The arithmetic mean in perhaps the most commonly used statistical mean to measure the central tendency of data.

The arithmetic mean is also called the "average". It is used in most scientific experiments.

Mathematically, the arithmetic mean is given by:

$$\text{Arithmetic mean} = \frac{\text{Sum of all data-points}}{\text{Total number of data-points}}$$

38. Public libraries arose worldwide along with growth in education, literacy, and publications.

RRRLF: RRRLF is a central autonomous organization established and fully financed by the Ministry of Culture, Government of India. It is the nodal agency of the Government of India to support public library services and systems and promote public library movement in the country.

The Delhi public library deserves special mention. It was founded in 1951 as the first UNESCO Public Library Pilot Project under the joint auspices of UNESCO and Government of India.

39. The Shibboleth System includes two major software components: the Shibboleth Identity Provider (IdP) and the Shibboleth Service Provider (SP). These two components are deployed separately but work together to provide secure access to Web-based resources.

The OpenID standard is a mechanism for using one digital identity on the Web. A user first registers with an OpenID *provider* and generates on OpenID *identifier.* A Web site that adopts this authentication process asks users for their *identifier* and redirects them to the provider to enter their password. The provider checks the password and sends a message back to the site to confirm the login.

40. PRECIS consist of two inter-related sets of working procedures:

1. Syntactical
2. Semantic

- The PRECIS is based on two principles

1. Principle of Context Dependency
2. Principle of One-to-One Relationship

- To achieve the principle of context-dependency, Two-Line-Three-Part entry structure is followed in PRECIS.

41. (*a*) The first official list of subject headings published by the National Library of Medicine appeared in 1954 under the title Subject Heading Authority List. It was based on the internal authority list that had been used for publication of Current List of Medical Literature which in turn had incorporated headings from the Library's Index-Catalogue and from the 1940 Quarterly Cumulative Index Medicus Subject Headings. With the inception of Index Medicus in 1960, a new and thoroughly revised Medical Subject Headings appeared.

(*b*) Sears List of Subject Headings offers a core list of headings as well as patterns and instructions for creating new subject headings as they are needed. EBSCO offers a practical solution. Since 1923, this resource has served the unique cataloging needs of small and medium-sized libraries by providing a flexible, extendable vocabulary in natural language.

(c) Librarians at the Library of Congress in Washington created the list of subject headings to describe the contents of materials in their collections. Development of the system began in 1898 and publication of the first edition began in 1909.

(*d*) AGROVOC, developed by FAO and the Commission of the European Communities, is one of the most important knowledge organization systems (KOS) in the fields of agriculture, forestry, fisheries, food, and other related domains. First published in 1982 as a thesaurus in English, French and Spanish, it has been used by libraries and documentation centers for indexing and retrieving agricultural information resources.

43. Work, expression, manifestation, and item are all defined by Functional Requirements for Bibliographic Records as entities.

46. (*a*) The *Bibliothèque nationale de France* is the National Library of France, located in Paris. It is intended to be the repository of all that is published in France. The current president of the library is Bruno Racine. It is established on 1461; 554 years ago.

(*b*) The Library of Congress was established by an act of Congress on On April 24, 1800 when President John Adams signed a bill providing for the transfer of the seat of government from Philadelphia to the new capital city of Washington.

(*c*) The Imperial Library was founded in 1891 by combining a number of Secretariat libraries. Of these, the most important and interesting was the library of the Home Department, which contained many books formerly belonging to the libraries of East India College, Fort William, and the East India Board in London. But the use of the library was restricted to the superior officers of the Government.

(*d*) The British Library was created on 1 July 1973 as a result of the British Library Act 1972. Prior to this, the national library was part of the British Museum, which provided the bulk of the holdings of the new library, alongside smaller organisations.

48. (*i*) Choice is a monthly publication of the Association of College and Research Libraries, a Division of the American Library Association".

(*ii*) Reference and User Services Quarterly is a peer-reviewed academic journal covering library science. It is the official journal of the Reference and User Services Association and is published by the American Library Association. The journal was established as the Reference Quarterly in 1961 and obtained its current name in 1997.

(*iii*) Information Outlook, Special Library Association's online digital magazine, helps information professionals stay abreast of trends and issues in the information profession.

(*iv*) Chartered Institute of Library and Information Professionals is a Professional body of UK librarians and information scientists. Provides advocacy, education, and information; publishes the monthly magazine *CILIP Update* and various books.

50. (*i*) Ekaswa is an Indian patent database. The coverage areas of the databases are given below:

- Ekaswa A database – Patent applications filed in India as published in the issues of the *Gazette of India.*
- Ekaswa B database – Patent applications notified for opposition in the *Gazette of India.*
- Ekaswa C database – Patent applications published in the official *Journal of Patent Office* published from January 2005 onward.

(*ii*) The Traditional Knowledge Digital Library (TKDL) is an Indian digital knowledge repository of the traditional knowledge, especially about medicinal plants and formulations used in Indian systems of medicine.

(*iii*) "Shodhganga" is the name coined to denote digital repository of Indian Electronic Theses and Dissertations. The word "Shodh" originates from Sanskrit and stands for research and discovery. The 'Ganga' is the holiest, largest and longest of all rivers in Indian subcontinent. The Ganga is the symbol of India's age-long culture and civilisation, ever-changing, ever-flowing, ever-loved and revered by its people, and has held India's heart captive and drawn uncounted millions to her banks since the dawn of history. Shodhganga stands for the reservoir of Indian intellectual output stored in a repository hosted and maintained by INFLIBNET Centre.

(*iv*) Vidwan is the premier database of profiles of scientists/researchers and other faculty members working at leading R & D Organisation and other Academic Institutions involved in teaching and research in India. It provides important information about expert's background, contact address, skills and accomplishments.

56. The simplest web page is just an HTML file. Just one valid HTML file on your computer and a web browser are the only things you need.

A Web server is a program that uses HTTP to store the files that form Web pages to users, in response to their requests, which are forwarded by their computers' HTTP clients.

A website represents a centrally managed group of web pages, containing text, images and all types of multimedia files presented to the attention of the Internet users in an aesthetic and easily accessible way. All websites enabled through the Internet constitute the World Wide Web (WWW).

A web browser is a software application for retrieving, presenting, and traversing information resources on the World Wide Web. It act like a navigator.

Previous Paper (Solved)

UGC–NET Library and Information Science, December–2014

PAPER-II

Note : *This paper contains **fifty (50)** objective type questions, each question carries **two (2)** marks. All questions are compulsory.*

1. Who introduced the concept of 'knowledge industry'?

A. Peter Drucker B. Fritz Machlup
C. Marc Porat D. William Saffady

2. When the last print version of Encyclopaedia Britannica was published?

A. 2009 B. 2010
C. 2011 D. 2012

3. Identify the place where IFLA was first found.

A. The Hague, Netherlands
B. Edinburgh, Scotland
C. Helsinki, Finland
D. London

4. Information For All Programme (IFAP) was launched by:

A. IFLA
B. Library of Congress
C. OCLC
D. UNESCO

5. A cross reference that gives an indexer complete control over the cross references of an index is known as:

A. see also cross reference
B. check also cross reference
C. see cross reference
D. inverted cross reference

6. DMAIC is the acronym for:

A. Define, Measure, Access, Improve and Control
B. Define, Measure, Analyse, Improve and Control
C. Describe, Measure, Analyse, Improve and Control
D. Define, Measure, Access, Instruct and Control

7. A template is a:

A. Structured specification
B. Recursive routine
C. Assembler program
D. I/O measure

8. The mode of displaying graphic information pixel by pixel with bits in main memory is:

A. Bit handling B. Bit mapping
C. Bit pattern D. Bit matrix

9. 'Delphi Technique' was first discussed in a monograph by:

A. O. Helmer B. E. Nagel
C. D.M. Potter D. J.H. Shera

10. The service that helps the students to acquire soft skills, writing skills and job-oriented skills is:

A. Reader's advisory B. Career guidance
C. Referral service D. User education

11. Skill Development Programme (SDP) for public librarians in India is initiated by

A. Ministry of Human Resource Development, Govt. of India
B. Directorate of Library Services, Govt. of West Bengal
C. Raja Ram Mohan Roy Library Foundation
D. Indian Library Association

12. Which of the following concepts are associated with professional ethics?
(*i*) Accountability
(*ii*) Unique training
(*iii*) High quality service
(*iv*) Professional independence
Codes:
A. (*i*), (*ii*) and (*iii*) are correct
B. (*i*) and (*iii*) are correct
C. (*i*), (*ii*) and (*iv*) are correct
D. (*iii*) and (*iv*) are correct

13. Which of the following are characteristics of a review?
(*i*) Analyses research topic
(*ii*) Indicates inter-relation of ideas
(*iii*) Presents an integrated picture of development and program
(*iv*) Provides only current information
Codes:
A. (*ii*), (*iii*) and (*iv*) are correct
B. (*i*), (*iii*) and (*iv*) are correct
C. (*i*), (*ii*) and (*iii*) are correct
D. (*i*), (*ii*) and (*iv*) are correct

14. An alerting service in the digital environment is offered through:
(*i*) RSS feeds
(*ii*) E-mail
(*iii*) Blogs
(*iv*) Bulletin Board
Codes:
A. (*i*) and (*iii*) are correct
B. (*ii*), (*iii*) and (*iv*) are correct
C. (*i*), (*ii*) and (*iii*) are correct
D. (*i*), (*ii*) and (*iv*) are correct

15. The important methods of measuring impact factor of any information retrieval system are:
(*i*) Expression Rate
(*ii*) Precision Rate
(*iii*) Recall Rate
(*iv*) Depression Rate
Codes:
A. (*i*) and (*iii*) are correct
B. (*ii*) and (*iv*) are correct
C. (*ii*) and (*iii*) are correct
D. (*iii*) and (*iv*) are correct

16. Which of the following are standard TQM tools?
(*i*) Pie chart
(*ii*) Zigzag chart
(*iii*) Fishbone diagram
(*iv*) Pareto chart
Codes:
A. (*i*) and (*iv*) are correct
B. (*ii*), (*iii*) and (*iv*) are correct
C. (*i*), (*iii*) and (*iv*) are correct
D. (*iii*) and (*iv*) are correct

17. Which of the following organizations are contributing to the implementation of standards for networked information system?
(*i*) CNI
(*ii*) W3C
(*iii*) IANA
(*iv*) IEEE
Codes:
A. (*i*) and (*iii*) are correct
B. (*ii*) and (*iv*) are correct
C. (*ii*) and (*iii*) are correct
D. (*i*) and (*ii*) are correct

18. Identify content management software from the following:
(*i*) Evergreen
(*ii*) Drupal
(*iii*) Joomla
(*iv*) New Genlib
Codes:
A. (*i*) and (*ii*) are correct
B. (*ii*) and (*iii*) are correct
C. (*iii*) and (*iv*) are correct
D. (*i*) and (*iv*) are correct

19. Identify open source softwares for library management.
(*i*) New Genlib
(*ii*) SOUL
(*iii*) LIBSYS
(*iv*) KOHA
Codes:
A. (*i*) and (*ii*) are correct
B. (*ii*) and (*iii*) are correct
C. (*iii*) and (*iv*) are correct
D. (*i*) and (*iv*) are correct

20. Assertion (A): The value of information depends on its age and the time it is sold.
Reason (R): Newer information tends to have more value.
Codes:
A. Both (A) and (R) are true
B. Both (A) and (R) are false
C. (A) is false, but (R) is true
D. (A) is true, but (R) is false

21. Assertion (A): Library legislation is not a pre-requisite for providing free library service.
Reason (R): There are states/union territories that are advanced in public library services without library legislation.
Codes:
A. (A) is true, but (R) is false
B. (A) is false, but (R) is true
C. Both (A) and (R) are true
D. Both (A) and (R) are false

22. Assertion (A) : Data stored in bibliographic database comprise inputs of bibliographic details of a document for identification, storage and retrieval purpose.
Reason (R) : Most of the bibliographic databases consist of indexing and abstracting series.
Codes:
A. (A) is false, but (R) is true
B. Both (A) and (R) are true
C. (A) is true, but (R) is false
D. Both (A) and (R) are false

23. Assertion (A) : Abstracts are precise representation of the content of a document.
Reason (R) : Researcher have time constraints to go through the original articles.
Codes:
A. (A) is true, but (R) is false
B. Both (A) and (R) are true
C. (A) is false, but (R) is true
D. Both (A) and (R) are false

24. Assertion (A) : To increase the specificity, we need to accept long notations.
Reason (R) : An important quality of notation is brevity.
Codes:
A. Both (A) and (R) are true and (R) is the correct explanation of (A)
B. (A) is false, but (R) is true
C. (A) is true, but (R) is false
D. Both (A) and (R) are true, but (R) is not the correct explanation of (A)

25. Assertion (A) : Knowledge organisation and knowledge management are conceptually one and the same.
Reason (R) : Simple Knowledge Organisation System (SKOS) is designed for knowledge management.
Codes:
A. (A) is true, but (R) is false
B. (R) is true, but (A) is false
C. Both (A) and (R) are true
D. Both (A) and (R) are false

26. Assertion (A) : One of the key lessons of the web 2.0 era is that users can add value.
Reason (R) : Web 2.0 serve communities of people and are created and maintained by and for the people.
Codes:
A. Both (A) and (R) are true
B. Both (A) and (R) are false
C. (A) is true and (R) is false
D. (R) is true and (A) is false

27. Assertion (A) : RSS is considered as an alternative to the current awareness service.
Reason (R) : RSS feeds enable us to syndicate data automatically.
Codes:
A. Both (A) and (R) are true
B. Both (A) and (R) are false
C. (A) is false, but (R) is true
D. (A) is true, but (R) is false

28. Assertion (A) : In a particular study, we may reject the alternative hypothesis.
Reason (R) : In the same study the null hypothesis is not rejected.
Codes:
A. (A) is true, but (R) is false
B. (A) is false, but (R) is true

C. Both (A) and (R) are true and (R) is the correct explanation of (A)
D. Both (A) and (R) are true, but (R) is not the correct explanation of (A)

29. **Assertion (A):** An electronic library may have both born digital and converted digital documents.
Reason (R): A document stored in Unicode is same as storing the scanned image of the document.
Codes:
A. (A) is false, but (R) is true
B. (A) is true, but (R) is false
C. Both (A) and (R) are true
D. Both (A) and (R) are false

30. Arrange the following in chronological order:
(*i*) Right to Information Act (India)
(*ii*) Information Technology Act (India)
(*iii*) Indian Copyright Act
(*iv*) Digital Millennium Copyright Act (US)
Codes:
A. (*i*) (*ii*) (*iii*) (*iv*)
B. (*iv*) (*i*) (*ii*) (*iii*)
C. (*ii*) (*iii*) (*iv*) (*i*)
D. (*iii*) (*iv*) (*ii*) (*i*)

31. Arrange the following Public Library Acts according to their year of enactment:
(*i*) Chhattisgarh Public Library Act
(*ii*) Gujarat Public Library Act
(*iii*) Orissa Public Library Act
(*iv*) Uttar Pradesh Public Library Act
Codes:
A. (*ii*) (*iii*) (*iv*) (*i*)
B. (*iii*) (*ii*) (*iv*) (*i*)
C. (*iv*) (*ii*) (*i*) (*iii*)
D. (*iii*) (*iv*) (*ii*) (*i*)

32. Arrange the stages in the preparation of State-of the Art Report.
(*i*) Consultation with subject expert
(*ii*) Scope determination
(*iii*) Appraisal of information
(*iv*) Identification of the collection
Codes:
A. (*ii*) (*iv*) (*iii*) (*i*)
B. (*iv*) (*ii*) (*iii*) (*i*)
C. (*iii*) (*i*) (*iv*) (*ii*)
D. (*i*) (*ii*) (*iii*) (*iv*)

33. Arrange the following in chronological order:
(*i*) FRBR
(*ii*) UNIMARC
(*iii*) ONIX for books
(*iv*) MARC-21
Codes:
A. (*ii*) (*iv*) (*iii*) (*i*)
B. (*i*) (*ii*) (*iii*) (*iv*)
C. (*iv*) (*iii*) (*ii*) (*i*)
D. (*ii*) (*iv*) (*i*) (*iii*)

34. Arrange the following web browsers in chronological order:
(*i*) Safari
(*ii*) Chrome
(*iii*) Netscape Navigator
(*iv*) Firefox
Codes:
A. (*iv*) (*i*) (*ii*) (*iii*)
B. (*i*) (*ii*) (*iii*) (*iv*)
C. (*ii*) (*i*) (*iv*) (*iii*)
D. (*iii*) (*i*) (*iv*) (*ii*)

35. Arrange the following in chronological order:
(*i*) MEDLINE
(*ii*) Pub-Med
(*iii*) Index Medicus
(*iv*) MEDLARS
Codes:
A. (*iii*) (*iv*) (*i*) (*ii*)
B. (*iv*) (*i*) (*iii*) (*ii*)
C. (*i*) (*iii*) (*ii*) (*iv*)
D. (*iii*) (*ii*) (*iv*) (*i*)

36. Arrange the following according to their year of origin:
(*i*) Statistical Bibliography
(*ii*) Librametery
(*iii*) Bibliometrics
(*iv*) Webometrics
Codes:
A. (*ii*) (*iii*) (*i*) (*iv*)
B. (*iii*) (*ii*) (*i*) (*iv*)
C. (*i*) (*ii*) (*iii*) (*iv*)
D. (*ii*) (*i*) (*iii*) (*iv*)

37. Arrange the following according to their year of establishment:
(*i*) Khuda Bakhsha Oriental Public Library
(*ii*) Sahitya Akademi Library, Delhi
(*iii*) Rampur Raza Library
(*iv*) The Asiatic Society

Codes:

A.	(*ii*)	(*iv*)	(*i*)	(*iii*)
B.	(*iii*)	(*i*)	(*iv*)	(*ii*)
C.	(*i*)	(*iv*)	(*ii*)	(*iii*)
D.	(*iv*)	(*i*)	(*ii*)	(*iii*)

38. Match the following electronic applications of information society with relevant service:

List–I	*List–II*
(*a*) E-Commerce	(*i*) Saakshat
(*b*) E-Governance	(*ii*) Living progress
(*c*) E-Education	(*iii*) G2C initiatives
(*d*) E-Health	(*iv*) SnapDeal

Codes:

	(*a*)	(*b*)	(*c*)	(*d*)
A.	(*iii*)	(*iv*)	(*i*)	(*ii*)
B.	(*ii*)	(*iii*)	(*iv*)	(*i*)
C.	(*iv*)	(*iii*)	(*i*)	(*ii*)
D.	(*iv*)	(*ii*)	(*i*)	(*iii*)

39. Match the following:

List–I	*List–II*
(*a*) Books are for use.	(*i*) Adopting to future needs
(*b*) Every reader his/her book.	(*ii*) Long operating hours
(*c*) Every book its reader.	(*iii*) Freedom of access to information & knowledge
(*d*) Library is a growing organism.	(*iv*) Reference Desk

Codes:

	(*a*)	(*b*)	(*c*)	(*d*)
A.	(*ii*)	(*iii*)	(*iv*)	(*i*)
B.	(*iv*)	(*i*)	(*ii*)	(*iii*)
C.	(*i*)	(*ii*)	(*iii*)	(*iv*)
D.	(*iii*)	(*iv*)	(*i*)	(*ii*)

40. Match the following:

List–I	*List–II*
(*a*) Biographical source	(*i*) Full text sources online
(*b*) Encyclopaedia	(*ii*) ODLIS
(*c*) Directory	(*iii*) Linkedin
(*d*) Dictionary	(*iv*) Liswiki

Codes:

	(*a*)	(*b*)	(*c*)	(*d*)
A.	(*i*)	(*ii*)	(*iii*)	(*iv*)
B.	(*ii*)	(*iii*)	(*i*)	(*iv*)
C.	(*iv*)	(*ii*)	(*iii*)	(*i*)
D.	(*iii*)	(*iv*)	(*i*)	(*ii*)

41. Match the following:

List–I	*List–II*
(*a*) ETC	(*i*) UK
(*b*) NTC	(*ii*) India
(*c*) BLLD	(*iii*) USA
(*d*) NISCAIR	(*iv*) Netherland

Codes:

	(*a*)	(*b*)	(*c*)	(*d*)
A.	(*iv*)	(*iii*)	(*i*)	(*ii*)
B.	(*ii*)	(*i*)	(*iii*)	(*iv*)
C.	(*iii*)	(*iv*)	(*ii*)	(*i*)
D.	(*i*)	(*ii*)	(*iv*)	(*iii*)

42. Match the following:

List–I	*List–II*
(*a*) Systematic indexing	(*i*) Derek Austin
(*b*) PRECIS	(*ii*) Mortimer Taube
(*c*) Uniterm	(*iii*) J. Kaiser
(*d*) Chain Procedure	(*iv*) S.R. Ranganathan

Codes:

	(*a*)	(*b*)	(*c*)	(*d*)
A.	(*ii*)	(*i*)	(*iv*)	(*iii*)
B.	(*iv*)	(*iii*)	(*ii*)	(*i*)
C.	(*i*)	(*ii*)	(*iii*)	(*iv*)
D.	(*iii*)	(*i*)	(*ii*)	(*iv*)

43. Match the following:

List–I	*List–II*
(*a*) Meta search engine	(*i*) HotBot
(*b*) Web directory	(*ii*) Search Engine
(*c*) Subject gateway	(*iii*) Galaxy
(*d*) Archie	(*iv*) Library Spot

Codes:

	(*a*)	(*b*)	(*c*)	(*d*)
A.	(*i*)	(*iii*)	(*iv*)	(*ii*)
B.	(*iii*)	(*ii*)	(*i*)	(*iv*)
C.	(*ii*)	(*iv*)	(*i*)	(*iii*)
D.	(*i*)	(*iii*)	(*ii*)	(*iv*)

44. Match the following:

List–I	*List–II*
(*a*) Nominal variable	(*i*) Temperature in centigrade
(*b*) Interval variable	(*ii*) Students and Faculty
(*c*) Ordinal variable	(*iii*) Classification of gender
(*d*) Ratio	(*iv*) Grades of students

Codes:

	(*a*)	(*b*)	(*c*)	(*d*)
A.	(*ii*)	(*iii*)	(*i*)	(*iv*)
B.	(*iii*)	(*i*)	(*iv*)	(*ii*)
C.	(*i*)	(*iv*)	(*iii*)	(*ii*)
D.	(*iv*)	(*ii*)	(*iii*)	(*i*)

45. Match the following:

List–I	*List–II*
(*a*) Internet	(*i*) Knowledge navigation
(*b*) Computing	(*ii*) Collection of E-resources
(*c*) WWW	(*iii*) Tools and Techniques for accessing
(*d*) Digital Library	(*iv*) Delivery Mechanism

Codes:

	(*a*)	(*b*)	(*c*)	(*d*)
A.	(*iv*)	(*i*)	(*iii*)	(*ii*)
B.	(*iv*)	(*iii*)	(*i*)	(*ii*)
C.	(*ii*)	(*i*)	(*iii*)	(*iv*)
D.	(*iii*)	(*iv*)	(*ii*)	(*i*)

Direction : *Read the following passage carefully and answer the questions that follows:*

According to Peter Walsh (2003), knowledge production has historically been based on the expert paradigm in which bodies of knowledge are controlled by groups of experts.

The differentiation between interior and exterior, expert and layperson, producer and consumer, creates what Walsh (2003) called "Knowledge Hegemony" in which control over the creation and distribution of knowledge and information is monopolized in the hands of the few. However, advances in information technology–from the printing press to the World Wide Web–have led to the steady erosion of this hegemony in so far as they have allowed greater numbers of people to participate in knowledge production. The printing press, for example, undermined one of the key elements of the medieval Church's knowledge hegemony: the control of book production and libraries. Mass publishing and the spread of literacy formed the basis the Reformation, the Age of Enlightenment, and the Scientific Revolution.

Today, the web is undermining the knowledge hegemony of a number of fields such as journalism, publishing, education, and museums. Echoing sentiments similar to those expressed by Benjamin in his essay "The Work of Art in the Age of Mechanical Reproduction" (1936/1968), Walsh (2003) argued that loss of physical control over art, owing to new technological means of mass production and distribution, undermines the ability of museums to control what types of art are made accessible to the public, the context in which they are seen, and the types of discourses about them that are considered "appropriate". The availability of easy to use digital technologies for reproducing, creating, and distributing content – artistic, literary, informational, or otherwise – has effectively weakened existing knowledge hegemonies by lowering the barriers to participation in knowledge production. Participatory cultures therefore produce a counter-hegemonic effect in so far as they "erode monopolistic positions held by professions, educational institutions, and experts, and they increase the diversity of perspectives on the way the world is and the way it could be".

46. According to Walsh, knowledge production has been historically based on:

A. Participatory culture
B. Application of technology
C. Expert paradigm
D. Collective intelligence

47. In knowledge hegemony control over creation of knowledge and information is:

A. in the printing press
B. in the world wide web
C. in the libraries
D. in the hands of a few

48. The main reason for the erosion of the knowledge hegemony of the medieval church was:
A. the printing press
B. world wide web
C. the libraries
D. action of a few

49. One of the important factors that helped to usher in the age of enlightenment was:
A. world wide web
B. monopoly of information
C. spread of literacy
D. control of libraries

50. The diversity of perspective is increased by:
A. knowledge hegemony
B. digital technology
C. control of book production
D. participatory culture

ANSWERS

1	2	3	4	5	6	7	8	9	10
B	B	B	D	D	B	A	B	A	B
11	**12**	**13**	**14**	**15**	**16**	**17**	**18**	**19**	**20**
C	B	C	D	C	D	D	B	D	A
21	**22**	**23**	**24**	**25**	**26**	**27**	**28**	**29**	**30**
C	B	B	D	D	C	A	C	B	D
31	**32**	**33**	**34**	**35**	**36**	**37**	**38**	**39**	**40**
A	A	D	D	A	C	D	C	A	D
41	**42**	**43**	**44**	**45**	**46**	**47**	**48**	**49**	**50**
A	D	D	B	A	C	D	A	C	D

PAPER-III

Note : *This paper contains* ***seventy five (75)*** *objective type questions, each question carries* ***two (2)*** *marks. All questions are compulsory.*

1. Name the characteristics of information in which the more information we have, the more we use, the more it becomes useful.
A. Synergetic Characteristics
B. Diffusive Characteristics
C. Compressible Characteristics
D. Shareable Characteristics

2. MIS provides all sorts of information required for:
A. Management of Organisation
B. Preparation of Budget
C. Administration
D. Decision making

3. Identify the correct sequence of elements of communication:
A. Channel-Decoder-Destination-Encoder-Message-Source
B. Decoder-Channel-Destination-Message-Source-Encoder
C. Source-Encoder-Message-Channel-Decoder-Destination
D. Encoder-Decoder-Source-Message-Channel-Destination

4. Who has recommended the establishment of district, taluka, town and village libraries?
A. S.R. Ranganathan
B. Velaga Venkatappayya
C. Fyzee Report
D. Library Advisory Committee

5. From which year the Encyclopaedia Britannica ceased its print version?
A. 2009 B. 2010
C. 2011 D. 2012

6. 'Indian Citation Index' (ICI) is developed by:
A. Informatics India
B. Veeru's technologies
C. DELNET
D. Knowledge Foundation

7. The class index entries which are derived from the class number of a document are based upon:
A. Unsought links B. Missing links
C. False links D. Sought links

8. Which of the followings does not belong to the set of canons for the characteristics?
A. Canon of Differentiation
B. Canon of Ascertainability
C. Canon of Currency
D. Canon of Relevance

9. Semouv Lubutzsky and Mary Piggot are associated with which of the following?
A. Classification B. Cataloguing
C. Indexing D. Management

10. Who advocated the seven basic statistical tools for quality control?
A. Joseph Juran B. Phillip Crosby
C. Kauro Ishikawa D. C.A. Cutter

11. LOCKSS (Lots of Copies Keep Stuff Safe) project was launched by:
A. Mellon Foundation
B. Stanford University
C. University of California
D. OCLC

12. KOHA is written in which of the following languages?
A. C, C++ B. Java
C. Karel++ D. Pearl

13. Which of the followings is an example of URN?
A. URL B. URI
C. DOI D. ISBN

14. The CIP (India) Project is an initiation of:
A. RRRLF
B. Delhi Public Library
C. NISCAIR
D. National Library of India

15. Identify the founders of Wikipedia from the followings:
(*i*) Michael E Davis
(*ii*) Jimmy Wales
(*iii*) Richard Stallman
(*iv*) Larry Sanger
Codes:
A. (*ii*) and (*iii*) are correct
B. (*i*) and (*ii*) are correct
C. (*i*) and (*iii*) are correct
D. (*ii*) and (*iv*) are correct

16. Alerting service is provided
(*i*) Before and after the publication of primary source
(*ii*) For specific search formulation by user
(*iii*) For retrieval of information
(*iv*) For individuals as well as groups
Codes:
A. (*i*) and (*ii*) are correct
B. (*i*) and (*iv*) are correct
C. (*ii*) and (*iii*) are correct
D. (*iii*) and (*iv*) are correct

17. Hierarchical relationship among concepts indicates:
(*i*) Genus-species relationship
(*ii*) Equivalance relationship
(*iii*) Whole-part relationship
(*iv*) Associate relationship
Codes:
A. (*ii*) and (*iv*) are correct
B. (*iii*) and (*ii*) are correct
C. (*i*) and (*iii*) are correct
D. (*iv*) and (*i*) are correct

18. The 'Principle of Facet Sequence' includes:
(*i*) Cow-calf principle
(*ii*) Wall-picture principle
(*iii*) Whole organ principle
(*iv*) Principle of osmosis

Codes:

A. (*i*), (*ii*) and (*iv*) are correct
B. (*i*), (*ii*) and (*iii*) are correct
C. (*i*), (*iii*) and (*iv*) are correct
D. (*ii*) and (*iv*) are correct

19. Identify the assistive softwares:

(*i*) Cybrarian (*ii*) Dragon
(*iii*) Jaws (*iv*) Librarian

Codes:

A. (*i*) and (*ii*) are correct
B. (*i*) and (*iii*) are correct
C. (*ii*) and (*iii*) are correct
D. (*iii*) and (iv) are correct

20. Which of the following are features of 'Open Journal System'?

(*i*) License to access content
(*ii*) Access restricted to limited group
(*iii*) Online submission
(*iv*) Subscription module with delayed open access options

Codes:

A. (*i*) and (*ii*) are correct
B. (*ii*) and (*iii*) are correct
C. (*iii*) and (*iv*) are correct
D. (*ii*) and (*iv*) are correct

21. Identify the types of OCR technology:

(*i*) Matrix matching
(*ii*) Instructional analysis
(*iii*) Feature extraction
(*iv*) Structural analysis

Codes:

A. (*i*), (*ii*) and (*iv*) are true
B. (*i*), (*ii*) and (*iii*) are true
C. (*ii*), (*iii*) and (*iv*) are true
D. (*i*), (*iii*) and (*iv*) are true

22. Match the following search techniques with their relevant example:

List–I	***List–II***
(*a*) Truncation	(*i*) Wom?n
(*b*) Wild cards	(*ii*) Comput*
(*c*) Proximity	(*iii*) edu AND biochemistry AND antibodies
(*d*) Field searching	(*iv*) "content collection"/5

Codes:

	(*a*)	(*b*)	(*c*)	(*d*)
A.	(*ii*)	(*iii*)	(*iv*)	(*i*)
B.	(*iv*)	(*iii*)	(*ii*)	(*i*)
C.	(*i*)	(*ii*)	(*iii*)	(*iv*)
D.	(*ii*)	(*i*)	(*iv*)	(*iii*)

23. Which of the following are features of flash memory?

(*i*) Erasable & Programmable Read Only Memory
(*ii*) Non-volatile memory
(*iii*) Temporary storage unit
(*iv*) Dynamic RAM

Codes:

A. (*i*), (*ii*) and (*iii*) are correct
B. (*i*), (*ii*) and (*iv*) are correct
C. (*i*) and (*ii*) are correct
D. (*ii*) and (*iv*) are correct

24. SQL is based on which of the following?

(*i*) Query string
(*ii*) Relational algebra
(*iii*) Relational calculus
(*iv*) Web search queries

Codes:

A. (*i*) and (*ii*) are correct
B. (*ii*) and (*iii*) are correct
C. (*iii*) and (*iv*) are correct
D. (*ii*) and (*iv*) are correct

25. What are the approaches to plagiarism check of academic publications?

(*i*) String matching
(*ii*) Bag of words analysis
(*iii*) Citation analysis
(*iv*) Parse trees

Codes:

A. (*ii*) and (*iv*) are correct
B. (*i*), (*ii*) and (*iii*) are correct
C. (*i*) and (*iv*) are correct
D. (*i*), (*iii*) and (*iv*) are correct

26. Identify the technology of digitization.

(*i*) Bit-depth
(*ii*) Resolution
(*iii*) Manipulation
(*iv*) Image enhancement

Codes:
A. (*ii*), (*iii*) and (*iv*) are correct
B. (*i*), (*iii*) and (*iv*) are correct
C. (*i*), (*ii*) and (*iv*) are correct
D. (*i*), (*ii*) and (*iii*) are correct

27. Which of the following are the types of validity of measurement?
(*i*) Construct
(*ii*) Current
(*iii*) Content
(*iv*) Predictive
Codes:
A. (*i*), (*ii*) and (*iii*) are true
B. (*ii*), (*iii*) and (*iv*) are true
C. (*i*), (*iii*) and (*iv*) are true
D. (*i*), (*ii*) and (*iv*) are true

28. Which are not open source library softwares?
(*i*) Bibliosys
(*ii*) Evergreen
(*iii*) New Genlib
(*iv*) Virtua
Codes:
A. (*i*) and (*ii*) are correct
B. (*i*) and (*iii*) are correct
C. (*i*) and (*iv*) are correct
D. (*ii*) and (*iv*) are correct

29. Identify the abilities of an information literate person:
(*i*) the ability to find information
(*ii*) the ability to prepare bibliographic description of information
(*iii*) the ability to use information
(*iv*) the ability to evaluate information
Codes:
A. (*i*), (*ii*) and (*iii*) are correct
B. (*i*), (*iii*) and (*iv*) are correct
C. (*i*), (*ii*) and (*iv*) are correct
D. (*ii*), (*iii*) and (*iv*) are correct

30. Which of the following are threats to information security?
(*i*) Personal firewalls
(*ii*) Compromise to IPR
(*iii*) Anti-spyware
(*iv*) Acts of espionage
Codes:
A. (*i*), (*ii*) and (*iii*) are correct
B. (*ii*) and (*iii*) are correct
C. (*ii*) and (*iv*) are correct
D. (*ii*), (*iii*) and (*iv*) are correct

31. Identify the compression protocols:
(*i*) TIFF
(*ii*) JPEG
(*iii*) ZIFF
(*iv*) LZW
Codes:
A. (*i*), (*iii*) and (*iv*) are correct
B. (*i*), (*ii*) and (*iv*) are correct
C. (*ii*), (*iii*) and (*iv*) are correct
D. (*i*), (*ii*) and (*iii*) are correct

32. Which of the following are sources for review of reference books?
(*i*) American Book Reference Annual
(*ii*) Publishers Weekly
(*iii*) Times Literary Supplement
(*iv*) Booklist
Codes:
A. (*i*) and (*ii*) are correct
B. (*i*), (*ii*) and (*iii*) are correct
C. (*i*), (*iii*) and (*iv*) are correct
D. (*i*), (*ii*) and (*iv*) are correct

33. Assertion (A): Multilingual dictionaries provide equivalent words in three or more languages.
Reason (R): They generally do not define the words but they give equivalent words in one or more foreign languages.
Codes:
A. Both (A) and (R) are true
B. Both (A) and (R) are false
C. (A) is true, but (R) is false
D. (A) is false, but (R) is true

34. Assertion (A): Wikis have provided everybody an opportunity for authoring, editing and publishing.
Reason (R): Web has provided very generic rules for creation, maintenance and development of Wikis.

Codes:

A. (A) is true, but (R) is false
B. (A) is false, but (R) is true
C. Both (A) and (R) are true
D. Both (A) and (R) are false

35. Assertion (A): Webliographies are bibliographic tools for print and electronic documents.
Reason (R): Webliography denotes an enumerative list of hypertext links surrounding a common subject following standard citation styles.

Codes:

A. (A) is true, but (R) is false
B. (A) is false, but (R) is true
C. Both (A) and (R) are true
D. Both (A) and (R) are false

36. Assertion (A): An ISO 2709 : 2008 record structure and review format has 'Record Label', 'Directory', 'Data fields' and 'Record Separator'.
Reason (R): ISO 2709 is a subset of MARC.

Codes:

A. (A) is true, but (R) is false
B. (A) is false, but (R) is true
C. Both (A) and (R) are true
D. Both (A) and (R) are false

37. Assertion (A): Knowledge Management is an extension of conventional library management.
Reason (R): Knowledge Management deals with elements like content, technology and culture.

Codes:

A. (A) is true, but (R) is false
B. Both (A) and (R) are true
C. (A) is false, but (R) is true
D. Both (A) and (R) are false

38. Assertion (A) : Precision ratio is a measure of the efficiency of an indexing system.
Reason (R) : Presence of relevant terms increases the precision ratio.

Codes:

A (A) is true, but (R) is false
B. Both (A) and (R) are true, but (R) is not the correct explanation of (A)
C. Both (A) and (R) are true and (R) is the correct explanation of (A)
D. (A) is false, but (R) is true

39. Assertion (A): The objective of "Cross Ref" is to improve access to publish scholarly works through collaborative technologies.
Reason (R): "Cross Ref" is a non-profit membership association founded and directed by publishers.

Codes:

A. Both (A) and (R) are true
B. Both (A) and (R) are true, but (R) is not the correct explanation
C. (A) is true, but (R) is false
D. (A) is false, but (R) is true

40. Assertion (A): Traditional Management process differ from the 'Quality Management'.
Reason (R): 'Quality Management' focuses on 'customer' in the management process.

Codes:

A. (A) is true, but (R) is false
B. (A) is false, but (R) is true
C. Both (A) and (R) are false
D. Both (A) and (R) are true

41. Assertion (A): DOI is the identification system for the intellectual property in the digital environment.
Reason (R): DOI is developed by WIPO.

Codes:

A. (A) is true, but (R) is false
B. Both (A) and (R) are true
C. Both (A) and (R) are false
D. (R) is true, but (A) is false

42. Assertion (A): Social networking tools are very effective for marketing of library products and services.
Reason (R): It does not help to reach out the patrons any where any time.

Codes:

A. (A) is true, but (R) is false
B. (A) is false, but (R) is true
C. Both (A) and (R) are true
D. Both (A) and (R) are false

43. Assertion (A): A database can be searched with a query language.
Reason (R): A database can store a large amount of data.
Codes:
A. Both (A) and (R) are true, but (R) is not the correct explanation of (A)
B. Both (A) and (R) are true and (R) is the correct explanation of (A)
C. (A) is true, but (R) is false
D. (A) is false, but (R) is true

44. Assertion (A): To increase accessibility to information for differently abled users we need to accept assistive technologies.
Reason (R): Information for all.
Codes:
A. Both (A) and (R) are true, but (R) is not the correct explanation of (A)
B. Both (A) and (R) are true and (R) is the correct explanation of (A)
C. (A) is true, but (R) is false
D. (A) is false, but (R) is true

45. Assertion (A): The plagiarism detection software implements a generic detection approach for all types of materials.
Reason (R): There is no difference between text and source code plagiarism.
Codes:
A. (A) is true, but (R) is false
B. (A) is false, but (R) is true
C. Both (A) and (R) are true
D. Both (A) and (R) are false

46. Assertion (A): UGC notification (2009) mandates submission of electronic theses and dissertations by the researchers in universities to facilitate open access.
Reason (R): UGC wants to monitor the quality of research through open access.
Codes:
A. (A) is true, but (R) is false
B. (A) is false, but (R) is true
C. Both (A) and (R) are true
D. Both (A) and (R) are false

47. Assertion (A): Bibliometric study is the popular area of research on which maximum number of Ph.D degree have been awarded in India.
Reason (R): Bibliometric study adds to the extension of fundamental research.
Codes:
A. Both (A) and (R) are true
B. (A) is true, but (R) is false
C. Both (A) and (R) are false
D. (R) is true, but(A) is false

48. Assertion (A): According to National Knowledge Commission, 'The library and information services sector in India has not kept pace with the paradigmatic changes taking place in society'.
Reason (R): There is no proportionate growth in library resources.
Codes:
A. Both (A) and (R) are true
B. (A) is true, but (R) is false
C. Both (A) and (R) are false
D. (A) is false, but (R) is true

49. Arrange the following in chronological order:
(*i*) Delivery of Books and Newspapers Act
(*ii*) RTI Act
(*iii*) Imperial Library Act
(*iv*) IT (Amendment) Act
Codes:
A. (*i*), (*iv*), (*ii*), (*iii*) B. (*iii*), (*i*), (*ii*), (*iv*)
C. (*iii*), (*ii*), (*i*), (*iv*) D. (*iv*), (*iii*), (*i*), (*ii*)

50. Arrange the following in chronological order:
(*i*) Rome convention
(*ii*) WIPO copyright treaty
(*iii*) Universal copyright convention
(*iv*) Berne convention
Codes:
A. (*i*), (*iv*), (*iii*), (*ii*) B. (*iv*), (*i*), (*ii*), (*iii*)
C. (*iv*), (*iii*), (*i*), (*ii*) D. (*iii*), (*i*), (*iv*), (*ii*)

51. Arrange the following in chronological order:
(*i*) UNESCO Public Library Manifesto
(*ii*) A.A.A. Fyzee Report
(*iii*) Library Advisory Committee Report
(*iv*) Raja Ram Mohan Roy Library Foundation

Codes:

A. (*i*), (*ii*), (*iii*), (*iv*) B. (*ii*), (*iii*), (*iv*), (*i*)
C. (*i*), (*iv*), (*ii*), (*iii*) D. (*iii*), (*i*), (*ii*), (*iv*)

52. Arrange the following bibliographics in the order of their chronological development:

(*i*) Universal (*ii*) Subject
(*iii*) Trade (*iv*) Webliography

Codes:

A. (*i*), (*ii*), (*iii*), (*iv*) B. (*iii*), (*i*), (*ii*), (*iv*)
C. (*ii*), (*iii*), (*i*), (*iv*) D. (*iv*), (*ii*), (*iii*), (*i*)

53. Arrange the following according to the year of origin:

(*i*) Encyclopaedia Britannica
(*ii*) World Book Encyclopaedia
(*iii*) Wikipedia
(*iv*) Encyclopaedia Americana

Codes:

A. (*iv*), (*i*), (*ii*), (*iii*) B. (*i*), (*iv*), (*ii*), (*iii*)
C. (*ii*), (*iv*), (*i*), (*iii*) D. (*i*), (*ii*), (*iv*), (*iii*)

54. Arrange the following in correct classified order as per C.C.

(*i*) A (*ii*) 2:5
(*iii*) 2a (*iv*) 234

Codes:

A. (*iii*), (*i*), (*iv*), (*ii*) B. (*i*), (*iii*), (*ii*), (*iv*)
C. (*iii*), (*ii*), (*iv*), (*i*) D. (*ii*), (*i*), (*iii*), (*iv*)

55. Arrange the following according to the procedural steps:

(*i*) Receipt of recommendations
(*ii*) Preparing master card
(*iii*) Checking titles of and bibliographical details
(*iv*) Duplication checking from library catalogue

Codes:

A. (*i*), (*ii*), (*iii*), (*iv*) B. (*i*), (*iii*), (*ii*), (*iv*)
C. (*iii*), (*i*), (*iv*), (*ii*) D. (*iv*), (*iii*), (*i*), (*ii*)

56. Arrange the following according to their publication year:

(*i*) Sears' list of subject headings
(*ii*) Panizzi code
(*iii*) AACR-I
(*iv*) CCC

Codes:

A. (*iv*), (*ii*), (*iii*), (*i*) B. (*i*), (*iii*), (*ii*), (*iv*)
C. (*ii*), (*i*), (*iv*), (*iii*) D. (*iii*), (*iv*), (*i*), (*ii*)

57. Arrange the following according to their date of origin:

(*i*) Librametry
(*ii*) Statistical bibliography
(*iii*) Statistical analysis
(*iv*) Bibliometrics

Codes:

A. (*i*), (*iii*), (*ii*), (*iv*) B. (*ii*), (*iii*), (*i*), (*iv*)
C. (*iii*), (*i*), (*ii*), (*iv*) D. (*iii*), (*ii*), (*i*), (*iv*)

58. Arrange the following activities in the order as given by Ellis in his model of information seeking behaviour:

(*i*) Browsing
(*ii*) Monitoring
(*iii*) Extracting
(*iv*) Differentiating

Codes:

A. (*ii*), (*i*), (*iv*), (*iii*) B. (*i*), (*iv*), (*ii*), (*iii*)
C. (*iii*), (*ii*), (*i*), (*iv*) D. (*ii*), (*i*), (*iii*), (*iv*)

59. Arrange the sequence of the following steps followed in classifying a document according to colon classification:

(*i*) Title with standard facet terms
(*ii*) Analyzed title
(*iii*) Kernel title
(*iv*) Transformed title

Codes:

A. (*ii*), (*iv*), (*i*), (*iii*) B. (*i*), (*ii*), (*iii*), (*iv*)
C. (*iii*), (*ii*), (*iv*), (*i*) D. (*iv*), (*iii*), (*ii*), (*i*)

60. Arrange the following steps in the order of accessioning the book:

(*i*) Arrange books as per bill
(*ii*) Check books as per order placed
(*iii*) Enter the accession number in the register
(*iv*) Write accession number on back of title page of other relevant pages

Codes:

A. (*i*), (*ii*), (*iii*), (*iv*)
B. (*ii*), (*iii*), (*i*), (*iv*)
C. (*iii*), (*i*), (*ii*), (*iv*)
D. (*ii*), (*i*), (*iii*), (*iv*)

61. Match the following:

List–I	**List–II**
(*a*) Infringement	(*i*) Unauthorized use of I.P.
(*b*) Enforcement	(*ii*) Criminal penalties
(*c*) Mis-appropriation	(*iii*) Breach of trade secret
(*d*) Counterfeit	(*iv*) Intentional forgery

Codes:

	(*a*)	(*b*)	(*c*)	(*d*)
A.	(*ii*)	(*iii*)	(*iv*)	(*i*)
B.	(*i*)	(*ii*)	(*iii*)	(*iv*)
C.	(*iii*)	(*iv*)	(*i*)	(*ii*)
D.	(*iv*)	(*i*)	(*iii*)	(*ii*)

62. Match the following:

List–I	**List–II**
(*a*) ALA	(*i*) 1909
(*b*) CILIP	(*ii*) 1933
(*c*) SLA	(*iii*) 1876
(*d*) ILA	(*iv*) 2002

Codes:

	(*a*)	(*b*)	(*c*)	(*d*)
A.	(*iv*)	(*ii*)	(*iii*)	(*i*)
B.	(*iii*)	(*iv*)	(*i*)	(*ii*)
C.	(*i*)	(*ii*)	(*iv*)	(*iii*)
D.	(*ii*)	(*iv*)	(*ii*)	(*i*)

63. Match the following:

List–I	**List–II**
(*a*) Sayaji Rao Gayakwad	(*i*) Revision of salary scale
(*b*) D.P. Chattopadhyaya	(*ii*) Library building
(*c*) K.D. Metcalf	(*iii*) Public libraries
(*d*) B.S. Kesavan	(*iv*) Librarian of national library

Codes:

	(*a*)	(*b*)	(*c*)	(*d*)
A.	(*ii*)	(*i*)	(*iii*)	(*iv*)
B.	(*i*)	(*ii*)	(*iii*)	(*iv*)
C.	(*iii*)	(*i*)	(*ii*)	(*iv*)
D.	(*iv*)	(*iii*)	(*i*)	(*ii*)

64. Match the following publishers with the relevant databases:

List–I	**List–II**
(*a*) Elsevier	(*i*) Academic search
(*b*) Thomson Reuters	(*ii*) Aerospace & high technology
(*c*) EBSCO	(*iii*) Scopus
(*d*) ProQuest	(*iv*) Web of knowledge

Codes:

	(*a*)	(*b*)	(*c*)	(*d*)
A.	(*ii*)	(*i*)	(*iv*)	(*iii*)
B.	(*i*)	(*iii*)	(*ii*)	(*iv*)
C.	(*iii*)	(*iv*)	(*i*)	(*ii*)
D.	(*iv*)	(*ii*)	(*iii*)	(*i*)

65. Match the following:

List–I	**List–II**
(*a*) Informing about best books	(*i*) Support service
(*b*) Guidance to use citation manual	(*ii*) Bibliography
(*c*) Providing prints for downloads	(*iii*) Readers advisory
(*d*) Providing list of URLs	(*iv*) Users education

Codes:

	(*a*)	(*b*)	(*c*)	(*d*)
A.	(*ii*)	(*iii*)	(*i*)	(*iv*)
B.	(*iii*)	(*iv*)	(*i*)	(*ii*)
C.	(*iv*)	(*ii*)	(*iii*)	(*i*)
D.	(*ii*)	(*iv*)	(*iii*)	(*i*)

66. Match the following:

List–I	**List–II**
(*a*) Market segmentation	(*i*) User behaviour
(*b*) Consumer analysis	(*ii*) Market mix
(*c*) Market positioning	(*iii*) Category of users
(*d*) Market program	(*iv*) Prioritising users

Codes:

	(*a*)	(*b*)	(*c*)	(*d*)
A.	(*i*)	(*iii*)	(*ii*)	(*iv*)
B.	(*iii*)	(*i*)	(*iv*)	(*ii*)
C.	(*ii*)	(*iv*)	(*i*)	(*iii*)
D.	(*iv*)	(*ii*)	(*iii*)	(*i*)

67. Match the following:

List–I	**List–II**
(*a*) India	(*i*) Agglomeration
(*b*) Agriculture of wheat	(*ii*) Fusion
(*c*) Bio-chemistry	(*iii*) Denudation
(*d*) Biological sciences	(*iv*) Lamination

Codes:

	(a)	(b)	(c)	(d)
A.	(iii)	(iv)	(ii)	(i)
B.	(iv)	(ii)	(iii)	(i)
C.	(ii)	(iii)	(i)	(iv)
D.	(i)	(ii)	(iv)	(iii)

68. Match the following:

List–I	***List–II***
(a) Standing order	(i) For serial publications till cancellation
(b) Blanket order	(ii) Routine publications on order
(c) Firm order	(iii) For publications on recommendation
(d) Approval order	(iv) For supply of institutional publications as and when published

Codes:

	(a)	(b)	(c)	(d)
A.	(iv)	(ii)	(i)	(iii)
B.	(iii)	(ii)	(i)	(iv)
C.	(i)	(iv)	(ii)	(iii)
D.	(ii)	(iv)	(i)	(iii)

69. Match the following:

List–I	***List–II***
(a) HTML	(i) Interpretation by web browser
(b) XML	(ii) Describes data
(c) UNICODE	(iii) Display data
(d) VB Script	(iv) Platform independent

Codes:

	(a)	(b)	(c)	(d)
A.	(i)	(ii)	(iii)	(iv)
B.	(iii)	(iv)	(i)	(ii)
C.	(ii)	(iv)	(i)	(iii)
D.	(iii)	(ii)	(iv)	(i)

70. Match the following national organizations with their relevant mission:

List–I	***List–II***
(a) National Mission on Libraries	(i) Digitization of AYUSH literature
(b) National Mission for Manuscripts	(ii) Nurturing of talent
(c) T.K.D.L.	(iii) Capacity building
(d) NME-ICT	(iv) Connects India's past with present

Codes:

	(a)	(b)	(c)	(d)
A.	(i)	(ii)	(iii)	(iv)
B.	(iii)	(iv)	(i)	(ii)
C.	(iv)	(iii)	(ii)	(i)
D.	(ii)	(i)	(iii)	(iv)

71. Match the following:

List–I	***List–II***
(a) Simple random	(i) Natural order
(b) Systematic random	(ii) Representative
(c) Stratified random	(iii) Equal chance
(d) Judgement	(iv) Sub-groups

Codes:

	(a)	(b)	(c)	(d)
A.	(ii)	(i)	(iii)	(iv)
B.	(iii)	(i)	(iv)	(ii)
C.	(iv)	(ii)	(i)	(iii)
D.	(iii)	(ii)	(iv)	(i)

72. Match the following:

List–I	***List–II***
(a) Semantic differential scale	(i) Graded structure
(b) Thurston scale	(ii) Opposition positions
(c) Interval scale	(iii) Group of Judgement
(d) Likert scale	(iv) Equal units of measurement

Codes:

	(a)	(b)	(c)	(d)
A.	(iv)	(iii)	(i)	(ii)
B.	(i)	(iv)	(iii)	(ii)
C.	(iii)	(ii)	(i)	(iv)
D.	(ii)	(iii)	(iv)	(i)

73. Match the following:

List–I	***List–II***
(a) Barren Hypothesis	(i) Indian men marry at 26-28 years age
(b) Idiographic Hypothesis	(ii) Seema will top this year
(c) Nomothetic Hypothesis	(iii) Loss of limbs
(d) Crude Hypothesis	(iv) Quality of collection

Codes:

	(a)	(b)	(c)	(d)
A.	(iv)	(iii)	(i)	(ii)
B.	(iii)	(ii)	(iv)	(i)
C.	(ii)	(i)	(iii)	(iv)
D.	(i)	(iv)	(ii)	(iii)

74. Match the following:

List–I	*List–II*
(a) Multiple choice questions	(i) Personal opinion of interviewer
(b) Loaded questions	(ii) No sets of answers
(c) Contingency questions	(iii) Alternative answers
(d) Open ended questions	(iv) Sub-group of respondents

Codes:

	(a)	(b)	(c)	(d)
A.	(i)	(iv)	(iii)	(ii)
B.	(iv)	(ii)	(iii)	(i)
C.	(iii)	(i)	(iv)	(ii)
D.	(ii)	(iii)	(i)	(iv)

75. Match the following:

List–I	*List–II*
(a) Mean	(i) $\sum \frac{(O-E)^2}{E}$
(b) Degree of freedom (df)	(ii) $\frac{n+1}{2}$
(c) Median	(iii) $(r-1)(c-1)$
(d) Chi-square (χ^2)	(iv) $\frac{\Sigma x}{n}$

Codes:

	(a)	(b)	(c)	(d)
A.	(ii)	(iv)	(i)	(iii)
B.	(iii)	(ii)	(i)	(iv)
C.	(iv)	(iii)	(ii)	(i)
D.	(i)	(ii)	(iv)	(iii)

ANSWERS

1	2	3	4	5	6	7	8	9	10
A	D	C	C	D	D	D	C	B	C
11	**12**	**13**	**14**	**15**	**16**	**17**	**18**	**19**	**20**
B	D	D	A	D	B	C	B	C	C
21	**22**	**23**	**24**	**25**	**26**	**27**	**28**	**29**	**30**
D	D	C	B	B	C	C	C	B	C
31	**32**	**33**	**34**	**35**	**36**	**37**	**38**	**39**	**40**
B	C	A	A	B	B	C	B	A	D
41	**42**	**43**	**44**	**45**	**46**	**47**	**48**	**49**	**50**
A	A	B	B	D	A	B	B	B	C
51	**52**	**53**	**54**	**55**	**56**	**57**	**58**	**59**	**60**
B	B	B	C	B	C	D	B	C	D
61	**62**	**63**	**64**	**65**	**66**	**67**	**68**	**69**	**70**
B	B	C	C	B	B	A	C	D	B
71	**72**	**73**	**74**	**75**					
B	D	B	C	C					

Previous Paper (Solved)

UGC-NET Library and Information Science, June 2014

PAPER-II

Note: *This paper contains* ***fifty*** *(50) objective type questions of* ***two*** *(2) marks each.* ***All*** *questions are compulsory.*

1. Books of Unknown or doubtful authorship is known as :
   A. Apograph
   B. Incunabulla
   C. Apocryphal books
   D. Blue Books
2. If we plot 'recall' and precision on 'X' and 'Y' axis to draw a graph, then we get a
   A. Downward sloping straight line
   B. Upward sloping straight line
   C. 'α' shaped curve
   D. Hyperbola
3. The term 'Literary warrant' for book classification was introduced by
   A. W.C.B. Sayers B. Wyndham Hulme
   C. J.D. Brown D. H.E. Bliss
4. Under which approach of Wersig-Neveling's information theory, information is seen as static relations between physical objects which may be perceived or not?
   A. The meaning approach
   B. The structural approach
   C. The process approach
   D. The knowledge approach
5. Which information theory focuses on the purpose of communication is, to inform, instruct or motivate the receiver?
   A. Shannon's Theory
   B. Weaver's Theory
   C. Ackoff's Theory
   D. Yovit's Theory
6. 'Noise' in Information retrieval is due to
   A. Precision
   B. Recall
   C. Relevant Information
   D. Redundant Information
7. In which scheme of classification, special auxiliaries denote locally recurrent characteristics?
   A. Deuey Decimal Classification
   B. Universal Decimal Classification
   C. Bibliographic Classification
   D. Colon Classification
8. Which of the following makes a network insecured?
   A. Encryption
   B. Network Interface Card (NIC)
   C. Password Capture
   D. Static Keys
9. Whose model of communication of knowledge suggests that communication is an open system?
   A. G. Garbner
   B. Juger Hebermans
   C. Shannon and Weaver
   D. M. Foucault
10. 'Trans Border Data Flow' means
    A. Exchange of documents between countries
    B. Free flow of information between countries
    C. Flow of information between countries
    D. Exchange of electronic information between countries
11. Which of the following three types of basic languages are used in computer programming?

A. Procedural, Non-procedural and Unconditional
B. Zero, Low and High levels
C. Machine, Assembly and High level languages
D. COBOL, BASIC and C

12. FRBR Model consist of which of the following four entities?
A. Personality, Matter, Energy, Space
B. Work, Expression, Manifestation, Item
C. Book, Form, Availability, Type
D. Action, Place, Impact, Category

13. The primary distinction between RDA and AACR is
A. Structural B. Relational
C. Non-structural D. Combinational

14. Which of the following are reasons for obsolescence of information?
(*i*) Information is considered invalid.
(*ii*) Information is valid but mostly available online.
(*iii*) Works are extensively cited.
(*iv*) Information is valid but inadequate for exploration.
Codes :
A. (*i*) and (*ii*) are correct.
B. (*ii*) and (*iii*) are correct.
C. (*i*) and (*iv*) are correct.
D. (*ii*) and (*iv*) are correct.

15. Which of the following are news summaries?
(*i*) Data India
(*ii*) Times of India Index
(*iii*) New York Times Index
(*iv*) Asian Recorder
Codes :
A. (*i*), (*ii*) and (*iii*) are correct.
B. (*ii*) and (*iii*) are correct.
C. (*ii*) (*iii*) and (*iv*) are correct.
D. (*i*) and (*iv*) are correct.

16. Which of the following are Web-zine?
(*i*) Email Magazine
(*ii*) E-Conference
(*iii*) Online Bulletin
(*iv*) Electronic News Letter
Codes :
A. (*i*), (*iii*) and (*iv*)
B. (*i*), (*ii*) and (*iii*)
C. (*ii*), (*iii*) and (*iv*)
D. (*i*), (*ii*) and (*iv*)

17. Which of the following are not the Models of communication?
(*i*) Vintage Model
(*ii*) Lasswell's Model
(*iii*) Epidemic Model
(*iv*) Garbner's Model
Codes :
A. (*i*) and (*iv*) are correct.
B. (*ii*) and (*iii*) are correct.
C. (*i*) and (*iii*) are correct.
D. (*iii*) and (*iv*) are correct.

18. In reference service, assimilation means :
(*i*) Recording the retrieved information
(*ii*) Sharing reference service experience with colleagues
(*iii*) Furnishing the exact information
(*iv*) Acquaintance with reference material
Codes :
A. (*i*) and (*ii*) are correct.
B. (*i*) and (*iv*) are correct.
C. (*ii*) and (*iii*) are correct.
D. (*ii*) and (*iv*) are correct.

19. The notation used to increase the capacity of an array are :
(*i*) Empty digit (*ii*) Emptying digit
(*iii*) Indicator digit (*iv*) Speciator
Codes :
A. (*i*) and (*ii*) are correct.
B. (*iii*) and (*iv*) are correct.
C. (*i*), (*ii*) and (*iii*) are correct.
D. (*i*), (*ii*) and (*iv*) are correct.

20. Which of the following are the functions of the physical layer in OSI Model?
(*i*) Defines protocol for flow control.
(*ii*) Reliable sending of data packets.
(*iii*) Defines electrical specifications.
(*iv*) Functional and procedural means of transferring data.
Codes :
A. (*iii*) and (*iv*) are correct.
B. (*ii*), (*iii*) and (*iv*) are correct.
C. (*i*) and (*iv*) are correct.
D. (*i*) and (*iii*) are correct.

21. Rich Text Format (RTF) is concerned with
(*i*) Formatting features like Font type, size, etc.
(*ii*) Transporting text documents across different computers.
(*iii*) Multimedia formatting.
(*iv*) Formatting based on binary concept.
Codes :
A. (*ii*) and (*iii*) are correct.
B. (*iii*) and (*iv*) are correct.
C. (*i*) and (*ii*) are correct.
D. (*i*) and (*iv*) are correct.

22. Which of the following are non-probability sampling?
(*i*) Quota sampling
(*ii*) Judgement Sampling
(*iii*) Cluster Sampling
(*iv*) Multi-stage sampling
Codes :
A. (*i*) and (*iv*) are correct.
B. (*ii*) and (*iii*) are correct.
C. (*i*) and (*ii*) are correct.
D. (*iii*) and (*iv*) are correct.

23. Arrange the following in the ascending order of their first year of publication :
(*i*) BNB
(*ii*) INB
(*iii*) Compendex
(*iv*) Roget's Thesaurus of English words
Codes :
A. (*iv*), (*iii*), (*i*) and (*ii*)
B. (*iii*), (*ii*), (*iv*) and (*i*)
C. (*ii*), (*iv*), (*i*) and (*iii*)
D. (*i*), (*iii*), (*ii*) and (*iv*)

24. Arrange the following ISBDs according to their year of formulation :
(*i*) ISBD (PM) (*ii*) ISBD (CF)
(*iii*) ISBD (M) (*iv*) ISBD (S)
Codes :
A. (*iii*), (*ii*), (*i*) and (*iv*)
B. (*iii*), (*iv*), (*i*) and (*ii*)
C. (*iv*), (*i*), (*iii*) and (*ii*)
D. (*iv*), (*ii*), (*iii*) and (*i*)

25. Arrange the following in the chronological order of their first year of publication :
(*i*) Arts and Humanities Index
(*ii*) Social Science Citation Index
(*iii*) ISI Web of Science
(*iv*) Science Citation Index
Codes :
A. (*iv*), (*ii*), (*i*) and (*iii*)
B. (*ii*), (*iii*), (*iv*) and (*i*)
C. (*iii*), (*ii*), (*i*) and (*iv*)
D. (*iv*), (*i*), (*iii*) and (*ii*)

26. Arrange the following Library Acts according to the year of their enactment :
(*i*) Arunachal Pradesh
(*ii*) Bihar
(*iii*) Lakshadweep
(*iv*) Rajasthan
Codes :
A. (*ii*), (*iv*), (*iii*) and (*i*)
B. (*iv*), (*i*), (*ii*) and (*iii*)
C. (*ii*), (*iii*), (*i*) and (*iv*)
D. (*iv*), (*iii*), (*ii*) and (*i*)

27. Arrange the following processes of research in order :
(*i*) Theory Building
(*ii*) Reflecting and Integrating of Idea
(*iii*) Research Design
(*iv*) Review of Literature
Codes :
A. (*iv*), (*iii*), (*ii*) and (*i*)
B. (*iii*), (*i*), (*iv*) and (*ii*)
C. (*ii*), (*iv*), (*iii*) and (*i*)
D. (*i*), (*ii*), (*iv*) and (*iii*)

28. Match the following :

List-I	List-II
(*a*) CILIP	(*i*) 1972
(*b*) ASLIB	(*ii*) 2002
(*c*) ALA	(*iii*) 1876
(*d*) COMLA	(*iv*) 1924

Codes :

	(*a*)	(*b*)	(*c*)	(*d*)
A.	(*ii*)	(*iv*)	(*iii*)	(*i*)
B.	(*iv*)	(*iii*)	(*ii*)	(*i*)
C.	(*iii*)	(*iv*)	(*i*)	(*ii*)
D.	(*ii*)	(*iii*)	(*iv*)	(*i*)

29. Match the following :

List-I	List-II
(*a*) Phenomenon	(*i*) Physical Media for grouping of Information
(*b*) Spectrum	(*ii*) Facts or Occurrence

(*c*) Modes (*iii*) Transfer Process
(*d*) Diffusion (*iv*) A broad range of varied but related ideas

Codes :

	(*a*)	(*b*)	(*c*)	(*d*)
A.	(*i*)	(*iii*)	(*iv*)	(*ii*)
B.	(*ii*)	(*iv*)	(*i*)	(*iii*)
C.	(*ii*)	(*iii*)	(*iv*)	(*i*)
D.	(*iv*)	(*i*)	(*iii*)	(*ii*)

30. Match the following :

List-I	List-II
(*a*) Union Catalogue	(*i*) Primary sources
(*b*) Pamphlets & Brochures	(*ii*) Unpublished sources
(*c*) Indexing & Abstracting Sources	(*iii*) Tertiary sources
(*d*) Memoirs of diaries	(*iv*) Secondary sources

Codes :

	(*a*)	(*b*)	(*c*)	(*d*)
A.	(*iv*)	(*iii*)	(*ii*)	(*i*)
B.	(*ii*)	(*iv*)	(*iii*)	(*i*)
C.	(*iii*)	(*i*)	(*iv*)	(*ii*)
D.	(*i*)	(*ii*)	(*iv*)	(*iii*)

31. Match the following :

List-I	List-II
(*a*) Fundamentals of Reference Service	(*i*) A.J. Walford
(*b*) Introduction to Reference works	(*ii*) S.R. Ranganathan
(*c*) Reference service	(*iii*) F.N. Cheney and W.J. Williams
(*d*) Guide to Reference Books	(*iv*) William A Katz

Codes :

	(*a*)	(*b*)	(*c*)	(*d*)
A.	(*ii*)	(*i*)	(*iv*)	(*iii*)
B.	(*iii*)	(*iv*)	(*i*)	(*ii*)
C.	(*iv*)	(*ii*)	(*iii*)	(*i*)
D.	(*iii*)	(*iv*)	(*ii*)	(*i*)

32. Match the following :

List-I	List-II
(*a*) Information on important recent happenings of India	(*i*) India – A Reference Annual
(*b*) Total number of foreigners visited in India in 2012	(*ii*) Keesing's Record of World Events
(*c*) Name of Prime Minister of India	(*iii*) Statistical Yearbook
(*d*) Postal Address of Anna Hazare	(*iv*) Who's Who

Codes :

	(*a*)	(*b*)	(*c*)	(*d*)
A.	(*iv*)	(*i*)	(*ii*)	(*iii*)
B.	(*ii*)	(*iii*)	(*i*)	(*iv*)
C.	(*iii*)	(*ii*)	(*i*)	(*iv*)
D.	(*i*)	(*iv*)	(*iii*)	(*ii*)

33. Match the following :

List-I	List-II
(*a*) Scaler Chain	(*i*) Direct dealing with subordinates
(*b*) Espirit de Corps	(*ii*) Production, efficiency and prevention of waste
(*c*) Scientific Management	(*iii*) Emphasis on Team Work
(*d*) Span of control	(*iv*) Top to Bottom

Codes :

	(*a*)	(*b*)	(*c*)	(*d*)
A.	(*iv*)	(*iii*)	(*ii*)	(*i*)
B.	(*iii*)	(*iv*)	(*i*)	(*ii*)
C.	(*iv*)	(*ii*)	(*iii*)	(*i*)
D.	(*ii*)	(*iii*)	(*i*)	(*iv*)

34. Match the following :

List-I	List-II
(*a*) Check Card	(*i*) Reader's Ticket
(*b*) Kardex	(*ii*) Three Card System
(*c*) Newark System	(*iii*) Periodicals
(*d*) Browne System	(*iv*) Borrower's Card

Codes :

	(*a*)	(*b*)	(*c*)	(*d*)
A.	(*ii*)	(*iii*)	(*iv*)	(*i*)
B.	(*iii*)	(*iv*)	(*i*)	(*ii*)
C.	(*ii*)	(*iv*)	(*iii*)	(*i*)
D.	(*iv*)	(*i*)	(*ii*)	(*iii*)

35. Match the following :

List-I	List-II
(*a*) Skewness	(*i*) Numbers of frequently appearing variables

(*b*) Modality	(*ii*) Degree of association between two/ more variables
(*c*) F-distribution	(*iii*) Structure of distribution
(*d*) Correlation	(*iv*) Ratio of two Chi-square variables

Codes :

	(*a*)	(*b*)	(*c*)	(*d*)
A.	(*i*)	(*iv*)	(*ii*)	(*iii*)
B.	(*iii*)	(*i*)	(*iv*)	(*ii*)
C.	(*iv*)	(*ii*)	(*iii*)	(*i*)
D.	(*ii*)	(*iii*)	(*i*)	(*iv*)

36. Assertion (A) : Mail survey, a data collection technique in which questionnaires are mailed to potential respondents, who in then fill and return at their convenience become obsolete.

Reason (R) : Survey-Monkey, the free online survey tool has totally replaced the traditional Mail survey.

Codes :

A. (A) is true, but (R) is false.
B. (A) is false, but (R) is true.
C. Both (A) and (R) are true.
D. Both (A) and (R) are false.

37. Assertion (A) : Case situations are seldom comparable and as such the information gathered in case studies is often not comparable.

Reason (R) : The subject under case study are usually described in terms of the characteristics exhibited by the subject/case itself.

Codes :

A. Both (A) and (R) are true.
B. Both (A) and (R) are false.
C. (A) is true, but (R) is false.
D. (A) is false, but (R) is true.

38. Assertion (A) : Intellectual Property Rights facilitate free flow of information.

Reason (R) : Effective free flow of information is the pre-requisite for knowledge society.

Codes :

A. (A) is true, but (R) is false.
B. (A) is false, but (R) is true.
C. Both (A) and (R) are true.
D. Both (A) and (R) are false.

39. Assertion (A) : The total output of Indian publications is reflected in 'Indian National Bibliography'.

Reason (R) : A number of publishers in India are defaulters and do not deposit their publications as per Delivery of Books and Newspapers (Public Libraries) Act.

Codes :

A. Both (A) and (R) are true.
B. Both (A) and (R) are false.
C. (A) is true, but (R) is false.
D. (A) is false, but (R) is true.

40. Assertion (A) : No library is self sufficient in terms of resources even in electronic age.

Reason (R) : Resource sharing and consortia initiatives are essential to meet user needs.

Codes :

A. (A) is true and (R) is false.
B. (A) is false and (R) is true.
C. Both (A) and (R) are true.
D. Both (A) and (R) are false.

41. Assertion (A) : Interviewing is essential to supplement the research data collected through questionnaire.

Reason (R) : Interview is the most suitable technique to collect data as all respondents cooperate more during interview.

Codes :

A. (A) is false, but (R) is true.
B. Both (A) and (R) are true.
C. Both (A) and (R) are false.
D. (A) is true, but (R) is false.

42. Assertion (A) : Indexing and abstracting services fulfil the 4th Law of Library Science.

Reason (R) : These services serve as the substitute to the primary journals.

Codes :

A. (A) is true, but (R) is false.
B. Both (A) and (R) are false.
C. Both (A) and (R) are true.
D. (A) is false, but (R) is true.

43. Assertion (A) : All classification schemes adopt 'phase relations'.

Reason (R) : Subject formation by loose assemblage leads to complex subjects and isolates.

Codes :

A. (A) is true, but (R) is false.
B. Both (A) and (R) are true.
C. Both (A) and (R) are false.
D. (A) is false, but (R) is true.

44. Assertion (A) : RSS (Rich Site Summary) is considered as an alternate to the SDI Service.

Reason (R) : RSS Feeds enable us to syndicate data automatically.

Codes :

A. Both (A) and (R) are true.
B. Both (A) and (R) are false.
C. (A) is false, but (R) is true.
D. (A) is true, but (R) is false.

45. Assertion (A) : Majority of academic libraries in India are lagging behind in switching over as technology-oriented service institutions.

Reason (R) : The apex academic bodies and library Associations have not taken the lead role to devise standards and policies.

Codes :

A. (A) is true, (R) is false.
B. (A) is false, (R) is true.
C. Both (A) and (R) are true.
D. Both (A) and (R) are false.

Directions: *Read the passage given below and answer the questions based on your understanding of the passage (Question Nos. 46 – 50) :*

As the global information landscape increasingly facilitate the sharing, repurposing and dissemination of information, the ways in which students are accustomed to interacting with information resources are also changing. For some new students to universities, their understanding of referencing is based solely on fear (McGowan, 2005) and many are familiar wit the basic concept of plagiarism. Some students bring with them the academic process that served them well at school – however, these are not suitable at Universities (Chanock, 2008). Students understand they should not copy words without referencing, but fail to grasp the reasons why; the reasons are not explicit and often cloaked in unfamiliar and impenetrable academic language. Pak's (2003) review of literature proved as a handy summation of the investigations, research, and thinking about plagiarism prior to the implementation of various plagiarism detection software products. There are three main schools of thought in referencing and plagiarism discourse. A punitive approach which focuses on the idea that students often deliberately engage in plagiarism and that the appropriate response is one of punishment (Blum, 2009; Sutherland – Smith, 2010; Bilic – Zulle, *et. al.* 2008). A Restorative Justice approach, however, suggests that plagiarism is in fact an act against a community (in this case, a community of students), and that steps need to be taken to restore a level of balance (Wenzel; *et. al.* 2010; Karp and Conrad, 2005; Karp, 2009; Dickson, *etc. al.* 2009). An educational approach that espouses that the best method of reducing plagiarism is to educate and support students. Marking criteria and assessment tasks should be linked to building referencing skills (especially in the first year) and ensure that the students learn these skills in a discipline related context (Jaschik; 2008). The approach of both the University of Southern Queensland (USQ) and Swinburne University of Technology is clearly aligned with the third school of thought. Students lack proper understanding of the purposes of referencing. For them, referencing and citing is linked to just words, not ideas (Jackson, 2006), so referencing is regarded as separate to the writing process, instead of an integral part. To help students develop good writing and referencing practices, it is useful if universities help them understand the research culture of tertiary study. Faculties need to make their referencing rules explicit and lectures should provide useful exemplars within courses.

46. Understanding of new students on Referencing is based on

A. Plagiarism
B. Fear
C. Ability to write
D. Insatiable desire to learn

47. An appropriate response to deliberate act of plagiarism according to punitive school of thought is
A. to debar the student from library use
B. to orient the student about plagiarism
C. to award punishment
D. to make him learn about referencing

48. To restore a 'level of balance' is advocated/reflected in
A. Deterrent Approach
B. Reformative Approach
C. Punitive Approach
D. Restorative Approach

49. 'Educational approach' which aims at reducing plagiarism should be linked with
A. building referencing skills of the students
B. inculcating reading habits of the students
C. building students as information literate
D. ignorance of the students on methods of social research

50. Lack of understanding of students about referencing is linked to their
A. Ideas B. Words
C. Experience D. Intuition

ANSWERS

1	2	3	4	5	6	7	8	9	10
C	D	A	B	C	D	B	C	A	C
11	**12**	**13**	**14**	**15**	**16**	**17**	**18**	**19**	**20**
D	B	A	C	D	A	C	A	A	D
21	**22**	**23**	**24**	**25**	**26**	**27**	**28**	**29**	**30**
C	C	A	B	A	D	A	A	B	C
31	**32**	**33**	**34**	**35**	**36**	**37**	**38**	**39**	**40**
D	B	A	A	B	D	A	B	D	C
41	**42**	**43**	**44**	**45**	**46**	**47**	**48**	**49**	**50**
D	A	D	A	C	B	C	D	A	A

PAPER-III

ote: *This paper contains* **seventy five** *(75) objective type questions of* **two** *(2) marks each.* **All** *questions are compulsory.*

1. Damodaran Committee was appointed in 1971 to review working of
A. Medical College Libraries
B. National Science Libraries
C. Agriculture Libraries
D. Polytechnic Libraries

2. Which form of reasoning is the process of drawing a specific conclusion from a set of premises?
A. Rationalism
B. Deductive reasoning
C. Inductive reasoning
D. Probabilistic

3. A non-linear model of information seeking behaviour was presented by
A. T.D. Wilson B. Ellis
C. Kulthou D. Allen Foster

4. Which of the following programming language is exclusively used for Artificial Intelligence?
A. C B. J2EE
C. Prolog D. JAVA

5. To make a program safe, one should take care of
A. Strong authentication and access controls
B. Error checking controls

C. Do risk analysis
D. Vendor's credibility

6. In CDS/ISIS 'delimiters' means
A. Field address B. Field repeatability
C. Field format D. Subfield indicators

7. A systematic method and process of studying and evaluating whether the expenditure for products, materials, or services is justified by the benefits is
A. Break Even Analysis
B. Cost-Effective Analysis
C. System Analysis
D. Administrative Analysis

8. What is the relationship between ISBD and cataloguing codes?
A. They are not related to each other
B. ISBD includes cataloguing rules
C. ISBD can replace cataloguing rules
D. Anglo-American codes include bibliographic description

9. Who first used the phrase 'Bibliographical Control'?
A. Paul Otlet B. Henry La Fontaine
C. Luther Evans D. Konrad Gesner

10. Cost recovery and profit making aspects in relation to gathering information, organization, services and usage, etc. refer to
A. Economy evaluation
B. Coverage evaluation
C. Workforce evaluation
D. User evaluation

11. Joseph W Lippincott Award is presented to the librarians for
A. promoting love for books and reading.
B. advanced study in the field of children's library.
C. achievements in classification and cataloguing.
D. outstanding participation in professional library associations.

12. LIPHIS (Linked Phrase Indexing System) was developed by
A. T.C. Craven B. J. Farradane
C. J.C.R. Yeats D. P. Ekern

13. Which of the following gives complete contro over the cross references of an index to th Indexer?
A. See also cross reference
B. check also cross reference
C. See cross reference
D. Inverted cross reference

14. LIS Gateway is maintained by
A. ILA B. IASLIC
C. SIS D. IATLIS

15. A situation where a digital resource is n longer readable is called
A. Digital Divide
B. Digital Representation
C. Digital Rendering
D. Digital Obsolescence

16. What type of bibliography is 'Indian Nationa Bibliography'?
A. Enumerative B. Analytical
C. Descriptive D. Textual

17. EUAL stands for
A. E-monitoring library for Academics
B. End User Logistics Association
C. Electronic Usage of Library Acquisitior
D. End User License Agreement

18. WIPO Academy deals with
A. Patent Cooperation Treaty
B. Courses on Intellectual Property
C. Trademarks Gateway
D. All of the above

19. Public Library Association (PLA) is a divisic of
A. ALA B. ILA
C. IFLA D. IASLIC

20. Which of the following are the characterist features of Postcoordinate indexing systen
(*i*) Index terms are pre-determined
(*ii*) Coordination of terms done by users
(*iii*) No fixed citation order
(*iv*) Multiple entries prepared for eac document

Codes :
A. (*i*) and (*ii*) are correct.
B. (*ii*) and (*iii*) are correct.

C. (*i*) and (*iii*) are correct.
D. (*ii*) and (*iv*) are correct.

21. The three leadership styles identified by Koontz and others are
(*i*) Autocratic (*ii*) Democratic
(*iii*) Trait approach (*iv*) Free-reign
Codes :
A. (*i*), (*ii*) and (*iii*) are correct.
B. (*ii*), (*iii*) and (*iv*) are correct.
C. (*iii*), (*iv*) and (*i*) are correct.
D. (*i*), (*ii*) and (*iv*) are correct.

22. Which of the following are not the features of ISDN?
(*i*) Simultaneous Digital Transmission
(*ii*) Set of communication standards
(*iii*) Creates and combines packets
(*iv*) Program to visit web pages
Codes :
A. (*i*) and (*ii*) are correct.
B. (*ii*) and (*iii*) are correct.
C. (*iii*) and (*iv*) are correct.
D. (*i*) and (*iv*) are correct.

23. Which of the following facilitate formal communication on the web?
(*i*) Wikis
(*ii*) Chat
(*iii*) RSS feeds
(*iv*) Split screens
Codes :
A. (*i*) and (*ii*) are correct.
B. (*ii*) and (*iii*) are correct.
C. (*i*) and (*iii*) are correct.
D. (*iii*) and (*iv*) are correct.

24. Semantic Web is based on which of the following :
(*i*) RDF
(*ii*) Ontologies
(*iii*) URL
(*iv*) Cloud seeding
Codes :
A. (*i*), (*ii*) and (*iii*) are correct.
B. (*ii*), (*iii*) and (*iv*) are correct.
C. (*i*), (*iii*) and (*iv*) are correct.
D. (*i*), (*ii*) and (*iv*) are correct.

25. Which of the following are not web 2.0 Tools?
(*i*) Ontologies
(*ii*) Facebook
(*iii*) Intelligent Web
(*iv*) RSS Feeds
Codes :
A. (*i*) and (*ii*) are correct.
B. (*i*) and (*iii*) are correct.
C. (*ii*) and (*iii*) are correct.
D. (*iii*) and (*iv*) are correct.

26. Who are associated with the development of OSI Model?
(*i*) Charles Buchman
(*ii*) ISO
(*iii*) MIT, USA
(*iv*) UCLA, California
Codes :
A. (*i*) and (*iv*) are correct.
B. (*i*) and (*iii*) are correct.
C. (*i*) and (*ii*) are correct.
D. (*ii*) and (*iii*) are correct.

27. Which of the following source(s) you refer to get information on old name for 'Zaire'?
(*i*) Encyclopaedias (*ii*) Yearbooks
(*iii*) Gazetteers (*iv*) Directories
Codes :
A. (*i*) and (*ii*) are correct.
B. (*i*), (*ii*) and (*iii*) are correct.
C. (*i*) and (*iii*) are correct.
D. (*ii*), (*iii*) and (*iv*) are correct.

28. The objectives of Empowered Committee under the chairmanship of D.P. Chattopadhyay submitted in 1986 were
(*i*) To find out the implications of recommendations of NIP 1986.
(*ii*) To recommend decision points for Government regarding libraries.
(*iii*) To initiate a national commission on libraries.
(*iv*) To develop a system of national libraries.
Codes :
A. (*i*) and (*ii*) B. (*i*), (*ii*) and (*iii*)
C. (*ii*) and (*iv*) D. (*iii*) and (*iv*)

29. Which of the following are plagiarism detection software?
(*i*) Turnitin

(*ii*) Ithenticate
(*iii*) Tulips
(*iv*) Veri Guide

Codes :

A. (*i*) and (*ii*) B. (*i*), (*ii*) and (*iii*)
C. (*i*), (*ii*) and (*iv*) D. (*ii*) and (*iii*)

30. Which of the following methods are adopted for offering information literacy?

(*i*) Stand alone course
(*ii*) Integrated with curriculum
(*iii*) Online course
(*iv*) Internship

Codes :

A. (*i*) and (*ii*) B. (*i*), (*ii*) and (*iii*)
C. (*ii*) and (*iv*) D. (*i*), (*ii*) and (*iv*)

31. Which of the following are direct methods of user study?

(*i*) Reading habits
(*ii*) Analysis of library records
(*iii*) Service preferences
(*iv*) User needs

Codes :

A. (*ii*) and (*iii*) B. (*ii*) and (*iv*)
C. (*i*) and (*iv*) D. (*iii*) and (*iv*)

32. Which of the following are the steps in operational research process?

(*i*) Construction of mathematical model
(*ii*) Deriving solution from the model.
(*iii*) Graphic representation of work on a time scale.
(*iv*) Developing network diagram showing interrelationships.

Codes :

A. (*i*) and (*ii*) are correct.
B. (*ii*) and (*iii*) are correct.
C. (*iii*) and (*iv*) are correct.
D. (*iv*) and (*i*) are correct.

33. Which of the following are statistical programming software?

(*i*) GAUSS (*ii*) SAS
(*iii*) SPSS (*iv*) SLIM

Codes :

A. (*i*), (*iii*) and (*iv*) B. (*i*), (*ii*) and (*iii*)
C. (*i*), (*ii*) and (*iv*) D. (*ii*), (*iii*) and (*iv*)

34. Which of the following organizations are involved in providing translation services in India?

(*i*) NISCAIR
(*ii*) National Library of India
(*iii*) IASLIC
(*iv*) IATLIS

Codes :

A. (*ii*) and (*iv*) are correct.
B. (*ii*) and (*iii*) are correct.
C. (*i*) and (*iv*) are correct.
D. (*i*) and (*iii*) are correct.

35. Which of the following are Internationa Referral Centres for Scholarly Information?

(*i*) DARE
(*ii*) INFOTERRA
(*iii*) International Referral Network
(*iv*) Information Referral

Codes :

A. (*ii*) and (*iv*) are correct.
B. (*i*) and (*iv*) are correct.
C. (*i*) and (*ii*) are correct.
D. (*ii*) and (*iii*) are correct.

36. Which of the following are the works relate to IFLA's Committee on Freedom of Acces to Information and Freedom of Expressio (FAIFE)?

(*i*) Publish reports, participate in nationa and international conferences an organize workshops.
(*ii*) Monitor the state of intellectual freedo within the library community world-wid and publish newsletters and online news
(*iii*) Respond to violations of free access t information and freedom of expressio and make press releases.
(*iv*) Cross-association activities, to brin participants together.

Codes :

A. (*i*), (*iii*) and (*iv*) are correct.
B. (*ii*), (*iii*) and (*iv*) are correct.
C. (*i*), (*ii*) and (*iv*) are correct.
D. (*i*), (*ii*) and (*iii*) are correct.

37. Shannon's model of information theory i criticized for which of the following reasons

(*i*) Concern on semantic issues
(*ii*) Engineering bias
(*iii*) Concern for technical transmission
(*iv*) Emphasis on effectiveness

Codes :
A. (*i*) and (*ii*) are correct.
B. (*ii*) and (*iii*) are correct.
C. (*iii*) and (*iv*) are correct.
D. (*i*) and (*iii*) are correct.

38. Arrange the following Library Acts according to their year of enactment :
(*i*) Uttarakhand (*ii*) Orissa
(*iii*) Manipur (*iv*) Goa
Codes :
A. (*iv*), (*i*), (*ii*), (*iii*) B. (*i*), (*ii*), (*iii*), (*iv*)
C. (*iii*), (*iv*), (*ii*), (*i*) D. (*ii*), (*iii*), (*i*), (*iv*)

39. Arrange the following stages of knowledge representation in order :
(*i*) Gather data
(*ii*) Knowledge database
(*iii*) Codification
(*iv*) Content mapping
Codes :
A. (*iv*), (*iii*), (*i*), (*ii*) B. (*iii*), (*i*), (*iv*), (*ii*)
C. (*ii*), (*iv*), (*i*), (*iii*) D. (*i*), (*iii*), (*ii*), (*iv*)

40. Arrange the following according to their year of emergence :
(*i*) ERNET (*ii*) NICNET
(*iii*) C-DOT (*iv*) C-DAC
Codes :
A. (*ii*), (*iii*), (*i*), (*iv*) B. (*iii*), (*ii*), (*iv*), (*i*)
C. (*iv*), (*ii*), (*iii*), (*i*) D. (*i*), (*iv*), (*iii*), (*ii*)

41. Arrange the following steps in Flow-Chart in order :
(*i*) Modularity
(*ii*) Data Structure
(*iii*) Identifying problems into subproblems
(*iv*) Loops and Termination of loops
Codes :
A. (*iii*), (*iv*), (*i*), (*ii*) B. (*iii*), (*ii*), (*iv*), (*i*)
C. (*ii*), (*iii*), (*iv*), (*i*) D. (*iv*), (*ii*), (*i*), (*iii*)

42. Arrange the following libraries according to their year of origin :
(*i*) Asiatic Society Library, Bombay
(*ii*) Connemara Public Library, Madras
(*iii*) Delhi Public Library, Delhi
(*iv*) National Library of India, Calcutta
Codes :
A. (*i*), (*ii*), (*iv*), (*iii*) B. (*i*), (*iii*), (*iv*), (*ii*)
C. (*ii*), (*iv*), (*iii*), (*i*) D. (*iv*), (*iii*), (*ii*), (*i*)

43. Arrange the following according to their year of origin :
(*i*) Bowker Annual
(*ii*) Europa World Yearbook
(*iii*) India : a reference annual
(*iv*) Stateman's yearbook
Codes :
A. (*iv*), (*i*), (*ii*), (*iii*) B. (*i*), (*ii*), (*iv*), (*iii*)
C. (*iv*), (*iii*), (*i*), (*ii*) D. (*ii*), (*i*), (*iv*), (*iii*)

44. Arrange the following in the order of development :
(*i*) GML (*ii*) Hypermedia
(*iii*) SGML (*iv*) Memex
Codes :
A. (*i*), (*ii*), (*iii*), (*iv*) B. (*iv*), (*ii*), (*i*), (*iii*)
C. (*ii*), (*iii*), (*iv*), (*i*) D. (*iii*), (*ii*), (*i*), (*iv*)

45. Arrange in sequence the following committees workshop in order of their year of constitution:
(*i*) UGC Committee for Development of University and College Libraries (S.R. Ranganathan)
(*ii*) UGC Committee on National Network System for University Libraries (Dr. Yashpal)
(*iii*) UGC Review Committee on Library Science (S.R. Ranganathan)
(*iv*) UGC Workshop on Standards for College Libraries
Codes :
A. (*iii*), (*iv*), (*i*), (*ii*) B. (*iii*), (*ii*), (*i*), (*iv*)
C. (*i*), (*iii*), (*iv*), (*ii*) D. (*i*), (*ii*), (*iv*), (*iii*)

46. Match the following tools used in Total Quality Management :

	List-I		List-II
(*a*)	Statistical Quality Control	(*i*)	Conformance and Maintain sticks
(*b*)	Check Sheets	(*ii*)	To identify relationship between problem and cause
(*c*)	Pareto Charts	(*iii*)	Checking variables
(*d*)	Fishbone diagram	(*iv*)	To identify intensity of problem

Codes :

	(*a*)	(*b*)	(*c*)	(*d*)
A.	(*ii*)	(*i*)	(*iv*)	(*iii*)
B.	(*iii*)	(*i*)	(*iv*)	(*ii*)

C. (*i*) (*iii*) (*ii*) (*iv*)
D. (*iv*) (*i*) (*iii*) (*ii*)

47. Match the following :

List-I (Hypothesis)	List-II (Characteristics)
(*a*) Null	(*i*) Statement of expectations
(*b*) Working (Directional)	(*ii*) Relational propositions
(*c*) Explanatory	(*iii*) No relation between variables
(*d*) Descriptive	(*iv*) Existence of variables

Codes :

	(*a*)	(*b*)	(*c*)	(*d*)
A.	(*i*)	(*iv*)	(*ii*)	(*iii*)
B.	(*iii*)	(*iv*)	(*ii*)	(*i*)
C.	(*iii*)	(*ii*)	(*i*)	(*iv*)
D.	(*iii*)	(*i*)	(*ii*)	(*iv*)

48. Match the following :

List-I	List-II
(*a*) Theory of Hygiene and Motivation	(*i*) Likerts
(*b*) Maturity Theory	(*ii*) Vroom and Lawler
(*c*) Expectancy Theory	(*iii*) Herzberg
(*d*) Analysis Theory	(*iv*) Argyris

Codes :

	(*a*)	(*b*)	(*c*)	(*d*)
A.	(*ii*)	(*iii*)	(*iv*)	(*i*)
B.	(*iii*)	(*iv*)	(*ii*)	(*i*)
C.	(*ii*)	(*i*)	(*iii*)	(*iv*)
D.	(*iv*)	(*i*)	(*ii*)	(*iii*)

49. Match the following :

List-I	List-II
(*a*) Harrold Koontz	(*i*) MBO
(*b*) Rensis Likert	(*ii*) Three leadership styles
(*c*) Peter Drucker	(*iii*) Four systems management
(*d*) George Haber	(*iv*) Problem solving vs. Decision making

Codes :

	(*a*)	(*b*)	(*c*)	(*d*)
A.	(*i*)	(*ii*)	(*iii*)	(*iv*)
B.	(*iii*)	(*iv*)	(*i*)	(*ii*)
C.	(*iv*)	(*iii*)	(*ii*)	(*i*)
D.	(*ii*)	(*iii*)	(*i*)	(*iv*)

50. Match the following :

List-I	List-II
(*a*) Information Literacy Competency Standards for Higher Education	(*i*) IFLA
(*b*) Seven Pillars of Information literacy	(*ii*) CAUL
(*c*) Guidelines on Information Literacy for Life Long Learning	(*iii*) ACRL
(*d*) Information Literacy Working Group	(*iv*) SCONUL

Codes :

	(*a*)	(*b*)	(*c*)	(*d*)
A.	(*iii*)	(*iv*)	(*i*)	(*ii*)
B.	(*iv*)	(*ii*)	(*iii*)	(*i*)
C.	(*iii*)	(*i*)	(*ii*)	(*iv*)
D.	(*ii*)	(*iii*)	(*i*)	(*iv*)

51. Match the following theories with the respectively profounders :

List-I	List-II
(*a*) Cybernetics	(*i*) Charles Osgood (1916)
(*b*) Human information processing	(*ii*) Marshal C. Yovits
(*c*) Psychological approach to message transmission	(*iii*) Nobert Wiener (1894-1964)
(*d*) General Information System	(*iv*) R.L. Ackoff

Codes :

	(*a*)	(*b*)	(*c*)	(*d*)
A.	(*i*)	(*iii*)	(*ii*)	(*iv*)
B.	(*i*)	(*ii*)	(*iv*)	(*iii*)
C.	(*iii*)	(*i*)	(*iv*)	(*ii*)
D.	(*iii*)	(*ii*)	(*i*)	(*iv*)

52. Match the following :

List-I	List-II
(*a*) N. Grogan	(*i*) Scientific and Technical Libraries
(*b*) J. Saha	(*ii*) Scientific and technical libraries; an introduction to literature

(*c*) Nilfred Ashworth — (*iii*) Handbook of special librarianship and information work

(*d*) L.J. Strauss — (*iv*) Special libraries and information services in India and USA

Codes :

	(*a*)	(*b*)	(*c*)	(*d*)
A.	(*ii*)	(*iv*)	(*iii*)	(*i*)
B.	(*i*)	(*ii*)	(*iv*)	(*iii*)
C.	(*ii*)	(*i*)	(*iii*)	(*iv*)
D.	(*iv*)	(*ii*)	(*i*)	(*iii*)

53. Match the following :

List-I	List-II
(*a*) Behaviour Science	(*i*) Cognitive Process of Information
(*b*) Philosophical Studies	(*ii*) Studies on Epistomology
(*c*) Ontology	(*iii*) Information Processing in living things
(*d*) Biological Science	(*iv*) Study of nature of existence

Codes :

	(*a*)	(*b*)	(*c*)	(*d*)
A.	(*iv*)	(*iii*)	(*i*)	(*ii*)
B.	(*iii*)	(*ii*)	(*iv*)	(*i*)
C.	(*ii*)	(*i*)	(*iii*)	(*iv*)
D.	(*i*)	(*ii*)	(*iv*)	(*iii*)

54. Match the following implications with the respective laws of library science :

List-I	List-II
(*a*) Location of the library	(*i*) Second Law
(*b*) Obligation of the State	(*ii*) Third Law
(*c*) Publicity	(*iii*) Fifth Law
(*d*) Strength of Library Staff	(*iv*) First Law

Codes :

	(*a*)	(*b*)	(*c*)	(*d*)
A.	(*iv*)	(*ii*)	(*i*)	(*iii*)
B.	(*iv*)	(*i*)	(*ii*)	(*iii*)
C.	(*ii*)	(*i*)	(*iii*)	(*iv*)
D.	(*ii*)	(*iii*)	(*iv*)	(*i*)

55. Match the following biographical publications from India with the respective compilers:

List-I	List-II
(*a*) India, Who's Who	(*i*) S.P. Sen
(*b*) Who's Who in India	(*ii*) J.S. Sharma
(*c*) Dictionary of Indian Biography	(*iii*) Business Press, Mumbai
(*d*) National Biographical Dictionary of India	(*iv*) INFA Pub., New Delhi

Codes :

	(*a*)	(*b*)	(*c*)	(*d*)
A.	(*iii*)	(*iv*)	(*ii*)	(*i*)
B.	(*i*)	(*ii*)	(*iii*)	(*iv*)
C.	(*ii*)	(*iii*)	(*i*)	(*iv*)
D.	(*iv*)	(*iii*)	(*i*)	(*ii*)

56. Match the following for locating the information :

List-I	List-II
(*a*) Information on recent Nobel Prize winners	(*i*) Bibliographic Service
(*b*) Current developments in Library and Information Science	(*ii*) Indexing Services
(*c*) Books on Economic Policies of India	(*iii*) Trend Sources
(*d*) Articles on Cloud Computing	(*iv*) Digest Services

Codes :

	(*a*)	(*b*)	(*c*)	(*d*)
A.	(*iv*)	(*iii*)	(*i*)	(*ii*)
B.	(*iii*)	(*i*)	(*iv*)	(*ii*)
C.	(*ii*)	(*iii*)	(*iv*)	(*i*)
D.	(*i*)	(*ii*)	(*iii*)	(*iv*)

57. Match the following :

List-I	List-II
(*a*) Principle of Osmosis	(*i*) Security
(*b*) Theory of Literary Warrants	(*ii*) Sinha Committee
(*c*) Public Libraries are stagnating pools of books	(*iii*) Reclassification
(*d*) Firewall	(*iv*) Dr. S.R. Ranganathan

Codes :

	(a)	(b)	(c)	(d)
A.	(iv)	(ii)	(iii)	(i)
B.	(iii)	(iv)	(ii)	(i)
C.	(iv)	(iii)	(i)	(ii)
D.	(i)	(ii)	(iv)	(iii)

58. Match the following :

List-I	List-II
(a) Referral	(i) Support
(b) SDI	(ii) Reaching out
(c) Extension	(iii) Directing
(d) Reprography	(iv) Anticipating

Codes :

	(a)	(b)	(c)	(d)
A.	(iii)	(iv)	(ii)	(i)
B.	(iv)	(ii)	(iii)	(i)
C.	(i)	(iv)	(ii)	(iii)
D.	(ii)	(iii)	(i)	(iv)

59. Match the following :

List-I	List-II
(a) Similar activities are grouped	(i) Bureaucratic System
(b) Grouping activities into divisions	(ii) Functional System
(c) Integration of projects into functional system	(iii) Departmentalisation
(d) Control and Supervision through hierarchy of positions	(iv) Matrix structure

Codes :

	(a)	(b)	(c)	(d)
A.	(iv)	(i)	(ii)	(iii)
B.	(iii)	(ii)	(iv)	(i)
C.	(i)	(ii)	(iii)	(iv)
D.	(ii)	(iii)	(iv)	(i)

60. Match the following :

List-I	List-II
(a) Virtua	(i) Veeru Technologies (KIIKM)
(b) Alice	(ii) Infotech Consultants Pvt. Ltd.
(c) Libsys	(iii) Softlink, Australia
(d) New Genlib	(iv) VTLS, Virginia

Codes :

	a	b	c	d
A.	(i)	(iii)	(ii)	(iv)
B.	(ii)	(iv)	(i)	(iii)
C.	(iv)	(ii)	(iii)	(i)
D.	(iv)	(iii)	(ii)	(i)

61. Match the following file formats with the creators :

List-I	List-II
(a) RTF	(i) Sun Micro System
(b) PDF	(ii) Aldus
(c) TIFF	(iii) Microsoft
(d) AU	(iv) Adobe

Codes :

	(a)	(b)	(c)	(d)
A.	(iv)	(iii)	(ii)	(i)
B.	(iii)	(iv)	(ii)	(i)
C.	(ii)	(iii)	(iv)	(i)
D.	(i)	(ii)	(iv)	(iii)

62. Match the following MARC 21 tags with respective fields :

List-I	List-II
(a) 020	(i) Publication and Distribution
(b) 100	(ii) Series Statement
(c) 260	(iii) ISBN
(d) 440	(iv) Personal name

Codes :

	(a)	(b)	(c)	(d)
A.	(i)	(ii)	(iii)	(iv)
B.	(ii)	(iv)	(iii)	(i)
C.	(iii)	(ii)	(iv)	(i)
D.	(iii)	(iv)	(i)	(ii)

63. Assertion (A) : Social networking tools are very effective for marketing of Library products and services.

Reason (R) : They help to reach out the patrons anywhere and at any time.

Codes :

A. Both (A) and (R) are true.
B. Both (A) and (R) are false.
C. (A) is true, but (R) is false.
D. (A) is false, but (R) is true.

64. Assertion (A) : There is no need for libraries to invest on reference collection.

Reason (R) : Web is a treasure of all types of information that can replace reference desk.

Codes :

A. Both (A) and (R) are true.
B. Both (A) and (R) are false.
C. (A) is true, but (R) is false.
D. (A) is false, but (R) is true.

65. Assertion (A) : UGC has devised performance indicators for the promotion of faculty and librarians.

Reason (R) : Performance Appraisal is an important tool for merit rating.

Codes :

A. (A) is true, but (R) is false.
B. (A) is false, but (R) is true.
C. Both (A) and (R) are true.
D. Both (A) and (R) are false.

66. Assertion (A) : All unabridged dictionaries provide word meaning, antonyms, synonyms and places, etc.

Reason (R) : All dictionaries provide information on antonyms and homonym, etc.

Codes :

A. (A) is true, but (R) is false.
B. Both (A) and (R) are true.
C. (A) is false, but (R) is true.
D. Both (A) and (R) are false.

67. Assertion (A) : Information Literacy is a technique and skill known by the information literate for utilizing the wide range of information sources and tools.

Reason (R) : It discourages the use of libraries and information centres and makes the patron independent in identifying, locating and using information sources without depending upon an intermediary.

Codes :

A. Both (A) and (R) are true.
B. Both (A) and (R) are false.
C. (A) is true, but (R) is false.
D. (A) is false, but (R) is true.

68. Assertion (A) : Inverse document frequency is the logarithm of the reciprocal of the number of documents in a collection that contains a given term.

Reason (R) : Inverse document frequency measure is computed from term frequency and inverse document frequency.

Codes :

A. Both (A) and (R) are true.
B. Both (A) and (R) are false.
C. (A) is true, but (R) is false.
D. (A) is false, but (R) is true.

69. Assertion (A) : Subject gateways are suitable for all types of users for finding their information.

Reason (R) : Subject gateways are developed by subject and computer experts.

Codes :

A. (A) is true, but (R) is false.
B. (A) is false, but (R) is true.
C. Both (A) and (R) are true.
D. Both (A) and (R) are false.

70. Assertion (A) : The principle of canonical sequence states when subjects in a array of subjects are traditionally referred to in a specific sequence, it will be convenient to conform to this traditional sequence.

Reason (R) : In classification scheme, the principle of canonical sequence is mainly followed to arrange the array of subjects.

Codes :

A. Both (A) and (R) are true.
B. (A) is false, but (R) is true.
C. (A) is true, but (R) is false.
D. Both (A) and (R) are false.

71. Assertion (A) : Acceptance of First Law of library Science "Books are for Use" has brought forth far reaching change in the present digital environment.

Reason (R) : Online access, open access, virtual reference are the results of this acceptance.

Codes :

A. (A) is true, but (R) is false.
B. (A) is false, but (R) is true.
C. Both (A) and (R) are false.
D. Both (A) and (R) are true.

72. Assertion (A) : PANDEX is a indexing system which sometimes allows changing the lead term to a standard form in order to provide better collocation of terms.

Reason (R) : It facilitates the first input string to be truncated after 18 characters and second after 11 characters.

Codes :

A. Both (A) and (R) are true.
B. Both (A) and (R) are false.
C. (A) is false, but (R) is true.
D. (A) is true, but (R) is false.

73. Assertion (A) : SGML is an international standard that describes the relationship between a document's content and its structure.

Reason (R) : Its primary purpose is to facilitate the sharing of data across different information systems particularly via Internet.

Codes :

A. Both (A) and (R) are false.
B. (A) is true, but (R) is false.
C. Both (A) and (R) are true.
D. (A) is false, but (R) is true.

74. Assertion (A) : In the digital environment, the users expect from the library the ability to connect broad range of information resources in a variety of formats with a single point access.

Reason (R) : Libraries already have much of what is required in the digital environment.

Codes :

A. (A) is true, but (R) is false.
B. Both (A) and (R) are true.
C. Both (A) and (R) are false.
D. (A) is false, but (R) is true.

75. Assertion (A) : The diary technique enables the researcher to keep record of information activities of the users for a specified period of time.

Reason (R) : The diary technique is the most suitable technique of user studies over other techniques.

Codes :

A. Both (A) and (R) are false.
B. (A) is true, but (R) is false.
C. Both (A) and (R) are true.
D. (A) is false, but (R) is true.

ANSWERS

1	2	3	4	5	6	7	8	9	10
D	B	D	C	A	D	B	D	C	A
11	**12**	**13**	**14**	**15**	**16**	**17**	**18**	**19**	**20**
D	A	D	A	D	A	D	B	A	B
21	**22**	**23**	**24**	**25**	**26**	**27**	**28**	**29**	**30**
D	C	C	A	B	C	C	A	C	B
31	**32**	**33**	**34**	**35**	**36**	**37**	**38**	**39**	**40**
C	A	B	D	C	D	B	C	D	C
41	**42**	**43**	**44**	**45**	**46**	**47**	**48**	**49**	**50**
B	A	C	B	C	B	D	B	D	A
51	**52**	**53**	**54**	**55**	**56**	**57**	**58**	**59**	**60**
C	A	D	B	D	A	B	A	D	D
61	**62**	**63**	**64**	**65**	**66**	**67**	**68**	**69**	**70**
B	D	A	B	C	A	C	A	B	C
71	**72**	**73**	**74**	**75**					
D	D	B	A	B					

Previous Paper (Solved)

UGC-NET Library and Information Science, December 2013

PAPER-II

Note: *This paper contains fifty (50) objective type questions of two (2) marks each. All questions are compulsory.*

1. Name the scientist who said that Information Science is cluster of many disciplines where in the central core is 'Information'.

A. B.C. Brooks B. Fritz Machlup
C. Daniel Bell D. N.J. Belkin

2. Which committee recommended that imperial library be designated as copyright library?

A. Fayzee Committee, 1939
B. Richey Committee, 1926
C. Statham Committee, 1932
D. Sadler Committee, 1916

3. Who was the first Librarian of Imperial Library, Calcutta?

A. John MacFarlane
B. Harinath De
C. B.S. Kesavan
D. S.R. Ranganathan

4. Who coined the phrase 'Information Retrieval'?

A. Calvin Mooers B. S.R. Ranganathan
C. J.D. Brown D. H.P. Luhan

5. In colon classification which indicator has been used for indicating interpolation?

A. Comma B. Hyphen
C. Astericks D. Ampersand

6. What is Denudation ?

A. Is dividing classes to decrease the extension.
B. Is dividing classes to increase the extension.
C. Is dividing classes to increase intension and decrease extension.
D. Is dividing classes to decrease intension.

7. The International Body that coordinates the assignment of unique domain names, protocol address is

A. IGF B. IANA
C. ICANN D. ISP

8. Name the Indian Librarian who was honoured with the title of "Khan Bahadur" in 1935 by the British Government.

A. S.R. Ranganathan
B. B.S. Kesavan
C. K.M. Asadullah
D. D.R. Kalia

9. Which approach of information is not given by Wersig and Neveling?

A. Structural Approach
B. Knowledge Approach
C. Meaning Approach
D. Technique Approach

10. Which of the following citation style manuals are from the same publisher?

(i) A.P.A. (ii) Turabian
(iii) Chicago (iv) M.L.A.

Codes :

A. (i) and (ii) are correct.
B. (ii) and (iii) are correct.
C. (iii) and (iv) are correct.
D. (ii) and (iv) are correct.

11. Pre co-ordinate Indexing system perceives:

(i) Syntax (ii) Semantic
(iii) Context (iv) Relation

Codes :

A. (i) and (iv) are correct
B. (i), (ii) and (iii) are correct

C. (ii), (iii) and (iv) are correct
D. (ii) and (iv) are correct

12. An indispensable function of Thesaurus is to
(i) Knowledge Classification
(ii) Grouping the words together according to similarity of meaning
(iii) Representation of Relationship between concepts
(iv) Knowledge Engineering
Codes :
A. (i) and (ii) are correct
B. (ii) and (iii) are correct.
C. (iii) and (iv) are correct.
D. (i) and (iv) are correct.

13. Which of the following are the basic components of expert system?
(i) User interface
(ii) Knowledge base
(iii) Inference Mechanism
(iv) Schema
Codes :
A. (i), (ii) and (iii)
B. (ii), (iii) and (iv)
C. (iii), (iv) and (i)
D. (iv), (iii) and (ii)

14. Which of the following are the types factors studies under ANOVA?
(i) Fixed (ii) Frequency
(iii) Calculated (iv) Random
Codes :
A. (ii) and (iii) are correct.
B. (i) and (iv) are correct.
C. (i) and (iii) are correct.
D. (ii) and (iv) are correct.

15. Which of the following are the models of communication?
(i) Economic Theory Model
(ii) Stock Adjustment Model
(iii) Shanon Weaver Model
(iv) Schramm Model
Codes :
A. (iii) and (iv) are correct.
B. (ii) and (iii) are correct.
C. (i) and (ii) are correct.
D. (ii) and (iv) are correct.

16. Which of the following are criteria for Web evaluation?
(i) Revision (ii) Response time
(iii) Format (iv) Archiving facility
Codes :
A. (i) and (ii) are correct.
B. (ii) and (iv) are correct.
C. (i) and (iii) are correct.
D. (ii) and (iii) are correct.

17. Which of the following countries do not have a code of Ethics for library profession?
(i) America (ii) Sri Lanka
(iii) India (iv) China
Codes :
A. (i) and (ii) are correct.
B. (i) and (iv) are correct.
C. (iii) and (ii) are correct.
D. (iii) and (iv) are correct.

18. Which of the following are the components of Search Engine?
(i) Spider
(ii) TCP/IP
(iii) Search Mechanism
(iv) Index
Codes :
A. (iv), (i) and (ii)
B. (iii), (ii) and (i)
C. (i), (iii) and (iv)
D. (ii), (iv) and (iii)

19. When the permission of copyright owner is not needed?
(i) Criticism or review
(ii) Translation
(iii) Research purpose
(iv) Photocopy for sale
Codes :
A. (i) and (iii) are correct.
B. (i) and (iv) are correct.
C. (iii) and (iv) are correct.
D. (ii) and (iii) are correct.

20. Which of the following are Library net works?
(i) Internet
(ii) Indonet
(iii) INFLIBNET
(iv) OCLC

Codes :

A. (i) and (ii) are correct.
B. (ii) and (iv) are correct.
C. (iii) and (iv) are correct.
D. (i) and (iv) are correct.

21. Arrange the following University Libraries according to the year of their establishment:

(i) Madras University Library
(ii) Delhi University Library
(iii) Calcutta University Library
(iv) Bombay University Library

Codes :

A. (iv) (ii) (iii) (i)
B. (ii) (i) (iv) (iii)
C. (i) (iii) (ii) (iv)
D. (iii) (iv) (i) (ii)

22. What is the correct sequence of the following sections of the main entry as per classified catalogue code (CCC)?

(i) Note Section
(ii) Leading Section
(iii) Heading Section
(iv) Title Section

Codes :

A. (i) (iv) (iii) (ii)
B. (ii) (iii) (iv) (i)
C. (iii) (iv) (ii) (i)
D. (iv) (i) (iii) (ii)

23. Arrange the following indexing sources according to the year of their first publication:

(i) Biological Abstracts
(ii) Chemical Abstracts
(iii) Index Medicus
(iv) Poole's Index to Periodical Literature

Codes :

A. (i) (ii) (iii) (iv)
B. (iv) (iii) (ii) (i)
C. (iv) (ii) (i) (iii)
D. (i) (iv) (iii) (ii)

23. Arrange the following library associations according to their year of emergence:

(i) CILIP (ii) ALA
(iii) SLA (iv) ASLIB

Codes :

A. (iii) (iv) (i) (ii)
B. (iii) (iv) (ii) (i)
C. (ii) (iii) (iv) (i)
D. (ii) (iv) (i) (iii)

25. Match the following:

	List–I		List–II
a.	Library Advisory Committee	i.	1962
b.	Review Committee	ii.	1963
c.	DRTC	iii.	1957
d.	Sarada Ranganathan Endowned	iv.	1961

Codes :

	a	b	c	d
A.	iv	iii	ii	i
B.	iii	iv	i	ii
C.	ii	i	iii	iv
D.	i	iv	iii	ii

26. Match the following:

	List–I		List–II
a.	Facts on File	i.	Periodical Directory
b.	World of Learning	ii.	Index
c.	Concordance	iii.	Newspaper Digest
d.	Willing's Press Guide	iv.	Directory

Codes :

	a	b	c	d
A.	i	iii	iv	ii
B.	ii	i	iii	iv
C.	iii	iv	ii	i
D.	iv	ii	i	iii

27. Match the following:

	List–I		List–II
a.	McGroger Theory X	i.	Less External Control
b.	McGroger Theory Y	ii.	PERT
c.	Unity of Command	iii.	Workers' Participation in Decision Making
d.	Time and Cost	iv.	All Powers in One Person

Codes :

	a	b	c	d
A.	iii	i	iv	ii
B.	iv	i	iii	ii
C.	ii	iv	iii	i
D.	i	iii	ii	iv

28. Match the following:

	List–I		List–II
a.	User Education	i.	James I Wyer
b.	Conservative, Liberal and Moderate Theory of Reference Service	ii.	Patricia B. Knapp
c.	Minimum, Middling and Maximum Theories of Reference Service	iii.	Eugene P. Sheehy
d.	Guide to Reference Book	iv.	Samuel Rothstein

Codes :

	a	b	c	d
A.	ii	i	iv	iii
B.	i	ii	iv	iii
C.	iii	ii	iv	i
D.	iv	iii	i	ii

29. Match the following:

	List–I		List–II
a.	W. Edward Deming	i.	Quality Control Circles
b.	Joseph M. Juran	ii.	TQM
c.	Armand V. Feigenbaum	iii.	Planning, Control, Improvement
d.	Kaoru Ishikava	iv.	Plan, Do, Check, Act (PDCA)

Codes :

	a	b	c	d
A.	ii	iii	iv	i
B.	iv	ii	i	iii
C.	iii	iv	i	ii
D.	iv	iii	ii	i

30. Match the following:

	List–I		List–II
a.	Encyclopaedia of Associations	i.	Secondary sources
b.	Whitaker's Almanac	ii.	Primary sources
c.	LISA	iii.	Directories
d.	Economic Times	iv.	Yearbooks

Codes :

	a	b	c	d
A.	iii	iv	i	ii
B.	iv	iii	i	ii
C.	ii	i	iv	iii
D.	i	iv	iii	ii

31. Match the following:

	List–I		List–II
a.	Books in Print	i.	National Bibliography
b.	Social Science : A Bibliography of Doctoral Dissertations	ii.	Trade Bibliography
c.	Asian Social Science Bibliography	iii.	National & Trade Bibliography
d.	Cumulative Book Index	iv.	Subject Bibliography

Codes :

	a	b	c	d
A.	ii	i	iv	iii
B.	i	iii	ii	iv
C.	iv	i	ii	iii
D.	iii	ii	i	iv

32. Match the following:

	List–I		List–II
a.	Dictionary	i.	Foreign Language
b.	Glossary	ii.	Synonymous terms
c.	Thesaurus	iii.	Words, Synonyms
d.	Lexicon	iv.	Specific subjects

Codes :

	a	b	c	d
A.	iii	iv	ii	i

B. iv iii i ii
C. i ii iv iii
D. ii iv iii i

33. Match the following:

List–I	List–II
a. Curriculum Development Committee (P.N. Kaula)	i. 2001
b. Curriculum Development Committee (C.R. Karrisidappa)	ii. 1992
c. Working Group on Libraries	iii. 1910
d. Library Movement in Baroda	iv. 1964

Codes :

	a	b	c	d
A.	ii	i	iv	iii
B.	i	ii	iv	iii
C.	iv	ii	iii	i
D.	iii	iv	ii	i

34. Match the following:

List–I	List–II
a. Current Biography	i. Russia
b. Index Translationum	ii. University of Illinois
c. VINITI	iii. U.S.A.
d. Library Trends	iv. UNESCO

Codes :

	a	b	c	d
A.	iii	iv	i	ii
B.	iv	i	ii	iii
C.	i	ii	iii	iv
D.	ii	iii	iv	i

35. Match the following:

List–I	List–II
a. Herbert Hicks	i. The Elements of Administration
b. F.W. Taylor	ii. The Management of Organisation
c. Henry Fayol	iii. Scientific Management
d. Colonel L. Urwick	iv. Administrative Management

Codes :

	a	b	c	d
A.	i	iv	ii	iii
B.	iv	ii	iii	i
C.	ii	iii	iv	i
D.	iii	iv	i	ii

36. Assertion (A) : In the study of History, as an academic discipline, a primary source is an artefact, a document, a recording or other source of information that was created during the event or immediately after the event.

Reason (R) : Primary sources are considered as original material or evidences about the topic and are fundamental to history.

Codes :

A. (A) is true, but (R) is false.
B. (A) is false, but (R) is true.
C. Both (A) and (R) are true.
D. Both (A) and (R) are false.

37. Assertion (A) : Indian National Bibliography is the most comprehensive source of Indian publications.

Reason (R) : National Library of Kolkata is entitled to receive one copy of each Indian publication under Delivery of Book Act.

Codes :

A. (A) is true, but (R) is false.
B. (A) is false, but (R) is true.
C. Both (A) and (R) are true.
D. Both (A) and (R) are false.

38. Assertion (A) : As per the generally accepted principles of construction of statistical tabulation, every table should have a clear, concise and adequate title so as to make the table intelligible without reference to the text and this title should always be placed just below the body of the table.

Reason (R) : A statistical table which reflects its title just above the table and supply information about several interrelated characteristics of data makes the table unwield and inconvenient.

Codes :

A. Both (A) and (R) are true.
B. Both (A) and (R) are false.
C. (A) is true, but (R) is false.
D. (A) is false, but (R) is true.

39. Assertion (A) : Knowledge Management involves a number of assets and value added to them.

Reason (R) : Knowledge Management is the core activity of information transfer.

Codes :

A. (A) is true, but (R) is false.
B. (A) is true, but (R) is partially true.
C. Both (A) and (R) are true.
D. (A) is partially true but (R) is true.

40. Assertion (A) : According to Horton and Merchant, information is a commodity like other resources.

Reason (R) : Information is a tangible commodity.

Codes :

A. (A) is true, but (R) is false.
B. Both (A) and (R) are false.
C. Both (A) and (R) are true.
D. (A) is false, (R) is true.

41. Assertion (A) : Reference section in a Library became insignificant.

Reason (R) : The Web. 2.0 services replaces the reference desk services.

Codes :

A. (A) is true, but (R) is false.
B. Both (A) and (R) are true.
C. Both (A) and (R) are false.
D. (A) is false and (R) is true.

42. Assertion (A) : Newspaper Digests are the best sources of information to get current and authentic information like books.

Reason (R) : These sources are compiled by going through various newspapers.

Codes :

A. Both (A) and (R) are true.
B. (A) is partially true but (R) is true.
C. Both (A) and (R) are false.
D. (A) is true but (R) is partially true.

43. Assertion (A) : Encyclopaedias have been regarded as the substitute of all categories of reference sources as these provide all types of information.

Reason (R) : Encyclopaedias provide comprehensive information on all aspects which otherwise are scattered in different categories of reference sources.

Codes :

A. (R) is true but (A) is false.
B. Both (A) and (R) are true.
C. (A) is true but (R) is false.
D. Both (A) and (R) are false.

44. Assertion (A) : Chi-square is an important non-parametric test which does not require rigid assumptions in respect of the type of population being studied.

Reason (R) : Since χ^2 is a non-parametric test, it requires only the degrees of freedom (implicitly, the size of the population) for using the test.

Codes :

A. (A) is true, but (R) is false.
B. Both (A) and (R) are true.
C. (A) is false but (R) is true.
D. Both (A) and (R) are false.

45. Assertion (A) : Information is commodity.

Reason (R) : Commodity is a marketable item produced to satisfy human wants or needs.

Codes :

A. (A) is false, and (R) is true.
B. (R) is false and (A) is true.
C. Both (A) and (R) are false.
D. Both (A) and (R) are true.

Directions (Qs. No. 46 to 50): *Read the passage given below and answer the questions based on your understanding of the passage.*

According to Wikipedia 'social media' is media designed to be disseminated through social interaction, created using highly accessible and scalable publishing techniques. According to search engine partner, the term social media describes media that is posed by the user and can take many different forms. Some type of social media are forums, message boards, blogs, wikis and podcarts. Social media applications include Google, Facebook and You tube. In social media, communication takes place through messages, status updates, voice chats etc. or through photos/videos sharing, games, virtual goods etc. Antony Mayfield in his e-book titled 'What is Social Media'? has defined social media as online media, which encourages contributions and feedback from everyone who is interested, is open to feedback and participation, is a two way conversation, allows communities to form quickly and communicate effectively to share common interests and thrive on their connectedness.

The growth of social media is phenomenal. It is being used by all netizens all over the world to a great extent in all areas including business, government, fashion etc. A research conducted by the Institute for Prospective Technological Studies (IPTS) indicates that high take up of social media application outside formal educational settings provides new opportunities for innovation and modernisation.

With this growing trend, political leaders have also realized its importance as an effective tool to spread awareness and to reach out their voters. Democratic presidential candidate Barack Obama used it during the Presidential elections. Since then, social media is being highly used by a number of politicians all over the world. Myspace has more than 7400 discussion groups related to politics. According to a survey by manpower, 29% of the companies in America and 20% of companies worldwide have a social media policy.

People even update themselves through micro-blogging on every aspect of human life including the natural and human diasters. In China, Twitter became the first media in the world to break the news of the Wenzhou earthquake. Social media is being used in fashion industry as well to generate interest in a brand through publicity across online communities and websites.

India is one of the most culturally, linguistically and genetically diverse regions having more than one billion people. It is ranked third in Asia in terms of the internet users and quite a number of them are using social media. In fact, approximately 60 millions to 65 millions netizens in India open most of their time on social media/networking sites.

46. Who defined social media as 'online media' which encourages contributions and feedback from everyone who is interested?

A. Wikepedia

B. Institute for Prospective Technological Studies (IPTS)

C. Myspace

D. Antony Myfield

47. Who used the social media for conversing during recent Presidential Election in U.S.A.?

A. Jimmy Carter B. Barack Obama

C. George Bush D. John F. Kennedy

48. In China, which social media became the first media to break the news of earthquake?

A. Facebook B. Youtube

C. Twitter D. Myzamana

49. In Asia, which country is ranked third in terms of using social media by the people?

A. China B. Pakistan

C. Japan D. India

50. Which social website has more than 7400 discussion groups relate to politics?

A. Orkut B. Myspace

C. Facebook D. Twitter

ANSWERS

1	2	3	4	5	6	7	8	9	10
B	B	A	A	C	C	D	C	D	B

11	12	13	14	15	16	17	18	19	20
C	B	A	B	A	B	D	C	A	C
21	**22**	**23**	**24**	**25**	**26**	**27**	**28**	**29**	**30**
D	B	B	C	B	C	A	A	D	A
31	**32**	**33**	**34**	**35**	**36**	**37**	**38**	**39**	**40**
A	A	A	A	C	C	B	B	B	A
41	**42**	**43**	**44**	**45**	**46**	**47**	**48**	**49**	**50**
B	B	C	B	D	D	B	C	D	B

PAPER-III

Note: *This paper contains seventy five (75) objective type questions of two (2) marks. All each questions are compulsory.*

1. A Boolean query using only AND and NOT is
A. Fuzzy query
B. Conjunctive query
C. Routing query
D. Probabilistic query

2. In which year Janet (U.K.) was established?
A. 1957 B. 1983
C. 1987 D. 1989

3. Who developed Repertory Grid Technique for assessing how the users view the world from their own perspective?
A. A. Delphi
B. Calvin Mooer
C. J. Belkin
D. George Kelley

4. A chart in which some figures are broken down into its constituent parts is
A. Bar chart B. Column chart
C. Pie chart D. Band chart

5. OAISTER is an example of digital libraries architecture based on
A. CORBA
B. Software Agents Architecture
C. Federated Database System
D. Metadata Harvesting

6. RSS feed is a tool of
A. Web 2.0
B. Web 1.0
C. Web 3.0
D. Graphic Design

7. The use of more words or symbols than are necessary to convey a meaning results in
A. Efficiency B. Accuracy
C. Redundancy D. Precision

8. A rubber stamp impressed on the verso of title page giving information concerning the records and processing of each individual book acquired is called
A. Book stamp
B. Process stamp
C. Date stamp
D. Accession stamp

9. Ontology is
A. A Documentation service
B. An Indexing method
C. Classification of Internet based documents
D. Cataloguing of Internet based documents

10. In colon classification, which mnemonic is displayed in the use of digit '4' as for pathology, disease, transport, hybrid etc.?
A. Seminal B. Systematic
C. Scheduled D. Alphabetical

11. Name the similarity measure in which similarity of a document is adjusted such that the similarity of a document to itself is 1.
A. Cosine measure
B. Distance measure
C. Swet's measure
D. Normalised similarity measure

12. Which law states that "An information retrieval system will tend not to be used whenever it is more painful and troublesome for a customer to have information than for him not to have it" ?

A. Bradford's Law
B. Mooer's Law
C. Ziff's Law
D. Lotka's Law

13. Who is the compiler of Web-Bibliography of Rabindranath Tagore?

A. Bengal Library Association
B. RRRLF
C. National Library of India
D. IASLIC

14. Who are the publishers of 'Year Book on Human Rights'?

A. United Nations
B. Ministry of Law, Govt. of India
C. Europa Publishers
D. R.R. Bowker

15. ASTINFO stands for

A. Asian Scientific and Technological Information Network
B. Association of Scientific and Technological Information Scientists in Asia
C. International Network for Exchange of Science and Technology Information
D. Regional Network for the Exchange of Information and Experience in Science and Technology in Asia and the Pacific

16. IFLA's programme for capacity building of library associations is named as

A. BSLA B. ALP
C. CLM D. PAC

17. The measure of certainty or predictability is called as

A. Entropy B. Feedback
C. Redundancy D. Distortion

18. A characteristic in which information tends to leak and the more it leaks, the more we have, is

A. Synergetic characteristics
B. Diffusive characteristics
C. Compressible characteristics
D. Shareable characteristics

19. Which of the following organizations are associated with the concept of '1000 crore plan to link 9000 libraries in India'?

(i) National Library of India
(ii) National Mission on Libraries
(iii) INFLIBNET
(iv) RRRLF

Codes :

A. (ii) and (iii) are correct.
B. (iii) and (iv) are correct.
C. (i) and (iv) are correct.
D. (ii) and (iv) are correct.

20. Which of the following are the core content of ISI web of knowledge?

(i) Current Contents
(ii) ISI proceedings
(iii) Derwent Information Index
(iv) AGRICOLA

Codes :

A. (i), (iv) and (iii)
B. (i), (ii) and (iii)
C. (ii), (iii) and (iv)
D. (i), (ii) and (iv)

21. Which of the following are value added information services?

(i) Aggregator Service
(ii) Referral Service
(iii) Document Delivery Service
(iv) Research Reports/Market Survey Reports

Codes :

A. (i) and (iii) are correct
B. (ii) and (iv) are correct
C. (ii) and (iii) are correct
D. (i) and (iv) are correct

22. Identify the methods used for plagiarism detection:

(i) Term occurrence analysis
(ii) API Testing
(iii) Citation-based plagiarism detection
(iv) Local similarity assessment

Codes :

A. (i), (ii) and (iv) are correct.
B. (i), (iii) and (iv) are correct.
C. (ii), (iii) and (iv) are correct.
D. (i), (ii) and (iii) are correct.

23. Which of the following are the main role operators of PRECIS?
(i) Key System
(ii) Action
(iii) Performer of action
(iv) Form of Document
Codes :
A. (i), (ii) and (iii)
B. (ii), (i) and (iv)
C. (i), (iii) and (iv)
D. (ii), (iii) and (i)

24. Which of the following are the advantages of RFID technology in libraries?
(i) Tags can be read inside a case.
(ii) Hundred of tags can be read at a time.
(iii) Cheaper than Barcode
(iv) More security and Privacy
Codes :
A. (i) and (iii) are correct
B. (i) and (ii) are correct
C. (ii) and (iii) are correct
D. (iii) and (iv) are correct

25. Which of the following are not Change Management Models?
(i) Kurtlewin's Model
(ii) Beer's Model
(iii) Lasswell's Model
(iv) Epidemic Model
Codes :
A. (i) & (iii) are correct.
B. (ii) & (iii) are correct.
C. (iii) & (iv) are correct.
D. (ii) & (iv) are correct.

26. Which of the following are the International Cooperative Serials Control Program?
(i) CONSER (ii) BIBCO
(iii) SERLINE (iv) CATLINE
Codes :
A. (i) & (ii) are correct.
B. (ii) & (iii) are correct.
C. (i) & (iii) are correct.
D. (ii) & (iv) are correct.

27. Which of the following are called 'path finders' to the literature?
(i) Bibliography
(ii) Catalogue
(iii) Shelf List
(iv) Indices and Abstracts
Codes :
A. (i) & (ii) are correct
B. (i), (ii) & (iv) are correct
C. (i) & (iv) are correct
D. (ii) & (iii) are correct

28. Which of the following facilitate informal communication on the web?
(i) Split Screens
(ii) Chat
(iii) Wikis
(iv) RSS feeds
Codes :
A. (i) & (iii) are correct
B. (ii) & (iii) are correct
C. (iii) & (iv) are correct
D. (i) & (ii) are correct

29. Which of the following associations have sponsored the Text Encoding Initiatives (TEI)?
(i) ACL (ii) ACRL
(iii) ALLC (iv) ACH
Codes :
A. (i), (ii) and (iii) are correct
B. (ii), (iii) and (iv) are correct
C. (i), (iv) and (ii) are correct
D. (i), (iii) and (iv) are correct

30. Which of the following are limitations of digital libraries?
(i) Full text searching
(ii) Operational costs
(iii) Rights management
(iv) Hyper text linking
Codes :
A. (ii), (iii) and (iv) are correct
B. (ii) and (iii) are correct
C. (i), (ii) and (iv) are correct
D. (i) and (iv) are correct

31. The sources of hypothesis, as enunciated by P.V. Young are
(i) Genealogy (ii) Culture
(iii) Experiment (iv) Analogy

Codes :

A. (i), (ii) and (iii) are correct
B. (i), (iii) and (iv) are correct
C. (i), (ii) and (iv) are correct
D. (ii), (iii) and (iv) are correct

32. "Women are more in library profession than men." Identify the variable in the statement.

(i) Men and women are independent variables.
(ii) Men and women are dependent variables.
(iii) Library profession is a dependent variable.
(iv) Library profession is an independent variable.

Codes :

A. (i) and (iii) are correct
B. (i) and (iv) are correct
C. (ii) and (iii) are correct
D. (ii) and (iv) are correct

33. Systematic sampling is

(i) A type of probability sampling.
(ii) A type of non-probability sampling.
(iii) In which first unit is selected randomly.
(iv) Selected on the basis of specified characteristics.

Codes :

A. (i) and (iii) are correct
B. (i) and (iv) are correct
C. (iii) and (iv) are correct
D. (ii) and (iv) are correct

34. Who are associated with the digitization of the collection of Rabindra Bhavan, Vishav Bharati?

(i) RRRLF
(ii) C-DAC
(iii) NIC
(iv) National Library of India

Codes :

A. (i) and (iii) are correct
B. (i) and (ii) are correct
C. (ii) and (iv) are correct
D. (iii) and (iv) are correct

35. Which of the following are the Pillars of SCONUL Seven Pillar Model?

(i) Recognising Information need
(ii) Locating and accessing information
(iii) Using information technology for assessing information need.
(iv) Comparing and evaluating information.

Codes :

A. (i), (ii) and (iii) are correct
B. (i), (ii) and (iv) are correct
C. (ii), (iii) and (iv) are correct
D. (i) and (iv) are correct

36. Resource Description Framework consists which of the following?

(i) Subject (ii) Thread
(iii) Predicate (iv) Object

Codes :

A. (i), (ii) and (iii)
B. (ii), (iii) and (iv)
C. (iii), (iv) and (i)
D. (iv), (i) and (ii)

37. Arrange the following factors of TQM in the order of their implementation:

i. Development of Human Resource Management
ii. Standardisation of Work process
iii. Improvement in Internal Organisation Management
iv. Quality Management Procedures

Codes :

A. ii iii i iii
B. iii iv ii i
C. iv iii ii i
D. ii iv iii i

38. Arrange the following according to their year of emergence:

i. ADINET ii. SIRNET
iii. MANLIBNET iv. DELNET

Codes :

A. i iv ii iii
B. iv ii iii i
C. iv iii ii i
D. iii i iv ii

39. Arrange the following according to their year of origin:

i. Indian National Bibliography
ii. British National Bibliography

iii. Cumulative Book Index
iv. Books in Print

Codes :

A. i ii iv iii
B. iii iv ii i
C. ii iii iv i
D. iv i ii iii

40. Arrange the following according to their levels:
i. Canons of Cataloguing
ii. Laws of Library Science
iii. General Normative Principles
iv. Principles of Cataloguing

Codes :

A. ii iv i iii
B. i iii ii iv
C. iv i iii ii
D. iii ii i iv

41. Arrange the following according to their year of emergence:
i. LISA
ii. Dissertation Abstracts International
iii. Indian Science Abstracts
iv. Indian Library & Information Science Abstracts

Codes :

A. iii iv ii i
B. iv iii i ii
C. ii i iii iv
D. i ii iii iv

42. Arrange the following according to their year of emergence:
i. INIS ii. AGRIS
iii. NATIS iv. UNISIST

Codes :

A. iii iv ii i
B. iv i iii ii
C. ii iv i iii
D. i iii iv ii

43. Arrange in sequence the following Model Public Library Acts/Bills in India:
i. Model Public Library Bill by M.D. Sen Committee
ii. Model Public Library Act by S.R. Ranganathan
iii. Model Public Library Act of ILA
iv. Model Public Library Bill by working group of Planning Commission

Codes :

A. i ii iii iv
B. ii i iv iii
C. iii iv i ii
D. iv iii ii i

44. Arrange in sequence the medium used for 'Virtual Reference' in the order of their progress.
i. Web form
ii. Ask a Service
iii. E-mail
iv. Social Networking

Codes :

A. i ii iii iv
B. ii iii iv i
C. iii i ii iv
D. iv ii i iii

45. Arrange in order the process of stock rectification and stock verification as suggested by S.R. Ranganathan:
i. Checking with charged tray
ii. Shelf Rectification
iii. Shelf checking
iv. Deciding the Quota

Codes :

A. iii i iv ii
B. iv i ii iii
C. iv ii iii i
D. ii iv i iii

46. Match the following:

	List–I		List–II
a.	Outdated Information	i.	Information Diffusion
b.	Condensed Information	ii.	Obsolete Information
c.	Message	iii.	Compressible Information
d.	Vintage model	iv.	Understanding

Codes :

	a	b	c	d
A.	iv	iii	ii	i
B.	i	ii	iv	iii
C.	iii	iv	ii	i
D.	ii	iii	iv	i

47. Match the following:

	List–I		List–II
a.	Technique for identifying the theme of a document	i.	Cataloguing
b.	Prussian Instruction	ii.	Standard for encoding data on CD-ROM
c.	ISO-9960	iii.	Data Transmission Speed
d.	Baud	iv.	Bibliographic coupling

Codes :

	a	b	c	d
A.	iv	i	ii	iii
B.	i	ii	iii	iv
C.	ii	iii	iv	i
D.	iii	ii	i	iv

48. Match the following:

	List–I		List–II
a.	Maurice B. Line	i.	Resource Management in Academic Libraries
b.	David Baker	ii.	Planning Academic and Research Library Buildings
c.	Peter Brophy	iii.	Academic Library Management
d.	K.D. Metcalf	iv.	The Academic Libraries

Codes :

	a	b	c	d
A.	iii	i	iv	ii
B.	i	ii	iii	iv
C.	iv	i	ii	iii
D.	ii	iii	i	iv

49. Match the following :

	List–I		List–II
a.	Digital	i.	Collections are Library stored in electronic media formats and accessible via computers
b.	Hybrid Library	ii.	Access to electronic information in a variety of remote locations through a local online catalogue or other gateway
c.	Virtual Library	iii.	Provides services in a mixed mode electronic and paper environment
d.	Electronic Library	iv.	Collection of electronic resources that provides direct/indirect access to a systematically organised collection of digital objects

Codes :

	a	b	c	d
A.	iv	iii	ii	i
B.	i	iii	iv	ii
C.	iii	i	ii	iv
D.	iv	ii	i	iii

50. Match the following:

	List–I		List–II
a.	Survey of requirements	i.	Design phase
b.	Determining cost efficiency and effectiveness	ii.	Installation phase
c.	Review of the programs and their goals	iii.	Analysis phase
d.	Complete change over basics of system	iv.	Evaluation phase

Codes :

	a	b	c	d
A.	i	ii	iii	iv
B.	ii	iii	iv	i
C.	iii	iv	i	ii
D.	iv	i	ii	iii

51. Match the following:

	List–I		List–II
a.	Nadir to Ascending	i.	Hypothesizing

b. Ascending to Zenith — ii. Verification
c. Zenith to Descending — iii. Deductive
d. Descending to Nadir — iv. Empirical

Codes :

	a	b	c	d
A.	i	iii	ii	iv
B.	ii	iv	i	iii
C.	iii	i	iv	ii
D.	iv	i	iii	ii

52. Match the following characteristics of DBMS with respective activity:

List–I	List–II
a. Reduction of redundancy	i. Encryption
b. Data sharing	ii. Centralized control
c. Data integrity	iii. No. of application programs
d. Data security	iv. Accurate and consistent data

Codes :

	a	b	c	d
A.	ii	iii	iv	i
B.	iv	iii	ii	i
C.	iii	iv	i	ii
D.	i	ii	iv	iii

53. Match the following:

List–I	List–II
a. XML	i. Joe Becker
b. METS	ii. Defence Organizations
c. UNICODE	iii. W3C
d. Cryptography	iv. Library of Congress

Codes :

	a	b	c	d
A.	i	ii	iii	iv
B.	iii	iv	i	ii
C.	ii	iii	iv	i
D.	iv	i	ii	iii

54. Match the following:

List–I	List–II
a. Social Microscope	i. Cluster Technique
b. Fundamental Research	ii. No control over variance
c. Ex-post facto research	iii. Case study method
d. Multi stage random sampling	iv. Knowledge for knowledge sake

Codes :

	a	b	c	d
A.	i	ii	iii	iv
B.	iii	iv	ii	i
C.	ii	iii	i	iv
D.	iv	i	ii	iv

55. Match the following:

List–I	List–II
a. Estimation of future expenditure on the basis of previous year expenditure	i. Programme
b. ₹ 15 per student and ₹ 200/- per teacher	ii. Comparison
c. 6.5%-10% of university budget for the development of library	iii. Per capita
d. Activities to be accomplished by the library	iv. Proportional

Codes :

	a	b	c	d
A.	ii	iii	iv	i
B.	i	ii	iii	iv
C.	iii	iv	i	ii
D.	iv	i	ii	iii

56. Match the following:

List–I	List–II
a. Identification of user categories	i. Market positioning
b. Prioriting user groups and services	ii. Segmentation
c. Information seeking behaviour of users	iii. Marketing Mix

d. Product, price, place, promotion — iv. Consumer analysis

Codes :

	a	b	c	d
A.	i	ii	iii	iv
B.	ii	i	iv	iii
C.	iii	iv	i	ii
D.	iv	iii	ii	i

57. Match the following:

List–I	List–II
a. FRBR	i. Paul Otlet
b. POPSI	ii. IFLA
c. UDC	iii. G. Bhattacharya
d. www	iv. Tem Berners-Lee

Codes :

	a	b	c	d
A.	ii	i	iii	iv
B.	ii	iii	i	iv
C.	ii	iv	i	iii
D.	iv	ii	iii	i

58. Match the following:

List–I	List–II
a. Index Translationum	i. NISCAIR
b. Translation Register Index (TR-I)	ii. NTC, Chicago
c. World Trans Index	iii. UNESCO
d. Commonwealth Index of Unpublished Transtations	iv. ITC, Delft, Netherlands
	v. ASLIB

Codes :

	a	b	c	d
A.	ii	iii	i	iv
B.	iii	ii	iv	v
C.	v	iii	i	ii
D.	iv	ii	v	iii

59. Match the following evaluation criteria of print materials:

List–I	List – II
a. Authority	i. Typography
b. Scope	ii. Stated purpose
c. Format	iii. Publisher's reputation
d. Arrangement	iv. Cross references

Codes :

	a	b	c	d
A.	ii	iii	i	iv
B.	i	iv	ii	iii
C.	iii	ii	i	iv
D.	iii	iv	ii	i

60. Match the following:

List–I	List–II
a. Measure of similarity between two documents	i. Proportion of coefficient association
b. Similarity measure based on overlap in terms between two documents	ii. Rectangular distance coefficient
c. Document similarity based solely on the occurrence of words	iii. Coefficient of association
d. Similarity measure which is based on the city block distance between two documents	iv. Lexical similarity

Codes :

	a	b	c	d
A.	i	iii	ii	iv
B.	iii	i	ii	iv
C.	iii	i	iv	ii
D.	ii	iii	iv	i

61. Match the following authors with their statements on information characteristics:

List–I	List–II
a. Peter Drucker	i. Human and shareable
b. Borlando Cleveland	ii. Quantity, Quality, Life
c. K.J. McGarry	iii. Natural and man-made physical resources
d. Williams	iv. Resources by analogy with classic resources of labour

Codes :

	a	b	c	d
A.	iii	i	iv	ii
B.	iii	ii	i	iv
C.	i	iii	iv	ii
D.	i	iv	ii	iii

62. Match the following:

List–I	**List–II**
a. Saraswati Mahal Library, Tanjavur (1535)	i. Lord Curzon
b. Khuda Baksh Oriental Public Library, Patna (1876)	ii. Telugu Nayakas
c. Library of Asiatic Society of Bengal (1784)	iii. Maulana M.B. Khan
d. Impèrial Library, Calcutta (1901)	iv. Sir G. William Jones

Codes:

	a	b	c	d
A.	iii	ii	iv	i
B.	ii	iii	i	iv
C.	ii	iii	iv	i
D.	iii	ii	i	iv

63. Assertion (A) : With the introduction of Internet, need for reference librarians has been minimised to fulfil the users reference needs.

Reason (R) : FAQ facility on internet is substituting the need for human interface in libraries.

Codes :

A. Both (A) and (R) are partially true.
B. Both (A) and (R) are true.
C. Both (A) and (R) are false.
D. (A) is true but (R) is false.

64. Assertion (A) : Approaches to Research is not dependent on Epistemologies.

Reason (R) : Scientific research relies on the application of the scientific method.

Codes :

A. Both (A) and (R) are true.
B. Both (A) and (R) are false.
C. (A) is true and (R) is false.
D. (R) is true and (A) is false.

65. Assertion (A) : According to the Third Law of Librarianship given by Michael Gorman, we need to use technology intelligently to enhance service.

Reason (R) : Technology is used to solve problems and improve services and achieve cost-effectiveness rather than adopted for its own sake.

Codes :

A. (A) is true, but (R) is false.
B. Both (A) and (R) are true, but (R) is not correct explanation of (A).
C. Both (A) and (R) are false.
D. Both (A) and (R) are true.

66. Assertion (A) : All reference sources provide uptodate information in their respective categories.

Reason (R) : As these are compiled from primary sources of information.

Codes :

A. Both (A) and (R) are true.
B. Both (A) and (R) are false.
C. (A) is false but (R) is partially true.
D. (A) is true but (R) is false.

67. Assertion (A) : The hierarchy based classification schemes have a major role in the organization of the web.

Reason (R) : The 'hotlists' retrieved by robots based search engines use the technique of relevance of subject descriptors.

Codes :

A. (A) is true, but (R) is false.
B. (A) is false, but (R) is true.
C. Both (A) and (R) are correct.
D. Both (A) and (R) are wrong.

68. Assertion (A) : Performance Based Budgeting demands that the objectives and goals of agency be clear and performance measures and target to put in place.

Reason (R) : The key to success firmly rely upon its clear sense of mission and objectives which the funding agencies have proposed to reach them.

Codes :

A. (A) is true, but (R) is false.
B. (A) is false, but (R) is true.
C. Both (A) and (R) are true.
D. Both (A) and (R) are false.

69. Assertion (A) : Majority of University Libraries in India are not fully automated.

Reason (R) : University Libraries in India are meddling with automation of circulation activities.

Codes :

A. (A) is true but (R) is false.
B. (A) is false but (R) is true.
C. Both (A) and (R) are true.
D. Both (A) and (R) are false.

70. Assertion (A) : Mean, median and mode are the simple techniques to get exact averages for data analysis in research.

Reason (R) : These are the well accepted statistical techniques of research for data analysis of historical data.

Codes :

A. (A) is false, but (R) is true.
B. Both (A) and (R) are true.
C. (A) is true but (R) is false.
D. Both (A) and (R) are false.

71. Assertion (A) : Online Reference Service can be offered using IMs, SMs, VoIP, Video, Blogs, Websites and host of such other mechanisms.

Reason (R) : Majority of academic libraries in India are equipped with required infrastructure.

Codes :

A. Both (A) and (R) are true.
B. (A) is true, (R) is false.
C. (A) is false, (R) is true.
D. Both (A) and (R) are false.

72. Assertion (A) : Semantic web is an extension of www in which web contents cannot be expressed in natural language.

Reason (R) : Semantic web can be easily associated with spider web.

Codes :

A. Both (A) and (R) are false.
B. (A) is true, but (R) is false.
C. Both (A) and (R) are true.
D. (A) is false, but (R) is true.

73. Assertion (A) : BIOS is a set of programs that handles startup operations in a computer such as power on, self tested and low level control for hardware.

Reason (R) : The graphical display at the beginning of the program prolongs the life of monitor.

Codes :

A. Both (A) and (R) are true.
B. (A) is false, but (R) is true.
C. Both (A) and (R) are false.
D. (A) is true, but (R) is false.

74. Assertion (A) : For providing an effective reference service, best & up to date reference collection is not as important as is the competent reference librarian.

Reason (R) : An efficient reference librarian can serve the users more effectively even in the absence of best reference collection.

Codes :

A. (A) is true but (R) is false.
B. Both (A) and (R) are true.
C. (A) is false but (R) is true.
D. Both (A) and (R) are false.

75. Assertion (A) : India's contribution to LIS literatures is decreasing.

Reason (R) : Authors find it more convenient to get their articles published in open access journals.

Codes :

A. Both (A) and (R) are true.
B. (A) is false, but (R) is true.
C. Both (A) and (R) are false.
D. (A) is true but (R) is false.

ANSWERS

1	2	3	4	5	6	7	8	9	10
B	B	D	C	D	A	C	D	C	A
11	12	13	14	15	16	17	18	19	20
D	B	B	A	D	A	C	B	D	B
21	22	23	24	25	26	27	28	29	30
D	B	A	B	C	C	C	D	D	B
31	32	33	34	35	36	37	38	39	40
C	A	A	A	B	B	D	B	B	D
41	42	43	44	45	46	47	48	49	50
C	B	B	C	B	D	A	A	A	C
51	52	53	54	55	56	57	58	59	60
D	A	B	B	A	B	B	B	C	C
61	62	63	64	65	66	67	68	69	70
A	C	A	A	D	C	A	C	C	C
71	72	73	74	75					
B	A	D	B	B					

Previous Paper (Solved)

UGC-NET LIBRARY AND INFORMATION SCIENCE, JUNE 2013

PAPER-II

Note: *This paper contains* ***fifty*** *(50) objective type questions, each question carrying* ***two*** *(2) marks. Attempt* ***all*** *the questions.*

1. The distinct characteristic(s) of digital objects are
   A. Physical medium
   B. Logical process
   C. Conceptual recognition and transaction
   D. All the above
2. 'Who's who in India', an irregular publication is published by
   A. Business Press, Bombay
   B. Sterling, New Delhi
   C. Tradesman & Men Asia, Delhi
   D. Sahitya Samsad, Calcutta
3. Which department of the Government of India deals with Public Libraries?
   A. Department of Archaeology
   B. Department of Culture
   C. Department of Primary Education
   D. Department of Science and Technology
4. Information on Prime Minister of Bangladesh can be found in
   A. International Who's Who
   B. Who's Who in Bangladesh
   C. Current Biography
   D. Statesman's Yearbook
5. 'Eradication of Malaria in India 1990-1999' – a report can be categorised under
   A. Trend Report
   B. Review Report
   C. State of the Art Report
   D. Research Report
6. Which is not a reprographic service ?
   A. Micro Copying B. Blue Printing
   C. Paper Printing D. Thermo Copying
7. ERIC is sponsored by
   A. US National Health Institute
   B. Health and Rehabilitation Services Division, A LA
   C. Department of Health Education & Welfare, Government of USA
   D. Health Science Information Centre, USA
8. In the library hierarchy which level of management is responsible for execution of policies?
   A. Middle level B. Operational level
   C. Top level D. Lower level
9. METS stands for
   A. Machine Encoded Transmission System
   B. Metadata Encoded for Textual Sources
   C. Machine Encoded Textual Standard
   D. Metadata Encoding Transmission Standard
10. Sector Device is an extension of
    A. Gap Device
    B. Empty Device
    C. Octave Device
    D. Group Notation Device
11. "Control, Disease, Malaria, Brain" indicates that it is
    A. Raw Title B. Expressive Title
    C. Kernel Title D. Transformed Title
12. A graphical representation using symbols to represent operations, data, flow, etc. is
    A. Logical Chart
    B. Flow Chart
    C. System Flow Chart
    D. Network Chart

13. The 12 rules for relational database were given by
A. E.F. Codd B. Charles Babbage
C. James Weyer D. Tim Berners Lee

14. A technique displaying graphic information on screen, pixel by pixel with bits held in main memory is
A. Bit handling B. Bit mapping
C. Bit pattern D. Bit matrix

15. ZOTERO is a ______.
A. Content Management System
B. Reference Management System
C. Serials Management System
D. Bibliographic Reference Management System

16. A network in which the host computer controls different nodes which further control other nodes, is known as
A. Star Network
B. Ring Network
C. Hierarchical Network
D. Multipoint Network

17. Impact factor is devised by
A. Eugene Garfield B. Alan Pritchard
C. David Hume D. Louis Brandeis

18. A skilful method of providing means, mechanism and structural elements to streamline organizational work is known as
A. Role Analysis
B. Strategic Planning
C. Work Culture
D. Autonomous Planning

19. Financial allocation made to a library for purchase of furniture and equipments usually comes under the budget head
A. Recurring grant
B. Endowments
C. Non-recurring grant
D. Annual grant

20. Historical/Government records related to an organization are maintained in
(*i*) Archieves
(*ii*) Museums
(*iii*) Repositories
(*iv*) Government libraries

Codes:
A. (*i*) and (*ii*) are correct.
B. (*ii*) and (*iii*) are correct.
C. (*i*) and (*iii*) are correct.
D. (*ii*) and (*iv*) are correct.

21. Major elements of a profession are
(*i*) Philosophy
(*ii*) Body of knowledge
(*iii*) Publicity
(*iv*) Status

Codes:
A. (*i*), (*ii*), (*iv*) are correct.
B. (*i*), (*ii*), (*iii*) are correct.
C. (*ii*), (*iii*), (*iv*) are correct.
D. (*i*), (*iii*), (*iv*) are correct.

22. Which of the following states don't have library legislation?
(*i*) Haryana (*ii*) Delhi
(*iii*) J & K (*iv*) Manipur

Codes:
A. (*i*) and (*ii*) are correct.
B. (*ii*) and (*iii*) are correct.
C. (*i*) and (*iv*) are correct.
D. (*ii*) and (*iii*) are correct.

23. Which of the following principles are associated with library building planning?
(*i*) Principle of Uniformity
(*ii*) Principle of Comfortability
(*iii*) Principle of Simplicity
(*iv*) Principle of Continuity

Codes:
A. (*i*), (*ii*) and (*iii*) are correct.
B. (*ii*), (*iii*) and (*iv*) are correct.
C. (*i*), (*ii*) and (*iv*) are correct.
D. (*iii*), (*iv*) and (*i*) are correct.

24. ETD database in India is maintained by
(*i*) Shodhgangotri
(*ii*) Vidyanidhi
(*iii*) Shodhganga
(*iv*) INDEST-AICTE consortium

Codes:
A. (*i*) and (*iii*) are correct.
B. (*ii*), (*iii*) and (*iv*) are correct.
C. (*ii*) and (*iii*) are correct.
D. (*iii*) and (*iv*) are correct.

25. Vocabulary in a database is controlled by
(*i*) Thesaurus files
(*ii*) Dictionary files
(*iii*) Standard files
(*iv*) Authority files

Codes:
A. (*i*) and (*ii*) are correct.
B. (*iii*) and (*iv*) are correct.
C. (*i*) and (*iii*) are correct.
D. (*i*) and (*iv*) are correct.

26. Limitations of Bibliometrics is/are
(*i*) Analysing research and development trends
(*ii*) Describing text, not necessarily meaning and context
(*iii*) Identifying the active areas of research
(*iv*) Citation bias

Codes:
A. (*ii*) and (*iv*) are correct.
B. (*i*) and (*iii*) are correct.
C. (*i*), (*ii*) and (*iv*) are correct.
D. (*ii*) and (*iii*) are correct.

27. Identify the technique(s) to collect the data regarding the number of persons visited the periodical section of the library at different hours of the day.
(*i*) Questionnaire (*ii*) Interview
(*iii*) Observation (*iv*) Library records

Codes:
A. (*i*) and (*ii*) are correct.
B. (*ii*) and (*iii*) are correct.
C. (*iii*) and (*iv*) are correct.
D. (*ii*) and (*iv*) are correct.

28. Which of the following are prohibited under copyright?
(*i*) Downloading a document, printing multiple copies
(*ii*) Placing a copyright protected document on web-server
(*iii*) Downloading a document and save it in folder
(*iv*) Downloading a document with license to use and E-mailing it

Codes:
A. (*i*), (*iii*) and (*iv*) are correct.
B. (*i*), (*ii*) and (*iii*) are correct.
C. (*iii*), (*iv*) and (*ii*) are correct.
D. (*i*), (*ii*) and (*iv*) are correct.

29. The professional ethics help to ____.
(*i*) Get the right direction
(*ii*) Enhance image
(*iii*) Get more salaries
(*iv*) Resolve day to day issues

Codes:
A. (*ii*) and (*iii*) are correct.
B. (*i*) and (*iv*) are correct.
C. (*i*) and (*ii*) are correct.
D. (*ii*) and (*iv*) are correct.

30. Match the following :

List-I	***List-II***
(*a*) Systematic Bibliography	(*i*) List of macro/micro ideas of articles
(*b*) Analytical or Critical Bibliography	(*ii*) Investigation of physical nature of books
(*c*) Historical Bibliography	(*iii*) Listing of items with minimum details
(*d*) Documentary Bibliography	(*iv*) Concerned with art of writing, printing and binding

Codes:

	(*a*)	(*b*)	(*c*)	(*d*)
A.	(*i*)	(*iv*)	(*iii*)	(*ii*)
B.	(*ii*)	(*i*)	(*iv*)	(*iii*)
C.	(*iii*)	(*ii*)	(*iv*)	(*i*)
D.	(*ii*)	(*iv*)	(*iii*)	(*i*)

31. Match the following queries with their appropriate category of reference source

List-I	***List-II***
(*a*) Enrolment of students in a university	(*i*) Yearbook
(*b*) Weather of Denmark	(*ii*) Statistical source
(*c*) No. of foreigners visited World Book Fair in 2011	(*iii*) Directory
(*d*) No. of hospitals in China	(*iv*) Geographical source .

Codes:

	(a)	(b)	(c)	(d)
A.	(iv)	(ii)	(i)	(ii)
B.	(i)	(iii)	(ii)	(iv)
C.	(ii)	(iv)	(i)	(iii)
D.	(iii)	(iv)	(i)	(ii)

32. Match the following :

List-I	List-II
(a) 1st Law of Library Science	(i) Real time access
(b) 2nd Law of Library Science	(ii) Search engine & subject gateways
(c) 3rd Law of Library Science	(iii) Web access to resources
(d) 4th Law of Library Science	(iv) Open access initiatives

Codes:

	(a)	(b)	(c)	(d)
A.	(iii)	(iv)	(ii)	(i)
B.	(iv)	(i)	(ii)	(iii)
C.	(i)	(iii)	(ii)	(iv)
D.	(ii)	(iv)	(i)	(iii)

33. Match the following :

List-I	List-II
(a) Douglas McGregor	(i) Scientific Management School
(b) Abraham Maslow	(ii) Theory of Authority Structure
(c) F.W. Taylor	(iii) Self Actualisation Needs
(d) Max Weber	(iv) Theory X and Theory Y

Codes:

	(a)	(b)	(c)	(d)
A.	(iv)	(iii)	(i)	(ii)
B.	(ii)	(iii)	(i)	(iv)
C.	(iii)	(iv)	(ii)	(i)
D.	(i)	(iv)	(ii)	(iii)

34. Match the following DDC numbers :

List-I	List-II
(a) Education	(i) 770
(b) Medicine	(ii) 370
(c) Photography	(iii) 610
(d) Astronomy	(iv) 520

Codes:

	(a)	(b)	(c)	(d)
A.	(iii)	(i)	(iv)	(ii)
B.	(ii)	(iii)	(i)	(iv)
C.	(i)	(iv)	(iii)	(ii)
D.	(iv)	(ii)	(i)	(iii)

35. Match the following :

List-I	List-II
(a) Key to a given collection	(i) Abstract
(b) Key to literary sources on a subject	(ii) Index
(c) Representation of subject concept	(iii) Catalogue
(d) Condensation of a document	(iv) Bibliography

Codes:

	(a)	(b)	(c)	(d)
A.	(iii)	(iv)	(ii)	(i)
B.	(ii)	(iii)	(iv)	(i)
C.	(i)	(ii)	(iii)	(iv)
D.	(iv)	(i)	(ii)	(iii)

36. Match the following :

List-I	List-II
(a) Unity of command	(i) Specialization
(b) Unity of direction	(ii) Strength in unity
(c) Esprit de corps	(iii) Orders from only one person
(d) Division of work	(iv) One boss, one plan

Codes:

	(a)	(b)	(c)	(d)
A.	(iv)	(iii)	(ii)	(i)
B.	(ii)	(iv)	(iii)	(i)
C.	(iii)	(iv)	(ii)	(i)
D.	(i)	(iv)	(iii)	(ii)

37. Give in sequence, the following in order of their origin :

i. National Library
ii. Calcutta Public Library
iii. Imperial Library Act
iv. Imperial Library

Codes:

A. (ii) (iii) (iv) (i)
B. (i) (ii) (iii) (iv)
C. (iii) (i) (iv) (ii)
D. (ii) (iv) (iii) (i)

38. Arrange the following according to year of publication :

i. Colon Classification
ii. Prolegomena to Classification
iii. Five Laws of Library Science
iv. Classified Catalogue Code

Codes:

A. (iii) (iv) (i) (ii)
B. (iv) (ii) (i) (iii)
C. (iii) (i) (iv) (ii)
D. (i) (ii) (iv) (iii)

39. Assertion (A) : Digitization has proved to be possible for every format and medium held by library.

Reason (R) : All libraries are making their text and visual collections digitized.

Codes:

A. (A) is true, but (R) is false.
B. (A) is false, but (R) is true.
C. Both (A) and (R) are true.
D. Both (A) and (R) are false.

40. Assertion (A) : In spite of political, economic and technological support, the growth of Public Library System is lopsided.

Reason (R) : The public libraries are totally depending on cess/tax amounts.

Codes:

A. Both (A) and (R) are true.
B. Both (A) and (R) are false.
C. (A) is true, but (R) is false.
D. (A) is false, but (R) is true.

41. Assertion (A) : 'Pay and Use' concept has not been accepted in libraries of India.

Reason (R) : Library staff do not possess the essential skills required for product development and promotion.

Codes:

A. Both (A) and (R) are true.
B. (A) is true but (R) are false.
C. (R) is true, but (A) is false.
D. Both (A) and (R) are false.

42. Assertion (A) : Library Science profession in India enjoys the status at par with medical, legal and management professions.

Reason (R) : S.R. Ranganathan's contributions and teachings for Indian librarianship secured a status to the profession.

Codes:

A. (A) is true, but (R) is false.
B. (A) is false, but (R) is true.
C. Both (A) and (R) are true.
D. Both (A) and (R) are false.

43. Assertion (A) : In conducting research, Social Sciences are not considered at par with natural sciences.

Reason (R) : Research in Social Sciences can't be performed so rigorously as can be in Natural Sciences.

Codes:

A. Both (A) and (R) are true.
B. Both (A) and (R) are false.
C. (A) is true, but (R) is false.
D. (A) is false, but (R) is true.

44. Assertion (A) : Research starts in mind first and then in laboratories.

Reason (R) : Systematically conducted research leads to generalization.

Codes:

A. (A) is true, but (R) is false.
B. (A) is false, but (R) is true.
C. Both (A) and (R) are true.
D. Both (A) and (R) are false.

45. Assertion (A) : Systematic and efficient use of statistical tools in research helps in precise interpretation of research results.

Reason (R) : Statistical tools cannot give specific explanations of the data.

Codes:

A. Both (A) and (R) are true.
B. (A) is true and (R) is false.
C. Both (A) and (R) are false.
D. (A) is false and (R) is true.

Directions (Qs. Nos. 46 to 50): *Read the following passage and answer the questions.*

While Boyd allows that some people consider email or discussion lists to be Social Software, he makes an important distinction between traditional communication software and Social Software. He explains that traditional software places people into groups with a top-down approach; in other words, it assigns membership. However, Social Software takes a bottom-up approach, which enables people to organize themselves into a network based on their preferences. Therefore, with a bottom-up approach, people can sign up for a system and build communities using their personal preferences (Marenzi *et al.,* 2008). In contrast, traditional communication software uses a top-down approach where people are assigned into a specific organization or groups. Social Software is based on supporting individuals who interact socially with people who have similar interests (Marenzi *et al.,* 2008). In addition, users typically enjoy Social Software itself and work with various Social Software applications voluntarily. For example, the authors of social media enjoy content that they have created themselves, content that is copied from other media, and mash-ups that contain a mix of content that could possibly be from several authors (Ahonen and Lietsala, 2007). The popularity of social technologies is attributed to the increase in low-cost tools and the critical mass of millions of people who are now connected to the Internet and to the people's need to feel like part of a community (Avram, 2006). These users tend to rely more on their own personal social networks than on traditional business structures. (Vinson 2005) describes additional features of Social Software tools: they allow people to easily participate (by both contributing and reading) in the activities; they provide the opportunity for networking and allow for the self-forming of networks since people are usually both consumers and producers; and each individual can be a member on several networks simultaneously (Avram, 2006).

46. People are assigned into specific organization or groups in ______ approach.
A. Top-down approach
B. Down-top approach
C. Top-bottom system approach
D. Down-top system approach

47. The basic feature(s) of social software is/are :
A. Social interaction
B. Personal interaction
C. Enjoying social software
D. (A) and (C) are correct.

48. Authors of social media enjoy ______ of contents.
A. Self created contents
B. Contents from magazines
C. Contents from many formats
D. Contents from many languages

49. The reason/s attributed to the popularity of social networking is/are :
A. Masses have started using internet.
B. All have free access to internet.
C. All are technology literates.
D. Stimulation of on-line communities over the traditional communities.

50. The social software tools allow.
A. Easy participation
B. Quick networking
C. Consumer networking
D. Both (A) & (B)

ANSWERS

1	2	3	4	5	6	7	8	9	10
D	A	B	D	A	C	C	A	D	C
11	**12**	**13**	**14**	**15**	**16**	**17**	**18**	**19**	**20**
C	B	A	B	D	C	A	B	C	C
21	**22**	**23**	**24**	**25**	**26**	**27**	**28**	**29**	**30**
A	B	B	C	B	A	C	D	C	C

31	32	33	34	35	36	37	38	39	40
D	A	A	B	A	A	D	C	A	C
41	42	43	44	45	46	47	48	49	50
A	B	A	C	A	A	D	A	A	D

PAPER-III

Note: *This paper contains* **seventy five** *(75) objective type questions of* **two** *(2) marks each.* **All** *questions are compulsory.*

1. "Poole's Index to Periodical Literature" was brought out by
A. William Frederick B. F.W. Lancaster
C. Van Rijsbergen D. H.P. Luhn

2. Walford's Guide to Reference Material is published by
A. American Library Association, Chicago
B. R.R. Bowkar, London
C. Library Association Publishing, London
D. Learned Information Ltd., New Jersey

3. Starting, Chaining, Browsing, Differentiating, Monitoring, Extracting, Verification and Ending are important stages of which information seeking behaviour model?
A. Dervin's Model
B. Ellis Model
C. Marchionnini Model
D. Kuhlthan Model

4. What kind of arrangement is followed in LISA?
A. Alphabetical B. Chronological
C. Classified D. Geographical

5. Webform is used in
A. Synchronous Virtual Reference Service
B. Asynchronous Virtual Reference Service
C. Both (A) & (B)
D. None of the above

6. An online search in which all aspects of the records in natural language may be used as sought terms is
A. Alphabetical collateral search
B. Multi-aspect search
C. Free text searching
D. Streaming search

7. Science Abstracts published by
A. INSPEC (Institute of Electrical Engineering)
B. Institute of Physics, London
C. American Institute of Physics
D. PSOJ (Physical Society of Japan)

8. Work study, standardised tools, selecting and training of workers are the contributions of
A. Louis Brandeis B. F.W. Taylor
C. Henry Fayol D. Lyndall Urwick

9. When the population is heterogenous, which of the following methods give better results?
A. Purposive Sampling
B. Quota Sampling
C. Random Sampling
D. Stratified Random Sampling

10. Which of the following is/are not database object(s)?
A. Tables B. Queries
C. Relationships D. Reports

11. What is the process of transferring software programme from secondary storage media to the hard disc called?
A. Download B. Upload
C. Installation D. Storage

12. Name a technique used for searching sorted data in a database
A. Boolean operator B. Inverting file
C. Indexing D. Binary

13. Information about Government of India's stand on 'FDI' can be found in
A. Gazetteer of India
B. Britannica Book of the Year
C. Statesman's Yearbook
D. Asian Recorder

14. "Anomalous State of Knowledge (ASK) Model", one of the user centered models of information retrieval was proposed by

A. P. Ingwersen B. T. Saracevic
C. J.N. Belkin D. D. Ellis

15. The 'Cranefield Test', associated with evaluation of information retrieval system was carried under the direction of ________.

A. C. W. Cleverdon
B. G. Salton
C. D. C. Blair & M.E. Maron
D. E. Voorhees

16. LAMP stands for

A. Library Archives Management Programme
B. Laser Analysis and Multimedia Performance
C. Linux Apache.MySQL Perl
D. Library Automation Management Protocol

17. "Information Literacy Competency Standards for Higher Education" is prepared by

A. AASL B. IFLA
C. SCONUL D. ACRL

18. Name the storage medium (compatible with speed of CPU) for storing instructions or data temporarily during processing

A. RAM B. ROM
C. Cache D. EPROM

19. "Scitation" is the online host service of

A. American Institute of Physics
B. University of Maryland
C. Society for Industrial Research
D. Oxford University

20. The process of surrogation, repackaging and compaction of the primary literature that results in creation of secondary journals, is

A. Newsletter
B. Abstracting and Indexing Periodical
C. House Journals
D. Electronic Journal

21. Which of the following is not a language of DBMS ?

A. DDL B. DML
C. PASCAL D. PLI

22. How do we render the name 'Bernardo Augustine De Voto'?

A. Voto, Bernardo, Augustine De
B. De Voto, Augustine, Bernardo
C. Bernardo Augustine, De Voto
D. De Voto, Bernardo Augustine

23. Which reference tool defines Reference service as ".... that phase of work which is directly concerned with assistance to readers in securing information and in using the resources of the library in study and research"?

A. Encyclopaedia of Librarianship
B. Encyclopaedia of Library and Information Science
C. ALA Glossary of Library Terms
D. ALA World Encyclopaedia of Library & Information Services

24. Indian National Advisory Board for Libraries was setup in 1966 by

A. Association of Indian Universities
B. Ministry of Education
C. Planning Commission
D. University Grants Commission

25. The process of establishing headings and providing 'Cross references' is called

A. Access points
B. Headings
C. Authority control
D. Bibliographic Records

26. Which set of rules is applicable for exchange of files over Internet?

A. FTP/IP B. HTTP
C. HTML D. HYPERLINK

27. The first printed works are called

A. Impensis B. Incunabula
C. Impression D. Imprimatur

28. Which Law of Library Science, restated with emphasis on information as a dynamic, continuum and never ending phenomenon?

A. Fifth Law B. Fourth Law
C. Third Law D. Second Law

29. Andrew Carnegie donated two million pounds for development of ________.

A. Library Collection
B. Library Building

C. Library Furniture
D. Library Staff

30. Whose model of communication of knowledge suggests that communication as an open system may be regarded as subjective, selective, variable and yet unpredictable?
A. G. Gerbner
B. Juger Hebermans
C. E Shanon & Weaver
D. M. Foucault

31. Which Committee/Commission recommended that Imperial Library be designated as Copyright Library?
A. Fayzee Commission, 1939
B. Riche Committee, 1926
C. Statham Committee, 1932
D. Sadler Committee, 1916

32. What are the four entities of FRBR model?
A. Personality, Matter, Energy, Space
B. Books, Form, Availability, Type
C. Work, Expression, Manifestation, Item
D. Discipline, Entity, Action, Personality

33. Who said that information is both a product and process?
A. S.R. Ranganathan B. J. Martin
C. D.J. Foskett D. S.C. Bradford

34. The process of planning, allocating, organizing and evaluating library tasks and activities within the framework of major objectives, mission and policy refers to
A. Functional control
B. Functional Classification
C. Functional Approach
D. Functional Authority

35. One of the authorized user makes bulk downloading of a Journal using robots and consequently licensor blocks access of the journal. What may be the most appropriate action(s) that librarian should initiate?
(*i*) Cancellation of authentication of the said user.
(*ii*) Asking the licensor for blocking up the access without prior information.
(*iii*) Investigate and take corrective measures.
(*iv*) Notify user community of user restrictions.

Codes:
A. (*ii*), (*iv*) are correct.
B. (*ii*), (*iii*) are correct.
C. (*i*), (*iii*) are correct.
D. (*i*), (*ii*) are correct.

36. The purposes of Metadata are
(*i*) Unique identification
(*ii*) Authentication of records
(*iii*) Shelf arrangement
(*iv*) Shows the collection of a library

Codes:
A. (*i*), (*ii*) are correct.
B. (*ii*), (*iii*) are correct.
C. (*iii*), (*iv*) are correct.
D. (*iv*), (*i*) are correct.

37. The primary difference between knowledge classification and library classification are
(*i*) Knowledge classification arranges knowledge itself.
(*ii*) Library classification arranges the expression of knowledge in the form of documents.
(*iii*) Knowledge classification is the basis of Library Classification.
(*iv*) Knowledge classification follows system of numbers, called notation.

Codes:
A. (*i*) and (*ii*) are correct.
B. (*ii*) and (*iii*) are correct.
C. (*i*), (*ii*) and (*iv*) are correct.
D. (*i*), (*ii*) and (*iii*) are correct.

38. Which of the following activities are supported by UGC ?
(*i*) Facilitating increased access to information.
(*ii*) Monitoring the implementation of revised curriculum.
(*iii*) Making policies for human resource development.
(*iv*) Funding all academic libraries.

Codes :
A. (*i*) and (*ii*) are correct.
B. (*i*) and (*iii*) are correct.
C. (*ii*) and (*iii*) are correct.
D. (*i*) and (*iv*) are correct.

39. Which of the following methods are suitable to achieve quality of teaching, learning in LIS?

(*i*) Research-led teaching
(*ii*) State of the art computer lab
(*iii*) Problem-based learning
(*iv*) Introducing the course at degree level

Codes :

A. (*ii*) and (*iv*)
B. (*i*), (*iii*) and (*iv*)
C. (*i*) and (*iii*)
D. (*iii*) and (*iv*)

40. Poor 'Accessibility' and less 'affordability' of journal subscription in print era led to

(*i*) High allocation of funds for serials
(*ii*) Open access movement
(*iii*) Decrease in subscription of journals
(*iv*) E-journal consortia subscription

Codes:

A. (*i*) & (*ii*) are correct.
B. (*i*), (*ii*), (*iv*) are correct.
C. (*ii*), (*iv*) are correct.
D. (*i*), (*ii*), (*iii*) are correct.

41. The alternatives and modifications to H-Index are

(*i*) I-index
(*ii*) Pure-h Index
(*iii*) Scimgo Journal Rank
(*iv*) European Impact Factor

Codes:

A. (*i*) & (*iii*) are correct.
B. (*i*) & (*ii*) are correct.
C. (*i*) and (*iv*) are correct.
D. (*ii*) & (*iii*) are correct.

42. Digitization of various cultural resources is possible through

(*i*) Scanners
(*ii*) Digital cameras
(*iii*) Video cameras
(*iv*) Smart & Mobile phones

Codes:

A. (*i*), (*ii*) are correct.
B. (*iv*), (*iii*) are correct.
C. (*iii*), (*iv*) are correct.
D. (*i*), (*ii*), (*iii*) & (*iv*) are correct.

43. What is/are not common feature/s between RFID & Barcode Technology?

(*i*) Read more than one item at a time
(*ii*) Able to locate specific items on shelves
(*iii*) Programmable
(*iv*) Read while item is moving

Codes:

A. (*i*), (*ii*) are correct.
B. (*iii*), (*iv*) are correct.
C. (*ii*), (*iv*) are correct.
D. All the above are correct.

44. When a librarian has to show the rationale for the purchase of more e-resources, which of the following/s will help to support his/her stand?

(*i*) Collection development policy
(*ii*) Indent from users
(*iii*) Book selection tools
(*iv*) All the above

Codes:

A. (*i*) and (*ii*) are correct.
B. (*i*) and (*iii*) are correct.
C. (*ii*) and (*iii*) are correct.
D. (*iv*) is correct.

45. Assertion (A) : Machine translation is not a fully dependable service.

Reason (R) : The semantics of languages are not fully encoded in algorithms.

Codes:

A. (A) is true, but (R) is false.
B. Both (A) & (R) are true.
C. (A) is false, but (R) is true.
D. Both (A) & (R) are false.

46. Match the following :

	List-I		*List-II*
a.	INFLIBNET	i.	Digital Library
b.	INDESTAICTE	ii.	Resource aggregator
c.	DELNET	iii.	E-consortia
d.	e-Gyankosh	iv.	Organisation

Codes:

	(*a*)	(*b*)	(*c*)	(*d*)
A.	(*i*)	(*ii*)	(*iii*)	(*iv*)
B.	(*iv*)	(*iii*)	(*ii*)	(*i*)
C.	(*iii*)	(*ii*)	(*i*)	(*iv*)
D.	(*ii*)	(*iii*)	(*iv*)	(*i*)

47. Match the following :

List-I	List-II
(*a*) Amenable to further algebraic treatment	(*i*) Mean deviation
(*b*) Estimated without knowing values of extreme items	(*ii*) Median
(*c*) Mathematically and logically incorrect	(*iii*) Inter-quartile deviation
(*d*) The dispersion does not cover all items of a series	(*iv*) Arithmetic means

Codes:

	(*a*)	(*b*)	(*c*)	(*d*)
A.	(*iv*)	(*ii*)	(*i*)	(*iii*)
B.	(*iii*)	(*ii*)	(*i*)	(*iv*)
C.	(*ii*)	(*iv*)	(*iii*)	(*i*)
D.	(*i*)	(*iii*)	(*iv*)	(*ii*)

48. Match the following :

List-I	List-II
a. Trade Publisher	i. UNESCO
b. Subject book publisher	ii. American Psychological Society
c. Government Press	iii. Harper Collins
d. Scholarly Publisher	iv. W.B. Saunders

Codes:

	(*a*)	(*b*)	(*c*)	(*d*)
A.	(*ii*)	(*iv*)	(*iii*)	(*i*)
B.	(*iv*)	(*iii*)	(*i*)	(*ii*)
C.	(*i*)	(*iv*)	(*iii*)	(*ii*)
D.	(*iii*)	(*iv*)	(*i*)	(*ii*)

49. Match the following :

List-I	List-II
(*a*) Statistical Quality/Process Control (SQC/SPC)	(*i*) Identify the intensity of each problem in the production process
(*b*) Check Sheets	(*ii*) Selected variables checked
(*c*) Pareto Chart	(*iii*) Identify the relationship between problems and causes
(*d*) Fish Bone Diagram	(*iv*) Record variables in the production process

Codes:

	(*a*)	(*b*)	(*c*)	(*d*)
A.	(*ii*)	(*iv*)	(*i*)	(*iii*)
B.	(*iv*)	(*ii*)	(*iii*)	(*i*)
C.	(*iii*)	(*iv*)	(*i*)	(*ii*)
D.	(*i*)	(*ii*)	(*iv*)	(*iii*)

50. Match the following :

List-I	List-II
(*a*) Sinha Committee	(*i*) Library staff strength
(*b*) Dr. S.R. Ranganathan Committee	(*ii*) Central Medical Library
(*c*) Report of Dr. Shaw and Dr. D. B. Krishna Rao	(*iii*) Libraries at Panchayat, Block, District and State level
(*d*) Dr. J. Bhore Committee	(*iv*) National Agricultural System of Agriculture Libraries

Codes:

	(*a*)	(*b*)	(*c*)	(*d*)
A.	(*iii*)	(*i*)	(*ii*)	(*iv*)
B.	(*iv*)	(*iii*)	(*ii*)	(*i*)
C.	(*iii*)	(*i*)	(*iv*)	(*ii*)
D.	(*i*)	(*iii*)	(*ii*)	(*iv*)

51. Match the following :

List-I	List-II
(*a*) Finding solution to the problem of pilferage in libraries	(*i*) Historical Research
(*b*) Implementation of cloud computing services in special libraries	(*ii*) Action Research

(*c*) A study of mathematician turned librarian — (*iii*) Experimental Research

(*d*) Use of web resources in Central Universities of India — (*iv*) Survey Research

Codes:

	(*a*)	(*b*)	(*c*)	(*d*)
A.	(*ii*)	(*iii*)	(*i*)	(*iv*)
B.	(*iii*)	(*ii*)	(*iv*)	(*i*)
C.	(*iv*)	(*i*)	(*ii*)	(*iii*)
D.	(*i*)	(*iv*)	(*iii*)	(*ii*)

52. Match the following :

	List-I		*List-II*
(*a*)	Internal Files	(*i*)	.WPD
(*b*)	Universal File Format	(*ii*)	.OeB
(*c*)	Corel's Word Perfect	(*iii*)	.HTML
(*d*)	Microsoft Reader	(*iv*)	.RTF

Codes:

	(*a*)	(*b*)	(*c*)	(*d*)
A.	(*i*)	(*iii*)	(*ii*)	(*iv*)
B.	(*ii*)	(*iv*)	(*iii*)	(*i*)
C.	(*iv*)	(*ii*)	(*i*)	(*iii*)
D.	(*iii*)	(*iv*)	(*i*)	(*ii*)

53. Match the following :

	List-I		*List-II*
(*a*)	Classical Models	(*i*)	Ruesch and Bateson's Functional Model
(*b*)	Linear Model	(*ii*)	Aristotle
(*c*)	Non-linear Model	(*iii*)	Lasswell
(*d*)	Multidimensional	(*iv*)	Westley and Mackan's Conceptual Model

Codes:

	(*a*)	(*b*)	(*c*)	(*d*)
A.	(*ii*)	(*iii*)	(*iv*)	(*i*)
B.	(*ii*)	(*iv*)	(*i*)	(*iii*)
C.	(*i*)	(*ii*)	(*iii*)	(*iv*)
D.	(*iii*)	(*ii*)	(*iv*)	(*i*)

54. Match the following :

	List-I		*List-II*
(*a*)	Henri La Fontaine	(*i*)	Expansive Classification
(*b*)	H.E. Bliss	(*ii*)	Bibliographic Classification
(*c*)	C.A. Cutter	(*iii*)	LC
(*d*)	J.C.M. Hansar	(*iv*)	UDC

Codes:

	(*a*)	(*b*)	(*c*)	(*d*)
A.	(*iv*)	(*ii*)	(*i*)	(*iii*)
B.	(*iii*)	(*ii*)	(*iv*)	(*i*)
C.	(*ii*)	(*iv*)	(*i*)	(*iii*)
D.	(*i*)	(*iii*)	(*ii*)	(*iv*)

55. Match the following :

	List-I		*List-II*
(*a*)	PDFA	(*i*)	High colour depth images
(*b*)	HTML	(*ii*)	Rules for encoding documents electronically
(*c*)	TIFF	(*iii*)	File format for long term archiving
(*d*)	XML	(*iv*)	Language for web pages

Codes:

	(*a*)	(*b*)	(*c*)	(*d*)
A.	(*ii*)	(*iii*)	(*i*)	(*iv*)
B.	(*iii*)	(*iv*)	(*i*)	(*ii*)
C.	(*i*)	(*iii*)	(*ii*)	(*iv*)
D.	(*iv*)	(*ii*)	(*iii*)	(*i*)

56. Match the books against their authors :

	List-I		*List-II*
(*a*)	Introduction to Modern Information Retrieval (McGraw Hill)	(*i*)	H. Borko & C. Bernier
(*b*)	Indexing Concepts and Methods (Academic Press)	(*ii*)	G. Salton & M.J. McGill
(*c*)	Thesaurus Construction : A Practical Manual (Aslib)	(*iii*)	J.E. Rowley & R. Hartley

(*d*) Organising Knowledge : An Introduction to Managing Access to Information (Ashgate) — (*iv*) J. Aitchison & A. Gilchrist

Codes:

	(*a*)	(*b*)	(*c*)	(*d*)
A.	(*i*)	(*ii*)	(*iii*)	(*iv*)
B.	(*ii*)	(*i*)	(*iv*)	(*iii*)
C.	(*iv*)	(*i*)	(*ii*)	(*iii*)
D.	(*iii*)	(*i*)	(*iv*)	(*ii*)

57. Match the following :

List-I	*List-II*
(*a*) Papyrus	(*i*) Assyria & Babylonia
(*b*) Handmade paper	(*ii*) Egypt
(*c*) Clay tablets	(*iii*) Medieval Europe
(*d*) Vellum/ Parchment	(*iv*) China

Codes:

	(*a*)	(*b*)	(*c*)	(*d*)
A.	(*ii*)	(*iv*)	(*i*)	(*iii*)
B.	(*iv*)	(*ii*)	(*iii*)	(*i*)
C.	(*iii*)	(*iv*)	(*i*)	(*ii*)
D.	(*iii*)	(*ii*)	(*iv*)	(*i*)

58. Match the following :

List-I	*List-II*
(*a*) Icon	(*i*) Character strings
(*b*) Menus	(*ii*) Select objects on the screen
(*c*) Dialogue Bou	(*iii*) Bit mapped region
(*d*) Pointing devices	(*iv*) Obtain information from the end users

Codes:

	(*a*)	(*b*)	(*c*)	(*d*)
A.	(*i*)	(*ii*)	(*iii*)	(*iv*)
B.	(*iii*)	(*iv*)	(*ii*)	(*i*)
C.	(*ii*)	(*iii*)	(*iv*)	(*i*)
D.	(*iii*)	(*i*)	(*iv*)	(*ii*)

59. Match the following :

List-I	*List-II*
(*a*) Resource Description	(*i*) MARC
(*b*) Resource Discovery	(*ii*) ISO 10160/10161
(*c*) Resource Exchange	(*iii*) Dublin Care
(*d*) Interlibrary Loan	(*iv*) Z 39.50

Codes:

	(*a*)	(*b*)	(*c*)	(*d*)
A.	(*ii*)	(*i*)	(*iv*)	(*iii*)
B.	(*iv*)	(*ii*)	(*i*)	(*iii*)
C.	(*iii*)	(*iv*)	(*ii*)	(*i*)
D.	(*iii*)	(*iv*)	(*i*)	(*ii*)

60. Match the following :

List-I	*List-II*
(*a*) Public Library Extension	(*i*) KD Metcalf
(*b*) Academic Library Management	(*ii*) M A Gelfand
(*c*) University Libraries for Developing Countries	(*iii*) L R McColvin
(*d*) Planning Academic and Research Library Buildings	(*iv*) M B Line

Codes:

	(*a*)	(*b*)	(*c*)	(*d*)
A.	(*iii*)	(*iv*)	(*ii*)	(*i*)
B.	(*iv*)	(*ii*)	(*i*)	(*iii*)
C.	(*iii*)	(*i*)	(*iv*)	(*ii*)
D.	(*ii*)	(*iii*)	(*i*)	(*iv*)

61. Match the following :

List-I	*List-II*
(*a*) Indian Cultural Heritage	(*i*) TKDL
(*b*) Race & Brittle documents	(*ii*) IGNCA
(*c*) Traditional Knowledge	(*iii*) C-DAC
(*d*) Mobile Digital Library	(*iv*) National Library

Codes:

	(*a*)	(*b*)	(*c*)	(*d*)
A.	(*i*)	(*iv*)	(*iii*)	(*ii*)
B.	(*iv*)	(*iii*)	(*ii*)	(*i*)
C.	(*ii*)	(*iv*)	(*i*)	(*iii*)
D.	(*iii*)	(*ii*)	(*iv*)	(*i*)

62. Match the following :

List-I	*List-II*
(*a*) Carol Kuhlthau	(*i*) 8 stages
(*b*) David Ellis	(*ii*) ISB is a 6 stage process
(*c*) M.J. Belkin	(*iii*) ISB is of 8 key activities
(*d*) Marchionnini	(*iv*) ISB is 4 dimension characteristic

Codes:

	(*a*)	(*b*)	(*c*)	(*d*)
A.	(*ii*)	(*iii*)	(*iv*)	(*i*)
B.	(*ii*)	(*iii*)	(*i*)	(*iv*)
C.	(*iii*)	(*i*)	(*iv*)	(*ii*)
D.	(*iv*)	(*ii*)	(*i*)	(*iii*)

63. Assertion (A) : Colon classification is popular in online catalogues.

Reason (R) : Traditional classification systems are used in online searching advantageously.

Codes:
A. (A) is true, but (R) is false.
B. Both (A) & (R) are true, but (R) is not the correct explanation ofA.
C. (A) is false, but (R) is true.
D. Both (A) & (R) are true.

64. Assertion (A) : Technical writing standards, style manuals and citation standards are very essential in structuring the research report.

Reason (R) : Value will get enhanced by standardising the structure of research report.

Codes:
A. (A) is true and (R) is partially true.
B. Both (A) and (R) are true.
C. Both (A) and (R) are false.
D. (A) is true and (R) is false.

65. Assertion (A) : The encouraging environment of all time, full reading halls with the students in the libraries is diminishing day by day.

Reason (R) : All the reading material is easily available and accessible on Internet to all the students.

Codes:
A. Both (A) and (R) are true.
B. Both (A) and (R) are false.
C. (A) is true, but (R) is false.
D. (A) is false, but (R) is true.

66. Assertion (A) : There is a tremendous increase in number of doctoral degrees being awarded in library and information science.

Reason (R) : Any academician in LIS holding a Ph.D degree is entitled to supervise research programme.

Codes:
A. (A) is true and (R) is partially true.
B. Both (A) and (R) are true.
C. Both (A) and (R) are false.
D. (A) is false and (R) is true.

67. Assertion (A) : The information seeking behaviour research at the current times is on the social and cultural context of human interaction with information.

Reason (R) : Attempt is being made to interpret social and cultural experiences of individuals with respect to their information seeking and searching experiences.

Codes:
A. (A) is true and (R) is false.
B. Both (A) and (R) are false.
C. (A) is false and (R) is true.
D. Both (A) and (R) are true.

68. Assertion (A) : With the emergence of Internet, there is no need for reference service in this technology-based era.

Reason (R) : Internet has allowed access to every one to seek his/her information from anywhere, any time.

Codes:
A. Both (A) and (R) are true.
B. Both (A) and (R) are false.
C. (A) is false but (R) is partially true.
D. (A) is true, but (R) is false.

69. Assertion (A) : Micrographic services have lost acceptance for preservation and dissemination of archival material.

Reason (R) : ICT has brought in cost effective alternatives and replaced micrographic services.

Codes:
A. (A) is true and (R) is partially true.
B. Both (A) & (R) are false.
C. (A) is true, (R) is false.
D. (A) is false, (R) is true.

70. Assertion (A) : Institutions generate information through research and development activities.

Reason (R) : All such generated information forms the grey literature.

Codes:

A. Both (A) and (R) are true.
B. Both (A) and (R) are false.
C. (A) is true, (R) is partially true.
D. (A) is false, (R) is true.

71. Assertion (A) : Maximizing the access to information in higher education is the motto of UGC INFONET Project.

Reason (R) : The financial grants of UGC-INFONET are not being fully utilized by all University Libraries for the assigned purpose.

Codes:

A. Both (A) and (R) are false.
B. (A) is true and (R) is partially true.
C. (A) is true and (R) is false.
D. (A) is false and (R) is true.

72. Assertion (A) : The effective reprographic service in libraries indirectly demotivates the user for tearing/theft of reading material.

Reason (R) : The user gets the photocopy of reading materials free of cost.

Codes:

A. (A) is false and (R) is true.
B. Both (A) and (R) are true.
C. (A) is true and (R) is false.
D. Both (A) and (R) are false.

73. Assertion (A) : RFID technology is still not widely installed in Indian Library Environment.

Reason (R) : The standardization, application and innovation are constantly changing.

Codes:

A. Both (A) & (R) are true and (R) is the correct explanation of (A).
B. Both (A) & (R) are true, but (R) is not the correct explanation of (A).
C. (A) is true, but (R) is false.
D. (A) is false, but (R) is true.

74. Assertion (A) : Gap device is a non-scientific solution to the problem of growing universe.

Reason (R) : A classificationist cannot forecast the areas/ subjects wherein some new ones may emerge.

Codes:

A. (A) and (R) are true.
B. (A) is true and (R) is false.
C. (A) is false and (R) is true.
D. (A) and (R) are false.

75. Assertion (A) : All the states in India have enacted library legislation.

Reason (R) : NKC recommends for the enactment of library legislation in all the states.

Codes:

A. Both (A) and (R) are true.
B. Both (A) and (R) are false.
C. (A) is true, but (R) is false.
D. (A) is false, but (R) is true.

ANSWERS

1	2	3	4	5	6	7	8	9	10
A	C	B	C	B	C	A	B	D	C
11	**12**	**13**	**14**	**15**	**16**	**17**	**18**	**19**	**20**
C	D	D	C	A	C	D	C	A	B
21	**22**	**23**	**24**	**25**	**26**	**27**	**28**	**29**	**30**
C	D	C	B	C	B	B	A	B	A
31	**32**	**33**	**34**	**35**	**36**	**37**	**38**	**39**	**40**
B	C	B	C	D	A	D	B	C	C
41	**42**	**43**	**44**	**45**	**46**	**47**	**48**	**49**	**50**
B	D	D	A	B	B	A	D	A	C
51	**52**	**53**	**54**	**55**	**56**	**57**	**58**	**59**	**60**
A	D	A	A	B	D	A	D	D	A
61	**62**	**63**	**64**	**65**	**66**	**67**	**68**	**69**	**70**
C	A	C	A	C	A	D	C	A	C
71	**72**	**73**	**74**	**75**					
B	C	B	A	D					

Previous Paper (Solved)

UGC-NET LIBRARY AND INFORMATION SCIENCE, DECEMBER 2012

PAPER-II

Note: *This paper contains **fifty** (50) objective type questions, each question carrying **two** (2) marks. Attempt **all** the questions.*

1. According to Machlup the difference between information and knowledge is

A. Information increases with use, whereas knowledge is constant.

B. Information is stimulatory, whereas knowledge is practical.

C. Information is shareable, whereas knowledge is one's property.

D. Information is piecemeal, fragmented, particular, whereas knowledge is structured, coherent and universal.

2. "Web of Science" is

A. A Citation Index

B. A Bibliography

C. An Abstracting Service

D. All of the above

3. *"Facts on File"* can be grouped under

A. Primary source B. Secondary source

C. Tertiary source D. None of the above

4. In MARC 21, subject access fields are

A. 3xx B. 4xx

C. 5xx D. 6xx

5. Transformation of traditional libraries to hybrid / digital libraries is

A. Crisis Management

B. Re-engineering

C. Change Management

D. Project Management

6. Which one of the following is not a switching system?

A. Packet B. Circuit

C. Router D. Message

7. Access to back volumes of E-journals is known as ______.

A. Random Access

B. Perpetual Access

C. Online Access

D. Retrospective Access

8. The chi-square technique is used to compare the observed data with that of

A. Collected raw data B. Expected data

C. Analysed data D. Graphical data

9. 'Parry Committee' (UK) was set up to advise

A. School Libraries

B. Public Libraries

C. Special Libraries

D. University Libraries

10. FRBR is developed by

A. LC B. UNESCO

C. IFLA D. FID

11. Who were involved in Public Library Movement in India?

(*i*) Sayaji Rao Gaekwad II

(*ii*) C.D. Deshmukh

(*iii*) S. Radhakrishnan

(*iv*) S.R. Ranganathan

Codes :

A. (*i*) & (*iii*) are correct

B. (*ii*) & (*iv*) are correct

C. (*i*) & (*iv*) are correct

D. (*ii*) & (*iii*) are correct

12. Which of the following are library networks?

(*i*) Internet (*ii*) DELNET

(*iii*) NICNET (*iv*) OCLC

Codes:

A. *(i)* and *(ii)* are correct.
B. *(ii)* and *(iv)* are correct.
C. *(i)* and *(iii)* are correct.
D. *(i)* and *(iv)* are correct.

13. Which of the following are review type services?

(i) Current Awareness
(ii) Trend Reports
(iii) News Clippings
(iv) State of the Art Report

Codes:

A. *(i)*, *(ii)*, *(iii)* are correct.
B. *(i)*, *(iii)*, *(iv)* are correct.
C. *(ii)* & *(iv)* are correct.
D. *(ii)* & *(iii)* are correct.

14. The basic characteristics of a system are

(i) Interrelated components
(ii) Independent and can stand alone
(iii) Arranged in hierarchical order
(iv) Inputs, processes, outputs & feed back

Codes:

A. *(i)*, *(ii)*, *(iii)* are correct.
B. *(i)*, *(ii)*, *(iv)* are correct.
C. *(ii)*, *(iii)*, *(iv)* are correct.
D. *(i)*, *(iii)*, *(iv)* are correct.

15. The general image file formats are :

(i) TIFF *(ii)* JPEG
(iii) MPEG *(iv)* PNG

Codes:

A. *(i)*, *(ii)* and *(iii)* are correct.
B. *(i)*, *(iii)* and *(iv)* are correct.
C. *(i)*, *(ii)* and *(iv)* are correct.
D. *(ii)*, *(iii)* and *(iv)* are correct.

16. Which of the following are common types of protocols?

(i) HTTP *(ii)* FTP
(iii) Telnet *(iv)* Gopher

Codes:

A. *(i)* and *(ii)* are correct.
B. *(i)*, *(ii)* and *(iv)* are correct.
C. *(iii)* and *(iv)* are correct.
D. *(i)*, *(ii)* and *(iii)* are correct.

17. Which of the following are not the elements of DOI system?

(i) Policies
(ii) Subject
(iii) Description
(iv) Resolution

Codes:

A. *(i)*, *(ii)* and *(iii)* are correct.
B. *(i)*, *(iii)* and *(iv)* are correct.
C. *(i)*, *(ii)* and *(iv)* are correct.
D. *(ii)*, *(iii)* and *(iv)* are correct.

18. Which of the following are Trade Bibliographies?

(i) Books-in-Print
(ii) Indian Books-in-Print
(iii) Indian National Bibliography
(iv) British National Bibliography

Codes:

A. *(i)* and *(iii)* are correct.
B. *(ii)* and *(iv)* are correct.
C. *(i)* and *(ii)* are correct.
D. *(ii)* and *(iii)* are correct.

19. Assertion (A) : Distance education for LIS courses is gaining ground in India.

Reason (R) : Majority of people prefer it as an alternative channel of education.

Codes:

A. (A) is true but (R) is false.
B. (A) is false but (R) is true.
C. Both (A) and (R) are correct.
D. Both (A) and (R) are wrong.

20. Assertion (A) : Indian libraries are making optimum use of social networking.

Reason (R) : Social networking has wider role in dissemination of information.

Codes:

A. (A) is true but (R) is false.
B. (A) is false but (R) is true.
C. (A) and (R) both are true.
D. (A) and (R) both are false.

21. Assertion (A) : Knowledge is growing exponentially.

Reason (R) : Number of researchers have increased.

Codes:

A. Both (A) & (R) are true.
B. Both (A) and (R) are false.

C. (A) is false but (R) is true.
D. (A) is true but (R) is false.

22. Assertion (A) : Present decade has accepted E-journals as channels of fast communication.

Reason (R) : E-publications have added enormous quantity of literature but affected the quality of research.

Codes:
A. (A) is true but (R) is false.
B. (A) is false but (R) is true.
C. Both (A) and (R) are true and (R) is the correct explanation.
D. Both (A) and (R) are true, but (R) is not a correct explanation.

23. Assertion (A) : Library & Information centres are knowledge/management centres.

Reason (R) : Libraries handle tacit knowledge.

Codes:
A. Both (A) and (R) are true.
B. (A) is partially true, but (R) is false.
C. (A) is false, but (R) is true.
D. Both (A) and (R) are false.

24. Assertion (A) : Metadata hold much promise for information retrieval and access in the digital age.

Reason (R) : Metadata can save a number of functions including description, resource discovery and management of resources.

Codes:
A. (A) is true, but (R) is false.
B. (A) is false, but (R) is true.
C. Both (A) and (R) are true.
D. Both (A) and (R) are false.

25. Assertion (A) : Training methods through brain storming stimulate idea generation.

Reason (R) : Training methods do not provide opportunity to unskilled to become skilled.

Codes:
A. (A) is false but (R) is true.
B. Both (A) and (R) are false.
C. Both (A) and (R) are true.
D. (A) is true but (R) is false.

26. Assertion (A) : Random samples are not representative of the whole population.

Reason (R) : Random numbers are used in forming a random sample.

Codes:
A. (A) is true, but (R) is false.
B. (A) is false, but (R) is true.
C. Both (A) and (R) are true.
D. Both (A) and (R) are false.

27. Assertion (A) : Information Literacy is a basic skill essential for work environment in 21st century.

Reason (R) : Information Literacy helps to train the users to make use of ICT.

Codes:
A. Both (A) and (R) are true.
B. Both (A) and (R) are false.
C. (A) is true, but (R) is false.
D. (A) is false, but (R) is true.

28. Arrange the following according to their year of first publication:
(*i*) Bliss Classification
(*ii*) Dewey Decimal Classification
(*iii*) Library of Congress Classification
(*iv*) Universal Decimal Classification.

Codes :
A. (*i*), (*ii*), (*iii*), (*iv*) B. (*i*), (*iii*), (*ii*), (*iv*)
C. (*iii*), (*i*), (*iv*), (*ii*) D. (*ii*), (*iv*), (*i*), (*iii*)

29. Arrange the following IFLA programmes according to their year of commencement :
(*i*) UBC
(*ii*) UAP
(*iii*) ISBD
(*iv*) International MARC Office

Codes:
A. (*i*), (*iv*), (*iii*), (*ii*) B. (*ii*), (*iv*), (*i*), (*iii*)
C. (*iv*), (*i*), (*ii*), (*iii*) D. (*iii*), (*i*), (*ii*), (*iv*)

30. Arrange the following according to their year of origin:
(*i*) Indian National Bibliography
(*ii*) British National Bibliography
(*iii*) Cumulative Book Index
(*iv*) Books in Print

Codes:

A. (*i*), (*iii*), (*iv*), (*ii*) B. (*ii*), (*i*), (*iii*), (*iv*)
C. (*iv*), (*iii*), (*ii*), (*i*) D. (*iii*), (*iv*), (*ii*), (*i*)

31. Arrange the following in a chronological order according to their year of establishment :

(*i*) Library of Congress
(*ii*) NISCAIR
(*iii*) Delivery of Books Act
(*iv*) National Library of India

Codes:

A. (*iii*), (*iv*), (*ii*), (*i*) B. (*ii*), (*iii*), (*i*), (*iv*)
C. (*i*), (*iv*), (*iii*), (*ii*) D. (*iv*), (*i*), (*iii*), (*ii*)

32. Arrange the following bibliographical standards according to their year of development:

(*i*) ISBD (*ii*) MARC
(*iii*) Dublin Core (*iv*) RDF

Codes:

A. (*i*), (*iii*), (*ii*), (*iv*) B. (*ii*), (*i*), (*iv*), (*iii*)
C. (*iii*), (*ii*), (*iv*), (*i*) D. None of these

33. Arrange the following according to their year of origin :

(*i*) UNICODE (*ii*) XML
(*iii*) HTML (*iv*) SGML

Codes:

A. (*iv*), (*iii*), (*i*), (*ii*) B. (*iii*), (*iv*), (*ii*), (*i*)
C. (*ii*), (*iv*), (*i*), (*iii*) D. (*i*), (*ii*), (*iii*), (*iv*)

34. Arrange the following in order of their year of establishment :

(*i*) INIS (*ii*) AGRIS
(*iii*) MEDLARS (*iv*) UNESCO

Codes:

A. (*iii*), (*i*), (*iv*), (*ii*) B. (*ii*), (*iv*), (*i*), (*iii*)
C. (*iv*), (*iii*), (*ii*), (*i*) D. None of these

35. Arrange the following according to their year of enactment :

(*i*) Tamil Nadu Public Library Act
(*ii*) Kerala Public Library Act
(*iii*) Maharashtra Public Library Act
(*iv*) Orissa Public Library Act

Codes:

A. (*i*), (*iii*), (*ii*), (*iv*) B. (*ii*), (*iii*), (*iv*), (*i*)
C. (*ii*), (*iii*), (*i*), (*iv*) D. (*iv*), (*iii*), (*ii*), (*i*)

36. Match the following :

List-I	*List-II*
(*a*) 'Guide to Use of Books and Libraries'	(*i*) F.W. Lancaster
(*b*) 'If You Want to Evaluate Your Library'	(*ii*) A.C. Foskelt
(*c*) 'Cuneiform to Computer : A History of Reference Sources'	(*iii*) Jean K. Gates
(*d*) 'Subject Approach to Information'	(*iv*) William A. Katz

Codes:

	(*a*)	(*b*)	(*c*)	(*d*)
A.	(*ii*)	(*iii*)	(*iv*)	(*i*)
B.	(*i*)	(*iv*)	(*iii*)	(*ii*)
C.	(*iii*)	(*i*)	(*iv*)	(*ii*)
D.	(*iv*)	(*ii*)	(*i*)	(*iii*)

37. Match the following :

List-I	*List-II*
(*a*) Directory	(*i*) Information Please Almanac
(*b*) Annuals	(*ii*) Keesing's Record of World Events
(*c*) Bibliography	(*iii*) Encyclopaedia of Associations
(*d*) News paper Digest	(*iv*) Publishers' Weekly

Codes:

	(*a*)	(*b*)	(*c*)	(*d*)
A.	(*iii*)	(*i*)	(*iv*)	(*ii*)
B.	(*i*)	(*iii*)	(*iv*)	(*ii*)
C.	(*iii*)	(*ii*)	(*iv*)	(*i*)
D.	(*iv*)	(*i*)	(*ii*)	(*iii*)

38. Match the following :

List-I	*List-II*
(*a*) Guiding users to the place of information	(*i*) Digest
(*b*) Guiding users in the use of information	(*ii*) User orientation

(c)	Alerting users with the latest arrivals	(iii)	Referral
(d)	Providing users with summarised information	(iv)	Current Awareness

Codes:

	(a)	(b)	(c)	(d)
A.	(iii)	(iv)	(i)	(ii)
B.	(iii)	(ii)	(iv)	(i)
C.	(iv)	(i)	(iii)	(ii)
D.	(ii)	(i)	(iii)	(iv)

39. Match the following:

	List-I		List-II
(a)	B.S. Kesvan	(i)	School of librarianship
(b)	Paul Otlet	(ii)	National Library of India
(c)	W.C.B. Sayers	(iii)	UDC
(d)	M. Taube	(iv)	Uniterm Indexing

Codes:

	(a)	(b)	(c)	(d)
A.	(ii)	(iii)	(i)	(iv)
B.	(iii)	(ii)	(i)	(iv)
C.	(ii)	(iii)	(iv)	(i)
D.	(iv)	(ii)	(iii)	(i)

40. Match the following:

	List-I		List-II
(a)	Theory of Motivation	(i)	Factor of planning
(b)	Unity of Command	(ii)	Efficiency and waste prevention
(c)	MBO	(iii)	Maslow
(d)	Forecasting	(iv)	Peter Drucker

Codes:

	(a)	(b)	(c)	(d)
A.	(i)	(ii)	(iii)	(iv)
B.	(iv)	(i)	(ii)	(iii)
C.	(ii)	(iii)	(iv)	(i)
D.	(iii)	(iv)	(i)	(ii)

41. Match the following:

	List-I		List-II
(a)	Classification	(i)	LISA
(b)	Cataloguing	(ii)	UDC
(c)	Subject Heading	(iii)	AACR
(d)	Library Science Abstracts	(iv)	LCSH

Codes:

	(a)	(b)	(c)	(d)
A.	(ii)	(i)	(iv)	(iii)
B.	(ii)	(iii)	(iv)	(i)
C.	(iv)	(iii)	(i)	(ii)
D.	(ii)	(iv)	(i)	(iii)

42. Match the following:

	List-I (Budgetary technique)		List-II (Limitation of budgetary technique)
(a)	Line	(i)	Detailed information required
(b)	Formula	(ii)	Time consuming
(c)	PPBS	(iii)	Do not permit variation
(d)	Zero-based	(iv)	Do not suggest future

Codes:

	(a)	(b)	(c)	(d)
A.	(ii)	(i)	(iv)	(iii)
B.	(iii)	(ii)	(i)	(iv)
C.	(iv)	(iii)	(i)	(ii)
D.	(i)	(iv)	(ii)	(iii)

43. Match the following :

	List-I		List-II
(a)	File transfer protocol	(i)	Data transmission capacity
(b)	Multimedia	(ii)	Integration of text, colour, sound and animation
(c)	Bandwidth	(iii)	Bulletin Board
(d)	Electronic Notice Board	(iv)	Internet

Codes:

	(a)	(b)	(c)	(d)
A.	(iv)	(ii)	(i)	(iii)
B.	(i)	(iii)	(ii)	(iv)
C.	(ii)	(i)	(iv)	(iii)
D.	(i)	(iv)	(ii)	(iii)

44. Match the following:

	List-I		List-II
(a)	ISDN	(i)	Web page
(b)	URL	(ii)	Video Conferencing

(*c*) Firewall (*iii*) Internet Standard for Information Transmission

(*d*) HTTP (*iv*) Protecting unauthorised access internet

Codes:

	(*a*)	(*b*)	(*c*)	(*d*)
A.	(*iii*)	(*iv*)	(*i*)	(*ii*)
B.	(*iv*)	(*i*)	(*iii*)	(*ii*)
C.	(*ii*)	(*i*)	(*iv*)	(*iii*)
D.	(*i*)	(*iii*)	(*ii*)	(*iv*)

45. Match the following:

List-I	***List-II***
(*a*) OCLC	(*i*) Bio-Med
(*b*) INFLIBNET	(*ii*) Web-Dewey
(*c*) IISC	(*iii*) N-List
(*d*) NLM	(*iv*) Digital Library of India

Codes:

	(*a*)	(*b*)	(*c*)	(*d*)
A.	(*ii*)	(*iii*)	(*iv*)	(*i*)
B.	(*iii*)	(*i*)	(*ii*)	(*iv*)
C.	(*iv*)	(*ii*)	(*iii*)	(*i*)
D.	(*i*)	(*iii*)	(*iv*)	(*ii*)

Directions (Qs. Nos. 46 to 50): *Read the passage given below, and answer the questions based on your understanding of the passage.*

With the realization across the world that the global economy is going to be increasingly knowledge-based, science and technology have become the subject of discussion not just in classical ministries but also in ministries as diverse as commerce, industry and finance, and in case of United States, even in the State Department. In India, the Prime Minister has made frequent statements about the need to step up scientific research in the country.

Several large companies, including multi-nationals are outsourcing R & D programmes to India. This is partly because scientists are cheaper in India dollar for dollar, but also because India has a large pool of trained scientists. Industry data shows that R & D is now the third-largest segment in India's export of Information Technology (IT) services. Foreign companies have invested over $ 1 billion in research operations in India from 1998 to 2003 and another estimated $ 5 billion are in the pipeline. The United States is the biggest investor followed by Germany, France, Denmark and UK. Japan and China have also begun to invest in research programmes in India. Most foreign investment is being directed to research in computer sciences, pharmaceuticals, molecular chemistry, drug discovery, engineering and automotive design and biotechnology, including plant breeding.

Whereas, flow of foreign investments has enthused research institutions that are targeted for collaboration, there is also cause for concern. Although, India now attracts considerable foreign investment in R & D, it has no system in place for assessing how this investment is affecting the country's technological development. Nor is there any mechanism to monitor the impact of such investment on aspects such as skill development, sectoral capacity building etc. Do such foreign – funded research programmes benefit only the scientists and technicians in the form of better salaries and perks or do they also produce benefits for the country as a whole?

46. Focus on science and technology has increased because

A. Indian commerce and Finance Ministries are giving great importance to it.

B. World economy has become knowledge based.

C. US State Department gives priority on S & T.

D. Knowledge Commission has identified it as one of the potential area of development.

47. The following group of countries are the biggest investors in research:

A. U.S., Germany, India, Russia

B. Britain, France, U.S., India

C. France, Denmark, U.S.A., U.K.

D. Japan, China, India, Denmark

48. What is the cause of concern regarding foreign investment in research?

A. Scientists and technicians involved in research are not paid well.
B. There are insufficient institutions that can be targeted for research collaboration.
C. The benefit of such investments doesn't get transferred to India.
D. Sufficient methods to assess and evaluate the impact of such investment are not available.

49. Most foreign investment is being made in the area of
A. Microbiology and life sciences.
B. Computer science and automotive design.
C. Physical sciences and planting.
D. Grafting and biology.

50. Foreign companies are outsourcing R & D programmes to India because
A. Quality of research is quite high in India.
B. Outsourcing is cost effective for foreign companies.
C. There is scarcity of skilled manpower in those countries.
D. None of the above.

ANSWERS

1	2	3	4	5	6	7	8	9	10
D	A	B	D	C	C	B	B	D	C
11	**12**	**13**	**14**	**15**	**16**	**17**	**18**	**19**	**20**
C	B	C	D	C	D	B	C	C	B
21	**22**	**23**	**24**	**25**	**26**	**27**	**28**	**29**	**30**
A	C	B	C	D	B	C	A	D	D
31	**32**	**33**	**34**	**35**	**36**	**37**	**38**	**39**	**40**
C	D	A	D	A	C	A	B	A	D
41	**42**	**43**	**44**	**45**	**46**	**47**	**48**	**49**	**50**
B	C	A	C	A	B	C	D	B	B

PAPER-III

Note: *This paper contains seventy five (75) objective type questions of two (2) marks each. All questions are compulsory.*

1. Who categorized the user studies into the following three categories?
(*i*) Behaviour studies
(*ii*) Use studies
(*iii*) Information flow studies
A. Maurice B Line
B. Menzel
C. Cronin
D. Voigt

2. Which one of the following is not a virtual library?
A. Without walls.
B. With distributed physical locations.
C. Providing integrated and unified remote access to geographically distributed collections.
D. Which does not exist in reality.

3. In 1974, Zurkowski used for the first time which of the following term?
A. Digital Literacy
B. Media Literacy
C. Computer Literacy
D. Information Literacy

4. Who defined "to be information literate, a person must be able to recognize when information is needed and have the ability to locate, evaluate and use effectively the needed information"?

A. SLA B. ALA

C. IFLA D. CILIP

5. Which of the factor is not helping in limiting the external validity?
A. Reactive effect
B. Ecological validity
C. Interaction between selection bias of experimental variables
D. Ecological effect

6. Semantic differential scale is concerned with
A. Pool of items
B. Selection from two opposite positions
C. Five point scale
D. Selection from a check list

7. In spiral of scientific method, the span of Zenith to descendent is
A. Empirical phase
B. Hypothesizing phase
C. Deductive phase
D. Verification phase

8. Which of the following variable cannot be expressed in quantitative terms?
A. Socio-Economic status
B. Marital status
C. Numerical Aptitude
D. Professional Attitude

9. National Knowledge Network is to be implemented by
A. National Knowledge Commission
B. Information and Library Network
C. National Information Centre
D. Department of Information Technology

10. Metadata Dublin core refers to
A. Data elements in database
B. Bibliographic elements in database
C. Field elements in database
D. Subject elements in database

11. E-Journal articles can be identified with the help of
A. Digital Journal Identifier
B. Journal Source Identifier
C. Journal Article Identifier
D. Digital Object Identifier

12. Z39.50 is a standard for
A. Communication formats
B. Search and Retrieval services
C. Cataloguing Web Resources
D. Library Management Services

13. In context to modulation, PCM stands for
A. Pulse Code Modulation
B. Phase Control Modulation
C. Popular Code Modulation
D. Penultimate Code Modulation

14. ISO 9000 standard denotes the
A. consistence confirmance of a product or service to a given set of standard or expectations
B. Total customer satisfaction
C. Representation of stakeholders issues.
D. Detailed list of measuring techniques

15. The stages in the product life cycle curve are
A. Introduction, Growth, Maturity, Decline
B. Introduction, Growth, Maturity, Profit
C. Growth, Maturity, Profit, Decline
D. Introduction, Growth, Maturity, Saturation

16. The physical and chemical treatment of materials to retard their further deterioration refers to

A. Conservation B. Rescuing

C. Prevention D. Restoration

17. Read the following example and indicate the name of the indexing system used :

'Remuneration of teachers in French universities.'

The index headings are set as the following two lines :

France

Universities • Teachers • Remuneration

Universities • France

Teachers • Remuneration

A. Chain procedure
B. POPSI
C. PRECIS
D. KWIC

18. Research in automatic classification for information retrieval of term or cluster of terms is called
A. Evaluation theory
B. Theory of clumps
C. Time binding theory
D. Dynamic theory

19. As specified by AACR-II (R), the source of information for machine readable data file is
A. Internal user label
B. Title page
C. Colophone
D. Title frame

20. NICRYS is information system for
A. Machine tools B. Food science
C. Crystallography D. Drugs

21. The national convention regularly organized by DELNET is known as
A. CALIBER B. ICDL
C. NACLIN D. DELNETCON

22. Report on 'the development of digital libraries of the past decade' is categorized as
A. Review Report
B. Trend Report
C. Research Report
D. State of the Art Report

23. Name of the President of Sri Lanka can be found in
A. International who's who
B. Stateman's Yearbook
C. Who's who in the world
D. Wilson Biographies

24. Which of the following has stopped publishing in the print from since 2012?
A. Europa World Yearbook
B. Times of India Directory
C. New Encyclopedia Britannica
D. Keesing's Contemporary Archives

25. Which of the following is not providing encyclopedia type of information?
A. Encyclopedia of Associations
B. Compton's Encyclopedia
C. Worldbook Encyclopedia
D. Encyclopedia Americana

26. Who used the phrase 'control-access-directional type sources'?
A. R.E. Bopp B. B.C. Wynar
C. W.A. Katz D. R. Balay

27. Raja Rammohan Roy Library Foundation (RRRLF) was established by
A. Indian Library Association
B. Department of Culture, Govt. of India
C. Govt. of West Bengal
D. Ministry of Home Affairs, Govt. of India

28. Which State Public Library Act has the provision to collect library fund through land tax?
A. Tamil Nadu B. Karnataka
C. Andhra Pradesh D. None of these

29. Association of College and Research Libraries (ACRL) (USA) is a
A. Division of American Library Association
B. Independent Association for Academic & Research Libraries
C. Division of Special Libraries Association (USA)
D. Division of IFLA

30. Which of the following is not an implication of Fourth Law of Library Science?
A. Classified arrangement
B. Stack-room-guides
C. Issue Methods
D. Rural Library Services

31. Which one of the following is not a recommendation of National Knowledge Commission (India)?
A. Preparation of a National Census of Library
B. Encourage greater community participation in library management
C. Raja Rammohan Roy library foundation to act as the National co-ordination agency
D. Facilitate donation and maintenance of private collection

32. Digital library function incorporate :
(*i*) Creating and capturing
(*ii*) Storage and management
(*iii*) Search and access
(*iv*) Abstracting and reviewing

Codes:

A. (*i*), (*ii*) and (*iii*) are correct.
B. (*i*), (*iii*) and (*iv*) are correct.
C. (*ii*), (*iii*) and (*iv*) are correct.
D. (*i*), (*ii*) and (*iv*) are correct.

33. Which topology of computer network provides faster server access?

(*i*) BUS Network Topology
(*ii*) RING Network Topology
(*iii*) MULTIPLE RING Network Topology
(*iv*) STAR Network Topology

Codes:

A. (*i*) and (*ii*) are correct.
B. (*i*) and (*iii*) are correct.
C. (*ii*) and (*iii*) are correct.
D. (*ii*) and (*iv*) are correct.

34. Which of the following are ISDN services?

(*i*) RSS
(*ii*) Teletext
(*iii*) Voice mail
(*iv*) Video conference

Codes:

A. (*i*), (*iii*) and (*iv*) are correct.
B. (*i*), (*ii*) and (*iv*) are correct.
C. (*ii*), (*iii*) and (*iv*) are correct.
D. (*i*), (*ii*) and (*iii*) are correct.

35. Vocabulary in a database is controlled by :

(*i*) Thesaurus files
(*ii*) Import files
(*iii*) Standard files
(*iv*) Authority files

Codes:

A. (*i*) and (*ii*) are correct.
B. (*iii*) and (*iv*) are correct.
C. (*i*) and (*iii*) are correct.
D. (*ii*) and (*iii*) are correct.

36. CCF for bibliographic record refers to

(*i*) Data transfer
(*ii*) Data storage
(*iii*) Standard tags of data identification
(*iv*) Formatting of records

Codes:

A. (*i*) and (*iii*) are correct.
B. (*i*), (*ii*) and (*iv*) are correct.
C. (*ii*) and (*iii*) are correct.
D. (*iii*), (*i*) and (*ii*) are correct.

37. Which of the following are not reference service?

(*i*) Preparation of user profile
(*ii*) Initiation of freshman
(*iii*) Compilation of documentation list
(*iv*) Readers Advisory

Codes:

A. (*i*) and (*ii*) B. (*ii*) and (*iii*)
C. (*i*) and (*iii*) D. (*iii*) and (*iv*)

38. Which of the following functions are analysed by ALA as reference service functions?

(*i*) Consultation function
(*ii*) Guidance function
(*iii*) Instruction function
(*iv*) Bibliographic function

Codes:

A. (*i*), (*ii*) and (*iii*) are correct.
B. (*ii*), (*iii*) and (*iv*) are correct.
C. (*i*), (*ii*) and (*iv*) are correct.
D. (*i*), (*iii*) and (*iv*) are correct.

39. Which of the following are the scientists' approach according to Melvin J. Voigt (1961)?

(*i*) Current Approach
(*ii*) Everyday Approach
(*iii*) Exhaustive Approach
(*iv*) 'Catching up' or 'brushing up' approach.

Codes:

A. (*ii*), (*iii*) and (*iv*)
B. (*i*), (*iii*) and (*iv*)
C. (*i*), (*ii*) and (*iv*)
D. (*i*), (*ii*) and (*iii*)

40. Magazines are suitable for

(*i*) Leisure and entertainment
(*ii*) Scholarly information
(*iii*) Popular information
(*iv*) Subject information

Codes:

A. (*i*), (*ii*) and (*iii*) are correct.
B. (*ii*), (*iii*) and (*iv*) are correct.
C. (*i*) and (*iii*) are correct.
D. (*ii*) and (*iv*) are correct.

41. Planting the virus 'Trojan Horse' in computer network is

(*i*) Hacking
(*ii*) Tampering
(*iii*) Decryption
(*iv*) Intrusion

Codes:

A. (*i*), (*iii*) and (*iv*) are correct
B. (*ii*), (*iii*) and (*iv*) are correct
C. (*i*), (*ii*) and (*iii*) are correct
D. (*i*), (*ii*) and (*iv*) are correct

42. Which of the following are the fundamental conditions for a subject to be protected by IPR?

(*i*) The work must be original
(*ii*) The work must be man made
(*iii*) The work must be intelligible
(*iv*) The work must be recorded/fixed

Codes:

A. (*i*), (*ii*) and (*iii*) are correct.
B. (*i*), (*iii*) and (*iv*) are correct.
C. (*ii*), (*iii*) and (*iv*) are correct.
D. (*i*), (*ii*) and (*iv*) are correct.

43. Which of the following are the problems of present information environment?

(*i*) Information indiscipline
(*ii*) Information literacy
(*iii*) Information overload
(*iv*) Information technology

Codes:

A. (*i*), (*iii*) are correct
B. (*i*) and (*iv*) are correct
C. (*ii*) and (*iv*) are correct
D. (*i*) and (*ii*) are correct

44. Assertion (A) : Qualitative measures must be made quantifiable in order to be convincing.

Reason (R) : Qualitative measures are a necessary complement to quantitative measures.

Codes:

A. (A) is true, (R) is false.
B. (A) is false, (R) is true.
C. Both (A) & (R) are true.
D. Both (A) & (R) are false.

45. Which of the following are not partners of National Programme on Technology Enhanced Learning (NPTEL)?

(*i*) IIT Madras
(*ii*) IIT Delhi
(*iii*) IIIT Bangalore
(*iv*) NIT Rourkela

Codes:

A. (*iii*) and (*iv*)
B. (*i*) and (*iv*)
C. (*ii*) and (*iii*)
D. (*i*) and (*ii*)

46. Assertion (A) : Internet can replace libraries.

Reason (R) : Google searches will satisfy the maximum users needs.

Codes:

A. Both (A) and (R) are true.
B. Both (A) and (R) are false.
C. (A) is true but (R) is false.
D. (A) is false but (R) is true.

47. Assertion (A) : Federated search technique is an integral component of an information portal.

Reason (R) : 'Content Index' contains content that is find by the search server.

Codes:

A. Both (A) and (R) are true.
B. Both (A) and (R) are false.
C. (A) is true but (R) is false.
D. (A) is false but (R) is true.

48. Assertion (A) : A combination of hypertext and Hypermedia contains text, images, sounds and other information.

Reason (R) : Hypermedia information is represented in a linear fashion.

Codes:

A. (A) is true and (R) is false.
B. Both (A) and (R) are true.
C. (A) is false and (R) is true.
D. Both (A) & (R) are false.

49. Assertion (A) : Book selection should be done judiciously.

Reason (R) : A library should acquire important and latest book selection tools.

Codes:

A. (A) is true but (R) is false.
B. (A) is false but (R) is true.
C. Both (A) & (R) are true, but (R) is not the correct explanation of (A).
D. Both (A) & (R) are true and (R) is the correct explanation of (A).

50. **Assertion (A) :** TQM promotes the way in which a library is organised and perform its ICT functions.

Reason (R) : TQM is seen as a hindrance to library and information services.

Codes:

A. Both (A) and (R) are true.
B. Both (A) and (R) are false.
C. (A) is false and (R) is true.
D. (A) is true and (R) is false.

51. **Assertion (A) :** The array of classes 11, 12, 13 and the array of classes 31, 32, 33 are said to be collateral arrays.

Reason (R) : They are derived from the original universe 'O'.

Codes:

A. (A) is false, (R) is true.
B. (A) is true, (R) is false.
C. Both (A) & (R) are true.
D. Both (A) & (R) are false.

52. **Assertion (A) :** RDF supports the use and exchange of metadata on the web.

Reason (R) : Bibliographic standards are the means to create and disseminate secondary information.

Codes:

A. (A) is true, (R) is false.
B. (A) is false, (R) is true.
C. Both (A) & (R) are correct.
D. Both (A) & (R) are false.

53. **Assertion (A) :** Informative abstracts provide a concise summary of the subject content of an article.

Reason (R) : These are title-oriented than finding-oriented.

Codes :

A. Both (A) and (R) are true.
B. (A) is true but (R) is false.
C. (A) is false but (R) is true.
D. Both (A) and (R) are false.

54. **Assertion (A) :** E-publications have added enormous quantity of literature but adversely affected the quality of literature.

Reason (R) : Present decade has accepted E-publication as channels of fast communication.

Codes:

A. (A) is true (R) is false.
B. (A) is false, but (R) is correct.
C. Both (A) & (R) are false.
D. Both (A) & (R) are true.

55. **Assertion (A) :** Encyclopedias are not relevant for finding geographically information.

Reason (R) : Encyclopedias are the substitute for all categories of reference sources.

Codes:

A. (A) is false but (R) is true.
B. Both (A) and (R) are true.
C. Both (A) and (R) are false.
D. (A) is true but (R) is false.

56. **Assertion (A) :** LIS profession is not considered at par with medical and legal professions.

Reason (R) : There is no constitutional body for LIS profession like Medical Council of India (MCI) and Bar Council of India (BCI).

Codes:

A. Both (A) and (R) are true.
B. Both (A) and (R) are false.
C. (A) is true but (R) is false.
D. (A) is false but (R) is true.

57. **Assertion (A) :** Dr. S.R. Ranganathan has been called 'Father of Library and Information Science' in India.

Reason (R) : Library Science education in India was started by Dr. S.R. Ranganathan.

Codes:
A. (A) is false but (R) is true.
B. (A) is true but (R) is false.
C. Both (A) and (R) are true.
D. Both (A) and (R) are false.

58. **Assertion (A) :** The exclusive rights conferred by Intellectual property rights can generally be transferred / licenced to third parties.

Reason (R) : The creators want to make monetary benefits out of their intellectual product.

Codes:
A. (A) is true but (R) is false.
B. (A) is false but (R) is true.
C. Both (A) & (R) are true.
D. Both (A) & (R) are false.

59. Which is the correct sequence of the national libraries in the order of their year of establishment?
(*i*) British Library (formerly British Museum Library)
(*ii*) Library of Congress (Washington D.C.)
(*iii*) Lenin Library (Moscow)
(*iv*) Bibliotheque Nationale (Paris)

Codes:
A. (*i*), (*ii*), (*iii*), (*iv*)
B. (*ii*), (*iii*), (*i*), (*iv*)
C. (*iii*), (*ii*), (*iv*), (*i*)
D. (*iv*), (*iii*), (*ii*), (*i*)

60. What is the correct order of SCONUL's "Seven Pillar Model of Information Skills"?
(*i*) Recognise information need
(*ii*) Construct strategies for locating
(*iii*) Compare and evaluate
(*iv*) Locate and access

Codes:
A. (*i*), (*ii*), (*iii*), (*iv*)
B. (*ii*), (*iii*), (*iv*), (*i*)
C. (*i*), (*ii*), (*iv*), (*iii*)
D. (*ii*), (*iii*), (*i*), (*iv*)

61. Identify the correct order as per increasing data storage capacity:
A. CDROM, DVD, Cartridge, BlueRay Disc
B. DVD, Cartridge, BlueRay Disc, CDROM
C. Cartridge, CDROM, DVD, BlueRay Disc
D. BlueRay Disc, DVD, Cartridge, CDROM

62. Identify the correct order of the LIS Associations as per their year of establishment
A. CLA, ALA, SLA, IASLIC
B. ALA, SLA, CLA, IASLIC
C. SLA, IASLIC, ALA, CLA
D. CLA, SLA, IASLIC, ALA

63. Arrange the following State Library Acts in chronological order:
(*i*) Karnataka Public Library Act
(*ii*) Uttar Pradesh Public Library Act
(*iii*) Goa Public Library Act
(*iv*) Bihar Public Library Act

Codes:
A. (*i*), (*iii*), (*ii*), (*iv*)
B. (*i*), (*ii*), (*iii*), (*iv*)
C. (*ii*), (*iii*), (*iv*), (*i*)
D. (*iii*), (*i*), (*iv*), (*ii*)

64. Match the following:

List-I	*List-II*
(*a*) Mean	(*i*) Most frequently occurring value
(*b*) Mode	(*ii*) Average
(*c*) Median	(*iii*) Measure of dispersion
(*d*) Standard Deviation	(*iv*) Middle value

Codes:

	(*a*)	(*b*)	(*c*)	(*d*)
A.	(*iii*)	(*iv*)	(*i*)	(*ii*)
B.	(*ii*)	(*i*)	(*iv*)	(*iii*)
C.	(*iv*)	(*iii*)	(*i*)	(*ii*)
D.	(*ii*)	(*iii*)	(*iv*)	(*i*)

65. Match the following:

List-I	*List-II*
(*a*) Bradford	(*i*) Citation indexing
(*b*) Lotka	(*ii*) Distribution of articles published in periodicals
(*c*) Zipf	(*iii*) Scientific productivity of author
(*d*) Garfield	(*iv*) Frequency of word occurrence in a text

Codes:

	(a)	(b)	(c)	(d)
A.	(iv)	(i)	(iii)	(ii)
B.	(ii)	(iii)	(iv)	(i)
C.	(iii)	(iv)	(i)	(ii)
D.	(iv)	(iii)	(ii)	(i)

66. Match the following:

List-I	List-II
(a) Altavista	(i) Subject search engine
(b) Lycos	(ii) Meta search engine
(c) Geoindex	(iii) Regional search engine
(d) Savvy search	(iv) General search engine

Codes:

	(a)	(b)	(c)	(d)
A.	(iii)	(ii)	(i)	(iv)
B.	(ii)	(iv)	(ii)	(i)
C.	(iv)	(iii)	(i)	(ii)
D.	(iv)	(i)	(ii)	(iii)

67. Match the following :

List-I	List-II
(a) Pen drive	(i) Communication device
(b) i-Pad	(ii) Web server device
(c) Wifi Modem	(iii) Storage device
(d) Cloud computing	(iv) Computing device

Codes:

	(a)	(b)	(c)	(d)
A.	(i)	(iii)	(ii)	(iv)
B.	(iii)	(iv)	(i)	(ii)
C.	(iv)	(iii)	(ii)	(i)
D.	(iii)	(ii)	(i)	(iv)

68. Match the following :

List-I	List-II
(a) Informix	(i) Image software
(b) Omni page	(ii) Remote login software
(c) TIFF viewer	(iii) DBMS software
(d) Team viewer	(iv) OCR software

Codes:

	(a)	(b)	(c)	(d)
A.	(ii)	(i)	(iii)	(iv)
B.	(iii)	(iv)	(i)	(ii)
C.	(i)	(ii)	(iii)	(iv)
D.	(iv)	(iii)	(ii)	(i)

69. Match the following:

List-I	List-II
(a) Means of improving operations and services	(i) Preservation
(b) Preparation of to-do-list	(ii) Standards
(c) Performance guidelines	(iii) Time management
(d) Reinforce the spines of books	(iv) Evaluation

Codes:

	(a)	(b)	(c)	(d)
A.	(iv)	(iii)	(ii)	(i)
B.	(iv)	(ii)	(iii)	(i)
C.	(ii)	(iv)	(iii)	(i)
D.	(iii)	(ii)	(i)	(iv)

70. Match the following :

List-I	List-II
(a) Chain indexing	(i) Derek Austin
(b) Relational indexing	(ii) S.R. Ranganathan
(c) Subject Indexing	(iii) J.E.L. Farradane
(d) PRECIS	(iv) E.J. Coats

Codes:

	(a)	(b)	(c)	(d)
A.	(i)	(ii)	(iv)	(iii)
B.	(ii)	(iii)	(iv)	(i)
C.	(i)	(ii)	(iii)	(iv)
D.	(ii)	(iv)	(i)	(iii)

71. Match the following :

List-I	List-II
(a) Collateral classes	(i) Class comprising two or more entities

(*b*) Multiple classes — (*ii*) Classes of the same order but not belonging to one in the same order

(*c*) Chain of classes — (*iii*) A subject fixed with others in the universal of subject

(*d*) Co-ordinate classes — (*iv*) A sequence of classes made up of any given class and its universe

Codes:

	(*a*)	(*b*)	(*c*)	(*d*)
A.	(*ii*)	(*iv*)	(*i*)	(*iii*)
B.	(*i*)	(*iii*)	(*ii*)	(*iv*)
C.	(*ii*)	(*i*)	(*iv*)	(*iii*)
D.	(*i*)	(*iv*)	(*ii*)	(*iii*)

72. Match the following :

List-I	***List-II***
(*a*) William Martin	(*i*) Little Science Big Science
(*b*) Alvin Toffler	(*ii*) Information society
(*c*) Eric J de Solla Price	(*iii*) Documentation
(*d*) S.C. Bradford	(*iv*) The Third Wave

Codes:

	(*a*)	(*b*)	(*c*)	(*d*)
A.	(*ii*)	(*iv*)	(*iii*)	(*i*)
B.	(*iv*)	(*ii*)	(*iii*)	(*i*)
C.	(*ii*)	(*iv*)	(*i*)	(*iii*)
D.	(*i*)	(*iv*)	(*ii*)	(*iii*)

73. Match the following :

List-I	***List-II***
(*a*) Communication Barrier	(*i*) Radio
(*b*) Communication Medium	(*ii*) Shanon & Weaver
(*c*) Communication Model	(*iii*) Video-conferencing
(*d*) Interactive Communication	(*iv*) Noise

Codes:

	(*a*)	(*b*)	(*c*)	(*d*)
A.	(*i*)	(*ii*)	(*iii*)	(*iv*)
B.	(*iv*)	(*i*)	(*ii*)	(*iii*)
C.	(*ii*)	(*iii*)	(*iv*)	(*i*)
D.	(*iii*)	(*ii*)	(*i*)	(*iv*)

74. Match the following :

List-I	***List-II***
(*a*) Osgood and Schramm	(*i*) General Model
(*b*) Berlo	(*ii*) Mathematical Model
(*c*) Shannon and Weaver	(*iii*) Circular Model
(*d*) George Gerbner	(*iv*) S-M-C-R Model

Codes:

	(*a*)	(*b*)	(*c*)	(*d*)
A.	(*i*)	(*ii*)	(*iii*)	(*iv*)
B.	(*ii*)	(*iii*)	(*iv*)	(*i*)
C.	(*iii*)	(*iv*)	(*ii*)	(*i*)
D.	(*iv*)	(*i*)	(*ii*)	(*iii*)

75. Match the following :

List-I	***List-II***
(*a*) Information contribution to the GNP of a nation	(*i*) Social information
(*b*) Information that changes human activity	(*ii*) Technological information
(*c*) Information that establishes interaction between government and people	(*iii*) Economic information
(*d*) Information that forms a modern society	(*iv*) Political information

Codes:

	(*a*)	(*b*)	(*c*)	(*d*)
A.	(*iii*)	(*i*)	(*iv*)	(*ii*)
B.	(*i*)	(*iii*)	(*iv*)	(*ii*)
C.	(*iv*)	(*ii*)	(*i*)	(*iii*)
D.	(*ii*)	(*iii*)	(*iv*)	(*i*)

ANSWERS

1	2	3	4	5	6	7	8	9	10
B	B	D	B	D	B	C	D	C	A
11	**12**	**13**	**14**	**15**	**16**	**17**	**18**	**19**	**20**
D	B	A	A	A	A	C	B	A	C
21	**22**	**23**	**24**	**25**	**26**	**27**	**28**	**29**	**30**
C	B	B	C	A	C	B	D	A	D
31	**32**	**33**	**34**	**35**	**36**	**37**	**38**	**39**	**40**
C	A	D	C	B	A	C	B	D	C
41	**42**	**43**	**44**	**45**	**46**	**47**	**48**	**49**	**50**
B	D	A	C	A	B	C	A	C	D
51	**52**	**53**	**54**	**55**	**56**	**57**	**58**	**59**	**60**
B	C	B	D	B	A	B	C	A	C
61	**62**	**63**	**64**	**65**	**66**	**67**	**68**	**69**	**70**
C	B	A	B	B	C	B	B	A	B
71	**72**	**73**	**74**	**75**					
C	C	B	C	A					

Previous Paper (Solved)

UGC-NET LIBRARY AND INFORMATION SCIENCE, JUNE 2012

PAPER-II

Note: *This paper contains **fifty (50)** objective type questions, each question carrying **two (2)** marks. Attempt **all** the questions.*

1. Who was the Chairman of 'National Policy on Library & Information Systems' (1986)?
A. D. N. Banerjee
B. D. P. Chattopadhyay
C. Sam Pitroda
D. Kalpana Dasgupta

2. The significance of the year 2011 for LIS education in India is
A. Golden Jubilee year
B. Platinum Jubilee year
C. Diamond Jubilee year
D. Centenary year

3. Digital Reference Service can be offered through
A. FAX
B. OPAC
C. Ask your librarian
D. Consortia

4. "Biotechnology" is formed as a result of
A. Fusion B. Lamination
C. Fission D. Agglomeration

5. The order of significance of "Thing, Material and Action" among various components of a compound subject was expanded by
A. J. Kaiser B. E. J. Coates
C. J. R. Sharp D. J. E. L. Farradane

6. Relational Database is
A. A work which has some relationship to another work
B. A symbol representing relationship between two concepts
C. Manipulation commands which relate records in different fields
D. All of the above

7. "Shodhganga" is a repository of
A. E-Resources B. E-Thesis
C. E-Journals D. E-Books

8. Which of the following tests can be employed for hypothesis testing ?
A. F-test B. Chi-square test
C. t-test D. All of the above

9. 'RRRLF' falls under the:
A. Ministry of Human Resource Development
B. Ministry of Information & Broadcasting
C. Ministry of Culture
D. Ministry of Science & Technology

10. "Internet Public Library" is being maintained by
A. MIT, Massachusettes
B. University of Michigan
C. University of Arizona
D. Drexal University

11. What are the major driving forces behind an 'Information society'?
(i) R T I (ii) I. C. T.
(iii) Internet (iv) I. T. ACT
Codes:
A. (ii) & (i) are correct
B. (ii) & (iv) are correct
C. (i) & (iv) are correct
D. (ii) & (iii) are correct

12. Which libraries are functioning as depository libraries?
(i) Delhi Public Library
(ii) Connemara Public Library
(iii) British Council Library
(iv) Central Reference Library

Codes:

A. (i), (iii), (iv) are correct
B. (i) & (iii) are correct
C. (i) & (ii) are correct
D. (ii) & (iii) are correct

13. Which of the following are 'Inclusive geographical sources'?

(i) Maps (ii) Atlases
(iii) Encyclopaedias (iv) Yearbooks

Codes:

A. (i) & (ii) are correct
B. (iii) & (iv) are correct
C. (ii) & (iii) are correct
D. (ii) & (iv) are correct

14. Which principles are corollary to Wallpicture principle?

(i) Cow-calf principle
(ii) Principle of later-in-time
(iii) Whole-organ principle
(iv) All of the above

Codes:

A. (i) and (ii) are correct
B. (ii) and (iii) are correct
C. (i) and (iii) are correct
D. (i) and (iv) are correct

15. The factors that influence computer file organisation are

(i) Speed of access
(ii) Storage space
(iii) Fixed length fields
(iv) File volatility

Codes:

A. (i), (ii) and (iii) are correct
B. (i), (ii) and (iv) are correct
C. (ii), (iii) and (iv) are correct
D. (i), (iii) and (iv) are correct

16. Major problems of 'Information Communication Technology' are

(i) Information overload
(ii) Information insecurity
(iii) Lack of innovative technologies
(iv) Lack of control over communication

Codes:

A. (ii) and (iv) are correct
B. (i) and (iv) are correct
C. (i), (ii) and (iv) are correct
D. (i), (ii) and (iii) are correct

17. Which of the following are 'Open Source Content Management Systems'?

(i) Drupal (ii) Atex
(iii) Joomla (iv) OpenCms

Codes:

A. (i), (ii) and (iv) are correct
B. (i), (ii) and (iii) are correct
C. (ii), (iii) and (iv) are correct
D. (i), (iii) and (iv) are correct

18. Which of the following are not styles of citation?

(i) Anglo American Cataloguing Rules
(ii) MLA Handbook for Writers of Research Papers
(iii) Chicago Manual of Style
(iv) Little Science Big Science

Codes:

A. (i) and (ii) are correct
B. (iii) and (iv) are correct
C. (i) and (iv) are correct
D. (ii) and (iii) are correct

19. Which of the following are Schools of Management thought?

(i) Scientific Management School
(ii) Human Behavioural School
(iii) Classical School
(iv) School of Authority

Codes:

A. (ii) and (iv) are correct
B. (i), (ii) and (iv) are correct
C. (iii) and (iv) are correct
D. (i), (ii) and (iii) are correct

20. Assertion (A) : Users can have access to large number of e-journals.

Reason (R) : Users are not aware of using e-journals.

Codes:

A. (A) is true, but (R) is false
B. Both (A) and (R) are true, but (R) is not the correct explanation of (A)
C. (A) is false, (R) is true
D. Both (A) and (R) are true and (R) is the correct explanation of (A)

21. **Assertion (A) :** Book selection must be done judiciously.

Reason (R) : Resource sharing is the need of the hour.

Codes:

A. Both (A) and (R) are true, but (R) is not the correct statement of (A)
B. (A) is false, but (R) is true
C. (A) is true, but (R) is false
D. Both (A) and (R) are false

22. **Assertion (A) :** Primary sources provide most authentic information for research.

Reason (R) : Primary sources are highly unorganised.

Codes:

A. (A) is false, but (R) is true
B. (A) is true, but (R) is false
C. Both (A) and (R) are correct and (R) is the correct explanation of (A)
D. Both (A) and (R) are correct, but (R) is not the correct explanation of (A)

23. **Assertion (A) :** Abstracting services facilitate literature review.

Reason (R) : Literature review summarises major findings of various studies.

Codes:

A. (A) is true, but (R) is false
B. (A) is false, but (R) is true
C. Both (A) and (R) are true
D. Both (A) and (R) are false

24. **Assertion (A) :** "Name Authority File" should be used in a library.

Reason (R) : All works of an author should be collocated.

Codes:

A. (A) is true, but (R) is false
B. Both (A) and (R) true and (R) is the correct explanation of (A).
C. (A) is false, but (R) is true
D. Both (A) and (R) are false

25. **Assertion (A) :** Classification plays a significant role in online retrieval.

Reason (R) : Classification played an important role in manual system.

Codes:

A. (A) is true, but (R) is false
B. Both (A) and (R) are false
C. Both (A) and (R) are true
D. (A) is false, but (R) is true

26. **Assertion (A) :** If changes cannot be adopted to its framework, the organisational equilibrium will be imbalanced.

Reason (R) : Organisation works in an environment which is marked by dynamic characteristics.

Codes:

A. (A) is true, but (R) is false
B. (A) is false, but (R) is true
C. Both (A) and (R) are true
D. Both (A) and (R) are false

27. **Assertion (A):** There is need to continuous evaluation and appreciation of value of libraries.

Reason (R) : There is economic pressure on public budget.

Codes:

A. Both (A) and (R) are true
B. Both (A) and (R) are false
C. (A) is true, but (R) is false
D. (A) is false, but (R) is true

28. **Assertion (A) :** System analysis identifies the flow of work.

Reason (R) : System analysis is not necessary if the library is automated.

Codes:

A. (A) is false, but (R) is true
B. (A) is true, but (R) is false
C. Both (A) and (R) are false
D. Both (A) and (R) are true

29. Arrange the following associations according to their year of establishment:

(i) IASLIC (ii) ASLIB
(iii) ALA (iv) SLA

Codes:

A. (iv), (ii), (iii), (i)
B. (ii), (iii), (iv), (i)
C. (iii), (iv), (ii), (i)
D. (i), (iv), (ii), (iii)

30. Arrange the following according to their year of enactment in India:

(i) Freedom of Information Act
(ii) Right to Information Act
(iii) Copyright Act (Revised)
(iv) Information Technology Act

Codes:

A. (iv), (ii), (i), (iii)
B. (iii), (iv), (i), (ii)
C. (ii), (iii), (iv), (i)
D. (i), (iv), (ii), (iii)

31. Arrange the following publications according to their year of origin.

(i) Social Science Citation Index
(ii) L I S A
(iii) Library Literature and Information Science
(iv) Library Journal

Codes:

A. (i), (iii), (iv), (ii)
B. (ii), (i), (iii), (iv)
C. (iv), (iii), (ii), (i)
D. (iii), (ii), (iv), (i)

32. Arrange the following according to their year of origin:

(i) Broad System of Ordering
(ii) Classification in Online Systems
(iii) Automated Keyword Classification
(iv) Classification Research Group

Codes:

A. (iv), (iii), (i), (ii)
B. (i), (ii), (iv), (iii)
C. (iii), (i), (ii), (iv)
D. (ii), (iv), (iii), (ii)

33. Arrange the following according to their year of origin:

(i) Bradford's Law
(ii) Lotka's Law
(iii) Statistical Bibliography
(iv) Zipf's Law

Codes:

A. (i), (iii), (iv), (ii)
B. (i), (ii), (iv), (iii)
C. (iv), (iii), (i), (ii)
D. (iii), (ii), (iv), (i)

34. "Prevention of Cholera in India" generates following index terms according to modified 'Chain Indexing', arrange them in correct order

(i) India (ii) Cholera
(iii) Disease (iv) Treatment
(v) Medicine

Codes:

A. (iii), (iv), (i), (ii), (v)
B. (ii), (i), (iii), (iv), (v)
C. (iv), (iii), (ii), (v), (i)
D. (i), (iii), (iv), (v), (ii)

35. Arrange the following according to their year of first publication:

(i) Encyclopaedia Britannica
(ii) Encyclopaedia Americana
(iii) Encyclopaedia of Library and Information Science
(iv) McGraw-Hill Encyclopaedia of Science and Technology

Codes:

A. (iv), (iii), (i), (ii)
B. (i), (ii), (iv), (iii)
C. (iii), (i), (iv), (ii)
D. (ii), (iv), (i), (iii)

36. Arrange the following according to their year of establishment:

(i) NIC (ii) DESIDOC
(iii) NISCAIR (iv) NASSDOC

Codes:

A. (i), (iii), (ii), (iv)
B. (iii), (i), (iv), (ii)
C. (iv), (i), (iii), (ii)
D. (ii), (iv), (i), (iii)

37. Arrange the following Public Library Acts according to their year of enactment:

(i) Uttar Pradesh PL Act
(ii) Arunachal Pradesh PL Act
(iii) Orissa PL Act
(iv) Gujarat PL Act

Codes:

A. (iv), (iii), (i), (ii)
B. (ii), (iii), (i), (iv)
C. (ii), (i), (iv), (iii)
D. (iii), (ii), (i), (iv)

38. Match the following:

List-I	List-II
(a) Obligation of the State	(i) First Law
(b) Shelf Arrangement & Catalogue	(ii) Second Law
(c) Open Access & Shelf Arrangement	(iii) Third Law
(d) Library location/ hours	(iv) Fourth Law

Codes:

	(a)	(b)	(c)	(d)
A.	(ii)	(iv)	(iii)	(i)
B.	(iv)	(iii)	(ii)	(i)
C.	(i)	(iii)	(iv)	(ii)
D.	(iii)	(ii)	(i)	(iv)

39. Match the following:

List-I	List-II
(a) Asian Recorder	(i) Location of specific volume of journal
(b) Union Catalogue of Scientific Serials	(ii) Articles on Green Revolution
(c) Books-in-Print	(iii) Obituary of Dev - Anand
(d) Social Science Index	(iv) Availability of books

Codes:

	(a)	(b)	(c)	(d)
A.	(iv)	(iii)	(i)	(ii)
B.	(i)	(iv)	(ii)	(iii)
C.	(iii)	(i)	(iv)	(ii)
D.	(ii)	(iv)	(iii)	(i)

40. Match the following:

List-I	List-II
(a) User orientation	(i) Bibliographic service
(b) Information repackaging	(ii) Reference service
(c) Translation	(iii) Digest series
(d) Indexing	(iv) Support service

Codes:

	(a)	(b)	(c)	(d)
A.	(i)	(iv)	(iii)	(ii)
B.	(iii)	(ii)	(i)	(iv)
C.	(iv)	(i)	(ii)	(iii)
D.	(ii)	(iii)	(iv)	(i)

41. Match the following:

List-I	List-II
(a) Textual representation	(i) Pascal
(b) Computer language	(ii) Gopher
(c) Network tool	(iii) Boolean operators
(d) Searching technique	(iv) ASCI

Codes:

	(a)	(b)	(c)	(d)
A.	(iv)	(i)	(ii)	(iii)
B.	(i)	(iv)	(iii)	(ii)
C.	(iii)	(ii)	(iv)	(i)
D.	(ii)	(iv)	(iii)	(i)

42. Match the following:

List-I	List-II
(a) Law of Parsimony	(i) Classification
(b) Principle of Osmosis	(ii) F. W. Lancaster
(c) Paperless Society	(iii) Overall economy
(d) APUPA pattern	(iv) Reclassification

Codes:

	(a)	(b)	(c)	(d)
A.	(ii)	(i)	(iv)	(iii)
B.	(iv)	(ii)	(i)	(iii)
C.	(iii)	(iv)	(ii)	(i)
D.	(i)	(iii)	(ii)	(iv)

43. Match the following:

List-I	List-II
(a) Hubs	(i) A physical layer device used to interconnect the media segments of an extended network
(b) Repeater	(ii) A physical layer device that connects multiple computers each via a dedicated cable

(c) Bus Topology	(iii)	Multiple bridges known for transfer of data between different parts
(d) Switches	(iv)	A straight line data highway that carries network information from one network station to another

Codes:

	(a)	(b)	(c)	(d)
A.	(iii)	(iv)	(ii)	(i)
B.	(ii)	(i)	(iv)	(iii)
C.	(iv)	(i)	(iii)	(ii)
D.	(i)	(iii)	(ii)	(iv)

44. Match the following:

List-I	List-II
(a) RRRLF	(i) Delhi
(b) Connemara Public Library	(ii) Patna
(c) NISCAIR	(iii) Kolkata
(d) Khuda Baksh Oriental Public Library	(iv) Chennai

Codes:

	(a)	(b)	(c)	(d)
A.	(iv)	(iii)	(ii)	(i)
B.	(ii)	(iii)	(iv)	(i)
C.	(iii)	(iv)	(i)	(ii)
D.	(iv)	(i)	(ii)	(iii)

45. Match the following:

List-I	List-II
(a) Right man at right library	(i) Annual financial statement
(b) Budget	(ii) Deployment
(c) Journal	(iii) TQM
(d) Identifying user's views and expectations	(iv) ISSN

Codes:

	(a)	(b)	(c)	(d)
A.	(iii)	(i)	(ii)	(iv)
B.	(ii)	(i)	(iv)	(iii)
C.	(iv)	(ii)	(iii)	(i)
D.	(i)	(iii)	(iv)	(ii)

Directions (Qs Nos. 46-50) : *Read the passage given below, and answer the questions based on your understanding of the passage.*

The primary concern with the longevity of digital documents is the "viewing problem" (Besser, 2000). Unlike analog or physical information, which tends to exist independent of human involvement, digital information needs constant intervention to survive. History has shown that digital documents are problematic by default. Whereas we can actually look at the Sistine Chapel ceiling, painted 500 years ago, it is difficult if not impossible to simply view documents on 8-inch floppy disks created in the last 20 years, even if there has been an immediate, proactive role in preserving them. Without concerted effort on the part of archivists and preservationists, digital objects quickly become obsolete or inaccessible due to unforeseen, although anticipated, advances in information technology.

The variable media art community currently utilizes four digital preservation strategies, all focused on the end product. The first three methods have technical origins and are based on general digital preservation practices. Related to "the viewing problem", they are : *refreshing*, the upgrade of storage mechanisms; *migration,* the premeditated upgrade of file formats; and *emulation*, which focuses on development of operating systems able to run obsolete media. The fourth option, developed by and for the new media art community, is *reinterpretation* (Depocas et al., 2003), where the curators attempt to recreate a work given comprehensive documentation of the original artefact.

Migration and *emulation* are the two primary methods in managing the problem of obsolete file formats (Waters & Garrett, 1996). Migration focuses on the files themselves, periodically updating files in new software formats. The second method of preservation is emulation, which can be either at the system or the software level. System emulation focuses on developing systems that mimic the hardware used to create or run the original artefact.

46. Why digital objects become inaccessible quickly?

A. Because of unforeseen advancement of technology
B. It is independent of human intervention
C. It is independent of any technological advancement
D. None of the above

47. Reinterpretation is a digital preservation strategy where curator intends to
A. Upgrade file formats
B. Upgrade storage mechanism
C. Recreate a work
D. Upgrade operating system

48. What is the focus of system emulation?
A. Developing systems that mimic hardware
B. Developing systems that mimic software
C. Developing systems that mimic file formats
D. None of the above

49. Which of the following is true about migration preservation strategy?
A. Migration is not related to the viewing problem
B. Migration is related to the viewing problem
C. Migration requires comprehensive documentation
D. Migration does not have a technical origin

50. Refreshing preservation strategy focuses on
A. Comprehensive documentation of original artefact
B. Development of operating system
C. Not on viewing problem
D. Upgradation of storage mechanism

ANSWERS

1	2	3	4	5	6	7	8	9	10
B	D	C	A	B	C	B	D	C	D
11	**12**	**13**	**14**	**15**	**16**	**17**	**18**	**19**	**20**
D	C	B	C	B	C	D	C	D	B
21	**22**	**23**	**24**	**25**	**26**	**27**	**28**	**29**	**30**
A	D	C	B	D	C	A	B	C	B
31	**32**	**33**	**34**	**35**	**36**	**37**	**38**	**39**	**40**
C	A	D	C	B	D	A	A	C	D
41	**42**	**43**	**44**	**45**	**46**	**47**	**48**	**49**	**50**
A	C	B	C	B	A	C	A	B	D

PAPER-III

Note : *This paper contains seventy five (75) objective type questions of two (2) marks each.* ***All*** *questions are compulsory.*

1. The initiation, selection, exploration, formulation, collection and presentation are two stages of which model of information seeking behaviour
A. Ellis Model B. Krikelas Model
C. Kuhlthou Model D. Wilson Model

2. Jubilee Project is associated with what?
A. Evaluation of electronic information services
B. Public library survey
C. Strategic management of libraries
D. Scale development

3. The publisher of "Information Power: Building Partnership for Learning" is
A. AASL B. AECT
C. ALA D. ILA

4. In 1974, Zurkowski used for the first time which of the following term?

A. Digital Literacy
B. Media Literacy
C. Computer Literacy
D. Information Literacy

5. Inference Engine is a part of which information system?
A. Management information System
B. Decision Support System
C. Expert System
D. Open System

6. Which of the following is not related to case study approach in a research design?
A. Indepth Study
B. Study of one/limited cases
C. General study
D. Little concern about generalisation to a large population

7. "Students' visit to Library is influenced by the availability of Internet". State "Students' visit to library" is which kind of variable?
A. Independent Variable
B. Intervening Variable
C. Dependent Variable
D. Intercept Variable

8. Idiographic hypothesis is directed towards predicting the behaviour of
A. An Individual
B. Group of People
C. Masses
D. People from same school of thought

9. In the process of reasoning when we start with a specific statement, and conclude to a general statement, it is called
A. Deductive Reasoning
B. Inductive Reasoning
C. Abnormal Reasoning
D. Transcendental Reasoning

10. Solomon Four group design is related to
A. Field studies
B. Pretest-post test control group design
C. Data Analysis Model
D. Statistical Technique

11. The information network that connects Universities and Colleges in United Kingdom:
A. JANET B. SERCNET
C. OCLC D. BONET

12. Internet filtering is
A. A form of censorship
B. Acceptable user policy
C. Access to inappropriate material
D. Blocking internet facility

13. Which one of the following is a Bulletin Board Service on Internet?
A. Picaso B. Google talk
C. Blog D. Oovoo

14. Virus is a software which can
A. Manipulate data
B. Replicate itself
C. Damage computer
D. All the above

15. Which one of the following protocol is used in file transfer over internet?
A. FTP B. SMTP
C. POP D. TCP/IP

16. Scaler chain shows
A. Authority structure
B. Scale of performance of staff
C. Chain for locating racks
D. A link in the chain

17. Blair and Maron evaluation study on retrieval effectiveness of full text search is called
A. SMART Retrieval Experiment
B. MEDLARS evaluation study
C. STAIRS project
D. Cranefield-II Project

18. In cataloguing, the square brackets [ ] are used
A. to enclose information taken from outside
B. to enclose the details of printed/ manufacturer
C. to enclose series statements .
D. to enclose statement of accompanying material

19. Which Section of AACR-II (R) deals with serial publications?
A. Part-A, Section-3
B. Part-B, Section-3
C. Part-A, Section-12
D. Part-B, Section-12

20. When two or more basic subjects having same relational approach form a specific subject, the relation is termed as
A. Speciater relation
B. Co-ordinate relation
C. Phase relation
D. Hierarchical relation

21. The concept of 'Stopword' list is relevant in the context of
A. Uniform Indexing
B. Citation Indexing
C. Chain Indexing
D. Keyword Indexing

22. A version of KWIC augmented with author/ name is called
A. WADEX B. KWOC
C. KWAC D. KWIC

23. 'Segmentation' is associated with
A. Reference Service
B. Market Survey Report
C. Digest Service
D. Indexing Service

24. State of the art report generally highlights
A. General Aspects
B. Technical Aspects
C. Administrative Aspects
D. All of the above

25. Who propounded "Minimum, Middling and Maximum Theories" of reference service?
A. C.M. Winchell B. James I. Wyer
C. Samuel Rothstein D. D.W. Lewis

26. Even though 'Xerography' is a photocopying method, but it is called
A. Diazographic B. Thermographic
C. Electrofax D. Electrostatic

27. 'CODEN' is connected with
A. Books B. Serials
C. Reports D. Gray Literature

28. Roget's International Thesaurus is a
A. Classified List of Words
B. Book of Synonyms
C. List of Standard Terms
D. List of Scientific Terms

29. Information about scale and projection can be found in
A. Encyclopaedias
B. Hand books of Manuals
C. Geographical sources
D. Directories

30. Who of the following is not the author of any reference book?
A. C.M. Winchell B. William A Katz
C. Louis Shores D. Maurice B. Line

31. Identify the odd one out.
A. ANSI B. BIS
C. BSI D. ESPN

32. Which of the following is not a part of word treatment in language dictionaries?
A. Gloss
B. Vernacular
C. Etymology
D. Grammatical information

33. Where the first M. Phil programme in Library and Information Science was started in India?
A. University of Madras
B. University of Delhi
C. University of Mysore
D. University of Bombay

34. Corollary for Second Law of Library Science is
A. Books for all
B. Free Books Service
C. Free Library Service
D. Books every where

35. Which of the following is not the prerequisite for a National Information Policy?
A. Legislative Frame work
B. Production of National Bibliography
C. Advisory and Administrative body
D. ICT infrastructure facilities

36. World Intellectual Property Organization is related to
A. UNESCO
B. United Nations
C. U.S. Organization
D. International Law Organization

37. Redundancy of information is
A. Unnecessary and should be eliminated
B. Unnecessary but cannot be avoided
C. Necessary and sometimes useful
D. Necessary and always desirable

38. Which sources would you consult to know the "Impact Factor" of Journal publications?
(i) Web of Science
(ii) Science Direct
(iii) SCOPUS
(iv) EBSCO
Codes:
A. (i) and (iv) B. (ii) and (iii)
C. (i) and (iii) D. (iii) and (iv)

39. Research is conducted to:
(i) Generate new knowledge
(ii) Develop a theory
(iii) Develop communication skills
(iv) Re-interpret existing knowledge
Codes:
A. (i), (iii) and (ii) are correct
B. (iii), (ii) and (i) are correct
C. (i), (ii) and (iv) are correct
D. (i), (iii) and (iv) are correct

40. Radio Frequency Identification is used in library for:
(i) Circulation of Documents
(ii) Cataloguing of Documents
(iii) Security of Documents
(iv) Acquisition of Documents
Codes:
A. (i) and (ii) are correct
B. (ii) and (iv) are correct
C. (iii) and (ii) are correct
D. (i) and (iii) are correct

41. BIOS contains:
(i) Operating System Program
(ii) Bootstrap Program
(iii) Application System Program
(iv) Convert Character to Code Program
Codes:
A. (i) and (ii) are correct
B. (ii) and (iii) are correct
C. (iii) and (iv) are correct
D. (ii) and (iv) are correct

42. Science Citation Index is published by
A. Thomson Reuters B. H.W. Wilson
C. Whitaker D. R.R. Bowker

43. In the information transfer cycles, internet is acting as
(i) Primary Publisher
(ii) Secondary Publisher
(iii) Tertiary Publisher
(iv) Primary Distributor
Codes:
A. (i), (iii) and (iv) are correct.
B. (i), (ii) and (iv) are correct.
C. (ii), (iii) and (iv) are correct.
D. (i), (ii) and (iii) are correct.

44. Methods and Techniques of Human Resource Planning includes
(i) Selection and Recruitment
(ii) Induction and Placement
(iii) Quality Management
(iv) Performance Evaluation
Codes:
A. (i), (iv) & (ii) are correct.
B. (iv), (iii) & (i) are correct.
C. (i), (ii) & (iv) are correct.
D. (iii) and (i) are correct.

45. Assertion (A) : Netiquette mandates that you do your best to act within the laws of cyberspace and society.

Reason (R) : Failing to respect other people's privacy is bad Netiquette.
Codes:
A. Both (A) and (R) are false.
B. Both (A) and (R) are true.
C. (A) is true, but (R) is false.
D. (A) is false, but (R) is true.

46. Assertion (A) : Modern Integrated Library Management Softwares offer user friendly Graphical User Interfaces (GUI) on the web.

Reason (R) : Almost every module of modern Integrated Library Management Software is accessible through the internet.
Codes:
A. Both (A) and (R) are correct.
B. (A) is correct but (R) is wrong.

63. Match the following:

List-I	List-II
(a) Thurston scale	(i) Sharing individual preference in a group
(b) Semantic Differential Scale	(ii) Group of Judges
(c) Likert Scale	(iii) Selection from two opposite position
(d) Sociometric scale	(iv) Intensity structure

Codes:

	(a)	(b)	(c)	(d)
A.	(i)	(iv)	(ii)	(iii)
B.	(ii)	(iii)	(iv)	(i)
C.	(iv)	(i)	(iii)	(ii)
D.	(iii)	(ii)	(iv)	(i)

64. Match the following:

List-I	List-II
(a) Vidyanidhi	(i) Institutional Repository
(b) TKDL	(ii) Electronic Theses & Dissertations
(c) DOAJ	(iii) Digital Library of Journals
(d) E-Prints @ IISc	(iv) Digital Archive

Codes:

	(a)	(b)	(c)	(d)
A.	(ii)	(iv)	(iii)	(i)
B.	(iii)	(ii)	(i)	(iv)
C.	(iv)	(iii)	(ii)	(i)
D.	(i)	(ii)	(iv)	(iii)

65. Match the following:

List-I	List-II
(a) HTML File	(i) Text Format
(b) PDF File	(ii) Film Format
(c) JPG File	(iii) Web Format
(d) AVI File	(iv) Image Format

Codes:

	(a)	(b)	(c)	(d)
A.	(i)	(ii)	(iv)	(iii)
B.	(iii)	(i)	(iv)	(ii)
C.	(i)	(iv)	(ii)	(iii)
D.	(iv)	(iii)	(i)	(ii)

66. Match the following:

List-I	List-II
(a) DRUPAL	(i) Integrated Library Management Software
(b) Moodle	(ii) Digital Library Software
(c) D space	(iii) Content Management Software
(d) New Gen Lib	(iv) Learning Management Software

Codes:

	(a)	(b)	(c)	(d)
A.	(iv)	(iii)	(ii)	(i)
B.	(ii)	(i)	(iv)	(iii)
C.	(iii)	(iv)	(ii)	(i)
D.	(i)	(ii)	(iii)	(iv)

67. Match the following:

List-I	List-II
(a) Face Book	(i) Video Networking site
(b) Research Gate	(ii) Social Networking site
(c) Oovoo	(iii) Academic Networking site
(d) Flicker	(iv) Photo Networking site

Codes:

	(a)	(b)	(c)	(d)
A.	(i)	(iii)	(ii)	(iv)
B.	(iv)	(i)	(ii)	(iii)
C.	(ii)	(iii)	(i)	(iv)
D.	(iii)	(iv)	(i)	(ii)

68. Match the following:

List-I	List-II
(a) Small set of dependent activities that form longest path of activity network	(i) PERT
(b) Delighting the customer by fully meeting their needs	(ii) CPM
(c) Interconnecting networks depicting tasks, duration and dependency	(iii) Delphi